THE COLLECTED WORKS OF
SAMUEL TAYLOR COLERIDGE · 16

POETICAL WORKS

General Editor: KATHLEEN COBURN
Associate Editor: BART WINER

THE COLLECTED WORKS

THE COLLECTED WORKS OF

Samuel Taylor Coleridge

Poetical Works

II

Poems (Variorum Text): PART 1

EDITED BY

J. C. C. Mays

⚜BOLLINGEN SERIES LXXV
PRINCETON UNIVERSITY PRESS

This edition of the text by Samuel Taylor Coleridge is
copyright © 2001 by Princeton University Press

The Collected Works, sponsored by Bollingen Foundation,
is published by Princeton University Press, Princeton, New Jersey
ISBN 0-691-00484-6
LCC 00-021206

Library of Congress Cataloging-in-Publication Data
Coleridge, Samuel Taylor, 1772–1834.
Poetical works / edited by J.C.C. Mays.
p. cm.—(Bollingen series; 75) (The collected works
of Samuel Taylor Coleridge; 16)
Includes bibliographical references and index.
Contents: v. 1, pt. 1. Poems (reading text)—v. 2, pt. 1.
Poems (Variorum text)—v. 3, pt. 1. Plays
ISBN 0-691-00483-8 (v. 1, pt. 2: alk. paper)—
ISBN 0-691-00484-6 (v. 2, pt. 2: alk. paper)—
ISBN 0-691-09883-2 (v. 3, pt. 2: alk. paper)
I. Mays, J.C.C. II. Title. III. Series.
PR4470 .F84 vol. 16   821'.7–dc21

The Collected Works constitutes
the seventy-fifth publication in Bollingen Series

The present work, number 16 of the Collected Works,
is in 3 volumes, this being 16:II pt 1

Typeset by John Waś, Oxford, UK

Printed in the United States of America
1 3 5 7 9 10 8 6 4 2

THIS EDITION
OF THE WORKS OF
SAMUEL TAYLOR COLERIDGE
IS DEDICATED
IN GRATITUDE TO
THE FAMILY EDITORS
IN EACH GENERATION

IN THE PREPARATION OF
THESE VOLUMES THE EDITOR IS
INDEBTED FOR SPECIAL KNOWLEDGE
AND CO-OPERATION
TO
Lorna Arnold
Joyce Crick

CONTENTS

═══════ **II** ═══════

vii

Contents

1795

Contents

Contents

PART 2

Contents

1807

Contents

LIST OF ILLUSTRATIONS

EDITORIAL PRACTICE, SYMBOLS, AND ABBREVIATIONS

ARRANGEMENT AND TRANSCRIPTION

THE present volume contains all of the poems included in the edition, with the exception of the plays (Volume Three). Poems of doubtful or misattributed authorship, projected works, and fragments too inconsiderable to be presented in the Reading Text are interpolated into the main sequence by means of .X numbers, as explained in the corresponding section of Volume One. When there is only one known text of a poem, it is given in full in Volume One, and only additional details are given here.

Throughout the present volume (in contrast to Volume One) Coleridge's regular use of "it's" in autograph manuscripts has been tacitly normalised to accord with modern usage: this follows the rule observed throughout the *Collected Coleridge*, and has the advantage of avoiding some overloading of the Variorum Text with variants; however, the spelling "it's" is preserved in the collation when it appears in a transcript in another hand or in a printed text. Holograph "it's" and (with equal frequency) "its'" are given uniformly as "it's".

Other of Coleridge's (and sometimes of his printers') usages have been normalised according to modern practice. No attempt has been made, for example, to represent such variations in the forms of letters as the long s (ſ), or the use of roman forms for some Greek capitals, especially U for Υ; J has been distinguished from I; the Greek ligatures that Coleridge regularly used for στ and ου have been expanded; erratic word-spacing has been normalised. This latter has led to a distinction Coleridge did not himself make clearly, and which may affect the prosody, between elision of a final vowel before a word beginning with a vowel and the merging of two vowels in this position (crasis); spacing has been closed up in the latter case. Accents, however, in all languages, have been transcribed as accurately as possible, favouring normal modern practice where the angle is doubtful or where they float between two vowels in manuscript. In Greek, the breathings and accents which Coleridge often placed above initial capitals have been given in

xli

their usual position, in front of the letter. Typographical ornaments such as swelled rules and drop initials (together with capitalisation of first words) are only occasionally noted.

See the corresponding section of Volume One, and the introduction to that volume, for fuller discussion and elucidation of the practice of the present edition.

CONVENTIONS USED IN TRANSCRIPTION
AND IN TEXTUAL NOTES

⟨thus⟩	A word or passage inserted between lines or marked by C for insertion from another place. More lengthy insertions are given in a note
⟨h1⟩	The reported variant occurs in MS h1 as an insert
⸍ d̶	A deleted mark of punctuation or single letter
t̶h̶u̶s̶	A deleted word
t̶h̶u̶s̶ s̶o̶	Continuous deletion of words
t̶h̶i̶s̶ t̶h̶u̶s̶	Successive deletions of alternative words and phrases
h̶1̶	The reported variant was written and then deleted in MS h1
⟨h̶1̶⟩	The reported variant was inserted and then deleted in MS h1
h̶1̶res	The reported variant was deleted but then restored in MS h1
?⸍ ?d̶	Deletion of an uncertainly read mark of punctuation or single letter
?t̶h̶u̶s̶ or ?t̶h̶u̶s̶/t̶h̶i̶s̶	Deletion of an uncertainly read word
?Brothers	An uncertain reading
?And/?Mind	Suggested readings of a difficult manuscript text

Note. The following entries concerning the use of the full point in reported readings indicate the practice of the present volume where it seems possible to guess at the number of missing or illegible characters. See the corresponding list in vol I for the practice adopted in other cases.

⌐.⌐	A completely illegible mark of punctuation or single letter
⌐. . . . .⌐	A completely illegible series of five letters
[.]	A deleted illegible mark of punctuation or single letter
[. . . . .]	A deleted illegible series of five letters
⌐thus⌐	Text supplied editorially to supplement a defective or lacunose source
|	Indicates line-division
soft mild	Used selectively in vol II to clarify cases where a
←mild→	variant consisting of a single word is centred on a variant which is generally much longer and consists of several words

24⁺	Reference to material excluded from the line-numbering (often a line-space) immediately following line 24. Also used to introduce material not admitted to the main text, occurring in the reported source at a point just after the line numbered 24 in the main text
⁻24	Reference to material excluded from the line-numbering (often a line-space) immediately preceding line 24
24a	The first half of line 24
24b	The second half of line 24
29.1	First alternative version of line 29 (vol II only)
358.1.1	First line of the first sequence of extra lines appearing between lines 358 and 359 in the Reading Text lineation (vol II only)
358.2.1	First line of the second sequence of extra lines appearing between lines 358 and 359 in the Reading Text lineation (vol II only)
1 2 3 or MSS 1 2 3	Sigla for manuscripts, numbered chronologically
1 2 3 or PR *1 2 3*	Sigla for printed texts, numbered chronologically
TEXTS *1* 1 2–*4* 2 3 5	A series of printed and manuscript sources in their presumed chronological order
3ⁱᵐᵖ	TEXT 3 is imperfect, most often lacking the RH edge
3ᵛᵃʳ	TEXT 3 as printed here differs from previous *CL/CN* printings
□	All of the sources which are being collated in the poem or play in question
⊠ *1* 3	All of the sources which are being collated in the poem or play in question, *with the exception of* PR *1* and MS 3
example,] *1* exanple, • 2 exemple,	Reading "example," adopted in the text, but variant "exanple," found in PR *1* and variant "exemple," in MS 2

Deletions of larger blocks of text are shown with a large cross, where necessary accompanied by an editorial note describing how the deletion was made (heavily, hurriedly, with a single careful line, as part of a process of successive revision, etc).

Brackets, in addition to their use to indicate illegible deletions (see above), are used to contain the names of authors who published anonymously: "[Thomas Allsop]". And they are used on a few occasions to mark off various kinds of interpolated editorial comment. The varying use of the same symbol should not in practice lead to confusion, and a note is added where it might.

ABBREVIATIONS

The place of publication is London unless otherwise noted.

Adelung	Johann Christian Adelung *Versuch eines vollständigen grammatisch-kritischen Wörterbuches der Hochdeutschen Mundart, mit beständiger Vergleichung der übrigen Mundarten, besonders aber der Oberdeutschen* (1st ed in 5 pts Leipzig 1774–86; 2nd ed in 4 pts Leipzig 1793–1801)
AG	Anne Gillman, wife of James Gillman
Allsop	[Thomas Allsop] *Letters, Conversations and Recollections of S. T. Coleridge* (2 vols 1836)
als	autograph letter signed
AR (1825, 1831)	S. T. Coleridge *Aids to Reflection* (1825, 2nd ed 1831)
AR (CC)	S. T. Coleridge *Aids to Reflection* ed John Beer (London & Princeton 1993) = *CC* IX
AV	The Authorised Version—or "King James Version"—of the Bible, in modern orthography
BA	Friedrich Schiller *Sämtliche Werke* (Berliner Ausgabe) ed H.-G. Thalheim et al (Berlin & Weimar 1980–) IV *Wallenstein, Maria Stuart, Die Jungfrau von Orleans* ed Anita and Jochen Golz (Berlin & Weimar 1984)
BCP	*The Book of Common Prayer and Administration of the Sacraments and Other Rites and Ceremonies of the Church according to the Use of the Church of England*
BL (1817)	S. T. Coleridge *Biographia Literaria; or, Biographical Sketches of my Literary Life and Opinions* (2 vols 1817)
BL (1847)	S. T. Coleridge, *Biographia Literaria* ed HNC and SC (2 vols 1847)
BL (1907)	S. T. Coleridge *Biographia Literaria* ed John Shawcross (2 vols Oxford 1907)
BL (CC)	S. T. Coleridge *Biographia Literaria* ed James Engell and W. Jackson Bate (2 vols London & Princeton 1983) = *CC* VII
BL&J	*Byron's Letters and Journals* ed Leslie A. Marchand (12 vols and suppl London & Cambridge, Mass 1973–82, 1994)
Bl Mag	*Blackwood's Edinburgh Magazine* (Edinburgh 1817–1980)
BM	British Library, formerly Library of the British Museum
BNYPL	*Bulletin of the New York Public Library* (New York 1897–1977), continued as *Bulletin of Research in the Humanities*
BPL	Avon Reference Library, formerly Bristol Public Library, College Green, Bristol
B Poets	*The Works of the British Poets* ed Robert Anderson (13 vols Edinburgh & London 1792–5; XIV 1807)

Bristol LB	George Whalley "The Bristol Library Borrowings of Southey and Coleridge" *Library* IV (Sept 1949) 114–32
C	Samuel Taylor Coleridge
C&SH	George Whalley *Coleridge and Sara Hutchinson and the Asra Poems* (1955)
Carlyon	Clement Carlyon *Early Years and Late Reflections* (4 vols 1836–58)
C Bibl (Haney)	John L. Haney *A Bibliography of S. T. Coleridge* (Philadelphia 1903)
C Bibl (Wise)	T. J. Wise *A Bibliography of the Writings in Prose and Verse of Samuel Taylor Coleridge* (1913) and *Supplement* (1919)
C Bibl (Wise TLP)	T. J. Wise *Two Lake Poets . . . William Wordsworth and Samuel Taylor Coleridge* (1927)
CC	*The Collected Works of Samuel Taylor Coleridge* general ed Kathleen Coburn (London & Princeton 1969–)
CG	Theatre Royal, Covent Garden
Christensen	Lorenzo Francis Christensen "Three Romantic Poets and the Drama" (diss Harvard 1934; HUL Archives HU90-2600)
C in Germany	Edith J. Morley "Coleridge in Germany (1799)" in *Wordsworth and Coleridge: Studies in Honor of George McLean Harper* ed E. L. Griggs (Princeton 1939)
CL	Charles Lamb
CL	*Collected Letters of Samuel Taylor Coleridge* ed Earl Leslie Griggs (6 vols Oxford & New York 1956–71)
C Life (G)	James Gillman *The Life of Samuel Taylor Coleridge* (1838)
CM	S. T. Coleridge *Marginalia* ed George Whalley and H. J. Jackson (6 vols London & Princeton 1980–) = *CC* XII
CN	*The Notebooks of Samuel Taylor Coleridge* ed Kathleen Coburn, Merton Christensen, and Anthony J. Harding (5 double vols New York, Princeton, & London 1957–)
Coffman	Ralph J. Coffman *Coleridge's Library: A Bibliography of Books Owned or Read by Samuel Taylor Coleridge* (Boston, Mass 1987)
Cottle *E Rec*	Joseph Cottle *Early Recollections; Chiefly Relating to the Late Samuel Taylor Coleridge* (2 vols 1837)
Cottle *Rem*	Joseph Cottle *Reminiscences of Samuel Taylor Coleridge and Robert Southey* (1847)
CRB	*Henry Crabb Robinson on Books and their Writers* ed Edith J. Morley (3 vols 1938)
CRC	*The Correspondence of Henry Crabb Robinson with the Wordsworth Circle* ed Edith J. Morley (2 vols Oxford 1927)
DC	Derwent Coleridge

DCL	Wordsworth Library, formerly Dove Cottage Library, Grasmere
DeQ	Thomas De Quincey
DeQ Works	*The Collected Writings of Thomas De Quincey* ed David Masson (14 vols Edinburgh 1889–90)
DL	Theatre Royal, Drury Lane
DNB	*Dictionary of National Biography* (1885–)
Dr	*Wallenstein: Ein dramatisches Gedicht von Schiller* (2 vols Tübingen 1800) (1st edition)
DW	Dorothy Wordsworth
DWJ	*Journals of Dorothy Wordsworth* ed E. de Selincourt (2 vols 1941)
DWJ (M)	*Journals of Dorothy Wordsworth: The Alfoxden Journal 1798* [and] *The Grasmere Journals 1800–1803* ed Mary Moorman (Oxford 1971)
EC	editorial commentary accompanying reading text of poems in vol I and text of plays in vol III
EC	Edward Coleridge, C's nephew
Ed Rev	*The Edinburgh Review* (Edinburgh & London 1802–1929)
EHC	E. H. Coleridge
ELG	Earl Leslie Griggs
EOT	S. T. Coleridge *Essays on his Own Times* ed Sara Coleridge (3 vols 1850)
EOT (*CC*)	S. T. Coleridge *Essays on his Times in "The Morning Post" and "The Courier"* ed David V. Erdman (3 vols London & Princeton 1978) = *CC* III
Folger	The Folger Shakespeare Library, Washington, DC
Friend (*CC*)	S. T. Coleridge *The Friend* ed Barbara Rooke (2 vols London & Princeton 1969) = *CC* IV
GC	George Coleridge, C's brother
Göttingen LB	A. D. Snyder "Books Borrowed by Coleridge from the Library of the University of Göttingen, 1799" *MP* xxv (1928) 377–80
Grantz	Carl Leon Grantz "Letters of Sara Coleridge: A Calendar and Index to her Manuscript Correspondence in the University of Texas Library" (diss University of Texas at Austin 2 vols 1966)
Grimm	Jakob and Wilhelm Grimm *Deutsches Wörterbuch* (16 vols Leipzig 1854–1961)
HC	Hartley Coleridge
HCR	Henry Crabb Robinson

HEHL	The Henry E. Huntington Library and Art Gallery, San Marino
HM	Huntington Manuscript
HNC	Henry Nelson Coleridge
HRC	Harry Ransom Humanities Research Center, University of Texas, Austin
HUL	The Houghton Library, Harvard University
H Works	*The Complete Works of William Hazlitt* ed P. P. Howe (21 vols 1930–4)
IS (1979)	*Inquiring Spirit: A New Presentation of Coleridge* ed Kathleen Coburn (rev ed Toronto 1979)
JDC	James Dykes Campbell
JDC facsimile	*Coleridge's Poems: A Facsimile Reproduction of the Proofs and MSS. of Some of the Poems* ed James Dykes Campbell (1899)
Jesus LB	J.C.C. Mays "Coleridge's Borrowings from Jesus College Library, 1791–94" *Transactions of the Cambridge Bibliographical Society* VIII (1985) 557–81
JG	James Gillman
Johnson	Samuel Johnson *A Dictionary of the English Language, in Which the Words are Deduced from their Originals, and Illustrated in their Different Significations by Examples from the Best Writers; to Which are Prefixed a History of the Language, and an English Grammar* (3rd ed 2 vols 1765)
JTC	John Taylor Coleridge
KC	Kathleen Coburn
Lawrence	Berta Lawrence *Coleridge and Wordsworth in Somerset* (Newton Abbot 1970)
LB	William Wordsworth and Samuel Taylor Coleridge *Lyrical Ballads* (various)
LCL	Loeb Classical Library
Lects 1795 (*CC*)	S. T. Coleridge *Lectures 1795: On Politics and Religion* ed Lewis Patton and Peter Mann (London & Princeton 1971)= *CC* I
Lects 1808– 1819 (*CC*)	S. T. Coleridge *Lectures 1808–1819: On Literature* ed Reginald A. Foakes (2 vols London & Princeton 1987)= *CC* V
LH	left-hand (e.g. left-hand page or left-hand end of verse lines)
LL	*The Letters of Charles Lamb, to Which are Added those of his Sister Mary Lamb* ed E. V. Lucas (3 vols 1935)
LL (M)	*The Letters of Charles and Mary Anne Lamb, 1796–1817* ed Edwin W. Marrs Jr (3 vols Ithaca 1975–8)

Lockhart	Friedrich Schiller *Wallenstein: A Dramatic Poem* tr C.G.N. Lockhart (Edinburgh & London 1887)
Logic (CC)	S. T. Coleridge *Logic* ed J. R. de J. Jackson (London & Princeton 1981) = *CC* XIII
LR	*The Literary Remains of Samuel Taylor Coleridge* ed Henry Nelson Coleridge (4 vols 1836–9)
LS (CC)	S. T. Coleridge *Lay Sermons* [being *The Statesman's Manual* and *A Lay Sermon*] ed R. J. White (London & Princeton 1972) = *CC* VI
L Works	*The Works of Charles and Mary Lamb* ed E. V. Lucas (6 vols 1912)
M Chron	*The Morning Chronicle* (1769–1962)
MH	Mary Hutchinson, later wife of WW
Migne *PL*	*Patriologiae Cursus Completus . . . Series Latina* ed J. P. Migne (221 vols Paris 1844–64)
Minnow	*Minnow among Tritons: Mrs S. T. Coleridge's Letters to Thomas Poole, 1799–1834* ed Stephen Potter (1934)
Misc C	*Coleridge's Miscellaneous Criticism* ed T. M. Raysor (1936)
ML	Mary Lamb
MLN	*Modern Language Notes* (Baltimore 1886–)
MLR	*Modern Language Review* (1905–)
MP	*Modern Philology* (Chicago 1903–)
M Post	*The Morning Post* (1772–1937)
M Rev	*The Monthly Review* (1749–1845)
Mrs C	Sara Coleridge née Fricker, wife of C
MS	a manuscript text of any title, e.g. *Love* MS 1
MW	Mary Wordsworth née Hutchinson, wife of WW
N	Notebook of Samuel Taylor Coleridge (numbered or lettered) in ms. References are given by folio
N&Q	*Notes and Queries* (1849–)
Newlyn	Lucy Newlyn *Coleridge, Wordsworth, and the Poetry of Allusion* (Oxford 1986)
NYPL	New York Public Library
OED	*The Oxford English Dictionary, Being a Corrected Reissue . . . of "A New English Dictionary on Historical Principles"* (12 vols Oxford 1970)
Omniana	*Omniana; or, Horae Otiosiores* [ed RS with articles by C] (2 vols 1812)
P&DW (RHS)	S. T. Coleridge *Poetical and Dramatic Works* ed R. H. Shepherd (4 vols 1877–80)
PEGS	*Publications of the English Goethe Society* NS (1924–)

Pforzheimer	The Carl H. Pforzheimer Library, New York (now part of NYPL)
PL	John Milton *Paradise Lost* (see also Migne above)
P Lects (1949)	*The Philosophical Lectures of Samuel Taylor Coleridge* ed Kathleen Coburn (London & New York 1949)
PM	Prime Minister
PML	The Pierpont Morgan Library, New York
PMLA	*Publications of the Modern Language Society of America* (New York 1884–)
Poems	Samuel Taylor Coleridge *Poems* (various: see annex B)
Poole	M. E. Sandford *Thomas Poole and his Friends* (2 vols 1888)
PR	a printed text of any title, e.g. *Love* PR 2
Prelude	William Wordsworth *The Prelude or Growth of a Poet's Mind* ed Ernest de Selincourt rev Helen Darbishire (Oxford 1959)
PW	S. T. Coleridge *Poetical Works* (various: see annex B)
PW (EHC)	*The Complete Poetical Works of Samuel Taylor Coleridge* ed E. H. Coleridge (2 vols Oxford 1912)
PW (JDC)	*The Poetical Works of Samuel Taylor Coleridge* ed J. D. Campbell (1893)
PW (RG)	*Poems of Samuel Taylor Coleridge* ed Richard Garnett (1898)
Reed I	Mark L. Reed *Wordsworth: The Chronology of the Early Years, 1770–1799* (Cambridge, Mass 1967)
Reed II	Mark L. Reed *Wordsworth: The Chronology of the Middle Years, 1800–1815* (Cambridge, Mass 1975)
RES	*Review of English Studies* (Oxford 1925–)
RH	right-hand (e.g. right-hand page or right-hand end of verse lines)
RHS	Richard Herne Shepherd
Robberds	J. W. Robberds *A Memoir of the Life and Writings of the Late William Taylor of Norwich* (2 vols 1843)
RS	Robert Southey
RT	reading text of poems (= vol I)
RX	John Livingston Lowes *The Road to Xanadu* (rev ed Boston, Mass 1930)
SB	*Studies in Bibliography* (Charlottesville, Va 1948–)
SC	Sara Coleridge (daughter of C and wife of HNC)
SCB	*Southey's Common-place Book* ed J. W. Warter (4 vols 1849–51)

Scott L	*The Letters of Sir Walter Scott* ed H.J.C. Grierson (12 vols 1932–7)
SH	Sara Hutchinson
Shaver	Chester L. Shaver and Alice C. Shaver *Wordsworth's Library: A Catalogue* (New York 1979)
Sh C	*Coleridge's Shakespearean Criticism* ed T. M. Raysor (2nd ed 2 vols 1960)
SH's Poets	"Sara Hutchinson's Poets": SH's commonplace book (DCL)
SL	S. T. Coleridge *Sibylline Leaves* (1817)
S Letters (Curry)	*New Letters of Robert Southey* ed Kenneth Curry (2 vols New York & London 1965)
S Letters (Warter)	*A Selection from the Letters of Robert Southey* ed J. W. Warter (4 vols 1856)
S Life (CS)	*Life and Correspondence of Robert Southey* ed C. C. Southey (6 vols 1849–50)
SM (*CC*)	S. T. Coleridge *The Statesman's Manual* in *Lay Sermons* ed R. J. White (London & Princeton 1972) = *CC* VI
Sonnets (1796)	Untitled collection of sonnets from various authors [ed C (?Bath/Bristol 1796)]
Stephens	Fran Carlock Stephens "Cottle, Wise, and 'MS. Ashley 408'" *Publications of the Bibliographical Society of America* LXVIII (1974) 391–406
SW&F (*CC*)	S. T. Coleridge *Shorter Works and Fragments* ed H. J. Jackson and J. R. de J. Jackson (2 vols London & Princeton 1995) = *CC* XI
TEXTS	both manuscript and printed texts of any title, e.g. *Love* TEXTS 1 2
TLS	*The Times Literary Supplement* (London 1902–)
TN	Variorum text of poems in vol II and textual notes to plays in vol III
TP	Thomas Poole
TT (1835)	*Specimens of the Table Talk of Samuel Taylor Coleridge* ed H. N. Coleridge (2 vols 1835)
TT (*CC*)	S. T. Coleridge *Table Talk* ed Carl R. Woodring (2 vols London & Princeton 1990) = *CC* XIV
TWC	*The Wordsworth Circle* (Philadelphia 1970–)
Two Letters	Peter Mann "Two Autograph Letters of S. T. Coleridge" *RES* NS XXV (1974) 312–17
UTQ	*University of Toronto Quarterly* (Toronto 1930–)
V&A	The Library, Victoria and Albert Museum
VAR	Variorum text of poems (= vol II)

VCL	The Coleridge Collection, Victoria College Library, University of Toronto
Watchman (CC)	S. T. Coleridge *The Watchman* ed Lewis Patton (London & Princeton 1970)=*CC* II
WEPF	William Wordsworth *Early Poems and Fragments 1785–1797* ed Carol Landon and Jared Curtis (Ithaca & London 1997)
WL (*E* rev)	*Letters of William and Dorothy Wordsworth: The Early Years* ed Ernest de Selincourt rev Chester L. Shaver (Oxford 1967)
WL (*L* rev)	*Letters of William and Dorothy Wordsworth: The Later Years* ed Alan G. Hill from the ed by Ernest de Selincourt (4 vols Oxford 1978–88)
WL (*M* rev)	*Letters of William and Dorothy Wordsworth: The Middle Years* ed Ernest de Selincourt rev Mary Moorman and Alan G. Hill (2 vols Oxford 1969–70)
wm	watermark
Woltmann	[Professor Karl Ludwig Woltmann] "Ueber das Schauspiel, *die Piccolomini*, und die Vorstellung desselben auf dem Nazionaltheater zu Berlin" *Jahrbücher der preußischen Monarchie* (Mar 1799) 278–313
Woodring	Carl R. Woodring *Politics in the Poetry of Coleridge* (Madison 1961)
Woof	R. S. Woof "Wordsworth's Poetry and Stuart's Newspapers: 1797–1803" *SB* XV (1962) 148–89
W Prose	*The Prose Works of William Wordsworth* ed W.J.B. Owen and J. W. Smyser (3 vols Oxford 1974)
WPW	*The Poetical Works of William Wordsworth* ed Ernest de Selincourt and Helen Darbishire (rev ed 5 vols Oxford 1952–9)
WRCP	William Wordsworth *The Ruined Cottage; The Pedlar* ed James Butler (Ithaca & Hassocks 1979)
WW	William Wordsworth

POEMS
(VARIORUM TEXT)

1. "FIRST ATTEMPT AT MAKING A VERSE"

A. DATE

1782–3? *C Life* (G) 18 records that the poem was C's "first attempt at making a verse", when C was "about eight years of age"—i.e. c 1780–1. However, JG also describes how it was written while C was at Christ's Hospital—which C entered in 1782 at the age of nine years and nine months—presumably soon after he arrived in Jul, and possibly before he moved from Hertford to the main school in London (Sept).

B. TEXT

Quoted in *C Life* (G) 18.

1–4. JG "O Lord . . . *tad*,"

2. FRAGMENTS OF AN ODE ON PUNNING

A. DATE

After 1785? C's later references to the poem (*CL* VI 629fn: to JG Jr [22 Oct 1826]; Notebook 42 ff 71ᵛ–72ʳ) are to a schoolboy performance. Another, however, in 1803, refers to the poem as still to be written (*CL* II 999: to Sir George and Lady Beaumont 1 Oct 1803).

B. TEXT

BM Add MS 47537=Notebook 42 ff 71ᵛ–72ʳ, Dec 1829.

C. GENERAL NOTE

C twice gave the title as "an Ode on Punning" (in the Notebook version and in *CL* II 999), and once as "an Ode to PUNNING" (*CL* VI 629fn). The RT exactly reproduces the fragments quoted in the Notebook, where they are separated not by asterisks but by linking explanation.

In *CN* III 3542n KC asserts that the opening, "SPELLING . . ." (q *CL* II 999=PML MA 1581–4), should be "HELL in a slave state", and so it indeed

3

appears at the present time, though the letters forming KC's "n a slave" are not completely legible. However, the passage was written with gout medicine instead of ink, was faded when ELG transcribed it, and must have faded further in the interval between his and KC's reading, as it has in the time between KC's reading and the present editor's (1988). It is reasonable to assume that ELG might have preserved the original reading of the opening words—one which coincides with the notebook he is unlikely to have seen and which undoubtedly makes better sense.

3. DURA NAVIS

A. DATE

1786–7? Possibly 1790–1? C says in one of his two notes on the poem of 1823–4 that it was written at school when he was fourteen. He none the less told J. H. Green that a prose exercise which makes use of the same simile of the current and maelstrom was also written when he was fourteen (*CL* VI 934: [7 Apr 1833])—even though it was not copied out until Jun 1788 (*SW&F—CC—*3–4).

B. TEXT

BM Add MS 34225 ff 1–4. Four leaves, 10.8×18.8 cm; wm Britannia in oval surmounted by crown; chain-lines 2.6 cm; versos blank. Fair copy in C's very early hand, unsigned.

C's two notes dating from 1823–4 are written in the large spaces at the foot of ff 1^r and 2^r.

title. ms *Dura Navis* **6.** ms ⌐Schemes **15.** ms ~~majestie~~ destructive
36. ms ⟨ardor⟩ **40.** ms ~~arn~~ fires **62.** ms ⌐Love **64.** ms Life

8$^+$, 16$^+$, 24$^+$, 40$^+$, 56$^+$. MS has rules.
41, 42. The commas at the end of each line both look like full points; the second has the force of a colon.

4. GREEK EPIGRAM ON APHRODITE
AND ATHENA

A. DATE

1786–7? 1788–9? 1790–1?

B. TEXT

Library of Congress (Manuscript Division) John Davis Batchelder Autograph Collection f 316ʳ. Single leaf, 16.2×11.4 cm; fragmentary wm; no chain-lines (wove). The leaf has at some time been folded in two and sealed with wax (by C?), which has mutilated it. Fair copy signed "S. T. C. | Ætat suæ 15—". A far from accurate translation is written, in an unknown 19th-century hand, beneath each line.

C. GENERAL NOTE

The fair copy is in C's late hand, and was perhaps made in the 1820s. Other schoolboy poems he recalled from that early time are often dated one or two years too early. Given that James Boyer sometimes set exercises on the same themes as those set for the Browne Medals at Cambridge, it might even date from after late Jan 1790, when the subject for Greek and Latin epigrams was "Artis est artem celare" (tr "The art is to hide art"). If it does date from 1790–1, it may be the same Ποιημάτιον which C sent to GC in Feb–Mar 1791 (=poem **22.X2**).

The RT reproduces the untitled ms exactly.

4.X1. TRANSLATIONS OF SYNESIUS

C claimed in *BL* to have translated at least one of Synesius' *Hymns* "from the Greek into English Anacreontics before my 15th year" (*BL* ch 12—*CC*—ɪ 247fn). Copies of *BL* (1817) differ at this point, reading either "the eight Hymn" or "the eight Hymns", and C perhaps dictated, or intended to write, "the first eight", for there are in fact ten hymns. In 1794, however, he told his brother GC that he had taken Canter's edition of Synesius with him when he left Cambridge to join the Dragoons, along with Barbou's *Casimir* (*CL* ɪ 76–7: to GC [26 Mar 1794]), because he intended to translate them. It appears from this that Synesius was to have been included in the volume of translations of "the best Lyric

Poems from the Greek" which C began to plan from Jan 1793 onwards (*CL* I 46; cf **50.X1** *Imitations from the Modern Latin Poets*).

The edition C possessed and was forced to sell at Reading in 1794 comprises the Greek text with Latin translations of four prose works and the ten hymns: Synesius *De dono ad Paeonium . . . Hymni* ed W. Canter (Basle 1567). The other edition of Synesius' *Hymns* which he is known to have owned is in *Poetae Graeci Veteres Tragici, Comici, Lyrici, Epigrammatarii* ed P. de la Rovière (2 pts in 1 Geneva 1614), which was sent to him with its companion volume from Keswick in 1813 and used for *BL*. The hymns are differently numbered in the two editions (the first eight in Canter's system are 3–6, 2, 7, and 9 in the other; the first eight in the other are 9, 5, 1–4, and 7 in Canter; the more recent modern editions return to Canter's numbering). In Canter's *Hymn* 8 (otherwise 9), Πολυήρατε . . ., Synesius invokes Christ and describes his descent to hell and return to heaven with the souls he has delivered. *Hymn* 8 in the other system (7 in Canter) is a much less likely choice: also addressed to Christ, it is a prayer for Synesius himself and his family, and for the chastity of his wife.

There is evidence that in his Christ's Hospital days C was interested in theological controversy, and precocious in his Greek reading (cf *L Works* II 24–5 q *BL*—*CC*—I 15n). The somewhat self-conscious and complicated way in which he asserts his youth suggests the greater claim, to have translated eight hymns (these would amount to some eighteen or nineteen pages in the English translation by Augustine Fitzgerald: Synesius *Essays and Hymns*—2 vols Oxford 1930—II 372–92), but the sixty-five-odd lines of the eighth (or ninth) hymn might be considered achievement enough for a boy of thirteen. However that may be, translations made then may well have been lost or appeared unsatisfactory in 1793–4. It may be relevant too that in 1796 C showed a degree of disrespect in describing Synesius as a "hyper-platonic Jargonist", though he was not then referring to the *Hymns* (*CN* I 200), and that he appears not to have mentioned his name again until 1813–15 (*CN* III 4189). It is possible that fragments of the Synesius translations will come to light, just as imitations of Casimir have survived (poems **67–8**), and that such translations will date from c 1794 rather than from 1786. See also **50.X1** *Imitations from the Modern Latin Poets*, **55.X1** *Laus Astronomiae*.

5. EASTER HOLIDAYS

A. DATE

Apr–May 1787. Easter fell on 8 Apr; the first known version of the poem is included in a letter of 12 May.

B. TEXT

C copied out the stanzas in an als to his brother Luke, dated 12 May 1787. *CL* I 3–4 printed them from the ms in the possession of A. D. Coleridge. The ms was not among those afterwards acquired by HRC from A. D. Coleridge, and it is not in the possession of his family. Its present whereabouts is unknown.

The RT reproduces the printed version of the ms, though it should be noted that ELG may not reproduce ms details such as superscripts exactly.

6. NIL PEJUS EST CAELIBE VITÂ

A. DATE

Before 12 May 1787.

B. TEXTS

1. BM MS Ashley 3506=James Boyer's *Liber Aureus* vol I ff 29ᵛ–30ʳ. Fair copy in C's hand, signed "Samuel Taylor Coleridge 1787".

2 [=RT]. C copied out the stanzas in an als to his brother Luke on 12 May 1787. *CL* I 4–5 printed them from the ms in the possession of A. D. Coleridge (present whereabouts unknown).
The beginning of line 9 (the first five letters of the first word) is missing. ELG might not reproduce exactly such details of the ms as indentation, superior letters, and ligatures.

title. □ Nil pejus est cælibe vitâ.

```
⁻1 □              Verse 1ˢᵗ
 1 □  What pleasures shall he ever find?
 2 □  What joys shall ever glad his heart?
 3 □  Or who shall heal his wounded mind,
 4 □  If tortur'd by misfortune's smart?
 5 □  Who Hymeneal bliss will never prove,
 6 □  That more than friendship, friendship mix'd with love.
       [Line-space]
⁻7 □              Verse 2ᵈ
 7 □  Then without child or tender wife,
 8 1  To drive away each care, each ⟵—sigh,—⟶
    2        soothe              woeborn sigh
 9 □  Lonely he treads the paths of life,
10 □  A stranger to Affection's tye:
11 □  And when from death he meets his final doom,
```

12 □ No mourning wife with tears of love shall wet his tomb.
       [*Line-space*]
‾13 □   Verse, 3ᵈ
13 □ Tho' Fortune riches, honours, pow'r
14 □ Had giv'n with every other toy,
15 □ Those gilded trifles of the hour,
16 □ Those painted Nothings sure to cloy;
17 □ He dies forgot, his name no son shall bear
18 □ To shew, the man so blest once breath'd the vital air.

title. 2 caelibe vitâ   ‾**1.** 2 1st   **5.** 2 Hymaeneal   ‾**7.** 2 2d   **7.** 2 wife
9. 2ⁱᵐᵖ y he   2 life   **10.** 2 tye;   ‾**13.** 2 Verse 3d   **13.** 2 Fortune,
14. 2 giv'n,   2 toy;   **16.** 2 nothings   2 cloy: **17.** 2 bear,

5–6, 11–12, 17–18. MS 1 gives these pairs stepped indentation.

7. DE MEDIO FONTE LEPORUM
SURGIT ALIQUID AMARI

A. DATE

1789.

B. TEXT

BM MS Ashley 3506=James Boyer's *Liber Aureus* vol ɪ ff 40ʳ–41ʳ. Fair copy
in C's hand, signed "Sam: T. Coleridge 1789".
   This is the second poem C copied into the book. It was printed (var) by
William Trollope *A History of the Royal Foundation of Christ's Hospital* (1834)
192, undoubtedly without C's knowledge.

title. ms De medio fonte leporum surgit aliquid amari.   **27.** wooes] ms woes

8. OH! MIHI PRÆTERITOS
REFERAT SI JUPITER ANNOS!

A. DATE

1789.

BM MS Ashley 3506=James Boyer's *Liber Aureus* vol I f 41^{r-v}. Fair copy in C's hand, signed "S. T. Coleridge 1789".

This is the third poem C copied into the book.

title. ms Oh! mihi præteritos referat si Jupiter annos!   **6⁺, 12⁺**. MS has rules

9. SONNET: TO MY MUSE

A. DATE

1789? 1789–91? PR *1* appends the date 1789; but C's recollection of early dates was frequently a year or more too early. Also, though it begins the sequence of sonnets in MS 1 below, it constitutes a general reflection on the kind of poetry which the subsequent sonnets represent, and is placed fairly well on in the PR *1* sequence of Juvenile Poems.

B. TEXTS

1 [=RT]. BM Add MS 47551=Ottery Copy Book f 25^r. Fair copy in C's hand.

1. PW (1834).

C. GENERAL NOTE

PW (JDC) 562A cites an undated ms, signed "S. T. Coleridge", which appears to have been lost.

title. 1 Sonnet 1. To my Muse. • *1* TO THE MUSE.

1	□	Though no bold flights to thee belong,
2	□	And though thy lays with conscious fear
3	□	Shrink from Judgement's eye severe,
4	□	Yet much I thank thee, Spirit of my song!
		[*Line-space*]
5	1	For, lowly Muse! thy sweet employ
	1	lovely
6	□	Exalts my soul, refines my breast,
7	□	Gives each pure pleasure keener zest,
8	□	And softens Sorrow into pensive Joy.
		[*Line-space*]
9	□	From thee I learnt the wish to bless,
10	□	From thee to commune with my heart,

11 □   From thee, dear Muse! the gayer part
12 □   To laugh with pity at the crouds, that press
13 □   Where Fashion flaunts her robes by Folly spun,
14 □   Whose hues gay-varying wanton in the Sun!
14⁺*1* 1789.

1. *1* Tho' *1* belong;   **2.** *1* tho' *1* fear,   **3.** *1* Judgment's   **8.** *1* sorrow
9. *1* learn'd   **10.** *1* heart;   **11.** *1* part,   **12.** *1* Pity *1* crowds,   **14.** *1* gay
1 sun.

4⁺, 8⁺. No line-space in PR *1*.

10. SONNET: "AS LATE I JOURNEY'D O'ER TH' EXTENSIVE PLAIN"

A. DATE

Sept 1789? early summer 1791? See vol I headnote for doubts concerning the dates that C himself gives with MSS 1 and 2.

B. TEXTS

1. In the possession of Erwin Schwarz (Jul 1982). Single large folded leaf, 46.0×36.2/37.9 cm overall; wm horn within shield beneath crown I C T TAY-LOR; countermark Q R; chain-lines 4.5 cm. Written on the last of four pages, which also contain **30** *Happiness*, as part of a letter to GC of 22 Jun 1791 (*CL* I 14). There is a photocopy of the complete letter in BM RP 2277 (i).

C says that he includes the poem because he accidentally found it as he looked over his papers, "and by the date of it see that I wrote it just after my return from the country" (*CL* I 11). He dates the poem (at the end) "Sept: 1789." The transcript by John May Jr in the Green Ottery Copy Book f 16ʳ⁻ᵛ (VCL S MS Fl.3) has no textual significance.

2 [=RT]. BM Add MS 47551 = Ottery Copy Book f 26ʳ. Transcript by C. The sonnet is second in a sequence of at least ten transcribed by C. It is described, after the title, as "Written Septembʳ 1789."

3. University of Pennsylvania Library (Special Collections) MS Eng 13 = JTC's Commonplace Book p 163. Transcript by JTC; subscribed "S.T.C.".

One might assume that JTC's transcript was a careless conflation of MS 2 and PR *1*, except that its probable date and JTC's habits of transcription make this unlikely. Other transcripts by JTC also represent versions a little later than the Ottery Copy Book texts, and have independent interest.

1. PW (1834).

The coincidence between MS 3 and PR *1* in line 8 lends authority to the PR *1* reading of line 14. One might otherwise have been tempted to dismiss the PR *1* variations from MSS 1 2 as being entirely due to HNC.

title. 1 3 Sonnet. • 2 Sonnet 2 • *1* LIFE.

1	1	As late I journey'd ~~o'er~~ o'er th' extensive plain,
	⊠1	o'er
2	☐	Where native Otter sports his scanty stream,
3	☐	Musing in torpid Woe a Sister's pain—
4	☐	The glorious prospect woke me from the dream.
5	☐	At every step it widen'd to my sight—
6	1	Woods, meadows, verdant hills, and barren steep
	2 *1*	Wood, Meadow, Hill, dreary
	3	& ←steep→
7	☐	Following in quick succession of Delight –
8	1 2	Till all—at once my ravish'd eye did sweep!
	3 *1*	did my eye ravish'd
9	☐	May this (I cried) my course thro' life pourtray!
10	☐	New scenes of Wisdom may each step display,
11	⊓	And Knowlege open, as my days advance:
12	1	Till, when Death pours at length th' undarken'd ray,
	⊠1	what time Death shall pour
13	☐	My eye shall dart thro' infinite expanse,
14	1	While Thought suspended lies in Transport's blissful trance!
	2 3	Rapture's
	1	And lie
14⁺	1	Sept: 1789.

title. 3 Sonnet **1.** *1* journied 3 *1* the ⊠1 plain **2.** 2 stream **3.** 3 *1* woe *1* sister's ⊠1 pain, **4.** *1* dream **5.** ⊠1 sight, **6.** 3 meadow, 3 Hill 2 Steep • *1* Steep. **7.** 2 delight; • 3 delight • *1* delight, **8.** ⊠1 once— **9.** *1* through ⊠1 Life 2 pourtray, • 3 pourtray • *1* portray! **10.** 2 Scenes 3 *1* wisdom **11.** 3 *1* knowledge open ⊠1 advance! **12.** ⊠1 Till 3 *1* the 2 ray **14.** 3 *1* thought 3 Raptures • *1* rapture's 2 Trance! • 3 Trance • *1* Trance.

MS 3 indents lines 2, 4, 8, 11, 13; PR *1* indents lines 2, 4, 6, 8, 11, 13.
4⁺, 8⁺. ⊠1 have line-spaces.

11. THE NOSE: AN ODAIC RHAPSODY

A. DATE

Sept–Nov 1789. The additional stanza (lines 30.1.1–10) was perhaps drafted separately and brought into the poem nearer the date of MS 2 (summer 1791).

B. TEXTS

1 [=**RT**]. VCL S LT Fl.3 = Green Ottery Copy Book ff 12^v–13^r. Transcript in the hand of John May Jr. Subscribed "S. C. aet: 17."

Though the transcript was made c 1820, it is likely to be from an original sent to GC before MS 2 was transcribed. The original has not been recovered.

2. BM Add MS 47551 = Ottery Copy Book ff 13^v–15^r. Fair copy in C's hand.

1. M Post (2 Jan 1798), stanza 3 only. Unsigned.

2. PW (1834). Subscribed "1789."

C. GENERAL NOTE

See vol I headnote for the relation between the four texts and the date.

title. 1 The Nose. An Odaic Rhapsody • 2 The Nose a Rhapsody— • *1 TO THE LORD MAYOR'S NOSE.* • 2 THE NOSE.

```
 ⌐1  1                    1
  1  ⊠1   Ye souls! unus'd to lofty verse,
  2  ⊠1   Who sweep the Earth with lowly wing,
  3  ⊠1   Like sand before the blast, disperse!
  4  ⊠1   A Nose, a mighty Nose I sing.
  5  1    As er'st from Heaven Prometheus stole th' Fire
     2 2            Prometheus stole from heaven
  6  ⊠1   To animate the wonder of his hand,
  7  1    Thus with unhallow'd hand, O Muse, aspire,
     2 2                    hands,
  8  ⊠1   And from my subject snatch a burning brand.
  9  ⊠1   So like the Nose, I sing, my verse shall glow.
 10  1    Like Phlegethon, my verse in fiery   waves shall flow.
     2 2                        waves of fire
          [Line-space]
 ⌐11 1                    2
 11  ⊠1   Light of this once all darksome spot,
 12  ⊠1   Where now their glad course Mortals run!
 13  ⊠1   First born of Sirius! begot
 14  ⊠1   Upon the Focus of the Sun!
 15  1    I'll call  the  G—ll! for such thy earthly name.
     2            thee  Gill!
     2                   —— !
 16  1    What name so great, but what too low must be?
     2 2                high
 17  ⊠1   Comets, when most they drink the Solar flame,
 18  ⊠1   Are but faint types and images of *Thee.*
 19  ⊠1   Burn madly, Fire! o'er ¢Earth in ravage run,
```

20   1^{imp}   Then blush more red for shame by fiercer G—ll outdone.
    2   for Shame more red   Gill
    2   ——
       [*Line-space*]
⁻21   1   3
21   ⊠*1*   I saw, when from the Turtle feast
    1   at
22   1 2   The thick, dank smoke in volumes rose,
    1 2   dark
23   □   I saw, the darkness of the mist
24   □   Encircle thee O Nose.
25   1   Shorn of thy beams thou shot'st a fearful gleam
    2 2   rays
    1   sent'st
26   □   (The Turtle quiver'd with prophetic fright)
27   ⊠*1*   Gloomy and sullen thro' the night of steam.
    1   Sullen   sad across the murky
28   □   So *Satan*'s nose, when Dunstan urg'd to flight,
29   □   Glowing from gripe of red-hot pincers dread
30   □   Athwart the smokes of Hell disastrous twilight shed.
       [*Line-space*]
30.1.1   2 2   The furies to madness my brain devote!
30.1.2   2 2   In robes of ice my body wrap!
30.1.3   2 2   On billowy flames of fire I float!
30.1.4   2 2   Hear ye my entrails, how they snap?
30.1.5   2 2   Some power unseen forbids my lungs to breath—
30.1.6   2 2   What fire-clad meteors round me whizzing fly?
30.1.7   2 2   I vitrify thy torrid zone beneath
30.1.8   2 2   Proboscis fierce! I am calcin'd, I die!
30.1.9   2   Thus like great Pliny in th' Ætnean fire,
    2   Vesuvius'
30.1.10   2 2   I perish in the blaze, while I the blaze admire.

1. 2 Souls! • *2* souls   **2.** 2 2 earth   2 wing—   **3.** *2* blast disperse—
4. *2* Nose! a   2 2 sing!   **5.** 2 2 erst   2 2 the fire   **6.** 2 2 wonder   2 hand;— •
2 hand;   **7.** 2 muse,   **8.** 2 brand— • 2 brand!   **9.** *2* Nose   2 sing,— • 2 sing—
2 glow, • *2* glow—   **10.** *2* Phlegethon   2 flow!   **11.** *2* spot   **12.** 2 2 mortals
2 run; • *2* run,   **13.** *2* First-born   *2* Sirius   **14.** 2 2 focus   *2* sun—
15. 2 2 name—   **16.** *2* high,   **17.** *2* Comets   *2* solar   2 2 flame
18. 2 2 thee!   **19.** *2* madly   2 fire!   2 2 earth   2 run;   **20.** *2* shame
2 outdone!   **21.** *2* saw   *1 2* turtle   2 Feast • *1* feast,   **22.** ⊠1 thick
1 rose; • *2* rose!   **23.** ⊠1 saw   **24.** ⊠1 thee,   2 2 Nose! • *1* N o s e ！
25. *1* rays,   2 shott'st   *1* gleam,   **26.** *1 2* turtle   **27.** 2 *1* steam: •
2 steam:—   **28.** ⊠1 Satan's   2 Nose, • *2* Nose   **29.** 2 2 red hot   *1* pincer's
30. *1 2* shed!   **30.1.1.** *2* devote—   **30.1.3.** *2* float,   **30.1.4.** *2* ye,   2 entrails
30.1.5. *2* breathe!   **30.1.6.** *2* fly!   **30.1.8.** *2* calcin'd!   **30.1.9.** *2* Thus,
2 Pliny,   **30.1.10.** *2* blaze while

1–4, 5–8, 9–10, etc. ⊠*1* distinguish first two quatrains and concluding couplet of each stanza by indentation.

24⁺. PR *1* has line-space.

30.1.1–10. There are reasons to believe that these lines were added to the poem after it was originally conceived. They have something in common with the verses that follow line 30 in the Green Ottery Copy Book (MS 1, which concludes with line 30), entitled "A FEW LINES SELECTED FROM SOME PIECES WRITTEN BY LEE WHEN MAD." It may be significant that the lines first appear in the Ottery Copy Book, which C copied out in Devon during the summer months of 1791. See also **16** *A Few Lines Written by Lee when Mad* headnote.

12. CONCLUSION TO A YOUTHFUL POEM

A. DATE

1789–91? It is possible that the lost poem incorporated earlier material, or material used elsewhere: cf vol I headnote.

B. TEXT

BM Add MS 47551=Ottery Copy Book f 5ʳ. See vol I headnote for further details and discussion.

The RT reproduces the untitled ms exactly.

13. AN ODE ON THE DESTRUCTION OF THE BASTILE

A. DATE

1789–91. The earliest possible date is late Oct 1789, the latest summer 1791; most likely is the six months following late Oct 1789 (see vol I headnote).

B. TEXTS

1 [=RT]. BM Add MS 47551=Ottery Copy Book ff 6ᵛ–8ʳ. Transcript by C. Each stanza fills a page, and stanzas 2 and 3 are missing because a page has dropped out or has been removed from between ff 6ᵛ and 7ʳ. See **12** RT headnote.

1. PW (1834).

title. 1 An Ode on the destruction of the Bastile. • *1* DESTRUCTION OF THE BASTILE.

⁻1 ☐   1
1 ☐ Heard'st thou yon universal cry,
2 1 And d̶o̶s̶ dost thou linger still on Gallia's shore?
  1   dost
3 ☐ Go, Tyranny! beneath some barbarous sky
4 ☐ Thy terrors lost, and ruin'd power deplore!
5 ☐ What! tho' thro' many a groaning age
6 ☐ Was felt thy keen-suspicious rage,
7 ☐ Yet Freedom rous'd by fierce Disdain
8 ☐ Has wildly broke thy triple chain,
9 ☐ And like the Storm, which Earth's deep entrails hide,
10 ☐ At length has burst its way, and spread the ruins wide.
    [*Line-space*]
10⁺ *1*   *   *   *   *   *
⁻31 ☐   4
31 ☐ In sighs their sickly breath was spent: each gleam
32 1 Of Hope had ceas'd the live-long day to cheer:
  1   long long
33 ☐ Or if, delusive, in some flitting dream
34 ☐ It gave them to their friends and children dear—
35 ☐ Awaké'd by lordly Insult's sound
36 ☐ To all the doubled horrors round
37 ☐ Oft shrunk they from Oppression's band,
38 ☐ While Anguish rais'd the desperate hand
39 ☐ For silent death; or, lost the Mind's controll,
40 ☐ Thro' every burning vein would tides of Frenzy roll!
    [*Line-space*]
⁻41 ☐   5
41 ☐ But cease! ye pitying bosoms! cease to bleed!
42 ☐ Such scenes no more demand the tear humane.
43 ☐ I see! I see! glad Liberty succeed
44 ☐ With every patriot Virtue in her train!
45 ☐ And mark yon Peasant's raptur'd eyes!
46 ☐ Secure he views his harvests rise.
47 ☐ No fetter vile the Mind shall know,
48 ☐ And Eloquence shall fearless glow—
49 ☐ Yes! Liberty, the soul of Life, shall reign,
50 ☐ Shall throb in every pulse, shall flow thro' every vein.
    [*Line-space*]
⁻51 ☐   6
51 ☐ Shall France alone a Despot spurn?
52 1 S̶h̶a̶l̶l̶ ̶S̶h̶e̶,̶ ̶O̶ ̶F̶r̶e̶e̶d̶o̶m̶,̶ ̶A̶L̶L̶ ̶a̶l̶l̶ ̶t̶h̶y̶ ̶b̶l̶e̶s̶s̶i̶n̶g̶s̶ ̶s̶h̶a̶r̶e̶?̶
   ☐ Shall she, alone, O Freedom, boast thy care?
53 ☐ Lo! round thy standard Belgia's heroes burn,
54 ☐ Tho' Power's blood-stain'd streamers fire the air.
55 ☐ And wider yet thy influence spread,

56 □ Nor e'er recline thy weary head,
57 □ Till every land from pole to pole
58 □ Shall boast one independant soul!
59 □ And still, as erst, let favor'd Britain be
60 □ First ever of the first, and freeest of the free!

⁻1. *l* I.   5. *l* What   *l* through   6. *l* keen   9. *l* storm   *l* earth's
10. *l* way   ⁻31. *l* IV.   31. *l* spent;   32. *l* cheer;   33. *l* if   *l* dream,
35. *l* Awak'd   36. *l* round,   37. *l* band   38. *l* anguish   39. *l* or
l mind's control,   40. *l* roll.   ⁻41. *l* V.   41. *l* cease,   *l* bosoms,
42. *l* humane;   43. *l* I see, I see!   44. *l* virtue   45. *l* peasant's rap-
tured eyes;   46. *l* rise;   47. *l* mind   48. *l* glow.   49. *l* Liberty
l Life   50. *l* vein!   ⁻51. *l* VI.   52. *l* she   53. *l* Lo,   54. *l* air,
58. *l* independent   60. *l* first   *l* freest

2, 4, 5–8, etc. PR *l* indents lines 2 and 4, □ indent more deeply lines 5–8, in each
stanza.
10⁺. Asterisks in PR *l* indicate the missing stanzas.

14. SONNET: TO THE EVENING STAR

A. DATE

1789–90? See the discussion in vol I headnote.

B. TEXTS

1 [=RT]. BM Add MS 47551 = Ottery Copy Book f 30ʳ. Part-transcript in
C's hand. The leaf has at some time been torn in half, leaving less than the first
half of each line.

2. Transcript in JTC's 1807 Notebook, as printed in *P&DW* (RHS) II 359*.
This version appears to be a transcript of MS 1, but of course it provides the
complete text. JTC's transcripts are accurate, though he sometimes substituted
his own punctuation and capitalisation, as did RHS.

title. 1 Sonnet 8 To ⌈. . . .⌉ • 2 TO THE EVENING STAR

1 □ O meek attendant of Sol's setting blaze,
2 □ I hail, sweet Star, thy chaste effulgent glow;
3 □ On thee full oft with fixed eye I gaze
4 □ Till I methinks all spirit seem to grow.
     [*Line-space*]
5 1 O first and f̶i̶r̶sairest of the starry choir,
  2   fairest

6 ☐ O loveliest mid the daughters of the night,
7 ☐ Must not the Maid, I love like thee inspire
8 ☐ *Pure* Joy and *calm* Delight?
   [*Line-space*]
9 ☐ Must she not be as is thy placid sphere
10 ☐ Serenely brilliant? Whilst to gaze a while
11 ☐ Be all my wish 'mid Fancy's high career
12 ☐ Ev'n till she quit this scene of earthly toil;
13 ☐ Then Hope perchance might fondly sigh to join
14 ☐ Her Spirit in thy kindred orb, O star benign!

2. 2 star,   **4.** 2 I, methinks,   **6.** 2 'mid   **7.** 2 maid   **8.** 2 joy   **9.** 2 be,
12. 2 E'en   **14.** 2 spirit

title. The title given in the list of poems JTC transcribed from MS 1 in 1807 is "Sonnet to the Evening Star" (see vol I annex A 3).
2, 4, etc. MS 2 indents alternate lines.

15. SONNET: COMPOSED IN SICKNESS

A. DATE

1789–90? (see vol I headnote).

B. TEXTS

1. University of Pennsylvania Library (Special Collections) MS Eng 13 = JTC's Commonplace Book p 165. Transcript by JTC; subscribed "S.T.C."
   The title corresponds to that given by JTC in the list of C ms poems in his possession in Jun 1809, now at DCL (MS A Coleridge, J T 11). JTC's habitual use of the contractions "ye" and "&" is not recorded in the collation here.
   PW (JDC) 563B, followed by *PW* (EHC) I 17, appears to refer to the original ms on which JTC's copy was based, but this has not been located.

2. VCL S MS Fl.1. Single leaf, 31.5×38.2 cm; wm quartered medallion surmounted by crown; chain-lines 2.5 cm. Transcript in C's hand on the verso, which also contains **16** *A Few Lines Written by Lee when Mad*; the recto contains **18** *Nemo Repente Turpissimus.*
   The transcript in the hand of John May Jr in the Green Ottery Copy Book f 13ᵛ, made about 1820 and subscribed "S.C." (VCL S LT Fl.3), derives from MS 2 and is therefore not collated. It does, however, suggest that MS 2 was a copy sent by C to GC.

3 [=RT]. DCL Letters Coleridge p 32. Single leaf, 16.00×19.55 cm, the

inner edge irregular as if torn from an album; no wm; chain-lines 2.6 cm; verso
blank. Transcript in C's youthful hand on the recto.

4. BM Add MS 47551 = Ottery Copy Book f 32ʳ. Transcript in C's hand.

The top half of the page has been torn away, leaving only the last eight lines
complete and the first word of line 6. The damage is likely to have been done
before 1834, since PR *1* provides the only occasion on which HNC did not draw
on the Ottery Copy Book for such a poem.

C's hand on this and the preceding f 31ʳ is more cursive, slightly larger, and
less careful than in the rest of the book—which bears on the supposition that
the MS 3 version might have been removed after it had been copied and MS 4
substituted. But there are objections to such a thesis: see in general vol I annex
A 3.

1. PW (1834).
The text (but not the title) derives from MS 1.

title. 1 Sonnet compos'd in Sickness • 2 Pain a Sonnet • 3 Sonnet 9 • *1* PAIN.

1	⊠4	Once could the Moórn's first beams, the healthful breeze,
2	⊠4	All Nature charm—and gay was every hour;
3	1 *1*	But ah! not Music's self nor fragrant bower
2		nor splendid feasts,
3		Music sweet
4	⊠3	Can glad the trembling sense of wan disease.
3		charm
5	⊠4	Now that the frequent pangs my frame assail,
6	⊠4	Now that my sleepless eyes are sunk and dim,
7	☐	And seas of pain seem waving thro' each limb—
8	☐	Ah! what can all life's gilded scenes avail.
9	⊠3	I view the Crowd whom youth and health inspire,
3		see
10	☐	Hear the loud laugh and catch the sportive lay,
11	☐	Then sigh and think—I too could laugh and play
12	1 *1*	And gayly sport it on the Muses lyre
2–4		festive
13	☐	Ere Tyrant Pain had chas'd away delight,
14	☐	Ere the wild pulse throbb'd anguish thro' the night.

1. 2 3 *1* Morn's   **2.** 2 3 Nature, • *1* nature   2 3 charm; • *1* charm,   2 hour. •
3 hour: • *1* hour:—   **3.** *1* self,   **4.** 3 "the   2 'wan   3 Disease.   **7** 2–4 Seas of
Pain   3 *waving*   2 *1* through   2 limb,   **8.** 2 Oh!   *1* Ah   3 4 *1* Life's   ⊠1 avail?
9. 2 *1* crowd, • 3 croud • 4 crowd   2–4 Youth and Health   **10.** 2 *1* laugh,   4 lay—
11. 2 laugh &   2–4 play,   **12.** 3 *1* gaily   *1* Muse's   ⊠1 lyre,   **13.** 2 3 Delight,
14. 4 th   3 Pulse   3 Anguish   2 through   3 Night! • 4 *1* night!

4⁺. MSS 2 3 have line-space.
8⁺. MSS 2–4 have line-space.

16. A FEW LINES WRITTEN
BY LEE WHEN MAD

A. DATE

1789–90, on the basis of the other poems accompanying it in the ms and parallels with poems dating from these years (see vol I headnote).

B. TEXTS

1 [=RT]. VCL S MS Fl.1. Verso of a single leaf, 31.5×38.2 cm; wm quartered medallion surmounted by crown; chain-lines 2.5 cm. Transcript in C's hand.

The lines immediately precede **15** *Composed in Sickness*, and the recto of the same leaf contains **18** *Nemo Repente Turpissimus*. The poems must have been sent to GC, at Mr Sparrow's in Hackney, since they were in GC's possession for John May Jr to transcribe them c 1820. John May's transcript (VCL S LT Fl.3 = Green Ottery Book f 13^r) has no textual authority, and the few variations (a comma, two apostrophes) are not recorded here. John May does supply a title, which was presumably given him by GC or passed on by a member of the family: "A few lines selected from some pieces written by Lee when mad."

2. BM Add MS 47523 = Notebook 25 f 100^{v-r} (*CN* IV 4931).

"Lee's rapturous Lines" are quoted by NÖUS, in a dialogue with ANTINÖUS on the subject of transcendental logic and mysticism, as an example of unintelligibility.

1 ☐ O! that my mouth could bleat, like butter'd peas,
2 ☐ Engendring windmills in the Northern seas—
3 ☐ Coaches and Waggons rumble down my Nose,
4 1 Whilst green iniquity flows off in prose:
  2 And   blue   flow
5 1 Then run full tilt against the Subjunctive mood,
  2   at   your
6 ☐ And fatten padlocks on Antarctic food.

1. 2 O   2 Mouth 2 bleat 2 Peas   **2.** 2 Engendering Windmills 2 s͵eas͵
3. 2 &   **4.** 2 pro̸se—   **5.** 2 Mood,   **6.** 2 Padlocks 2 Food—

17. SONNET: GENEVIEVE

A. DATE

1786–7? 1789–90? In PR *1* below and in the Fitzwilliam copy of PR *5* the poem is dated "Ætatis 14", i.e. 1786–7. PR *3 4* both have a note: "This little Poem was written when the Author was a boy." C consistently placed it first in the section of Juvenile Poems in his last three collections. On the other hand, in an undated letter to an unknown correspondent (*CL* I 128–9) he says he wrote the poem two years before he left school, i.e. in 1789–90. The Christ's Hospital tradition, that the poem describes C's feelings for Jenny Edwards, daughter of his school nurse, favours the later date, since C spent much of the year 1789–90 in the sick-ward (*C Life*—G—33).

B. TEXTS

1. VCL (uncatalogued in 1978). Ann Frances Bacon's Commonplace Book f 38ᵛ. Transcript in AFB's hand. Subscribed "S. T. Coleridge".

2. VCL S LT Fl.3 = Green Ottery Copy Book f 1ʳ. Transcript in the hand of John May Jr. Subscribed "S. C."

3 [=RT]. BM Add MS 47551 = Ottery Copy Book f 27ʳ. Transcript in C's hand.

1. M Chron (15 Jul 1793). Signed "C.—— Ætatis 14."

4. Princeton University Library Robert H. Taylor Collection. Recto of a single leaf (verso blank), 18.5×23.0 cm; wm (in part) horn with fleur-de-lis and possibly entwined letters below; chain-lines 2.5 cm. Transcript in C's hand. Signed "S. T. C."

The transcript is accompanied by some musical scoring, in a hand other than C's. The scoring is not necessarily that of Charles Hague, whose setting of the poem as a glee for four voices was published in *A Collection of Glees and Rounds . . . Composed by the Members of the Harmonic Society of Cambridge* (Cambridge n.d.) 31–5, since it is for lines 12 and 13, whereas only the first eight lines were printed with Hague's setting. Compare, however, the setting by William Carnaby in *Six Songs* (n.d.) 24–8.

2. Cambridge Intelligencer (1 Nov 1794). Signed "S. T. C. | *Jes. Coll.*"

5. BPL B 22189 = Estlin Copy Book f 18ʳ. Transcript in C's hand.

3. Poems (1796).
Rpt *The Port Folio* (Philadelphia) II (28) (17 Jul 1802) 224.

4. Poems (1803).
The version of the poem on p 31 of JTC's Commonplace Book at the Uni-

versity of Pennsylvania Library (Special Collections) MS Eng 13 is merely a transcript of PR *4*.

5. *PW* (1828).

In the large-paper copy in the Fitzwilliam Museum, Cambridge (Marlay Bequest 1912), C has written underneath the text "Æt. 14."

6. *PW* (1829).

7. *PW* (1834).

C. GENERAL NOTE

The sequence of texts is particularly uncertain. Firstly, MS 1 might derive from an original written before or after the original of PR *1*. Secondly, the sequence of MS and PR texts 4 *2* 5 is vague, and MS 4 could postdate PR *2*. C told Mary Evans in Feb 1793 that Charles Hague was to set **51** *The Complaint of Ninathoma* to music (*CL* I 51–2), yet when Hague came to print his setting of **51** he appears to have drawn on *Poems* (1796) (see **51** VAR).

title. 1 *2* A Sonnet— • 3 Sonnet 3 • *1* IRREGULAR SONNET. • *2* SONNET. • 5 Ode • *3* EFFUSION XVII. • *4–7 GENEVIEVE.*

1 □	Maid of my Love! sweet Genevieve!
1fn *3 4*	This little Poem was written when the Author was a boy.
2 ⊠*3–7*	In Beauty's light thou glid'st along;
3–7	you glide
3 1–3 *1*	Thy eye is like the star of Eve;
4 *2* 5	Thine
3–7	Your
4 1 *2 1*	Thy voice is soft as Seraph's song.
3	sweet
4 *2* 5	lovely as the
3–7	And sweet your Voice, as
5 1	Yet not thy heavnly charms could give,
2 3 *1* 2 5	beauty gives
4	But
3–7	Yet your
6 □	This heart with passion soft to glow!
7 ⊠*3–7*	Within thy soul a Voice there lives—
3–7	your
8 1–3 *1*	It bids thee hear the *tale* of *woe*—
4 *2* 5	tearful Plaint of Woe.
3–7	you tale of Woe.
9 □	When sinking low the sufferer wan
10 1–3	Beholds no hand stretch'd out to save,
1 3–7	out-stretched
4 *2* 5	friendly hand, that saves—
11 □	Fair as the Bosom, of the Swan,

12 1–3 *1 3–7* That rises graceful o'er the   Wave,
    4 2 5   quick-rolling Waves,
13 ⊠*3–7* I've seen thy breast with pity heave,
    3–7   your
14 1   And therefore do I love sweet Genevieve!—
    2 *1* 3 4 2 5   love thee,
    3–7   you,

title. 2 Sonnet. • *5–7* GENEVIEVE.   **1.** *1* love! • *2* 5 *5–7* Love, *1 3–*
6 GENEVIEVE! • *2* GENEVIEVE!   **2.** *1* beauty's   4 5 Light   3 glids't •
4 glid*1*s't   2 *3–7* along: **3.** 4 5 Eye   4 5 Star   2 Eve, • 3 eve; • *1 3–7* eve,
4. 4 5 Voice   *1* seraph's   5 Song.   **5.** ⊠*1* 4 heavenly • 4 heav'nly   3–5 *3–*
7 Beauty   **6.** 5 Heart   ⊠1 glow: **7.** 5 Soul   *1* 2 voice • *3–6* VOICE   2 lives, •
3–7 lives!   **8.** 5 thee ~~the~~ hear   2 3 *1* tale   2 plaint   2 3 Woe. • *1* woe. • 5 Woe!
9. *1* low,   3–5 *5–7* Sufferer • *3* 4 Suff'rer   **10.** 5 hand   2 3 stretcht   *3–*
7 outstretcht   2 saves; • 5 saves,   **11.** 2 5 *3–7* Fair,   2 4 5 Bosom • 3 *1* 2–7 bosom
3–5 *3–7* Swan • *1* 2 swan   **12.** 2 oer   2 Wave • 3 *1 3–7* wave, • 2 waves,
13. 5 Breast   4 Pity   *1* 4 5 heave—   **14.** 5 *3–6 therefore*   2–5 7 Genevieve! •
1 3–6 GENEVIEVE! • *2* GENEVIEVE!

    title. In the PR *3* list of contents the title is given as "Effusion 17, to Genevieve,"
    1fn. PR *3* has the cross-reference "Note 5.—Page 62.", the notes being printed at the end of the 1796 volume.
    2, 4, 6, etc. Alternate lines indented in PR *1 2*.
    4⁺, 8⁺. TEXTS 3 4 *2* 5 have line-space.
    14. C gives, as an alternative reading written under the line in MS 3, the MS 1 reading "do I love".

18. NEMO REPENTE TURPISSIMUS

A. DATE

1789–90. MS 1 is dated 1790. John May's description at the head of his transcript—"S. C. ætatis 16" (see MS 2)—would place the date at 1788–9 and is probably less accurate. The other two poems accompanying the MS 2 text date from 1789–90.

B. TEXTS

    1 [=RT]. BM MS Ashley 3506=James Boyer's *Liber Aureus* vol I f 47ʳ. Transcript in C's hand, signed "S. T. Coleridge I 1790".
    The poem has only two stanzas in this version. It is the fifth and last poem that C copied into the book. Facsimile reproduction in *C Bibl* (Wise *TLP*) facing 53.

2. VCL S MS Fl.1. Recto of a single leaf, 31.5×38.2 cm; wm quartered medallion surmounted by crown; chain-lines 2.5 cm. Transcript in C's hand. The verso contains **16** *A Few Lines Written by Lee when Mad* and **15** *Composed in Sickness*.

The copy in the hand of John May Jr in the Green Ottery Copy Book f 12^r (VCL S LT Fl.3), made c 1820, derives from MS 2 and is not collated. It does, however, suggest that MS 2 was sent by C to GC.

3. BM Add MS 47551 = Ottery Copy Book f 4^{r-v}. Transcript in C's hand.

1. PW (1834).

title. 1 2 *Nemo repente turpissimus* • 3 The progress of Vice—an Ode. •
1 PROGRESS OF VICE.

1	1 2	Deep in the gulph of guilt and woe
	3 *1*	Vice
2	□	Leaps Man at once with headlong throw?
3	1 2	Him innate Truth and Virtue guide,
	3 *1*	~~im~~inborn
4	□	Whose guards are Shame and conscious Pride.
5	□	In some gay hour Vice steals into the breast;
6	□	Perchance she wears some softer Virtue's vest:
7	□	By unperceiv'd degrees she tempts to stray,
8	1–3	'Till far from Virtue's paths she leads the feet away.
	1	path

[*Line-space*]

9	1	Yet still the heart to disenthrall
	2	~~Y~~But
	3	~~But~~ Then swift soul
	1	Then
10	□	Will Memory the past recall;
11	□	And Fear before the Victim's eyes
12	1 2 ˙	Bid future woes and dangers rise.
	3	Bids ills
	1	Bid
13	1	But hark! their charms the Voice, the lyre combine—
	2	Then
	3 *1*	But the voice, the lyre their charms
14	□	Gay sparkles in the Cup the generous Wine—
15	1	The mazy dance, [. . .] and frail young Beauty fires—
	2	←the→ fair Nymph inspires,
	3 *1*	Th' inebriate fair frail
16	1	And Virtue ⟨vanquish'd,⟩ scorn'd, with hasty flight retires.
	2 3 *1*	vanquish'd,

[*Line-space*]

16.1.1 2 3 *1* But soon to tempt the Pleasures cease—
16.1.2 2 3 *1* Yet Shame forbids return to Peace—
16.1.3 2 3 *1* And stern Necessity will force

16.1.4 2 3   Still on to urge the desperate course.
    1   to urge on
16.1.5 2   The dreer black paths of life the wretch must try,
    3 *1*   Vice
16.1.6 2 3 *1*   Where Conscience flashes horror on each eye,
16.1.7 2   Where Hate, where Murder scowls, where starts Affright—
    3 *1*   scowl—
16.1.8 2 3   Ah! close the scene—for   dreadful   is   the   sight.
    1   —ah! close—for dreadful is the sight.

title. Not underlined in MS 2   **1.** 3 *1* Woe   **2.** *1* man   **3.** *1* inborn
4. *1* shame   *1* pride;   **5.** 2 breast— • 3 breast: **6.** 2 vest— • 3 *1* vest.
8. 2 3 *1* Till   2 Paths   **10.** *1* recall,   **11.** *1* fear   2 victim's   **13.** 2 hark—
1 lyre,   2 combine;   **14.** 2 3 *1* cup   2 wine— • 3 Wine. • *1* wine;
15. 3 *1* dance—   *1* nymph   **16.** *1* vanquish'd—   2 3 scorn'd • *1* scorn'd
16.1.1. *1* pleasures   *1* cease;   **16.1.2.** *1* shame   3 Peace,— • *1* peace,
16.1.3. *1* necessity   **16.1.5.** 3 *1* drear   3 Wretch   **16.1.6.** 3 Horror   3 eye—
16.1.7. *1* Hate—   *1* Affright!   **16.1.8.** 3 scene, • *1* scene,—   3 sight!

1–4, 5–7, 8. □ indent.
8⁺, 16⁺. MSS 1–3 have rules.

19. SONNET: ANNA AND HARLAND

A. DATE

1790? 1794? The evidence of MS 1 suggests that the poem might have been contained in the Ottery Copy Book, and therefore written before 1791. The evidence of PR *1* suggests, on the contrary, that it might have been written in 1794. Although the style and possible echoes of other writers might support the later date (see vol I headnote), the circumstantial evidence on behalf of the earlier date is difficult to dismiss.

B. TEXTS

1 [=RT]. Transcript in JTC's 1807 Notebook, as printed in *P&DW* (RHS) II 359*–360*. Neither the original from which JTC copied nor this particular notebook has survived.

The other two poems by C in the notebook—**14** *To the Evening Star* and **82** *Monody on the Death of Chatterton*—appear to have been copied from the Ottery Copy Book, and the present sonnet might well have been one of the two removed from it (see vol I annex A 3).

JTC's transcripts are accurate, although he sometimes substituted his own capitalisation and punctuation. In this case, of course, such details might have been further modified by the editor and publisher.

1. Cambridge Intelligencer (25 Oct 1794). Signed "S. T. C. | *Jes. Coll.*"

title. 1 ANNA AND HARLAND. • *1* SONNET.

1 1 Within these wilds was Anna wont to rove
   1 Along this glade
2 1 While Harland told his love in many a sigh,
   1   HENRY
3 1 But stern on Harland rolled her brother's eye,
   1   dark   HENRY
4 ☐ They fought, they fell—her brother and her love!
   [*Line-space*]
5 1 To Death's dark house did grief-worn Anna haste,
   1   her   cold   grave   woe-worn
6 1 Yet here her pensive ghost delights to stay;
   1   stray,
7 1 Oft pouring on the winds the broken lay—
   1   a
8 ☐ And hark, I hear her—'twas the passing blast.
   [*Line-space*]
9 1 I love to sit upon her tomb's dark grass,
   1   dank
10 1 Then Memory backward rolls Time's shadowy tide;
   1 There
11 1 The tales of other days before me glide:
   1   forms
12 ☐ With eager thought I seize them as they pass;
13 ☐ For fair, though faint, the forms of Memory gleam,
14 1 Like Heaven's bright beauteous bow reflected in the stream.
   1   bow   reflected   on

1. *1* ANNA *1* rove,   **2.** *1* sigh: **3.** *1* roll'd *1* eye: **4.** *1* fell,
5. *1* ANNA haste;   **7.** *1* lay: **8.** *1* hark! *1* her!—'Twas   **10.** *1* memory
11. *1* glide;   **12.** *1* them, *1* pass: **13.** *1* tho' *1* memory

2–3, 6–7, 10–11. ☐ indent.
13–14. Used as the last lines of **87** *On Hope* and **128** *Recollection.*

20. THE ABODE OF LOVE

A. DATE

Before Jul 1790.

B. TEXT

The World (26 Jul 1790). Signed "S. T. C." The poem was reprinted, similarly signed, in *Cambridge Chronicle* (31 Jul 1790); the only variant is an obvious correction at the end of line 7.

C. GENERAL NOTE

C's authorship is not absolutely certain; see vol I headnote.

The RT reproduces the *World/Cambridge Chronicle* text exactly, except that both give the title in the form "*The* ABODE *of* LOVE.", and in the first of these there is no punctuation at the end of line 7.

21. MONODY ON A TEA KETTLE

A. DATE

1790? See TEXTS 1 *1*.

B. TEXTS

1. Printed from a holograph ms in *PW* (JDC) 12–13. JDC 563B describes the ms, which has not been traced, as one "sent or taken home by Coleridge from Christ's in 1790", and as containing also **82** *Monody on the Death of Chatterton* and **22** *An Invocation*. The allusion to GC in line 33 of this version suggests, on the other hand, that it was sent to GC, who was then living in Hackney.

2 [=RT]. BM Add MS 47551 = Ottery Copy Book ff 12ʳ–13ʳ. Transcript in C's hand.

1. PW (1834). Subscribed "1790."

title. 1 Monody the Second, occasioned by a very recent Calamity. • 2 *1* Monody on a Tea kettle

1 1	Muse that late sang another's poignant pain,
2 *1*	O Muse! who sangest late another's pain,
2 ☐	To griefs domestic turn thy coal-black steed!
3 1	In slowest steps the funeral steeds shall go,
2 *1*	With thy steed must
4 1	Nodding their heads in all the pomp of woe:
2 *1*	his head
5 1	Wide scatter round each ◄——deadly——► weed,
2 *1*	dark and deadly,

6 □　And let the melancholy dirge complain,
7 1　(Whilst bats shall shriek and dogs shall howling run)
　2 *1*　(While
8 1 2　His tea-kettle is spoilt and Coleridge is undone!
　1　The
　[*Line-space*]
9 1　Your cheerful song, ye unseen crickets, cease!
　2 *1*　　　　　　songs,
10 □　Let songs of grief your alter'd minds engage!
11 □　For he who sang responsive to your lay,
12 □　What time the joyous bubbles 'gan to play,
13 □　The *sooty swain* has felt the fire's fierce rage;—
14 □　Yes, he is gone, and all my woes increase;
15 1 2　I heard the water hissing from the wound—
　1　　　　　　issuing
16 1　No more the Tea shall throw its fragrant steam around!
　2　　　　　　pour　　　　　steams
　1　　　　　　　flagrant
　[*Line-space*]
17 □　O Goddess best beloved! Delightful Tea!
18 1　With whom compar'd what yields the madd'ning Wine?
　2 *1*　　　thee　　　　　　　　　　　　vine?
19 1　Sweet power! that know'st to spread the calm delight,
　2 *1*　　　　　who
20 □　And the pure joy prolong to midmost night!
21 1　Ah! must I all thy various charms resign?
　2 *1*　　　　　varied　sweets
22 □　Enfolded close in grief thy form I see
23 1 2　No more wilt thou expand thy willing arms,
　1　　　　　extend
24 □　Receive the *fervent Jove*, and yield him all thy charms!
　[*Line-space*]
25 1　How low the mighty sink by Fate opprest!—
　2 *1*　　　sink　　　low
26 □　Perhaps, O Kettle! thou by scornful toe
27 □　Rude urg'd t' ignoble place with plaintive din,
28 □　May'st rust obscure midst heaps of vulgar tin;—
29 1　As if no joy had ever chear'd my breast
　2 *1*　　　　　　seiz'd
30 1　When from thy spout the stream did arching flow,—
　2　　　　　　streams
　1　　　　　　　　　fly,—
31 1　As if, inspir'd, thou ne'er hadst known t' inspire
　2 *1*　　　infus'd
32 □　All the warm raptures of poetic fire!
　[*Line-space*]
33 1　But hark! or do I fancy *Georgian* voice—
　2 *1*　　　　　　　the　glad

34   1   'What tho' its   form did wondrous charms disclose—
       2 *1*   the swain
35   ☐   (Not such did Memnon's sister sable drest)
35fn   2   A Parenthetical Reflection of the Author's—
36   ☐   Take these bright arms with royal face imprest,
37   ☐   A better Kettle shall thy soul rejoice,
38   1   And with Oblivion's wing o'erspread thy woes!'
       2 *1*   wings
39   ☐   Thus Fairy Hope can soothe distress and toil;
40   ☐   On empty Trivets she bids fancied Kettles boil!

title. *1* MONODY ON A TEA-KETTLE.   **1.** *1* muse   **2.** 2 steed:
3. 2 go   **4.** 2 Woe: **6.** 2 complain   **7.** 2 *1* Bats   2 *1* Dogs   **8.** 2 "His
Tea Kettle   **9.** 2 cheerful   2 Crickets! • *1* crickets   2 cease—   **11.** 2 He,
2 lay   **13.** 2 *1* sooty swain   2 rage!   **14.** 2 Yes! He • *1* Yes he   2 gone—&
2 encrease!   **15.** 2 *1* Water   2 *1* Wound—   **17.** 2 belov'd! Delightful •
1 beloved, delightful   **18.** 2 mad'ning   **19.** 2 Power—   **20.** 2 Joy   2 night,
22. 2 see— • *1* see;   **24.** 2 *1* fervent Jove   2 charms.   **25.** 2 opprest!
26. *1* Perhaps   2 Toe   **27.** 2 din   **28.** 2 'midst   2 Tin—   **29.** 2 Joy
2 breast,   **30.** 2 Spout   2 flow—   **31.** 2 if— • *1* if   2 had'st   2 to inspire
33. 2 voice?   **34.** 2 *1* "What   2 disclose?   **35.** 2 Sister sable-drest!)
36. 2 "Take   2 imprest—   **37.** 2 "A   2 rejoice   **38.** 2 "And   2 woes. •
1 woes!"   **39.** 2 sooth   2 toil—   **40.** 2 *she*

     title. 1 Monody the Second] The previous poem in MSS 1 2 is **82** *Monody on the Death of Chatterton* (referred to also in lines 1–2).
     7–8 etc. The following lines are offset to the left: 7–8 (MS 2), 8 (MS 1), 16 (TEXTS 1 2 *1*), 23–4 (TEXTS 1 *1*), 40 (MSS 1 2).
     8⁺, 16⁺, 24⁺. MS 2 has rules (not at 32⁺, which falls at the bottom of f 12ᵛ).
     8⁺. No line-space in PR *1*.
     32⁺. No line-space in PR *1*.

22. AN INVOCATION

A. DATE

1790–1? The other poems in the same ms appear to date from C's last year at school.

B. TEXT

First printed in *PW* (JDC) 10B, "from the autograph copy which accompanied the *Monody* on Chatterton and *Monody on a Tea-Kettle*", "in the handwriting of the poet, and sent from school to his brother George" (563B, 562B).
     This ms has not been traced, and apparently EHC did not see it either (cf

PW—EHC—I 16). The final sentence of JDC's note on **21** *Monody on a Tea Kettle* (563B) suggests that the title was his own invention.

The RT reproduces JDC's text exactly.

22.X1. EPITAPH: BY A SON
ON HIS DECEASED FATHER

The Gazetteer and New Daily Advertiser (London) (27 Jan 1791): "ORIGI-NAL EPITAPH. I BY A SON ON HIS DECEASED FATHER. I (NEVER PRINTED.) I To thee, blest shade, this humble stone we raise" (18 lines). Signed "S. T."

The copy of the newspaper in the library of the University of California, Los Angeles, is catalogued with the C materials (Δ *PR 4480 069), and "Coleridge" is written in pencil after the initials. The recollection of the librarians in 1975 was that the attribution was by ELG; the newspaper championed peace and reform from a middle-class point of view. The epitaph might be the same as **22.X2,** having been sent on to the newspaper by GC, but this is entirely speculative.

22.X2. SCHOOLBOY POEM SENT TO
GEORGE COLERIDGE

In a letter written to GC from Christ's Hospital in Feb–Mar 1791 C says: "I have inclosed the Ποιημάτιον, which I should have sent before, had not business prevented" and adds "I have enclosed with it a Latin Ode" (*CL* I 6; see **23** *Honos Alit Artes*). If C is alluding, as is possible, to a "little poem" in Greek, it has not been preserved in the several collections of GC's papers.

There are three possibilities. (1) The poem became detached from GC's papers and exists in a collection where its provenance is unknown. It might, for example, be **4** *Greek Epigram on Aphrodite and Athena*, especially if that poem dates from later in the sequence than its position in the present edition (e.g. 1790–1); or it might be **40** *Greek Epitaph on an Infant*, which may date from 1791 (though the only known version dates from 1795). (2) C's Greek word refers to an English poem such as **17** *Genevieve*, which he referred to as a "little Poem" (see **17** VAR headnote sec A) and which John May Jr copied into the Green Ottery Copy Book from a lost original sent to GC; or to e.g. **22.X1** *By a Son on his Deceased Father*, which GC then sent to the newspaper (supposing C's letter to him to have been written up to a month earlier than ELG has it). (3) The poem has been lost.

23. HONOS ALIT ARTES

A. DATE

Feb–Mar 1791 (ELG's dating).

B. TEXT

In the possession of Sir Charles Cave (Oct 1981). Two conjoint leaves, each 18.5×22.5 cm, folded; wm crown above horn-in-oval above GR; chain-lines 2.5 cm. Comprising the larger part of an als to GC, Feb–Mar 1791 (*CL* I 6).

The title was inserted after the lines were transcribed, in the form "⟨Honos alit artes.⟩" Otherwise the RT reproduces the ms exactly.

24. PROSPECTUS AND SPECIMEN OF A TRANSLATION OF EUCLID

A. DATE

Mar 1791. The references in lines 57–63 make it likely that the poem was written earlier in the month in which it was sent to GC. The epigraph and prospectus are likely to have been written after the poem itself, on the spur of the occasion of sending the poem to GC. See vol I headnote.

B. TEXTS

1 [=RT]. NYPL Berg Collection. Two conjugate leaves, each 22.5× 36.5 cm; wm crown above horn-in-oval above GR; countermark G TAYLO[R]; chain-lines 2.5 cm. With an introductory letter, the whole of an als to GC, 31 Mar 1791 (*CL* I 7–9).

The "contemporary copy" cited in *PW* (JDC) 564A is probably this one: one cannot be sure because, despite what JDC asserts, he prints from PR *1* below. The transcripts by John May Jr in the Green Ottery Copy Book ff 17ᵛ–20ʳ (VCL S LT Fl.3) and, less accurately, by JTC in his Commonplace Book pp 178–80 (University of Pennsylvania Library (Special Collections) MS Eng 13) are from this als and have not been collated.

1. PW (1834).

title. 1 Prospectus and Specimen of a Translation of Euclid in ⟨a series of⟩ Pindaric Odes. • *1* Mathematical Problem.

epigraph
⁻**1.1** □ If Pegasus will let *thee* only ride him
⁻**1.2** 1 Spurning my clumsi̶l̶y̶ efforts to o'erstride him,
  1   clumsy
⁻**1.3** □ Some fresh expedient the Muse will try,
⁻**1.4** □ And walk on stilts, although she cannot fly.

prospectus [present in TEXTS 1 *1*; all PR *1* variants are given in the apparatus register below]

Dear Brother—   ⁻1.5
 I have often been surprized, that Mathematics, the Quintessence of Truth, should have found admirers so few and so languid—Frequent consideration and minute scrutiny have at length unravelled the cause— Viz—That, though Reason is feasted, Imagination is starved: whilst Reason is luxuriating in its proper Paradise, Imagination is wearily travelling ⁻1.10 over a dreary desart. To assist *Reason* by the stimulus of *Imagination* is the *Design* of the following Production. In the *execution* of it much may be objectionable. The verse (particularly in the introduction of the Ode) may be accused of unwarrantable liberties; but they are liberties equally homogeneal with the exactness of Mathemat: disquisition and ⁻1.15 the boldness of *Pindaric* Daring. I have three strong champions to defend me against the attacks of Criticism: the Novelty, the Difficulty, and the Utility of the work. I may justly plume myself, that I *first* have drawn the Nymph Mathesis from the visionary caves of Abstracted Idea, and caused her to ?a̶s̶s̶a̶u̶l̶t̶ unite with Harmony. The ?o̶f̶ first-born of this union I now ⁻1.20 present to you: with interested motives indeed, as I expect to receive in return the more valuable offsprings of your Muse—

              Thine ever
              S. T. Coleridge—
March 31ˢᵗ. 1791.   ⁻1.25

 1 □ This is now—This was erst
 2 □ Proposition the first and Problem the first.
   [*Line-space*]
⁻**3** □   1
 3 □ On a given finite Line,
 4 □ Which must no way incline,

  5 □ To describe an equi—
  6 □ —lateral TRI
  7 □ A EN GEE EL E
7fn 1 Poetice ⟨for⟩ Angle.
         [*Line-space*]
  8 □ Now let A B
  9 □ Be the given Line,
10 □ Which must no way incline,
11 □ The Great Mathematician
12 □ Makes this Requisition,
13 □ That we describe an equi—
14 □ —lateral Tri—
15 □ —angle on it.
16 □ Aid us Reason! Aid us, Wit!
        [*Line-space*]
⁻**17** □   2.
17 □ From the centre A. at the distance A B
18 □ Describe the circle B C D.
19 □ At the distance B A from B, the centre
20 □ The round A C E to describe boldly venture.
21 □ (Third Postulate see)
22 □ And from the point C,
23 □ In which the Circles make a pother
24 □ Cutting and slashing one another,
25 □ Bid the straight lines a journeying go,
26 □ C A, C B those lines will show
27 □ To the points, which by A B are reckon'd;
28 □ And Postulate the second
29 □ For authority ye know.
30 □ A B C
31 □ Triumphant shall be
32 □ An Equilateral Triangle—
33 1 Not Peter Pindar carp, no*t*r Zoilus can wrangle.
    1   nor
     [*Line-space*]
⁻**34** □   3ʳᵈ
34 □ Because the point A is the centre
35 □ Of the circular B C D;
36 □ And Because the point B is the centre
37 □ Of the circular A C E;
38 1 A C to C B and C B to C A
    1 A. C.   A. B.   B. C.   B. A.
39 □ Harmoniously equal for ever must stay.
40 □ Then C A and B C
41 □ Both extend the kind hand
42 □ To the Basis A. B.
43 1 ~~Harmon~~ Unambitiously join'd in Equality's band.
    1 ←—Unambitiously—→

44 1 ~~Both~~ But to the same power when two powers are equal—
 1 But   powers,
45 □ My Mind forebodes the sequel:
46 □ My mind does some celestial impulse teach,
47 □ And equalizes each to each.
48 □ Thus C A with B C strikes the same sure alliance,
49 1 Which C A and B C had with A B before:
 1 That
50 1 And in mutual reliance,
 1   affiance
51 □ None attempting to soar
52 □ Above another
53 □ The unanimous Three,
54 □ C A and B C and A B—
55 □ *All* are equal, each to his Brother.
56 □ Preserving the balance of Power so true:
57 1 Ah! the like would the proud Autocratorix do!
 1   Autocratix
57fn 1 The ⌞Title of⌟ the ⌞Empress of Russia.⌟
 1 Empress of Russia.
58 □ At taxes impending not Britain would tremble,
59 □ Nor Prussia struggle her fear to dissemble,
60 □ Nor the Mah'met-sprung Wight,
61 □ The Great Musselman
62 □ Would stain his Divan,
63 □ With Urine, the soft-flowing Daughter of Fright.
 [*Line-space*]
⁻64 □   4ᵗʰ
64 □ But rein your stallion in, too daring Nine!
65 □ Should Empires bloat the scientific line?
66 □ Or with dishevell'd hair all madly do ye run
67 □ For Transport, that your task is done?
68 □ For done it is—the cause is try'd!
69 □ And Proposition, gentle maid,
70 □ Who soothly ask'd stern Demonstration's aid,
71 □ Has prov'd her right: and A B C
72 1 ~~With~~ Of angles three
 1 Of
73 □ Is shewn to be of equal side.
74 □ And now our weary steed to rest in fine,
75 □ 'Tis rais'd upon A B, the straight, the given line.

epigraph. ⁻1.1 *1* thee *1* him, **prospectus.** ⁻1.5. *1* DEAR BROTHER,
⁻1.6. *1* surprised *1* quintessence ⁻1.7. *1* languid. ⁻1.8. 1 cause— • *1* case;
⁻1.9. *1* viz. that *1* starved; ⁻1.11. 1 over • *1* on *1* Reason *1* Imagination
⁻1.12 *1* design *1* production. *1* execution ⁻1.14. *1* ode) *1* liberties, but
⁻1.15. *1* Mathematical disquisition, ⁻1.16. *1* Pindaric daring. ⁻1.17. *1* Criticism;
⁻1.18. *1* first ⁻1.19. *1* nymph *1* abstracted ⁻1.20. 1 ?~~assault~~ unite • *1* unite
1 The ?of first-born • *1* The first-born *1* Union ⁻1.21. *1* you; *1* indeed—

⁻**1.22.** 1 offsprings • *1* offspring   *1* Muse.   ⁻**1.23.** *1* ever,   ⁻**1.24.** 1 S. T. Coleridge— • *1* S. T. C.   ⁻**1.25.** *1* prints at LH of ⁻1.23, and adds at the LH of ⁻1.24: To the Rev. G. C.   *1* 31,   **1.** *1* —this was erst,   **2.** *1* first—and ⁻**3.** *1* I.   **3.** *1* line   **4.** *1* incline;   **6.** *1* Tri—   **7.** *1* —A, N, G, E, L, E. **8.** *1* A. B.   **9.** *1* line   **10.** *1* incline;   **11.** *1* great   **13.** *1* Equi-   **15.** *1* it: **16.** *1* Reason—aid us   ⁻**17.** *1* II.   **17.** *1* A. B.   **18.** *1* B. C. D.   **19.** *1* B. A. from B.   **20.** *1* A. C. E.   **21.** *1* postulate see.)   **22.** *1* C.   **23.** *1* circles **25.** *1* go.   **26.** *1* C. A. C. B.   **27.** *1* A. B.   *1* reckon'd,   **28.** *1* postulate **29.** *1* Authority   **30.** *1* A. B. C.   **32.** *1* Triangle,   ⁻**34.** *1* III.   **34.** *1* A. **35.** *1* B. C. D.   **36.** *1* because   *1* B.   **37.** *1* A. C. E.   **39.** *1* stay; **40.** *1* C. A. and B. C.   **42.** *1* basis A. B,   **43.** *1* Band.   **44.** *1* equal, **45.** *1* mind   *1* sequel;   **48.** *1* C. A. with B. C.   **49.** *1* C. A. and B. C. *1* A. B. before;   **52.** *1* another,   **53.** *1* three   **54.** *1* C. A. and B. C. and A. B.   **55.** *1* All   *1* brother,   **56.** *1* power   **59.** *1* dissemble;   **60.** *1* wight **61.** *1* Mussulman   **62.** *1* Divan   **63.** *1* Urine   *1* daughter   ⁻**64.** *1* IV. **67.** *1* transport   **68.** *1* tried!   **71.** *1* right, and A. B. C.   **72.** *1* Angles **73.** *1* shown   *1* side;   **75.** *1* raised   *1* A. B.

title. In PR *1* this appears only in the list of contents (as "Mathematical Problem"). **2⁺, 7⁺, 16⁺, 33⁺, 63⁺.** MS 1 has rules. It looks as if the numbers were inserted later. **7⁺.** No line-space in PR *1*. **20.** 1 boldly venture] MS 1 underlines, and deletes "*boldly*". C then wrote alongside: "delendus pene—" tr "almost to be deleted". **33.** 1 no*f*r] JTC read the amended word as "not", John May as "nor". **50.** 1 reliance, • *1* affiance] Though the word is clear in MS 1, JTC and John May both misread it as "alliance". **57fn.** C's note on "Autocratorix" in MS 1 has been torn away; John May's and JTC's transcripts have the same note as PR *1*.

25. SONNET: ON RECEIVING AN ACCOUNT THAT MY SISTER'S DEATH WAS INEVITABLE

A. DATE

Late 1790? early 1791? See vol I headnote on the personal circumstances behind the poem.

B. TEXTS

1 [=RT]. BM Add MS 47551 = Ottery Copy Book f 28ʳ. Transcript in C's hand.

The copies of MS 1 in JTC's Commonplace Book (University of Pennsylvania

Library (Special Collections) MS Eng 13) p 163 and in the Coleridge family album in the BM (Add MS 47554 f 42ᵛ) are of no textual interest.

1. PW (1834).

title. 1 Sonnet 5 On receiving an account that my Sister's Death was inevitable. •
1 ON RECEIVING AN ACCOUNT I THAT HIS ONLY SISTER'S DEATH WAS INEVITABLE.

1 □ The tear, which mourn'd a brother's fate, scarce dry,
2 □ Pain after pain, and woe succeeding woe,
3 □ Is my heart destin'd for another blow?
4 1 O my sweet Sister! must   *thou*   die?
  1   and must thou too die?
   [*Line-space*]
5 □ Ah! how has Disappointment pour'd the tear
6 □ O'er infant Hope destroy'd by early frost?
7 1 How are ye flown, whom most my soul held dear?
  1   gone,
8 □ Scarce had I lov'd you, ere I mourn'd you lost!
   [*Line-space*]
9 1 Say—is this hollow eye—oh! heartless pain!—
  1   this
10 1 Destin'd to rove thro' life's wide cheerless plain,
  1   Fated
11 1 Nor Mother, Brother, Sister meet its ken?
  1   father,   meets
12 □ My woes, my joys unshar'd? Ah! long ere then
13 □ On me thy icy dart, stern Death, be prov'd!
14 □ Better to die, than live and not be lov'd.

1. *1* tear   *1* fate   *1* dry—   **2.** *1* woe—   **4.** *1* sister!   **6.** *1* frost!   **7.** *1* dear!
8. *1* lost;   **9.** *1* Say,   *1* pain   **10.** *1* Life's   *1* plain—   **11.** *1* brother, sister
1 ken—   **12.** *1* unshar'd!   **13.** *1* prov'd;—   **14.** *1* lov'd!

4⁺, 8⁺. No line-space in PR *1*.

26. SONNET: ON SEEING A YOUTH
AFFECTIONATELY WELCOMED
BY HIS SISTER

A. DATE

Following Mar 1791, when Ann Coleridge died; and before Aug 1791, when C left Christ's Hospital (and soon afterwards, presumably, transcribed the sonnet into the Ottery Copy Book).

B. TEXTS

1 [=**RT**]. University of Pennsylvania Library (Special Collections) MS Eng 13 = JTC's Commonplace Book p 164. Transcript in the hand of JTC.

It is likely that JTC took his text from the Ottery Copy Book, perhaps through an intermediary copy he took in 1807. See vol I annex A 3. JTC's "y^e" for "the" is silently expanded here.

1. PW (1834).

title. 1 On seeing a Youth affectionately welcom'd by his Sister. • *1* ON SEEING A YOUTH | AFFECTIONATELY WELCOMED BY A SISTER.

1 □ *1* too a Sister had! Too cruel Death!
2 □ How sad remembrance bids my bosom heave!
3 □ Tranquil her soul as sleeping Infant's breath;
4 □ Meek were her manners as a vernal eve.
    [*Line-space*]
5 □ Knowlege that frequent lifts the bloated mind,
6 1 Gave HER the treasure of a lovely breast;
  1   lowly
7 □ And Wit to venom'd malice oft assign'd
8 □ Dwelt in *her* bosom in a turtle's nest.
    [*Line-space*]
9 1 Cease busy Memory! cease to deep the dart,
  1   urge
10 □ Nor on my soul her love to me impress!
11 □ For oh I mourn in anguish—and my heart
12 □ Feels the keen pang, th' unutterable distress.
13 □ Yet wherefore grieve I that her sorrows cease,
14 □ For life was misery, & the grave is peace!

1. *1* I   *1* sister   *1* too   **3.** *1* soul,   **4.** *1* Eve.   **5.** *1* Knowledge,   **6.** *1* her
1 breast,   **7.** *1* Malice   *1* assign'd,   **8.** *1* her   *1* Turtle's   **9.** *1* Cease,   *1* dart;
14. *1* Life   *1* and   *1* Grave   *1* Peace!

4⁺, 8⁺. MS 1 has rules. No line-space in PR *1*.
13–14. Offset in both MS 1 and PR *1*.

26.X1. VERSION OF AN EPITAPH
ON A YOUNG LADY

A. DATE

Spring–summer 1791? Mar 1797?

B. TEXTS

1. VCL S MS F3.58. Two conjoint leaves, each 20.8×32.5 cm; wm Britannia in oval surmounted by crown; countermark G I; chain-lines 2.6 cm. Quoted in C's second autobiographical letter to TP, Mar 1797 (*CL* I 311).

2. University of Pennsylvania Library (Special Collections) MS Eng 13= JTC's Commonplace Book p 54. Transcribed in the hand of JTC, with the title "Epitaph on an amiable Girl". Unsigned.

C. GENERAL NOTE

C quoted the lines to TP apropos of his sister Ann, who died in 1791. In fact they are variants of an epitaph which seems to have been current at the time. The variants always appear in the first of the two lines, the second being the same as in both C versions. Cf also *WEPF* 98–9, 402–4.

The closest analogue to the MS 1 version was reported in Tenby parish church, to the memory of Elizabeth Prosser, by Richard Warner *A Second Walk through Wales in August and September 1798* (2nd ed Bath 1800) 351. The first line reads "Rest, gentle lamb! to wait th' Almighty's will,".

The closest analogue to the MS 2 version—from Cheltenham churchyard on a Miss Forder—was collected by William Shenstone: the first line reads "Soft sleep thy dust, & wait th' almightys will," (*Shenstone's Miscellany 1759–1763* ed Ian A. Gordon—Oxford 1952—44; cf 147). Another, entitled *On the tomb of a beautiful girl*, in which the first line reads "Sleep, sleep, fair form: await the Almighty's will:", was published in *The Oriental Asylum* (Calcutta 1788) (q Bertram Dobell "Coleridgeana" *Athenaeum* 9 Jan 1904 p 53; original unlocated). Yet another, set as a glee for five voices by Dr Callcott and beginning "Sleep! soft fair form, await th' Almighty's will", was published in *The Words of the Most Favourite Pieces, Performed at the Glee Club, the•Catch Club, and Other Public Societies* comp Richard Clark (1814) 405. Yet another, from Harrow churchyard, entitled *On a Young Lady*, in which the first line reads "Sleep on thou fair, and wait the Almighty's will", was published in *A Select Collection of Epitaphs* (Ipswich 1806) 95. Of course, MS 2 may well be from yet another printed version, and may not have been connected to C by his nephew; it is one of a number of pieces which JTC transcribed without attributing authorship.

The lines, in the variant forms in which C quotes them, might be considered "adaptations". But so much is uncertain that they are not given here as such. Cf **105.X1** *Lines Probably Borrowed from John Gaunt.*

1 1 Rest, gentle Shade! & wait thy maker's will;
   2 Sleep soft in dust! wait the Almighty's will!
2 ☐ Then rise *unchang'd*, and be an Angel still!

2. 2 unchang'd!   2 &   2 angel

27. ARDUA PRIMA VIA EST

A. DATE

1791? The lines appear in the same ms as **28** *Greek Imitation of "A Winter Piece"*, which is dated 1791. In spite of some elementary blunders, they appear to date from C's later years at school, and the evidence of the paper suggests that they were transcribed around Whitsun (May) 1791 (see **28** VAR headnote sec A). Alternatively, it could be argued that they were written any time after Richards won the Chancellor's Prize for Latin Verse at Oxford (1787).

B. TEXT

In the possession of Sir Charles Cave (Oct 1981). On the recto of the first of two conjoint leaves, each 22.7×37.1 cm; wm T TAYLOR and (on the other leaf) a bugle within a shield, surmounted by a crown and all above G R; chain-lines 2.6 cm. Transcript in C's hand.

The verso of the same first leaf is filled with C's transcription of some English lines headed "A Winter Piece from Enfield's Speaker". The recto of the second leaf contains C's Greek imitation of the English lines (poem **28**). The verso of the second leaf is blank, apart from some later mathematical calculations.

The RT reproduces the ms, except for:

title. ms Ardua prima via est—Ovid—   **10.** Gradus] ms ǥGradus   **15.** macilentâ] ms ~~quondam~~ macilentâ

16⁺. C's spacing in the ms is slightly erratic here and elsewhere, but no extra space (for stanza division) is intended.

28. GREEK IMITATION OF
A WINTER PIECE

A. DATE

1791? This date is given along with C's signature at the end of the ms, and the paper is identical to that of his letter to GC of 17 May 1791 (*CL* I 9–11). There is room for doubt, however, because the Greek is not as advanced as one might have expected—in common with the Latin of **27** *Ardua Prima Via Est* in the same ms—though it could be argued that C would have corrected the poems when he copied them if he had been aware of their limitations. The paper is also identical to that of a letter which ELG assigns to 26 May 1789 (*CL* I 5), but again, ELG's grounds for adopting the earlier date are not compelling. The handwriting closely resembles that of the mss of **47** *Greek Epitaph for Howard's Tomb* and **48** *Sors Misera Servorum*, which date from Mar–Jul 1792.

B. TEXT

In the possession of Sir Charles Cave (Oct 1981). The recto of the second of two conjoint leaves, each 22.7×37.1 cm; wm C TAYLOR and (on the other leaf) a bugle within a shield, surmounted by a crown and all above GR; chain-lines 2.6 cm. Transcript in C's hand. Signed Ὁ Κόληρος [C's signature, "Kolēros", idiomatically preceded by the definite article], with the date αψϥά.

The first page of the ms is filled by C's Latin lines on a theme from Ovid, **27** *Ardua Prima Via Est*. The second page (verso of the first leaf) is filled by C's transcription of the English original of his Greek, headed "A Winter Piece from Enfield's Speaker" (see vol I headnote). The fourth page (verso of the second leaf) is blank, apart from some later mathematical calculations.

The transcript in another, 19th-century, hand in the folio letter-book at HRC (MS (Coleridge, S T) Letters I pp 255–6) has no textual authority, although it confirms some readings which have become rubbed and faint in the holograph.

The RT reproduces the ms, except for:

title. ms An imitation of the Winter Piece   **2.** ἐμβρέμετ'] ms 'ἐμβρέμετ'
6. θέλουσ'] ms θέλουσ'ά   **16.** ἄπαντ'] ms ἄπαντ'ά   **17.** πέσε,] ms ἔπεσε,

2, 4, etc. The elegiac couplets, whose alternate lines are indented as usual, are grouped as four-line stanzas separated by rules. C's word-spacing is erratic in some respects, and has been normalised.

29. O CURAS HOMINUM! O QUANTUM EST IN REBUS INANE!

A. DATE

1790–1? Internal evidence suggests that the poem dates from late in C's school career. The date of MS 1 provides a *terminus ante quem*.

B. TEXTS

1 [=RT]. BM Add MS 47551 = Ottery Copy Book ff 15ᵛ–17ᵛ. Transcript in C's hand.

1. PW (1834).

title. ☐ O Curas hominum—o quantum est in rebus inane—

1 ☐ The fervid Sun had more than halv'd the Day,
2 ☐ When gloomy on his couch Philedon lay:
3 ☐ His feeble frame consumptive as his purse;
4 ☐ His aching head did Wine and Women curse;
5 1 His fortunes ruin'd and his health decay'd,
   1   fortune   wealth
6 ☐ Clamorous his Duns, his gaming debts unpaid—
7 ☐ The Youth indignant seized his Taylor's bill,
8 ☐ And on its back thus wrote with moral quill:
    [*Line-space*]
9 ☐ Various as colours in the rainbow shewn,
10 1 ~~And~~ Or similar in emptiness alone,
   1   Or
11 ☐ How false, how vain are Man's pursuits below!
12 ☐ Wealth, Honor, Pleasure—what can ye bestow?
13 ☐ Yet see, how high and low and young and old
14 ☐ Pursue the all delusive power of Gold!
15 ☐ Fond Man! should all Peru thy empire own,
16 ☐ For thee tho' all Golconda's jewells shone,
17 ☐ What greater bliss could all this Wealth supply?
18 ☐ What, but to eat and drink and sleep and die?
19 ☐ Go—tempt the stormy sea, the burning soil—
20 ☐ Go—waste the night in thought, the day in toil!
21 1 ~~Bla~~ Dark frowns the rock, and fierce the tempests rave—
   1   Dark
22 ☐ Thy ingots go th' unconscious deep to pave:
23 ☐ Or thunder at thy door the midnight train:
24 1 Or Death shall knock, who never knocks in vain!
   1   that
    [*Line-space*]

25 1 Next Honor's Sons come bustling in amain—
  1   on
26 □ I laugh with Pity at the idle train.
27 □ Infirm of Soul! who think'st to lift thy name
28 □ Upon the waxen wings of human fame—
29 □ Who for a sound—*articulated breath*—
30 □ Gazest undaunted in the face of Death;
31 1 What art ⟨thou⟩ but ~~me~~ a meteor's glaring light,
  1   thou   a
32 □ Blazing a moment and then sunk in night?
33 □ Caprice, which rais'd thee high, shall hurl thee low,
34 1 And Envy blast the Laurels on thy brow.
  1 Or
    [*Line-space*]
35 □ To such poor Joys could ancient Honor lead,
36 1 When empty fame was toiling Merit's meed.
  1   mead;
37 □ To modern Honor other lays belong,
38 □ Profuse of Joy and Lord of Right and Wrong,
39 □ *Honor* can game, drink, riot in the Stew,
40 □ Cut a friend's throat—what cannot *Honor* do?
41 □ Ah! me—the storm within can Honor still
42 □ For Julio's death—whom Honor made me kill?
43 1 Or will my Honor kindly tell the way
  1   this lordly Honor
44 1 To pay the debts, which Honor makes me pay?
  1   those
45 □ Or if with pistol and terrific threats
46 □ I make some Traveller pay my Honor's debts,
47 □ A medicine for this *Wound* can Honor give?
48 □ Ah no! my Honour dies to make my Honour live!
    [*Line-space*]
49 1 ~~No~~ But see young Pleasure and her train advance,
  1   But
50 □ And Joy and Laughter wake th' inebriate dance.
51 □ Around my neck she throws her fair white arms—
52 □ I meet her loves and madden at her charms.
53 □ For the gay grape can Joys celestial move;
54 □ And what so sweet below as Woman's Love?
55 □ With such high transport every moment flies—
56 □ I *curse* Experience, that he makes me wise.
57 □ For at *his* frown the dear deliriums flew,
58 □ And the chang'd scene now wears a gloomy hue.
59 □ An hideous hag th' Enchantress Pleasure seems,
60 1 And all her Joys appear but feverish dreams—
  1   feverous
61 □ The vain resolve still broken, and still made—
62 □ Disease, and Loathing and Remorse invade;
63 □ The charm is vanish'd, and the bubble's broke—

64 □ A Slave to Pleasure is a Slave to Smoke.
   [*Line-space*]
65 □ Such lays repentant did the Muse supply,
66 1 When, as the Sun ⟨was⟩ hastening down the Sky,
   1   was
67 □ In glittering state twice fifty guineas come—
68 □ His Mother's Plate antique had rais'd the sum—
69 □ Forth leap'd Philedon of new life possest:
70 1 'Twas Brooke's till   two—twas Hacketts' all the rest
   1   all till two,—
70fn 1 Brooke's—a famous gaming house in St James' Street.
   Hacketts'—a brothel under the Covent-garden Piazzas.

title. *1* O, Curas hominum! O, *1* inane!   **1.** *1* day,   **2.** *1* lay;   **3.** *1* purse,
4. *1* wine and women   **6.** *1* unpaid,   **7.** *1* youth *1* seiz'd *1* tailor's
9. *1* "Various *1* colors *1* shown,   **13.** *1* low,   **14.** *1* Gold.   **15.** *1* man!
16. *1* jewels   **17.** *1* wealth   **19.** *1* Go,   **20.** *1* Go, *1* toil,   **22.** *1* the
1 pave!   **23.** *1* train,   **24.** *1* death *1* knock *1* vain.   **25.** *1* sons *1* amain;
26. *1* pity   **27.** *1* soul!   **28.** *1* fame,—   **29.** *1* sound, articulated breath—
30. *1* death!   **31.** *1* Meteor's *1* light—   **33.** *1* Caprice *1* high   **34.** *1* envy
1 laurels   **35.** *1* joys *1* lead   **37.** *1* Modern *1* belong;   **38.** *1* joy *1* right
1 wrong,   **39.** *1* Honor *1* stew,   **40.** *1* throat;— *1* Honor   **41.** *1* Ah me—
42. *1* death,   **46.** *1* traveller   **47.** *1* med'cine *1* wound   **48.** *1* Ah, *1* Honor
1 Honor live.   **49.** *1* see! *1* Pleasure,   **50.** *1* joy *1* laughter *1* the *1* dance;
51. *1* arms,   **52.** *1* loves,   **53.** *1* joys *1* move,   **54.** *1* love?   **55.** *1* flies,
56. *1* curse experience, *1* wise;   **57.** *1* his   **59.** *1* A   **60.** *1* joys *1* dreams.
61. *1* Resolve *1* broken *1* made,   **62.** *1* Disease *1* loathing *1* remorse
63. *1* vanish'd *1* broke,—   **64.** *1* slave *1* pleasure *1* slave *1* smoke!"
65. *1* supply;   **66.** *1* When *1* sky,   **67.** *1* come,—   **68.** *1* plate *1* sum.
69. *1* possest:—   **70.** *1* Brookes's *1* 'twas Hackett's *1* rest!

title. The list of contents in PR *1* gives the title as "Honor."
8⁺, 24⁺, 34⁺, 48⁺, 64⁺. No line-space in PR *1*.

30. HAPPINESS: A POEM

A. DATE

Early summer (May–Jun?) 1791.

B. TEXTS

1. In the possession of Erwin Schwarz (Jul 1982). Single large folded leaf, 46.0×36.2/37.9 cm overall; wm horn within shield beneath crown | C T TAY-LOR; countermark Q R; chain-lines 4.5 cm. In two columns down to line 41,

the four closing lines (102–3, 104–5) doubled up; the remainder in a single column. Comprises the larger part of an als to GC, 22 Jun 1791 (*CL* I 11–14). The first page of the letter and lines 1–41 of the poem are reproduced in Sotheby's Catalogue (17 Dec 1981) 113. There is a photocopy of the complete letter in BM RP 2277 (i).

C's letter begins: "This is the Poem, you wished to see—". There is a transcript by John May Jr in the Green Ottery Copy Book ff 13ᵛ–16ʳ (VCL S LT Fl.3), headed "Upon the Author's leaving school and entering into Life" and containing alternative readings in lines 25, 57, and 77fn. These variants are recorded here, but it is unlikely that they possess any authority (the version of 77fn is contradicted by the sense of the poem).

2 [=RT]. BM Add MS 47551=Ottery Copy Book ff 18ʳ–21ʳ. Transcript in C's hand.

The text improves several details of MS 1; but its replacement of lines 91.1.1–5 by line 91 attains dignity at the cost of rhyme and sense.

1. PW (1834).

title. 2 Happiness a Poem • *1* HAPPINESS.

1 ☐	On wide or narrow scale shall Man
2 ☐	Most happily describe Life's plan?
3 ☐	Say, shall he bloom and wither there,
4 ☐	Where first his infant buds appear?
5 ☐	Or upwards dart with soaring force,
6 1	And dare some more ambitious course?
2	tempt ~~wide~~ more
1	more

[*Line-space*]

7 1 *1*	Obedient now to Hope's command
2	~~Ano~~ Obedient
8 ☐	I bid each humble wish expand—
9 ☐	And fair and bright Life's prospects seem,
10 1	When Hope displays her cheering beam,
2	While ~~Fa~~ *Hope*
1	Hope
11 ☐	And Fancy's vivid colourings stream.
11.1.1 1	How pants my breast, before my eyes
11.1.2 1	While Honour waves her radiant prize,
12 1	And Emulation stands me nigh,
2 *1*	While
13 ☐	The Goddess of the eager eye!

[*Line-space*]

14 ☐	With foot advanc'd and anxious heart
15 ☐	Now for the fancied goal I start—
16 ☐	Ah! why will Reason intervene
17 ☐	Me and my promis'd joys between?
18 ☐	She stops my course, she chains my speed,

19 ☐   While thus her forceful words proceed.
        [*Line-space*]
20 ☐   Ah! listen, Youth, ere yet too late,
21 1 *1* What evils on thy course may wait—
    2   in
22 1   To bend the head, to bow the knee,
    2 *1*   bow   bend
23 ☐   A Minion of Servility;
24 1 2 At low Pride's frequent frown to sigh
    1   frowns
25 ☐   And watch the glance in Folly's eye—
26 ☐   To toil intense—yet toil in vain!
27 ☐   And feel, with what an hollow pain
28 ☐   Pale Disappointment hangs her head
29 ☐   O'er darling Expectation dead.
        [*Line-space*]
30 ☐   The scene is chang'd—& Fortune's gale
31 ☐   Shall belly out each prosp'rous sail!
32 ☐   Yet sudden Wealth, full well I know,
33 ☐   Did never Happiness bestow—
34 ☐   That wealth, to which we were not born,
35 ☐   Dooms us to Sorrow or to Scorn—
36 1 *1* Behold yon flock, which long had trod
    2   who
37 1   O'er the short grass of ~~Lincoln's~~ Devon's sod,
    2 *1*   ←—Devon's—→
38 ☐   To Lincoln's rank rich meads transferr'd—
39 ☐   And in their Fate thy own be fear'd.
40 ☐   Thro' every limb Contagions fly;
41 1 2 Deformed,   choak'd—they burst and die.
    1   and
        [*Line-space*]
42 ☐   When Luxury opens wide her arms,
43 ☐   And smiling wooes thee to those charms,
44 ☐   Whose fascination thousands own—
45 1 2 Shall *thy* brow wear the Stoic frown?
    1   brows
46 ☐   And when her goblet she extends,
47 ☐   Which mad'ning myriads press around,
48 ☐   What pow'r divine thy soul befriends,
49 ☐   That *Thou* should'st dash it to the ground?
        [*Line-space*]
50 1   ⟨No—⟩ *Thou* shalt drink, and *thou* shalt know
    2 *1*   "No—
51 ☐   Her transient bliss, her lasting woe
52 ☐   Her maniac joys, that know no measure,
53 1   With Riot rude and painted Pleasure:
    2 *1*   "And
54 ☐   Till (sad reverse!) th' Enchantress vile

55 1 To frowns converts her wonted smile—
 2 *1*   magic
56 ☐ Her train impatient to destroy
57 1 Observe the ~~train~~ frown with gloomy joy—
 2   frown
 1   her
58 ☐ On thee with harpy fangs they seize—
59 ☐ The hideous offspring of Disease—
60 ☐ Swoln Dropsy ignorant of Rest;
61 ☐ And Fever garb'd in scarlet vest;
62 ☐ Consumption driving the quick hearse;
63 ☐ And Gout, that howls the frequent curse;
64 ☐ With Apoplex of heavy head,
65 ☐ That surely aims his dart of Lead.
   [*Line-space*]
66 ☐ But say—Life's Joy's unmix'd were given
67 ☐ To Thee, some favourite of Heaven;
68 1 Without, within— tho' all were Health—
 2 *1* "Within—without—
69 ☐ Yet what e'en thus are Fame, Pow'r, Wealth,
70 1 ?~~Barth~~ But sounds, that variously express
 2 *1* "But
71 1 ?𝔅What's thine already—Happiness.
 2 *1* "What's
72 ☐ 'Tis thine the converse deep to hold
73 ☐ With all the famous Sons of Old—
74 ☐ And thine the happy waking dream,
75 ☐ While Hope pursues some favorite theme,
76 1 As oft, when Night o'er heaven has spread,
 2 *1*   is
77 ☐ Round this maternal seat you tread,
77fn 2 Christ's Hospital
78 ☐ Where far from Splendor, far from Riot,
79 ☐ In Silence wrapt sleeps car⟨e⟩less Quiet.
80 1 *1* 'Tis thine with Fancy oft to talk;
 2   ⟨with⟩
81 ☐ And thine the peaceful Evening Walk;
82 ☐ And what to thee the sweetest are,
83 ☐ The setting sun, the evening star,
84 1 The tints that live along the sky,
 2 *1*   which
85 1 *1* And moon, that meets thy 'raptur'd eye [. . .],
 2   my
86 1 2 Where oft the tear does grateful start—
 1   shall
87 ☐ Dear silent Pleasures of the Heart!
88 ☐ Ah! being blest! for Heaven shall lend
89 ☐ To share thy simple joys—a friend.
90 ☐ Ah! doubly blest! if Love supply

90.1.1 1   Lustre to this now heavy eye,
90.1.2 1   And with unwonted Spirit grace—
90.1.3 1   That fat vacuity of face.
90.1.4 1   Or if e'en Love, the mighty Love
90.1.5 1   Shall find this change his power above,
  91 2 *1* "His influence to complete thy joy;
  92 1   Some lovely maid perchance thou'lt find
     2 *1* "If chance some lovely maid thou find
  93 ☐   To read thy visage in thy mind.
         [*Line-space*]
  94 ☐   One blessing more demands thy care:
  95 ☐   Once more to Heaven address the prayer.
  96 ☐   For humble Independence pray,
  97 ☐   The Guardian Genius of thy way;
  98 ☐   Whom (sages say) in days of yore
  99 ☐   Meek Competence to Wisdom bore.
100 ☐   So shall thy little vessel glide
101 1   With a fair breeze adown Life's tide,
     2 *1*   the
102 ☐   And Hope, if e'er thou 'gin'st to sorrow,
103 ☐   Remind thee of some fair to-morrow,
104 ☐   Till Death shall close thy tranquil eye,
105 ☐   While Faith proclaims, "Thou shalt not die."

1. *1* wide,   **2.** *1* life's   2 Plan?   **3.** 2 there;   **4.** *1* appear;   **7.** *1* command,
8. 2 expand. • *1* expand,   **11.** *1* colorings   2 stream! • *1* stream,   **12.** *1* nigh
13. *1* eye.   **15.** *1* start:—   **17.** *1* promised   *1* between!   **19.** 2 proceed:
20. 2 *1* "Ah!   2 listen—Youth—   *1* youth,   2 late—   **21.** 2 "What
2 wait: • *1* wait!   **22.** 2 "To   2 head.   2 knee—   **23.** 2 ("A   2 *1* minion
2 Servility:) • *1* Servility,   **24.** 2 "At   2 *1* Pride's   2 sigh; • *1* sigh,   **25.** 2 "And
2 *1* eye;   **26.** 2 "To   *1* intense,   2 vain; • *1* vain,   **27.** 2 "And   2 *1* feel
1 a   **28.** 2 "Pale   **29.** 2 "O'er   2 *1* dead!   **30.** *1* "The   2 chang'd, •
1 changed   2 *1* and   **31.** 2 *1* prosperous sail.   **32.** 2 "Yet   2 Wealth— •
1 wealth   2 know— • *1* know   **33.** 2 "Did   2 *1* bestow.   **34.** 2 "That
Wealth,   *1* born   **35.** 2 "Dooms   2 *1* sorrow   2 *1* scorn.   **36.** 2 "Behold
1 flock   **37.** 2 "O'er   2 sod   **38.** 2 "To   *1* transferr'd,   **39.** 2 "And
2 *1* fate   *1* fear'd;   **40.** 2 "Thro' • *1* Through   *1* contagions   2 fly— • *1* fly,
41. 2 "Deformed, • *1* Deform'd   2 choak'd • *1* chok'd   2 die!   **42.** 2 *1* "When
43. 2 "And   2 charms   **44.** 2 "Whose   2 *1* own,   **45.** 2 "Shall   *1* thy
2 *1* stoic   **46.** 2 "And   *1* extends   **47.** 2 "Which   *1* madd'ning   **48.** 2 "What
2 *1* power   2 *1* befriends   **49.** 2 "That   2 *thou* • *1* thou   *1* shouldst   *1* ground?—
50. *1* No,   2 *thou* shalt drink, and *thou* • *1* thou shalt drink, and thou   **51.** 2 "Her
2 *1* woe,   **52.** 2 "Her   **53.** *1* And riot   2 rude,   2 Pleasure; • *1* pleasure;—
54. 2 "Till   2 reverse!   *1* the   **55.** 2 "To   2 smile: • *1* smile;   **56.** 2 "Her
1 destroy,   **57.** 2 "Observe   2 joy: • *1* joy;   **58.** 2 "On   *1* seize   **59.** 2 "The
2 Disease: • *1* Disease,   **60.** 2 "Swoln • *1* Swoll'n   2 rest; • *1* Rest,   **61.** 2 "And
1 vest,   **62.** 2 "Consumption   *1* hearse,   **63.** 2 "And   *1* Gout   2 curse: •
1 curse,   **64.** 2 "With   *1* head   **65.** 2 "That   *1* lead.   **66.** 2 *1* "But
1 say,   2 *1* joys   **67.** 2 "To thee, • *1* To thee   2 *1* favorite   *1* Heaven:

68. *1* Within, without,   *1* health—   **69.** 2 "Yet   2 *1* Power,   2 Wealth
70. *1* But   2 *1* sounds   *1* express,   **71.** *1* What's   *1* Happiness!   **72.** 2 "Tis
73. 2 "With   *1* sons   2 old: • *1* old;   **74.** 2 "And   *1* dream   **75.** 2 "While
2 theme;   **76.** 2 "As   *1* oft   2 *1* Heaven   **77.** 2 "Round   **78.** 2 "Where
1 splendour,   2 Riot • *1* riot,   **79.** 2 "In   *1* silence   2 *1* careless   *1* quiet.
80. 2 "Tis   *1* fancy   *1* talk,   **81.** 2 "And   2 *1* evening   *1* walk;   **82.** 2 "And
1 are—   **83.** 2 "The   2 Sun,   *1* star—   **84.** 2 "The tints • *1* The tints,
85. 2 "And   2 *1* Moon   2 *1* raptur'd eye,   **86.** 2 "Where   *1* start,   **87.** 2 "Dear
2 *1* pleasures   **88.** 2 "Ah!   *1* Being   2 blest— • *1* blest,   **89.** 2 "To   2 *1* joys
a friend!   **90.** 2 "Ah!   2 blest— • *1* blest,   **91.** *1* His   *1* joy,   **92.** *1* If
93. 2 "To   2 mind!   **94.** 2 *1* "One   2 care— • *1* care:—   **95.** 2 "Once
2 *1* prayer: **96.** 2 "For   *1* independence pray   **97.** 2 "The   2 *1* guardian
genius   2 way,   **98.** 2 "Whom   **99.** 2 "Meek   *1* competence   *1* wisdom bore,
100. 2 "So   2 vessell   **101.** 2 "With   **102.** 2 "And   *1* 'ginst   *1* sorrow
103. 2 "Remind   **104.** 2 "Till   *1* death   *1* eye   **105.** 2 "While   *1* proclaims
2 Thou   *1* "thou   2 die!   *1* die!"

19⁺. No line-space in TEXTS 2 *1*.
25. □ in] Green Ottery Copy Book f 14ʳ [John May Jr's transcript] of
49⁺. No line-space in TEXTS 2 *1* (the first uncertain).
57. Green Ottery Copy Book f 15ʳ [John May Jr's transcript] ~~frown~~ ⟨fiend⟩
65⁺. No line-space in MS 2.
77fn. Green Ottery Copy Book f 15ʳ [John May Jr's transcript] ⟨Ottery Saint Mary in
Devonshire⟩   The addition is quite misleading.
80–105. C wrote out an adapted version of these lines in a letter to RS, 13 Jul 1794,
as if extempore (ms at PML: MA 1848 (2); cf *CL* I 85–6):

> 'Tis thine with faery forms to talk,
> And thine the ~~pensive~~ philosophic Walk,
> And (what to thee the sweetest are)
> The setting Sun, the Evening Star,
> The tints, that live along the Sky,
> And Moon, that meets thy raptur'd eye,
> Where grateful oft the big drops start—
> Dear silent Pleasures of the Heart!
> But if thou pour one votive Lay,
> For humble Independence pray,
> Whom (sages say) in days of yore
> Meek Competence to Wisdom bore.
> So shall thy little Vessel glide
> With a fair Breeze adown the Tide—
> Till Death shall close thy tranquil eye
> While Faith exclaims "Thou shalt not die!

90.1.3. Green Ottery Copy Book f 15ᵛ [John May Jr's transcript, added as fn]: ⟨The
Author was at this time æt. 17. remarkable for a plump face.⟩

31. AN ANTHEM FOR THE CHILDREN OF CHRIST'S HOSPITAL

A. DATE

1789–91. PR *1* appends the date 1789, and the poem was inscribed in MS 1 by the summer of 1791. If it owes anything to a pamphlet by Bowles published in Mar 1790 (for which see vol I headnote), it was composed closer to the later date.

B. TEXTS

1 [=RT]. BM Add MS 47551 = Ottery Copy Book ff 5ᵛ–6ʳ. Transcript in C's hand.

1. PW (1834).

title. 1 An Anthem • *1* ANTHEM | FOR THE CHILDREN OF CHRIST'S HOSPITAL.
title fn. 1 This Anthem is written, as if intended to have been sung by the Children of Xts' Hospital.

1 1 Seraphs! around th' Eternals' seat who throng
   1   Eternal's
2 ☐ With tuneful extacies of Praise:
3 1 O teach our feeble tongues, like you, the song
   1   yours
4 ☐ Of fervent gratitude to raise—
5 ☐ Like you, inspir'd with holy flame
6 ☐ To dwell on that ⱡAlmighty Name.
7 ☐ Who bade the Child of Woe no longer sigh,
8 1 And Joy in tears o'erspread the Widows' eye.
   1   Widow's
   [*Line-space*]
9 ☐ Th' All gracious Parent hears the Wretch's prayer:
10 ☐ The meek tear strongly pleads on high:
11 ☐ Wan Resignation struggling with Despair
12 ☐ The Lord beholds with pitying eye—
13 ☐ Sees cheerless Want unpitied pine,
14 1 Disease its head on earth recline,
   1   on earth its head
15 ☐ And bids Compassion seek the realms of Woe
16 ☐ To heal the Wounded, and to raise the low.
   [*Line-space*]
17 ☐ She comes! she comes! the meek-ey'd power I see—
18 ☐ With liberal hand, that loves to bless!
19 ☐ The clouds of Sorrow at Her presence flee!

20 1   ←—Rejoice,—→ ye Children of Distress!
   1   Rejoice! rejoice!
21 ☐   The beams, that play around her head,
22 ☐   Thro' Want's dark vale their radiance spread:
23 ☐   The young uncultur'd mind imbibes the ray,
24 1   And Vice reluctant quits the ~~promised~~' expected prey.
   1   ←—th'—→
    [Line-space]
25 1   Cease, thou ~~lonern~~ Mother! cease thy wailings drear!
   1   lorn
26 ☐   Ye Babes! th' unconscious sob forego!
27 ☐   Or let full Gratitude now prompt the tear,
28 ☐   Which erst did Sorrow force to flow.
29 ☐   Unkindly cold, and tempest shrill
30 ☐   In Life's Morn oft the Traveller chill:
31 ☐   But soon his path the Sun of Love shall warm,
32 ☐   And each glad scene look brighter for the Storm.

2. *1* praise: **3.** *1* O!   *1* tongues   **6.** *1* Almighty name   **7.** *1* child of
woe   **9.** *1* all-gracious   *1* wretch's prayer;   **10.** *1* high;   **11.** *1* despair
12. *1* eye;   **13.** *1* want   **15.** *1* compassion   *1* woe   **16.** *1* wounded,
17. *1* meek ey'd   *1* see   **18.** *1* hand   *1* bless;   **19.** *1* sorrow   *1* her   *1* flee;
20. *1* children   *1* distress!   **21.** *1* beams   *1* head   **22.** *1* want's   **24.** *1* vice
25. *1* mother!   *1* drear;   **26.** *1* babes! the   *1* forego;   **27.** *1* gratitude   *1* tear
28. *1* sorrow   **29.** *1* cold   **30.** *1* life's morn   *1* traveller chill,   **31.** *1* sun
1 warm;   **32.** *1* storm!

2, 4, etc. MS 1 indents as in RT; PR *1* indents slightly differently.
8⁺, 16⁺, 24⁺. MS 1 has rules.

32. SONNET: SENT TO MRS ——
WITH FIELDING'S *AMELIA*

A. DATE

1789–91. The poem was almost certainly written after 1789, when C was intro-
duced to Bowles's *Sonnets*. Perhaps it dates from about the time he left Christ's
Hospital, when he might have made such a gift to Mrs Evans. It must have been
written before the summer of 1791, the date of MS 1 (EHC's suggested 1792 is
too late).

B. TEXTS

1 [=**RT**]. BM Add MS 47551 = Ottery Copy Book f 29ʳ. Transcript in C's hand.

The first word of lines 1 and 2 has been torn away.

1. PW (1834).

title. 1 Sonnet 7 Sent to Mʳˢ —— with an Amelia. • *1* WITH FIELDING'S AMELIA.

1	1ⁱᵐᵖ *1*	ˌVirtuˌes and Woes alike too great for Man
2	1ⁱᵐᵖ	ˌInˌ the soft tale oft claimṣ the *useless* sigh;
	1	claim
3	☐	For vain th' attempt to realize the plan;
4	☐	On Folly's Wings must Imitation fly.
		[*Line-space*]
5	☐	With other aim has Fielding here display'd
6	☐	Each social Duty, and each social Care;
7	1	With ~~warm~~ just yet vivid colouring pourtray'd
	1	just
8	☐	What *every* Wife *should* be * what *many are.*
		[*Line-space*]
9	☐	And sure the Parent of a race so sweet
10	1	With doubled pleasure on the page shall dwell;
	1	double
11	☐	Each scene with sympathizing breast shall meet,
12	☐	While Reason still with smiles delights to tell
13	☐	Maternal Hope, that her lov'd Progeny
14	☐	In all but sorrows shall Amelias be!

1. *1* man   **2.** *1* useless   **3.** *1* the attempt   *1* plan,   **4.** *1* folly's wings   *1* imitation   **6.** *1* duty   *1* care; .   **7.** *1* coloring   *1* portray'd   **8.** *1* every wife should be, what many are.   **10.** *1* dwell,   **13.** *1* hope,   **14.** *1* Sorrows

2, 4, 6, 8. Indented in PR *1*.
4⁺, 8⁺. No line-space in PR *1*.

33. SONNET: ON QUITTING CHRIST'S HOSPITAL

A. DATE

Jul–Aug 1791.

B. TEXTS

1 [=RT]. BM Add MS 47551 = Ottery Copy Book f 31ʳ. Transcript in C's hand.

1. PW (1834).

title. 1 Sonnet 9 On quitting Christ's Hospital • *1* SONNET. ǀ ON THE SAME.

1 ☐ Farewell! Parental scenes! a sad farewell—
2 ☐ To you my grateful heart still fondly clings,
3 ☐ Tho' fluttering round on Fancy's burnish'd wings
4 ☐ Her tales of future Joy Hope loves to tell.
    [*Line-space*]
5 ☐ Adieu—Adieu—Ye much-lov'd Cloysters pale.
6 ☐ Ah! would those happy days return again
7 ☐ When 'neath your arches free from every stain
8 1 ~~Her tales of~~ I heard of Guilt and wonder'd at the Tale!
  1 ←——I——→
    [*Line-space*]
9 ☐ Dear haunts! where oft my simple lays I sang
10 ☐ Listning meanwhile the echoings of my feet—
11 ☐ Lingring I quit you with as great a pang
12 ☐ As when erewhile my weeping Childhood torn
13 ☐ By early Sorrow from my native seat
14 1 Mingled its tears with her's—my ~~weeping~~ widow'd Parent lorn!
  1   ←——widow'd——→

1. *1* Farewell parental   *1* sad farewell!   **5.** *1* Adieu, adieu! ye much lov'd cloisters pale!   **6.** *1* again,   **7.** *1* arches, *1* stain,   **8.** *1* guilt *1* tale!   **9.** *1* sang, **10.** *1* Listening *1* feet,   **11.** *1* Lingering *1* you, *1* pang,   **12.** *1* ere while, *1* childhood,   **13.** *1* sorrow *1* seat,   **14.** *1* hers—   *1* lorn.

title. The poem which precedes PR *1* in *PW* (1834) is "ABSENCE. ǀ A FAREWELL ODE ON QUITTING SCHOOL FOR JESUS COLLEGE, CAMBRIDGE." (the later title of **39** *Absence: An Ode*). The title given in the list of contents in *PW* (1834) is "Sonnet. On Leaving School."
4⁺, 8⁺. No line-space in PR *1*.

34. ODE TO SLEEP

A. DATE

17 Aug 1791 (see subtitle in ms, given below). PR *1* appends the incorrect date 1790.

B. TEXTS

1 [=**RT**]. BM Add MS 47551 = Ottery Copy Book ff 21ᵛ–22ʳ. Transcript in C's hand.

1. PW (1834).

title. 1 Ode to Sleep— | Travelling in the Exeter Coach with three other Passengers over Bagshot heath after some vain endeavors to compose myself I compos'd this ode—August 17ᵗʰ, 1791 • *1* INSIDE THE COACH.

  1 1 'Tis harder on Bagshot heath to try
      1   hard
  2 □ Unclos'd to keep the weary eye;
  3 1 But ah! oblivious nod to get
      1   Oblivion's
  4 □ In rattling Coach is harder yet!
      [*Line-space*]
  5 □ Slumbrous God of half-shut eye,
  6 □ Who lov'st with limbs supine to lie;
  7 □ Soother sweet of toil and care—
  8 □ Listen, listen to my prayer,
  9 □ And to thy votary dispence,
 10 □ Thy soporific influence!
      [*Line-space*]
 11 □ What tho' around thy drowsy head
 12 □ The seven-fold Cap of Night be spread,
12fn 1 vulge y-clept night-cap.
 13 1 Yet lift thy drowsy head awhile,
      1   that
 14 □ And *yawn* propitiously a smile:
 15 □ In drizzly rains poppæan dews
 16 □ O'er the tir'd inmates of the Coach diffuse!
      [*Line-space*]
 17 □ And when thou'st charm'd our eyes to rest
 18 □ Pillowing the chin upon the breast,
 19 □ Bid many a dream from thy Dominions
 20 1 Wave their various-painted Pinions,
      1   its
 21 □ Till—ere the splendid visions close—
 22 □ We snore *quartettes* in extacy of Nose!
      [*Line-space*]
 23 □ While thus we urge our aery course,
 24 □ Ah! may no jolt's electric force
 25 □ Our fancies from their steeds unhorse;
 26 1 And calls us from thy faery reign
      1   call
 27 □ To dreary Bagshot heath again!

1. *1* Heath   **4.** *1* coach *1* yet.   **5.** *1* half shut eye!   **6.** *1* Limbs   **7.** *1* care

8. *1* prayer;   **9.** *1* dispense   **12.** *1* cap   *1* night   **13.** *1* awhile   **14.** *1* yawn
1 smile;   **15.** *1* poppean   **16.** *1* diffuse;   **19.** *1* dominions   **20.** *1* pinions,
21. *1* Till   *1* close   **22.** *1* quartettes   *1* nose.   **23.** *1* airy   **24.** *1* Oh
25. *1* unhorse,   **26.** *1* fairy   **27.** *1* Heath

1–4. Indented in TEXTS 1 *1*; PR *1* is thereafter variously indented.
4⁺, 10⁺, 16⁺, 22⁺. No line-space in PR 1.

35. PLYMTREE ROAD

A. DATE

18 Aug 1791 (PR *1* appends the incorrect date 1790).

B. TEXTS

1 [=RT]. BM Add MS 47551 = Ottery Copy Book ff 22ᵛ–23ʳ. Transcript in
C's hand.
The transcript is continuous with the preceding poem on ff 21ᵛ–22ʳ, **34** *Ode
to Sleep*.

   1. PW (1834).

title. *1* DEVONSHIRE ROADS.

⁻**1.1** ☐ Th' indignant bard compos'd this furious ode,
⁻**1.2** ☐ As tir'd he dragg'd his Way thro' Plymtree road.
⁻**1.2⁺** 1   August 18ᵗʰ 1791.
       [*Line-space*]
   1 ☐ Crusted with filth and stuck in mire
   2 ☐ Dull sounds the Bard's bemudded lyre,
   3 ☐ Nathless Revenge and Ire the Poet gode
   4 ☐ To pour his imprecations on the road.
       [*Line-space*]
   5 ☐ Curst road! whose execrable way
   6 ☐ Was darkly shadow'd out in Milton's lay,
   7 ☐ When the sad fiends thro' Hell's sulphureous roads
   8 ☐ Took the first survey of their new abodes:
   9 ☐ Or when the fall'n Archangel fierce
  10 ☐ Dar'd thro' the realms of Night to pierce,
  11 ☐ What time the Bloodhound lur'd by human scent
  12 1   Thro' ←—Chaos'—→ quagmires floundering went!
   1   all Confusion's
       [*Line-space*]
  13 ☐ Nor cheering pipe, nor bird's shrill note
  14 ☐ Around thy dreary paths shall float;

15 ☐ Their boding songs shall screech-owls pour
16 ☐ To fright the guilty Shepherds sore
17 ☐ Led by the fwandering fires astray
17fn 1 Jack o' lanthorns
18 ☐ Thro' the dank horrors of thy way!
　　　　[*Line-space*]
19 ☐ While they their mud-lost sandals hunt,
20 ☐ May all the curses, which they grunt
21 ☐ In raging moan, like goaded hog,
22 ☐ Alight upon thee, damned Bog!

⁻**1.1.** *1* The　*1* Bard　**0.1.2** *1* way　*1* Plimtree road!　**2.** *1* lyre;　**3.** *1* goad
8. *1* abodes;　**10.** *1* through　**11.** *1* Blood Hound　*1* Human　**12.** *1* went.
13. *1* Bird's　**15.** *1* scritch owls　**16.** *1* shepherds sore,　**17.** *1* wandering
19. *1* hunt　**21.** *1* moan

⁻**1.1–2.** Printed as the first two lines of text in PR *1*. In MS 1 the lines stand almost as the title.
1–4, 5–11, 12, etc. Different patterns of indentation in PR *1*.
3. gode] MS 1 underlines, adding "goad" in the margin.
4⁺. No line-space in PR *1*.
17fn. Cued to "wandering fires" in MS 1.
18⁺. Line-space not certain in either text.

36. ODE ON THE OTTERY AND TIVERTON CHURCH MUSIC

A. DATE

Aug 1791? The poem was probably written following a visit to Tiverton, soon after C arrived home in Ottery from Christ's Hospital. Its burlesque parodic style, allusions to Milton's octosyllabics, and other internal features resemble those of the two poems **34–5** that C wrote on the journey homewards.

B. TEXTS

1 [=**RT**]. BM Add MS 47551=Ottery Copy Book ff 23ᵛ–24ʳ. Transcript in C's hand.

1. PW (1834).

title. 1 Ode on the Ottery and Tiverton Church Music. • *1* MUSIC.

1 ☐ Hence—soul-dissolving Harmony!

2 1   Who lead'st th' oblivious soul awstray:
   1   That   astray—
3 1   Tho' you sphere-descended be,
   1   thou
4 □   Hence! away!
       [*Line-space*]
5 □   Thou, Mightier Goddess, thou demand'st my lay.
6 □   Born when Earth was seiz'd with Colic,
7 □   Or as more sapient sages say,
8 □   What time the Legion Diabolic
9 □   Compell'd their beings to enshrine
10 □   In bodies vile of herded swine
11 □   Precipitate adown the steep
12 □   With hideous rout were plunging in the deep,
13 1   ~~Then if aright old~~ And Hog and Devil mingling grunt & yell
   1   And Hog and Devil mingling grunt & yell
14 □   Seiz'd on the ear with horrible obtrusion,
15 □   Then, if aright old legendaries tell,
16 □   Wert thou begot by Discord on Confusion!
       [*Line-space*]
17 □   What tho' no name's sonorous power
18 □   Was given thee at thy natal hour,
19 □   Yet oft I feel thy sacred might,
20 □   While Concords wing their distant flight:
21 □   Such power inspires thy holy Son,
22 □   Sable Clerk of Tiverton!
23 □   And oft where Otter sports his stream
24 □   I hear thy banded Offspring scream—
25 □   Thou—Goddess! Thou inspir'st each throat!
       [*Line-space*]
26 □   Tis thou, who pour'st the screech-owl note!
27 □   Transported hear'st thy children all
28 □   Scrape, and blow and squeek and squall—
29 □   And while Old Otter's steeple rings
30 □   Clappest hoarse thy raven wings!
30⁺ 1 ~~Cetera desunt.~~

1. *1* Hence, *1* Harmony   **3.** *1* Though *1* sphere *1* be—   **4.** *1* Hence away!—   **5.** *1* Thou mightier *1* lay,   **6.** *1* earth *1* cholic;   **8.** *1* diabolic   **9.** *1* Compelled   **10.** *1* swine,   **13.** *1* hog and devil *1* and   **14.** *1* obtrusion;—   **15.** *1* Then   **18.** *1* hour!—   **20.** *1* concords *1* flight.   **21.** *1* son   **22.** *1* clerk *1* Tiverton.   **23.** *1* stream,   **24.** *1* offspring scream.   **25.** *1* Thou Goddess! thou *1* throat;   **26.** *1* 'Tis thou *1* scritch owl   **28.** *1* Scrape *1* squeak *1* squall,   **29.** *1* old *1* rings,

1, 3, 4, 6. RT gives MS 1 indentation. The pattern of indentation in PR *1* is more elaborate.
4⁺. No line-space in PR *1*.
25⁺. Line-space perhaps doubtful in MS 1; no line-space in PR *1*.

30⁺. Cetera desunt.] Tr "The rest is missing."

37. EPIGRAM ON MY GODMOTHER'S BEARD

A. DATE

Aug–Sept 1791? summer 1792? In his note accompanying MS 1 C says that he wrote the lines when he was eighteen—i.e. in 1790–1. He was in Ottery during the summers of 1789 and 1791, and the poem is more likely to have been written on the later occasion. If, on the other hand, C dated the poem a year too early, as he often did with early poems, it would have been written during the summer vacation of 1792. Poems **49** and **50** are similar in spirit.

B. TEXTS

1 [=RT]. BM C 45 a 4 = JG's copy of *Omniana* II 55–7. In C's hand in the margins; signed "S. T. C." One word in the title and parts of lines 3, 4, 11, and 12 have been trimmed away. *CM* (*CC*) III 1073 (var).

A note on p 157 of the same volume is dated 27 Dec 1819; C appears to have annotated the copy of *Omniana* specifically for JG at about that time.

2. [John Payne Collier] *An Old Man's Diary, Forty Years Ago . . . 1832–1833* (2 vols in 4 pts 1871–2) I (1) 34–5. Recited to Collier shortly before 5 Mar 1832.

Collier introduces the lines thus: "Coleridge recently recited to me the following, not very good, epigram by him on his godmother's beard; the consequence of which was that she struck him out of her will."

title. 1ⁱᵐᵖ Epigram on my Godmother's beard, wh . . . she had the *barbarity* to revenge by striking me out of her will—

1 □	So great the charms of Mʳˢ Munday,
2 □	That men grew rude a kiss to gain:
3 1ⁱᵐᵖ	This so provok'd the Dame that one . . .
2	day,
4 1ⁱᵐᵖ	. . . . did she complain.
2	To Wisdom's power she did
	[*Line-space*]
5 □	Nor vainly she address'd her prayer,
6 □	Nor vainly to that Power applied:
7 □	The Goddess bade a length of Hair
8 □	In deep recess her muzzle hide.
	[*Line-space*]
9 □	Still persevere! to Love be callous!
10 □	For I have your petition heard:

11 1^{imp} To snatch a kiss were vain (cried Pallas . .
  2   Pallas),
12 1^{imp} Unless you first should shave your be . . . .
  2   beard.

1. 2 Mrs.   **2.** 2 kiss   **3.** 2 dame,   **6.** 2 power   **7.** 2 goddess   2 hair,
9. 2 persevere—   2 love   2 callous,   **10.** 2 heard;   **11.** 2 kiss

2, 4, etc. RT indentation follows MS 2; indentation is irregular in MS 1 (lines 3, 4, 6, 8 only) owing to the cramped conditions.
4. *PW* (EHC) II 976 No 1 gives line 4 (from MS 1) as follows: "To Pallas chaste she did complain:". EHC might have seen the untrimmed copy, or he might have supplied the beginning of the line (note that he mistakenly transposes the fourth and fifth words).

38. ON IMITATION

A. DATE

Summer 1791? The nature of MS 1 below suggests that the lines might have been composed not long before the Ottery Copy Book was made. Or perhaps they are a reworking of part of a school exercise.

B. TEXTS

1 **[=RT]**. BM Add MS 47551 = Ottery Copy Book f 5^r. Transcript in C's hand.

1. PW (1834).

title. □ *On Imitation*

1 □ All are not born to soar—& ah! how few
2 1 In ~~paths~~ tracks where Wisdom leads, their paths pursue:
  1   tracks,
3 □ On Folly every fool his talent tries—
4 □ It asks some toil to imitate the wise.
5 □ Tho' few like Fox can speak, like Pitt can think;
6 1 Yet all ~~P~~like Fox can game, ~~can~~ like Pitt can drink.
  1   like   like
7 □ Contagious when to Wit or Wealth allied
8 □ Folly and Vice diffuse their venom wide.

title. *1* ON IMITATION.   **1.** *1* and   **2.** *1* pursue!   **3.** *1* tries;   **4.** *1* wise;
5. *1* speak—   *1* think—   **6.** *1* game—   **7.** *1* wit *1* wealth *1* allied,

3–6. Transposed to end of poem in PR *1*.

39. ABSENCE: AN ODE

A. DATE

Oct 1791? 1793? In a letter which ELG dates Nov 1794 C claimed that the poem was written "about this time *three* years ago" (*CL* I 128–9)—i.e. about the time he went up to Cambridge in 1791. When the poem was included in C's last three collections it carried the subtitle "A Farewell Ode on Quitting School for Jesus College, Cambridge"; and in *PW* (1834) it was placed immediately before **33** *On Quitting Christ's Hospital*. There is, however, a possibility that the poem was written in 1793, despite C's asseveration and the later title. See vol I headnote.

B. TEXTS

1. The Weekly Entertainer (Sherborne) XXII (21 Oct 1793) 406. Signed "S. T. COLERIDGE. I *Ottery St. Mary, October* 12, 1793."

C's later recollections concerning the publication of the poem suggest that it was not submitted by himself (*CL* I 129: to an unknown correspondent [6 Nov 1794]). It could have been submitted by one of his family (his brother Edward, who was a member of the circle C shared with Ann Bacon) or by a friend of Fanny Nesbitt (to whom he might have presented it when he returned to Cambridge). The publication in the following number of the same newspaper of **60** *Absence: A Poem* suggests some kind of a local joke.

2. Cambridge Intelligencer (11 Oct 1794) 4. Signed "S. T. C. I *Jes. Coll. Wednesday, Oct.* 8."

1 [=RT]. BPL B 22189 = Estlin Copy Book f 11^{r-v}. Transcript in C's hand.

2. HRC MS (Coleridge, S T) Works B. Single leaf, 15.0×27.5 cm, imperfect; wm COLES; chain-lines 2.5 cm; verso blank. Transcript in C's hand. Bound into Rugby Manuscript p 35/f 14^r.

3. Poems (1796).

The reprint in *Universal Magazine* XCIX (Dec 1796) 432 has no textual significance.

4. Poems (1803).

5. PW (1828).

6. PW (1829).

7. PW (1834).

C annotated the poem in the HEHL copy (Book No 109531) by numbering each stanza and commenting, alongside lines 16–17, "Here should have been a blank interspace." The printing error in PR 7 reveals that copy was provided by PR 5 or 6, where stanza 3 is on a separate page.

C. GENERAL NOTE

C told his unknown correspondent in Nov 1794 (?) that he had given a ms copy to Robert Lovell three months previously (*CL* I 129)—i.e. at the time of his first visit to Bristol, when he became engaged to Sara Fricker. The line he quotes from this lost version coincides with PR *1* (and MS 1), and predates PR 2.

title. *1* 1 ABSENCE: AN ODE. • *2* 2 ABSENCE. • *3* 4 ABSENCE. | A FARE-WELL ODE. • *5–7* ABSENCE. | A FAREWELL ODE ON QUITTING SCHOOL FOR JESUS COLLEGE CAMBRIDGE.

1 *1*	Where grac'd with many a classic sport	
⊠*1*		spoil,
2 ⊠2	Cam rolls his reverend	stream along,
2		~~wave~~ stream
3 *1* 1	I haste to woo	the learned toil,
2	Once more I	
2	I haste to ~~woo~~ urge	
3–7		urge
4 □	That sternly chides my love-lorn song;	
5 ⊠2	Ah me! too mindful of the days	
2		day
6 ⊠2	Illum'd by passion's orient rays,	
2		ray,
7 *1* 2 1	When friendship,	gaiety, and health,
2 *3–7*		Peace, and Chearfulness,
8 □	Enrich'd me with the best of wealth.	
	[Line-space]	
9 □	Ah fair delights! that o'er my soul	
10 *1* 2 1	On mem'ry's wings, like shadows, fly!	
2 *3–7*		wing,
11 □	Ah flowers! which joy from Eden stole,	
12 □	While innocence stood smiling by!	
13 *1* 2	Oh cease, fond heart! thy bootless moan—	
⊠*1* 2	But	this
14 □	Those hours, on rapid pinions flown,	
15 □	Shall yet return—by absence crown'd,	
16 □	And scatter livelier roses round.	
	[Line-space]	
17 □	The sun, who ne'er remits his fires,	
18 □	On heedless eyes may pour the day:	
19 □	The moon, that oft from heaven retires,	
20 □	Endears her renovated ray.	
21 □	What tho' she leave the sky unblest,	

22 *1*   Awhile to mourn in murksome vest,
   ⊠*1* 1 5 To mourn awhile   murky
   1   Awhile to mourn
   5   To mourn awhile the
23 □   When she relumes her lovely light,
24 □   We bless the wanderer of the night!

title. 1 Absence, an Ode. • 2 Absence • *4 ABSENCE,* I • *5 6* COLLEGE,   **1.** *5–*
7 graced 1 Spoil • *3–7* spoil   **2.** *2* CAM • *2 3–6* CAM 2 along;   **3.** 1 2 Toil •
3–7 toil   **4.** 1 Song— • *2 3–7* song: **5.** 1 2 Days   **6.** *5–7* Illumed
2 1 *7* Passion's • *2 3–6* PASSION's 2 *orient* 1 Rays,   **7.** 1 Friendship,
Gaiety, *7* peace, *5–7* Cheerfulness, 2 health • 1 2 *4–7* Health • *3* Healt   **8.** *5–*
7 Enriched 1 Wealth! • 2 Wealth.   **9.** ⊠*1 2* 2 Delights! • 2 *d*DELIGHTS!
1 Soul   **10.** 2 memory's • 1 *5–7* • Memory's • 2 MEM'RY's • *3 4* Mem'ry's
1 Shadows, • *5–7* shadows   **11.** ⊠*1 2* 2 Flowers! • 2 FLOWER's ⊠*1* 2 Joy •
2 JOY ⊠*1* stole   **12.** ⊠*1* 2 Innocence • 2 INNOCENCE 2 *3–7* by!—   **13.** *1* O
⊠*1 2 4* Heart! 1 Moan— • *2 3 4* moan. • *5–7* moan: **14.** ⊠*1 2 4* Hours •
2–4 hours ⊠*1* 2 Pinions ⊠*1* flown   **15.** 2 1 2 return • *3–7* return, 1 2
5–7 Absence • *3 4* ABSENCE 1 2 crown'd • *5–7* crowned,   **16.** 1 R livelier
1 Roses   **17.** 1 Sun, • *2 3 4* SUN, • *5 6* SUN • *7* Sun 2 *3–7* fires   **18.** 1 Eyes
1 Day: **19.** 1 *7* Moon, • *2 3–6* MOON, 2 2 heav'n • 1 *5–7* Heaven •
3 4 Heav'n   **20.** 2 *Endears* 1 *f*Ray.   **21.** 2 *5–7* though 1 Sky 1 2 *3–*
7 unblest   **22.** ⊠*1* vest?   **23.** 2 *3–7* Light,   **24.** 1 *bless* • 2 *3–6* BLESS
⊠*1* 2 Wanderer 1 Night! • 2 *3–7* Night.

2, 4, 12, 18, 20. Indented in PR *1 2.*
7. PR *3* Healt] An "h," is written into some copies (e.g. at VCL).
16⁺. No line-space in PR *7,* undoubtedly because line 17 heads a new page in PR *5 6.*

40. GREEK EPITAPH ON AN INFANT

A. DATE

1791? Reasons for placing the poem at this point in the sequence are given in
vol I headnote.

B. TEXT

BPL B 22189 = Estlin Copy Book f 15ʳ. Fair copy in C's hand.

The ms title is "Epitaph on a Infant." Otherwise the RT reproduces the ms as
closely as possible.

40.X1. TRANSLATIONS OF ANACREON

A. DATE

In a letter to GC from Cambridge written in early Nov 1791 C boasts of "composing Greek verse, like a mad dog":

> At my Leisure hours I translate Anacreon—I *have* translated the first, the second, the 28th, the 32nd, the 43rd, and the 46th—Middleton thinks I have translated the 32nd ('Άγε ζωγραφῶν ἄριστε) very well—I think between us both, we might translate him entirely—You *have* translated 6 or 7, have you not? (*CL* I 17).

No edition has been found in which 'Άγε ζωγράφων ἄριστε is numbered 32. It is 28 in the old system established by Henricus Stephanus (Paris 1554) in the first edition, and it is now 15 (16 in LCL), C's version appears below as **62** *To a Painter*, where details of the LCL edition are given. The other poems he mentions are: "the first" (now 23) Θέλω λέγειν Ἀτρείδας; "the second" (now 24) Φύσις κέρατα ταύροις; "the 32nd" (now 13, LCL 14) Εἰ φύλλα πάντα δένδρων; "the 43rd" (now 32, LCL 34) Μακαρίζομέν σε τέττιξ ("The Grasshopper"); and "the 46th" (now 27b, LCL 29) Χαλεπὸν τὸ μὴ φιλῆσαι. C's versions of these have not survived, but versions of two others appear below as **41** *An Ode in the Manner of Anacreon* and **56** *On Presenting a Moss Rose*. For editions of Anacreon see vol I **41** headnote.

The genuine poems and fragments of Anacreon (c 570–c 485 B.C.) which are known through quotation in later authors such as Athenaeus and Stobaeus are not to be found in the collection of imitations known under his name in C's time. The latter, which are now usually called the *Anacreontea*, were still generally thought to be Anacreon's genuine works, though some had already been queried on such grounds as language, metre, and allusions to later events.

For C's continuing regard for "Anacreon" see *BL* ch 16 (*CC*) II 34, where "The Grasshopper" (C's "43rd" = 32 = LCL 34) is specially mentioned.

41. AN ODE IN THE MANNER OF ANACREON

A. DATE

Before 13 Feb 1792. The poem was almost certainly written after Nov 1791, and possibly after Christmas. It might have been written only shortly before C sent it to Mary Evans.

B. TEXT

Pforzheimer MS Misc 67. Single folio leaf, 22.8×37.2 cm; wm posthorn in shield above G R; countermark C TAYLOR; chain-lines 2.7 cm. The first of three unsigned poems in the body of an als to Mary Evans, 13 Feb 1792 (*CL* I 28).

The RT follows the ms exactly, except for:

title. ms An Ode in the manner of Anacreon.   **8.** ~~about~~ within

42. A WISH WRITTEN IN JESUS WOOD

A. DATE

10 Feb 1792 (given in ms title).

B. TEXT

Pforzheimer MS Misc 67. Single folio leaf, 22.8×37.2 cm; wm posthorn in shield above G R; countermark C TAYLOR; chain-lines 2.7 cm. The poem was included, unsigned, as the second of three in the body of an als to Mary Evans, 13 Feb 1792 (*CL* I 28–9).

The RT follows the ms exactly, except for:

title. ms A Wish written in Jesus Wood Feb: 10th 1792

43. A LOVER'S COMPLAINT
TO HIS MISTRESS

A. DATE

Before 13 Feb 1792.

B. TEXT

Pforzheimer MS Misc 67. Single folio leaf, 22.8×37.2 cm; wm posthorn in shield above G R; countermark C TAYLOR; chain-lines 2.7 cm. The last of three unsigned poems included in an als to Mary Evans, 13 Feb 1792 (*CL* I 29).

The RT reproduces the ms exactly, except for:

title. ms A lover's complaint to his Mistress, who deserted him in quest of a more wealthy Husband in the East Indies.

44. TO DISAPPOINTMENT

A. DATE

Before 13 Feb 1792. Though ELG prints the letter in which the poem appears before that containing poems **41–3,** it bears the same date. The poem itself would appear to be more spontaneous than the other three.

B. TEXT

Pforzheimer MS Misc 65. Single folio leaf, 22.6×37.5 cm; wm posthorn in shield above G R; countermark C TAYLOR; chain-lines 2.5 cm. Unsigned in the body of an als to Mrs Evans, 13 Feb 1792 (*CL* I 23).

The RT reproduces the ms exactly, except for:

title. ms To Disappointment   **14.** ms ∅ sweet   **28.** ms corn-cloath'd

45. FRAGMENT FOUND IN A MATHEMATICAL LECTURE ROOM

A. DATE

Late Mar 1792. C introduces the lines in the ms, with "I wrote the following the other day . . .".

B. TEXTS

1. Eton College (College Library). Large folded leaf, 37.6×46.4 cm overall; wm horn within oval surmounted by crown; chain-lines 2.5 cm. Transcribed in an als to GC of 2 Apr 1792 (*CL* I 34–5).

2 [=RT]. BPL B 22189=Estlin Copy Book f 16ʳ. Transcript in C's hand.

title. 1 Fragment found in a Lecture Room • 2 Fragment I found in a Mathematical Lecture Room.

1 1 Where deep in mud Cam rolls his slumbrous stream,
    2   reverend
2 □ And Bog and Desolation reign supreme,
3 □ Where all Bœtia clouds the misty brain,
4 □ The Owl Mathesis pipes her loathsome strain.
5 1 Far far aloof the frighted Muses fly,
    2   th' affrighted
6 □ Indignant Genius scowls and passes by:
7 □ The frolic Pleasures start amid their dance,
8 □ And Wit congealed stands fix'd in Wintry trance.
9 1 But to the sounds with duteous haste repair
    2   at   sound
10 □ Cold Industry, and wary-footed Care,
11 □ And Dullness dosing on a couch of Lead
12 1 Pleas'd with the song uplifts her heavy head,
     2 Sooth'd   uprears
13 1 The sympathetic numbers lists awhile,
     2 Its
14 □ Then yawns propitiously a frosty smile.

1. 2 Stream   **2.** 2 supreme,—   **3.** 2 Bœotia 2 Brain,—   **4.** 2 MATHESIS
2 strain!   **6.** 2 by!   **7.** 2 Dance,   **8.** 2 congeal'd 2 wintry Trance!
10. 2 Industry 2 Care;   **12.** 2 th   Song 2 head;   **13.** 2 Numbers
14. 2 Smile!—

4⁺, 8⁺. MS 2 perhaps intends line-spaces.

4⁺, 8⁺. MS 2 perhaps intends line-spaces.
14. C added in MS 1, at the end of the line: "⟨. . . . . . | Cetera desunt.⟩" ("The rest is missing").

46. ON A LADY WEEPING

A. DATE

Feb–Jun 1792? *PW* (EHC) I 17–18 suggests 1790, but see sec C below.

B. TEXTS

1 [=RT]. VCL S LT Fl.3 = Green Ottery Copy Book f 21ʳ. Transcript by John May Jr, subscribed "S. C."

1. The Weekly Entertainer (Sherborne) xx (9 Jul 1792) 48. Unsigned; dated "*June* 26, 1792."

2. VCL (uncatalogued in 1978). Ann Frances Bacon's Commonplace Book f 39ʳ. Transcript by AFB, subscribed "S. T. Coleridge".

C. GENERAL NOTE

MS 1 was transcribed c 1820 from a version sent to GC which is no longer extant. It may be presumed that it was sent at about the same time that the original of PR *1* was sent either to C's brother Edward Coleridge, or to an acquaintance at Ottery or Exeter. MS 1 and PR *1* are clearly closer to one another than either is to MS 2, which must have been transcribed from a version made in the summer months of 1793, when C was himself in Devon. Though the originals of TEXTS 1 *1* may be presumed to predate MS 2, therefore, it is possible that the original of PR *1* predates the original of MS 1.

title. 1 On a Lady weeping | Imitation from the Latin of Nicolaus Archius • *1* ON A LADY WEEPING. | (From the Latin of NICHOLAUS ARCHIUS.) • 2 On Laura's weeping at taking leave of a female Friend—

1	□	Lovely gems of radiance meek
2	□	Trembling down my Laura's cheek,
3	1	As the streamlets silent glide
	1	Like little streams that
4	1	Thro' the Mead's enamell'd pride,
	1	meadow's flowery
3.1	2	As the streamlet silent flows
4.1.1	2	Moist'ning the Lily and the Rose,
5	□	Pledges sweet of pious Woe,
6	□	Tears, which Friendship taught to flow,
7	1	Sparkling in yon humid light
	2	your
8	1 2	Love embathes his pinions bright:
9	1	There amid the glitt'ring show'r
	2	glist'ning
10	1 2	Smiling sits th*é*' insidious Power,
9.1	*1*	Glitt'ring in your chrystal show'r,
10.1	*1*	Wantons love's insidious pow'r:
7.1	*1*	Sparkling in your lucid light,
8.1	*1*	There he waves his pinions bright,
11	1 *1*	As some winged warbler oft,
	2	Like the warbling bird, that
12	1 *1*	When Spring-clouds shed their treasures soft,
	2	fragrance
13	1 *1*	Joyous tricks his plumes anew,
	2	its
14	1 2	And flutters in the fos't'ring dew.
	1	heavenly

1. *1* meek,   **2.** 2 *Laura*'s   **4.** *1* pride.   **5.** *1* woe, • 2 *woe*,   **6.** *1* 2 Tears *1* 2 friendship   *1* flow; • 2 flow!   **8.** 2 *Love*   **9.** 2 shower,   **10.** 2 th' 2 power,   **12.** *1* spring-clouds   **13.** 2 anew   **14.** 2 fost*é*'ring dew.—

3. *1* streams] The final "s" is missing in some copies of the newspaper owing to loose type.

4⁺. PR *1* gives a line-space. Could this indicate that C intended to suggest a sonnet in couplets?

7–10. Replaced in PR *1* by an alternative version which transposes the two couplets (hence the order of the decimal numbering above), as well as rewording.

47. GREEK EPITAPH FOR HOWARD'S TOMB

A. DATE

Mar 1792.

B. TEXT

Eton College (School Library). Large folded leaf, 37.6×46.4 cm overall; wm horn within oval surmounted by crown; chain-lines 2.5 cm. Copied at the end of an als to GC, 2 Apr 1792 (*CL* I 35–6).

The transcripts by John May Jr in the Green Ottery Copy Book f 9ᵛ (VCL S LT Fl.3) and in another, later 19th-century, hand in the Folio Letter Book at HRC (MS (Coleridge, S T) Letters I p 66) have no textual authority.

The RT reproduces the ms exactly, except for:

title. ms An Epitaph for Howard's tomb on the Banks of the Dnieper.   **5.** ms Αμ-φεπολη↓σ'

48. SORS MISERA SERVORUM IN INSULIS INDIÆ OCCIDENTALIS

A. DATE

Feb–May 1792. C announced his intention to try for the prize in Greek lyric in Nov 1791 (*CL* I 17: to GC [early Nov 1791]), but he cannot have begun the poem until after 27 Jan 1792, when the subjects for the three Browne prizes were announced (*Cambridge Chronicle* 28 Jan 1792). On the evening of Monday 2 Apr he wrote that he was writing for all three Browne Medals, and that his Greek ode was, he thought, his *chef d'œuvre*. The date of the letter is fixed by the allusion to his matriculation "last Saturday" (*CL* I 34: to GC [2 Apr 1792]; C matriculated on 31 Mar). The college tradition (recorded by A. Gray "Coleridge at Jesus, 1791–1794" *The Chanticleer*—Jesus College Cambridge—xvi—Oct Term 1890—1–13 at 3) that he had to be shut up by his friends to finish in time is not inconsistent with the implication that a version existed on 2 Apr, and is consistent with the continued rewriting in the versions we have.

C reported that "The prize medals will be adjudged about the beginning of June" (*CL* I 34). MS 1 is dated 16 Jun, which is probably after the submission date and definitely before the announcement of the awards on 22 Jun (*Cambridge Chronicle* 23 Jun 1792). The poem was copied into the official record book on 3 Jul (Commencement Day).

B. TEXTS

1. In the possession of Sir Charles Cave (Oct 1981). Three large leaves, 24.4×38.9 cm, folded and sewn to make a twelve-page booklet; wm (outer leaf) CURTEIS & SONS, (inner leaves) bugle within a shield surmounted by a crown; chain-lines 2.5 cm. Fair copy in C's hand, signed "S. T. Coleridge June 16 1792". The poem is transcribed on the rectos of the six leaves; the versos are blank. There are four ms additions in pencil: line 33 a misguided attempt at emendation; lines 49–50 two breathings added; line 60 a note in EHC's (?) hand. See below.

The copy was sent by C to GC probably after the submission date. It may be a discarded version, since it differs substantially from the version C copied in the official book (MS 2).

There is a transcript in the hand of John May Jr in the Green Ottery Copy Book ff 1ᵛ–3ᵛ (VCL S LT Fl.3), where it is followed by May's transcript of a poem to C by GC, "being vastly pleased by the composition, thinking it would be a sort of compliment to the Superior Genius of his Brother" (f 3ᵛ; GC's poem is printed in *PW*—JDC—653ʙ–654ᴀ). There is another transcript of C's poem in the Folio Letter Book at HRC (MS (Coleridge, S T) Letters I pp 66–70). Neither transcript has any authority.

2 [=RT]. Cambridge University Library Archives Charters 1. 4, ms volume "Browne Medals: Odes and Epigrams: Vol. II 1788–1808" pp 230–3; signed "Samuel Taylor Coleridge, Coll. Jes. Scholaris." Dated (following the title): "In maximis Comitiis Jul. 3. 1792." There are a few pencil markings and clarification of letters in a later hand (not recorded here).

The copy was made in accordance with Sir William Browne's will, which required it to be "fairly written, dated and subscribed by the author(s) in a book to be laid on the register's table for public inspection at the commencement".

There is a transcript among the collection of Greek and Latin prize poems written between 1780 and 1800, mostly copied by J. J. Conybeare, in the Bodleian (MS Top Oxon C 216 ff 80ʳ–81ᵛ), but this has no textual authority.

1. C quoted lines 1–16 (var) in 1795, in **110** *Contributions to "Joan of Arc"*

II 428fn. Almost all breathings, accents, and iotas subscript are omitted, and not all of the textual variants are improvements.

A note on the lines in red pencil in William Hood's copy of *Joan of Arc* (NYPL Berg Collection Copy 2), which C annotated in Jun 1814 (?), is given at line 2EC. (C's remaining notes on his contribution are given with poem **110**, and his notes on RS's volume overall in *CM—CC—*v.)

2. Lines 1–16 are repeated verbatim from the *Joan of Arc* fn in the *SL* printing of **139** *The Destiny of Nations* 438fn.

C made corrections and comments on the lines in the copy of *SL* which belonged to HNC (HUL *AC 85 L 8605 Zy 817c), and there is a correction in JG's hand in the copy C presented to William Hood (Columbia X 825C67 W3 1817). See line 2EC, and **139**.438fn VAR.

3. Lines 1–16 are repeated (var) in the *PW* (1828) printing of **139** *The Destiny of Nations* 439fn. The variations are minor.

C made two small changes to line 13 (see EC) in the copy of *PW* (1828) at the Fitzwilliam Museum, Cambridge (Marlay Bequest 1912).

4. Lines 1–16 are repeated (var) in the *PW* (1829) printing of **139** *The Destiny of Nations* 439fn. The variations are minor.

5. Lines 1–16 are repeated in the *PW* (1834) printing of **139** *The Destiny of Nations* 439fn, with accents, breathings, and iotas subscript supplied afresh, presumably by HNC and without recourse to MS 2. C would no doubt have approved of the absence of concessions to Aeolic practice, since he had already removed some Aeolic forms in MS 2, and more in the earlier printed versions.

C. GENERAL NOTE

The variants in lines 1–16 are displayed in the customary way. Thereafter, only MS 1 is given here complete, since MS 2 already appears verbatim in vol I and there are no other authoritative texts. The two versions do not differ much in wording but there are very many differences of capitalisation, punctuation, pointing, and minor dialectal forms, to which no special attention is drawn in the apparatus criticus following the main sequence below.

The differences of wording between MSS 1 and 2 occur in the following lines: 19; RT 21–8 (which replace a single stanza in MS 1: lines 23.1, 25.1, 27.1, 28.1 below); 43; and 73. In line 42 MS 2 substitutes a more familiar form for a particularly uncommon Aeolic one; and there are changes in word-order in lines 63 and 89–90.

title. 1 Sors misera servorum in insulis Indiæ occidentalis. • 2 Sors misera Servorum in insulis Indiæ occidentalis. I In maximis Comitiis Jul. 3. 1792.

1 □   Ω σκοτω πυλας, **Θανατε**, προλειπων

2 1 2 Ες γενος σπευδων ιθι ζευχθεν ατα·
1–5 σπευδοις υποζευχθεν Ατα,
3 ☐ Ου ξενισθηση γενυων σπαραγμοῖς
4 ☐ Ουδ' ολολυγμῳ,
[*Line-space*]
5 1 2 Αλλα δ' αυ κυκλοισι χοροιτυπόισιν,
1–5 και
6 1 Κ'ασματων χαρᾳ· φοβερος γαρ εσσι,
☒1 μὲν
7 ☐ Αλλ' ομως **Ελευθερίᾳ** συνοικεῖς,
8 ☐ Στυγνε Τυραννε.
[*Line-space*]
9 1 2 Δασκιοις τὲυ αιρομενοι πτεροισι
1–4 επει πτερυγεσσι σησι
5 επὶ
10 1 2 Τραχυ μακρω Ωκεανω δι' οιδμα
1–5 Α! θαλασσιον καθορωντες
11 1 2 Αδονᾶν φιλας ες εδρας *πέτωνταί*,
1–5 Αιθεροπλαγτοις υπο ποσσ' ανεισι
12 1 2 Γαν τε πατρωαν.
1–5 Πατριδ ἐπ' αιαν.
[*Line-space*]
13 ☐ Ενθα μαν ερασται ερωμενησι,
14 1 2 Αμπι κρουνοισιν κιτριων υπ' αλσῶν,
1–5 πηγησιν κιτρινων
15 1 2 Οια προς βροτων επαθον βροτοι, τα
1–5 Οσσ' υπο βροτοις
16 ☐ Δεινα λεγοντι.

Note. The following reproduces MS 1 literatim: see sec C above. Apart from the few lines which exhibit substantial changes in wording from MS 2, there are minor discrepancies passim, and MS 2 lacks the footnotes.

17 Φευ· κορω **Νασοι** φονιω γεμουσαι
18 Δυσθεατοις αμφιθαλεις κακοισι,
19 Πα νοσει **Νηστις**, βρεμεται τε πλαγα
20 Αιματοεσσα,

[21–8=MS 2: see RT]

23.1 Ποσσακις κ'αμα κραδια στεναξεν
25.1 Δουλιαν γενναν φρασιν εννοευντος
27.1 Ως πονων διναις στυγερων κυκλουνται,
28.1 Τεκνα **Αναγκας**.
[*Line-space*]
29 Αμερησ' ἐπει γ' αφιλησιν αμπι
30 **Καυμα**, και **Λοιμος**, **Καματος** τ' αφερτος
31 Μαρναται, και **Μναμοσυνας** τα πικρα
32 Φασματα λυγρας.
[*Line-space*]
33 Φευ· καμοντας **Μαστις** αγρυπνος ορμᾶ,
34 Αλιον πιρν αν επεγειρεν **Αως**·

35	Κ'Άματος δυνει γλυκυδερκες αστρον,
36	Πενθεα δ' ανθει

[*Line-space*]

37	Εις αεν· ψυχαν γαρ αωρονυκτα
38	Δειματ' εμπληττει, κοτον εμπνεοντα·
39	Ομμα κοιμᾶται μελεοις, **Φοβος** δε
40	Ουδεποτ' υπνôι.

[*Line-space*]

41	Ει δε τι ψευδος μεθεπωντι αδυ
42	Ελπιδος σκιαις πεδ' ονειροφαντοις,
43	Αικιᾶν ανισταμενοι ταχ' οιστροις
44	Αλιθιωνται.

[*Line-space*]

45	Ω κακοισι Δουλοσυνας χλιοντες,
46	Αθλιων ω βοσκομενοι διοιγμοις,
47	**Παιδες Ὑβρισται Κορω,** αυταδελφον
48	Αιμα δρεποντες,

[*Line-space*]

49	Ου ρα προσδερκει ταδ' αφυκτον **Ομμα;**
50	Ου ρα κ'αμειψιν **Νεμεσις** τινασσει
51	Πυρπνοαν· ακουετ'; η ουκ ακουετ';
52	Ως χθονα παλλει
52fn 1	Tempestatibus αινιττω, quas "Hurricanes" Anglici dicunt.

[*Line-space*]

53	Πνευματ' εκ ριζων, και υποστενοντι
54	Γας μυχοι, βυθοι τε μυκῶνται αινως,
55	Εγκοτειν τους νερθεν υπεγγυωντες
56	Τοις κτανεουσιν!

[*Line-space*]

57	Αλλα τις μ' αχω μελιγαρυς, οιαι
58	Δωριαν ριπαι κιθαρᾶν, προσεπτα;
59	Τίς ποτισταζει ψιθυρισμον αδυν
60	Μαλθακα φωνα;

[*Line-space*]

61	Οι! ορω **Κηρυκ' Ελεω,** κλαδοισιν
62	Ως κατασκιον κεφελαν ελαιας!
63	Οι! τεων λογων γανος, Ιλβρεφορσεῦ
63fn 1	Gotho-græce pro Wilberforce.
64	Χρυσεον αιω!

[*Line-space*]

65	"Παγα Δακρυων οσια, σταλαγμων
66	"Νυν αλις τεων; στερποπα ξεναρκεῖ
67	"Τᾶς **Δικας** ατυζομενον τεθναξει
68	"Πημα δαμασθεν.

[*Line-space*]

69	"Εμπεσει δ' ακταις Λιβυκῃσιν ουκετ'
70	"Α χαρις χρυσω αχαρις, βδελυκτα,
71	"Οια γ' ιππευει καπυροῖς αηταις
72	"Εκπνοα Λοιμου.

[*Line-space*]
73 "Νηστιος πλαγησιν υπ᾽ Υβρεως τε
74 "Γηρας ου μοχθοις ανομοις παλαισει
75 "Τω βιω ποιφυγματα δυντος αι· αι·
76 　　　　　　"Αγρια φυσων.

[*Line-space*]
77 "Ου φοβῳ Ματηρ αμα θεσπιωδῳ
78 "Σταθεσιν βρεφος πελασει πινωδες·
79 "Ου περισσως εκτεταται γαρ ηδη
80 　　　　　　"Δουλιον Αμαρ.

[*Line-space*]
81 "Οιτινες, δουλοι βλοσυρων δυναστων,
82 "Δακρυον τεγγειν Ελεω παρειαν
83 "Ουδαμως ιδον, μελεοι παθοντες
84 　　　　　　"Θραυματ᾽ ακουειν,

[*Line-space*]
85 "Υμμι ται Παιδες Θεμιτος γενουνται
86 "Ανθεμιζουσαι βροδα τας Γαλανας,
87 "Ιρον ηδ᾽ **Ελευθεριας** σεβας δὴ,
88 　　　　　　"Ματρος αεθλων.

[*Line-space*]
89 Τοι᾽ επεμψαν ιμεροεντα αὖραι
90 Μᾶλλον, η **Νικας** περ᾽ οχος βραδυνθεν
91 Των ανηριθμων ιαχαι, Θριαμβω
92 　　　　　　Αματι τερπνῳ.

[*Line-space*]
93 Χαιρ᾽, ος ευ νωμᾶς Ελεω τον οιακ᾽!
94 Εργματων καλων **Αγαπα** πτεροισι
95 Δακρυων εντοσθε γελωτα θεισα
96 　　　　　　Σε στεφανωσει.

[*Line-space*]
97 Ηδε **Μοισα,** τᾶν **Αρετᾶν** οπαδος,
98 Σειο **μεμνα** μεμνασθαι συνεχως φιλησει·
99 Τλαμονων ηδ᾽ ευλογιαις προς αιθερ᾽
100 　　　　　　Ουνομ᾽ αιξει.

1. 5 °Ω　2 σκότω • *1–4* σκοτου • 5 σκότου　2 πύλας, • 5 πύλας　2 **Θάνατε,** •
5 Θάνατε,　2 5 προλείπων　**2.** 2 5 'Ες γένος　2 σπεύδων ἴθι ζεύχθεν •
5 σπεύδοις ὑποζευχθὲν　2 ἄτᾳ· *1 2* Ατᾳ. • *3 4* Ατᾳ· • 5 'Ατᾳ·　**3.** 2 'Ου •
5 Οὐ　2 5 ξενισθήσῃ γενύων　*1–4* σπαραγμοις, • 5 σπαραγμοῖς,　**4.** 2 'Ουδ' •
5 Οὐδ'　2 ὀλολυγμῷ, • *1–4* ολολυγμω, • 5 ὀλόλυγμῳ,　**5.** 2 5 Ἀλλὰ　2 αὖ •
5 καὶ　2 5 κύκλοισι　*1–4* χοροιτυποισι • 5 χοροιτύποισι,　**6.** 2 5 ἀσμάτων
2 5 χαρᾷ· • *1* χαρα·　2 Φοβερὸς • *1* Φοβερος • 5 φοβερὸς　*1–4* μεν　2 ἐσσὶ, •
3–4 εσσι • 5 ἐσσὶ　**7.** 2 5 Ἀλλ᾽　2 ὁμῶς • 5 ὁμῶς　2 **Ελευθερία** • *1–*
4 Ελευθερια • 5 'Ελευθερία　*3 4* συνοικεῖς　**8.** 2 5 Στυγνὲ　2 Τύραννε. • *1–*
4 Τυραννε! • 5 Τύραννε!　**9.** 2 5 Δασκίοις　2 ἀιρομένοι πτερόισι　5 πτερύ-
γεσσι σῇσι　**10.** 2 τραχὺ μακρῶ Ωκεανῶ　5 °Α! θαλάσσιον καθορῶντες
2 5 οἶδμα　**11.** 2 Ἀδονᾶν φίλας ἐς ἕδρας πέτωνται,　5 Αἰθεροπλάγκτοι ὑπὸ
ποσσ᾽ ἀνεῖσι　*1* ποσσ`　**12.** 2 Γᾶν　2 πατρώαν　*3 4* Πατριδ᾽ • *5* Πατρίδ᾽

2–5 ἐπ’ 5 αἶαν.   13. 2 5 ῎Ενθα μὰν 2 ἔρασται • *1 2* Ερασται • *3 4* Ερασαι •
5 ῎Ερασαι 2 ἐρωμένησιν • *1–4* Ερωμενησιν • *5* ᾽Ερωμενῆσιν   14. 2 ᾽Αμπι • *1–
4* Αμφι • *5* ᾽Αμφὶ 2 κρουνὸισιν *5* πηγῃσιν 2 κιτρίων • *5* κιτρίνων 2 ὕπ’ • *5* ὑπ’
2 ἀλσῶν • *5* ἄλσων   15. 2 Οἶα πρὸς βροτῶν • *5* ῏Οσσ᾽ ὑπὸ βροτοῖς 2 5 ἔπαθον
2 βροτὸι, • *5* βροτοὶ, 2 5 τὰ   16. 2 5 Δεινὰ λεγόντι. • *4* Δεινὰ λεγοναι.

1. PR *3* misprints as Ωσκοτου (one word).
4, 8, 12, etc. The last line of each stanza indented in all texts.
6. It is unclear whether the initial letter of φοβερος in PR *3 4* is meant to be capitalised.
6, 7, 11, 15. PR *1 2* use the grave accent instead of the apostrophe.
33. In MS 1 a letter has been inserted in pencil, suggesting (unconvincingly) Μναστις "Memory" for Μαστις "whip".
49–50. In MS 1 breathings have been added in pencil, inconsistently: ῥα and ρα respectively.
62. In MS 2 C repeated his error κεφελαν for κεφαλάν from MS 1, only adding the accent.
73. In MS 2 C repeated his error συνομαιμενων for συνομαιμόνων from MS 1, only adding the accent.
92. In MS 1 C had some difficulty with the fourth letter of τερπνῳ ("glad"), and wrote the word again in the margin, making it qualify "day" instead of "festival".

48.X1. CAMBRIDGE PRIZE POEMS, 1792

The subjects for the Browne Medals were announced on 27 Jan 1792, and in a letter to GC written on 2 Apr C says: "I have been writing for *all* the prizes— namely—the Greek Ode, the Latin Ode, and the Epigrams" (*CL* I 34). Though he had nurtured ambitions to win the Greek prize almost from the moment he went to Cambridge, and of course did win it, there is no reason to suppose that he did not submit entries in the other classes as well. The Latin ode was to be in imitation of Horace, on the same subject as the Greek—in this instance, on the miseries of the slaves in the West Indies. The subject for the Greek and Latin epigrams—after the model of the *Greek Anthology* and Martial, respectively— was "Purpura vendit I Causidicum" (Juvenal *Satires* 7.135–6 tr "It is the purple robe that gets the lawyer custom").

Samuel Butler (St John's), C's successful rival for the Craven Scholarship the following year, won the prize for his Latin ode, and John Belcher (Clare) won the prize for epigrams.

49. A SIMILE; WRITTEN AFTER A WALK BEFORE SUPPER

A. DATE

Jul–early Aug 1792.

B. TEXTS

1 [=RT]. In the possession of Mrs Denise Coleridge (Mar 1980). Two conjoint leaves, each 18.5×23.4 cm; wm horn design above LVG; chain-lines 2.5 cm. An als to GC, 6 Aug 1792 (*CL* I 37–8).

2. HRC MS (Coleridge, S T) Works B. Verso and recto of two leaves, each 19.7×32.6 cm; wm (on each) Britannia in oval surmounted by crown; chain-lines 2.5 cm. Bound into Rugby Manuscript pp 82 3/ff 35ᵛ–36ʳ. Transcript in C's hand, which served as copy for PR *1*.

1. Poems (1796).

introduction/title. 1 I have nothing more to say—so shall fill up the Letter with a Simile, which I wrote after an Evening Walk before Supper—I had met Smerdon and Spouse. • 2 Epistle III | Written after a walk before supper time. • *1* EPISTLE III. | WRITTEN AFTER | A WALK BEFORE SUPPER.

1 1	Tho' much averse at ←—folk—→ to flicker,	
2	dear ~~Friend~~! Jack!	
1	←—Jack,—→	
2 1	To find a Simile for Vicar	
2 *1*	Likeness for friend Vicker,	
3 ☐	I've made thro Earth, and Air, and Sea	
4 ☐	A Voyage of Discovery—	
5 ☐	And let me add (to ward off strife)	
6 1	For Vicar & for Vicar's Wife.	
2 *1*	Vicker Vicker's	
7 1	She, gross & round beyond belief,	
2 *1*	large	
8 ☐	A Superfluity of Beef:	
9 1	Her mind and body of a ~~piece~~ piece,	
2 *1*	piece,	
10 ☐	And both compos'd of Kitchen Grease—	
11 ☐	In short, Dame Truth might safely dub her	
12 1	"Vulgarity enclos'd in Blubber.	
2 *1*	enshrin'd	
13 ☐	He, meagre Bit of Littleness,	
14 ☐	All Snuff, and Musk, and Politesse,	
15 ☐	So thin, that strip him of his cloathing	

16 □   He'd totter on the Edge of Nothing—
16fn 1   *a good Line*
17 □   In case of Foe he well might hide
18 □   Snug in the Collops of *her* side.
19 1   Ah—then—what simile can suit?
  2 *1*   will
20 □   Spinde Leg in great Jack Boot?
21 □   Pismire crawling in a Rutt?
22 □   Or a Spiggot in a Butt?
23 1   So I Ha'd and Hem'd awhile,
  2 *1* Thus humm'd   ha'd
24 1   When Mrs Memory with a smile
  2 *1*   Madam
25 □   Thus twitch'd my Ear "Why sure, I ween
26 □   In London Streets thou oft hast seen
27 □   The very image of this Pair,
28 1   A Little Ape with large she bear
  2 *1*   huge
29 1   Tied   by hapless chain together,
  2 *1* "Link'd
30 □   An unlick'd mass the One—the other
31 1   An Antic lean with nimble crupper—
  2 *1*   huge
32 □   But stop, my Muse! for here comes Supper.

1. 2 *1* averse,   **2.** *1* likeness *1* V—ker,   **3.** 2 *1* thro' 2 Earth 2 Air
1 Sea,   **4.** 2 *1* Discovery!   **6.** *1* V—ker 2 *1* and *1* V—ker's 2 *1* Wife—
7. 2 *1* S**HE** 2 *1* and   **8.** 2 *1* superfluity 2 *1* Beef!   **10.** 2 Kitchen-
grease. • *1* kitchen-grease.   **12.** 2 *1* Vulgarity 2 *1* blubber!   **13.** 2 *1* H**E**,
14. 2 *1* snuff, *1* musk, 2 *1* politesse;   **15.** 2 *1* cloathing,   **16.** 2 *1* edge
2 *1* N**OTHING**!   **17.** 2 Foe, • *1* foe,   **18.** 2 *1* collops 2 *1* her 2 Side.
19. 2 *1* Ah then 2 Simile   **20.** 2 *1* Spindle leg 2 jack boot? • *1* jack-boot?
21. 2 Rut? • *1* rut?   **22.** 2 spiggot • *1* spigot *1* butt?   **25.** 2 *1* ear— 2 *1* ween,
26. 2 *1* "In 2 *1* streets   **27.** 2 *1* "The 2 *1* Pair: **28.** 2 *1* "A little 2 *1* She
Bear   **29.** 2 Chain 2 *1* together: **30.** 2 *1* "An 2 Mass 2 *1* one—
31. 2 *1* "An antic

16fn. Actually in the margin of M**S** 1.
⁻**19.** M**S** 2 [above the line, as a direction to Cottle's printer] a white Line. • P**R** *1* has
line-space.
31. Erratum in P**R** *1* reads: "For Antic huge read *antic small*."

50. LATIN LINES ON OTTERY'S INHABITANTS

A. DATE

24 Aug 1792 or earlier.

B. TEXT

In the possession of Sir Charles Cave (Oct 1981). Two conjoint leaves, each 18.5×23.2 cm; wm IV; chain-lines 2.5 cm. Part of a letter wholly in Latin to GC, 24 Aug 1792 (*CL* I 39).

The RT reproduces the untitled ms exactly.

50.X1. IMITATIONS FROM THE MODERN LATIN POETS

C originally intended to include Greek as well as Latin lyrics in this collection. He mentioned to GC in Jan 1793 his plan to translate "the best Lyric Poems from the Greek, and the modern Latin Writers", and to publish them by the middle of the year to pay off his debts (*CL* I 46: to GC [13 Jan 1793]). He was translating Casimir in the Dragoons at Reading in Dec 1793–Feb 1794 (*CL* I 76–7: to GC [26 Mar 1794]); he borrowed Buchanan after he had returned to Cambridge, in May (*Jesus LB* No 31); and advertisements began to appear a month later, in the *Cambridge Intelligencer*, for *Imitations from the Modern Latin Poets*, to include "a copious Selection from the Lyrics of Casimir, and a new Translation of the Basia of Secundus" (14 Jun, 26 Jul, 22 Sept 1794; cf *CL* I 82n). The same prospectus was reissued bound up with copies of **76.X1** *The Fall of Robespierre*, and is given in full in *SW&F* (*CC*) 24–5. Cf also C's list of projected works in *CN* I 161 (a).

The *Imitations* were to have filled two quarto volumes, and C and his friends worked to obtain a total of 450 subscribers (see *CL* I 82n; 101: to RS [11 Sept 1794]; 152: to George Dyer [late Feb 1795]; 154: to George Dyer 10 Mar 1795). However, C lost his Casimir on the way back to Cambridge (*CL* I 97: to RS [1 Sept 1794]), and admitted to feeling depressed by the project in Oct (*CL* I 116: to RS 21 Oct [1794]). The volumes had been announced for "shortly after the next *Christmas*", but they were postponed; and C's last reference to them is in

Oct 1795, when he speculated on returning to Cambridge to finish off his "great work of Imitations in 2 vols" (*CL* I 161: to TP [7 Oct 1795]).

C clearly did very much less work on the project than he pretended. At the same time, there is evidence that he did more than is often supposed. See poems **42, 46, 57, 67, 68;** and poems **43, 44,** and **53** might well turn out to be imitations of untraced originals. Also, Latin originals by John Owen and others lie behind some of the epigrams he translated at the time he returned from Germany, in 1799 (e.g. poems **221, 239**). For the Greek lyrics see poem **4.X1** and the references given in poem **40.X1**.

50.X2. SONNET TO THE EARL OF LAUDERDALE

M Chron (7 Feb 1793): "*SONNET* | to the | EARL OF LAUDER-DALE. | occasioned by a very recent conversation repor-ted | in the morning chronicle. | Maitland, accept the verse a muse would pay,". Signed "one of the people"; dated "Feb. 5, 1793."

Suggested by L. Werkmeister and P. M. Zall "Possible Additions to Coleridge's 'Sonnets on Eminent Characters'" *Studies in Romanticism* (Boston) VIII (1969) 121–7. James Maitland, 8th Earl of Lauderdale (1759–1839), a lawyer, former MP, and now Scottish representative peer, was a vigorous opponent of Pitt's government in the Lords, and was afterwards to be taken to task (with the Duke of Bedford) by Burke in *A Letter to a Noble Lord* (1796). C reviewed Burke's *Letter* in the first number of *The Watchman* (*CC* 29–39), and alluded to it in **145** *The Raven*. He was also critical of Lauderdale's later reactionary opposition to reform: see **568** *Greek Couplet on Lauderdale*. However, more than circumstantial evidence of C's authorship of the present sonnet would be required before it could be accepted into the canon.

51. THE COMPLAINT OF NINATHOMA

A. DATE

Shortly before 7 Feb 1793? See *CL* I 51–2.

1. VCL (uncatalogued in 1978). Ann Frances Bacon's Commonplace Book ff 39ᵛ–40ʳ. Transcript by AFB in five stanzas. Subscribed "S. T. Coleridge".

One reason for thinking that this version was made from one earlier than MS 2 below is that the headnote is closer to the story told in Ossian than the headnote in MS 2. Ninathóma was the daughter of Torthóma (though he was still alive), and she was marooned on a desert island (though she was not confined in a cave—despite the passage C quotes as a note to the title in PR 2 3). It could be argued, on other grounds, that this version should follow MS 2; and Ann Bacon appears to have obtained the bulk of the poems she copied later, during the summer of 1793 (after PR 1).

2. Pforzheimer MS Misc 70. Two quarto conjoint leaves, the first 18.6× 22.9 cm overall, the second 18.6×22.5 cm overall; wm ELGAR & SON; chain-lines 2.6 cm. Transcript by C in five stanzas in an als to Mary Evans, 7 Feb 1793 (CL I 52).

In his letter C told Mary Evans that his friend Charles Hague would set the lines to music, and it appears in *A Second Collection of Glees, Rounds, & Canons* (Cambridge n.d.) 14–17. The text which accompanies Hague's music is not that of MS 2 or PR 1; it might even have been taken, with a few variations of punctuation and capitalisation, from PR 2.

1. M Chron (18 Jul 1793). Unsigned. This version is also in five stanzas but omits the original third stanza; it closes the poem by repeating the first stanza. The change in line 5 appears to be a deliberate clarification (Torthóma was Ninathóma's father, Cathlóma was the district he ruled over), others (e.g. line 10 "mornbeams") look like errors. In all, the authority of this version is uncertain.

3. In the possession of J.C.C. Mays (1999). Verso of a single sheet, approx. 17.6×10.7 cm; wm fragmentary; chain-lines 2.7 cm. Facsimile reproduction in Christie's Catalogue (22 Oct 1980) 55. Fragment (titled) in C's hand, in which stanzas 1 and 2 are combined. The recto contains **55** *Imitated from Ossian* 9–17.

The fragment appears to have been cut from the Quarto Copy Book (PML MA 1916), which was used in the preparation of PR 2. An accompanying letter from SC to Mrs Auriol, dated 25 Nov 1845, makes it clear that it was sent in response to a request for a scrap of C's handwriting.

2 [=RT]. *Poems* (1796). This and all subsequent versions omit the third stanza, as in PR 1, and combine the first two and last two, but do not carry forward the other changes.

3. Poems (1803). The inclusion of the poem was undoubtedly due to CL, who protested against C's omitting it from the 1797 collection (LL—M—I 65).

4. PW (1828).

5. *PW* (1829).

6. *PW* (1834).

headnote/title. 1 Ninathóma was the daughter of the king of Cathlóma, a district in the highlands of Scotland: her father having been killed in an engagement with a neighbouring Chief, the young Princess according to the customs of the Age and Country was confined in a Cave, on the shore of a desert Island—The following is her supposed Complaint.— • 2 Cathlóma, who reigned in the Hig⟨h⟩lands of Scotland about 200 years after the birth of our Saviour, was defeated and killed in a war with a neighbouring Prince—and Nina-thoma, his Daughter (according the custom of those times and that country) was imprisoned in a cave by the Sea Side: this is supposed to be her Complaint.— • *1* (FROM OSSIAN.) | *NINA-THOMA.* • 3 Effusion ~~31~~ 30. | The Complaint of ‡Ninathoma • 2 EFFUSION XXX. | THE | *COMPLAINT OF NINATHOMA.*• • *3–6* THE | *COMPLAINT of NINATHOMA.** **title**
fn. *2 3* How long will ye roll around me, blue-tumbling waters of ocean? My dwelling was not always in caves, nor beneath the whistling tree. My feast was spread in Torthoma's Hall. The youths beheld me in my loveliness. They blessed the dark-haired Nina-thomà.—BERRATHON.

1 □	How long will ye round me be swelling,	
2 ⊠*1*	O ye blue-tumbling waves of the Sea?	
1	Ye	
3 □	Not always in Caves was my dwelling,	
4 □	Nor beneath the cold blast of the tree!	
	[*Line-space*]	
5 ⊠2 *1*	Thro' the high-sounding Halls of Cathlóma	
2	Hall	
1	halls Torthóma,	
6 □	In the steps of my beauty I stray'd:	
7 1	The warrior beheld Nina thóma,	
⊠1	Warriors	
8 1 2 *1*	And they blessed the dark-tressed Maid!	
3 *2–6*	white-bosom'd	
	[*Line-space*]	
8.1.1 1 2	By my friends, by my Lovers discarded	
8.1.2 1	Like the flower of the rock, O! I waste,	
2	now	
8.1.3 1 2	That lifts its fair head unregarded	
8.1.4 1 2	And scatters its Leaves on the blast.	
	[*Line-space*]	
9 ⊠*1*	A Ghost! by my cavern it darted!	
1	window started,	
10 ⊠3 *1*	In moonbeams the spirit was drest!	
1	morn-beams	
11 ⊠3	For lovely appear the departed,	
12 ⊠3	When they visit the dreams of my rest—	
	[*Line-space*]	

13	1 2 *1*	But dispers'd by the Tempest's commotion
	2–6	disturb'd
14	⊠3	Fleet the shadowy forms of delight:
15	⊠3 *1*	Ah! cease, thou shrill blast of the ocean,
	1	rude
16	⊠3 *1*	To howl thro' my cavern by night!
	1	at
		[Line-space]
16.1.1	*1*	Oh! how long will ye round me be swelling,
16.1.2	*1*	Ye blue-tumbling waves of the sea!
16.1.3	*1*	Not always in caves was my dwelling,
16.1.4	*1*	Nor beneath the cold blast of the tree!

title. *4* THE COMPLAINT OF NINATHÓMA, • *5 6* THE COMPLAINT OF NINATHÓMA. **title fn.** [see commentary below] 2[proof note] [=Rugby MS p 52/f 22ᵛ, HRC MS (Coleridge, S T) Works B] Waters Ocean? Dwelling Tree. Feast Youths 2[proof note] *3* Nina-thomà [with "BERRATHON." on separate line] **2.** 3 Waves *1* sea! • *6* sea? **3.** 2 *1 6* caves 3 Dwelling, **4.** 2 3 *2–5* Tree. • *6* tree. **5.** *4–6* Through *2–6* halls **6.** 2 3 *2–5* Beauty 3 *1–3* stray'd; • *4–6* strayed; **7.** *1 6* warriors 2 Nina thoma, • *1* Nina-thoma, • *2–6* Ninathóma, **8.** *4–6* white-bosomed 2 Maid. • *1* maid. **8.1.1.** 2 Friends, **8.1.2.** 2 Flower 2 Rock **8.1.3.** 2 unregarded, **8.1.4.** 2 leaves **9.** *1* —A ghost!— • *2–5* A GHOST! • *6* A Ghost! *2–5* Cavern **10.** 2 *2–6* moon-beams 2 *2–6* Spirit 2 *2–6* drest— • *1* drest: **11.** *2–5* DEPARTED • *6* departed **12.** 2 Rest. • *1* rest. • *2–5* Rest! • *6* rest! **13.** *4–6* disturbed 2 *1 6* tempest's *1* commotion, **14.** 2 Delight: • *2–5* Delight— • *6* delight— **15.** *2–6* Ah *1* cease 2 Blast 2 *2–6* Ocean! • *1* ocean **16.** *4–6* through 2 *2–5* Cavern 2 *6* night. • *2–5* Night.

title fn. MS 3 title has the footnote indicator only. C added the footnote (preserved in the Rugby Manuscript cited in the apparatus above) at the proof stage of PR 2. The note appears at the end of the volume in PR 2, where it is headed "Note 9.—Page 86.", and at the foot of the page in PR 3.

2, 4, 6, etc. Alternate lines indented in TEXTS *1* 3 *2–6*.

4⁺ etc. MS 1 has rules.

4⁺. No line-space in TEXTS 3 *2–6*.

9. Indented in MS 1.

12⁺. No line-space in PR *2–6*.

52. TWO LINES ON THE POET LAUREATE

A. DATE

7 Feb 1793.

Pforzheimer MS Misc 70. Two quarto conjoint leaves, the first 18.6×22.9 cm overall, the second 18.6×22.5 cm overall; wm ELGAR & SON; chain-lines 2.6 cm. Transcript by C in an als to Mary Evans, 7 Feb 1793 (*CL* I 50).

The RT reproduces the untitled ms exactly, except for:

2. ms ~~flow.~~ grow.—

53. O TURTLE-EYED AFFECTION!

Early Feb 1793.

Pforzheimer MS Misc 70. Single quarto leaf, the first 18.8×22.9 cm; wm ELGAR & SON; chain-lines 2.6 cm. Transcript by C in an als to Anne Evans, 10 Feb 1793 (*CL* I 55).

The RT reproduces the ms exactly, except for:

title. ms O Turtle-eyed Affection!—

54. LATIN VERSES, SENT TO GEORGE COLERIDGE

Before 18 Feb 1793.

In the possession of Sir Charles Cave (Oct 1981). Two conjoint leaves, each 18.5×22.8 cm; wm PAINE & SONS; chain-lines 2.5 cm. Part of a letter to GC, postmarked 18 Feb 1793 (*CL* I 56).

The RT reproduces the untitled ms exactly, except for:

1. ms pro?~~eut~~cul

55. IMITATED FROM OSSIAN

A. DATE

Shortly before Feb 1793? Feb–Jul 1793? Dec 1794–Apr 1795? See vol I headnote.

B. TEXTS

1. BPL B 22189=Estlin Copy Book f 19ʳ⁻ᵛ. Transcript in C's hand.

2. PML MA 1916=Quarto Copy Book f 8ᵛ. First two stanzas only, on the bottom half of a tipped-in leaf. Transcript in C's hand.

The transcript was clearly preparatory to PR *1* below (see note on the title), though it might not have served as printer's copy.

3. In the possession of J.C.C. Mays (1999). Single sheet, 17.6×10.7 cm approx; wm fragmentary; chain-lines 2.7 cm. Lines 9–17 only, in C's hand. The verso contains the first two stanzas of **51** *The Complaint of Ninathoma*.

The fragment appears to have been cut from the same Quarto Copy Book as MS 2, whose text it continues. An accompanying letter from SC to Mrs Auriol (25 Nov 1845) makes it clear that it was sent in response to a request for a scrap of C's handwriting.

1 [=RT]. *Poems* (1796).

2. *Poems* (1803).

3. *PW* (1828).

4. *PW* (1829).

5. *PW* (1834).

title. 1 Ode • 2 Effusion no 30 29 | Imitated* from Ossian • *1* EFFUSION XXIX. | IMITATED* | *FROM OSSIAN.* • *2–5* IMITATED | *FROM OSSIAN,*   **title**
fn. *1 2* The flower hangs its head waving at times to the gale. Why dost thou awake me, O Gale! it seems to say, I am covered with the drops of Heaven. The time of my fading is near, the blast that shall scatter my leaves. To-morrow shall the traveller come, he that saw me in my beauty shall come. His eyes will search the field, they will not find me. So shall they search in vain for the voice of Cona, after it has failed in the field.—BERRATHON, see Ossian's Poems, vol. 2.

1 ⊠3   The stream with languid murmur creeps
2 ⊠3   In Lumin's flow'ry Vale;
3 ⊠3   Beneath the Dew the Lily weeps
4 ⊠3   Slow-waving to the Gale.
         [*Line-space*]
5 ⊠3   "Cease, restless Gale! it seems to say—

6	⊠3	"Nor wake me with thy sighing;
7	⊠3	"The Honors of my vernal Day
8	⊠3	"On rapid wing are flying!
		[*Line-space*]
9	⊠2	"To morrow shall the Traveller come
10	1	"That erst beheld me blooming:
3	*1–5*	"Who late
11	⊠2	"His searching Eye shall vainly roam
12	⊠2	"The dreary Vale of Lumin!
		[*Line-space*]
13	⊠2	With eager gaze and wetted Cheek
14	⊠2	My wonted Haunts along,
15	1	Thus, lovely Maiden! *thou* shalt seek
3		~~lo~~ faithful
1–5		faithful
16	1	The youth of ~~simplest~~ gentle Song.
3	*1–5*	simplest
		[*Line-space*]
17.1	3	~~But I along the breeze shall roll~~
17.2	3	~~B~~
17	1	But I along the Breeze ~~will~~ shall roll
3	*1–5*	shall
18	1 *1–5*	The voice of feeble power,
19	1 *1–5*	And dwell, the Moonbeam of thy Soul,
20	1 *1–5*	In Slumber's nightly Hour!

title. *3–5* IMITATED FROM OSSIAN.   **1.** 2 Murmur   *1–5* creeps,   **2.** 2 *1–4* LUMIN's   2 *1–4 flowery* • 5 flowery   2 *1–5* vale: **3.** *1–5* dew   **4.** *1–5* gale.   **5.** *1–5* gale!   2 *1* say • *2–5* say,   **6.** 5 Nor   2 Sighing! • *1–5* sighing!   **7.** 5 The   *2 1* 2 honors • *3–5* honours   *1–5* day   **8.** 5 On   2 ? ~~res~~rapid   2 *1–5* flying.   **9.** 2 5 "To-morrow   3 *1* 2 Trav'ller   **10.** 5 Who   **11.** 5 His   *1–5* eye   **12.** 5 The   3 *1–4 dreary*   3 *1–5* vale   3 LUMIN • *1–4* LUMIN." • 5 Lumin."   **13.** 3 *1–5* cheek   **14.** *1–5* haunts   **15.** 5 thou   **16.** 3 *1–5* Youth   *1–5* song.   **17.** 3 *1–5* breeze   **18.** *1–5* power;   **19.** *1–5* Moon-beam   *1–5* soul,   **20.** *1–5* hour.

    title fn. The portion of the Rugby Manuscript in which one might expect to find the note cued in the title of MS 2 is imperfect. The note is given at the end of the volume in PR *1* and at the foot of the page in PR 2, where it is headed "Note 8.—Page 84.", and reads identically in both texts.

    2, 4, 6, etc. Alternate lines indented in all texts.

    17.1, 17.2. The deletions were prompted by C's attempt to get the spacing right.

55.X1. LAUS ASTRONOMIAE

Although subjects for the Browne competition were announced in the *Cambridge Chronicle* on 19 Jan 1793, C did not tell GC that the odes were to be in praise of astronomy ("Thesis nobis Odica Laus Astronomiae") until a month later (*CL* I 56: to GC 18 Feb 1793). He learned in early Jun that John Keate had won the Greek prize. It is not known on what authority C is said to have been placed second (*CL* I 56n), since the prescribed procedure preserved the anonymity of all candidates except, eventually, the single prizewinner in each section. Nor is there any record of C's progress with the poem, or of its final text apart from the translation given below. The Greek text has not come to light in records at Cambridge, RS's papers, or family manuscripts.

C found a way to interpret the subject which made it more than a mere exercise. In Jul 1797 he described it as the finest poem he ever wrote—*"too good"* to win the prize (*CL* I 330: to Joseph Cottle [c 3 Jul 1797]; the reference in *CL* I 80 (to GC 1 May 1794) may or may not be to the same)—but his many other preoccupations may have interfered with his concentration. There was the project, to be completed before the end of Jun, to translate a selection of Greek and Latin lyrics in the hope of earning enough to pay off his debts, made more urgent by the failure to win the Craven (*CL* I 46: to GC 13 [Jan 1793]; see **50.X1** *Imitations from the Modern Latin Poets*). He was also distracted by the trial of William Frend, the Fellow of Jesus with whom he had struck up an acquaintance in his first term, and by other commitments. His library borrowings suggest a strong interest in contemporary travel and include only one book of obvious relevance—R. G. Boscovich *De Solis ac Lunae Defectibus* (1760) (*Jesus LB* No 24)—and even this would be more relevant to the Latin than to the Greek ode, being a scientific treatise on solar and lunar eclipses in Latin dactylic hexameters, in five books.

C had already been deeply impressed by his father's conversation about the stars at the age of eight, and particularly remembered him talking about the great distance of Jupiter (*CL* I 354: to TP [16 Oct 1797]). This and his later "sky-gazing in 'ecstatic fit'" at Christ's Hospital must have had some influence on the poem (see **289** *A Letter to* —— 62; cf **171** *Frost at Midnight* 53), apart from the importance of astronomy, with mathematics, as a subject of study at Cambridge.

The form of the translation, with its irregular rhyme and metre, is that of a "Pindaric", not a Sapphic, ode. It probably gives a better impression of ecstatic spontaneity, and must have minimised any need for divergences from the original in other respects, but precise influences are difficult to pin down. The rare and astonishing words and phrases in which Greek is so rich and which made sources detectable in **48** *Sors Misera Servorum* are not so identifiable from their English equivalents. Some possible connections are pointed out in the notes that follow the translation. The ascent to heaven in the second half of the poem comes in other forms in the closing paragraph of the Christ's Hospital version of **82** *Monody on the Death of Chatterton*, and in **101** *Religious Musings* 35–63, 409 et seq. It is a Neoplatonic and Christian commonplace, much to C's taste, and was perhaps inspired here by Synesius *Hymn* 9.108–34, the conclusion (this is *Hymn* 1 in Synesius *Essays and Hymns* tr Augustine Fitzgerald—2 vols Oxford 1930—II 372–92); cf also the conclusions of *Hymns* 2 (4) and 1 (3). It seems that C at first intended to include Synesius in the *Imitations* he had begun to plan in Jan 1793; indeed, he afterwards took the Canter edition with him when he joined the Dragoons (cf **4.X1** *Translations of Synesius* and **50.X1** *Imitations from the Modern Latin Poets*). He might also have looked for Greek inspiration in Hesiod *Theogony*, Aratus *Phenomena* (c 300 B.C., the first didactic poem on astronomy), and "Orpheus" *Hymns*, addressed to *Night*, *Heaven* (*Ouranos*), *Aether*, *Sun*—all mentioned below in the notes. What little astronomical detail is given owes nothing to ancient sources.

In C's poem the praise of astronomy is implicit rather than explicit. It can be compared to the winning odes, inscribed as decreed in the volume in Cambridge University Library (Archives Charters 1.4), and published in *Musae Cantabrigienses* (1810)—the Greek on pp 114–20, the Latin on pp 15–20. One might also compare the English *Ode to Astronomy*, signed "J.", in *Academical Contributions of Original and Translated Poetry* published by Benjamin Flower (Cambridge 1795) 37–40. The winning Greek and Latin versions, by Keate and Butler, mention the benefits to navigation and agriculture, at least in passing, as well as the approach through knowledge of God's works to knowledge of God. C's poem moves in a different direction, and exemplifies a remark of Synesius he could have found in the first work of the Canter edition he had been reading, *De dono*. It may be translated: "Astronomy is a most venerable science and might become a stepping stone to . . . mystic theology."

The translation given below appeared, unsigned, in *M Post* (28 Nov 1801), and was reprinted in *The Port Folio* (Philadelphia) II (18) (8 May 1802) 144; *The Weekly Entertainer* (Sherborne) XXXIX (21 Jun 1802) 499–500; *Poems by Robert Southey* (3rd ed 2 vols Bristol 1806) II 1–9; *The Minor Poems of Robert Southey* (3 vols 1815) I 206–12, etc. RS contributed items to *M Post* on a regular basis during 1798–9, but he ceased to do so at the beginning of 1800, and contributed only occasionally after his return from Portugal. C, however, was sending a good many contributions to *M Post* at the end of 1801, and it is just possible that he sent in the translation of his poem. If he did, he almost certainly revised what he sent.

The *M Post* version is given verbatim below. The translation appears in subsequent collections by RS, where the capitalisation and punctuation are successively revised. The subsequent versions also contain minor improvements of phrasing, but these are unlikely to have been made with reference to the original ms, and the variations have not been collated.

TRANSLATION
OF A
GREEK ODE on ASTRONOMY.

WRITTEN FOR THE PRIZE AT CAMBRIDGE,
1793.
(*Never before published*)

Hail, venerable Night!
O thou, the first created, hail!
Thou who art doom'd in thy dark breast to hide
    The dying beam of light,
    The eldest and the latest, thou   5
Hail, venerable Night! O Goddess, hail!
    Around thine ebon brow
    Glittering plays with lightning rays
    A wreath of flow'rs of fire;
The varying clouds with many a hue attire   10
    Thy many-tinted veil.
Holy are the blue graces of thy zone!
    But who is he whose tongue could tell
The dewy lustres that thine eyes adorn?
Lovely to some the blushes of the morn!   15
    To some the glitter of the day,
    When blazing in meridian ray
The gorgeous Sun ascends his highest throne;
But I with solemn and severe delight
Still watch thy constant car, immortal Night!   20

For then to the celestial palaces
    Urania leads, Urania, she
        The goddess who alone
        Stands by the blazing throne
Effulgent with the light of deity.   25
Whom wisdom, the creatress, by her side
    Plac'd on the heights of yonder sky,
And, smiling with ambrosial love, unlock'd
    The depths of Nature to her piercing eye.
Angelic myriads struck their harps around,   30
    And with triumphant song
    The host of stars, a beauteous throng,
    Around the Ever-living Mind,

In jubilee their mystic dance begun,
  When at thy leaping forth, O Sun,   35
  The Morning started in affright,
Astonish'd at thy birth, her Child of Light!

   Hail, O Urania, hail!
Queen of the Muses! mistress of the song!
For thou didst deign to leave the heav'nly throng. 40
  As earthward thou thy steps wert bending,
A ray went forth and harbinger'd thy way.
  All ether laugh'd with thy descending,
  Thou hadst wreath'd thy hair with roses,
  The flower that in the immortal bower   45
   Its deathless bloom discloses.
Before thine awful mien, compell'd to shrink,
Fled Ignorance abash'd, and all her broods,
  Dragons, and hags, of baleful breath,
   Fierce dreams that wont to drink   50
   The sepulchre's black blood,
   Or on the wings of storms
   Riding in fury forms,
Shriek'd to the mariner the shriek of Death.

I boast, O Goddess, to thy name   55
That I have rais'd the pile of fame!
   Therefore to me be giv'n
  To roam the starry path of heav'n,
  To charioteer with wings on high,
And to rein in the tempests of the sky.   60

  Chariots of happy Gods! fountains of light!
   Ye angel temples bright;
May I, unblam'd, your flamy threshold tread?
   I leave Earth's lovely scene,
   I leave the Moon serene,   65
   The lovely Queen of Night,
   I leave the wide domains,
Beyond where MARS his fiercer light can fling
   And JUPITER's vast plains
   (The many-belted King),   70
Even to the solitude where SATURN reigns,
Like some stern tyrant to just exile driv'n:
  Dim seen the sullen pow'r appears,
   In that cold solitude of Heav'n,

And slow he drags along   75
The mighty circle of long ling'ring years.

Nor shalt thou escape my sight,
Who at the threshold of the sun-trod domes
Art trembling, youngest daughter of the Night!
And ye—ye fiery-tressed strangers! ye   80
    Comets who wander wide,
Will I along your pathless way pursue,
    Whence bending, I may view
The worlds whom elder Suns have vivified.

For hope with loveliest visions soothes my mind,   85
    That even in Man, life's winged pow'r,
    When comes anew the natal hour,
    Shall, on Heaven-wand'ring feet,
      Spring to the blessed seat,
      In undecaying youth;   90
    Where round the fields of truth,
    The fiery essences for ever feed,
    And o'er th' ambrosial mead,
    The gales of calm serenity,
    Silent and soothing, glide for ever by.   95

There, hireless Priest of Nature, dost thou shine,
NEWTON! a King among the Kings divine,
    Whether with harmony's mild force,
    He guides along its course
The axle of some beauteous star on high,   100
    Or gazing in the Spring,
    Ebullient with creative energy,
Feels his pure breast with rapt'rous joy possest,
    Inebriate in the holy ecstacy!

I may not call thee mortal then, my soul!   105
    Immortal longings lift thee to the skies,
Love of thy native home inflames thee now
    With pious madness wise.
Know then thyself, expand thy plumes divine,
Soon mingled with thy fathers thou shalt shine   110
    A star amid the starry throng,
    A GOD the Gods among!

2. On Night as first in ancient cosmogonies, C may have had in mind his early reading in Thomas Stanley's *History of Philosophy* (1701) 5, 7 (cf *CL* VI 843: to JG Jr [11 Aug 1830]). See also Hesiod *Theogony* 123 etc; "Orpheus" *Hymn to Night*; Gen 1.2.

22, 38. Urania ("Heavenly" one), listed as one of the Muses by Hesiod, was first specifically associated with astronomy much later, in the time of Aratus. She sometimes merges with Aphrodite Urania as Celestial Venus, Heavenly Love. To Boscovich she gives instruction on the discovery of Astronomy by Prometheus and how he was conveyed to the skies by Athena's winged steeds. None the less, C must surely have had Milton in mind. The links between Urania, Wisdom, and Creation are made in *PL* VII 1–39 (cf I 6–26).

26. wisdom, the creatress] See Prov 8, esp 22–30, and cf σοφία κοσμοτεχνῖτις in Synesius *Hymn* 5.30 (though several other synonyms were available).

70. The belts were already correctly explained as cloud formations in the atmosphere of the planet.

77–9. So far, C would have called the planets by their Greek names—Ares, Zeus, and Cronos—but there would be a problem in introducing the Georgium Sidus (Georgian Planet), discovered in 1781 by William Herschel. It was already known especially in Prussia as Uranus (Greek Ouranos), to which name the objection was made that it meant primarily the whole sky itself as well as, in anthropomorphic myth, the father of Cronos. Urania, favoured by the Austrians, was obviously equally unsuitable here. The two moons (or more, as he thought) of Uranus had also been observed by Herschel in 1787. Keate clarified his allusion to "stars in the outermost recesses" with a footnote "Georgium Sidus" (p 19).

88–9. Shall, . . . Spring] Here C may have written Αἰθεροπλάγκτοις ὑπὸ πόσσ᾽ ἀίξει. The line seems to have strayed into the version of the opening stanzas of **48** *Sors Misera Servorum* which C quoted in his footnote to **110** *Contributions to "Joan of Arc"*. Cf **48.**11EC. Ἄνεισι would mean "shall rise" in this context; ἀίξει, the last word in poem **48,** is suggested by the translation "shall spring".

97. NEWTON] Both Keate and Butler particularly mention his connection with Cambridge.

109. Know then thyself] Γνῶθι σεαυτόν (cf **700** *"E Cælo Descendit"*) would do for the last line of a sapphic stanza.

110, 112. Cf Synesius *Hymn* 9.132–4, addressing his soul, tr "Soon, mingling with thy father, thou mayst move as god, in god." C's father coined the word "instellation" to describe the same process in *Miscellaneous Dissertations* (1768) 247—citing Diodorus Siculus, Philo Judaeus, Hesiod, and others as authorities on "The original of starry Gods". (The first usage recorded by *OED* is John Wilson in 1832.)

55.X2. CAMBRIDGE PRIZE POEMS, 1793

C told GC that he was entering for all three Browne Medals in 1792 and in 1794 (*CL* I 34: [2 Apr 1792]; 80: 1 May 1794). The record of his undergraduate academic reading (*Jesus LB*) and his letters suggest strongly that he still nurtured ambitions to excel at Cambridge, and it is likely that he worked on entries for the other categories besides the Greek ode. The topic for the Latin ode, to be composed "in imitation of Horace", was, as usual, the same as for the Greek, "Astronomiae Laus", the "Praise of Astronomy". There is a hint of a Latin poem in **54** *Latin Verses, Sent to George Coleridge* 13 "Camænæ", C's first response to the competition. The Latin medal was won by Samuel Butler of St John's, who had also won it the previous year and who had been ranked above C in the Craven Scholarship. The topic for the epigrams, one "after the Model of Anthologia", the other "after the Model of Martial", was Ὕστερον πρότερον, "last first"—a rhetorical figure and, more importantly, a fallacy in logic, indicating a reversal of the normal order, in which C came to take a particular interest. John Keate of King's won the medals for his epigrams and Greek ode.

56. ON PRESENTING A MOSS ROSE
TO MISS F. NESBITT

A. DATE

Jun 1793 or earlier. The composition of the poem might have been less spontaneous than C told GC (*CL* I 57–8; see vol I headnote). The lines are an expansion of Anacreon 19, and C had been imitating "Anacreon" in such a way since before Feb 1792 (see poems **40.X1, 41, 62**).

B. TEXTS

1. Present location unknown. Facsimile of the verses only in Sotheby Catalogue (25 Jul 1978), facing p 270. Sold at Sotheby's, lot 360 (to Bonner for £1,900). Included in an als to GC, 28 Jun 1793 (*CL* I 58).

ELG based his text on a transcript in the Folio Copy Book at HRC (MS (Coleridge S T) Letters I pp 80–1). In the original lines 21–2 and 23–4 are written abreast to fit them on to the page. The postmark in the original advances ELG's date by one month.

2 [=RT]. BM Add MS 47552 f iii^{r–v}. In pencil, signed "S T Coleridge". Transcript in C's hand on a rear flyleaf of Langhorne's edition of *The Poetical Works of William Collins* (1781). *CM* (*CC*) II 94, 95–6.

Another poem transcribed into the same volume (**57** *Cupid Turn'd Chymist*) is dated "Friday Evening—July 1793".

3. VCL (uncatalogued in 1978). Ann Frances Bacon's Commonplace Book f 41^{r–v}. Transcript by AFB, subscribed "S. T. Coleridge.—"

4. BPL B 22189=Estlin Copy Book f 9^{r–v}. Fair copy in C's hand.

5. HRC MS (Coleridge, S T) Works B. Single leaf, 19.1×32 cm; wm Britannia in oval surmounted by crown; chain-lines 2.5 cm. Bound into Rugby Manuscript p 49/f 21ʳ. Transcript in C's hand, submitted as copy for PR *1* below.

1. Poems (1796); rpt *The Port Folio* (Philadelphia) I (37) (12 Sept 1801) 296; *The Lyre of Love* (2 vols 1806) II 119–20.

2. Poems (1797); rpt *Poetical Beauties of Modern Writers* (1798; 2nd ed 1803) 36–7.

In a letter of 6 Jan 1797 (*CL* I 300) C asked J. Cottle to omit the definite article in line 8, which had appeared in TEXTS 5 *1*.

3. Poems (1803).

4. PW (1828).

5. PW (1829).

6. PW (1834).

title. 2 —On presenting a Moss Rose to Miss F. Nesbitt • 3 On presenting a moss rose to Miss Nesbitt • 4 Ode. • 5 Effusion 28 • *1* EFFUSION XXVII. • *2–6 THE ROSE.*

1 □	As late each Flower that sweetest blows	
2 □	I pluck'd, the Garden's pride;	
3 □	Within the petals of a Rose	
4 ⊠3	A sleeping Love I spy'd	
3	sleepy	
	[Line-space]	
5 1–3	Around his brows a lucid wreath	
4	lucent	
5 *1–6*	beamy	
6 1 2	Of many a mingled hue;	
3	vivid	
4	changing	
5	~~That~~ Of lucent	
1–6	Of	
7 1	And purple glow'd his Cheek beneath	
⊠1	All	
8 ⊠5 *1*	Inebriate with Dew.	
5 *1*	the Dew.	
	[Line-space]	
9 □	I softly seiz'd th' unguarded Power,	
10 ⊠3	Nor scar'd his balmy rest,	
3	gentle	
11 □	And plac'd him cag'd within the Flower	
12 1 3	On Angelina's Breast.	
2	lovely Nesbitt's	
4	spotless Anna's	
5 *1–6*	SARA'S

[*Line-space*]

13　1 2　　　But when all reckless of the Guile
　　3　　　　　　　　unknowing
　　4 5 *1–6*　　　　　unweeting
14　1 2　　　Awoke the Slumberer sweet,
　　☒1 2　　　　　　pris'ner
15　1　　　He struggled to escape as awhile,
　　☒1　　　　　　　　awhile
16　1 2　　　And stamp'd his angry feet
　　3　　　　　　　　elfin
　　4 5 *1–6*　　　　　faery

[*Line-space*]

17　☐　　Ah! soon the ʄsoul-entrancing Sight
18　☐　　Subdued th' impatient Boy:
19　☐　　He gaz'd, he thrill'd with deep delight,
20　☐　　Then clapt his Wings for Joy.

[*Line-space*]

21　1　　　And—oh! he cried what J̶o̶y̶s̶ Charms refin'd,
　　2–5　　　　　　　　charms
　　1–6　　　　　　"Of　　magic　　kind
22　1–5　　This　　　magic Throne endear!
　　1–4 6　　　"What charms this
　　5　　　　　　　charm
23　1　　　　Another　Love may Venus find—
　　☒1　　　Some other　　let
24　☐　　I'll fix my empire here!—

title. *4–6* THE ROSE.　　**1.** 2 flow'r • 3 5 *1–6* flower　　**2.** *4–6* plucked,
2 3 garden's　5 *1–6* pride!　　**3.** 4 Petals　　**4.** 3 *Love*　2 spy'd. • 3 'spy'd •
4 5 *1* 'spied. • *2–6* spied.　　**5.** 3 5 Brows　4 Wreath　　**6.** 4 Hue;　　**7.** *4–*
6 glowed　2 3 cheek • 4 *1–6* cheek, • 5 Cheek,　4 5 *1–6* beneath,　　**8.** 2 *1–*
6 dew. • 3 Dew.—　　**9.** 4 *4–6* seized　*1* 6 the　3 unguarded　2 power, •
3 power • 4 Power　　**10.** *4–6* scared　3 5 *1–4* rest; • 4 Rest; • *5* 6 rest:　　**11.** *4–*
6 placed　4 5 *1–6* him,　2 cagd • *4–6* caged　2 3 flower • 4 Flower, • 5 *1–6* flower,
12. *4 5* Spotless　6 Sara's　☒1 breast.　　**13.** 3 when— • 5 when,　2 3 *1–6* guile •
5 guile,　　**14.** 2 slumberer　4 Pris'ner • *4–6* prisoner　5 sweet;　　**16.** *4–*
6 stamped　☒1 feet.　　**17.** ☒1 soul-entrancing　3 sight, • *1–6* sight　　**18.** *4–6* the
2 3 5 Boy! • *1–6* boy!　　**19.** 2–4 gaz'd— • 5 *1–3* gaz'd! • *4–6* gazed!　*4–6* thrilled
3 delight　• 4 Delight— • 5 delight—! • *1–6* delight!　　**20.** 2–5 *1–3* clapp'd • *4–*
6 clapped　☒1 wings　4 Joy! • *2–6* joy.　　**21.** 2–5 *1–3* And　*4–6* "And O!" •
4 o! • 5 *1–3* ô!　3 (he cry'd) • 2 he cry'd, • 4 5 *1–6* he cried—　4 What • 5 "ẁWhat
6 "of　*3–5* refin'd　　**22.** 6 What　3 throne　4 endear?　　**23.** *1–5* "Some
3 *Love* • 5 *1–5* LOVE　3 *Venus* find　　**24.** *1–5* "I'll　*3–5 1–5* my*　2 Empire
2 3 here.— • 4 *here!* • 5 3 here. • *1* 2 *4–6* here."

2, 4, 6, etc. Alternate lines indented in MSS 1–5.

4. Love] In slightly larger letters in MS 1, perhaps indicating that it should be read as
bold text.

4+, 8+, etc. MS 2 has rules.

20⁺. No line-space in PR *6*.
21–2, 23–4. The couplets written abreast in MS 1.
23. Love] Slightly larger letters in MS 1 (as line 4); perhaps also in MS 4.

57. CUPID TURN'D CHYMIST

A. DATE

Jul 1793 or earlier.

B. TEXTS

1. BM Add MS 47552 ff ii^{r-v}, 1^v. In pencil on two front flyleaves of Langhorne's edition of *The Poetical Works of William Collins* (1781). Transcript in C's hand, signed "S T Coleridge | Friday Evening—July 1793." *CM* (*CC*) II 94–5.

2. VCL (uncatalogued in 1978). Ann Frances Bacon's Commonplace Book f 42^r. Transcript in the hand of AFB; the footnote subscribed "S. T. Coleridge.—".

3 [=RT]. For sale by Roy Davids Ltd Catalogue 4 (Jun 1998) item 29 (£4500). I examined this ms when it was in the possession of Sir Charles Cave (Oct 1981). Two conjoint leaves, 18.5×23.6 cm; no wm; chain-lines 2.5 cm. Included in an als to GC, 5 Aug 1793 (*CL* I 60).

C introduces the poem by saying: "I stayed at Tiverton about 10 days, and got no small κῦδος among the young Belles by complimentary effusions in the poetic Way—". He writes afterwards: "Do you know Fanny Nesbitt? She was my fellow-traveller in the Tiverton diligence from Exeter.—I think a very pretty Girl.—" Sara Besly (or Besley) might have been another of the Tiverton girls: cf **60** *Absence: A Poem* TEXT PR *1*.

4. BPL B 22189=Estlin Copy Book f 18^v. Fair copy in C's hand.

5. HRC MS (Coleridge, S T) Works B. Single leaf, 18.8×32 cm; wm Britannia in oval surmounted by crown; chain-lines 2.5 cm. Bound into Rugby Manuscript p 50/f 21^v. Transcript in C's hand, submitted as copy for PR *1* below.

5*. HRC MS (Coleridge, S T) Works B. C's note for the poem, submitted as copy for PR *1* below. Single leaf, 18×11 cm; wm fragment of a curly ornament unlike any other on paper in the same volume; chain-lines 2.35 cm. Verso blank, except for the tag "Effinxit, quondam blandum" and some calculations (both in C's hand). Bound into Rugby Manuscript p 53/f 23^r.

At the foot of a previous page of notes (p 52/f 22ᵛ) C has written the direction: "Note 7ᵗʰ—Print from the annexed Strip of Paper".

1*. Two proof copies (A) and (B) of PR *1* below contain the note in slightly variant form, and are corrected or have comments in C's hand. A is BM Ashley 408 f 40ʳ⁻ᵛ (*JDC facsimile* 75–6 var); B is MH's copy, now at the Alexander Turnbull Library, Wellington, New Zealand (R Eng COLE Poems (1796)).

1. Poems (1796).

2. Poems (1797), included in the Supplement to the vol; rpt *Poetical Beauties of Modern Writers* (1798; 2nd ed 1803) 42–3.

3. Poems (1803).

title. 1 *Cupid turn'd Chymist* • 2 Cupid turn'd Chymist I a Poem • 3 ⟨A Specimen—⟩ I Cupid turned Chymist.— • 4 The Compound • 5 Effusion 27 I ~~Imitate Distantly imitated from the Latin~~ • *1* EFFUSION XXVI. • *2 The COMPOSITION of a KISS.* • *3 KISSES*.

1	1	Cupid (if ancient legends tell aright)
	⊠1	storying
1fn	5* *1** *1–3*	Effinxit quondam blandum meditata laborem
		Basia lascivâ Cypria Diva manû.
		Ambrosiæ succos occultâ temperat arte,
		Fragransque infuso nectare tingit opus.
		Sufficit et partem mellis, quod subdolus olim 5
		Non impune favis surripuisset Amor.
		Decussos violæ foliis admiscet odores
		Et spolia æstivis plurima rapta rosis.
		Addidit illecebras, et mille et mille lepores,
		Æt quot Acidalius guadia Cestus habet. 10
		Ex his composuit Dea basia; et omnia libans
		Invenias nitidæ sparsa per ora Cloës.
		[L. Thomas]
2	⊠5	Once fram'd a rich Elixir of Delight:
	5	ꞔ a
3	1–3	A cauldron o'er love-kindled flames he fix'd,
	4 5 *1–3*	Chalice
4	□	And in it Nectar and Ambrosia mix'd:
5	□	With these the magic dews, which Evening brings,
6	⊠3	Brush'd from th' Idalian Star by fairy wings;
	3	stom
6fn	1	Idalian Star—Venus, the Evening Star: a planet, which from its superior Beauty, and the time of its Appearance has been (time out of mind) appropriated to Love.
	2	The *Idalian Star* i.e. the evening star, a planet which from its beauty, & the time of its appearance has been ever held sacred to *Love*
	3	The planet Venus, the Evening Star.
7	□	Each tender pledge of sacred Faith he join'd,

8 □	Each gentler pleasure of th' unspotted mind,	
10.1 1	Fond Hopes, the blameless parasites of woe,	
9 1	And　Dreams, whose tints with　beamy　brightness glow.	
2–4	Gay	
5	~~Gay~~ Day-	beaming
1–3	Day-	sportive
10 ⊠1	And *Hope*, the blameless parasite of *Woe*.	
11 1 4	With joy he view'd the chymic process rise,	
2 3	his	
5 *1–3*	The eyeless Chemist heard the	
12 1 3	The　steaming　cauldron bubbled up in sighs	
2	stre⟨a⟩ming	
4	steaming　Chalice	
5 *1–3*	steamy	
13 □	Sweet sounds transpired—as when th' enamour'd Dove	
14 1–3	Pours the soft　murmurs　of responsive Love.	
4 5 *1–3*	Murm'ring	
15 1–3	The finish'd work not Envy's self could blame,	
4	might	
5	~~The finish'd work not Envy's self might~~	
5 *1–3*	The finish'd Work might Envy vainly blame,	
16 ⊠5 *1 3*	And "Kisses" was the　precious　compound's name.	
5	~~lovely~~ precious Compounds'	
1 3	precious	
17 1–4	With　part　the God his Cyprian Mother blest,	
5	~~part~~ half	
1–3	half	
17fn 2	*Cyprian mother* i.e. Venus, so called from the Island of Cyprus, in which she was more particularly worshipped	
18 1 3	And breath'd on　Nesbitt's　lovely　lips the rest—	
2	B—tfl—r's	
4	Mary's　lovelier	
5 *1–3*	Sᴀʀᴀ's	

1. 3–5 *1–3* Cupid, if　2 Ledends • 3–5 *1–3* Legends　3–5 *1–3* aright,
1fn1. *1**ᴀ *1* 2 "Effinxit　**1fn2.** *1** *1–3* manâ　**1fn4.** *1** tinquit • *1**ᴀ [C's hand] tingit　**1fn6.** *1** amor • *1**ᴀ [C's hand] Amor　**1fn8.** *1** pulrima • *1**ᴀ [C's hand] plurima　**1fn9.** *1**ᴀ *1–3* Addit et　*1** illecebra • *1**ᴀ [C's hand] *1–3* illecebras　**1fn10.** *1** *1–3* Et　*1**ᴀ *1* habet."　**1fn12.** 2 Cloës."
2. 2 *delight*: • 3–5 *1 3* Delight. • 2 delight.　**3.** 4 Flames　**4.** 2 *Nectar*　2 *Ambrosia*　4 mix'd;　**5.** 3–5 Dews, • *3* dews　3 wch　2 evening　**6.** *1–3* the　2 *Idalian*　*1–3* star　5 *1–3* faery　3 5 *1–3* wings:　**7.** 3–5 Pledge　2 3 faith　**8.** 3–5 *1–3* Pleasure　2 mind: • 3 4 mind; • 5 Mind— • *1–3* mind—　**9.** 2 5 *1–3* dreams,　5 Tints　2–5 *3* glow, • *1* 2 glow　**10.** 3–5 *1–3* Hope, 3–5 *1–3* Parasite　3 woe. • 4 Woe! • 5 *1–3* Woe.　**11.** 4 chemic　2 5 rise— • 4 rise;　**12.** 3 Cauldron bubb[?]led　4 up—　2 *sighs*— • 3 Sighs, • 4 sighs! • 5 *1–3* sighs;　**13.** 2 *sounds* • 3 4 Sounds　2–4 *1–3* transpir'd, • 5 transpird, 5 *1–3* the　4 enamor'd　2 dove • *3* Dove,　**14.** 3 Murmurs • 5 *1–3* murm'ring　2 *Love*: • 4 love!　**15.** *1* 2 finished　2 work, • 3 4 Work • *1–3* work　2 envy's

3 blame—   **16.** 2 *"Kisses"*   3 4 2 Compound's   2 name: • 4 Name.   **17.** 2 god
2 *Cyprian*   2 3 mother   **18.** 2 4 5 Lips   2 4 rest! • 3 5 *1–3* rest.

title. PR *1* Contents gives "Effusion 26, on a Kiss,"
1fn. Printed at the end of the volume in PR *1*, where it is headed "Note 7.—Page ",
and at the foot of the page in PR *2 3*.
*1**A has three caret marks at the head of the Latin text, and the following description
at the foot of the page, which C subsequently deleted: "~~From the Carmina Quadra-~~
~~gesimalia / Vol II. To the Copy in the Bristol Library there is a manuscript signature of L.~~
~~Thomas to this beautiful composition.~~"
*1**B has, at the head of the Latin text, "From Carm. Qua" (the rest cropped).
1–3 have the following ascription at the end of the text (*2* prints in italic): "Carm.
Quad. vol. II."
1fn2. manû] In MS 5 the last letter looks very like "â", the misprint found in *1* 1–3*.
6fn. In MS 1 the note is cued to "Idalian" and is written on f 1ᵛ (the verses are on f
iiʳ⁻ᵛ). In MS 2 the note is cued to "*Idalian* star".
14⁺. Line-space in MS 4.
18. 2 B—tfl—r's] I.e. "Doutflowcr's". Scc **64** *Songs of the Pixies* headnote.

58. AN EXTEMPORE

A. DATE

26 Jun 1793.

B. TEXT

Present location unknown. Sold at Sotheby's, 25 Jul 1978, lot 360 (to Bonner
for £1,900). Included in an als to GC, 28 Jun 1793 (*CL* I 58).

ELG printed his text from a transcript in the Folio Copy Book at HRC (MS
(Coleridge, S T) Letters I p 81). The postmark on the original letter advances
the date by one month.

The RT reproduces the ms exactly. The title derives from the letter, where C
describes the lines as "An Extempore."

58.X1. ADAPTATION OF
JOHN BAMPFYLDE'S *TO EVENING*

A. DATE

Between ? Jul 1793 and late Oct 1796.

C's adaptation seems more likely to be based on a version published in 1792 than on earlier printed versions or an original ms (see sec C below). This provides a *terminus ad quem*. The sonnet on the verso of MS 1, **61** *To the Autumnal Moon*, is meanwhile exactly as it appears in Ann Bacon's Commonplace Book, and probably represents a version which dates from the summer vacation of 1793. C was in Exeter from 28 Jun to about 20 Jul, when he moved in literary circles (*BL* ch 1—*CC*—I 19–20; Christopher Wordsworth *Social Life at the English Universities in the Eighteenth Century*—Cambridge 1874—589). The changes C introduced into the Bampfylde sonnet echo the spirit of poems of his own, written at that time.

On the evidence of the paper, MS 1 itself could have been written later—e.g. Sept 1795 (see **61** *To the Autumnal Moon* TEXT MS 1). PR *1* was put together and published rather on the spur of the moment, in late Oct–early Nov 1796.

B. TEXTS

1. Christ's Hospital (School Library). Single leaf, 19×23 cm; wm J WHAT-MAN; chain-lines 2.5 cm. The other side contains the sonnet **61** *To the Autumnal Moon*, signed "S. T. C." Transcript in C's hand, signed "**S T** C". It is uncertain whether C meant to amend the first two initials (to "B"?), or to replace the first two by "C", or instead to cancel all three.

1. A Sheet of Sonnets (1796). Signed "BAMFIELD."

The sonnet is the only one in the collection of twenty-eight for which C failed to supply the author's first name or initials and misspelled the surname. It should be noted that C's probable source (Polwhele's 1792 anthology: see sec C below) signs the poem "B. E." (only). It is also the only sonnet in *A Sheet of Sonnets* which does not have the fourteen lines that C argues in his Preface any sonnet should have. This might be taken as evidence that PR *1* depends on MS 1 and not on a fresh look at Bampfylde's original—though PR *1* does restore Bampfylde's original reading in MS 1. For the other sonnets—by RS, Charles Lloyd, CL, C himself, and other authors—C draws on materials available to him since late 1794 as well as on a good deal which came to hand at the time he put the collection together.

C. GENERAL NOTE

John Bampfylde (1754–96) was born in Devon and had matriculated at Trinity Hall in 1771. He went to London, fell in love and afterwards into dissipation, wrote and published verse, and passed the last seventeen years of his life in a madhouse before dying of consumption. He was a friend of William Jackson of Exeter, who afterwards became his literary executor. Besides the poems published in the collections described below, others remained uncollected or unpublished until the edition of *The Poems of John Bampfylde* by Roger Lonsdale (Oxford 1988). C was undoubtedly struck by the real or imagined coincidences between Bampfylde's career and his own (cf his identification with Lee in poem **16** above), as well as Bampfylde's quite unusual powers of observation in verse. The odd signature in MS 1 may reflect this; cf the signature in **70.X1** *Adaptation of "I shall behold far off thy barren crest"*, in which Joseph Hucks may have collaborated in a rewriting of Bowles.

An early version of the original, which differs in lines 3 and 11 and in punctuation, is preserved among transcripts by William Jackson now at HUL. There are two printed versions, which differ in lines 1 and 11 (differently from Jackson's ms), as well as in details of punctuation and capitals: (*a*) [John Bampfylde] *Sixteen Sonnets* (1778) 14; rpt in *Specimens of the Later English Poets* ed RS (3 vols 1807) III 434–5; (*b*) [Richard Polwhele (ed)] *Poems Chiefly by Gentlemen of Devon and Cornwall* (2 vols Bath 1792) I 179; rpt in Thomas Park (ed) *The Works of the British Poets* (42 vols 1808) XLI 12; *The British Poets* (100 vols Chiswick 1822) LXXIII 192–3. Jackson complained of Polwhele's editorial interference with the texts, but C appears none the less to have followed version (*b*), and to have introduced other extensive changes of his own.

Version (*b*) in Polwhele's text reads as follows:

> What numerous tribes beneath thy shadowy wing,
> O mild and modest evening, find delight!
> First, to the grove, his lingering fair to bring,
> The warm and youthful lover, hating light,
> Sighs oft for thee. And next, the boistrous string 5
> Of school-imps, freed from dame's all-dreaded sight,
> Round village cross, in many a wanton ring,
> Wishes thy stay. Then too with vasty might,
> From steeple's side to urge the bounding ball,
> The lusty hinds await thy fragrant call. 10
> I, general friend, by turns am join'd with all,
> Lover, and elfin gay, and harmless hind;
> Nor heed the proud, to real wisdom blind,
> So as my heart be pure, and free my mind.

title. 1 To Evening. • *1* SONNET VII. | *To EVENING*.

1 1   What   various   Tribes beneath thy shadowy Wing,
  1   numerous
2 1   O ~~mild~~ meek and modest Evening, find delight!
  1   meek
3 □   First to the Grove his ling'ring fair to bring
4 □   The warm and youthful Lover hating Light
5 □   Sighs oft for thee. And next the boisterous String
6 □   Of School-Imps, freed from Dame's all-dreaded Sight,
7 □   Round village-cross, in many a wanton ring,
8 1   Wishes thy Stay. And last with vasty might
  1   active
9 □   The lusty hinds urge the rebounding Ball.
10 □   I, general Friend! by turns [?] am mix'd with all,
11 □   Lover, and Elfin gay, and harmless Hind;
12 □   Nor heed the proud to real Wisdom [?] blind,
13 □   So as my Heart be pure, and free my Mind.

1. *1* tribes   *1* wing,   **2.** *1* EVENING,   *1* delight: **5.** *1* thee; and   *1* string
6. *1* School-Imps   *1* all dreaded sight,   **7.** *1* village cross   *1* ring   **8.** *1* stay;
and   *1* might,   **9.** *1* Hinds   *1* Ball;   **10.** *1* am   **11.** *1* Hind,   **12.** *1* proud,
1 wisdom blind,   **13.** *1* Mind!

2, 4, 6, 8, 10. Indented in PR *1*.

59. ELEGY

A. DATE

Jul–Sept 1793? Jul–Sept 1794? MS 1 appears to antedate PR *1*, and is likely to represent a version Ann Bacon obtained when C was at Ottery during the summer months of 1793. *PW* (EHC) I 69–70 dates the poem tentatively to 1794, and PR *1* below provides a *terminus ante quem*.

B. TEXTS

1. VCL (uncatalogued in 1978). Ann Frances Bacon's Commonplace Book ff 37ᵛ–38ʳ. Transcript by AFB, subscribed " S. T. Coleridge".

1. M Chron (23 Sept 1794). Unsigned.

2 [=RT]. *The Watchman* III (17 Mar 1796) 77–8. Signed "T." (the two poems following are signed "C." and "S."). *Watchman* (*CC*) 104 (var).

C's copy in the BM (Ashley 2842) has the following marginal note on the poem: "Rhymified by me, S.T.C. from the much nobler blank Verse Poem of Akenside.", and he corrected the punctuation in line 6.

3. *SL* (1817).

4. *PW* (1828).

5. *PW* (1829).

6. *PW* (1834).

title. 1 For an Inscription • *1* AN ELEGY. • *2* ELEGY. • *3–6 ELEGY*, | Imitated from one of Akenside's Blank-verse Inscriptions.

1	⊠*1*	Near the lone Pile with Ivy overspread
	1	yon
2	1 *1*	Fast by the Riv'lets peace persuading sound
	2–6	sleep-
3	☐	Where sleeps the moon-light on yon verdant bed—
4	1	Ah! humbly press *that* consecrated ground!
	⊠1	O,
		[*Line-space*]
5	1	For there does *Edmund* lie, the learned swain!
	⊠1	rest—
6	1	And there his pale-eyed phantom joys to rove:
	1	loves
	2–6	spirit most delights
7	☐	Young Edmund! fam'd for each harmonious strain
8	1	And the sore wound of ill-requited Love.
	⊠1	wounds
		[*Line-space*]
9	1	Like some tall Plant, that spreads its branches wide,
	⊠1	tree,
10	1 *1*	And loads the Zephyr, with its soft perfume,
	2–6	West-wind
11	1 *1*	His manhood blossom'd—ere the faithless Pride
	2–6	till
12	1 *1*	Of fair Lucinda sunk him to the Tomb.—
	2–6	Matilda
		[*Line-space*]
13	1 *1*	But soon did righteous Heav'n her crime pursue
	2–6	guilt
14	1 *4–6*	Wheree'er with 'wilder'd step she wander'd pale,
	1–3	steps,
15	☐	Still *Edmund*s image rose to blast her view,
16	☐	Still *Edmund*s voice accus'd her in each gale—
		[*Line-space*]
17	1 *1*	With keen remorse & tortur'd guilt's alarms
	2–6	regret, conscious
18	☐	Amid the pomp of *affluence* she pin'd;
19	☐	Nor all that lur'd her faith from *Edmund*'s arms,

20 1   Could sooth the frenzied *horrors* of her mind.
  1   conscious
  2   lull   wakeful
  3–6   horror
        [*Line-space*]
21 □   Go, Traveller! tell the Tale with sorrow fraught—
22 1 *1*   Some lovely Maid perchance, or blooming Youth,
  2–6   tearful
23 □   May hold it in remembrance, and be taught
24 □   That *Riches* cannot pay for *Love* or *Truth*.

title. *4 5* ELEGY, | IMITATED FROM ONE OF AKENSIDE'S BLANK VERSE
INSCRIPTIONS. • *6* ELEGY, | IMITATED FROM ONE OF AKENSIDE'S
BLANK- | VERSE INSCRIPTIONS.   **1** *1* pile, • *3–6* pile   ⊠1 ivy overspread,
2. *1 2* riv'let's • *3–6* rivulet's   *1* peace-persuading   ⊠1 sound,   **3.** *2–
6* "sleeps   *1* moonlight • *2* moonlight," • *3–6* moonlight"   **4.** *2–6* O   *1 3–
6* that   **5.** *1* EDMUND rest • *2–6* Edmund rest,   *1* learn'd   **6.** *1* -ey'd   *2* rove.
7. *1* EDMUND,   *4–6* famed   ⊠1 strain,   **8.** *1 3–6* love.   **9.** *2–6* tree
1 wide;   **10.** *1* zephyr   *3–6* west-wind   *1* perfume—   **11.** *1* blossom'd, •
2 3 blossom'd; • *4* blossomed; • *5 6* blossomed: ⊠1 pride   **12.** *1* LUCINDA
2–6 sank   ⊠1 tomb.   **13.** *2–6* Heaven   *1* pursue: • *2* pursue!— • *3–
6* pursue!   **14.** *1* Where'er, • *4–6* Where'er   *1* wilder'd • *3–6* wildered
2 3 steps   *2–6* wandered   **15.** *1* EDMUND's • *2–6* Edmund's   *1* rose,   *1* view—
16. *1* EDMUND's • *2–6* Edmund's   *3–6* accused   ⊠1 gale.   **17.** *1* Remorse,
⊠1 and   *1* Guilt's   ⊠1 alarms,   **18.** *1* Affluence • *2–6* affluence   *2* pin'd: •
3–6 pined;   **19.** *3–6* lured   *1* EDMUND's • *2–6* Edmund's   *1 3–6* arms
20. *1 2* horrors   **21.** *1 2* Trav'ller!   ⊠1 tale   ⊠1 fraught: **22.** *1* Maid, • *3–
6* maid   *2* Youth • *3–6* youth,   **23.** *2–6* remembrance;   *1* taught—   **24.** *1–
5* Riches • *6* riches   ⊠1 Love   *1* Truth! • *2–6* Truth.

2, 4, 6, etc. Alternate lines indented in TEXTS ⊠1.
6. PR *2* rove.] C corrected the punctuation in the BM copy to "rove:".
11. PR *5* blossomed:] The punctuation may well be a semicolon with a broken tail.

60. ABSENCE: A POEM

A. DATE

Aug 1793. Vol I headnote describes the circumstances which led to the writing
of the poem, after C left Tiverton and arrived at Ottery (see also *CL* I 57: to GC
[24?] Jul 1793; 60: to GC 5 Aug 1793). Christopher Wordsworth records that C
read the PR *1* version to a party of college friends on 7 Nov (*Social Life at the
English Universities in the Eighteenth Century* 589).
    While it is of course likely that C improved on the poem during the summer
before its publication, it is possible that the extensive revision represented by

later versions is continuous with the first version. The reason for suggesting this is that when C rewrote the poem he incorporated a quotation from WW's *An Evening Walk* which he had enthused over in Exeter earlier that summer and which had been discussed by Christopher Wordsworth and his Cambridge friends (cf Christopher Wordsworth, above; *BL* ch 1—*CC*—I 19–20; below on lines 22.1.3–4, 22.2.7–8). The rewriting continued through to 1795–6 and beyond.

B. TEXTS

1 [=RT]. *The Weekly Entertainer* (Sherborne) XXII (28 Oct 1793) 430–2. Signed "S. T. C——RIDGE. | *Ottery St. Mary*."

Publication was almost certainly prompted by the publication in the previous week of **39** *Absence: An Ode*. The earlier poem was submitted by someone other than C (Edward Coleridge?), perhaps with mischievous intent. If this was indeed the case, the present poem could have been submitted by way of reply by another mutual friend of Fanny Nesbitt and C.

A transcript of the *Weekly Examiner* text in an unknown hand addressed to "Miss S. Besly" was offered for sale by Pickering & Chatto (London) during Jun–Jul 1991. From accompanying materials, it appears she was the daughter of William Besley of Tiverton. Had she been one of the "young Belles" C entertained with "complimentary effusions in the poetic Way" when he lingered in the town earlier that summer (*CL* I 60: to GC 5 Aug 1793)?

1. BPL B 22189=Estlin Copy Book ff 13ʳ–14ᵛ (lines 1–16, 22.1.1–8, 23– 32, 71–84, 87–106 only). Transcript of a much-abridged and -revised version in C's hand.

PW (EHC) I 49–50 wrongly describes this as a "First Draft". EHC was perhaps misled by the title, which backdates the period of composition by exactly one year, probably because of C's engagement to Sara Fricker.

2. HRC MS (Coleridge, S T) Works B. Single leaf, 19.6×33 cm; wm Britannia in oval surmounted by crown; chain-lines 2.52 cm; verso blank. Bound into Rugby Manuscript p 67/f 29ʳ. Revised version of lines 1–16, 22.2.1–8 only.

3. HRC MS (Coleridge, S T) Works B. Two leaves, written on both sides. The first 19.6×32.6 cm; wm small crown surmounting small GR; chain-lines 2.5 cm. The second 19.6×32.8 cm; wm Britannia within oval surmounted by crown; chain-lines 2.5 cm. Bound into Rugby Manuscript pp 71–4/ff 31ʳ–31bisᵛ. Transcript in C's hand, which served as copy for PR 2.

The position of the transcript in the Rugby Manuscript—immediately following C's fair copy of the conclusion to **115** *The Eolian Harp* (TEXT MS 5)—suggests that it was submitted while PR 2 was already printing. It is headed with the instruction: "(to be printed the last of the Effusions next to 'My pensive Sara'.)"

2*. Two proof copies (A and B) of PR *2* contain C's note on line 57 in slightly variant form, and are corrected in his hand. A is BM Ashley 408 ff 41–2 (*JDC facsimile* 77–9); B is MH's copy, now at the Alexander Turnbull Library, Wellington, New Zealand (R Eng COLE Poems (1796)).

2. *Poems* (1796).

3. *Poems* (1797); the poem was included in the Supplement to the vol.

4. *Poems* (1803); the last two paragraphs of this text rpt in *The Parnassian Garland* (1807) 143–4.

5. *PW* (1828).

6. *PW* (1829).

JG's (?) copy at NYPL (Berg Collection) contains two corrections which might possess some authority.

7. *PW* (1834).

title. *1* ABSENCE: A POEM. • 1 An Effusion at Evening— | Written in August 1792 • 2 Effusion | (A Poem wWritten in early youth) • 3 Effusion ⟨36⟩ | Written in *early Youth—The Time, a Summer Evening.an autumnal Evening. • 2 EFFUSION XXXVI. | WRITTEN | IN EARLY YOUTH, | THE TIME, | *AN AUTUMNAL EVENING.* • *3* AN EFFUSION | *On an AUTUMNAL EVENING.* | WRITTEN IN EARLY YOUTH. • *4* WRITTEN | *IN EARLY YOUTH.* | THE TIME | AN AUTUMNAL EVENING. • *5–7* LINES ON AN AUTUMNAL EVENING.

1 *1* 1	Imagination!　mistress　of　my　lore!	
2	O Fancy! check thy wilder ~~fl song~~ plume: no*t* more	
3 *2–7*	thou wild FANCY, check thy wing! No	
2 *1* 1	Where　shall　mine　eye　thy　elfin　haunt explore?	
2	Yon　beauteous　Clouds　with　elfin　eye	
3 *2–7*	Those thin white Flakes, those purple Clouds,	
3 *1* 1	Dost thou on yon rich cloud thy pinions bright	
2	Nor there with happy Spirits wing thy flight	
3 *2–7*	speed	
4 *1* 1	Embathe　in　　amber-glowing floods of light?	
2	Embath'd	
3 *2–7*	Bath'd　　rich	
5 *1*	Or,　wild　of　　plume,　　pursue　the　track　of day	
1	~~wing~~ speed,	
2	Nor　in　that　Gleam,　where　slow　descends　the	
3 *2–7*	yon	
6 *1* 1	In　other　worlds　to hail the morning ray?	
⊠*1* 1	With western Peasants	
7 *1* 1	'Tis　　thine　　to bid the shadowy pleasures move	
2	~~Tis thine~~ Ah! rather　　　perish'd	
3 *2–7*	Ah　　　　rather	
8 *1* 1	On mem'ry's wings across the soul of love;	
⊠*1* 1	A　shadowy　train,	

9	*1*	And thine o'er winter's ice-clad plains to fling
	1	icy
	2	o'er the wintry waste of Sorrow
	3 2–7	O'er Disappointment's wintry Desart
10	*1*	Each flower, that binds the breathing locks of spring,
	1	flowers ~~or,~~
	2	flower, ~~bin~~ wreath'd dewy
	3 2–7	wreath'd
11	*1*	When blushing, like a bride, from violet bower
	1	primrose Bower*s*
	2	bower
	3 2–7	Hope's trim
12	*1* 1	She ◄——starts,——► awaken'd by the pattering shower.
	2	~~starts, a started,~~ leapt,
	3 2–7	◄——leapt,——►
		[*Line-space*]
13	*1*	Now sheds the unseen sun a purple gleam,
	1	setting
	2	richer
	3 2–7	sinking deeper
14	*1* 1 2	Aid, lovely sorceress! aid the poet's dream!
	3 2–7	thy
15	*1* 1	With fairy wand oh! bid *my* *love* arise,
	2 2–7	the Maid
	3	~~my~~ the
16	*1* 1	The dewy brilliance dancing in her eyes,—
	☒*1* 1	Chaste Joyance bright blue
17	*1*	Oh! bid her come in meek compassion's vest,
18	*1*	And heed the sigh that swells my secret breast!
19	*1*	And lo! the faded scenes their tints renew—
20	*1*	With raptur'd gaze the absent maid I view!
21	*1*	When th' orient hour, in robe of roses dight,
22	*1*	Studs the relumin'd east with gems of light,
22.1.1	1	As erst she woke with soul-entrancing Mien
22.1.2	1	The thrill of Joy extatic yet serene,
22.1.3	1	When link'd with Peace I bounded o'er the Plain
22.1.4	1	And Hope itself was all I knew of Pain!
		[*Line-space*]
22.1.5	1	Propitious Fancy hears the votive sigh—
22.1.6	1	The absent Maiden flashes on mine Eye!
22.1.7	1	When first the matin Bird with startling Song
22.1.8	1	Salutes the Sun his veiling Clouds among,
22.2.1	2	As erst ~~she wak'd with look~~ they beam'd when Learning's Prize was mine,
22.2.2	2	~~And her hand~~ What time she weav'd ~~the~~ a sportive la*w*urel twine,
22.2.3	2	While thro' my frame shot rapid the thrill'd heart,
22.2.4	2	And every nerve confess'd the electric dart.
22.2.5	2	Yes, Fancy, yes! I see the Maid arise,
22.2.6	2	Chaste Joyance dancing in her bright blue Eyes,

22.2.7	2	As erst when glad I caroll'd on the plain
22.2.8	2	"And Hope itself was all I knew of Pain.
22.3.1	3 *2–7*	As erst, when from the Muses' calm abode
22.3.2	3 *2–7*	I came, with Learning's meed "not unbestow'd:
22.3.3	3 *2–7*	When, as ſshe twin'd a Laurel round my Brow,
22.3.4	3 *2–7*	And met my Kiss, and half-return'd my Vow,
22.3.5	3 *2–7*	O'er all my frame shot rapid my thrill'd Heart,
22.3.6	3 *2–7*	And every nerve confess'd th' electric dart!
		[*Line-space*]
22.3.7	3	~~Joy to my soul!~~ O dear Deceit! I see the MAIDEN rise,
	2–7	O dear Deceit!
22.3.8	3 *2–7*	Chaste Joyance dancing in her bright blue Eyes!
22.3.9	3 *2–7*	When first the Lark high-soaring swells his throat,
22.3.10	3 *2–7*	Mocks the tir'd Eye, and scatters the loud note;
23	☒1 2	I trace her footsteps on th' accustom'd lawn,
	1	the steaming
24	*1 5–7*	I mark her glancing 'mid the gleam of dawn.
	1	view ~~mid~~ in gleams
	3 *2–4*	mark mid
25	☒2	When the bent flower beneath the night-dew weeps,
26	☒2	And on the lake the silver lustre sleeps,
27	☒2	Amid the paly radiance soft and sad,
28	☒2	She meets my lonely path in moon-beams clad.
29	☒2	With *her* along the streamlet's brink I rove,
30	☒2	With *her* I list the warblings of the grove,
31	*1*	And seems on ev'ry gale *her* voice to float
	☒*1* 2	in each low wind
32	☒2	Lone-whispering pity in each soothing note.
		[*Line-space*]
33	*1*	Spirits of love! that people the hush'd air,
	3 *2–7*	ye heard her Name! Obey
34	*1*	On white-rein'd breezes to my haunt repair!
	3 *2–7*	The powerful Spell, and
35	*1*	Float round my lyre, while Nesbitt's charms I sing,
36	*1*	And with light fingers touch each trembling string!
36.1.1	3 *2–7*	Whether on clust'ring Pinions ye are there,
36.1.2	3 *2–7*	Where rich Snows blossom on the Myrtle Trees,
36.1.3	3 *2–7*	Or with fond Languishment around my Fair
36.1.4	3 *2–7*	Sigh in the loose Luxuriance of her Hair;
36.1.5	3 *2–7*	O heed the spell, and hither wing your way,
36.1.6	3 *2–7*	Like far-off Music, voyaging the Breeze!
37	*1*	To you, a precious charge, was Nesbitt given,
	3 *2–7*	SPIRITS! to you the infant Maid was
38	*1*	Form'd by the magic alchemy of Heaven.
	3 *2–7*	wondrous
39	*1*	No lovelier maid does love's wide empire know,
	3	fairer doth ~~Beauty's~~ Love's
	2–7	does Love's

40 *1*		No lovelier maid e'er heav'd the bosom's snow.
	3 2–7	fairer
41 *1*		A thousand loves her gentle face adorn,
42 *1*		Fair as the blushes of a summer morn:
43 ☒1 2		A thousand loves around her forehead fly,
44 ☒1 2		A thousand loves sit melting in her eye:
45 *1 3 5–7*		Love lights her smile—in joy's red nectar dips
	3 2 4	bright
46 *1*		The opening rose, and plants it on her lips!
	3 2 4	flamy
	3 5–7	His myrtle flower,
47 *1 3 2 4*		Tender, serene, and all devoid of guile,
48 *1 3 2*		Soft is her soul, as sleeping infants' smile
	4	infant's
49 *1*		She speaks! and baffled art repines to see
50 *1*		Th' unweeting triumph of simplicity!
51 *1*		She speaks! and hark that lip-bedewing song!
	3 2–7	passion-warbled
52 *1 3 2 4*		Still, fancy! still those mazy notes prolong!
	3 5–7	that voice, those
53 *1 3 2 4*		Sweet as th' angelic harps, whose rapt'rous falls
	3 5–7	As sweet as when that voice with
54 *1 3 2 4*		Awake the soften'd echoes of Heaven's halls,
	3 5–7	Shall wake
55 *1*		They bid the vernal buds of pleasure bloom,
56 *1*		As showers at eve the blossom's soft perfume.
57 ☒1 2		Oh! (have I sigh'd) were mine the wizard's rod,

57fn *2* 2   I entreat the Public's pardon for having carelessly suffered to be printed such intolerable stuff as this and the thirteen following lines. They have not the merit even of originality: as every thought is to be found in the Greek Epigrams. The lines in this poem from the 27th to the 36th, I have been told are a palpable imitation of the passage from 5 the 355th to the 370th line of the Pleasures of Memory part 3. I do not perceive so striking a similarity between the two passages; but if it exist, at all events, I had written the Effusion several years before I had seen Mr. Rogers' Poem.—It may be proper to remark that the tale of Florio in "the Pleasures of Memory" is to be found in Lochlever; 10 a Poem of great merit, by Michael Bruce.—In Mr. Rogers' Poem the names are FLORIA and JULIA; in the Lochlera Lomond and Levina— and this is all the difference. We seize the opportunity of transcribing from the Lochlever of Bruce the following exquisite passage, describing the effects of a fine day on the human heart. 15

> Fat on the plain and mountain's sunny side
> Large droves of oxen and the fleecy flocks
> Feed undisturbed, and fill the echoing air
> With Music grateful to their Master's ear.
> The Traveller stops and gazes round and round   20
> O'er all the plains that animate his heart

With Mirth and Music. Even the mendicant
Bow-bent with age, that on the old gray stone
Sole-sitting suns himself in the public way,
Feels his heart leap, and to himself he sings.   25

58 ☒1 2   Or mine the power of Proteus, changeful God!
59 *1*   A flow'r-entangled ◄——arbour——► would I seem,
   3   ~~MYRTLE~~ ARBOR
   2–7   ◄—ARBOUR—► I would
60 ☒1 2   To shield my love from noontide's sultry beam;
61 ☒1 2   Or bloom a myrtle—from whose od'rous boughs
62 ☒1 2   My love might weave gay garlands for her brows.
63 *1–7*   When   twilight stole across the   fading   vale,
   3   da Twilight   ~~dewy~~ fading
64 ☒1 2   To fan my love I'd be the evening gale:
65 *1*   Sigh in the loose folds of her floating vest,
   3 2–7   Mourn   soft   swelling
66 ☒1 2   And flutter my faint pinions on her breast.
67 *1*   On   rosy   wing I'd float—a dream, by night,
   3   ~~rosy~~ seraph
   2–7   seraph
68 ☒1 2   To soothe my love with shadows of delight:
69 ☒1 2   Or soar aloft, to be the spangled skies,
70 *1*   And gaze upon her with unnumber'd eyes.
   3 2–7   a thousand
[*Line-space*]
71 *1* 1   As oft, in climes beyond the western main,
72 *1* 1   Where boundless spreads the wildly-silent plain,
73 *1* 1   The savage hunter, who his drowsy frame
   3 2–7   As when the Savage,
74 ☒2   Had bask'd beneath the sun's unclouded flame;
75 *1* 1   Awakes amid the tempest-troubled air,
   3 2–7   troubles of the
76 *1* 1   The thunder's peal, and lightning's lurid glare;
   3   skiey Deluge and ~~blue~~ white Lightning's
   2–7   white
77 *1* 1   Aghast he hears the rushing whirlwind's sweep,
   3 2–7   scours before the tempest's
78 ☒2 3   And sad recalls the sunny hour of sleep:
   3   sun[?]ny
79 ☒2   So, tost by storms along life's wild'ring way,
80 *1*   Mine eye reverted views the cloudless day,
   ☒*1* 2   that
81 *1*   When, Isca! on thy banks I joy'd to rove,
   1   ——!
   3   by my native ~~stream~~ Brook I wont
   2–7   ◄—brook—►
81fn *1* The river Exe, which flows by Tiverton.
82 ☒2   While hope with kisses nurs'd the infant love.

83	*1*	Dear Tiverton! where pleasure's streamlet glides
	1	Sweet ————!
84	*1*	←—Fann'd—→ by soft winds to curl in mimic tides;
	1	~~Taught~~ Fann'd
84.1.1	3	Dear native ~~Haunts!~~ Brook! like PEACE, so placidly
	2–7	←—brook!—→
84.1.2	3 2–7	Smoothing thro' fertile fields thy current meek!
84.1.3	3 2–7	Dear native Brook! where first young POESY
84.1.4	3	Star'd wildly-eager in ~~his~~ her noontide dream,
	2–7	her
84.1.5	3	Where BLAMELESS ~~MIRTH~~ PLEASURES ~~with fair transparent Cheek,~~
		dimple*s* ~~soft~~ QUIET's Cheek,
	2–7	Where BLAMELESS PLEASURES dimple QUIET's cheek,
84.1.6	3	~~Dimpled the surface of TRANQUILLITY,~~
84.1.7	3 2 4	As water-lillies ripple a slow stream!
	3 5–7	thy
85	*1*	Where genius warbles sweet his gladdest strain,
86	*1*	And wildly-cinctur'd bounds across the plain;
87	*1*	Where mirth and health beguile the blameless day;
	1	~~Health~~ Mirth and Peace
	3 2–7	Dear native Haunts! where Virtue still is gay;
88	*1* 1	Where friendship's fixt star beams a mellow'd ray;
	3	Where ~~mellow'd~~ FRIENDSHIP's ~~beams~~ Fixt-star [?]sheds […]
		a mellow'd ray
	2–7	Where Friendship's fix'd-star sheds a mellow'd ray;
89	⊠2	Where love a crown of thornless roses wears;
90	⊠2	Where soften'd sorrow smiles within her tears;
91	*1* 1	And mem'ry, with a vestal's meek employ,
	3	~~meek~~ chaste
	2–7	chaste
92	⊠2	Unceasing feeds the lambent flame of joy!
93	*1*	No more thy sky-larks melting from the sight
	1	less'ning my
	3 2–7	your melting the
94	*1*	Shall thrill the attuned nerve with pure delight:
	⊠*1* 2	Heartstring delight;
95	*1* 1	No more shall deck thy "pensive pleasures" sweet
	3 2–7	your
96	⊠2	With wreaths of sober hue my evening seat!
97	*1* 1	Yet dear to fancy's eye thy varied scene
	3	sw dear your
	2–7	dear
98	*1*	Of wood, hill, vale, and sparkling brooks between;
	1 2–7	Dale Brook
	3	brooks
99	*1*	And sweet to fancy's ear the earliest song
	⊠*1* 2	Yet warbled

100 *1*	That floats on morning's wings thy	fields among!
1	soars	wing
3 *2–7*		your vales
101 *1*	Scenes of delight! my aching heart ye leave,	
⊠*1* 2	my Hope! the	Eye
102 *1* 1	Like those rich ←—hues—→ that paint the clouds of eve!	
3	yon bright ~~Tints~~ Hues,	
2–7	←—hues—→	
103 ⊠2	Tearful, and sadd'ning with the sadden'd blaze,	
104 ⊠2	Mine eye the gleam pursues with wistful gaze,	
105 *1*	Sees shades on shades with deeper tints impend,	
1	~~tint~~ Shades	tint
3 *2–7*	shades	
106 ⊠2	Till chill and damp the moonless night descend.	

1. 1 Imagination, Mistress *2 3* Thou *7* Fancy, 1 Lore! **2.** 1 Eye *2–7* flakes, *2–7* clouds 2 explore; • 3 *2–7* explore! **3.** 1 Cloud *2–7* spirits 3 Flight **4.** *5–7* Bathed 1 3 Floods 1 Light? • 2 Light; • 3 Light! • *2–7* light; **5.** *2–7* gleam, 1 Day • 2 3 Day, • *2–7* day, **6.** *2–7* peasants 1 Ray? • 2 3 Ray! • *2–7* ray! **7.** 1 Tis *2–7* Ah! *5–7* perished 1–3 Pleasures 2 3 *2–7* move, **8.** 1 Mem'ry's 3 Train, 1–3 Soul 1 Love; • 2 Love, • 3 *2–7* Love! **9.** 1 *Winter*'s *2–4* desart • *5–7* desert **10.** 3 Flower, • *5–7* flower *5–7* wreathed 1–3 Locks 1 *Spring*, • 2 3 *2–6* SPRING, • *7* Spring, **11.** 2 3 Bride, 3 Bower **12.** *5–7* awakened 1 3 Shower! • 2 Shower. **13.** 1–3 *2–7* Sun **14.** 1 3 Sorc'ress! • 2 *2–7* Sorceress! 1–3 *2–7* Poet's 1 dream. • 2 Dream. **15.** ⊠*1* faery ⊠*1* 1 2* O 1 2 my Love 3 *2–6* MAID **16.** 3 *2–7* bright-blue 1 3 Eyes; • 2 Eyes • *2–7* eyes; **22.3.1.** *2–7* erst **22.3.2.** *2–7* not *5–7* unbestowed; **22.3.3.** *3 5–7* When *2–7* she *5–7* twined *2–7* laurel *2–7* brow, **22.3.4.** *2–7* kiss, *2–7* half *5–7* returned *2–7* vow, **22.3.5.** *5–7* thrilled *2–7* heart, **22.3.6.** *5–7* confessed *2–7* the *2–7* dart. **22.3.7.** *2–7* Maiden **22.3.8.** *3 5–7* bright- *2 4* Eyes, • *7* eyes! **22.3.9.** *2–7* lark *5–7* high **22.3.10.** *5–7* tired *2–7* eye, *2–7* note, **23.** 3 *2–7* the *5–7* accustomed 1 3 Lawn, **24.** ⊠*1* 1 mid 1 3 Dawn! **25.** 1 3 Flower 1 *5–7* night • 3 Night 1 *2–7* weeps **26.** 1 3 Lake 1 3 Lustre 3 sleeps; **27.** 1 3 Radiance 1 3 *2 4* sad **28.** 3 path, 1 3 moon beams 3 clad! **29.** 3 Her • *2–7* her 1 3 *2–7* rove; **30.** 3 Her • *2–7* her 1 3 Grove; • *2–7* grove; **31.** 3 ~~Her~~ HER • *2–7* her 3 Voice *7* float, **32.** 3 -whisp'ring • *5–7* whispering 1 *2–7* Pity 1 Note! • 3 *2–7* note! **33.** 3 *2–6* SPIRITS OF LOVE! • *7* Spirits of Love! *2–7* name! **34.** *2–7* spell, 3 Haunt repair; • *2 3 5–7* haunt repair. • *4* haunt repair, **36.1.1.** *5–7* clustering *2–7* pinions **36.1.2.** *2–7* snows *2–7* trees, **36.1.3.** *2–7* languishment *2–7* fair **36.1.4.** *2–7* luxuriance *2–7* hair; **36.1.6.** *2–7* music, *2–7* breeze! **37.** *7* Spirits! 3 *2–7* given **38.** *5–7* Formed *2–4* wond'rous • *5–7* wonderous 3 *2–7* Alchemy 3 *2–7* Heaven! **39.** 3 *2–7* Maid 3 Empire **40.** 3 *2–7* Maid 3 Bosom's **43.** 3 LOVES • *2–7* Loves 3 ~~f~~Forehead 3 *2–7* fly; **44.** 3 LOVES • *2–7* Loves 3 Eye; • *2–7* eye; **45.** 3 LOVES 3 smile! 3 *2–7* Joy's **46.** 3 Rose, 3 Lips. • *3 5–7* lips. **47.** 3 Guile, **48.** 3 Infants' 3 Smile! • *2 4* smile: **51.** 3 hark— *3 5* passion 3 Song! • *2–7* song— *52.* *3* Still 3 FANCY! • *2–7* Fancy! 3 still, 3 prolong— • *2–7* prolong. **53.** 3 Harps, *2 4–7* rapturous 3 Falls •

3 5 falls,   **54.** *5–7* softened   3 ~~Echo~~ Echoes   3 *2–7* Halls!   **57.** 3 O! •
2–7 O   *5–7* sighed)   3 Wizard's Rod,   **57fn7–13.** *2** but if it exist, . . . all
the difference.] *2**B deletes   **57fn7.** *2** but if it exist,] In *2**A deleted by C • *2*
omits   **57fn10.** *2** found in Lochlever; • *2**A, B [corrections in C's hand] *2* found
in Lochleven;   **57fn11.** *2* merit   **57fn12.** *2** FLORIA • *2**A, B [corrections in
C's hand] *2* FLORIO   *2** Lochlera • *2**A, B [corrections in C's hand] *2* Lochleven
57fn14. *2** Lochlever • *2**A, B [corrections in C's hand] *2* Lochleven   *2** describing •
2 expressing   **58.** 3 Power   **59.** 3 *2–7* flower-   7 Arbour   *2–7* seem
60. 3 MY LOVE • *2–7* my Love   3 *2–7* Noontide's   *2–7* beam: **61.** 3 MYRTLE •
2–6 MYRTLE, • 7 Myrtle,   3 ⟨whose⟩ 3 *5–7* odorous   3 Boughs   **62.** 3 MY
LOVE   *2–7* Love   3 Brows.   **63.** *2–7* Twilight   **64.** 3 MY LOVE •
2–7 my Love   3 *2–6* EVENING GALE; • 7 Evening Gale;   **65.** 3 Vest,
66. 3 Pinions   3 Breast! • *2–7* breast!   **67.** *2–7* Seraph   *2–7* float   3 *2–*
4 DREAM, • *5 6* DREAM • 7 Dream   **68.** 3 *3 5 6* sooth   3 MY LOVE   *2–*
7 Love   3 delight; • *2–7* delight:—   **69.** 3 *2–7* aloft   3 SPANGLED • *2–*
6 SPANGLED • 7 Spangled   3 *2–6* SKIES, • 7 Skies,   **70.** 3 Eyes! • *2–7* eyes!
71. 1 oft   1 Main   **72.** 1 Plain,   **73.** 1 Hunter,   *7* savage,   **74.** *5–7* basked
1 3 *2–7* Sun's   1 Flame, • 3 *2–7* flame,   **76.** 1 Thunder's Peal   *2–7* deluge,
1 Lightning's • *2–7* lightning's   1 *2–7* glare— • 3 Glare;   **77.** 1 Whirlwind's
Sweep,   **78.** 1 hour of Sleep! • 3 Hour of Sleep: • *2–7* hour of sleep:—
79. ⊠*1* 2 So   *5–7* tossed   ⊠*1* 2 Life's   *5–7* wildering   1 Way • 3 *2 4* way
80. 1 3 Eye   1 3 Day,   **81.** 3 *2–7* When   *2–6* rove   **82.** 1 *2–4* 7 Hope •
3 *5 6* HOPE   3 Kisses   *5–7* nursed   *2–7* Infant   1 Love! • 3 LOVE! • *2–7* Love.
83. 1 Pleasure's   **84.1.1.** *6* 7 Peace,   **84.1.2.** *5–7* through   **84.1.3.** *2–*
7 brook!   7 Poesy   **84.1.4.** *5–7* Stared   *6* 7 dream!   **84.1.5.** *5–7* blameless
pleasures   7 Quiet's   **84.1.7.** *2–7* -lilies   **87.** *2–7* haunts!   1 Day;   *2–*
4 gay: • *5–7* gay,   **88.** 1 Friendship's   *3 4* 7 fix'd • *5 6* fixed   *5–7* mellowed
1 Ray; • *5–7* ray,   **89.** 1 *7* Love • 3 *2–6* LOVE   1 3 *2 3 5–7* Roses   *2–*
4 wears: • *5–7* wears,   **90.** *5–7* softened   1 *7* Sorrow • 3 *2–6* SORROW   3 Tears;
91. 1 *7* Memory, • 3 *5 6* MEMORY, • *2–4* Mem'ry,   1 *Vestal*'s • 3 *2–6* VESTAL'S •
7 Vestal's   **92.** 1 *2 4* Joy! • 3 JOY!   **93.** 1 Sky Larks • 3 SKY-LARKS
94. 1 3 *2–4* th'   3 heartstring • *2–7* heart-string   *2 4* delight:— • *3 5–7* delight—
95. 1 *2–7* pensive • 3 PENSIVE   1 *2–7* Pleasures • 3 PLEASURES   **96.** 3 wreathes
2–7 seat.   **97.** 1 *2–7* Fancy's • 3 FANCY'S   1 3 Eye   **98.** 1 3 Wood, Hill,
2–7 dale,   *2–7* brook   1 between. • 3 *2–7* between!   **99.** 1 *2–7* Fancy's •
3 FANCY'S   1 3 Ear   1 3 *2–7* song,   **100.** 1 3 *2–7* Morning's   3 *2–*
7 among.   **101.** 3 *2–4* aking   3 *2–7* eye   3 *2–7* leave   **102.** 1 Hues   1 3 Eve!
103. ⊠*1* 2 Tearful   1 *5–7* saddening • 3 *2–4* sad'ning   *5–7* saddened   1 3 Blaze •
2–7 blaze   **104.** 1 3 Eye   1 Gaze— • *3 2 3 5–7* gaze: • 4 gaze;   **105.** 1 on
Shades   **106.** 1 3 Night descend!

6⁺. MS 1 perhaps has line-space.

7. 1 shadowy] C has written "faded" above, and put a cross at the beginning of the
line.

8. 1 Mem'ry's] C has written "shadowy" above.

10. 2 3 *2–7* dewy locks] *PL* v 56 (Eve describing Satan).

12⁺. PR *5–7* have no line-space, perhaps an error deriving from PR *3*, where there is a
page-break.

22.1.3–4, 22.2.7–8. The two lines (not merely the phrase in quotation-marks) derive from WW's *An Evening Walk* (1793)=*WPW* I 6:

> When link'd with thoughtless Mirth I cours'd the plain,
> And hope itself was all I knew of pain.
> (Errata, becoming lines 31–2)

Further references to C's enthusiasm for WW's poem are given in sec A above.

22.1.4. Two small portions have been cut out of MS 1—before "Hope" and before the exclamation-mark—which might have contained quotation-marks (cf 22.2.8).

22.1.7–8. Perhaps from Bowles's "carol of the matin bird | Salute his lonely porch" (*Sonnet XVIII* 3–4, in *Sonnets*—3rd ed Bath 1794—21).

22.2.1. when Learning's Prize was mine] This claim, added in 1796 but later modified, has only a general application. C's first version of the poem was written immediately following his failure to win Browne Medals (cf **55.X1** *Laus Astronomiae*, **55.X2** *Cambridge Prize Poems, 1793*).

22.3.2. "not unbestow'd] Source not traced.

22.3.6⁺. PR *4* has no line-space.

23. 1 steaming] C has written "accustom'd" above.

30–1. The later readings echo Bowles's line "In each low wind I seem thy voice to hear" (*On Leaving a Place of Residence* 16).

36.1.6⁺. PR *6 7* have line-space, perhaps resulting from the line-space at 38⁺.

38⁺. PR *5* has line-space (coincides with page-break in PR *3*).

50⁺. There is extra space following line 50 at the bottom of the page in PR *2*, but it is probably adventitious.

56⁺. TEXTS 3 *2–7* have line-space.

57fn. Printed at the end of the volume in PR 2* *2*, with the cross-reference "Page 105." (only) and line 57 quoted in italic. No cue appears on p 105. Cf **90** *To Burke* 9fn for the only other instance of an uncued note in the 1796 volume. Both notes are of some length and of a more emotionally driven character than the others. Were they an opportunistic addition? The present note draws attention to a passage in Rogers *The Pleasures of Memory* (1792) II 354–70 (C mistakenly refers to a non-existent part III), which he probably read (or reread) in *Anthologia Hibernica* I (Jan 1793) 60–5, (Feb 1793) 137–42, as PR *2* was going to press (*Bristol LB* No 76). There are thematic and occasional verbal parallels between the whole of his and Rogers's poem, but the respective dates of publication bear out C's claim that they are fortuitous.

The quotation from *Lochleven* may be found (var) in Michael Bruce *Poems on Several Occasions* (Edinburgh 1770) 89. CL reported that Rogers was hurt by C's accusation of unoriginality (*LL*—M—I 98), and C withdrew the note and apologised in the Advertisement to the relevant section of PR *3* (*Poems*—1797—244–5; see vol I annex B 3). Why C made the accusation, which is peculiar, is another question. It may have been prompted by an embarrassed sense of his own, complicated obligations.

57fn7–13. but if it exist, . . . all the difference.] The deletion in 2*B is marked with a single slanting line.

57fn22–5. Even the mendicant . . . he sings.] 2*B marks with a vertical line in the RH margin, with the comment "exqᵢ?uisiteⱼ".

73–82, 84.1.1–2. Used (var) in **128** *Recollection* 1–12.

75. PR *6* troubles] In JG's (?) copy the "s" is underlined, and a question-mark is added in the margin.

76. 3 2–7 skiey] Revived from *Measure for Measure* iii i 9? The examples cited by *OED* suggest that the word afterwards became a stock item of Romantic poetic diction.
81. PR 6 rove] In JG's (?) copy a comma is added.
84⁺. C indicates a line-space in MS 3; this is given in PR 2–7.
88. MS 1 Where] C has written "and" above; it is just conceivable that he meant it to be an alternative to the same word in line 87.
89–90. In MS 1 marked with a line in the LH margin.
100⁺. C indicates a line-space in MS 3; this is given in TEXTS 1 2–7.

61. SONNET: TO THE AUTUMNAL MOON

A. DATE

1789–95; perhaps Scpt 1793? C placed the poem second (following **17** *Genevieve*) among his Juvenile Poems in PR *3–5*, and dated it 1788–9 in the annotated copy of PR *3*. However, C's dating on such late occasions habitually errs towards a date which is too early. If the poem had been in existence before 1792, it would surely have been included in ms collections such as that transcribed by John May Jr from the poems C sent to GC or the Ottery Copy Book, or would have been included in JTC's list of 20 Jun 1809 (for which see vol I annex A 3). Also, it may be noted, the rhyme-scheme in part follows that of a Shakespearean sonnet: Bowles, C's model in 1789 and after, never wrote a Shakespearean sonnet, whereas Charlotte Smith, whom C praised in *Sonnets from Various Authors*, for the most part followed the Shakespearean pattern.

The adaptation of Bampfylde that appears on the verso of MS 1 is of a version first published in 1792, which C perhaps arrived at during the summer months of 1793 (see **58.X1**). The evidence of the paper suggests an even later date for MS 1—perhaps Sept 1795—but the poems which accompany MS 2 appear to have been collected by Ann Bacon in Aug–Sept 1793.

B. TEXTS

1. Christ's Hospital (School Library). Recto of a single leaf, 19×23 cm; wm (imperfect) J WHATMAN; chain-lines 2.5 cm. The verso contains the sonnet **58.X1** *Adaptation of Bampfylde's "To Evening"*. Transcript in C's hand, signed "S T C".

2. VCL (uncatalogued in 1978). Ann Frances Bacon's Commonplace Book f 37ʳ. Transcript by AFB, subscribed "S. T. C.—"
The transcript is possibly an inaccurate copy of MS 1. The punctuation and spelling are almost certainly Ann Bacon's.

1 [=RT]. *Poems* (1796).

The poem was excluded from *Poems* (1797), despite CL's remonstrances (*LL*—M—I 65, 66).

2. Poems (1803).

3. PW (1828).
The poem was omitted from the list of contents. In the copy in the Fitzwilliam Museum, Cambridge (Marlay Bequest 1912) C has written "Æt. 16." at the end of the text.

4. PW (1829).

5. PW (1834).

title. 1 To the Moon ⟨in Autumn—⟩ • 2 *To the Moon—* • *1* EFFUSION XVIII. I *TO THE AUTUMNAL MOON.* • *2 SONNET XVIII.* I TO THE AUTUMNAL MOON. • *3–5* SONNET. I TO THE AUTUMNAL MOON.

1 1 2 Hail, softly-beaming Wand'rer of the Night!
   1–5 Mild Splendor of the various-vested Night!
2 □ Mother of wildly-working Visions, hail!
3 ⊠2 I watch thy gliding, while with watry light
   2   the
4 □ Thy weak Eye glimmers thro' a fleecy Veil;
5 1 2 And when thou lov'st thy paly form to shroud
   1–5   pale orb
6 1   Amid the gather'd Blackness lost on high;
   2   gathering
   1–5 Behind   gather'd
7 □ And when thou dartest from the wind-rent cloud
8 1 2 Thy placid Lightnings o'er th' awaken'd Sky!
   1–5   lightning
9 1 2 Ah! such is **Hope,** and such her radiance fair—
   1–5   as changeful and as
10 □ Now dimly peering on the wistful sight;
11 1 2 Now hid unneath the dragon-wing'd **Despair;**
   1–5   behind
12 1   Anon shall she relume her ~~beamingy~~ might,
   2   beamy
   1–5 But soon emerging in her   radiant
13 1 2 And o'er the woe-benighted Breast of Care
   1–5 She o'er the sorrow-clouded
14 1 2   Sail, like a Meteor kindling in its flight.
   1–5 Sails,

1. *3–5* Splendour 2 wanderer **2.** *1–5* visions! **3.** *3–5* watery **4.** ⊠1 eye
3–5 through ⊠1 veil; **5.** *1–5* lovest **6.** *3–5* gathered ⊠1 blackness
7. 2 Cloud. **8.** 2 Lightnings, *3–5* the awakened 2 Sky.— • *1–5* sky. **9.** *1–*
5 Ah 2 *Hope*! • *1–4* HOPE! • 5 Hope! ⊠1 fair! **10.** 2 sight, **11.** 2 un'neath

3–5 -winged   2 *Despair*: • *1–5* Despair: **12.** *1–5* might   **13.** ⊠1 breast   2 care
14. ⊠1 meteor   *1* it's   2 flight—

9. MS 1 **Hope,**] Written as if to be read as bold.
11. MS 1 **Despair;**] Written as if to be read as bold.

61.X1. EST QUÆDAM FLERE VOLUPTAS

University of Pennsylvania Library (Special Collections) MS Eng 13=JTC
Commonplace Book p 95. "*Est quædam flere voluptas.* | To sigh when sor-
row loads the breast,". 2 4-line stanzas. Unsigned.

The attribution is tentatively suggested by Bertram Dobell, who once owned
the Commonplace Book, in some notes on the list of contents loosely inserted.
Dobell did not, however, mention the suggestion in his article "Coleridgeana"
Athenaeum 9 Jan 1904 p 53. No evidence to confirm the suggestion has come
to light.

62. TO A PAINTER

A. DATE

Oct–Nov 1791? revised Aug 1793? See vol I headnote.

B. TEXT

VCL (uncatalogued in 1978). Ann Frances Bacon's Commonplace Book ff 40ᵛ–
41ʳ. Transcript by AFB, subscribed "S. T. Coleridge.—"

The RT reproduces the ms exactly, except for:

title. ms To a Painter—

63. TO MISS DASHWOOD BACON
OF DEVONSHIRE

A. DATE

Sept 1793.

B. TEXT

VCL (uncatalogued in 1978). Ann Frances Bacon's Commonplace Book f 7^v. Transcript by AFB, subscribed "S T Coleridge".

The RT reproduces the ms exactly, except for:

title. ms To Miss Dashwood Bacon of Devonshire— | Sep^{br}. 1793—   **8. the]** ms y^e.

64. SONGS OF THE PIXIES

A. DATE

Aug–Sept 1793. C asked Joseph Cottle to put the date "August, 1793" at the end of the PR *2* version of the poem (*CL* I 300: to J. Cottle [6 Jan 1797]), which Cottle failed to do. C's comment on lines 40–1 in the HEHL copy of PR *6* claims that the poem was written on his earlier visit to Ottery (1789), and at the same time opens the possibility that it might have even earlier origins. The date in MS 1 (Sept 1793) is likely to be the most accurate.

B. TEXTS

1. VCL (uncatalogued in 1978) Ann Frances Bacon's Commonplace Book ff 42^v–45^r. Transcript by AFB, dated "Set^{br} 1793—", subscribed "S. T. Coleridge". Divided into eight (not nine) strophes.

2. BPL B 22189 = Estlin Copy Book ff 4^r–8^v. Transcript in C's hand.
   The poem is the first that C transcribed into the book, a separate and separately headed page being used for each strophe.

3 [=RT]. PML MA 1916 = Quarto Copy Book ff 1^r–3^v. Transcript in C's hand.
   The poem is the first that C transcribed into the book. Special care has been taken with the indenting of lines and the capitalisation of certain words. It provided copy for PR *1* below, possibly through an intermediate version.

1. Poems (1796).

C's own copy, in which he carried the errata into the text of the poem, is now at the NYPL (Berg Collection).

2. Poems (1797).

The title is given on a separate half-title page. Printer's copy was provided by PR *1*, amended according to the instructions C sent to Joseph Cottle in Jan 1797 (*CL* I 299–300). In the copy that once belonged to William Bowles—now in the possession of Erwin Schwarz (1982)—C has written, above the additional title, "Stuff I S. T. C."

3. Poems (1803).

The title is given on a separate half-title page. The reprint in *The Port Folio* (Philadelphia) III (50) (10 Dec 1803) 399–400 has no textual significance.

4. PW (1828).

C has corrected a misprint in this poem in the large-paper copy now at the Fitzwilliam Museum, Cambridge (Marlay Bequest 1912).

5. PW (1829).

6. PW (1834).

C's own copy, now at HEHL (Book No 109531), carries corrections, and a comment on lines 40–1 (see vol I headnote).

title/divisional title. 1 3 *1–6* Songs of the Pyxies • 2 The Songs of the Pixies, an irregular Ode.

introduction

   1   On the occasion of Miss Beautfleur's &c's Visit to the Pyxies Parlour near Ottery St Mary Devon— I Set^{br} 1793—

   2 The lower order of people in Devonshire have a superstition concerning the existence of "Pixies"—a race of fairy beings, supposed to be invisibly small, and harmless, or friendly to Man. At a small distance from a village in that county, half way up a Hill, is a large Excavation, called the "Pixies' Parlour. The Roots of the Trees growing above it form its ceiling—and on its sides are engraved innumerable ⁻1.5 Cyphers—among which the Author descried his own and those of his Brothers, cut by the rude hand of their Childhood. ~~Beneath~~ At the ~~bottom~~ foot of the Hill flows the River Otter.

     To this place the Author had the Honor of conducting a party of young Ladies during the summer Months—on which occasion the following Poem was written. ⁻1.10

3 *1–6*   The PIXIES, in the superstition of Devonshire, are a race of be-
         ings, invisibly small—and harmless or friendly to man. At a small
         distance from a village in that county, half-way up a wood-cover'd
         Hill, is an Excavation, called the Pixies' Parlour. The roots of
         old Trees form its ceiling—and on its sides are innumerable   ⁻1.5
         Cyphers, among which the author descried his own Cypher and
         those of his Brothers, cut by the hand of their Childhood. At the
         foot of the Hill flows the River Otter.

To this place the Author conducted a party of young Ladies
during the summer months of the year, 1793—one ~~whom~~ of whom (of   ¯1.10
stature elegantly small, and of complexion colourless yet clear)
was proclaimed the Fairy Queen—on which occasion the follow-
ing Irregular Ode was written.—

additional title. 2 The Songs of the Pixies. • 3 *1–3* Songs of the Pixies.

¯1.15 □		1
1 □		Whom the untaught Shepherds call
2 □		Pyxies in their Madrigal,
3 □		Fancy's children here we dwell:
4 □		Welcome Ladies! to our cell.—
5 1		Here the Thrush of softest note
2		TWren
⊠1 2		Wren
6 1 2		Builds her nest and warbles well;
⊠1 2		its
7 □		Here the blackbird strains his throat—
8 □		Welcome Ladies! to our cell.—
		[*Line-space*]
¯9 □		2
9 ⊠6		When fades the moon all shadowy pale:
6		to
10 1		And flits the scud before the gale,
⊠1		scuds the Cloud
11 ⊠6		Ere Morn with living gems bedight
6		the Morn, all gem-bedight,
12 1 2 3		Streaks the east with purple light,
2 3 *1 4 5*	Purples th'	streaky
6		Hath streak'd the East with rosy
13 □		We sip the furze flowr's fragrant dews,
14 □		Clad in robes of rainbow hues
15 ⊠*5* 6		Richer than the deepen'd bloom
16 1–3 *1 4*		That glows on Summer's lily-scented plume:
2 3		scented
17 ⊠6		Or sport amid the rosy gleam
6		shooting gleams
18 ⊠6		Sooth'd by the distant-tinkling team,
6		To the tune of teams,
19 □		While lusty *Labour* scouting sorrow
20 □		Bids the *Dame* a glad *good Morrow*,
21 □		Who jogs th' accustom'd road along
22 1 2		Timing to Dobbin's foot her cheery song.—
3		~~"Timing to Dobbin's foot her cheery song"~~ /
		And paces ~~to~~ cheery foot to her cheering song.
1–6		cheery
		[*Line-space*]

‾23 □		3
23	1 2	But not the filmy pinion
	3 *1–6*	our
24 □		We scorch amid the blaze of day,
25 □		When noontide's fiery-tressed minion
26 □		Flashes the fervid ray.—
27 □		Aye from the sultry heat
28 □		We to the cave retreat,
29 ☒2		O'er canopied by huge roots intertwin'd
2		with
30 □		With wildest texture, blacken'd o'er with age;
31 □		Round them their mantle green the Ivies bind,
32 ☒3		Beneath whose foliage pale
3		~~Beneath whose~~ Beneath whose
33 □		Fann'd by th' unfrequent gale
34 ☒*1*		We shield us from the tyrant's midday rage.
1		Tyrants'

[*Line-space*]

‾35 □		4
35 □		Thither, while the murmuring throng
36 □		Of *wild-bees* hum their drowsy song,
37	1 2	By ◄——rapture-beaming——► Fancy brought
	3	~~rapture/beaming~~ Indolence and
	1–6	◄———Indolence———►
38 □		A youthful Bard "unknown to fame"
39	1 2	Oft wooes the Queen of solemn thought,
	☒1 2	Wooes
40 □		And heaves the gentle *Misery* of a *sigh*
41 □		Gazing with tearful eye,
42 □		As round our sandy grot appear
43	1	Full many a rudely-sculptur'd name
	☒1	Many
44 □		To pensive *Memory* dear:
45 □		Weaving gay *dreams* of sunny-tinctur'd hue,
46 □		We glance before his view;
47 □		O'er his hush'd soul our soothing witcheries shed,
48	1	And twine our faery chaplets round his head.
	☒1 *6*	garlands
	6	the future garland

[*Line-space*]

‾49 □		5
49 □		When *Evening*'s dusky car
50 □		Crown'd with her dewy star
51	1	Steals o'er the fading sky with shadowy flight,
	☒1 3	in
	3	⟨sky⟩
52 □		On leaves of aspen trees
53 □		We tremble to the breeze
54 □		Veil'd from the grosser ken of mortal sight:

55	1	◄——Or——► at the silent visionary, Hour
	2	O̶r̶ i̶n̶ o̶u̶t̶ r̶u̶d̶e̶ ̶A̶ Or
	3	Or a̶t̶ t̶h̶e̶ s̶i̶l̶e̶n̶t̶ haply
	1–6	Or, haply,
56	1	◄——Along——► the ◄——wild——► sequester'd walk
	2	our ◄——rude——►
	3	A̶l̶o̶n̶g̶ o̶u̶r̶ w̶i̶l̶d̶ Along wildly-bower'd,
	1 4–6	◄——Along——►
	2 3	◄——wild——►
57	1	We list the swain's impassion'd talk,
	2	th' enamour'd Shepherd's
	3 1–6	listen to th' enamour'd Rustic's
58	1	Heave with the heavings of the Virgin's breast,
	⊠1	Maiden's
59	⊠6	Where young-eyed *Loves* have built their turtle-nest,
	6	hid
60	1 2	Or guide with soul-subduing pow'r
	⊠1 2	of [eye
61	⊠3 6	◄————Th'————► electric *flash*, that from the ◄——melting——►
	3	T̶h̶'̶ e̶l̶e̶c̶t̶r̶i̶c̶ F̶l̶a̶s̶h̶,̶ t̶h̶a̶t̶ Th'
	6	◄————The————► glance, half-confessing
62	⊠6	Darts the fond question, and the soft reply:
	6	or
	[*Line-space*]	
⁻63	⊠1	6
63	1	Or haply in the flower-embroider'd dale
	2	vale
	3	h̶a̶p̶l̶y̶ i̶n̶ thro' the m̶a̶z̶y̶ c̶i̶r̶e̶ mystic ringlets of the
	1–6	◄——thro'——► ◄——mystic——►
64	1 2	We ply our airy feet in gamesome prank:
	⊠1 2	flash faery
65	1 2	Or pay our wonted court
	3	O̶r̶ ◄—— haply ——► p̶a̶y̶ o̶u̶r̶
	3	O̶r̶ i̶n̶ d̶e̶f̶t̶ h̶o̶m̶a̶g̶e̶ p̶a̶y̶ o̶u̶r̶ s̶i̶l̶e̶n̶t̶ c̶o̶u̶r̶t̶
	3	Or ⟨silent sandal'd D̶a̶n̶c̶e̶r̶s̶⟩ pay our ⟨defter⟩ court
	1–6	◄——silent-sandal'd,——► defter
66	□	Circling the *spirit* of the *western gale*
67	1 2	Where tir'd with ◄——vernal——► sport
	⊠1 2	wearied his flower-caressing
68	□	Supine he slumbers on a violet bank:
69	1	Or with quaint music hymn the parting gleam
	2	O̶r̶ Then
	3 1–6	Then
70	1 2	By lonely *Otter*'s peace-persuading stream,
	3	p̶e̶a̶c̶e̶ sleep-persuading
	1–6	sleep-persuading

71	1	Or where its frothing wave with merry song
	2	his
	3	~~frothing~~ waves loud unquiet
	1	←—waves,—→
	2–6	←—wave—→
72	1 2	Dash'd o'er the rough rock lightly leaps along,
	3	~~ring~~ rocky channel froths
	1–3 6	rocky
	4 5	froth
73	1	Or where, its silver waters smooth'd to rest,
	⊠1	his
74	1	The tall tree's shadow sleeps upon its breast.—
	⊠1 *1*	his
	1	trees'

[*Line-space*]

⁻75	1	6
	⊠1	7
75	□	Hence! thou Lingerer Light!
76	□	Eve saddens into *night*.
77	1 2	Mother of wildering dreams! thy course pursue
	⊠1 2	wildly-working we view
78.1	1	The sombre hours, a duteous band;
79.1	1	With downcast eyes around thee stand,
79.2	2	With downcast Eyes around thee stand
78.2	2	The sombre Hours, a duteous band!
78	⊠1 2	The SOMBRE HOURS, that round thee stand
79	⊠1 2	With down-cast eyes, a duteous Band,
80	□	Their dark robes dripping with the heavy Dew
82.1	1	Thy power the Elfin Pyxies own,
81.1	1	Sorceress of the Ebon throne!
81	⊠1	Sorc'ress of the ebon Throne!
82	⊠1	Thy power the Pixies own,
83	□	When round thy raven brow
84	□	Heaven's lucent roses glow,
85	1	And clouds in humid colors drest
	⊠1	watry
86	□	Float in light drapery o'er thy sable vest,
87	□	What time the pale Moon sheds a softer day
88	1	Mellowing the woods beneath her pensive beam,
	⊠1	its
89	□	For 'mid the quivering Light 'tis our's to play
90	□	Aye dancing to the cadence of the Stream.

[*Line-space*]

⁻92	1	7
	⊠1	8
91	□	Welcome, Ladies! to the cell
92	□	Where the blameless Pyxies dwell!
93	□	But thou, sweet nymph! proclaim'd our *faery Queen*
93fn	1	Miss Boutflour.

94 ⊠3 *1*	With what obeisance meet	
3 *1*	obedience	
95 ☐	Thy presence shall we greet?	
96 1	For lo! around thee move	
2	thy steps are seen	
⊠1 2	attendant on	
97 ☐	Graceful ease in artless stole,	
99.1 1	And *honor*'s soften'd mien,	
98.1 1	And white-robed *purity* of soul;	
98 ⊠1	And white-rob'd Purity of Soul	
99 2	With Honor's gentler mien;	
3	~~meeker~~ softer	
1–6	⟵softer⟶	
100 ☐	*Mirth* of the loosely-flowing hair,	
101 1	And soft-eyed *Pity* eloquently fair,	
2	meekest	
⊠1 2	meek-eyed	
102 ⊠2 3	Whose tearful cheeks are lovely to the view	
2	Cheek is	
3	Cheeks are ~~as~~ to	
103 1	As Jasmine wet with dew.	
⊠1	Snowdrop	
	[Line-space]	
⁻**104** 1	8	
⊠1	9	
104 ☐	Unboastful Maid! tho' now the Lily pale	
105 ☐	Transparent grace thy beauties meek;	
106 1	Yet ere again th' impurpled vale	
2	purpling	
3	~~elfin~~ impurpled	
1–6	along the impurpling	
107 1–3	⟵——And——⟶ Elfin-haunted Grove	
1–6	The purpling vale and	
108 1–3	Young Zephyr with fresh flowrets strews,	
1–6	his fresh flowers profusely throws,	
109 ☐	We'll tinge with livelier hues thy cheek,	
110 1 2	And haply from the Nectar-dropping *rose*,—	
⊠1 2	-breathing	
111 1	By chymic *art* extract a *blush* for *Love*.—	
⊠1	⟵——Extract——⟶	

title/divisional title. 3 PIXIES. • *1* SONGS | OF | THE PIXIES. • *2 3* ~~Songs~~ |
OF | ~~The Pixies~~. • *4–6* SONGS OF THE PIXIES.   **introduction.** PR *2 3* give
in italic throughout   ⁻**1.1–2.** *1–6* beings   ⁻**1.2.** *1–6* small,   ⁻**1.3.** *1 2 4–*
6 half way • *3 half-way* *4–6* -covered   ⁻**1.4.** *1–6* hill,   *1–4* excavation, •
5 6 excavation   ⁻**1.5.** *1–6* trees *1* cieling; • *2–6* ceiling;   ⁻**1.6.** *1–6* cyphers,
1–3 Author *2 3* descried • *1 4–6* discovered • *2 3 discovered* 3 his own Cypher •
1 4 5 his own cypher • *2 3 his own cypher* • *2 6* his own   ⁻**1.7.** *1–6* brothers, *1–*
6 childhood.   ⁻**1.8.** *1–6* hill *1–6* river   ⁻**1.9–10.** 3 *1 4–5* the Author . . .

1793—one • *2 3 the Author . . . 1793—one* • *6* the Author, during the Summer
months of the year 1793, conducted a party of young ladies; one ⁻**1.9.** *1–5*
Ladies, ⁻**1.10.** *1 2 4–6* Summer *1–5* year 1793; 3 one ~~whom~~ • *1–6* whom,
⁻**1.11.** *1–6* clear, ⁻**1.12.** *5 6* Faery *1–4* Queen: On • *5 6* Queen. On 2 3 *1 4–
6* occasion the • *2 3 occasion, and at which time, the* ⁻**1.13.** *1–6* written.
additional title. *1* SONGS | OF | THE PIXIES. • *2 3* SONGS | OF | *THE
PIXIES*. ⁻**1.15.** 1–3 1 • *1–6* I. **2.** 2 6 Pixies • 3 *1–5* PIXIES ☒1 madrigal,
3. 2 3 Children, • *1–6* children, **4.** ☒1 Welcome, 3 *1 2 4 5* LADIES! 2 Cell! •
☒1 2 cell. **5.** *1–6* wren **6.** *1–3* it's **7.** 2 3 Blackbird 2 *1–4* throat: •
3 Throat: • *5 6* throat; **8.** ☒1 2 Welcome, 2 Ladies • 3 *1–5* LADIES! 2 cell! •
3 *1–6* cell. ⁻**9.** *1–6* II. **9.** 2 Moon 2 shadowy pale, • 3 6 shadowy-pale, •
1–5 shadowy-pale **10.** *1–6* cloud 2 Gale, **11.** 3 *1–3* MORN 2 Gems
12. 3 *1 4 5* the 2 3 *1 4 5* East **13.** 2 3 *4–6* furze-flower's • *1–3* furze-
flowr's 2 Dews • ☒1 2 dews **14.** 2 Robes *5 6* hues: **15.** 3 *1* Richer,
4 deepened *1* bloom, **16.** 2 lilly- 2 plume! • 3 Plume: **17.** *1* Or,
18. *4 5* Soothed 2 Team, **19.** 2 3 Labor • *1–3* LABOR • *4–6* Labour
2 Sorrow **20.** 2 3 *4–6* Dame • *1–3* DAME 2 good morrow, • ☒1 2 good-
morrow, **21.** *4–6* the *4–6* accustomed *1–6* along, **22.** 2 "Timing
2 song. ⁻**23.** *1–6* III. **23.** 2 Pinion **24.** 2 Day, **25.** 2 *4–6* Noontide's •
3 *1–3* NOONTIDE's 2 3 *3* Minion **26.** *5* ferved ☒1 ray. **28.** 2 3 Cave
☒1 retreat **29.** ☒1 3 O'ercanopied *4–6* intertwined **30.** *4–6* blackened
☒1 age: **31.** *1–6* ivies **33.** *4–6* Fanned *1–6* the **34.** ☒1 *1* Tyrant's
1–6 mid-day 2 Rage. ⁻**35.** *1–6* IV. **35.** 2 3 *1–3* murm'ring 2 Throng
36. 2 wild bees • 3 *3–6* wild-bees • *1 2* wild-bees, 2 Song, **37.** *1–6* brought,
38. 2 6 Bard, • 3 *1–5* BARD, 2 3 fame", • *1–6* Fame," **39.** *2–6* Solemn 3 *2–
6* Thought, **40.** 2 Misery • 3 *1–3* mis'ry • *4–6* misery 2 Sigh • 3 *ⁿ*Sigh • *1–
6* sigh **41.** 2 Eye, **42.** 2 Grot **43.** *1–6* rudely *4–6* sculptured 2 3 Name
44. 2 *4–6* Memory • 3 *1–3* MEM'RY ☒1 dear! **45.** ☒1 dreams *4–6* -tinctured
2 Hue • ☒1 2 hue **46.** ☒1 view: **47.** 2 Soul 2 Witcheries • 3 Witch'ries •
1–3 witch'ries 3 *5 6* shed ⁻**49.** *1–6* V. **49.** 2 6 Evening's • 3 *1–5* EVENING's
2 3 Car **50.** *4–6* Crowned 2 3 Star **51.** 2 Sky *1–6* flight; **52.** 2 Aspen
Trees **53.** 2 Breeze • *2 3* breeze, **54.** *4–6* Veiled 2 Sight: • ☒1 2 sight.
55. ☒1 visionary 3 hour • *1–6* hour, **56.** *1* -bow'rd, • *4* -bowered, • *5 6* -bowered
1–3 sequestred • *4–6* sequestered 2 Walk • *1–6* walk, **57.** *4–6* the enamoured
2 Shepherd's Talk, • 3 Rustic's Talk; • *1–6* rustic's talk; **58.** *1–6* maiden's
2 3 Breast **59.** 2 -ey'd • *5* eyed 2 6 Loves • 3 *1–5* LOVES 2 3 nest, • *1–6* nest;
60. ☒1 3 power • 3 Power **61.** *1–5* The 2 Flash • 3 Flash, • *1–6* flash, 2 3 Eye
62. 2 3 Question • *1–6* question 2 Reply! • 3 Reply: • *1–6* reply. ⁻**63.** *1–
6* VI. **63.** *4–6* through **64.** 2 aery ☒1 prank; **65.** *1–6* Or, 2 3 Court •
6 court, **66.** 2 6 Spirit • 3 *1–5* SPIRIT 2 6 Western Gale, • 3 *1–5* WESTERN
GALE, **67.** *1–4* Where, *1–6* sport, **68.** 2 Bank; • ☒1 2 bank; **69.** 2 Music
2 Gleam • *1–4* gleam, **70.** 2 6 Otter's • 3 *1–5* OTTER's 2 "peace-persuading"
1–6 stream; **71.** 2 Wave 2 Song **72.** 2 "Dash'd • *4–6* Dashed 2 Rock
2 along"; • *1–6* along; **73.** 2 Waters *4–6* smoothed **74.** 2 3 Tree's
Shadow 2 Breast. • ☒1 2 breast. ⁻**75.** *1–6* VII. **75.** 2 Hence, • *5 6* Hence
2 3 Lingerer, • *1–6* lingerer, *1–5* LIGHT! **76.** 3 *1–5* EVE 2 6 Night. • 3 *1–
5* NIGHT. **77.** 2 wild'ring Dreams! • 3 wildly-working Dreams! 2 pursue—
78. *1–5* SOMBRE HOURS, • *6* sombre hours, **79.** *1–6* eyes (a *1–5* band!) •
6 band)! **80.** 2 3 Dew. • *1–6* dew. **81.** 3 *1* SORC'RESS • *2–5* SORCERESS •

6 Sorceress *1–6* throne!   **82.** 3 *1–5* Pixies   **83.** 3 Brow   **84.** 2 Roses
85. 2 3 Clouds • *1–4* clouds,   *4–6* watery 2 Colours • *1–6* colours *1–*
5 drest,   **86.** 2 3 Drapery 2 2 *3* vest; • 3 *1* *4–6* vest: **87.** ⊠1 2 moon
2 Day   **88.** 2 Woods   ⊠1 beam: **89.** ⊠1 3 mid ⊠1 2 quiv'ring *1–*
6 light   3 tis *3 6* ours   ⊠1 2 play,   **90.** 3 *1 2* Aye- 2 Cadence 2 Stream! •
⊠1 2 stream.   ⁻**91.** *1–6* VIII.   **91.** 3 *1–5* Ladies!   2 Cell, • 3 Cell • *1–*
3 cell,   **92.** 2 6 Pixies • 3 *1–5* Pixies 3 *1–3* dwell. • *4–6* dwell: **93.** *1 4* thou
⊠1 Nymph!   *4–6* proclaimed 2 3 Fairy • *1–6* Faery 2 3 Queen— • *1–6* Queen,
95. 2 great?   **97.** 2 6 Ease • 3 *1–5* Ease   **98.** *4–6* -robed 3 *1–5* Purity
1–6 soul,   **99.** 3 *1–3* Honor's • *4 5* Honour's • 6 Honour's 3 *3* mien: •
1 2 mein: *4* mein;   **100.** 2 6 Mirth • 3 *1–5* Mirth   2 Hair • 3 Hair,   **101.** *1–*
3 ey'd • *4 5* eyed 2 Pity, • 3 *1–5* Pity • 6 Pity 2 fair! • 3 fair   **102.** *1–6* view,
103. ⊠1 2 snow-drop 2 Dew.   ⁻**104.** *1–6* IX.   **104.** 2 *4–6* though *1–5* Lily
105. 2 3 meek,   **106.** 2 3 the • 2 *3* th' 2 3 Vale • *1–6* vale,   **107.** ⊠1 elfin- *1–*
6 grove,   **109.** 2 3 Cheek; • *1 2 4–6* cheek; • *3* cheek!   **110.** *1–6* And, haply,
⊠1 nectar- 2 3 6 Rose • *1–5* Rose   **111.** 2 6 Blush • 3 *1–5* Blush 2 6 Love! •
3 *1–5* Love!

title/divisional title. ms 2 has the running headline "Songs of the Pixies." on all pages.
pr *2 3* give the Gothic divisional title on a separate page.

introduction. pr it 2 3 give on a separate recto page, following the divisional title.

2 etc. The patterns of indentation in different texts are too various to be specified.

4⁺. texts 2 3 *1* have line-space (but in pr *1* the line begins at the head of a page).

19. 2 Labor] The word might be written as if to be printed bold.

30. *6* With] In the HEHL copy C emended the word to "In".

32. C adjusted the indentation in ms 3.

34. 3 Tyrant's • *1* Tyrants'] The positioning of C's apostrophe explains the composi-
tor's misreading.

59. 2 Loves] The word might be written as if to be printed bold.

61. C adjusted the indentation in ms 3.

62⁺. texts ⊠1 have line-space.

65. The two deleted lines in ms 3 appear to follow the revised version that C eventually
settled on.

71–2. Erratum in pr *1* reads: "For froths read *froth*, and omit the comma at waves."
C made the corrections in his own copy, now at NYPL (Berg Collection). It was one of
those he asked Cottle to make in Jan 1797 (*CL* i 299–300).

74. 3 Tree's • *1* trees'] The positioning of C's apostrophe explains the compositor's
misreading.

78. *6* hours,] In the HEHL copy C emended to "Hours,".

94. Erratum in pr *1* reads: "For obedience read *obeisance*." C made the correction in
his own copy, now at NYPL (Berg Collection).

99. *4* mein;] In the Fitzwilliam copy C has written alongside the misprint "*mien*".

110. 2 Rose] The word might be written as if to be printed bold.

111. 2 Love] The word might be written as if to be printed bold.

64.X1. TO THE RT HON C. J. FOX

M Chron (3 Oct 1793): "TO THE RIGHT HONOURABLE C. J. FOX. | Fox—thy bright Virtues, in degenerate days,". 14 lines. Unsigned.

Suggested by Werkmeister and Zall "Possible Additions to Coleridge's 'Sonnets on Eminent Characters'" 125–6. The evidence is insufficient to prove that C was the author.

65. TO FORTUNE, ON BUYING A TICKET IN THE IRISH LOTTERY

A. DATE

Early Nov 1793.

B. TEXT

M Chron (7 Nov 1793). Signed "S. T. C." *CL* I 61 reproduces the following introductory note (only):

Sir,
    The following Poem you may perhaps deem admissable into your jour-
nal—if not, you will commit it εἰς ἱερὸν μένος Ἡφαίστοιο. I am,
    With more respect and gratitude than I ordinarily feel for Editors of
Papers, your obliged, &c.,

Cantab.—S. T. C.

C's Greek derives from Homer *Odyssey* 8.359 tr "to the sacred power of Hephaestus" (i.e. the fire). The poem was reprinted in *Gentleman's Magazine* LXIII (Dec 1793) 1133.

C. GENERAL NOTE

Christopher Wordsworth appears to refer to a ms of the poem in the possession of William Rough of Trinity, which has not survived (*Social Life at the English Universities in the Eighteenth Century* 590).

The RT reproduces the *M Chron* version exactly, except for the typography of the title:

TO FORTUNE, | ON BUYING A TICKET IN THE IRISH LOTTERY.

65.X1. A SOLILOQUY OF ROBERSPIERRE

Reading Mercury (10 Mar 1794): "A SOLILOQUY | Of the *famous or infamous* ROBERSPIERRE, | The Present Chief Ruler of FRANCE, | Overheard by DEBORAH SWEEPHOUSE | Power usurp'd like stol'n delight,". 58 lines. Unsigned.

Very tentatively suggested by David Erdman, in a letter to the present editor dated 1 Nov 1979. C was working for the *Reading Mercury* in Mar 1794, and the lines are a striking exception to the lack of writing beyond advertisements in the newspaper at the time. The style, on the other hand, constitutes very strong evidence against C's authorship, and the poem should not be accepted unless further evidence comes to light.

However, even if C was not the author, he might have taken a hand in including the poem in the newspaper—especially if the author was one of the local radicals he met through William Shield—in which case he almost certainly tampered with the text.

Compare the ms novel entitled *The Son of Robespierre* (dated early 1800), for which see **76.X1** *The Fall of Robespierre* introduction sec B.

66. DOMESTIC PEACE

A. DATE

Apr 1794? late Aug–early Sept 1794? The poem may have been one of four songs set to music by Walter Clagett in Apr 1794 (cf *CL* I 79: to GC [7 Apr 1794]), though it has not been traced in Clagett's published or unpublished collections, several of which contain his music only. Or perhaps it was written as part of **76.X1** *The Fall of Robespierre* (I 214–27) in late Aug–early Sept.

B. TEXTS

1. The Fall of Robespierre (1794) 13–14 = I 214–27.

The song is sung by Adelaide—a character created for this her song, it has been conjectured, though she does have her counterpart in Tallien's real-life mistress, Thérésa de Cabarrús.

2. Cambridge Intelligencer (25 Oct 1794). Signed ". . . by S. T. COLE-
RIDGE."

The printing is more likely to be an advertisement for the play, which the
same publisher brought out some weeks before, than to possess independent
authority.

3. Poems (1796).

4 [=RT]. *Poems* (1797).

5. Poems (1803).

6. PW (1828).

7. PW (1829).

8. PW (1834).

C. GENERAL NOTE

Different texts of the poem were reprinted with and without C's name. For
example, see *The Universal Magazine* CI (Jul 1797) 45; *Poetical Beauties of
Modern Writers* 40; *A Selection of Poems, Designed Chiefly for Schools and
Young Persons* ed Joseph Cottle (1804) 197–8 (later eds 1815, 1823, 1836);
The Parnassian Garland (1807) 184; *The Bristol Gazette and Public Advertiser*
(19 May 1814); *The Weekly Entertainer* (Sherborne) LIV (5 Sept 1814) 720;
The Penny Magazine I (20 Oct 1832) 288.

The poem was set to music by William Carnaby some time before 1802
(advertisement on p 6 of his setting of "Hear sweet Spirit!", *Invocation to a
Spirit*—London: C. Mitchell for the Author, May 1802). I have not seen this
version; it may be the same as the setting for "In a Cottag'd vale she dwells"—
Song on Peace (1825)—a copy of which is in the BM.

There is also a setting by William Horsley, as a glee for four voices, in *A
Second Collection of Glees, Madrigals, &c &c* (n.d.) 1–6. The text follows the
PR *3* and later versions in line 4 ("wings"); line 9 has "While" for "Still"; it
omits lines 11–12; and line 13 has "mindful" for "conscious". The same text
(without music) is reprinted under Horsley's name, with "While still" in line
9, in *The Words of the Most Favourite Pieces, Performed at the Glee Club,
the Catch Club, and Other Public Societies* comp Richard Clark (1814) 321.
It is not known if the Carnaby or Horsley versions have any textual authority,
though it will be noticed that the reading in line 13 is shared with the Plumtre
version cited below.

The text (only) is reprinted in James Plumtre *A Collection of Songs* (3 vols
1806–8) II 208, a collection in which C's Cambridge friend Charles Hague
assisted. In view of their friendship (Hague set **17** *Genevieve* and **51** *The Com-
plaint of Ninathoma*), the following variations may be significant: the title
"PEACE"; line 4 "Far on fearful wing she flies"; line 5 "From the tyrant's

scepter'd state"; line 13 "And, mindful of the past, employ". The first verse is headed "RECITATIVE", and the second verse "AIR". The variations are, however, more likely to be a corruption of PR *1* or *2*.

title. *1* SONG. • *2* SONG. | (From the FALL of ROBESPIERRE, an Historic Drama, by S. T. COLERIDGE.) • *3* EFFUSION XXV. • *4–8 DOMESTIC PEACE.*

1 ☐	Tell me, on what holy ground	
2 ☐	May domestic peace be found?	
3 ☐	Halcyon daughter of the skies,	
4 *1 2*	Far on fearful wing she flies,	
3–8	wings	
5 ☐	From the pomp of scepter'd state,	
6 ☐	From the rebel's noisy hate.	
	[*Line-space*]	
7 ☐	In a cottag'd vale she dwells	
8 ☐	List'ning to the Sabbath bells!	
9 ☐	Still around her steps are seen,	
10 ☐	Spotless honor's meeker mein,	
11 ☐	Love, the sire of pleasing fears,	
12 ☐	Sorrow smiling through her tears,	
13 ☐	And conscious of the past employ,	
14 ☐	Memory, bosom-spring of joy.	

title. *6–8* DOMESTIC PEACE.   **2.** *3–7* DOMESTIC PEACE • *8* Domestic Peace *8* found—   **3.** *3–8* Daughter   *8* skies!   **5.** *6 7* Sceptered • *8* sceptered   *3–8* State,   **6.** *3–8* Rebel's   **7.** *3–8* cottaged   *3–8* She   **8.** *2 6–8* Listening • *5* Lst'ning   **9.** *3–8* seen   **10.** *3–5* HONOR'S • *6 7* HONOUR'S • *8* Honour's *2* mien; • *3–8* mien,   **11.** *3–7* LOVE,   **12.** *3–7* SORROW   **13.** *3–8* employ   **14.** *3–7* MEMORY,   *3* Joy.

title. In the PR *3* list of contents the title is given as "Effusion 25, to Domestic Peace,". **6+.** No line-space in PR *4–8*.

66.X1. SONNET: ON READING MIRANDA'S SONNET TO A SIGH

M Chron (28 Jun 1794): "SONNET. | ON READING MIRANDA'S SONNET TO A SIGH. | Thy plaintive voice, so eloquent and meek,". 14 lines. Unsigned; dated "Dec. 9, 1793."

The sonnet is a response to Miranda's/Mrs Robinson's sonnet published in *M Chron* (9 Dec 1793). It reads as follows:

Thy plaintive voice, so eloquent and meek,
  Poor Child of Wretchedness! I never hear,
  But silently I turn t' indulge the tear
Which Pity gives! To me thine accents speak—

Haply of him, who knows no friend, the fate;
  Or one to dark Despondency consign'd,
  Or cast to the cold mercy of mankind,
On Life's bleak waste. Thee too, all desolate,

I mourn, MIRANDA! for thy tender tale
  Bespeaks thy suff'ring, whosoe'er thou art,
  And Anguish deep, that wrings the heavy heart:—
Yet may thy sigh, so sweetly breath'd, avail,
  While gen'rous Love, engag'd on Pity's part,
Shall plead thy cause, nor leave thee drooping, sad, and pale!

Very tentatively suggested by D. V. Erdman et al "Unrecorded Coleridge Variants: Additions and Corrections" *SB* XIV (1961) 236–45 at 238.

If C was the author, he might have been encouraged to write the sonnet by the literary circle he found himself in at Reading and Henley. William Shields, for one, is known to have been sympathetic to Mrs Robinson. An anecdote recorded by George Bellas Greenough in his diary for 27 Jun 1799 might also be taken into account:

> Coleridge had one day been abusing Mrs. T. Robinson's poetry more than he thought it deserved—he therefore agreed with his friends that by way of atonement he should publish a sonnet in praise of that lady in the public papers. He filled his sonnet with the most extravagant eulogy. A few days later he received a most highly complimentary letter from Mrs. Robinson in which she begged his acceptance of all her works, handsomely bound and printed on wire-woven paper. (*C in Germany* 230–1)

The fact that C's attitude towards Mrs Robinson changed and became more simply appreciative after he returned from Germany (cf **271** *A Stranger Minstrel*; *CL* I 562–3: to RS 25 Jan 1800; etc), and that he made no reference then to earlier, more dismissive, attitudes or to an "encounter", is not evidence against him being the author of the present sonnet. None the less, the positive evidence remains slender. The anecdote recorded by Greenough might refer to **165** *The Apotheosis* if one allows either a very loose description of "a sonnet" or a misremembering—alternatives which do not exclude one another, perhaps almost consciously.

67. SONG: IMITATED FROM CASIMIR

A. DATE

Mar–Aug 1794. See vol I headnote.

B. TEXTS

1. The Watchman II (9 Mar 1796) 49–50 (*CC*) 69–70.

The Latin original, C's "Imitation", and an alternative "Translation" by POR-
TIUS were published in *The Bristol Gazette and Public Advertiser* (22 Oct
1807), where C's text is taken directly from PR *1* and has no textual authority.

1 [=RT]. BPL B 22189=Estlin Copy Book f 17^{r-v}. Transcript in C's hand.

title. *1* IMITATION. • 1 Song.

The words and indentation in the two texts of the poem are identical; only punctuation
and capitals vary. The RT reproduces MS 1 exactly except for the deletion at line 9 (see
below). Although PR *1* precedes MS 1, the printed text is taken here to be a variant of the
MS.

1. *1* air   **2.** *1* lay!   **3.** *1* Poplar branch suspended,   **4.** *1* eye   **7.** *1* lying,
8. *1* waterfall   **9.** 1 ~~In~~ In *1* -roaring,   **10.** *1* sound—   **11.** *1* louring!
13. *1* measure,   **15.** *1* flatterer,

title. PR *1* is preceded by the original Latin poem, entitled "*AD LYRAM.*" MS 1 adds
at the end of the poem: "*Note.* | Imitated from Casimir."
9. The deletion in MS 1 is because C wanted a wider space between stanzas 2 and 3.

67.X1.CAMBRIDGE PRIZE POEMS, 1794

C told GC, at the beginning of Mar 1794 from High Wycombe, "The moments I
can abstract from more interesting and more intrusive thoughts I am dedicating
to the Cambridge Odes" (*CL* I 70); and, following his return to Cambridge, that
he had "been engaged in finishing a Greek Ode—I mean to write for all the
Prizes" (*CL* I 80: [1 May 1794]). Despite his expressed intention and his good
reasons for working at the project—"*if* I should be so *very lucky* as to win one
of the Prizes, I could *comfortably* ask the Dr's Advice concerning the *time* of
my degree"—there is no evidence, in the Jesus library borrowings or elsewhere,
that C completed or submitted any entries. See poems **48, 48.X1, 55.X1,** and
55.X2 for his entries and supposed entries in previous years.

It is noticeable that C assured GC that he was busy with such academic tasks even while he told him about **50.X1** *Imitations from the Modern Latin Poets* (*CL* I 56: [18 Feb 1793]; 80: [1 May 1794]), and that he was considerably less forthcoming about **76.X1** *The Fall of Robespierre.* The Browne prizes were gold medals worth £5, no more, and C was in considerable financial difficulty.

The topics for the Browne Medals in 1794 were as follows. For the Greek and Latin odes, "Graiis ingenium Graiis dedit ore rotundo I Musa loqui" (Horace *Ars Poetica* 323–4 tr H. R. Fairclough—LCL rev 1929—477 "To the Greeks the Muse gave native wit, to the Greeks she gave speech in well-rounded phrase"). The Greek prize was won by Samuel Butler, the Latin by John Keate. The topic for Greek and Latin epigrams was "Simplex munditiis" (Horace *Odes* 1.5.5 tr Milton "plain in neatness"), the prize for which was won by C's fellow scholar at Jesus George Caldwell.

68. TO A FRIEND IN ANSWER TO A MELANCHOLY LETTER

A. DATE

Mar–Aug 1794? 1795? See vol I headnote.

B. TEXTS

1 [=RT]. HRC MS (Coleridge, S T) Works B. Recto of a single leaf 21.0× 32.6 cm; wm Britannia in rounded oval, surmounted by crown; chain-lines 2.5 cm; verso blank. Rugby Manuscript p 81/f 35^r. Transcript in C's hand, intended as copy for PR *1* below.

The notes C sent Joseph Cottle to include in PR *1* contain a deleted instruction which appears to refer to this poem: "~~Page 119 / Print from the Strip of Paper /~~" (bound into Rugby Manuscript p 124/f 56^v). Cf the deleted title in MS 1. Did C intend to give the Casimir "original" in a note, and then, in Mar 1796 (see *CL* I 193: to J. Cottle [late Mar 1796]), change his mind?

1. Poems (1796).

2. Poems (1803).

3. PW (1828).

The copy at the Fitzwilliam Museum, Cambridge (Marlay Bequest 1912) contains a comment on the poem (see vol I headnote) and a correction to line 13 (see below).

4. PW (1829).

5. PW (1834).

title. 1 Epistle II. | (Imitated from Casimir) To a Friend. | In answer to a melancholy Letter | , from a Fri • *1* EPISTLE II. | *TO A FRIEND,* | IN ANSWER TO | A MELANCHOLY LETTER. • *2 To a FRIEND,* | IN ANSWER TO | A MELANCHOLY LETTER. • *3–5* LINES | TO A FRIEND IN ANSWER TO A MELANCHOLY | LETTER.

The RT reproduces MS 1 exactly (except that it does not record the minor deletions in lines 7, 13, and 18). The five printed texts have the same words as the RT, with variant punctuation and spelling.

1. ⊠1 looks,   *1 2* lab'ring • *3–5* labouring   ⊠1 sigh,   **2.** ⊠1 offspring
3. ⊠1 power,   **4.** *5* gamester   **5.** *5* sun   ⊠1 gleam   **6.** ⊠1 clouds,
7. ⊠1 To-morrow   *3–5* -coloured   1 main/ • ⊠1 main   **9.** *3–5* the   ⊠1 gust,
⊠1 hand   *5* Time   **10.** *1 3–5* lyre: • 2 lyre!   ⊠1 dance   **11.** *3–5* The   *1–4* groupes • *5* groups   **13.** 1 ᵬBears • ⊠1 Bears   ⊠1 its   ⊠1 hour   *3* Fate, • *4 5* Fate;   **14.** *3–5* swain,   ⊠1 who,   *3–5* lulled   ⊠1 murmurs,   **15.** ⊠1 oxen
16. ⊠1 To-day   **18.** 1 Haply sSurvey • ⊠1 Survey   *1–4* Despot's • *5* despot's
19. *5* pageant   ⊠1 height   **20.** ⊠1 isle.   **22.** *3–5* tired   ⊠1 limbs   **23.** *3–5* mixed   ⊠1 and   **24.** *1–4* food, • *5* food   ⊠1 jewels

13. 1 ᵬBears] C's correction is an attempt to preserve a wider space between stanzas 3 and 4.

3 Fate,] C corrected the punctuation in the Fitzwilliam copy to "Fate!"

68.X1. LINES WRITTEN IN A PRAYER BOOK: AFTER BOWLES

A. DATE

c 1794 (George Whalley's dating); perhaps after C returned to Cambridge in Apr, following his months in the army. C's adaptation of the sonnet "I shall behold far off thy barren crest" (poem **70.X1**) reveals that he was familiar with Bowles's third edition before Jul.

B. TEXT

Printed in *LR* I 34, with the description: "These lines were found in Mr. Coleridge's hand-writing in one of the Prayer Books in the chapel of Jesus College, Cambridge." The edition of the Book of Common Prayer is not specified, and the copy has not been traced. The description may well be an invented title, and there may never have been an annotated book. *CM (CC)* I 700.

C. GENERAL NOTE

The opening lines of the text comprise the last five and a half lines of W. L. Bowles's elegy *On the Death of Mr. Headley*, which was first published in 1794 (in the 3rd ed of Bowles's *Sonnets*, p 43). C has made minor adjustments of phrasing, punctuation, and capitalisation. Bowles's lines read as follows:

> —I, alas! remain
> To mourn the hours of youth (yet mourn in vain)
> That fled neglected.—Wisely thou hast trod
> The better path; and that High Meed, which GOD
> Ordain'd for Virtue, towering from the dust,
> Shall bless thy labours, spirit! pure and just.

C's last six lines directly echo but do not follow so directly the opening paragraph of the next poem in Bowles's 1794 volume, *On Mr. Howard's Account of Lazarettos* (p 49). They may be read as a commentary on the first six lines, in which case the relation would be clearer if the first six lines were placed in quotation-marks.

The new entity made up of the two sets of lines is as much an "original" composition as several adaptations which are given in vol I. It is not included there because of the doubt which lingers over the *LR* text.

> —I yet remain
> To mourn the hours of youth (yet mourn in vain)
> That fled neglected: wisely thou hast trod
> The better path—and that high meed which God
> Assign'd to virtue, tow'ring from the dust,   5
> Shall wait thy rising, Spirit pure and just!
>
> O God! how sweet it were to think, that all
> Who silent mourn around this gloomy ball
> Might hear the voice of joy;—but 'tis the will
> Of man's great Author, that through good and ill   10
> Calm he should hold his course, and so sustain
> His varied lot of pleasure, toil, and pain!

69. FROM *PERSPIRATION:*
A TRAVELLING ECLOGUE

A. DATE

5–6 Jul 1794.

B. TEXT

PML MA 1848 (1). Single folded leaf, 37.4×29.3 cm overall; wm coat of arms of Great Britain in round frame surmounted by crown; countermark LLOYD; chain-lines 2.6 cm. The two extracts are contained in the same als to RS, 6 Jul 1794 (*CL* I 84).

The RT reproduces the ms exactly, except for:

9. Emblem] ms ~~Image~~ Emblem

70. LINES ON THE "MAN OF ROSS"

A. DATE

6 Jul 1794, at Ross-on-Wye (see MS 1 below).

B. TEXTS

1. PML (uncatalogued in Jul 1978) (R–V Autographs Misc). One of two conjoint leaves, each 20.4×32.0 cm; no wm; chain-lines 2.5 cm. Transcript in the hand of Joseph Hucks, in ink, subscribed after the Introduction "S. T. Coleridge—", with corrections in C's hand in pencil.

The poem is one of three complete poems transcribed on the sheet, the others being **70.X1** *Adaptation of "I shall behold far off thy barren crest"* and **73.X1** *The Faded Flower*; it also contains **72** *Stanzas from an "Elegy on a Lady"*. The transcript must date from 12 Jul (the date affixed to the adaptation of Bowles) or after. It might even postdate MS 2, since C's pencil corrections are later still—possibly contemporary with MS 3.

Joseph Hucks and C parted company between 1 and 4 Aug, and the corrections were probably made before then. It is not easy to decide whether the transcript was made from another or from dictation.

2. PML MA 1848 (2). Single folded leaf, 40.2×25.2 cm overall; wm J. STE-

VENS; chain-lines 2.7 cm. The lines are written two abreast. Included as part of an als to RS, 13–15 Jul 1794 (*CL* I 87).

This version is identical in all but small details with the uncorrected MS 1. The transcript made by RS in his letter to Grosvenor Bedford of 20 Jul 1794 (Bodleian MS Eng lett c 22 f 120ʳ) has no textual significance.

3. University of Kentucky Libraries, Lexington (Special Collections) W. Hugh Peal Collection. Bound into a volume, the eight letter-pages of which measure 20×32 cm; wm present but difficult to decipher; chain-lines 2.5 cm. The end of the last six lines in this version have been cut away with the seal. Included as part of an als to Henry Martin, 22 Jul 1794 (*CL* I 95).

The poem is the first of two transcribed, the other being **73.X1** *The Faded Flower*. Lines 5–10 of MSS 1 2 have been dropped, to be incorporated (var) in the version of **82** *Monody on the Death of Chatterton* published soon afterwards (see **82** VAR TEXT PR *1*).

4. Pforzheimer MS Misc 83. Recto of a leaf, 11.4×18.5 cm; wm BUTTAN-SHAW; chain-lines 2.7 cm; verso blank. Transcript in C's hand (the attribution is not absolutely certain).

The poems transcribed in the same group of leaves are **78.X3** *On Bala Hill* and **75** *The Sigh* (here entitled "Song"). The group of leaves formed part of the 1919 Morrison Sale and are thereby associated with Mary Evans. It is worth noting that C had seen her at Wrexham on 13–14 Jul, just before beginning his second letter to RS and copying out the first extant versions of the poem.

MS 4 follows the corrected version of MS 1, and two details suggest that it might postdate MS 3 and even PR *1*. First, C apparently hesitated whether to transcribe the shorter, fourteen-line version, which was in his mind while **82** *Monody on the Death of Chatterton* included the six omitted lines. Second, CL associated the poem with the Salutation and Cat, having "the mark of the beast 'Tobacco' upon it" (*LL*—M—II 113: to C [28] May 1803; the related transcripts of **75** *The Sigh* appear to date from the same period).

The ms might have been sent to Mary Evans any time between Jul and Dec; C was at the Salutation and Cat from early Nov.

1. *Cambridge Intelligencer* (27 Sept 1794). Signed "*S.T.C.* I *Jes. Coll.*"
This version follows the corrected version of MS 1, in twenty lines.

2. Joseph Hucks *A Pedestrian Tour through North Wales* (1795) 16.
This twenty-line version includes a reading ("virgins" in line 9) found also in MS 5 and PR *3*, which suggests that it might derive from a text later than the tour itself—e.g. from between 17 Sept and 8 Nov, when C and Hucks were together at Cambridge.

5. BPL B 22189=Estlin Copy Book f 22ʳ⁻ᵛ. Transcript in C's hand.

3. Charles Heath *The Excursion down the Wye from Ross to Monmouth* (Monmouth 1799) 64.

The status of this version, and its relation to other versions, is something of a mystery. Heath implies that the text was taken from "a volume of POEMS, written by Mr. *Coleridge*", yet it was taken neither from PR *4* nor from PR *5*, nor from any other single known source. Heath omits the first two lines (which is perhaps not significant), then follows the general pattern of the longer versions before PR *5*, though he shares the reading "Virgins" (line 9, his seventh) only with PR *2* and MS 5; line 11 (his ninth) is shared only with PR *4 5*.

It is possible that PR *3* represents a ms version given to Heath in the first half of 1795, C telling him that it would be published in his forthcoming *Poems*— which it was, but differently. Heath claimed to be acquainted with C: they did not know each other in Aug 1794 (*CL* I 96–7: to C. Heath 29 Aug 1794) and probably did not meet until C returned to Bristol in Jan 1795. Heath's brother, a Bristol apothecary, had been a convert to pantisocracy.

It is possible that this version has no textual authority whatsoever.

6. Cornell WORDSWORTH Bd. Cottle=Joseph Cottle's Album ff 5^v–6^r. Signed "Samuel Taylor Coleridge". Transcript in C's hand, dated 6 Jun 1795.
The twenty-line version, with minor variations.

7. PML MA 1916=Quarto Copy Book f 4^r. Transcript in C's hand.
The fourteen-line version which might have served as copy for PR *4* through an intermediate version.

4. Poems (1796).
Further small changes were introduced (e.g. "Beneath" for "If 'neath"), and the six omitted lines were incorporated (var) into **82** *Monody on the Death of Chatterton* 41–6.

5 [=RT]. *Poems* (1797).
RS's copy, now at Yale (In 678 797 Copy 1), contains a correction in C's hand.
The twenty-line version, but in a different form from any other text, apparently because of a mistake by Joseph Cottle. C asked him in early Apr 1797 to reinstate the six lines following line 4, and to begin a new paragraph thereafter in which further revisions were to be made (*CL* VI 1007–8 var; see commentary on 4.1.1–4 below). Cottle reinstated the six lines at a later point in the text, in a form which partially follows the version in C's letter and partially follows the previously published versions of **82** *Monody on the Death of Chatterton*. The error concerning the order of lines is cited in the Errata.
The RT given in vol I supplies the text which C instructed Cottle to print in 1797.

6. Poems (1803).
A reversion to the fourteen-line poem, closer to MS 7 than to PR *4*. CL was responsible for omitting the six lines, even though he had earlier thought them necessary (*LL*—M—II 114; cf ibid I 20, 67). The transcript of this version in

JTC's Commonplace Book (University of Pennsylvania (Special Collections) MS Eng 13) p 33 has no textual significance.

7. *PW* (1828).
This version follows PR *4* and earlier texts in restoring the six lines to their proper place, but in their PR *5* form (derived from **82** *Monody on the Death of Chatterton*).

8. *PW* (1829).

9. *PW* (1834).

title/introduction. 1 Written at the King's Arms, Ross. 16 Miles from Gloucester— once the house of the celebrated M^r. Kirley July 6 1794 • 2 At Ross (16 miles from Gloucester) we took up our quarters at the King's Arms, once the House of Kyrle, the M. of R. I gave the window-shutter the following Effusion. • 3 Lines written at Ross, at the King's Arms'—once th House of Mr Kyrle. • 4 Written at the King's Arms, Ross—once the House of Mr Kyrle, the "Man of Ross."— • *1* LINES | *Written at the King's Arms*, ROSS, *formerly the House | of the* "MAN OF ROSS." • *2* We slept at the King's Arms at Ross, which was formerly the habitation of that celebrated character who usually goes by the name of the "Man of Ross." . . . I cannot omit sending you a few lines which my fellow traveller scribbled upon a window shutter, unlike the general style of composition which such places abound with: • 5 Lines written at the King's Arms, Ross—formerly the House of Mr Kyrle, the "Man of Ross. • *3* Lines, | Written at | The King's Arms, Ross, | Formerly the House of | "The Man of Ross." • 6 Lines written at the King's Arms, Ross— | formerly the residence of Mr Kyrle, the "Man of Ross" celebrated by *Pope* | • 7 Lines written at the King's *4*Arms, Ross—th formerly the House of the "Man of Ross." • *4–9* LINES | WRITTEN | *AT THE KING'S ARMS, ROSS,* | FORMERLY THE HOUSE OF THE | "MAN OF ROSS."

1 1 2 4 *1* 2 5 6 6	Richer than misers	o͞er	their countless hoards,
3		brood o'er	
7		o'er	the his
4 5 7–9		MISER	his
2 ⊠*3*	Nobler than Kings, or king-polluted Lords,		
3 ⊠*3*	Here dwelt the Man of Ross! O Traveller—hear—		
3			Stranger,
4 1–3	"Departed Merit claims the Glistening Tear."		
4 *1* 2 5 6			reverent
3 7 4–9		a	
4.1.1 *4 5*	Beneath this roof if thy cheer'd moments pass,		
4.1.2 *4 5*	Fill to the good man's name one grateful glass:		
4.1.3 *4 5*	To higher zest shall MEM'RY wake thy soul,		
4.1.4 *4 5*	And VIRTUE mingle in th' ennobled bowl.		
5 ⊠3 4 7 4 6	←—Friend—→ to the friendless, to the sick man health		
4	If 'neath Friend	poor	Wealth
6 ⊠3 7 4 6	With generous joy he view'd his modest wealth.		
7 ⊠3 7 4–8	He heard the Widow's heaven breath'd prayer of praise,		
5 7 8	hears		

8 ⊠3 7 *4–7*	He mark'd the shelter'd Orphan's tearful gaze;	
5 7	marks	
9 *1 2*	And o'er the dowried Maiden's glowing cheek	
4	snowy	
1 2 3 5	Virgin's	
6	portion'd Maiden's	
10 ⊠3 7 *4–9*	Bade bridal love suffuse its blushes meek—	
10.1.1 *5 7–9*	Or where the sorrow-shrivel'd captive lay,	
10.1.2 *5 7 8*	Pours the bright blaze of Freedom's noon-tide ray.	
9	Pour'd	
	[*Line-space*]	
11 ⊠*3 4 5 7–9*	If 'neath this roof thy wine cheer'd moments pass,	
3 7–9	Beneath if thy	
12 ⊠4 5 *4 5*	Fill to the goodman's name one ⟵grateful⟶ glass.	
4 5	~~cheerful~~ grateful	
13 *1*	To higher rest shall memory wake thy soul,	
⊠1 *4 5*	zest	
14 *1 2*	And Virtue mingle in the sparkling Bowl.	
⊠1 2 *4 5*	th' ennobled	
	[*Line-space*]	
15 ⊠*6*	But if, like me, thro' Life's distressful scene	
6	mine,	
16 *1*	Lonely & sad thy Pilgrimage ha~~s~~th been,	
⊠1	hath	
17 ⊠*7*	⟵And⟶ if, thy ~~br~~ Breast with heartsick Anguish fraught	
7	~~Here ch~~ And	
18 □	Thou journeyest onward tempest tost in thought,	
19 □	Here cheat thy cares: in generous Vision's melt,	
20 □	And *dream* of Goodness, thou hast never felt!—	

title. *5 6* LINES | *Written at the KING's-ARMS, ROSS,* | Formerly the House of the | *"MAN OF ROSS."* • *7 8* LINES WRITTEN AT THE KING'S-ARMS, | ROSS, | FORMERLY THE HOUSE OF THE "MAN OF ROSS." • *9* LINES | WRITTEN AT THE KING'S ARMS, ROSS, FORMERLY | THE HOUSE OF THE "MAN OF ROSS."   **1.** 2 3 4 *1* 5 6 Misers • 7 6 MISERS • *9* Miser   ⊠1 *3* o'er   7 Hoards,   **2.** 2–4 *1* 5 Kings • 2 kings • 7 *4–8* KINGS,   2 lords; • 7 *4–8* LORDS,   **3.** 4 "Man • *3* 7 *4–8* MAN   *3* 7 *4–8* OF   *1 2* Ross. • *3* 7 *4–8* ROSS!   2 Trav'ler, • 5–7 *4–6* Trav'ller, • *3* Trav'ller • 4 *1* 7–9 Traveller, • 2 traveller   ⊠1 2 hear! • 2 hear,   **4.** ⊠1 Departed   2 merit   3 th'   2 3 glistening • 2 rev'rend   2 4 *1* 5 6 Tear. • *3* 3 7 *4–9* tear. • 2 tear;   **5.** 5 sick-   2 4 5 Man   2 6 Health • *1* 5 Health, • *2* 3 5 7–9 health,   **6.** 2 gen'rous • 6 *generous*   *1* 5 6 Joy   2 3 7–9 viewed   4 5 wealth— • *1–3* wealth: • 6 Wealth: • 5 7–9 wealth;   **7.** 4 2 3 5 7–9 widow's   2 *1–3* heav'n-breath'd • 4 heavnbreath'd • 5 6 *5* heaven-breath'd • 7–9 heaven-breathed   *1* 5 6 Prayer   2 *1* 5 6 Praise,   **8.** *8 9* marked   7–9 sheltered   2 3 5 7–9 orphan's   2 gaze— • 4 Gaze— • *1* 7–9 gaze, • 5 6 Gaze,   **9.** *2 3* virgins   5 snowy-   *1–3* cheek, • 5 6 Cheek   **10.** 6 *bridal*   *1* 5 6 Love   *1* it's   2 meek • 4 *1* 2 5 *3* meek. • 6 meek!   **10.1.1.** 7 8 sorrow-shrivelled • *9* sorrow shrivelled   **11.** 3 *1* 6 Roof   2–4 *1* 5–7 6 wine-   7–9 cheered   *1* 5–7 Moments   **12.** *1* 2 5 *3* 7 4 6–

9 good • 6 Good   *1* 6 Man's • *2 5 3 7 4 6–9* man's   *1* Name   5 ~~chearful~~
grateful   2 glass! • *1* Glass. • 2 glass, • 4 6 Glass— • 5 Glass! • *3 5* glass; •
7 *4 6–9* glass: **13.** *1* Zest   2–4 *1 5 9* Memory • 2 mem'ry • *3 4 6* Mᴇᴍ'ʀʏ •
6 Mem'ry • 7 [?]Mᴇᴍ'ʀʏ • *7 8* Mᴇᴍᴏʀʏ   2 *1 5* 6 Soul,   **14.** 2 virtue • *3 6–*
8 Vɪʀᴛᴜᴇ • *9* Virtue   2 *7–9* the   *2–9* bowl. • 6 Bowl! • 7 [?]bowl.   **15.** 2 *3* if
1 me, • 2 me   4 6 7 *7–9* through   *2–9* life's   2 3 6 Scene • 4 2 scene, • *1* Scene,
16. 2–4 *1* 2 5 *3–9* and   4 *2–9* pilgrimage   2 *1 3* 7 *4–9* been; • 4 been—
17. 2 *8 9* if   ☒1 3 *1* breast • *3 1* Breast   ☒1 2 4 5 heart-sick   ☒1 4 *1* anguish   ☒1–
4 *1* fraught,   **18.** ☒1 *7–9* tempest-tost • *7–9* tempest-tossed   2 4 5 thought—
• *3* 7 *4–9* thought;   **19.** 4 6 *Here*   2 2 cares— • 3 cares; • 4 5 7 Cares! •
1 Cares— • *3–9* cares!   2 *1* 5 Visions • 4 2 3 6 7 *4–9* visions   2 melt— • 4 melt
20. 4 2 *3* 7 *4–9* dream   2 goodness   2 *1* 2 felt. • *3 felt* • 4 5 3 6 7 *4–9* felt!

title. In the ᴘʀ *5* list of contents the title is given as "Lines on the Man of Ross,".
4. ᴍs 1 Glistening] C has corrected the word, in pencil, to "reverent".
4.1.1–4. These lines in ᴘʀ *5* were never intended by C to appear in this position,
indeed in this form. He wrote to Joseph Cottle, early in Apr 1797, with the proofs
obviously in hand:

> Friend to the friendless, to the sick man Health,
> With generous joy he view'd his modest wealth;
> He heard the Widow's heaven-breath'd prayer of praise;
> He mark'd the shelter'd Orphan's tearful gaze;
> And o'er the portion'd Maiden's snowy cheek
> Bade bridal *I*Love suffuse its blushes meek.

Then a new paragraph &

> If near this roof thy wine-cheer'd moments pass
> Fill to the Good Man's name one ~~gta cheerful glass.~~
>   grateful glass:
> To higher zest shall ʌᴛʜMemory wake thy soul,
> And Virtue mingle in th' ennobled bowl!
> But if, like mine, thro' Life's &c.—

But never mind it—the poem may, perhaps, be reprinted in the *Errata*.—
  (University of Birmingham Library, Special Collections; *CL* ᴠɪ 1007–8 var)

The ᴘʀ *5* volume has, in the Errata at the end of the volume:

In the Poem to the Mᴀɴ of Rᴏss, from the *fifth* to the *eighth* line should have
been placed after the *fourteenth*.—Two or three typographical errors the reader will
correct as they occur.

9. ᴍs 1 glowing] C has corrected the word, in pencil, to "snowy".
10⁺. ᴛᴇxᴛs 1 3 4 *1* 5 6 (only) have line-space.
11. ᴍs 4 ~~cheerful~~ grateful] The correction is in pencil, and not certainly by C.
13. ᴍs 1 rest] C has corrected the word, in pencil, to "zest".
13. ᴍs 1 memory] C has corrected the first letter, in pencil, to "Memory".
14. ᴍs 1 sparkling] C has corrected the word, in pencil, to "ennobled".
14⁺. ᴍss 1 3 5 and perhaps ᴍs 6 (only) have line-space.
15–20. ᴍs 3 is imperfect (the end of the lines has been cut away with the seal).

15. PR *5* me,] C has emended to "mine," in RS's copy.

70.X1. ADAPTATION OF BOWLES'S "I SHALL BEHOLD FAR OFF THY BARREN CREST"

A. DATE

11 Jul 1794? The ms is headed "North Wales— | Bala—July 12. 1794". But C and Joseph Hucks had left Bala on 11 Jul, to spend the night at Druid, and on Sunday 12 Jul had travelled from Druid to Wrexham via Llangollen. The first letter of Hucks's *Pedestrian Tour through North Wales* is dated "BALA, North Wales, July 11, 1794", and there are further reasons to think that the date on the ms is incorrect (see sec C below).

B. TEXT

PML (uncatalogued in Jul 1978) (R–V Autographs Misc). On one of two conjoint leaves, each 20.4×32.0 cm; no wm; chain-lines 2.5 cm. Transcript in the hand of Joseph Hucks, signed "S.J.C." The poem is one of three transcribed by Hucks, the others being **70** *Lines on the "Man of Ross"* (dated 6 Jul 1794) and **73.X1** *The Faded Flower* (dated 10 Jul 1794), all of them addressed to Miss A. Evans; Hucks also transcribed **72** *Stanzas from an "Elegy on a Lady"*, and C jotted down **70.X2** *Fragmentary Adaptation of a Welsh Sonnet*. The peculiar signature might be compared with the signature to **58.X1** *Adaptation of Bampfylde's "To Evening"*.

C. GENERAL NOTE

The transcript constitutes a modified version of sonnet XXVII in the third edition of W. L. Bowles's *Sonnets* (Bath 1794) 30. The title—"WRITTEN | AT MALVERN, | JULY 11, 1793"—helps explain why the transcript was made as a commemorative exercise, transferring the application of the lines from Malvern to the mountains encircling Bala. The variations from Bowles's text are as follows: in line 1 Bowles has "tow'ring" for "barren"; in line 3 "distant" for "winding" and "homeward" for "weary"; in line 7 "life's bitter losses" for "Love's disappointments"; in line 13 "shades" for "mists". There are also variations of punctuation and spelling: in line 2 "Mountain:" and "stray,"; in line 3 "vale"; in line 4 "breast,"; etc.

C knew the third edition of Bowles's *Sonnets*, and quoted from other poems in the collection in the present poem, if this text is to be taken as genuine, but he regretted some of its omissions (*CL* I 318–19: to W. L. Bowles [16 Mar 1797]).

The initials with which the transcript is signed might suggest that Hucks helped with the adaptation. At the same time, the changes are similar to the kind C made later to Bowles's originals, in *Sonnets from Various Authors.*

title. North Wales— | Bala—July 12. 1794

1 I shall behold far off thy barren crest,
2 Proud mountain! from thy heights as slow I stray
3 Down thro' the winding Vale my weary way,
4 I shall behold, upon thy rugged breast
5 The parting Sun sit smiling: me the while
6 Escapd the croud, thoughts full of heaviness
7 May visit, as Love's disappointments press
8 Hard on my ~~breast~~ Bosom! But I shall beguile
9 The thing I am—& think, that (ēēn as thou
10 Dost lift in the pale Beam thy forehead high,
11 Proud Mountain! whilst the scatter'd vapours fly
12 Unheeded round thy Breast!) so with calm brow
13 The mists of sorrow I may meet, & wear
14 The smile unchanged of Peace, tho' prest by Care.

    title. It is not certain whether Hucks's heading is meant to constitute a title. Its closeness to Bowles's original title, in form, suggests that it might be. Amending the date to the anniversary of the date of Bowles's poem (11 July 1793) would make the allusion more definite.

70.X2. FRAGMENTARY ADAPTATION
OF A WELSH SONNET

A. DATE

Jul–Aug 1794. C undoubtedly came across a copy of Edward Jones's book, which his lines closely follow, on his tour in Wales. He is likely to have jotted down the lines in a bookshop or in someone's home from the new edition. The dates on Hucks's transcript of other lines in the same ms are 6, 10, and 12 Jul (see the references in sec B): either Hucks was using a piece of paper C had already used, or (more likely) the lines were added after C's meeting with Mary Evans at Wrexham on 13 July (*CL* I 87: to RS 13–15 Jul 1794), on a poetical message in a hand unknown to Anne and Mary Evans which was never delivered. C and Hucks parted company between 1 and 4 Aug.

PML (uncatalogued in Jul 1978) (R–V Autographs Misc). On one of two conjoint leaves, each 20.4×32.0 cm; no wm; chain-lines 2.5 cm. Draft in C's hand, in pencil.

C wrote the lines on a page containing (at right angles to them, in the hand of Joseph Hucks, in ink) the name "Miss A Evans". Four other poems are transcribed on the other pages, in Hucks's hand—**70** *Lines on the "Man of Ross"*, **70.X1** *Adaptation of "I shall behold far off thy barren crest"*, **72** *Stanzas from an "Elegy on a Lady"*, and **73.X1** *The Faded Flower*.

C. GENERAL NOTE

The lines might represent a scribbled attempt to copy an untitled "Welsh Sonnet" translated by Edward Jones *Musical and Poetical Relicks of the Welsh Bards* (1784) 34 (2nd ed—1794—65) in unfavourable circumstances, or to retrieve the lines, after having read them, by memory:

> Sad and heavy sinks the stone,
> On the lake's smooth surface thrown;
> Man oppress'd by sorrow's weight
> Sadly sinks beneath his fate;
> But the saddest thing to tell,
> Is to love, and bid farewell!

farewell!] 1794 farewel!

The difference of wording in the first two lines suggests that they might represent the beginning of an adapation like **73** *Imitated from the Welsh*, which is based on another "sonnet" from a previous page of Jones. Several words in subsequent lines are too faint to be legible, and the version given here avoids adjusting them to match the printed original.

1 Sad & heavy falls the stone
2 On the Lake's smooth surface shows
3 Man opp...... by......... ......
4 Sadly sits .... beneath the .....
5 But this modest thing to .....
6 .. .. .jasi....

5. modest] The reading is particularly uncertain. The first letters are obscure, and the last four might read "dost".

71. LATIN LINES ON MARY EVANS

A. DATE

Jul 1794?

B. TEXTS

1 [=RT]. PML MA 1848 (2). Single folded leaf, 40.2×25.2 cm overall; wm J. STEVENS; chain-lines 2.7 cm. Included in an als to RS, 13–15 Jul 1794 (*CL* I 87–8).

2. University of Kentucky Libraries, Lexington (Special Collections) W. Hugh Peal Collection. Bound into a volume, the eight letter-pages of which measure 20×32 cm; wm difficult to decipher; chain-lines 2.5 cm. Included in an als to Henry Martin, 22 Jul 1794 (*CL* I 92).

The words in the two texts of the poem are identical; only punctuation and capitals vary.

1. 2 Vivit,   **3.** 2 valetæ   2 insomnia Mentis,

72. STANZAS FROM AN *ELEGY ON A LADY*

A. DATE

14 Jul 1794? Soon afterwards? C claimed in MS 3 that the stanzas date from before his fifteenth year. However, although they may be associated with feelings he had at school or soon afterwards (cf e.g. **39** *Absence: An Ode*), they were probably not composed until later. **574** *First Advent of Love*, which accompanies the stanzas in MS 3, can be proved to have been written later. The fact that MS 1 dates from very close to when C's feelings for Mary Evans had been reawakened suggests that the stanzas may date from that time. Cf C's similar description of his feelings to RS in *CL* I 87–8 (13–15 Jul 1794).

B. TEXTS

1 [=RT]. PML (uncatalogued in Jul 1978) (R–V Autographs Misc). On one of two conjoint leaves, each 20.4×32.0 cm; no wm; chain-lines 2.5 cm. Transcript in the hand of Joseph Hucks.

The other poems on the two leaves are **70** *Lines on the "Man of Ross"* (dated 6 Jul 1794), **70.X1** *Adaptation of "I shall behold far off thy barren crest"* (dated

12 Jul 1794), **73.X1** *The Faded Flower* (borrowed from RS 10 Jul 1794), and also six lines, undated, in C's hand in pencil (**70.X2** *Fragmentary Adaptation of a Welsh Sonnet*)—the whole addressed to "Miss A Evans".

The two stanzas, untitled but numbered 15 and 16, fill up a page which contains **73.X1** *The Faded Flower*.

2. BM Add MS 35343 f 247^r. On one of two conjoint leaves, each 16.4× 20.7 cm; no wm; chain-lines 2.5 cm. Transcript of the second stanza only (unnumbered) in a letter to TP, 1 Feb 1801 (*CL* II 669).

C introduced the lines as a comment on the recently dead Mrs "Perdita" Robinson: "O Poole! that that Woman had but been married to a noble Being, what a noble Being she herself would have been. Latterly, she felt this with a poignant anguish.—Well!—"

3. Transcript of the second stanza only (unnumbered) in a memorandum headed "Relics of my School-boy Muse; i.e. fragments of poems composed before my fifteenth year." Signed "S.T.C. *Sept*. 1827."

Quoted in *The Poems of Samuel Taylor Coleridge* ed DC and SC (1852) 379. The original has not been recovered.

The fragment is described as "The concluding stanza of an Elegy on a Lady, who died in early youth". The other fragment C claimed to have written at school is "Love's First Hope" (**574** *First Advent of Love*). He also transcribed the much later fragment **593** *"Dewdrops are the Gems of Morning"*.

title. 3 Elegy on a Lady, who died in early youth:—

```
⁻1 1                 15
 1 1     On me her lingering gaze she seem'd to roll,
 2 1     And still she clasp'd me with convulsive throes;
 3 1     My sick heart dies within me & my soul
 4 1     Withers beneath th unutterable woes
         [Line-space]
⁻5 1                 16
 5 1     Oer the pilé'd earth the Gales of Evening sigh;
   2         her       grave              sighś;
   3         the raised earth              sigh;
 6 1     Blooms the white Daisy on its grassy slope—
   2     And flowers will grow upon
   3     And see a Daisy peeps upon its
 7 1     I wipe the starting anguish from mine Eye;
   2              dimming Water              eyes—
   3              waters                     eye;
 8 1 2 Een in the cold Grave dwells the Cherub Hope.—
   3       on                   lights
```

5. 2 3 O'er   2 pil'd   2 3 gales   2 3 evening   **6.** 2 Slope. • 3 slope!   **8.** 2 Ev'n • 3 Even   2 3 Hope!

6, 8. MS 3 indents.

73. IMITATED FROM THE WELSH

A. DATE

Jul 1794, or in the months following. Cf **70.X2** *Fragmentary Adaptation of a Welsh Sonnet*, which appears to have been jotted down while C was still in Wales and represents the beginning of such a poem as the present, developed imitation.

B. TEXTS

1 [=RT]. PML MA 1848 (11). Included in an als to RS, 11 Dec 1794 (*CL* I 137).

2. BPL B 22189=Estlin Copy Book f 11ᵛ. Transcript in C's hand.

1. Poems (1796).

2. Poems (1803).

3. PW (1828).

4. PW (1829).

5. PW (1834).

description/title. 1 . . . a little Song of mine, which has no other Merit than a pretty simplicity of silliness. • 2 Song. • *1* EFFUSION XXXI. I IMITATED I *FROM THE WELCH.* • *2–5* IMITATED I *FROM THE WELCH.*

The words in both ms texts and all five printed texts are identical; only punctuation and capitalization vary. The RT reproduces MS 1 exactly, except for:

4. *You.*] ms ǂ*You.*

description/title. *3–5* IMITATED FROM THE WELSH.   **1.** 2 If   *1–5* passion 2 impart   **3.** ⊠1 hand   ⊠1 heart—   **4.** *1–5* Feel   2 *you!* • *1–4 you!* • *5* you! **5.** ⊠1 no!   ⊠1 claim   **7.** *1–5* touch   2 Flame • *1–5* flame,   **8.** ⊠1 discover.

2, 4, 6, 8. Indented in all texts.

73.X1. THE FADED FLOWER

"The Faded Flower. | Ungrateful he, who pluck'd thee from thy stalk,". 14 lines. Pub—along with the letter by C to Henry Martin, 22 Jul 1794, in which C copied it out—as "A Letter from Wales by the Late S. T. Coleridge" *New Monthly Magazine* XLVII (Aug 1836) 420–4. Cf *CL* I 95. The original is now at the University of Kentucky Libraries, Lexington (Special Collections) W. Hugh Peal Collection. Included in *PW* (JDC) 31B–32A; *PW* (EHC) I 70–1.

The poem is by RS. There is a transcript in his hand, together with a sonnet dated Dec 1793 and "To a Frog", the whole signed "R. Southey | Balliol College | Oxford", in NYPL (Berg Collection). RS transcribed it as his own in a letter to Grosvenor Bedford of 20 Jul 1794 (Bodleian Library MS Eng lett c 22); the letter (only) is printed in *S Letters*—Curry—I 60–4. The poem was printed as by Bion in Robert Lovell and RS *Poems* (Bath 1795) 68—Bion being identified as RS on p viii of the Preface.

    The poem was borrowed by C during his Welsh tour because it struck a particularly responsive chord (cf *CN* I 15). Though he might at the time have misled two friends about its authorship, he never went so far as to claim it as his own. A fair copy and a more hurried transcript, both in Joseph Hucks's hand, are at PML (uncatalogued in Jul 1978; R–V Autographs Misc). Both are dated 10 Jul 1794, are subscribed "S.T.C.", and are on the same kind of paper; the fair copy is one of several in a ms which embodies C's corrections, addressed to "Miss A Evans". In the version C copied out for Henry Martin on 22 Jul he changed the name "Emma" in line 11 to "Abra". It was probably included to fill up space on the last page of the letter, following **70** *Lines on the "Man of Ross"*, and there is no claim to authorship.

    RS did not include the poem in later editions of his *Poems*, and C of course never did. The attribution to C by JDC and EHC rests on a misunderstanding of the version printed in the *New Monthly Magazine*, because they were not aware of the ms and printed versions over RS's name. The modifications in C's transcript are so very minor that he can hardly be said to have adapted it or to have collaborated in it.

73.X2. SONNET: TO AN INFANT
AT THE BREAST

M Post (25 Jul 1794): "*SONNET* | TO AN INFANT AT THE BREAST. | Dear, lovely Babe! equal in birth to all,". 14 lines. Signed "C."

Very tentatively suggested by Erdman et al "Unrecorded Coleridge Variants: Additions and Corrections" 238. More evidence would be required before it could be accepted.

74. LINES TO A BEAUTIFUL SPRING
IN A VILLAGE

A. DATE

Shortly before 21 Aug 1794. See vol I headnote.

B. TEXTS

1. BPL B 22189=Estlin Copy Book f 21^{r-v}.
There may well be a previous ms or published version which has not been traced. RS told Grosvenor Bedford on 21 Aug 1794 that the poem "will soon be published and you will see it then" (*S Letters*—Curry—I 69).

2. PML MA 1916=Quarto Copy Book ff 4^v–5^r. Transcript in C's hand.
This version appears to have served as copy for PR *1*, perhaps through an intermediate version. (If not, three corrections were made in proof.)

1 [=RT]. *Poems* (1796).
Rpt (var) *The Annual Register for 1796* XXXVIII (1800) 494–5.

2. *Poems* (1797).
C emended the text in RS's copy, now at Yale (In 678 797 Copy 1). Rpt (var) *Poetical Beauties of Modern Writers* (1798; 2nd ed 1803; etc) 40–1; *Beauties of British Poetry* ed Sidney Melmoth (Huddersfield 1801 etc) 119–20.

3. *Poems* (1803).

4. *PW* (1828).

5. *PW* (1829).
Rpt (var) *The Golden Lyre: Second Series* ed J. Macray (1830) [unpaginated].

6. *PW* (1834).

title. 1 Lines addressed to a ~~Forest~~ Spring in the Village of Kirkhompton near Bath. • 2 *1–6* Lines I To a beautiful Spring in a Village.

  1 □   Once more, sweet Stream! with slow foot wandering near
  2 □   I bless thy milky waters cold and clear:
  3 ⊠2 Escap'd the Flashing of the noontide hours
    2   flashings

4 □	With one fresh garland of Pierian Flowers	
5 □	(Ere from thy zephyr-haunted Brink I turn)	
6 □	My languid hand shall wreathe thy mossy Urn.	
	[Line-space]	
7 1	For not thro' pathless groves in murmurs rude	
2	grove ~~in~~ with murmur	
1–6	with	
8 □	Thou soothest the sad Wood nymph, Solitude:	
9 □	Nor thine unseen in cavern depths to well,	
10 □	The hermit fountain of some dripping cell—	
11 □	Pride of the Vale! thy useful streams supply	
12 ⊠2	The scatter'd Cots and peaceful Hamlet nigh!	
2	Cot	
13 □	The elfin tribe around thy friendly banks	
14 ⊠5	With infant Uproar and soul-soothing Pranks	
5	age	
15 ⊠2	(Releas'd from school, their little hearts at rest)	
2	Schools,	
16 □	Launch paper Navies on thy waveless Breast.	
	[Line-space]	
17 □	The Rustic here at Eve with pensive Look	
18 □	Whistling lorn Ditties leans upon his Crook;	
19 □	Or starting pauses with hope-mingled dread	
20 □	To list the much-lov'd Maid's accustom'd tread;	
20.1.1 1	And now essays his simple Faith to prove	
20.1.2 1	By all the soft Solicitude of Love.	
21 ⊠2	←——She,——→ vainly mindful of her Dame's command,	
2	~~She vain vain~~ She,	
22 □	Loiters, the long-fill'd Pitcher in her Hand.	
	[Line-space]	
23 □	Unboastful Stream! thy fount with pebbled falls	
24 □	The faded Form of past Delight recalls,	
25 □	What time the Morning Sun of Hope arose	
26 □	And all was Joy—save when another's Woes	
27 □	A transient gloom upon my soul imprest,	
28 1	Like ~~transient~~ passing Clouds impictur'd on thy breast!	
⊠1	←——passing——→	
28.1.1 1	But ah! too brief is ~~y~~Youth's enchanting reign,	
28.1.2 1	Ere Manhood wakes th' unweeting heart to pain.	
28.1.3 1	Silent & soft thy silver Waters glide:	
28.1.4 1	So glided Life, a smooth & equal Tide.	
28.1.5 1	Sad Change! for now by choking Cares withstood	
28.1.6 1	It hardly bursts its way, a turbid boist'rous Flood!	
29 2	~~How Then~~ Life's Current ?~~or~~ then ran sparkle~~ing~~ to the Noon	
1–6	←——Life's——→ then sparkling	
30 2	Or ~~silv'ry stole beneath the pensive Moon.~~ ~~smooth'd its silv'ry course~~	
	~~beneath~~ silver'd its smooth course beneath the Moon.	
1–6	Or silv'ry stole beneath the pensive Moon.	

31 2   Ah! now it ~~works creeps~~ works ~~the thorny brakes among,~~ rude brakes &

thorns among,

1–6 Ah! now it works rude brakes and thorns among,

32 ☒1   Or o'er the rough rock bursts and foams along.

title. *1* LINES | TO A | BEAUTIFUL SPRING | *IN A VILLAGE.* •
2 3 LINES | *TO A BEAUTIFUL SPRING* | IN A VILLAGE. •
4 5 LINES TO A BEAUTIFUL SPRING IN | A VILLAGE. • *6* LINES |
TO A BEAUTIFUL SPRING IN A VILLAGE.   **1.** 2 *1–3* wand'ring *3–*
6 near,   **2.** ☒1 clear.   **3.** *4–6* Escaped *1–6* flashing *3 6* hours,   **4.** *1–*
6 flowers   **5.** ☒1 brink   **6.** ☒1 wreath   ☒1 urn.   **7.** *4–6* through
8. 2 Wood- • *1–6* wood-   2 *Solitude:* • *1–3* SOLITUDE: • *4 5* SOLITUDE; •
6 Solitude;   **10.** 2 *1–5* HERMIT-FOUNTAIN • *6* hermit-fountain   2 Cell! • *1–*
6 cell!   **11.** 2 Streams   **12.** *4–6* scattered   *1–6* cots   *1–6* hamlet   ☒1 nigh.
13. 2 Tribe   **14.** ☒1 uproar   ☒1 pranks,   **15.** 2 *1–3* Releas'd • *4–6* Released
2 Hearts   ☒1 rest,   **16.** 2 ~~Laun~~ Launch   ☒1 navies   ☒1 breast.   **17.** *1–6* rustic
☒1 eve   ☒1 look   **18.** ☒1 ditties   ☒1 crook,   **20.** *4–6* -loved   *1–6* maid's
4–6 accustomed   2 Tread: • *1–6* tread: **21.** *1 2 4 6* dame's   2 Command,
22. *4–6* -filled   *1–6* pitcher   ☒1 hand.   **23.** *3* stream!   *1* Thy   **24.** ☒1 form
1–6 delight   **25.** ☒1 morning   *1–6* sun   ☒1 arose,   **26.** 2 Joy; • *1–6* joy;
2 Another's   ☒1 woes   **28.** *1–6* clouds   *4–6* impictured   ☒1 breast.   **29.** *1–*
6 current   *1–3* noon • *4–6* noon,   **30.** *4–6* silvery   *3–6* Moon: **32.** *1–6* along!

title. 1 Kirkhompton near Bath.] There is no such village. The deleted word "Forest"
reinforces other evidence on behalf of Chilcompton, where the spring rose in a "rich
woody vale" (John Collinson *The History of Somersetshire* —3 vols Bath 1791—II 126).
The mistake with the place-name might begin with the local pronunciation of it.

6⁺. No line-space in PR *2–6*. PR *1* has page-division (also at 22⁺), which is probably
why the divisions of the poem were lost.

11, 12. In RS's copy of PR *2* C emended "useful streams supply" to "social Bubblings
clear", and "nigh." to "near."

14. In RS's copy of PR *2* C emended "uproar and soul-soothing" to "shouts and
angel-guarded".

16⁺. No line-space in PR *2–6*.

22⁺. No line-space in PR *2–5*.

75. THE SIGH

A. DATE

Jun–Sept 1794. If the poem was written in Jun 1794 (as TEXTS 4 *1–6* state), it
must have been written after 15 Jun, in the weeks at Oxford when pantisocracy
was born. Internal evidence makes it more likely that it was written after 13
Jul, when C saw Mary Evans at Wrexham; or even later, at a time when C was
regretting the understanding he had come to with Sara Fricker. CL says that he

thought of it as a Salutation and Cat poem, i.e. associated with autumn 1794 (*LL*—M—I 18). The date appended to all published versions had to be before August, when C's understanding with his future wife was formed.

B. TEXTS

1. PML MA 1848 (9). Single folded leaf, 58.0×45.5 cm; no wm; chain-lines 2.5 cm. Subscribed "S.T.C." Transcribed in an als to RS, 3 Nov 1794 (*CL* I 124).

2. Pforzheimer MS Misc 83. Recto only of two leaves, each 11.4×18.5 cm; wm BUTTANSHAW; chain-lines 2.7 cm. Transcript in C's hand (the attribution is not absolutely certain).

Two lines are written in pencil on the verso of the second leaf:

> Why are you wandering here I pray.—
> I will na halt in sith attire—

The other leaves in the same set contain **70** *Lines on the "Man of Ross"* and **78.X3** *On Bala Hill.*

3. BPL B 22189=Estlin Copy Book ff 24^v–25^r. Transcript in C's hand.

4. HRC MS (Coleridge, S T) Works B. Single leaf, 20×32 cm; wm G P&J; chain-lines 2.5 cm. Bound into Rugby Manuscript p 55/f 24^r. Transcript in C's hand, intended as copy for PR *1* below.

1 [=RT]. *Poems* (1796).
The transcript in JTC's Commonplace Book (University of Pennsylvania Library (Special Collections) MS Eng 13 p 90) has no textual significance. Nor have the reprintings in *The Universal Magazine* XCIX (Apr 1796) 282 and *The Weekly Entertainer* (Sherborne) XXVII (20 Jun 1796) 500.

2. Poems (1797).
RS's copy, now at Yale (In 678 797 copy 1) contains a correction in C's hand. Rpt *Poetical Beauties of Modern Writers* (1798; 2nd ed 1803; etc) 35–6; *Beauties of British Poetry* ed Sidney Melmoth (Huddersfield 1801) 167–8.

3. Poems (1803).
Rpt *The Poetical Album* ed Alaric A. Watts (1828) 252.

4. PW (1828).

5. PW (1829).

6. PW (1834).

C. GENERAL NOTE

The poem was set to music by William Carnaby some time before 1802: see
the Advertisement on p 6 of his setting of "Hear sweet Spirit!", *Invocation to a
Spirit* (London: C. Mitchell for the Author, May 1802) (=**66** *Domestic Peace*).

title. 1 2 Song • 3 Ode • 4 Effusion 3~~42~~ ~~June, 1794~~ I *The Sigh.* • *1* EFFUSION
XXXII. I *THE SIGH.* • *2–6 THE SIGH.*

⁻1	1 *3*	1
1	□	When Youth his faery reign began,
2	⊠4	Ere Sorrow had proclaim'd me—Man;
	4	proclaim'd
3	□	While Peace the *present* Hour beguil'd,
4	□	And all the lovely *Prospect* smil'd;
5	□	Then, Mary! mid my lightsome glee
6	⌐	I heav'd the painless sigh for thee!
		[*Line-space*]
⁻7	1 *3*	2
7	1–3	And when along the wilds of Woe
	4	~~along~~ when waves
	1 2 4–6	when,
	3	as toss'd on
8	□	My harrass'd Heart was doom'd to know
9	⊠*3*	The frantic burst of Outrage keen,
	3	the
10	□	And the slow Pang that gnaws unseen;
11	□	Then shipwreck'd on Life's stormy Sea
12	□	I heav'd an anguish'd Sigh for thee!
		[*Line-space*]
⁻13	1 *3*	3
13	1–3	But soon Reflection's hand imprest
	4	ℏpower
	1–6	power
14	□	A stiller sadness on my breast;
15	⊠2	And sickly Hope with waning Eye
	2	?~~Eyes~~ Eye
16	□	Was well content to droop and die!
17	□	I yielded to the stern Decree,
18	1	Yet heav'd the languid Sigh for thee!
	⊠1	a
		[*Line-space*]
⁻19	1 *3*	4
19	□	And though in distant climes to roam
20	□	A Wanderer from my native home
21	1	I fain would woo a gentle Fair
	2 3	soothe the aching Care
	4 *1–6*	sense of

22	1	To soothe the aching sense of Care,
	⊠1	And lull to sleep the Joys that were!—
23	1	Thy Image may not banish'd be*é*—
	⊠1	be—
24	☐	Still, Mary! still I sigh for thee!
24⁺	4 *1–6*	June, 1794.

title. 2 *Song* • *4–6* THE SIGH.   ⁻**1.** *3* I.   **1.** 3 fairy   2 Reign   ⊠1 *3* began
2. *6* sorrow   *4–6* proclaimed   2 3 *1–6* me   2 3 Man, • 4 *1–6* man;   **3.** *1–
6* present   3 4 *1–6* hour   2 3 beguil'd • *4–6* beguiled,   **4.** *1–6* Prospect
2 3 smil'd— • *4–6* smiled;   **5.** *5 6* Then   4 *1–5* MARY!   2 *1–6* 'mid
2 Glee   **6.** *4* heaved   2 3 *6* Sigh • 4 *1–5* SIGH   4 Thee! • *2–6* thee.   ⁻**7.** *3* II.
7. 3 woe • *1–6* woe,   **8.** 4 hararass'd • *1 2* harass'd • *4–6* harassed   *4–6* doomed
4 know?   **9.** 2 4 *1 2 4 5* Burst • *3* Burst,   2 4 keen   **10.** 4 Pang,   2 3 unseen—
11. *4–6* shipwrecked   *1–6* sea   **12.** *4–6* heaved   *4–6* anguished   4 *1–5* SIGH
4 Thee!   ⁻**13.** *3* III.   **14.** 2 Breast; • 3 breast,   **15.** *5 6* hope   4 *1–6* eye
16. 2 droop—   2 die!— • 3 die— • 4 *1–6* die: **17.** 2 Decree • 4 *1–6* decree,
18. *4–6* heaved   4 *1–5* SIGH   4 Thee!   ⁻**19.** *3* IV.   **19.** 2–4 *1–3* tho'
3 4 Climes   *1–6* roam,   **20.** *4–6* wanderer   2 Home • *1–6* home,   **21.** 4 *1–
5* sooth   4 6 Care,   **22.** 3 4 *1–3* Joys,   4 *1–5* were! • *6* were,   **23.** *4–6* banished
3 be,   **24.** 4 *1–5* MARY!   4 *1–5* SIGH   4 Thee. • *1–6* thee.   **24⁺.** *1–3 JUNE,* •
4–6 June,

⁻**1,** ⁻**7,** ⁻**13,** ⁻**19.** The stanzas are numbered only in MS 1 and PR *3*; there are rules
between stanzas in MS 2. The text is printed continuously, without line-spaces, in PR *2 4*.
C marked line-spaces and inserted numbers into Charles Lloyd's copy of PR *2*.
    15. MS 3 Hope] Written larger, perhaps to be read as bold.

76. THE KISS

A. DATE

Aug 1794? See vol I headnote. Though the lines have something in common
with those addressed to Fanny Nesbitt the previous summer, Ann Bacon's tran-
script is from PR *2* below, and significantly not from some previous ms.

B. TEXTS

1. BPL B 22189 = Estlin Copy Book f 10ʳ⁻ᵛ. Transcript in C's hand.
    There is probably a previous ms (or published version) which has not been
traced, or which is no longer extant.

2. PML MA 1916 = Quarto Copy Book f 8ʳ. Transcript of a reworked portion
of lines 9–19 in C's hand.
    Folio 8ʳ is a half-leaf of the same paper as the rest of the Quarto Copy Book,

tipped in to the first of the stubs where thirty-nine leaves have been removed. It is clear that a line or more of deleted verse preceded, since some of the downstrokes indicating deletion have carried on to this surviving portion of the leaf. The verso contains part of **55** *Imitated from Ossian*.

1 [=RT]. *Poems* (1796).

2. Poems (1797).
Transcribed (var) by Ann Frances Bacon in her Commonplace Book ff 23ᵛ–24ʳ (VCL uncatalogued in 1978); this transcript has no textual significance. Rpt *Poetical Beauties of Modern Writers* (1798; 2nd ed 1803; etc.) 37–8; *Beauties of British Poetry* ed Sidney Melmoth (Huddersfield 1801 etc) 201–2.

3. Poems (1803).
Rpt *The Lyre of Love* (2 vols 1806) II 118–19.

4. PW (1828).

5. PW (1829).

6. PW (1834).

title. 1 Ode • *1* EFFUSION XXVIII. • *2 4–6 THE KISS.* • *3 TO SARA.*

1	☒2	One kiss, dear Maid! I said & sigh'd—
2	☒2	Your scorn the little Boon deny'd.
3	☒2	Ah! why refuse the blameless Bliss?
4	☒2	Can Danger lurk within a kiss?
		[*Line-space*]
5	☒2	Yon viewless Wanderer of the Vale,
6	☒2	The Spirit of the Western Gale,
7	☒2	At Morning's break, at Evening's close
8	☒2	Inhales the sweetness of the Rose,
9	☐	And hovers o'er th' uninjur'd Bloom
10	☐	Sighing back the soft Perfume.
11.1	2	~~Vigor to on~~ o'er ⟨on o'er⟩ ~~his languid wing~~ the ZEPHYR'S ~~wing~~ fling
12.1	2	~~The Roses fragrant~~ Her nectar-breathing KISSES ~~bring~~ fling
13.1	2	And He o'er all ~~her brighten'd Hue the~~ Glitters of the Dew
14.1	2	Shed ~~the Glitter of the Dew.~~ on the ROSE's brighten'd Hue.
		Earthward ~~she bends~~ hangs her bashful head,
15.1	2	~~And darts~~ a Blush of deeper Red!
11	1	Vigor to his languid Wing
	2	Vigor ~~o'er~~ to the ZEPHYR's wing
	1–6	to
12	1	The Rose's fragrant kisses bring;
	☒1	Her nectar-breathing KISSES fling,
13	1	And He o'er all her brighten'd Hue
	2	And He the Glitter of the Dews
	1–6	Dew

14 1   Flings the Glitter of the Dew.

      2   Scatters on the ROSE's Hue~~s~~.

    1–6   hue.

15 1   See! she bends her bashful head,

      2   ~~To Earth she han~~

    ⊠1   Bashful lo! she bends her head,

16 □   And darts a Blush of deeper Red!

         [*Line-space*]

17 □   Too well those lovely Lips disclose

18 1   The fragrant Triumphs of the Rose:

    ⊠1   triumphs of the op'ning

19 □   O fair! O graceful! bid them prove

20 ⊠2   As passive to the Breath of Love!

         [*Line-space*]

21 ⊠2   In tender accents faint & low

22 ⊠2   Well-pleas'd I hear the whisper'd, "No"!

23 ⊠2   The whisper'd, "No"! how little meant—

24 ⊠2   Sweet Falsehood, that endears Consent!

25 ⊠2   For on those lovely Lips the while

26 1   Dawn'd the soft relenting Smile,

    1–6   Dawns

27 1   That tempts with feign'd Dissuasion coy

    1–6   And

28 ⊠2   The gentle Violence of Joy!

title. PR *4–6* THE KISS.   **1.** *6* maid!   *1–6* and   *4–6* sighed—   **2.** *1–6* boon   *1 2 4–6* denied.   **3.** *1–6* Ah   *1–6* bliss?   **4.** *1 2 4–6* danger   **5.** *1–3* Wand'rer   *1–6* vale,   **6.** *1–5* SPIRIT   **7.** *3* close,   **8.** *1–5* ROSE,   **9.** *4–6* the uninjured   **10.** *1–6* perfume.   **11.** *4–6* Vigour   *1–6* Zephyr's   **12.** *6* Kisses   *1–6* fling;   **13.** *1–6* glitter   **14.** *6* Rose's   **16.** *1–6* blush   **17.** *1–6* lips   **18.** *1–5* Triumphs   *4–6* opening Rose;   **19.** *2* 6O   **20.** *1–6* breath   *1–6* Love.   **21.** *1–6* accents,   *1–6* and low,   **22.** *4–6* -pleased   *1–3* whisper'd • *4–6* whispered   *1–6* "No!"   **23.** *1–3* whisper'd • *4–6* whispered   *1–6* "No"—   *1–6* meant!   **24.** *4–6* Falsehood   **25.** *1–6* lips   **26.** *1–6* smile,   **27.** *4–6* feigned   *1–6* dissuasion   **28.** *1–6* violence   *1 2 4–6* Joy. • *3* joy.

title. The change in PR *3* was brought about by CL's objection that the PR *2* title confused the poem with **57** *Cupid Turn'd Chymist*—in PR *2* entitled "*The COMPOSI-TION of a KISS*"—which immediately preceded it in the same volume (*LL*—M—II 111). The revival of the old title in PR *4–6* followed the omission of poem **57**.

10, 14, 16. Indented in MS 1.

11.1–15.1. The much-revised draft in MS 2 is cancelled with diagonal lines and a clearer draft written alongside.

20⁺. No line-space in PR *1–6*. Given the tangled state of the text C might have submitted (MS 2), this may be a mistake introduced by Joseph Cottle and subsequently unnoticed by C.

76.X1. THE FALL OF ROBESPIERRE

(with Robert Southey)

DATE
Aug–Sept 1794.

See vol III.

77. TWO VERSIONS OF AN EPITAPH
ON AN INFANT

A. DATE

Version (*a*) dates from before Sept 1794. C spoke of the poem as "very youthful" to William Rowan Hamilton, at their meeting in Mar 1832, and dated it a year or so "(or some such period)" before **388** *Time, Real and Imaginary* (R. P. Graves *Life of Sir William Rowan Hamilton*—3 vols Dublin 1882–91—I 540–1), which he thought of as a Christ's Hospital poem, though the written versions are later in date. On the other hand, on this late occasion C was clearly intent on deprecating the present poem. However, it might well date from any time between 1789 and 1794. All the texts below, except MS 3, are of this version.

Version (*b*) was extemporised on one of the two occasions when Hamilton visited C, i.e. on 20 or 23 Mar 1832. See MS 3 below.

B. TEXTS

1. M Chron (23 Sept 1794). Unsigned.

1 [=RT(a)]. BPL B 22189=Estlin Copy Book f 15^r (where it follows **40** *Greek Epitaph on an Infant*). Transcript in C's hand.

2. PML MA 1916=Quarto Copy Book f 5^r. Transcript in C's hand.
This appears to have served as copy for PR 2 below, perhaps through an intermediate version.

2. Poems (1796).

3. The Watchman IX (5 May 1796) 270 (*CC*) 316. Signed "S.T.C."

4. Poems (1797).
In RS's copy (Yale In 678 797 Copy 1) the poem is followed by **448** *Another Epitaph on an Infant*, in two stanzas copied in C's hand, dating from Apr 1809 (?).

5. *Poems* (1803).

6. *PW* (1828).

7. *PW* (1829).

3 [=RT(b)]. Alternative version (*b*) transcribed by William Rowan Hamilton. Graves *Life of Sir William Rowan Hamilton* I 540.

Hamilton, on behalf of Lady De Vere, asked C for a copy of the poem in its author's handwriting. C forwarded the lines with a letter to Hamilton in Mar 1832 (*CL* VI 893–4), but spoke slightingly of the poem when Hamilton visited him. "He extemporised an altered set of lines, on the same subject, of which I have just found a pencilled note in shorthand, and shall translate and transcribe it here."

8. *PW* (1834).

C. GENERAL NOTE

The transcript of version (*a*) by JTC in his Commonplace Book p 3 (University of Pennsylvania (Special Collections) MS Eng 13) could be from several of the texts above (probably PR 5), and has no textual significance. This is also true of the reprintings of (*a*) in *Elegant Selections, in Prose and Verse* (Doncaster 1801) 3; *The Weekly Entertainer* (Sherborne) (26 Jul 1802) 80; *Felix Farley's Bristol Journal* (7 Apr 1804) 4; *A Selection of Poems . . .* ed Joseph Cottle (1804) 168 (new eds 1815, 1823, 1836); *The Words of the Most Favourite Pieces, Performed at the Glee Club, the Catch Club, and Other Public Societies* comp Richard Clark (1814) 79, where the unsigned words are given as a glee for three voices by William Linley; *The Poetical Album* ed Alaric A. Watts (1828) 131; etc.

The unsigned reprinting of (*a*) in *The Bath Herald* (8 Sept 1804) is entitled "ON A CHILD. | (IN A COUNTRY CHURCH-YARD IN NORFOLK)". This casts a faint shadow of doubt over C's authorship, but it should be borne in mind that the same newspaper carried **212** *The British Stripling's War-song* on 21 Apr 1804, and poems by WW and RS during the same period (24 Nov 1804, 16 Mar 1805, 6 Apr 1805).

title. *1–8* EPITAPH, | ON AN INFANT. • 1 Epitaph on an Infant | (First published in the Morning Chronicle) • 2 ~~On a~~ Epitaph on an Infant.

(*a*) **1** ⊠3 Ere Sin could blight, or Sorrow fade,
(*a*) **2** ⊠3 Death came, with friendly care:
(*a*) **3** ⊠3 The op'ning Bud to Heav'n convey'd—
(*a*) **4** ⊠3 And bade it blossom there.

(*b*) **1** 3 This lovely bud, so young, so fair,
(*b*) **2** 3 Called hence by early doom,
(*b*) **3** 3 Just came to show how sweet a flower

(*b*) **4** 3   In paradise would bloom.

title. *2* EPITAPH | ON | AN INFANT. • *4 EPITAPH* | ON | *AN INFANT.* •
5 EPITAPH | ON | *AN INFANT.* • *6–8* EPITAPH ON AN INFANT.
1. 1 2 2 *4–8* blight   **2.** *2* D EATH   1 2 2*–8* came   1 Care; • 2 2*–8* care;
3. 1 2 2*–8* opening   2 *4–8* bud   1 2 2*–8* Heaven   1 *3 8* conveyed, • 2 2 *4 5* con-
vey'd • *6 7* conveyed   **4.** *3* Blossom   1 *3* there!

(*a*) **2,** (*a*) **4,** (*b*) **2,** (*b*) **4.** Indented in all texts.

77.X1. THE TRIUMPHS OF THE NEW CABINET

M Chron (4 Sept 1794): "THE TRIUMPHS OF THE NEW CABINET, |
AN ODE. | ADDRESSED TO THE DUKE OF PORTLAND. | The
polish'd Greeks, renown'd in fame,". 12 6-line stanzas. Unsigned.

Included without explanation by T. J. Wise in *Coleridgeiana: Being a Supple-
ment to The Bibliography of Coleridge* (1919) 32–4; cited but not collated by
Erdman et al "Unrecorded Coleridge Variants: Additions and Corrections" 148.
Evidence would be required before the poem could be accepted.

78. SONNET ON PANTISOCRACY
(with Samuel Favell)

A. DATE

Sept 1794. See vol I headnote, which also comments on the extent of C's
collaboration with Samuel Favell.

B. TEXTS

1. PML MA 1848 (4). Single folded leaf, 40.0×30.5 cm overall; wm Britan-
nia in round frame surmounted by crown | E&P; chain-lines 2.7 cm. Included
in an als to RS, 18 Sept 1794 (*CL* I 104).

2. BM Add MS 30927 f 4ᵛ. Final verso of two conjoint leaves, each 20.7×
31.8 cm; wm Britannia in oval, surmounted by crown; countermark GR; chain-
lines 2.5 cm. Transcript by RS in a letter to his brother Thomas, 19 Oct 1794 (*S*

Life—CS—I 224—with changes of punctuation, and misreadings in lines 8, 10, and 14).

The status of this transcript is uncertain. RS may be transcribing MS 1, with his own improvements, or he may be transcribing another ms text, perhaps given him by Favell.

3 [=RT]. BPL B 22189 = Estlin Copy Book f 24^r. Transcript in C's hand.

description/title. 2 you may perhaps like this sonnet on the subject of our emigration by Favell. • 3 Sonnet

1   1 2   No more my Visionary Soul shall dwell
   3   the
2   ☐   On Joys, that were! No more endure to weigh
3   ☐   The Shame and Anguish of the evil Day,
4   ☐   Wisely forgetful! O'er th Ocean swell
5   ☐   Sublime of Hope I seek the cottag'd Dell,
6   ☐   Where Virtue calm with careless step may stray,
7   ☐   And dancing to the moonlight Roundelay
8   ☐   The Wizard Passions weave an holy Spell.
9   1 3   Eyes that have ach'd with Sorrow! ye shall weep
   2   anguish!
10   1   Tears of doubt-mingled Joy, like their's who start
   2   as
   3   they,
11   ☐   From Precipices of distemper'd Sleep,
12   1 2   On which the fierce-eyed Fiends their Revels keep,
   3   revel
13   ☐   And see the rising Sun, & feel it dart
14   ☐   New Rays of Pleasance trembling to the Heart.

1. 2 3 visionary   2 soul   **2.** 2 joys   2 were.   2 3 no   **3.** 2 shame & anguish
2 day,   **4.** 2 o'er   2 3 the   2 ocean swell, • 3 Ocean Swell   **5.** 2 Hope,
2 cottaged dell   **6.** 3 stray   **7.** 2 roundelay   **8.** 2 3 wizard   2 passions
2 3 spell.   **9.** 3 Eyes,   2 ached • 3 ak'd   3 sorrow! Ye   **10.** 2 joy— •
3 Joy—   2 theirs   **11.** 2 3 precipices   2 distemperd sleep • 3 distemper'd Sleep
12. 2 fiends   2 revels   **13.** 2 sun—& • 3 Sun and   **14.** 2 3 rays   2 Pleasance—
2 heart.

78.X1. SONNET: ON ESTABLISHING
PANTISOCRACY IN AMERICA

The Co-operative Magazine and Monthly Herald I (4) (Apr 1826) 133: "SON-NET, | *On the Prospect of establishing a Pantisocracy in America* | Whil'st pale anxiety, corrosive care,". 14 lines. Unsigned; dated "*Sept.* 1794."

The sonnet was contributed by "AN OLD DISCIPLE OF CO-OPERATION." in a letter to the magazine dated "*London, March* 6, 1826." It is included in *PW* (EHC) I 69, but is unlikely to be by C; cf also Woodring 69. If the author of the poem was the author of the letter, the pantisocrat alive and living in London in 1826 is likely to have been George Dyer (1755–1841). Educated at Christ's Hospital, he had come to know C's subsequent mentor, William Frend, at Cambridge in the 1780s. His book *Complaints of the Poor People of England* was published in 1793, he was a Unitarian, and he had been excited by pantisocracy (see *CL* I 97–8: to RS [1 Sept 1794]). C was in his mind in the mid-1820s: he presented him with a copy of his two-volume *Privileges of the University of Cambridge* in 1824, and afterwards with a copy of his *Academic Unity* (1827): *CM* (*CC*) VI Appendix of Marked Books.

78.X2. REVISIONS TO VARIOUS
EARLY POEMS BY ROBERT SOUTHEY

A. DATES

(*a*) Sept–Dec 1794; (*b*) early May 1795; (*c*) Oct–Dec 1796 and Jul 1797; and probably at other times.

B. TEXTS

(*a*)

C made extensive revisions to the poems RS sent him during Sept–Dec 1794 (*CL* I 103–4: to RS 18 Sept 1794; 134–5: to RS [11 Dec 1794]; 138–40: to RS 17 Dec 1794; 146: to RS [29 Dec 1794]). The most radical were to three poems: *The Pauper's Funeral, To the Chapel Bell,* and the sonnet "With wayworn feet"; but since RS's original versions have not survived, the extent of C's rewriting cannot be measured exactly.

C revised *The Pauper's Funeral* in a way that required him to copy out the complete poem again in its different form (*CL* I 134; the original is in PML MA

1848 (11)). RS published the revised version in his *Poems* (Bristol 1797) 47–8; 2nd ed (Bristol 1797) 143–4; etc. Though C's letter is dated 11 Dec 1794, RS afterwards dated the poem 1795: see *Poetical Works* (14 vols 1814–18) XI 228 and *Poetical Works* (10 vols 1837–8) II 217.

In *To the Chapel Bell* C altered two lines in the first stanza, cancelled another stanza altogether, and rewrote five lines in the last stanza (*CL* I 135; the ms revisions—in PML MA 1848 (11)—differ in some matters of detail). Most of the revisions were adopted in the version RS printed in *Poems* (Bristol 1797) 149–51; 2nd ed (Bristol 1797) 84–6; etc. In later collections—*Poetical Works* (1815) XI 173 and *Poetical Works* (1837–8) II 144—the poem is dated 1793.

In his letter to RS written some two weeks later C rewrote entirely the sonnet "With wayworn feet" (*CL* I 146; the original is in PML MA 1848 (13)). It was reprinted thus—with changes only in lines 2 ("road" for "Steep") and 13 ("'Mid" for "With")—in the unnumbered preliminary pages of RS's *Poems* (Bristol 1797); 2nd ed (Bristol 1797); etc. When the poem was collected in *Poetical Works* (1815) XI ix and *Poetical Works* (1837–8) II xix, many further changes were made and the date 1796 was appended. It is not known whether the 1815 and later versions constitute a reversion to RS's original or further, later improvements.

(b)

C's contribution in early May 1795 of the third of the four stanzas which make up RS's dactylics *The Soldier's Wife*, published in RS's *Poems* (Bristol 1797 etc) is collated separately as poem **106** below.

(c)

In Oct–Nov 1796 C revised four sonnets by RS in his collection of *Sonnets from Various Authors*. The sonnets were "With many a weary step" (No 2), "Hard by the road,' (No 15), "Oh he is worn with toil!" (No 16), and "Mild arch of promise!" (No 19). C perhaps saw the originals as they went to press, and was possibly shown them by Joseph Cottle rather than RS. His revisions involve one or two words apiece in three of the four sonnets, as well as changes of punctuation and capitalisation. None of the revisions appeared in RS's *Poems* (Bristol 1797) or subsequent editions. Details are given in vol I annex B 2.

When RS's 1797 *Poems* became available in Dec 1796, C sent RS a list of "faults" (*CL* I 290–2: [27 Dec 1796]). C suggested the cancellation of the last stanza of *To the Genius of Africa* and of the last four lines of *To my Own Miniature Picture*—both of which suggestions RS adopted in the second edition, published by Cottle during the late summer of 1797. RS ignored C's other suggestions, concerning individual lines in *To Contemplation* and *Musings on a Landscape by Gaspar Poussin*. He also ignored C's more extensive revisions of *Hymn to the Penates*.

C sent a suggestion concerning *Mary, Maid of the Inn* in Jul 1797 (*CL* I 333–

4: to RS [c 17 Jul 1797]). It arrived after the first edition had been exhausted, but apparently too late to be incorporated in the second edition. RS did incorporate it in the fifth edition (London 1808).

Whether or not RS's greater selectivity in accepting C's revisions after their quarrel in Aug–Sept 1795 is on personal or on literary grounds is an open question.

78.X3. ON BALA HILL

"On Bala Hill. | With many a weary step at length I gain". 14 lines.

First published as C's in *PW* (JDC) 33B, 571B from an unsigned autograph ms among the Morrison–Evans papers (now Pforzheimer Misc 83); included in *PW* (EHC) I 56–7. However, the poem was published (var) as sonnet VIII in RS *Poems* (Bristol 1797) 114, and C previously referred to it as RS's in a letter to him dated 18 Sept 1794 (*CL* I 103). It would appear that RS sent the poem to C with a number of others early in Sept 1794, and that C substituted "Bala" for RS's "Lansdown", made a few other changes (noted by EHC), and then sent a copy to Mary Evans. It should be noted that C did not actually claim the poem as his own, although Mary Evans might have received and preserved it as such; also that, even after the revisions, RS's falling leaves and autumnal weather are allowed to remain in a poem supposedly composed in early July.

79. TO ANN BRUNTON: IMITATED FROM THE LATIN OF FRANCIS WRANGHAM

A. DATE

18–26 Sept 1794. Ipswich Fair, at which the Bruntons appeared with the Norwich Company, was proclaimed on 18 Sept, the day after C returned to Cambridge (Henry Gunning *Reminiscences of the University, Town and County of Cambridge, from the Year 1780*—2 vols 1854—I 172–3; *CL* I 105: to RS 19 Sept 1794).

B. TEXT

University of Kentucky Libraries, Lexington (Special Collections) W. Hugh Peal Collection. Leaves 20.5×32.0 cm, folded; wm present but difficult to decipher; chain-lines 2.7 cm. Transcribed in an als to Francis Wrangham, 26 Sept 1794 (*CL* I 107–9).

C's transcript is of the original he sent to Eliza Brunton on Wrangham's behalf, which has not survived. It has been marked up and emended by Wrangham, so as to provide copy for his *Poems* (1795). The changes are mainly of punctuation and capitalisation, though a few words are also changed. These alterations have no authority and are not recorded.

C's version faces Wrangham's original on pp 79, 81, and 83 of the printed volume. It is headed "TRANSLATED I BY A FRIEND.", and C is identified by name in the Advertisement (p v). Despite the date on the title-page of the printed volume, it is made up of sheets dated 1795, 1797, and 1801, and appears to have been issued in 1802. There is no evidence that C knew that his version had been published here or in Wrangham's *Works* (3 vols 1816) III 471, 473, and these printed versions are not recorded here.

It is worth mentioning that the translation of Wrangham's French stanzas, in *Poems* (1795) 106–11, was by WW, and that WW and Wrangham planned a joint volume of satirical pieces at about this time. In *Works* (1816) C is described as "B.A.", and it is noted that "The Rev. A. H. Trollope also, now of Christ's Hospital, honoured these lines with an elegiac version in blank verse."

The RT reproduces the ms exactly, except for:

title. ms To Miss Brunton (now Mrs Merry) I on her departure from Cambridge—Oct. 1790 I (Imitated from the Latin of the reverend F. Wrangham)   **3.** Praise] ms **Praise** **5.** Pity] ms **Pity**   **7.** thy] ms ~~her~~ thy   **14.** Loves] ms **Loves**   **16.** Passions] ms **Passions**   **19.** from] ms ~~o'er~~ from   **28.** same!"] ms same"!

3, 5, 14, 16. The four words written larger (see above) may have been meant to be printed bold, but this is not certain.

80. TO ELIZA BRUNTON, ON
BEHALF OF FRANCIS WRANGHAM

A. DATE

20–6 Sept. See **79** *To Ann Brunton* VAR SEC A.

B. TEXT

University of Kentucky Libraries, Lexington (Special Collections) W. Hugh Peal Collection. Leaves 20.5×32.0 cm, folded; wm present but difficult to decipher; chain-lines 2.7 cm. Transcribed in an als to Francis Wrangham, 26 Sept 1794 (*CL* I 108–9).

C's transcript is of the original he sent to Eliza Brunton, on Wrangham's behalf, which has not survived. It has been marked up and emended by Wrangham in a way similar to poem **79**, which it follows in the ms. It was published in Wrangham's *Poems* (1795) 83n (though not in his 1816 *Works*), but this text has no authority.

The RT reproduces the untitled ms exactly. C follows his imitation with an explanation: "I prefixed to it the following poemation—which is very pretty, but rather silly or so."

81. TO A YOUNG LADY, WITH A POEM ON THE FRENCH REVOLUTION

A. DATE

Sept–Oct 1794. PR *3 4* append the date "*September*, 1794." The copy of **76.X1** *The Fall of Robespierre* in which the lines were inscribed must have been given to the young lady, Ann Brunton, after 27 Sept, when the book finished printing, and before 8 Oct, when she left the vicinity of Cambridge. PR *5–7* append the date "September, 1792.", which appears to be a mistake—though the poem incorporates earlier verses and describes events which took place at the earlier time. The earlier date positions the poem well before C met his future wife and also before line 25 could bear a regicidal meaning (see EC).

B. TEXTS

1. PML MA 1848 (7). Two folded leaves, the first 58×45 cm and the second 36.9×22.3 cm (overall dimensions). First leaf: no wm; chain-lines 2.7 cm. Second leaf: wm BUTTANSHAW; chain-lines 2.5 cm. Signed "S.T.C. | Jes. Coll. Cambridge". Transcript in an als to RS, 21 Oct 1794 (*CL* I 117–18).

2. BPL B 22189=Estlin Copy Book ff 22ᵛ–23ᵛ. Transcript in C's hand.

1. The Watchman I (1 Mar 1796) 15–16 (*CC*) 27–9.
Watchman I exists in two issues, the second of which includes a correction to line 5 (insertion of "by").

3. PML MA 1916=Quarto Copy Book ff 6ᵛ–7ᵛ. Transcript in C's hand. Folio 7ᵛ is reproduced in *Watchman* (*CC*) facing p 28.

4. HRC MS (Coleridge, S T) Works B. Verso of a single leaf, 19.6×32.6 cm; wm Britannia in large oval surmounted by crown; chain-lines 2.6 cm. Bound into Rugby Manuscript p 34/f 13ᵛ. Transcript in C's hand of the notes, intended

as copy for PR 2 below. (The transcript was made after printed pages were available.)

2*. C's note on line 10 as it appears in the two extant proof copies of PR 2: (*a*) MH's copy in the Alexander Turnbull Library, Wellington, New Zealand (R Eng COLE Poems (1796)); and (*b*) Joseph Cottle's in the BM (Ashley 408) (*JDC facsimile* 69). (*b*) has a minor correction in C's hand.

2. *Poems* (1796).

3 [=RT]. *Poems* (1797).

4. *Poems* (1803).

5. *PW* (1828).

6. *PW* (1829).

7. *PW* (1834).

description/title. 1 I presented a Copy to Miss Brunton with these Verses in the blank Leaf.— • 2 Verses addressed to a Lady with a poem relative to a recent Event in the French Revolution. • *1* TO A YOUNG LADY, I *WITH A POEM ON THE FRENCH REVOLUTION.* • 3 ~~Lines addressed t~~To a young Lady together with a Poem on the French Revolution. • *2–7* TO A I YOUNG LADY I WITH I A POEM I ON I *THE FRENCH REVOLUTION.*

NB. The symbol □ excludes TEXTS 4 2* in the following collation.

1 □	Much on my early Youth I love to dwell	
2 1 2	Ere yet I bade that guardian Dome farewell,	
⊠1 2	friendly	
3 ⊠2	Where first beneath the echoing Cloysters pale	
2	its	
4 □	I heard of Guilt, and wonder'd at the tale!	
5 ⊠2 *1*	Yet, tho' the hours flew by on careless wing,	
2	rosy	
1	flew	
6 □	Full heavily of Sorrow would I sing.	
7 □	Aye as the Star of Evening flung its beam	
8 □	In broken Radiance on the wavy stream,	
9 1	My pensive Soul amid the twilight gloom	
⊠1	soul amid the pensive	
10 □	Mourn'd with the Breeze, O Leé Bo! o'er thy tomb.	
10fn *1*	LEE BOO, son of ABBA THULE, chief of the Pelew Islands. He came over to England with Captain Wilson, died of the small pox, and is buried in Greenwich Church-yard.	
4 2* *2–7*	LEE BOO, the Son of Abba Thule, Prince of the Pelew Islands came over to England with Captain Wilson, died of the small-pox, and ~~was~~ is buried in Grenwich Church-yard. See Keate's Account.	
11 □	Where'er I wander'd, Pity still was near,	

12	1	Breath'd from the Heart, and glitter'd in the tear:
	⊠1	glisten'd
13	1 2	No knell, that toll'd, but fill'd my anguish'd Eye,
	⊠1 2	anxious
14	□	"And suffering Nature wept that *one* should die"!
14fn	3	Put as a note the fourteenth Line of this Poem these Lines.

But When eager patriots fly the news to spread
Of glorious conquest and of thousands dead;
All feel the mighty glow of victor's Joy:

— — — — — — —

But if extended on the gory plain
And snatch'd in conquest some lov'd friend be dead—
Affection's tears will dim the sorrowing Eye
And suff'ring Nature [?]grieve that one should die.

From fThe Retrospect by Robert Southey—
published by Dilly.

	4	And ~~suffering pitying Nature weeps that one should die!~~ ~~Southey's retrospect.~~
	4 2* 2	And suffering Nature weeps that *one* should die. Southey's Retrospect.
	3–7	Southey's Retrospect.

[*Line-space*]

15	□	Thus to sad Sympathies I sooth'd my breast
16	⊠2	Calm, as the Rainbow in the weeping West;
	2	Bright
17	⊠6	When slumb'ring Freedom rous'd by high Disdain
	6	with
18	□	With giant fury burst her triple Chain.
19	□	Fierce on her Front the blasting Dogstar glow'd;
20	□	Her banners, like a midnight meteor, flow'd;
21	□	Amid the yelling of the storm-rent Skies
22	□	She came, and scatter'd Battles from her Eyes!
23	1 2	Then Exultation woke the patriot fire
	1–7	waked
	3	~~woke~~ waked
24	1	And swept with wilder hand th' empassion'd Lyre.
	⊠1 7	Alcœan
	7	wild Tyrtæan
25	1	Red from the Tyrant's wounds I shook the Lance,
	2 3 *5–7*	Wound
	1–4	Tyrants'
26	□	And strode in Joy the reeking plains of France!

[*Line-space*]

27	⊠*3–7*	In ghastly horror lie th' Oppressors low—
	3–7	Fall'n is th' oppressor, friendless, ghastly, low,
28	□	And my Heart akes tho' Mercy struck the Blow!

29	1	With wearied thought I seek the Amaranth Shade
	2	sad and wearied thought I seek the
	☒1 2	wearied thought once more
30	1 2	Where peaceful Virtue weaves her *myrtle* Braid.
	☒1 2	the
31	☐	And O! if Eyes, whose holy Glances roll–/
32	☒*3–7*	The eloquent Messengers of the pure Soul;
	3–7	Swift messengers, and eloquent of
33	☐	If Smiles more winning and a gentler Mien,
34	☐	Than the love-wilder'd Maniac's brain hath seen
35	☐	Shaping celestial forms in vacant air;
36	1	If *these* demand the wond'ring Poet's care—
	☒1	th' empassion'd
37	☐	If Mirth and soften'd Sense, and Wit refin'd,
38	☐	The blameless Features of a lovely Mind;
39	☐	Then haply shall my trembling Hand assign
40	1 2	No *fading* Flowers to Beauty's saintly Shrine.
	☒1 2	wreath
41.1	1	Nor, BRYNTON! thou the blushing Wreath refuse;
	2	——!
41.1	1	Though harsh her Notes, yet guileless is my Muse.
	2	song, the
43.1	1 2	Unwont at Flattery's Voice to plume her wings,
44.1	1 2	A Child of Nature, as she feels, she sings.
41	*1–7*	Nor, SARA! thou these early flowers refuse—
42	*1–7*	Ne'er lurked the snake beneath their simple hues:
43	*1–7*	No purple bloom the Child of Nature brings
44	*1–7*	From Flatt'ry's night-shade: as he feels, he sings.
41.2	3	~~Nor, Sara! thou these~~ sinful early ~~flowers refuse:~~
42.2	3	No Serpent ~~lurks~~ beneath their ~~simple~~ hues.
43.2	3	~~From~~ No purple ~~blooms from~~ Flatt'ry's Night-shade ~~no sick blooms~~
		I bring / bring
44.2	3	~~A~~The Child of Nature/: as ~~I~~he feels, ~~I~~he sings.
41.3	3	Nor, SARA! thou these *early* flowers refuse
42.3	3	Ne'er lurk'd the Snake beneath their simple hues.
43.3	3	Nature's pure Child from Flatt'ry's night-shade brings
44.3	3	No blooms rich-purpling: as he feels, he sings.

title. *3* TO A | *YOUNG LADY*, | WITH A POEM | *On the FRENCH RE-VOLUTION.* • *4* TO A | *YOUNG LADY*, | *With a* POEM *on the* FRENCH REVOLUTION. • *5 6* TO A YOUNG LADY, WITH A POEM ON | THE FRENCH REVOLUTION. • *7* TO A YOUNG LADY, | WITH A POEM ON THE FRENCH REVOLUTION.   **1.** ☒1 youth   ☒1 2 dwell,   **2.** ☒1 2 dome
3. ☒1 2 first,   2 Cloisters • ☒1 2 cloisters   ☒1 2 pale,   **4.** 2 3 Guilt • *1* guilt, •
2–7 guilt   *5–7* wondered   2 tale.   **5.** ☒1 *1* Yet   3 *5–7* though   2 Hours
2 wing   **6.** 3 sing: **7.** *1* Aye,   ☒1 2 star   ☒1 2 evening   **8.** ☒1 radiance
9. *1* soul,   *1* gloom,   **10.** *5–7* Mourned   ☒1 2 breeze,   *1–6* O LEE BOO! •
3 7 Lee Boo!   2 3 Tomb.   **10fn.** 7 Lee Boo,   2* *2–6* ABBA THULE,
3–7 Islands,   *2* 2–7* is   2*(*b*) Gre⟨e⟩nwich • *2–7* Greenwich   *5–7* church-

11. 2 3 Where e'er   *1 5–7* wandered,   *1* 3 *2–6* PITY   **12.** *5–7* Breathed
2 Heart • ⊠1 2 heart   *5–7* glistened   2 Tear.   **13.** ⊠1 knell   2 toll'd • *5–
7* tolled,   2 Eye • *1–7* eye,   **14.** ⊠1 And   *1–3* suff'ring   7 one   ⊠1 die!
15. *1* Thus,   ⊠1 2 sympathies   *5–7* soothed   *3–7* breast,   **16.** *1* Calm
⊠1 2 rainbow   2 West, • ⊠1 2 West: **17.** *1* slum'bring • *5–7* slumbering   *1* 3 *2–
6* FREEDOM   *5–7* roused   *1* 3 *2–6* DISDAIN   **18.** 2 Fury   ⊠1 2 chain!
19. ⊠1 front   2 Dog star • ⊠1 2 Dog-star   *5–7* glowed;   **20.** *1* 3 *2–6* Banners,
⊠1 7 Meteor,   *5–7* flowed;   **21.** *1* 3 *2–5* 7 skies • *6* skies!   **22.** *5–
7* scattered   ⊠1 2 battles   ⊠1 2 eyes!   **23.** ⊠1 2 7 EXULTATION   *2–
4* wak'd   *4* fire,   **24.** 7 the   *1* 3 Alcæan   *1–7* lyre: • 3 Lyre: **25.** ⊠1 2 wound
2 Lance • ⊠1 2 lance,   **26.** ⊠1 2 joy   2 Plains   **27.** *5–7* Fallen   *5–7* the
2 low • ⊠1 2 low,   **28.** ⊠1 heart   2 3 *2 3* akes, • *1 5–7* aches,   *5–7* though
⊠1 2 7 MERCY   ⊠1 blow.   **29.** 2 3 Shade, • *1–7* shade,   **30.** 2 7 myrtle •
1 Myrtle • 3 MYRTLE • *2–6* MYRTLE   ⊠1 2 braid.   **31.** 2 3 *2–4* ô! •
1 oh!   *1* 3 *2–4* EYES, • *5 6* EYES • *7* Eyes   *1–7* glances   2 roll • ⊠1 2 roll,
32. *1 2* messengers   *1–7* soul;   **33.** *1* 3 *3–6* SMILES • *2* SMILES   ⊠1 2 winning,
1 3 *2–4* MIEN, • *5 6* MIEN • *7* Mien   **34.** *1* love wilder'd • *5–7* love-wildered
3 Brain   *1* seen,   **35.** *3–7* air,   **36.** ⊠1 these   *5–7* the   *5 6* cmpassioned •
7 impassioned   **37.** *1* 3 *2–5* MIRTH, • *6* MIRTH   *5–7* softened   *2 7* Sense •
1 3 *2–5* SENSE, • *6* SENSE   *1* 3 *2–6* WIT   *5–7* refined,   **38.** ⊠1 2 features
⊠1 2 mind;   **39.** ⊠1 2 hand   **40.** ⊠1 fading   *1* 3 *2–6* BEAUTY's   2 Shrine! •
⊠1 2 shrine.   **41.1.** 2 refuse—   **42.1.** 2 Tho'   2 Muse!   **43.1.** 2 voice
2 wings   **41.** 7 Sara!   **42.** *2–4* lurk'd   *5–7* hues;   **44.** *3* Flatt'rys •
5–7 Flattery's   *5–7* feels

5. PR *1* flew] The second issue of PR *1* gives "flew by"

9. MS 1 twilight] C has underlined the word, and written "*shadowy*" in the margin.

10. MS 3 has a footnote indicator, but no note is supplied.

10fn, 14fn. PR *2** 2 have the cross-references "Note 1—Page 37." and "Note 2.—Page 37." respectively, referring to the notes at the end of the volume. The notes are printed at the foot of the page in PR *3–7*.

16. MS 1 Calm,] C has written underneath: "(Bright?)"

25. MSS 1–3 Tyrant's] The word can be read as "Tyrants'" (plural) in all three texts (see EC): the apostrophe appears over the "s", even slightly to the right of it. However, C's habit in writing was to place plural apostrophes unambiguously much further to the right. His signification of the singular possessive is nearly always potentially misleading; of the plural, never.

30. MS 1 Virtue] Written larger, perhaps to be read as bold.

33. MS 1 Smiles . . . Mien,] Written larger, perhaps to be read as bold.

34. MS 1 Maniac's] Written larger, perhaps to be read as bold.

37. MS 1 Mirth . . . Sense, . . . Wit] Written larger, perhaps to be read as bold.

44.1. MS 1 Child . . . Nature] Written larger, perhaps to be read as bold.

82. MONODY ON THE DEATH
OF CHATTERTON

A. DATE

The original version of the poem was written at Christ's Hospital, and dates from 1790. This would have a place in the present sequence between poems **9** and **10**. It may have been written as a theme on the lines from Gray prefixed to MS 1 below; and some lines may be associated with material from even earlier in C's schooldays, perhaps from 1785–6 onwards (cf on PR *6* below and **12** *Conclusion to a Youthful Poem* headnote). From the original version, at intervals during C's whole life, sprang a succession of revisions.

C's dating of the revisions is confusing. PR *3 4* are dated Oct 1794, though in reality they belong as much to 1796, 1797, or 1803, and the substantially altered PR *6 7* are placed in a class of Juvenile Poems. Confusion can be reduced if the poem is considered to exist in three basic forms: a school exercise in the form of an irregular Pindaric ode dating from 1790, a Romantic ode written at Bristol and Cambridge in 1794 and successively expanded and modified in subsequent collections, and an elegy in couplets dating from 1829–34. The three stages do not enlarge and modify a continuous impulse. The impulse itself changed direction as C's identification with Chatterton changed.

B. TEXTS

Stage 1

This stage is represented by three mss, which differ from one another only within individual lines.

1. BM MS Ashley 3506=James Boyer's *Liber Aureus* vol I ff 44^r–46^v. Fair copy in C's hand, signed "S. T. Coleridge I 1790". Folio 46^v (lines 88.1–91.1, 91/143.1.1–9, 91.1.10–11 below) is reproduced in *C Bibl* (Wise *TLP*) facing p 52.

This is the fourth of the five poems C copied into the book. The lines are divided into eight stanzas, separated by rules, as follows: ‾1.1–4 (st 1), 14.1.1–8 (st 2), 23.1–26.1, 26.1.1–4, 32.1, 32.1.1–2 (st 3), 33.1–44.1, 44.1.1–5 (st 4), 48.1.1–15 (st 5), 67.1–81.1 (st 6), 81.1.1, 82.1–91.1 (st 7), 91/143.1.1–9, 91.1.10–11 (st 8).

2. VCL S LT Fl.3 =Green Ottery Copy Book ff 10^r–11^v. Subscribed "S.C.", and described in the title as "written by the Author at the age of sixteen." Transcript in the hand of John May Jr, made c 1820.

May has added the following initialled note of his own to the antepenultimate line (line 91/143.1.9 below): "Altho' this latter reflection savours of Suicide, it will easily meet with the indulgence of the considerate reader, when he reflects that the Author's Imagination was at that time enflam'd with the idea of his beloved Poet, and perhaps utter'd ~~at that time~~ a Sentiment, which in his cooler moments he would have abhor'd the thoughts of."

The lines are divided into seven stanzas as follows: ⁻1.1–4, 14.1.1–8 (st 1), 23.1–26.1, 26.1.1–4, 32.1, 32.1.1–2 (st 2), 33.1–44.1, 44.1.1–5 (st 3), 48.1.1– 15 (st 4), 67.1–81.1 (st 5), 81.1.1, 82.1–91.1 (st 6), 91/143.1.1–9, 91.1.10–11 (st 7).

3. BM Add MS 47551 = Ottery Copy Book ff 8ᵛ–11ᵛ. Transcript in C's hand.

The lines are divided into seven stanzas—differently from MS 2 and separated by rules, as in MS 1—as follows: ⁻1.1–4 (st 1), 14.1.1–8 (st 2), 23.1–26.1, 26.1.1–4, 32.1, 32.1.1–2 (st 3), 33.1–44.1, 44.1.1–5 (st 4), 48.1.1–15 (st 5), 67.1–81.1, 81.1.1, 82.1–91.1 (st 6), 91/143.1.1–9, 91.1.10–11 (st 7). The substitution for the last three lines (see the collation) is in a smaller, neater hand, and was possibly made later. Note (*h*) below bears on this.

1*. A revision of MSS 1–3 in the form of a cancelland version of PR *1*. Only one such copy—of the large-paper issue—is known: HUL *97-391. A discard copy of the same large-paper issue, containing portions of the same text in offset and now at the BM (uncatalogued in Feb 1992), had earlier been reported by Arthur Freeman and Theodore Hofmann "The Ghost of Coleridge's First Effort: 'A Monody on the Death of Chatterton'" *The Library* 6th ser XI (1989) 328 35. The readings of the HUL and incomplete BM copies coincide, although this does not rule out the possibility, raised by Freeman and Hofmann (333n), that more than one setting of the cancellanda exist.

The 72-line revision is essentially an abridgement of the MS 1 version comprising lines 23.1–32.1 (st 1), 33.1–40.1, 43.1–44.1, 44.1.4–44.1.5 (st 2), 48.1.1–48.1.15 (st 3), 67.1–81.1 (st 4), 81.1.1–91.1 (st 5), 91/143.1.1–91.1.11 (st 6); that is, it omits the epigraph, the two opening stanzas, and six further lines. C might have worked from a copy of MS 1 obtained by the editor of PR *1*, who was Boyer's nephew, or a few coincidences with MSS 2 3 might suggest that he reconstructed the poem from memory. Whatever the case, his abridgement appears to be opportunistic, to fit his lines into the restricted space available. There are some patent errors, and the few verbal changes were not carried forward, which suggests that the revision was perfunctory and quickly overtaken by the enlargement represented by PR *1*. Cf Note (*b*) below and fur ther on PR *1*.

Notes on Stage 1

(*a*) PW (JDC) 562ʙ describes a ms of this poem and of **22** *An Invocation* and **21** *Monody on a Tea Kettle* "in the handwriting of the poet, and sent from school to his brother George". It might predate the MSS 2 3 versions— indeed, it is likely to have been the original of MS 2—but it has not proved possible to trace it.

(*b*) Anna Seward, writing to H. F. Cary on 4 Mar 1798 (*Letters*—6 vols Edinburgh 1811—v 56), reported that, "Some four years since, Mr Coleridge's friend, Kennedy, gave me C's Monody on Chatterton in manuscript." This version appears to have been of the first form of the poem (PR *1**), though this is not certain and it may have been closer to PR *1*. Rann Kennedy (1772–1851), a lifelong opponent of intolerance and bigotry and a friend of WW as well as of C, was an undergraduate at St John's at the time (see *DNB*).

(*c*) The transcript of MS 1, with variants from MS 2, in the hand of EHC at VCL (LT 16) and the transcript of MS 3, with C's earlier version of the last three lines, in JTC's 1807 notebook, as given in *PW* (RHS) II 355*–358*, are of no textual interest. These readings—along with PR *1**—have not been collated.

(*d*) The indentation of lines in MS 1 is not always certain, and TEXTS 2 3 *1** differ in their indentation. The uncertainties and the differences are not recorded here.

Stage 2

This stage of the poem is made up of ms and printed texts in an evolving relation to one another.

1. Poems, Supposed to Have Been Written at Bristol, by Thomas Rowley, and Others, in the Fifteenth Century ed Lancelot Sharpe (Cambridge 1794) xxv–xxviii. C's poem was introduced by the following note: "The Editor thinks himself happy in the permission of an ingenious Friend, to insert the following Monody." Unsigned.

Lancelot Sharpe was educated privately by his uncle Dr Boyer of Christ's Hospital until he proceeded to Pembroke College Cambridge, where he graduated BA in 1796. He later attacked C in *The Satirist* as Sam Spitfire. The printer of the present volume was the radical editor of the *Cambridge Intelligencer*, Benjamin Flower.

The lines are divided into ten stanzas as follows: 1–8 (st 1), 9–14 (st 2), 15–22 (st 3), 23–32 (st 4), 33–48 (st 5), 49–60 (st 6), 61–6 (st 7), 67–91 (st 8), 92–9 (st 9), 100–7 (st 10). Only 17 of the 90 lines of MSS 1–3 are carried forward unchanged, the remainder being either abandoned or rewritten. Lines 41–4 were embodied in a version of **70** *Lines on "The Man of Ross"* copied for RS on 13 Jul 1794 (*CL* I 87), and published in *Cambridge Intelligencer* on 27 Sept. The same lines were omitted from a sonnet version of *The Man of Ross* sent to Henry Martin on 22 Jul (*CL* I 95); and the composition of PR *1* dates from the months during and after these trials and uncertainties.

Freeman and Hofmann point out (pp 334–5) that C's revision of PR *1** was evidently constrained by the physical limit of the new quarter-sheet: 107 lines were squeezed into four pages which previously held 72, and further enlargement was not possible. They suggest, therefore, that the enlarged conclusion contained in MSS 4 5 might have been in C's mind at the earlier time. "Coleridge's first appearance in book form, despite its bibliographical and biographical importance, may be a compromised text."

PR *1* is reprinted in the *University Magazine* (Cambridge) II (Feb 1795) 129–32, where its author is identified as "S. T. COLERIDGE, JESUS COLLEGE." The magazine is one with which C had been involved since its inception (Christopher Wordsworth *Social Life at the English Universities in the Eighteenth Century* 589–92) and with which he kept in touch (*CN* I 47; *RX* 457–8 n 56), but the reprinting has no textual significance and has not been collated.

4. HRC MS (Coleridge, S T) Works B. Single leaf, 18.1×23.8 cm; no wm; chain-lines 2.5 cm. Written on both sides. Bound into Rugby Manuscript pp 27–8/f 11^{r-v}. Transcript of enlarged conclusion (lines 108–31, 133.1.1–6, 137.1–143.1) in C's hand, with revisions, headed "begin here".

The addition incorporates the octave of **78** *Sonnet on Pantisocracy*, which C included in a letter to RS dated 18 Sept 1794 (*CL* I 104). In *Poems* (1797, 1803)=PR *3 4* below C dated the present poem Oct 1794, which suggests that the MSS *4 5* addition was conceived quickly after the PR *1* expansion, even though MSS *4 5* appear not to have been transcribed until a year later, whereas in MS *6* below (1822?) C declared that the addition was written in 1795, at Bristol. See on TEXTS *1* 1* above for the suggestion that the enlargement might have been in C's mind at proof stage and that he was prevented from incorporating it because of the constraints of space.

5. HRC MS (Coleridge, S T) Works B. Two leaves, 18.0×23.4 cm; no wm; chain-lines 2.5 cm. The first leaf written on both sides, the second on the recto only. Bound into Rugby Manuscript pp 29–31/ff 12^{r}–12bis^{r}. Fair copy of MS *4* (lines 108–43) in C's hand.

5*. HRC MS (Coleridge, S T) Works B. Single leaf, 20.0×32.6 cm; wm Britannia in large oval surmounted by crown; chain-lines 2.6 cm. Bound into Rugby Manuscript pp 33–4/f 13^{r-v}. Note for the poem in C's hand, evidently transcribed after the text of PR *2* below was set. The note continues on to the verso, where it is followed by other notes.

C. G. Martin (see note on title fn) suggests reasons for thinking that the note was among those written out in Mar 1796 (*CL* I 193: to J. Cottle [late Mar 1796]).

2*. Two proof copies of PR *2* below print the note as in MS *5**, which C cancelled before publication. They are MH's copy at the Alexander Turnbull Library, Wellington, New Zealand (R Eng COLE Poems (1798)) and Joseph Cottle's in BM Ashley 408 (*JDC facsimile* 67–8). The first is a complete proof copy (lacking only sig A), the second is fragmentary and bound misleadingly with other material. C's note in both copies is amended.

2 [=RT]. *Poems* (1796).

C borrowed a copy of PR *1* from the Bristol Library between 21 Jul and 21 Sept 1795, while PR *2* was being set by the printer (*Bristol LB* No 65). Printer's copy was perhaps provided by a lightly revised PR *1*, complemented by MS *4* ("begin here") and MS *5* for the enlarged conclusion. JDC told EHC, in a letter dated 17 Aug 1890 (HRC, uncatalogued in 1976), that he was to be loaned a ms of the poem in the handwriting of Sarah Poole (Mrs King), TP's sister. This possibly dates from Sept 1795, when C was with TP at Stowey, being a copy of C's revised version of PR *1*, but it has not come to light.

The lines are divided into fourteen stanzas as follows: 1–8 (st 1), 9–14 (st 2), 15–22 (st 3), 23–32 (st 4), 33–48 (st 5), 49–60 (st 6), 61–6 (st 7), 67–82 (st 8), 83–91 (st 9), 92–107 (st 10), 108–17 (st 11), 118–25 (st 12), 126–33 (st 13), 134–43 (st 14).

3. Poems (1797). Dated "*October*, 1794."

C's letter to Cottle of 6 Jan 1797 (*CL* I 299) shows that printer's copy was supplied by a list of emendations to PR *2*. Cottle did not make all the changes C requested, and C repeated one of them in Jul (*CL* I 331: to J. Cottle [c 3 Jul 1797]), which was again ignored. C later said that the poem was included only at Cottle's request (*CL* I 381–2; to the Editor of the *Monthly Magazine* [Jan 1798]; cf 333: to RS [c 17 Jul 1797]; *LL*—M—I 82).

The lines are divided into thirteen stanzas as follows: 1–8 (st 1), 9–14 (st 2), 15–22 (st 3), 23–32 (st 4), 33–40 (st 5), 49–60 (st 6), 61–6 (st 7), 67–82 (st 8), 83–91 (st 9), 92–117 (st 10), 118–25 (st 11), 126–33 (st 12), 134–43 (st 13).

Four copies contain C's ms corrections: the copy he presented to GC (Princeton, Robert H. Taylor Collection); W. L. Bowles's copy (in the possession of Erwin Schwarz, 1982); William Roskilly's copy (in the possession of J.C.C. Mays, 1999); and RS's copy (Yale In 678 797 Copy 1).

4. Poems (1803). Dated "*October*, 1794." The last four stanzas of this version are reprinted in *The Parnassian Garland* (1807) 155–6, but the reprinting has no textual significance.

The lines are divided into thirteen stanzas—differently from PR *3*—as follows: 1–8 (st 1), 9–14 (st 2), 15–22 (st 3), 23–32 (st 4), 33–40 (st 5), 61–6 (st 6), 67–82 (st 7), 83–91 (st 8), 92–107 (st 9), 108–13 (st 10), 118–25 (st 11), 126–33 (st 12), 134–43 (st 13).

5. PW (1828).

The lines are divided into fourteen stanzas exactly as in PR *2*.

Stage 3

This stage of the poem comprises the following three texts.

6. PW (1829).

The first four lines of the enlarged beginning had been sent to correspondents over ten years previously, where they were described as schoolboy verses, "*composed in the thirteenth year of my Age*" (*CL* III 499: to J. Cottle 27 May 1814; IV 937n: to W. Worship 22 Apr 1819). The original of the letter to William Worship of 22 Apr 1819, for which ELG in the second reference cites a transcript, is at the Fondation Martin Bodmer, Geneva.

The lines are divided into fifteen stanzas as follows: 8.1.1–6 (st 1), 8.1.7–15 (st 2), 9.1–10.1, 10.1.1–4, 12.1–14.1 (st 3), 15.1–22.1 (st 4), 23.2–26.2, 27.1–31.1, 32.2 (st 5), 33.2–37.2, 37.1.1–4 (st 6), 37.1.5–10, 41.1, 43.2, 43.1.1–4, 47.1–48.1 (st 7), 66.1.1–6, 61.1–66.1 (st 8), 67.2–71.2, 72.1, 73.2–82.2 (st 9), 83.2–91.2 (st 10), 143.1.12/92–143.1.27/107 (st 11), 143.1.28/108–143.1.37/117 (st 12), 143.1.38/118–143.1.45/125 (st 13), 143.1.46/126–143.1.53/133 (st 14), 143.1.54/134–143.1.63/143 (st 15).

6. C's ms revision of the poem in the large-paper copy of PR *5* at the Fitz-william Museum, Cambridge (Marlay Bequest 1912).

C's ms revision is written across the foot of each page, and in the margin of p 17. It is prefaced with an instruction which dates it after PR *6* (the "second" edition of C's *PW*): "Substitute from the 2nd Edition (or rather in great part restore from the original School-exercise) the following:—" The most likely date is 1832. C has added a note following line 91.2: "(So far a School Exercise, æt. 17: the remaining five §§phs, at Bristol, æt. 23.)"

The revision affects stanzas 1 and 2, 4 (from line 37.2 onwards), and 5 of the PR *5* text. The remainder is unrevised and is therefore not incorporated as MS 6 in the collation elsewhere. It should be noted that, though C marked paras 4 and 5 for substitution (i.e. down to line 66/66.1.5), he copied out a revised text only down to line 43.2. Cf lines 8.1.1–6, 8.1.7–15, 9.1–10.1, 10.1.1–4, 12.1–14.1, 15.1–22.1, 37.2, 37.1.1–10, 41.1).

AG's copy of PR *5* (in the possession of Erwin Schwarz) contains a verbatim transcript of this version, but is of no textual significance.

7. *PW* (1834).

The lines reintroduced from MSS 1–3 are likely to have been reinstated on the initiative of HNC: see vol I annex B 6.

The lines are divided into fifteen stanzas—differently from PR *6*—as follows: 8.1.1–6 (st 1), 8.1.7–15 (st 2), 9.1–10.1, 10.1.1–4, 12.1–14.1 (st 3), 15.1–22.1 (st 4), 23.2–26.2, 27.1–31.1, 32.2 (st 5), 33.2–37.2, 37.1.1–4 (st 6), 37.1.5–10, 41.1, 43.2, 43.1.1–4, 47.1–48.1 (st 7), 66.1.1–6, 61.1–66.1 (st 8), 67.2–71.2, 72.1, 73.2–82.2 (st 9), 83.2–91.2 (st 10), 143.1.1–11 (st 11), 143.1.12/92–143.1.27/107 (st 12), 143.1.28/108–143.1.37/117 (st 13), 143.1.38/118–143.1.45/125 (st 14), 143.1.46/126–143.1.63/143 (st 15).

divisional title. *3 4* 𝔐onody I on the I 𝔇eath of 𝔠hatterton.

title. 1 3 *1–7* Monody on the Death of Chatterton. • 2 A Monody on Chatterton, who poison'd himself at the age of eighteen; written by the Author at the age of sixteen.

title fn [present in TEXTS 5* 2*]

Notes
Monody on Chatterton. Poor Chatterton! Herbert Croft has written with feeling concerning him; and Vicesimus Knox has ATTEMPTED to write with feeling. Hayley [?] [. . .] who (so ⟨future⟩ Antiquarians will inform our Posterity) has written sundry things ~~which being in rhyme are by courtesy of the land deemed Poetry~~ in the reign of King George 5 the Third, describes the death of Chatterton in ~~some well-meaning lines~~ his Essay ~~of~~ on

Poetry—describes him as *tearing the strings of his Lyre in the agonies of Death!!*—By
far the best poem on this subject ~~was~~ ~~w~~ is "Neglected Genius or Tributary Stanzas to the
Memory of the unfortunate Chatterton" written by Rushton, a blind Sailor.
 Walpole writes thus—"All the House of Forgery are Relations. ~~All the House of~~ 10
~~Forgery are Relations.~~ Although it be but just to CHATTERTON's Memory to say, that
his Poverty never made him claim kindred with the more enriching Branches, yet he
who could so ingeniously counterfeit styles & (the ~~Editor~~ Asserter believes) Hands,
might easily have been led to the more facile Imitation of prose promissory Notes!"—O
ye, who honor the name of MAN, rejoice that this Walpole is called a LORD!—Milles 15
too, the Editor of his Poems—a Priest who tho' only a DEAN, in dullness and malignity
was most *episcopally* eminent, ~~has most~~ foully culumniated ~~the~~ him—An Owl mangling
a poor dead Nightingale!—

    Most inspired Bard!—
    To him alone in this benighted Age   20
    Was that divine Inspiration given,
    Which glows in MILTON's and in SHAKESPEARE's Page,
    The Pomp & Prodigality of Heaven!—

⁻1.1	1	Cold penury repress'd his noble rage,
⁻1.2	1	And froze the genial current of his soul.
		[*Line-space*]
⁻1.3	1–3	Now prompts the Muse poetic lays,
⁻1.4	1–3	And high my bosom beats with love of Praise.
⁻1.5	1–3	But, Chatterton! methinks, I hear thy name!
⁻1.6	1–3	For cold my Fancy grows, and dead each Hope of Fame.
1	*1–5*	When faint and sad o'er Sorrow's desart wild,
2	*1–5*	Slow journeys onward, poor Misfortune's child,
3	*1–5*	When fades each lovely form by Fancy drest,
4	*1–5*	And inly pines the self-consuming breast;
5	*1–5*	No scourge of Scorpions in thy right arm dread,
6	*1–5*	No helmed Terrors nodding o'er thy head,
7	*1–5*	Assume, O DEATH! the Cherub Wings of PEACE,
8	*1–5*	And bid the heart-sick Wanderer's Anguish cease!
8.1.1	*6 6 7*	O what a wonder seems the fear of death,
8.1.2	*6 6 7*	Seeing how gladly we all sink to sleep,
8.1.3	*6 6 7*	Babes, Children, Youths and Men,
8.1.4	*6 6 7*	Night following night for threescore years and ten!
8.1.5	*6 7*	But doubly strange, where life is but a breath
	6	O
8.1.6	*6 6 7*	To sigh and pant with, up Want's rugged steep.
		[*Line-space*]
8.1.7	*6 6 7*	Away, Grim Phantom! Scorpion King, away!
8.1.8	*6 7*	Reserve thy terrors and thy stings display
	6	sting
8.1.9	*6 6 7*	For coward Wealth and Guilt in robes of State!
8.1.10	*6 6 7*	Lo! by the grave I stand of one, for whom
8.1.11	*6 6 7*	A prodigal Nature and a niggard Doom
8.1.12	*6 6 7*	(*That* all bestowing, *this* withholding all,)
8.1.13	*6 6 7*	Made each chance knell from distant spire or dome

8.1.14 *6 6 7*	Sound like a seeking Mother's anxious call,
8.1.15 *6 6 7*	Return, poor Child! Home, weary Truant, home!
	[*Line-space*]
9 *1–5*	Thee, CHATTERTON! yon unblest Stones protect
10 *1–5*	From Want, and the bleak freezings of Neglect!
11 *1–5*	Escap'd the sore wounds of Affliction's rod,
12 *1–5*	Meek at the Throne of Mercy, and of God,
13 *1–5*	Perchance thou raisest high th' enraptur'd hymn
14 *1–5*	Amid the blaze of Seraphim!
9.1 *6 6 7*	Thee, CHATTERTON! these unblest stones protect
10.1 *6 7*	From want, and the bleek freezings of neglect.
6	Proud Spirit, from the
10.1.1 *6 6 7*	Too long before the vexing Storm-blast driven
10.1.2 *6 6 7*	Here hast thou found repose! beneath this sod!
10.1.3 *6 6 7*	Thou! O vain word! *thou* dwell'st not with the clod!
10.1.4 *6 6 7*	Amid the shining Host of the FORGIVEN
12.1 *6 6 7*	Thou at the throne of Mercy and thy God
13.1 *6 6 7*	The triumph of redeeming Love dost hymn
14.1 *6 6 7*	(Believe it, O my Soul!) to harps of Seraphim.
	[*Line-space*]
14.1.1 *1–3*	When Want and cold Neglect had chill'd thy soul,
14.1.2 *1*	Athirst for Death I see thee drench the bowl!
2 3	drain
14.1.3 *1–3*	Thy corpse of many a livid hue
14.1.4 *1–3*	On the bare ground I view,
14.1.5 *1–3*	Whilst various passions all my mind engage;
14.1.6 *1–3*	Now is my breast distended with a sigh,
14.1.7 *1–3*	And now a flash of Rage
14.1.8 *1 3*	Darts through the tear, that glistens in my eye.
15. *1 2 5*	Yet oft ('tis Nature's bosom-startling call)
3 4	←——call)——→
16 *1–5*	I weep, that heaven-born Genius *so* should fall,
17 *1–5*	And oft in Fancy's saddest hour my soul
18 *1–5*	Averted shudders at the poison'd Bowl.
19 *1–5*	Now groans my sickening Heart, as still I view
20 *1*	The Corse of livid hue;
2–5	Thy
21 *1–5*	And now a Flash of Indignation high
22 *1–5*	Darts thro' the Tear, that glistens in mine Eye!
	[*Line-space*]
15.1 *6 6 7*	Yet oft, perforce, ('tis suffering Nature's call)
16.1 *6 7*	I weep, that heaven-born Genius *so* should fall;
6	haughty
17.1 *6 7*	And oft, in Fancy's saddest hour, my soul
6	sadder moods,
18.1 *6 6 7*	Averted shudders at the poisoned bowl.
19.1 *6 7*	Now groans my sickening heart, as still I view
6	And now I groan, thy Corse of livid hue

20.1	*6 7*	Thy corse of livid hue;
	6	Outstretch'd before my view:
21.1	*6 7*	Now indignation checks the feeble sigh,
	6	chides
22.1	*6 7*	Or flashes through the tear that glistens in mine eye!
	6	And swelling fills my
		[*Line-space*]
23.1	*1–3 1**	Is this the land of liberal Heart?
24.1	*1–3 1**	Is this the land, where Genius ne'er in vain
25.1	*1–3 1**	Pour'd forth her soul-enchanting strain?
26.1	*1–3 1**	Ah me! Yet Butler, 'gainst the bigot foe
26.1.1	*1–3 1**	Well-skill'd to aim keen Humour's dart,
26.1.2	*1–3 1**	Yet Butler felt Want's poignant sting;
26.1.3	*1–3 1**	And Otway, Master of the Tragic Art,
26.1.4	*1–3 1**	Whom Pity's self had bade to sing,
32.1	1	Sunk beneath a load of Woe.
	2 3 *1**	the
32.1.1	1	This ever can the generous Briton hear,
	2	Which
	3	can the generous Briton ever
32.1.2	*1–3*	And starts not in his eye th' indignant tear?
23	*1–5*	Is this the Land of song-ennobled Line?
24	*1–5*	Is this the Land, where Genius ne'er in vain
25	*1*	Pour'd forth her lofty strain?
	2–5	his
26	*1–5*	Ah me! yet Spenser, gentlest Bard divine,
27	*1*	Beneath chill Disappointment's deadly shade
	2–5	shade,
28	*1–5*	His weary Limbs in lonely Anguish lay'd!
29	*1–5*	And o'er her Darling dead
30	*1–5*	*Pity* hopeless hung her head,
31	*1*	While "mid the pelting of that pitiless storm,"
	2–5	merciless
32	*1–5*	Sunk to the cold Earth Otway's famish'd form!
23.2	*6 7*	Is this the land of song-enobled line?
24.2	*6 7*	Is this the land, where Genius ne'er in vain
25.2	*6 7*	Poured forth his lofty strain?
26.2	*6 7*	Ah me! yet SPENSER, gentlest bard divine,
27.1	*6 7*	Beneath chill Disappointment's shade,
28.1	*6 7*	His weary limbs in lonely anguish lay'd.
29.1	*6 7*	And o'er her darling dead
30.1	*6 7*	PITY hopeless hung her head,
31.1	*6 7*	While "mid the pelting of that merciless storm,"
32.2	*6 7*	Sunk to the cold earth OTWAY's famished form!
		[*Line-space*]
33.1	*1–3 1**	Elate of Heart and confident of Fame,
34.1	*1–3 1**	From vales, where Avon sports, the minstrel came.
35.1	*1–3 1**	Gay, as the Poet hastes along,
36.1	*1–3 1**	He meditates the future song,

37.1	1 2 *1**	How Ælla battled with his country's foes,
	3	Countries'
38.1	1–3 *1**	And, whilst Fancy in the Air
39.1	1–3 *1**	Paints him many a vision fair,
40.1	1–3 *1**	His eyes dance rapture, and his bosom glows.
42.1	1 2	With generous joy he views th' ideal gold:
	3	the rising
43.1	1–3	He listens to many a Widow's prayers,
	1*	many
44.1	1–3 *1**	And many an Orphan's thanks he hears;
44.1.1	1–3	He sooths to peace the careworn breast,
44.1.2	1	He bids the Debtor's eyes know rest,
	2	too
	3	⟨eyes⟩
44.1.3	1–3	And Liberty and Bliss behold:
44.1.4	1–3 *1**	And now he punishes the heart of Steel,
44.1.5	1–3 *1**	And her own iron rod he makes Oppression feel.
33	*1–5*	Sublime of Thought and confident of Fame,
34	*1–5*	From Vales, where Avon winds, the Minstrel came,
34fn	*2–5*	Avon, a river near Bristol; the birth place of Chatterton.
35	*1 2 5*	Light-hearted Youth! aye, as he hastes along,
	3 4	he hastes along,
36	*1 2 5*	He meditates the future Song,
	3 4	And
37	*1*	How dauntless Ælla fray'd the Danish foes;
	2–5	Dacyan
38	*1 2 5*	And as floating high in air,
	3 4	See,
39	*1–5*	Glitter the sunny Visions fair,
40	*1–5*	His eyes dance rapture, and his bosom glows!
41	*1 2 5*	Friend to the friendless, to the sick man Health;
42	*1 2 5*	With generous Joy he views th' *ideal* Wealth;
43	*1 2 5*	He hears the Widow's heaven-breath'd prayer of Praise;
44	*1 2 5*	He marks the shelter'd Orphan's tearful gaze;
45	*1 2 5*	Or, where the sorrow-shrivell'd Captive lay,
46	*1 2 5*	Pours the bright Blaze of Freedom's noon-tide Ray:
47	*1 2 5*	And now indignant grasps the patriot steel,
48	*1 2 5*	And her own iron rod he makes Oppression feel.
33.2	*6 7*	Sublime of thought, and confident of fame,
34.2	*6 7*	From vales where Avon winds the MINSTREL came.
34.2fn	*6 7*	Avon, a river near Bristol; the birth-place of Chatterton.
35.2	*6 7*	Light-hearted youth! aye, as he hastes along,
36.2	*6 7*	He meditates the future song,
37.2	*6 6 7*	How dauntless Ælla fray'd the Dacyan foe;
37.1.1	*6 6 7*	And while the numbers flowing strong
37.1.2	*6 6 7*	In eddies whirl, in surges throng,
37.1.3	*6 7*	Exulting in the spirits' genial throe
	6	Exultant

37.1.4	6 7	In tides of power his life-blood seems to flow.
	6	His life-blood seems in tides of power
		[*Line-space*]
37.1.5	6 7	←—And—→ now his cheeks with deeper ardors flame,
	6	~~And~~ But lo! keener
37.1.6	6 6 7	His eyes have glorious meanings, that declare
37.1.7	6 6 7	More than the light of outward day shines there,
37.1.8	6 6 7	A holier triumph and a sterner aim!
37.1.9	6 6 7	Wings grow within him; and he soars above
37.1.10	6 6 7	Or Bard's, or Minstrel's lay of war or love.
41.1	6 6 7	Friend to the friendless, to the Sufferer health,
43.2	6 7	He hears the widow's prayer, the good man's praise;
43.1.1	6 7	To scenes of bliss transmutes his fancied wealth,
43.1.2	6 7	And young and old shall now see happy days.
43.1.3	6 7	On many a waste he bids trim Gardens rise,
43.1.4	6 7	Gives the blue sky to many a prisoner's eyes;
47.1	6 7	And now in wrath he grasps the patriot steel,
48.1	6 7	And her own iron rod he makes Oppression feel.
		[*Line-space*]
48.1.1	1–3 *1**	Fated to heave sad Disappointment's sigh,
48.1.2	1–3 *1**	To feel the Hope now rais'd, and now deprest,
48.1.3	1 2 *1**	To feel the burnings of an injur'd breast,
	3	With all
48.1.4	1 2	From all thy Fate's deep sorrows keen
	3	Lo! from thy fate's dark
	1*	And all the
48.1.5	1–3	In vain, O youth, I turn th' affrighted eye;
	1*	O youth, in vain,
48.1.6	1 2 *1**	For powerful Fancy evernigh
	3	busy
48.1.7	1–3 *1**	The hateful picture forces on my sight.
48.1.8	1 3	There, Death of every dear delight,
	2	dear
	1*	foe to every dear
48.1.9	1–3	Frowns Poverty of Giant mien!
	1*	squalid
48.1.10	1–3 *1**	In vain I seek the charms of youthful grace,
48.1.11	1	Thy sunken eye, thy haggard cheeks it shews,
	2	looks
	3	cheek~~s~~ she
	1*	cheek it
48.1.12	1–3 *1**	The quick emotions struggling in thy Face,
48.1.13	1–3 *1**	Faint index of thy mental throes,
48.1.14	1–3 *1**	When each strong Passion spurn'd controll,
48.1.15	1–3 *1**	And not a Friend was nigh to calm thy stormy soul.
49	*1* 2 5	Clad in Nature's rich array,
	3	Yes! Clad
50	*1–3* 5	And bright in all her tender hues,
51	*1–3* 5	Sweet Tree of Hope! thou loveliest Child of Spring!

52 *1 2 5*		How fair didst thou disclose thine early bloom,
3		Most
53 *1–3 5*		Loading the west-winds with its soft perfume!
54 *1*		And Fancy hovering round on shadowy wing,
2 3 5		elfin　form　of　gorgeous
55 *1–3 5*		On every blossom hung her fostering dews,
56 *1–3 5*		That changeful wanton'd to the orient Day!
57 *1*		Ah! soon upon thy poor unshelter'd Head
2 3 5		But
58 *1–3 5*		Did Penury her sickly mildew shed:
59 *1–3 5*		And soon the scathing Lightning bade thee stand,
60 *1–3 5*		In frowning Horror o'er the blighted Land!

[*Line-space*]

61 *1*		Whither　are fled the charms of vernal Grace,
2–5		Ah! where
62 *1 2 5*		And Joy's wild gleams, that lighten'd o'er thy face!
3 4		light-flashing
63 *1–5*		Youth of tumultuous Soul, and haggard Eye!
64 *1–5*		Thy wasted form, thy hurried steps I view:
65 *1–5*		On thy cold forehead starts the anguish'd Dew:
66 *1–5*		And dreadful was that bosom-rending Sigh!
66.1.1 *6 7*		Sweet Flower of HOPE! free Nature's genial child!
66.1.2 *6 7*		That didst so fair disclose thy early bloom,
66.1.3 *6 7*		Filling the wide air with a rich perfume!
66.1.4 *6 7*		For thee in vain all heavenly aspects smil'd;
66.1.5 *6 7*		From the hard world brief respite could they win—
66.1.6 *6 7*		The frost nipp'd sharp without, the canker prey'd within!
61.1 *6 7*		Ah! where are fled the charms of vernal Grace,
62.1 *6 7*		And Joy's wild gleams that lightened o'er thy face?
63.1 *6 7*		YOUTH of tumultuous soul, and haggard eye!
64.1 *6 7*		Thy wasted form, thy hurried steps I view,
65.1 *6 7*		On thy wan forehead starts the lethal dew,
66.1 *6 7*		And oh! the anguish of that shuddering sigh!

[*Line-space*]

67.1 *1– 3 1**		Such was the sad and gloomy hour,
68.1 *1– 3 1**		When anguish'd Care of sullen brow
69.1 *1– 3 1**		Prepar'd the poison's death-cold power.
70.1 *1– 3 1**		Already to thy lips was rais'd the bowl,
71.1 *1–3*		When Filial　Pity stood thee by,
*1**		Pity shuddering
73.1 *1*		Thy fixed eye she bade thee roll
2		eyes
*3 1**		The　eye
74.1 *1 1**		On scenes, that well might melt thy soul:
2		To
3		On　which
75.1 *1–3 1**		Thy native cot she held to view,
76.1 *1–3 1**		Thy native cot, where Peace ere long

77.1	1 3	Had listen'd to thy evening song,
	2	Evening's
	*1**	hearkened evening
78.1	1–3 *1**	Thy Sister's shrieks she bade thee hear,
79.1	1	And mark thy Mother's [?]thrilling tear,
	2	frequent
	3 *1**	thrilling
80.1	1 *1**	She made thee feel her deep-drawn sigh,
	2 3	bade
81.1	1–3 *1**	And all her silent agony of Woe.
		[Line-space]
81.1.1	1–3 *1**	And from *thy* Fate shall such Distress ensue?
82.1	1–3 *1**	Ah! dash the poison'd chalice from thy Hand!
83.1	1	And thou had'st dash'd it ⟨at⟩ her soft command,
	2 3 *1**	at
84.1	1–3 *1**	But that **Despair** and **Indignation** rose,
85.1	1–3 *1**	And told again the story of thy Woes,
86.1	1–3 *1**	Told the keen insult of th' unfeeling heart,
87.1	1–3 *1**	The dread dependance on the low-born mind,
88.1	1–3 *1**	Told every woe, for which thy breast might smart,
89.1	1–3 *1**	Neglect and grinning Scorn, and Want combin'd.
90.1	1 *1**	Recoiling back thou sent'st the friend of Pain
	2	send'st
	3	bad'st
91.1	1	To roll a tide of Death through every freezing vein.
	2	in icening
	3	Quick thro'
	*1**	To the freezing
67	*1–3* 5	Such were the struggles of the gloomy Hour,
	4	that
68	*1–5*	When Care of wither'd brow
69	*1 2* 5	Prepar'd the Poison's death-cold power:
	3 4	←—power:—→
70	*1–5*	Already to thy Lips was rais'd the Bowl,
71	*1–5*	When near thee stood Affection meek,
72	*1–5*	(Her Bosom bare, and wildly pale her Cheek)
73	*1–5*	Thy sullen gaze she bade thee roll
74	*1–5*	On Scenes that well might melt thy Soul;
75	*1–5*	Thy native Cot she flash'd upon thy view,
76	*1–5*	Thy native Cot, where still at close of Day
77	*1–5⁻*	Peace smiling sate, and listen'd to thy Lay;
78	*1–5*	Thy Sister's shrieks she bade thee hear,
79	*1 2* 5	And mark thy Mother's thrilling tear;
	3 4	←—tear;—→
80	*1–5*	See, see her Breast's convulsive throe,
81	*1–5*	Her silent Agony of Woe!
82	*1–5*	Ah! dash the poison'd Chalice from thy Hand!
83	*1–5*	And thou had'st dash'd it at her soft command,
84	*1–5*	But that Despair and Indignation rose,

85 *1–5*	And told again the Story of thy Woes;	
86 *1–5*	Told the keen Insult of th' unfeeling Heart,	
87 *1*	The dread Dependence on the low-bred mind,	
2–5	low-born	
88 *1*	Told every pang, at which thy Soul might smart,	
2–5	with	must
89 *1–5*	Neglect, and grinning Scorn, and Want combin'd!	
90 *1–5*	Recoiling quick thou bad'st the Friend of Pain,	
91 *1*	Roll the dark tide of Death thro' every freezing Vein!	
2–5	black	
67.2 *6 7*	Such were the struggles of the gloomy hour,	
68.2 *6 7*	When CARE, of withered brow,	
69.2 *6 7*	Prepared the poison's death-cold power:	
70.2 *6 7*	Already to thy lips was raised the bowl,	
71.2 *6 7*	When near thee stood AFFECTION meek	
72.1 *6 7*	(Her bosom bare, and wildly pale her cheek)	
73.2 *6 7*	Thy sullen gaze she bade thee roll	
74.2 *6 7*	On scenes that well might melt thy soul;	
75.2 *6 7*	Thy native cot she flashed upon thy view,	
76.2 *6 7*	Thy native cot, where still, at close of day,	
77.2 *6 7*	PEACE smiling sate, and listened to thy lay;	
78.2 *6 7*	Thy Sister's shrieks she bade thee hear,	
79.2 *6 7*	And mark thy Mother's thrilling tear;	
80.2 *6 7*	See, see her breast's convulsive throe,	
81.2 *6 7*	Her silent agony of woe!	
82.2 *6 7*	Ah! dash the poisoned chalice from thy hand!	
	[*Line-space*]	
83.2 *6 7*	And thou had'st dashed it, at her soft command,	
84.2 *6 7*	But that DESPAIR and INDIGNATION rose,	
85.2 *6 7.*	And told again the story of thy woes;	
86.2 *6 7*	Told the keen insult of the unfeeling heart;	
87.2 *6 7*	The dread dependence on the low-born mind;	
88.2 *6 7*	Told every pang, with which thy soul must smart,	
89.2 *6 7*	Neglect, and grinning Scorn, and Want combined!	
90.2 *6 7*	Recoiling quick, thou bad'st the friend of pain	
91.2 *6 7*	Roll the black tide of Death through every freezing vein!	
	[*Line-space*]	
91/143.1.1 1 2 *1**	←—O—→ Spirit blest!	
3	~~O Being~~ O	
91/143.1.2 1	Whether the ~~endless'~~ eternal throne around	
2	←—the—→ endless	
3	←—th'—→ Eternal's	
*1**	eternal	
91/143.1.3 1 2 *1**	Amidst the blaze of Cherubim	
3	Seraphim	
91/143.1.4 1–3 *1**	Thou pourest forth the grateful hymn,	
91/143.1.5 1 *1**	Or soaring through the vast domain	
2 3	blest	
91/143.1.6 1–3 *1**	Enraptur'st angels with thy strain,	

91/143.1.7 1–3 *1**	Grant me, like thee, the lyre to sound,
91/143.1.8 1–3 *1**	Like thee, with fire divine to glow;
91/143.1.9 1 *1**	But, ah! when rage the Waves of Woe,
2	Like thee
3	~~Like thee, when rage the waves of woe,~~
3	But ah! when rage the waves of woe,
91.1.10 1 *1**	Grant me with firmer breast t' oppose their hate,
2	To leave behind Contempt and Want and Hate
3	~~To leave behind Contempt, and Want, and Hate,~~
3	Grant me with firmer breast to meet their hate,
91.1.11 1 *1**	And soar beyond the Storm with upright eye elate.
2	And seek in other worlds an happier fate.
3	~~And seek in other Worlds an happier Fate.~~
3	And soar beyond the Storm with upright eye elate!
92 *1–5*	Ye Woods! that wave o'er Avon's rocky steep,
93 *1–5*	To Fancy's ear sweet is your murm'ring deep!
94 *1–4*	For *here* she loves the Cypress Wreath to weave,
5	wave;
95 *1–5*	Watching with wistful eye the sad'ning tints of Eve.
96 *1–5*	Here far from Men amid this pathless grove,
97 *1–5*	In solemn thought the Minstrel wont to rove,
98 *1*	Like Star-beam on the rude sequester'd Tide,
2–5	slow
99 *1*	Lone-glittering, thro' the Forest's murksome pride.
2–5	high tree branching wide.
	[*Line-space*]
100 *1–5*	And here in Inspiration's eager Hour,
101 *1–5*	When most the big soul feels the mad'ning Power,
102 *1–5*	These wilds, these caverns roaming o'er,
103 *1–5*	Round which the screaming Sea-gulls soar
104 *1–5*	With wild unequal steps he pass'd along,
105 *1–5*	Oft pouring on the winds a broken song:
106 *1–5*	Anon upon some rough Rock's fearful Brow,
107 *1–5*	Would pause abrupt—and gaze upon the waves below.
	[*Line-space*]
108 4 5 *2–5*	Poor Chatterton! *he* sorrows for thy F A T E
109 4 5 *2–5*	Who would have prais'd & lov'd thee, ere too late.
110 4 5 *2–5*	Poor Chatterton! farewell! Of darkest hues
111 4 5 *2 3 5*	This Chaplet cast I on thy unshap'd tomb—
4	shapeless
112 4	~~No~~ But longer dare Inot on such sad theme muse
5	On such sad Theme I dare no longer
2–5	But dare no longer on the sad theme
113 4	Lest kindred woe persuade a kindred doom
5	woes ~~impel~~ persuade
2–5	persuade
113.1.1 4	What time, with ~~sinking heart~~ sick'ning soul, at close of day
113.1.2 4	I lay me down, and think of happier years;
113.1.3 4	Of Joys that glimmer'd in Hope's twilight ray,

113.1.4 4	Then left me darkling in a vale of tears.	

114 4 5 *2 3 5*   For oh! big gall-drops shook from Folly's wing

115 4   Have ~~fal~~ blasted the fair promise of my spring—

   5 2 3 5   blacken'd

116 4   And sterner Fate ~~pursues~~ has touch'd with   icy   dart

   5   the   stern   F A T E   transpierc'd   mortal

   2 3 5   viewless

117 4 5 *2 3 5*   The last pale Hope, that shiver'd at my heart—!

   [*Line-space*]

118 4   Hence, gloomy Thoughts! No more the Soul shall dwell

   5 *2–5*   my

119 4 5 *2–5*   On Joys, that were! No more endure to weigh

120 4 5 *2–5*   The shame and anguish of the evil day,

121 4 5 *2–5*   Wisely forgetful! O'er the Ocean swell

122 4   ~~Iseek My~~ Our Cots shall stand in some far distant Dell,

   5 *2–5*   Sublime   of   hope   I   seek   the   cottag'd

123 4 5 *2–5*   Where V I R T U E calm with *careless* step may stray,

124 4 5 *2–5*   And dancing to the moonlight roundelay,

125 4 5 *2–5*   The wizard P A S S I O N S weave an holy spell!

   [*Line-space*]

126 4 5 *2–5*   O Chatterton! that thou wert yet alive!

127 4   Sure thou wouldst spread thy Canvass to the gale,

   5 *2–5*   the

128 4   And love with us th'~~unwearied~~⟨e⟩ tinkling Team to drive

   5 *2–5*   ←——the——→

129 4   O'er ←——mild-eyed——→ Freedom's undivided dale—

   5   ~~mild-eyed~~ peaceful

   2–5   ←——peaceful——→

130 4   And we at ⟨sober⟩ eve would round thee throng,

   5 *2–5*   sober

131 4   And hang enraptur'd on thy minstrel song!

   5 *2–5*   Hanging   stately

132 5 *2–5*   And greet with smiles the young-eyed P O E S Y

133 5 *2–5*   All deftly mask'd, as hoar A N T I Q U I T Y.

   [*Line-space*]

133.1.1 4 5   Eyes⸝! that did ~~ache~~ ake with anguish! ye had wept

133.1.2 4   Tears of doubt-mingled Joy: as ~~to~~ one who leapt

   5   one,

133.1.3 4 5   From Precipices of distemper'd Sleep,

133.1.4 4   On which the fierce-eyed Fiends their   revel   keep

   5   revels

133.1.5 4   And ~~se~~   saw the rising Sun, and felt him dart

   5   ~~see~~ saw

133.1.6 4   New ~~beams~~ rays of Pleasance, trembling to the heart.

   5   rays

   [*Line-space*]

137.1 4   ⟨Vain Thought!⟩ Yet there, when Susquianna wide

139.1 4   In calmer murmurs rolls his mighty Tide,

140.1 4   ~~A ceno~~ A rustic cenotaph I'll raise to Thee,

141.1	4	Sweet Harper of time-honor'd Minstrelsy!
142.1	4	And there, sooth'd sadly by the moaning wind,
143.1	4	Muse on the sore Ills, I have left behind.
134	5 2–5	Alas! vain Phantasies—the fleeting Brood
135	5 2–5	Of Woe self-solac'd in her dreamy mood!
136	5	Yet ~~oft~~ will I ~~indulge the~~ love to frame the lonely Dream,
	2–5	will I love to follow the sweet
137	5 2–5	Where Susquiannah pours his untam'd stream;
138	5 2–5	And on some Hill, whose forest-frowning Side
139	5 2–5	Waves o'er the murmurs of his calmer Tide,
140	5 2–5	Will raise a Solemn CENOTAPH to Thee,
141	5 2–5	Sweet Harper of time-shrouded Minstrelsy!
142	5 2–5	And there, sooth'd sadly by the dirgeful wind,
143	5 2–5	Muse on the sore Ills, I had left behind.

[*Line-space*]

143.1.1	7	O Spirit blest!
143.1.2	7	Whether the Eternal's throne around,
143.1.3	7	Amidst the blaze of Seraphim,
143.1.4	7	Thou pourest forth the grateful hymn;
143.1.5	7	Or soaring thro' the blest domain
143.1.6	7	Enrapturest Angels with thy strain,—
143.1.7	7	Grant me, like thee, the lyre to sound,
143.1.8	7	Like thee with fire divine to glow;—
143.1.9	7	But ah! when rage the waves of woe,
143.1.10	7	Grant me with firmer breast to meet their hate,
143.1.11	7	And soar beyond the storm with upright eye elate!

[*Line-space*]

143.1.12/92	6 7	Ye woods! that wave o'er Avon's rocky steep,
143.1.13/93	6 7	To Fancy's ear sweet is your murmuring deep!
143.1.14/94	6 7	For here she loves the cypress wreath to weave
143.1.15/95	6 7	Watching, with wistful eye, the saddening tints of eve.
143.1.16/96	6 7	Here, far from men, amid this pathless grove,
143.1.17/97	6 7	In solemn thought the Minstrel wont to rove,
143.1.18/98	6 7	Like star-beam on the slow sequestered tide
143.1.19/99	6 7	Lone-glittering, through the high tree branching wide.
143.1.20/100	6 7	And here, in INSPIRATION's eager hour,
143.1.21/101	6 7	When most the big soul feels the mastering power,
143.1.22/102	6 7	These wilds, these caverns roaming o'er,
143.1.23/103	6 7	Round which the screaming sea-gulls soar,
143.1.24/104	6 7	With wild unequal steps he passed along
143.1.25/105	6 7	Oft pouring on the winds a broken song:
143.1.26/106	6 7	Anon, upon some rough rock's fearful brow
143.1.27/107	6 7	Would pause abrupt—and gaze upon the waves below.

[*Line-space*]

143.1.28/108	6 7	Poor CHATTERTON! *he* sorrows for thy fate
143.1.29/109	6 7	Who would have praised and loved thee, ere too late.
143.1.30/110	6 7	Poor CHATTERTON! farewell! of darkest hues
143.1.31/111	6 7	This chaplet cast I on thy unshaped tomb;
143.1.32/112	6 7	But dare no longer on the sad theme muse,

143.1.33/113 *6 7*	Lest kindred woes persuade a kindred doom:
143.1.34/114 *6 7*	For oh! big gall-drops, shook from FOLLY's wing,
143.1.35/115 *6 7*	Have blackened the fair promise of my spring;
143.1.36/116 *6 7*	And the stern FATE transpierced with viewless dart
143.1.37/117 *6 7*	The last pale Hope that shivered at my heart!
	[*Line-space*]
143.1.38/118 *6 7*	Hence, gloomy thoughts! no more my soul shall dwell
143.1.39/119 *6 7*	On joys that were! No more endure to weigh
143.1.40/120 *6 7*	The shame and anguish of the evil day,
143.1.41/121 *6 7*	Wisely forgetful! O'er the ocean swell
143.1.42/122 *6 7*	Sublime of Hope I seek the cottaged dell
143.1.43/123 *6 7*	Where VIRTUE calm with careless step may stray;
143.1.44/124 *6 7*	And, dancing to the moon-light roundelay,
143.1.45/125 *6 7*	The wizard PASSIONS weave an holy spell!
	[*Line-space*]
143.1.46/126 *6 7*	O CHATTERTON! that thou wert yet alive!
143.1.47/127 *6 7*	Sure thou would'st spread the canvass to the gale,
143.1.48/128 *6 7*	And love, with us the tinkling team to drive
143.1.49/129 *6 7*	O'er peaceful Freedom's undivided dale;
143.1.50/130 *6 7*	And we, at sober eve, would round thee throng,
143.1.51/131 *6*	Hanging, enraptured, on thy stately song!
7	Would hang,
143.1.52/132 *6 7*	And greet with smiles the young-eyed POESY
143.1.53/133 *6 7*	All deftly masked, as hoar ANTIQUITY.
	[*Line-space*]
143.1.54/134 *6 7*	Alas vain Phantasies! the fleeting brood
143.1.55/135 *6 7*	Of Woe self-solaced in her dreamy mood!
143.1.56/136 *6 7*	Yet will I love to follow the sweet dream,
143.1.57/137 *6 7*	Where Susquehannah pours his untamed stream;
143.1.58/138 *6 7*	And on some hill, whose forest-frowning side
143.1.59/139 *6 7*	Waves o'er the murmurs of his calmer tide,
143.1.60/140 *6 7*	Will raise a solemn CENOTAPH to thee,
143.1.61/141 *6 7*	Sweet Harper of time-shrouded MINSTRELSY!
143.1.62/142 *6 7*	And there, soothed sadly by the dirgeful wind,
143.1.63/143 *6 7*	Muse on the sore ills I had left behind.

title. 3 death • *1 2* MONODY | ON THE | DEATH OF CHATTERTON. • *3 4* MONODY | ON THE | *DEATH of CHATTERTON.* • *5 6* MONODY ON THE DEATH OF | CHATTERTON. • *7* MONODY ON THE DEATH OF CHATTERTON. **title fn1.** *5* 2** NOTES **title fn2.** *5** Monody on Chatterton. • *2** ON THE | *MONODY TO CHATTERTON.* | *2** POOR CHATTERTON! *2** HERBERT CROFT **title fn3.** *2** VICESIMUS KNOX *2** feeling.— *2** —HAYLEY **title fn 3–4.** *5** [?] [. . .] who • *2** who **title fn4.** *5** ⟨future⟩ • *2** future *2** posterity) **title fn4– 5.** *5** which . . . Poetry in • *2** in **title fn6.** *5** some . . . lines his • *2** his *5** of on • *2** on **title fn7.** *5** Poetry—describes him as • *2** Poetry—as *2** *lyre* *2** *death!!*— **title fn8.** *5** was-w is • *2** is *2** Tributary **title fn9.** *2** memory *2** Chatterton," *2** RUSHTON, **title fn10.** *2** WALPOLE *2** thus. *2** All *2** house **title fn10–11.** *5** Relations. All . . . Relations.

Although • *2** relations. Although   **title fn12.** *2** poverty   *2** branches
title fn13. *2** styles and   5* ~~Editor~~ Asserter • *2** asserter   *2** hands,   **title
fn14.** *2** imitation   *2** notes!"   **title fn15.** *2** ye who   *2** LORD!   5* Milles •
*2** [new para] MILES   **title fn16.** *2** though only   **title fn17.** *5** ~~has most~~
foully • *2** fouly   5* ~~the~~ him— • *2** him—   **title fn19.** *2** Bard!   **title
fn20.** *2** age   **title fn22.** *2** page,   **title fn23.** *2** pomp and prodigal-
ity of Heaven.   ⁻**1.1.** 2 Lays,   ⁻**1.2.** 2 Love   2 praise;   ⁻**1.3.** 2 3 But
2 3 methinks   2 name,   ⁻**1.4.** 2 3 hope   **1.** *5* desert   *2–5* wild   **2.** *2–
5* onward   *2–5* child;   **5.** *3 4* (No   *2–5* scorpions   **6.** *2–5* terrors   *3 4* head,)
7. *2–5* cherub wings   **8.** *2–5* anguish   **8.1.2.** 6 Sleep,   **8.1.3.** *7* Youths,
8.1.4. 6 night,   **8.1.5.** 6 Life   6 Breath,   **8.1.6.** 6 with   6 Steep!
8.1.7. 6 grim   **8.1.8.** 6 terrors,   **8.1.9.** 6 state!   **8.1.10.** 6 One,
8.1.12. *7* (That   *7* this   6 all)   **8.1.14.** 6 Sound,   6 call: **9.** *2–
5* CHATTERTON!   *2–5* stones   **10.** *2–5* Freezings   *2–5* neglect!   **11.** *2 3* rod
12. *4* God   **13.** *2–5* Perchance,   *5* the enraptured   **9.1.** *7* Chatterton!   6 Stones
protect,   **10.1.** *7* bleak   **10.1.1.** 6 storm-   **10.1.3.** 6 Thou?   6 word!—
7 thou   **10.1.4.** *7* Forgiven   **14.1.1.** 2 Soul,   **14.1.2.** 2 A thirst   2 Death,
14.1.3. 2 *t*Corse • 3 corse   **14.1.4.** 2 view: • 3 view—   **14.1.5.** 3 While
3 engage: **14.1.6.** 2 Sigh,   **14.1.7.** 3 rage   **14.1.8.** 2 3 thro'   2 Eye.
15. *2–4* nature's   **16.** *2–5* fall;   **17.** *2–5* oft,   *2–5* hour,   **18.** *5* poisoned
2–5 bowl.   **19.** *2–5* heart,   **20.** *2–5* corse   **21.** *2–5* flash of indignation
22. *5* through   *2–4* tear, • *5* tear   *2–5* eye!   **16.1.** *7* so   **18.1.** 6 poison'd
21.1. 6 Indignation   6 sigh   **22.1.** 6 thro'   6 tear,   6 eye.   **23.1.** 3 *this*
2 Land   2 Liberal   3 *1** heart?   **24.1.** 3 *this*   2 Land   2 *Genius* • *1** genius
25.1. *1** soul-enchanting   **26.1.** 2 3 *1** yet   *1** Butler   **26.1.1.** 2 *1** Well
2 humour's • *1** Humor's   2 dart;   **26.1.2.** 2 *want*'s • 3 want's   3 sting:
26.1.3. 2 Otway master   3 *1** art,   **26.1.4.** 2 sing   **32.1.** 2 3 Woe, •
*1** woe.   **32.1.1.** 2 hear   **32.1.2.** 2 tear.   **23.** *2–5* land   *2 5* line?
24. *2–5* land,   **25.** *5* Poured   **26.** *2–5* SPENSER,   *2–5* bard   **28.** *2–
5* limbs   *2–5* anguish   *2 5* lay'd • *3 4* lay'd: **29.** *2–5* darling   **30.** *2–
5* PITY   **32.** *2–5* earth   *2–5* OTWAY'S   *5* famished   **23.2.** *7* -ennobled
26.2. *7* Spenser,   **28.1.** *7* laid;   **30.1.** *7* Pity   **32.2.** *7* Otway's
33.1. *1** heart   2 3 Fame   **34.1.** 2 3 *1** vales   2 3 *1** sports   2 Minstrel
*1** came: **35.1.** 2 3 *1** Gay   *1** poet   2 3 *1** along   **36.1.** 2 song—
37.1. 2 3 Alla   2 Country's foes • 3 Countries' foes— • *1** country's foes;
38.1. 2 And (whilst • 3 And while • *1** And, while   2 *Fancy*   2 3 *1** air
39.1. 2 fair) • 3 fair—   **40.1.** 2 *1** rapture   2 glows, • 3 glows! • *1** glows:
42.1. 2 3 Joy   2 Gold • 3 gold—   **43.1.** 2 widow's prayers   **44.1.** 2 hears •
3 hears— • *1** hears,   **44.1.1.** 2 3 care-worn   2 breast • 3 breast—
44.1.2. 2 debtor's   **44.1.3.** 2 behold • 3 behold:—   **44.1.4.** 2 Steel •
3 *1** steel,   **44.1.5.** 2 *Oppression*   3 feel!   **33.** *2–5* thought,   *2–
5* fame,   **34.** *2–5* vales   *4* AVON   *2–5* winds   *2–5* MINSTREL   *2 3* came.
34fn. *3 4 Avon*,   *5* birth-place   **35.** *2–5* youth!   **36.** *2–5* song,   **37.** *5* frayed
38. *2 5* And,   *2–5* air   **39.** *2–5* visions   **41.** *2 5* health,   **42.** *2 5* joy   *5* the
2 5 wealth;   **43.** *2 5* widow's   *5* -breathed   *2 5* praise;   **44.** *5* sheltered
2 5 orphan's   **45.** *5* -shrivelled   *2 5* captive   **46.** *2 5* blaze   *2 5* ray:
47. *2 5* now, indignant, "grasps   *2 5* steel,"   **34.2.** *7* Minstrel   **37.2.** 6 foe:
37.1.1. 6 Numbers   **37.1.5.** 6 Cheeks   6 flame!   **37.1.6.** 6 declare,
37.1.9. 6 him!   **37.1.10.** *7* Bard's   **41.1.** 6 Friendless,   **48.1.2.** 3 hope

2 3 *1** rais'd   2 depress'd • 3 deprest   **48.1.3.** 3 *burnings*   2 breast •
3 breast—   **48.1.4.** 3 sorrow*l*s   *1** keen,   **48.1.5.** 3 Youth,   *1** the   3 eye—
48.1.6. 2 *Fancy* • *1** fancy   2 3 *1** ever nigh   **48.1.7.** 3 sight!— • *1** sight:
48.1.9. 2 *Poverty*   2 3 giant   2 Mien • *1** mien: **48.1.10.** 2 Youthful Grace •
3 youthful grace—   **48.1.11.** 2 eye   *1** shows,   **48.1.12.** 2 strugling   3 *1** face,
48.1.13. 2 *1** Index   2 *Mental* throes,— • 3 mental *throes*,   **48.1.14.** 3 passion
2 Controul • *1** control,   **48.1.15.** 2 *1** friend   2 *Soul.* • 3 soul!   **51.** 2 *3 5* tree
2 *3 5* child   2 *3* Spring   **54.** 2 *3 5* Fancy,   **56.** 2 *3* That,   2 *3 5* changeful,
5 wantoned   2 *3 5* day!   **57.** 2 *3 5*   unsheltered   2 *3 5* head   **59.** *3* Light'ning
2 *3 5* stand   **60.** 2 *3 5* horror   2 *3 5* land!   **61.** *5* Ah   **62.** *5* gleams
5 lightened   2–5 face?   **63.** 2–5 YOUTH   2–5 soul,   2–5 eye!   **64.** 2–
5 view,   **65.** *5* anguished   2–4 dew: • *5* dew,   **66.** 2–5 sigh!   **66.1.1.** *7* Hope!
62.1. *7* lighten'd   **63.1.** *7* Youth   **67.1.** 2 Hour   **68.1.** 2 *Care*   2 Brow •
*1** brow,   **69.1.** 2 3 *1** Poison's   2 Death-cold Power; • *1** death-cold power,
70.1. 3 Lips   2 bowl   **71.1.** 2 filial *Pity*   2 by • 3 by— • *1** by;   **73.1** *1** She
74.1. 2 *1** scenes   2 Soul, • 3 soul— • *1** soul,   **75.1.** 2 Cot • *1** cot   *1** peace
2 view   **76.1.** 2 Cot • *1** cot   *1** peace   2 e'er   **77.1.** 2 song   **78.1.** 2 hear
79.1. 2 *Mother's*   2 tear; • 3 tear—   **80.1.** 2 Sigh   3 -drawn*/*   **81.1.** 2 3 Agony
*1** woe.   **81.1.1.** 3 *1** "And   *1** thy   2 *1** fate   2 3 *1** distress   2 ensue!
82.1. *1** "Ah,   2 Chalice   2 3 hand! • *1** hand!"   **83.1.** 2 *her*   2 Command •
3 command—   **84.1.** 2 3 *1** Despair   2 3 *1** Indignation   2 rose   **85.1.** 3 Story
2 woes • 3 Woes— • *1** woes;   **86.1.** 3 Insult   2 Heart   **87.1.** 3 dependence
*1** low-born   2 mind   **88.1.** 2 Woe   2 smart   **89.1.** 3 Neglect,   2 Grinning
2 *1** Scorn   2 combin'd • 3 combin'd—   **90.1.** 2 3 Friend   *1** Pain,
91.1. 2 ev'ry   **67.** 2–5 hour,   **68.** 2 *3 5* CARE, • *4* CARE   5 withered
2–5 brow,   **69.** *5* Prepared   2–5 poison's   **70.** 2–5 lips   5 raised   2–5 bowl,
71. 2–5 AFFECTION meek   **72.** 2–5 bosom   2–5 cheek)   **74.** 2–5 scenes
2–5 soul;   **75.** 2–5 cot   5 flashed   **76.** 2–5 cot,   2–5 still,   2–5 day,
77. 2–5 PEACE   5 listened   2–5 lay;   **80.** 2 *5* breast's   **81.** 2–5 agony
2–5 woe!   **82.** *5* poisoned   2–5 chalice   2–5 hand!   **83.** *4* hadst   5 dashed
2–5 it,   **84.** 2–5 DESPAIR and INDIGNATION   **85.** 2–5 story   2–5 woes;
86. 2–5 insult   5 the unfeeling   2–5 heart;   **87.** 2–5 dependence   2–5 mind;
88. *4* ev'ry   2–5 soul   **89.** 5 combined!   **90.** 2–5 quick,   2–5 friend
of pain   **91.** *5* through   2–5 vein!   **68.2.** *7* Care,   **71.2.** *7* Affection
77.2. *7* Peace   **79.2.** *7* mother's   **84.2.** *7* Despair and Indignation   **91/**
143.1.1 *1** O!   2 Blest   **94/143.1.2.** *1** around,   **91/143.1.4.** 2 Hymn • 3 hymn—
91/143.1.5. 2 3 *1** thro'   3 Domain • *1** domain,   **91/143.1.6.** 2 3 Angels
2 Strain,   **91/143.1.7.** 2 *me*   2 *thee*   2 Lyre   2 sound   **91/143.1.8.** 2 *thee*
2 glow • 3 glow—   **91/143.1.9.** *1** waves   2 Woe • *1** woe,   **91.1.10.** *1** storm
*1** elate!   **92.** 2–5 woods!   **93.** *5* murmuring   **94.** *5* here   2–5 cypress
wreath   2–4 weave;   **95.** 2–5 Watching,   2–5 eye,   5 saddening   2–
5 eve.   **96.** 2 *3 5* Here,   2–5 men,   **98.** 2–5 star-   5 sequestered   2–5
tide   **99.** *5* through   **100.** 2–5 here,   2–5 INSPIRATION's   2–5 hour,
101. 2 madning pow'r, • *3–4* mad'ning pow'r, • 5 maddening power,   **103.** 2–5 sea-
2–5 soar,   **104.** *5* passed   2–5 along   **106.** 2–5 Anon,   2–5 rock's   2–5 brow
107. 2 below   **108.** 5 2–5 CHATTERTON!   5 2–5 fate   **109.** *5* praised   5 2–
5 and   5 loved   5 late!   **110.** 5 2–5 CHATTERTON!   2–5 of   **111.** 2–5 chaplet
5 unshaped   5 Tomb. • 2–5 tomb;   **112.** 5 2–5 muse,   **113.** 5 doom. •
2 *3 5* doom: • *4* doom!   **114.** 5 2 *3 5* -drops,   5 2 *3 5* FOLLY's   2 *3 5* wing,

115. 5 blackened   5 Promise   5 Spring; • *2 3 5* spring;   **116.** *5* transpierced
117. *5* Hope   *5* shivered   5 *2 3 5* heart!   **118.** *2–5* thoughts!   *2–5* no
2–5 soul   **119.** 5 Joys • *2–5* joys   5 *were*!   5 no   **121.** 5 *2–5* ocean
122. *2–5* Hope   *5* cottaged   5 dell, • *2–5* dell   **123.** 5 *2–5* careless   5 stray •
2–5 stray;   **124.** *2–5* And,   *2 3 5* moon-light   5 Roundelay   **125.** *2–5* PAS-
SIONS   5 spell.   **126.** *2* O,   *2–5* CHATTERTON!   **127.** *2–5* would'st
2–5 canvass   5 Gale,   **128.** *2–5* love,   *2–5* us,   5 *2–5* team   **129.** 5 *2–
4* UNDIVIDED   5 dale; • *2–5* dale;   **130.** *2–5* we,   *2–5* eve,   5 [?]throng
131. *2–5* Hanging,   *2–4* enraptur'd, • 5 enraptured,   5 song,   **133.** *5* masked,
133.1.1. 5 Eyes,   5 ake   **133.1.3.** 5 precipices   5 sleep   **133.1.4.** 5 fierce
eyed   5 keep,   **133.1.5.** 5 sun,   **133.1.6.** 5 pleasance   5 heart!   **134.** *2–
5* Alas   *2–5* Phantasies!   *2–5* brood   `135.` *5* -solaced   **136.** *2–5* dream,
137. *2–5* Susquehannah   *5* untamed   **138.** *2–5* hill,   *2–5* side   **139.** *2–5* tide,
140. *2–5* solemn   *2–5* thee,   **141.** *2–5* MINSTRELSY!   **142.** *5* soothed
143. *2–5* ills   **143.1.20/100.** *7* Inspiration's   **143.1.24/104.** *7* along,
143.1.28/108. *7* Chatterton!   7 he   **143.1.30/110.** *7* Chatterton!   **143.1.34/**
114. *7* Folly's   **143.1.36/116.** *7* Fate   **143.1.43/123.** *7* Virtue   **143.1.45/**
125. *7* passions   *7* a   **143.1.46/126.** *7* Chatterton!   **143.1.48/128.** *7* love
143.1.51/131. *7* song,   **143.1.52/132.** *7* Poesy   **143.1.53/133.** *7* Antiquity.
143.1.54/134. *7* Alas,   **143.1.57/137.** *7* Susquehana   **143.1.60/140.** *7* Cenotaph
143.1.61/141. *7* Minstrelsy!

title fn. Herbert Croft was the author of *Love and Madness* (1780), part of which
was based on letters sent to Croft by Chatterton's mother; Vicesimus Knox had written
sympathetically about Chatterton in "On the Poems Attributed to Rowley" *Essays Moral
and Literary* (2 vols 1782) II 247–51; William Hayley's lines on Chatterton occur in
A Letter to the Editor of the Miscellanies of T. Chatterton (Strawberry Hill 1779) rpt
Gentleman's Magazine LIII (Apr 1782) 189–95 (C's quotation differs in details); Dean
Jeremiah Milles's edition of *Poems, Supposed to Have Been Written at Bristol, in the
Fifteenth Century by Thomas Rowley, . . . with a Commentary in Which the Antiquity
of Them is Considered, and Defended* (1782) was an answer to Tyrwhitt's 3rd ed of the
Rowley poems (1778). The references are given by C. G. Martin "Coleridge, Edward
Rushton, and the Cancelled Note to the 'Monody on the Death of Chatterton'" *RES*
NS XVII (1966) 391–402, who describes how Rushton (1756–1814) moved in the same
circles in Liverpool that C became acquainted with in his *Watchman* tour.
    Jeremiah Milles (1714–84) had been Dean of Exeter since 1762, President of the
Society of Antiquaries since 1768, and had considerable social pretensions. He appears
not to have moved in the same scholarly or ecclesiastical circles as C's father, but C's
dislike might well have been based on personal acquaintance. Cottle *Rem* 24 claims the
note was cancelled because C feared to offend Milles's son-in-law, one Captain Blake,
who was a member of Bristol Corporation and, as a dragoon, wore a very large sword.
Deeper and more personal reasons are suggested by C. G. Martin.
    In MH's copy of *2** C has deleted the passage "O ye who honor the name of MAN,
rejoice that"; corrected "MILES" to "Milles"; and deleted the verse quotation at the end.
In Joseph Cottle's copy C has deleted the latter part of the title ("ON THE | *MONODY
TO CHATTERTON.*"), as well as the whole of the running headline on the verso of
sig N; italicised "ATTEMPTED"; deleted the passage "who (so future . . . George the
Third," and the phrase "the death of"; supplied opening quotes before "All the house";

deleted the passage "O ye . . . called a LORD!"; corrected "MILES" to "MILLES", and "fouly" to "foully"; and again deleted the verse quotation.

⁻**1.1–2** (MS 1)=Gray's *Elegy in a Country Churchyard* 51–2, with "Cold" for "Chill" and the pronouns adapted. The epigraph was omitted in PR *1*.

⁻**1.3 et seq.** The very complex patterns of indentation are not described here.

8.1.1–4. In 1814 and 1819 C described the lines as schoolboy verses. See on PR *6* above.

8.1.9. C gives as a queried alternative in a footnote in MS 6 "For Wealth, the Coward, and Guilt in robes of state!"

14.1⁺. No line-space in MS 2.

41–8. A number of these lines were included in the version of the **70** *Lines on the "Man of Ross"* copied for RS on 13 Jul 1794 (*CL* I 87) and published in the *Cambridge Intelligencer* on 27 Sept. They were not included in the version of poem **70** published in *Poems* (1796), but they were reclaimed for the 1797 volume, perhaps at the prompting of CL (*LL*—M—I 19, and cf 98). See on poem **70** above.

49. The reading in PR *3* is Cottle's mistake. C had asked him to revise PR 2 to read "Yes! in Nature's rich array," (*CL* I 299: to J. Cottle [6 Jan 1797]).

62. In GC's, Bowles's, and Roskilly's copies of PR *3* C emended " flashing" to " flush-ing". The emendation had been included in the list of errata C sent Cottle on 6 Jan and again c 3 Jul 1797 (*CL* I 299, 331).

65. In RS's copy of PR *3* C emended "anguish'd" to "mortal".

81.1⁺. No line-space in MS 3.

67. The line heads a page (p 23) in PR *3*; it is debatable whether a preceding line-space is to be understood.

82⁺. Line-space in PR *2–5*.

91⁺. C inserted an asterisk in MS 6, adding at the foot of the page: "(* So far a School Exercise, æt. 17: the remaining five §§phs, at Bristol, æt. 23)".

91/143.1.9, 91.1.10–11. In MS 3 the three lines are cancelled together, with two sets of crossed lines.

99⁺. No line-space in PR *2–5*.

107⁺. No line-space in PR *3*.

118–25. The lines incorporate the octave of **78** *Sonnet on Pantisocracy*, which C included in a letter to RS dated 18 Sept 1794 (*CL* I 104), and which he copied into the Estlin Copy Book but never published.

133⁺. No line-space in MS 5.

143.1.12/92–143.1.63/143. PR *6 7* follow lines 92–143 of PR *5*, with only two dif-ferences of wording (at lines 143.1.14/94, 143.1.21/101) and differences of capitalisation and punctuation.

143.1.46/126. The line heads a page in PR *7*, where it seems unlikely that a preceding line-space is to be understood.

143.1.62/142–143.1.63/143. Quoted (var) *The Friend* XI (26 Oct 1809) (*CC*) II 146 (also I 224).

143.1.53/133⁺. No line-space in PR *7*.

83. SONNET: TO MY OWN HEART

A. DATE

Mid-Oct 1794. C told Wrangham that the poem was occasioned by a letter he received from Mary Evans in the week or so before 21 Oct (*CL* I 121: to F. Wrangham 24 Oct 1794; cf 112–13: to RS 21 Oct [1794]). CL remembered it afterwards as one of several Salutation and Cat poems (*LL*—M—I 18).

B. TEXTS

1. PML MA 1848 (7). Two folded leaves, the first 58×45 cm and the second 36.9×22.3 cm (overall dimensions). First leaf: no wm; chain-lines 2.7 cm. Second leaf: wm BUTTANSHAW; chain-lines 2.5 cm. Transcribed in an als to RS, 21 Oct 1794 (*CL* I 115–16).

2 [=RT]. HUL fMS Eng 947. Single folded leaf (now in two pieces, with a hole in the middle), originally 36.7×22.0 cm overall; wm BUT‚TAN‚SHAW; wm 2.3 cm. Transcribed in an als to Francis Wrangham, 24 Oct 1794 (*CL* I 121, which omits the poem).

1. Poems (1796).

2. Sonnets from Various Authors (1796). Signed "S. T. COLERIDGE."

3. Poems (1797).

4. Poems (1803).

5. PW (1828).

6. PW (1829).

7. PW (1834).

title. 1 2 Sonnet • *1* EFFUSION XIX. • *2* SONNET XIV. | *On a Discovery made too late.* • *3 4 SONNET II.* | *On a Discovery made too late.* • *5–7* SONNET XI.

1.1 1   ~~My Heart! thou~~ bleedest/ And thy ~~sore~~ distress
2.1 1   I ponder with a ~~faint and~~ anguish'd Smile
3.1 1   ~~And sternly probe~~ Probing thy ?~~dim~~ sore wound ⟨sternly;⟩ though the while
4.1 1   ~~My swelling Eye be~~ ine Eye be swoln and dim with heaviness.
  1 ☐   Thou bleedest, my poor Heart! & thy Distress
  2 1 2 Doth Reason ponder with an anguish'd smile
    1–7 Reas'ning I   a   scornful
  3 1 2   Probing thy sore Wound sternly, tho' the while
    1–7 And probe
  4 1 2 Her Eye be swoln and dim with heaviness.
    1–7 Swoln be mine eye

5 □	Why didst thou *listen* to Hope's whisper bland?	
6 1	Or, listening, why *forget* its ←—healing—→ Tale,	
2	soothing healing	
1–7	the ←—healing—→	
7 ⊠7	When Jealousy with feverish Fancies pale	
7	feverous	
8 □	Jarr'd thy fine fibres with a Maniac's hand?	
9 □	Faint was that Hope and rayless: yet 'twas fair	
10 □	And sooth'd with many a dream the Hour of Rest!	
11 □	Thou should'st have lov'd it most when most opprest,	
12 □	And nurs'd it with an Agony of Care,	
13 □	Ev'n as a Mother her sweet infant heir	
14 1 2	That pale and sickly droops upon her Breast.	
1–7	wan	

title. 2 Sonnet. • *4 DISCOVERY . . . TOO LATE.* **1.** *1–6* HEART! ⊠1 and
⊠1 distress **2.** *5–7* Reasoning 2 Smile • 7 smile, **3.** ⊠1 wound *5–
7* though **4.** 2 Heaviness. **5.** *1–7* listen **6.** *3 4* Or 2 *1–4* list'ning,
1–7 forget 2 tale • *1–7* tale, **7.** *1–4* fev'rish ⊠1 fancies **8.** *5–7* Jarred
1–7 maniac's **9.** *1–6* HOPE, • 7 Hope, ⊠1 rayless!—Yet 7 fair, **10.** *5–
7* soothed ⊠1 hour ⊠1 rest: **11.** *4 7* shouldst *5–7* loved *1–7* most,
2 opprest • *3 4* opprest. **12.** *5–7* nursed *1–7* agony 7 care, **13.** *5–7* Even
2–4 heir, **14.** 2 Breast!— • *1–7* breast!

title. In the PR *1* list of contents the title is given as "Effusion 19, to my own heart,".
2–3, 6–7, 10–1, 14. Indented in PR *2–4*.
7. MSS 1 2 Jealousy] Written larger, perhaps to be read as bold.

84. TO A YOUNG ASS, ITS MOTHER BEING TETHERED NEAR IT

A. DATE

MS 1 is dated 24 Oct 1794; PR 3 4 append the date "*December*, 1794."

B. TEXTS

1. HUL bMS Am 1622 (36). Two conjoint leaves, 18.8×22.8 cm; wm
CURTEIS & SONS; chain-lines 2.5 cm. Verso of second leaf blank. Ini-
tialled "S.T.C. | Jes. Coll. | Oct. 24th | 1794." Transcript in C's hand, given to
William Smyth.
   The ms is described by E. [=H. M.] Vaughan "Coleridgianum" *The Chan-
ticleer* (Jesus College Cambridge) XVIII (Easter Term 1891) 22–4 at 22: "The
original MS. came into my possession through the late Professor Smythe [*sic*]

of St. Peter's College, Cambridge, my great [great] uncle, who was a personal friend of Coleridge."

William Smyth (1765–1849) had been eighth wrangler in 1787, and was, at the time C gave him the poem, private tutor to Thomas Sheridan, elder son of R. B. Sheridan, living with his pupil at Wanstead, Bognor, and Cambridge. C also presented him with a copy of *The Plot Discovered* (Bristol 1795): see John F. Fleming Sale, Christie's (New York), 18 Nov 1988, lot 78 and Catalogue p 49. Smyth published a volume of *English Lyrics* in 1797, and was appointed Regius Professor of Modern History in 1807.

2. PML MA 1848 (12). Single folded leaf, 46.5×37.7 cm; wm horn within shield surmounted by crown, above GR | 1794; countermark J LARKING | 1794; chain-lines 2.5 cm. The lines are written continuously, two and three abreast. Transcribed in an als to RS, 17 Dec 1794 (*CL* I 142–3).

1. M Chron (30 Dec 1794). Signed "S.T.C."

3. HRC MS (Coleridge, S T) Works B. Two leaves. Folio 24^v: 20.1× 32.0 cm; wm GP&J; chain-lines 2.5 cm. Folio 25^r: 19.9×31.9 cm; wm Britannia in small and rounded oval; chain-lines 2.5 cm. Bound into Rugby Manuscript pp 56–7/ff 24^v–25^r. Transcript in C's hand, which served as copy for PR 2 below.

2. Poems (1796).

3 [=RT]. *Poems* (1797).

Rpt *Poetical Beauties of Modern Writers* (1798; 2nd ed 1803; etc) 38–9; *Beauties of British Poetry* ed Sidney Melmoth (Huddersfield 1801) 21–2.

4. Poems (1803).

The transcript in JTC's Commonplace Book (University of Pennsylvania (Special Collections) MS Eng 13) p 32 is of no textual significance.

5. PW (1828).

6. PW (1829).

7. PW (1834).

title. 1 **Monologue** | to a young Jackass in Jesus Piece—its Mother | ıNear it chained to a Log. • 2 Address to a young Jack Ass & its *tethered* Mother. • *1* ADDRESS TO A YOUNG JACK-ASS, AND | ITS *TETHER'D* MOTHER, | IN FAMILIAR VERSE. • 3 Effusion 33 | To the Foal of an Ass | To a young Ass, its Mother being tethered near it. • *2* EFFUSION XXXIII. | TO | *A YOUNG ASS,* | IT'S MOTHER BEING TETHERED NEAR IT. • *3–7 TO A YOUNG ASS.* | ITS MOTHER BEING TETHERED NEAR IT.

1 ☐   Poor little Foal of an oppressed Race!
2 ☐   I love the languid Patience of thy Face;

3 ⊠2 *1* And oft with gentle hand I give thee Bread,
  2 *1*   friendly
4 1   And And clapped thy ragged Coat, and scratch thy head.
  ⊠1 *1* ◄——Clap——►   pat
  1   scratch
5 1 2 *1* But what thy dulled Spirit hath dismay'd,
  3 2–7   Spirits
6 ⊠2 *1* That never thou dost sport along the glade—
  2 *1*   upon
7 □   And (most unlike the nature of things young)
8 1   That still   to   earth   thy   moping head of is young hung?
  2 *1*   is   hung?
  3 2–7   [?]earth-ward still thy moveless
9 1   Doth thy prophetic Soul anticipate
  ⊠1   Do   Fears
10 □   Meek Child of Misery! thy future fate,
11 □   The starving Meal and all the thousand aches
12 1 2   "That   patient Merit of th' unworthy takes?
  ⊠1 2 Which "patient
13 □   Or is thy sad heart thrill'd with filial pain
14 ⊠2 *1* To see thy wretched Mother's shorten'd Chain?
  2 *1*   lengthen'd
15 □   And truly, very piteous is her lot
16 1 2 *1* Chain'd to a Log   upon   a narrow Spot
  3   upon within
  2–7   within
17 ⊠2   Where the   close-eaten   Grass is scarcely seen,
  2   sw close-eaten
18 ⊠3   While   sweet around her waves the tempting green!
  3   Whereile
19 ⊠3 2 Poor Ass! thy master should have learnt to shew
  3 2   her
20 □   Pity best taught by fellowship of woe:
21 ⊠3 2 For much I fear me, that He lives, like   thee,
  3 2   fear,   ev'n as She,
22 □   Half-famish'd in a Land of Luxury.
              [*Line-space*]
23.1 1   H
23 1   How *askingly* it Its   steps   toward me bend!—
  2 *1*   its
  3   íIts footsteps
  2   It's
  3–7   hither
24 □   It seems to say, "And have I then *one* Friend?
25 1   Innocent Foal, despised   and   forlorn!
  ⊠1   thou poor despis'd Forlorn!—
26 □   I hail thee *Brother*, spite of the fool's scorn;

27 1	And fain	I'd take thee with me to the Dell,
2 *1*		in
3 *2–7*	would	
28 1	Where	high-soul'd PANTISOCRACY shall dwell!
2	Of	to
1–7		Peace and mild Equality
3	~~Of high-soul'd~~ Of lofty-soul'd ISOCRACY

30.1 1	Where Mirth shall tickle Plenty's ribless side*l*,
29.1.1 1	~~Where~~ And Smiles from Beauty's Lip on sunbeams glide;
29.1.1fn 1	This is a truly poetical Line, of which the Author has assured us, that he did not *mean* it to have any *meaning*. Edit.
29.1 1	Where Toil shall wed young Health, that charming Lass!
30.1.1 1	And [?]use his sleek Cows for a looking-glass;
30.1.2 1	Where Rats shall mess with Terriers, hand in glove—
30.1.3 1	And Mice with Pussy's whiskers sport in love!
31.1 1	How thou would'st toss thy heels in gamesome Play,
32.1 1	And frisk about, as Lamb or Kitten, gay!
33.1 1	Yea—and more musically sweet to me
34.1 1	Thy dissonant harsh Bray of Joy would be?[?]
35.1 1	Than Handel's softest airs, that soothe to rest
36.1 1	The tumult of a scoundrel Monarch's Breast.

29 ⊠1	Where Toil shall call the charmer Health his Bride,
30 ⊠1	And Laughter tickle Plenty's *ribless* side!
31 2	How thou would'st toss thy ~~Heal~~ Heels in gamesome Play
⊠1 2	heels,
32 ⊠1	And frisk about, as Lamb or Kitten, gay—
33 ⊠1	Yea—and more musically sweet to me
34 ⊠1	Thy dissonant harsh Bray of Joy would be
35 2	Than *Banti*'s warbled airs, that sooth to rest
⊠1 2	warbled Melodies,
36 2	The Tumult of a scoundrel Monarch's Breast!—
1 3 2	some
3–7	aching of pale FASHION's vacant

title. *4 To a YOUNG ASS*, | • *5–7* TO A YOUNG ASS. | **1.** *1* Foal,   2 Race, • *1* race!   **2.** *1* patience   2 Face! • *1* face; • 3 Fface; • *2–7* face: **3.** *1* oft,   *1* hand, *1* bread— • 3 *2–7* bread,   **4.** ⊠1 2 clap   2 Coat • *1* coat,   2 &   2 Head. • *1* head!   **5.** *1* spirit   *5–7* dismayed,   **6.** 2 Glade, • *1* glade; • 3 *2–7* glade? **7.** 2 3 Nature   2 Things • 3 Thin[?]gs   2 3 Young)   **8.** 2 Earth ward • *2–4* earth-ward • *5–7* earthward   2 3 Head   *4* hung!   **9.** *1* fears   ⊠1 anticipate, **10.** 2 Fate, • *1* fate; • 3 *2–5* fate?— • *6* 7 fate?   **11.** *1–7* meal, • 3 Meal,   2 & 2 Aches, • *1* 3 aches,   **12.** 2 That "patient • 3 *2–7* "Which patient   2 the' • *4–7* the   ⊠1 2 Unworthy   2 3 takes"? • *1–3 5–7* takes?"   **13.** *5–7* thrilled *1* pain,   **14.** 3 *2–6* MOTHER's   *5–7* shortened   **15.** *1* 7 And,   2 7 truly ⊠1 7 *her*   2 Lot • *1* lot— • 3 *2–7* Lot—   **16.** *5–7* Chained   *1* 7 spot, • 3 *2–6* spot   **17.** *1* grass   **18.** 2 Green. • *1* Green? • 3 *2–7* Green!   **19.** ⊠1 7 Master 7 show   **20.** ⊠1 Pity—   2 Fellowship   2 Woe: • 3 2 woe! • *3–7* Woe!   **21.** *5–7* me 2   *1* he • *3–6* He   *6* 7 lives   2 thee • *1 thee*,   2 she,   **22.** *5–7* Half famished   3 *2–7* land   ⊠1 3 2 Luxury! • 3 2 luxury!   **23.** 7 askingly   3 it's •

4–7 its   *1* towards • 3 2 t'ward   2 bend—• 3 2–6 bend? • 7 bend,   **24.** 2 say—
1 I, then,   *7* one   2 Friend?—• *1–7* Friend?"   **25.** ⊠1 Foal!   *1* poor,   *5–*
7 despised   ⊠1 2 Forlorn!   **26.** 2 Brother, • 3 *2–6* BROTHER—• *7* Brother—
1 'spite   2 *1* Fool's   2 Scorn! • 3 *2–7* scorn!   **27.** ⊠1 2 me,   *1* dell • 3 *2–7* Dell
28. 2 Pantisocracy   2 *1* dwell; • 3 *2–7* dwell,   **29.** ⊠1 2 7 TOIL   *1* Charmer,
HEALTH, • 3 *2–6* charmer HEALTH   *7* bride,   **30.** ⊠1 2 7 LAUGHTER
⊠1 2 7 PLENTY's   ⊠1 2 ribless   **31.** *2–7* wouldst   3 *2–7* heels   *1* play—•
3 *2–7* play,   **32.** *7* lamb   ⊠1 2 7 Kitten • *7* kitten   ⊠1 2 gay!   **33.** *1* Yea; •
3 *2–7* Yea!   **34.** *7* bray   *7* joy   3 *2–7* be,   **35.** 3 *2–6* Melodies • *7* melodies
1 7 soothe   **36.** *1* 3 2 tumult   *1* Scoundrel • 2 SCOUNDREL   *7* Fashion's
1–7 breast! • 3 breast!—

title. C added the following instruction to MS 3: "as small as 'In the'—page 73." The
reference is to p 73 of *Poems* (1796), which contains the title of "EFFUSION XXIV. |
IN THE | *MANNER OF SPENSER*.
8. moping/moveless] CL criticised C's revision in a letter of Dec 1796 (*LL*—M—I
67).
22⁺. No line-space in PR *3–7*.
23.1. The false start is because C wanted a wider space between stanzas in MS 1.

85. LINES ON A FRIEND, WHO DIED
OF A FRENZY FEVER, INDUCED
BY CALUMNIOUS REPORTS

A. DATE

Early Nov 1794? Though Smerdon had died on 1 Aug, C appears to have
learned of his death from GC only in late Oct–early Nov (see MS 2 description/
title below).

B. TEXTS

1. PML 1848 (9). Single folded leaf, 58.0×45.5 cm; no wm; chain-lines
2.5 cm. The lines are written two abreast. Signed "S.T.C." Transcribed as part
of an als to RS, 3–4 Nov 1794 (*CL* I 121–4, which omits these verses).

2. In the possession of Sir Charles Cave (Oct 1981). Two conjoint leaves,
each 29.0×44.5 cm; no wm; chain-lines 2.5 cm. The end of the last four lines
is worn away. Transcribed as part of an als to GC, 6 Nov 1794 (*CL* I 127–8).

3. BPL B 22189=Estlin Copy Book ff 26ʳ–27ʳ. Fair copy in C's hand.

4. PML MA 1916=Quarto Copy Book ff 5ᵛ–6ᵛ. Transcript in C's hand.
Copy for PR 1 below was perhaps prepared from this text.

1. Poems (1796).

2. Poems (1797). With the date appended "*November*, 1794."
RS's copy (Yale In 678 797 Copy 1) contains an emendation in C's hand.

3 [=RT]. *Poems* (1803). With date appended "*November*, 1794."

4. PW (1828).

5. PW (1829).

6. PW (1834).

description/title. 1 A Friend of mine hath lately departed this Life in a frenzy fever induced by Anxiety! poor fellow—a child of frailty like me: yet he was amiable—! I poured forth these incondite Lines in a moment of melancholy dissatisfaction: • 2 Poor Smerdon! the reports concerning His literary plagiarism (as far as concerns *my* assistance) are falsehoods. I have felt much for him—and on the morning I received your Letter, poured forth these incondite Rhymes—of course, they are meant for a *Brother's* Eye!— • 3 On the Death of a Friend, who died of a Frenzy fever brought on by Anxiety. • 4 Lines on ~~the Dead~~ a Friend, who died of a frenzy fever induced by ~~Anxiety.~~ calumnious Reports. • *1–6* LINES I ON I A FRIEND I WHO DIED OF A FRENZY FEVER I ɪɴᴅᴜᴄᴇᴅ ʙʏ I CALUMNIOUS REPORTS.

1	1	——! thy grave with aching Eye I scan
	2	Smerdon!
	☒1 2	Edmund!
2	☐	And inly groan for Heaven's poor Outcast, Man!
3	1–3	Tis Tempest all—or Gloom! In earliest Youth
4	*1–6*	early
4	☐	If gifted with th' Ithuriel Lance of Truth
5	1–4 *1*	He force to start amid her feign'd Caress
	2–6	We
6	☐	Vice, Siren Hag! in native Ugliness,
7	1–4	A Brother's Fate shall haply rouse the Tear—
	1–6	will
8	1–4 *1*	And on he goes in heaviness and fear!
	2 4–6	we go
	3	Onward move
9	1–4 *1*	But if his fond Heart call to Pleasure's Bower
	2–6	our hearts
10	☐	Some pigmy Folly in a careless Hour,
11	1–3	The faithless Guest quick stamps th' inchanted Ground,
	4	~~quick~~ soon
	1–6	shall stamp
12	1 2	And mingled forms of Misery threaten round:
	☒1 2	rise around—
13	1	~~Remor~~ Heart-fretting with pallid look Aghast,
	☒1	Heart-fretting Fear
14	☐	That courts the future Woe to hide the past;
15	☐	Remorse, the poison'd Arrow in his side—

16 □	And loud lewd Mirth to Anguish close allied;	
17 1 2	Till Frenzy, ◄——frantic——► Child of moping Pain,	
3	~~frantic~~ fierce-eyed	
4 *1–6*	fierce-eyed	
18 □	Darts her hot lightning flash athwart the Brain!	
	[Line-space]	
19 ⊠2 3	Rest, injurd Shade! shall Slander squatting near	
2 3	couching	
20 □	Spit her cold Venom in a dead man's Ear?	
21 □	'Twas thine to feel the sympathetic glow	
22 □	In Merit's Joy and Poverty's meek Woe;	
23 □	Thine all that cheer the moment as it flies,	
24 □	The zoneless Cares and smiling Courtesies.	
25 1 2	Nurs'd in thy Heart the generous Virtues grew—	
3	manly	
4 *1–6*	firmer	
26 □	And in thy Heart they wither'd!—such chill dew	
27 □	Wan Indolence on each young Blossom shed ;	
28 □	And Vanity her filmy network spread	
29 1–3	With Eye, that prowl'd around in asking gaze	
4 *1–6*	roll'd	
30 □	And Tongue, that traffick'd in the trade of Praise!	
31 □	Thy follies such—! the hard World mark'd them well—	
32 □	Were they more wise, the Proud who never fell?	
33 ⊠4 *1*	Rest, injur'd Shade! the poor Man's grateful Prayer	
4 *1*	Prayer of Praise	
34 1 2–6	On heaven-ward wing thy wounded Soul shall bear!	
2	wound	
3	heaven-~~win~~ward wounded	
4 *1*	heaven-ward	raise.
35 1 2	As oft in Fancy's thought thy grave I pass,	
⊠1 2	at twilight gloom	
36 ⊠*3*	And sit me down upon its recent grass,	
3	oft sit	
37 □	With introverted Eye I contemplate	
38 □	Similitude of soul—perhaps of Fate!	
39 1–3	To me hath Heaven with liberal hand assign'd	
4 *1–6*	bounteous	
40 □	Energic Reason and a shaping Mind,	
41 1	The daring Soul of Truth, the Patriot's part,	
⊠1	ken	
42 □	And Pity's sigh that breathes the gentle Heart—	
43 ⊠4	Sloth-jaundic'd all! and from my graspless hand	
4	⟨my⟩	
44 □	Drop Friendship's precious pearls, like Hour-glass sand.	
45 □	I weep—yet stoop not!—the faint anguish flows,	
46 ⊠6	A dreamy Pang in Morning's fev'rish doze!	
6	feverous	
	[Line-space]	

47　1 3　　Is that pil'd Earth our Being's passless Mound?
　　2^{imp}　　　　　　　　　　　　　Mound⌐.⌐
　　4 *1–6*　this　　　　　　　　　　　　Mound?
48　☒2　　Tell me, cold Grave! is Death with poppies crown'd?
　　2^{imp}　　　　　　　　　　　　　crown'd⌐.⌐
49　1　　Tir'd Centinel, with fitful starts I nod—
　　2^{imp}　　　　　　　　　　　⌐. . . .⌐
　　☒1 2　　　　　　mid　　　　　nod,
50　☒2　　And fain would sleep, though pillow'd on a Clod!
　　2　　　　　　　　⌐. . . . .⌐

description/title. *2 3* LINES | *On a FRIEND,* | WHO DIED OF A FRENZY
FEVER, | *Induced by Calumnious Reports.* • *4* LINES ON A FRIEND, | WHO DIED
OF A FRENZY FEVER INDUCED BY | CALUMNIOUS REPORTS. • *5* LINES ON
A FRIEND. | WHO DIED OF A FRENZY FEVER INDUCED BY | CALUMNIOUS
REPORTS. • *6* LINES ON A FRIEND | WHO DIED OF A FRENZY FEVER
INDUCED BY | CALUMNIOUS REPORTS.　　**1.** 4 *1–6* EDMUND!　2 Grave •
3 [?]grave　3 4 *1* aking　4 *1–6* eye　☒1 scan,　　**2.** *1–3* outcast, • *4–6* outcast—
3. 3 *1–6* 'Tis　☒1 2 tempest all　2 Gloom!— • 3 gloom!— • 4 *1–6* gloom:
☒1 in　4 *1–6* youth　　**4.** *3* wirh　4 *1–6* the　*1–6* lance　4 Truth—　　**5.** *4–*
6 feigned　*1–6* caress　　**6.** 4 *1–5* VICE,　4 *1–6* siren-hag!　3 4 *1–3* ugliness, •
4–6 ugliness;　　**7.** 4 *1–6* fate　4 Tear • *1* 2 *4–6* tear, • *3* tear:　　**8.** 4 &
fear—!　　**9.** *1* heart　4 *1–5* PLEASURE'S　*1–6* bower　　**10.** 4 *1–5* FOLLY
☒1 2 hour,　　**11.** 2 faith[?]less　*1–6* guest　*4–6* the enchanted　2 4 *1–5* ground •
3 Ground • 6 ground,　　**12.** 2–4 Forms　4 *1–3* Mis'ry　2 round; • 4 *1–6* around:
13. 4 *1–5* FEAR, • 6 Fear,　2 Look aghast • ☒1 2 look aghast,　　**14.** *1–6* woe
15. 4 *1–5* REMORSE,　*4–6* poisoned　4 *1–6* arrow　2–4 *1–3* side; • *4–6* side,
16. 4 *1–5* MIRTH, • 6 Mirth,　☒1 3 allied:　　**17.** 4 *1–5* FRENZY,　*1–3* fierce-ey'd
1–6 child　*1–6* pain,　　**18.** 6 lightning-flash • 2 3 lightning Flash　4 Brain. • *1–*
6 brain.　　**19.** ☒1 *4* injur'd • *4* injured　*1–6* shade!　☒1 2 Shall　*1–5* SLANDER
20. 4 *1–6* venom　4 DEAD • *1–5* DEAD　3 6 Man's • 4 *1–5* MAN'S　*1–6* ear?
21. 3 4 Twas　　**22.** 2 3 Joy, • 4 *1–6* joy,　2 Woe, • ☒1 2 woe;　　**23.** 4 *1–6* all,
24. 4 *1–5* *zoneless* CARES, • 6 zoneless Cares,　2 Courtesies! • 4 *1–5* COURTESIES.
25. *4–6* Nursed　☒1 2 heart　4 *1–6* grew,　　**26.** ☒1 2 heart　4 *1–3* wither'd!
Such • *4–6* withered! Such　　**27.** 4 *1–5* INDOLENCE　2 *1–6* blossom　2 3 shed, •
4 *1–6* shed;　　**28.** 4 *1–5* VANITY　4 *1–6* net-work　*1–6* spread,　　**29.** *1–6* eye
4–6 rolled　3 Gaze • 4 *1–6* gaze,　　**30.** 3 Tongue • *1–6* tongue　*4–6* trafficked
2 Trade　3 4 Praise. • *1–6* praise.　　**31.** ☒1 3 such!　*1–6* world　*4–6* marked
3 5 6 well!　　**32.** 2 *more*　4 *1* PROUD • 2–5 PROUD • 6 proud　　**33.** *4–6* injured
1–6 shade!　3 Poor　*1–6* man's　*1* prayer of　*2–6* prayer　*1* praise　　**34.** *1–*
6 soul　3 2–6 bear.　　**35.** 2 3 Grave　　**36.** *1* its'　2 Grass—　　**37.** *1–6* eye
38. 2 3 Soul—perhaps • 4 Soul, perhaps • *1–6* soul, perhaps　4 *1–6* of—　6 fate;
39. *4–6* assigned　　**40.** 2 &　4 *1–6* mind,　　**41.** 3 Ken　2 4 patriot's　4 part
42. 2 3 Sigh, • 4 *1–6* sigh,　4 breaths　2 heart • 4 *1* 3 heart— • 2 *4–6* heart.
43. *4–6* Sloth-jaundiced　　**44.** 2–4 Pearls,　☒1 6 hour glass • 6 hour-glass　3 Sand.
45. ☒1 2 weep,　☒1 3 not! the　2–4 Anguish　　**46.** *1–6* pang　*3* morning's
3 *4* 5 feverish　2 3 Doze! • 4 Doze. • *1–6* doze.　　**47.** *4–6* piled　2–6 earth　*1–*
6 mound?　　**48.** *1–6* grave!　6 death　2 3 Poppies　*4–6* crowned?　　**49.** *4–*
6 Tired　4 *1–5* Centinel! • 6 Sentinel!　　**50.** 3 tho'　*4–6* pillowed　*1–6* clod!

6. MS 1 Vice] C writes the word as if it should perhaps be printed in bold.

8. PR 2 on we go] In RS's copy C has emended to "we creep on".

18⁺. No line-space in PR 6. PR *4 5* have page-break at this point.

24. MS 4 *zoneless*] C first wrote "ZONELESS" and subsequently deleted one of the underlinings.

27. MS 1 Indolence] C writes the word as if it should perhaps be printed in bold.

34⁺. TEXTS 3 4 *1* have line-space.

46⁺. Apparently no line-space in MS 2.

86. SONNET: TO THE AUTHOR OF
THE ROBBERS

A. DATE

The reading of Schiller which C describes in his note took place on 3–4 Nov 1794 (*CL* I 122: to RS). The poem was probably composed soon afterwards.

B. TEXTS

1. Yale In C678 796 P. Single leaf, 16.1×7.4 cm; no wm; chain-lines 2.7 cm; verso blank. Transcript of the octave in C's hand, laid into a copy of PR 2 below.

The octave was clearly written on this scrap as it is; that is, the sestet has not been trimmed away, and must have been transcribed separately.

C added a footnote indicator before the first word ("*Schiller!") and, at the foot of the page, "*Note 5." Since the note on the poem in MS 1* and PR *1* below is numbered 6, the transcript must date from an early stage of the Rugby Manuscript material. Cf **88** *To an Old Man in the Snow* MS 2.

1*. HRC MS (Coleridge, S T) Works B. On recto of part of a single leaf, 19.5×18.5 cm; wm GR in circle; chain-lines 2.5 cm. The recto and verso contain other notes besides. Bound into Rugby Manuscript p 51/f 22ʳ. Note for the poem, evidently transcribed after the text of PR *1* below was set, perhaps in Mar 1796 (*CL* I 193: to J. Cottle [late Mar 1796]).

1. Poems (1796).

2. Sonnets from Various Authors (1796). Signed "S. T. COLERIDGE."

The copy C presented to Mrs Thelwall on 18 Dec 1796, now at the V&A (Dyce Collection 4ᵗᵒ 1298), contains two minor emendations, together with a comment given in vol II headnote.

2. Pforzheimer MS Misc 74. PR 2 corrected in C's hand (this half of the page only), with a fresh transcript of the first four lines. Endorsed by Joseph Cottle: "Autograph of S. T. Coleridge | *J.C.*"

This fragment clearly served as copy for PR *3* below. C has deleted "XXVIII" and replaced it with the arabic numeral 8. He has written 4 3 2 1, in that order, at the end of the first four lines; deleted the punctuation at the end of the printed line 2; emended the dash at the end of the printed line 4 to a comma; and written in the LH margin, against the lines: "Arrange the four first lines as they are in my first Edition, i.e. according to the figures here. Add the note from my notes." Only C's fresh transcript of the first four lines, at the foot of the page, is collated.

3 [=RT]. *Poems* (1797).

4. Poems (1803).

5. PW (1828).

6. PW (1829).

7. PW (1834).

title. *1* EFFUSION XX. I *TO THE AUTHOR OF THE "ROBBERS."* •
2 SONNET XXVIII. I *To the Author of the "Robbers."* • *3 SONNET VIII.* I *To the Author of "THE ROBBERS."* • *4 SONNET XV.* • *5–7* SONNET XII. I TO THE AUTHOR OF THE "ROBBERS."

1 ⊠*2*	Schiller! that hour I would have wish'd to die,
1fn *1* 1 3*	One night in Winter on leaving a⟨a college-⟩friend's Room, with whom I had
	supped, I carelessly took away with me "The R̶o̶o̶m̶sobbers" a Drama, the very name
	of which I had never before e̶v̶e̶n̶ heard of—. A winter midnight—the wind high—
	and "The Robbers" for the first time! The Reader of SCHILLER w̶e̶l̶l̶ m̶a̶y̶ will conceive
	what I felt. ∕̶ a̶n̶d̶ t̶h̶o̶s̶e̶ w̶h̶o̶ h̶a̶v̶e̶ n̶o̶t̶ r̶e̶a̶d̶ h̶i̶s̶ w̶o̶r̶k̶s̶ SCHILLER introduces
	no p̶r̶æ̶t̶e̶r̶ supernatural Beings; yet b̶y̶ his ? m̶e̶ human beings 5
	agitate and astonish more than "all the *goblin* Rout—even of Shakspeare.
2 *1*	If thro' the s̶t̶a̶r̶t̶l̶i̶ shudd'ring Midnight I had sent
⊠*1 2*	shudd'ring
3 ⊠*2*	From the dark dungeon of the Tower time-rent
4 ⊠*2*	That fearful Voice, a famish'd Father's cry—
4fn *4*	The Father of MOOR, in the Play of the *Robbers*.
4.1 *2*	That fearful voice, a famish'd Father's cry,
3.1 *2*	From the dark dungeon of the tower time-rent,
2.1 *2*	If thro' the shudd'ring midnight I had sent
1.1 *2*	SCHILLER! that hour I would have wish'd to die—
5 *1 1 5–7*	Lest in some after moment aught more mean
2–4	That no less vast
6 ⊠*2 2*	Might stamp me mortal! A triumphant Shout
2	human!
7 ⊠*2*	Black Horror scream'd, and all her *goblin* rout

7fn *2*　　　SCHILLER introduces no supernatural Beings.

8 1 *1 5–7* Diminish'd shrunk from the more with'ring scene!

　　2–4　　From the more with'ring scene diminish'd past.

9 *1–7*　　Ah Bard tremendous in sublimity!

10 *1–7*　Could I behold thee in thy loftier mood

11 *1–7*　Wand'ring at eve with finely-frenzied eye

12 *1–7*　Beneath some vast old tempest-swinging wood!

13 *1–7*　Awhile with mute awe gazing I would brood:

14 *1–7*　Then weep aloud in a wild extacy!

1. *1–3 5–7* SCHILLER!　*5–7* wished　*7* die　　**1fn1.** *1 3* Winter,　1* leaving a̸⟨a •
1 3 leaving a　1* college-⟩ • *1 3* College-　*1 3* room,　　**1fn2.** 1* R̶o̶o̶m̶sobbers" •
1 3 Robbers"　*1 3* drama,　　**1fn3.** 1* before e̶v̶e̶n̶ • *1 3* before　*1 3* heard of:—
1 3 Winter　　**1fn4.** *1 3* time!—　1* Reader • *1 3* readers　1* SCHILLER w̶e̶l̶l̶
m̶a̶y̶ • *1 3* SCHILLER　　**1fn5.** 1* felt.̶/̶a̶n̶d̶ . . . w̶o̶r̶k̶s̶ • *1 3* felt.　1* no p̶r̶æ̶t̶e̶r̶ •
1 3 n̶o̶　*1 3* heings;　1* b̶y̶ his ?̶m̶e̶ • *1 3* his　　**1fn6.** *3* astonish,　*1 3* all
1 3 rout—　　*1 3* Shakespeare.　　**2.** 2 thro • *5–7* through　*5–7* shuddering
1 3–7 midnight　　**3.** 2 *3 4* Dungeon　⊠1 *2 3 4* tower　　**4.** *1 3–7* voice,　*5–*
7 famished　　**6.** ⊠2 shout　　**7.** *1–6* HORROR　*2 3* scream'd • *5–7* screamed,
5–7 goblin　　**8.** *5–7* Diminished　*5–7* withering　　**9.** *2–4 7* Ah!　　**10.** *2–*
4 mood,　　**11.** *5–7* Wandering　*3–7* finely　　**13.** *2–4* brood,　　**14.** *5–7* ecstasy!

title. In the PR *1* list of contents the title is given as "Effusion 20, to Schiller,", in the PR *3* list of contents simply as "To Schiller,". MS 2 revises the title to the PR *3* version (substituting arabic numeral 8).

1fn. Printed at the end of the volume in PR *1*, with the cross-reference "Note 6.—Page 65.", and at the foot of the page in PR *3*.

1fn3. MS 1* e̶v̶e̶n̶] Deletion in pencil.

2–3, 6–7, 10, 12–13. Indented in PR *2–4*.

3.1, 2.1. In Mrs Thelwall's copy of PR 2 C deleted the comma at the end of line 3.1 and inserted a comma at the end of line 2.1.

87. SONNET: ON HOPE

(with Charles Lamb)

A. DATE

Nov–Dec 1794?

B. TEXTS

1. PML MA 1848 (11). Single folded leaf, 46.5×37.7 cm overall; wm horn within shield surmounted by crown, above GR | 1794; countermark J LARK-

ING | 1794; chain-lines 2.5 cm. Lines 13.1–14.1 are written abreast. Transcribed in an als to RS, 11 Dec 1794 (*CL* I 136).

The poem is one of several transcribed in part or in whole by C in the course of the letter. C introduces it with the remark, "the four *last* Lines were written by Lamb—a man of uncommon Genius".

2. BPL B 22189=Estlin Copy Book f 25ᵛ. Transcript in C's hand.

3. HRC MS (Coleridge, S T) Works B. Single leaf, 18.9×32.4 cm; wm Britannia in large oval; chain-lines 2.5 cm. Bound into Rugby Manuscript p 44/f 18ᵛ. Transcript in C's hand, which served as copy for PR *1* below.

1. Poems (1796).
Rpt *Flowers of Poesy* (Carlisle 1798) 56.

2 [=RT]. *Poems* (1797).

3. Poems (1803).

4. PW (1828).

5. PW (1829).

6. PW (1834).

title. 1 Sonnet. • 2 Irregular Sonnet. • 3 *1* EFFUSION 14 • *2 3* SONNET III. • *4–6* SONNET VIII.

1 1	O	gentle Look, that didst my Soul beguile,
2 3	ØThou	
1–6	Thou	
2 □	Why hast thou left me? Still in some fond Dream	
3 □	Revisit my sad Heart, auspicious Smile!	
4 □	As falls on closing Flowers the lunar Beam—.	
	[*Line-space*]	
5 1	What time in sickly Mood at ? e̶l̶o̶ parting Day	
2	e̶l̶o̶s̶e̶ ̶o̶f̶ parting	
3 *1–6*	←—parting—→	
6 □	I lay me down and think of happier Years—	
7 □	Of Joys, that glimmer'd in Hope's twilight Ray,	
8 □	Then left me darkling in a vale of Tears.	
	[*Line-space*]	
9 1 2 2 3	O pleasant Days of Hope, for ever flown!	
3 *1* 4–6	gone!	
10 □	Could I recall you—!—But that thought is vain.	
11 □	Availeth not Persuasion's sweetest Tone	
12 □	To lure the fleet-wing'd Travellers back again—	
13.1 1 2	On on they haste to everlasting Night,	
14.1 1 2	Nor can a Giant's arm arrest them in their Flight!	
13 ⊠1 2	Yet fair, tho' faint, their Images shall gleam	

14 3 *1 4–6* Like the bright Rainbow on a willowy stream.
   2 3   an evening

title. *1* EFFUSION XIV.   **1.** 3 *1–5* L O O K,   ⊠1 2 soul   **2.** 2 3 ~~lelf~~ left
⊠1 2 dream   **3.** ⊠1 2 heart,   *1–5* S M I L E!   **4.** ⊠1 2 flowers   2 Beam: •
⊠1 2 beam: **5.** ⊠1 2 time,   2 mood • ⊠1 2 mood,   ⊠1 2 day   **6.** 2 Years; •
⊠1 2 years;   **7.** *4–6* glimmered   ⊠1 ray,   **8.** 3 ~~le~~left   2 Tears! • ⊠1 2 tears.
9. ⊠1 2 days   2 Hope • ⊠1 2 Hope—   2 flown,   *6* gone!—   **10.** ⊠1 you!—
2 but   2 3 Thought   2 vain: **11.** ⊠1 3 tone   **12.** 2 fleetwing'd • *4–6* fleet-
winged   2 Trav'llers • ⊠1 2 Travellers   2 3 again. • *1–6* again: **14.1.** 2 ~~FLIGHT~~!
Flight!   **13.** *4–6* though   ⊠1 2 images

title. In the PR 2 list of contents, the title is given as "On Hope,".
1. 1 2 Look,] Written in MSS 1 2 as if it might be meant to be read as bold.
4⁺, 8⁺. The extra space in MS 3 is very slight, if it exists at all, and there are no
line-spaces in PR *1–6*.

88. SONNET: TO AN OLD MAN IN THE SNOW
(with Samuel Favell)

A. DATE

C refers to the poem in a letter to RS of 11 Dec 1794 (*CL* I 134). It was
probably written after early Sept 1794, when Samuel Favell became a convert
to pantisocracy (*CL* I 99: to RS [1 Sept 1794]), and probably after 8 Nov, when
C went down to London and spent time with Grecians keeping the school term.

B. TEXTS

1. BPL B 22189=Estlin Copy Book f 20ʳ. Transcript in C's hand.

2. HEHL HM 260. Single leaf, 18.4×17.7 cm; no wm; chain-lines 2.7 cm;
verso blank. Transcript in C's hand, endorsed by Joseph Cottle "(Autograph of
S. T. Coleridge. J.C)".

The ms is almost certainly the bottom half of a leaf, the top half of which
contains the collaborative sonnet **103** *Adaptation of "Pale Roamer thro' the
Night"* (with RS), submitted as copy for PR *1* below but divided, either when
C decided to make changes in poem **103** or, for reasons of his own, by Joseph
Cottle. Cf also **86** *To the Author of "The Robbers"* MS 1.

1. Poems (1796).
"For the rough sketch of Effusion XVI. I am indebted to Mr. F A V E L L."
(Preface p xi).

2. Sonnets from Various Authors (1796). Signed "S. T. COLERIDGE."

3 [=RT]. *Poems* (1797).
Rpt *Poetical Beauties of Modern Writers* (1798; 2nd ed 1803 etc) 41–2.

4. The Courier (16 Jul 1801). "(By Mr. COLERIDGE.)"
This is a reprinting of PR *3*, but it probably had C's authority.

5. Poems (1803).
The transcript by JTC, in his Commonplace Book (University of Pennsylvania (Special Collections) MS Eng 13) p 31, is probably from this text (possibly from PR *2* or *3*), and has no textual significance.

6. PW (1828).

7. PW (1829).

8. PW (1834).

title. 1 Ode | written in snowy Weather. • 2 *1* Effusion 16 • *2* SONNET XVII. • *3 SONNET VI.* • *4 TO AN OLD MAN.* • *5 SONNET V.* • *6–8* SONNET X.

1	⊠2	Sweet Mercy! how my very heart has ~~sigh~~ bled
	2	sigh bled
2	☐	To see thee, poor old Man! and thy grey hairs
3	☐	Hoar with the snowy Blast—while no one cares
4	☐	To cloath thy shrivell'd Limbs and palsied Head.
5	☐	My Father! throw away this tatter'd vest,
6	☐	That mocks thy Shiv'ring! take my garment—Use
7	⊠2 *1 6*	A young Man's Arm! I'll melt these frozen Dews,
	2 1 6	arms!
8	☐	That hang from thy white beard and numb thy Breast.
9	1	My Laura too shall tend thee, like a Child—
	⊠1 *5*	Sara
	5	fend
10	⊠	And thou shalt talk, in our fire side's recess,
11	⊠4	Of purple Pride that scowls on Wretchedness!
	4	and
12	⊠2 *2–5*	He did not so, the Galilæan mild,
	2	~~He did not so, the~~ And how, that He,
	2–5	He did not scowl,
13	1	Who met the Lazar turn'd from Dives' doors
	2	~~Who m~~Met the ⟨poor⟩ Lazars rich man's doors,
	1 6 7	Who met the
	2–5	Lazar
	8	Lazars men's
14	1 *2–5*	And call'd him Friend and wept upon his Sores.
	⊠1 *2–5*	them Friends, heal'd their noisome

title. *1* EFFUSION XVI.   **2.** ⊠1 *4 8* OLD MAN!   *8* old   ⊠1 *2–5* gray
4 Hairs   **3.** ⊠1 *2–5* blast: • *2–5* blast;   **4.** 2 *1–3 5* cloathe • *4 6–8* clothe

6–8 shrivelled ⊠1 limbs 2 & ⊠1 *4* head. • *4* head! **5.** *6–8* tattered
⊠1 *4* vest **6.** *1–3 5* shiv'ring! • *4* shiv'ring!— • *6–8* shivering! *4* Take
⊠1 use **7.** ⊠1 man's *2–5 7 8* arm! ⊠1 dews **8.** *4* beard, ⊠1 breast.
9. *1–3 5–7* SARA too • *4* Sarah, too, ⊠1 *4 5* Child: • *4 5* child: **10.** 2 Fire
side's • *4 8* fire-side's **11.** ⊠1 *4 8* Pride, • *4 8* pride, 2 *6 7* Wretchedness. •
1–3 5 Wretchedness.— • *4* wretchedness;— • *8* wretchedness. **12.** *1–3 5–*
7 GALILÆAN • *8* Galilean **13.** *6–8* turned **14.** *6–8* called 2 *3 5* Friend, •
4 friend, *6–8* healed 2 *1 6 7* Sores! • *2–5 8* sores!

title. In the PR *1* list of contents the title is continued as "to an Old Man,". In PR *3* it
is given simply as "To an Old Man,". In C's first reference to the poem, in his letter to
RS of 11 Dec 1794, he described it as "the 'Old Man in the snow'" (*CL* I 134).
2–3, 6–7, 10–11, 13–14. Indented in PR *2–4*.
4⁺, 8⁺. PR *4* has line-spaces.

89. SONNET: TO THE HON MR ERSKINE

A. DATE

Nov–Dec 1794. See vol I headnote.

B. TEXTS

1. M Chron (1 Dec 1794). Signed "S. T. C. I Jesus College, Cambridge."

1. HRC MS (Coleridge, S T) Works B. Recto of a single leaf, 18.5×31.1 cm;
wm COLES; chain-lines 2.5 cm. Bound into Rugby Manuscript p 39/f 16ʳ.
Transcript in C's hand, which served as copy for PR 2 below.

2 [=RT]. Poems (1796).

3. Poems (1803).
Rpt *Laura* ed Capel Lofft (5 vols 1813–14) III No 255.

4. PW (1828).

5. PW (1829).
JG's (?) copy at NYPL (Berg Collection) contains a correction.

6. PW (1834).

title. *1 SONNETS.* I No. I. I TO THE HONOURABLE MR. ERSKINE. •
1 Effusion 45 • *2* EFFUSION V. • *3 SONNET X.* • *4–6* SONNET IV.

1 ☐   When British Freedom for an happier land
2 ☐   Spread her broad wings, that fluttered with affright,
3 ☐   ERSKINE! thy voice she heard, and paus'd her flight—

4 *1*   Sublime of hope, where fearless thou didst stand,
⊠*1*   For dreadless
        [*Line-space*]
5 □   Thy censer glowing with the hallow'd flame,
6 *1*   An hireless Priest before her injur'd shrine,
⊠*1*   th' insulted
7 □   And at her altar pour'dst the stream divine
8 *1*   Of ◄——matchless——► eloquence! Therefore thy name
1   ~~matchless~~ unmatch'd
2–6   ◄——unmatch'd——►
        [*Line-space*]
9 ⊠*5*   Her sons shall venerate, and cheer thy breast
5   end
10 *1*   With heav'n-breath'd blessings; and, when late the doom
⊠*1*   blessings heaven-ward breath'd. And when
11 ⊠*3*   Of Nature bids thee die, beyond the tomb
3   rise
12 □   Thy light shall shine, as sunk beneath the West,
        [*Line-space*]
13 *1*   Though the great Sun not meets our wistful gaze,
⊠*1*   Summer Sun eludes our
14 *1*   Still glows wide Heav'n with his distended blaze!
⊠*1*   burns

1. 1 ~~F̶R̶E̶E̶D̶O̶M̶~~ Freedom *6* a   **2.** 1 *2 3* flutter'd   **3.** *6* Erskine! *4–6* paused
⊠*1* flight   **4.** ⊠*1* hope! ⊠*1* stand   **5.** ⊠*1* (Thy 1 Censer *4–6* hallowed
⊠*1* flame)   **6.** *6* A *4–6* the   **7.** 1 *2 3* pourd'st • *4–6* pour   **8.** *4–*
6 unmatched ⊠*1* eloquence.   **9.** 1 *3* Sons   **10.** *4–6* breathed.   1 Doom
12. 1 Light   ⊠*1* shine: ⊠*1* West   **13.** 1 *2 3* Tho'   **14.** ⊠*1* Heaven   ⊠*1* blaze.

    title. In the PR *2* list of contents the title is given as "Effusion 5, to Erskine,".
    1. The PR *4–6* lists of contents all give the first line as "When British Freedom from
an [*6* a] happier Land [*6* land]".
    2–3, 6–7, 10–11. Indented in PR *1*.
    4⁺, 8⁺, 12⁺. Only PR *1* has line-spaces.
    9. PR *5* end] Corrected to "and" in JG's (?) copy.

90. SONNET: TO BURKE

A. DATE

Nov–Dec 1794.

B. TEXTS

1. M Chron (9 Dec 1794). Signed "S. T. C. I Jesus College, Cambridge."

1. PML MA 1848 (12). Single folded leaf, 46.5×37.7 cm; wm horn within shield surmounted by crown, above GR I 1794; countermark J LARKING I 1794; chain-lines 2.5 cm. The lines are written out continuously, two and three abreast. Transcript in an als to RS, 17 Dec 1794 (*CL* I 142).

2. HUL fMS Eng 947.8. Verso of a single leaf, 17.5×21.3 cm; no wm; chain-lines 2.8 cm. Transcript in C's hand, which might have served as copy for PR 2 below.

The recto contains an intermediate version of the sonnet to Bowles ("*Effusion 1*"), and Katharine Southey's endorsement. See poem **95.**

2*. HRC MS (Coleridge, S T) Works B. Verso of a single leaf, 19.6× 32.6 cm; wm Britannia in large oval surmounted by crown; chain-lines 2.6 cm. Bound into Rugby Manuscript p 34/f 13ᵛ. Transcript in C's hand of the note to MS 2, which served as copy for PR 2* below.

C's instruction to print from the first number of *The Watchman* (*CC*) 37–9 indicates that the note was written after 1 Mar 1796.

2*. C's note as it appears in the two extant proof copies of PR 2: (A) MH's copy, in the Alexander Turnbull Library, Wellington, New Zealand (R Eng COLE Poems (1796)); (B) Joseph Cottle's copy, bound into BM Ashley 408 (*JDC facsimile* 69–73). Copy B has corrections in C's hand.

2 [=RT]. *Poems* (1796).

3. Poems (1803).
Rpt *Laura* ed Capel Lofft (5 vols 1813–14) II No 147.

4. PW (1828).

5. PW (1829).
JG's (?) copy at NYPL (Berg Collection) contains a correction.

6. PW (1834).

C. GENERAL NOTE

The transcript in the hand of Leigh Hunt, now at the Pforzheimer (LH 293), was made in the 1850s and has no textual significance.

title. *1 SONNETS* I ON I EMINENT CHARACTERS. I No. II. • 2 ~~Effusions~~ *Effusion 2* • 2 EFFUSION II. • *3 SONNET VII.* • *4–6* SONNET II.

1 ☒1   As late I lay   in   Slumber's shadowy vale,
1   roam'd thro' Fancy's
2 ☐   With wetted cheek and in a mourner's guise,

3 ☐ I saw the sainted form of FREEDOM rise:

4 ☐ She spake! Not sadder moans th' autumnal gale:—

[*Line-space*]

5 ⊠2 "Great Son of Genius!   sweet   to me thy name,

   2   ~~dear~~ sweet

6 ☐ "Ere in an evil hour, with alter'd voice,

7 ☐ "Thou bad'st Oppression's hireling crew rejoice,

8 ☐ "Blasting with wizard spell my laurell'd fame.

[*Line-space*]

9 ☐ "Yet never, BURKE! thou drank'st Corruption's bowl!

9fn 2*   Yet never, BURKE! thou drank'st Corruption's Bowl

               When I composed this line, I had not read the following paragraph in the Cambridge Intelligencer (of Saturday, November 21, 1795)—Print from Page 21st of the first number of the Watchman the passage marked between (crotchets) and likewise the paragraphs so marked 22 and 23rd pages— 5 Concluding with the word—PRIESTLEY! ~~Instead~~ See Number I of the WATCHMAN, a miscellany published every eighth day, by the Author of these Poems, and by Parsons, Pater-noster Row, London.—

     2* 2   *Yet never*, BURKE! *thou drank'st Corruption's Bowl!*

               When I composed this line, I had not read the following paragraph in the Cambridge Intelligencer (of Saturday, November 21, 1795.)

     2* 2   *When Mr. Burke first crossed over the House of Commons from the Opposition to the Ministry, he received a pension of* 1200*l. a-year charged* 5 *on the King's Privy Purse!* When he had completed his labors, it was then a question what recompence his service deserved. Mr. Burke wanting a present supply of money, it was thought that a pension of 2000l. per annum *for forty years certain*, would sell for eighteen years purchase, and bring him of course 36,000l. But this pension must, by the very unfortunate act, 10 of which Mr. Burke was himself the author, have come before Parliament. Instead of this Mr. Pitt suggested the idea of a pension of 2000l a-year *for three lives*, to be charged on the King's Revenue of the West India 4$\frac{1}{8}$ per cents. This was tried at the market, but it was found that it would not produce the 36,000l. which were wanted. In consequence of this a pension 15 of 2500l. per annum, *for three lives* on the 4$\frac{1}{2}$ West India Fund, the lives to be nominated by Mr. Burke, that he may accomodate the purchasers, is *finally* granted to this disinterested patriot! He has thus retir'd from the trade of politics, with pensions to the amount of 37000l. a-year.

     2*   We feel not for the Public in the present instance: we feel for the honor of 20 genius; and mourn to find one of her most richly-gifted children associated with the Youngs, Wynhams, and Reeveses of the day; "matched in mouth" with

               "Mastiff, bloodhound, mungril grim,

               Cur, and spaniel, brache, and lym,   25

               Bobtail tike and trundle-tail;"

And the rest of that motley pack, that open in most hideous concert, whenever out State-Nimrod provokes the scent by a trail of rancid plots and false insurrections! For of the *rationality* of those animals, I am inclined to entertain a doubt, a *charitable* doubt! since such is the system which 30 they support, that we add to their integrity whatever we detract from their understanding:

>—*Fibris increvit optimum*
>*Pingue: carent culpa.*

It is consoling to the lovers of human nature, to reflect that Edmund 35 Burke, the only writer of that faction "whose name would not sully the page of an opponent," learnt the discipline of genius in a different corps. At the flames which rise from the altar of Freedom, he kindled that torch with which he since endeavored to set fire to her temple. Peace be to his spirit, when it departs from us: this is the severest punishment I wish him—that 40 he may be appointed under-porter to St. Peter, and be obliged to open the gate of Heaven to Brissot, Roland, Concordet, Fayette, and Priestley!—See Number I. of the WATCHMAN, a miscellany published every eighth day, by the Author of these Poems, and by Parsons, Paternoster-Row, London.

10	⊠*5*	"Thee stormy Pity, and the cherish'd lure
	5	"The
11	☐	"Of Pomp, and proud Precipitance of soul
12	*1* 1	"Urg'd on with wild'ring fires. Ah, Spirit pure!
	⊠*1* 1	"Wilder'd with meteor
		[*Line-space*]
13	☐	"That Error's mist had left thy purged eye—
14	☐	"So might I clasp thee with a Mother's joy!"

1. *2–6* slumber's   1 Vale, • 2 vale   **2.** 1 2 Cheek   1 2 Mourner's   1 Guise, •
2 *2 3* guise   **3.** 1 Form   1 *6* Freedom   **4.** 1 spake!—   ⊠*1* not   1 saddenr
2–6 the   1 Autumnal   1 Gale. • 2 *2 3* gale. • *4–6* gale—   **5.** 1 Name, • 2 name
6. *6* Ere   1 Hour • ⊠*1* 1 hour   1 alterd • *4–6* altered   1 Voice*ı* • ⊠*1* 1 voice
7. *6* Thou   2 *4 5* badst   1 Crew   ⊠*1* rejoice   **8.** *6* Blasting   1 Spell   1 Lau-
rell'd • 2 ? laur laurell'd • *4–6* laurelled   **9.** *6* Yet   1 **Burke!** • *6* Burke!   1 Bowl!
9fn4. 2*ʙ 2 *"When*   **9fn19.** 2*ʙ 2 3700l. a-year."   **9fn28.** 2*ʙ our State-Nimrod
The last two paragraphs of 2*ʙ have been cancelled by C with a single vertical line; a
note in the ʀʜ margin of 2*ᴀ, beginning alongside the last paragraph and continuing
to the foot of the page, has been cropped almost completely   **10.** *6* Thee   1 **Pity** •
2 Pɪᴛʏ • *2–6* Pity   *4–6* cherished   1 2 Lure   **11.** *6* Of   1 **Pomp** • 2 Poᴍᴘ,
1 **Precipitance** • 2 Pʀᴇᴄɪᴘɪᴛᴀɴᴄᴇ   1 Soul,   **12.** *4 5* "Wildered • *6* Wildered
1 Fires.—Ah— • ⊠*1* 1 fires. Ah   **13.** *6* That   *2–6* error's   1 2 Eye— • *2–6* eye:
14. *6* So   1 Joy. • 2 *5* joy!

title. In the ᴘʀ 2 list of contents the title is given as "Effusion 2, to Burke,".
2–3, 6–7, 10, 12. Indented in ᴘʀ *1*.
4⁺, 8⁺, 12⁺. Only ᴘʀ *1* has line-spaces. In ᴍꜱ 1, where the lines are written out
continuously, two and more abreast, each stanza is begun as a new continuous paragraph.
9fn. When the note appeared in ᴘʀ 2* 2, it was not affixed to any line-number, but to
the poem in general, by a cross-reference—"Page 46." (only)—at the end of the volume.
There is no note-cue on p. 46; see **60** *Absence: A Poem* 57fn for a similar instance in the
1796 volume and a comment on its significance. *The Watchman* ɪ (1 Mar 1796) (*CC*)
37–9 has not been collated.
Fibris . . . culpa] Persius *Satires* 3.32–3 tr G. G. Ramsay *Juvenal and Persius* (LCL

1941) 347 "Their hearts are overlaid with fat lard; they have no sense of sin". (The Latin is misquoted.)

10. PR *5* "The] The missing "e" added in JG's (?) copy.

91. SONNET: TO PRIESTLEY

A. DATE

Early Dec 1794.

B. TEXTS

1. M Chron (11 Dec 1794). Signed "S. T. C."

1. PML MA 1848 (12). Single folded leaf, 46.5×37.7 cm; wm horn within shield surmounted by crown, above GR I 1794; countermark J LARKING I 1794; chain-lines 2.5 cm. Transcript in an als to RS, 17 Dec 1794 (*CL* I 140).

2 [=RT]. *Poems* (1796).

3. Poems (1803).

4. PW (1828).

5. PW (1829).

6. PW (1834).

C. GENERAL NOTE

The transcript in the hand of Leigh Hunt, now at the Pforzheimer (LH 293), was made in the 1850s and has no textual significance.

title. *1 SONNETS* I ON I EMINENT CHARACTERS.I No. III. • 1 Sonnet •
2 EFFUSION IV. • *3 SONNET IX.* • *4–6* SONNET III.

1 *1*	Tho' King-bred rage, with lawless uproar rude,	
1		Tumult
2–6	rous'd by that dark Vizir RIOT	
2 *1*	Hath driv'n our PRIESTLEY o'er the ocean swell;	
☒*1*	Have	
3 ☐	Tho' Superstition and her wolfish brood	
4 ☐	Bay his mild radiance, impotent and fell;	
	[*Line-space*]	
5 ☐	Calm, in his halls of brightness, he shall dwell!	
6 ☐	For, lo! RELIGION, at his strong behest,	

7 *1* 1   Disdainful   rouses from the Papal spell,
   2–6 Starts with mild anger
8 □   And flings to earth her tinsel-glitt'ring vest,
     [*Line-space*]
9 □   Her mitred State, and cumbrous Pomp unholy;
10 □   And JUSTICE wakes, to bid th' Oppressor wail,
11 *1*   That   ground th' ensnared soul of patient Folly;
  1   ~~Who~~ That
  2–6 Insulting   aye   the   wrongs
12 □   And from her dark retreat by Wisdom won,
13 □   Meek NATURE slowly lifts her matron veil,
14 □   To smile with fondness on her gazing Son!

1. *4–6* Though roused   1 king—   1 Rage   *4 5* RIOT • *6* Riot   ⊠*1* rude   **2.** *2–6* driven   1 **Priestley** • *2–5* PRIESTLY • *6* Priestly   1 Ocean   **3.** *4–6* Though *2–5* SUPERSTITION   1 &   1 Brood   **4.** 1 Radiance,   1 &   **5.** ⊠*1* Calm 1 Halls   1 *2–5* Brightness • *6* brightness   ⊠*1* dwell!   **6.** ⊠1 For   1 *2–5* RELIGION • *6* Religion   ⊠*1* behest   **7.** 1 papal spell   **8.** 1 *2–4* Earth   *2–6* -glittering   1 ⩘Vest,   **9.** 1 State • *2–6* state   1 &   *2–6* pomp   **10.** *6* Justice ⊠*1* wakes   *4–6* the   *2–6* wail   **11.** 1 Soul   *3* folly; • *6* Folly: **12.** ⊠*1* won **13.** *6* Nature   1 Veil, • *2–6* veil   **14.** *2–6* son!

title. In the PR *2* list of contents the title is given as "Effusion 4, to Priestley,".
2, 4, 6, 8, 10, 13. Indented in PR *1*.
4⁺, 8⁺. Only PR *1* has line-spaces.
12, 14. Double-indented in PR *1*.

92. SONNET: TO FAYETTE

A. DATE

Early Dec 1794. See the note from PR *1* in the collation below.

B. TEXTS

1. M Chron (15 Dec 1794). Signed "S. T. C."

1. HRC MS (Coleridge, S T) Works B. Recto of a single leaf, 18.0×31.2 cm; wm Britannia in smaller rounded oval; chain-lines 2.5 cm; verso blank. Bound into Rugby Manuscript p 41/f 17ʳ. Transcript in C's hand, which served as copy for PR *2* below.

2 [=RT]. *Poems* (1796).

3. Poems (1803).
Rpt *Laura* ed Capel Lofft (5 vols 1813–14) II No 133.

4. PW (1828).

5. PW (1829).

6. PW (1834).

title. *1 SONNETS* | on | EMINENT CHARACTERS. | No. IV. • 1 *Effusion 9* •
2 EFFUSION IX. • *3 SONNET XIII.* • *4–6* SONNET VII.

  1 ☐ As when far off the warbled strains are heard,
  2 ☐ That soar, on Morning's wing, the vales among,
  3 ☐ Within his cage th' imprison'd Matin Bird
  4 ☐ Swells the full Chorus with a gen'rous Song.—
     [Line-space]
  5 ☐ He bathes no pinion in the dewy light;
  6 ☐ No Father's joy, no Lover's bliss he shares;
  7 ☐ Yet still the rising radiance cheers his sight—
  8 ☐ His fellows' Freedom soothes the Captive's cares!
     [Line-space]
  9 ☐ Thou, FAYETTE! who didst wake, with startling voice,
 10 ☐ Life's better Sun from that long wintry night,
 11 ☐ Thus in thy Country's triumphs shalt rejoice—
 12 ☐ And mock, with raptures high, the Dungeon's might;
     [Line-space]
 13 ☐ For, lo! the Morning struggles into Day,
 14 ☒1 And   Slav'ry's   spectres shriek, and vanish from the ray!
   1   ~~Freed~~ Slavery's
14⁺fn. *1* The above beautiful Sonnet was written antecedently to the joyful account
of the Patriot's escape from the Tyrant's Dungeon.

1. 1 Strains ☒*1* heard **2.** ☒*1* soar ☒*1* wing **3.** 1 Cage *4–6* the imprisoned
2–6 matin bird **4.** *2–6* chorus ☒*1* generous song: **5.** ☒*1* light, **6.** 1 Joy,
1 Bliss ☒*1* shares, **7.** *4–6* sight; **8.** 1 fFellows' • *2–5* Fellows' ☒*1* freedom
6 captive's **9.** 6 Fayette! ☒*1* wake 1 Voice • *2–6* voice **10.** 2 4–
6 sun **11.** 1 Triumphs 1 *2–5* rejoice • 6 rejoice, **12.** ☒*1* mock ☒*1* high
☒*1* dungeon's might: **13.** ☒*1* For *2–6* morning *2–6* day, **14.** *2–6* Slavery's
1 Spectres ☒*1* shriek

  title. In the PR 2 list of contents the title is given as "Effusion 9, to Fayette,".
  2, 4, 6, 8, 10, 12. Indented in PR *1*.
  4⁺, 8⁺, 12⁺. Only PR *1* has line-spaces; no more than a slight indication of these
divisions is retained in MS 1.

93. SONNET: TO KOSCIUSKO

A. DATE

Early Dec 1794.

B. TEXTS

1. M Chron (16 Dec 1794). Signed "S. T. C."

1. PML MA 1848 (12). Single folded leaf, 46.5×37.7 cm; wm horn within shield surmounted by crown, above GR | 1794; countermark J LARKING; chain-lines 2.5 cm. Transcript in an als to RS, 17 Dec 1794 (*CL* I 140).

2 HRC MS (Coleridge, S T) Works B. Verso of a single leaf, 18.2×31.2 cm; wm COLES; chain-lines 2.5 cm. Bound into Rugby Manuscript p 40/f 16ᵛ. Transcript in C's hand, which served as copy for PR 2 below.

2 [=RT]. *Poems* (1796).

3. PW (1828).

4. PW (1829).
JG's (?) copy at NYPL (Berg Collection) contains a correction.

5. PW (1834).

title. *1 SONNETS* | ON | EMINENT CHARACTERS. | No. V. • 1 Sonnet •
2 *Effusion 8* • 2 EFFUSION VIII. • *3–5* SONNET VI.

1 □	O! what a loud and fearful shriek was there,	
1fn 2	When *Kosciusko* was observed to fall, the Polish ranks set up a shriek.	
2 □	As tho' a thousand souls one death-groan pour'd!	
3.1 *1* 1	Great KOSCIUSKO, 'neath an Hireling's sword,	
4.1 *1*	His Country view'd.—Hark! thro' the list'ning air,	
1	The Warriors	
3 2	~~Great *Kosciusk*~~ Ah me! they view'd beneath an hireling's sword	
2–4	←——— Ah———→	
5	saw	a
4 2	~~His Warriors view'd / Hark!~~ ṯ Fall'n *Kosciusko*! Thro' the wavy air	
2–4	←———————Fall'n————————→ KOSKIUSKO! Thro' burthen'd	
5	Their Kosciusko fall! Through swart	
	[*Line-space*]	
5 *1* 1	When pauses the tir'd Cossack's barb'rous yell	
2	~~Wh~~ (as	
2–5	(As	
6 □	Of Triumph, on the chill and midnight gale	
7 □	Rises with frantic burst, or sadder swell,	
8 □	The dirge of murder'd Hope: while Freedom pale	

[*Line-space*]
9 □   Bends in such anguish o'er her destin'd bier,
10 □   As if from eldest time some Spirit meek
11 □   Had gather'd in a mystic urn each tear
12 ⊠*3–5* That ever furrow'd a sad Patriot's cheek;
   3–5   on a Patriot's furrowed
      [*Line-space*]
13 *1* 1   And she had drench'd the sorrows of the bowl—
   2 2   drain'd
14 ⊠*3–5* E'en till she reel'd, intoxicate of soul!
13.1 *3–5* Fit channel found; and she had drained the bowl
14.1 *3–5* In the mere wilfulness, and sick despair of soul!

1. ⊠*1* O   1 2 Shriek   **2.** *3–5* though 1 Souls 1 Death groan *3–
5* poured!   **3.1.** 1 Kosciusko 1 hireling's sword   **4.1.** 1 view'd!— 1 Air
3. *3 4* viewed   **4.** *3 4* Fallen Koskiusko! Through *3 4* burthened   **5.** *3–
5* tired 2 *2–5* Cossac's 1 *3–5* barbarous 1 Yell   **6.** 2 *2–4* Triumph) •
5 triumph) 1 & 1 Gale   **7.** 1 *2–5* burst • 2 Burst 1 2 Swell • *2–5* swell
8. 1 2 "Dirge *3–5* murdered 1 Hope"!— • 2 Hope"! • *2–5* Hope!   **9.** 1 2 2 *such*
1 Anguish *3–5* destined 1 Bier,   **10.** 1 Time   **11.** *3–5* gathered 1 2 Urn
1 2 Tear   **12.** 1 2 cheek, • *3–5* cheek   **13.** 1 2 She 1 2 Sorrows 1 2 Bowl •
2 bowl   **14.** 1 2 2 Ev'n 1 Soul!— • 2 Soul!   **13.1.** *5* found,

title. In the PR *2* list of contents the title is given as "Effusion 8, to Kosciusko,".
2–3, 6, 8, 10, 12. Indented in PR *1*.
1fn. The note appears at the end of the volume with the cross-reference "Note 4.—
Page 52."
   The last seven words of the note are present at the head of the copy C submitted to J.
Cottle (HRC MS (Coleridge, S T) Works B p 51/f 22^r).
2–3, 6, 8, 10, 12. Indented in PR *1*.
4. PR *4* Koskiusko!] The spelling is emended to "Kosciusko! in JG's (?) copy.
4⁺, 8⁺, 12⁺. Only PR *1* has line-spaces.

94. SONNET: TO PITT

A. DATE

Early Dec 1794.

B. TEXTS

1. M Chron (23 Dec 1794). Signed "S. T. C."

2. The Watchman v (2 Apr 1796) 133 (*CC*) 166–7. Signed "S.T.C."

3 [=RT]. *Poems* (1796).
Rpt *The Universal Magazine* XCIX (Oct 1796) 276.

4. Poems (1803).

title. *1 SONNETS* I ON I EMINENT CHARACTERS. I No. VI • *2* TO
MERCY. I *SONNET* • *3* EFFUSION III. • *4 SONNET VIII.*

1 ⊠*2*   Not always should the tear's ambrosial dew,
  2   Tears'
2 □   Roll its soft anguish down thy furrow'd cheek;
3 □   Not always heav'n-breath'd tones of suppliance meek
4 □   Beseem thee, MERCY!—yon dark scowler view,
    [*Line-space*]
5 □   Who with proud words of dear-lov'd Freedom came,
6 □   More blasting than the mildew from the South—
7 □   And kiss'd his Country with Iscariot mouth
8 *1 2* (Staining most foul a godlike Father's name)!
  3 4 (Ah! foul apostate from his   fame!)
8fn *1*   Earl of CHATHAM.
    [*Line-space*]
9 □   Then fix'd her on the cross of deep distress,
10 □   And at safe distance marks the thirsty Lance
11 □   Pierce her big side! But, O! if some strange trance
12 □   The eyelids of thy stern-brow'd Sister press,
12fn *1 2* JUSTICE.
    [*Line-space*]
13 *1*   Seize thou, more terrible, th' avenging brand—
  ⊠*1*   MERCY! thou more terrible the
14 □   And hurl her thunderbolts with fiercer hand!

1. *2–4* dew   **2.** *3 4* cheek!   **3.** *2–4* heaven- *2* Tones *2 Suppliance*
4. *2–4* MERCY! Yon *2–4* Scowler   **5.** *3 4* came—   **6.** *3* blasting, *2–*
4 South!   **7.** *3 4* country *2 Iscariot*   **8.** *2* name)   **9.** *2* Cross *2* Distress,
10. *3 4* lance   **11.** *2–4* But *3 4* ô! *2* Trance   **12.** *2–4* eye-lids
12fn. *2* Justice.   **13.** *2–4* Seize, *2* Brand, • *3 4* brand,   **14.** *2* hand.

title. In the PR *3* list of contents the title is given as "Effusion 3, to Mercy,".
2–3, 6–7, 10–11. Indented in PR *1*.
4⁺, 8⁺, 12⁺. Only PR *1* has line-spaces.

95. SONNET: TO BOWLES

A. DATE

(*a*) Early Dec 1794; (*b*) 1796.

1. [=RT (*a*)]. *M Chron* (26 Dec 1794). Signed "S. T. C."

1. PML MA 1848 (11). Single folded leaf, 46.5×37.7 cm; wm horn within shield surmounted by crown, above GR I 1794; countermark J LARKING I 1794; chain-lines 2.5 cm. Lines 2.1–3.1, 6.1–7.1, 10.1–11.1 are written two abreast. Transcript in an als to RS, 11 Dec 1794 (*CL* I 136).

It is assumed that printer's copy for PR *1* antedates the transcript made for RS. It is natural to assume, but cannot be proved, that when C says in his letter (*CL* I 137) that he has written ten sonnets, he had in fact submitted them.

2. HUL fMS Eng 947.8. Recto of a single leaf, 17.5×21.3 cm; no wm; chain-lines 2.8 cm. Endorsed in Katharine Southey's hand: "S. T. Coleridge's writing.— I given me by his daughter Mrs. H. N. Coleridge. I Katharine Southey. I —1852." The verso contains **90** *To Burke*. Transcript in C's hand, which might have served as copy for PR *2* below.

The title suggests that this version served as copy for PR *2*, as the Burke sonnet on the verso appears to have done. On the other hand, the paper differs from any other paper known to have been used as copy, and lines 4, 9–12 of PR *2* differ considerably.

2 [=RT (*b*)]. *Poems* (1796).

A corrected copy of this volume (uncut), once owned by Winston H. Hagen, contained a "somewhat different form" of the poem in C's autograph, on an inserted loose leaf marked "First Version". See Anderson Galleries Catalogue (New York) No 1352 (13–16 May 1918), item 253; also vol I annex C 3.8.

3. Poems (1797).

4. Poems (1803).
Rpt *Laura* ed Capel Lofft (5 vols 1813–14) II No 114.

5. PW (1828).

6. PW (1829).

7. PW (1834).

PR *2* prints a four-line motto to the Effusions, facing the C poem, taken from Bowles's *Monody, Written at Matlock*. PR *5–7* mistakenly include the motto between the title and the text of the present sonnet. See vol I annex B 1.

title. *1 SONNETS* I ON I EMINENT CHARACTERS I No. VII. I TO THE REV. W. L. BOWLES. • 1 To Bowles. • 2 ~~Effusions~~ I *Effusion 1* I To the Revd W. L. Bowles. • 2 EFFUSION I. • *3–7 SONNET I*.

title fn [present in PR *1* only]

Author of Sonnets and other Poems, published by Dilly. To Mr.
BOWLES's Poetry I have always thought the following remark, from
MAXIMUS TYRIUS, peculiarly applicable: "Οὐ τοι λεγω τὴν τῳ τερπνῳ τῆς
ακοῆς τιμηθεισαν δεδεκασμένης τῆς ακοῆς, δεδεκασμένου καὶ του τῶν ἀλ-
λων αισθητηριων δικαστηριου· τὴν δὲ εκ του νοερου Ελικωνος Μουσαν, την   5
καὶ υψηλην καὶ ανθρωπινην καὶ επι τῇ ψυχῃ ιουσαν.—"I am not now treat-
ing of that Poetry, which is estimated by the pleasure it affords to the ear—the
ear having been corrupted, and the judgment-seat of the perceptions; but of that
which proceeds from the intellectual Helicon, that which is *dignified*, and ap-
pertaining to *human* feelings, and entering into the soul."—The 13th Sonnet for   10
exquisite Delicacy of painting; the 19th for tender simplicity; and the 25th for
manly Pathos, are compositions of, perhaps, unrivalled merit. Yet, while I am
selecting these, I almost accuse myself of causeless partiality; for surely never
was a Writer so equal in excellence!

S. T. C.   15

1.1 *1* 1		My heart has thank'd thee, BOWLES! for those soft strains,
2.1 *1* 1		That, on the still air floating, tremblingly
3.1 *1*		Wak'd in me Fancy, Love, and Sympathy!
1		Woke
4.1 *1* 1		For hence, not callous to a Brother's pains,
		[*Line-space*]
5.1 *1* 1		Thro' Youth's gay prime and thornless paths I went;
6.1 *1* 1		And, when the *darker* day of life began,
7.1 *1* 1		And I did roam, a thought-bewilder'd man!
8.1 *1* 1		Thy kindred Lays an healing solace lent,
		[*Line-space*]
9.1 *1* 1		Each lonely pang, with dreamy joys combin'd,
10.1 *1*		And stole from vain REGRET her scorpion stings;
1		~~And stole~~ And stole
11.1 *1* 1		While shadowy PLEASURE, with mysterious wings,
12.1 *1* 1		Brooded the wavy and tumultuous mind,
		[*Line-space*]
13.1 *1* 1		Like that great Spirit, who with plastic sweep
14.1 *1* 1		Mov'd on the darkness of the formless Deep!

1 ☒*1* 1		My heart has thank'd thee, BOWLES! for those soft strains
2 ☒*1* 1		Whose sadness soothes me, like the Murmuring
3 ☒*1* 1		Of wild-bees in the sunny showers of spring!
4 2		For mindful hence of each poor brother's pains
2–7		hence not callous to the mourner's
5 ☒*1* 1		Thro' Youth's gay prime and thornless paths I went:
6 2 2–4		And when the *darker* Day of Life began
5–7		mightier Throes of mind
7 2 2–4		And I did roam, a thought-bewilder'd Man!
5–7		drove me forth,
8 ☒*1* 1		Their mild and manliest Melancholy lent

9.2	2	~~Such solace, as a while to Sleep consign'd tho' it the~~
	2	~~The keener pang, while~~
	2	~~Such tender thoughts, as oft~~
	2	A mingled Charm, that oft the tear renew'd
10.2	2	Yet the keen pang ~~awhile~~ to ⟨dreamy⟩ sleep consign'd;
12.2	2	Over the wavy and tumultuous mind
11.2	2	Bidding a strange mysterious PLEASURE brood,
9	2 5–7	A mingled charm, such as the pang consign'd
	3 4	which oft
10	2–7	To slumber, tho' the big tear it renew'd;
11	2 5–7	Bidding a strange mysterious PLEASURE brood
	3 4	such
12	2–7	Over the wavy and tumultuous mind,
13	⊠*1* 1	As the great SPIRIT erst with plastic ~~swe*a*ee~~p
14	2 2 5–7	Mov'd on the darkness of the unform'd Deep.
13.2	3 4	As made the soul enamour'd of her woe:
14.2	3 4	No common praise, dear Bard! to thee I owe!

title. *5–7* print in roman   **title fn6.** *1* ψυκη *1* "I   **1.1.** 1 Bowles! 1 Strains
2.1. 1 That 1 floating   **3.1.** 1 Love & Sympathy.   **4.1.** 1 hence 1 pains
5.1. 1 Paths 1 went   **6.1.** 1 And 1 Day 1 Life began   **7.1.** 1 Man!
8.1. 1 Solace   **9.1.** 1 Pang 1 Joys combin'd   **10.1.** 1 Regret 1 Scorpion
11.1. 1 Pleasure 1 wings   **12.1.** 1 Mind,   **13.1.** 1 Sweep   **1.** *5–7* thanked
7 Bowles!   **2.** *2–7* murmuring   **3.** *4* wild *4* snnny   **5.** *5–7* Through
6. *2–4* day 7 throes *2–4* life *2–7* began,   **7.** *5–7* -bewildered *2–6* man! •
7 man,   **8.** *2–7* melancholy   **9.** *5–7* consigned   **10.** *5–7* though *3 4* re-
new'd: • *5–7* renewed;   **11.** *3 4* pleasure • 7 Pleasure   **13.** 7 Spirit *2 5–7* sweep
14. *5–7* Moved *5–7* unformed *2 5–7* deep.

   title. In the PR *2* list of contents the title is given as "Effusion 1, to Bowles,"; in the
PR *3* list of contents, as "To W. L. Bowles,".
   2.1–3.1, 6.1–7.1, 10.1–11.1. Indented in PR *1*; written two abreast in MS 1.
   4.1⁺, 8.1⁺, 12.1⁺. Only PR *1* has line-spaces.
   10.1. MS 1 ~~And stole~~] Deleted because C was intent on setting out the poem with the
couplets abreast in one continuous line. He deleted the phrase to begin the line further
to the left.

96. SONNET: TO MRS SIDDONS
(with Charles Lamb)

A. DATE

Dec 1794.

B. TEXTS

1. M Chron (29 Dec 1794). Signed "S. T. C."

1. HRC MS (Coleridge, S T) Works B. Verso of a single leaf, 18.2×31.2 cm; wm COLES; chain-lines 2.5 cm. Bound into Rugby Manuscript p 40/f 16ᵛ. Subscribed "C. Lamb C.L." Transcript in C's hand, which served as copy for PR *2* below.

2 [=RT]. *Poems* (1796). Signed "C.L."

3. Poems (1797).
The last of the "POEMS BY CHARLES LAMB"

4. Poems (1803).

title. *1 SONNETS* | ON | EMINENT CHARACTERS. | No. VIII. • 1 Effusion *6*•
2 EFFUSION VII. • *3 SONNET VIII.* • *4 SONNET XII.*

1 □   As when a Child, on some long Winter's night,
2 □   Affrighted, clinging to its Grandame's knees,
3 □   With eager wond'ring and perturb'd delight
4 *1* Listens dark tales of fearful strange decrees
 ⊠*1*   strange   dark
    [*Line-space*]
5 □   Mutter'd to Wretch by necromantic spell
6 *1*   Of Warlock Hags, that, at the 'witching time
 1   And Or of those   who
 2–4 Or
7 □   Of murky Midnight, ride the air sublime,
8 *1*   Or mingle foul embrace with Fiends of Hell—
 ⊠*1* And
    [*Line-space*]
9 □   Cold Horror drinks its blood! Anon the tear
10 □ More gentle starts, to hear the Beldam tell
11 □ Of pretty Babes, that lov'd each other dear—
12 □ Murder'd by cruel Uncle's mandate fell:
    [*Line-space*]
13 □ E'en such the shiv'ring joys thy tones impart;—
14 *1–4* E'en so thou, SIDDONS! meltest my   sad   heart!
 1   fond sad

1. 1 Child • *2–4* child *2–4* winter's 1 Night • *2–4* night **2.** ⊠*1* Affrighted *2–4* Grandam's ⊠*1* knees **5.** 1 Wret[?]ch • *2–4* wretch ⊠*1* spell; **6.** ⊠*1* hags, ⊠*1* witching **7.** ⊠*1* midnight **8.** 1 ffffoul ⊠*1* fiends 1 Hell • *2–4* Hell: **9.** 1 *2* it's 1 Tear **10.** ⊠*1* Beldame **11.** 1 bab Babes, • *2–4* babes, ⊠*1* dear, **13.** ⊠*1* Ev'n 1 Joys 1 Tones ⊠*1* impart, **14.** ⊠*1* Ev'n 1 Heart!

title. In the PR *2* list of contents the title is given as "Effusion 7, to Siddons,".
2, 4, 6–7, 10, 12. Indented in PR *1*.

4⁺, 8⁺, 12⁺. Only PR *1* has line-spaces.

97. SONNET: TO WILLIAM GODWIN,
AUTHOR OF *POLITICAL JUSTICE*

A. DATE

Dec 1794.

B. TEXTS

1 [=RT]. *M Chron* (10 Jan 1795). Signed "S. T. C."

1. PML MA 1848 (12). Single folded leaf, 46.5×37.7 cm; wm horn within shield surmounted by crown, above GR ‖ 1794; countermark J LARKING ‖ 1794; chain-lines 2.5 cm. The lines are written two abreast. C's transcript of the sestet (only) in an als to RS, 17 Dec 1794 (*CL* I 141).

For C's introductory remarks and the octave composed by RS see vol I headnote.

The RT reproduces TEXTS *1* 1 exactly, with the following exceptions:

title. *1 SONNETS* ‖ ON ‖ EMINENT CHARACTERS. ‖ No. IX. ‖ *TO WILLIAM GODWIN,* ‖ AUTHOR OF "POLITICAL JUSTICE."   **9.** 1 bless
10. 1 lay,   **11.** 1 Voice,   1 Day,   **13.** 1 Form   1 Way,   **14.** 1 **Happiness!**

In addition, MS 1 lacks a title and has no indentation in the sestet.

98. SONNET: TO ROBERT SOUTHEY, OF
BALIOL COLLEGE, OXFORD, AUTHOR OF
THE "RETROSPECT," AND OTHER POEMS

A. DATE

Dec 1794.

B. TEXTS

1 [=RT]. *M Chron* (14 Jan 1795). Signed "S. T. C."

1. PML MA 1848 (12). Single folded leaf, 46.5×37.7 cm; wm horn within shield surmounted by crown, above GR | 1794; countermark J LARKING | 1794; chain-lines 2.5 cm. The lines are written two abreast. Transcript in an als to RS, 17 Dec 1794 (*CL* I 143).

The RT reproduces TEXTS *1* 1 exactly, with the following exceptions:

title. *1 SONNETS* | ON | EMINENT CHARACTERS. | No. X. | *TO ROBERT SOUTHEY,* | OF BALIOL COLLEGE, OXFORD, AUTHOR OF THE | "RETRO-SPECT," AND OTHER POEMS.   **1.** 1 Southey!   1 Melodies   1 Ear
2. 1 Joyance   1 Murmuring   **3.** 1 Showers   **4.** 1 Import   **5.** 1 Breast, 1 Tear.   **6.** 1 hope-   1 Fancy   **7.** 1 Showers   1 Fragrance   **8.** 1 Till 1 Passion's   **9.** 1 But ô!   1 thrill'd   **10.** 1 Mem'ry's dream   **11.** 1 arise—
12. 1 soft   1 Love's   1 Cheek   1 Gleam   **13.** 1 smiles, as faint

In addition, MS 1 lacks a title, has no indentation, and does not have a space at 8⁺. Line 6 "fancy" is written as if it might be meant to be read as bold.

99. SONNET: TO RICHARD BRINSLEY SHERIDAN, ESQ.

A. DATE

Dec 1794.

B. TEXTS

1. M Chron (29 Jan 1795). Signed "S. T. C."

1. PML MA 1848 (12). Single folded leaf, 46.5×37.7 cm; wm horn within shield surmounted by crown, above GR | 1794; countermark J LARKING | 1794; chain-lines 2.5 cm. The lines are written two abreast. Transcript in an als to RS, 17 Dec 1794 (*CL* I 141–2).

C has inserted, just before his transcript of the poem, an observation from which the note in TEXTS 2 *2* 2 3* developed: "(You have read S's poetry—and know that the Fancy displayed in them is sweet and *delicate* to the highest degree.)"

2. BPL B 22189=Estlin Copy Book f 27ᵛ. Transcript in C's hand.
The poem is the last in the book, which is otherwise filled with poems written after C left school and while he was at Cambridge.

3. HRC MS (Coleridge, S T) Works B. Recto of a single leaf, 18.5×31.1 cm; wm COLES; chain-lines 2.5 cm. Bound into Rugby Manuscript p 39/f 16ʳ. Transcript in C's hand, which served as copy for PR 2 below.

3*. HRC MS (Coleridge, S T) Works B. Verso of a single leaf, 19.6×
32.6 cm; wm Britannia in large oval surmounted by crown; chain-lines 2.6 cm.
The remainder of the verso and the recto contain other notes. Bound into Rugby
Manuscript p 34/f 13ᵛ. Transcript in C's hand of the beginning of the note to MS
2, which served as copy for PR 2 below.

2 [=RT]. *Poems* (1796).

3. Poems (1803).
Rpt *Laura* ed Capel Lofft (5 vols 1813–14) III No 289.

4. PW (1828).

5. PW (1829).

6. PW (1834).

title. *1 SONNETS* I ON I EMINENT CHARACTERS. I No. XI. I *TO RICHARD
BRINSLEY SHERIDAN, ESQ.* • 1 To R. B. Sheridan Esq.— • 2 To Sheridan •
3 *Effusion 3•* 2 EFFUSION VI. • *3 SONNET XI.* • *4–6* SONNET V.

1.1 *1*	Was it some Spirit, SHERIDAN! that breath'd	
1 2	Some winged Genius,	imbreath'd
2.1 *1* 1	His *various* influence on thy natal hour?—	
3.1 *1* 1	My Fancy bodies forth the Guardian Power	
4.1 *1* 1	His temples with Hymettian flowrets wreath'd;	
4.1fn *1*	Hymettus, a mountain of Attica, famous for Honey.	
1 3	? TIt was some ~~great~~ Spirit, SHERIDAN! that breath'd	
2–6	It	spirit,
2 2	O'er thy young Soul ~~such~~ a wildly-various power!	
3 2–6		mind such
3 2	My Fancy meets thee in ~~it~~ her shaping hour,	
3 2–6		Soul hath mark'd her
4 ⊠*1* 1	Thy Temples with Hymettian Flowrets wreath'd:	

4fn *3*   Hymettus, a mountain near Athens, famous for honey—an allusion to Mʳ
Sheridan's classical attainments. The four Lines immediately following are
intended to designate the inimitable sweetness & almost Italian Delicacy
of his Poetry.

3*   Hymettian Flowrets. Hymettus a mountain near Athens celebrated for its
honey—This alludes to Mʳ Sheridan's classical ⟨attainments⟩ and the fol-
lowing 4 lines to ⟨the⟩ exquisite sweetness & almost *Italian* Delicacy of his
Poetry.—In Shakespeare's "Lover's Complaint" there ~~some~~

2 *3*   Hymettian Flowrets. Hymettus a mountain near Athens, celebrated for its
honey. This alludes to Mr. Sheridan's classical attainments, and the fol-
lowing four lines to the exquisite sweetness and almost *Italian* delicacy of
his Poetry.—In Shakespeare's "Lover's Complaint" there is a fine stanza
almost prophetically characteristic of Mr. Sheridan.   5

> So on the tip of his subduing tongue
> All kind of argument and question deep,
> All replication prompt and reason strong

For his advantage still did wake and sleep,
To make the weeper laugh, the laugher weep: 10
He had the dialect and different skill,
Catching all passions in his craft of will:
That he did in the general bosom reign
Of young and old.

[*Line-space*]

5 *1* 1   And sweet his voice, as when, o'er LAURA's Bier,
⊠*1* 1   thy
6 ⊠3   Sad   Music trembled thro' Vauclusa's glade;
3   S̶o̶f̶t̶ Sad
7 □   Sweet as, at dawn, the love-lorn Serenade,
8 *1* 1 2   That bears soft Dreams to SLUMBER's list'ning ear.
3 *2–6*   wafts

[*Line-space*]

9 *1* 1 2   Now Patriot Zeal and Indignation high
3 *2–6*   Rage
10 *1* 1   Swell the full tones;—and now his eye-beams dance
⊠*1* 1   thine
11 □   Meanings of Scorn, and Wit's quaint revelry!
12 *1*   While inly writhes, from the Soul-probing glance,
3 *2–6* Writhes inly from the bosom-probing

[*Line-space*]

13 □   Th' Apostate by the brainless rout ador'd—
12.1 1 2   Writhes inly from the bosom-probing Glance,
14 *1*   As   erst   that other Fiend beneath great MICHAEL's Sword!
1 2   nobler
3   e̶l̶d̶ erst   elder
2–6   erst

1.1. 2 *Genius*, 1 2 Sheridan!   **2.1.** 1 Influence 1 hour: **3.1.** 1 Power,
4.1. 1 Flowrets   **1.** *4–6* Spirit, *6* Sheridan! *4–6* breathed   **2.** *4–*
6 wildly   **3.** *2–6* soul *4–6* marked   **4.** 3 *2–6* temples *2 3* flowrets • *4–*
6 flow'rets   **4fn** [PR *2 3*] **4.** *3* Stanza   **5.** 1 2 Voice, ⊠*1* when ⊠*1* Laura's
⊠*1* 2 bier • 2 Bier   **6.** *2–6* music *2 4–6* through 1 Glade, • 2 Glade;
7. 1 Sweet • ⊠*1* 1 Sweet, ⊠*1* as   1 2 Dawn • 3 *2–6* dawn ⊠*1* Serenade
8. 2 *2–6* dreams ⊠*1* Slumber's   3 listning • *4–6* listening 1 Ear! • 2 3 Ear.
9. ⊠*1* patriot *6* rage *2* & *6* indignation   **10.** *1–3* Tones! • *2–6* tones!
⊠*1* 2 And • 2 —And 1 2 Eye beams   **11.** ⊠*1* Scorn *1–3* Revelry!   **12.** 3 *2–*
6 glance   **13.** *4–6* The *1–3* Rout 1 2 ador'd • 3 *2 3* ador'd, • *4–6* adored,
14. ⊠*1* Michael's *2–6* sword.

title. In the PR *2* list of contents the title is given as "Effusion 6, to Sheridan,".
2–3, 6–7, 10, 12. Indented in PR *1*.
4.1⁺, 8⁺, 12⁺. PR *1* has line-spaces; MS 2 has line-spaces at 4⁺, 8⁺; no line-spaces in
other texts.
4fn. TEXTS 3* 2 have the cross-reference "Note 3.—Page 50.", the notes being printed
at the end of the 1796 volume. The notes appear at the foot of the page in TEXTS 3 *3*.

100. TO A FRIEND, TOGETHER
WITH AN UNFINISHED POEM

A. DATE

Late Dec 1794. The "unfinished poem" of the title is **101** *Religious Musings*, begun on Christmas Eve 1794. PR *2 3* below append the date "*December,* 1794."

B. TEXTS

1. PML MA 1848 (13). Single folded leaf, 46.5×37.7 cm. overall; wm horn within shield surmounted by crown, above GR I 1794; countermark J LARKING I 1794; chain-lines 2.5 cm. Transcribed in an als to RS, 29 Dec 1794 (*CL* I 147–8).

2. HRC MS (Coleridge, S T) Works B. Single leaf, 19.7×32.1 cm; wm Britannia in large oval; chain-lines 2.5 cm. Bound into Rugby Manuscript pp 45–6/f 19ʳ⁻ᵛ. Transcript in C's hand, which served as copy for PR *1* below.

1 [=RT]. *Poems* (1796).
Note that the poem is here included among the "Effusions", not among the "Epistles".

2. Poems (1797).
RS's copy (Yale In 678 797 Copy 1) contains ms corrections by C.

3. Poems (1803).

4. PW (1834).
Lines 12–19 only, printed under the title "THE SAME.", following the sonnet **26** *On Seeing a Youth Welcomed by his Sister*.

The same lines are transcribed (from PR *3*?) in JTC's Commonplace Book (University of Pennsylvania (Special Collections) MS Eng 13) p 164, where again they follow the sonnet and where they are headed "Of his Sister he thus speaks in another Poem.—" The transcript appears to have no textual significance.

title. 1 To C. Lamb • 2 Effusion 22 I To a friend together with ~~a Poem.~~ an unfinished Poem. • *1* EFFUSION XXII. I TO I A FRIEND I TOGETHER WITH I *AN UNFINISHED POEM.* • *2 3 To a FRIEND,* I TOGETHER WITH I *AN UNFINISHED POEM.*

1 1   Thus far my sterile Brain hath   fram'd   the Song
    2   scanty   ~~fram'd~~ built   rhyme
    1–3   ←—built—→
2 1   Elaborate & swelling—but the Heart
    ⊠1 *4*   yet

3	⊠4	Not owns it. From thy spirit-breathing powers
4	⊠4	I ask not now, my Friend! the aiding Verse
5	1	Tedious to thee, and from my anxious thought
	⊠1 4	thy
6	⊠4	Of dissonant Mood. In Fancy, well I know,
7	⊠1 4	From business wand'ring far, and local cares,
8	⊠4	Thou creepest round a dear-lov'd Sister's Bed
9	⊠2 4	With　　noiseless　　step, and watchest the faint Look
	2	? ~~one~~ noiseless
10	1	Soothing each Pang with fond Solicitudes
	⊠1 4	solicitude
11	⊠4	And tenderest Tones medicinal of Love.
12	□	I too a Sister *had*—an only Sister—
13	1	She loved m~~y~~e dearly—and I doted on her—
	⊠1	me
13.1.1	1	~~It~~ On her soft Bosom I repos'd my Cares
13.1.2	1	And gain'd for every wound an healing Tear.
14	□	To her I pour'd forth all my puny Sorrows,
15	1	~~As~~ (As a sick Patient in his Nurse's arms)
	⊠1 4	(As
	4	a
16	□	And of the Heart those hidden Maladies
17	⊠3 4	That shrink asham'd from even Friendship's Eye.
	3 4	even from Friendship's eye will shrink asham'd.
18	⊠4	O! I have woke at midnight, and have wept
	4	wak'd
19	□	Because she was not!—Cheerily, dear Charles!
20	⊠4	Thou thy best Friend shalt cherish many a year—
21	1	Such high　presages feel I of [?]warm Hope!
	2 *1* 2	warm　　　　　　high
	3	presagings
22	⊠4	For not uninterested the dear Maid
23	⊠4	I've viewed, her Soul affectionate yet wise,
24	⊠4	Her polish'd Wit as mild as lambent Glories
25	1	That play around an　holy Infant's head.
	⊠1 4	a sainted
26	1	He knows (the Spirit who in secret sees,
	⊠1 4	that
27	⊠4	Of whose omniscient & all-spreading Love
28	⊠4	Aught to implore were Impotence of Mind)
28fn	2 3	I utterly recant the sentiment contained in the Lines

Of whose omniscient and all-spreading Love
Aught to *implore* were impotence of mind,

it being written in Scripture, "*Ask*, and it shall be given you," and my human reason being moreover convinced of the propriety of offering *petitions* 5 as well as thanksgivings to Deity.

| 29 | 1 | That my m~~á~~ute Thoughts are sad before his Throne, |
| | ⊠1 4 | mute |

30 ☒*4*   Prepar'd, when he his healing Ray vouchsafes,
31 ☒*4*   To pour forth Thanksgiving with lifted heart
32 ☒*4*   And praise him gracious with a Brother's Joy!

1. 2 *1–3* brain   **2.** 2 *1–3* and   2 [?]swelling: • *1–3* swelling: 2 *1–3* heart
4. 2 *1–3* friend!   2 verse • *1–3* verse,   **6.** 2 *1–3* mood.   2 *1–3* fancy (2 *1–3* know)   **7.** *1–3* far   **8.** 2 *1–3* bed   **9.** 2 *1–3* look,   **10.** 2 *1–3* pang   *1–3* solicitude,   **11.** 2 *1–3* tones   2 *1–3* love.   **12.** 2 *1–3* SISTER • *4* sister   2 *1–4* had,   2 Sister*l*— • *4* sister;—   **13.** ☒1 lov'd   2 *1–3* dearly, • *4* dearly   *1* her •   2 *2 3* her! • *4* her;   **14.** ☒1 sorrows,   **15.** *4* patient   *4* nurse's   **16.** ☒1 heart   2 Ma[?]ladies • *1–4* maladies   **17.** *4* e'en   2 *1 2* eye.   **18.** *4* midnight   2 *1–3* wept,   **19.** 2 SHE WAS NOT!— • *1–3* SHE WAS NOT!— • *4* she was not.—   2 *1–3* CHARLES!   **20.** 2 *1–3* friend   2 *1–3* year: **21.** 2 *1–3* Hope.
22. 2 *1 2* maid   **23.** 2 *1–3* view'd—   2 *1–3* soul   2 affectionate*ı*   **24.** *1–3* wit   2 *1–3* glories,   **25.** 2 *1–3* infant's   **26.** 2 *1–3* SPIRIT   2 sees*ı*,   **27.** 2 *1–3* and   2 all   **28.** 2 *1–3* *implore*   2 *1–3* impotence   2 mind,) • *1–3* mind)
28fn1. *3* lines   **28fn4.** *3* It   **29.** *1–3* thoughts   2 *1–3* throne,   **30.** 2 Prepar'd   2 *1–3* ray   2 vouchsafes   **31.** 2 *1–3* thanksgiving   2 *1–3* heart,   **32.** 2 *1–3* Him Gracious   2 *1–3* BROTHER'S

title. In the PR *1* list of contents the title is given simply as "To a Friend with an unfinished Poem,".
13. C emended RS's copy of PR 2 to "and on her I doted!"
17. C emended RS's copy of PR 2 to "That, ev'n from Friendship's eye oft shrink asham'd."

101. RELIGIOUS MUSINGS

A. DATE

24 Dec 1794–28 Mar 1796; Jan–Jul 1797.

C first referred to the poem in a letter to RS of 29 Dec 1794 (*CL* I 147). Citations, parallels, and drafts appear in published and unpublished writing throughout the following months (*Lects 1795—CC—*70, 82, 106, 352, etc; *CN* I 23, 30, 124) until Oct 1795, when C told Cottle that the poem had grown to 300 lines (*CL* I 162). C continued to work on the poem up to the last moment while the 1796 volume was being printed (Cottle *E Rec* II 52, and see e.g. MSS 6(a–c) or 9–12 below). C told TP that he had finished it in a letter of 30 Mar 1796, and the receipt of Cottle's payment is in fact dated two days before (*CL* I 195 and n). The date prefixed to the text in all versions refers to the day of the poem's conception.

1. HRC MS (Coleridge, S T) Works B. Four identical leaves, 16.6×20.4 cm; no wm; chain-lines (horizontal) 2.5 cm; written on both sides. Bound into Rugby Manuscript pp 95–102/ff 42^r–45^v. Copy for lines 1–118 of PR *3* below (=VAR 1.1–14.1.5, 23–34b, 35–70, 71–84.1, 85–104), in C's hand.

Various printer's marks prove that the ms was used as printer's copy. At the end of the text is written, in faint pencil, "Bristol". Each page is numbered, as are the lines from "5" to "115".

2. Kenneth Spencer Research Library, University of Kansas, Lawrence MS P76: 2a. Single leaf, 15.7×18.5 cm; wm (imperfect) crown surmounting oval; chain-lines 2.5 cm; verso blank. Copy for lines 119–35 of PR *3* below (=VAR 105–21), in C's hand.

The lines are numbered from "120" to "135", and are endorsed at the head in Joseph Cottle's younger hand: "Extract from 'Religious Musings' in Mr Coleridge's Hand-Writing". (There is no Cottle-number.)

3. HRC MS (Coleridge, S T) Works B. Three identical leaves, 16×20 cm; wm (imperfect) crown and top of oval on the two first, bottom of oval containing Britannia on last; chain lines (horizontal) 2.5 cm; versos blank. Bound into Rugby Manuscript pp 103–8/ff 46^r–48^v. Copy for lines 152–205 of PR *3* below (=VAR 137.1–141.1, 142–85), in C's hand.

Various printer's marks prove that the ms was used as printer's copy. The lines are numbered from "155" to "185" on the first two leaves, not on the last (covering lines 189–205 in PR *3*'s version).

A fragment of autograph ms in C's hand sold at Christie's (London) 24 Jun 1987 lot 104 (to Quaritch for £600) might fit in here. It is described as comprising seven lines beginning with the present line 186. The fragment measures 16.0×7.5 cm, is tipped on to stiff paper, and is accompanied by a one-page letter on mourning paper from JG to an anonymous addressee, Highgate, 26 Jul [1834], announcing that the "dear, valued and beloved friend, is no longer capable of answering your note. Alas, he is no more." But there is no way of of knowing, without examination, whether the fragment continues MS 3, or is in fact earlier or later.

4. Maine Historical Society, Portland, Maine, Fogg Autograph Collection Vol 27. Single leaf, 15×18 cm; no wm; chain-lines 2.5 cm; verso blank. Transcript in C's hand, corresponding to lines 211–25 of PR *3* below (=VAR 191–205).

The lines are numbered from "115" to "125", a difference of exactly 100 from the PR *3* numbering. Cf the similar misnumbering of MS 6(c) below. There are no printer's markings. The verso is endorsed in Joseph Cottle's shaky hand: "Autograph of Coleridge | (part of 'Religious Musings.') | J.C."; but there is no Cottle-number on the recto.

1. Quoted in *The Watchman* IV (25 Mar 1796) 101 (*CC*) 131, corresponding to lines 226–44 of PR *3* below (=VAR 206–22, 224–5), with differences of verb-tense and capitalisation.

What status this printing has is uncertain. It may have been set from corrected sheets of PR *3*, which shows signs of having been set from an unrecorded ms at this point (for example, PR *3* line 232 =VAR 212 supplies an apostrophe in "it's"). At the same time, PR *1* has C's characteristic capitalisation.

5. BM Add MS 35343 f 66^{r-v}. Single leaf, 20.5×33.7 cm; no wm; chain-lines 2.5 cm; written on both sides. Transcript in C's hand, corresponding to lines 329–73 (var) of PR *3* below (=VAR 309–323a.1, 323–355.1).

The transcript breaks off, leaving 12.5 cm to the foot of the second page. Up-side down in this space TP has written: "Fragment of the | Religious musings | as first written". It is not possible to say whether the transcript predates TEXTS 1–4 *1 2*. Some extra lines are elsewhere to be found only in MS 6(c) below, some readings are closer to PR *3*, and some are unique to this ms.

6(a). HRC MS (Coleridge, S T) Works B. Single leaf, 19.8×24.2 cm; wm (traces only, along outer margin); chain-lines (horizontal) 2.7 cm; written on both sides. Bound into Rugby Manuscript pp 109–10/f 49^{r-v}. Transcript in C's hand, corresponding to lines 243–78 of PR *3* below (=VAR 224–59).

Numbered with a large "3" in top RH corner of recto. The lines are numbered from "245" to "275", the first three numbers having been corrected from "145", "150", and "155". Cf the similar misnumbering of MS 4.

6(b). HRC MS (Coleridge, S T) Works B. Single leaf, 18.2×30.4 cm; wm Britannia in smaller rounded oval; chain-lines (vertical) 2.5 cm; written on both sides. Bound into Rugby Manuscript pp 111–12/f 50^{r-v}. Transcript in C's hand, corresponding to lines 279–312 (var) of PR *3* below (=VAR 260–291a.1).

The lines are numbered from "280" to "310".

6(c). HRC MS (Coleridge, S T) Works B. Single leaf, 20.0×24.1 cm; wm (bottom of design only along longer margin); chain-lines (horizontal) 2.7 cm; written on both sides. Bound into Rugby Manuscript pp 113–14/f 51^{r-v}. Tran-script in C's hand, corresponding to lines 313–42 (var) of PR *3* below (=VAR 291a.2–294.1.1, 296–308.1.1, 309–322b.1/323a.1).

Printer's marks prove that the ms was used as printer's copy. The lines are numbered only at line 330 (=line 329 of PR *3*). The blank space following the transcript on the verso contains the description "M.S. 2 Religious Musings". Each of the three leaves of MS 6(a–c) ends with a variatim text on the verso, followed by blank space, as if C was submitting copy a leaf at a time, reckoning to smooth the transitions in proof.

2. Quoted in *The Watchman* II (9 Mar 1796) 45–7 (*CC*) 64–7, under the title "*THE PRESENT STATE OF SOCIETY*." and followed by the note "(Extract from 'Religious Musings,' one of the 'Poems by S. T. Coleridge.')", corresponding to lines 279–378 of PR *3* below (=VAR 260–89, 290.2–292.2,

293.1.1–2, 296–300, 301-3, 304–21, 322a–327, 328–348.1, 349–57). Some of the variations from MSS 5 and 6 were taken into PR *3*, others not.

7. Rosenbach Museum and Library, Philadelphia, MS 386/21. Single leaf, 19.7×19.4 cm; wm Britannia; chain-lines 3.6 cm; recto only (at some time roughly backed with brown paper). Draft in C's hand, corresponding to lines 379–87 of PR *3* below (=VAR 358.1–359a.1, 359b.1/360a.1–363b.1).

Endorsed: "(Autograph of S. T. Coleridge.—Part of his 'Religious Musings.') | J.C." Cottle's own number at the head of the page is 53.

8. Reported by H.G.T. of Launceston, "Coleridge's 'Religious Musings'" *N&Q* III (68) (15 Feb 1851) 115. Single leaf ("on a detached piece of paper"); no other details known. Transcript in C's hand, corresponding to lines 379–87 of PR *3* below (=VAR 358.1–360a.1, 360b.1–363b.1).

H.G.T. of Launceston was almost certainly Henry George Tomkins (1826–1907), who was at the time an undergraduate of Trinity College Cambridge. A fairly extensive search among his documents has failed to locate the ms.

9. HRC MS (Coleridge, S T) Works B. Single leaf, 20.4×23.2 cm; wm Britannia in smaller rounded oval; chain-lines (vertical) 2.5 cm. Written on both sides to foot of verso, where there is a cross—as if a key for further lines—which matches the cross-heading VAR 403–8 in MS 12. Bound into Rugby Manuscript pp 121–2/f 55^{r-v}. Transcript in C's hand, corresponding to lines 379–428 of PR *3* below (=VAR 358.2–377.1, 378.1–383b.3, 384.2–393b.1, 394.2–396a.1, 399b.1–402).

There are numerous deletions, and the lines are not numbered. It is possible that this text up to line 428 (=VAR 402) was used as printer's copy for PR *3*, although a different fair copy may have been employed.

The sequence of MSS 9–12 given here follows the order of Cottle's numbering (Cottle has numbered this leaf 122). The sequence bound into the Rugby Manuscript arranges the mss in the order 10, 12, 11, 9. The correct order might in fact be 10, 11, 9, 12; this must remain uncertain.

10. HRC MS (Coleridge, S T) Works B. Single leaf, 20.2×31.7 cm; wm Britannia in small oval; chain-lines (vertical) 2.5 cm; verso blank. Bound into Rugby Manuscript p 115/f 52^r. Transcript in C's hand, corresponding to lines 379–400 (var) of PR *3* below (=VAR 358.3–375.2).

Cottle has numbered this leaf 123.

11. HRC MS (Coleridge, S T) Works B. Single leaf, 20.7×32.6 cm; no wm; chain-lines (vertical) 2.5 cm. Written on both sides (ending half way down verso). Bound into Rugby Manuscript pp 119–20/f 54^{r-v}. Transcript in C's hand, corresponding to lines 379–407 (var) of PR *3* below (=VAR 358.4–377.2, 379a.3/380b.6–380b.7).

MSS 10 and 11 appear to be separately drafted alternatives to MSS 9 and 12. MS 11 is more heavily revised, and neither ms numbers the lines. Cottle has numbered this leaf 126. (It should be noted that two leaves appear to have been dropped from the Cottle sequence, between MSS 10 and 11, although possibly they may not have contained verse.)

12. HRC MS (Coleridge, S T) Works B. Single leaf, 20.2×32.9 cm; no wm; chain-lines (vertical) 2.5 cm; written on both sides (to foot of verso). Bound into Rugby Manuscript pp 117–18/f 53^{r-v}. Transcript in C's hand, corresponding to lines 379–421 (var) and 429–34 of PR *3* below (=VAR 358.5–377.3, 378.2–395b.2/396.2, 403–8). The verso is reproduced in facsimile in Sotheby's Catalogue (15 May 1967) facing p 73.

Lines 379–421 (=VAR 358.5–377.3, 378.2–395b.2/396.2) were afterwards cancelled with a single vertical stroke. C has written in the space corresponding to lines 421–8 of PR *3*: "Room for ~~six eight lines~~ sixteen lines". (In fact, it turned out that he inserted seventeen lines.) Cottle has numbered this leaf 127.

12*. HRC MS (Coleridge, S T) Works B. Two leaves, each 20.5×32.6 cm; wm (first) GR countermark, (second) Britannia in large oval; chain-lines (vertical) 2.5 cm; verso of second leaf blank. Bound into Rugby Manuscript, pp 125–7/ff 57^r–58^r. Notes for the poem in C's hand, evidently written after 9 Mar 1796 (PR 2 above), headed "Notes on RELIGIOUS MUSINGS".

3. Poems (1796).

C's own copy at the NYPL (Berg Collection Copy 7) contains the pencilled memorandum at the end of the text "No Notes to this to be printed". All versions of the poem contain notes, and this was perhaps written soon after PR *3*, the first complete printing, was published.

It is indeed curious that no known copies of PR *3* incorporate the revisions C was prompted to make in the poem very soon after publication, and together with other evidence this suggests that a second edition might even have been agreed upon at the time of the first printing. The one copy described in sales catalogues as containing notes and corrections, including twenty-six draft or inserted lines of *Religious Musings*, is almost certainly a phantom. See vol I annex C 3E, 3.7, etc.

13. BM MS Ashley 408 ff 5^r–30^v. C's revision of PR *3* in the form of an interleaved and corrected version, submitted as copy for PR *4*.

The collation records insertions, corrections, and deletions, but ignores unchanged PR *3* readings altogether; thus, where MS 13's reading is not recorded, it can be taken to be identical with the recorded PR *3* reading at that point. C's emendations of the line-numbering are also omitted (as an instance of his muddle about line-numbers, the fn given here at line 33 is cued to line "32").

JDC facsimile 6–58 can be consulted for a clearer picture of the relation between deleted, revised, and inserted passages, though it is inaccurate in details. JDC does not record that one interleaf containing corrections or redrafting between ff 20 and 21 has been removed. The corrections blotted on to f 20^v and f 21^r (i.e. pp 156 and 157 of PR *3*) and would have concerned the text between the present lines 233 and 264. Alternatively, C might have drafted revisions on the interleaf, thought better of them, and removed the leaf himself.

C had pinned his poetical ambitions on the poem, and eagerly received the criticism of his friends (e.g. *CL* I 207: to TP 5 May 1796; 216: to J. Thelwall 13 May 1796). He told Cottle that he had "monstrously" revised it in the New Year of 1797 (*CL* I 309), and he appears to have sent this revised version with his next letter, which ELG dates c 10 Feb.

In early Apr 1797 C asked Cottle to make two changes in the text as it had been printed (*CL* VI 1008). Later, in early Jul, he asked for a number of errata to be incorporated, but too late (*CL* I 331–2).

13*. BM MS Ashley 408 ff 7^r–35^r. C's notes as first intended to accompany MS 13, comprising ms revisions of the PR *3* notes to the poem. Besides cancelling and revising some notes following the text, C wrote additional notes and new versions on the pages interleaved with the printed text. Cf *JDC facsimile* 11–66.

C cancelled four notes (to line 8/VAR 5.1; line 235/VAR 215; line 294/VAR 275; line 335/VAR 315). He keyed the remainder to the emended line-numbering (of TEXTS 13 *4*), introducing corrections and additions into three of them. Only these three corrected or enlarged notes have been recorded here.

4 [=RT]. *Poems* (1797).

C sent two sets of errata which affect the poem to Cottle (*CL* VI 1007–8: early Apr 1797; I 331–2: c 3 Jul 1797), but too late to be included. Five copies contain corrections which overlap with these errata: W. L. Bowles's copy, in the possession of Erwin Schwarz (1982); the Abbé Barbey's copy, now in the BM (c 126 b 1); William Roskilly's copy, in the possession of J.C.C. Mays (1999); C's own copy (?), described by J. Rogers Rees "Coleridge Items" *N&Q* ser 10 IX (213) (25 Jan 1908) 63–4 at 63 (and cf "Coleridge Items" ibid 133–4); RS's copy, now at Yale (In 678 797 Copy 1). The fact that three copies were presented to clergymen may bear on C's concern to emend this poem in particular.

5. Poems (1803).

C told Cottle in Mar 1798 that "My alterations in the Religious Musings will be considerable, & will lengthen the poem" (*CL* I 391). But the alterations did not add much to the length, perhaps because not all of those which C had in mind were included.

The transcript of lines 1–28 in this version in JTC's Commonplace Book (University of Pennsylvania (Special Collections) MS Eng 13) p 34, and the reprint of lines 377–420 in *The Parnassian Garland* (1807) 208–10, are of no textual interest.

6. PW (1828).

The copy at the Fitzwilliam Museum, Cambridge (Marlay Bequest 1912), contains corrections in C's hand.

7. *PW* (1829).

JG's (?) copy at NYPL (Berg Collection) contains a single correction.

8. *PW* (1834).

The copy at HEHL (109531) contains corrections in C's hand.

C. GENERAL NOTE

The pattern of rewriting and revision is particularly complicated in this poem. For this reason, the decimalised system of connecting VAR and RT lines has been extended by the use of lettering (a, b, c) to show connected part-lines (14a.2, 34b.1, etc). Even so, it has not been possible to correlate certain much-reworked passages exactly.

divisional title. *3–5* Religious Musings.

⁻1.1	*3–5*	What tho' first,
⁻1.2	*3–5*	In years unseason'd, I attun'd the Lay
⁻1.3	*3–5*	To idle Passion and unreal Woe?
⁻1.4	*3–5*	Yet serious Truth her empire o'er my song
⁻1.5	*3–5*	Hath now asserted: Falshood's evil brood,
⁻1.6	*3–5*	Vice and deceitful Pleasure, She at once
⁻1.7	*3–5*	Excluded, and my Fancy's careless toil
⁻1.8	*3–5*	Drew to the better cause!
⁻1.9	*3–5*	AKENSIDE.

⁻**1.10** *3–5*   ARGUMENT.

Introduction. Person of Christ. His Prayer on the Cross. The process of his Doctrines on the mind of the Individual. Character of the Elect. Superstition. Digression to the present War. Origin and Uses of Government and Property. The present State of Society. French Revolution. Millenium. Universal Redemp- ⁻1.15 *tion. Conclusion.*

title. 1 *3* Religious Musings | a desultory Poem written on Christmas Eve in the year of our Lord, 1794.   *1* RELIGIOUS MUSINGS.   13 *4–8* Religious Musings, a desultory Poem written on the Christmas Eve of 1794.

1.1	1 *3*	This is the Time, when most divine to hear,
3.1	1	As with an An Cherub's "loud uplifted" Trump
	3	a Cherub's
2.1	1 *3*	The Voice of Adoration my thrill'd Heart
3.1.1	1 *3*	Rouses! And with the rushing Noise of Wings
3.1.2	1 *3*	Transports my Spirit to the favor'd fields
3.1.3	1 *3*	Of Bethlehem, there in shepherd's guise to sit
3.1.4	1 *3*	Sublime of extacy, and mark entranc'd
5.1	1 *3*	The glory-streaming VISION throng the Night.
5.1fn	12* *3*	And suddenly there was with the Angel a Multitude of the

heavenly Host, praising God and saying Glory ~~the~~ to God in
the Highest and on Earth Peace.

Luke II. 13.

5.1.1	1 *3*	Ah not more radiant, nor loud harmonies
6.1	1 *3*	Hymning more unimaginably sweet
6.1.1	1 *3*	With choral songs around th' ETERNAL MIND
6.1.2	1 *3*	The constelled Company of WORLDS
6.1.3	1 *3*	Danc'd jubilant: what time the startling East
6.1.4	1 *3*	Saw from her dark Womb leap her flamy Child!
6.1.5	1 *3*	Glory to God in the Highest! PEACE on Earth!
		[*Line-space*]
7.1	1	Yet Thou, than all th' Angelic Blaze, more bright,
	3	more bright than all that Angel Blaze,
9.1	1 *3*	Despised GALILÆAN! Man of Woes!
9.1.1	1	When poor and mean and hungry thou didst roam
9.1.2	1	Placeless to hide thy all unshelter'd Head,
9.1.3	1	Where slept the nested Bird and cavern'd Brute.
12.1	1 *3*	For chiefly in th' oppressed Good Man's Face
10.1	1 *3*	The great Invisible (by symbols seen)
11.1	1 *3*	Shines with peculiar & concenter'd light,
12.1.1	1 *3*	When all of Self regardless the scourg'd Saint
14.1	1 *3*	Mourns for th' Oppressor. O thou meekest Man!
14.1.1	1 *3*	Meek Man and lowliest of the Sons of Men!
14.1.2	1 *3*	Who thee beheld, thy imag'd Father saw.
14.1.2fn	12* *3*	~~Philip saith unt~~ Philip saith unto him—Lord! shew us the Fa-
		ther.—and it sufficeth us. Jesus saith unto him, Have I been so
		long time with you, and yet hast thou not known me, Philip?
		He that hath seen me hath seen the Father.—

John XIV. 9 5

14.1.3	1	For Power & Wisdom from thy aweful Eye
	3	His
14.1.4	1 *3*	Blended their beams, and loftier Love sate there
14.1.5	1 *3*	Musing on human Weal, and that dread hour
1	13 *4–8*	This is the time, when most divine to hear
2	13 *4–8*	The Voice of Adoration rouses me,
3	13	As with a Cherub's trump: till high upborne
	4–8	and
4	13 *4–8*	Yea, mingling with the Quire, I seem to view
5	13 *4–8*	The Vision of the heavenly Multitude,
6	13	That hymn'd the song of Peace o'er Bethlehem's fields.
	4–8	Who
6.2.1	13	~~Making the midnight glorious~~
	13	~~Yet more bright,~~
7	13 *5*	Yet thou more bright than all the Angel Host
	4 6–8	blaze,
8	13 *4–8*	That harbingerd thy birth, thou, Man of Woes!
9	13 *4–8*	Despised Galilæan! For the Great
10	13 *4–8*	Invisible (by symbols only seen)
11	13 *4–8*	With a peculiar and surpassing Light

12 13	Shines from the visage off th' oppress'd Good Man,
4–8	of
7.2 13	Yet thou more bright than all the Angel Blaze
8.1 13	That harbinger'd thy birth, thou, Man of Woes.
9.2 13	Despised GALILÆAN! For the Great
10.2 13	Invisible (by symbols only seen)
11.2 13	Seems with peculiar & unsullied light
12.2 13	To shine from forth th' oppressed Good Man's face,
13 13 *4–8*	When heedless of himself the scourged Saint
14a.2 13	Mourns for the' Oppressor. Son of the most high
14b.2 13	Preeminent! Fair is the Vernal mead,
14 *4–8*	Mourns for th' Oppressor. Fair the vernal Mead,
15 13	Fair the high in the high Grove, the Sea, the Sun, the Stars;
4–8	the high Grove,
15.1 13	Yet nor high Grove nor many-colorsor'd mead,
16.1 13	⟨Bright Impress each of their creating Sire!⟩
16 *4–8*	True Impress each of their creating Sire!
17 *4–8*	Yet nor high Grove, nor many-coloured Mead,
18 13 *4–8*	Nor the green Ocean with his thousand Isles
19 13 *4–8*	Nor the starr'd Azure, nor the sovran Sun
20 13 *4–8*	E'er with such majesty of portraiture
21 13	Imag'd the unimaginable God
4–8	supreme beauty uncreate,
22 13	As thou, meek Savioriour! at thate fearful hour
4–8	the
23.1 13	When thy insulted Anguish &c.
23 1 *3–8*	When thy insulted Anguish wing'd the Prayer
24 1 *3–8*	Harp'd by Archangels, when they sing of Mercy!
25 1 *3–8*	Which when th' ALMIGHTY heard, from forth his Throne
26 1 *3*	Diviner Light flash'd extacy o'er Heaven!
13 *4–8*	fill'd Heaven with extacy—
27 1 *3–8*	Heaven's hymnings paus'd: and Hell her yawning Mouth
28a 1 *3–8*	Clos'd a brief moment.
	[*Line-space*]
28b 1 *3–8*	Lovely was the Death
29 1 *3–8*	Of Him, whose Life was Love! Holy with power
30 1 *3–8*	He on the thought-benighted Sceptic beam'd
31 1 *3–8*	Manifest Godhead, melting into day
32 1 *3*	What Mists dim-floating of Idolatry
13 *4–8*	floating Mists of dark
33 1 *3*	Split and misshap'd the Omnipresent Sire:
13 *4–8*	Broke
33fn 13* *4–7*	Τὸ Νοητὸν διῃρήκασιν εἰς πολλῶν Ι Θεῶν ἰδιότητας. Damas.
	de myst.
	Ægypt.
34a.1 1 *3*	And first by TERROR, Mercy's startling prelude,
34b.1 1 *3*	Uncharm'd the spir Spirit spell-bound with earthy Lusts,
34a.2 13	And first by TERROR, Mercy's startling prelude,
34b.2 13	Uncharm'd the Soul spell-bound with earthy lusts

34a.3	13	Renewer of the ancient Truth! And first
34b.3	13	By Terror he uncharm'd the slumb'ring Spirit,
34	13 *4–8*	And first by Fear uncharm'd the droused soul,
35	1 *3* 13[imp]	
	4–8	Till of its nobler Nature It 'gan feel
36	1 *3–8*	Dim recollections; and thence soar'd to Hope:
37	1 *3–8*	Strong to believe whate'er of mystic Good
38	1 *3* 13 *4–8*	Th' Eternal dooms for his immortal Sons.
39	1 *3*	From Hope and stronger Faith to perfect Love
	13 *4–8*	firmer
40	1 *3–8*	Attracted and absorb'd: and center'd there
41	1 *3–8*	God only to behold, and know, and feel,
42	1 *3–8*	Till by exclusive Consciousness of God
43	1 *3–8*	All self-annihilated It shall make
43fn	13* *4*	See this *demonstrated* by ⟨vide Hartley & Pistorius⟩ Hartley, Vol. I. p. 114. & Vol. II[d]. p. 329. See it likewise proved, and freed from the charge of mysticism, by Pistorius in his Notes & Additions to part second of Hartley on Man. Addition the 18th: the 653rd page of the third Volume of Hartley.—Octavo Edition.—
44	1 *3–8*	God Its Identity: God all in all!
45a.	1 *3–8*	We and our Father One!
		[*Line-space*]
45b.	1 *3–8*	And blest are They,
46	1	Who in this fleshly World, the Elect of Christ, Heaven,
	3–8	←—Heaven, —→
47	1 *3–8*	Their strong eye darting thro' the deeds of Men
48	1 *3–8*	Adore with stedfast unpresuming Gaze
49	1	Creation's Him Nature's Essence, Mind, and Energy!
	3–8	←—Him, —→
50	1 *3–8*	And gazing, trembling, patiently ascend
51	1 *3–8*	Treading beneath their Feet all visible Things
52	1 *3–8*	As Steps, that upward to their Father's Throne
53	1 *3–8*	Lead gradual—else nor glorified nor lov'd.
54	1 *3–8*	They nor Contempt imbosom nor Revenge:
55	1 *3–8*	For They dare know of what may seem deform
56	1 *3–8*	The Supreme Fair Sole Operant: in whose sight
57	1 *3–8*	All Things are pure, his strong controlling Love
58	1 *3–8*	Alike from all educing perfect Good.
		[*Line-space*]
59	1 *3–8*	Their's too celestial Courage, inly arm'd—
60	1 *3–8*	Dwarfing Earth's giant Brood, what time they muse
61	1 *3–8*	On their great Father, great beyond compare:
62	1 *3–8*	And marching onwards view high o'er their heads
63	1 *3–8*	His waving Banners of Omnipotence!
		[*Line-space*]
64	1 *3* 4 *6–8*	Who the Creator love, created might
65	1 *3* 4 *6–8*	Dread not: within their Tents no Terrors walk.

66	1 *3* 4 6–8	For TThey are Holy Things before the Lord
67	1 *3* 4 6–8	Aye-unprofan'd, tho' Earth should league with Hell!
68	1 *3* 4 6–8	God's Altar grasping with an eager Hand
69	1 *3* 4 6–8	FEAR, the wild-visag'd, pale, eye-starting Wretch,
70	1 *3* 4 6–8	Sure-refug'd hears his hot-pursuing fiends
64–5.1	*5*	They cannot dread created might, who love
64a.1	*5*	God, the Creator!—fair and lofty thought!
65.1.1	*5*	It lifts and swells my heart! And as I muse,
65.1.2	*5*	Behold! a VISION gathers in my soul,
65.1.3	*5*	Voices and shadowy shapes! In human guise
69.1	*5*	I seem to see the phantom, FEAR, pass by,
69.1.1	*5*	Hotly-pursued, and pale! From rock to rock
69.1.2	*5*	He bounds with bleeding feet, and thro' the swamp,
69.1.3	*5*	The quicksand, and the groaning wilderness,
69.1.4	*5*	Struggles with feebler and yet feebler flight.
68a.1	*5*	But lo! an altar in the wilderness,
68b.1	*5*	And eagerly yet feebly lo! he grasps
69.1.5	*5*	The altar of the living God! and there
69.1.6	*5*	With wan reverted face the trembling wretch
70.1	*5*	All wildly list'ning to his Hunter-fiends
70.1.1	*5*	Stands, till the last faint echo of their yell
71	1 *3* 4 6–8	Yell at vain distance. Soon refresh'd from heaven
	5	Dies in the
72	1 *3–8*	He calms the Throb and Tempest of his Heart.
73	1 *3–8*	His Countenance settles: a soft solemn Bliss
74	1 *3* 4 6–8	Swims in his Eye: his swimming Eye uprais'd:
	5	eyes: eyes
75	1 *3* 4 6–8	And Faith's whole armour glitters on his limbs.
	5	girds his limbs! And thus
76	1 *3* 4 6–8	And thus transfigur'd with a dreadless Awe,
	5	Transfigur'd, with a meek and
77	1 *3* 4 6–8	A solemn Hush of Soul, meek he beholds
	5	Spirit
78.1	1 *3*	All Things of terrible Seeming. Yea, and there,
78.1.1	1 *3*	Unshudder'd, unaghasted, he shall view
80b.1	1 *3*	E'en the SEVEN SPIRITS, who in the Latter Day⌇
80b.1fn	12* *3*	And I heard a great Voice out of the Temple saying to the Seven Angels, ~~saying~~, pour out the Vials of the Wrath of God upon the Earth.
		Revelation XVI. 1.
80a.1	1 *3*	Will shower hot pestilence on the Sons of Men.
	13	~~Will shower hot blasting on the Sons of Men.~~
80.1.1	1	For He ~~shall~~ doth know, his Heart ~~shall~~ doth understand,
	3	shall shall
81.1	1 *3*	That kindling with intenser Deity
82.1	1 *3*	They from the MERCY-SEAT—like rosy Flames
82.2	1 *3*	From God's celestial MERCY-SEAT will flash,
	13	~~From God's celestial MERCY-seat leapt forth~~
83.1	1 *3*	And at the Wells of renovating LOVE

84.1	1	Fill'd their SEVEN S̶P̶I̶R̶I̶T̶S̶ VIALS with salutary Wrøath,
	3	Fill ←——Vials——→ wrath,
78	13 *4–8*	All things of terrible seeming: yea, unmov'd
79	13 *4–8*	Views e'en th' immitigable Ministers
80	13 *4–8*	That shower down vengeance on these latter days.
80.2.1	*5*	For even these on wings of healing come,
81	13 *4 6–8*	For kindling with intenser Deity
	5	Yea,
82	13 *4 6–8*	From the celestial MERCY-SEAT they come,
	5	speed,
83	13 *4–8*	And at the renovating Wells of LOVE
84	13 *4–8*	Have fill'd their Vials with salutary Wrath
85	1 *3–8*	To sickly Nature more medicinal
86	1 *8*	Than what soft Balm the weeping Good Man pours
	3 4 6 7	That
	5	Than sweet
87	1 *3–8*	Into the lone despoiled Trav'ller's Wounds!
88.1	1	T̶h̶u̶s̶ ̶f̶r̶o̶m̶ ̶t̶h̶
		[Line-space]
88	1 *3–8*	Thus from thé' Elect, regenerate thro' faith,
89	1 *3–8*	Pass the dark Passions and what thirsty Cares
89fn	13* *4 5*	Our evil passions under the influence of Religion become in-nocent &
		may be made to animate our virtues—in the same manner as the thick mist melted
		by the Sun increases the Light, which it had before excluded. In the preceding
		paragraph agreeably to this Truth we had allegorically narrated the transfigura-
		tion of Fear into holy Awe. 5
90	1	Drink up the spirit and the t̶h̶i̶r̶s̶t̶y̶ dim Regards
	3–8	dim
91	1 *3–8*	Self-center. Lo—they vanish! or acçquire
92	1 *3–8*	New names, new features—by supernal Grace
93	1 *3–8*	Enrob'd with Light, and naturaliz'd in Heaven.
94	1	S̶As when the Shepherd on a vernal morn
	3–8	As a
95	1 *3–8*	Thro' some thick Fog creeps tim'rous with slow foot,
96	1 *3 4 6–8*	Darkling he fixes on th' immediate Road
	5	with earnest eyes he traces out
97	1 *3 4 6–8*	His downward eye: all else of fairest kind
	5	Th' immediate road,
98	1 *3 4 6–8*	Hid or deform'd.̶/̶But lo—the bursting Sun!
	5	burning
99	1 *3–8*	Touch'd by th' Enchantment of that sudden Beam
100	1	Strait the black Vapor melteth—and w̶i̶t̶h̶ in globes
	3–8	in
101	1 *3–8*	Of dewy Glitter gems each Plant and Tree.
102	1 *3–8*	On every Leaf, on every Blade it hangs!

103	1 *3–8*	Dance glad the new-born intermingling Rays,
104	1 *3–8*	And wide around the Landscape streams with Glory!
		[*Line-space*]
105	2 *3–8*	There is one Mind, one omnipresent Mind,
106	2 *3–8*	Omnific. His most holy name is LOVE.
107	2 *3–8*	Truth of subliming import! with the which
108	2 *3–8*	Who feeds and saturates his constant soul,
109	2 *3–8*	He from his small particular Orbit flies
110	2 *3–8*	With blest Outstarting! From HIMSELF he flies,
111	2 *3–8*	Stands in the Sun, & with no partial gaze
112	2 *3–8*	Views all creation, and he loves it all,
113	2 *3–8*	And blesses it, and calls it very good!
114	2 *3–8*	This is indeed to dwell with the most High!
115	2 3 4 *6–8*	Cherubs and rapture-trembling Seraphim
	5	The Cherubs and the trembling
116	2 *3–8*	Can press no nearer to th' Almighty's Throne.
117	2 *3–8*	But that we roam unconscious, or with hearts
118	2 *3–8*	Unfeeling of our universal Sire,
119	2	And that in his vast family ? áno Cain
	3 4 6–8	no
120	2 *3 4 6–8*	Injures uninjur'd ⟨()in her best-aim'd blow
121	2 *3 4 6–8*	Victorious MURDER a blind Suicide—⟨)⟩
122	*3–8*	Haply for this some younger Angel now
123	*3–8*	Looks down on Human Nature: and, behold!
124	*3–8*	A sea of blood bestrew'd with wrecks, where mad
125	*3–8*	Embattling INTERESTS on each other rush
126a	*3–8*	With unhelm'd Rage!
		[*Line-space*]
126b	*3–8*	'Tis the sublime of man,
127	*3–8*	Our noontide Majesty, to know ourselves
128	*3–8*	Parts and proportions of one wond'rous whole:
129	*3–8*	This fraternizes man, this constitutes
130	*3–8*	Our charities and bearings. But 'tis God
131	*3–8*	Diffus'd thro' all, that doth make all one whole;
132	*3–8*	This the worst superstition, him except,
132fn	1 *3* * *4 5*	If to make aught but the supreme Reality ~~our ruling Passion~~
		the object of final pursuit, be
		Superstition; if ~~falsely to~~ the attribut⟨é⟩ing of sublime properties
		to things or persons, which
		those things or persons neither do or can possess, be Supersti-
		tion; then Avarice
		& Ambition are Superstitions: and he, who wishes to estimate
		the evils of
		Superstition, should transport himself, not to the temple⟨s⟩of
		~~Mex~~ the Mexican Deities,
		but ⟨to⟩ the plains of Flanders, or the coast of Africa.—Such
		is the sentiment
		conveyi~~ng~~ed in this & the subsequent Lines.—
133	*3–8*	Aught to desire, SUPREME REALITY!

5

134 *3–8*		The plenitude and permanence of bliss!
135.1 *3*		O Fiends of SUPERSTITION! not that oft
136.1 *3*		Your pitiless rites have floated with man's blood
137.1 3 *3*		The skull-pil'd Temple, not for this shall Wrath
138.1 3 *3*		Thunder against you from the Holy One!
138.1.1 3 *3*		But (whether ye th' unclimbing Bigot mock
138.1.2 3 *3*		With secondary Gods, or if more pleas'd
138.1.3 3 *3*		Ye petrify th' imbrothell'd Atheist's Heart,
13		~~imbrothell'd~~
139a.1 3 *3*		The Atheist, your worst Slave!) I o'er some plain
140a.1–		
139c.1 *3*		Peopled with Death, and to the silent ~~Moon~~ Sun
3		Sun
139b.1 3 *3*		Steaming with tyrant-murder'd Multitudes;
140b.1 3 *3*		Or where mid groans and shrieks loud-laughing TRADE
141.1 *3*		More hideous packs her Bales of ←—living—→ Anguish;
3		his
13		~~living~~ human
135 13 *4–8*		O Fiends of SUPERSTITION! not that, oft
136 13 *4–8*		The erring Priest hath stain'd with Brother's blood
137 13 *4–8*		Your grisly Idols, not for this may Wrath
138 13 *4–8*		Thunder against you from the Holy One!
139 13 *4–8*		But o'er some plain, that steameth to the Sun
140 13 *4–8*		Peopled with Death; or where more hideous TRADE
141 13 *4–8*		Loud-laughing packs his bales of human anguish;
142 3 *3–8*		I will raise up a Mourning, O ye Fiends!
143 3 *3* 13 *4–8*		And curse your spells, that film the Eye of Faith,
144 3 *3* 13 *4–8*		Hiding the *present* GOD, whose presence lost,
145 3 *3–8*		The moral worlƀd's Cohesion, we become
146 3 *3–8*		An Anarchy of Spirits! ʄToy-bewitch'dʃ,
147 3 *3–8*		Made blind by Lusts, disherited of Soul,
148 3 *3–8*		No common center Man, no common Sire
149 3 *3–8*		Knoweth! A sordid solitary Thing,
150 3 *3–8*		Mid countless Brethren with a lonely Heart
151 3 *3–8*		Thro' Courts and Cities the smooth Savage roams
152 3 *3–8*		Feeling Himself, his own low Self the Whole,
153 3		When he by ~~holy~~ sacred Sympathy might make
3–8		sacred
154 3 *3–8*		The Whole ONE SELF! SELF, that no Alien knows!
155 3 *3–8*		SELF, far diffus'd as Fancy's wing can travel!
156 3 *3–8*		SELF, spreading still! Oblivious of its own*l*,
157 3 *3–8*		Yet all of All possessing! This is FAITH!
158 3 *3–8*		This the MESSIAH's destin'd Victory!
		[*Line-space*]
159 3 *3–8*		But first offences needs must come! Even now
159fn 13* *4–8*		January 21ˢᵗ, 1794, in the debate on the Address to his Ma-
		jesty, on the
		Speech from the Throne, the Earl of Guildford moved an
		amendment to the

following effect: "That the House hoped, His Majesty would
seize the earliest
opportunity to ~~a~~conclude a peace with France &c." ~~Op~~ This
motion was opposed by
the Duke of Portland, who "considered the war to be merely
grounded on one   5
principle—the preservation of the CHRISTIAN RELIGION.
May 30th, 1794,
the Duke of Bedford moved a number of Resolutions with a
view to the es-
tablishment of a Peace with France. He was opposed (among
others) by Lord
Abingdon in these remarkable words: "The best road to Peace,
my Lords! is
WAR: and WAR carried on in the same manner, in which we
are taught to wor-   10
ship our CREATOR, namely, with all our souls, and with all
our minds, &
with all our hearts, & with all our strength."

160 3 *3–8*	(Black Hell laughs horrible—to hear the scoff!)	
161 3 *3–8*	THEE⸝ to defend, meek Galilæan! THEE	
162 3 *3–8*	And thy mild Laws of Love unutterable,	
163 3	[?]Mistrust and Enmity have burst the bands	
3–8	Mistrust	
164 3 *3–8*	Of social Peace; and list'ning Treachery lurks	
165 3 *3–8*	With *pious* fraud to snare a Brother's Life;	
166 3 *3–8*	And childless Widows o'er the groaning Land	
167 3 *3–8*	Wail numberless; and Orphans weep for Bread!	
168 3 *3–8*	THEE to defend, dear Saviour of Mankind!	
169 3 *3–8*	THEE, Lamb of God! THEE, blameless Prince of Peace!	
170 3 *3–8*	From all sides rush the thirsty brood of War!	
171 3 *3–8*	AUSTRIA, and that foul WOMAN of the NORTH,	
172 3 *3–8*	The lustful Murd'ress of her wedded Lord!	
173 3 *3–8*	And he, connatural Mind! whom (in their songs	
173fn 12* *3* 13*	That ~~Man~~ Despot who received the wages of an Hireling that he might act the part of a Swindler; and who skulked from his impotent attacks on the Liberties of France to perpetrate more successful iniquity in the plains of *Poland*.	
174 3 *3–8*	So Bards of elder Time had haply feign'd)	
175 3 *3–8*	Some Fury fondled in her Hate to Man,	
176 3	Bidding her ~~sp~~serpent hair in tortuous folds	
3	serpent	
13 4–8	mazy surge	
177 3	Lick⸍ his young Face, and at his Mouth imbreathe	
3 8	Lick	
13 4–7	inbreathe	
178 3 *3–8*	Horrible Sympathy! And leagued with These⸝	
179 3 *3–8*	Each petty German Princeling, nurs'd in gore!	
180 3 *3–8*	Soul-harden'd Barterers of human Blood!	

180fn 12* *3*	The Father of the present Prince of Hesse Cassell supported himself and his strumpets at Paris ~~for~~ by the vast sums which he received from the British Government during the American War for ~~human~~ the flesh of his Subjects.—
181 3 *3–8*	Death's prime Slave-merchants! Scorpion-whips of Fate!
182 3 *3–8*	Nor least in Savagery of Holy Zeal
183 3 *3–8*	Apt for the yoke, the race degenerate,
184 3 *3–8*	Whom Britain erst had blush'd to call *her* Sons!
185 3 *3–8*	THEE to defend the Moloch Priest prefers
186 *3–8*	The prayer of hate, and bellows to the herd
187 *3–8*	That Deity, ACCOMPLICE Deity
188 *3–8*	In the fierce jealousy of waken'd wrath
189 *3–8*	Will go forth with our armies and our fleets
190 *3–8*	To scatter the red ruin on their foes!
191 4 *3–8*	O blasphemy! to mingle fiendish deeds
192 *4* 3 13 *4–8*	With blessedness! Lord of unsleeping love,
192fn 12* *3* 13* *4–8*	Art thou not from everlasting, O Lord, mine Holy One?—We shall not die. O
	Lord! thou hast ordained them for Judgement—&c Habakkuk I. 12. In this para-
	graph the Author recalls himself from his indignation against the instruments of
	Evil, to contemplate the *uses* of these Evils in the great process of divine Bene-
	volence. In the first age Men were innocent from ignorance of vice; they fell, 5
	that by the knowledge of consequences they might attain intellectual security—
	i.e. ~~which~~ Virtue, which is a wise & strong-nerv'd Innocence.—
193 4 *3–8*	From everlasting Thou! We shall not die.
194 4 *3–8*	These, even these, in mercy didst thou form,
195 4 *3–8*	Teachers of Good thro' Evil, by brief wrong
196 4 *3–8*	Making Truth lovely, and her future might
197 4 *3–8*	Magnetic o'er the fix'd untrembling heart.
	[*Line-space*]
198 4 *3–8*	In the primæval Age a dateless while
199 4 *3* 8	The vacant Shepherd wander'd with his flock
200 4 *3–8*	Pitching his tent where e'er the green Grass wav'd.
201 4 *3–8*	But soon Imagination conjur'd up
202 4 *3–8*	An host of new desires: with busy aim,
203 4 *3–8*	Each for himself, Earth's eager Children toil'd.
204 4 *3–8*	So PROPERTY began, twy-streaming Fount,
205 4	Whence ~~Virtu~~ Vice and Virtue flow, honey and gall.
3–8	Vice
206 *1* *3–8*	*Hence* the soft Couch and many-colour'd Robe,
207 *1* *3–8*	The Timbrel and arch'd Dome and costly Feast
208 *1*	With all th' inventive Arts that nurse the Soul
3–8	nurs'd

209 *1 3–8*	To forms of Beauty; and by sensual wants
210 *1*	Unsensualize the mind, which in the *Means*
3–8	Unsensualiz'd
211 *1*	Learns to forget the grossness of the *End*,
3–8	Learnt
212 *1 3–8*	Best-pleasur'd with its own activity.
213 *1 3–8*	And *hence* DISEASE that withers manhood's arm,
214 *1 3–8*	The dagger'd ENVY, spirit-quenching WANT,
215 *1 3–8*	WARRIORS, and LORDS, and PRIESTS—all the sore ills
215fn *12* 3*	~~We~~ I deem that the teaching of the Gospel for Hire is wrong;

because it gives the Teacher an improper bias in favor of
particular opinions on a subject where it is of the last ~~imp~~ im-
portance that the Mind should be perfectly unbiassed—Such
is my private opinion; but I mean not to censure all hired 5
Teachers, many among whom I know, and venerate as the
best and wisest ~~&~~of men—God forbid that I should think of
these, when I use the word PRIEST—a name, after which
~~all other~~ ~~every other~~ any other term⊀ of abhorrence would ap-
pear an ~~Anti~~ Anti-climax. By a PRIEST I mean a Man who 10
holding the scourge of Power in ~~the~~ his Right Hand and a
Bible (*translated by Authority*) in ~~the other;~~ his Left, doth
necessarily ~~cause~~ make the Bible & the Scourge to be as-
sociated Ideas, and so produces that temper of mind ~~which~~
that leads to Infidelity—Infidelity which ~~having been taught~~ 15
~~mysterious doctrines~~ judging of ~~Christianity~~ Revelation by the
doctrines and ~~establishment~~ practices of established Churches
honors God by rejecting Christ. See ~~Conciones ad Populum,~~
~~my~~ "Addresses to the People"—Page 57—sold by Parsons,
Pater-noster Row. 20

216 *1 3–8*	That vex and desolate our mortal life.
217 *1 3–8*	Wide-wasting ills! yet each th' immediate source
218 *1 3–8*	Of mightier good! Their keen necessities
219 *1 3–8*	To ceaseless action, goading human thought
220 *1 3–8*	Have made Earth's reasoning Animal her Lord,
221 *1 3–8*	And the pale-featur'd SAGE's trembling hand
222 *1 3 13 4–8*	Strong as an Host of armed Deities!
223 *13 4 6–8*	Such as the blind Ionian fabled erst.
224 *1 6(a) 3 13*	
4–8	From Avarice thus, from Luxury, and War
225 *1 6(a) 3–8*	Sprang heavenly SCIENCE, and from Science FREEDOM!
226 *6(a) 3–8*	O'er waken'd Realms Philosophers and Bards
227 *6(a) 3–8*	Spread in concentric circles: they whose souls
228 *6(a) 3–8*	Conscious of their high dignities from God
229 *6(a) 3–8*	Brook not Wealth's rivalry; and they, who long
230 *6(a) 3–8*	Enamour'd with the charms of order, hate
231 *6(a) 3–8*	Th' unseemly Disproportion; and who' e'er
232 *6(a) 3–8*	Turn with mild sorrow from the victor's car
233 *6(a) 3–8*	And the low puppetry of thrones, to muse
234 *6(a) 3–8*	On that blest triumph, when the patriot Sage

234fn	12* 3	DR FRANKLIN.
235	6(a) 3–8	Call'd the red lightnings from th' o'er rushing Cloud
236	6(a) 3–8	And dash'd the beauteous terrors on the earth
237	6(a) 3–8	Smiling majestic. Such a Phalanx ne'er
238	6(a) 3–8	Measur'd firm paces to the calming sound
239	6(a) 3–8	Of Spartan Flute! These on the fated day,
240	6(a) 3 13 4–8	When stung to Rage by Pity eloquent men
241	6(a) 3–8	Have rous'd with pealing voice th' unnumber'd tribes
242	6(a) 3–8	That toil and groan and bleed, hungry and blind,
243	6(a) 3–8	These hush'd awhile with patient eye serene
244	6(a) 3–8	Shall watch the mad careering of the storm;
245	6(a) 3–8	Then o'er the wild and wavy chaos rush
246	6(a) 3–8	And tame th' outrageous mass, with plastic might
247	6(a) 3–8	Moulding Confusion to such perfect forms,
248	6(a) 3–8	As erst were wont, bright Visions of the Day!
249	6(a) 3–8	To float before them, when, the summer noon,
250	6(a) 3–8	Beneath some arch'd romantic Rock reclin'd
251	6(a) 3–8	They felt the Sea-breeze lift their youthful locks,
252	6(a) 3–8	Or in the month of blossoms at mild Eve
253	6(a) 3–8	Wand'ring with desultory feet inhal'd
254	6(a) 3 4 6–8	The wafted perfumes, and the flocks, and woods,
	5	gazing on the
255	6(a) 3 4 6–8	And many-tinted streams, and setting Sun
	5	The
256	6(a) 3–8	With all his gorgeous company of clouds
257	6(a) 3 4 6–8	Extatic gaz'd! then homeward as they stray'd
	5	In extacy!
258	6(a) 3–8	Cast the sad eye to earth, and inly mus'd
259	6(a)	Whence there was Misery in a world so fair.
	3–8	Why

[*Line-space*]

260	6(b) 2–8	Ah far remov'd from all that glads the sense,
261	6(b)	From all that softens or ennobles ~~life~~ Man,
	2–8	man,
262	6(b) 2–8	The wretched Many! Bent beneath their loads
263	6(b) 2–8	They gape at pageant Power, nor recognize
264	6(b) 3–8	Their Cots' transmuted plunder! From the tree
	2	Cot's
265	6(b) 2–8	Of Knowledge, ere the vernal sap had risen,
266	6(b) 2 3	Rudely disbranch'd! O *blest* Society!
	13 4 6–8	*Blessed*
	5	Evil
267	6(b) 2–8	Fitliest depictur'd by some sunscorcht ~~w~~Waste,
268	6(b) 2–8	Where oft majestic thro' the tainted noon
269	6(b) 2–8	The SIMOOM sails, before whose purple pomp
269fn	2 3 13*	"At eleven o'clock, while we contemplated with great pleasure

the rugged top of Chiggre, to which we were fast approaching,
and where we were to solace ourselves with plenty of good
water, Idris cried out, with a loud voice, 'Fall upon your faces,

for here is the Simoom.' I saw from the S.E. an haze come 5
on, in colour like the purple part of the rainbow, but not so
compressed or thick. It did not occupy twenty yards in breadth,
and was about twelve feet high from the ground. We all lay
flat on the ground, as if dead, till Idris told us it was blown
over. The meteor, or purple haze, which I saw, was indeed 10
passed; but the light air that still blew was of heat to threaten
suffocation."

(BRUCE's Travels, Vol. 4, page 557.)

270	6(b) *3–8*	Who falls not prostrate dies! And where, by night,
	2	at
271	6(b) *2–8*	Fast by each precious fountain on green herbs
272	6(b) *2–8*	The Lion couches; or Hyæna dips
273	6(b) *2–4 6–8*	Deep in the lucid stream his bloody jaws;
	5	gore-stain'd
274	6(b) *3*	Or Serpent rolls his vast moon-glittering bulk,
	2 13 4–8	plants
275	6(b) *2–8*	Caught in whose monstrous twine Behemoth yells,
275fn	*2 3*	Used poetically for a very large quadruped; but in general it designates the Elephant.
	13* 4–8	Behemoth in Hebrew signifies wild-beasts in general. Some believe it is the
		elephant, some the Hippopotamus, some affirm it is the wild-bull.—Poetically,
		it designates any large Quadruped.
276a	6(b) *2–8*	His bones loud-crashing!
		[*Line-space*]
276b	6(b)	Ƴe O ye numberless,
	2–8	O
277	6(b) *2–4 6–8*	Whom foul Oppression's ruffian gluttony
	5	Ye, whom
278	6(b) *2–4 6–8*	Drives from Life's plenteous feast! O thou poor wretch,
	5	the Feast of Life!
279	6(b)	That Who nurs'd in darkness and made wild by want
	2–8	Who
280	6(b)	Dost roam for prey, or thy unnatural hand
	2 13 4–8	Roamest yea
	3	Dost roam
281	6(b)	Liftest to midnight slaughter! Thou pale form,
	2	Dar'st lift deeds of blood! O pale-eyed Form!
	3	Liftest
	13 4–8	Dost lift
282	6(b)	Seduction's victim, that shalt never know
	2–8	The Victim of Seduction, doom'd to
283	6(b)	One innocent hour throughout the livelong years,
	2–4 6–8	Polluted nights and days of blasphemy;
	5	Nights of Pollution,

284 6(b)   But in loath'd orgies with lewd Wassailers
     2–4 6–8   Who
     5   thy   loath'd
285 6(b) 2–8   Must gaily laugh, while thy remember'd Home
286 6(b)   Gnaws ₄, like a Viper, at thy secret heart!
     2–8   Gnaws,
287 6(b)   O wretched Mothers, ye who weekly catch
     2–8   aged   Women!
288 6(b) 2–8   The Morsel tost by law-forc'd Charity,
289 6(b) 2–8   And die so slowly, that none call it murder!
290.1 6(b)   O loathly-visag'd Suppliants, ~~that~~ ye that oft
290.1.1 6(b)   Rack'd with disease, no earthly comforts your's,
292.1 6(b)   From the full Lazar-houses, unreceiv'd,
291a.1 6(b)   Totter heart-broken!
290.2 2   O loathly-visag'd   Supplicants!   that oft
     3   Suppliants! ye
290.2.1 2 3   Rack'd with disease from the unopen'd gate
292.2 2 3   Of the full lazar-house heart-broken crawl!
291a.2 6(c)   Totter heart-broken! Ye ~~that~~ to fields of Death
293.1.1 2   O ye that steaming to the silent Noon
293.1.2 2   People with Death red-eyed Ambition's plains!
293b.1 3   O ye to scepter'd Glory's gore-drench'd field
294a.1 6(c) 3   Forc'd or ensnar'd, who swept by Slaughter's scythe,
294.1.1 6(c) 3   (Stern Nurse of Vultures!) steam in putrid heaps!
290 13 4–8   O loathly Suppliants! ye, that unreceiv'd
291 13 4–8   Totter heart-broken from the closing Gates
292 13 4–8   Of the full Lazar-house; or gazing, stand
293 13 4–8   Sick with despair! O ye to Glory's field
294 13 4–8   Forc'd or ensnar'd, who, as ye gasp in death
295 13 4–8   Bleed with new wounds beneath the Vulture's Beak!
296 6(c)   And thou poor Widows, who in dreams dost view
     2   O   wretched   Widow
     3–8   O thou poor
297 6(c)   The   mangled   corse, and from uneasy sleep
     2–8   Thy Husband's mangled corse—   short   doze
298 6(c) 2–8   Start'st with a shriek: or in thy half-thatch'd Cot
299 6(c) 2–8   Wak'd by the wintry night-storm, wet and cold
300 6(c)   Cowr'st o'er thy screaming Babe! ~~O rest aw~~ O rest awhile,
     2 3 13 4–8   baby! ◄——Rest——►
304.1 6(c)   The Lamb of God hath open'd the fifth Seal:
305.1 6(c)   From the four quarters of the earth ascend
306.1 6(c)   Th' innumerable multitude of Wrongs
307.1 6(c)   By man on man inflicted! Rest awhile,
301 6(c) 2–8   Children of Wretchedness! More groans must rise,
302 6(c) 2–5   More blood must steam, or ere your wrongs be full.
     6–8   stream,
303 6(c) 2–8   Yet is the day of Retribution nigh:
308b.1 6(c)   The Hour approaches: soon shall Tyranny
308.1.1 6(c)   Burst self-destroyed thro' wild excess of Ill.

304 *2–8*	The Lamb of God hath open'd the fifth seal,
304fn *2 3*	See the sixth Chapter of the Revelation of St. John the Divine. "And I looked and beheld a pale Horse; and his name that sat on him was Death, and Hell followed with him. And power was given unto them over the FOURTH part of the Earth, to kill with sword, and with hunger, and with pestilence, and with 5 the beasts of the Earth.—And when he had opened the fifth seal, I saw under the altar the souls of them that were slain for the word of God, and for the testimony which they held: and white robes were given unto every one of them; and it was said unto them, that they should rest yet for a little season, 10 until their fellow-servants also, and their brethren, that should be killed as they were, should be fulfilled. And I beheld, when he had opened the sixth seal, the stars of Heaven fell unto the Earth, even as a fig-tree casteth her untimely figs, when she is shaken of a mighty wind: And the Kings of the Earth, and the 15 great men, and the rich men, and the chief captains," &c.
305 *2*	And upwards spring on swiftest plume of fire
3–8	rush wing
306 *2–8*	The innumerable multitude of wrongs
307 *2–8*	By man on man inflicted! Rest awhile,
308 *2–8*	Children of Wretchedness! the hour is nigh:
309 *5 6(c) 2–8*	And lo! the Great, the Rich, the Mighty Men
310 *5*	W̶i̶t̶ The Kings, and the Chief Captains of the World
6(c) 2–8	The
311 *5 6(c) 2–8*	With all that fixt on high like stars of Heaven
312 *5 2–8*	Shot baleful influence, shall be cast to earth
6(c)	dash'd
313 *5 2–8*	Vile and downtrodden, as the untimely fruit
6(c)	like
314 *5 2–8*	Shook from the fig-tree by a sudden storm.
6(c)	a the
315 *5*	Even now the Storm begins: ◄——each——► gentler Name,
6(c)	m̶e̶e̶k̶ P̶I̶E̶T̶Y̶ each gentle
2–8	◄——each——►
315fn *12* 3*	The French Revolution.
13 4 5*	This passage alludes to the French Revolution: and the subsequent ⟨paragraph⟩ to the downfall of Religious Establishments. I am convinced, that the Babylon of the Apocalypse does not apply to Rome exclusively; but to the union of Religion with Power & Wealth, wherever it is found.
6–8	Alluding to the French Revolution.
316 *5 2–8*	Faith & meek Piety with fearful Joy
6(c)	e̶a̶c̶h̶ g̶e̶n̶t̶l̶e̶ N̶a̶m̶e̶ meek PIETY,
317 *5 6(c) 2–8*	Tremble far off—for lo! the Giant Frenzy
318 *5 6(c) 2–8*	Uprooting empires with his whirlwind arm
319 *5 6(c) 2–8*	Mocketh high Heaven, burst hideous from the Cell

320 5 6(c) *2–8*	Where the old Hag, unconquerable, huge
321 5 6(c) *2–8*	CREATION's eyeless drudge, black RUIN sits
322.1 5 6(c)	Nursing th' impatient earthquake, and with dreams
322.1.1 5 6(c)	Of shatter'd cities & the promisd day
322.1.2 5 6(c)	Of central fires thro' nether seas upthundring
322b.1/	
323a.1 5 6(c)	Soothes her fierce solitude—Return, pure Faith!
322a *2–8*	Nursing th' impatient Earthquake.
322fn 12* *3* 13*	And there came one of the Seven Angels which had the Seven Vials and talked with me, saying unto me, Come hither! I will shew unto thee the Judgment of the great Whore, that sitteth upon many waters: with whom the Kings of the Earth have committed fornication &c. Revelation of S. John the Divine, Chapter the Seventeenth. This (the 17th) & the thirteenth Scaliger deem'd the only intelligible Chapters of the whole Apocalypse. Scaligerianis II. pag. 14 & 15. 5
12*	In a circular Letter to the Welch Clergy Bishop Horsley declares the Church-men of Rome to be much more their 10 Brethren than the Protestant Dissenters. God forbid, it should be otherwise! They who perceive any real difference between the Church of Rome & that of England possess microscopic optics, to which I have no pretension!—Are they not both of them "arranged in ~~gold~~ purple and scarlet colour, & decked 15 with gold"? Are they not both allied with the Powers of this World? On the Foreheads of both is there not written "MYSTERY"? Do they not both sell the Gospel? Nay—Nay! They neither *sell*, nor is it the *Gospel*—but forcibly tear the tenth part of the poor Man's Subsistence from his Mouth in re- 20 turn for having crammed their lying Legends down his throat! But ~~for~~ "their Sins have reached unto Heaven—Babylon hath fallen and is falling. "And the Kings of the Earth who have committed fornication and lived deliciously with her, shall bewail her and lament for her." 25
	[Line-space]
322b *2–8*	O return!
323 5	Return, meek PIETY! Th' abhorred FORM,
2–8	Pure FAITH! meek PIETY!
324 5 *2–8*	Whose scarlet Robe was stiff with earthly pomp,
325 5 *2–8*	Who drank iniquity in cups of gold,
326 5 *2–8*	Whose names were many & all blasphemous [cry,
327 5	Hath met the horrible Judgment! ~~She hath fallen,~~ Whence that
2–8	←——— Whence ———→
327.1.1 5	~~A whore~~
328 5 *2–8*	The mighty army of foul Spirits shriek'd
329 5 *3–8*	Disherited of earth! For ~~ʃ~~She hath fallen
2	Disperited
330 5 *2–8*	On whose black front was written MYSTERY;
331 5	She that reel'd heavily, drunken with blood;
2–8	whose wine was

332 5 2–8	She that work'd whoredom with the DÆMON POWER,
333 5 2–8	And from the dark embrace all evil things
334 5 2–8	Brought forth & nurtur'd mitred ATHEISM,
335 5	And patient Folly, ~~that~~ who on bended knee
2–8	who
336 5	Gives back the steel that stabbd him; and pale Fears
2–8	FEAR
337 5 2 3	Hunted by ghastlier Terrors, than surround
13 4–8	shapings,
338 5 2–8	Moon-blasted Madness, when he yells at midnight.
339 5 2–8	Return, pure Faith! Return, meek Piety!
340 5 2–8	The Kingdoms of the world are your's: each Heart
341 5 2–8	Self-govern'd, the vast Family of Love
342 5	Rais'd ~~by~~ from the common earth by common toil
2–8	from
343 5 2–8	Enjoy the equal produce. Such delights
344 5	As ~~steal~~ float to earth, permitted Visitants,
2–8	float
345.1 5	When on some ⟨solemn⟩ Jubilee of ~~blessed~~ Saints
2 3	solemn ←—Saints—→
346.1 5	The sapphire-color'd gates of Paradise
2 3	-blazing
347.1 5	Are thrown wide open, and forth undulate
2 3	thence voyage forth
348.1 5	Detachment wild of seraph-warbled Airs
2 3	Detachments
349.1 5	And Odors snatch'd from beds of Amaranth,
350.1 5	And gentle Winds that from the river of Life
351.1 5	Spring up on freshen'd passion. The Good man
345 13	When ~~on~~ in some ~~high &~~ hour of solemn jubilee
4–8	in ←—hour—→
346 13	The ~~mighty~~ massy Gates of Paradise are thrown
4–8	←—massy—→
347 13 4–8	Wide open, and forth come in fragments wild
348 13 4–8	Sweet echoes of unearthly melodies,
349 13 2–8	And Odors snatch'd from beds of Amaranth,
350 2–8	And they, that from the chrystal river of life
351 2–8	Spring up on freshen'd wing, ambrosial gales!
352 2–8	The favour'd good Man, in his lonely walk,
353 2–8	Perceives them, and his silent spirit drinks
354 2–8	Strange bliss, which he shall recognize in Heaven.
355 2–7	And such delights, such strange beatitude,
8	beatitudes
356 2	Have seiz'd my young anticipating heart,
3–8	Seize on
357 2–8	When that blest Future rushes on my view!
	[*Line-space*]
358.1 7 8	For in his own and in his Father's Might,
359a.1 7 8	Heaven blazing in his train, the SAVIOUR comes!

359.1.1	8	To solemn symphonies of Truth and Love
359b.1/		
360a.1	7 8	The THOUSAND ɏYEARS lead up their mystic dance
379.1	7	And sweep before the rapt prophetic Gaze
381.1	7	Bright as what Glories from the Jasper Throne
382a.1/		
380b.1	7	Reflective glitter on the eye-veiling plumes
380b.2	7	Of Spirits adoring. ~~So Lo! their blissful reign~~ Lo! reparadis'd
361a.1/		
360b.1	7 8	Old Ocean claps his hands; the Desert shouts;
360.1.1	7 8	And vernal breezes wafting seraph sounds
361b.1	7	Melt the primæval poles! The mighty Dead
	8	North.
362.1	7	Leap from their Tombs, who e'er in ages past
	8	Rise from earliest time
363.1	7	~~Conscious have join'd~~
		With conscious zeal ha~~ve~~d aided the vast plan
	8	had
363b.1	7 8	Of Love Almighty.—
		[*Line-space*]
358.2	9 *3*	For in his own and in his Father's might
359a.2	9 *3*	The SAVIOUR comes! While as to solemn strains
359b.2/		
360a.2	9 *3*	The THOUSAND YEARS lead up their mystic dance,
361a.2/		
360b.2	9 *3*	Old OCEAN claps his hands! the DESERT shouts!
360.2.1	9	And ~~vernal Breezes wafting seraph sounds~~
		soft Gales wafted from the haunts of Spring
	3	And soft gales wafted from the haunts of Spring
361b.2	9 *3*	Melt the primæval North! The Mighty Dead
362.2	9	Rise to new life, ~~with recompacted frames,~~
		who e'er from earliest time
	3	Rise to new life, whoe'er from earliest time
362b.3/		
372b.1	9	~~Who e'er from earliest time, Patriot, or Sage~~
363.2	9	With conscious Zeal had ~~aided the vast plan~~
		urg'd Love's wondrous plan,
	3	With conscious zeal had urg'd Love's wond'rous plan
364.1	9	~~Of God most high.~~ Co-adjutors of God! To MILTON's ~~angel~~
		trump
	3	Coadjutors of God. trump
365.1	9 *3*	The odorous groves of Earth reparadis'd
366.1	9 *3*	Unbosom their glad echoes: inly hush'd
367.1	9 *3*	Adoring NEWTON his serener eye
368.1	9	Raises to Heaven; ~~and he with him~~ & he of mortal kind
	3	and he
369.1	9	Wisest, he first who [?]mark'd the ideal ~~trains~~ tribes
	3	mark'd tribes
369.1fn	9 *3*	David Hartley

370.1 9 *3*		Down the fine fibres from the sentient brain
371.1 9 *3*		Roll subtly-surging. Pressing on his steps
372.1 9		Patriot, and Saint, and Sage, lo! Priestley smiles,
	3 13	Lo! Priestley there, Patriot, and Saint, and Sage,
372.1.1 9 *3*		Whom that my fleshly eye hath never seen
372.1.2 9 *3*		A childish pang of impotent regret
373.1 9 *3*		Hath thrill'd my heart. Him from his native land
374.1 9 *3*		Statesmen blood-stain'd and Priests idolatrous
375.1 9		~~With~~ By dark lies mad'ning the blind multitude
	3	By
376.1 9 *3*		Drove with vain hate. Calm, pitying he retir'd
377.1 9 *3*		And mus'd expectant on these Promis'd Years.

[*Line-space*]

358 *4–8*		For in his own and in his Father's might
359 13 *4–8*		The S A V I O U R comes! While as the T H O U S A N D Y E A R S
359fn 13* *4 5*		The Millenium: in which I suppose that man will continue to enjoy the
		highest glory, of which his human nature is capable. That all who in past ages
		have endeavoured to ameliorate the state of man, will rise & enjoy the fruits
		& flowers, the imperceptible seeds of which they had sown in their former
		Life: and that the wicked will during the same period be suffering the remedies 5
		adapted to their several bad habits ~~that~~. I suppose that this period will be followed
		by the passing away of this Earth, & by our entering ~~on~~ the state of pure intellect;
		when all Creation shall rest from its labors.
360 13 *4–8*		Lead up their mystic dance, the D E S E R T shouts!
361 13 *4–8*		Old O C E A N claps his hands! The mighty Dead
362 *4–8*		Rise to new life, whoe'er from earliest time
363 *4–8*		With conscious zeal had urg'd Love's wondrous plan,
364 *4–8*		Coadjutors of God. To M I L T O N's trump
365 13 *4–8*		The high Groves of the renovated Earth
366 *4–8*		Unbosom their glad echoes: inly hush'd
367 *4–8*		Adoring N E W T O N his serener eye
368 *4–8*		Raises to heaven: and he of mortal kind
369 *4–8*		Wisest, he first who mark'd the ideal tribes
369fn *4–8*		David Hartley.
370 13 *4–8*		Up the fine fibres thro' the sentient brain
371 *5*		Pass in fine surges. Pressing on his steps
372 *4–8*		Lo! P R I E S T L E Y there, Patriot, and Saint, and Sage,
373 *4–8*		Him, full of years, from his lov'd native land
374 *4–8*		Statesmen blood-stain'd and Priests idolatrous
375 *4–8*		By dark lies mad'ning the blind multitude
376 *4–8*		Drove with vain hate. Calm, pitying he retir'd,
377 *4–8*		And mus'd expectant on these promis'd years.

[*Line-space*]

358.3	10	For in his own and in his Father's Might
359a.3	10	The SAVIOUR comes! While as to solemn strains
359b.3/		
360a.3	10	THOUSAND YEARS lead up their mystic dance,
361a.3/		
360b.3	10	Old Ocean claps his hands, the Desert shouts,
360.3.1	10	And vernal Breezes wafting seraph sounds
361b.3	10	Melt the primæval North. The Mighty Dead
362.4	10	~~Leap~~ Rise from their Tombs, who e'er ~~in Ages past~~
		from earliest time
363.3	10	With conscious zeal had aided the vast plan
363b.2/		
363.1.1	10	Of Love Almighty. There to PLATO's gaze
363.1.2	10	Sweep brighter Visions ~~than in elder days~~ time
363.1.3	10	Wilder'd his wildly-working phantasy;
381.2	10	[?]Bright as what Glories from Heaven's Jasper Throne
382a.2	10	Glitter reflective on the gorgeous Plumes
380.3	10	That veil the faces of Adoring Spirits!
364–5.2	10	~~There Milton o'e~~ To Milton's ~~bowers~~ song Earth's Bowers
		reparadis'd
366–7.2	10	Unbosom their glad echoes; Newton smiles,
367.1.1	10	And with him in most blest communion join'd
369.2	10	HARTLEY, ~~divinest~~ that humblest Sage! who first of Men
370.2	10	Untwisted all the finely-fibred Mind
372a.2	10	Making Thought palpable, & Priestley there
372.2.1	10	Whom that my fleshly eye hath never seen
372.2.2	10	A childish pang of impotent Regret
373.2	10	Hath thrill'd my heart.—Him from his native land
374.2	10	Statesmen blood-stain'd and Priests idolatrous
375.2	10	With dark lies mad'ning the blind Multitude
358.4	11	For in his own and in his Father's Might,
359a.4	11	Heaven blazing in his train, the SAVIOUR comes!
359.2.1	11	~~To the sweet blended strains of Truth and Love~~
359b.4/		
360a.4	11	The THOUSAND YEARS lead up their mystic Dance,
381.3	11	Bright as the Glori~~ie~~es of the Jasper Throne
382a.3	11	Flashing reflected from those gorgeous plumes
380.4	11	That veil the faces of th' adoring Blest.
361a.4/		
360b.4	11	Old Ocean claps his hands! The Desert shouts!
360.4.1	11	And vernal Breezes wafting solemn sounds
362a.4	11	Melt the primæval North! Rise from their sleep
361b.3	11	With recompacted frames the Mighty Dead,
362b.4/		
372b.3	11	Who e'er from earliest time, Patriot or Sage,
363.4	11	Aided with conscious zeal ⟨have aided⟩ the ~~wondrous~~ ⟨vast⟩
		plan

363b.5/		
363.2.1	11	~~Of Love Almighty! He of ancient days Name~~
363.2.2	11	~~Wisest, nor haply uninspir'd of God,~~
363.2.3/		
364b.3	11	~~Mild Socrates. To Milton's deeper song~~
365.3	11	~~The odorous Groves of Earth reparadis'd~~
366a.3	11	~~Unbosom their mild Echoes.~~
364b.4	11	~~Of God most high.~~ To Milton's angel trump
365.4	11	The Odorous groves of Earth reparadis'd
366.4	11	Unbosom their ~~mild~~ glad echoes. ~~Hush'd~~ Inly hush'd
367.3	11	Adoring Newton his serene eyes
368.2	11	Raises to Heaven; and He of mortal men
369a.3	11	Wisest nor haply uninspir'd of God
369b.3	11	HARTLEY, meek sage! who ~~first with palest thought~~ th' ideal tribes of Mind
370.3	11	Untwisted, ~~all the finely,~~ fibres of the Heart
372a.3	11	Making ʃThought palpable—& Priestly there, saw the ʃnascent, thought,
371.2	11	Roll subtly-surging o'er the passive brain
370a.4	11	Down thro' the finely-~~frib~~fibred
369b.4	11	Hartley, ~~meek sage! who~~ whose ~~keen eye~~ mark'd th Ideal tribes
370.5	11	Down each fine fibre from the sentient brain
371.3/		
372a.4	11	Roll subtly-surging! ~~Pressing on his steps~~ es close behind
		~~Lo Priestley~~
		And mild PRIESTLY there
		~~Lo Priestley~~
372b.4	11	Lo! ~~the blest~~ That meek Preacher, Patriot, and Sage, and Saint
		Lo! the meek Preacher ~~presses close behind,~~ Patriot, Sage, & Saint
372.3.1	11	Whom that my fleshly eye hath never seen
372.3.2	11	A childish pang of impotent Regret
373.3	11	Hath thrill'd my heart. Him from his native land
374.3	11	Statesmen blood-stain'd & Priests idolatrous
376.2	11	Have vainly driven.—Calm, pitying he retir'd
377.2	11	And mus'd expectant on these mystic days.
358.5	12	For in his own and in his Father's Might
359a.5	12	The Saviour comes! To solemn-breathing strains
359b.5/		
360a.5	12	The THOUSAND YEARS lead up their mystic Dance.
361a.5/		
360b.5	12	Old Ocean claps his hands⸍! the Desert shouts!
360.5.1	12	And vernal Breezes wafting seraph sounds
361b.4	12	Melt the primæval North! The Mighty Dead
362a.5	12	Rise from strange sleep with recompacted frames,
362b.5/		
372b.5	12	Who e'er from earliest time, Patriot or Sage,
363.5	12	With conscious zeal have aided the vast plan
364.5	12	Of the Most High. To MILTON's angel trump

365.5	12	The Odorous Groves of Earth reparadis'd
366.5	12	Unbosom their glad echoes! Inly hush'd
367.4	12	Adoring NEWTON his serener eye
368.3	12	Raises to Heaven! And He of mortal men
369a.5	12	Wisest nor haply uninspir'd of God
369b.5	12	H̶A̶R̶T̶L̶E̶Y̶,̶ ̶w̶h̶o̶s̶e̶ first b̶e̶h̶e̶l̶d̶ t̶h̶' I̶d̶e̶a̶l̶ t̶r̶i̶b̶e̶s̶ w̶i̶t̶h̶ ̶w̶o̶n̶d̶r̶o̶u̶s̶
		e̶y̶e̶ ̶s̶e̶r̶e̶n̶e̶
		D̶o̶w̶n̶ ̶e̶a̶c̶h̶ ̶f̶i̶b̶r̶e̶
		Meek HARTLEY, first who mark'd th Ideal Tribes
370.6	12	Down each fine fibre from the sentient brain
371a.4/		
372b.5	12	Roll subtly-surging. Patriot, Sage, and Saint
372a.5	12	Lo! Priestly presses onward—wondrous man,
372.4.1	12	Whom that my fleshly hath never seen,
372.4.2	12	A childish pang of impotent regret
373.4	12	Hath thrill'd my heart. Him from his native land
374.4	12	Statesmen blood-stain'd and Priests idolatrous
375.3	12	With dark lies mad'ning the blind multitude
376.3	12	Idly have driven. Calm, pitying he retir'd
377.3	12	And mus'd expectant on these mystic Years!
		[*Line-space*]
378.1	9 *3*	O Years! the blest Preeminence of Saints!
379.2	*3*	Sweeping before the rapt prophetic Gaze
381.4	9	Bright as what Glories f̶r̶o̶m̶ of the Jasper Throne
	3	of
380a.5	9 *3*	Stream from the gorgeous & face-veiling plumes
380b.5	9	Of hymning Spirits! Ye, blest Years! must end,
	3	Spirits adoring!
383.1	9	A̶n̶d̶ ̶a̶l̶l̶ beyond is darkness! h̶e̶i̶g̶h̶t̶s̶ theme t̶o̶o̶ ̶v̶a̶s̶t̶
383.1.1	9	For mortal s̶o̶a̶r̶i̶n̶g̶. My stretcht I̶n̶t̶e̶l̶l̶e̶c̶t̶
383b.2	9	Akes as with growing p̶a̶i̶n̶s̶!̶ ̶F̶r̶o̶m̶ ̶s̶u̶c̶h̶ ̶s̶t̶r̶a̶n̶g̶e̶ ̶h̶e̶i̶g̶h̶t̶s̶
		So strange the Height
384.1	9	W̶h̶e̶n̶c̶e̶ Fancy falls, first flutt'ring her vain w̶i̶n̶g̶.
383b.3	9	Heights most strange
383.4	*3* 13	And all beyond is darkness! Heights most strange!
384.2	9	Whence ? F̶Fancy falls, fast-fluttering her vain wing.
	3	Fancy fluttering her idle
385.1	9 *3*	For who of woman born may paint the Hour,
386.1	9 *3*	When seiz'd in his mid course the Sun shall wane
387.1	9 *3*	Making Noon ghastly? Who of woman born
388.1	9	May image in his wildly-working brain,
	3	thought,
389.1	9 *3*	How the black-visag'd, red-eyed Fiend outstretcht
390.1	9 *3*	Beneath th' unsteady feet of Nature groans
391.1	9 *3*	In feverish slumbers—destin'd then to wake,
392.1	9 *3*	When fiery whirlwinds thunder his dread name
393a.1/		
394b.1	9	And Angels shout, DESTRUCTION! H̶i̶g̶h̶ ̶i̶n̶ ̶a̶i̶r̶
394a.1	9	T̶h̶e̶ ̶S̶p̶i̶r̶i̶t̶ ̶l̶i̶f̶t̶i̶n̶g̶,̶ ̶h̶i̶s̶ ̶s̶t̶r̶o̶n̶g̶ ̶a̶r̶m̶ ̶h̶a̶t̶h̶ ̶s̶w̶o̶r̶n̶

393b.1	9	How his arm
393.2	*3*	And Angels shout, DESTRUCTION! How his arm
394.2	9 *3*	The Mighty Spirit lifting high in air
395.1	9	~~Sweareth~~ Shall swear by ~~h~~Him, the everliving ONE,
	3	Shall swear by Him,
396a.1	9 *3*	TIME IS NO MORE!
379a.3/		
380b.6	11	Visions! that sweep before the prophet's eyes
381.5	11	Bright as ~~what~~ the ~~Glories~~ what Hues before the Jasper Throne
380a.7	11	Flash from the gorgeous & face-veiling Plumes
380b.7	11	Of Spirits adoring!—
378.2	12	O years! the blest Preeminence of Saints!
379.4	12	Sweeping before the rapt prophetic Gaze
381.6	12	Bright as what Glories of the Jasper Throne
380a.8	12	~~Dart~~ Stream from the gorgeous & face-veiling Plumes
380b.8	12	Of Spirits adoring! Ye, blest Years! must end—
383.2.1	12	But ~~the~~ my soul tires, and my stretch'd Intellect
383.2.2	12	Akes, as with growing pains, and Fancy~~'s song~~ now
383.2.3	12	~~Upsoaring thro' the infinite of Truth~~
383b.5	12	From ~~that~~ these unmeasur'd and stupendous heights
384.3	12	Fast-fluttering her vain pinions, falls to earth
385b.2	12	And there lies panting—else would I paint the Hour,
386.2	12	When seiz'd in his mid course the Sun shall wane
387.2	12	Making Noon ghastly; and bid some Spirit tale,
389.2	12	Where the black-visag'd red-eyed fiend outstretchd
390.2	12	Beneath the unsteady feet of Nature groans
391.2	12	In feverish slumbers—destin'd then to wake,
392.2	12	When fiery whirl~~s~~-winds thunder his dread name,
393a.3	12	And Angels shout, DESTRUCTION! Like a Dream
393.1.1	12	Corporeal things shall vanish—and the Clouds
393.1.2	12	Sudden retiring, from the throne of God
393.1.3	12	Shall flash one blaze of all-~~pervading~~restoring Light
393.1.4	12	Involving Earth, & Heaven, & deepest Hell!
393.1.5	12	The mighty Angel shall descend, and fix
393.1.7	12	His right foot on the Sea, his left on earth,
393.1.7	12	Seven Thunders utter their dread voices—He
394b.3/		
395a.2	12	Lifts up his hand to Heaven, & swears by him
395b.2/		
396.2	12	The ~~aye-living One~~ ever-living God—Time is no more!
378	*4–8*	O Years! the blest preeminence of Saints!
379a.4/		
382a.4	13	~~Ye sweep before me in as lovely Hues~~
382a.5/		
380b.9	13	~~As stream, reflected, from the veiling plumes~~
381b.7	13	~~Of them, that aye before the Jasper Throne~~
380b.10/		
381a.7/		
382b.1	13	~~Adoring bend. Blest Years! ye too depart.~~

381b.7fn 13*   ~~The~~ Revel. Ch. IV. v. 2 & 3ʳᵈ.—And immediately I was in the Spirit: and behold a Throne was set in Heaven, and one sat on the throne. And he that sat was to look like a jasper & sardine stone &c.

379 *4–8*   Ye sweep athwart my gaze, so heavenly-bright,

380 *4–7*   The wings that veil the adoring Seraph's eyes,

     8   Seraphs'

381 *4–7*   What time he bends before the Jasper Throne

     8   they bend

381fn *4–8*   Rev. Chap. iv, v. 2, and 3.—And immediately I was in the Spirit: and

              behold, a Throne was set in Heaven, and one sat on the Throne. And he that sat

              was to look upon like a jasper and sardine stone, &c.

382 *4–8*   Reflect no lovelier hues! yet ye depart,

383 *4–8*   And all beyond is darkness! Heights most strange,

384 *4–8*   Whence Fancy falls, fluttering her idle wing.

385 *4–8*   For who of woman born may paint the hour,

386 *4–8*   When seiz'd in his mid course, the Sun shall wane

387 *4–8*   Making noon ghastly! Who of woman born

388 13   May image in the workings of his ~~Spirit,~~ Thought,

     4 6–8   ←—thought, —→

     5   how the red-eyed Fiend outstretcht

389 *4 6–8*   How the black-visag'd, red-eyed Fiend outstretcht

389fn 13 *4–8*   The final Destruction impersonated.

390 *4–8*   Beneath the unsteady feet of Nature groans,

391 *4–7*   In feverish slumbers—destin'd then to wake,

     8   feverous

392 *4–8*   When fiery whirlwinds thunder his dread name

393.1 *5*   DESTRUCTION! when the Sons of Morning shout,

393 *4 6–8*   And Angels shout, DESTRUCTION! How his arm

     5   The

394 13 *4–8*   The last great Spirit lifting high in air

395 *4–8*   Shall swear by Him, the ever-living ONE,

396a *4–8*   TIME IS NO MORE!

399b.1 9   Sudden the Clouds retire,

400.1 9   And lo! the Throne of the redeeming God

401.1 9   Forth-flashing unimaginable Days

402.1 9   Wraps in one Blaze Earth, Heaven, & deepest Hell!

396a.2 9   TIME IS NO MORE!

396b 9 *3–8*   Believe thou, O my soul!

396fn 13* *4 5*   This paragraph is intelligible ~~who~~ to those, who, like the Author, believe &

              feel the sublime system of Berkley; & the doctrine of the final Happiness of

              all men.

397 9 *3–8*   Life is a Vision shadowy of Truth,

398 9 *3–8*   And Vice, and Anguish, and the wormy Grave

399 9 *3–8*   Shapes of a Dream! The veiling Clouds retire,

400	9 *3–8*	And lo! the Throne of the redeeming God
401	9 *3 4 6–8*	Forth flashing unimaginable Day
402	9 *3 4 6–8*	Wraps in one blaze Earth, Heaven, & deepest Hell.
	5	Light
		[*Line-space*]
403	12 *3–8*	Contemplant Spirits! ye that hover o'er
404	12 *3–8*	With untir'd gaze th' immeasurable fount
405	12 *3–8*	Ebullient with creative Deity!
406	12 *3–8*	And ye of plastic power, that interfus'd
407	12 *3–8*	Roll thro' the grosser & material mass
408	12 *3–8*	In organizing surge! Holies of God!
409	*3–8*	(And what if Monads of the infinite mind?)
410	*3–8*	I haply journeying my immortal course
411	*3–8*	Shall sometime join your mystic choir! Till then
412	*3–7*	I discipline my young noviciate thought
	8	and novice
413	*3–8*	In ministeries of heart-stirring song,
414	*3–8*	And aye on Meditation's heaven-ward wing
415	*3–8*	Soaring aloft I breathe th' empyreal air
416	*3–8*	Of LOVE, omnific, omnipresent LOVE,
417	*3–8*	Whose day-spring rises glorious in my soul
418	*3–8*	As the great Sun, when he his influence
419	*3–8*	Sheds on the frost-bound waters—The glad stream
420	*3–8*	Flows to the ray and warbles as it flows.

⁻**1.6** *4 5* she   ⁻**1.11** *5 prayer*   ⁻**1.15–16** *5 redemption.*   **title.** *3* RELIGIOUS MUSINGS | *A DESULTORY POEM*, | WRITTEN | *ON CHRISTMAS' EVE*, | IN THE YEAR OF OUR LORD, 1794. • *4 RELIGIOUS MUSINGS.* | A | *DESULTORY POEM*, | Written on the Christmas Eve of 1794. • *5 RELIGIOUS MUSINGS.* | A DESULTORY POEM, | Written on the Christmas Eve of 1794. • *6 7* RELIGIOUS MUSINGS; | A DESULTORY POEM, | WRITTEN ON THE CHRISTMAS EVE OF 1794. • *8* RELIGIOUS MUSINGS; | A DESUL- TORY POEM, WRITTEN ON THE CHRISTMAS | EVE OF 1794.   **1.1.** *3* time, **3.1.** *3* trump   **2.1.** *3* voice   *3* heart   **3.1.1.** *3* noise   *3* wings   **3.1.2.** *3* spirit **5.1.** *3* night.   **5.1fn1.** *3* multitude   **5.1fn2.** 12* Glory ~~the~~ to • *3* glory to   **5.1fn3.** *3* highest   *3* earth peace.   **5.1fn4.** *3* LUKE   **6.1.1.** *3* MIND, **6.1.2.** *3* company   **6.1.4.** *3* womb   **7.1.** *3* Thou   **12.1.** *3* the   *3* face **10.1.** *3* Great   **11.1.** *3* and concentred   **14.1.2.** *3* beheld   **14.1.2fn1.** 12* ~~Philip saith unt~~ Philip • *3* Philip   *3* him,   **14.1.2fn1–2.** *3* Father.   **14.1.2fn5.** *3* JOHN **14.1.3.** *3* and   *3* awful eye.   **14.1.5.** *3* weal,   **1.** *4 5* when,   *4–8* hear, **2.** *4–8* voice   *8* adoration   **3.** *4–8* upborne,   **4.** *4–7* Choir, • *8* choir,   **5.** *4– 8* vision   *4–8* multitude,   **6.** *6–8* hymned   *8* peace   *4–8* fields!   **7.** *8* angel *5* Host,   **8.** *4 5* harbinger'd • *6–8* harbingered   *4–8* Thou,   **9.** *4–7* GREAT • *8* great   **10.** *4–7* INVISIBLE   **11.** *4–8* light   **12.** *6–8* the oppressed   *4– 8* good   *8* man,   **14.** *6–8* the   *8* oppressor.   *8* mead,   **15.** *8* grove,   *8* sea, *8* sun,   *8* stars;   **16.** *8* impress   **17.** *8* grove,   *8* mead,   **18.** *4–7* Isles, • *8* isles,   **19.** *5–8* starred   *8* azure,   *4–7* Sun, • *8* sun,   **21.** *6–8* Imaged **22.** *4–8* Saviour!   **23.** *8* anguish   *6–8* winged   *3–8* prayer   **24.** *6–8* Harped *8* mercy!   **25.** *5–8* the   *8* Almighty   *6–8* heard   *4–6* Throne, • *8* throne

26. *3* 12 *4–8* light   *6–8* filled   *4 5* extacy! • *6* ecstacy! • *7 8* ecstasy!   **27.** *3–*
5 Heav'n's   *6–8* paused: *3–8* mouth   **28a.** *6–8* Closed   **28b.** *8* death
29. *6–8* Him   *8* life   **30.** *6–8* beamed   **32.** *4–8* mists   *8* idolatry   **33.** *6–*
8 misshaped   *8* omnipresent   **33fn.** *4–7* print the Greek without accents, breathing,
or iota subscript; in MS 13* C had to begin a new line with Θεῶν, for reasons
of space, and it is so printed, as if it were a line of verse, in PR *4–7*   **33fn1–**
2. *4–7* DAMAS. DE MYST. ÆGYPT.   **34b.1.** *3* Spirit   *3* lusts   **34.** *8* Fear
6–8 uncharmed   *8* drowsed   *4 5* Soul, • *6–8* Soul.   **35.** *3* it's   *8* nature   *3–*
8 it   **36.** *6–8* soared   *3 4 6 7* HOPE, • *5* HOPE • *8* Hope,   **37.** *3–8* good
38. *6–8* The   13 *4–8* Eternal   *3* IMMORTAL • 13 *4 5* Immortal • *6–8* immortal
8 sons.   **39.** *8* Hope   *8* Faith   *8* Love   **40.** *6–8* absorbed: *6–7* centered •
8 centred   **41.** *8* God   **42.** *8* consciousness   *4–8* God   **43.** *3–8* it
43fn1. 13* ⟨vide Hartley & Pistorius⟩ Hartley, Vol. I. • *4* Hartley, vol. 1.   *4* and vol. 2,
43fn2. *4* Mysticism,   **43fn3.** *4* Notes and   *4* 18th,   **43fn4.** *4* 653d   *4* Hartley.
4 Edition.   **44.** *8* God   *3* it's • *4–8* its   *8* identity: **45a.** *3–7* ONE! •
8 one!   **45b.** *6 7* blessed   *3–8* they,   **46.** *3–8* elect   **47.** *6–8* through
4–7 Men, • *8* men,   **48.** *6 8* steadfast   *3–8* gaze   **49.** *6–8* Him   *8* essence,
mind, and energy!   **51.** *3–8* feet   *3* *8* things   **52.** *3–8* steps,   *5 8* throne
53. *6–8* loved.   **54.** *8* They   *8* contempt   *6–8* embosom   *8* revenge: **55.** *3–*
7 THEY • *8* they   **56.** *8* Supreme Fair   *3–8* sole   *3–7* Operant: • *8* operant:
57. *3–8* things   **58.** *3–8* good.   **59.** *3–8* courage,   *5* arm'd, • *6–8* armed—
60. *3–8* brood,   **61.** *3–8* compare!   **63.** *8* banners   *3–8* Omnipotence.
64. *6* Love,   **65.** *3 4 6–8* tents   *8* terrors   **66.** *3 4 6–8* they   *8* holy things
67. *6–8* Aye unprofaned, though   *6–8* Hell;   **68.** *3 4 6 7* GOD's   *8* altar
3 4 6–8 hand   **69.** *8* Fear,   *6–8* -visaged,   *3 4 6–8* wretch,   **70.** *6–8* -refuged
3–8 hot pursuing   **71.** *6–8* refreshed   *3–8* Heaven   **72.** *3–8* throb   *3–8* tempest
3–8 heart.   **73.** *3–8* countenance   *7 8* settles;   *3–8* bliss   **74.** *3 4* his eye: •
6–8 his eye—   *3 4 6–8* swimming eye   *6–8* upraised: **75.** *3 4 6–8* limbs!
76. *3 6–8* transfigured   *3–8* awe,   **77.** *3–8* hush   *3 4 6–8* soul,   **78.1.** *3* things
3 seeming.   **80b.1.** *3* latter day   **80b.1fn1.** *3* voice   **80b.1fn2.** 12* Seven
Angels, saying, pour • *3* seven Angels, pour   *3* vials   *3* wrath   **80b.1fn3.** *3* earth.
80b.1fn4. *3* REVELATION   **80a.1.** *3* 12 sons   *3* 12 men.   **80.1.1.** *3* he
3 heart   **82.1.** *3* MERCY-SEAT—   *3* flames,   **83.1.** *3* wells   **84.1.** *3* Seven
78. *6–8* unmoved   **79.** *6–8* the   *4–8* ministers   **82.** *5* MERCY SEAT • *8* Mercy-
seat   **83.** *8* wells   *8* Love   **84.** *6–8* filled   *8* vials   *4–7* Wrath, • *8* wrath,
86. *3–8* balm   *3–8* good man   **87.** *5* lone,   *3–5* trav'ller's • *6–8* traveller's
3–8 wounds!   **88.** *3–5* th' • *6–8* the   *6–8* through   **89fn1.** *4 5* Passions
4 5 Religion,   *4 5* innocent, and   **89fn2.** 13* virtues— • *4 5* virtue—
89fn3. *4 5* Sun,   *4 5* light   13* In the preceding] *4 5* run on in same paragraph
89fn4. *4 5* paragraph,   *4 5* truth,   **90.** *8* Spirit,   *3–8* regards   **91.** *6–8* -centre.
3–8 Lo   *3–8* acquire   **92.** *3–8* grace   **93.** *6–8* Enrobed   *5–8* naturalized
94. *8* shepherd   **95.** *6–8* Through   *3–8* fog   *6–8* timorous   **96.** *6–8* the
3 4 6–8 road   **98.** *6–8* deformed.   *3–8* But   *3* lo, • *4–8* lo!   **99.** *6–8* Touched
5–8 the   *3–8* enchantment   *3–8* beam   **100.** *6–8* Straight   *3 4* vapor •
5–8 vapour   *3–8* melteth,   **101.** *3–8* glitter   *3–8* plant   *3* tree: • *4–8* tree;
102. *3–8* leaf,   *3–8* blade   *5* hangs;   **103.** *3–8* rays,   **104.** *3–8* landscape
3–8 glory!   **106.** *8* Love.   **109.** *3–8* orbit   **110.** *6 7* blessed   *3–8* outstarting!
4–7 HIMSELF • *8* Himself   **111.** *8* sun,   *3–8* and   **112.** *4–8* creation;
114. *5* Most   **116.** *6–8* the   **120.** *6–8* uninjured   *3 4 6–8* (in   *6–8* -aimed

121. *8* murder *3 4 6 7* Suicide) • *8* suicide)   **123.** *8* human nature: **124.** *6–*
8 bestrewed   **125.** *8* interests   **126a.** *6–8* unhelmed *8* rage!   **127.** *8* majesty
128. *6 7* wonderous • *8* wondrous *4–8* whole!   **131.** *6–8* Diffused through
132. *4–8* except   **132fn.** *13** cues to line 134   **132fn1.** *13** supreme Reality
~~our ruling Passion~~ the • *4 5* Supreme Reality the   **132fn2.** *5* Superstition: *13** if
~~falsely to~~ the attribut~~é~~ing • *4 5* if the attributing   **132fn3–4.** *4 5* Avarice and
132fn5. *13** temple~~s~~of ~~Mex~~ the • *4 5* temple of the   **132fn6.** *13** but ⟨to⟩ the •
4 5 but to the   **132fn7.** *13** convey~~ing~~ed • *4 5* conveyed *4 5* this and *4 5* lines.
133. *8* Supreme Reality!   **137.1.** *3* wrath   **138.1.3.** *3* heart,   **139a.1.** *3* Atheist
3 slave)   **139b.1.** *3* multitudes;   **140b.1.** *3* TRADE   **141.1.** *3* bales
3 anguish;   **135.** *8* Superstition! *4–8* that   **136.** *8* priest *6–8* stained
8 brother's   **137.** *4–8* idols, *7 8* wrath   **139.** *4–8* plain *4–7* Sun, • *8* sun,
140. *8* death; *8* Trade   **142.** *3–8* mourning,   **143.** *3* 13 *4–8* eye *3* Faith; •
13 Faith*í*,   **144.** *3* 13 *4–8* present *3* God, • 13 *4–8* God;   **145.** *3–8* world's
3–8 cohesion,   **146.** *8* anarchy *3–8* Toy- *3–5* -bewitch'd, • *6–8* -bewitched,
147. *3–8* lusts, *3* soul • *4–8* soul,   **148.** *6–8* centre *3–8* sire   **149.** *3–*
8 thing,   **150.** *3–8* brethren *3–8* heart   **151.** *6–8* Through *3–8* courts
3–8 cities *8* savage   **152.** *3–8* himself, *8* self *3* whole, • *4–8* whole;
153. *3–8* sympathy   **154.** *3–8* whole *3–7* ONE SELF! SELF, • *8* one self!
self, *3–8* alien   **155.** *8* Self, *6–8* diffused   **156.** *8* Self, *3* it's *3–8* own,
157. *3–8* of all *8* Faith!   **158.** *8* Messiah's *6–8* destined *3–8* victory!
159fn1. *4–7* 21st. • *8* 21st, *8* address   **159fn2.** *4–8* speech *4–7* Amendment
159fn3. *6* effect; • *7 8* effect:— *4–8* hoped his   **159fn4.** *13** to *í*conclude •
4–8 to conclude *7 8* France," &c. *13** ~~Op~~ This • *4–8* This   **159fn5.** *6* Portland,
who,   **159fn6.** *8* Christian *4–7* RELIGION." • *8* Religion." *4–8* 30th,
159fn7. *4–7* Resolutions, • *8* resolutions,   **159fn7–8.** *4–7* Establishment
159fn8. *8* peace   **159fn9.** *4–8* Lords,   **159fn9–10.** *4–7* is WAR! and WAR •
8 is War! and War   **159fn10.** *4–8* manner   **159fn11.** *8* Creator, *4–8* minds,
and   **159fn12.** *4–8* hearts, and   **161.** *3–7* THEE to • *8* Thee to *8* Galilean!
Thee   **162.** *3–8* laws   **163.** *8* enmity   **164.** *8* peace; *6–8* listening
8 treachery   **165.** *8* pious *3–8* brother's life;   **166.** *3–8* widows *3–*
6 8 land • *7* land!   **167.** *3–8* orphans *3–7* bread! • *8* bread   **168.** *8* Thee
8 mankind!   **169.** *8* Thee, Lamb *8* Thee, *8* peace!   **170.** *3* war! • *6 7* War? •
8 War,—   **171.** *8* Austria, *8* Woman *8* North,   **172.** *6 7* Murderess •
8 murderess *8* lord!   **173.** *8* mind!   **173fn1.** *12** ~~man~~ Despot • *3* Despot •
13* Despot, *3* 13* hireling   **173fn2.** *3* 13* swindler,   **173fn3.** *3* 13* liberties
174. *3–8* bards *3–8* time *6–8* feigned)   **175.** *3–8* hate *3–8* man,   **177.** *3–*
8 face, *3–8* mouth   **178.** *3–8* sympathy! *3–8* these   **179.** *4–8* princeling,
6–8 nursed   **180.** *6–8* -hardened *3–8* barterers *3–8* blood!   **180fn2.** *12** ~~for~~
by • *3* by   **180fn4.** *12** War for ~~human~~ the • *3* war for the *12* 3* subjects.
181. *8* slave-   **182.** *3–8* savagery *3–8* holy zeal,   **184.** *6–8* blushed *3–8* her
sons!   **185.** *8* Thee *8* priest   **187.** *8* accomplice   **188.** *6–8* wakened
192. *3* 13 *4–8* Love,   **192fn1.** *12* 3* 13* *4–7* O Lord, mine Holy • *8* O Lord, my
God, mine Holy *3* 13* *4–8* One? We   **192fn2.** *13* 4–8* Lord, thou *13** has
3 8 judgment, &c. • *13* 4–7* Judgment, &c. *3* HABBAKUK I. 12. • *13** Habakkuk,
I. 12. • *4 5* Habakkuk, I. 12. • *6–8* *Habakkuk.* TEXTS *12* 3 6–8* end the note here.
TEXTS *13* 4 5* continue in the same paragraph *4 5* In   **192fn4.** *4* these Evlis
192fn5. *4 5* age,   **192fn6.** *4 5* security,   **192fn7.** *13** ~~which~~ Virtue, • *4 5* Virtue,
4 5 wise and *4 5* Innocence.   **195.** *6–8* through   **197.** *6–8* fixed   **198.** *3–*

8 primeval age   **199.** *6–8* wandered   *8* flock,   **200.** *3–8* where'er   *3–8* grass
5–8 waved.   **201.** *6–8* conjured   **202.** *8* A   **203.** *3–8* children   *6–8* toiled.
204. *8* Property   *3–8* fount,   **206.** *3–8* Hence   *3–8* couch,   *6–8* -coloured
3–5 8 robe, • *6 7* robe   **207.** *3–8* timbrel,   *6 7* arched   *3–8* dome   *3* feast •
4–8 feast,   **208.** *6–8* the   *3–8* arts,   *6–8* nursed   *3–8* soul   **209.** *3–8* beauty,
210. *6–8* Unsensualized   *3–8* means   **211.** *5* Learn'd   *3–8* end,   **212.** *4–8* Best
6–8 pleasured   *3* it's   **213.** *3–8* hence Disease   **214.** *6–8* daggered   *3–8* Envy,
3–8 Want,   **215.** *3–8* Warriors,   *3–8* Lords,   *3–8* Priests—   **215fn1.** *12* ~~We~~
I • *3* I   *3* gospel   *3* hire   **215fn2.** *3* teacher   **215fn3–4.** *12* ~~imp~~ importance •
3 importance   **215fn4.** *12* *3* mind   *3* unbiassed.   **215fn6.** *12* *3* teachers,
215fn7. *12* ~~áof~~ • *3* of   **215fn8.** *3* word PRIEST,   **215fn9.** *12* ~~all other~~
~~every other~~ any • *3* any   *12* ~~terms~~ • *3* term   **215fn10.** *12* ~~Anti~~ Anti- •
3 anti-   *3* man   **215fn11.** *3* power   *12* ~~the~~ his Right Hand • *3* his right
hand   **215fn12.** *12* Bible *(translated by Authority)* in ~~the other,~~ his Left, • *3* bible
(translated by authority) in his left,   **215fn13.** *12* ~~cause~~ make • *3* cause   *3* bible
and   *3* scourge   **215fn14.** *3* ideas,   **215fn14–15.** *12* ~~which~~ that • *3* that
215fn15–16. *12* which ~~having been taught mysterious doctrines~~ judging of ~~Christianity~~
Revelation • *3* which judging of Revelation   **215fn17.** *12* ~~establishment~~ practices •
3 practices   **215fn18–19.** *12* See ~~Conciones ad Populum, my~~ "Addresses •
3 See "Address   **215fn19.** *3* People,"   *3* 57,   **215fn20.** *3* Paternoster-
Row.   **216.** *5* life: **217.** *6–8* the   **218.** *3–8* good.   **219.** *3–8* action
220. *3–8* animal   *3–8* Lord;   **221.** *6–8* -featured   *3–8* Sage's   **222.** *8* a
3 13 4–8 host   *13 4 6–8* Deities, • *5* Deities.   **224.** 6(a) Av'rice • *8* avarice
3 13 4–7 Luxury • *8* luxury   *8* war   **225.** 6(a) *3* Science: • *3–7* Science; • *8* science;
6(a) *3–7* Science Freedom. • *8* science freedom.   **226.** *6–8* wakened   *3–8* realms
227. *6–8* souls,   **228.** *6–8* God,   **229.** *8* wealth's   *6–8* rivalry!   *3 4 6–*
8 they   **230.** *6–8* Enamoured   *3–8* order   **231.** *6–8* The   *3* disproportion; •
4–8 disproportion: *3–8* whoe'er   **234.** *3–7* PATRIOT SAGE   **234fn.** *3* DR.
235. *6–8* Called   *6–8* the   *3–8* -rushing cloud   **236.** *6–8* dashed   *3–7* Terrors
237. *3–8* phalanx   **238.** *6–8* Measured   **239.** *3–8* flute!   **240.** 13 *4–8* When,
3 13 4–8 rage   13 *4–7* Pity, • *8* pity,   **241.** *6–8* roused   *6–8* the unnumbered
242. *6 7* blind. • *8* blind,—   **243.** *6–8* hushed   **246.** *6–8* the   **247.** *8* confusion
248. *8* wont,—   *3–8* visions   *3–7* day! • *8* day!—   **249.** *3–7* Summer
250. *6 7* arched   *3–8* rock   *6–8* reclined   **251.** *3–5* sea- • *6–8* sea   *4–8* locks;
252. *3–8* blossoms,   *3–8* eve,   **253.** *3–8* Wandering   *6–8* inhaled   **254.** *3 4 6–*
8 flocks   *3 4 6–8* woods   **255.** *3 4 6–8* streams   *8* sun   **256.** *5* clouds,
257. *6–8* Ecstatic gazed!   *6–8* strayed   **258.** *6–8* mused   **259.** *8* misery
260. *2 8* Ah!   *6–8* removed   **261.** *3–8* Man,   **263.** *2* PAGEANT POWER,
8 recognise   **264.** *3–8* cots'   **265.** *4–8* risen   **266.** *8* Blest   *2* disbranch'd. •
6–8 disbranched!   **267.** *6–8* depictured   *2* sun-scorch'd • *3–5* sun-scorcht •
6–8 sun-scorched   *2–8* waste,   **268.** *6–8* through   **269.** *8* Simoom
269fn1. *3* 13* At   **269fn4.** *3* 13* IDRIS   *2 3* 13* out   **269fn7.** *3* 13* thick.—
269fn8. *3* 13* ground.—   **269fn9.** *3* 13* IDRIS   **269fn12.** *3* 13* suffocation.
269fn13. *3* 13* BRUCE'S   *3* 13* vol. 4.   *3* 13* 557.   **270.** *2* dies: and   *7 8* where
272. *2* LION • *3–8* lion   *2* HYÆNA • *3–8* hyæna   **274.** *2* SERPENT • *3* 13 *4–*
8 serpent   **275.** *2* BEHEMOTH   **275fn1.** *6–8* Behemoth,   *6–8* Hebrew,
4–8 wild   **275fn2.** *4 5* Elephant,   *4 5* Hippopotamus; • *6–8* hippopotamus;
4 5 Wild-Bull. • *6–8* wild bull.   **275fn3.** *6–8* quadruped.   **276a.** *2* loud-
crashing. • *3* loud crashing!   **276b.** *2* numberless   **277.** *2* OPPRESSION'S •

8 oppression's   **278.** *3 4 6–8* life's   *2–5* Wretch, • *6 7* Wretch • *8* wretch
279. *6–8* nursed   *8* want,   **281.** *3–7* Form, • *8* form,   **282.** *3–8* victim
3–8 seduction,   *6–8* doomed   **283.** *5* Days   *5* Blasphemy;   **284.** *6–*
8 loathed   *3–8* wassailers   **285.** *4* rememember'd • *6–8* remembered   *2 8* home
286. *3–8* Gnaws   *3–8* viper   *2* heart.   **287.** *8* women!   **288.** *2–8* morsel
6–8 tossed   *6–8* -forced   *8* charity,   **290.2.1.** *3* disease,   **292.2.** *3* Lazar-house,
294.1.1. *3* nurse   **290.** *8* suppliants!   *4 6–8* unreceived   **291.** *4–8* gates
292. *7 8* -house: *4–8* or,   **293.** *8* glory's   **294.** *6–8* Forced   *6–8* ensnared,
4–8 death,   **295.** *8* vulture's   *4–8* beak!   **296.** *3–7* Widow • *8* widow,
297. *8* husband's   *3–8* corse,   **298.** *2* shriek! • *7 8* shriek;   *2* half thatch'd •
6–8 half-thatched   *2* cot, • *3–8* cot   **299.** *6–8* Waked   *2–8* cold,   **300.** *2 6–*
8 Cow'rst • *3* Cow'rest   *7 8* awhile   **301.** *8* wretchedness!   **303.** *8* retribution
304. *6–8* opened   *3–8* seal: **304fn1.** *3* chapter   **304fn1–2.** *3* Divine.—
And   **304fn2.** *3* horse;   **304fn4.** *3* Earth to   **304fn6.** *3* earth.—And
304fn11. *3* fellow servants   **304fn12.** *3* were should   *3* beheld   **304fn14.** *3* fig
tree   *3* figs   **304fn15.** *3* earth, and   **304fn16.** *3* captains, &c.   **305.** *3–*
8 upward   **306.** *3–5* Th'   *3–8* Wrongs   **308.** *8* wretchedness!   *3–8* The
6–8 nigh;   **309.** *8* great,   *8* rich,   *8* mighty   *6(c) 3–8* Men, • *2* men,
310. *6(c) 2–8* Kings   *8* chief   *6(c) 2–8* World,   **311.** *2* all,   *6(c) 2–5* fix'd •
6–8 fixed   *2* high,   *2* Heaven,   **312.** *6(c) 3–8* earth,   **313.** *2–8* down-
trodden,   *6(c)* th'   **315.** *6(c) 2–5* Ev'n   *2–8* storm   *2* begins!   *2* Each
6(c) Name • *2–8* name,   **315fn1.** *4 5* And   **315fn1–2.** *13** subsequent ⟨para-
graph⟩ • *4 5* subsequent paragraph   **315fn2.** *4 5* convinced   **315fn4.** *4 5* and
316. *6(c)* Faith,   *6(c) 2–8* and   *2–8* Piety,   *2* Joy, • *3–8* joy   **317.** *6(c) 3 4 6–*
8 far-off—For • *2* far-off. For   *2 7* GIANT • *8* giant   *6(c) 3–7* FRENZY • *2* FRENZY,
318. *6(c) 2* Empires   *2* arm,   **319.** *6(c) 2–8* Heaven;   *6(c) 3–8* cell • *2* cell,
320. *2* Old   *6(c) 2–8* huge,   **321.** *2–8* Creation's   *2* Drudge,   *6(c)* Ruin •
3–5 RUIN, • *6 7* RUIN, • *8* ruin,   **322.1.** *6(c)* earthquake—   **322.1.1.** *6(c)* and
6(c) promis'd   **322b.1/323a.1** *6(c)* solitude!   **322a.** *6–8* the   *3–8* earthquake.
322fn1. *3 13** seven Angels   **322fn1–2.** *3 13** seven vials   **322fn2.** *3 13** come
322fn3. *3 13** judgment   **322fn4.** *3 13** earth   **322fn5.** *3 13** fornication,
3 13* St.   **322fn6.** *3 13** chapter   *3 13** seventeenth.   TEXTS *12* 3* end paragraph
here, the rest of the paragraph appearing in MS *13** only   **323.** *8* Faith!   *8* Piety!
2–8 The   *2* Form, • *3–8* Form   **324.** *2–8* robe   *2* pomp;   **325.** *2* gold; •
4–7 Gold,   **326.** *2–8* and   *2* blasphemous; • *3–8* blasphemous,   **327.** *2 4–*
8 judgment! • *3* judgement!   *2–8* cry?   **328.** *2* spirits   *2–5* shriek'd, • *6–8* shrieked
329. *2–4* She • *5–8* she   *2* fallen,   **330.** *8* Mystery;   **331.** *6–8* reeled
332. *6–8* worked   *6 7* DŒMON • *8* Demon   *3–7* POWER • *8* Power,   **334.** *2–*
8 and   *2–5* nurtur'd: • *6–8* nurtured: *2–6* ATHEISM; • *7* ATHEISM! • *8* atheism!
335. *2* FOLLY, • *3–7* FOLLY • *8* Folly   **336.** *4 5* Steel   *2–5* stabb'd • *6–8* stabbed
8 Fear   **337.** *3* terrors   *6–8* shapings   **338.** *2–8* Madness   *2–8* midnight!
339. *3–8* Return   *2–7* FAITH!   *2–8* return   *2–7* PIETY!   **340.** *2–*
8 kingdoms   *2* World   *8* yours: *2–8* heart   **341.** *6–8* -governed,   *3–8* family
2 Love,   **342.** *6–8* Raised   *2* toil,   **344.** *2–8* visitants!   **345.1.** *3* jubilee
348.1. *2 3* airs,   **346.** *4–8* gates   **349.** *2–5* odors snatch'd • *6–8* odours snatched
2–3 8 amaranth,   **350.** *6–8* crystal   **351.** *6–8* freshened   **352.** *3–5* favor'd •
6–8 favoured   *3–8* man   *3–8* walk   **354.** *3–8* bliss   *8* recognise   *3–8* heaven.
355. *3–7* beatitude   **356.** *3–8* heart   **357.** *3–8* future   **358.1.** *8* own,
359b.1/360a.1. *8* dance,   **361a.1/360b.1.** *8* hands,   *8* shouts,   **360.1.1.** *8* Breezes

361b.1. 8 Mighty   **362.1.** 8 tombs, 8 whoe'e   **363b.1.** 8 Almighty.   **359b.2/**
360a.2. *3* THOUSAND YEARS   **361b.2.** *3* primœval *3* mighty   **365.1.** *3* earth
368.1. *3* heaven: **369.1fn.** *3* Hartley.   **372.1.** 13 PRIESTLEY   **376.1.** *3* hate:
calm, *3* retir'd,   **377.1.** *3* promis'd years.   **359.** *8* Saviour *8* Thousand Years
359fn1. *4 5* Millenium:— *4 5* suppose, *4 5* Man will   **359fn2.** *4 5* capable.—
359fn3. *4 5* and enjoy   **359fn4.** *4 5* and flowers,   **359fn5.** *4 5* period,
359fn6. 13* habits ~~that~~. I • *4 5* habits. I   **359fn7.** *4 5* and by 13* ~~on~~ the • *4 5* the
359fn8. *4 5* labours.   **360.** *8* Desert   **361.** *8* Ocean   **363.** *6–8* urged
364. *8* Milton's   **365.** *8* groves   **366.** *6–8* hushed,   **367.** *8* Newton
369. *6–8* marked   **370.** *6–8* through *4 6–8* brain.   **372.** *8* Priestley *8* patriot,
8 saint, *5* Sage! • *8* sage,   **373.** *6–8* loved   **374.** *6 7* blood-stained • *8* blood
stained *8* priests   **375.** *6–8* maddening   **376.** *6–8* retired,   **377.** *6–*
8 mused *6–8* promised   **378.1.** *3* preeminence   **381.4.** *3* glories *3* jasper
throne   **380a.5.** *3* and   **383.4.** 13 strange,   **385.1.** *3* hour,   **387.1.** *3* noon
3 ghastly!   **394.2.** *3* mighty   **395.1.** *3* ever-living   **378.** *7 8* pre-eminence
379. *7 8* heavenly bright,   **381.** *5* Throne,   **381fn1.** *8* chap. *7 8* iv. *5 2.*
and *3.*— • *7 8 2* and *3.*—   **381fn2.** *8* Heaven   **381fn3.** *4–7* and • *8* and
a   **382.** *8* Yet   **386.** *6–8* seized   **388.** *5* image,   **389.** *6–8* -visaged,
6–8 outstretched   **389fn.** 13 *4–7* Destruction • *8* destruction   **391.** *5–8* destined
392. *5* Whirlwinds *5* name,   **393.** *8* Destruction! *5* —How   **395.** *5* him,
8 One,   **396a.** *8* Time is no more!   **396b.** *3–8* soul,   **396fn1.** 13* ~~who~~
to • *4 5* to *5* belive   **396fn1–2.** 13* *4 5* and feel   **396fn2.** *4 5* and the
397. *3–8* vision *4–8* Truth;   **398.** *3–8* vice, *3–8* anguish, *3–8* grave,
399. *3–8* dream! *3–8* clouds   **401.** *3 4 6–8* day   **402.** *3–8* earth, heaven, and
3–8 hell.   **404.** *6–8* untired *6–8* the   **406.** *6–8* interfused   **407.** *6–8* through
3–8 and   **409.** *6* mind, • *7 8* mind)   **411.** *6 7* choir? • *8* choir.   **415.** *6–8* the
416. *8* Love . . . Love,

¯**1.1–9.** PR *3 5* print on a separate page, following the divisional title. PR *4* prints on
the same page, below the divisional title.
5.1fn. Deleted in the MS 13* revision of PR *3*. The note actually comprehends Luke
2.13 and all but the last phrase of 2.14.
The PR *3* notes follow the poem in a separate section, which precedes the main body
of notes. Line-references ("LINE 8." etc) are prefixed to the notes, and there are no cues
in the text of the poem, with the exception of line 369.1fn, which appears at the foot of
the page, cued with an asterisk. In PR *4–8* the notes appear at the foot of the page.
14.1.2fn. The false start in MS 12* is because C was trying to get the spacing right.
The note actually comprehends John 14.8 and all but the last phrase of 9.
1–23.1. Lines 12.1.1–14.1.5 are deleted in MS 13, and replaced by VAR 1–23.1, which
are cancelled in turn by a single vertical stroke.
6⁺. PR *4 5* begin a new paragraph.
7. In a letter written during early Apr 1797 C told Cottle to alter the line in PR *4* to
read: "Yet thou more glorious, than the Angel Host," (*CL* VI 1008).
13. In a letter written during early Apr 1797 C told Cottle to alter the line in PR *4* to
read: "What time his Spirit with a brother's love" (*CL* VI 1008).
33fn. C consistently miscued the note to line 34 (owing to his emendation of the
line-numbering in MS 13*).
58⁺. PR *7 8* have no line-space (owing to a misunderstanding of PR *6*).
64–77. C has deleted these lines in Bowles's copy of PR *4*, adding the instruction:

"See the blank page of this volume: at the end." The page referred to, which contained C's draft replacement, has been removed, and a later version or fair copy in his hand is tipped in to p 123 (see vol I annex C 6.2 for details). 2.75 cm of the RH margin of the tipped-in leaf has broken off and been lost, so that the lines C wrote are now incomplete:

> They cease to dread created might, [
> God the Creator. A thrice holy [
> It lifts & swells the heart: and a [
> Imaginations, that embody Truth [
> Gather within me, and a Vision [
> Voices & shadowy Shapes! In [
> I seem to see the Phantom FEA[
> Hotly-pursued and pale: from ro[
> He leaps with bleeding feet, & o'e[
> The quicksand & the hissing wil[
> Hurries, a mad-ey'd Wretch! but [
> The Altar of the living God—& [
> All wildly list'ning to the Hun[
> Stands, till the last faint ech[
> Dies in the distance. Soon refres[
> He calms the throb & tempest of h[
> His countenance settles; a soft [
> Swims in his eye; his swimming [
> While Faith's whole armour girds h[
> Transfigur'd, with a deep & drea[
> A solemn hush of spirit, &c [

In Roskilly's copy of PR *4* C has corrected VAR 69 to read:

> FEAR, a wild visag'd man with starting eye,

and VAR 75–7 to read:

> While Faith's whole armour girds his limbs! And thus
> Transfigur'd, with a deep and dreadless awe,
> A solemn hush of spirit, he beholds

C had told Cottle to record the same changes in lines 69 and 75–7 in the list of errata he sent him during early Jul 1797 (*CL* I 331).

In the Fitzwilliam copy of PR *6* C corrected 64 "Love," to "love," and 67 "Hell;" to "Hell!", and indicated that line 68 should be preceded by a line-space.

80b.1fn. C actually omits a phrase from the middle of the verse.

78. Before drafting lines 78–84 in MS 13, in PR *3* C changed 80a.1 "pestilence" to "blasting" and 82.2 "will flash" to "leapt forth"; he then cancelled from 78.1 "Yea, and there," to 84.1 "wrath," altogether.

114–15. In Barbey's copy of PR *4* C revised the lines to read:

> All very good! This is indeed to dwell
> With the most high! Cherubs & Seraphim

132. PR *4* except] In RS's copy C substituted "beyond".
In the HEHL copy of PR *8* C emended the line and added to it thus:

> This is the worst superstition, save *in* Him,
> Or as *his* Image, and *his* Sword pronounc'd,
> (And in his Light each Dew-drops hath its Sun)

134⁺. In the HEHL copy of PR *8* C indicated "New Paragraph"

135. Before drafting lines 135–41 in MS 13, in PR *3* 138.1.3 C deleted "imbrothell'd" and changed 141.1 "living" to "human", both in pencil; he then cancelled lines 135.1–141.1 altogether.

166. PR *7* land!] The exclamation-mark is deleted in JG's (?) copy.

170. PR *6* War?] In the Fitzwilliam copy C substituted "War—".

192. TEXTS 13* *4–8* begin a new paragraph at "Lord".

192fn. The PR *8* reading of Habakkuk is the correct one.

215fn. Deleted in the MS 13* version of PR *3*.

222–3. In Barbey's copy of PR *4* C substituted an exclamation-mark for the comma after "Deities", and deleted line 223.

223⁺. TEXTS 13* *4–8* have a line-space.

223–4. In RS's copy of PR *4* the lines have been revised to read:

> Such as the blind Ionian fabled!

> Thus
> From Avarice, from Luxury, and from War

It is not absolutely certain that the revision is in C's hand.

259. C's pen snagged in MS 6(a), with the result that three of the first four words are overwritten.

259⁺. No line-space in PR *4* *6–8*. C has indicated in RS's copy of PR *4*, the Fitzwilliam copy of PR *6*, and the HEHL copy of PR *8* that line 260 should begin "A new Paragraph."

269fn. MS 12* has the instruction "Print the Note ✳ in the 45th page of the Watchman." MS 13* adds at the end: "The Simoom is here introduced as emblematical of the pomp & powers of Despotism".

275fn. MS 12* has the instruction "Print the note † in the 45th page of the Watchman." The PR *3* footnote was previously deleted in MS 13⁺.

281. PR *4* Dost] In RS's copy C emended to "Dar'st".

290. Before drafting lines 290–5 in MS 13*, C cancelled lines 290.2–292.2, 293b.1–294.1.1 in PR *3*.

292. PR *6* the full] In the Fitzwilliam copy C emended to "th' o'er-fill'd".

304fn. MS 12* has the instruction "Print Note ✳ in the 46th page of the Watchman."

315fn. The PR *3* footnote was previously deleted in MS 13*.

321. PR *8* ruin,] In the HEHL copy C emended to "Ruin,".

321–3. There is a pencil mark in the LH margin of MS 5 against these lines. Cf on line 331 below.

322b.1/323a.1. MS 6(c) gives only the first half of the line.

322fn. PR *2* has an indicator but no note. The second paragraph of the note, quoting phrases from the same chapter of Revelation, occurs in MS 12* only, where it has been deleted with a single vertical line.

331. There is a pencilled cross in the LH margin of MS 5, as there is against lines 346.1, 347.1, 350.1, 351.1 in the same ms. Cf on lines 321–3.

345–9. Before drafting these lines in MS 13*, C deleted lines 345.1–349.1 in PR *3*. Joseph Cottle had written "saintly" at the end of line 345.1.

357⁺. No line-space in PR *4–8*. (In PR *3* line 358.2 falls at the top of a page.)

375.1. When C drafted MS 13*, he deleted this line in PR *3*, before cancelling the whole block of lines 371.1–377.1, 378.1–380b.5. See below on 379a/382a.4-380b.10/ 381a.7/382b.1.

360–1. C first tried out the possibility in MS 13 of following the present line 360 with the revised line "And soft breezes of an equal Spring" (see line 360.2.1 for the PR *3* reading), but then rejected it and continued as here.

369. In the Fitzwilliam copy of PR *6* C emended "marked" to "traced".

370–2. In Bowles's copy of PR *4* C emended the full point following "brain" to a comma, and inserted the following line before 372: "Roll subtly-surging. Pressing on his steps,". He made the same changes in Barbey's and Roskilly's copies, where he also emended the punctuation at the end of 371 (to a full point in Barbey's, to a colon in Roskilly's). In his own (?) copy, as described by J. Rogers Rees, he deleted the full point following "brain", but did not replace it with any other punctuation; he inserted the same line; and he emended 373 "years," to "days,".

372–7. The corresponding passage in MS 13 (lines 371.1–377.1) is deleted, although C had previously marked 372.1 "Priestley" for cap and small caps, and had struck out line 375.1.

372. In the Fitzwilliam copy of PR *6* C emended "Sage" to "Sage!"

374. In the Fitzwilliam copy of PR *6* C emended "idolatrous" to "idolatrous,".

375. In the Fitzwilliam copy of PR *6* C emended "multitude" to "multitude,".

381.3–380.4. Deleted in MS 11 with a vertical stroke.

358.5–377.3, 378.2–395b.2/396.2. Deleted in MS 12 with a single vertical stroke.

379a.3/380b.6. No preceding line-space in MS 11.

381.5. C first substituted "the" for "what", but failed to cancel "the" when he cancelled "Glories".

378.2. No preceding line-space in MS 12.

378. PR *4–8* have preceding line-space.

379a.4/382a.4–380b.10/381a.7/382b.1. The cancelled lines in MS 13 were intended to replace lines 379.2–380b.5 in PR *3*. (C in the end cancelled the whole block of lines 371.1–377.1, 378.1–380b.5 with two large strokes.)

380, 381. In the Fitzwilliam copy of PR *6* C has inserted a comma after "wings" and after "Throne".

389–90. In Roskilly's copy of PR *4* and in the Fitzwilliam copy of PR *6* C has added a comma after "Fiend" and after "Nature", and deleted the comma after "groans". He also deleted the comma after "groans" (only) in Barbey's copy of PR *4*.

389fn. Cued to line 388 in PR *5*.

396b. MS 9 has the written instruction above "Believe thou": "new paragraph"; PR *3–8* have a line-space before the half-line.

398. PR *4* grave,] In Barbey's copy C substituted "guilt,".

401–2. C deleted the lines in the Fitzwilliam copy of PR *6*, adding an exclamation-mark after "God" at the end of line 400.

409. C emended the punctuation in the Fitzwilliam copy of PR *6* to read "mind?", and he placed the line within brackets.

411. C emended the punctuation in the Fitzwilliam copy of PR *6* to read "choir."

101.X1. SONNET: TO MRS SIDDONS

M Chron (29 Jan 1795): "SONNET. I TO MRS. SIDDONS. I 'Tis not thy fascinating charms to trace." 14 lines. Signed "FONTROSE."

Attribution: D. V. Erdman "Newspaper Sonnets Put to the Concordance Test: Can they be Attributed to Coleridge?" (I) *BNYPL* LXI (1957) 508–16. See also Erdman "Unrecorded Coleridge Variants" *SB* XI (1958) 143–62 at 149. Further evidence is required before the sonnet can be accepted as by C.

101.X2. SONNET: TO LORD STANHOPE

M Chron (31 Jan 1795): "TO LORD STANHOPE, I ON READING HIS LATE PROTEST IN THE HOUSE OF I LORDS. I STANHOPE! I hail, with ardent Hymn, thy name!" 14 lines. Signed "ONE OF THE PEOPLE".

The sonnet was included in *PW* (JDC) 42–3, 575–6, the editor arguing that it is the original of the sonnet to Stanhope in *Poems* (1796, 1803). JDC was followed by EHC in *PW* (EHC) I 89; and in more recent years by D. V. Erdman "Newspaper Sonnets Put to the Concordance Test: Can they be Attributed to Coleridge?" (II) *BNYPL* LXI (1957) 611–20, and L. Werkmeister and P. M. Zall "Possible Additions to Coleridge's 'Sonnets on Eminent Characters'" *Studies in Romanticism* (Boston) VIII (1969) 121–7. Arguments against accepting the poem as Coleridge's are advanced by ELG in *CL* I 156n and Woodring 108–9, 248–9 n 24.

101.X3. SONNET: TO GILBERT WAKEFIELD

In the Gutch Notebook list of poems from which the collection of *Poems* (1796) apparently grew, C included the title *Wakefield* (*CN* I 305; Woodring 226–7). All the other poems in the list, except for the sonnet to Stanhope, can be proved to have been written by the time the list was made, in Jul 1795; all of the sonnets contributed to *M Chron* in Dec 1794–Jan 1795 are there, except for the one on Pitt. C certainly did not write as many sonnets as he planned (*CL* I 137: to RS 11 Dec 1794; 155–6: to G. Dyer 10 Mar 1795), and whether or not he wrote and published the one to Stanhope is also uncertain.

Wakefield had previously subscribed to C's projected *Imitations from the Modern Latin Poets* (*CL* I 101; poem **50.X1** above), and C maintained an acquaintance with him through George Dyer (*CL* I 153: to G. Dyer [late Feb 1796]; 156). When *Poems* (1796) was published, C planned to send a copy to Wakefield with a sonnet written on the blank preliminary (*CL* I 201: to J. Cottle [early Apr 1796])—as he intended to do with copies to Mrs Barbauld, Dr Beddoes, Francis Wrangham, and George Augustus Pollen (C's junior by a year at Cambridge and, at that time, still an "advocate for the Rights of the People": see *Watchman—CC*—115 and n). None of these copies, if they were sent, has survived either.

101.X4. SONNET: WRITTEN ON CONTEMPLATING A VERY FINE SETTING SUN. TO LORD STANHOPE

Cambridge Intelligencer (21 Feb 1795): "SONNET, | *Written on contemplating a very fine setting Sun.* | Inscribed to LORD STANHOPE. | Behold yon splendid Orb, whose dazzling rays". 14 lines. Unsigned.

Tentative attribution by Erdman "Newspaper Sonnets Put to the Concordance Test" (II); Erdman "Unrecorded Coleridge Variants" 149. Further evidence is required before the sonnet can be accepted as by C.

102. SONNET: TO LORD STANHOPE

A. DATE

Between 10 Mar and Jul (?) 1795. See vol I headnote.

B. TEXTS

1. HRC MS (Coleridge, S T) Works B. Recto of single leaf, 18.0×31.2 cm; wm Britannia in small rounded oval; chain-lines 2.5 cm. Bound into Rugby Manuscript p 41/f 17^r. Transcript in C's hand, which served as copy for PR *1* below.

   1 [=RT]. *Poems* (1796). Rpt Allsop I 217.

2. *Poems* (1803).

The poem is vigorously deleted in SH's copy, now at Cornell (WORDS-WORTH PR 4252 B91R9 1813 Copy 2); C's accompanying comment is given in vol I headnote. Rpt *Laura* ed Capel Lofft (5 vols 1813–14) III No 331.

title. *1 Effusion 10ᵗʰ • 1 EFFUSION X. • 2 SONNET XVI.*

1 ☐   Not, STANHOPE! with the Patriot's doubtful name
2 ☐   I mock thy worth—Friend of the human race!
3 ☐   Since scorning Faction's low and partial aim
4 ☐   Aloof thou wendest in thy stately pace
5 1   Thyself redeeming from th*é*at leprous stain,
   1 2   that
6 1   ~~Of LORDAGE:~~ NOBILITY! and ~~unbrib'd~~ aye unterrify'd
   1 2   ←——NOBILITY:——→   ←—aye—→
7 1   Raisest thine Abdiel Warnings to the ~~trai~~ Train
   1 2 Pourest   on   train
8 1   ~~Idly complotting~~ Who complot idly with rebellious pride
   1 2 That   sit   complotting
9 1   'Gainst Her, ~~who~~ that from the Almighty's Bosom leapt,
   1 2   who
9fn *1 2* Gallic Liberty.
10 1   Saviour of Man! the First born of his Love!
   1 2 With whirlwind arm, fierce Minister of
11 ☐   Wherefore, ere Virtue o'er thy tomb hath wept,
12 ☐   Angels shall lead thee to the Throne above*;*:
13 1   And Thou from forth his Clouds shalt hear the Voice,
   1 2   it's
14 1   "Champion of Freedom & of God! Rejoice!—
   1 2   her

2. *1 2* FRIEND OF THE HUMAN RACE!   **4.** *1 2* pace,   **7.** 1 *1 2* warnings
9. *1* her, • *2 Her*, *1 2* bosom   *1 2* leapt   **12.** *1 2* above: **13.** *1 2* thou
1 2 clouds   *1 2* voice,   **14.** *1 2* Champion   *1 2* FREEDOM and   *1 2* rejoice!

title. In the PR *1* list of contents the title is given as "Effusion 10, to Earl Stanhope,".

14. In MS 1 "Freedom" is underlined twice (for capitalisation), and "her" is substituted for "of". The changes are made in pencil.

102.X1. TRANSLATION OF FOUR LINES
IN FRENCH

The Times (23 Mar 1795): "TRANSLATIONS | TO THE FOUR LINES IN FRENCH, IN OUR PAPER | OF FRIDAY LAST. | Oh People!

whither are you led,".. 4 lines. Signed "C." This is the first of four translations, the last ("Is it for this that France has bled,") being signed "R. S."

Tentatively suggested by Erdman et al "Unrecorded Coleridge Variants: Additions and Corrections" 239. The original French lines were published in *The Times* (20 Mar 1795). This translation cannot be accepted as by C unless further evidence comes to light.

103. ADAPTATION OF ROBERT SOUTHEY'S SONNET "PALE ROAMER THRO' THE NIGHT!"

A. DATE

Dec 1794–Jul 1795. RS's original poem was written before 17 Dec 1794, when C criticised it in some detail in a letter (*CL* I 139–40). C had rewritten six lines by 12 May 1795 (MS 1 below), and he extended his rewriting in the months thereafter (TEXTS 2 *1* below). He had come to think of it as his own by about Jul 1795 (*CN* I 305, under the title "Prostitute", and cf 297).

B. TEXTS

1. Bodleian MS Eng lett c 22 f 149ʳ. Transcript headed "Sonnet. the 6 last lines by Coleridge." in RS's hand in a letter to Grosvenor Bedford (12 May 1795). *S Letters* (Curry) I 95–6 gives the letter only.

2. Alexander Turnbull Library, Wellington, New Zealand MS Papers 1646. Single leaf, 18.2×14.2 cm; no wm; chain-lines 2.7 cm; verso blank. Transcript in C's hand, endorsed as by C by Joseph Cottle.

There are traces of glue and/or fragments of paper round all edges, and the number "96" appears in Cottle's hand at the top RH. The transcript is almost certainly the top half of a leaf, the bottom half of which contained **88** *To an Old Man in the Snow*, submitted as copy for PR *1* below, and even incorporated into the Rugby Manuscript sequence, but then replaced by Cottle. When the Turnbull Library acquired the transcript, it was loosely inserted in a defective copy of PR *1* (Turnbull Library R Eng COLE Poems 1796), but the insertion appears not to have been made until 1899–1902. For further details see vol I annex C 3B.

1. Poems (1796).

"And the first half of Effusion XV. was written by the Author of 'Joan of Arc,' an Epic Poem" (Preface, p xi).

2. Poems (1797).

Two copies contain ms emendations by C: Thomas Hutchinson's, in the possession of Jonathan Wordsworth (1980); and RS's (?), at Yale (In 678 797 Copy 1). A further comment by C in RS's copy is quoted in vol I headnote.

3 [=**RT**]. *Poems* (1803).

The transcript by JTC in his Commonplace Book (University of Pennsylvania (Special Collections) MS Eng 13) p 31 is from this text and has no significance.

4. PW (1828).

5. PW (1829).

6. PW (1834).

title. 1 Sonnet. the 6 last lines by Coleridge. • 2 EFFUSION 15 • *1* EFFUSION XV. • *2 SONNET VII.* • *3 SONNET VI.* • *4–6* SONNET IX.

1	1 2	Poor Wanderer of the Night! thou pale forlorn!
	1–6	Pale Roamer thro' poor
2	☐	Remorse that man on his death-bed possess,
3	1	Who in the hour of credulous tenderness
	☒1	credulous hour of
4	1	Betrayed & left thee to the hard worlds scorn.
	2	then
	1–6	cast thee forth to Want and
5	1	The hard world scoffs thy woes! the chaste Ones pride
	2	hard World marks thy woes / is pityless: fair Chaste
	1–6	←world→ ←——is——→ Chaste
6	1	Mimic of Virtue mocks thy keen distress,
	2	mocks thy keen scowls on thy
	1–6	←——scowls——→
7	☒*3*	Thy Loves & they that envied thee, deride,
	3	kindred, when they see thee, turn aside,
8	☐	And Vice alone will shelter Wretchedness.
9	☒*6*	Oh I am sad to think—that there should be
	6	could weep
10	☒*3*	Cold-bosomed lewd Ones, who endure to place
	3	Men, born of woman,
11	1	Foul offerings at the shrine of Misery
	☒1	on
12	1	Forcing from Famines arms the embrace of Love.
	☒1	And force from FAMINE caress
13	1 2 *1 2* 4	May he shed healing on thy sore disgrace
	3	Man has no feeling for
	5	May he shed feeling on the
	6	healing
14	1	He, the great Comforter who rules above.
	☒1 *3*	that
	3	Keen blows the Blast upon the moulting Dove!

1. *4–6* through   *6* night!   ⊠1 *3* Forlorn!   **4.** 2 Betrayed—•⊠1 2 *3* Betrayed,•
3 Betray'd,   *6* want   2 World's scorn!   *1 2 4 5* Scorn!•*3 6* scorn!   **5.** *2 3* pity-
less;•*4–6* pitiless: *6* chaste   2 *1–6* one's   2 Pride•*1 4–6* pride•*2 3* pride,
6. *2 3* Virtue,   ⊠1 *3* distress:•*3* distress;   **7.** ⊠1 *3* and they,   ⊠1 *3* deride:
8. 2 *1–4* Wretchedness!•*5 6* wretchedness!   **9.** 2 O•*1–6* O!   ⊠1 think,
10. 2 *1 2* -bosom'd   2 *1 4 5* Lewd   ⊠1 *3* ones,   **11.** 2 Offerings   ⊠1 *6* Misery,•
6 misery,   **12.** *6* famine   2 *1–3* LOVE!•*4 5* LOVE;•*6* Love;   **13.** ⊠1 *3* He
⊠1 *3* disgrace,•*3* Disgrace: **14.** *1 2 4 5* COMFORTER   ⊠1 *3* above!

title. C's title in the list on the last page of the Gutch Notebook was "Prostitute" (*CN*
I 305)—if the present poem is indeed the one referred to.
7. In Thomas Hutchinson's copy of PR 2 C deleted the whole line and substituted
"Thy kindred, when they see thee, turn aside,".
10. In both Thomas Hutchinson's and RS's copies of PR 2 C deleted "Cold-bosom'd
lewd ones," and substituted "Men, born of Woman,".
13. In Thomas Hutchinson's copy of PR 2 C deleted "May He shed" and substituted
"Go! seek thou"; he also deleted "on" and substituted "for".
14. In Thomas Hutchinson's copy of PR 2 C deleted "He," and substituted "From".

104. ADAPTATION OF CHARLES LAMB'S SONNET *WRITTEN AT MIDNIGHT, BY THE SEA-SIDE*

A. DATE

Dec 1794–Apr 1795. C had seen a copy of the poem before 11 Dec 1794 (*CL*
I 136: to RS), and Mrs Estlin wrote the date "April 1795" on the album that
contains MS 1 below.

B. TEXTS

1. BPL B 22189=Estlin Copy Book f 20ᵛ. Transcript in C's hand, subscribed
"Lamb."
    The poem is one of three in the collection not by C himself—the others being
by Samuel Favell and John Gaunt (?).

2. HRC MS (Coleridge, S T) Works B. Verso of single leaf, 18.8×32.4 cm;
wm Britannia in large oval; chain-lines 2.5 cm. Transcript in C's hand, which
served as copy for PR *1* below. Subscribed "C.L." (the last of three poems, all
signed thus). The same page contains C's collaboration with CL, **87** *On Hope*,
and there are two sonnets by CL on the recto. Bound into Rugby Manuscript p
44/f 18ᵛ.

    1 [=RT]. *Poems* (1796). Signed "C. L."

2. *Sonnets from Various Authors* (1796). Signed "CHARLES LAMB."

title. 1 Written by the Sea side • 2 *Effusion 13* | ⟨Written at midnight, by the sea-side, after a Voyage.⟩ • *1* EFFUSION XIII. | WRITTEN | AT MIDNIGHT, | BY THE | *SEA-SIDE, AFTER A VOYAGE.* • *2* SONNET XXV.

1 1	O I could laugh to hear the midnight winds	
⊠1		wind
2 1	That rushing on their way with careless sweep	
⊠1		its
3 1	Scatter the Ocean Waves, and I could weep	
⊠1	Scatters	
4 1	Ev'n like a Child!—For now to my rapt mind	
⊠1	as	
5 □	On wings of Winds comes wild-eyed **Phantasy**,	
6 1	And her strange Visions give a ~~rude~~ dread delight.	
⊠1	dread	rude
7 □	O winged Bark! how swift along the Night	
8 □	Pass'd thy proud Keel! Nor shall I let go by	
9 □	Lightly of that drear hour the Memory	
10 □	When wet and chilly on thy deck I stood	
11 □	Unbonnetted, and gaz'd upon the Flood,	
12 □	And almost wish'd it were no crime to die!	
13 □	How Reason reel'd! What gloomy Transports rose!	
14 1	Till the rude Dashings rock'd ~~me~~ them to repose.	
⊠1		them

1. 2 O! • *1 2* Oh!   **2.** 2 *1* it's • *2* its   **3.** 2 Waves— • *1 2* waves—   *1 2* weep,
4. *1 2* child! For   **5.** ⊠1 winds   *1 2* wild-ey'd   ⊠1 Phantasy,   **6.** *1 2* visions
⊠1 delight!   **7.** ⊠1 night   **8.** *1 2* keel!   **9.** ⊠1 memory,   **10.** 2 Deck
11. ⊠1 flood,   **13.** *1 2* transports   2 rose   **14.** *1 2* dashings   2 Repose.

2–3, 10–11, 13–14. Indented in PR 2.

105. TO AN INFANT

A. DATE

Jan (?)–Apr 1795.

B. TEXTS

1. Lilly Library, Indiana University, Bloomington, Coleridge Collection. Single leaf, 19.1×22.5 cm approx (the top and bottom of the leaf have been trimmed irregularly); wm (in part) horn above small scroll design; chain-lines 2.5 cm; verso blank. Transcript in C's hand, signed "S T C."

What there is of the wm appears to indicate a paper made by J. Whatman (see Edward Heawood *Watermarks*—Hilversum 1960—Nos 2755, 2760). Whatman supplied Joseph Cottle, and paper made by him was used for printing and transcribing poems by C, so that MS 1 may in fact postdate MS 2 below. If this is the case, the interval between the two texts is likely to be short.

2. BPL B 22189 = Estlin Copy Book f 15ᵛ. Transcript in C's hand.

3. HRC MS (Coleridge, S T) Works B. Single leaf, 19.8×32.0 cm; wm Britannia in smaller rounded oval; chain-lines 2.5 cm; verso blank. Bound into Rugby Manuscript p 59/f 25bisʳ. Transcript of an expanded version in C's hand, submitted as copy for PR *1* below.

1. Poems (1796).

2 [=RT]. "Supplement" to *Poems* (1797).

3. Poems (1803).
JTC's transcript in his Commonplace Book (University of Pennsylvania (Special Collections) MS Eng 13) p 33 has no textual significance; nor has the reprint in *The Parnassian Garland* (1807) 145.

4. PW (1828).

5. PW (1829).

6. PW (1834).

title. 2 Verses to an Infant. • 3 *1* Effusion 34 | To an Infant. • *2–6 TO AN INFANT.*

‾**1.1**	1	How yon sweet Babe my bosom's grief beguiles
	2	Child
‾**1.2**	1 2	With soul-subduing Eloquence of smiles!
‾**1.3**	1	Ah lovely Child! in thee myself I scan—
	2	Babe!
‾**1.4**	1	Thou weep'st—! alas! those Tears proclaim thee—Man!
	2	sure
1	☒1 2	Ah cease thy Tears and Sobs, my little Life!
2	☒1 2	I did but snatch away the unclasp'd [?]Knife—
3	1	But　lo! some glittering Toy arrests thine Eye,
	2	And now
	☒1 2	Some　safer　Toy　will　soon　arrest
4	1	And to quick Laughter turns　the peevish E̶y̶e̶ Cry!
	2	cry.
	☒1 2	change this
5	☐	P̶Poor Stumbler on the rocky Coast of Woe,
6	1	Tutor'd by Pain　the　source of p̶a̶i̶n̶ Pain to know,
	2	Pain
	☒1 2	each
7	☐	Alike the foodful Fruit, and scorching Fire

8	⊠2	Awake thy eager Grasp, and young Desire;
	2	Or rouse thy screams or wake thy
8.1.1	1 2	Alike the Good, the Ill thy aching Sight
	⊠1 2 2	offend thy
8.1.2	1	May scare with keen Emotions of Affright!
	2	Scare with the
	⊠1 2 2	And rouse the stormy Sense of shrill
9	1	Untaught, yet wise! mid all thy short alarms
	2	? WUntaught, brief
	⊠1 2 2	Untaught
	2	Yet art thou wise, for mid
10	□	Thou closely clingest to thy Mother's Arms,
11	1	Nestling thy little Face in the fond Breast,
	⊠1	that
12	1	Whose kindly heavings lull thy fears to Rest.
	2	cares
	⊠1 2	anxious thee to thy

[*Line-space*]

13	⊠1 2	Man's breathing Miniature! thou mak'st me sigh—
14	⊠1 2	A Babe art thou—and such a Thing am I!
15	⊠1 2	To anger rapid and as soon appeas'd,
16	⊠1 2	For trifles mourning and by trifles pleas'd,
17	3	Break Friendship's Mirror with a ~~bl~~ tetchy blow
	1 3–6	tetchy
	2	fretful
18	⊠1 2	Yet snatch what Coals of Fire on Pleasure's Altar glow!
19	3	O thou ~~who~~ that rearest with celestial aim
	1–6	that
20	⊠1 2	The future Seraph in my mortal frame,
21	⊠1 2	Thrice holy FAITH! whatever Thorns I meet
22	⊠1 2	As on I totter with unpractic'd feet,
23	3	Still ~~may I~~ let me stretch my arms and cling to Thee,
	1–6	let
24	⊠1 2	Meek Nurse of Souls thro' their long Infancy!

title. *1* EFFUSION XXXIV. | *TO AN INFANT.* • *4–6* TO AN INFANT.
⁻**1.2.** 2 Smiles!   ⁻**1.3.** 2 weepest!   2 thee   **1.** *6* Ah!   *6* tears   *6* sobs,   **2.** *4–6* unclasped   *1–5* Knife: • *6* knife: **3.** 2 glitt'ring   *6* toy   *3 1 2 4 5* eye • *3 6* eye,   **4.** *6* laughter   3 *1–6* cry!   **5.** ⊠1 Poor   *6* stumbler   3 *1–6* coast   *6* woe,   **6.** *4–6* Tutored   *6* by pain   3 Source   *6* of pain   ⊠1 know!   **7.** 2 Fruit • ⊠1 2 fruit   *1 3–6* fire • *2* fire,   **8.** 2 Grasp • ⊠1 2 2 grasp   3 Desire: • *1–4* desire: • *5 6* desire;   **8.1.1.** ⊠1 2 sight,   **8.1.2.** 2 emotions   *6* sense   *6* affright!   **9.** *1 3–6* Untaught,   3 Alarms   **10.** 2 closely-clingest   2 Arms • *1–6* arms,   **11.** *1–6* face   ⊠1 2 breast   **12.** ⊠1 *6* Heavings   2 Rest! • ⊠1 2 rest!   **15.** *4–6* appeased,   **16.** *4–6* pleased,   **17.** *6* mirror   *1 3–6* blow,   **18.** *1–6* coals   *1–6* fire   *1–6* altar   **21.** *6* Faith!   *1–6* thorns   **22.** *1–3* unpractis'd • *4–6* unpractised   **23.** *1–6* thee,   **24.** *6* nurse   *6* souls   *4–6* through   *6* infancy!

4⁺. MS 2 appears to have a line-space. C's repositioning of the line in MS 1 (hence P Poor) may also suggest some such break.

6. MS3 rest] The initial letter is written large, as if C might have intended a capital.

12⁺. MS 3 has line-space. Line 13 heads a new page in PR *1* (also PR *3 6*), and there is no way of telling whether a line-space is intended; PR *2 4 5*, which derive from PR *1*, have no line-space.

18⁺. PR *1–6* have line-space—a feature which is undoubtedly related to the obscured or revised break at line 13⁺.

105.X1. LINES PROBABLY BORROWED FROM JOHN GAUNT

A. DATE

Before Apr 1795. The references in st 3 to France's "alter'd Eye of Conquest" and in st 4 to the pursuit of peace suggest a date in 1794. The debt was probably acquired in Sept–Nov 1794, just before C left Cambridge (see sec C below).

B. TEXTS

1. BPL B 22189 = Estlin Copy Book f 12ʳ⁻ᵛ. Transcript in C's hand.

1. The Watchman IV (25 Mar 1796) 110 (*CC*) 141–2. Signed "G.A.U.N.T."

C. GENERAL NOTE

The fact that C included the poem in Mrs Estlin's Album as if it were his own does not mean that he claimed authorship. The other two poems in the Album which are not by him are attributed, but perhaps only because of his closer relation to both Favell and CL. C attributed the poem to another author when it was made generally public, and he never afterwards included it in his own collections. The attribution in *The Watchman* appears to be to John Gaunt of Clare Hall, who was his slightly older contemporary at Cambridge and who had literary ambitions (see *CC* 141n). The curious separation of letters by full points may be a half-hearted attempt to preserve Gaunt's anonymity, or it may indicate that C had intervened to revise the poem somewhat.

No evidence has emerged to suggest that C and Gaunt were acquainted, but they certainly moved in the same circles. Gaunt's projected translation of Lucretius was announced in the same *University Magazine* to which William Rough contributed and which Benjamin Flower published. Rough had been a member of the literary society to which C also belonged during Michaelmas Term 1793 and a presentation copy of his *Poems, Miscellaneous and Fugitive* (1816) is now at VCL (Book No 76). Flower was the publisher of **76.X1** *The*

Fall of Robespierre and the *Cambridge Intelligencer*, and was to have been the publisher of C's *Imitations*.

The poem is collated here because the differences between the two texts prove that C revised it in some measure when he printed it (as he had, almost certainly, when he previously transcribed it). It is not included in vol I because so much about C's authorship is uncertain. Compare the similar case of **26.X1** *Version of an Epitaph on a Young Lady*.

title. 1 Ode • *1* A MORNING EFFUSION.

```
 1  □   Ye Gales, that of the Lark's repose
 2  □   The impatient Silence break,
 3  □   To yon poor Pilgrim's wearying Woes
 4  1   Your gentle Comfort speak!
    1                solace
 5  □   He heard the midnight whirlwind die—
 6  □   He saw the sun-awaken'd Sky
 7  □   Resume its slowly-purpling Blue.
 8  □   And ah! he sigh'd—that I might find
 9  □   The cloudless Azure of the Mind
10  □   And Fortune's brightning Hue!
        [Line-space]
11  □   Wheree'er in waving Foliage hid
12  □   The Bird's gay Charm ascends,
13  1   Or by the  fretful  Current chid
    1             fretting
14  □   Some giant Rock impends—
15  □   There let the lonely Cares respire
16  1   While As small airs thrill the mourning Lyre
    1      As                     lonely
17  1   And teach the Soul her native Calm;
    1                its
18  1   While Passion with a languid Eye
    1                waning
19  1   Hangs o'er the fall of Harmony
    1   Bends
20  □   And drinks the sacred Balm.
        [Line-space]
21  1   Slow as  the  fragrant  whisper creeps
    1   As slow the whispered measure
22  1   Along the   lilied   Vale,
    1               steaming
23  □   The alter'd Eye of Conquest weeps,
24  1   And ruthless War grows pale
    1                turns
25  □   Relenting that his Heart forsook
26  □   Soft Concord of auspicious Look,
27  □   And Love, and social Poverty;
28  □   The Family of tender Fears,
```

29 ☐ The Sigh, that saddens and endears,
30 ☐ And Cares, that sweeten Joy.
  [*Line-space*]
31 1 Then cease, thy frantic Tumults cease,
  1   outrage
32 1 Ambition,   Sire   of War!
  1 Thou scepter'd Demon,
33 ☐ Nor o'er the mangled Corse of Peace
34 ☐ Urge on thy scythed Car.
35 1 And oh! that Reason's voice might swell
  1   ah!
36 ☐ With whisper'd Airs and holy Spell
37 ☐ To rouse thy gentler Sense,
38 1 As bending o'er the   chilly   bloom
  1   flowret's
39 ☐ The Morning wakes its soft Perfume
40 ☐ With breezy Influence.

2. *1* Th' *1* silence   **3.** *1* pilgrim's *1* woes   **4.** *1* speak.   **5.** *1* die,
6. *1* -awakened sky   **7.** *1* blue: **8.** *1* (he sigh'd)   **9.** *1* azure *1* mind,
10. *1* fortune's brightening hue.   **11.** *1* Where-e'er *1* foliage   **12.** *1* bird's
1 charm   **13.** *1* current   **14.** *1* rock impends;   **15.** *1* cares respire,
16. *1* lyre,   **17.** *1* soul *1* calm;   **18.** *1* *Passion* *1* eye   **19.** *1* harmony,
20. *1* balm.   **22.** *1* vale, · **23.** *1* eye *1* Conquest   **24.** *1* War *1* pale;
25. *1* heart   **26.** *1* concord *1* look,   **27.** *1* love, *1* poverty.   **28.** *1* family
1 fears,   **29.** *1* sigh   **30.** *1* cares *1* joy.   **32.** *1* War!   **33.** *1* corse
34. *1* car.   **36.** *1* airs *1* spell   **37.** *1* sense;   **39.** *1* morning *1* perfume
40. *1* influence.

2, 4, etc. Alternate lines indented in PR *1*; there are traces of erratic indentation in MS 1.

106. CONTRIBUTION TO *THE SOLDIER'S WIFE*, BY ROBERT SOUTHEY

A. DATE

Before 12 May 1795.

B. TEXTS

1 [=RT]. Bodleian MS Eng lett c 22 f 149ʳ. Fair copy in RS's hand. The poem was one of several copied for Grosvenor Bedford, in an als sent on 12 May 1795; only the letter is given in *S Letters* (Curry) I 95–6.

1. RS *Poems* (Bristol 1797) 145–6. Whether or not the variants are due to RS's or to C's second thoughts is not known. I have not collated subsequent versions—in RS *Poems* (2nd ed Bristol 1797) 81; *Poetical Works* (1814–18) xi 168; *Poetical Works* (1837–8) ii 140. These versions differ only in punctuation.

title. 1 The Soldier's Wife | Written with Coleridge. • *1 The SOLDIER's WIFE. | DACTYLICS.*

title fn 1   read this aloud & accent it
    1 ☐ Weàry way-wànderer! lànguid & sìck at heart
    2 ☐ Tràvelling paìnfully òver the rùgged road,
    3 ☐ Wìld-visagd Wànderer! àh for thy heàvy chance!
      [Line-space]
    4 ☐ Sòrely thy lìttle one dràgs by thee bàre-footed
    5 1 But àh for the bàby that hàngs at thy bènding back
    1 Cold   is
    6 ☐ Meàgre & lìvid & screàming its wrètchedness.
      [Line-space]
    7 ☐ Woè-begone mòther half ànger half àgony,
  7fn *1* This stanza was supplied by S. T. COLERIDGE.
    8 1   Òver thy shoùlder thou tùrnest to hùsh the babe
    1 As over   lookest
    9 1 Bleàkly the blìnding snow drìfts in thy hàgged cheek.
    1   beats   face.
      [Line-space]
  10 ☐ Thy hùsband will nèver retùrn from the wàr again
  11 ☐ Còld is thy hòpeless heart—èven as Chàrity!
  12 ☐ Còld are thy fàmishd babes—Gòd help thee wìdowd One!

1. *1* way-wanderer languid and   **3.** *1* Wild-visag'd   **4.** *1* bare-footed,
6. *1* and livid and   **7.** *1* mother, *1* anger,   **8.** *1* babe,   **10.** *1* again,
11. *1* heart *1* Charity—   **12.** *1* famish'd *1* thee, widow'd

title fn. By RS.
1 et seq. Stress-marks are omitted throughout PR *1*.
7fn. By RS.

107. ALLEGORIC VISION

A. DATE

May 1795; recast Aug 1811 and 1817.

B. TEXTS

1. VCL BT 5. Transcript by EHC in a bound volume entitled (on the spine) *Lectures and Sermons 1795–6*, ff 4^r–10^r. As the opening of C's first lecture on revealed religion, delivered in Bristol during May 1795 = *Lects 1795* (*CC*) 89–93.

The originals from which EHC made his transcript were given to him by JG's granddaughter, Lucy Watson, and have since disappeared. *Lects 1795* (*CC*) 76–9 comments on the accuracy of the transcript as a whole. EHC collated the "*MS. 1795*" in *PW* (EHC) II 1091–6: the omission of "stern and" in line 78 is probably a simple error, although the insertion of commas elsewhere in EHC's *PW* collation is probably intentional.

1. The Courier (31 Aug 1811) = *EOT* (*CC*) II 262–70. Signed "S. T. C." The errata following C's initials are given in the textual notes. There is also a good deal of faulty setting and broken type, most of which is silently corrected here.

The *CC* text corrects misprints, which are particularly plentiful in the quotation from Petrarch (lines 171.1.14 –19); these have been left uncorrected in the text below.

2. Conclusion of the Introduction to *A Lay Sermon* (1817) xix–xxxi = *LS* (*CC*) 131–7.

Five copies contain corrections and notes on this passage in C's own hand: C's own copy (NYPL Berg Collection); J. G. Lockhart's (HUL HEW 2. 1. 15); RS's (Texas Christian University, Mary Couts Burnett Library); John Anster's (BM Ashley 2853); and EC's (HUL 19476.345.4*). The annotations in JG's copy (NYPL Berg Collection) appear to be in JG's hand; those in SC's copy (Wellesley College Library Special Collections) appear to be in HNC's hand. Further details are given in *LS* (*CC*) 238–9.

LS (1839) incorporates most of the revisions found in C's own copy, some of them variatim. The *CC* text records further variants unique to *LS* (1839), which may or may not have the authority of a lost corrected copy.

3 [=RT]. *PW* (1829).

4. PW (1834).

C. GENERAL NOTE

Lines 1–51a give the PR *2* text, with PR *3 4* variants keyed to it; lines 51b–130.1.32   the MS 1 text, with PR *1–4* variants keyed to it; and lines 126–end the PR *1* and PR *2* texts, with later PR variants keyed to them. Decimal numeration (see e.g. lines 18.1–20.1 below, corresponding to lines 18–20 of the RT) is used to indicate places where the VAR sequence differs markedly from the RT. The textual notes in this instance contain variants of wording as well as of spelling and punctuation: the RT version of lines 18–20 is thus to be found in the textual notes rather than the main sequence, which has no lines numbered simply 18–20. It should be noted that references in the commentary at the end are sometimes keyed to variant readings contained in the textual notes, not to the main line-numbered sequence. In this instance strict adherence to the normal conventions of the volume would have created an even more complicated apparatus.

Annotation of material not included in the RT, based on PR *3*, is provided by the other *CC* volumes.

title. 1 Lecture on Origin of Evil. • *1 SUPERSTITION, RELIGION, ATHEISM.* | (AN ALLEGORIC VISION.) • *2–4* ALLEGORIC VISION.

1 *2–4* A feeling of sadness, a peculiar melancholy, is wont to take possession
2 *2–4* of me alike in Spring and in Autumn. But in Spring it is the melancholy
3 *2–4* of Hope: in Autumn it is the melancholy of Resignation. As I was jour-
4 *2–4* neying on foot through the Appennine, I fell in with a pilgrim in whom
5 *2–4* the Spring and the Autumn and the Melancholy of both seemed to have
6 *2–4* combined. In his discourse there were the freshness and the colors of
7 *2–4* April:
8 *2–4*   Qual ramicel a ramo,
9 *2–4*   Tal da pensier pensiero
10 *2–4*   In lui germogliava.
11 *2–4* But as I gazed on his whole form and figure, I bethought me of the not
12 *2–4* unlovely decays, both of age and of the late season, in the stately elm; af-
13 *2–4* ter the clusters have been plucked from its entwining vines, and the vines
14 *2–4* are as bands of dried withies around its trunk and branches. Even so
15 *2–4* there was a memory on his smooth and ample forehead, which blended
16 *2–4* with the dedication of his steady eyes, that still looked—I know not,
17 *2–4* whether upward, or far onward, or rather to the line of meeting where
18.1 *2–4* the sky rests upon the distance. But how may I express—the breathed
19.1 *2–4* tarnish, shall I name it?—on the lustre of the pilgrim's eyes?
20.1 *2–4* Yet had it not a sort of strange accordance
21 *2–4* with their slow and reluctant movement, whenever he turned them to
22 *2–4* any object on the right hand or on the left? It seemed, methought, as
23 *2–4* if there lay upon the brightness a shadowy presence of disappointments
24 *2–4* now unfelt, but never forgotten. It was at once the melancholy of hope
25 *2–4* and of resignation.
26 *2–4*   We had not long been fellow-travellers, ere a sudden tempest of wind
27 *2–4* and rain forced us to seek protection in the vaulted door-way of a lone
28 *2–4* chapelry: and we sate face to face each on the stone bench along-side the
29 *2–4* low, weather-stained wall, and as close as possible to the massy door.
30 *2–4*   After a pause of silence: Even thus, said he, like two strangers that
31 *2–4* have fled to the same shelter from the same storm, not seldom do Despair
32 *2–4* and Hope meet for the first time in the porch of Death! All extremes
33 *2–4* meet, I answered; but your's was a strange and visionary thought. The
34 *2–4* better then doth it beseem both the place and me, he replied. From a
35 *2–4* VISIONARY wilt thou hear a VISION? Mark that vivid flash through
36 *2–4* this torrent of rain! Fire and water. Even here thy adage holds true, and
37 *2–4* its truth is the moral of my Vision. I entreated him to proceed. Sloping
38 *2–4* his face toward the arch and yet averting his eye from it, he seemed to

39	*2–4*	seek and prepare his words: till listening to the wind that echoed within
40	*2–4*	the hollow edifice, and to the rain without,
41	*2–4*	Which stole on his thoughts with its two-fold sound,
42	*2–4*	The clash hard by and the murmur all round,
43	*2–4*	he gradually sunk away, alike from me and from his own purpose, and
44	*2–4*	amid the gloom of the storm and in the duskiness of that place he sate
45	*2–4*	like an emblem on a rich man's sepulchre, or like an aged mourner on the
		sod-
46	*2–4*	ded grave of an only one, who is watching the wained
47	*2–4*	moon and sorroweth not. Starting at length from his brief trance of ab-
48	*2–4*	straction, with courtesy and an atoning smile he renewed his discourse,
49	*2–4*	and commenced his parable.
50	*2–4*	During one of those short furlows from the service of the Body, which
51a	*2–4*	the Soul may sometimes obtain even in this, its
51b	☐	militant state, I found
52	☐	myself in a vast Plain, which I immediately knew to be the Valley
53	☐	of Life. It possessed a great diversity of soils and here was a
54	☐	sunny spot and there a dark one just such a mixture of sunshine
55	☐	and shade as we may have observed on the Hills óin an April
56	☐	Day when the thin broken Clouds are scattered over the heaven. Almost in
57	☐	the very entrance of the Valley stood a large and gloomy pile into which
58	☐	I seemed constrained to enter—every part of the building was crowded
59	☐	with tawdry Ornament and fantastic Deformity—on every window was
60	☐	pourtrayed in ⟨in⟩elegant and glaring Colours some horridble tale or preter-
61	☐	natural action—so that not a ray of light could enter untinged by the
62	☐	medium through which it passed. The Place was full of
63	☐	People some of them dancing about in
64	☐	strange ceremonies and antic merriment while others seemed convulsed
65	☐	with horror or pining in mad Melancholy—intermingled with all these I
66	☐	observed a great number of men in Black Robes who appeared
67.1	☐	now marshalling the various Groups &
67.1.1	☐	now collecting with scrupulous care the Tenths of every Thing
67.1.2	☐	that grew within their reach.
71	☐	I stood wondering a while what these Things might be when
72	☐	one of these men approached me ⟨&⟩ with a reproach-
73	☐	ful Look bade me uncover my Head for that the Place into which I had
74	☐	entered was the Temple of *Religion*—in the holier recesses
75	☐	of which the great Goddess resided.
76	☐	Awestruck by the
77	☐	name I bowed before the Priest and
78	☐	entreated him to conduct me into her Presence—he assented—offerings
79	☐	he took from me, with mystic Sprinklings of Water he pu-
80	☐	rified me and then led me
81	☐	through many a dark and winding alley the dew damps of which chilled
82	☐	and its hollow echoes beneath my feet
83	☐	affrightedned me till at last we entered a large Hall
84.1	☐	where not even a Lamp glimmered.
85.1	☐	Around its walls I observed a
86.1	☐	number of phosphoric Inscriptions—each one

89	☐	of the Words separately I seemed to understand but when I read
90	☐	them in sentences they were riddles incomprehensible and contradictory.
91	☐	Read
92	☐	and believe said my Guide—These are mysteries. In the middle of the Hall
93	☐	the Goddess was placed—her features blended with darkness rose
94	☐	to my view terrible yet vacant. I prostrated myself before her, and then
95	☐	retired with my guide wond'ring and dissatisfied.
96	☐	As I reentered the body of the Temple I heard a deep Buz as of Dis-
97	☐	content, a few whose Eyes were piercing,
98	☐	and whose Foreheads
99	☐	spoke Thought, amid a
100	☐	much larger number who were enraged by the severity
101	☐	of the Priests in exacting their Tenths, had collected in a
102	☐	group, and exclaiming. This is the Temple of
103	☐	Superstition, after much contumely & much mal-
104	☐	treatment they rushed out of it. I joined
105	☐	them—
106	☐	we travelled from the Temple with hasty steps and had now nearly
107	☐	gone round half the Valley when we were addressed by a Woman
114.1	☐	clad in white garments of simplest Texture
107.1.1	☐	the Air was mild yet majestic,
110.1	☐	and her Countenance displayed deep Reflection ani-
111	☐	mated by ardent Feelings.
115	☐	We enquired her name. My name is Religion—she said
116	☐	The greater part of our Company affrighted by the
117	☐	sound and sore from recent impostures hurried on-
118	☐	wards and examined no farther. A few struck by the
119	☐	difference of her form & manners
120	☐	agreed to follow her although with cau-
121	☐	tious circumspection. She led us to an Eminence in the midst of the
122	☐	Valley, on the Top of which we could command the whole Plain, and
123	☐	observe the Relation of its different Parts, each one to the other.
124	☐	She then gave us an optic Glass which
125	☐	assisted without contradicting our natural Vision and enabled
126.1	1	us to see far beyond the Valley—
130.1	1	(and now with the rapid Transition of a Dream I had
130.1.1	1	

∧ ∧ ∧ ∧
∧ ∧ ∧

of Superstition and went to sleep in its
darkest cloisters—but there were many however who lost not the
impression of Hatred towards their Oppressors and never looking 130.1.5
back had in their eagerness to recede from Superstition completed
almost the whole of the Circle, and were already in the Precincts
of the Temple when they abruptly entered a Vast and dusky Cave.
At the mouth of it sate two Figures the first, a female whom by
her dress & gestures I knew to be Sensuality the second from 130.1.10
the fierceness of his Demeanor and the brutal Scornfulness of his
Looks declared himself to be the Monster Blasphemy—he uttered
big words, yet ever and anon I observed that he turned pale at his

own Courage. We entered—the climate of the place was unnatu-
rally cold in the midst was an old dim eyed Man   130.1.15

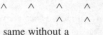

same without a
which was written—   the Old man was continually
applying his Microscope, and seemed greatly delighted in counting   130.1.20
the Irregularities which were made visible by it on the polished
surface of the Marble! He spoke in diverse Tongues (and) unfolded
many Mysteries, and among other strange Things he talked much
about an infinite Series of Causes—which he explained to be—A
string of blind men of which the last caught hold of the skirt of   130.1.25
the one before him, he of the next, and so on till they were all
out of sight; and that they all walked straight without making one
false step. We enquired, Who there is at the head to guide them.
He answered No one, but that the string of blind men went on for
ever without a beginning for though one blind man could not move   130.1.30
without stumbling, yet that infinite Blindness supplies the want of
sight. I burst into Laughter at this strange exposition and awoke—

126 ☒1   us to see far beyond the limits of the Valley of Life: though our eye
127 ☒1   even thus assisted permitted us only to behold a light and a glory, but
128 ☒1   what we could not descry, save only that it *was*, and that it was most
129 ☒1   glorious.
130 ☒1   And now with the rapid transition of a dream, I had overtaken and
131 ☒1   rejoined the more numerous party, who had abruptly left us indignant
132 ☒1   at the very name of religion. We journed on, goading each other with
133 ☒1   remembrances of past oppressious, and never looking back, till in the
134 ☒1   eagerness to recede from the Temple of Superstition, they had rounded
135 ☒1   the whole circle of the valley. And lo! there faced us the
136 ☒1   perpendicular side of a lofty rock, the in-
137 ☒1   terior side of which, unknown to them, and unsuspected, formed the
138 ☒1   extreme and backward wall of the Temple. And here they, and I with them,
139 ☒1   entered a vast and dusky cave, which was the only perforation of
140 ☒1   this vast precipice. At the mouth of the Cave sate two figures; the first, by
141a ☒1   her dress and gestures, I knew to be SENSUALITY;
140.1.1 1   on her bosom she wore the image of a snail with its horns, or
         organs of touch, protruded, and its eyes in its horns; and beneath
         the motto—Believe that alone which thou doest at once, see and
         feel. Her adoration, however, seemed directed to a picture before
         her of two snails connected together by a linked chain, proceeding   140.1.5
         from both, and by which each was to other at once both male and
         female.

141b ☒1   The second form,
142 ☒1   from the fierceness of his demeanour, and the brutal scornfulness of
143 ☒1   his looks, declared himself to be the Monster BLASPHEMY. He uttered
144 ☒1   big words, and yet ever and anon I observed that he turned pale at his
145 ☒1   own courage. We entered. Some remained in the opening of the cave,
146 ☒1   with the one or the other of its guardians. Others and I among them,
147 ☒1   pressed on, til we reached an ample chamber, that seemed the centre

148 ☒1 of the rock. The climate of the place was unnaturally cold.
148.1.1 *1* Scarcely had we entered it, before we were dwarfed into one half
of our former size and faculties. But if this BLASPHEMY had pre-
informed us under the name, "*riddance of prejudices:*" at the same
time that he presented to us an emblem of philanthropic justice,
in which was figured a murdered body, and beside it the assassin 148.1.5
before the judgment seat, on which philosophy was imaged sitting,
with a label from her mouth, sentencing the dagger to be hung,
because neither less nor more guilty than the assassin whom fate
had necessitated to necessitate his dagger to stab his friend, the
idea of whose wife or wealth had formed the irresistible motive: 148.1.10
yet the dagger rather than the man: for pain alone is evil, and the
man would but the steel will not feel pain.
149 ☒1   In the midst of the chamber sate an old dim-eyed man, por-
150 ☒1 ing with a microscope over the Torso of a statue, which had
151 ☒1 neither basis, nor feet, nor head; but on its breast was carved, NATURE!
152 ☒1 To this he continually applied his glass, and seemed enraptured with
153 ☒1 the various inequalities which it rendered visible on the seemingly
154 ☒1 polished surface of the marble.—Yet evermore was this delight and
155 ☒1 triumph followed by expressions of hatred, and vehement railing
156 ☒1 against a Being, who yet, he assured us, had no existence. This
157 ☒1 suddenly recalled to me what I had read in the Holiest Recess
158 ☒1 of the Temple of *Superstition*. The old man spoke in divers tongues,
159a ☒1 and continued to utter other and strange mysteries;
159.1.1 ☒1 as, that those only were rightfully wise and virtuous, and entitled
to power, who were chosen to be such by the ignorant and vi-
cious; that the base of every pillar, inasmuch as it is the base and
159.1.4 *1* support of the whole, ought therefore to be its capital; that his il-
lumined disciples, who denied to the Power, which legislates for 159.1.5
each particular country, all sanction, but that of their own good
liking *pro tempore*, ought, while they despised their prejudices,
to coalesce with, in order to use as tools, those who held a su-
pernatural sanction *against* that Power. He warned us against an
imposter, who called herself Religion, and declaimed concerning 159.1.10
a Supreme Reason, at once holy and all-powerful that revealed its
will to man, wholly and exclusively through his conscience and
his understanding; but bade us tolerate and unite with a crazy sis-
ter of his, whose silly phantasms had gained for her the name of
SUPERSTITION; but which contained nothing incompatible with 159.1.15
his principles, and in all ages had led by similar means to the same
end. For as blind Nature has produced the worm and the man, so
it may have produced not only men but Devils and Gods. I re-
peat the latter, because I have never even seen, much less touched
them, and despise them, therefore, as my sister's dreams. But in 159.1.20
the one great thing we are unanimous, in exercising that ghost, the
conscience: she, by making it depend on the sounds received from
a mountebank's jargon, and I, more wisely, on all the stimulants
by which Nature awakens our appetites. This, I remember, was the
practical part of his harangue. He then   159.1.25

159b ☒1 became more speculative, and more sublime. Among
160 ☒1 other strange things he talked much and vehemently concerning an
infinite series
161 ☒1 of causes and effects, which he explained to be—a string of blind
162 ☒1 men, the last of whom caught hold of the skirt of the one before
163 ☒1 him, he of the next, and so on till they were all out of sight: and
164 ☒1 that they all walked infallibly straight, without making one false
165 ☒1 step, though all were alike blind. Methought I borrowed cour-
166 ☒1 age from surprize, and asked him—Who then is at the head to guide
167 ☒1 them? He looked at me with ineffable contempt, not unmixed with
168 ☒1 an angry suspicion, and then replied, "No one. The string of blind
169 ☒1 men went on for ever without any beginning: for although one
170 ☒1 blind man could not move without stumbling, yet infinite blindness
171 ☒1 supplied the want of sight." I burst into laughter, which instantly turned
171.1.1 *1* to terror—for lo! a crowd of fiends rushed in on me, sometimes
in the feverish confusion of my thought appearing as figures, here
French faces, some with red caps and with crosses, and behind
them an Hibernian variety of the Centaur genus, composed of
a deranged man and mad *bull*; and sometimes as mere words 171.1.5
and notions of the Irish massacre, and St. Bartholomew's, and
the Septembrizers, and the whole Pandemonium of persecutors,
from the ST. DOMINIC, to the Atheists MARAT, CARRIER, and
BONAPARTE. Need I say, that awaking from such a night-mare,
I rejoiced at my deliverance; and by a glass of peppermint water 171.1.10
eliminated from my stomach the gas from indigestion, the pressure
of which on the lungs and blood-vessels had produced the painful
sensations, which had interpreted themselves under these forms—
"Nec me fallit, ut in corporibus hominum sic inanimis multiplici
passione affectis, medicamenta verborum multis inefficacia visum 171.1.15
iri, sed nec illud quoque me præterit, ut invisibiles, animorum mor-
bis, sic invisibilla esse *remedia*. Falsis opinionibus eris circumventi
veris sententlls liberandi sunt, ut qui andiendo ceciderent, audiendo
consurgat."—*Petrarcha in libro de remediis utriusque fortunæ*.
172 *2–4* to terror—for as he started forward in rage, I caught a glance of him from
173 *2–4* behind; and lo! I beheld a monster bi-form and Janus-headed, in the hin-
174 *2–4* der face and shape of which I instantly recognized the dread countenance
175 *2–4* of SUPERSTITION—and in the terror I awoke.

2. *4* spring   *4* autumn.   *4* spring   **3.** *4* hope: *4* autumn   *4* resignation.
5. *4* spring   *4* autumn   *4* melancholy   **12.** *3 4* elm,   **18.1–21.** *2* But how . . .
their slow • *3 4* But how may I express that dimness of abstraction which lay on the
lustre of the pilgrim's eyes like the flitting tarnish from the breath of a sigh on a
silver mirror! and which accorded with their slow   **28.** *4* chapelry;   **30.** *4* even
33. *4* yours   **35.** *4* Visionary   *4* Vision?   **43.** *4* sank   **44.** *4* place,
45. *2* an aged mourner • *3 4* a mourner   **46.** *2* an only one, who is watching • *3 4* an
only one—an aged mourner, who is watching   *4* waned   **50–2.** *2–4* During . . .
found myself • 1 *1* It was towards Morning [*1* morning,] when the Brain [*1* dream]
begins to reassume [*1* re-assume] its waking state, and our dreams approach to
[*1* imitate] the regular trains of fReality, [*1* reality, shot through by the dawn of the

re-ascending reason,] that I found myself   **50.** *4* furloughs   *4* body,   **51a.** *4* soul
4 this   **52.** *1–4* plain,   **52–3.** *1–3* VALLEY OF LIFE.   **53.** 1 a great • *1–4* an
astonishing   1 soils and • *1–3* soils: and • *4* soils: **54.** *1–4* spot,   1 one • *1–4* one,
forming   *1* sun-shine   **55.** *1–4* shade,   1 Hills • *1–4* mountains' side   *1–4* in
1 *2–4* April • *1* April's   **56.** *1–4* day,   *1–4* clouds   1 the heaven • *1–4* heaven.
57. *1–4* valley   *1–4* pile,   **58.** *1–4* enter. Every   **59.** 1 Ornament • *1–*
4 ornaments   *1–4* deformity. On   **60.** *1–3* pourtrayed, • *4* portrayed,   1 ⟨in⟩elegant
and glaring • *1* inelegant and glaring • *2–4* glaring and inelegant   *1* colours, •
2–4 colors,   1 horrdble • *1–4* horrible   *1–4* tale,   **61.** 1 action— • *1–4* incident,
1–4 enter,   **62.** 1 Place • *1–4* body of the building   **63.** *1–4* people,   *1–*
4 dancing,   1 about in • *1* in and out in unintelligible figures, with • *2–4* in and
out, in unintelligible figures, with   **64.** *1–4* merriment,   **65.** *1–4* horror,   *1–*
4 melancholy. Intermingled   1 with all • *1–4* with   *1–4* these,   **66–67.1.2.** 1 a
great number . . . within their reach. • *1* a number of men, clothed in ceremonial robes,
who appeared now to marshal the various groupes, and to direct their movements,
and now with menacing countenances, to drag some reluctant victim to a vast idol,
framed of iron bars intercrossed, which formed at the same time an immense cage,
and yet represented the form of a human Colossus. On the base of this statue I read
engraven the words: "To Dominic, holy and merciful, the preventer and the avenger
of soul-murder." But below I saw the dim reliques of Runic characters, which seemed
to imply a greater antiquity, and the whole form of the statue was probably first
impressed on my fancy by the wicked idol of Woden, which, as children, we have
all seen pictured in the common history-books of our rude ancestors. • *2–4* a number
of men, clothed in ceremonial robes, who appeared now to marshal the various
groups, and to direct their movements; and now with menacing countenances, to
drag some reluctant victim to a vast idol, framed of iron bars intercrossed, which
formed at the same time an immense cage, and the form [*3 4* shape] of a human
Colossus.   **71.** 1 wondering a while • *1* 2 for a while lost in wonder, • *3* 4 for a
while lost in wonder   *1–4* things   **71–2.** 1 be when one • *1–4* mean; when lo! one
72. 1 these men approached me ⟨&⟩ • *1–4* the Directors [*4* directors] came up to me,
and   **72–3.** 1 reproachful • *1–4* stern and reproachful   **73.** *1–4* look   1 2 head; •
3 4 head,   *1* 2 place, • *3* 4 place   **74.** *1* 2 entered,   1 the Temple of *Religion—* •
1–4 the temple of the only true Religion,   **75.** 1 resided. • *1* herself resided. •
2–4 personally resided.   **76.** 1 Awestruck • *1–4* Himself too he bade me reverence,
as the consecrated Minister of her Rites. [*4* minister of her rites.] Awe-struck
76–7. 1 the name • *1–4* the name of Religion,   **77.** *1–3* Priest, • *4* priest,   **77–**
8. 1 and entreated • *1–4* and humbly and earnestly intreated   **78.** *1–4* presence. He
assented. Offerings   **79.** *1–4* sprinklings   1 Water he • *1–4* water and with salt he
79–80. 1 purified me and • *1–4* purified, and with strange sufflations he exercised
[*2 3* exorcized • *4* exorcised] me; and   **81.** *1–4* alley,   *1–4* dew-damps   1 chilled •
1–4 chilled my flesh,   **82.** 1 its hollow • *1–4* the hollow   1 beneath • *1–4* under
82–3. 1 feet affrightedned me till at last we • *1–4* feet, mingled, methought, with
moanings, affrighted me. At length we   **83–95.** 1 a large Hall . . . and dissatisfied. •
1 2 a large hall where not even a single lamp glimmered. It was made half visible by
the wan phosphoric light [*2* rays] which proceeded from inscriptions on the walls,
in letters of the same pale and visionary [*2* sepulchral] light. I could read them,
methought; but though each one of the words taken separately I seemed to understand,
yet when I took them in sentences, they were riddles and incomprehensible. [*2 omits*
following] Two only of very many remained in my memory, after I awoke. Of the

one these were the words: "Accursed be the persecutor, that withholds the poisoned dagger from the holy ones, who would stab him therewith." The other was: "Separate and yet combine the object and the pretext: for the life of the crab is not in its shell or claws, but the one is its safeguard, and the other its tools." [*2 resumes*] As I stood meditating on these hard sayings, my guide thus addressed me—the [*2* The] fallible becomes infallible, and the infallible remains fallible. Read and believe: these are MYSTERIES!—In the middle of the vast hall the Goddess was placed. Her features [*2* features,] blended with darkness, rose out to my view, terrible, yet vacant. No definite thought, no distant image, [*2* distinct image] was afforded me: all was uneasy and obscure feeling. I prostrated myself before her, and then retired with my guide, soul-withered, and wondering, and dissatisfied. • *3 4* a large hall, without window, or spiracle, or lamp. The asylum and dormitory it seemed of perennial night—only that the walls were brought to the eye by a number of self luminous inscriptions in letters of a pale pulchral [*4* sepulchral] light, that [*4* which] held strange neutrality with the darkness, on the verge of which it kept its rayless vigil. I could read them, methought; but though each one of [*4* each of] the words taken separately I seemed to understand, yet when I took them in sentences, they were riddles and incomprehensible. As I stood meditating on these hard sayings, my guide thus addressed me—Read [*4* "Read] and believe: these are MYSTERIES!—[*4* mysteries!"*—] At the extremity of the vast hall the Goddess was placed. Her features, blended with darkness, rose out to my view, terrible, yet vacant. I prostrated myself before her, and then retired with my guide, soul-withered, and wondering, and dissatisfied.   **83.** *1 2* hall • *3 4* hall, **96.** *1–4* re-entered   *1–4* temple,   *1–3* buz • *4* buzz   **96–7.** *1–4* discontent. A **97–105.** 1 Eyes were piercing, . . . joined them— • *1–4* eyes were bright, and either piercing or steady, and whose ample foreheads, with the weighty bar, ridge-like, above the eye-brows, [*3 4* eyebrows,] bespoke observation followed by meditative thought; and a much larger number [*3 4* number,] who were enraged by the severity and insolence of the priests in exacting their offerings, [*2* offerings;] had collected in one tumultuous groupe, [*4* group,] and with a confused outcry of "this [*4* "This] is the Temple of SUPERSTITION!" [*4* Superstition!"] after much contumely, and turmoil, and cruel mal-treatment on all sides, rushed out of the pile: and I, methought, joined them.   **106.** 1 we travelled • *1–4* We speeded   *1–4* steps,   **107.** *1– 4* valley,   **107–15.** 1 a Woman clad . . . she said • *1–4* a woman, tall beyond the stature of mortals, and with a something more than human in her countenance and mien, which yet could by mortals be only felt, not conveyed by words or intelligibly distinguished. Deep reflection, animated by ardent feelings, was displayed in them: and hope, without its uncertainty, and a something more than all these, which I understood not, [*2* not;] but which yet seemed to blend all these into a divine unity of expression. Her garments were white and matronly, and of the simplest texture. We enquired her name. My name, she replied, is RELIGION. [*4* "My name," she replied, "is Religion."]   **107.** *1–4* woman,   **116.** 1 greater • *1–4* more numerous   *1– 4* company,   **116–17.** 1 the sound • *1–4* the very sound,   **117.** 1 impostures • *1– 4* impostures or sorceries,   **118.** 1 few • *1–4* few of us,   **119.** 1 difference • *1– 4* manifest opposition   *1–4* and   **119–20.** 1 manners agreed • *1* manners, agreed • *2–4* manners to those of the living Idol, whom we had so recently abjured,   **120.** *1– 4* her,   1 although • *1–4* though   **121.** *1–4* eminence   **122.** *1–4* valley,   1 on • *1–4* from   *1–4* top   *1–4* plain,   **123.** *1–4* relation   1 its • *1–4* the   1 Parts, each one to the other. • *1* parts, each to the other, and to the whole, and of all to each. • *2 3* parts, [*3* parts] of each to the other, and of each to the whole, and of all to each. •

4 parts to each other, and of each to the whole, and of all to each.   **124.** *1–4* glass
125. *1–4* vision,   **126.** *4* Life;   **128.** *4* was,   **131.** *2–4* us,   **132.** 1 We •
1–4 They   *2–4* journied   **133.** *2–4* oppressions,   **134.** *2–4* Superstition
136. *1* perpendicular side of a lofty rock, • *2–4* mouth of a vast cavern, at the base of
a lofty and almost perpendicular rock,   **138.** *1* And here . . . with them, • *2–4* An
impatient crowd, we   **139.** *1* a • *2–4* the   **140.** *1* this vast • *2–4* the   *2–4* cave
141a. *4* Sensuality;   **141b.** *1* The • *2–4* the   **143.** *3 4* monster   *4* Blasphemy.
146. *1* Others • *2–4* The rest,   **147.** *2–4* till   **149.** *1* midst • *2–4* furthest
distance   **150.** *4* torso   *3 4* statue   *1 2 4* had • *3* hath   **151.** *3 4* carved
4 Nature!   **156.** *1* This • *2–4* This mystery   **157.** *4* holiest recess   **158.** *2–
4* temple   *4* Superstition.   *4* spake   **159a–160.** *1* strange mysteries; . . . Among
other strange things • *2–4* most strange mysteries. Among the rest   **163.** *4* sight;
166. *4* surprise,   **168.** *2–4* one."   **169.** *4* beginning;   **171.** *2–4* sight.
172. *2 4* forward • *3* forwarded   *1–3* glance • *4* glimpse   **174.** *4* recognised
175. *4* Superstition—

title. The MS 1 title of course applies to the whole lecture.

13. PR 2 the vines] In Lockhart's copy *C* added "themselves".

18.1–21. PR 2 how may I . . . accordance with] In his own copy C emended to read
"how may I express that dimness of Abstraction, which lay on the lustre of the pilgrim's
eyes like the flitting varnish from the Breath of a Sigh on a Silver Mirror! and which
accorded with".

20.1–22. PR 2 Yet had it not . . . on the left?] Deleted in JG's copy.

20.1. PR 2 Yet had it not] In Lockhart's copy C emended to "Yet even this, methought,
had".

22. PR 2 left?] In Lockhart's copy C emended to "left."

PR 2 , methought,] Deleted by C in Lockhart's copy.

36. PR 2 true, and] In Lockhart's copy C substituted "true. EXTREMES MEET. And".

37. PR 2 I entreated] In Lockhart's copy C noted: "*A new paragraph should have
commenced here.*"

45VAR. PR 2 an aged mourner] C emended his own copy to what became the PR *3 4*
reading.

46VAR. PR 2 who is watching] C corrected his own copy to what became the PR *3 4*
reading. He corrected Lockhart's copy, differently, to "one—a mourner".

49. C added a "*Private* note" in RS's copy of PR *2*: "I myself feel that this introduction
is too ~~myst~~ romantic and (if I may dare whisper my own thoughts) too good for the
semi-real, semi-verbal Allegory, or Metaphorage, that follows. To an experienced Taste
it betrays the fact, that the two parts were composed at different Times—not smartly
struck off, like a gun-flint."

50–2VAR. Erratum to PR *1*: "for dream, read brain".

65–67.1.2VAR. Erratum to PR *1*: "for wicked, read wicker". In C's own and SC's
copies of PR *2* the variant reading "form" is emended to the PR *3 4* reading "shape".
Anster's, EC's, JG's, and Lockhart's copies of PR *2* are emended to read "semblance".

71. Only PR *1–4* begin a new paragraph with "I stood".

73. □ for that the] In his collation of "*MS. 1795*" in *PW* II 1093n EHC gives "for
the".

74VAR. In Lockhart's copy of PR *2* C underlined "Religion" twice.

80VAR. Erratum to PR *1*: "for exercised, read exorcised".

83–95VAR. Erratum to PR *1*: "for light read rays". C emended his own version of PR

2 in a way that anticipates the PR *3 4* version. The first alteration proceeded through two phases. He emended the opening phrase and first complete sentence of the text given above to read "hall ~~without~~ where was neither Lamp nor window: and ~~only seen by means~~ which I saw only by å sundry self luminous inscriptions on the walls, in letters of pale & sepulchral light, that did indeed render the darkness visible." Then he wrote the following, on a slip covering the first six lines of *LS* (1817) xxv: "Hall, without window or spiracle, ~~and where not~~ or lamp. The Asylum and Dormitory it seemed of perpetual Night—only that ~~its~~ the Walls were brought to the eye by a number of self luminous Inscriptions in letters of a pale sepulchral Light, that held strange neutrality with the Darkness on the verge of which it kept its rayless Vigil." In the sixth complete sentence of the text given above he deleted "The fallible . . . remains fallible." In the eighth sentence he changed "In the middle" to "At the extremity" (a change also made in SC's copy). And he deleted the tenth sentence, "No definite . . . obscure feeling."

96. Only PR *1–4* begin a new paragraph with "As I".

106. Only PR *1–4* begin a new paragraph with "We".

111. Only PR *1–4* begin a new paragraph with "The".

130.1.32⁺. MS 1 continues with a fresh paragraph concerned with other matter.

131. Erratum to PR *1*: "a comma after 'us'".

132. PR *2–4* religion.] Emended to "RELIGION." in Lockhart's copy of PR *2*.

148. The paragraph ends in PR *2–4* with "cold." The text continues in PR *1* without a break. In Lockhart's copy of PR *2* C indicated that "The climate" should begin a new paragraph, and that the sentence thus beginning should be run on as part of the new paragraph.

148.1.2 . Erratum to PR *1*: "for if, read of".

159.1.18–19. PR *1* "repeat" is an obvious misprint for "reject", but it is not cited in the Errata.

159.1.21. Erratum to PR *1*: "for exercising, read exorcising".

171.1.14–19. The obvious, uncorrected misprints in the Latin are: "inanimis" for "in animis"; erroneous comma after "invisibiles"; "morbis" for "morbos"; "invisibilla" for "invisibilia"; "eris" does not represent any word in the original; "sententlls" for "sententiis"; "andiendo" for "audiendo"; "consurgat" for "consurgant"; "ceciderent" for "ceciderant".

C transcribed the passage in Feb 1809, along with others, from Petrarch *Opera Quae Extant Omnia* (4 vols Basle 1581). Cf "Epistolaris praefatio" (I 3) and *CN* III 3467 f 63ʳ. He used it as one of the epigraphs for Essay VII of the 1818 *Friend*, where it is translated as follows: "I am well aware, that words will appear to many as inefficacious medicines when administered to minds agitated with manifold passions, as when they are muttered by way of charm over bodily ailments. But neither does it escape me, on the other hand, that as the diseases of the mind are invisible, invisible must the remedies likewise be. Those who have been entrapped by false opinions are to be liberated by convincing truths: that thus having imbibed the poison through the ear they may receive the antidote by the same channel" (*Friend—CC*—I 51–2).

175. The last words close the Introduction in PR *2*.

108. COMPOSED WHILE CLIMBING THE LEFT ASCENT OF BROCKLEY COOMB, IN THE COUNTY OF SOMERSET

A. DATE

May 1795 (included in the full title).

B. TEXTS

1 [=RT]. *Poems* (1796).
There are suggestions (the spelling "brouze" in line 6, the form "it's" in lines 8 and 9) that copy was provided by C's lost ms.

2. Poems (1797).
Thomas Hutchinson's copy, in the possession of Jonathan Wordsworth (1980), contains one emendation.

3. Poems (1803).
SH's copy (Cornell WORDSWORTH PR 4252 B91R9 1813 Copy 2) contains one correction.

4. PW (1828).

5. PW (1829).

6. PW (1834).

The wording of all six texts is identical with PR *1*, as given in the RT, except for:

title. *1* EFFUSION XXI. | COMPOSED | WHILE CLIMBING THE LEFT ASCENT | OF | *BROCKLEY COOMB,* | IN THE | COUNTY OF SOMERSET, | *MAY,* 1795. • *2 SONNET V.* | Composed while climbing the left ascent of | *BROCKLEY-COOMB,* | IN THE COUNTY OF SOMERSET, | MAY, 1795 • *3 SONNET XIV.* | COMPOSED WHILE CLIMBING THE LEFT ASCENT OF | *BROCKLEY-COOMB,* | IN THE COUNTY OF SOMERSET, | MAY, 1795. • *4–6* LINES | COMPOSED WHILE CLIMBING THE LEFT ASCENT | OF BROCKLEY COOMB, SOMERSETSHIRE, | MAY, 1795.   **7.** ⊠6 forc'd] *6* deep   **8.** ⊠*3* tree] *3* trees

title. *5 6* ASCENT OF | BROCKLEY   **4.** *4–6* the   **6.** *2–5* browze: • *6* browse:
7. *4 5* forced   **8.** *2–6* its   **9.** *2–6* its   **11.** *4–6* rest:—and   *4–6* gained
13. *6* towers,   *6* cots   *2 3* me;   **14.** *4* -shadowed   *6* fields,   *3* Sea; • *6* sea!
16. *6* Sara

title. In the PR *1* list of contents the title is given as "Effusion 21, on Brockley Coomb,".

8. In SH's copy of PR *3* C has deleted the second "s" in "bursts!"

15. In Thomas Hutchinson's copy of PR *2* C has deleted the line and substituted "I am alone, and cannot check the Tears—".

109. TO THE REV W.J.H. WHILE TEACHING A YOUNG LADY SOME SONG-TUNES ON HIS FLUTE

A. DATE

Summer 1795? The poem would probably have found a place in the Estlin Copy Book if it had been written before Apr 1795.

B. TEXT

Poems (1796).

The RT reproduces the *Poems* text exactly, with the exception of the title:

TO THE | Rev. W. J. H. | WHILE TEACHING A YOUNG LADY | SOME SONG-TUNES | *ON HIS FLUTE.*

22. away!] The exclamation-mark is missing from some copies of *Poems* (1796).

110. CONTRIBUTIONS TO *JOAN OF ARC*, BY ROBERT SOUTHEY

A. DATE

Mid-May to mid-Aug 1795. See vol I headnote.

B. TEXTS

1. BM Add MS 28096. 317 leaves, each measuring 14.5/16.5×20.0/21.0 cm; wm COLES 1794; chain-lines 2.6 cm; the larger number of leaves written on the rectos only. Fair copy of the larger part of the text as published in 1796, in

RS's hand with some emendations by C in pencil and ink. Emendations in C's hand are to be found on ff 7^r, 8^r, 9^r, 10^r, 11^r, 12^r, 12^v, 15^r, 24^r, 26^r, 27^r, 28^v–29^r, 34^r, 35^v, 94^r, 96^r, 97^r, 108^v–109^r, 119^v, 120^v, 123^r, and perhaps elsewhere. While the ms of Book I is scrappy, markings by Joseph Cottle in subsequent books show that they were received by him as printer's copy for PR *1*. (The ms was sold as the "Printer's Copy" in the Cottle Sale, Sotheby's—13 Mar 1865—lot 113.)

The portions of the ms composed or clearly emended by C are set out in more detail in sec C below. Even single-word and very minor emendations to MS 1 are given here so as to make the record as complete as possible. Angle-brackets are employed freely to indicate C's alterations to RS's original as clearly as possible.

Other single leaves of the ms, which have nothing to do with C's contribution and which were separated before MS 1 was foliated, are to be found at NYPL (Berg Collection), Cornell (Joseph Cottle Album ff 17^r and 19^v: WORDSWORTH Bd Cottle), and HUL (bMS Eng 265.2). They are in RS's hand, on the same paper as the BM ms, and those at Cornell and HUL are endorsed by Cottle.

2. NYPL Berg Collection. Two leaves, 15.7×20.0 cm; wm 1794; chain-lines 2.6 cm. Fair copy of the Argument to Book II (1796) and lines 1–12, in RS's hand, with some minor emendations by C.

The first leaf contains the Argument only; the second, the twelve lines of verse on the recto and a fair copy of line 19 on the verso. The two leaves fit between ff 25 and 26 of MS 1. The fair copy of line 19 is to replace a cancelled passage on f 26^r of MS 1.

3. HRC MS (Coleridge, S T) Works B. Single leaf, 16.5×20.0 cm; wm COLES 1794; chain-lines 2.6 cm; written on both sides. Fair copy of Book II (1796) lines 271–301, in RS's and C's hands. Bound into Rugby Manuscript pp 93–4 /f 41^{r-v}.

The leaf is bound into the Rugby Manuscript with material for C's *Poems* (1796). The first one and a half lines are in RS's hand, the remainder in C's.

4. Single leaf (?), "endorsed and signed by Joseph Cottle". Fair copy (?) of Book II (1796) lines 436–41, in C's hand. The description is derived from S. J. Davey *Catalogue 31* (1889) item 2981 (at 15*s*); Davey's bookshop was at 47 Great Russell Street, opposite the BM. The lines are quoted in the catalogue, and the paper on which they are written and the format of the lines is presumably similar to, if not identical with, MSS 3 and 5 here. The original has not been recovered.

5. HRC MS (Coleridge, S T) Works Hanley II B. Single leaf, 21.1×11.0 cm; no wm; chain-lines 2.5 cm; verso blank. Fair copy of Book II (1796) lines 442–52, in C's hand.

The leaf is torn off across the bottom, tight against line 452, as if more lines followed. It is endorsed "Coleridge's — — Autograph J Cottle | (from Religious Musings". Cottle's muddle (as in his classifying of MS 3) was undoubtedly encouraged by C's changes of mind while submitting copy for **101** *Religious Musings*. At the same time, it suggests that Cottle was more used to receiving copy for *Joan of Arc* in RS's hand.

1 [=RT]. Robert Southey *Joan of Arc* (1796).

There was an unauthorised reprint of this first edition by the American firm of Joseph Nancrede (Boston) in 1798. Subsequent editions, as explained in vol I headnote, omit the bulk of C's contribution.

A copy of PR *1* annotated for William Hood, probably in Jun 1814 (see *CL* III 510: to J. J. Morgan [16 Jun 1814]), is at the NYPL (Berg Collection Copy 2). Here only those annotations which bear directly on C's contribution are recorded, and others are given in vol I. The provenance of the book and the full set of annotations will be given in *CM* (*CC*) v. The majority of annotations are in red pencil, others are in ordinary pencil, and others (not cited here) are in ink.

The notes which accompany the Hood copy at NYPL relate to C's contribution to MS 1, and the copy of PR *1* at DCL (SOU (a) 1796) contains JDC's transcriptions from the Hood copy. Neither JDC's notes nor his copy are of independent textual interest, although the first helps with the identification of C's contributions and the second with readings in the Hood copy that have become faint or rubbed.

Another copy, on occasions described as having been given to C by RS but apparently not, is described in vol I annex C 2.

C. GENERAL NOTE

Three main sources throw light on how C contributed to the revision of the first four books, or perhaps the first five: (1) the copy submitted to Joseph Cottle (MSS 1–4), although it is not complete; (2) RS's Preface to PR *1*, although it passes over C's minor contributions; and (3) the copy of PR *1* marked up for William Hood, although C did this nearly twenty years after his involvement with the poem, in 1814. The three sources confirm one another for the most part, as follows:

(1)	(2)	(3)
Corrections and additions to MSS 1–4 indubitably in C's hand	Passages acknowledged by RS in the Preface to PR *1* (p vi)	Passages picked out by C in W. Hood's copy of PR *1*
(*a*)		I 34–51, where revised and further corrected by C
(*b*)		I 59
(*c*) I 163 (MS 1 f 7ʳ)		
(*d*) I 198 (MS 1 f 8ʳ)		

(*e*) I 223 (MS 1 f 9ʳ)		I 221–3
(*f*) I 229, 231 (MS 1 f 10ʳ)		
(*g*) I 240 (MS 1 f 10ʳ)		
(*h*) I 246, 248 (MS 1 f 11ʳ)		
(*i*) I 262 (MS 1 f 12ʳ)		
(*j*) I 274, 276 (MS 1 f 12ᵛ)		I 269–80
(*k*) I 294 (MS 1 f 15ʳ)		
(*l*) I 457 etc (MS 1 f 24ʳ)		I 454–60
(*m*)		I 484–96

(*n*) II 1–59 (MS 2; MS 1 ff 26ʳ, 27ʳ, 28ᵛ–29ʳ) — II 1–140
(*o*) — II 144–7 } II 1–147

(*p*) II 195–269 (MS 1 ff 32ʳ, 34ʳ, 35ᵛ) — II 223–65 — II 223–66

(*q*) II 272–301 (MS 3) } II 273–85 — II 272–90
(*r*) II 442–52 (MS 4) } II 292–450 — II 292–452, where revised and further corrected by C

(*s*) — III 75–82

(*t*) IV 66 (MS 1 f 94ʳ)		
(*u*) IV 112 (MS 1 f 96ʳ)		
(*v*) IV 125 (MS 1 f 97ʳ)		
(*w*) IV 331–5 (MS 1 ff 108ᵛ–109ʳ)		IV 330–3
(*x*) IV 489fn (MS 1 ff 119ᵛ, 120ᵛ)		
(*y*) V 47 (MS 1 f 123ʳ)		

Some of the discrepancies and obscurities in this tabulation are repaired by RS's Brixton Manuscript (HUL MS Eng 265.3), written before he met C, and by other references given below.

(*a*) Book I lines 34–51

C drew a line alongside this passage in W. Hood's copy of PR *1*, and marked it "*S.T.C.*" (both in ordinary pencil). There is a similar passage in RS's Brixton Manuscript, f 5ʳ⁻ᵛ, but it has been so heavily revised that C's claim has some colour. Besides, the simile in lines 47–51 is entirely new in PR *1*, and was specifically said to be C's by Cottle (*Rem* 141–2).

The RT reproduces PR *1* exactly.

37. not slept,] C has corrected Hood's copy (in ordinary pencil) to "slept not,".

39. red] C has underlined the word in Hood's copy, and written "*S*" alongside in the RH margin (both in red pencil). S, according to C's set of abbreviations on p [4], means "pseudo-poetic Slang, generally, too, not English".

46. Firm] C has underlined the word in Hood's copy, and written in the RH margin "Not English" (both in red pencil).

(*b*) Book I, line 59

The line is marked "S.T.C." (in red pencil) in the LH margin of Hood's copy of PR *1*. There is no equivalent for the line in the Brixton Manuscript (f 5ᵛ), though there are equivalents for/approximations to the lines before and after. It therefore seems likely that line 59 was inserted by C.

58 *1* Erichtho mingled on Pharsalia's field,
59 *1* Making the soul retenant its cold corse,
60 *1* More potent; thro' his frame with force divine

(*c*) Book I line 163

The substitution in MS 1 is in C's hand, in pencil. The equivalent line in RS's Brixton Manuscript reads "Who lovd my sire preservd his infant child" (f 8ᵛ).

163 1 "My fallen father, saved his ~~orphan~~ ⟨helpless⟩ child.
    1   ←—helpless—→

(*d*) Book I line 198

The suggested alteration in MS 1 is written in C's hand, in pencil. The equivalent line in RS's Brixton Manuscript reads "Mark yonder fawn how frolick in the sun" (f 9ᵛ).

198 1 "How frolic in the sun that little fawn
    1   yon

    198. C has underlined "that" and written "yon" in the RH margin. A line four lines further on in MS 1 (with no equivalent in the Brixton Manuscript) has also been underlined in pencil: I 202 "Who could endure to gore his innocent side!" But the line appears thus, unchanged, in PR *1*.

(*e*) Book I lines 221–223

In Hood's copy of PR *1* the lines are marked, and C has written "S. T. C." alongside, both in red pencil. Nothing resembling the entire passage in which these lines appear is to be found in RS's Brixton Manuscript (f 10ʳ), and the revision of line 222 in MS 1 is in C's hand.

221 1 *1*   . . . the groves of Paradise
222 1   ~~"Reechoed to the choral song of joy~~
       1 *1* Gave their mild echoes to the choral song
223 1 *1* "Of new-born beings; . . .

222. *1* "Gave   **223.** *1* beings:

(*f*) Book I line 229–231

Lines 229, 231, and 231.1.1 are revised in C's hand—in pencil (line 229) and in ink (lines 230–231.1.1)—in MS 1. There is no equivalent for the whole passage which ends with these lines in the Brixton Manuscript (f 10ʳ).

229 1 "Till Christ ~~descending~~ ⟨expiring⟩ on the sacred cross
1   ←——expiring——→
230 1 "Pourd forth the atoning ~~blood~~ life; the tears ran down
1   life;
231 1 "His aged cheeks ~~& woe &~~ ⟨with woe-mixt⟩ gratitude⟨.⟩
1   with   woe-mixt   gratitude.
231.1.1 1 ~~"Proclaimed this more than mortal still was man.~~

229. *1* "'Till   **230.** *1* "Pour'd

230. 1 [~~Blood~~ life;] This revision (only) is in RS's hand, and was made as the text was copied—not afterwards, like C's.
231.1.1. It is possible that the line was deleted by RS, not C.

(*g*) Book I line 240

The revised version of the line in MS 1 is in C's hand. There are unrevised approximations to the lines before and after in RS's Brixton Manuscript (f 10ʳ), and RS appears to have added the unrevised line 240 to MS 1.

238 1 *1*   "One morn it chanced
239 1 *1* "As wandering thro the wilds my steps strayed on
240 1   ~~"Brushing ⟨from⟩ the high grass the morning dew~~
      1   And ~~brush'd~~ from the high grass brush'd the morning dew,
      1   ←—from—→
241 1 *1* "The track of blood alarm'd me. . . .

238. *1* chanc'd,   **239.** *1* thro'   *1* stray'd on,   **240.** *1* "And   *1* brushed
241. *1* me;

240. MS 1 ⟨from⟩] The insertion in the original, deleted version of MS 1 is in C's hand.

(*h*) Book I lines 246, 248

The suggested revision to line 246 and the second revision of line 248 are in C's hand in MS 1. RS's Brixton Manuscript reads at this point (f 10ᵛ):

            Nor long I sought ere on this reeking ground
            These eyes beheld a youth—his auburn hair
            Clotted with gore & from his side welld forth
            The stream of life—pale—~~cold~~ wan his cheek convulsd
            Reekd with the cold damp dews—. . .

Considered alongside RS's own revisions, and the further slight emendation in PR *1*, it would seem that C's intervention was part of a continuous process of revision.

246 1 *1* "It led me where outstretchd on the red earth
247 1 *1* "There lay a youth wounded & faint: his hair
248 1   "Clotted with gore—fast from his side ~~rusht welld~~ ⟨stream'd⟩ out
   1   ←——stream'd——→
249 1   "The blood ⟨on his pale cheek⟩—the cold dews ~~reekd on his cold cheek~~ started,
   1   blood;   on   his   pale   cheek   the   cold   dews   stood,
250 1 *1* "And from his hand the blood-staind sword had falln.

246. *1* outstretch'd   **247.** *1* wounded, and faint;   **248.** *1* gore;   **250.** *1* -stain'd
1 fall'n.

   246. MS 1 on] C has underlined the word and written "upon" alongside, in the RH margin (both in pencil).
   248. MS 1 ~~welld~~ ⟨stream'd⟩] This, not the previous emendation in the same line, is in C's hand (in ink).

(*i*) Book I line 262

The suggested alteration in MS 1 is written in C's hand, in pencil. The whole passage in MS 1 is much revised in RS's hand, and C's suggestion (which was not adopted) would have brought the line closer to what it had been in RS's Brixton Manuscript: "His frame revivd | To former vigour—" (f 11ʳ).

261 1   . . . his frame ~~revivd~~ the temperate current rolld
   1   the
262 1 *1* "Of former strength, . . .

261. *1* roll'd   **262.** *1* strength:

   262. 1 strength] C has underlined the word, and written "vigor" alongside in the LH margin.

(*j*) Book I lines 269–280

C marked the lines in Hood's copy of PR *1*, and wrote "S.T.C." alongside, both in red pencil. Although the lines in MS 1 are in RS's hand, they rewrite an abandoned passage and continue on the verso of a leaf (f 12ᵛ), and hence were probably a later addition; they also contain two markings, apparently in C's hand. They replace a passage in the Brixton Manuscript (f 11ʳ⁻ᵛ) which is related in content but very different in phrasing.

The RT reproduces PR *1* exactly (this departs from the normal practice of printing the earliest text and showing later readings as variants).

269. 1 hamlets,—   1 widows groan   **270.** 1 orphans   **272.** 1 oer
1 framd   **273.** 1 &   1 crownd   **274.** 1 dogs   **276.** 1 escaped   1 stretchd
277. 1 "Seemd   **279.** 1 glowd   1 cheek:/

274. MS 1 merciless] Underlined in pencil, apparently by C.
276. MS 1 then] The word has been underlined and "ex" is written beneath it in C's hand, both in pencil. Excising the word would bring the reading closer to the Brixton Manuscript: "his arm outstretchd".

(*k*) Book I line 294

The substitution in MS 1 is in C's hand, in pencil. RS's Brixton Manuscript reads at the equivalent place (f 11ᵛ) "his ~~slender~~ wasted lamp of life | Gently ~~dissolves~~ expires in peace."

293 1 *1*   . . . his wasted lamp of Life
294 1   "Gently ~~give~~ ⟨go⟩ out."
    1   go

293. *1* life

(*l*) Book I lines 454–460

C marked the lines in Hood's copy of PR *1* and wrote "S.T.C." alongside, both in red pencil. The substitution in line 457 of MS 1 is in his hand, and he may have made the deletion in lines 454a.1–454b.1. There is no equivalent to the last part of Book II in RS's Brixton Manuscript (between the two sides of f 17).

454a.1 1   "My soul grew sick within me ~~& my cheek~~
454b.1 1   "~~Reddend with indignation~~: then methought
    454 *1*   "My soul grew sick within me: then methought
    455 1 *1* "From a dark lowering cloud the womb of tempests
    456 1 *1* "A giant arm burst forth, & dropt a sword
    457 1   "That ~~fell~~ ⟨pierc'd⟩ like lightning thro the midnight air.
    1   pierc'd
    458 1 *1* "Then was there heard a voice, which in mine ear
    459 1 *1* "Shall echo at that hour of dreadful joy
    460 1 *1* "When the pale foe shall wither in my rage.

455. *1* cloud,   *1* tempests,   **456.** *1* and   **457.** *1* thro'   **459.** *1* echo, (*m*) Book I lines 484–496

C marked the lines rather tentatively with red pencil in Hood's copy of PR *1*, as if to designate his authorship; and marked again lines 485–8 and 491–4. Against lines 485–8, he wrote in red pencil in the LH margin: "Suggested and in part worded by S.T.C."

Only line 486 appears in MS 1—in RS's hand, but alone on f 17ᵛ in a way that suggests that the passage underwent revision. At the same time, although there is no equivalent to the last part of Book I in RS's Brixton Manuscript, some earlier lines in that ms (f 15ʳ) bear a similarity to those claimed by C:

> —how abhorrent to my soul
> That loved these scenes of bliss—the dingles bed
> The primrosed bank where hung the fallen trunk
> In antic wildness of the stream hoarse broke
> Rough rolling oer the stones—

The RT reproduces PR *1* exactly.

(*n*) Book II lines 1–140

The lines are ascribed to C by RS in the Preface to PR *1*, and C marked them as his in Hood's copy of the same. MSS 1 2 are in RS's hand, but contain corrections and additions in C's. There is of course no equivalent for this part of Book II in RS's Brixton Manuscript.

argument. 2 *1* Argument. | Preternatural agency. Joan & Dunois rest at a cottage. their host speaks of the battle of Azincour & the massacre of the prisoners after that defeat. the siege of Rouen related & the miseries of the besieged. the useless inhabitants sent out of the town. behaviour of Henry to them. capture of Rouen & execution of Allain Blanchard its gallant defender.   **title.** 2 *1* JOAN OF ARC | Book the second.

> 1 2 *1* No more of Usurpation⟨'⟩s doom⟨'⟩d defeat,
> 2 2 *1* Ere we the deep preluding strain have pourd
> 3 2 *1* To the Great Father, ONLY RIGHTFUL KING,
> 4 2 *1* Eternal Father! King Omnipotent!
> 5 2   Beneath whose shadowing banners wide unfurld
>   *1*   shadowy
> 6 2 *1* Justice leads forth her tyrant-quelling Hosts.
> 7 2 *1* Such Symphony requires best Instrument.
> 8 2 *1* Seize then, my Soul! from FREEDOM's trophied Dome
> 9 2   The Harp that, hanging high between the shields
>   *1*   which
> 10 2 *1* Of Brutus & Leonidas, oft gives
> 11 2 *1* A fitful music to the breezy touch
> 12 2 *1* Of patriot Spirits that demand their fame.
> 13 1 *1* For what is Freedom, but the unfetterd use
> 14 1 *1* Of all the Powers which God for use had given?
> 15 1 *1* But chiefly this: with holiest habitude

16 1   Of constant Faith, ~~the~~ ⟨him⟩ First, ~~the~~ ⟨him⟩ Last to view
    1   him   him
17 1 *1* Thro meaner powers & secondary things
18 1 *1* Effulgent, as thro clouds that veil his blaze.
29.1 1   ~~Yet there are those who deem themselves most free~~
30.1 1   ~~When they within this gross and visible sphere~~
31.1 1   ~~Chain down the winged thought, scoffing ascent~~
32.1 1   ~~Proud in their meanness, but all Motion round~~
19 2 *1* For all that meets the bodily sense I deem
20 1   Symbolical, ⟨one~~ ~~vast~~ mighty alphabet
    1   one   mighty
21 1 *1* For infant minds; & we in this low world
22 1 *1* Placed with our backs to bright ʄReality,
23 1   That we may learn with young unwounded ~~eyes~~ ken
    1   ken
24 1 *1* Things from their shadows. know thyself, my Soul!
25 1 *1* Confirmd thy strength, thy pinions fledged for flight
26 1 *1* Bursting this shell & leaving next thy nest
27 1   Soon ~~shalt thou~~ upward soaring ⟨shalt thou⟩ fix intense
    1   ←—upward—→   shalt thou
28 1 *1* Thine eaglet eye on Heavens eternal Sun!
29 1 *1* But some there are who deem themselves most free,
30 1 *1* When they within this gross & visible sphere
31 1 *1* Chain down the winged Thought, scoffing ascent
32 1 *1* Proud in their meanness. & themselves they cheat
33 1 *1* With noisy emptiness of learned phrase,
34 1 *1* Their subtile fluids, impacts, essences,
34fn 1 *1* ~~Sir~~ Isaac Newton at the end of the last edition of his Optics, sup-
           poses
           that a very subtile & elastic fluid, which he calls æther, is diffused
           thro the
           pores of gross bodies, as well as thro the open spaces that are void
           of gross
           matter. he supposes it to pierce all bodies, & to touch their least
           particles,
           acting on them with a force proportional to their number or to the
           matter of the   II 34fn5
           body on which it acts. he supposes likewise, that it is rarer in the
           pores of bodies
           than in open spaces, & even rarer in small pores & dense bodies,
           than in large
           pores & rare bodies; & also that its density increases in receding
           from gross
           matter; so for instance as to be greater at the $\frac{1}{100}$ of an inch from the
           surface of
           any body than at its surface; & so on. to the action of this æther he
           ascribes the   II 34fn10
           attractions ~~& repulsions~~ of gravitation & cohæsion, the attraction &
           repulsion of electrical

bodies, the mutual influences of bodies & light upon each other, the effects &

communication of heat, & the performance of animal sensation & motion.

David Hartley from whom this account of æther is chiefly borrowed makes it

the instrument of propagating those vibrations or configurative motions which   II 34fn15

are ideas. as it appears to me, no hypothesis ever involved so many contradictions.

for how can the same fluid be both dense & rare in the same body at one time?

yet in the Earth as gravitating to the Moon, it must be very rare; & in the Earth

as gravitating to the Sun, it must be very dense. for, as ~~Baxter~~ Andrew Baxter well

observes, it doth not appear sufficient to account how this fluid may act with a   II 34fn20

force proportional to the body to which another is impelled, to assert that is

rarer in great bodies than in small ones: it must be farther asserted that this fluid

is rarer or denser in the same body, whether small or great, according as the

body to which that is impelled is itself small or great. but whatever may be the

solidity of this objection, the following seems unanswerable.   II 34fn25

   If every particle thro the whole solidity of a heavy body, receive its impulse

from the particles of this fluid, it should seem that the fluid itself must be as dense

as the very densest ~~bo~~ heavy body, gold for instance; there being as many impinging

particles in the one, as there are gravitating particles in the other which receive

their gravitation by being impinged upon: so that, throwing gold or any heavy   II 34fn30

body upward, against the impulse of this fluid, would be like throwing gold *thro*

gold. and as this æther must be equably diffused over the whole sphere of its

activity, it must be as dense when it impels cork as when it impels gold: so that

to throw a piece of cork upward, would be as if we endeavourd to make cork

penetrate a medium as dense as gold. & tho we were to adopt the extravagant   II 34fn35

opinions which have been advancd concerning the progression of pores, yet

however porous we suppose a body, if it be not all pore/ the argu-
ment holds

equally; the fluid must be *as* dense as the body in order to give
every particle its

impulse.

    it has been asserted that Sir Isaac Newtons philosophy leads in its
conse-   II 34fn40

quences to Atheism: perhaps not without reason. for if matter by
any powers or

properties *given* to it, can produce the order of the visible world, &
even gen-

erate thought; why ~~might~~ may it not have possessed such properties
by *inherent* right?

& where is the necessity of a God? matter is, according to the
mechanic phi-

losophy—capable of acting most wisely & most beneficently with-
out consciousness of Wisdom   II 34fn45

or Benevolence; & what more does the Atheist assert? if matter
could possess these

properties, why might it not possess them from all eternity? Sir
Isaac

Newtons Deity seems to be alternately operose & indolent, to have
delegated

t so much power as to ~~leave~~ make it inconceiveable what he can
have reserved. he is

dethroned by Vice-regent second causes.   II 34fn50

    We seem placed here to acquire a knowledge of *effects*. Whenever
we would

pierce into the *Adyta* of Causation, we bewilder ourselves—and all,
that laborious

Conjecture can do, is to fill up the gaps of Imagination. We are
restless, because

invisible things are not the objects of vision—and philosophical
Systems, for the

most part, are received not for their Truth, but in [?]proportion as
they ~~enable our~~ gives   II 34fn55

to Causes a susceptiblility of being *seen*, [?]whenever our visual
organs shall have

become sufficiently [?]powerful.

35	1	*1*	Self-working Tools, uncausd Effects, & all
36	1	*1*	Those ~~B~~blind Omniscients, those Almighty ~~s~~Slaves,
37.1	1		~~That would untenant Heaven of God~~
37	1		Untenanting Creation of its Maker.
	1		God.
38	1	*1*	But Properties are God: the naked mass
39	1	*1*	Acts only by its inactivity.
40	1	*1*	Here we pause humbly. others boldlier think
41	1	*1*	That as one body is the aggregate

42 1   Of atoms numberless, ~~all~~ each organized;
    1   each
43 1 *1* So by a strange & dim similitude,
44 1 *1* Infinite myriads of self-conscious minds
45 1   Form one all-conscious Spirit, that directs
    1   who
46 1 *1* With absolute ubiquity of thought
47 1   All his component monads, that all seem
    1   yet
48 1 *1* With various province & apt agency
49 1 *1* Each to pursue its own self-centering end.
50 1 *1* Some nurse the infant diamond in the mine,
51 1 *1* Some roll the genial juices thro the oak,
52a.1/
53b.1 1 ~~Some form the Monsoon, & with whirlwind speed~~
52 1   Y̶Some drive the mutinous clouds to clash in air
    1   Some
53 1 *1* And rushing on the storm with whirlwind speed
54 1 *1* Yoke the red lightning to their vollying car
55 1   Thus they pursue their never-varying course,
    1   these
56 1 *1* No eddy in their stream. others more wild,
57 1 *1* With complex interests weaving human fates,
58 1 *1* Duteous or proud, alike obedient all,
59 1 *1* Evolve the process of eternal good.

60–140, including footnotes, occur in PR *1* only, reproduced exactly in the RT, except that the following misprints are silently corrected in the RT: 71fn "altitudinis", misprinted as "altudinis"; 75fn9 "quo", misprinted as "quod"; 112fn1 "Torngarsuck;", misprinted as "Torngarsuck"; 112fn2 "spirit is", misprinted as "spiritis"; 112fn7 "ascend", misprinted as "asceed".

argument and title. For the different typography, spelling, and punctuation of PR *1* see RT   **1.** *1* Usurpation's doom'd   **2.** *1* pour'd   **3.** *1* Only Rightful King,   **5.** *1* unfurl'd   **8.** *1* then   *1* Freedom's   **10.** *1* and   **13.** *1* unfetter'd   **15.** *1* this,   **17.** *1* Thro'   *1* and   **18.** *1* thro'   **21.** *1* and   **22.** *1* Reality,   **24.** *1* Know thyself   **25.** Confirm'd   **26.** *1* and   **28.** *1* Heaven's   **30.** *1* and   **31.** *1* thought,   **32.** *1* meanness: and   **34.** *1* subtle   **34fn1.** 1 S̶i̶r̶ Isaac Newton • *1* Sir Isaac Newton   **34fn2.** *1* and   *1* thro'   **34fn3.** *1* thro' *1* spaces,   **34fn4.** *1* matter;   *1* and   **34fn6.** *1* He   **34fn7.** *1* and . . . and   **34fn8.** *1* and . . . and   **34fn10.** *1* body,   *1* and   *1* To   **34fn11.** 1 attractions & ~~repulsions~~ of • *1* attractions of   *1* and . . . and   **34fn12.** *1* and . . . aud   **34fn13.** *1* and . . . and   **34fn14.** *1* borrowed,   **34fn16.** 1 as it appears • *1* It appears   *1* contradictions;   **34fn17.** *1* and   **34fn18.** *1* and   **34fn19.** *1* For, 1 as ~~Baxter~~ Andrew • *1* as Andrew   **34fn21–2.** 1 that is rarer • *1* that it is rarer   **34fn24.** *1* But   **34fn25.** *1* unanswerable: **34fn26.** *1* thro'   *1* body   **34fn28.** 1 densest b̶o̶ heavy body • *1* densest heavy body   **34fn32.** *1* *thro'* gold;   **34fn34.** *1* endeavoured   **34fn35.** *1* gold: *1* and tho'   **34fn36.** *1* advanced   *1* progession   **34fn37.** *1* pore,   **34fn38.** *1* as   **34fn40.** *1* It   *1* Newton's

34fn41. *1* For   **34fn42.** *1* and   **34fn43.** 1 why ~~might~~ may • *1* why may
34fn44. *1* and   **34fn44–5.** *1* philosophy   **34fn45.** 1 without consciousness
of Wisdom • *1* without Wisdom   *1* and   **34fn46.** *1* and   1 if matter could
possess these • *1* if matter possess those   **34fn47.** 1 why might it not possess •
1 why might it not have possessed   **34fn48.** *1* Newton's   *1* and indolent;
34fn49. *1* so   1 as to ~~leave~~ make • *1* as to make   *1* He   **34fn51–7.** 1 We seem . . .
sufficiently powerful.] While the first three paragraphs are entirely in RS's hand,
this last is entirely in C's   **34fn52.** *1* ourselves;   **34fn53.** *1* imagination.
34fn54. *1* systems,   **34fn55.** *1* proportion   1 ~~enable our~~ give*s* • *1* attribute
34fn56. *1* susceptibility   *1* whenever   **34fn57.** *1* powerful   **35.** *1* uncaus'd
1 and   **36.** *1* blind   *1* Slaves,   **40.** *1* Others   **42.** *1* organiz'd;   **43.** *1* and
48. *1* and   **50.** *1* mine;   **51.** *1* thro'   *1* oak;   **52.** *1* air;   **54.** *1* car.
56. *1* Others

1. The apostrophes in MS 2 were probably inserted by C. RS's practice is habitually to
omit them, and they have not been inserted elsewhere in MS 1.

16. The substitutions in MS 1 are in C's hand.

19. The line is written in the middle of an otherwise blank page of MS 2. The recto of
the same leaf contains lines 1–12 above, all of which suggests that the line was drafted
immediately following the cancellation of lines 29.1–32.1.

27. The substitution in MS 1 is in C's hand.

55. MS 1 they] Underlined.

56. MS 1 their] Underlined.

59. MS 1 ends quarter-way down f 29^r, and it therefore appears that RS was prevented
from continuing his transcript by C's addition of a fourth paragraph to the footnote on
line 34. RS had begun the footnote on f 26^v, and continued it on ff 27^v and 28^v. C
continued it to the bottom of f 28^v and across to f 29^r, immediately following line 59 of
the text.

136–40. C bracketed the lines in Hood's copy of PR *1*, with the instruction in the RH
margin (both in ordinary pencil) "Transcribe". The annotation is connected with **139** *The
Destiny of Nations*.

(*o*) Book II lines 144–147

The lines are ascribed to C by RS in the Preface to PR *1*. C marked the first 147
lines of Book II as his in Hood's copy of PR *1* (the claim there to lines 141–3
being, presumably, an oversight).

The RT reproduces PR *1* exactly.

(*p*) Book II lines 223–266

Lines 223–65 are ascribed to C by RS in the Preface to PR *1*. C marked lines
223–66 as his, in Hood's copy of PR *1*, with a line in red pencil down the LH
margin. In the same copy he put a bracket at the beginning of the passage and
deleted lines 267–72, with the remark (in ordinary and in red pencil): "These
Lines Southey's". MS 1 contains emendations in C's hand.

223	1 *1*	"Maid beloved of Heaven."
224	1 *1*	To her the tutelary Power exclaimd,
225	1 *1*	"Of CHAOS the adventurous progeny
226	1 *1*	"Thou seest, foul missionaries of foul sire
227	1 *1*	"Fierce to regain the losses of that hour
228	1	"When LOVE rose glittering, & his gorgeous wing
	1	wings
229	1	"Over the dark womb fluttered, with ~~glad~~ such noise,
	1	abyss　　　　　such glad
230	1 *1*	"As what time after long & pestful calms
231	1 *1*	"With slimy shapes & miscreated life
232	1 *1*	"Poisoning the vast ꝑPacific,—the fresh breeze
233	1 *1*	"Wakens the merchant sail, uprising. NIGHT
234	1 *1*	"An heavy un*á*imaginable moan
235	1 *1*	"Sent forth, when she the PROTOPLAST beheld
236	1 *1*	"Stand beauteous on Confusion's charmed wave.
237	1 *1*	"Moaning she fled, & entered the ꝑProfound
238.1	1	"That leads with mazy windings many & dark
240.1	1	"To that strange cave below the massy root
241.1	1	"Of Hell. there many an age the Beldame lurkd
242.1	1	~~⟨And⟩ Trembling~~
238	*1*	"That leads with downward windings to the Cave
239	*1*	"Of darkness palpable, desart of Death,
240	*1*	"Sunk deep beneath GEHENNA's massy roots.
241	*1*	"There many a dateless age the Beldame lurk'd
242	1 *1*	"And trembled: till engenderd by fierce HATE,
243	1 *1*	"Fierce HATE & gloomy HOPE, a DREAM arose
244	1 *1*	"Shapd like a black cloud markd with streaks of fire.
245	1	"It rousd the beldame. she the dew damps wipd
	1	Hell-hag:
246	1 *1*	"From off her brow, & thro the uncouth maze
247.1	1	"Retraced her ~~fugitive~~ ⟨exile⟩ steps. but ere she reachd
248.1	1	"The mouth of that drear labyrinth, she pausd
249.1	1	"Shuddering, nor to reenter Chaos dared.
247	*1*	"Retraced her steps; but ere she reach'd the mouth
248	*1*	"Of that drear labyrinth, shudd'ring she paus'd
249	*1*	"Nor dar'd re-enter the diminish'd Gulph.
250	1 *1*	"As thro the dark vaults of some moulderd tower
251	1	"(Which fearful to approach at ~~evening~~ the hind
	1	the　　evening
252	1 *1*	"Circles at distance in his homeward way)
253	1	"The winds ~~groan~~ breathe hollow, deemd the plaining groan
	1	breathe
254	1 *1*	"Of prisond spirits, with such fearful voice
255	1 *1*	"NIGHT murmurd, & the sound thro Chaos went.
256	1 *1*	"Leapt at the call her hideous-fronted brood!
257	1 *1*	"A dark behest they heard, & rushd on earth,
258	1 *1*	"Since that sad hour in camps & courts adored

259 1   "Rebels from God & Monarchs ~~of~~ ⟨o'er⟩ Mankind.
     1   o'er
260 1 *1* "These are the fiends that oer thy native land
261 1   "~~Have scattered~~ ⟨Spread Guilt &⟩ Horror, Maid beloved of Heaven
     1 "Spread   Guilt   and
262 1 *1* "~~Darest~~'st thou ~~inspired~~'d by the holy flame of Love
263 1 *1* "Encounter such fell shapes, nor fear to meet
264 1 *1* "Their wrath, their wiles. O Maiden—dar*é*'st thou die
          [*Line-space*]
265 1 *1* "FATHER OF HEAVEN! I will not fear," she said
266 1 *1* "My arm is weak—but mighty is thy sword.

223. *1* Heaven!"   **224.** *1* (To *1* exclaimed)   **225.** *1* CHAOS   **226.** *1* seest;
1 sire,   **228.** *1* and   **229.** *1* flutter'd   **230.** *1* and   *1* Calms   **231.** *1* and
232. *1* "Pois'ning *1* Pacific,   **234.** *1* unimaginable   **237.** *1* and   *1* Profound
242. *1* engender'd   **243.** *1* and   **244.** *1* "Shap'd *1* mark'd   **245.** *1* rous'd
1 dew-damps *1* wip'd   **246.** *1* and thro'   **250.** *1* thro' *1* moulder'd
251. *1* approach,   **253.** *1* deem'd   **254.** *1* prison'd spirits;   **255.** *1* murmur'd,
and *1* thro'   **257.** *1* and rush'd   **258.** *1* and   **259.** *1* and *1* Mankind!
260. *1* o'er   **261.** *1* belov'd *1* Heaven!   **262.** *1* "Dar'st *1* inspir'd
264. *1* wiles? *1* Maiden, dar'st *1* die?   **265.** *1* fear,"   **266.** *1* weak,

235. For C's comment in red pencil in Hood's copy of PR *1* see vol I EC.
237, 247.1, 259, 261, 262, 264. The emendations and corrections in MS 1 are in C's hand.

(*q*) Book II lines 272–290 [+291–3]

Lines 273–85 are ascribed to C by RS in the Preface to PR *1*. C marked the lines as his in Hood's copy of PR *1*, with a line in red pencil, although he extended his claim as far as line 290 (lines 286–7 and lines 291–2 are marked "S", which may stand for pseudo-poetic slang, as C explained on p [4], or here for RS). Line 271 and the first half of line 272 in MS 3 are in RS's hand, which is thereafter (to line 301) in C's. C's ascription of lines 277–93 to RS in the proofs of *SL* is his reason for not reprinting them, but only lines 291–3 have any parallel in RS's Brixton Manuscript (where they appear in Book IV).

272 3 *1*   . . . From his obscure haunt
273 3 *1* Shriek'd FEAR, the ghastliest of AMBITION's throng,
274 3 *1* Fev'rish yet freezing, eager-pac'd yet slow;
275 3 *1* As she that creeps from forth her swampy reeds
276 3 *1* AGUE, the biform Hag! when early Spring
277 3 *1* Beams on the marsh-bred vapours. "Lo! she goes!
278 3 *1* "To Orleans lo! she goes—the Mission'd Maid!
279 3 *1* "The Victor Hosts wither beneath her arm—
280 3 *1* "And what are Crecy, Poictiers, Azincour
281 3 *1* "But noisy echoes in the ear of Pride?

282 3 *1* AMBITION heard and startled on his Throne;
283 3 *1* But strait a Smile of savage Joy illum'd
284 3 *1* His gri⟨e⟩sly features, like the sheety Burst
285 3 *1* Of Lightning o'er th' awaken'd midnight clouds
286 3 *1* Wide-flash'd. For lo! a flaming Pile reflects
287 3 *1* Its red light fierce and gloomy on the face
288 3 *1* Of SUPERSTITION and her goblin Son
289 3 *1* Loud-laughing CRUELTY, who to the Stake
290 3 *1* A female fix'd, of bold and beauteous mien,
291 3 *1* Her snow-white Limbs by iron fetters bruis'd,
292 3 *1* Her breast expos'd. JOAN saw, she saw and knew
293 3 *1* Her perfect image. . . .

274. *1* eager paced,   279. *1* arm!   281. *1* Pride?"   282. *1* throne;
283. *1* smile *1* joy   284. *1* grisly   285. *1* the   286. *1* pile   288. *1* Son,
289. *1* stake

277–93. Lo! she goes! . . . Her perfect image.] The lines appear in the first set of proofs of **139** *The Destiny of Nations*, in John Evans's proof copy of *SL* (Yale In C678 817 sa). C deleted them, and added the two comments: "None of mine, thank God!"; "Blessings on us! Why these are not mine." See on II 398 below for further comment on the grounds of C's rejection.

(*r*) Book II lines 292–452

Lines 292–450 are ascribed to C by RS in the Preface to PR *1*. C marked the lines as his in Hood's copy, introducing a few minor changes and adding comments. MS copy up to line 301 and for lines 436–52 is in his hand (MSS 3–5).

292   3 *1*   . . . JOAN saw, she saw and knew
293   3 *1* Her perfect image. Nature thro' her frame
294   3 *1* One pang shot shiv'ring; but, that frail pang soon
295   3 *1* Dismiss'd, "Ev'n so (the exulting Maiden said)
296   3 *1* "The sainted Heralds of Good Tidings fell,
296fn   3   Ευαγγελιον *f*The Gospel i.e. Good Tidings.
297   3 *1* "And thus *they* witness'd God! But now the Clouds
298   3 *1* "Treading, and Storms beneath their feet, they soar
299   3 *1* "Higher, and higher soar, and soaring sing
300   3   "Th' eternal Pæan! "Triumphal harmonies! The Loud Songs of Triumph!
                                                              Spirits of Air, God,
        3 *1* "Loud Songs of Triumph! O ye Spirits of God,
301.1   3   "Who hover o'er my mortal agonies,
301.1.1 3   "Assist me*1*, in that hour!

301–435, including footnotes, occur in PR *1* only, reproduced exactly in the RT, except for line 339, where the misprint "hotss," is silently corrected in the RT.

436 4 *1* "Soon shall the morning struggle into Day,

437 4   "The stormy morning into endless noon.
1   cloudless
438 4 *1* "Much has't thou seen, nor all can'st understand,
439 4 *1* "But this be thy best omen, *Save thy Country*.
440 4 *1* "Thus saying from the answ'ring maid he pass'd
441 4 *1* "And with him disappear'd the goodly vision."
          [*Line-space*]
442 5   Glory to thee, FATHER of ~~Heaven~~ Earth and Heaven!
1   ←—Earth—→
443 5 *1* All-conscious PRESENCE of the Universe!
444 5 *1* Nature's vast ever-acting ENERGY!
445 5 *1* In Will, in deed, IMPULSE of All to all.
446 5 *1* Whether thy Law with unrefracted ray
447 5   Beams on the PROPHET's purged Eye, or if
1   "Beam
448 5 *1* Diseasing Realms th' ENTHUSIAST wild of thought
449 5 *1* Scatter new Ffrenzies on th*ě*' infected throng,
450 5 *1* Thou ƀBOTH inspiring, and predooming BOTH,
451 5 *1* Fit instruments and best of perfect End.
452 5 *1* Glory to thee, FATHER of Earth & Heaven!

295. *1* "Even so"   **297.** *1* they   **436.** *1* Morning   **437.** *1* Morning
1 Noon.   **438.** *1* hast   *1* understand—   **439.** *1* Omen, SAVE THY COUNTRY!"
440. *1* Thus   *1* saying,   *1* answering MAID   *1* pass'd,   **441.** *1* And   *1* Vision.
442. *1* "Glory   **443.** *1* "All-   **444.** *1* "Nature's   **445.** *1* "In will,   *1* to all;
446. *1* "Whether   *1* LAW   *1* Ray   **448.** *1* "Diseasing   *1* the   **449.** *1* "Scatter
1 frenzies   *1* the   *1* Throng,   **450.** *1* "THOU Both   *1* Both,   **451.** *1* "Fit
INSTRUMENTS   *1* END.   **452.** *1* "Glory   *1* Father   *1* and Heaven!"

302–12, 317 et seq. A fragment possibly related to these lines, and having something in common with **101** *Religious Musings* 166–7, occurs on the verso of a ms prospectus for C's *Six Lectures on Revealed Religion* (Yale Tinker 656; *Lects 1795—CC—*82):

> When as he told of her fair cities burnt
> Her fruitful fields laid waste/—her hamlet hearths
> Silent or echoing to the widows ~~long~~ groan
> Or the pale orphans ⟨feeble⟩ cry ~~that asks~~ for bread
> *JOAN*
> *JOAN*
> Wast husht, ~~was the sound [. . .] on the trembling~~ air

The first lecture was probably delivered on 19 May 1795, at about the time RS decided that his poem needed to be rewritten.

304. PR *1* calmy] In Hood's copy C emended to "calmest" (in red pencil).
316–17. Anticipated in the Gutch Notebook (*CN* I 55 [1795–6]):

> Broad-breasted Rock.
> hanging cliff that glasses
> His rugged forehead in the calmy sea.

Apropos of calmy (see C's revision in line 304 above), KC remarks that it is Spenser's word (*Faerie Queene* II xii 30).

339. hosts,] PR *1* misprints as "hotss,".

364. foul] In a copy of *PW* (1828) now at the Fitzwilliam Museum, Cambridge (Marlay Bequest 1912) C has underlined the word in the corresponding passage of **139** *The Destiny of Nations*, writing alongside: "*Southeyan* | a vile Line. S.T.C." At the same time, he has encircled lines 363–8 (to "why") for deletion, and rewritten the beginning of line 368.

387–90. The image is jotted down in prose form in the Gutch Notebook (*CN* I 54): "The Whale followed by *Waves*—I would glide down the rivulet of quiet Life, a Trout!" KC connects it with Erasmus Darwin *The Botanic Garden* II i 257–66, and there are associations with the treacherous Leviathan of *PL* I 200–8.

398. C has put a cross in red pencil in the RH margin of Hood's copy of PR *1* against this line. It is perhaps related to his comment at the foot of the page (also in red pencil), some fourteen lines further on (see vol I EC). The comment may also explain or bear on C's deletion of lines 409–11 (in ordinary pencil).

418. For C's comment see vol I EC. It is written alongside, in the RH margin of Hood's copy of PR *1*, in red pencil.

421. PR *1* those, the] C substituted "hiss'd" in Hood's copy (in ordinary pencil). He also underlined "locust" and "crawl'd" in red pencil, adding a comment in the RH margin, for which see II 398EC.

428fn. For C's comment see vol I EC. It is given in the RH margin against the second line, in red pencil, in Hood's copy of PR *1*.

In line 11 of the Greek PR *1* misprints ποσσ' as ποσσ`. This passage, including the footnote, was afterwards repeated in **139** *The Destiny of Nations* (to line 439), in *SL*, and in *PW* (1828, 1829, 1834). The repeated versions of the Greek poem are collated at **48** *Sors Misera Servorum* 1–16 above.

431–3. C quoted the lines at *The Watchman* I (1 Mar 1796) (*CC*) 33.

444–5. For C's comment see vol I EC. It is given in red ink in Hood's copy of PR *1*.

(*s*) Book III lines 75–82

The lines are marked with a red pencil in Hood's copy of PR *1*, signifying that they are C's. They are quoted (var) in *The Watchman* I (1 Mar 1796) (*CC*) 22, where, apart from some differences in punctuation, line 75 is omitted, 80 "love" is replaced by "Peace", and 81 "act" is replaced by "Deed".

The corresponding passage in MS 1 (ff 60ʳ–61ʳ), in RS's hand, is entirely different, so perhaps C intervened to alter the text at the proof stage of PR *1*. There is no equivalent for either MS 1 or the PR *1* passage in the original Brixton Manuscript (at f 62ᵛ). MS 1 reads as follows:

> martyrd patriots—spirits pure
> Wept by the good ye fell! yet not in vain
> Living & labouring for your fellow men,
> That better part survives the eternal mind
> Immutable incorruptible Truth
> To beam hereafter sun-surpassing splendor

> To illumine & to bless mankind, a band
> Of brethren in the unity of peace
> The bond of Love.

The RT reproduces PR *1* exactly.

Note. There are no equivalents for sections (*t*)–(*y*) in the original, Brixton Manuscript.

(*t*) Book IV line 66

The substitution in MS 1 is in C's hand.

66 1 The ~~shadowy~~ Shapes of ⟨holy⟩ Phantasy. by her
    1 ◄—shapes—►   holy

66. *1* fantasy. By

(*u*) Book IV line 112

The substitution in MS 1 is in C's hand.

112 1 Of Maximin, on whose ~~fierce brow~~ ⟨rais'd Lip⟩ Revenge
    1   rais'd   lip

(*v*) Book IV line 125

The substitution is in C's hand.

125 1 With lifted arm & trump as ~~tho to blow~~ ⟨she would blow⟩
    1   she   would   blow

125. *1* and

(*w*) Book IV lines 331–335

C marked lines 330–3 as his, with a red pencil line in the LH margin, in Hood's copy of PR *1*. His correction of and insertion into RS's text in MS 1 suggest that he should have marked lines 331–5. First he emended lines 330–335a.1/334b.1 as RS had written them on f 109ʳ, then he drafted the insertion of lines 332–5 on the facing page, f 108ᵛ.

331 1   She thought of Arc, ~~the dingle bosomd brook,~~ ⟨and of the dingled brook,⟩
    1   and   of   the   dingled   brook,
335a.1/
334b.1 1   ~~And~~ ⟨Of⟩ that old oak ~~that~~ ⟨which⟩ on the glassy ~~stream~~ ⟨lake⟩
    332 1 *1* Whose Waves oft leaping on their craggy course

333 1 *1* Made dance the low-hung Willow's dripping twigs,
334 1   And, where it spread into a ~~smoother Stream~~ glassy Lake,
     1   glassy   Lake,
335 1 *1* Of that old Oak, which on the smooth Expanse
336 1   Imaged his hoary mossy-mantled boughs.
     1   its

332. *1* waves   333. *1* willow's *1* twigs;   334. *1* And *1* lake,   335. *1* oak,
1 expanse

(*x*) Book IV lines 489fn

The footnote is entirely in C's hand in MS 1 (it is endorsed at the end by Cottle: "Coleridge's writing J.C."). The emendations suggest that it derives variatim from the text (var) of *Conciones ad Populum*, as C prepared it for publication some time after Jun 1795. Cf *Lects 1795 (CC)* 65–6 and, on the date, 22, 66n.

489fn 1 *1* If they who mingled the Cup of Bitterness, drank it's Contents, we
             might look with a calm compassion on the wickedness of great
                Men: but alas! the Storm,
             which they raise, falls ~~beats heaviest on the unprotected~~ exposed
                ~~Innocent~~ "Beats heaviest on the exposed Innocent" and the
                Cottage of the
             Poor Man is stripped of *every* comfort before the Oppressors who
                send forth the
             mandate of Death are amerc/ed of one Luxury or one Vice. If
                Calamities succeed   IV 489fn5
             each other in a long series, they deprecate the anger of Heaven by
                a FAST: which
             word (being interpreted) seems to signify—Prayers of Hate to the
                God of Love,
             and then a Turbot Feast to the Rich and their usual scanty meal to
                the Poor—if
             indeed debarred from their usual Labor they can procure even this!
                But if the
             Cause be crowned by victory,   IV 489fn10

                         —they o'er the ravag/ed Earth
                  As at an Altar wet with human blood
                  And flaming with the fire of Cities burnt
                  Sing their mad hymns of Triumph—Hymns to God
                  O'er the destruction of his gracious ∀Works,   IV 489fn15
                  Hymns to the Father o'er his slaughter'd Son.

             See "Conciones ad Populum. or Addresses to the People by S. T. Cole-
             ridge.

1. *1* "If *1* its *1* contents,   **2.** 1 with a calm compassion • *1* with compassion
1 men: But *1* storm   **3.** 1 raise, ~~falls . . . Innocent~~ "Beats • *1* raise, "beats

1 innocent," *1* cottage *1* poor man   **4.** *1* comfort,   *1* Oppressors,   **5.** *1* death,
1 amerced *1 one* Luxury, *1 one 1* calamities   **6.** *1* FAST;   **8.** *1* turbot
feast *1* rich, *1* poor,   **9.** *1* indeed, *1* labor,   **10.** *1* cause be crowned by
victory,   **11.** *1* "They *1* ravaged earth,   **12.** *1* altar *1* blood,   **13.** *1* cities
burnt,   **14.** *1* Hymns *1* God,   **15.** *1* works,   **16.** *1* father *1* son."
17. *1* CONCIONES AD POPULUM, or,   *1* People,   **17–18.** *1* S. T. COLERIDGE.

(*y*) Book v line 47

The substitution in MS 1 is in C's hand. Although C wrote at the end of Book
IV, in Hood's copy of PR *1* (p 151) (in red pencil), "All the preceeding I gave
my best advice in correcting. From this time Southey & I parted.—S.T.C.", he
also wrote in a letter at about the same time: "I looked over the 5 first Books
of the 1st. (Quarto) Edition of Joan of Arc Yesterday . . . in order to mark the
lines written by me" (*CL* III 510: to J. J. Morgan [16 Jun 1814]).

47 1 ~~Fast~~ ⟨There,⟩ by a streamlet⟨,⟩ on its mossy bank
   1   There,

47. *1* streamlet,

110.X1. UNTITLED STANZAS ON GRACE

In Jan 1999 some papers came to light in the archive of C. T. Jefferies, a book-
seller and printer of Redcliffe Street, Bristol (Bristol Record Office, 'B' Bond
Warehouse, Smeaton Road, Bristol BS1 6XN). They include a letter to Jefferies
from Joseph Cottle, dated 6 May 1847, which refers to enclosed samples of the
writing of RS and C. The RS sample is a page of the ms copy of *Joan of Arc*
which Cottle published in 1796 (IX 439–59), authenticated by Cottle in a way
identical to other pages now in public collections (e.g. NYPL Berg Collection).
Cottle's sample of C's writing comprises five unpunctuated 4-line stanzas be-
ginning "Down to the gloomy shades of death". However, the hand is not C's,
neither are the sentiments (summed up in the final line of each stanza: "A sinner
saved by grace") during the time he was a Unitarian, nor is the style. To add to
the confusion, the lines are accompanied by another note in Jefferies' (?) hand:
"A few lines of the Writing of My late friend Cottle wherein he presents Me
with the MS of Southey and Wordsworth"; but the lines are not in WW's hand
either, and are not characteristic of his style or thinking at any period. No other
version of the same lines has been located, and the hand remains unidentified.

Cf **159** *To a Lady* for another poem of mysterious Cottle provenance but
which is more likely to be by C.

110.X2. REPORT ON MR COTTEL

Richard Monkton Milnes, first Baron Houghton (1809–85), copied the follow-
ing lines into the margin of a manuscript commonplace book he used during
1838–9 (Trinity College Cambridge Houghton G1 p 24):

> Dear Mr Cottel (Cottle)
> Who appears very well
> Has another Poema indited
> ⟨Of⟩ Called John the Baptizer,
> Whʰ will make you no wiser,
> How can you be over delighted.

> *Coleridge*—at the end of a letter from Bristol

Joseph Cottle published his first collection, entitled *Poems, Containing John
the Baptist*, in 1795, i.e. within a year of meeting C. If C wrote the lines during
this period, they were most probably addressed to CL or RS; otherwise, they
have something in common with later doggerel notes to TP (see **146** *To Thomas
Poole*). See also **117** *Lines to Joseph Cottle* and **642** *Couplet on Joseph Cottle*.

Monkton Milnes called at Highgate in 1828, while he was an undergraduate
at Cambridge. His tutor was the Coleridgean Connop Thirlwall, and he later
associated with such disciples of Coleridge as F. D. Maurice and John Sterling;
he was to purchase the manuscript of **178** *Kubla Khan* at auction in 1859 (for
£1 15*s*). Cottle's *E Rec* was published in 1837, and it is possible that the lines
were invented at the later time, during the ensuing controversy and gossip.

111. IN THE MANNER OF SPENSER

A. DATE

PR *2* and PR *3* below are followed by the date "*July*, 1795."

B. TEXTS

1. HRC MS (Coleridge, S T) Works B. Single leaf, 20×32 cm; wm GP&J;
chain-lines 2.5 cm; written on both sides. Bound into Rugby Manuscript pp 47–
8/f 20ʳ⁻ᵛ. Transcript in C's hand, submitted as copy for PR *1* below.

1. Poems (1796).
C himself made the correction (listed in the Errata) in the text of his own copy
(NYPL Berg Collection Copy 7). The poem was reprinted in *The Universal
Magazine* XCIX (Jul 1796) 56–7.

2 [=RT]. Supplement to *Poems* (1797).

3. Poems (1803).

4. PW (1828).

5. PW (1829).

6. PW (1834).

C's own copy at HEHL (Book No 109531) carries the comment, keyed to the title: "i.e. Little Potatoes in the *Manner* of the Pine Apple. I S. T. Coleridge I April, 1834".

C. GENERAL NOTE

The lines continued to please CL more than C, it seems, and would have been dropped from PR *3* but for CL's prompting (*LL*—M—I 12, 17, 66). CL included them in PR *3* on WW's "authority" (*LL*—M—II 114).

title. 1 *Effusion 25* I In the manner of Spenser. • *1* EFFUSION XXIV. I IN THE I *MANNER OF SPENSER.* • *2 3 In the MANNER of SPENCER.* • *4–6* LINES I IN THE MANNER OF SPENSER.

1	□	O PEACE, that on a lilied bank dost love
2	1	To rest thy head beneath an Olive Tree,
	⊠1	thine
3	□	I would that from the Pinions of thy Dove
4	□	One quill withouten pain ypluck'd might be!
5	□	For ô! I wish my SARA's frowns to flee,
6	□	And fain to her some soothing song would write,
7	1	Lest she ~~disprove~~ resent my rude discourtesy,
	⊠1	←—resent—→
8	□	Who vow'd to meet her ere the morning light
9	1	But broke my plighted faith—ah! false and recreant Wight!
	⊠1	word—
		[*Line-space*]
10	□	Last night as I my weary head did pillow
11	□	With thoughts of my dissever'd fair engross'd,
12	1	~~Sad~~ Chill Fancy droop'd, wreathing herself with willow,
	⊠1	Chill
13	□	As tho' my breast entomb'd a pining ghost.
15.1	1	Hither, soft Slumber! (inly did I say)
14	⊠1	"From some blest couch, young Rapture's bridal boast,
15	⊠1	"Rejected SLUMBER! hither wing thy way;
16	□	But leave me with the matin hour, at most;
17	1	Like ~~crocus~~ snowdrop opening to the solar ray,
	1	Like snowdrop opening to the solar ray,
	2–6	"As night-clos'd flowret to the orient ray,
18	1	My sad heart will expand ~~with~~, when I my Fair survey.
	⊠1	when the Maid

		[*Line-space*]
19	☐	But LOVE, who heard the silence of my thought,
20	☐	Contriv'd a too successful Wile, I ween:
21	☐	And whisper'd to himself, with malice fraught—
22	1	"Too long our Bard the Maiden's smiles hath seen:
	☒1	Slave Damsel's
23	1	"To morrow shall he mark her alter'd mien!
	☒1	ken
24	1	He smil'd, and ambush'd lay, till on my bed
	☒1	spake,
25	☐	The Morning shot her dewy glances keen,
26	1	When as I 'gan arouse my drowsy head—
	1 4–6	to lift
	2 3	uplift
27	☐	"Now, Bard! I'll work thee woe! the laughing Elfin said.
		[*Line-space*]
28	☐	SLEEP, softly-breathing God! his downy wing
29	☐	Was flutt'ring now, as quickly to depart;
30	☐	When twang'd an Arrow from LOVE's mystic string—
31	☐	With pathless wound it pierc'd him to the heart.
32	☐	Was there some Magic in the Elfin's dart?
33	☐	Or did he strike my couch with wizard Lance?
34	☐	For strait so fair a Form did upwards start,
35	☐	(No fairer deck'd the Bowers of old Romance)
36	☐	That SLEEP enamour'd grew, nor mov'd from his sweet Trance!
		[*Line-space*]
37	☐	My SARA came, with gentlest Look divine;
38	☐	Bright shone her Eye, yet tender was its Beam:
39	☐	I felt the pressure of her Lip to mine—!
40	☐	Whisp'ring we went, and Love was all our theme—
41	☐	Love pure and spotless, as at first, I deem,
42	☐	He sprang from Heaven! Such joys with Sleep did 'bide,
43	☐	That I the living Image of my Dream
44	☐	Fondly forgot. Too late I woke, and sigh'd—
45	☐	O! how shall I behold my Love at eventide!

1. *1 2* PEACE,   **2.** *6* olive tree,   **3.** ☒1 *3* would,   ☒1 pinions   *6* dove
4. *4–6* yplucked   **5.** *4–6* O!   *6* Sara's   **8.** *4–6* vowed   ☒1 light,   **9.** *4–*
6 wight!   **11.** *2–6* dissevered   ☒1 Fair   *4 5* engrossed, • *6* engrost,   **12.** *1–*
3 droop'd • *4–6* drooped   **13.** *4–6* though   *4–6* entombed   **15.** *6* Rejected
Slumber!   **16.** ☒1 *6* "But   ☒1 most!   **17.** *3 6* As   *1* "Like   *4–6* -closed
4 5 Floweret • *6* floweret   **18.** ☒1 *3 6* "My   *4–6* survey."   **19.** *6* Love,
2 3 "heard   *2 3* thought,"   **20.** *4–6* Contrived   ☒1 wile,   **21.** *4–6* whispered
22. ☒1 *6 smiles*   **23.** ☒1 *6* "To-morrow • *6* To-morrow   *4–6* altered   ☒1 mien!"
24. *4–6* ambushed   **25.** *4–6* morning   **27.** ☒1 woe!"   **28.** *6* Sleep,
29. *3–6* fluttering   **30.** *4–6* twanged   ☒1 arrow   *3 6* Love's   ☒1 string,
31. *4–6* pierced   **32.** *6* magic   **33.** ☒1 lance?   **34.** *4–6* straight   ☒1 start
35. *4–6* decked   *6* bowers   **36.** *2 3 6* Sleep   *4–6* enamoured   *4–6* moved
6 trance!   **37.** *6* Sara   *3* LOOK • *6* look   **38.** *6* eye,   ☒1 beam: **39.** *4–6* lip

⊠1 mine!   **40.** *4–6* Whispering   **42.** *3* bide   **43.** *6* image   *6* dream
45. ⊠1 "O!   ⊠1 even-tide!"

9⁺. No line-space in PR *2*, undoubtedly because line 10 heads a new page in PR *1*.

17. Erratum in PR *1*: "For Like snowdrop opening to the solar ray read *As night-clos'd Flowret to the orient ray*." C made the correction himself in his own copy (NYPL Berg Collection Copy 7).

36⁺. No line-space in PR *6*, undoubtedly because line 37 heads a new page in PR *4 5*.

112. TO THE NIGHTINGALE

A. DATE

Summer 1795? late Aug–early Sept 1795? The slightly later date is suggested by the connection between lines 18–22 and a variant of **115** *The Eolian Harp* 19–19.1.1 (see the commentary there), as well as MS 1 of **139** *The Destiny of Nations*.

B. TEXTS

1 [=**RT**]. *Poems* (1796).

2. Poems (1803).

The two texts differ only in line 12 and in matters of punctuation. The RT gives PR *1* exactly.

title. *1* EFFUSION XXIII. I *TO THE NIGHTINGALE.* • *2* TO THE I *NIGHTINGALE.*   **8.** *2* Queen   **12.** *2* I have   **23.** *2* sweet

113. ADAPTATION OF
CHARLES LAMB'S SONNET
"WAS IT SOME SWEET DEVICE
OF FAERY LAND...?"

A. DATE

Aug 1795–late Feb 1796. C might have had a copy of CL's original in his possession any time from c Nov 1794 onwards. MS 1 below might have been prepared for Cottle any time between Aug 1795 and late Feb 1796. C seems to have introduced his changes at this time.

B. TEXTS

1. HRC MS (Coleridge, S T) Works B. Single leaf, 18.8×32.4 cm; wm Britannia in large oval; chain-lines 2.5 cm. Transcript in C's hand, which served as copy for PR *1* below. Subscribed "C.L." (the first of three poems, all subscribed thus). The same page contains another sonnet by CL which C rewrote (poem **114**); and there are two sonnets (the first being poem **104** above) on the verso. Bound into Rugby Manuscript p 43/f 18ʳ.

1 [=**RT**]. *Poems* (1796).
Signed "C. L."

2. Sonnets from Various Authors (1796).
Signed "CHARLES LAMB."

C. GENERAL NOTE

CL's version of his own sonnet is given in vol I headnote.

title. 1 *1* EFFUSION 11 • *2* SONNET XII.

1 ☐   Was it some sweet Device of faery land
2 ☐   That mock'd my steps with many a lonely glade,
3 ☐   And fancied wand'rings with a fair-hair'd Maid?
4 ☐   Have these Things been? Or did the wizard Wand
5 ☐   Of Merlin wave, impregning vacant air,
6 1   ~~Lightning~~ And kindle up ~~a fondly *vision'd*~~ the Vision of a Smile
   1 2 ←—And—→   ←———the———→
7 1   In those blue eyes, that ~~sti~~ seem'd to speak the while
   1 2   seem'd
8 ☐   Such tender things, as might enforce Despair
9 ☐   To drop the murth'ring knife, and let go by
10 ☐   His fell resolve?—Ah me! the lonely glade
11 ☐   Still courts the footsteps of the fair-hair'd Maid,
12 ☐   Among whose locks the west-winds love to sigh:
13 ☐   But I forlorn do wander, reckless where,
14 ☐   And mid my wand'rings find no ANNA there!

title. *1* EFFUSION XI.   **1.** *1 2* device   **3.** *1 2* maid?   **4.** *1 2* things
1 2 wand   **6.** *1* vision • *2 vision   1 2* smile   **10.** *1 2* resolve? Ah
11. *1 2* maid,

2–3, 6–7, 10–11, 13–14. Indented in PR *2*.

114. ADAPTATION OF
CHARLES LAMB'S SONNET
"METHINKS, HOW DAINTY SWEET IT WERE"

A. DATE

Aug 1795–late Feb 1796. MS 1 below might have been prepared for Cottle any time between Aug 1795 and late Feb 1796. Other poems were demonstrably revised as copy was prepared, and changes might have been introduced at this time. On the other hand, the poem might have been in C's possession, and changes made, any time from c Nov 1794 onwards.

B. TEXTS

1. HRC MS (Coleridge, S T) Works B. Single leaf, 18.8×32.4 cm; wm Britannia in large oval; chain-lines 2.5 cm. Transcript in C's hand, which served as copy for PR *1* below. Subscribed "C. L." (the second of three poems, all subscribed thus). The same page contains another sonnet by CL which C rewrote (poem **113**); and there are two sonnets (the first being poem **104**) on the verso. Bound into Rugby Manuscript p 43/f 18ʳ.

1 [=RT]. *Poems* (1796).
Signed "C. L."

C. GENERAL NOTE

CL's version of his own sonnet is given in vol I headnote.

The words in the two texts of the poem are identical: the only differences are two capital letters and an italicised word. The RT reproduces PR *1* exactly (and therefore the readings of the earlier MS 1 are, exceptionally, given as variants in the four discrepancies recorded below).

title. 1 EFFUSION 12ᵗʰ • *1* EFFUSION XII.   **3.** 1 he   **5.** 1 Maid!
8. 1 Shade.   **9.** *1 fancied*

115. THE EOLIAN HARP: COMPOSED
AT CLEVEDON, SOMERSETSHIRE

A. DATE

Aug–Oct 1795; also Feb (?) 1796. The date given in earlier versions of the title is misleading, and applies to the first version of the poem only. Sunday 20 Aug is perhaps the date on which the Clevedon cottage was chosen, in anticipation of C's marriage on 4 Oct, and the short initial ms version celebrates this occasion.

The poem was expanded either very soon afterwards, in late Aug–Oct 1795, or after an interval (perhaps again) in Feb 1796. One set of mss suggests that the entire process of expansion took place in the earlier period, while the mss which supplied copy for the first printed version suggest that it occurred later. Either way, the major developments in the evolution of the poem were at the ms stage, although C continued undecided over whether to include certain ideas and emotions he had entertained.

B. TEXTS

1. HRC MS (Coleridge, S T) Works B. Single leaf, 15.95×20.00 cm; no wm; chain-lines (horizontal) 2.5 cm; verso blank. Transcript of a short version in C's hand, headed "Effusion 35. | Clevedon, August 20th, 1795." Bound into Rugby Manuscript p 61/f 26^r.

This is probably the copy which C first submitted for inclusion in the volume that Cottle was printing.

2. Haverford College Library Charles Roberts Autograph Letters Collection, 115. Single leaf, 20.5×16.5 cm; wm (fragmentary) Britannia (?) in small oval; chain-lines (horizontal) 2.5 cm; verso blank. Revised version of the same text in C's hand, headed "Effusion 35 | Composed August 20th—Clevedon, Somersetshire." There is a facsimile in Barbara Rosenbaum and Pamela White *Index of English Literary Manuscripts* IV (*1800–1900*) pt 1 (Arnold–Gissing) (1982) pl 14.

C has written "Unfinish'd" at the end; alongside of which is written "Autograph of | S. T. Coleridge | Joseph Cottle". Cottle has also numbered it at the head 104 (MSS 1 and 3 being numbered 103 and 105 respectively).

3. HRC MS (Coleridge, S T) Works B. Two leaves: the first, 19.45×24.30 cm (trimmed at bottom edge); wm GP&J; chain-lines (vertical) 2.5 cm; written on both sides; the second, 19.65×31.65 cm; wm Britannia in oval, surmounted by crown; chain-lines (vertical) 2.55 cm; verso blank. Transcript of an expanded version in C's hand, with numerous cancellations, headed simply "Effusion". The last two pages (lines 23b.1–64 below) printed with facsimile in

Autograph Poetry in the English Language ed P. J. Croft (2 vols 1973) II 97–8. Bound into Rugby Manuscript pp 63–5/ff 27ʳ–28ʳ.

This ms might predate mid-Sept, when C left the proofs of the printed version at Stowey, if ELG's dating of *CL* I No 92 is correct. If it does, C probably provided copy for the beginning of the poem as printed in sig G of *Poems* (1796)—viz down to and including line 8—the printed text differing thereafter according to MSS 3 and 4. *CL* I No 92 might, however, date from Feb 1796.

4. Cornell WORDSWORTH Bd Cottle. Single leaf, 19.7×24.0 cm (trimmed at bottom edge); wm Britannia; chain-lines (vertical) 2.6 cm; written on both sides, much reworked on verso. Unheaded transcript apparently deriving from MS 3, but reworked towards the first published form (lacking only five lines), in C's hand. Endorsed "(Coleridge. J. C.)" in Cottle's hand. The leaf is accompanied by two related scraps, here designated 4* and 4†. 4* measures 15.9×6.2 cm; no wm; chain-lines (horizontal) 2.6 cm; verso blank. 4† measures 15.9×11.1 cm; wm Britannia; chain-lines (horizontal) 2.6 cm; written on both sides; endorsed "Coleridge. J. C." in Cottle's hand. The three pieces are inserted loosely into Joseph Cottle's Album, between ff 14 and 15.

The paper is the same as that used throughout the Cottle Album. Though 4* and 4† were not acquired by Cornell until 1966 (see Sotheby's Sale 20 Jul 1965 lot 802), they fit together and otherwise correspond, making up an Album page conjugate with 4. C perhaps began to transcribe this later version of his poem in the Album, tore out the page and trimmed it as he reworked, and at the same time used portions of the detached conjoint leaf to make fair copies of his reworking. Cottle says that C read the poem on the occasion following his visit to Clevedon on 7 Oct (*Rem* 41, 63), and the Album version might date from this time, in mid or late October. If it does, it adds to the likelihood that the major expansion of the poem took place in Aug–Oct 1795. It is none the less possible that C inscribed the lines as late as Feb 1796.

5. HRC MS (Coleridge, S T) Works B. Single leaf, 19.5×32.4 cm; countermark small crown over GR; chain-lines (vertical) 2.5 cm; written on both sides. Transcript in C's hand, headed with the description "Serenely brilliant (such should Wisdom be.) | the end of the [?]sixth sheet | the seventh to proceed." Bound into Rugby Manuscript pp 69–70/f 30ʳ ᵛ.

The evidence of the direction at the head, and the fact that the ms presents a clean text of the readings arrived at in MS 4, with the additional five lines as printed, show that it provided copy for the continuation of the poem on sig H (p 97) in PR *1*. It could be referred to in C's undated letter to Cottle published in *CL* I 162–3. (ELG dates the letter Oct 1795; it could be as late as Feb 1796.)

5*. HRC MS (Coleridge, S T) Works B. Verso of part of a single leaf, 19.5× 18.5 cm; wm GR in circle; chain-lines 2.5 cm. Note for the poem, evidently transcribed after the text of PR *1* was set, perhaps in Mar 1796 (cf *CL* I 193: to J. Cottle [late Mar 1796]). The verso and recto contain other notes besides; the transcription of the French is in a noticeably careful hand. Bound into Rugby Manuscript p 52/f 22ᵛ.

1. Poems (1796).
Both proof copies—Cottle's own (BM Ashley 408—*JDC facsimile* 77) and that given to MH (Alexander Turnbull Library, Wellington, New Zealand)— annotate the note extracted from Mme Roland.

2. Poems (1797).
Four copies contain C's ms corrections to this poem: W. L. Bowles's (in the possession of Erwin Schwarz, 1982); William Roskilly's (in the possession of J.C.C. Mays, 1999); Thomas Hutchinson's (in the possession of Jonathan Wordsworth, 1980); and RS's (Yale In 678 797 Copy 1). The last also contains an initialled comment (given in vol I headnote).

3. Poems (1803).

4. SL (1817).
It should be noted that the present poem is the only one from PR *1* included in this volume. Three copies contain ms corrections by C: Francis Wrangham's (?) (sold at Christie's 13 Jun 1979); an untraced copy of which I have only two photocopied pages (133 and 176), acquired by George Whalley; and HNC's (HUL *AC 85 L 8605 Zy 817c).
For some reason, C has numbered every 5th line in Wrangham's (?) copy, making allowance for his ms addition of the "One Life" passage. This copy also contains a comment (given in vol I headnote).
There are further corrections in the following copies: TP's (Brown PR 4478 A1 1817 Koopman Collection); Martha Fricker's (HUL Lowell *EC8 C6795 817s); an uninscribed copy (Yale In C678 817s Copy 2); WW's (Cornell WORDSWORTH PR 4480 S5 1817 copy 1); William Hood's (Columbia X 825 C67 W3 1817); and the emended part copy (HUL *EC8 C6795 817s (D)). These are all in AG's and JG's hands, not C's, and merely copy out the passage given in the printed errata (apparently via the the annotated copy of which I have two photocopied pages). They are not recorded here.
Rpt *Spirit of Contemporary Poetry* (3 vols Boston, Mass 1827) I 17–19.

*4*ᵉʳʳ. Erratum to lines 26–33 included in PR *4*.

5 [=RT]. *PW* (1828).
Printer's copy for this poem may have been provided by a corrected copy of sigs G4–O3 of PR *4* (HUL *EC8 C6795 817s (D)), the corrections in this instance being in JG's hand. There is a single minor correction in the annotated copy at the Fitzwilliam Museum, Cambridge (Marlay Bequest 1912).

6. PW (1829).

7. PW (1834).

Tempt to repeat the wrong!   And now, its strings
Boldlier swept, the long sequacious notes
Over delicious surges sink and rise,
Such a soft floating witchery of sound
As twilight Elfins make, when they at eve
Voyage on gentle gales from Fairy-Land,
Where Melodies round honey-dropping flowers,
Footless and wild, like birds of Paradise,
ɤ ˅ ˅   Nor pause, nor perch, hovering on untamed wing!
~~Methinks, it should have been impossible~~
~~Not to love all things in a world like this,~~
~~Where even the breezes, and the common air,~~
~~Contain the power and spirit of Harmony!~~

And thus, my love! as on the midway slope
Of yonder hill I stretch my limbs at noon,
Whilst thro' my half-closed eye-lids I behold
The sunbeams dance, like diamonds, on the main,
And tranquil muse upon tranquillity;
Full many a thought uncall'd and undetain'd,
And many idle flitting phantasies,
Traverse my indolent and passive brain,
As wild and various as the random gales
˅˅˅ *Insert*   That swell and flutter on this subject lute!

O the one Life within us, and abroad,
Which meets all Motion and becomes its soul,
A Light in Sound, a sound-like power in Light,
Rythm in all Thoughts, and Joyance every where,—
Methinks, it should have been impossible
Not to love all things in a World so filled
Where the breeze warbles, and the mute still air
Is Music slumbering on its instrument!

1(*a*). Page 176 of *Sibylline Leaves* (1817) corrected by Anne Gillman

Tempt to repeat the wrong ! And now, its strings
Boldlier swept, the long sequacious notes
Over delicious surges sink and rise,
Such a soft floating witchery of sound
As twilight Elfins make, when they at eve
Voyage on gentle gales from Fairy-Land,
Where Melodies round honey-dropping flowers,
Footless and wild, like birds of Paradise,
Nor pause, nor perch, hovering on untamed wing!
Methinks, it should have been impossible
Not to love all things in a world like this,
Where even the breezes, and the common air,
Contain the power and spirit of Harmony.

And thus, my love ! as on the midway slope
Of yonder hill I stretch my limbs at noon,
Whilst thro' my half-closed eye-lids I behold
The sunbeams dance, like diamonds, on the main,
And tranquil muse upon tranquillity ;
Full many a thought uncall'd and undetain'd,
And many idle flitting phantasies,
Traverse my indolent and passive brain,
As wild and various as the random gales
That swell and flutter on this subject lute !

Insert

O the one Life within us, and abroad,
Which meets all Motion and becomes its soul,
A Light in Sound, a sound-like power in Light,
Rhythm in all Thought, and Joyance every where—
Methinks, it should have been impossible
Not to love all things in a World so fill'd
Where the breeze warbles, and the mute still Air
Is Music slumb'ring on its instrument !

1(*b*). Page 176 of *Sibylline Leaves* (1817) corrected by James Gillman

Tempt to repeat the wrong! And now, its strings
Boldlier swept, the long sequacious notes
Over delicious surges sink and rise,
Such a soft floating witchery of sound
As twilight Elfins make, when they at eve
Voyage on gentle gales from Fairy-Land,
Where Melodies round honey-dropping flowers,
Footless and wild, like birds of Paradise,
Nor pause, nor perch, hovering on untamed wing!
~~Methinks, it should have been impossible~~
~~Not to love all things in a world like this,~~
~~Where even the breezes, and the common air,~~
~~Contain the power and spirit of Harmony.~~

And thus, my love! as on the midway slope
Of yonder hill I stretch my limbs at noon,
Whilst thro' my half-closed eye-lids I behold
The sunbeams dance, like diamonds, on the main,
And tranquil muse upon tranquillity;
Full many a thought uncall'd and undetain'd,
And many idle flitting phantasies,
Traverse my indolent and passive brain,
As wild and various as the random gales
That swell and flutter on this subject lute!

Insert:

O the one Life within us, and abroad,
Which meets all motion and becomes its soul,
A Light in Sound, a sound-like power in Light,
Rhythm in all Thought, and Joyance every where —
Methinks, it should have been impossible
Not to love all things in a world so fill'd;
Where the Breeze warbles, and the mute still Air
Is Music slumbering on its instrument!

1(*c*). Page 176 of *Sibylline Leaves* (1817) corrected by Coleridge

title. 1 Effusion 35 | Clevedon, August 20th, 1795. • 2 Effusion 35 | Composed
August 20th—Clevedon, Somersetshire. • 3 Effusion • *1* EFFUSION XXXV. |
COMPOSED | *AUGUST* 20*th*, 1795, | AT CLEVEDON, SOMERSETSHIRE. •
2 3 COMPOSED at *CLEVEDON,* | *SOMERSETSHIRE.* • *4–7 THE EOLIAN
HARP.* | *Composed at Clevedon, Somersetshire.*

1	⊠5	My pensive SARA! thy soft Cheek reclin'd
2	1	Thus on my arm, how soothing sweet it is
	2	~~mine~~ my most
	3 4	my
	1–7	mine
3	1 2	Beside our Cot to sit, our Cot o'ergrown
	⊠1 2 5	To sit beside our Cot,
4	1	With white-flowr'd Jasmine and the blossom'd Myrtle
	2	~~an~~ the broad-leav'd
	⊠1 2 5	the
5	⊠5 *3*	(Meet emblems they of Innocence & Love!)
6	⊠4 5	And watch the Clouds, that late were rich with light,
	4	~~mark~~ watch
7	⊠1 5	Slow-sad'ning round, and mark the Star of eve
8.1	1	Serenely brilliant, like thy polish'd Sense,
9.1	1	Shine opposite. What snatches of perfume
10.1	1	The noiseless ~~Breeze~~ Gale from yonder bean-field ~~walfts,~~ wafts!
11.1	1	The stilly Murmur of the far-off Sea
12.1	1	Tells us of Silence! And behold, my love!
13.1	1	In the half-closed w[e]indow we will place the Harp,
14.1	1	Which by the desultory ~~wind~~ Breeze caress'd,
15.1	1	Like some coy Maid half willing to be woo'd,
16.1	1	Utters such sweet Upbraidings, as perforce
17a.1	1	Tempt to repeat the wrong!
8.2	2	Serenely brilliant (such should Wisdom be)
9.2	2	Shine opposite! What snatches of Perfume
10.2	2	The noiseless Gale from yonder bean-field wafts!
11.2	2	The still⟨y⟩ murmur of the far-off Sea
12.2	2	Tell? ~~ins~~ us of Silence! ~~Hark!~~ And the Harp, my Love
13.2	2	~~Which~~ Plac'd sideways in the half-clos'd Casement, ~~plaed~~ harks!
14.2	2	~~And~~ How by the desultory Breeze caress'd
15.2	2	? ~~With~~ Like some coy Maid half-yielding to her Lover,
16.2	2	~~Utter~~ It pours such sweet upbraidings, as ~~porerf⟨e⟩orce~~
17a.2	2	Tempt to repeat the wrong!
8	⊠1 2 5 *3*	Serenely brilliant (such should WISDOM be!)
9	⊠1 2	Shine opposite. How exquisite the Scents
10	⊠1 2	Snatch'd from yon Bean-field! And the World *so* hush'd!
11	3 4	The stilly murmur of the far-off Sea
	⊠1–4 *3*	distant
	3	Hark! the still
12	⊠1 2 *3*	Tells us of Silence! And that simplest Lute
	3	th' Eolian
13	⊠1 2 *3*	Plac'd lengthways in the clasping ₵casement, hark!

14	☒1 2	How by the desultory Breeze caress'd,
15	☒1 2	⟨(Like some coy Maid half-yielding to her Lover)⟩
16	3–5 *1–4*	It pours such sweet Upbraidings, as must needs
	5–7	upbraiding,
17	☒1 2	Tempt to repeat the Wrong.—And now its strings
18	☒1 2	Boldlier swept, the long sequacious Notes
19	☒1 2	Over delicious Surges sink and rise
19.1.1	3 4	In aëry voyage, Music such as erst
19.1.2	3	Round rosy bowers (so Legendaries tell)
20.1	3	To sleeping Maids came floating witchingly
22.1	3	By wand'ring West winds stoln from Faery land,
23a.1	3	Where on some magic Hybla MELODIES
23.1.1	3	————————⟨ambrosial⟩————————
23b.1	3	Round many a newborn honey-dropping Flower
20	4* 5 *1–7*	Such a soft floating Witchery of sound
21	4* 5 *1 2 4–7*	As twilight Elfins make, when they at eve
22	4* 5 *1 2 4–7*	Voyage on gentle gales from Faëry Land.
22.2	4	~~Might~~ Would wand'ring Winds have stoln ~~from Faëry Land,~~
23	4	Where MELODIES, ~~like Birds of Paradise~~ round honey-dropping
		Flowers
	5 1 2 4–7	←———round———→
24	3 *5 1 2 4–7*	Footless and wild, like Birds of Paradise,
	4	~~round honey dropping flowers,~~ like Birds of Paradise,
25	3	Nor pause nor perch, warbling on untir'd wing.
	4	untam'd
	5 1 2 4–7	hov'ring
26	*4*err *5–7*	O! the one Life, within us and abroad,
27	*4*err *5–7*	Which meets all Motion, and becomes its soul,
28	*4*ell *5–7*	A Light in Sound, a sound-like power in Light,
29	*4*err *5–7*	Rhythm in all Thought, and Joyance every where—
30	*3–7*	Methinks, it should have been impossible
31	*3 4*	Not to love all things in a World like this,
	*4*err *5–7*	so fill'd,
32	*3*	Where e'en the Breezes of the simple Air
	4	and the common
	*4*err *5–7*	the breeze warbles mute still
33	*3*	Possess the power and Spirit of Melody!
	4	Contain Harmony.
	*4*err	Is Music slumbering on its instrument.
	5–7	her
		[*Line-space*]
34	☒1 2	And thus, my Love! as on the midway Slope
35	☒1 2	Of yonder Hill I stretch my limbs at noon
36	☒1–4	While thro' my half clos'd Eyelids I behold
37	☒1–4	The sunbeams dance, like diamonds, on the Main,
38	☒1 2	And tranquil muse upon Tranquillity,
39	☒1 2	~~Ful~~ Full many a Thought uncall'd and undetain'd—
40	☒1 2	And many idle flitting Phantasies

41	3	Traverse my idolent and passive Mind
	⊠1–3	Brain
42	3	As wild, as various, as the random Gales
	4	wild~~ly~~/ and
	⊠1–4	wild and
43	3–5 *1–3*	That swell or flutter on this subject Lute.
	4–7	and
44	3 4	And what if All of animated Life
	⊠1–4	nature
45	3	~~But to~~ Be but as Instruments diversly fram'd
	4	Be ~~as~~ but organic Harps ~~fram'd~~ strung
	⊠1–4	but fram'd,
46	3	←——That——→ tremble into thought, while thro' them breathes
	4	~~That Which~~ That as ~~thro' them breathes,~~
		o'er them sweeps,
	⊠1–4	←——That——→ ←———o'er———→
47	3	One infinite and intellectual Breeze?
	4	~~One infinite and~~ Plastic and vast, one
	⊠1–4	←———Plastic———→
47.1.1.	3	~~And all i~~ In diff'rent ~~stations~~ Heights so aptly ~~plac'd~~ hung, ~~that All~~
47.1.2	3	~~So that the low For~~ In half-heard Murmurs and loud ~~Bursts~~ sublime,
47.1.3	3	Shrill Discords and most soothing Melodies
47.1.4	3	~~Creation's~~ Raise one great ~~harmonious Concert form'd~~ Concert
47.1.5	3	Thus God, the only universal Soul,
47.1.6	3	~~Organiz'd Body~~ Mechaniz'd Matter ~~is~~ the ~~Instrument~~ Organic Harps,
47.1.7	3	And each one's Tunes are that, which each calls I—
47.2.1	3	⟨And all⟩ In different Heights so aptly hung, ~~that all~~
47.2.2	3	~~In~~ That Murmurs indistinct and Bursts sublime,
47.2.3	3	Shrill Discords and most soothing Melodies,
47.2.4	3	Harmonious from Creation's vast concért?
47.2.5	3	Thus GOD would be the universal Soul,
47.2.6	3	~~And m~~ matter Mmechaniz'd ⟨as⟩ th*é* organic harps,
47.2.7	3	And each one's Tunes be that, which each calls **I**.—
47.3.1	4	~~That sweeps the Instruments, it éŕŕł had's passage fram'd,~~
48	⊠1–3	At once the Soul of each, and God of All?
		[*Line-space*]
49	3	But thy more serious Look a mild Reproof
	⊠1–3	Eye
50	3	Darts, O beloved Woman! and thy words
	4† 5 *1–7*	nor such Thoughts
51.1	3	Pious and calm check these unhallow'd Thoughts,
55.1	3	These shapings of the unregen'rate Soul,
56.1	3	Bubbles, that glitter as they rise & break
57.1	3	On vain Philosophy's aye-bubbling Spring!
52.1	3	Thou biddest me walk humbly with my God!
53.1	3	Meek Daughter in the family of Christ,
54.1	3	Wisely thou sayest, and holy are thy words!
51	4† 5 *1–7*	Dim and unhallow'd dost thou not reject,
52	4† 5 *1–7*	And biddest me walk humbly with my God.

[*Line-space*]

53 4† 5 *1–7*	Meek Daughter in the Family of Christ,
54 4† 5 *1–7*	Well hast thou said and holily disprais'd
55 4† 5 *1–7*	These Shapings of the unregen'rate Mind,
56 4† 5 *1–7*	Bubbles that glitter as they rise and break
57 4† 5 *1–7*	On vain Philosophy's aye-babbling Spring.
58 3	Nor may I unblam'd or speak or think of Him,
4†	⋈For never guiltless may I
⊠ 1–4†	For speak
59 3 4† 5 *1–7*	Th' INCOMPREHENSIBLE! save when with ⋈Awe
60 3 4† 5 *1–7*	I praise ⟨him,⟩ and with Faith that inly feels,
60fn 5* *1–3*	L'athee n'est point a mes yeux un faux esprit; je puis vivre avec lui aussi bien et mieux qu'avec le devot, car il raisonne davantage, mais il lui manque un sens, et mon ame ne se fond point entierement avec la sienne; il est froid au spectacle le [?]plus ravissant, et il cherche un syllogisme lorsque je rends une action de grace. 5
	Appel a l'impartiale posteritè postérité, par la Citoyenne Roland troisieme partie. p. 113.
61 3 4† 5 *1–7*	Who with his saving Mercies healed me,
62 3 4† 5 *1–7*	A sinful and most miserable Man
63 3 4† 5 *1–7*	Wilder'd and dark, and gave me to possess
64 3 4†	PEACE and this COT, and THEE, my best-belov'd!
5 *1–7*	heart-honor'd Maid!

title. *5–7* THE EOLIAN HARP. | COMPOSED AT CLEVEDON, SOMERSETSHIRE.   **1.** *4–7* Sara! *1–7* cheek *4–7* reclined   **3.** *1–7* cot, *1–7* cot *1–3* oe'r grown   **4.** 2–4 *1–4* -flower'd • *5–7* -flowered 2 3 *1–6* Jasmin, • 4 Jasmin • 7 jasmin, *3* broad leav'd • *5–7* broad-leaved *1–6* Myrtle, • 7 myrtle, **5.** 2–4 Emblems 3 *1* 2 4–7 and   **6.** *1–7* clouds, 2 4 Light,   **7.** *4–7* Slow 3 ~~sadning~~ sadd'ning • 4 sad'ning • *5–7* saddening *1–7* star 3 ~~Eve~~ eve • 4 Eve **8.** 5 *1* Wisdom • 2 4–7 wisdom 4 *1* 2 4–7 be)   **9.** *1–7* opposite! *1–7* scents **10.** *5–7* Snatched 5 beanfield! • *1–7* bean-field! *1–7* and *1–7* world *4–7* so *5–7* hushed!   **11.** 5 Murmur 5 ⋈Sea • *3* 7 sea   **12.** 4 Silence— • 5 *1* 2 4– 6 Silence. • 7 silence. *4–6* Lute, • 7 lute,   **13.** *4–7* Placed *1* 2 4–7 length-ways 4 5 *1* 2 4–7 casement,   **14.** 4 *1–7* breeze *5–7* caressed,   **15.** 4 5 *1–7* Like 4 ~~eoy~~ coy *4–7* maid *4–7* half yielding 4 4–7 lover, • 5 *1–3* Lover,   **16.** 4 *1–* 4 upbraidings,   **17.** 4 *1–7* wrong! • 5 wrong. *1–7* And *1–7* now,   **18.** *1–* 7 notes   **19.** 4 5 *1–7* surges 4 & 4 5 *1* 3–7 rise,   **20.** *1–7* witchery 5 Sound • *3* sound—   **22.** 5 Gales 5 Faery-Land, • *1* 2 Faery Land, • *4–7* Fairy-Land,   **23.** 5 MELODIES • *1* 2 *Melodies* • *4–7* Melodies *1* 2 flowers • *4–7* flowers, **24.** *1* 2 4–7 birds   **25.** *4–7* pause, 4 perch *4–7* hovering *4–7* untamed 4 4–7 wing!   **26.** *5–7* O *5–7* life   **27.** *5–7* motion   **28.** *5–7* light *5–7* sound, *5–7* light   **29.** *5–7* thought, *5–7* joyance   **31.** *4–7* world *5–7* filled;   **32.** *4* even 4 breezes, *5–7* warbles, 4 5 air, • 6 7 air   **33.** *4* spirit **34.** *4–7* love! 4 *1–7* slope   **35.** *1–7* hill 5 2–7 noon,   **36.** *1–7* Whilst *5–7* through 5 *1–3* -clos'd • *4–7* -closed *1–3* eyelids • *4–7* eye-lids   **37.** *1–* 7 main,   **38.** 4 tranquillity, • 5 *1–7* tranquillity;   **39.** 4 5 *1–7* Full *1–7* thought *5–7* uncalled 4 *1–4* undetain'd, • 5 undetain'd • *5–7* undetained,   **40.** 4 Fantasies, • 5 ⋈Phantasies, • *1–7* phantasies,   **41.** *1* brain • 2–7 brain,   **42.** 2–7 various

4 5 *1–7* gales   **43.** 4 5 *1–3* Lute! • *4–7* lute!   **44.** 4 *1–7* all   **45.** *4–7* harps
5 *5–7* diversely   *3* fram'd • *5–7* framed,   **46.** *4–7* sweeps   **47.** 4 Breeze •
1–3 5 Breeze, • *4–7* breeze,   **48.** 5 All?— • *1 3* all? • *2* all?—   **49.** *1–7* eye
4 5 *1–7* reproof   **50.** *4–7* woman! 5 *1–7* thoughts   **51.** *5–7* unhallowed
53. *4–7* daughter *4–7* family 5 *4–7* Christ!   **54.** 5 said, *5–7* dispraised
55. *1–7* shapings 5 *1–7* unregenerate *1–4* mind, • *5–7* mind;   **56.** 5 [?]Bubbles
5 glitter,   **57.** 5 *1–7* spring.   **58.** 4† *think* *4–7* him,   **59.** *5–7* The *4–*
7 Incomprehensible! 4 Awe • 5 *1–7* awe   **60.** 4† him • 5 *1–7* him, 5 *3* faith
5 *2 3 feels*; • *1 feels;* • *4–7* feels;   **60fn1.** *1–3* athée *1–3* à   **60fn2.** *1–3* dévot,
60fn3–4. *1–3* entièrement   **60fn4.** *1 2* sienne: *1–3* plus   **60fn5.** *2 3* un action
60fn6. *1–3* "Appel *1–3* postérité, 1–3 Roland,"   **60fn7.** *2 3* partic, *1–3* p. 67.
61. 4† 5 *1–7* mercies   **62.** 5 *4–6* Man, • *1–3* man • *7* man,   **63.** *5–7* Wildered
5 dark!   **64.** 4† 5 *1–3* P E A C E, • *4–7* Peace, *4–6* Cot, • *7* cot, *4* Thee, • *5–7* thee,
5–7 -honoured

title. In the PR *1* list of contents the title is given as "Effusion 35, written at Cleveden,".

5. C deleted the line in Thomas Hutchinson's copy of PR 2.

10.1. The uncertainty over the spelling of "waft" is likewise evident in a fragment related to lines 19–25 in the Gutch Notebook (*CN* I 51 q vol I 19–25EC). The fragment dates from before 20 Aug 1795.

9.2. The beginning of the line is marked in MS 2, and an indecipherable comment written alongside in the LH margin. The comment refers to to the changed lines that follow, or to their replacement by the MS 3 version.

8. C deleted the line in Thomas Hutchinson's copy of PR 2.

12. C indicated a new paragraph with "And" in RS's copy of PR 2. PR *4–7* begin a new paragraph at this point.

19–19.1.1a. This line and a half coincides with the beginning of a five-line fragment preserved at Cornell (uncatalogued in 1980):

> Which o'er delicious Surges sink and rise
> In aery voyage, tho' they sweeter be
> Than sad airs from a white-arm'd Lady's Lute,
> What time the Languishment of lonely Love
> Melts in her eye, and heaves her breast of snow—

The fragment has been cut from the bottom of a page and measures 16.9×5.5 cm; no wm; chain-lines (horizontal) 2.7 cm; verso blank. It has nothing in common with other mss of *The Eolian Harp*. It would fit over lines 22.2–25 in MS 4, which did once have something glued over them. (At present it has traces of grey paper on the verso, as if it had been glued into an album at some stage.) However, it may instead be connected with **112** *To the Nightingale*, with which it also has lines in common (see lines 18–22); but unless mss of that poem are recovered, the question must remain open.

19.1.1. The line has been deleted in MS 4, subsequent lines have been trimmed away, and a (missing) replacement has been keyed in.

23.1.1. The line, and perhaps others following, has been deleted and trimmed away at the foot of the page in MS 3. Only the insertion above the line remains.

21–5. C marked the lines in RS's copy of PR 2, and added:

This passage was altered in the 3rd Edition, but whether for the better, I doubt.

> Such a soft floating witchery of Sound—
> Methinks it should have been impossible
> Not to love all things in a World like this
> Where even the breezes and the common air
> Contain the power & Spirit of Harmony
> And thus, &c (omitting the 5 lines marked)

22.2–25. These four heavily revised lines are deleted in MS 4.

23–5. In the errata list for PR 2 in DW's hand which C sent to Cottle c 3 Jul 1797 he told him: "Scratch out these three lines" (*CL* I 331). Cottle ignored the direction. C deleted them himself in the copy of PR 2 he gave to Bowles, ending line 22 with an exclamation-mark; and again in Roskilly's copy, where he ended line 22 with a full stop. In RS's copy of PR 2, after making the substitution described above (on 21–5), he ended line 25 with an exclamation-mark.

26–33. The erratum in PR 4 is introduced with "from the 9th [=26th] line r. as follows:". C deleted lines 30–3 and made the substitution given in PR 4's erratum in his own hand both in Wrangham's copy and in the copy of which I have two photocopied pages. There are variations in capitalisation and punctuation, and line 31 in Wrangham's (?) copy reads "~~like this~~ so fill'd". C supplied caret-marks before line 30 in HNC's copy of PR 4, with the marginal instruction "Read from ERRATA." The erratum correction is made in JG's hand in the emended part copy of PR 4 used as copy for PR 5 (with "around" for "abroad" in line 26).

28. C added a comma at the end of the line in the Fitzwilliam copy of PR 5.

33+. No line-space in PR 2–4. C indicated insertion of a space in RS's (?) copy of PR 2.

43+. C indicated a line-space in RS's (?) copy of PR 2. This is given in PR 4–7.

44–8. Quoted in *P Lects* lect 13 (1949) 371; see vol I EC for the context; also in Notebook 37 (=BM Add MS 47532) f 28ᵛ.

44–7. Quoted with variations in punctuation and capitalisation in a letter to John Thelwall of 31 Dec 1796 (PML MA 77 (6); *CL* I 294). Some of C's comments are given in vol I headnote and 44–7EC.

47–8. The question of "one Breeze of Life—at once the soul of each & God of all?" is raised in a Malta note dated 13 Dec 1804 (*CN* II 2330).

47.1.1–7. The seven heavily revised lines in MS 3 are deleted, and the catchword "Breeze" (line 47) written underneath.

47.2.6. The words "matter" and "mechaniz'd" are marked for transposition.

48+. No line-space in TEXTS 5 *1–3*. C indicated one in RS's copy of PR 2.

52+. No line-space in PR 2–7. JG indicated one in the emended part copy of PR 4.

60fn. Printed at the end of the volume in PR *1*, with the cross-reference "Note 10.— Page 99.", and at the foot of the page in PR 2 3.

The extant proof copies of PR *1* differ slightly—dropping accents and reading "une actione". C has written in the margin of Cottle's copy: "Mr Cottle will carefully compare this with the Copy." and in the margin of the MH's copy he has drawn a line.

C transcribed the note from Marie Jean (Philipon) Roland de la Platière *Appel a l'impartiale postérité* (3 vols Paris 1795) II 113, dropping accents and changing the punctuation slightly. It is clear that Cottle followed his instructions, and went back to the original. The book was current reading in the circle of C's friends: see *Poole* I 167; *S Life* (CS) I 316–17; *WL* (*E* rev) 166. C read French only slowly at the time (*CL* I 260:

to J. Thelwall 19 Nov 1796), and perhaps owed the quotation to Thomas Beddoes (see *Watchman—CC—*23n). A translation and further gloss are given in vol I EC.

116. ODE TO SARA, WRITTEN AT SHURTON BARS, NEAR BRIDGEWATER, IN ANSWER TO A LETTER FROM BRISTOL

A. DATE

All titles state Sept 1795. C was probably at Stowey on 12 Sept, and certainly on 19 Sept. If he returned to Bristol a few days before WW left (on 25 or 26 Sept), the poem must have been written at the beginning of his vacation from Bristol, possibly 9 or 10 Sept.

B. TEXTS

1. HRC MS (Coleridge, S T) Works B. Three leaves: ff 32 and 33, 20.2× 32.6 cm; f 34, 20.1×32.5 cm; wm (ff 32 and 34) small crown surmounting GR, (f 33) Britannia in oval surmounted by crown; chain-lines (all folios) 2.5 cm. Transcript in C's hand which served as copy for PR *1* below. Bound into Rugby Manuscript pp 75–80/ff 32^r–34^v.

1*. HRC MS (Coleridge, S T) Works B. Notes for the poem in C's hand, evidently transcribed after the text of PR *1* below was set, perhaps during Mar 1796 (cf *CL* I 193: to J. Cottle [late Mar 1796]). The RH edge is imperfect, and some missing words and letters have been inserted in Joseph Cottle's hand. Bound into Rugby Manuscript p 124/f 56^v.

1. Two proof copies of PR *1* below print the first note from MS 1*, with C's revisions, and supply the second as intended. They are (A) MH's copy at the Alexander Turnbull Library, Wellington, New Zealand; and (B) Joseph Cottle's in BM Ashley 408 (*JDC facsimile* 79–82). (A) is a complete proof copy, (B) is fragmentary and bound misleadingly with other material.

1. Poems (1796).

2 [=RT]. *Poems* (1797).
RS's (?) copy (Yale In 678 797 Copy 1) contains a comment by C: see vol I 5fnEC.

3. Poems (1803).
This version omits the concluding stanza.

4. PW (1828).

5. *PW* (1829).

6. *PW* (1834).

title. Epistle 1 | Written at Shurton Bars, ⟨near Bridgewater,⟩ September 1795, in answer to a Letter from Bristol. • *1* EPISTLE I. | WRITTEN AT | SHURTON BARS, NEAR BRIDGEWATER, | *SEPTEMBER.* 1795, | IN ANSWER TO | A LETTER FROM BRISTOL. • *2 3* ODE TO SARA, | *Written at SHURTON BARS, near Bridgewater,* | SEPTEMBER, 1795, | IN ANSWER TO A LETTER | FROM BRISTOL. • *4–6* LINES | WRITTEN AT SHURTON BARS, NEAR BRIDGE- | WATER, SEPTEMBER, 1795, IN ANSWER TO | A LETTER FROM BRISTOL.   **prefatory note.** *2 3 Note.—The first Stanza alludes to a Passage in the Letter.*

1	☐	Nor travels my meand'ring Eye
2	☐	The starry wilderness on high;
3	☐	Nor now with curious sight
4	☐	I mark the Glow worm, as I pass,
5	☐	Move with "green radiance" thro' the grass,
5fn	**1***	Note ? XXI. Page 111.—The expression "green Radiance" is bor-

rowed from a Poem of Mr. Wordsworth, a Poet whose diversification
is occasionally harsh and his diction too frequently obscure: but he
is whom I deem unrivalled among the writers of the present day
in strong conceptions manly sentiment, novel imagery, and vivid   5
colouring.—His chief work is a Poem entitled "Descriptive Sketches
on of the Alps." The Reviewers have spoken with contempt of it. In
the style of Fable, which makes the inanimate "instinct with thought"
suppose ⟨that⟩ a small hollow Cylinder, thrown which had been fixed
into the midst channel of a mighty Stream, should judge of the tor-   10
rent by the Quantity of Water which passed through itself—Should
we wonder that the Cylinder should speak think contemptuously of
the Torrent?—A Gentleman near Bristol has made makes it an in-
variable rule to publish purchase every work that is violently abused
by the Reviewers: and with a few a very few exceptions I never saw   15
a be more judicious collection of recent Compositions, both in prose
and verse verse.

1* 1 2   The expression "green radiance" is borrowed from Mr. WORDS-
WORTH,
a Poet whose versification is occasionally harsh and his diction too
frequently
obscure: but whom I deem unrivalled among the writers of the pre-
sent day in
manly sentiment, novel imagery, and vivid colouring.

6	☐	An EMERALD of Light.
		[*Line-space*]
7	☐	O ever-present to my view!
8	☐	My wafted Spirit is with you,
9	☐	And soothes your boding fears:
10	☐	I see you all opprestst with gloom

11 □	Sit lonely in that cheerless Room—
12 □	Ah me! You are in tears!
	[*Line-space*]
13 □	Beloved Woman! did you fly
14 □	Chill'd Friendship's dark disliking eye,
15 □	Or Mirth's untimely din?
16 □	With cruel weight these Trifles press
17 □	A temper sore with tenderness,
18 □	When akes the Void within.
	[*Line-space*]
19 □	But why with sable wand unblest
20 □	Should Fancy rouse within my breast
21 □	Dim-visag'd Shapes of Dread?
22 □	Untenanting its beauteous Clay
23 □	My SARA's soul has wing'd its way,
24 □	And hovers round my head!
	[*Line-space*]
25 □	I felt it prompt the tender Dream,
26 □	When slowly sunk the day's last gleam;
27 □	You rous'd each gentler sense
28 1	As sighing o'er the Blossoms' bloom
1–6	Blossom's
29 □	Meek Evening wakes its soft perfume
30 □	With viewless influence.
	[*Line-space*]
31 □	And hark—my Love! The sea-breeze moans
32 □	Thro' yon reft house! O'er rolling stones
33 ⊠2 *3*	In bold ambitious sweep
2 3	With broad impetuous
34 ⊠2 *3*	The onward-surging tides supply
2 3	fast incroaching
35 □	The silence of the cloudless sky
36 □	With mimic thunders deep.
	[*Line-space*]
37 □	Dark-red'ning from the channel'd Isle
37fn 1 *1** *1–6*	The Holmes, in the Bristol Channel
38 □	(Where stands one solitary Pile
39 □	Unslated by the blast)
40 □	The Watchfire, like a sullen Star
41 □	Twinkles to many a dozing Tar
42 □	Rude-cradled on the Mast.
	[*Line-space*]
43 1	~~Ev*é*'n there*!* / beneath that Light-house Tower /~~
⊠1	Ev'n there—beneath that light-house Tower—
44 □	In the tumultuous evil hour
45 □	Ere Peace with SARA came,
46 □	Time was, I should have thought it sweet
47 □	To count the echoings of my feet,

48	☒2 *3*	And watch the storm-vext flame.
	2 3	troubled
		[*Line-space*]
49	☒*2*	And there in black soul-jaundic'd fit
	2	and jaundic'd
50	☐	A sad gloom-pamper'd Man to sit,
51	☐	And listen to the roar;
52	☐	When mountain surges bellowing deep
53	☐	With an uncouth monster Leap
54	☐	Plung'd foaming on the shore.
		[*Line-space*]
55	☐	Then by the Lightning's blaze to mark
56	☐	Some toiling tempest-shatter'd Bark;
57	☐	Her vain distress-guns hear:
58	☐	And when a second Sheet of light
59	☐	Flash'd o'er the Blackness of the night—
60	☐	To see *no* Vessel there!
		[*Line-space*]
61	☐	But Fancy now more gaily sings:
62	☐	Or if awhile she droop her wings,
63	☐	As sky-larks mid the Corn,
64	☐	On summer fields she grounds her breast;
65	☐	Th' oblivious Poppy o'er her nest
66	☐	Nods, till returning Morn.
		[*Line-space*]
67	☐	O mark those smiling Tears, that swell
68	☐	The open'd Rose! From heaven they fell,
69	☐	And with the sun beam blend.
70	☐	Blest Visitations from above,
71	☐	Such are the tender Woes of Love
72	☐	Fost'ring the heart, they bend!
		[*Line-space*]
73	☐	When stormy Midnight howling round
74	☐	Beats on our roof with clatt'ring sound,
75	☐	To me your Arms you'll stretch:
76	☐	"Great God! you'll say—"To us so kind,
77	☐	"O shelter from this loud bleak wind
78	☐	"The houseless friendless wretch!
		[*Line-space*]
79	☐	The Tears, that tremble down your cheek,
80	☐	Shall bathe my kisses, chaste and meek
81	☐	In Pity's Dew divine;
82	☐	And from your heart the Sighs that steal
83	☐	Shall make your rising bosom feel
84	☐	The answ'ring swell of mine!
		[*Line-space*]
85	☐	How oft, my Love! with shapings sweet
86	☐	I paint the moment, we shall meet!
87	☐	With eager speed I dart—

88 ☐	I seize you in the vacant air,
89 ☐	And fancy, with a Husband's Care
90 ☐	I press you to my Heart!
	[Line-space]
91 ⊠*3 6*	'Tis said, on Summer's evening hour
6	in
92 ⊠*6*	Flashes the golden-colour'd Flower
92fn⁻1 *1**	Note 13—Page 118. Print from the Encyclopædia—
92fn *1* 1 2*	LIGHT *from plants.* In Sweden a very curious phenomenon has been ob-

served on certain flowers by M. Haggern, lecturer in natural history. One evening

he preceived a faint flash of light repeatedly dart from a marigold. Surprized at

such an uncommon appearance, he resolved to examine it with attention; and, to

be assured it was no deception of the eye, he placed a man near him, with orders   5

to make a signal at the moment when he observed the light. They both saw it

constantly at the same moment. The light was most brilliant on marigolds of an orange or flame colour; but

scarcely visible on pale ones. The flash was frequently seen on the same flower two or three times in quick   10

succession; but more commonly at intervals of several minutes: and when sev-

eral flowers in the same place emitted their light together, it could be observed

at a considerable distance. This phenomenon was remarked in the months of July and August at sun-set,

and for half an hour, when the atmosphere was clear; but after a rainy day, or   15

when the air was loaded with vapours, nothing of it was seen. The following flowers emitted flashes, more or less vivid, in this order:

1. The Marigold, *galendula officinalis.*
2. Monk's-hood, *tropælum majus.*
3. The orange-lily, *lilium bulbiferum.*   20
4. The Indian pink, *tagetes patula & erecta.*

From the rapidity of the flash, and other circumstances, it may be conjectured

that there is something of electricity in this phenomenon.

93 ⊠*6*	A fair electric flame.
94 ⊠*6*	And so shall flash my love-charg'd Eye
95 ⊠*6*	When all the Heart's big ecstacy

96 ⊠6   Shoots rapid thro' the frame!

title. *3* ODE TO SARA, | *Written at SHURTON BARS, near Bridgewater,* |
September, 1795, | IN ANSWER TO A LETTER | FROM BRISTOL. •
5 LINES | WRITTEN AT SHURTON BARS, NEAR BRIDGEWATER, SEP-
TEMBER, 1795, | IN ANSWER TO A LETTER FROM BRISTOL. • *6* LINES |
WRITTEN AT SHURTON BARS, NEAR BRIDGEWATER, | SEPTEMBER, 1795, IN
ANSWER TO A LETTER | FROM BRISTOL.   **prefatory note.** *3 Note—*   **1.** *4–*
6 meandering   *1–6* eye   **4.** *1–6* glow-worm,   **5.** *4–6* through   **5fn2.** *2* harsh,
5fn3. *2* day,   **6.** *6* emerald   *6* light.   **7.** *4–6* ever present   **8.** *1–6* spirit
9. *3* fears;   **10.** *1–3* opprest • *4–6* oppressed   **11.** *1–6* room—   **12.** *3* you
14. *4–6* Chilled   **16.** *1–6* trifles   **17.** *1–3* Tenderness,   **18.** *4–6* aches
6 within   **19.** *4 5* unblessed   **20.** *6* breas   **21.** *3* Dim   *4–6* -visaged   *1–*
6 shapes   **22.** 1 *1* it's   *1–6* clay   **23.** *6* Sara's   *4–6* winged   1 *1 2* it's
25. *6* dream,   **26.** *6* sank   **27.** *4–6* roused   *6* sense,   **28.** *6* blossom's
3 -bloom   **29.** 1 *1 2* it's   **31.** *1–6* hark,   **32.** *4–6* Through   **33.** *6* sweep,
37. *4–6* Dark reddening   *4–6* channelled   **37fn.** *1* * *1–6* Channel.   **38.** *1–6* pile
40. *6* watchfire   *1 4–6* star • *2 3* star,   **41.** *6* tar   **42.** *1 4–6* Rude cradled   *1–*
6 mast.   **43.** *4–6* Even   *1–6* tower—   **45.** *6* Sara   **48.** *1* -vex'd • *4–6* -vexed
49. *4–6* -jaundiced   **50.** *4–6* -pampered   **51.** *1–6* roar: **52.** *1–5* Surges
53. *1 6* leap   **54.** *4–6* Plunged   **55.** *6* lightning's   **56.** *4–6* -shattered
1–3 bark: • *4–6* bark;   **57.** *4–6* hear;   **58.** *1–6* sheet   **59.** *4–6* Flashed   *1–*
6 blackness   **60.** *6* no vessel   **61.** *1 6* sings;   **63.** *3* sky larks   *4–6* 'mid
1–6 corn,   **64.** *1–6* breast: **65.** *4–6* The   *6* poppy   **66.** *1–6* morn.
67. *1–6* tears,   **68.** *4–6* opened   *6* rose!   **69.** *1–6* sun-beam   *2 3* blend;
70. *1–6* visitations   *2 3* above: **71.** *1–6* woes   **72.** *4–6* Fostering   *6* heart
74. *4–6* clattering   **75.** *1–6* arms   **76.** *1–6* Great   *1–6* To   **77.** *1–6* O
78. *1–6* The   *1–6* houseless,   **79.** *1–6* tears   **80.** *1–6* kisses   **81.** *1–*
6 dew   **82.** *1–6* sighs   **84.** *4–6* answering   **89.** *6* husband's   *1–6* care
90. *1–6* heart!   **92.** *4–6* -coloured   *1 2 4–6* flower   **92fn3.** *1 2* perceived
92fn11. *2* minutes;   **92fn16.** *1 2* vapours   **92fn16.** *1 2* marigold,   **93.** *2 4–*
6 flame: **94.** *4–6* -charged   *1 2 4–6* eye   **95.** *1 2 4–6* heart's   *5 6* ecstasy
96. *4–6* through

title. The PR *4–6* list of contents abbreviates the title to "Lines in Answer to a Letter
from Bristol".

prefatory note. PR *4–6* printed a four-line epigraph instead of the note. It is clear
from C's instructions to Cottle in MS 1 that this is a mistake, and that these four lines
were intended to be an epigraph to the whole Epistles section in PR *1*. For the epigraph
see **125** *Verse Motto.*

3, 6, etc. The third and sixth lines in each stanza are indented in all texts.

5fn, 92fn. Printed at the end of the volume in PR *1* * *1*, with the cross-references "Note
11.—Page 111." and "Note 13.—Page 118." respectively. PR *1* * *1* do not contain a Note
12, and print 37fn as a footnote. PR *2* prints all notes as footnotes.

5fn. William Poole might have been the "Gentleman" C refers to in the fuller version
of the note, although TP, his nephew, whom C met for the first time on this visit, is
a slightly more probable candidate. C has added a comment at the end of the shorter
version of the note in PR *1**(B), which was subsequently deleted: "There is a great deal
omitted here I insist on its insertion."

70. PR *2* above:] In the list of errata which C sent to Cottle c 3 Jul 1797 (*CL* I 331) he wrote: "For the colon put a comma."

92fn. C wrote between the third and fourth, fourth and fifth, and fifth and sixth paragraphs in PR *1**(B), respectively: "Good heavens! what a Gap!", "Good heavens! what a Gap!", "Good Heavens! what a Gap!" Then, at the foot of the last page (p 192): "From Monk's hood to phænomenon may very well be printed in the 191nd Page— and then let the Errata be occupy the last—". PR *1* reduces the spaces between all the paragraphs, and the errata occupy a separate page.

117. LINES TO JOSEPH COTTLE

A. DATE

Sept 1795–Feb 1796? The *terminus ante quem* depends on ELG's dating of *CL* I No 106; the letter might be earlier, e.g. Oct–Nov 1795.

B. TEXTS

1. HRC MS (Coleridge, S T) Works B. Two leaves, 20.2×32.5 cm and 20.3×32.5 cm; wm (first) Britannia in rounded oval, surmounted by crown, (second) small crown surmounting GR; chain-lines (both) 2.5 cm. Transcript in C's hand in the form of an als addressed to Joseph Cottle, which served as copy for PR *1* below. Cottle has corrected a line according to MS 2 below. Bound into Rugby Manuscript pp 85–7/ff 37^r–38^r.

2. HUL fMS Eng 947.2. Recto of a single leaf, 20.5×32.2 cm; wm F&H; chain-lines 2.9 cm. Additional stanza and correction to MS 1, in the form of an als to Joseph Cottle, late Feb 1796 (?) (*CL* I 186–7). The verso contains C's emendation of **119** *The Silver Thimble*.

1. Poems (1796).

C made three of the four errata corrections in his own copy (NYPL Berg Collection Copy 7).

2 [=RT]. Supplement to *Poems* (1797).

3. Poems (1803).

C made two corrections in SH's copy (Cornell WORDSWORTH PR 4252 B91R9 1813 Copy 2).

title. *1* Epistle 4 | To the Author of a collection of Poems published ⟨anonymously⟩ at | Bristol, in September / but without his Name / at Bristol—in September, 1795. • *1* EPISTLE IV. | TO THE | AUTHOR OF POEMS | PUBLISHED ANONYMOUSLY | AT BRISTOL, | *IN SEPTEMBER*, 1795. • *2* LINES | TO |

JOSEPH COTTLE. • *3* TO THE | *AUTHOR of POEMS,* | *Published anonymously at* BRISTOL, *in September,* 1795. **title fn.** *3* Mr. Joseph Cottle.

⁻1	1	1ˢᵗ
1	1	High-honor'd FRIEND Unboastful Bard High-honor'd FRIEND! whose
		verse concise yet clear
2	*1* 3	Unboastful Bard!
	2	My honor'd Friend!
2	⊠2	Tunes to smooth melody unconquer'd Sense—
3	⊠2	May your fame fadeless live, as never-sere ear
4	⊠2	The Ivy wreathes yon Oak, whose broad Defence
5	⊠2	Embow'rs me from Noon's sultry influence!
6	⊠2	For, like that nameless Riv'let stealing by,
7	⊠2	Your modest Verse to musing Quiet dear
8	⊠2	Is rich with tints *heaven-borrow'd*: the charm'd Eye
8fn	1	Alluding to the religious and scriptural nature of the two principal Poems.
9	⊠2	Shall gaze undazzled there, and love the soften'd Sky.
		[*Line-space*]
⁻10	1	2ᵈ
10	⊠2	Circling the Base of the poetic Mount
11	⊠2	A stream there is, which rolls in lazy Flow
12	⊠2	Its coal-black Waters from OBLIVION'S fount:
13	⊠2	The vapor-poison'd Birds, that fly too low,
14	⊠2	Fall with dead swoop, and to the bottom go.
15	⊠2	Escap'd that heavy stream on pinion fleet
16	⊠2	Beneath the Mountain's lofty-frowning Brow,
17	1	Ere aught of perilous Ascent you meet meet,
	1–3	meet,
18	⊠2	A Mead of mildest Charm delays th' unlab'ring Feet.
		[*Line-space*]
⁻19	1	3
19	1	Not there the cloud-climb'd subli Rock, sublime & vast,
	1–3	rock,
20	⊠2	That, like some giant King, o'er glooms the Hill;
21	⊠2	Nor there the Pine grove to the midnight Blast
22	⊠2	Makes solemn Music! But th' unceasing Rill
23	⊠2	To the soft Wren or Lark's descending Trill
24	⊠2	Murmurs sweet undersong mid jasmin bowers.
25	⊠2	In this same pleasant meadow at your will;
26	⊠2	I ween, *you* wander'd—there collecting Flowers
27	⊠2	Of sober tint, and Herbs of med'cinable powers!
		[*Line-space*]
⁻28	1	4
28	⊠2	There for the monarch-murder'd Soldier's Tomb
29	⊠2	You wove th' unfinish'd Wreath of saddest hues;
29fn	1 *1*–3	WAR, a fragment.
30	⊠2	And to that holier Chaplet added Bloom
30fn	1 *1*–3	John the Baptist, a Poem.
31	⊠2	Besprinkling it with JORDAN's cleansing dews.

32 ⊠2   But lo! your HENDERSON awakes the Muse—   [Oxford.
32fn 1 *1–3* Monody on ~~the Death of~~ John Henderson, ~~A.B. of Pembroke College,~~
33 ⊠2   His Spirit beckon'd from the mountain's Height!
34 1   You le~~av~~ft the Plain and soar'd ~~to bolder~~ mid richer Views!
    1–3   left   ⟵—'mid—⟶
35 1   So Nature mourn'd the   first   departed Light
    ⊠1   when sunk the First Day's
36 □   With stars, unseen before, spangling her robe of night
                                    [*Line-space*]
37 ⊠1   Still soar, my FRIEND! those richer views among,
38 ⊠1   Strong, rapid, fervent, flashing Fancy's beam!
39 2   Virtue and Faith shall love your gentler song;
    1–3   Truth
40 ⊠1   But Poesy demands th' impassion'd theme*l*.
41 ⊠1   Wak'd by Heaven's silent dews at Eve's mild gleam
42 ⊠1   What balmy sweets POMONA breathes around!
43 ⊠1   But if the vext air rush, a stormy stream,
44 ⊠1   Or Autu*n*mn's shrill Gust moan in plaintive sound,
45 ⊠1   With Fruits and Flowers she loads the tempest-honor'd ground.

1. *1 3* BARD!   **2.** *1 2* sense • *3* sense,   **3.** *1–3* "never-sere"   **4.** *1–3* defence
7. *1–3* verse   **8.** *1–3* heaven-borrow'd: *1–3* eye   **9.** *1–3* sky.   **10.** *1–3* base
1–3 Poetic mount   **11.** *1–3* flow   **12.** 1 *1* It's   *1–3* waters   **13.** *3* vapour—
16. *1–3* brow,   **17.** *1–3* ascent   **18.** *1–3* mead   *1–3* charm   *1 3* unlabring
1–3 feet.   **19.** *1–3* and   **20.** *1–3* That   *1–3* king,   *1–3* hill;   **21.** *1–3* -grove
1–3 blast   **22.** *1–3* music!   *1–3* rill   **23.** *1–3* trill   **25.** *1–3* meadow,   *2* will,
26. *1–3* you   *1–3* flow'rs   **27.** *1–3* herbs   **28.** *1–3* tomb   **29.** *1–3* wreath
29fn. *1 2* War, a Fragment. • *3* War a Fragment.   **30.** *1–3* chaplet   *1–3* bloom
30fn. *3* John the Baptist, a poem.   **32.** *1* lo   **32fn.** *1–3* Monody on John
Henderson.   **33.** *1–3* height!   **34.** *1–3* plain   *1–3* views!   **35.** *2 1–3* mourn'd,
2 sank   *1* Frst • *2* first   *3* day's   *2* Light, • *1 2* light, • *3* light   **36.** *2* Stars unseen
before   *2* night. • *1–3* night!   **37.** *1–3* soar   *1–3* FRIEND   **40.** *1* impasion'd
1–3 theme: **43.** *1–3* rush   *1 2* stream   **44.** *1–3* Autumn's   *1–3* gust   *1 2* sound
45. *1–3* fruits   *1–3* flowers   *1 2* honor'd

8fn. The deletion was made later.
18⁺. No line-space in PR *1*, but the PR *1* errata list instructs "Divide the third from the second Stanza." C indicated the division in his own copy.
25. Erratum in PR *1*: "For the semicolon after at your will; put a comma." C made the correction in his own copy.
26–7. Quoted in *The Friend* XI (26 Oct 1809) (*CC*) II 152 (cf I 23).
35. The MS 2 reading is written into MS 1 in Joseph Cottle's hand.
Erratum in PR *1*: "For Frst read *First*." C made the correction in his own copy.
35. In SH's copy of PR *3* C corrected "sunk" to "sank" and inserted a comma at the end of the line.
45. Erratum in PR *1*: "For tempest honor'd read *tempest-honor'd*."

118. TRANSLATIONS OF
HOMER *ILIAD* 1.34, 49

A. DATE

1795–6. The conversation which C recalls in his note ("In the 25th year of my age—1795 or 6, I forget which . . .": see vol I headnote) might have taken place on many occasions during the year he cites and is evidently at least in part fictitious. The location of the lines at this point in the chronological sequence is somewhat arbitrary.

B. TEXT

NYPL Berg Collection = Notebook Q f 70[¹⁻ᵛ].

The lines in the notebook bear no title (or letter-heading), and occur in the middle of a four-page prose commentary. The RT reproduces the ms exactly, except for:

(*a*) **2.** Of] ms of   (*b*) **4.** the] ms ~~his~~ the

119. THE SILVER THIMBLE
(with Sara Fricker Coleridge)

A. DATE

MS 1 is dated, following the signature, 17 Aug 1795; the emendation which constitutes MS 2 is dated by ELG to late Feb 1796, but may be earlier, e.g. Oct–Nov 1795.

B. TEXTS

1. HRC MS (Coleridge, S T) Works B. Two leaves, 20.2×31.9 cm and 20.3×31.9 cm; wm (first) Britannia in smaller rounded oval, surmounted by a crown, (second) GP&J; chain-lines (both) 2.5 cm. Transcript in the hand of Sara Fricker Coleridge, in the form of an als to Joseph Cottle, serving as copy for PR *1* below. Signed "Sara~~h~~ Fricker." Bound into Rugby Manuscript pp 89–91/ff 39[r]–40[r].

There are a number of corrections, not recorded here, where the same word has been copied out more legibly or an apostrophe repositioned. The original mistakes are of a kind that could derive from copying another person's (C's) hand, and the corrections in lines 23, 25.1, and 54 are indubitably in C's hand. Cottle has corrected the last lines according to MS 2 below.

2. HUL fMS Eng 947.2. Verso of a single leaf, 20.5×32.2 cm; wm F&H; chain-lines 2.9 cm. Title and emendation of the last lines of MS 1 in C's hand, in the form of an als to Joseph Cottle, late Feb 1796 (?) (*CL* I 187). Subscribed (in C's hand) "Sara". The recto contains C's additional stanza to **117** *Lines to Joseph Cottle*.

1 [=RT]. *Poems* (1796). Signed "SARA."

title and prefatory note. 2 Epistle V. I The production of a young Lady addressed to the I Author of the Poems alluded to in the preceding Epistle. I She had lost her thimble—and her complaints being I accidentally overheard by him, her friend, he I immediately sent her four silver thimbles, to take her I choice of.— • *1* EPISTLE V. I THE PRODUCTION OF I A YOUNG LADY, I ADDRESSED TO THE I *AUTHOR OF THE POEMS* I ALLUDED TO I IN THE PRECEEDING EPISTLE. I *She had lost her Silver Thimble, and her complaint being accidentally overheard by him, her Friend, he immediately sent her four others to take her choice of.*

1	1	*1*	As oft mine Eye with careless glance
2	1	*1*	Has gallop'd thro' some old Romance,
3	1	*1*	Of speaking Birds and Steeds with Wings,
4	1	*1*	Giants and Dwarfs and Fiends and Kings;
5	1	*1*	Beyond the rest with more attentive care
6	1	*1*	I've lov'd to read of elfin-favour'd Fair—
7	1	*1*	How if she long'd for aught beneath the Sky
8	1	*1*	And suffer'd to escape one votive sigh,
9	1	*1*	Wafted along on viewless pinions aery
10	1	*1*	It lay'd itself obsequious at her feet:
11	1		Such ⟨things,⟩ I thought, one might not hope to meet
		1	things,
12	1	*1*	Save in the dear delicious Land of Faëry!
13	1	*1*	But now (by proof I know it well)
14	1	*1*	There's still some peril in free Wishing—
15	1	*1*	*Politeness* is a licenc'd *Spell*
16	1	*1*	And *You*, dear Sir! the Arch-magician.
			[*Line-space*]
17	1	*1*	You much perplex'd me by the *various* set:
18	1	*1*	They were indeed an elegant quartette!
19	1	*1*	My mind went to and fro, and waver'd long;
20	1	*1*	At length I've chosen—(Samuel thinks me wrong)
21	1		*That* ~~one~~, around whose azure rim
		1	*That*,
22	1	*1*	Silver figures seem to swim,
25.1	1		~~Like~~ Or Ocean Nymphs with limbs of snowy hue
26.1	1		Slow-floating o'er the ~~waveless azure~~ calm cerulean plain;
23	1		~~Or~~ Like fleece-white Clouds, that on the Skiey Blue,
		1	Like

24	1	*1*	Wak'd by no breeze, the self-same shapes retain.
25		*1*	Or ocean Nymphs with limbs of snowy hue
26		*1*	Slow-floating o'er the calm cerulean plain.

[*Line-space*]

27	1	*1*	Just such a one, mon cher Ami!
28	1	*1*	(The finger-shield of Industry)
29	1	*1*	Th' inventive Gods, I deem, to Pallas gave—
30	1	*1*	What time the vain Arachne, madly brave,
31	1	*1*	Challeng'd the blue-eyed Virgin of the Sky
32	1	*1*	A duel in embroider'd work to try.
33	1	*1*	And hence the thimbled Finger of grave Pallas
34	1	*1*	To th' erring Needle's point was more than callous.
35	1	*1*	But ah the poor Arachne! She unarm'd
36	1	*1*	Blundring thro' hasty eagerness, alarm'd
37	1	*1*	With all a *Rival*'s hopes, a *Mortal*'s fears,
38	1	*1*	Still miss'd the stitch, and stain'd the web with tears.
39	1	*1*	Unnumber'd punctures small yet sore
40	1	*1*	Full fretfully the maiden bore,
41	1	*1*	Till she her lilly Finger found
42	1	*1*	Crimson'd with many a tiny wound;
43	1	*1*	And to her eyes suffus'd with watry woe
44	1	*1*	Her flower embroider'd Web danc'd dim, I wist,
45	1	*1*	Like blossom'd Shrubs in a quick-moving mist:
46	1	*1*	Till vanquish'd the despairing Maid sunk low!

[*Line-space*]

47		*1*	O Bard! whom sure no common Muse inspires,
48		*1*	I heard your Verse that glows with vestal fires
49	1	*1*	And *I* from unwatch'd needle's erring point
50	1		Should surely suffer on each Finger joint
		1	Had suffer'd
51	1	*1*	Those wounds, which erst did poor Arachne meet:
53.1	1		My bosom thrill'd with an enthusiast heat
52	1		When He, the much-lov'd object of my choice!
		1	While
53		*1*	(My bosom thrilling with enthusiast heat)
54	1		Shall read to me with ~~deep~~ his impressive voice,
		1	Pour'd on mine ear with deep
55	1	*1*	How the great Prophet of the Desart stood
56	1	*1*	And preach'd of Penitence by Jordan's fFlood;
57	1	*1*	On W A R ; or else the legendary Lays
58	1	*1*	In simplest measures hymn'd to A L L A 's Praise;
59	1	*1*	Or what the Bard from his Heart's inmost stores
60	1	*1*	O'er his *Friend*'s Grave in loftier numbers pours:
62.1	1		You were but *just*, when you the Thimble sent—
63.1	1		What ills your *Muse* might cause, your well-tim'd *Gifts* prevent!
61	2	*1*	Yes, Bard polite! you but obeyed the Laws
62	2	*1*	Of Justice, when the Thimble you had sent:
63	2	*1*	What wounds, your thought-bewild'ring Muse might cause,
64	2	*1*	Tis well, your finger-shielding Gifts prevent!

Those wounds, which erst did hoar Arachne meet:
My bosom thrill'd with an enthusiast heat
When He, the much-lov'd object of my choice!
Shall read to me with deep impressive voice,
How the great Prophet of the Desart stood
And preach'd of Penitence by Jordan's Flood;
Or War; or else the legendary Lays
In simplest measures hymn'd to Alla's Praise;
Or what the Bard from his Heart's inmost stores
Over his Friend's Grave in loftier numbers pours:
You were but just, when you the Thimble sent —
What ills your Muse might cause, your well-tim'd
                              Gifts prevent!

                              Sara Fricker

                    August 17th, 1795

Yes, Bard Polite! you but obeyed the laws
Of Justice, when the Thimble you had sent;
What wounds, your thought-bewildering Muse might cause
So well, your finger-shielding Gifts prevent

                    Sarah Fricker

2. *The Silver Thimble* MS 1: part of the "Rugby Manuscript", which served as
copy for Coleridge's 1796 *Poems*, in the hand of Mrs Coleridge with corrections
by Joseph Cottle

1. *1* eye   **2.** *1* romance,   **3.** *1* wings,   **4.** *1* Dwarfs,   **6.** *1* elfin-
favor'd   **7.** *1* sky   **10.** *1* Feet: **12.** *1* land   *1* Faery!   **14.** *1* wishing—
15. *1* spell   **16.** *1* you,   **17.** *1* various   **20.** *1* chosen (Samuel   **23.** *1* clouds,
1 skiey   **24.** *1* retain;   **25.** *1* ocean   **26.** *1* plain.   **27.** *1* mon cher
ami   **28.** *1* shield *1* industry)   **29.** *1* gave   **31.** *1* sky   **36.** *1* Blund'ring
37. *1* Rival's   **41.** *1* lily finger   **43.** *1* eyes, *1* woe,   **44.** *1* -embroider'd
web   **45.** *1* shrubs   **46.** *1* low.   **49.** *1* I   **50.** *1* finger   **51.** *1* meet;
52. *1* he, *1* Object *1* Choice,   **56.** *1* Flood;   **57.** *1* lays   **58.** *1* praise;
59. *1* heart's   **60.** *1* Friend's grave   **61.** *1* Polite! *1* laws   **62.** *1* thimble
1 sent;   **63.** *1* -bewildering *1* cause   **64.** *1* 'Tis *1* gifts prevent.

title. In the PR *1* list of contents the title is given as "Epistle 5, from a Young Lady,".
25.1–24. At the time the substitutions were made in MS 1, a note was added to change
the order of the lines (to the version printed in PR *1*), and to insert a space after line 26.
38. MS 1 has been trimmed, so that only the first three letters of "tears." remain.
57. MS 1 "On" could alternatively be read as "Or".
61–4. Cottle's transcript of MS 2 is added to MS 1 at this point, following the signature
and date.

120. FRAGMENTS OF AN EPISTLE TO THOMAS POOLE

A. DATE

A version of the poem was most probably in existence by Oct 1795–Feb 1796,
when C promised to send "The Epistle to Tom Poole . . . I think, one of my
most *pleasing* compositions" to Joseph Cottle (*CL* I 163). One would take C's
promise less seriously were it not for two lines from the poem in the Gutch
Notebook (MS 1 below) and his quotation of a further twelve lines in a letter to
John Thelwall of 31 Dec 1796 (MS 2 below).

The poem appears not to have been written down, however, apart from these
two incidental extracts. The other three known extracts are later and are found
in marginalia, written in two copies of *SL* (MSS 3 and 4 below) and in a copy
of Chalmer's *English Poets* (MS 5). MS 4 is the most extensive, but it adds a
further complication to the dating by claiming that the lines were written not at
but after leaving Stowey—contradicting the evidence of MSS 1 and 2.

Another question is raised by the lines on Donne (lines 6–9), added by the
three later texts. C had resolved to write "2 Satires in the manner of Donne"
at an early stage (*CN* I 171, which KC dates ?Oct 1796), but there is no sug-
gestion that the two satires were connected with the epistle to TP, unless one
plan overtook the other. Some similarities between the lines on Donne and C's
annotation of Donne's *Satires* in 1811 (see *CM—CC—*II 227, 228) might also
suggest that the lines postdated the annotation, although this is not a necessary

inference. The question of whether the lines on Donne were part of the original epistle is a moot one.

B. TEXTS

1. BM Add MS 27901 = Gutch Notebook f 87ᵛ. Untitled draft of lines 1.1.1, 3 in C's hand. The lines are written vertically from the binding. KC is able to date them only in the broad category 1796–8 (*CN* I 295).

2. PML MA 77 (6). Single folded leaf, 37.2×23.3 cm overall; wm horn within oval topped with three fleurs-de-lis | 1795; chain-lines 2.5 cm. Lines 11.1.1, 13–23 transcribed as part of a holograph letter to John Thelwall of 31 Dec 1796 (*CL* I 295).

C introduces the lines by saying: "—Joking apart, I would to God we could sit by a fireside & joke vivâ voce, face to face—Stella & Sara, Jack Thelwall, & I!—As I once wrote to my dear *friend*, T. Poole, 'repeating'". The lines are then written out two abreast. The punctuation at the end of some lines in the collation is questionable.

3. HUL *AC85 L8605 Zy 817c. Lines 4–5 copied into C's/HNC's copy of *SL* (1817) 269.

The lines are part of a comment on **482** *Human Life*, and are introduced as follows (the RH margin has been trimmed, and the end of some words is missing): "The preceding Lines, in ~~which~~ each of whic⌊h⌋ the utmost quantity of thought is condensed, far beyond what is consistent with the nature and purposes of poetry, are more in the style of t⌊he⌋ great Dʳ Donne (of Elizabeth & James the Iˢᵗ.'s time ⌜. . .⌝"

4 [=RT]. Present whereabouts unknown. Sold at Christie's 13 June 1979 lot 126. (Plate 18 of the catalogue, between pp 96 and 97, is a photograph of p 269 of the annotated copy.) Lines 1–20 copied in a copy of *SL* (1817) 269–70, given to Francis Wrangham (?). Signed "S.T.C.—".

This copy of *SL* was annotated over a number of years (see vol I annex C 17.5), and it is not known whether this particular annotation preceded or followed MS 4. The lines are again part of a comment on **482** *Human Life*, and are introduced thus: "These lines were written in purposed imitation of Donne—/ but Charles Lamb says, that he sees no other resemblance but that more thought is *packed* together than is compatible with poetry. This reminds me of some lines, I wrote a̶f̶fter leaving Stowey/⟨, in a poetic Epistle to my Friend, T. Poole: describing m̶y̶ our pursuits and conversations.⟩"

5. Untraced. Lines 4–7 added in pencil to commendatory verses on Donne in a copy of Chalmer's *English Poets* (21 vols 1810) v 126 (*CM—CC*—II 16, rpt from *LR* I 148).

HNC gives 1829 as the date of the Donne marginalia; see *CM* (*CC*) II 14.

1	4	Or while in too perverse a scorn Iwe hold
1.1.1	1	With skill that never Alchemist yet told
2	4	The *lengthy* poets who, like Gower of old,
3	1	Makesde drossy Lead as ductile as pure Gold
	4	Make
4	4	* * * * * * * * * * * *
5	4	* * * * * * * * * * * * *
6	3^imp	"While DONNE, whose Muse on Dromedary tr⌐ots,⌐
	4	With Like Verse trots,
	5	With muse
7	3^imp	Twists iron pokers into *true-love* kno⌐ts,⌐
	4 5	Wreathe knots,
8	4	Rhyme's sturdy Cripple-god, Wit's Maze and Clue,
	5	cripple, fancy's
9	4	Thought's Forge and Furnace, Mangle-press and Screw.
	5	Wit's fire-blast, meaning's press
10	4	? So / And now * * * * * * * * * *
11	4	* * * * * * * * * * * *
11.1.1	2	Such Verse as Bowles, heart-honour'd Poet, sang,
12	4	Inspir'd by Love that tender Lay I sang
13	2 4	That wakes the Tear yet steals away the Pang,
14	2	Then or with Berkley or with Hobbes romance it
	4	Now
15	2 4	Dissecting Truth with metaphysic lancet.
16	2	Or drawn from up those dark ←——unfathom'd——→ Wells
	4	forth unfathom sieve-bucket
17	2	In wiser folly clink the Cap & Bells.
	4	With
18	2 4	How many tales we told! What jokes we made!
19	2	Conundrum, Crambo, Rebus, or Charade;
	4	Rebus, Crambo, and
20	2 4	Ænigmas, that had driven the Theban mad,
20fn	2 4	Oedipus.
21	2 4	And Puns then best when exquisitely bad;
22	2 4	And I, if aught of archer vein I hit,
23	2 4	With my own Laughter stifled my own Wit.

3. 4 lead 4 gold,   6. 4 5 Donne, 4 5 dromedary   7. 4 5 true-love
5 knots;   8. 5 maze   5 clue,   9. 5 forge   5 screw.   13. 4 tear   4 pang—
15. 4 fTRUTH 4 Metaphysic Lancet: 17. 4 fFOLLY   4 and   18. 4 what
Jokes 4 made,   19. 4 Charade: 20. 4 Enigmas   4 mad   20fn. 4 Edipus.
21. 4 bad: 23. 4 laughter   4 wit!

4–5. For another version, perhaps dating from 1826–7, see vol I EC; also **490** *The Suicide's Argument* TEXT MS 2 and VAR line 11n.

121. SUMMARY VERSION OF HORACE

A. DATE

1–15 (?) Dec 1795.

B. TEXT

Quoted in the text of C's *Answer to "A Letter to Edward Long Fox, M.D."* (Bristol 1795) 7 = *Lects 1795 (CC)* 330.

The RT reproduces the lines exactly as they appear (without a title) in C's *Answer*.

122. FRAGMENTS FROM THE GUTCH NOTEBOOK

A. DATE

Various occasions during the years 1795–8. KC's sequence (which, exceptionally, follows the notebook sequence rather than attempting chronological order) and date for particular entries are adopted here.

B. TEXT

BM Add MS 27901 = Gutch Notebook, selected folios (pub *CN* I).

The RT reproduces the undeleted text of the ms. Deletions are recorded below.

> (*a*) f 11ʳ (*CN* I 90).
> (*b*) f 11ʳ (*CN* I 94) (Feb–Mar 1796). Written out continuously (as if prose) in the notebook.
> (*c*) f 11ᵛ (*CN* I 95). Written out continuously (as if prose) in the notebook.
> 2 ms ~~their~~ Thirst's
> (*d*) f 11ᵛ (*CN* I 96).
> (*e*) f 11ᵛ (*CN* I 97).
> (*f*) f 17ʳ (*CN* I 134). The wide spacing of the lines in *CN* is not supported by the ms, and it seems most probable that they are—somehow—intended to form part of a consecutive text.
> (*g*) f 17ᵛ (*CN* I 135). In pencil.
> (*h*) f 19ʳ (*CN* I 149).

(*i*) f 20ᵛ (*CN* I 160). KC remarks that there is some doubt about "Leanness". The correct reading may be "Meanness".

(*j*) f 26ᵛ (*CN* I 179) (22 Sept–12 Oct 1796).

(*k*) f 26ᵛ (*CN* I 181) (22 Sept–12 Oct 1796).

(*l*) f 28ʳ (*CN* I 196).

(*m*) f 28ᵛ (*CN* I 202). Written out continuously (as if prose) in the notebook.

(*n*) f 30ᵛ (*CN* I 213). Asterisks are used in the RT to separate fragments.

Fr 2 ms The ~~A~~brook

(*o*) f 31ʳ (*CN* I 214). Preceded by three lines cancelled with perpendicular strokes:

> And one or two poor melancholy Joys
> Pass by on flimsy wing in Hope's cold gleam,
> Moths in the Moonlight.—

4 ms ~~cold~~ pale   ms ~~gleams~~ light

(*p*) f 31ʳ (*CN* I 217). Written out continuously (as if prose) in the notebook.

(*q*) f 36ʳ (*CN* I 229) (winter 1797–8?).

(*r*) f 76ᵛ (*CN* I 264) (22 Sept–12 Oct 1796).

(*s*) f 76ᵛ (*CN* I 269) (22 Sept–12 Oct 1796).

(*t*) f 77ʳ⁻ᵛ (*CN* I 272) (22 Sept–12 Oct 1796).

Fr 13 ms ~~And Yesterday is~~ it

(*u*) ff 77ᵛ–78ʳ (*CN* I 273) (Nov–Dec 1796 (?)). It is not certain how the connection between the phrases is to be understood, but they are treated in the RT as consecutive lines, and what appears to be a pattern of indentation has been retained.

(*v*) f 87ʳ (*CN* I 293). The lines of verse begin from the outside margin and run parallel to it. On a recto, especially so near the end of the notebook, this would seem so inconvenient as to suggest that they were written before the leaf was incorporated in this position.

3 ms ~~if~~ when   ms ~~still~~ this   4 ~~red-hot~~ fiery

122.X1. HABENT SUA FATA—POETAE

"The Fox, the Statesman subtile wiles ensure,". 12 lines. Untitled.

Included at the end of a letter to Josiah Wade, from Lichfield c 10 Feb 1796, and known only from Cottle *E Rec* I 172; the whole signed "S. T. C." (see *CL* I 184–5). Included as *PW* (EHC) II 1089 P, with the title given here. In fact, the verses are put together from Robert Burns's poem *To Robert Graham of Fintry, Esq.* (1794). Unless C's original letter turns up, it would be foolish to speculate on whether or not he meant to mislead Wade into accepting the verses as his own. Burns was more widely read in advanced literary circles in Bristol then than now, and C's "quotation" is hardly obscure. C drew on the same poem in **521** *Contemporary Critics*.

123. THE HOUR WHEN WE SHALL MEET AGAIN

A. DATE

The poem was probably written during C's *Watchman* tour; indeed, its manner suggests that it was written after his meeting with Erasmus Darwin at Derby, on 23 or 24 Jan 1796. In PR *2 3* below it follows **124** *Lines on Observing a Blossom*, written on 1 Feb.

B. TEXTS

1. The Watchman III (17 Mar 1796) 78 (*CC*) 105. Signed "C."
C's own copy (BM Ashley 2842) contains his correction to line 15.

2 [=RT]. *Poems* (1797).
C emended the poem in the copies he gave to William Bowles (in the possession of Erwin Schwarz, 1982) and William Roskilly (in the possession of J.C.C. Mays, 1999), in accordance with an instruction he gave, too late to be incorporated, to Joseph Cottle c 3 Jul 1797 (*CL* I 331).

3. Poems (1803).

4. Table Talk (1835) II 358–9.
The poem is the first of those "*accidentally omitted in the Collection of Mr. Coleridge's Poetical Works lately published*". See vol I headnote for HNC's note on the text.

title. *1–3 THE HOUR WHEN WE SHALL MEET AGAIN.* | *(Composed during Illness, and in Absence.)* • *4* DARWINIANA. | THE HOUR WHEN WE SHALL MEET AGAIN. | *(Composed during illness and in absence.)*

1	☐	Dim Hour! that sleep'st on pillowing clouds afar,
2	☐	O rise and yoke the Turtles to thy car!
3	☐	Bend o'er the traces, blame each lingering Dove,
4	☐	And give me to the bosom of my Love!
5	☐	My gentle Love, caressing and carest,
6	☐	With heaving heart shall cradle me to rest;
7	☐	Shed the warm tear-drop from her smiling eyes,
8	☐	Lull with fond woe, and med'cine me with sighs:
8.1.1	⊠*3*	While finely-flushing float her kisses meek,
8.1.2	⊠*3*	Like melted rubies, o'er my pallid cheek.
9	☐	Chill'd by the night, the drooping Rose of May
10	☐	Mourns the long absence of the lovely Day:
11	☐	Young Day returning at her promis'd hour
12	☐	Weeps o'er the sorrows of her fav'rite flower;
13	☐	Weeps the soft dew, the balmy gale she sighs,

14 □   And darts a trembling lustre from her eyes.
15 *1*   Now life and joy th' expanding flow'ret feels:
⊠*1* New
16 □   His pitying Mistress mourns, and mourning heals!

title. *2 THE HOUR* | WHEN WE SHALL MEET AGAIN. | *(Composed during Illness, and in Absence.)* • *3 THE HOUR* | WHEN WE SHALL MEET AGAIN. | *(Composed during Illness, and in Absence.)*   **2.** *4* turtles   **3.** *4* dove,   **6.** *3* rest!
8. *3* sighs! • *4* sighs;   **10.** *2 3* Day;   **11.** *4* promised   **12.** *2 3* Flower;
15. *3* flowret   **16.** *4* mistress

8.1.1–2. C carefully scratched out these lines in the copies of PR *2* he gave to William Bowles and William Roskilly (see TEXT PR *2* above).
15. C corrected "Now" to "New" in his own copy of PR *1*, and asked John Edwards and TP to make the correction in letters of Mar and Apr 1796 (*CL* I 193, 203).

124. LINES ON OBSERVING A BLOSSOM

A. DATE

1 Feb 1796.

B. TEXTS

1. The Watchman VI (11 Apr 1796) 164–5 (*CC*) 202–3. Signed "S. T. C."

2. The Iris (Sheffield) (13 May 1796). Signed "S. T. C."

3 [=RT]. *Poems* (1797).
William Roskilly's copy (in the possession of J.C.C. Mays, 1999) has two corrections in C's hand.

4. Poems (1803).

5. SL (1817).
The proof sheets at Yale (In C678 817sa) show that copy was provided by PR *3* above, and that new readings were introduced at lines 22–3 and 26 while the text was in proof. This stage of the poem's evolution is not recorded.

6. PW (1828).

7. PW (1829).

8. PW (1834).

The transcript (var) of the first eight lines made from PR *6–8*, in an unknown hand at the Pforzheimer (MS Misc 87.5), is of no textual interest.

title. *1–4* LINES | On Observing a Blossom on the First of February, 1796. |
WRITTEN NEAR SHEFFIELD. • *5–8 ON OBSERVING A BLOSSOM | On the 1st
of February,* 1796.

1 □		Sweet Flower! that peeping from thy russet stem,
2 □		Unfoldest timidly—for in strange sort
3 *1–5*		This dark, freeze-coated, hoarse, teeth-chattering Month
6–8		frieze-coated,
4 □		Hath borrow'd Zephyr's voice, and gaz'd upon thee
5 □		With blue voluptuous eye—alas poor Flower!
6 □		These are but flatteries of the faithless Year.
7 □		Perchance escap'd its unknown polar cave
8 □		Ev'n now the keen North-East is on its way.
9 □		Flower, that must perish! shall I liken thee
10 □		To some sweet girl of too, too rapid growth
11 □		Nipp'd by Consumption mid untimely charms?
12 □		Or to Bristowa's Bard, the wond'rous boy!
12fn □		Chatterton.
13 *1 2*		An Amanarth, which Earth scarce seem'd to own,
⊠*1 2*		Amaranth,
14 *1–6*		Blooming mid poverty's drear wintry waste,
15 □		Till Disappointment came and pelting Wrong
16 □		Beat it to earth? Or with indignant grief
17 *1 2*		Shall I compare thee to poor POLAND's hopes,
3–8		Hope,
18 □		Bright flower of hope kill'd in the opening bud!
19 □		Farewell, sweet blossom! better fate be thine
20 □		And mock my boding! dim similitudes
21 □		Weaving in moral strains, I've stolen one hour
22 *1–4*		From black anxiety that gnaws my heart
23 *1–4*		For her who droops far off on a sick bed:
22.1 *5–8*		From anxious SELF, Life's cruel Task-Master!
24 □		And the warm wooings of this sunny day
25 □		Tremble along my frame, and harmonize
26 *1–4*		Th' attemper'd brain, that ev'n the saddest thoughts
5–8		organ, even
27 □		Mix with some sweet sensations, like harsh tunes
28 □		Play'd deftly on a soft-ton'd instrument.

title. *2 LINES,* | On Observing a Blossom on the 1st of February, | 1796. | WRITTEN
NEAR SHEFFIELD. • *3 4* LINES | *ON OBSERVING A BLOSSOM* | On the First
of February, 1796. | WRITTEN NEAR SHEFFIELD. • *6–7* ON OBSERVING A
BLOSSOM ON THE | FIRST OF FEBRUARY,1796. • *8* ON OBSERVING
A BLOSSOM ON THE | FIRST OF FEBRUARY, | 1796.   **1.** *5–8* stem
2. *3 4* timidly (for • *5–8* timidly, (for   **4.** *6–8* borrowed   *6–8* gazed   **5.** *4* "blue
2 eye—alas! • *3* eye) alas • *4* eye") alas • *5–8* eye) alas,   **6.** *5–8* year.   **7.** *5–*
8 Perchance, escaped   *5–8* cave,   **8.** *6–8* E'en   *2* north-east   **9.** *5–8* Flower
10. *2–4* Girl   *5–8* too too   *2* growth,   **11.** *6–8* Nipped   *2 8* consumption
12. *8* bard,   *5* wonderous • *6–8* wondrous   **12fn.** *2 Chatterton.*   **13.** *8* amaranth,

6–8 seemed   **14.** *6* 'mid   *2* Poverty's   **15.** *8* disappointment   *2 5–8* came,
2 wrong, • *5–8* wrong   **16.** *5–8* Earth?   *2* O   *5–8* or   **17.** *5–8* Poland's
8 hope,   **18.** *4* flow'r   *2* hope, • *5–8* Hope   *6–8* killed   *3–8* bud?   **19.** *2–*
4 Blossom!   **20.** *2–8* Dim   **23.** *4* far-off   **22.1.** *8* self,   *8* task-master!
25. *3–7* frame   **26.** *5–8* The attempered   **28.** *6–8* Played   *5–8* -toned

3. In Roskilly's copy of PR *3* C emended "freeze-" to "frieze-".
5. PR *3* alas] C added a comma in Roskilly's copy.

125. VERSE MOTTO TO POETICAL EPISTLES

A. DATE

Feb–Mar 1796? The dating depends on the point at which sig H of *Poems* (1796) was printed.

B. TEXTS

1. HRC MS (Coleridge, S T) Works B. Single leaf, 20.2×32.6 cm; wm small crown surmounting GR; chain-lines 2.5 cm; verso blank. Draft in C's hand, signed "Anon." Bound into Rugby Manuscript p 75/f 32ʳ.

The motto precedes the first of C's Epistles (**116** *Written at Shurton Bars*), and is introduced by the following instruction: "On the other side of the Leaf, in the middle THIS motto (in the same manner as in the title page of the Effusions)".

1 [=RT]. *Poems* (1796). Signed "ANON."

The lines are printed on a page by themselves, as an epigraph to the section "𝕻𝖔𝖊𝖙𝖎𝖈𝖆𝖑 𝕰𝖕𝖎𝖘𝖙𝖑𝖊𝖘.", facing p 111.

2. PW (1828). Signed "ANON."

In this text and the two following, the lines are printed as an epigraph to **116** *Written at Shurton Bars* alone (between the title and the first line).

3. PW (1829). Signed "ANON."

4. PW (1834). Signed "—ANON."

1 1   Good Verse, ~~then best,~~ *most* good, and bad Verse then seems better
   ⊠1   ←——*most*——→
2 1   ~~Sent from far~~ Receiv'd from absent friend by way of Letter.
   ⊠1   ←——Receiv'd——→
3 1   N̄ For ~~nought~~ what so sweet can ~~sweetest~~ labor'd Lays impart
   ⊠1   For   ←—what—→   ←—labor'd—→
4 ☐   As one rude rhyme warm from a friendly heart?

1. ⊠1 Good verse *4* most ⊠1 bad verse **2.** *2–4* Received **3.** *2–4* laboured ⊠1 lays

126. LINES ON THE PORTRAIT OF A LADY

A. DATE

Before 17 Mar 1796.

B. TEXT

In *The Watchman* III (17 Mar 1796) 78–9 (*CC*) 105–6, following two poems by C, signed respectively "T." and "C." The present poem is signed "S.", while a fourth poem is acknowledged in a brief introductory paragraph to be by John Logan (*The Braes of Yarrow*).

The RT reproduces the *Watchman* text (where the title is in italic capitals with concluding full point).

126.X1. LINES COMBINED FROM BOWLES

The Watchman III (17 Mar 1796) 88 (*CC*) 117: "Now past, and but remembered like sweet sounds". 5 lines. Untitled.

The lines are quoted in an essay on "Domestic Intelligence", without attribution. They were never claimed by C or his editors and in fact combine lines from two sonnets by W. L. Bowles. Lines 1–2 reproduce lines 4–5 of the first *May, 1793*, beginning "As o'er these hills I take my silent rounds"; and lines 3–5 constitute lines 8–10 (var) of *On Revisiting Oxford*, beginning "I never hear the sound of thy glad bells". C inserted quotation-marks at the beginning of his first three lines (only), inserted a comma in his line 3, introduced italic in lines 4–5, and substituted "Youth" for Bowles's "life". The originals were first collected in the third edition of Bowles's *Sonnets* (Bath 1794) 25 and 29 respectively, which C had drawn on when he combined other passages from Bowles in a similar way two years earlier. See poems **68.X1** and **70.X1.**

127. FROM AN UNPUBLISHED POEM

A. DATE

Before 25 Mar 1796.

B. TEXT

The Watchman IV (25 Mar 1796) 101 (*CC*) 132.

The RT reproduces the *Watchman* text, except for:

title. *Watchman* [printed at end of text] *From an unpublished Poem.*

127.X1. EPIGRAM: "SAID WILLIAM TO EDMUND ..."

The Watchman IV (25 Mar 1796) 113 (*CC*) 145: "EPIGRAM. I Said William to Edmund I can't guess the reason". 4 lines; signed "BRISTOLIENSIS"; dated "*March* 21, 1796". Rpt *The Port Folio* (Philadelphia) I (4) (24 Jan 1801) 32.

Included in *PW* (EHC) II 951 No 1. But as Lewis Patton points out (*Watchman—CC*—145n), C thanked "BRISTOLIENSIS" for his contribution in the previous issue (*CC* 125). There is no reason for C to have employed the pseudonym if he was the author. On the other hand, an element of doubt arises because of an unexplained discrepancy: the issue in which C acknowledged receipt is dated 17 Mar, while the epigram is dated 21 Mar.

Cf the eight-line variant quoted in a letter to SH (without reference to C) by CL in Jan 1825 (*LL* II 153).

127.X2. TO THE REV. W. L. BOWLES

Bath Chronicle (31 Mar 1796): "To the Rev. W. L. BOWLES. I When PROSPERO wav'd his magic wand in air,". 22 lines. Signed "F. P. C. I —— *Coll. Cambridge, March* 20."

The lines contain similarities to **95** *To Bowles*, and have been tentatively attributed to C by Geoffrey Little and Elizabeth Hall "Coleridge's 'To the Rev. W. L. Bowles': Another Version?" *RES* xxxii (May 1981) 193–6. Little and Hall suggest that "F. P. C." might be an acronym which represents (Samuel) Favell, (Thomas) Poole, and C—to which it might be added that no member of the University of Cambridge at that time had the initials F.P.C. The evidence for C's authorship none the less remains slender.

128. RECOLLECTION

A. DATE

Mar 1796.

B. TEXT

The Watchman v (2 Apr 1796) 133–4 (*CC*) 167–8. Signed "S. T. C."

The RT reproduces the *Watchman* text exactly (where the title is followed by a full point). See vol I headnote for the passages in other poems by C which make up the present text.

129. REFLECTIONS ON HAVING LEFT A PLACE OF RETIREMENT

A. DATE

Nov 1795–Sept 1796, most probably Mar–Apr 1796 (immediately following **101** *Religious Musings*).

Different versions of the title suggest that the poem was written after leaving the Clevedon cottage, and before C's plans to "enter active life" were modified: that is, after mid-Nov 1795–Mar 1796 and before the meeting with Charles Lloyd and the decision to move to Stowey, in Sept.

It was Mar 1796 before the Coleridges were settled in another home of their own in Bristol (Oxford Street, Kingsdown), and they did not finally quit the Clevedon cottage, therefore, until that time; there are parallels with the fourth number of *The Watchman*, which appeared on 25 Mar (*CC* 139–40); the "active life" contemplated was first that of a dissenting minister, and the poem follows on naturally from the conclusion of **101** *Religious Musings* (pub Apr 1796).

B. TEXTS

1. Monthly Magazine II (Oct 1796) 732. Signed "S. T. COLERIDGE." Rpt ("BY MR COLLERIDGE") *Ed Mag* NS VIII (Nov 1796) 388.

Another version of the poem, intended for a joint volume with Charles Lloyd, had been printed before Dec 1796, but the loose sheets have not survived. CL's references to it (*LL*—M—I 74–5; see also *CL* I 285: to J. Thelwall 17 Dec 1796) suggest a version longer than PR *1*, which it might have preceded.

1. Alexander Turnbull Library, Wellington, New Zealand R Eng COLE Poems (1796). Transcript in the hand of MH in her proof copy of C's *Poems* (1796), between sigs M and N.

The interleaved copy of *Poems* (1796) at DCL was broken up (into DC MS 28 and DC MS 30) in Oct–Dec 1800, and thereafter used by WW and DW for their own writing. MH's transcript might have been made between this time and Oct 1804, and if it was, probably in the period Nov 1803–Mar 1804. But it is more likely that it was made while MH was at Racedown (c 28 Nov 1796–4 Jun 1797), which C was to visit just after she had left (see Reed I 189, 198, etc), a period during which the poem influenced the way WW completed *Lines Left upon a Seat in a Yew-tree* (*WPW* I 92–4). It constitutes either a version midway between PR *1* and PR *2*, or else one predating PR *1*. For further details see vol I annex C 3.2.

2 [=RT]. *Poems* (1797).

C made a single correction to the poem in RS's (?) copy (Yale In 678 797 Copy 1).

3. Poems (1803).

JTC's transcript in his Commonplace Book (University of Pennsylvania Library (Special Collections) MS Eng 13) pp 50–1 has no textual significance.

4. SL (1817).

There are three emendations in JG's hand in the emended part copy at HUL (*EC8 C6795 817s (D)), one of which was carried forward to PR *5*. C quoted lines 47–59 in *AR* (1825) 52–3 (*CC*) 59 var, giving "*Sibylline Leaves*, p. 180" as his source, but with several minor and substantial variations. The same lines are emended in the copy of *AR* he presented to JTC (BM C 126 d 3).

5. PW (1828).

6. PW (1829).

7. PW (1834).

title. *1* REFLECTIONS ON ENTERING INTO | ACTIVE LIFE. | *A Poem, which affects not to be* POETRY. • *2–7 REFLECTIONS* | ON HAVING LEFT A PLACE OF RETIREMENT. **motto.** *2–7 Sermoni propriora.*—HOR.

1 ☐   Low was our pretty cot: our tallest rose

2 □		Peep'd at the chamber-window. We could hear
3 □		(At silent noon, and eve, and early morn)
4 □		The sea's faint murmur: in the open air
5 □		Our myrtles blossom'd, and across the porch
6 □		Thick jasmines twin'd; the little landscape round
7 □		Was green and woody, and refresh'd the eye.
8 □		It was a spot, which you might aptly call
9 □		The VALLEY of SECLUSION. Once I saw
10 □		(Hallowing his sabbath-day by quietness)
11 □		A wealthy son of Commerce saunter by,
12 *1* 1		BRISTOWA's citizen: he paus'd, and look'd,
2–7		Methought, it calm'd
13 *2–7*		His thirst of idle gold, and made him muse
14 *2–7*		With wiser feelings: for he paus'd, and look'd
15 □		With a pleas'd sadness, and gazed all around;
16 □		Then ey'd our cottage, and gaz'd round again,
17 *1* 1		And said, *it was a blessed little place!*
2–7		sigh'd, and said, *it was a blessed place.*
18 □		And we *were* blessed! Oft with patient ear
19 □		Long-list'ning to the viewless sky-lark's note,
20 □		(Viewless, or haply for a moment, seen
21 *1* 1 2 4		Gleaming on sunny wing) in whisper'd tones
3		"And such," I said,
5–7		wings) in whispered tones
22 *1* 1		I said to my beloved, "Such, sweet girl!
2 4–7		I've
23 □		Th' inobtrusive song of happiness:
24 □		Unearthly minstrelsy! then only heard
25 □		When the soul seeks to hear: when all is hush'd,
26a □		And the heart listens!"
		[*Line-space*]
26b □		But the time, when first
27 □		From that low dell steep up the stony mount
28 □		I climb'd with perilous toil, and reach'd the top,
29 □		O what a goodly scene! *Here* the bleak mount,
30 □		The bare bleak mountain speckl'd thin with sheep;
31 □		Grey clouds, that shadowing spot the sunny fields;
32 □		And river, now with bushy rocks o'erbrow'd,
33 □		Now winding bright and full with naked banks;
34 □		And seats, and lawns, the abbey, and the wood,
35 □		And cots and hamlets, and faint city-spire:
36 □		The channel *there*, the islands, and white sails,
37 *1* 1		Dim coast, and cloudlike hills, and shoreless ocean!
2–7		Coasts,
38 □		It seem'd like Omnipresence! God, methought,
39 □		Had built him there a temple! The whole world
40 *1* 1		Was *imag'd* in its vast circumference.
2–7		Seem'd
41 □		No wish profan'd my overwhelmed heart:

42 □	Blest hour! it was a luxury—*to be!*
	[*Line-space*]
43 □	Ah, quiet dell! dear cot! and mount sublime!
44 □	I was constrain'd to quit you. Was it right,
45 □	While my unnumber'd brethren toil'd and bled,
46 *1 2*	That I should dream away the trusted hours
1	wasted
3–7	entrusted
47 □	On rose-leaf beds, pamp'ring the coward heart
48 □	With feelings all too delicate for use?
49 □	Sweet is the tear, that from some HOWARD's eye
50 □	Drops on the cheek of one he lifts from earth:
51 □	And he that works me good with unmov'd face,
52 □	Does it but half: he chills me while he aids;
53 □	My benefactor, not my brother man!
54 □	Yet even this, this cold beneficence,
55 *1* 1 *2–4*	Seizes my praise, when I reflect on those,
5–7	Praise, praise it, O my Soul! oft as thou scann'st
56 □	The sluggard Pity's vision-weaving tribe!
57 ⊠1	Who sigh for wretchedness, yet shun the wretched,
1	but
58 □	Nursing in some delicious solitude
59 □	Their slothful loves and *dainty* sympathies!
60 □	I therefore go—and join head, heart, and hand,
61 □	Active and firm, to fight the bloodless fight
62 □	Of Science, Freedom, and the Truth in Christ.
63 □	Yet oft when after honourable toil
64 □	Rests the tir'd mind, and waking loves to dream,
65 □	My spirit shall revisit thee, dear cot!
66 □	Thy jasmin, and thy window-peeping rose,
67 □	And myrtles fearless of the mild sea-air,
68 □	And I shall sigh fond wishes—sweet abode!
69 □	Ah! had *none* greater, and that *all* had such!
70 ⊠*3*	It might be so—but the time is not yet;
71 ⊠*3*	Speed it, O Father! Let thy kingdom come!

title. *3 REFLECTIONS* | ON | HAVING LEFT A PLACE OF RETIREMENT. •
4 REFLECTIONS | *On having left a Place of Retirement.* • *5 6* REFLECTIONS
ON HAVING LEFT A PLACE | OF RETIREMENT. • *7* REFLECTIONS |
ON HAVING LEFT A PLACE OF RETIREMENT. **motto.** *4–7* Sermoni
propriora.— *7* HOR. **1.** 2 *4–7* Cot: • *3* Cot! *2–6* Rose **2.** *5–7* Peeped
3. *2–7* At 1 eve *2–7* morn, **4.** *2–6* Sea's *2–7* murmur. In **5.** 2–
6 Myrtles *2–4* blossom'd; • *5–7* blossomed; *4–6* Porch **6.** 1 Jas'mines •
2–4 Jasmins • *5–7* jasmins 1 *2 3* twin'd: • *4–7* twined: **7.** 1 & 2 *3* woody
1 & *5–7* refreshed **8.** *4–7* spot **9.** 1 valley • *7* Valley 1 Seclusion. •
2–6 SECLUSION! • *7* Seclusion! **10.** *2–7* Sabbath- **11.** *4–7* commerce
12. 1 Bristolwa's • *2–7* Bristowa's *4–7* methought, 1 & look'd *5–7* calmed
14. *5–7* paused, *5–7* looked **15.** *4–7* pleased 1 & *2 3* gaz'd *2–7* around,
16. *2–7* eyed *4–7* Cottage, 1 & *4–7* gazed **17.** *5–7* sighed, 1 it was *a*

blessed little place! • *4–7* it was a Blessed Place.   **18.** *7* were   *2–7* blessed.
19. ⊠*1* -listening   *2–7* note   **20.** 1 Viewless,   *2–7* moment   **21.** 1 (Gleaming
3 wing,)   **22.** *2* Beloved,   1 "Such   *2* Girl!   **23.** *2–6* "The   *4 5* inobstrusive
2 3 HAPPINESS—• *4–6* Happiness, • *7* happiness,   **24.** *2–6* "Unearthly   **25.** *2–*
6 "When   *2 3* Soul   *2–7* hear;   *2 3* hush'd • *5–7* hushed,   **26a.** *2–6* "And
2–6 Heart   **26b.** 1 time   **27.** *2 3* Dell • *4–6* Dell, • *7* dell,   *2–6* Mount
28. *5–7* climbed   *2–7* toil   1 &   *5–7* reached   **29.** *3–7* Oh!   *7* Here   *2–*
6 Mount,   **30.** *2–6* Mountain   ⊠*1* speckled   **31.** *7* Gray   *2 3* Clouds,
3 fields   **32.** *2–6* River,   *2 3* o'erbrow'd • *5–7* o'erbrowed,   **33.** 1 &   *2–7* full,
34. 1 seats₁ & • *2–6* Seats, and   *2–6* Lawns,   1 the₁ abbey & • *2–5* the Abbey, and •
6 7 the Abbey and   *2–6* Wood,   **35.** *2–6* Cots, • *7* cots,   1 &   *2–6* Hamlets,
1 &   *2–5* City-spire: • *6* City-spire; • *7* city-spire;   **36.** *2–7* Channel   *7* there,
2–7 Islands   1 &   *2–6* Sails,   **37.** *7* coasts,   1 & cloudlike-hills & • *2–6* and
cloud-like Hills, and • *7* and cloud-like hills, and   *2–7* Ocean—   **38.** *5–*
7 seemed   **39.** *2–6* Temple: • *7* temple: *2–7* the   *2–7* World   **40.** *5–7* seemed
1 imag'd • *5–7* imaged   *6 7* circumference,   **41.** *2–6* wish   *4* prophan'd •
5–7 profaned   *2–6* Heart. • *7* heart.   **42.** *2–7* It   *2 3* Luxury— • *4–6* Luxury,— •
7 luxury,—   *2–7* to be!   **43.** *2 3* Ah • *4–7* Ah!   *2 3* Dell!   *2 3* Cot! • *5–7* cot,
1 &   *2 3* Mount   **44.** *5–7* constrained   **45.** *5–7* unnumbered   *2 3* Brethren
5–7 toiled   1 &   **46.** *4* th'   *2 3* Hours   **47.** *2–6* Beds,   *4–7* pampering
2–6 Heart   **49.** *2 3* Tear • *4–7* tear   ⊠*1* Howard's   **50.** *2–4* One, • *5 6* One
4–6 Earth: **51.** *2–4* He, • *5 6* He   *5–7* unmoved   **52.** *2–7* aids,   **53.** *2–*
6 Benefactor,   *2–6* Brother Man!   **54.** *2–6* Beneficence • *7* beneficence
55. *2–4* Praise,   **56.** *4–6* Sluggard   *2–6* Tribe!   **57.** 1 wretchedness •
2–6 Wretchedness,   *2–4* Wretched,   **59.** 1 &   *2–7* dainty   1 sympathies. •
2–6 Sympathies!   **60.** *2–7* go, and   1 heart &   **61.** 1 &   **62.** *7* science,
freedom, and • 1 Science, Freedom &   *7* truth   *2 3* CHRIST.   **63.** 1 honorable
64. *5–7* tired   1 &   **65.** *2 3* Spirit   *2–7* Cot!   **66.** 1 jasmine & • *2–6* Jasmin
and • *7* jasmin and   *2–6* Rose,   **67.** *2–6* Myrtles   *2–7* -air.   **68.** *2–6* Abode!
69. *2 3* Ah— • *4–7* Ah!—   *2–7* none greater!   1 & • *2–7* And   *2–7* all   **70.** *2 4–*
7 yet.   **71.** *2* FATHER!   1 kindom • *2 4–6* Kingdom

title. In the PR *2* list of Contents the title is given as "*On leaving a Place of Resi-dence,*"; in the PR *5 6* list of Contents it is given as "Recollections on having left a place of Retirement".

12–14. The PR *2–7* revisions might represent the restoration of a passage which existed in a version referred to by CL (*LL*—M—I 74–5).

29. In the emended part copy of PR *4* at HUL the line is emended in JG's hand to "Oh! what a Joy of Surview! *Here* the Mount,".

42⁺. Apparently no line-space in MS 1.

46. C has corrected RS's copy of PR *2* to "th' entrusted".

47–59. The lines are given differently in *AR* (1825) 52–3 (*CC*) 59 var, although the source is given at the end as "*Sibylline Leaves*, p. 180." The *AR* version is:

> ———— pampering the coward heart
> With feelings all too delicate for use.
>
> Sweet are the Tears, that from a Howard's eye
> Drop on the cheek of one, he lifts from earth:
> And He, who works me good with unmoved face,

Does it but half. He chills me, while he aids,
My Benefactor, not my Brother Man.
But even this, this *cold* benevolence,
Seems Worth, seems Manhood, when there rise before me
The sluggard Pity's vision-weaving Tribe,
Who sigh for Wretchedness yet shun the wretched,
Nursing in some delicious Solitude
Their Slothful Loves and dainty Sympathies.

In the annotated copy which C presented to JTC he emended "benevolence" to "beneficence", "wretched" to "Wretched", and "Slothful" to "slothful".

55. Erratum in PR *4*: ". . . substitute *Praise, praise it, O my soul! oft as thou scann'st.*"
In the emended part copy at HUL JG has emended the line to conform to PR *5–7*.

59. PR *4* Sympathies!] In the emended part copy at HUL JG has emended to "sympathies!"

62⁺. Line-space in PR *4–7* (line 63 heads a page in PR *2*).

130. IRREGULAR SONNET:
TO JOHN THELWALL

A. DATE

Apr 1796. See sec C below.

B. TEXTS

1. HRC MS (Coleridge, S T) Works B. Single leaf, 18.5×23.7 cm; no wm;
chain-lines 2.5 cm. Draft in C's hand. Bound into Rugby Manuscript p 37/f 15ʳ.

2 [=RT]. HRC MS (Coleridge, S T) Works B. Verso of MS 1. Draft in C's
hand. Bound into Rugby Manuscript p 38/f 15ᵛ.

3. New York University, Heights Library Treasure Room. Lines 1–7, 15–16
quoted by John Thelwall in a marginal note to C's *BL* ch 10 (1817) I 177–8
(*CC*) I 187.

Thelwall describes the lines as part of a "sonnet", lines 15–16 being its
close. The complete marginalia are published by Burton R. Pollin and Redmond Burke "John Thelwall's Marginalia in a Copy of Coleridge's *Biographia
Literaria*" *BNYPL* LXXIV (Feb 1970) 73–94 (here 77, 82). The punctuation and
spelling are idiosyncratic and Thelwall's own; what authority the other variants
have is debatable. The version of lines 4–5 that Thelwall quotes in a letter to
C of 10 May 1796 (BM Add MS 35344 f 184ʳ) reinforces the independent
authority of MS 3, as well as the impression that Thelwall was casual over
details.

4. Lines 1–7 quoted in a report of the first of C's 1818–19 lectures on Shakespeare, in *The Champion* (21 Dec 1818), following the rhetorical question "Does Mr. C. recollect these lines—"; *Lects 1808–1819 (CC)* II 276. The report is subscribed "A. S." and, as R. A. Foakes remarks in *CC*, was probably written by John Thelwall, editor of the journal.

The lines are introduced in a way that connects them with the *BL* context, and therefore with MS 3. However, while "need" in line 1 might be a printer's error, line 6 goes behind MS 3 to C's holographs.

C. GENERAL NOTE

The sonnet has something in common with C's poems "on Eminent Characters" contributed to *M Chron* between Nov 1794 and Jan 1795, although its form is less regular. Thelwall's name may be one of those on the practically illegible list in the Gutch Notebook, a tentative order of poems to be included in the 1796 volume jotted down about Jul 1795 (*CN* I 305; see Woodring 226–7). The paper is compatible with that of other poems submitted as copy for the 1796 volume at about the same time (Effusions 5–8).

It is more likely that the sonnet was written a year later, at the beginning of C's friendship with John Thelwall. Thelwall quoted two lines in a letter dated 10 May 1796 (see MS 3 above), his letter being a reply to the first that he received from C together with a copy of *Poems* (1796) (*CL* I 204–5: to J. Thelwall [late Apr 1796]). Since the sonnet does not appear in C's letter, it is reasonable to assume that it was written in the volume itself; and it would have been appropriate for C to inscribe a recantation of his previous sonnet to Godwin as he addressed Thelwall for the first time (for the quarrel between Godwin and Thelwall see vol I headnote). The way in which C's lines contrast Thelwall with self-styled mimic patriots (like Godwin), and rewrite the Godwin sonnet to describe how Thelwall moves an admirer not to zeal but to action, certainly alludes to the quarrel. The same position is set out at greater length in C's second letter to Thelwall, of 13 May 1796 (*CL* I 212–16).

The inclusion of MSS 1 2 with the other materials contained in the Rugby Manuscript is not an indication that C intended to publish the sonnet in *Poems* (1797). One must suppose that the finished version represented by MS 3 was inscribed on a blank leaf of the presentation copy to Thelwall, and that Cottle retained the previous drafts as mementoes. If the poem was written impromptu, while C was in Bristol during the second half of Apr, he is unlikely to have kept a copy for himself, and it is in fact unlikely that the poem was ever intended to be published over his own name.

1	1		Some, Thelwall! to the patriot's ~~name~~ meed aspire
	2		Patriot meed
	3		patriot's
	4	********	need

```
2  1 2  Who in safe rage  without  or  rent or scar
   3 4       at      distance, without wound
3  1 2  Round pictur'd Strong-holds sketching mimic war
   3 4                  strong  walls  waging
4  1 2  Closet their valor. Thou mid thickest Fire
   3 4                  you midst
5  1 2  Leap'st on the wall: therefore shall Freedom chuse
   3 4  Leap         perilous  wall—Therefore  I
6  ⊠3  Ungaudy flowers, that chastest odours breathe,
   3    Unfading
7  1   And weave for thy young locks ~~the~~ her mural wreath:
   2                               her
   3 4  To                        the    civic
8  1   Nor thou this brief prelusive strain refuse.
   2          my song of grateful praise
11.1  1  From Him, whose youth thy fair example
9a.1  1  From ill-adventur'd Passion's feverish dream—
9b.1  1  And stretch'd at length by Cam's slow willowy stream
10.1  1  Pin'd for a woman's love in slothful woe
13.1  1  ~~Blest be thóue~~ hour, when first
      1  Starting I tore indignant from my brows
14.1  1  The myrtle ~~wreath~~ crown inwove with cypress boughs
9   2  My ill-adventur'd Youth by Cam's slow stream
10  2  Pin'd for a Woman's Love in slothful woe
11  2  First by thy fair example to glow
12  2  With patriot zeal: from Passion's feverish dream
13  2  Starting I tore ~~indign~~ disdainful from my brows
14  2  The Myrtle crown inwove with cypress boughs—
15  2  Blest if ~~in áftét future life to me~~ to me in Manhood's years belong
    3           to       my          maturer
16  2  Thy stern simplicity & vigorous song.
    3              nervous
```

1. 3 Some Thelwall 4 aspire, **2.** 4 Who, 4 scar, **3.** 2 strong- **4.** 3 Closset 2 valour. • 3 valour, • 4 valour: 4 you, 'midst 2 3 fire • 4 fire, **5.** 2 Wall: therefore • 4 wall. Therefore, ⊠1 choose **6** ⊠1 flowers 2 odors 3 breathe **7.** 2 *Mural* Wreath • 3 civic wreath • 4 civic wreathe **16.** 3 simplicity, 3 song—

4–5. Thelwall quoted the following version of these lines in his letter to C of 10 May 1796 (BM Add MS 35344 f 184ʳ):

> Thou, mid thickest fire,
> Leap'st on the perilous wall

7. 4 wreathe"] Followed by a dash and the words "etc. etc."

130.X1. EPIGRAM: ON A LATE MARRIAGE

The Watchman v (2 Apr 1796) 152 (*CC*) 188: "EPIGRAM | On a late Marriage between an OLD MAID and | French PETIT MAITRE. | Tho' Miss ——'s match is a subject of mirth,". 4 lines. Unsigned. Included in *LR* I 45; *PW* (EHC) II 952 No 2.

The epigram is by John Brenan, in *Anthologia Hibernica* I (Apr 1793) 307 (var), which C borrowed from the Bristol Library. See *Watchman* (*CC*) 188n.

130.X2. EPIGRAM: ON AN AMOROUS DOCTOR

The Watchman v (2 Apr 1796) 152 (*CC*) 188: "EPIGRAM | On an AMOROUS DOCTOR. | From Rufa's eye sly Cupid shot his dart". 8 lines. Unsigned. Included in *LR* I 46; *PW* (EHC) II 952 No 3.

The epigram is by John Brenan, in *Anthologia Hibernica* I (Apr 1793) 307, which C borrowed from the Bristol Library. See *Watchman* (*CC*) 188n.

130.X3. EPIGRAM: "OF SMART PRETTY FELLOWS IN BRISTOL ARE NUMBERS"

The Watchman v (2 Apr 1796) 159 (*CC*) 196: "Of smart pretty Fellows in Bristol are numbers, some". 4 lines. Unsigned. Included in *EOT* (1850) I 164; *PW* (EHC) II 952 No 4.

The untitled epigram adapts one by a Dr M'Donnell, in *Anthologia Hibernica* I (Feb 1793) 142, which C borrowed from the Bristol Library. See *Watchman* (*CC*) 196n.

130.X4. TO A PRIMROSE

The Watchman VIII (27 Apr 1796) 236 (*CC*) 277: "TO A PRIMROSE, | (The first seen in the Season.). | Thy smiles I note, sweet, early flower,". 5 4-line stanzas. Unsigned. Included in *LR* I 47; *PW* (JDC) 64–5; *PW* (EHC) I 149–50.

The poem is borrowed from *Anthologia Hibernica* I (Jan 1793) 60 (var), which C borrowed from the Bristol Library; there it is signed "S——" and dated 15 Feb 1791. In an annotated copy of *The Watchman*, now at the University of Kansas, C wrote underneath the poem "N.B. Not mine". See *Watchman* (*CC*) 277n.

130.X5. HALESWOOD POEM

On 28 May 1796 C sent a message via TP to Ellen Cruikshank, indicating that he would send his "Haleswood Poem" in his next parcel (*CL* I 218). One would suppose that Haleswood was in in the Quantocks—Ellen Cruikshank lived at Enmore—but there is no such place in the area, and names which look similar (Halswell, Halseway) are pronounced quite differently in Somerset (as "Has-well", "Holl-see", or "Hall-see"). Nor is there a Haleswood at or near any of the towns C had recently visited on his *Watchman* tour (Birmingham, Nottingham, Sheffield, etc). The title/description does not fit any poem C is known to have written, yet he appears to refer to a composition known by at least two other people.

The reference might possibly be connected with **120** *Fragments of an Epistle to Thomas Poole*, or the allusion may be to a copy of **82** *Monody on the Death of Chatterton*. C could have promised this to Ellen Cruikshank as a poem which answered or dealt differently with themes explored by the antiquary Joseph Haslewood (1769–1833). Haslewood interested himself in the Rowley controversy, and entered into a correspondence about it with Joseph Cottle. A further suggestion is that C may have been alluding to the *Halsewell*, an East India-man wrecked off Seacomb on 6 Jan 1786 and mentioned by Erasmus Darwin in *The Botanic Garden* I iv 213–32; the poem in question could then be **3** *Dura Navis*. If C did not have Darwin's poem in mind, he might have remembered the *Halsewell* from the description in William Crowe's *Lewesdon Hill* (Oxford 1788) 10–13, a poem which he had borrowed shortly before (*Bristol LB* No 72; cf No 38) and which he continued to think highly of long afterwards (*BL* ch 1—*CC*—I 17–18). By this circuitous route, the reference would then be to **129**

Reflections on Having Left a Place of Retirement, on which Crowe's poem had a formative influence.

130.X6. HYMNS TO THE ELEMENTS

C includes "Hymns to the Sun, the Moon, and the Elements—six hymns" in lists of projected works which he drew up in 1796 and Nov 1803 (*CN* I 174 (16); cf *CN* I 1646). CL several times asked after them in 1796–7 (*LL*—M—I 28, 57, 96). In 1820 C described to Thomas Allsop "the proud times when I planned, when I had present to my mind the materials as well as the Scheme of the Hymns, entitled Spirit, Sun, Earth, Air, Water, Fire, and Man" (*CL* v 28 [30 Mar 1830]). The project was admittedly a "mere Dream" by 1802 (*CL* II 829: to RS 29 Jul 1802), but the notebooks contain a good deal of material—observations and reading—relating to them: see *CN* indexes s.n. "Coleridge, S. T.—Projected Works"; their transformation into the *Ancient Mariner* is discussed in *RX* 74–9. The title is included here partly because of its importance as a shaping idea behind C's early verse, and partly because of its bearing on several untitled fragments. It is possible that further fragments will come to light—e.g. in letters to CL currently presumed lost.

131. TO THE PRINCESS OF WALES: WRITTEN DURING HER SEPARATION FROM THE PRINCE

A. DATE

The poem was written at the close of May or during the first half of Jun 1796. The Prince of Wales's renunciation of Princess Caroline took place on 30 Apr, but was not mentioned in *The Times* until 24 May. C alludes to those involved, displaying the same attitude as he exhibits in his poem, in a letter to John Fellows dated 31 May (*CL* I 219), while the scene alluded to in line 11 took place on 28 May and was reported in the newspapers a few days later. C sent a version of the poem (now lost) to CL, along with **132** *Poetical Address for Horne Tooke*, to be submitted to *M Chron* (*LL*—M—I 35), although James Perry, the editor, seems not to have been impressed.

The extant transcripts date from the time when C hoped that the poem might be published in *M Chron*, and are substantially similar. He appears to have lost interest in it soon afterwards.

1. BPL B 20895. Two conjoint leaves, each 25.0×39.5 cm; wm P I 1794; no chain-lines. Transcript signed "S. T. C.", in the body of an als to John Prior Estlin, 4 Jul 1796 (*CL* I 223–4).

The letter also contains **132** *Poetical Address for Horne Tooke.*

2. Cornell (WORDSWORTH). On the recto of two leaves, each 19.0× 25.7 cm, the LH margin being unevenly trimmed; first leaf has: no wm or chain-lines; second leaf: wm horn displayed in a crowned shield; chain-lines 2.3 cm. Transcript in C's hand, signed and dated "S. T. Coleridge I July 5th 1796". Endorsed on the recto of the second leaf: "This little Poem was read to my Mother by Coleridge at the Moment when it was written & given to her before she left the room—I *believe* it has never been published. Southy & Coleridge were at that time (& young Humphry Davey) constant visitors at my Fathers house. I Susan Coates."

Estlin's first wife, by whom he had a son, was a Miss Coates from Bristol. The person to whom C gave the transcript was probably Mrs Matthew Coates of Clifton.

3 [=RT]. Cornell WORDSWORTH Bd Cottle =Joseph Cottle's Album f 8ʳ. Transcript in C's hand, signed and dated "S. T. Coleridge I July, 1796". The ms is reproduced in *The Cornell Wordsworth Collection* ed George Harris Healey (Ithaca 1957) facing p 401.

1. Monthly Magazine II (Sept 1796) 647. Signed "S. T. COLERIDGE".

It is possible that this version resembles that sent to CL and Perry more closely than MSS 1–3. Rpt *Felix Farley's Bristol Journal* (2 Aug 1806), *The Poetical Register for 1806–1807* VI (1811) 365.

2. Felix Farley's Bristol Journal (8 Oct 1796). Signed "S. T. COLE-RIDGE".

It is difficult to know whether this text has separate authority. When C drew Thelwall's attention to the poem on 19 Nov (*CL* I 259), claiming that it was "written at the desire of a beautiful little Aristocrat", he referred only to the *Monthly Magazine* printing.

4. BPL B 21075. Single leaf, 12.2×19.7 cm, with imperfect conjoint leaf; wm J. PARSONS; chain-lines 2.4 cm; written on both sides. Transcript in the hand of John Prior Estlin, headed "Lines addressed to the Princess of Wales by Coleridge."

The pattern of variants suggests that this version might be a careless copy from a printed version; but this is not a necessary inference, and the transcript might even predate PR *1.*

title. 1 2 To an unfortunate Princess. • 3 To the Princess of Wales I written during her separation from the Prince. • *1 2* ON A LATE CONNUBIAL RUPTURE I IN HIGH LIFE.

1 ☐   I sigh, fair injur'd Stranger! for thy fate—
2 ☒4   But what shall Sighs avail thee? Thy poor Heart
4   ⟨can⟩
3 ☒4   Mid   all the pomp & circumstance of State
4   'Midst
4 ☐   Shivers in nakedness! Unbidden start
        [*Line-space*]
5 ☐   Sad Recollections of Hope's garish dream
6 ☒4   That shap'd a seraph form, and nam'd it Love—
4   call'd
7 ☒4   Its hues gay-varying,   as   the Orient Beam
4   ~~like~~ as
8 ☐   Varies the neck of Cytherea's Dove.
        [*Line-space*]
9 ☐   To one soft accent of domestic Joy
10 ☐   Poor are the Shouts that shake the high-arch'd Dome:
10fn 3   alluding to the Plaudits with which the Princess was received at the opera
        house during her separation.
11 1 2   The   Plaudits, that thy *public* path annoy;
☒1 2   Those
12 ☐   Alas! they tell thee—Thou'rt a Wretch *at home*!
        [*Line-space*]
13 1   Then o! retire and weep! Their very Woes
☒1   O then
14 ☐   Solace the guiltless. Drop the pearly Flood
15 ☒4   On thy sweet Infant, as the FULL-BLOWN Rose
4   O'er
16 ☒3 4 Surcharg'd   with dew bends o'er its neighb'ring BUD!
3   ~~O'er~~ Surcharg'd
4   Surcharg'd   it
        [*Line-space*]
17 1–3   And ah! that Truth some "holy spell" could lend
1 2   might
4   ⟨And⟩
18 ☒2   To lure thy Wanderer from the Syren's power:
2   the
19 ☒4   Then bid your Souls   inseparably blend,
4   hearts indissolubly
20 1 2   Like two bright Dew-drops ⟵—bosom'd—⟶ in   a   flower!
3   ~~bosom'd~~ meeting   ~~the~~ a
1 2 4   ⟵—meeting—⟶   a

title. 2 To an | Unfortunate Princess. • *2 On a late connubial Rupture in High Life.*
1. 4 sigh   *1 2* stranger! • 4 Stranger   *1* fate; • 2 fate, • 4 fate   **2.** 3 *1 2* sighs
1 2 thy   *1 2* heart, • 4 heart   **3.** 2 *1 2* 'Mid   3 "the pomp and circumstance" •
1 2 the "pomp and circumstance"   2 and   *1 2* state,   **4.** 3 *1* 4 nakedness. •
2 nakedness.—   *1* Unbidden,   **5.** 2 *1 2* 4 recollections   4 hope's   *1 2* dream,
6. 2 Seraph   4 form   3 4 &   2 3 LOVE, • *1 2* Love, • 4 love   **7.** 3 4 gay-varying
1 2 4 orient beam   **8.** 4 Neck   *1 2* 4 dove.   **9.** *1* 2 4 joy,   **10.** *1 2* 4 shouts

4 high arch'd   3 Dome; • *1 2* dome; • 4 dome   **11.** *1 2* plaudits, • 4 plaudits
4 publick   ☒1 annoy,   **12.** 4 thee thou'rt   *1 2* 4 wretch   2 *at home.* • 3 *1 2 at*
home! • 4 at home.   **13.** 4 Oh   *1 2* retire,   2 and weep! Their very woes •
1 2 and weep! *Their very woes* • 4 & weep—their very woes   **14.** 2 Solace the
ℊGuiltless. Drop • 3 Solace the Guiltless. Drop • *1 2 Solace the guiltless.* Drop •
4 Solace the guiltless—drop   ☒1 flood   **15.** *1* 4 infant,   3 *full-blown* • 4 full
blown   2 ROSE, • *1* rose, • 2 Rose, • 4 rose   **16.** *1 2* 4 dew,   3 *neighb'ring* •
4 neighbring   2 3 BUD. • *1 2* BUD. • 4 bud.   **17.** 4 Ah   4 truth   ☒1 holy spell
18. *1* wanderer • 4 Wand'rer   *1* syren's • 4 Syrens   2 *1 2* power; • 3 Power; • 4 power,
19. 2 *1 2* souls   3 4 blend   **20.** *1 2* dew-drops • 4 dew drops   2 *1 2* flower. •
3 Flower! • 4 flow'r.

2, 4, 6, etc. Alternate lines indented in PR *1 2.*
4⁺, 8⁺, 12⁺, 16⁺. Line-spaces uncertain in MSS 3 4.
6. MS 1 Love—] Possibly written a little larger, as if to be printed in bold.

132. POETICAL ADDRESS FOR
HORNE TOOKE

A. DATE

As C makes clear when introducing the lines to Estlin, they are "addressed to
Horne Tooke & the Company who met on June 28ᵗʰ to celebrate his Poll". The
poem had been received by CL in time to submit it, along with **131** *To the
Princess of Wales*, to James Perry of the *M Chron* before 30 Jun (*LL*—M—I
35), so it must have been written quickly in the preceding day or two. The fact
that C went back to the Gutch Notebook, combing it for phrases (see vol I EC),
again suggests hasty composition.

B. TEXTS

1. The Telegraph (9 Jul 1796): "By S. T. COLERIDGE."
This version must be close to the text sent to CL and rejected by Perry, now
lost. Capitals and punctuation are not C's, of course, and there appear to be a
few printer's errors. (Dropped type is not noted below.)

1 [=RT]. BPL B 20895. Two conjoint leaves, each 25.0×39.5 cm; wm P I
1794; no chain-lines. The lines are written two abreast. Transcript in the body
of an als to John Prior Estlin, 4 Jul 1796 (*CL* I 224–5).
The letter also contains **131** *To the Princess of Wales*.

title. *POETICAL ADDRESS,* I WRITTEN FOR I THE LATE MEETING OF
MR. TOOKE'S FRIENDS.

1 ☐ BRITONS! when last ye met, with distant streak,
1fn *1* Alluding to Horne Tooke's first contest for Westminster, and the comparatively small numbers, which he then polled.
2 ☐ So faintly promis'd the pale dawn to break,
3 *1* So dimly stain'd the precincts of the sky—
    1   dim it
4 *1* Hush'd expectation gaz'd with doubtful eye.
    1   E'en
5 ☐ But now such fair varieties of light
6 ☐ O'ertake the heavy-sailing clouds of night:
7 ☐ Th' horizon kindles with so rich a red,
8 ☐ That, tho' the sun still hides his glorious head,
9 ☐ Th' impatient mattin bird assur'd of day,
10 ☐ Leaves his low nest to meet it's earliest ray;
11 ☐ Loud the sweet song of gratulation sings,
12 ☐ And high in air claps his rejoicing wings.
      [*Line-space*]
13 *1* Yes, patriot sage! whose cleansing spirit first
    1   Patriot & Sage!   breeze-like
13fn *1* Diversions of Purley.
    1   Επεα πτεροεντα.
14 *1* The wordy pedant's lazy mist dispers'd,
    1   lazy mists of Pedantry
15a.1 *1* (That mist, within whose dim deceitful shade,
15.1.1 *1* Blighting with clammy dews each pleasant glade,
15b.1 *1* Decrepit *superstition's* pigmy band
15 1 (Mists, in which Superstition's *pigmy* band
16 ☐ Seem'd giant forms, the Genii of the land!)
17 1 Thy struggles soon shall wak'ning Britain bless,
18 1 And Truth & Freedom hail thy wish'd success.
19 ☐ Yes, TOOKE! tho' foul Corruption's wolfish throng
20 ☐ Out-malice Calumny's imposthum'd tongue,
17.1 *1* Thy struggles soon shall waken'd Britain bless,
18.1 *1* And truth and freedom hail thy wish'd success!
21 ☐ Thy country's noblest and *determin'd* choice,
22 ☐ Soon shalt thou thrill the Senate with thy voice;
23 ☐ With gradual dawn bid error's phantoms flit,
24 ☐ Or wither with the lightning flash of wit.
25 ☐ Or with sublimer mien and tones more deep
26 ☐ Charm sworded Justice from mysterious sleep—
27 ☐ By violated Freedom's loud lament,
28 ☐ Her lamps extinguish'd and her temple rent;
29 ☐ By the forc'd tears, her captive martyrs shed;
30 ☐ By each pale orphan's feeble cry for bread;
31 ☐ By ravag'd Belgium's corse-impeded flood,
32 ☐ And Vendee steaming still with brothers' blood!
33 ☐ And if amid the strong impassion'd tale
34 ☐ Thy tongue should faulter and thy lips turn pale;
35 ☐ If transient darkness film thy awful eye.

36 □ And thy tir'd bosom struggle with a sigh;
37 □ Science and freedom shall demand to hear
38 □ Who practis'd on a life so doubly dear;
39 *1* Infus'd the ←—secret—→ anguish drop by drop
   1   unwholesome
40 *1* Pois'ning the precious stream they could not stop;
   1   sacred
41 *1* Shall bid thee with recov'ring vigor shew
   1   recover'd strength relate
41.1.1 *1* Disease's gnawing pang unseen and slow,
41.1.2 *1* And the worse bodings of parental woe:
42 1 How dark & deadly is a Coward's Hate:
43 1 What seeds of Death by wan Confinement sown
44 1 When prison-echoes mock'd Diseases grown!
45 *1* Bid   thy   indignant   spirit flash dismay
   1 Shall bid th' indignant Father
46 □ And drag th' unnatural villain into day,
47 *1* Who to the sport of his flesh'd ruffians left
   1   sports
47fn 1 Dundas left thief-takers in Horne Tooke's House for three days—with his
       two Daughters *alone*; for Horne Tooke keeps no servant.—
48 *1* The helpless virgins of their sire bereft!
   1 Two lovely Mourners
49 □ 'Twas wrong like this, which Rome's first consul bore
49fn *1* Jun. Brutus.
50 □ So by th' insulted female's name he swore
51 *1* Ruin (and rais'd the reeking dagger high)
   1   her
52 *1* To strike the tyrants and the tyranny!
   1 Not   to   but

1. 1 Britons! 1 streak   **2.** 1 Dawn 1 break;   **3.** 1 Sky   **4.** 1 *Expectation*
1 Eye.   **5.** 1 Varieties 1 Light   **6.** 1 Clouds of Night;   **7.** 1 Horizon
8. 1 though 1 *Sun still hides*   **9.** 1 Matin-bird *assur'd of Day*   **11.** 1 Gratulation
12. 1 wings!   **13.** 1 Spirit   **16.** 1 Giant Forms, 1 Land!)   **19.** 1 *Tooke*!
20. 1 Outmalice 1 Tongue,   **21.** 1 Country's 1 & *determin'd* Choice,
23. 1 Dawn 1 Error's   **24.** 1 Wit;   **25.** 1 &   **26.** 1 Sleep,   **27.** 1 "By
1 Lament,   **28.** 1 "Her Lamps 1 & 1 Temple   **29.** 1 "By 1 Martyrs
30. 1 "By 1 Orphan's   **31.** 1 "By 1 Flood,   **32.** 1 "And   **33.** 1 Tale
34. 1 Tongue 1 falter & 1 Lips   **35.** 1 Dark͵ness͵ 1 aweful Eye,
36. 1 Bosom   **37.** 1 & Freedom 1 ͵shall͵   **38.** 1 Life   **39.** 1 unwholso͵me
a͵nguish   **40.** 1 stream, 1 stop!   **46.** 1 Villain 1 Day,   **47.** 1 Ruffians
48. 1 Sire   **49.** 1 wrong, 1 *first ₵Consul* bore—   **50.** 1 Female's 1 *he*
51. 1 &   **52.** 1 *Tyrants* 1 *Tyranny*!!

41–41.1.2. The triple rhyme is indicated by a brace in PR *1*.

132.X1. SONNET: TO POVERTY

Selection of Poems, Designed Chiefly for Schools and Young Persons ed Joseph Cottle (1st ed 1804) 198 = (2nd ed 1815) 152–3: "SONNET. I TO POVERTY. I Low in a barren vale I see thee sit". 14 lines. Unsigned.

The irregular (unrhymed) sonnet was printed in Cottle's volume following C's *Domestic Peace* (poem **66**). In the table of Contents of each edition there is a rule under C's name, which could be construed as a ditto-mark, indicating that C was also the author of *To Poverty*. G. W. Wright so construed it, and reported that EHC accepted his argument that the sonnet was by C and would have incorporated it in a second edition of *PW* ("A Sonnett by Coleridge?" *N&Q* CLII—12 Feb 1927—115–16). But C's authorship seems more than doubtful.

Although the poem does not appear in the first edition of Joseph Cottle's *Malvern Hills and Other Poems* (1798), it appears in later editions (3rd ed 1802 p 144; 4th ed 2 vols 1829 II 266) among a section of "Poems by the late Amos Cottle". Its authorship is so specified in the third edition of Joseph Cottle's *Selections* (1823 pp 157–8), and it is omitted altogether from the fourth edition (1836). G. W. Wright, and apparently EHC, thought that the evidence proved that Joseph Cottle could not properly recall who the author was and that, on internal grounds, the sonnet should be assigned to C. But the internal and external evidence rather proves that the author was Amos Cottle.

133. TO A FRIEND WHO HAD DECLARED HIS INTENTION OF WRITING NO MORE POETRY

A. DATE

Sept 1796. The focus of the poem on Burns (who died on 21 Jul 1796) and the implications of PR *1* below, might suggest that it was composed before C learned of the calamity that overtook CL on 22 Sept. It could have been sent to CL in a letter which arrived at the time of the calamity itself or immediately following—the title sadly anticipating or even provoking CL's expressions of impatience with the "the idle trade of versifying" in Sept–Nov 1796, unless it was added afterwards. CL certainly came to forbid C to mention poetry (*LL*— M—I 45; cf ibid 78), and it is also possible that the poem was written after the calamity, deliberately to rouse CL's feelings in a cause to which he had long been committed.

The addition of the date 1796 to the end of PR *2–6* is an unusual feature, explained by the fact that the Wedgwoods had assuaged C's complaints about patronage by the time the poem was republished.

1. V&A Dyce Collection 4to 1298. A corrected cutting bound up with a copy of W. L. Bowles *Sonnets* (1796) presented to Mrs Thelwall on 18 Dec 1796. Signed "S. T. COLERIDGE."

In his accompanying letter C says that the poem "was printed to be dispersed among friends" (*CL* I 286). Cottle *E Recs* I 244 implies that it was first published in a Bristol newspaper. The only one of the five Bristol newspapers it could have been published in is *Sarah Farley's Bristol Journal* (10 Sept 1796); the section torn from the only extant copy (BPL) would contain C's poem exactly, and the previous number carried "A Bard's Epitaph. By the late Robert Burns." However, the V&A cutting is from heavier stock than an ordinary newspaper, and the verso is blank. Peculiarities of spelling (e.g. 2 "wizzard", 29 "it's") might suggest that it was set from C's holograph, but are not decisive. The newspaper version was likewise signed with C's name (*S Letters*—Curry—I 207).

2. Annual Anthology ed RS (2 vols Bristol 1799–1800) II 103–5. Signed "*ES TEESI.* 1796." RS appears to have used the Bristol newspaper version as his copy, alhough C is responsible for the changed signature (*S Letters*—Curry—I 207).

3 [=RT]. *SL* (1817). Dated 1796.

The erratum has been taken in on the following copies: WW's (by AG) (Cornell WORDSWORTH PR 4480 S5 1817 Copy 1); TP's (by AG) (Brown PR 4478 A1 1817 Koopman Collection); JG's (by C overwritten by JG) (HUL *EC8 C6795 817s (C)); an unknown person's (by JG?) (Duke R.B.R. A-29 C693 SM); the emended part copy (by JG) (HUL *EC8 C6795 817s (D)).

4. PW (1828).

5. PW (1829).

6. PW (1834).

The copy at HEHL (109531) carries two minor corrections in C's hand.

title. *1–6 To a FRIEND who had declared his intention of* | *Writing no more Poetry.*

1 *1 2* Dear Charles! while yet thou wert a babe, I ween
   3–6 whilst
2 ☐ That GENIUS plung'd thee in that wizzard fount,
3 *1 2* Hight Castalie: and (sureties for thy faith)
   3–6 of
4 ☐ That PITY and SIMPLICITY stood by,
5 ☐ And promis'd for thee, that thou should'st renounce

6 □		The World's low cares and lying vanities,
7 □		Stedfast and rooted in the heavenly Muse,
8 □		And wash'd and sanctified to POESY.
9 □		Yes—thou wert plung'd, but with forgetful hand
10 □		Held, as by Thetis erst her warrior son:
11 □		And with those recreant unbaptized heels
12 □		Thou'rt flying from thy bounden ministeries—
13 □		So sore it seems and burthensome a task
14 □		To weave unwith'ring flowers! But take thou heed:
15 □		For thou art vulnerable, wild-eyed Boy!
16	*1 2*	And I have arrows mystically tipt,
	3–6	dipt,
16fn □		*Vide Pind. Olymp.* 2. *l.* 156.
17 □		Such as may stop thy speed. Is thy BURNS dead
18 □		And shall he die unwept and sink to earth
19 □		"Without the meed of one melodious tear?"
20 □		*Thy* BURNS, and Nature's own beloved Bard
21 □		Who to "th' Illustrious of his native land
22 □		So properly did look for patronage."
21–2fn □		*Verbatim from Burn's Dedication of his Poems to the Nobility and Gentry of the Caledonian Hunt.*
23 □		Ghost of Mæcenas! hide thy blushing face!
24 □		They snatch'd him from the sickle and the plough—
25a ⊠*3*		To gauge ale-firkins!
	3	guard
		[*Line-space*]
25b □		O for shame return!
26 □		On a bleak rock, midway th' Aonian mount,
27 □		There stands a lone and melancholy tree,
28 □		Whose aged branches to the midnight blast
29 □		Make solemn music: pluck it's darkest bough,
30 □		Ere yet th' unwholesome night-dew be exhal'd,
31 □		And weeping wreath it round thy poet's tomb.
32 □		Then in the outskirts, where pollutions grow,
33	*1 2*	Pick stinking hensbane, and the dusky flowers
	3–6	the rank
34 □		Of night-shade, or its red and tempting fruit.
35 □		These with stopp'd nostril and glove-guarded hand
36 □		Knit in nice intertexture, so to twine
37 □		Th' illustrious Brow of SCOTCH NOBILITY!

title. *2 3 To a FRIEND* | *Who had declared his intention of writing no more Poetry.* *4–6* TO A FRIEND | WHO HAD DECLARED HIS INTENTION OF WRITING | NO MORE POETRY. **1.** *2* CHARLES! *4 5* babe **2.** *3–6* Genius *2–6* plunged *2–6* wizard *3–6* fount **3.** *3–5* Castalie; **4.** *3–6* Pity and Simplicity **5.** *3–6* promised *3–6* shouldst **6.** *3–6* world's **7.** *4–6* Steadfast **8.** *4–6* washed *3–6* Poesy. **9.** *2–6* plunged, **10.** *3–5* Son: **11.** *3–5* Heels **12.** *3–5* Ministeries • *6* minist'ries— **14.** *2–6* unwithering **15.** *3–5* Boy, • *6* boy, **16.** *4 5* dipped, **16fn.** *2* Vide Pind. Olymp. 2. l. 156. • *3 4* Vide

Pind. Olym. ii. 1. 156. • *5* Vide Pind. Olymp. iii. 1. 156. • *6* Pind. Olymp. ii. 1. 150.
17. *3–6* Burns dead?   **18.** *3–6* unwept,   *3–5* Earth   **19.** *5* tear?   **20.** *3–6* Thy
Burns,   *3–5* Bard, • *6* bard,   **21.** *2* "the Illustrious • *3–6* the "Illustrious   *3–6* Land
22. *3–5* "So   *3–5* Patronage."   **21–2fn.** *2* Verbatim from Burn's Dedication of
his Poem to the Nobility and Gentry of the Caledonian Hunt. • *3—5* Verbatim from
Burns's dedication of his Poem to the Nobility and Gentry of the Caledonian Hunt. •
6 Verbatim from Burns' dedication of his Poem to the Nobility and Gentry of the
Caledonian Hunt.   **24.** *4–6* snatched   *3–5* Sickle   *3–5* Plough—   **25a.** *3–5* Ale-
Firkins. • *6* ale-firkins.   **25b.** *3–6* Oh!   **26.** *3–5* Rock,   *2–6* the   **29.** *2–6* its
30. *2–6* the   *3–6* unwholesome   *3–5* Night-dew   *3–6* exhaled,   **31.** *3–6* Poet's
3–5 Tomb.   **33.** *3* hensbane • *4–6* henbane   **34.** *5 6* fruit,   **35.** *3–6* stopped
36. *5 6* twine,   **37.** *2–6* The   *3–5* Illustrious   *3–6* Scotch Nobility.

title. In the HEHL copy of PR *6* C has inserted "Charles Lamb" after "TO".
3. PR *5* Castalie;] The tail of the semicolon is broken in all copies inspected, so that it
looks like a colon.
21–2fn. All texts in fact key the footnote to "Illustrious" in line 21.
25. Erratum in PR *3*: "for *guard* r. *guage*."
35. PR *1* nostril⟨s⟩] Insertion possibly by C.
37. In the HEHL copy of PR *6* C has altered to "Scotch".

134. SONNET: WRITTEN ON RECEIVING LETTERS INFORMING ME OF THE BIRTH OF A SON, I BEING AT BIRMINGHAM

A. DATE

It would appear the poem was written between 20 Sept 1796, when C learned
of his son's birth, and mid-Oct, when he was with TP. See vol I headnote.

B. TEXT

BM Add MS 35343 f 128ʳ. Two conjoint leaves, each 26.5×41.6 cm; wm
(each leaf) WATT & CO: | PATENT COPYING | PAPER | 1796; no chain-lines
(wove). The first of three sonnets by C enclosed in an als to TP of 1 Nov 1796,
each signed "S. T. Coleridge" (*CL* I 245–6). See Addenda, p 1374 below.
    For the other sonnets see poems **135, 136.**

The RT reproduces the ms exactly, except for:

title. ms Sonnet | written on receiving letters informing me of the birth of a Son, ⟨I
being at Birmingham⟩   **2.** ms spirit*t*!   **3.** ms ~~Seeking the throne of Mercy; but I
felt~~ Seeking

135. SONNET: COMPOSED ON A JOURNEY HOMEWARD, THE AUTHOR HAVING RECEIVED INTELLIGENCE OF THE BIRTH OF A SON

A. DATE

Sept–Oct 1796. The date given in later titles—20 Sept 1796—is confirmed from other sources (*CL* I 236: to TP 24 Sept 1796; 260–1: to J. Thelwall 19 Nov 1796), but it is the date of the genesis of the poem, not of its composition. The poem did not advance to its finished form until after C had left Poole at Stowey—i.e. late Oct (*CL* I 246: to TP 1 Nov 1796).

B. TEXTS

1. BM Add MS 35343 f 128ʳ. Two conjoint leaves, each 26.5×41.6 cm; wm (each leaf) WATT & CO: I PATENT COPYING I PAPER I 1796; no chain-lines (wove). The second of three sonnets by C enclosed in an als to TP of 1 Nov 1796, each signed "S. T. Coleridge" (*CL* I 246).

2. PML MA 77 (5). Two conjoint leaves, each 26.7×41.7 cm; wm WATT & CO: I PATENT COPYING I PAPER I 1796; no chain-lines (wove). Included as the first of two sonnets by C in an als to John Thelwall of 19 Nov 1796 (*CL* I 260–1).

2*. An alternative version of the first five lines, included in MS 2. For a revision of this alternative, sent to Thelwall on 17 Dec 1796 (*CL* I 278), see vol I headnote.

3. NYPL Berg Collection. Recto of a single leaf, 21.9×20.9 cm; wm Britannia in oval frame; chain-lines 2.6 cm. Transcript in C's hand, initialled "S T C" by Joseph Cottle (as a note by RS on the verso remarks). The verso contains the sonnet 136 *When the Nurse First Presented my Infant*. The two poems are headed "Sonnet 9" and "Sonnet 10", and clearly provided copy for PR *1* below.

1 [=RT]. *Poems* (1797).
There is a correction in C's hand in Thomas Hutchinson's copy (in the possession of Jonathan Wordsworth, 1980).

2. *Poems* (1803).
There is a correction in C's hand in SH's copy (Cornell WORDSWORTH PR 4252 B91R9 1813 Copy 2).

3. SL (1817).
The proof sheets at Yale (In C678 817sa) suggest that copy was provided by an uncorrected version of PR *1*.

4. PW (1828).

5. PW (1829).

6. PW (1834).

title. 1 Sonnet ǀ ⟨Composed on my journey home from Birmingham. • 3 Sonnet 9 ǀ Composed on a journey homeward. ⟨when⟩ the Author had received ǀ intelligence of the birth of a Son, Septemb. 20ᵗʰ, 1796. • *1 SONNET IX.* ǀ *Composed on a journey homeward; the Author having* ǀ *received intelligence of the Birth of a Son, September* ǀ *20, 1796.* • *2 SONNET XVII.* ǀ *Composed on a journey homward; the Author having received* ǀ *intelligence of the Birth of a Son, Sept. 20, 1796.* • *3–6 SONNET.* ǀ *Composed on a journey homeward; the Author having received* ǀ *intelligence of the birth of a Son, September 20, 1796.*

1.1	1 2	Oft of *some unknown Past* such Fancies roll
2.1	1 2	Swift o'er my brain, as make the Present seem,
2.1.1	1 2	For a brief moment, like a most strange dream
2.1.2	1 2	When, not unconscious that she dreamt, the Soul
1	2ᵗʰ	Oft o'er my brain mysterious Fancⅰes roll
3	*1–6*	does that strange Fancy
2	2*	That make the Present seem (the while they last)
3	*1–6*	Which makes the Present (while the Flash doth last)
3	2*	A dreary Semblance of some Unknown Past
3	*1–6*	Seem a mere
4	2*ⁱᵐᵖ	Mix'd with such feelings, as distress the ₍soul₎
3	*1–6*	perplex the soul
5	1 2	Questions herself in sleep! and Some have said
	2*	Half-reas'ning in her
3	*1–6*	Self-question'd
5fn	3 *1–6*	ἦν που ἡμῶν ἡ ψυχη πρὶν ἐν τῷδε τῷ ἀνθρωπίνῳ εἴδει γενέσθαι.
		Plat. in Phædon.—
6	1–3	We liv'd ere yet this *fleshly* robe we wore.
	1 2	fleshy
	3–6	robe of Flesh
7	□	O my sweet Baby! when I reach my door,
8	⊠*3–6*	If heavy Looks should tell me, thou wert dead,
	3–6	art
9	□	(As sometimes, thro' excess of Hope, I fear)
10	□	I think, that I should struggle to believe,
11	□	Thou wert a Spirit to this nether sphere
12	□	Sentenc'd, for some more venial crime to grieve—
13	□	Didst scream, then spring to meet Heaven's quick Reprieve,
14	□	While we wept idly o'er thy little Bier!

title. *4 5* SONNET. ǀ COMPOSED ON A JOURNEY HOMEWARD; THE ǀ AUTHOR

HAVING RECEIVED INTELLIGENCE | OF THE BIRTH OF A SON, SEPTEMBER 20, 1796. • *6* SONNET. | COMPOSED ON A JOURNEY HOMEWARD; THE AUTHOR | HAVING RECEIVED INTELLIGENCE OF THE | BIRTH OF A SON, SEPT. 20, 1796.   **1.1.** 2 some *Unknown Past* 2 fancies   **2.1.** 2 seem,   **2.1.2.** 2 Dream **1.** *1–6* fancy   **2.** *1–6* present *1–6* flash   **3.** 3 *1–6* semblance 3 *1–6* unknown 3 Past, • *1–6* past,   **4.** *4–6* Mixed   **5.** *4–6* -questioned 2 2* 3 *1–4* sleep: • *5* 6 sleep; 3 *1–6* some 2 3 said,   **5fn.** *1–5* omit all diacritics   **5fn1.** *1–* *5* Ἡν • *6* Ἡν *6* ψύχη *6* γενεσθαι.—   **5fn2.** *3–5* PLAT. • *6* Plat. 3 *6 in* • *4 5* IN *1* 2 Phædon. • *3 6 Phædon.* • *4 5* PHÆDON   **6.** 3 *1–3* liv'd, • *4–6* lived, 3 fleshly • 6 flesh   **7.** *3–6* baby! 2 Door   **8.** *1–6* looks *3–6* me 3 *1–* *3* dead   **9.** *4–6* through 3 *1–6* hope,   **10.** *4–6* think 2 *struggle* 2 *1–* 6 believe   **11.** 3 *1* 2 Spirit, • *3–6* spirit, 2 Sphere   **12.** 2 3 *1–3* Sentenc'd • *4–6* Sentenced   ☒1 grieve;   **13.** *3–6* Did'st 2 heaven's 2 reprieve • 3 *1–* 6 reprieve,   **14.** 3 *1 3–6* bier! 2 bier.

title. In the PR *1* list of Contents given as "*On the Birth of a Son*,".

2–3, 6–7, 11, 14. Indented in PR *2–6*.

5fn. See vol I headnote for C's earlier comment concerning Fénelon, written alongside lines 5–6 in MS 1; and for his reference to Plato in MS 2.

6. PR *1* 2 fleshly] In Thomas Hutchinson's copy of PR *1* C altered to "earthly"; in SH's copy of PR *2* he altered to "fleshly". The proof sheets of *SL* at Yale alter the line to conform to the reading of PR *3–6*.

136. SONNET: TO A FRIEND, WHO ASKED HOW I FELT, WHEN THE NURSE FIRST PRESENTED MY INFANT TO ME

A. DATE

Sept–Oct 1796. The poem represents C's feelings when he first saw HC, on 20 or 21 Sept 1796 (cf *CL* I 236: to TP 24 Sept 1796), but it was "in a rude & undrest state" when he stayed with TP in mid-Oct (*CL* I 246: to TP 1 Nov 1796).

B. TEXTS

1. BM Add MS 35343 f 128ʳ. Two conjoint leaves, each 26.5×41.6 cm; wm (each leaf) WATT & CO: | PATENT COPYING | PAPER | 1796; no chain-lines (wove). The third of three sonnets by C enclosed in an als to TP of 1 Nov 1796, each signed "S. T. Coleridge" (*CL* I 246–7). See Addenda, p 1374 below.

2. PML MA 77 (5). Two conjoint leaves, each 26.7×41.7 cm; wm WATT & CO: | PATENT COPYING | PAPER | 1796; no chain-lines (wove). Included as

the second of two sonnets by C in an als to John Thelwall of 19 Nov 1796 (*CL*
I 261).

3. NYPL Berg Collection. Verso of a single leaf, 21.9×20.9 cm; wm Britan-
nia in oval frame; chain-lines 2.6 cm. Transcript in C's hand, initialled "S T C"
by Joseph Cottle (as a note by RS testifies). The recto has the sonnet **135** *Com-
posed on a Journey Homeward*. The two poems are headed "Sonnet 9" (recto)
and "Sonnet 10" (verso), and clearly provided the copy for PR *1* below.

1 [=RT]. *Poems* (1797).
The copy C gave to William Roskilly (in the possession of J.C.C. Mays,
1999) and the copy he annotated for RS (?) (Yale In 678 797 Copy 1) contain
the correction (deletion of the point after "appear" in line 11) which C asked
Joseph Cottle to make in his letter of c 3 Jul 1797 (*CL* I 331).

The reprint in *Poetical Sketches of Modern Writers* (1798; 2nd ed 1803; etc)
157–8 is of no textual interest.

2. *Poems* (1803).
The transcript in JTC's Commonplace Book (University of Pennsylvania
Library (Special Collections) MS Eng 13) pp 51–2 is of this text, omitting
line 8.

3. SL (1817).

4. PW (1828).

5. PW (1829).

6. PW (1834).

C. GENERAL NOTE

In a letter to his wife from Germany C says that he made a German version of
the poem which was found pleasing, "& considerably dilated with new images
& much superior in the German to it's former dress" (*CL* I 429: 20 Oct 1798).
If such a version did indeed exist by 20 Oct 1799 (C was in the early stages of
learning German), it appears not to have been preserved.

title. 1 Sonnet | to a friend who wished to know *how I felt* when the Nurse first
present my Infant to me. • 2 Sonnet II | To a Friend who asked me *how* I felt when
the Nurse first presented the | Child to me. • 3 Sonnet 10th | To a Friend, who asked
how I felt, when the Nurse first | presented ~~me~~ my Infant to me.— • *1 SONNET
X.* | *To a Friend, who asked how I felt, when the Nurse first* | *presented my Infant to
me.* • *2 SONNET XIX.* | *To a FRIEND, who asked how I felt, when the Nurse first* |
presented my Infant to me. • *3–6 SONNET,* | *To a Friend, who asked how I felt, when
the Nurse first* | *presented my Infant to me.*

1 ☐   Charles! my slow Heart was only *sad*, when first
2 ☐   I scann'd that face of feeble Infancy:

3 □　　　For dimly on my thoughtful spirit burst
4 ⊠*3–6*　All I had been, and all my Babe might be!
　3–6　　　　　　　　　　　child
5 1 2　　But when I　watch'd　it on its Mother's arm
3　　　　　　　　　　~~watch'd~~ saw
1–6　　　　　　　　←—saw—→
6 □　　　And hanging at her bosom (she the while
7 ⊠2　　　Bent　　o'er its features with a tearful smile)
2　　　　~~Meant~~ Bent
8 □　　　Then I was thrill'd & melted, and most warm
9 □　　　Imprest *a Father's kiss*! And all beguil'd
10 □　　Of dark Remembrance and presageful Fear
11 ⊠*3–6*　I seem'd to see an Angel's form appear—
　3–6　　　　　　　　　　angel-form
12 □　　'Twas even thine, beloved Woman mild!
13 □　　So for the Mother's sake the Child was dear,
14 ⊠2　　And dearer was the Mother for the Child!
2　　　　　　　　　　　Mother

title. *4–6* SONNET. | TO A FRIEND WHO ASKED, HOW I FELT WHEN
THE | NURSE FIRST PRESENTED MY INFANT TO ME.　**1.** *1–6* heart　3 *1–*
6 sad,　3 first *I*　**2.** *4–6* scanned　*1–6* infancy:　**3.** 3 Spirit　**4.** 2 *1 2* babe
5. *6* mother's　3 *1–6* arm,　**6.** 2 (She　**8.** 2 *thrill'd*, & *melted*, • 3 *1–3* thrill'd
and melted, • *4–6* thrilled and melted,　**9.** 3 *1–3* Impress'd • *4–6* Impressed　2 a
Father's Kiss—and • 3 *1–5* a Father's kiss: and • *6* a father's kiss: and　*4–6* beguiled
10. 3 Remembrance, • *1 2* remembrance, • *3–6* remembrance　*1* fear • *2–6* fear,
11. 3 see?⸗　*4–6* seemed　3 *1* appear.—　**12.** *3–6* woman　**13.** *6* mother's
6 child　**14.** *6* mother　3 *1–5* Child. • *6* child.

　title. In the PR *1* list of Contents given as *"On first seeing my Infant,"*.
　2, 4, 6–7, 10–11, 13. Indented in PR *3–6*.
　11. PR *1* appear.—] C told Cottle to omit the full point when he sent him a list of
errata c 3 Jul 1797 (*CL* I 331). C deleted it himself in the copy he gave to William
Roskilly, and in RS's (?) copy.

137. SONNET: INTRODUCING
CHARLES LLOYD'S POEMS ON THE
DEATH OF PRISCILLA FARMER

A. DATE

Sept–Oct 1796. C met Lloyd in mid-Aug 1796, and Lloyd returned with C to
Bristol on 20–1 Sept. C's sonnet was written thereafter, as Lloyd put together
and published the volume in which the sonnet first appeared.

B. TEXTS

1. Charles Lloyd *Poems on the Death of Priscilla Farmer* (Bristol 1796) 3 (the first poem in the volume). Signed "S. T. COLERIDGE."

2 [=RT]. *Poems* (1797).
C's poem here (on p 193) introduces the same set of poems by Lloyd. Signed "*S. T. COLERIDGE.*" It is not listed in the table of Contents as being by C, which may explain its omission from later collections.

3. Charles Lloyd *Nugæ Canoræ* (3rd ed 1819) 145. Signed "*S. T. COLE-RIDGE.*"
C emended the poem (in pencil) in his own copy (BM C 45 a 22).

The RT reproduces PR *2* exactly. Only accidental variants are given here since the words and indentation are identical in all three texts.

title. *1* SONNET. • *2 SONNET.* • *3* SONNET.   **1.** *3* breath,   **3.** *3* dwelling; **4.** *3* death;   **9.** *3* recal

13. In the BM copy of PR *3* C emended the line to "Comforts on his late Eve, whose youthful breast".

138. TO CHARLES LLOYD, ON HIS PROPOSING TO DOMESTICATE WITH THE AUTHOR

A. DATE

Oct 1796. See vol I headnote.

B. TEXTS

1 [=RT]. *Poems* (1797).
The following three copies contain revisions, the first two indubitably in C's hand and the third apparently in RS's (or perhaps Charles Lloyd's): William Bowles's (in the possession of Erwin Schwarz, 1982); William Roskilly's (in the possession of J.C.C. Mays, 1999); RS's (?) (Yale In 678 797 Copy 1).

2. *Poems* (1803).

3. *SL* (1817).
The new readings in lines 8 and 16 were introduced in proof (see the proof

copy at Yale: In C678 817sa), the other changes having been made in the copy previously sent to the printer.

4. PW (1828).

5. PW (1829).

6. PW (1834).

title. *1 To C. LLOYD*, | ON HIS PROPOSING TO DOMESTICATE | WITH THE AUTHOR. • *2 To a FRIEND*, | ON HIS PROPOSING TO DOMESTICATE | WITH THE AUTHOR. • *3–6 TO A YOUNG FRIEND*, | *On his proposing to Domesticate with the Author*. | Composed in 1796.

1	☐	A mount, not wearisome and bare and steep,
2	☐	But a green Mountain variously up-pil'd,
3	☐	Where o'er the jutting rocks soft mosses creep
4	☐	Or color'd lichens with slow oozing weep;
5	☐	Where cypress and the darker yew start wild;
6	☐	And mid the summer torrent's gentle dash
7	☐	Dance brighten'd the red clusters of the ash;
8	*1*	Beneath whose boughs, by stilly sounds beguil'd,
	2	stillest
	3–6	those still
9	☐	Calm PENSIVENESS might muse herself to sleep;
10	☐	Till haply startled by some fleecy dam,
11	☐	That rustling on the bushy cliff above
12	☐	With melancholy bleat of anxious love
13	☐	Made meek enquiry for her wand'ring lamb:
14	☐	Such a green Mountain 'twere most sweet to climb
15	☐	E'en while the bosom ach'd with loneliness—
16	*1 2*	How heavenly sweet, if some dear Friend should bless
	3–6	more than
17	☐	Th' advent'rous toil, and up the path sublime
18	☐	Now lead, now follow; the glad landscape round,
19	☐	Wide and more wide, increasing without bound!
		[*Line-space*]
20	☐	O then 'twere loveliest sympathy, to mark
21	☐	The berries of the half up-rooted ash
22	☐	Dripping and bright; and list the torrent's dash—
23	☐	Beneath the cypress or the yew more dark,
24	☐	Seated at ease, on some smooth mossy rock;
25	☐	In social silence now, and now t' unlock
26	☐	The treasur'd heart; arm link'd in friendly arm,
27	☐	Save if the one, his muse's witching charm
28	☐	Mutt'ring brow-bent, at unwatch'd distance lag;
29	☐	Till high o'er head his beck'ning Friend appears,
30	☐	And from the forehead of the topmost crag
31	☐	Shouts eagerly: for haply *there* uprears
32	☐	That shadowing PINE its old romantic limbs,

33	☐	Which latest shall detain th' enamoured sight
34	☐	Seen from below, when Eve the valley dims,
35	☐	Ting'd yellow with the rich departing light;
36	☐	And haply, bason'd in some unsunn'd cleft,
37	☐	A beauteous spring, the rock's collected tears,
38	☐	Sleeps shelter'd there, scarce wrinkled by the gale!
39	☐	Together thus, the world's vain turmoil left,
40	☐	Stretch'd on the crag, and shadowed by the pine,
41	☐	And bending o'er the clear delicious fount,
42	*1*	Ah dearest LLOYD! it were a lot divine
	2	Charles!
	3–6	youth!
43	☐	To cheat our noons in moralizing mood,
44	☐	While west-winds fann'd our temples toil-bedew'd:
45	☐	Then downwards slope, oft-pausing, from the mount,
46	*1 2*	To some low mansion in some woody dale,
	3–6	lone
47	☐	Where smiling with blue eye DOMESTIC BLISS
48	☐	Gives *this* the husband's, *that* the brother's kiss!
		[*Line-space*]
49	☐	Thus rudely vers'd in allegoric lore,
50	☐	The hill of knowledge I essay'd to trace;
51	☐	That verd'rous hill with many a resting place,
52	☐	And many a stream, whose warbling waters pour
53	☐	To glad, and fertilize the subject plains;
54	☐	That hill with secret springs, and nooks untrod,
55	☐	And many a fancy-blest and holy sod
56	☐	Where INSPIRATION, his diviner strains
57	☐	Low-murm'ring, lay; and starting from the rocks
58	☐	Stiff evergreens, whose spreading foliage mocks
59	☐	Want's barren soil, and the bleak frosts of age,
60	*1 2*	And mad oppression's thunder-clasping rage!
	3–6	Bigotry's mad fire-invoking
61	☐	O meek retiring Spirit! we will climb,
62	☐	Cheering and cheer'd, this lovely hill sublime;
63	☐	And from the stirring world uplifted high
64	☐	(Whose noises faintly wafted on the wind
65	☐	To quiet musings shall attune the mind,
66	☐	And oft the melancholy *theme* supply)
67	☐	There while the prospect thro' the gazing eye
68	☐	Pours all its healthful greenness on the soul,
69	*1 2*	We'll laugh at wealth, and learn to laugh at fame,
	3–6	smile smile
70	☐	Our hopes, our knowledge, and our joys the same,
71	☐	As neighb'ring fountains image, each the whole:
72	*1*	Then when the mind has drank its fill of truth,
	3–5	hath
	6	drunk
73	⊠2	We'll discipline the heart to pure delight,

74 ⊠2   Rekindling sober joy's domestic flame.
75 *1*   She, whom I love, shall love thee. Honor'd youth,
   3–6 They
76 ⊠2   Now may Heaven realize this vision bright!

title. *4 5* TO A YOUNG FRIEND, | ON HIS PROPOSING TO DOMESTICATE WITH THE | AUTHOR. | COMPOSED IN 1796. • *6* TO A YOUNG FRIEND, | ON HIS PROPOSING TO DOMESTICATE WITH THE | AUTHOR. COMPOSED IN 1796. **1.** *2* Mount, **2.** *3–6* mountain *3–6* -piled, **3.** *3–6* creep, **4.** *4–6* coloured *3–6* oosing **6.** *3–6* 'mid **7.** *4–6* brightened **8.** *4–6* beguiled, **9.** *3–6* Pensiveness **11.** *3–5* clift *3–6* above, **12.** *3–6* love, **13.** *3–6* wandering **14.** *3–6* mountain *3–6* climb, **15.** *4–6* ached **16.** *3–6* friend **17.** *4–6* The adventurous **18.** *3–6* follow; **21.** *3–6* half-uprooted **22.** *3–6* dash,— **23.** *3–6* cypress, **25.** *4–6* to **26.** *4–6* treasured *4–6* linked **28.** *4–6* Muttering *4–6* unwatched **29.** *4–6* beckoning *3–6* friend **31.** *6* there **32.** *3–5* PINE • *6* pine *2* limbs **33.** *4–6* the **34.** *3–6* eve **35.** *4–6* Tinged **36.** *4–6* basoned *4–6* unsunned **38.** *4–6* sheltered **40.** *4–6* Stretched *2 3* shadow'd **42.** *3–6* Ah! **44.** *2* west winds *4–6* fanned *4–6* -bedewed: **45.** *3–6* oft pausing, **46.** *3–6* mansion, **47.** *3–6* eye, *3–5* DOMESTIC BLISS • *6* domestic bliss **48.** *6* this *3–5* Husband's, *6* that *3–5* Brother's **49.** *4–6* versed **50.** *3–6* Hill *3–6* Knowledge *4–6* essayed **51.** *4–6* verdurous *2* resting place • *3–6* resting-place, **53.** *6* glad **56.** *6* Inspiration, **57.** *3–6* Low murmuring, **60.** *6* bigotry's **61.** *3–6* spirit! **62.** *4–6* cheered, **63.** *3–6* up-lifted *3–6* high, **64.** *3–6* noises, *3–6* wind, **66.** *6* theme **67.** *3–6* There, *3–6* through **71.** *3–6* neighbouring *2* whole. **72.** *5 6* truth **75.** *3–6* love *6* thee, *4 5* Honoured • *6* honoured *3–6* youth!

2, 5, 8, 10, etc. PR *3–6* indent throughout to indicate rhyme.
33. In William Roskilly's copy of PR *1* C altered "detain th' enamoured sight" to "delay the swimming sight".
42. In RS's (?) copy of PR *1* "LLOYD" has been emended to "youth".
49–60. In the list of errata C sent Cottle c 3 Jul 1797 he wrote and then deleted the following instruction: "Scratch out the 14 lines beginning at 'Thus rudely vers'd' & ending with 'thunder-clasping rage!'" This deleted section is not included in *CL* I 331 (see HUL fMS Eng 947). This part of the letter is in DW's hand; "14" is an error for "12". C deleted the lines in Bowles's copy of PR *1* with a large, neat cross. For the trimmed marginal note see vol I EC.
60. In RS's (?) copy of PR *1* the line has been emended to the PR *3–5* reading.
69. In RS's (?) copy of PR *1* the line has been emended to the *3–6* reading.
75. In RS's (?) copy of PR *1* "She" has been emended to "They".

138.X1. NURSERY SONG

Untitled nursery song: "Did a very little babby make a very great noise?"

SC reported that the above "is the first line of a nursery song, in which Mr. Coleridge recorded some of his experience on this recondite subject" (*BL—* 1847—I 355). C appears to have sent a version of it, or more probably described it, to CL in a letter of Nov–Dec 1796. CL wrote: "[I] had rather hear you sing 'Did a very little baby' by your family fire-side, than listen to you when you were repeating one of Bowles's sweetest sonnets in your sweet manner" (*LL—* M—I 78). HC was born on 19 Sept 1796.

The song has not been found. It may adapt or be dependent on a traditional nursery rhyme. C plays with the punning possibilities of the name Didymus in a notebook entry of 21–2 May 1828 (Notebook 37—BM Add MS 47532—ff 67^v– 68^r), which may somehow be connected through metrical association. It may be echoed in HC's phrasing in a letter to Mrs C of 16 Apr 1831, speaking playfully of SC: "Dod-a-bless a little soul—does it read Greek with its good man [HNC] of a night? Lord love it. You see she never grows any older in my imagination" (*Letters of Hartley Coleridge* ed G. E. Griggs and E. L. Griggs—1937—132). Cf also C's adaptation of a traditional nursery rhyme in poem **298.**

139. THE DESTINY OF NATIONS: A VISION

A. DATE

C's work on the poem centres on two periods: May–Sept 1795, when he collaborated with RS on *Joan of Arc* (poem **110**) and perhaps began to draft the beginnings of a separate poem of his own, and Oct 1796–Jan 1797, when he worked on enlarging the projected separate poem, hoping to include it in *Poems* (1797). Some rewriting of the materials took place in 1815, for publication in *SL*, and at intervals thereafter as the poem was republished.

B. TEXTS

1. BM Add MS 34225 f 6^r. Single leaf, 22.2×33.2 cm; wm (partial) decorated shield; chain-lines 2.9 cm. Heavily revised draft of c 36 lines in C's hand. Text extends to the very bottom of the page.

The draft may or may not predate the point at which C ceased to contribute to *Joan of Arc* (c 20 Aug 1795). There are parallels between lines 14.1.1–14 and entries in the Gutch Notebook, which KC dates before and after that time (*CN* I 51, 174–8); and with **112** *To the Nightingale* and **115** *The Eolian Harp*, which date from Aug–Sept 1795.

On the other hand, textual evidence suggests that lines 14.1.1–14 might have been added on a different occasion, and it is possible that MSS 1–3 were not written in 1795 at all, but a year later. All begin with the new opening quoted in Nov 1796 (*CL* I 243: to TP 1 Nov 1796). The evidence from the paper used is not helpful.

2. BM Add MS 34225 f 6ᵛ (verso of MS 1 above), covering first half of page. Selective copy and development (17½ lines), in C's hand.

3. BM Add MS 34225 f 5ʳ⁻ᵛ. Single leaf, 19.4×25.1 cm; wm (partial) circular design; chain-lines 2.5 cm. Written on both sides, to very foot of verso. Revised copy and 60-line continuation of MSS 1 2, in C's hand.

The priority of MSS 1 2 over MS 3 is uncertain.

1. M Post (26 Dec 1797). Signed "by S. T. COLERIDGE."

C had written to TP and CL about his contributions to *Joan of Arc* in May–Jun 1796 (*CL* I 207; *LL*—M—I 3, 6, 11, 15–16), but was apparently stimulated to work on the material again only when Joseph Cottle called for a second edition of his *Poems*, in Oct 1796 (*CL* I 241, VI 1005–7: both to J. Cottle [18 Oct 1796]). C told TP and CL during Nov that he would begin the new edition with a revision of *Joan of Arc* (*CL* I 243; *LL*—M—I 66). He apparently meant to do this by cutting out pages from the 1796 *Joan of Arc*, altering them, and adding a new beginning (*CL* I 285: to J. Thelwall 17 Dec 1796).

At the same time, or very soon after, C set about adding to the poems. He told Thelwall in Dec that he had added 400 lines, and Cottle in Jan 1797 that the new poem would comprise about 820 lines (*CL* I 285; 297–8: to J. Cottle [6 Jan 1797]). In fact, he appears only to have added the 148-line "fragment" which makes up PR *1* (lines 121–271a below).

PR *1* draws on material published in *The Watchman* VII (19 Apr 1796) (*CC*) 238–41, and overlaps with C's sonnet written in Sept–Oct 1796 and with jottings in the Gutch Notebook from the same time (**133** *To a Friend Who had Declared his Intention of Writing No More Poetry*; *CN* I 180, 194, 197). Book IX of the original *Joan of Arc* had been entitled "Visions of the Maid", and described her descent into hell. C condemned this book specifically at the time he was writing his own "VISIONS" (*CL* I 293–4: to Thelwall 31 Dec 1796), and RS dropped it from later editions of *Joan of Arc*. It is impossible to say now whether C's lines were written with RS's in mind. C submitted an earlier but very similar version to CL in early Feb 1797, which CL so disapproved of that C abandoned further work on the poem (*LL*—M—I 94–5, 97–8, 100–3; *CL* I 309: to J. Cottle [c 10 Feb 1797]; *Two Letters* 313).

C's confidence in the poem returned just as the second edition of his poems came into print (*CL* I 329: to J. Cottle [late Jun 1797]; 330: to J. Cottle [c 3 Jul 1797]), and the publication of PR *1* in Dec 1797 reflects his renewed commitment. This continued into the spring of 1798, as a third edition was projected (*CL* I 387, 391), but thereafter it waned.

2 [=RT]. *SL* (1817).

C's interest in the poem was probably revived through marking up a copy of *Joan of Arc* for his friend William Hood, picking out his contributions, in

Jun 1814 (*CM—CC*—v). Although he belittled its worth in the marginalia, and although the attitude he expressed to John Gutch (in the *SL* proofs) and to John Morgan (*CL* III 510: [16 Jun 1814]) was dismissive, there is evidence of a returning interest and proprietary attitude (*CN* III 4202 = **508** *National Independence*; *BL* ch 7—*CC*—I 122–3). But he did not do any further work on the poem until the proof stage of *SL*, in May–Jun 1816.

The *SL* proofs (as distinct from the "Waste-Office Copy", which is lost) are at Yale (In C678 817sa), and the newly entitled poem appears on sigs T and U. Sig T arrived at Highgate on 15 May and was returned on the 24th; the first state of sig U arrived on 5 Jun and was returned the next day; the second state of sig U arrived on 14 Jun and was returned the next day. Comments by Gutch and C make it clear that initial copy was supplied by revised pages of *Joan of Arc*, supplemented by lines very close to PR *1*. The commentary below records substantial differences between the proof version and the text as printed (PR 2); differences between PR 2 and *Joan of Arc* are not recorded.

The following copies of PR 2 contain emendations in C's hand: Francis Wrangham's (?) (sold at Christie's 13 Jun 1979 lot 126); JG's (HUL *EC8 C6795 817s (C)); HNC's (HUL *AC85 L8605 Zy 817c). William Hood's copy (Columbia X825C67 W3 1817) has an emendation in JG's hand; WW's copy (Cornell WORDSWORTH 4480 S5 1817 Copy 1) has an emendation in AG's hand.

3. PW (1828).

The copy at the Fitzwilliam Museum, Cambridge (Marlay Bequest 1912) carries emendations to this poem. The general comment given in vol I headnote bears on the difficulties C had in revising the *Joan of Arc* text to make an independent poem, as well as on many of his subsequent adjustments of its meaning.

4. PW (1829).

5. PW (1834).

The first page of the PR *4* text (vol I p 104), emended in C's hand to conform to the PR *5* text, is at VCL (S MS Fl.13). Together with other small peculiarities of the PR *5* text, it suggests that copy was provided by marked-up pages of PR *4*.

C. GENERAL NOTE

C's contribution to bk II of RS's *Joan of Arc* (poem **110**) should be consulted for the original of which lines 1–120, 271b–467 are a reworking and revision; see **48** *Sors Misera Servorum* lines 1–16 for the Greek quoted at line 438fn.

title. *1 The VISIONS of the MAID of ORLEANS.* I A FRAGMENT, • *2–5 THE DESTINY OF NATIONS.* I A VISION.

290

The Pilgrim Man, who long since eve had watch'd
The alien Shine of unconcerning Stars,
Not seldom some a poor night-roaming man
Shouts to himself, there first the cottage Abbey-lights
Seen in Neufchatel's vale, *now slopes* adown
The bleak hill's further side, till at the base;
The winding sheep-track valeward; when, behold
In the first entrance of the level road
An unattended Team! A thwart-wain stopt her speed. The foremost horse
Lay with stretch'd limbs; the others, yet alive
But stiff and cold, stood motionless, their manes
Hoar with the frozen night-dews. Dismally
The dark-red dawn new glimmer'd; but its gleams
Disclosed no face of man. The maiden paused,
Then hail'd who might be near. No voice replied.
From the thwart wain at length there reach'd her Ear
At length she listened from the vehicle,
A sound so feeble that it almost seem'd
Distant—and feebly, with slow effort push'd,
A miserable man crept forth. His limbs
The silent frost had eat, scathing like fire.
Faint on the shafts he rested. She meantime
Saw crowded close beneath the coverture
A mother and her children—lifeless all,
Yet lovely! not a lineament was marr'd—
Death had put on so slumber-like a form!
It was a piteous sight; and one, a babe,
The crisp milk frozen on its innocent lips,
Lay on the woman's arm, its little hand
stretch'd on her bosom.

An unattended Team!
A victim did thwart her course.

3. Coleridge's revision of *The Destiny of Nations* 184.1.1–211a and 211b–234
in the proofs of *Sibylline Leaves* (1817) (see TEXT PR 2). See vol I annexes B 5
and C 17 for the positioning of the poem in the volume, which required it to be
revised, and for the proofs as a whole

Acutely questioning

~~The Maid gaz'd wildly at the living wretch.~~

~~Wildly pale, the Maid~~
Gazed at the living wretch, ~~mute~~ questioning.

He, his head feebly turning, on the group
Look'd with a vacant stare, and his eye spoke
The ~~????~~ calm that steals on worn-out anguish. _heavy/drowsy_
She shudder'd / but, each vainer pang subdued,
Quick disentangling from the foremost horse
The rustic bands, with difficulty and toil
The stiff/crampt team forced homeward. There arrived / _stiffly crampt_
Anxious she tended him with healing herbs,
And wept and pray'd—but the numb power of Death
Spread o'er his limbs; and ere the noon-tide hour,
The hov'ring spirits of his Wife and Babes
Hailed him immortal! Yet amid his pangs,
With interruptions long from ghastly throes,
His voice had falter'd out this simple tale.

The Village where he dwelt an Husbandman,
By sudden inroad had been seiz'd and fir'd
Late on the yester-evening. With his wife
And little ones he hurried his escape.
They saw the neighbouring Hamlets flame, they heard
Uproar and shrieks / and terror-struck / drove on
Through unfrequented roads, a weary way
But saw nor house nor cottage. All had quench'd

U 2

Mr. Coleridge   _Mr Gillman's Surgeon_

Highgate
Middx

1	⊠*1*	Auspicious Reverence! hush all meaner Song,
2	1	Ere we the deep prelusive strain have pour'd
	2 3	Till
	2–5	Ere preluding
3	⊠*1*	To the great Father, only rightful King
3fn	1	3ʳᵈ l.—i.e. jure suo, by any inherent Right.
4	1 2	~~Eternal~~ All-gracious Father, King Omnipotent!
	3 *2–5*	⟵——Eternal——
4.1.1	1	Mind! co-eternal Word! forth-breathing Sound!
4.1.2	1	⟨Aye-unconfounded, undivided Trine⟩
4.1.3	1	Birth. and Procession. ⟨ever-⟩reincircling Act!
4.1.4	1	God in God immanent, distinct yet one!
4.1.5	1	~~Aye unconfounded, undivided Trine~~!
	1	Omnific, Omniform! the Immoveable,
4.1.6	1	~~That goes~~ Immoveable! ~~that He~~ That goes forth & remaineth, &
		at once
4.1.7	1	~~That d~~ He Dawns, ⟨rises,⟩ ~~and~~ sets, and crowns the height of
		Heaven/!
4.2.1	2	To Him, the inseparate, unconfounded Tʀɪɴᴇ,
4.2.2	2	Mɪɴᴅ! Co-eternal Wᴏʀᴅ! Forth-breathing Sᴏᴜɴᴅ!
4.2.3	2	Bɪʀᴛʜ! and Pʀᴏᴄᴇssɪᴏɴ! Ever-circling Aᴄᴛ!
4.2.4	2	Gᴏᴅ in Gᴏᴅ immanent, distinct yet one!
4.2.5	2	⟨Sole Rest, ⟨&⟩ true Substance, of all finite Being!⟩
4.2.6	2	Omnific! Omniform! The Immovable,
4.2.7	2	That goes forth and remaineth: and at once
4.2.8	2	Dawns, rises, sets, and crowns the height of Heaven!
5	3	Beneath whose shadowing banners wide-unfurl'd
	2	shadowy
6	3 2	Justice leads forth her tyrant-quelling Hosts.
6.1.1	*3 4*	Tʜᴇ Wɪʟʟ, ᴛʜᴇ Wᴏʀᴅ, ᴛʜᴇ Bʀᴇᴀᴛʜ,—ᴛʜᴇ Lɪᴠɪɴɢ Gᴏᴅ.
6.2.1	*5*	To the Will Absolute, the One, the Good!
6.2.2	*5*	The I Aᴍ, the Word, the Life, the Living God!
7	1–3	Such Symphony demands best Instrument.
	2–5	requires
8	⊠*1*	Seize then, my Soul! from Freedom's trophied Dome
9	1–3	The Harp, that hanging high between the Shields
	2–5	which hangeth
10.1	1	Of Brutus and Leonidas, gives oft
9.1.1	1	A fateful music, when with breeze-like Touch
9.1.2	1	~~Departed Patriots with their sure & shr~~
	1	Pure Spirits—thrill its strings: the ~~Aged~~ Poet's heart
9.1.3	1	Listens, ~~with kindly heart, and inly knows~~
	1	and kindly knows that they demand
9.1.4	1	~~With sacred Influence the Poets Song.~~
13.1	1	~~For what is Freedom, but th' unfetter'd use~~
14.1	1	~~Of all the Powers, which God for use had given!~~
9.1.5	1	⟨~~That this demand once more to work by Fame,~~⟩
9.1.6	1	⟨~~And influence of spirit-stirring Song!~~⟩
9.1.7	1	Once more to live for Man, and work by Fame,

9.1.8	1	~~Send the~~ Thro the sweet Influence of ~~inspired Verse~~ harmonious
		Words.
10.2	2	Of Brutus and Leonidas, ~~gives~~ flashes forth
9.2.1	2	Starts of shrill music, when with breeze-like Touch
9.2.2	2	Departed Patriot's [?] thrill the
10.3	3	Of Brutus and Leonidas, ⟨oft⟩ gives ~~out~~
9.3.1	3	A fitful music, when with breeze-like Touch
9.3.2	3	~~Spirits of great men ask to work by Fame~~
	3	~~Great Spirits thrill its strings~~
	3	Great Spirits passing thrill its strings:
9.3.3	3	The Bard Listens, & knows, thy will to work by Fame.
10	2–5	Of Brutus and Leonidas! With that
11	2–5	Strong music, that soliciting spell, force back
12	2–4	Earth's free and stirring spirit that lies entranced.
5		Man's
13	⊠*1* 2	For what is Freedom but the unfetter'd use
14	⊠*1* 2	Of all the Powers, which God for use had given!
		[*Line-space*]
14.1.1	1	The ~~wild breeze~~ zephyr-travelld Harp, that flashes forth
14.1.2	1	Jets, and ~~wan~~ low wooings of ~~sad~~ wild Melody
14.1.3	1	That sally forth & seek the meeting ~~Sou~~ Ear
14.1.4	1	Then start away, half-wanton, half-afraid
14.1.5	1	Like the Red-breast forced by wintry snows
14.1.6	1	~~From the fair Hand, that feeds~~
	1	In the first visits by the genial Hearth
14.1.7	1	From the fair Hands, that tempt it to—
14.1.8	1	Or like a cone of flame, from the deep sigh
14.1.9	1	Of the idly musing Lover dreaming of his Love
14.1.10	1	With thoughts & hopes & fears, ~~as various~~ sinking, snatching upward
14.1.11	1	~~And as fluttering as itself~~ Bending, recoiling, fluttering as itself—
		[*Line-space*]
14.1.12	1	—And cheats us with false prophecies of sound,
14.1.13	1	—Shts mocks, shts promises, & mocks again
14.1.14	1	And dall~~iesi~~ance sweeter than frankincense.
15.1	3	But chiefly ~~him to view, first, midst and last~~
	3	this, him first to view, him last—
16.1	3	Thro' shapes, and sounds, and all the world of sense,
16.1.1	3	~~And~~ The change of empires, and the deeds of man
17.1	3	Translucent, as thro' clouds that veil his Light—
17.1.1	3	But most, O man! in thine unwarped Self
17.1.2	3	And the still growth of immortality
17.1.3	3	Image of God, and his Eternity—
15	2–5	But chiefly this, him First, him Last to view
16	2–5	Through meaner powers and secondary things
17	2–5	Effulgent, as through clouds that veil his blaze.
18	2–5	For all that meets the bodily sense I deem
19	2–5	Symbolical, one mighty alphabet
20	2–5	For infant minds; and we in this low world
21	2–5	Placed with our backs to bright Reality,

22	*2–5*	That we may learn with young unwounded ken
23.1	*2*	The substance from its shadow—Earth's broad shade
25.1/26.1	*2*	Revealing by Eclipse the Eternal Sun!
23	*3–5*	The substance from its shadow. Infinite Love
24	*3–5*	Whose latence is the plenitude of All,
25	*3–5*	Thou with retracted Beams, and Self-eclipse
26	*3–5*	Veiling, revealest thine eternal Sun.
27	*3*	But some there are who deem themselves most wise
	2–5	free
28	*3 2–5*	When they within this gross and visible sphere
29	*3*	Chain down the winged soul, scoffing ascent—
	2–5	thought,
30	*3*	Proud in their meanness—and themselves they mock
	2–5	cheat
31	*3 2–5*	With noisy emptiness of learned phrase,
32	*3 2–5*	Their subtle Fluids, impacts, essences,
33	*3 2–5*	Self-working Tools, uncaus'd effects, and all
34	*3 2–5*	Those blind Omniscients, those Almighty Slaves
35	*3 2–5*	Untenanting Creation of its God!
		[*Line-space*]
36	*3 2–5*	But Properties are God! the naked mass
37	*3*	(If mass there be, at best a guess obscure)
	2–5	fantastic Guess or Ghost)
38	*3 2–5*	Acts only by its inactivity.
39	*3*	Here we pause humbly. Others' boldlier dream,
	2–5	think
40	*3*	That as one body is the Aggregate
	2–5	seems
41	*3 2–5*	Of Atoms numberless, each organized,
42	*3 2–5*	So by a strange and dim Similitude
43	*3 2–5*	Infinite myriads of self-conscious minds
44	*3*	Form one all-conscious Spirit, who controlls
	2–5	Are which informs
45	*3 2–5*	With absolute ubiquity of thought
47.1	*3*	All his component Monads:—each evolving
47.1.1	*3*	In its own sphere its own entrusted powers.
47.1.2	*3*	Howe'er this be, or be it but a Dream
47.1.3	*3*	Fallacious, an illusion veiling Truth,
47.1.4	*3*	linked Minds,
47.1.5	*3*	Each in its own sphere evermore evolving
47.1.6	*3*	Its own entrusted powers.—Howe'er this be
47.1.7	*3*	Whether a Dream presumptious, caught from earth
47.1.8	*3*	And earthly form—or Vision veiling Truth,
47.1.9	*3*	Yet th Eternal ⟨Omnific?⟩ Father of all words Worlds,
47.1.10	*3*	God in God immanent, the eternal Word,
47.1.11	*3*	That gives forth, yet remains—Sun, that at once
47.1.12	*3*	Dawns, rises, sets, and crowns the Height of Heaven,
47.1.13	*3*	Generant and Full and Wane, yet remain
47.1.14	*3*	Equal and one

47.1.15	3	Great general Agent in all finite Souls,
47.1.16	3	Doth in that action put on finiteness,
47.1.17	3	For all his Thoughts are acts, and every Act
47.1.18	3	A Being & Substance/ God impersonal,
47.1.19	3	Yet in all worlds impersonate in all, .
47.1.20	3	Absolute Infinite, whose dazzling robe
47.1.21	3	Flows in rich folds, and darts in shooting Hues
47.1.22	3	Of infinite Finiteness/—he rolls each orb
47.1.23	3	Matures each plant, and Tree, & spread thro' all
47.1.24	3	Wields all the Universe of Life & Thought,
47.1.25	3	~~Yet leaves *to all the creatures meanest, highest, to all the meanest*~~
47.1.26	3	~~Angelic *privilege* Right, self-conscious Agency/~~
46	2–5	(His one eternal self-affirming Act!)
47	2–5	All his involved Monads, that yet seem
48	2–5	With various province and apt agency
49	2–5	Each to pursue its own self-centering end.
50	2–5	Some nurse the infant diamond in the mine;
51	2 5	Some roll the genial juices through the oak;
52	2–5	Some drive the mutinous clouds to clash in air,
53	2–5	And rushing on the storm with whirlwind speed,
54	2–4	Yoke the red lightning to their vollying car.
	5	lightnings
55	2–5	Thus these pursue their never-varying course,
56	2–5	No eddy in their stream. Others, more wild,
57	2–5	With complex interests weaving human fates,
58	2–5	Duteous or proud, alike obedient all,
59	2–5	Evolve the process of eternal good.
		[*Line-space*]
60	2–5	And what if some rebellions, o'er dark realms
61	2–5	Arrogate power? yet these train up to God,
62	2–5	And on the rude eye, unconfirmed for day,
63	2–5	Flash meteor-lights better than total gloom.
64	2–5	As ere from Lieule-Oaive's vapoury head
65	2–5	The Laplander beholds the far-off Sun
66	2–5	Dart his slant beam on unobeying snows,
67	2–5	While yet the stern and solitary Night
68	2–5	Brooks no alternate sway, the Boreal Morn
69	2–5	With mimic lustre substitutes its gleam,
70	2–5	Guiding his course or by Niemi lake
71	2–5	Or Balda-Zhiok, or the mossy stone
71fn	2–5	*Balda Zhiok*: i.e. mons altudinis, the highest mountain in Lapland.
72	2–5	Of Solfar-Kapper, while the snowy blast
72fn	2–5	*Solfar-Kapper*: capitium Solfar, hic locus omnium, quotquot veterum Lap-
		ponum superstitio sacrificiis religiosoque cultui dedicavit, celebratissimus erat, in
		parte sinus australis situs, semimilliaris spatio a mari distans. Ipse locus, quem

curiositatis gratia aliquando me invisisse memini, duabus prealtis
  lapidibus, sibi

invicem oppositis, quorum alter musco circumdatus erat, constabat.   5

LEEMIUS *De Lapponibus.*

73 *2–5*   Drifts arrowy by, or eddies round his sledge,
74 *2–5*   Making the poor babe at its mother's back
74fn *2–5*   The Lapland women carry their infants at their back in a piece of
      excavated

wood, which serves them for a cradle. Opposite to the infant's mouth
      there is a

hole for it to breathe through.—Mirandum prorsus est et vix credibile
      nisi cui

vidisse contigit. Lappones hyeme iter facientes per vastos montes,
      perque hor-

rida et invia tesqua, eo presertim tempore quo omnia perpetuis
      nivibus obtecta   5

sunt et nives ventis agitantur et in gyros aguntur, viam ad destinata
      loca absque

errore invenire posse, lactantem autem infantem, si quem habeat,
      ipsa mater in

dorso bajulat, in excavato ligno (Gieed'k ipsi vocant) quod pro cunis
      utuntur: in

hoc infans pannis et pellibus convolutus colligatus jacet.

LEEMIUS *De Lapponibus.* 10

75 *2–5*   Scream in its scanty cradle: he the while
76 *2–5*   Wins gentle solace as with upward eye
77 *2–5*   He marks the streamy banners of the North,
78 *2–5*   Thinking himself those happy spirits shall join
79 *2–5*   Who there in floating robes of rosy light
80 *2–5*   Dance sportively. For Fancy is the Power
81 *2–5*   That first unsensualizes the dark mind,
82 *2–5*   Giving it new delights; and bids it swell
83 *2–5*   With wild activity; and peopling air,
84 *2–5*   By obscure fears of Beings invisible,
85 *2–5*   Emancipates it from the grosser thrall
86 *2–5*   Of the present impulse, teaching Self-controul,
87 *2–5*   Till Superstition with unconscious hand
88 *2–5*   Seat Reason on her throne. Wherefore not vain,
89 *2–5*   Nor yet without permitted power impress'd,
90 *2 3 5*   I deem those legends terrible, with which
    4   deemed
91 *2–5*   The polar ancient thrills his uncouth throng:
92 *2–5*   Whether of pitying Spirits that make their moan
93 *2–5*   O'er slaughter'd infants, or that Giant Bird
94 *2–5*   VUOKHO, of whose rushing wings the noise
95 *2–5*   Is Tempest, when the unutterable shape
95fn *2–5*   Jaibme Aibmo.
96 *2–5*   Speeds from the mother of Death, and utters once
97 *2–5*   That shriek, which never Murderer heard, and lived.

98	*2–5*	Or if the Greenland Wizard in strange trance
99	*2–5*	Pierces the untravelled realms of Ocean's bed
100	*2–4*	(Where live the innocent as far from cares
101	*2–4*	As from the storms and overwhelming waves
102	*2–4*	Dark tumbling on the surface of the deep),
103	*2–5*	Over the abysm, even to that uttermost cave
104	*2–5*	By mis-shaped prodigies beleaguered, such
105	*2–5*	As Earth ne'er bred, nor Air, nor the upper Sea.
		[*Line-space*]
106	*2–4*	There dwells the Fury Form, whose unheard name
	5	Where
107	*2–5*	With eager eye, pale cheek, suspended breath,
108	*2–5*	And lips half-opening with the dread of sound,
109	*2–5*	Unsleeping SILENCE guards, worn out with fear
110	*2–5*	Lest haply escaping on some treacherous blast
111	*2–5*	The fateful word let slip the Elements
112	*2–5*	And frenzy Nature. Yet the wizard her,
113	*2–5*	Armed with Torngarsuck's power, the Spirit of Good,
113fn	*2–5*	They call the Good Spirit, Torngarsuck. The other great but malignant spirit
		is a nameless Female; she dwells under the sea in a great house, where she
		can detain in captivity all the animals of the ocean by her magic power. When
		a dearth befalls the Greenlanders, an Angekok or magician must undertake a
		journey thither: he passes through the kingdom of souls, over an horrible abyss 5
		into the Palace of this phantom, and by his enchantments causes the captive
		creatures to ascend directly to the surface of the ocean.
		See CRANTZ' *Hist. of Greenland, vol. i.* 206.
114	*2–5*	Forces to unchain the foodful progeny
115	*2–4*	Of the Ocean stream.—Wild phantasies! yet wise,
	5	thence thro' the realm of Souls,
115.1.1	*5*	Where live the Innocent, as far from cares
115.1.2	*5*	As from the storms and overwhelming waves
115.1.3	*5*	That tumble on the surface of the Deep,
115.1.4	*5*	Returns with far-heard pant, hotly pursued
115.1.5	*5*	By the fierce Warders of the Sea, once more,
115.1.6	*5*	Ere by the frost foreclosed, to repossess
115.1.7	*5*	His fleshly mansion, that had staid the while
115.1.8	*5*	In the dark tent within a cow'ring group
115.1.9	*5*	Untenanted.—Wild phantasies! yet wise,
116	*2–5*	On the victorious goodness of high God
117	*2–5*	Teaching Reliance, and medicinal Hope,
118	*2–5*	Till from Bethabra northward, heavenly Truth
119	*2–5*	With gradual steps winning her difficult way,
120	*2–5*	Transfer their rude Faith perfected and pure.

[*Line-space*]

121 *1–5*	If there be Beings of higher class than Man,
122 *1–5*	I deem no nobler province they possess
123 *1–5*	Than by disposal of apt circumstance
124 *1–5*	To rear up kingdoms: and the deeds they promp,
125 *1–5*	Distinguishing from mortal agency,
126 *1*	They chuse their ←—servants—→ from such mean estates
2	mortal ministers states
3–5	human
127 *1–5*	As still the Epic Song half fears to name,
128 *1*	Disdain'd by all the minstrelcies that strike
2–5	Repelled from
129 *1*	The palace roof, soothing the Monarch's pride.
2–5	and sooth

[*Line-space*]

130 *1–5*	And such perhaps the Spirit, who (if words
131 *1–5*	Witness'd by answering deeds may claim our faith,)
132 *1–5*	Held commune with that warrior-maid of France
133 *1*	Who scourg'd the invader. From her childish days
2–5	infant
134 *1–5*	With wisdom, mother of retired thoughts,
135 *1–5*	Her soul had dwelt; and she was quick to mark
136 *1–5*	The good and evil thing, in human lore
137 *1–5*	Undisciplined: for lowly was her birth,
138 *1–5*	And Heaven had doom'd her early years to toil,
139 *1–5*	That, pure from tyranny's least deed, herself
140 *1–5*	Unfear'd by fellow-natures, she might wait
141 *1–5*	On the poor lab'ring-man with kindly looks,
142 *1–5*	And minister refreshment to the tir'd
143 *1–5*	Way-wanderer, when along the rough-hewn bench
144 *1*	The sultry man had stretch'd him, and aloft
2–5	sweltry
145.1/146.1 *1*	Watch'd the gay sign-board on the mulberry bough
145 *2–5*	Vacantly watch'd the rudely pictured board
146 *2–5*	Which on the Mulberry-bough with welcome creek
147 *1*	Swing to the pleasant breeze! Here too the Maid
2–5	Swung
148 *1–5*	Learnt more than schools could teach, Man's shifting mind,
149 *1–5*	His vices and his sorrows; and full oft
150 *1–5*	At tales of cruel wrong, and strange distress,
151 *1–5*	Had wept and shiver'd. To the tott'ring Eld
152 *1*	Still as a daughter she would run; she plac'd
2–5	would she
153 *1–5*	His cold limbs at the sunny door, and lov'd
154 *1–5*	To hear him story in his garrulous sort
155 *1–5*	Of his eventful years, all come and gone.—
156 *1*	So twenty summers pass'd. The Virgin's form
2–5	seasons
157 *1–5*	Active and tall, nor sloth nor luxury

158	*1*	Had sicklied o'er; her front sublime and broad;
	2–5	shrunk or paled.
159	*1–5*	Her flexile eye-brows wildly hair'd and low;
160	*1*	And her large eye, now bright, now unillum'd,
	2–5	full
161	*1–5*	Spake more than woman's thought: and all her face
162	*1–5*	Was moulded to such features, as declar'd
163	*1–5*	That Pity there had oft and strongly work'd—
164	*1–5*	And sometimes Indignation! Bold her mien,
165	*1–5*	And like an haughty Huntress of the woods
166	*1–5*	She mov'd: yet sure she was a gentle Maid!
167	*1–5*	And in each motion her most innocent soul
168	*1*	Out-beam'd so brightly, that who saw would say,
	2–5	Beam'd forth
169	*1–5*	Guilt was a thing impossible in her.—
170	*1–5*	Nor idly would have said, for she had liv'd
171	*1–5*	In this bad world, as in a place of tombs,
172	*1–5*	And touch'd not the pollutions of the dead.

[*Line-space*]

173	*1–5*	'Twas the cold season, when the Rustic's eye
174	*1–5*	From the drear desolate whiteness of his fields
175	*1–5*	Rolls, for relief, to watch the skiey tints,
176	*1–5*	And clouds slow-varying their huge imagery;
177	*1–5*	When now, as she was wont, the healthful Maid
178	*1–5*	Had left her pallet, ere one beam of day
179	*1–5*	Slanted the fog-smoke. She went forth alone,
180	*1–5*	Urg'd by the indwelling Angel-guide, (that oft
181	*1–5*	With dim inexplicable sympathies,
182	*1*	Disquieting the heart, shapes out our course
	2–5	Man's
183	*1*	To some predoom'd adventure) and the ascent
	2–5	the Now
184	*1*	Now pass'd of that steep upland (on whose top
	2–5	She climbs
184.1.1	*1*	Not seldom some poor nightly-roaming man
185	*2–5*	The Pilgrim-Man, who long since eve had watch'd
186	*2–5*	The alien shine of unconcerning Stars,
187	*1*	Shouts to himself, there first the cottage lights
	2–5	Abbey-lights
188	*1*	Seen in Neufchatel's vale) she slop'd a-down
	2–5	now slopes
188.1.1	*1*	The bleak hill's further side, till at the base,
189	*2–5*	The winding sheep-track valeward: when, behold
190	*1–5*	In the first entrance of the level road,
191	*1*	A waggon stay'd her speed. Its foremost horse
	2–5	An unattended Team! The
192	*1–5*	Lay with stretch'd limbs: the others yet alive,
193	*1*	But stiff with cold, stood motionless, their manes
	2–5	and

194	*1–5*	Hoar with the frozen night-dews. Dismally
195	*1 5*	The dark-red dawn now glimmer'd; but its gleams
	2 3	new
	4	down now
196	*1–5*	Disclos'd no face of man. The Maiden paus'd,
197	*1*	And hail'd who might be near. No voice reply'd.
	2–5	Then
197.1.1	*1*	At length she listen'd, from the vehicle
198	*2–5*	From the thwart wain at length there reach'd her ear
199	*1*	A voice so feeble, that it almost seem'd
	2–5	sound
200	*1–5*	Distant: and feebly with slow effort push'd
201	*1*	A miserable man crawl'd forth: his limbs
	2–5	crept
202	*1–5*	The silent Frost had eat, scathing like fire!
203	*1*	Faint on the shafts he rested: she meanwhile
	2–5	mean time,
204	*1–5*	Saw crowded close beneath the coverture
205	*1–5*	A mother and her children, lifeless all,
206	*1–5*	Yet lovely: not a lineament was marr'd,
207	*1–5*	Death had put on so slumberlike a form!
208	*1–5*	It was a piteous sight! and one, a babe,
209	*2–5*	The crisp milk frozen on its innocent lips,
210	*1–5*	Lay on the woman's arm, it's little hand
211.1	*1*	Smooth on her bosom. Wildly pale the maid
212.1	*1*	Gaz'd at the living wretch, mute questioning.
211a	*2–5*	Stretch'd on her bosom.
		[*Line-space*]
211b	*2–5*	Mutely questioning,
212	*2–5*	The Maid gazed wildly at the living wretch.
213	*1–5*	He, his head feebly turning, on the group
214	*1–5*	Look'd with a vacant stare, and his eye spoke
215	*1–5*	The drowsy calm, that steals on worn out anguish.
216	*1–5*	She shudder'd; but each vainer pang subdu'd,
217	*1–5*	Quick disentangling from the foremost horse
218	*1–5*	The rustic bands, with difficulty and toil
219	*1–5*	The stiff cramp'd team forc'd homewards. There arriv'd,
220	*1*	Anxious she tended him with healing herbs
	2–5	Anxiously tends him she
221.1	*1*	And wept and pray'd; but green putridity
221	*2–5*	And weeps and prays—but the numb power of Death
222	*1*	Spread o'er his limbs, and ere the noontide hour
	2–5	Spreads
223	*1–5*	The hov'ring spirits of his wife and babes
224	*1*	Hail'd him immortal!—Yet amid his pangs
	2–5	Hail
225	*1*	With interruptions strange from ghastly throes
	2–5	long
226	*1–5*	His voice had falter'd out this simple tale.

227	*1–5*	The village where he dwelt, an husbandman,
228	*1*	By sudden foragers was seiz'd and fir'd
	2–5	inroad had been
229	*1–5*	Late on the yester-evening, with his wife
230	*1–5*	And little ones he hurried his escape.
231	*1–5*	They saw the neighbouring hamlets flame: they heard
232	*1–5*	Uproar and shrieks: and terror-struck drove on
233	*1–5*	Thro' unfrequented roads, a weary way,
234	*1–5*	But saw nor house nor cottage: all had quench'd
235	*1*	Their evening hearthfires; for the alarm had spread.
	2–5	hearth-fire:
236	*1–5*	The air clipp'd keen, the night was fang'd with frost,
237	*1–5*	And they provisionless; the weeping wife
238	*1*	Ill hush'd her children's cries—and still they cry'd,
	2–5	moans; moan'd,
239	*1–5*	Till fright, and cold, and hunger drank their life:
240	*1–5*	They clos'd their eyes in sleep, nor knew 'twas death!
241	*1–5*	He only, lashing his o'er wearied team,
242	*1–5*	Gain'd a sad respite, till beside the base
243	*1–5*	Of the high hill his foremost horse dropp'd dead.
244	*1–5*	Then hopeless, strengthless, sick for lack of food,
245	*1*	He crept beneath the coverture, and doz'd
	2–5	entranced,
246	*1–5*	Till waken'd by the maiden. Such his tale.

[*Line-space*]

247	*1–5*	Ah suffering to the height of what was suffer'd,
248	*1–5*	Stung with too keen a sympathy, the maid
249	*1–5*	Brooded with moving lips, mute, startful, dark;
250	*1–5*	And now her flush'd tumultuous features shot
251	*1–5*	Such strange vivacity as fires the eye
252	*1–5*	Of misery fancy-craz'd: and now once more
253	*1–5*	Naked, and void, and fix'd—and all within
254	*1–5*	The unquiet silence of confused thought
255	*1–5*	And shapeless feelings. For a mighty hand
256	*1–5*	Was strong upon her, till in th' heat of soul
257	*1–5*	To the high hill top tracing back her steps
258	*1*	Aside the beacon, down whose moulder'd stones
	2–5	up smoulder'd
259	*1–5*	The tender ivy-trails crept thinly, there
260	*1–5*	Unconscious of the driving element,
261	*1–5*	Yea, swallow'd up in th' ominous dream, she sate
262	*1–5*	Ghastly as broad-eyed slumber! a dim anguish
263	*1–5*	Breath'd from her look; and still with pant and sob
264	*1*	Inly she toil'd to fly, and still subdu'd,
	2–5	flee,
265	*1–5*	Felt an inevitable presence near!

[*Line-space*]

266	*1*	Thus as she toil'd in troubled ecstacy,
	2–5	troublous

267 *1–5*	An horror of great darkness wrapt her round,
268 *1–5*	And a voice utter'd forth unearthly tones
269 *1–5*	Calming her soul. "O thou of the Most High
270 *1–5*	Chosen, whom all the perfected in heaven
271a *1–5*	Behold expectant."
	[*Line-space*]
271a⁺ *2–5*	(The following fragments were intended to form part of the Poem when finished.)
271b *2–5*	"Maid belov'd of Heaven!
272 *2–5*	"(To her the tutelary Power exclaimed)
273 *2–5*	"Of CHAOS the adventurous progeny
274 *2–5*	"Thou seest; foul missionaries of foul sire,
275 *2–5*	"Fierce to regain the losses of that hour
276 *2–5*	"When LOVE rose glittering, and his gorgeous wings
277 *2–5*	"Over the abyss flutter'd with such glad noise,
278 *2–5*	"As what time after long and pestful calms,
279 *2–5*	"With slimy shapes and miscreated life
280 *2–5*	"Poisoning the vast Pacific, the fresh breeze
281 *2–5*	"Wakens the merchant-sail uprising. Night
282 *2–5*	"An heavy unimaginable moan
283 *2–5*	"Sent forth, when she the PROTOPLAST beheld
284 *2–5*	"Stand beauteous on Confusion's charmed wave.
285 *2–5*	"Moaning she fled, and entered the Profound
286 *2–5*	"That leads with downward windings to the Cave
287 *2–5*	"Of Darkness palpable, Desart of Death
288 *2–5*	"Sunk deep beneath GEHENNA's massy roots.
289 *2–5*	"There many a dateless age the Beldame lurk'd
290 *2–5*	"And trembled; till engender'd by fierce HATE,
291 *2–5*	"Fierce HATE and gloomy HOPE, a DREAM arose,
292 *2–5*	"Shap'd like a black cloud mark'd with streaks of fire.
293 *2–5*	"It rous'd the Hell-Hag: she the dew-damp wiped
294 *2–5*	"From off her brow, and thro' the uncouth maze
295 *2–5*	"Retraced her steps; but ere she reach'd the mouth
296 *2–5*	"Of that drear labyrinth, shuddering she paused,
297 *2–5*	"Nor dared re-enter the diminish'd Gulph.
298 *2–5*	"As thro' the dark vaults of some moulder'd Tower
299 *2–5*	"(Which, fearful to approach, the evening Hind
300 *2–5*	"Circles at distance in his homeward way)
301 *2–5*	"The winds breathe hollow, deem'd the plaining groan
302 *2–5*	"Of prison'd spirits; with such fearful voice
303 *2–5*	"NIGHT murmur'd, and the sound thro' Chaos went.
304 *2–5*	"Leapt at her call her hideous-fronted brood!
305 *2–5*	"A dark behest they heard, and rush'd on earth,
306 *2–5*	"Since that sad hour, in Camps and Courts adored,
307 *2–4*	"Rebels from God, and Monarchs o'er Mankind!
5	tyrants
307⁺ *2–5*	———————
308 *2–5*	From his obscure haunt

309	*2–5*	Shriek'd FEAR, of Cruelty the ghastly Dam,
310	*2–4*	Fev'rish yet freezing, eager-paced yet slow,
	5	Feverous
311	*2–5*	As she that creeps from forth her swampy reeds,
312	*2–5*	Ague, the biform Hag! when early Spring
313	*2–5*	Beams on the marsh-bred vapours.
313⁺	*2–5*	———————————
314	*2–5*	"Even so" (the exulting Maiden said)
315	*2–5*	"The sainted Heralds of Good Tidings fell,
316	*2–5*	"And thus they witness'd God! But now the clouds
317	*2–5*	"Treading, and storms beneath their feet, they soar
318	*2–5*	"Higher, and higher soar, and soaring sing
319	*2–5*	"Loud songs of Triumph! O ye spirits of God,
320	*2–5*	"Hover around my mortal agonies!"
321	*2–5*	She spake, and instantly faint melody
322	*2–5*	Melts on her ear, soothing and sad, and slow,
323	*2–5*	Such measures, as at calmest midnight heard
324	*2–5*	By aged Hermit in his holy dream,
325	*2–5*	Foretell and solace death; and now they rise
326	*2–5*	Louder, as when with harp and mingled voice
327	*2–5*	The white-robed multitude of slaughter'd saints
327fn	*2–5*	Revel. vi. 9, 11. And when he had opened the fifth seal, I saw under the
		altar the souls of them that were slain for the word of God, and for the testi-
		mony which they held. And white robes were given unto every one of them, that
		they should rest yet for a little season, until their fellow-servants also and their
		brethren, that should be killed as they were, should be fulfilled. 5
328	*2–5*	At Heaven's wide-open'd portals gratulant
329	*2–5*	Receive some martyr'd Patriot. The harmony
330	*2–5*	Entranced the Maid, till each suspended sense
331	*2–5*	Brief slumber seized, and confused extacy.
		[*Line-space*]
332	*2–5*	At length awakening slow, she gazed around:
333	*2–5*	And thro' a Mist, the relict of that trance,
334	*2–5*	Still thinning as she gaz'd, an Isle appear'd,
335	*2–5*	Its high, o'er-hanging, white, broad-breasted cliffs
336	*2–5*	Glass'd on the subject ocean. A vast plain
337	*2–5*	Stretch'd opposite, where ever and anon
338	*2–5*	The Plough-man following sad his meagre team
339	*2–5*	Turn'd up fresh sculls unstartled, and the bones
340	*2–5*	Of fierce hate-breathing combatants, who there
341	*2–5*	All mingled lay beneath the common earth,
342	*2–5*	Death's gloomy reconcilement! O'er the Fields
343	*2–5*	Stept a fair form, repairing all she might,
344	*2–5*	Her temples olive-wreath'd; and where she trod,

345 *2–5*   Fresh flowrets rose, and many a foodful herb.
346 *2–5*   But wan her cheek, her footsteps insecure,
347 *2–5*   And anxious pleasure beam'd in her faint eye,
348 *2–5*   As she had newly left a couch of pain,
349 *2–5*   Pale Convalescent! (Yet some time to rule
350 *2–5*   With power exclusive o'er the willing world,
351 *2–5*   That blest prophetic mandate then fulfill'd,
352 *2–5*   PEACE be on Earth!) An happy while, but brief,
353 *2–5*   She seem'd to wander with assiduous feet,
354 *2–5*   And heal'd the recent harm of chill and blight,
355 *2–5*   And nurs'd each plant that fair and virtuous grew.
　　　　　　[*Line-space*]
356 *2–5*   But soon a deep precursive sound moan'd hollow:
357 *2–5*   Black rose the clouds, and now, (as in a dream)
358 *2–5*   Their reddening shapes, transform'd to Warrior-hosts,
359 *2–5*   Cours'd o'er the Sky, and battled in mid-air.
360 *2–5*   Nor did not the large blood-drops fall from Heaven
361 *2–5*   Portentous! while aloft were seen to float,
362 *2*   Like hideous features blended with the clouds,
　　 3–5　　　　　　　　　booming on the mist,
363 *2–5*   Wan Stains of ominous Light! Resign'd, yet sad,
364 *2–5*   The fair Form bow'd her olive-crowned Brow:
365 *2–5*   Then o'er the plain with oft reverted eye
366 *2–5*   Fled till a Place of Tombs she reach'd, and there
367 *2–5*   Within a ruin'd Sepulchre obscure
368a *2–5* Found Hiding-place.
　　　　　　[*Line-space*]
368b *2–5*　　　　　　　　The delegated Maid
369 *2–5*   Gaz'd thro' her tears, then in sad tones exclaim'd,
370 *2–5*   "Thou mild-ey'd FORM! wherefore, ah! wherefore fled?
371 *2*   "The name of JUSTICE written on thy brow
　　 3–5　　　　Power　　　　　　like a name all Light,
372 *2*   "Resplendent   shone; but all they, who unblam'd
　　 3–5   "Shone from thy brow;
373 *2–5*   "Dwelt in thy dwellings, call thee HAPPINESS.
374 *2–5*   "Ah! why, uninjured and unprofited,
375 *2–5*   "Should multitudes against their brethren rush?
376 *2–5*   "Why sow they guilt, still reaping Misery?
377 *2–5*   "Lenient of care, thy songs, O PEACE! are sweet,
378 *2–5*   "As after showers the perfumed gale of eve,
379 *2–5*   "That flings the cool drops on a feverous cheek:
380 *2–5*   "And gay thy grassy altar pil'd with fruits.
381 *2–5*   "But boasts the shrine of Dæmon WAR one charm,
382 *2–5*   "Save that with many an orgie strange and foul,
383 *2–5*   "Dancing around with interwoven arms,
384 *2–5*   "The Maniac SUICIDE and Giant MURDER
385 *2–5*   "Exult in their fierce union! I am sad,
386 *2–5*   "And know not why the simple Peasants crowd
387 *2–5*   "Beneath the Chieftains' standard!" Thus the Maid.

[*Line-space*]

388	*2–4*	To her the tutelary Spirit replied:
	5	said:
389	*2–5*	"When Luxury and Lust's exhausted stores
390	*2–5*	"No more can rouse the appetites of KINGS;
391	*2–5*	"When the low flattery of their reptile Lords
392	*2–5*	"Falls flat and heavy on the accustom'd ear;
393	*2–5*	"When Eunuchs sing, and Fools buffoonery make,
394	*2–5*	"And Dancers writhe their harlot-limbs in vain:
395	*2–5*	"Then WAR and all its dread vicissitudes
396	*2–5*	"Pleasingly agitate their stagnant Hearts;
397	*2–5*	"Its hopes, its fears, its victories, its defeats,
398	*2–5*	"Insipid Royalty's keen condiment!
399	*2–5*	"*Therefore*, uninjur'd and unprofited,
400	*2–5*	"(Victims at once and Executioners)
401	*2–5*	"The congregated Husbandmen lay waste
402	*2–5*	"The Vineyard and the Harvest. As along
403	*2–5*	"The Bothnic coast, or southward of the Line,
404	*2–5*	"Though hush'd the Winds and cloudless the high Noon,
405	*2–5*	"Yet if LEVIATHAN, weary of ease,
406	*2–5*	"In sports unwieldy toss his Island-bulk,
407	*2–5*	"Ocean behind him billows, and before
408	*2–5*	"A storm of waves breaks foamy on the strand.
409	*2–5*	"And hence, for times and seasons bloody and dark,
410	*2–5*	"Short Peace shall skin the wounds of causeless War,
411	*2–5*	"And War, his strained sinews knit anew,
412	*2–5*	"Still violate th' unfinish'd works of Peace.
413	*2–5*	"But yonder look! for more demands thy view!"
414	*2–5*	He said: and straightway from the opposite Isle
415	*2–5*	A Vapor sail'd, as when a cloud, exhaled
416	*2–5*	From Egypt's fields that steam hot pestilence,
417	*2–5*	Travels the sky for many a trackless league,
418	*2–5*	'Till o'er some Death-doom'd land, distant in vain,
419	*2–5*	It broods incumbent. Forthwith from the Plain,
420	*2–5*	Facing the Isle, a brighter cloud arose,
421	*2–5*	And steer'd its course which way the Vapor went.

[*Line-space*]

422	*2–5*	The Maiden paus'd, musing what this might mean.
423	*2–5*	But long time pass'd not, ere that brighter Cloud
424	*2–5*	Returned more bright: along the Plain it swept;
425	*2–5*	And soon from forth its bursting sides emerg'd
426	*2–5*	A dazzling Form, broad-bosom'd, bold of eye,
427	*2–5*	And wild her hair, save where with laurels bound.
428	*2–5*	Not more majestic stood the healing God,
429	*2*	When from his brow the arrow sped that slew
	3–5	bow
430	*2–5*	Huge Python. Shriek'd AMBITION's giant throng,
431	*2–5*	And with them hiss'd the Locust-fiends that crawl'd
432	*2–5*	And glitter'd in CORRUPTION's slimy track.

433 *2–5*   Great was their wrath, for short they knew their reign:
434 *2–5*   And such commotion made they, and uproar,
435 *2–5*   As when the mad Tornado bellows through
436 *2–5*   The guilty islands of the western main,
437 *2–5*   What time departing from their native shores,
438 *2–5*   Eboe, or Koromantyn's plain of Palms,
438fn *2–5*   The Slaves in the West-Indies consider death as a passport to their native

country. This sentiment is thus expressed in the introduction to a Greek Prize-

Ode on the Slave-Trade, of which the ideas are better than the language in which

they are conveyed.

Ω σκοτου πυλας, Θανατε, προλειπων   5
Ες γενος σπευδοις υποζευχθεν Ατᾳ.
Ου ξενισθηση γεννων σπαραγμοις
          Ουδ᾽ ολολυγμω,

Αλλα και κυκλοισι χοροιτυποισι
Κ᾽ασματων χαρᾳ· φοβερος μεν εσσι,   10
Αλλ᾽ ομως Ελευθερια συνοικεῖς,
          Στυγνε Τυραννε!

Δασκιοις επει πτερυγεσσι σησι
Α! θαλασσιον καθορωντες οιδμα
Αιθεροπλαγτοις υπο ποσσ᾽ ανεισι   15
          Πατριδ ἐπ᾽ αιαν.

Ενθα μαν Ερασται Ερῳμενησιν
Αμφι πηγησιν κιτρινων υπ᾽ αλσων,
Οσσ᾽ υπο βροτοις επαθον βροτοι, τα
          Δεινα λεγοντι.   20

LITERAL TRANSLATION.

Leaving the Gates of Darkness, O Death! hasten thou to a Race yoked with

Misery! Thou wilt not be received with lacerations of cheeks, nor with funereal

ululation—but with circling dances, and the joy of songs. Thou art terrible in-

deed, yet thou dwelleth with LIBERTY, stern GENIUS! Borne on   25
thy dark pin-

ions over the swelling of Ocean, they return to their native country. There, by

the side of Fountains beneath Citron-groves, the lovers tell to their beloved what

horrors, being Men, they had endured from Men.

439 *2–5*   The infuriate spirits of the Murdered make
440 *2–5*   Fierce merriment, and vengeance ask of Heaven.

441 *2–5*   Warm'd with new influence, the unwholesome Plain
442 *2–5*   Sent up its foulest fogs to meet the Morn:
443 *2–5*   The Sun that rose on FREEDOM, rose in BLOOD!
         [*Line-space*]
444 *2–5*   "Maiden belov'd, and Delegate of Heaven!"
445 *2–5*   (To her the tutelary Spirit said)
446 *2–5*   "Soon shall the Morning struggle into Day,
447 *2–5*   "The stormy Morning into cloudless Noon.
448 *2–5*   "Much hast thou seen, nor all canst understand—
449 *2–5*   "But this be thy best Omen—SAVE THY COUNTRY!"
450 *2–5*   Thus saying, from the answering Maid he pass'd,
451 *2–5*   And with him disappear'd the Heavenly Vision.
         [*Line-space*]
452 *2–5*   "Glory to Thee, Father of Earth and Heaven!
453 *2–5*   "All conscious PRESENCE of the Universe!
454 *2–5*   "Nature's vast Ever-acting ENERGY!
455 *2–5*   "In Will, in Deed, IMPULSE of All to All!
456 *2–5*   "Whether thy Love with unrefracted Ray
457 *2–5*   "Beam on the PROPHET's purged eye, or if
458 *2–5*   "Diseasing Realms the ENTHUSIAST, wild of Thought,
459 *2–5*   "Scatter new Frenzies on the infected Throng,
460 *2–5*   "Thou Both inspiring and predooming Both,
461 *2–5*   "Fit INSTRUMENTS and best, of perfect End:
462 *2–5*   "Glory to Thee, Father of Earth and Heaven!"

462⁺ *2–5*   ————————————

463 *2–5*   And first a Landscape rose,
464 *2–5*   More wild, and waste, and desolate, than where
465 *2–5*   The white bear, drifting on a field of ice,
466 *2–5*   Howls to her sundered cubs with piteous rage
467 *2–5*   And savage agony.

title. *3–5* THE DESTINY OF NATIONS.   **1.** *2–4* AUSPICIOUS *2–4* REVERENCE! *2–5* Hush   3 *2–5* song,   **2.** 2 3 Strain *2–5* poured   **3.** *2–4* GREAT • 5 Great *2–4* FATHER, 2 RIGHTFUL • *3 4* RIGHTFUL • 5 Rightful   2 3 5 King, • *2–4* KING,   **4.** *2–4* ETERNAL FATHER! • 5 Eternal Father! *2–4* KING   3 omnipotent; • *2–4* OMNIPOTENT! • 5 Omnipotent!   **5.** 2 banners, wide unfurl'd,   **6.** 2 Tyrant-quelling   **7.** *2–5* symphony *2–5* instrument.   **8.** *2–5* Seize, *2–5* soul! *2–5* dome   **9.** 3 harp Harp, • *2–4* Harp • 5 harp 5 shields   **13.** 3 *2–4* Freedom, • 5 freedom, 3 unfetterd • *3–5* unfettered   **14.** *2–5* powers 3 given. • *2–5* given?   **15.** 5 first, 5 last 4 View   **21.** 5 reality,   **23.** 5 Love,   **24.** 5 all,   **25.** 5 beams, 5 self-eclipse   **29.** *2–4* ascent • 5 ascent,   **30.** *2–5* meanness: **32.** *2–5* fluids,   **33.** *2–5* tools, uncaused   **34.** 5 omniscients, 5 almighty *2–4* Slaves, • 5 slaves,   **35.** *2–5* creation *2–5* God.   **36.** *2–5* properties *2–5* God: **37.** 5 guess 5 ghost)   **39.** *2–5* Others   **40.** *2–5* aggregate   **41.** 5 atoms *2–5* organized;   **42.** *2–5* similitude   **46.** 5 act!)   **49.** 5 self-centring   **54.** *3–5* volleying   **60.** *3 4* rebellious, • 5 rebellious   **65.** 5 sun   **67.** 5 night   **71.** 5 Balda Zhiok, **71fn1.** *3 4* *Balda-Zhiok*; i.e. • 5 Balda Zhiok; i.e. *3–5* altitudinis,   **72.** *3–*

5 Solfar-kapper,   **72fn1.** *3 Solfar kapper*; • *4 Salfar Kapper*; • *5* Solfar Kapper; *4 5* omnium   **72fn3.** *4 5* situs   **72fn5.** *3–5* constabat.—   **72fn6.** *5 Leemius de*   **74fn4.** *3 4* vidisset   **74fn7.** *4 5* infantem   **74fn9.** *3–5* jacet.— **74fn10.** *5 Leemius de*   **80.** *5* power   **84.** *5* beings   **86.** *5* self-control, **89.** *3–5* impressed,   **93.** *2–5* slaughtered   *5* giant bird   **94.** *5* Vuokho, **95.** *5* tempest,   **97.** *5* murderer   **105.** *5* earth   *5* air,   *5* sea: **109.** *5* Silence **110.** *5* 'scaping   **111.** *5* elements   **113fn1.** *3–5* Spirit   **113fn2.** *3* Female: **113fn5.** *3–5* thither. He   *3* souls.   *5* a horrible   **113fn7.** *5* ocean.— **113fn8.** *5 Crantz's History   3–5* vol. i.   **115.** *4* Oceans stream,— • *5* Ocean stream;—   **117.** *5* reliance,   *3 4* Medicinal   *5* hope,   **119.** *5* steps, **121.** *5* beings   **122.** *2–5* possess,   **124.** *2–4* Kingdoms: *2–5* prompt, **126.** *5* choose   **127.** *4 5* song   **128.** *2–4* Minstrelsies • *5* minstrelsies   **129.** *2– 4* Palace-Roof • *5* palace-roof   *5* soothe   *5* monarch's   **130.** *2–5* such, perhaps, **131.** *2–5* Witnessed   *2–4* Faith) • *5* faith)   **133.** *3–5* scourged   *2* Invader.— • *3–5* Invader.   *2–5* days,   **134.** *2–5* Wisdom,   *2–4* Mother   *2–4* Thoughts, **137.** *2* Undisciplin'd. • *3–5* Undisciplined.   *2–5* For   *2–4* Birth,   **138.** *3–5* doomed *2–4* Toil • *5* toil   **139.** *2–5* That   *2–4* Tyranny's   **140.** *3–5* Unfeared   *2– 4* Fellow-natures,   **141.** *2* Lab'ring man • *3 4* Labouring man • *5* labouring man   **142.** *3–5* tired   **143.** *5* rough hewn   *2–4* Bench   **144.** *3–5* stretched **145.** *3–5* watched   **146.** *5* mulberry-bough   *3–5* creak   **147.** *2–5* breeze. Here, too,   **148.** *2–4* Schools   *2–5* teach: **149.** *2–4* Vices   *2–4* Sorrows! • *5* sorrows!   *2–5* And   **150.** *2–4* Tales   *2–4* Wrong • *5* wrong   *2–4* Distress • *5* distress   **151.** *3–5* shivered.   *2–5* tottering   *5* eld   **152.** *2–4* Daughter   *2– 5* run: *3–5* placed   **153.** *2–4* Limbs   *2–4* Door,   *3–5* loved   **154.** *2–5* story, *2–5* sort,   **155.** *2–5* gone.   **156.** *2–5* past.   *2–4* Form, • *5* form,   **157.** *2– 4* Sloth   *2–4* Luxury   **158.** *2–5* Her   *2–5* broad,   **159.** *3–5* haired   *2–5* low, **160.** *3–5* unillumed,   **161.** *2–5* Woman's   *2* Thought: • *3 4* Thought; • *5* thought; **162.** *2* Features, • *3 4* Features • *5* features   *2* declared, • *3–5* declared   **163.** *5* pity *2* work'd, • *3–5* worked,   **164.** *2–4* Indignation. • *5* indignation.   **165.** *5* a *5* huntress   **166.** *3–5* moved: *2–5* maid!   **168.** *3–5* Beamed   *3–5* say **169.** *2–5* her!   **170.** *3–5* said—   *3–5* lived   **171.** *2–5* World,   *2–4* Tombs **172.** *3–5* touched   *2–4* Dead.   **173.** *2–5* season   *5* rustic's   **175.** *2–5* Rolls *2–5* relief   *2–5* tints   **176.** *4 5* slow varying   **178.** *2–5* pallet   **179.** *3– 5* alone   **180.** *2–5* Urged   *2–5* angel-guide, that oft,   **181.** *2–5* sympathies **182.** *2–4* Heart,   **183.** *2–5* predoomed adventure.   **184.** *2–5* upland, on **185.** *5* Pilgrim-man,   *3–5* watched   **186.** *5* stars,   **188.** *2–5* vale;   *2–5* adown **189.** *4 5* vale-ward: **190.** *2–5* road   **191.** *5* team!   **192.** *3–5* stretched *2–5* limbs;   *2–5* others,   *2–5* alive   **194.** *5* night dews.   **195.** *3–5* glimmered; **196.** *2–5* Disclosed   *2–5* maiden paused,   **197.** *3–5* hailed   *2–5* replied. **198.** *3–5* reached   **199.** *2–5* feeble   *3–5* seemed   **200.** *2* Distant—   *2– 5* feebly,   *2* push'd, • *3–5* pushed,   **202.** *2–5* frost   *2–5* fire.   **203.** *2–5* rested. She,   **205.** *2–5* children—   **206.** *2–5* lovely!   *2* marr'd— • *3–5* marred— **207.** *2–5* slumber-like   **208.** *2–5* sight;   **210.** *2–5* its   **211.** *3–5* Stretched **214.** *3–5* Looked   **215.** *2–5* calm   *2–5* worn-out   **216.** *2* shudder'd: • *3 4* shuddered: • *5* shuddered;   *2–5* but,   *2–5* subdued,   **219.** *2* stiff, crampt • *3– 5* stiff cramped   *2–5* forced homeward.   *2* arrived • *3–5* arrived,   **220.** *2–5* herbs, **222.** *2–5* limbs;   *2–4* noon-tide   *2–5* hour,   **223.** *3–5* hovering   *2–4* Wife *2–4* Babes   **224.** *2–5* immortal! Yet   *2–5* pangs,   **225.** *2–5* throes,   **226.** *3– 5* faltered   **227.** *2–4* Village, • *5* village,   *2–5* dwelt   *5* a   *2–4* Husbandman,

228. *3–5* seized   *2–5* fired   **229.** *2–5* yester-evening. With   **231.** *2–*
4 Hamlets   *2–5* flame,   **232.** *2–5* shrieks!   **233.** *2–5* Through   *2–5* way!
234. *2–5* cottage. All   *3–5* quenched   **236.** *2–4* clipt • *5* clipped   *3–5* fanged
237. *2–5* provisionless! The   **238.** *2* Ill-hush'd • *3–5* Ill hushed   *3–5* moaned,
239. *2–4* Fright • *5* fright   *2–4* Cold • *5* cold   *2–4* Hunger   *2–5* life.   **240.** *2–*
5 closed   *2–4* Death. • *5* death.   **241.** *2–5* o'er-wearied   **242.** *2–5* Gained
243. *2* dropt • *3–5* dropped   **246.** *3–5* wakened   *2–5* maiden.—Such   **247.** *2–*
5 Ah!   *2–5* suffered,   **248.** *2–5* Maid   **249.** *2–5* dark!   **250.** *3–5* flushed
251. *2–5* vivacity,   **252.** *2* Fancy-craz'd! • *3 4* Fancy-crazed! • *5* fancy-crazed!
253. *2* fix'd, and • *3–5* fixed, and   *2* all, within,   **256.** *2–5* the   **257.** *2–5* hill-top
2–5 steps,   **258.** *3–5* smouldered   **259.** *2–5* there,   **261.** *2–5* swallowed
2–5 the   *2 3* sate,   **262.** *2–5* Slumber!   **263.** *3–5* Breathed   *2–5* look!
3–5 sob,   **264.** *2* subdued • *3–5* subdued,   **265.** *2–5* Presence near.   **266.** *3–*
5 toiled   *2* extacy, • *3–5* ecstasy,   **267.** *5* A   **268.** *2–5* uttered   *2–5* tones,
269. *2–5* soul,—"O Thou   **270.** *2–4* "Chosen,   *2–5* Heaven   **271a.** *2–4* "Behold
2–5 expectant—   **271a⁺.** *5* poem   **271b.** *3–5* beloved   **272.** *3–5* (To
273. *5* Of Chaos   **274.** *5* Thou   **275.** *5* Fierce   **276.** *5* When Love
277. *5* Over   *3–5* fluttered   **278.** *5* As   **279.** *5* With   **280.** *5* Poisoning
281. *5* Wakens   **282.** *5* A   **283.** *5* Sent   *5* Protoplast   **284.** *5* Stand
5 confusion's   **285.** *5* Moaning   **286.** *5* That   *5* cave   **287.** *5* Of   *3–*
5 darkness   *3 4* Desert • *5* desert   **288.** *5* Sunk   *5* Gehenna's   **289.** *5* There
5 beldam   *3–5* lurked   **290.** *5* And   *3–5* engendered   *5* Hate,   **291.** *5* Fierce
Hate   *5* Hope,   *5* Dream   **292.** *3 4* "Shaped • *5* Shaped   *3–5* marked   **293.** *5* It
3–5 roused   *4 5* dew damp   **294.** *5* From   *3–5* through   **295.** *5* Retraced
3–5 reached   **296.** *5* Of   **297.** *5* Nor   *3–5* diminished   *5* Gulf.   **298.** *5* As
3–5 through   *3–5* mouldered   *5* tower   **299.** *5* (Which,   *5* hind   **300.** *5* Circles
301. *5* The   *3–5* deemed   **302.** *5* Of   *3–5* prisoned   **303.** *5* Night   *3–*
5 murmured,   *3 4* through   **304.** *3 4* "Leaped • *5* Leaped   **305.** *5* A   *3–5* rushed
3–5 earth;   **306.** *5* Since   *5* camps   *5* courts   **307.** *5* Rebels   *3–5* Mankind!"
309. *3–5* Shrieked   *5* Fear,   *5* dam,   **310.** *3 4* Feverish   **312.** *5* hag!
314. *5* so (the   **315.** *5* The   *5* heralds   *5* good tidings   **316.** *5* And   *3–*
5 witnessed   **317.** *5* Treading,   **318.** *5* Higher,   **319.** *5* Loud   *5* triumph!
320. *5* Hover   **323.** *4* Measures,   **324.** *5* hermit   **327.** *3–5* slaughtered
327fn1. *5* Revalations,   **327fn3.** *2–4* them, that • *5* them, and it was said
unto them, that   **327fn4.** *3–5* fellow servants   **328.** *3–5* wide-opened
329. *5* patriot.   **331.** *3–5* ecstasy.   **333.** *3–5* through   *5* mist,   *5* relique
4 5 trance   **334.** *3–5* gazed,   *3–5* appeared,   **335.** *3 5* cliffs,   **336.** *3–*
5 Glassed   **337.** *3–5* Stretched   **338.** *5* plough-man   **339.** *3–5* Turned
342. *5* fields   **343.** *5* Form,   **344.** *3–5* olive-wreathed;   **345.** *3–5* flowerets
347. *3–5* beamed   **349.** *5* convalescent!   *4 5* (yet   **351.** *3 4* blessed
3 4 fulfilled • *5* fulfilled—   **352.** *5* Peace   *5* A   **353.** *3–5* seemed   **354.** *3–*
5 healed   **355.** *3–5* nursed   **356.** *3–5* moaned   **358.** *3–5* transformed
5 warrior-hosts,   **359.** *3–5* Coursed   *5* sky,   **360.** *5* heaven   **363.** *5* stains
5 light!   *3–5* Resigned,   **364.** *3–5* bowed   *3 4* Brow, • *5* brow,   **366.** *5* place
5 tombs   *3–5* reached,   **367.** *3–5* ruined   *5* sepulchre   **368.** *5* hiding-place.
369. *3–5* Gazed through   *3 4* exclaimed • *5* exclaimed;—   **370.** *3–5* mild-
eyed   *5* Form!   **371.** *5* The power   *5* Justice   *5* light,   **372.** *5* Shone
3–5 unblamed   **373.** *5* Dwelt   *5* Happiness.   **374.** *5* Ah!   **375.** *5* Should
376. *5* Why   *5* misery?   **377.** *5* Lenient   *5* Peace!   **378.** *5* As   **379.** *5* That

5 cheek; **380.** *5* And *3–5* piled **381.** *5* But *5* demon *3–5* War
382. *5* Save **383.** *5* Dancing **384.** *5* The maniac Suicide *5* giant Murder
385. *5* Exult **386.** *5* And *5* peasants **387.** *5* Beneath **389.** *5* luxury
5 lust's **390.** *5* No *5* kings; **391.** *5* When *5* lords **392.** *5* Falls
3–5 accustomed **393.** *5* When eunuchs *5* fools **394.** *5* And dancers
3–5 vain; **395.** *5* Then War **396.** *5* Pleasingly *5* hearts; **397.** *5* Its
398. *5* Insipid royalty's **399.** *4* "*Therefore* • *5* Therefore *3–5* uninjured
400. *5* (Victims *5* executioners) **401.** *5* The *5* husbandmen **402.** *5* The
vineyard *5* harvest. **403.** *5* The **404.** *5* Though *3–5* hushed *5* winds
5 noon, **405.** *5* Yet *5* Leviathan, **406.** *5* In *5* island-bulk, **407.** *5* Ocean
408. *5* A **409.** *5* And **410.** *5* Short **411.** *5* And **412.** *5* Still *3–*
5 the unfinished **413.** *5* But **415.** *3* Vapour • *4 5* vapour *3–5* sailed,
418. *5* Till *3 4* Death-doomed • *5* death-doomed **419.** *5* plain, **421.** *3–*
5 steered *3 4* Vapour • *5* vapour **422.** *3–5* paused **423.** *3–5* passed *5* cloud
424. *3–5* bright; *5* plain **425.** *3–5* emerged **426.** *3–5* form, broad-
bosomed, **430.** *5* Ambition's **431.** *3–5* hissed *5* locust-fiends *3–5* crawled
432. *3–5* glittered *5* Corruption's **433.** *3–5* reign; **435.** *5* tornado
438. *5* palms, **438fn3.** *2–4* ideas • *5* thoughts **438fn5–20.** PR *5* prints the
Greek with all diacritics in place **438fn5.** *3* Ωσκοτου **438fn6.** *3 4* Ατα· • *5* ῎Ατα·
438fn10. *3 4* Κ᾽ασματων • *5* Κ᾽ασμάτων *3 4* εσσι • *5* ἐσσὶ **438fn11.** *3 4* Αλλ᾽ •
5 ᾽Αλλ᾽ **438fn13.** *5* ἐπὶ **438fn15.** *3–5* ποσσ᾽ **438fn16.** *3 4* Πατριδ᾽ •
5 Πατρίδ᾽ **438fn17.** *3 4* Ερασαι • *5* ῎Ερασαι **438fn19.** *3 4* Οσσ᾽ •
5 ῍Οσσ᾽ **438fn20.** *4* λεγοναι **438fn22.** *5* gates *5* darkness, *5* race
438fn23. *5* misery! *5* funeral **438fn24.** *3–5* dances **438fn25.** *3–5* dwellest
5 Liberty, *5* Genius! **438fn27.** *5* fountains *5* citron-groves, **438fn28.** *5* men,
5 men. **439.** *5* murdered **441.** *3–5* Warmed *5* plain **442.** *5* morn:
443. *5* Freedom, *5* blood! **444.** *3–5* beloved, *4 5* Heaven! **446.** *5* Soon
5 morning *5* day, **447.** *5* The *5* morning *5* noon. **448.** *5* Much
449. *5* But *5* omen—Save thy Country!" **450.** *3–5* passed, **451.** *3–*
5 disappeared *5* heavenly **453.** *5* All *5* presence **454.** *5* Nature's
5 ever-acting energy! **455.** *5* In will, *5* deed, impulse **456.** *5* Whether *5* ray
457. *5* Beam *5* Prophet's **458.** *5* Diseasing realms *5* enthusiast, *5* thought,
459. *5* Scatter *5* frenzies *5* throng, **460.** *5* Thou both . . . both, **461.** *5* Fit
instruments *5* end: **462.** *5* Glory *4* Heaven! **463.** *5* landscape *4 5* rose
464. *3–5* wild *3–5* waste *3–5* desolate

title. The PR *1* title ("A FRAGMENT") applied to lines 121–271a. Other titles
canvassed by C were:

"the progress of European Liberty, a vision" (*CL* I 243: to TP 1 Nov 1796);
"the Visions of the Maid of Orleans" (*CL* I 275: to TP 13 Dec 1796);
"The Progress of Liberty—or the Visions of the maid of Orleans" (*CL* I 285: to John
Thelwall 17 Dec 1796);
"Visions of the Maid of Arc" (*CL* I 297: to Joseph Cottle [6 Jan 1797]);
"Progress of Liberty, or Visions of the Maid of Orleans" (*CL* I 329: to Joseph Cottle
[late Jun 1797]);
"The Vision of the Patriot Maiden" (VCL S MS Fl.7: ?19–24 Dec 1799);
"the Vision of the Maid of Orleans" (*CN* I 1577 f 53ᵛ: 19–20 Oct 1803).

C continued to entertain the possibility of such a title up to c Jun 1814, when he marked up his copy of *Joan of Arc* for William Hood. See also *CN* III 4202=**508** *National Independence*.

3fn. Written in the RH margin of MS 1. C's "any" is an error for "an" (see VAR **413** *On the Roots of a Tree* 2 for another unintentional "y").

4.2.5. In MS 2 this line was originally written after 4.2.7, before being transposed.

4.2.8⁺. MS 2 has line-space.

6⁺/6.1.1⁺/6.2.2⁺. PR *2–5* have line-space.

10–11. First printed in the PR 2 proofs as follows:

> Of Brutus and Leonidas! Force back
> With its strong music, that soliciting spell,

C revised the lines in proof.

12⁺. Line-space in PR *2–5*. The gap was introduced by C on the PR 2 proofs (there is no break here in the corresponding passage **110** *Contributions to "Joan of Arc"* II 12–13).

14⁺. No line-space in texts 3 *2–5*.

14.1.1–14. In MS 1 these lines follow on after a 4-cm space, in a slightly different ink and apparently written on a later occasion, which may bear on the question of their relevance to the preceding lines. They are paralleled by entries in the Gutch Notebook (*CN* I 51, 174 (8)), and by passages in **112** *To the Nightingale* and **115** *The Eolian Harp*.

14.1.13. MS 1 Shts . . . shts] C's abbreviation for "shoots" or "shouts"?

15. The line was printed as two lines in the PR 2 proofs (=**110** *Contributions to "Joan of Arc"* II 15–16):

> But chiefly this, with holiest habitude
> Of constant Faith, him First, him Last to view

C revised the lines in proof.

23.1–25.1/26.1. Erratum in PR 2: "substitute:

> The substance from its shadow. Infinite Love,
> Whose Latence is the plenitude of All,
> Thou with retracted Beams, and Self-eclipse
> Veiling revealest thy eternal Sun."

26⁺. Line-space in PR *2–5*.

27–30. Quoted (var) *The Friend* VI (21 Sept 1809) (*CC*) II 82 (also I 117), reading "free," in line 27 and "soul," in line 29.

36–9. In Francis Wrangham's (?) copy of PR 2 C's wrote alongside, in the LH margin: "Must be altered: as false in philosophy, ᵢaᵢnd subversive of ᵢrᵢeligion. The lines ᵢbᵢelow * are for ᵢtᵢrial, or rather ᵢfoᵢr hint and *memorandum*." The lines written at the foot of the two following pages are as follows:

> * What IS, ~~that~~ but as God IS! What Wing of Thought
> May overtaken, what spell of Words may bind
> The ~~dark smal~~ mockful fugitive Alien that exists
> Yet is not? Who declare the Cloud whose edge
> Refracts the Light into the showerless Air,
> ~~The~~ And unreceiving Void, that sends it back
> A gorgeous Spectre? O proud Soul of Man,
> Strong art thou in thy weakness, and dost make

The shifting limits of thy scanty ~~Being~~ Ken
A ~~second Sight~~ living outline, eddying ~~ceaseless~~ in ~~all~~ to form,
A second Sight, the Vision of a World:
Here Iwe pause humbly!

44–7. First printed as three lines in the PR 2 proofs (=**110** *Contributions to "Joan of Arc"* II 45–7, with the exception of the first word):

> Are one all-conscious spirit, who directs
> With absolute ubiquity of thought
> All his component monads, that yet seem

C revised the lines in proof.

47.1.9. MS 3 ⟨Omnific?⟩] The question-mark is C's.

60. Erratum in PR 2: "for *rebellions* r. *rebellious*". The correction is made in JG's copy at HUL, where a comma is also inserted after "some".

97⁺. Line-space in PR 5.

105⁺. The space was introduced in the PR 2 proofs (there is no break in the corresponding passage **110** *Contributions to "Joan of Arc"* II 105–6). No line-space in PR 5.

126. Erratum in PR 2: "for *mortal ministers* r. *human ministers*." The correction is taken in to WW's copy at Cornell, in AG's hand.

134. The line appears (var) in the Gutch Notebook, where it is followed by two Greek phrases, one from Homer, one from the Chaldean Oracles, which C found in Jeremy Taylor (*CN* I 180).

155⁺. Line-space in PR 2–5.

167–9. C quoted the lines (var) to Joseph Cottle c 3 Jul 1797, to describe DW (*CL* I 330).

171–2. Anticipated (var) in the Gutch Notebook (*CN* I 194: [1796]).

183–91. The first proof of PR 2 was closer to MS 1:

> To the predoomed adventure. And the ascent
> Now past of that steep upland, on whose top
> Not seldom some poor nightly-roaming man
> Shouts to himself, there first the cottage-lights
> Seen in Neufchatel's vale, she slop'd adown
> The bleak hill's further side, till at the base,
> In the first entrance of the level road,
> A thwart wain stopt her speed.

C revised the lines in the same, first proof.

195. PR 2 new] Corrected to "now" (ink over pencil) in JG's copy at HUL.

198–9. The first proof of PR 2 has PR *1*'s text (197.1.1, 199), revised by C on the proof.

211–12. The first proof of PR 2 opens the paragraph with PR *1*'s text (lines 211.1–2), revised by C on the proof. In JG's copy of PR 2 at HUL the lines are turned round as follows (ink over pencil):

> At the living Wretch,
> The Maid gazed wildly mutely questioning.

215. drowsy] The first proof of PR 2 read "dreary", which may or may not be a printer's mistake. C corrected the word on the proof.

220, 222, 224. The two sets of PR 2 proofs follow the PR *1* readings in these lines. C did not emend them until he saw the second set of proofs.

225. Deleted in JG's copy of PR 2 at HUL, apparently by C.

226⁺. Line-space in PR 2–5.

238. The first proof of PR 2 read "Ill-hush'd her children's cries; and still they moan'd," revised by C on the proof.

251–2. Anticipated (var) in the Gutch Notebook (*CN* I 197).

254–5. Identical with **134** *Written on Receiving Letters Informing me of the Birth of a Son 7–8.*

307. The line was followed in the first proof of PR 2 by seven more lines from **110** *Contributions to "Joan of Arc"* (II 260–6), which C deleted on the first proof.

309. The two sets of PR 2 proofs give the line as in **110** *Contributions to "Joan of Arc"* II 273. C did not emend it until he saw the second set of proofs.

313. The line was followed in the first proof of PR 2 by seventeen more lines from **110** *Contributions to "Joan of Arc"* (II 277–93), which C deleted on the proof with the comments "None of mine, thank God!" and "Blessings on us! Why these are not mine." Cf VAR **110** (*q*) commentary on the question of authorship.

332–4. Line 332 was not preceded by a line-space in the two sets of PR 2 proofs (no gap either at **110** *Contributions to "Joan of Arc"* II 312⁺), and lines 332–3 read as in *Contributions to "Joan of Arc"* II 313–14. C introduced the PR 2 readings into the second set of proofs.

335–6. Reworked from an entry in the Gutch Notebook (*CN* I 55):

> Broad-breasted Rock.
> hanging cliff that glasses
> His rugged forehead in the calmy sea.

359. Followed in the first proof of PR 2 by two more lines from **110** *Contributions to "Joan of Arc"* (II 341–2), which C deleted on the proof.

362–4. The first proof of PR 2 gave the lines as in **110** *Contributions to "Joan of Arc"* II 345–7. C revised them in two stages, in the successive proofs.

362. Erratum in PR 2: "for *blended with the clouds* r. *looming on the mist.*"

371–2. Erratum in PR 2: "substitute:

> The power of Justice, like a name all Light,
> Shone from thy brow;"

377. In JG's copy of PR 2 at HUL C rewrote the line to avoid the assonance of "sweet" and "cheek":

> ~~Thy Songs,~~ Sweet are thy Songs, O Peace! ~~are sweet~~ lenient of Care,

He did the same in the copy of PR *3* at the Fitzwilliam Museum:

> A grievous defect here in the rhyme—recalling Assonance of Peace, sweet, eve, cheek.—Better thus—

> Sweet are thy songs, O Peace! lenient of Care,

379. The first proof of PR 2 gave the line as in **110** *Contributions to "Joan of Arc"* II 361, revised by C on the proof.

381–6. In the Fitzwilliam copy of PR *3* C deleted the lines down to "And know not why". In the margin he described line 381 as "a vile Line. I S.T.C.", and underlined 382 "foul", adding in the margin "*Southeyian*". The lines correspond to **110** *Contributions to "Joan of Arc"* II 363–8. C rewrote line 386 to read "Ah! wherefore should the guileless Peasants crowd".

410. PR *3* Short] In the Fitzwilliam copy C substituted "Brief".

414. The line was followed in both sets of PR *2* proofs by five more lines from **110** *Contributions to "Joan of Arc"* (II 397–401). C did not delete them until he saw the second proof.

416. In JG's copy of PR *2* at HUL C has emended "hot" to "the".

429. The PR *2* reading "brow" is evidently a misprint which escaped C: cf **110** *Contributions to "Joan of Arc"* II 419.

430. giant] The two proofs of PR *2* give "ghastly", as in **110** *Contributions to "Joan of Arc"* II 420. C did not revise the reading until he saw the second PR *2* proof.

437. In the Fitzwilliam copy of PR *3* C changed "from" to "for" (=**110** *Contributions to "Joan of Arc"* II 427), which is surely the correct reading.

438fn. For a collation with the first version of the Greek text see VAR **48** *Sors Misera Servorum* 1–16.

438fn6. For C's comments on vowel quantities in HNC's copy of PR *2* at HUL and in an earlier printing of the Greek text, see **48** *Sors Misera Servorum* 2EC.

438fn17. For C's changes in the Fitzwilliam copy of PR *3* see **48** *Sors Misera Servorum* 13EC.

438fn25. In HNC's copy of PR *2* C corrected "dwelleth" to "dwellest". JG made the same correction in William Hood's copy at Columbia.

463–7. The only lines in *The Destiny of Nations* which have been transferred from their original position in **110** *Contributions to "Joan of Arc"*(II 136–40). The transposition from their equivalent position here, before line 271b, to the very end changes and even reverses their implications for the argument of the poem.

140. SONNET: TO THE RIVER OTTER

A. DATE

Aug–Nov 1796? 1793? It is possible that the poem dates from 1793, as JDC and EHC assumed. If it does, it was probably in a form different from the present version, one with which C was not satisfied. However, the absence of the poem from C's early ms collections is striking. The present version was probably arrived at between Aug and Nov 1796: see vol I headnote.

B. TEXTS

1. Sonnets from Various Authors (1796). Signed "S. T. COLERIDGE."
The poem is emended in the copy inscribed (in Dec 1800) to SH (DCL MS 14/2).

2. *Poems* (1797).

C listed errata for the poem in a letter to Joseph Cottle of c 3 Jul 1797 (*CL* I 331), which Cottle ignored. C made the changes himself in the copies he gave to his brother GC (Princeton University Library Robert H. Taylor Collection); to William Roskilly (in the possession of J.C.C. Mays, 1999); to William Bowles (in the possession of Erwin Schwarz, 1982); to Thomas Hutchinson (in the possession of Jonathan Wordsworth, 1980); and in RS's (?) copy (Yale In 678 797 Copy 1).

3. *Poems* (1803).

One of the group PR *1–3* was reprinted in *A Selection of Poems, Designed Chiefly for Schools and Young Persons* ed Joseph Cottle (1804) 195–6 (new eds 1815, 1823, 1836); *Laura* ed Capel Lofft (5 vols 1813–14) II No 105; *Specimens of the Lyrical, Descriptive, and Narrative Poets of Great Britain* ed John Johnstone (Edinburgh 1828) 487–8; *Specimens of English Sonnets* ed Alexander Dyce (1833) 175.

4 [=RT]. *SL* (1817).

C copied the errata into Francis Wrangham's (?) copy (sold at Christie's 13 June 1979 lot 126). They were copied into WW's copy by AG (Cornell WORDSWORTH PR 4480 S5 1817 Copy 1); and into the copy at Duke (R.B.R. A-29 C693 SM) by a person unknown. HNC's copy (HUL *AC85 L8605 Zy 817c) contains a change of punctuation. Rpt *Spirit of Contemporary Poetry* (3 vols Boston, Mass 1827) II 99.

5. *PW* (1828).

6. *PW* (1829).

Either PR *5* or PR *6* was reprinted in *The Talisman* ed Z. M. Watts (1832?) 248.

7. *PW* (1834).

title. *1* SONNET V. | *To the RIVER OTTER.* • *2 3* SONNET IV. | *To the River Otter.* • *4–7* SONNET TO THE RIVER OTTER.

1 □   Dear native Brook! wild Streamlet of the West!
2 □   How many various-fated Years have past,
3 *1–3* What blissful and what anguish'd hours, since last
   4–7   happy,   mournful
4 □   I skimm'd the smooth thin stone along thy breast,
5 □   Numbering its light leaps! Yet so deep imprest
6 □   Sink the sweet scenes of Childhood, that mine eyes
7 *1–3* I never shut amid the sunny blaze,
   4–7   ray,
8 ⊠*4* But strait with all their tints thy waters rise,
   4   their
9 *1–3* Thy crossing plank, thy margin's willowy maze,
   4–7   marge with willows grey,

10 ☐   And bedded sand that vein'd with various dies
11 *1–3* Gleam'd thro' thy bright transparence to the gaze!
  4–7   On my way,
12 ☐   Visions of Childhood! oft have ye beguil'd
13 ☐   Lone Manhood's cares, yet waking fondest sighs,
14 ⊠*4* Ah! that once more I were a careless Child!
  4   I were once more

title. *3 SONNET IV. | To the RIVER OTTER.* • *5–7* SONNET TO THE RIVER
OTTER.   **1.** *7* brook! *7* streamlet   **2.** *4–7* years   **4.** *5–7* skimmed
5. *4–7* yet *4* impresst   **6.** *4–7* childhood,   **8.** *5–7* straight   **10.** *7* that,
5–7 veined *7* dyes,   **11.** *5–7* Gleamed *4–7* through *4–7* transparence!
12. *4–7* childhood! *4–7* beguiled   **13.** *4–7* manhood's *4* sighs. • *5–7* sighs:
14. *4–7* child!

1–11. Previously used in **128** *Recollection* 13, 17–26.

2–3, 5–6, 8, 10, 12, 14. Indented in PR *1 2 4*; lines 2–3, 5, 8, 10, 12, 14 indented in
PR *3*; lines 2–3, 7, 9, 12, 14 indented in PR *5–7*.

3. In SH's copy of PR *1*, and in GC's, William Bowles's, William Roskilly's, Thomas
Hutchinson's, and RS's (?) copies of PR *2*, C emended "blissful" to "happy" and "an-
guish'd" to "mournful", as he asked Cottle to do in his letter of c 3 Jul 1797 (*CL* I
331).

7. In SH's copy of PR *1*, and in GC's, William Bowles's, William Roskilly's, Thomas
Hutchinson's, and RS's (?) copies of PR *2*, C emended "blaze" to "ray", as he had asked
Cottle to do (*CL* I 331).

8. In Francis Wrangham's (?) copy of PR *4* C emended "their" to "thy", as requested
in the PR *4* Errata.

9. In SH's copy of PR *1*, and in GC's, William Bowles's, William Roskilly's, Thomas
Hutchinson's, and RS's (?) copies of PR *2*, C emended "margin's willowy maze," to
"marge with willows grey" (a comma follows "grey" in the Bowles and Roskilly copies),
as he had asked Cottle to do (*CL* I 331).

11. In SH's copy of PR *1* and in GC's, William Bowles's, Thomas Hutchinson's, and
RS's (?) copies of PR *2*, C emended "transparence to the gaze!" to "transparence! on my
way," and in William Roskilly's he altered to "transparence.—On my way,". When C
asked Cottle to make the change (*CL* I 331), he specified a full stop after "transparence".

13. In SH's copy of PR *1* C emended "Lone Manhood's cares, yet" to "The cares of
Manhood". In HNC's copy of PR *4* the full stop at the end of the line has been emended
to a dash.

14. In Francis Wrangham's (?) copy of PR *4* C emended the line to conform to the
reading of other versions, as requested in the Errata.

141. ADAPTATION OF THOMAS DERMODY

A. DATE

Nov 1796? C's adaptation was probably made when he put together *Sonnets from Various Authors*, although it might have been composed mentally any time after May 1796.

B. TEXT

Sonnets from Various Authors (1796) No xxiv, signed "THOMAS DERMODY."

The RT reproduces the *Sonnets* text exactly, except for the title, given there simply as "SONNET XXIV."

142. ODE ON THE DEPARTING YEAR

A. DATE

Nov–Dec 1796. The printed texts date the poem variously between 23 and 27 Dec 1796. But C was engaged in writing it when he wrote to Benjamin Flower on 11 Dec (*CL* I 268), Catherine II of Russia died on 17 Nov, and the rheumatic illness referred to in the PR 2 prefatory epistle began in that month (*CL* I 249–50: to TP 5 Nov 1796; 276: to J. Thelwall 17 Dec 1796; 288: to TP [18 Dec 1796]). The poem draws on C's reading during these two months and earlier.

B. TEXTS

1. Cambridge Intelligencer (31 Dec 1796). Signed "S. T. COLERIDGE I *December* 27." Lines 1–110 only.
    Punctuation at the end of lines is not always clear.

2 [=RT]. *Ode on the Departing Year* I *By S. T. COLERIDGE.* Quarto pamphlet (1796).
    The prefatory epistle is dated 26 Dec, but this version extends the poem beyond line 110 and must therefore be considered later than PR *1*. The inscription on one of the two annotated copies (vol I annex C 5.1) is dated 30 Dec 1796.
    A variant state of this printing, represented by BM Ashley 4766, records what appears to be a later, trial version of lines 158–70: later, because another variant affecting **143** *Lines to a Young Man of Fortune* 9 suggests a different,

uncorrected state of the same printing; trial, because no other copy has come to light. See further vol I annex C 5.

1. Present whereabouts unknown. Revisions of fourteen lines and four notes, with the addition of an Argument, in an als to Joseph Cottle written some time between 6 Feb and 15 Mar 1797 (*Two Letters* 313–14), showing that printer's copy for PR *3* below was provided by PR *2* emended according to this letter. The first page is reproduced as an illustration to Christie's Catalogue (2 Apr 1975) lot 36, and the details differ slightly from J. P. Mann's transcription.

C took suggestions for several revisions from two letters by CL written in Jan 1797 (*LL*—M—I 80–2, 85–6). The collation below cites MS 1 only where C instructed Cottle to emend PR *2*; where no MS 1 reading is cited, the ms is identical with PR *2*.

3*. BM Ashley 408 ff 58^r–65^v, 66^r–72^v. Two proof copies of PR *3* below. The printed text is identical in each, although the second lacks the Argument. They are differently corrected in C's hand, and are here designated PR *3**A and PR *3**B. PR *3**A bears the date (in ms) "Decemb. 23rd I 1796" at the end of the printed text. Reproduced (var) in *JDC facsimile* 83–112; photographic facsimile of ff 58^v, 66^v, 65^r in *C Bibl* (Wise *TLP*) 63 and facing 63.

Proof A accompanied C's letter to Cottle of 15 Mar (*CL* I 315–16), while proof B contains, besides C's emendations and comments, Cottle's reactions to a number of these. C's letter to Cottle of 8 Jun 1797 (*CL* I 325) reveals that at least one correction in proof B was made after this date.

1*. HRC MS (Coleridge, S T) Works B. Single leaf, 18.0×11.5 cm; no wm; chain-lines (horizontal) 2.2 cm. Revised note on line 143 in C's hand, transcribed after C saw the second corrected proof, PR *3**B. Bound into Rugby Manuscript pp 25–6/f 10^{r-v}.

3. Poems (1797).

Three copies contain corrections to the poem in C's hand: William Bowles's (in the possession of Erwin Schwarz, 1982); Thomas Hutchinson's (in the possession of Jonathan Wordsworth, 1980); RS's (?) (Yale In 678 797 Copy 1).

4. Poems (1803).

It is possible, but not certain, that CL was responsible for the unique variants in this text. There is evidence that he had C's authority for at least some of them (see on lines 88–9 below).

5. SL (1817).

The proof copy at Yale (In C678 817sa) suggests that PR *5* was set from a revised copy of an earlier printed text; further revisions were introduced in proof, but this stage has not been recorded here. Three copies contain emendations by C to the poem: AG's (Stanford V 821.6 C69s); Francis Wrangham's (?) (sold at Christie's 13 Jun 1979 lot 126); an untraced copy quoted by JDC when it belonged to Stuart M. Samuel (*PW*—JDC—588), for which see the start of vol I headnote.

The Erratum was copied by JG into the copies owned by William Hood (Columbia X825C67 W 3 1817) and Martha Fricker (HUL Lowell *EC8 C6795 817s), and a copy at Duke (R.B.R. A-29 C693 SM); and by AG into the copies owned by TP (Brown PR 4478 A1 1817 Koopman Collection), WW (Cornell WORDSWORTH pr 4480 S5 1817 Copy 1), and a copy at Yale (In C678 817s Copy 2).

Rpt *Select British Poets* ed William Hazlitt (1824) 625–6; *Spirit of Contemporary Poetry* (3 vols Boston, Mass 1827) I 7–15.

6. *PW* (1828).

7. *PW* (1829).
JG's (?) copy at NYPL (Berg Collection) contains a single correction.

8. *PW* (1834).

C. GENERAL NOTE

John P. Anderson's bibliography in Hall Caine *Life of Samuel Taylor Coleridge* (1887) iiiʙ includes the title *Prospect of Peace* (4ᵗᵒ; London 1796), on the authority of Robert Watt's *Bibliotheca Britannica* (4 vols Edinburgh 1824) and W. T. Lowndes's *The Bibliographer's Manual of English Literature* (6 vols 1857–64). No such title has been traced, and it is almost certain that PR 2 above is intended. See poem **143.X1** below.

title/divisional title. *1* ODE I FOR THE LAST DAY OF THE YEAR,1796.•
2 3 *3 4* ODE I ON THE I 𝕯𝕰𝕻𝕬𝕽𝕿𝕴𝕹𝕲 𝖄𝕰𝕬𝕽. • *5–8* ODE I TO I THE
DEPARTING YEAR.

additional title/title. *2 3* *3–7* ODE I ON THE I *DEPARTING YEAR.*

additional title/title fn
*3*A   (Composed Decembʳ 23ʳᵈ, 1796)
*3*B *3–8* This Ode was written on the 24ᵗʰ 25ᵗʰ and 26ᵗʰ days of December, 1796; and
    published separately on the last day of the year.

epigraph
⁻**1.1** *2 3–8* Ἰου, Ἰου, ω ω κακα.
⁻**1.2** *2 3–8* Ὑπ' αυ με δεινος ορθομαντειας πονος
⁻**1.3** *2 3–8* Στροβει, ταρασσων φροιμιοις εφημιοις.
⁻**1.3⁺** *2 3–8* – – – – – – – – – – – –
⁻**1.4** *2 3–7* Το μελλον ηξει· και συ μην ταχει παρων
    8   μ' εν
⁻**1.5** *2 3–7* Αγαν γ' αληθομαντιν ←—μ'—→ ερεις.
    8   Αγαν γ' αληθομαντιν οικτειρας
⁻**1.6** *2 3–8*   ÆSCHY. AGAMEM. 1225.

prefatory epistle [PR 2 only]

To THOMAS POOLE, of Stowey.

MY DEAR FRIEND,

Soon after the commencement of this month, the Editor of the Cambridge Intelligencer (a newspaper conducted with so much ability, and such unmixed and ⁻1.10
fearless zeal for the interests of Piety and Freedom, that I cannot but think my
poetry honoured by being permitted to appear in it), requested me, by Letter, to
furnish him with some Lines for the last day of this Year. I promised him that I
would make the attempt; but, almost immediately after, a rheumatic complaint
seized on my head, and continued to prevent the possibility of poetic compo- ⁻1.15
sition till within the last three days. So in the course of the last three days the
following Ode was produced. In general, when an Author informs the Public
that his production was struck off in a great hurry, he offers an insult, not an
excuse. But I trust that the present case is an exception, and that the peculiar
circumstances, which obliged me to write with such unusual rapidity, give a ⁻1.20
propriety to my professions of it: nec nunc eam apud te jacto, sed et ceteris
indico; ne quis asperiore limâ carmen examinet, et a confuso scriptum et quod
frigidum erat ni statim traderem. (I avail myself of the words of Statius, and
hope that I shall likewise be able to say of any weightier publication, what *he*
has declared of his Thebaid, that it had been tortured* with a laborious Polish.) ⁻1.25
   For me to discuss the *literary* merits of this hasty composition, were idle and
presumptuous. If it be found to possess that Impetuosity of Transition, and that
Precipitation of Fancy and Feeling, which are the *essential* excellencies of the
sublimer Ode, its deficiency in less important respects will be easily pardoned
by those, from whom alone praise could give me pleasure: and whose minuter ⁻1.30
criticisms will be disarmed by the reflection, that these Lines were conceived
"not in the soft obscurities of Retirement, or under the Shelter of Academic
Groves, but amidst inconvenience and distraction, in sickness and in sorrow."
I am more anxious, lest the *moral* spirit of the Ode should be mistaken. You,
I am sure, will not fail to recollect, that among the Ancients, the Bard and ⁻1.35
the Prophet were one and the same character; and you *know*, that although I
prophesy curses, I pray fervently for blessings.
   Farewell, Brother of my Soul!

——— O ever found the same,
And trusted and belov'd! ⁻1.40

Never without an emotion of honest pride do I subscribe myself
Your grateful and affectionate Friend,

BRISTOL,   *S. T. COLERIDGE.*
December 26, 1796.

⁻**1.25fn** 2 Multâ cruciata limâ.

argument [present in TEXTS 1 *3**A 3–8*]

Argument ⁻1.45

The Ode commences with an address to the divine Providence that regulates into one
vast Harmony all the events of Time, however calamitous some of them may appear
to mortals:—the second Strophe calls on men to suspend their private joys & sorrows,
& devote them for a while to the cause of Human Nature in general. The first Epode

speaks of the Empress of Russia, who died of an apoplexy on the 17th of November, ⁻1.50
1797, having just concluded a subsidiary treaty ~~again~~ with the Kings combined against
France. The first & second Antistrophes describe the image of the Departing Year &c,
as seen in a Vision. The second Epode prophesies in anguish of spirit the downfall of
this country.—

⁻1.55	*1 2 3* 3 4*	STROPHE I.
	5–8	I.
1	⊠*4*	SPIRIT, who sweepest the wild harp of time!
	4	BEING!
2	☐	It is most hard with an untroubled ear
3	☐	Thy dark inwoven harmonies to hear.
4	*1*	But, mine eye fix'd on heaven's unchanged clime,
	2	Yet,
	*3**A–B	unchange~~ding~~
	3–8	unchanging
5	⊠*7*	Long had I listen'd, free from mortal fear,
	7	when
6	*1 2 3* 3 8*	With inward stillness and a bowed mind:
	4–7	submitted
7	*1–4*	When lo! far onwards waving on the wind
	*3**A–B	~~in~~ on
	5–8	its folds far
8	*1 2 3* 3 4*	I saw the skirts of the DEPARTING YEAR!
	5–8	train
9	☐	Starting from my silent sadness,
10	☐	Then with no unholy madness,
11	*1*	Ere yet he pierc'd the cloud and mock'd my sight,
	2 3* 3 4	the entered forbade
	5–8	foreclos'd
12	☐	I rais'd th' impetuous song, and solemniz'd his flight!
		[*Line-space*]
⁻13	*1 2 3* 3 4*	STROPHE II.
	5–8	II.
13	☐	Hither from the recent tomb,
14	☐	From the prison's direr gloom;
15	*1 2 3* 3 4*	From poverty's heart-wasting languish;
16	*1 2 3* 3–8*	From distemper's midnight anguish;
15.1	*5–8*	And thence, where Poverty doth waste and languish;
17	☐	Or where his two bright torches blending,
18	☐	Love illumines manhood's maze,
19	☐	Or where o'er cradled infants bending,
20	☐	Hope has fix'd her wishful gaze:
21	☐	Hither, in perplexed dance
22	*1*	Ye SORROWS, and ye JOYS advance!
	2 3* 3 4	WOES, and young-eyed
	5–8	ye
23	☐	By time's wild harp, and by the hand,
24	☐	Whose indefatigable sweep

25 *1 2 3* 3 4* Forbids it's fateful strings to sleep;
5–8 Raises from
26 □ I bid you haste, a mix'd tumultuous band!
27 □ From every private bower,
28 □ And each domestic hearth,
29 □ Haste for one solemn hour;
30 □ And with a loud, and yet a louder voice,
31 *1 2* O'er the sore travail of the common earth
1 *3* 3–8* Nature struggling in portentous birth
32 □ Weep and rejoice!
33 *1 2* Seiz'd in sore travail and portentous birth,
34 *1 2* (Her eye-balls flashing a pernicious glare,)
35 *1 2* Sick NATURE struggles, hark! her pangs increase,
36 *1 2* Her groans are horrible! but O! most fair
37 *1 2* The promis'd twins, she bears—EQUALITY and PEACE!
37.1.1 1 *3* 3–8* Still echoes the dread Name, that o'er the Earth
37.1.1fn *4* The Name of Liberty, which at the commencement of the French Revolution was both the occasion and the pretext of unnumbered crimes and horrors.
37.1.2 1 *3* 3–8* Let slip the Storm and woke the brood of Hell:
37.1.3 1 *3* 3–8* And now advance in saintly Jubilee
37.1.4 1 *3* 3 4* JUSTICE and TRUTH: they too have heard the spell,
5–8 thy
37.1.5 1 *3* 3–8* They too obey thy Name, divinest LIBERTY!
[*Line-space*]
⁻38 *1 2 3* 3 4* EPODE.
5–8 III.
38 □ I mark'd AMBITION in his war-array,
39 □ I heard the mailed Monarch's troublous cry,
40 *1 2 3** "Ah! ⟵whither⟶ does the NORTHERN CONQUERESS stay?
*3*B* ~~whither~~ wherefore
3–8 ⟵wherefore⟶
40fn *1* The Empress died, just as she had engaged to furnish more effectual aid to the powers combined against France.
2 Northern Conqueress.—A Subsidiary Treaty had just been concluded; and
Russia was to have furnished more effectual aid, than that of pious manifestoes,
to the powers combined against France. I rejoice—not over the deceased Wo-
man—(I never dared figure the Russian Sovereign to my imagination under the
dear and venerable character of WOMAN—WOMAN, that complex term for
Mother, Sister, Wife!) I rejoice, as at the disenshrining of a Dæmon! I rejoice,
as at the extinction of the evil Principle impersonated! This very day, six years

ago, the massacre of Ismail was perpetrated. THIRTY THOU-
SAND HUMAN
BEINGS, MEN, WOMEN & CHILDREN, murdered in cold
blood, for no other
crime, than that their Garrison had defended the place with per-
severance and   10
bravery! Why should I recall the poisoning of her husband, her
iniquities in
Poland, or her late unmotived attack on Persia; the desolating
ambition of her
public Life, or the libidinous excesses of her private Hours! I
have no wish to
qualify myself for the office of Historiographer to the King of
Hell—— !

                                        December 23, 1796.   15

41	*1 2 3* 3 4*	"Groans not her chariot o'er it's onward way?"
	5–8	on
42	☐	Fly, mailed Monarch, fly!
43	☐	Stunn'd by death's "twice-mortal" mace,
44	☒*7*	No more on MURDER'S lurid face,
	7	luric
45	*1*	That tyrant hag shall glote with frenzied eye!
	☒*1*	Th' insatiate drunken
46	☐	Manes of the unnumber'd slain,
47	☐	Ye that gasp'd on WARSAW'S plain!
48	☐	Ye that erst at ISMAEL'S tower,
49	☐	When human ruin choak'd the streams,
50	☐	Fell in conquest's glutted hour,
51	*1 2 3* 5*	'Mid women's shrieks and infant's screams;
	3*ʙ 3 4 6–8	Infant's'
52	*1 2 3* 3 4*	Whose shrieks, whose screams were vain to stir
53	*1 2 3* 3 4*	Loud-laughing, red-eyed massacre!
54	☐	Spirits of the uncoffin'd slain,
55	☐	Sudden blasts of triumph swelling,
56	☐	Oft, at night, in misty train,
57	☐	Rush around her narrow dwelling!
58	☐	The exterminating fiend is fled.
59	☐	(Foul her life, and dark her doom)
60	*1 2 3* 3 4*	Mighty army of the dead;
	5–8	armies
61	☐	Dance, like death-fires, round her tomb!
62	☐	Then with *prophetic* song relate,
63	*1 2 3* 3 4*	Each some scepter'd murderer's fate.
	5–8	tyrant-murderer's
64	*1 2 3**	When shall scepter'd SLAUGHTER cease,
65	*1 2 3**	Awhile he crouch'd, O victor France,
66	*1 2 3**	Beneath the light'ning of thy lance;
67	*1*	With treacherous dalliance courting PEACE.
	2 1 3*	wooing

67fn *2*   With treacherous dalliance wooing Peace.—To juggle this easily-juggled

people into better humour with the supplies (and themselves, perhaps, affrighted

by the successes of the French,) our Ministry sent an ambassador to Paris to

sue for Peace. The Supplies are granted: and in the mean time the Arch-duke

Charles turns the scale of Victory on the Rhine, and Buonaparte is checked   5

before Mantua. Straightways, our courtly Messenger is commanded to *uncurl*

his lips, and propose to the lofty Republic to *restore* all *its* conquests, and to suf-

fer England to *retain* all *hers*, (at least all her *important* ones) as the only terms

of Peace, and the ultimatum of the negociation!

Θρασυνει γαρ αισχρομητις   10
Ταλαινα ΠΑΡΑΚΟΠΑ πρωτοπημων.
ÆSCHYL. AG. 230.

The friends of Freedom in this country are idle. Some are timid; some are selfish;

and many the torpedo touch of hopelessness has numbed into inactivity. We

would fain hope, that (if the above account be accurate—it is only the French   15

account) this dreadful instance of infatuation in our ministry will rouse them to

one effort more; and that at one and the same time in our different great towns the

people will be called on to think solemnly, and declare their thoughts fearlessly,

by every method, which the *remnant* of the constitution allows.

1 3*   "With treacherous dalliance wooing peace" At the time this Ode was being composed, our Ambassador had returned from Paris, the French Directory professing to consider his ultimatum, as an insult to the Republic.

68 *1*   But soon   upstarting   from his coward trance,
    2 3*   up-springing   dastard
69 *1 2 3**   The boastful   bloody   son of pride betray'd,
    *3**ʙ   ~~bloody~~
70 *1*   His ancient hatred of the dove-eyed maid.
    2 3*   Hatred of the blest and blessing
71 *1*   A   cloud, O Freedom! cross'd thy orb of light,
    2 3*   One
72 *1*   And sure he deem'd that orb was   set   in night,
    2 3*   quench'd
73 *1 2 3**   For still does MADNESS roam on GUILT'S bleak dizzy height!

[*Line-space*]

⁻74 *1 2 3* 3 4*	ANTISTROPHE I.
5–8	IV.
74 *1*	DEPARTING YEAR! 'twas on an awful shore
⊠*1*	no earthly
75 □	My soul beheld thy vision. Where, alone,
75fn *2*	My Soul beheld thy Vision.—*i. e.* Thy Image in a Vision.
76 □	Voiceless and stern, before the cloudy throne,
77 *1 2 3* 3*	Aye MEMORY sits, there garmented with gore,
4	thy vest profan'd
5–8	robe inscrib'd
78 ⊠*4*	With many an unimaginable groan
4	Thou with
79 ⊠*4*	Thou storied'st thy sad hours! silence ensued,
4	Gav'st reck'ning of thy
80 *1*	Deep silence o'er the choired multitude,
⊠*1*	th' etherial
81 *1 2*	Whose purple locks with snow-white glories shone!
1 3* 3 4	wreathed
5–8	locks with wreaths, whose wreaths with
82 *1*	Then, his eye strange ardors glancing,
⊠*1*	wild
83 □	From the choired Gods advancing;
84 □	The SPIRIT of the EARTH made reverence meet,
85 □	And stood up beautiful before the cloudy seat.

[*Line-space*]

⁻86 *1 2 3* 3 4*	ANTISTROPHE II.
5–8	V.
86 *1 2 3* 3 4*	On every harp, on every tongue,
87 *1 2 3* 3 4*	While the mute enchantment hung,
88 *1 2 3* 3*	Like midnight from a thunder cloud,
4	Thunder midnight
89 *1*	The sudden spirit cry'd aloud;
2 3* 3 4	Spake the sudden SPIRIT loud—
89.1.1 *5–8*	Throughout the blissful throng,
89.1.2 *5–8*	Hush'd were harp and song:
89.1.3 *5–8*	Till wheeling round the throne the LAMPADS seven,
89.1.4 *5–8*	(The mystic Words of Heaven)
89.1.5 *5–8*	Permissive signal make;
89.1.6 *5–8*	The fervent Spirit bow'd, then spread his wings and spake!
90 □	"Thou in stormy blackness throning
91 □	"Love and uncreated light,
92 □	"By the earth's unsolac'd groaning
93 *1*	"Seize thy terrors, God of might!
2 3* 3–8	Arm
94 *1 2 3* 3 4*	"By BELGIUM's corse impeded flood!
94fn *1*	The Rhine.
2 3* 3 4	Belgium's corse-impeded flood.—The Rhine.
95 *1 2 3* 3 4*	"By VENDEE steaming brother's blood!

96	*1*	"By Peace with proffer'd insults scar'd,
	2 3* 3–8	insult
97	*1*	"And marked hate, and envying scorn,
	2 3* 3–8	"Masked
98	☐	"By years of havoc yet unborn;
99	*1*	"By hungers' bosom to the bleak winds bar'd!
	⊠*1*	"And frost-winds
100	☐	But chief by AFRIC's wrongs,
101	*1*	Most horrible and foul,
	⊠*1 6*	"Strange,
	6	"Stranger
102	*1*	And what deep guilt belongs
	⊠*1*	"By
103	*1 2 5–8*	"To the deaf Synod, full of gifts and lies,
	1 3* 3 4	Senate,
103fn	*1*	Gifts used in scripture for corruption.
104	☐	"By wealth's insensate laugh! by torture's howl:
105	☐	"Avenger! rise.
106	*1 2 3* 3 4*	"For ever shall the bloody island scowl?
	5–8	thankless
106fn	*2*	—*bloody island scowl?*
	1 2	"In Europe, the smoking Villages of Flanders and the putrified fields of La
		Vendee—from Africa the unnumbered victims of a detestable Slave Trade—in
		Asia, the desolated plains of Indostan, and the Millions whom a rice-contracting
		governor caused to perish—In America, the recent enormities of their Scalp- 5
		merchants—The four quarters of the globe groan beneath the intolerable iniquity
		of the nation." See "Addresses to the People," p. 46.
107	*1*	"For ever shall her vast and iron bow,
	2 3* 3 4	aye unbroken, shall her cruel
108	*1*	"Shoot famine's evil arrows o'er the world,
	2 3* 3 4	arrows o'er thy ravag'd
109	*1 2 3* 4*	"Hark! how wide nature joins her groans below:
110	*1*	"Rise, God of mercy, rise! why sleep thy bolts unhurl'd!
	2	Nature,
	1 3* 3 4	Ah why those
110.1.1	*5–8*	"Her quiver full, and with unbroken bow?
110.1.2	*5–8*	"Speak! from thy storm-black Heaven O speak aloud!
110.1.3	*5–8*	"And on the darkling foe
110.1.4	*5–8*	"Open thine eye of fire from some uncertain cloud!
110.1.5	*5–8*	"O dart the flash! O rise and deal the blow!
110.1.6	*5–8*	"The Past to thee, to thee the Future cries!
110.1.7	*5–8*	"Hark! how wide Nature joins her groans below!
110.1.8	*5–8*	"Rise, God of Nature! rise."
		[*Line-space*]

⁻111	*2 3* 3 4*	EPODE II.
	5–8	VI.
111	*2 3* 3 4*	The Voice had ceas'd, the Phantoms fled,
	5–8	vision
112	*2 3* 3–8*	Yet still I gasp'd and reel'd with dread.
113	*2 3* 3–8*	And ever when the dream of night
114	*2 3* 3 4*	Renews the vision to my sight,
	5–8	phantom
115	*2 3* 3 4*	Cold sweat-damps gather on my limbs,
	5–8	sweat-drops
116	*2 3* 3–8*	My Ears throb hot, my eye-balls start,
117	*2 3* 3–8*	My Brain with horrid tumult swims,
118	*2 3* 3–8*	Wild is the Tempest of my Heart;
119	*2 3* 3–8*	And my thick and struggling breath
120	*2 3* 3–8*	Imitates the toil of Death!
121	*2*	No uglier agony confounds
	1 3* 3–8	stranger
122	*2 3* 3–8*	The Soldier on the war-field spread,
123	*2 3* 3–8*	When all foredone with toil and wounds
124	*2 3* 3–8*	Death-like he dozes among heaps of Dead!
125	*2 3* 3–8*	(The strife is o'er, the day-light fled,
126	*2 3* 3–8*	And the Night-wind clamours hoarse;
127	*2 3* 3 4*	See! the startful Wretch's head
	5–8	starting
128	*2 3* 3–8*	Lies pillow'd on a Brother's Corse!)
⁻129	*5–8*	VII.
129	*2 3* 3 4*	O doom'd to fall, enslav'd and vile,
	5–8	Not yet enslav'd, not wholly
130	*2 3* 3–8*	O ALBION! O my mother Isle!
131	*2 3* 3–8*	Thy valleys, fair as Eden's bowers,
132	*2 3* 3–8*	Glitter green with sunny showers;
133	*2*	Thy grassy Upland's gentle Swells
	1 3*A–B 3–8	Uplands'
134	*2 3* 3–8*	Echo to the Bleat of Flocks;
135	*2 3* 3–8*	(Those grassy Hills, those glitt'ring Dells
136	*2 3* 3–8*	Proudly ramparted with rocks)
137	*2 3* 3–8*	And Ocean 'mid his uproar wild
138	*2 3* 3–8*	Speaks safety to his Island-child.
139	*2 3* 3–8*	Hence for many a fearless age
140	*2 3* 3–8*	Has social Quiet lov'd thy shore;
141	*2 3* 3*	Nor ever sworded Foeman's rage
	4	Warrior's
	5–8	proud Invader's
142	*2 3* 3–8*	Or sack'd thy towers, or stain'd thy fields with gore.
⁻143	*5–8*	VIII.
143	*2 3* 3*	Disclaim'd of Heaven! mad Av'rice at thy side,
	4	O abandon'd thy Guide
	5–8	Abandon'd
143fn	*1 3**	"Disclaim'd of Heaven!" We have been preserved by our in-

sular [?]situation from [?]suffering the actual horrors of War ourselves; and we have shewn our gratitude to Providence for this immunity by our eagerness to spread those horrors over nations less happily situated. Of the hundred and seven last years 5 50 have been years of War!—

1* *3 4*   "Disclaim'd of Heaven!" The poet from having considered the ⟨peculiar⟩ advantages, which this Country has enjoyed, ~~makes~~ ~~a~~ passes in rapid transition to the uses, which we have made of these advantages. We have been preserved by our insular situation from suffering the actual horrors of War ourselves, and 5 we have shewn our gratitude to Providence for this immunity by our eagerness to spread those horrors over nations less happily situa~~tioned~~.—In the midst of plenty & safety, we have raised or joined the yell for famine & blood. Of the one hundred & seven last years fifty have been years of war.—Such Wickedness 10 cannot pass unpunished. We have been proud & confident in our alliances & our fleets—but God has prepared the cankerworm, & ~~smote~~ will smite the *gourds* of our pride. "Art thou better than populous No, that was situate among the rivers, that had the waters round about it, whose rampart was ~~from~~ the Sea? 15 Ethiopia & Egypt was her strength, & it was infinite: Put & Lubim were her Helpers. Yet she was carried away, she went into captivity: and they cast lots for her honourable men, & all her great men were bound in chains. Thou also shalt be drunken: all thy strong-holds shall be like fig-trees with the first-ripe figs; 20 if they be shaken, they shall ever fall into the mouth of the Eater. Thou hast multiplied thy merchants above the stars of Heaven. Thy crowned are as the Locusts; and thy captains as the great Grasshoppers which camp in the hedges in the cool day; ~~and~~ but when the Sun ariseth, they flee away, and their place is not 25 known where they are. There is no healing of thy bruise; thy wound is grievous: all, that hear the report of thee, shall clap hands over thee: for upon whom hath not thy wickedness passed continually?"

Nahum. Chapt. III.   30

144 *2 3* 3*	At coward distance, yet with kindling pride—
4–8	cowardly kindling with
145 *2 3* 3*	Safe 'mid thy herds and corn-fields thou hast stood,
4	Mid thy Corn-fields and Herds thou in plenty
5–8	herds and thy corn-fields secure thou
146 *2 3* 3*	And join'd the yell of Famine and of Blood.
4	loud yellings of Famine and
5–8	wild yelling
147 *2 3* 3*	All nations curse thee: and with eager wond'ring
4 5	The
6–8	They
148 *2 3* 3–8*	Shall hear DESTRUCTION, like a vulture, scream!
149 *2 3* 3–8*	Strange-eyed DESTRUCTION, who with many a dream

150 *2*	Of central flames thro' nether seas upthund'ring	
3*A–B	~~flames~~ fires	
3–8	fires	
151 ⊠*1*	Soothes her fierce solitude, yet (as she lies	
152 *2*	Stretch'd on the marge of some fire-flashing fount	
1 3* *3*	By livid fount, or roar of blazing stream,	
4-8	red volcanic	
153 *2*	In the black chamber of a sulphur'd mount,)	
3*A–B	~~In the black chamber of a sulphur'd mount,~~	
154 ⊠*1*	If ever to her lidless dragon eyes,	
155 ⊠*1 4*	O ALBION! thy predestin'd ruins rise,	
4	Visions of	
156 ⊠*1* 1	The Fiend-hag on her perilous couch doth leap,	
157 ⊠*1* 1	Mutt'ring distemper'd triumph in her charmed sleep.	
	[*Line-space*]	
¯158 *5–8*	IX.	
158 ⊠*1*	Away, my soul, away!	
159 ⊠*1*	In vain, in vain, the birds of warning sing—	
160 *2 3**	And hark! I hear the famin'd brood of prey	
3–8	famish'd	
161 *2 3–8*	Flap their lank pennons on the groaning wind!	
3*A–B	~~dark~~ lank	
162 ⊠*1*	Away, my Soul, away!	
163 ⊠*1*	I unpartaking of the evil thing,	
164 ⊠*1*	With daily prayer, and daily toil	
165 *2*	Soliciting my scant and blameless soil,	
1 3* *3–8*	for food my scanty	
166 ⊠*1*	Have wail'd my country with a loud lament.	
167 ⊠*1*	Now I recenter my immortal mind	
168 *2 3**	In the long sabbath of high self-content;	
3*B	~~long~~ deep ~~high~~ blest	
3	deep blest	
4	blest high	
5–8	deep meek	
169 *2*	Cleans'd from the fleshly Passions that bedim	
1 3* *3*	fears and anguish	
4	bedimming Fear, and Anguish weak and blind.	
5–8	the vaporous passions that bedim	
170 ⊠*1 4*	God's Image, Sister of the Seraphim.	

title/divisional title. *1* Ode on the departing Year. • *3** *3 4* Ⓞ𝖉𝖊 | *on the* | 𝕯𝖊-𝖕𝖆𝖗𝖙𝖎𝖓𝖌 𝖄𝖊𝖆𝖗. • *8* ODE TO THE DEPARTING YEAR. **additional title/title.** *3** *3* ODE | on the | *DEPARTING YEAR.* • *4* ODE | ON THE | *DEPARTING YEAR.* • *5 ODE ON THE DEPARTING YEAR.* • *6 7* ODE ON THE DEPARTING YEAR. **additional title/title fn.** *3–8* 24th, 25th, and 26th *3**B *3 4 6–8* days of • *5* day of *5 6* December *7 8* 1796: *3**B *3 4* and published separately • *5–8* and was first published *3**B *3 4* of the • *5–8* of that *4* year.—   ¯**1.1.** *5–7* Ἰού, • *8* 'Ιού, • *5–8* ἰού, *5–8* ὦ ὦ κακά   ¯**1.2.** *5 8* 'Υπ' *5–8* αὖ *8* μὲ *5–7* δεινὸς ορθομαντείας πόνος   ¯**1.3.** *5–8* Στροβεῖ, ταράσσων

5 7 8 φροιμίοις • *6* φροιμίοις, *5* ἐφημίοις, • *6* ἐφημίοις • *7 8* ἐφημίοις. ⁻**1.4.** *5–8* Τὸ μέλλον ἥξει. Καὶ *5 8* σύ • *6 7* σὺ *5–8* τάχει παρών ⁻**1.5.** *6–8* Ἄγαν *5–8* ἀληθόμαντιν *5–8* ἐρεῖς. ⁻**1.6.** *5–7* ÆSCHYL. • *8* Æschyl. *5–8 Agam.* ⁻**1.45.** *3**A *3 ARGUMENT.* • *5–8* ARGUMENT. *3**A *3 5* print the argument in italic ⁻**1.46.** 1 *4* address to the • *3**A Address to the ⟨to⟩ that • *3 5–7* Address to the 1 divine Providence that regulates • *3**A Divine Providence, that which regulates • *3 5–8* Divine Providence, that regulates • *4* great BEING, or Divine Providence, who regulates ⁻**1.47.** *5–8* harmony *4* Events *3**A *5–8* time, • *3* time 1 *3**A *3 5–8* them may appear • *4* them appear ⁻**1.48.** *3**A *3–8* mortals. The *3* Second *4* Joys *3**A *3–8* and *4* Sorrows, ⁻**1.49.** *3**A *3–8* and 1 *3**A *3 5–8* devote them • *4* to devote their passions *3**A *3* awhile *3**A *3–8* human *3**A *3 5–8* nature ⁻**1.50.** 1 *3**A *3 5–8* speaks of the • *4* refers to the late *3**A *3 4* Apoplexy *6 7* 17th. *3**A *5 6* November ⁻**1.51.** 1 1797, • *3**A *3 5–8* 1796; • *4* 1796, *3**A *3–8* treaty with ⁻**1.52–4.** 1 *3**A *5–8* the first . . . country.— • *4* The first Antistrophe describes the Image of the Departing Year, as in a vision; and concludes with introducing the Planetary Angel of the Earth preparing to address the Supreme Being. . . . The Poem concludes with prophecying in anguish of Spirit the Downfall of this Country. ⁻**1.52.** *3**A *3 5–8* and 1 Antistrophes • *3**A *3 5–8* Antistrophe *3**A *3 5–8* Image *3**A *3* departing year, &c. • *5–8* Departing Year, &c. ⁻**1.53.** 1 as seen in • *3**A *3–8* as in *3**A *3 5–8* vision. *6* the second *3**A prophecies⟨,⟩ • *3* prophecies • *5–8* prophecies, *3**A *3 5–8* spirit, ⁻**1.54.** *3**A *3* Country. • *5–8* country. ⁻**1.55.** *4* STROPHE I. **1.** *2* SPIRIT, • *3** *3* SPIRIT! • *5–8* SPIRIT *2 3** *3–7* Harp *2 3** *3 4* Time, • *5–8* Time! **2.** *5–8* hard, *2 3** *3 4* Ear **3.** *2 3** *3 4* Harmonies *2 3** *3–8* hear! **4.** *2 3** *3 5* fixt • *6–8* fixed *2 3** *3–8* Heaven's *7* clime **5.** *3** *3 5–8* listened, **6.** *2 3** *3–8* stillness, *4* mind! • *5–8* mind; **7.** *5–8* wind, **8.** *2 3** *3–7* DEPARTING YEAR! • *8* departing Year! **9.** *2 3** *3–8* sadness • *3**A sadness⟨,⟩ **10.** *6 7* madness **11.** *5* enter'd *6–8* foreclosed **12.** *6–8* raised the *2 3** *3–8* solemnized his flight. ⁻**13.** *4* STROPHE II. **13.** *5–8* Hither, *2 3** Tomb; • *3 4* tomb; • *5–7* Tomb, **14.** *2 4–7* Prison's • *3**A ⸢Prison's *5–8* gloom, **15.** *2 3** *3 4* Poverty's **16.** *2 3** *3–7* Distemper's *2 3** *3 4* anguish: **15.1.** *8* poverty *8* languish! **17.** *5–8* where, *2 3** *3 4* blending **18.** *3**A–B illumine⸤s *2 3** *3–7* Manhood's *2 3** *3–8* maze; **19.** *2* Infants *2 3** *3–6 8* bending **20.** *6–8* fixed *5– 7* gaze. • *8* gaze; **21.** *2 3** *3–8* dance, **22.** *5–8* Woes! *2 3** *3 4* JOYS, • *5–8* Joys! **23.** *2 3** *3–6 8* Time's *2 3** *3 4* Hand • *5–8* hand **24.** *2 3** *3– 5* Sweep **25.** *2 3** *3 4 6–8* its *2 3** *3–8* sleep, **26.** *2 3** *3–5* mixt • *6–8* mixed **30.** *2 3** *3–8* loud *2 3** voice **31.** *3–8* birth, **32.** *3**A–B rejoice⸤! **33.** *2* birth **34.** *2* glare) **35.** *2* NATURE struggles! Hark— *2* increase! **36.** *2* But ô! **37.** *2* Twins, *2* EQUALITY and PEACE! **37.1.1.** *3**A name Name, • *3**B ⸢Name • *3* Name • *5* NAME, • *6 7* NAME • *8* name *3** *3–8* earth **37.1.2.** *3** *3 4* storm • *5–8* storm, *4* Hell! • *5 6* Hell. **37.1.3.** *3**A–B Jubilee⸤ • *8* jubilee **37.1.4.** *5–8* Justice *3**A TRUTH⸤. ⸢They • *5–8* Truth! They **37.1.5.** *3** *5–8* name, • *3**B ⸢Name, *5–7* Divinest *4* liberty! • *8* Liberty! ⁻**38.** *4* EPODE. **38.** *6–8* marked *2 3** *3–8* Ambition *2* war-array: • *3** *3 4* war- array; • *5–8* war-array! **39.** *2 3** *3–8* cry— **40.** *2 3** *3–8* Northern Conqueress *7 8* stay! **41.** *2 3** *3 4* Chariot *2 3** *3 4 6–8* its *2* way? **43.** *6– 8* Stunned *2 3** *3–8* Death's *2 3** *3 4* "twice mortal" • *5–8* twice mortal *2* mace **44.** *2 3** *3 4* MURDER'S • *5–7* Murder's • *8* murder's *2 3** *3–8* face **45.** *6–8* The *2 3** *3 4* Hag *3 4 6–8* gloat **46.** *2 3** *3–5* th' *2 3** *3 6–8* unnumbered

2 *3* 3 4* Slain! • *5–8* slain!   **47.** *6–8* gasped   *2 3* 3 5–7* WARSAW'S •
8 Warsaw's   **48.** *2 3* 3 5–7* ISMAIL'S • *8* Ismail's   **49.** *2 3** Ruin • *3**B Rruin
2 3* 3 4 chok'd • *6–8* choked   **50.** *2 3* 3 4* Conquest's   *2 3* 3 4* hour
51. *2 3* 3–8* Mid   *2 3* 3 4* Women's   *2 3** Infant's • *3 4* Infants' • *6–8* infants'
5–8 screams!   **53.** *2 3* 3 4* Massacre!   **54.** *2 3* 3 4* th'   *6–8* uncof-
fined   *2 3* 3 4* Slain,   **55.** *2 3* 3 4* Triumph swelling   **56.** *2* Oft •
*3**A–B Oft⟨,⟩   *2 3* 3 4* train   **57.** *2 3* 3 4* Dwelling!   **58.** *2 3* 3 4* Th'
2 3* 3 4 Fiend   *2 3* 3–8* fled—   **59.** *2 3* 3 4* Life   *2 3** Doom!) • *3 4* doom!)
60. *2 3* 3 4* Army   *2 3* 3 4* Dead, • *5* dead, • *6–8* dead   **61.** *5–7* Dance
2 3* 3 4 Death-fires, • *5–7* death-fires   *2 3* 3 4* Tomb!   **62.** *2 3* 3–8* prophetic
2 3* 3 4 relate   **63.** *3** sceptered   *2 3* 3 4* Murderer's   *2 3* 3–8* fate!
64. *3** sceptered   *2 3** SLAUGHTER   *2 3** cease?   **65.** *2 3** He   *3**A–
B crouch'd⟨,⟩ O   *2 3** Victor France!   **66.** *3** lightning   *2 3** Lance,
67. *2 3** PEACE.   **67fn** [1 *3** version] **1.** *3** prints cue in italic   *3* peace.*"—
2. *3** Paris;   **3.** *3** ultimatum   **68.** *2 3** trance   **69.** *2 3** boastful,
2 Son   *2 3** Pride   *2* betray'd • *3** betrayed   **70.** *3** hatred   *2 3** Maid.
71. *2 3**B Light • *3**A Light⟨,⟩   **72.** *2 3** sure,   *2 3** deem'd,   *2 3** Orb
2 3* night: **73.** *2 3** MADNESS   *2 3** GUILT'S   ⁻**74.** *4* ANTISTROPHE
I.   **74.** *2 3* 3 4* DEPARTING YEAR! • *5–8* Departing Year!   **75.** *2 3 4* Soul
2 3* 3 4 Vision. Where, • *5–8* vision! Where   **76.** *2 3* 3 4* Cloudy Throne
77. *2 3–7* MEMORY • *3* 8* Memory   *2 3* 3 4* sits; • *5–8* sits: *2 3* 3* there,
6–8 inscribed   **79.** *2 3* 3* storiedst   *2 3* 3 4* Hours! Silence • *5–8* hours! Silence
2 3* 3 4 ensued: **80.** *2 3** Silence • *3**B Ssilence   *6–8* the   *3 4 6–8* ethereal
2 3* 3 4 Multitude,   **81.** *2 3* 3 4* Locks   *2 3* 3 4* Glories   *2 3* 3–8* shone.
82. *5–8* ardours   **83.** *8* gods   *2 3* 3 5–8* advancing, • *4* advancing   **84.** *2 3* 3–*
7 SPIRIT • *8* Spirit   *2 3* 3–7* EARTH • *8* Earth   *2* meet   **85.** *5–8* up, beautiful,
2 3* 3 4 Cloudy Seat!   ⁻**86.** ANTISTROPHE II.   **86.** *2 3* 3 4* Harp,
2 Tongue • *3* 3 4* Tongue,   **87.** *2 3* 3 4* Enchantment   *2 3 4* hung; • *3**A hung*l*, •
*3**B hung*l*;   **88.** *2 3* 3* Midnight   *2* thundercloud, • *3**A–B thunder⟨-⟩cloud •
3 thunder-cloud,   **89.1.2.** *6–8* Hushed   **89.1.3.** *6 7* LAMPADS • *8* Lampads
89.1.5. *6–8* make: **89.1.6.** *6–8* bowed,   **90.** *2 3* 3 4* Blackness   **91.** *8* Love
2 3* 3–8 Light,   **92.** *8* By   *2 3* 3–8* Earth's   *3* 5–8* unsolaced   *5–8* groaning,
93. *8* Seize   *2 3* 3 4* Might!   **94.** *2 3* 3 4* Belgium's   *2 3* corse-impeded •
*3**A–B corse⟨-⟩impeded   **94fn.** *3* 3 4* print cue in italic   *3* 3 4* "*By   4 corse
impeded   3* 3 flood!*"—• *4 flood.*"—   **95.** *2 3* 3 4* Vendee   *2 3* 3 4* Brother's
96. *8* By   *2 3* 3 4* PEACE • *5 6* Peace, • *8* peace   *6–8* proffered   *6–8* scared,
97. *8* Masked   *3* 3 4 8* hate • *5–7* Hate   *2 3* 3 4 8* scorn! • *5–7* Scorn!   **98.** *8* By
2 3* 3–7 Years of Havoc   *5–8* unborn!   **99.** *8* And   *2 3* 3–7* Hunger's
5–8 bared!   **100.** *2 3* 3–7* "But   *2 3* 3–8* Afric's   *2 3* 3 4* wrongs
101. *8* Strange,   *2 3* 3–8* horrible,   *2 3* 3–8* foul!   **102.** *8* By   *2 3* 3 4* Guilt
103. *8* To   *2 3* 3 4* "full • *5–8* 'full   *2 3* 3 4* lies!" • *5–8* lies!'   **104.** *8* By
2 3* 3–7 Wealth's   *2* Laugh!   *2 3* 3 4* By   *2 3* 3–7* Torture's   *2* Howl! •
3* 3–8 howl!   **105.** *2 3* 3–7* "Avenger, rise! • *8* Avenger, rise!   **106.** *8* For
2 3* 3–8 Island   *4* scowl; • *5–8* scowl,   **106fn2.** *2* Europe   *2* smoking villages
106fn3. *2* Véndee   *2* Slave-trade   **106fn4.** *2* Asia   *2* Indostan   *2* million
106fn5. *2* Governor   *1* caused to perish—. • *2* destroyed by famine—   *2* —in Amer-
ica   *1* their • *2* our   **106fn5–6.** *2* scalp-merchants—the   **106fn7.** *1* the nation. •
2 this nation!"   *1* See "Addresses • *2* Addresses   *2* People,   **107.** *3* 3 4* aye,
2 3* 3 4 Bow   **108.** *2 3* 3 4* Famine's   *3* 3* ravaged   *2 3* 3* World? • *4* World!

109. *2 3* 3 4* NATURE   *2 3* 3 4* below—   **110.** 1 Nature!   *2* Why   *2* 1 *3** Bolts
2 3* 3 4 unhurl'd?   **110.1.1.** *8* Her   **110.1.2.** *8* Speak!   **110.1.3.** *8* And
110.1.4. *8* Open   **110.1.5.** *8* O   **110.1.6.** *8* The   *7* future   **110.1.7.** *8* Hark!
110.1.8. *8* Rise,   ⁻**111.** EPODE II.   **111.** *3* 3–8* voice   *5–8* ceased,   *5–8* fled;
112. *6–8* gasped   *6–8* reeled   *3**A dread/:   **113.** *5–8* ever,   **115.** *3**A–
B limbs/; • *3–8* limbs;   **116.** *5–8* ears   *3**A–B hot/; • *3–8* hot;   *3** eyeballs
*3**A–B start/; • *3–8* start;   **117.** *5–8* brain   *3* 3–8* swims;   **118.** *3* 3–8* tempest
5–8 heart;   **120.** *8* death!   **122.** *8* soldier   **123.** *3**A–B wounds/ • *5* wounds. •
6–8 wounds,   **124.** *5–8* dead!   **126.** *5 8* night-wind   *5–8* hoarse!   **127.** *5–*
8 wretch's   **128.** *6–8* pillowed   *5–8* brother's corse!)   **129.** *6–8* enslaved,
130. *5–8* Albion!   **131.** *5–7* vallies,   **133.** *5–7* uplands' • *8* uplands   *3* 3–*
8 swells   **134.** *5–8* bleat of flocks;   **135.** *5–8* hills,   *6–8* glittering   *5–8* dells
137. *5–7* OCEAN   *3* 3–8* mid   **138.** *7* saftety   *5–7* ISLAND-CHILD! •
8 island-child,   **139.** *5* Hence,   *5* age,   **140.** *6–8* loved   **141.** *8* invader's
142. *6–8* sacked   *6–8* stained   **143.** *6–8* Abandoned   *5–7* Avarice • *8* avarice
3* 3 side   *5–8* guide,   **143fn.** [1 *3** version] **1.** *3** *"Disclaim'd of Heaven!"*
4. *3** immunity,   **5.** 1 situated. • *3**A ~~situated.~~ circumstanced.   Of] *3** begins
a new paragraph   *3** years,   **6.** *3** fifty   *3** War.   **143fn.** [1* *3 4* ver-
sion] **1.** *3 4* print the cue in italic   *3* *"Disclaim'd* • *4* *"O abandon'd   3 4* Heaven!"—
3 4 Poet   **2.** *3 4* peculiar   **3.** *3 4* passes   **5.** *3 4* situation,   **8.** *3 4* situated.
3 4 and safety   **9.** *3 4* and . . . and   **10.** *3 4* years,   *3 4* wickedness
11. *3 4* and   **12.** *3 4* and   *3 4* canker-worm,   **13.** 1* & ~~smote~~ will • *3 4* and
will   **14.** *3 4* No,   **15.** 1* was ~~from~~ the • *3 4* was the   **16.** *3 4* and   1* was •
3 4 were   *3 4* and . . . and   **17.** *3 4* helpers.   **18.** *3 4* and   **20.** *4* strong holds
3 fig trees   *3 4* first ripe   **21.** 1* ever • *3 4* even   *3 4* eater.   **22.** *3 4* heaven.
23. *3 4* locusts;   **24.** *3 4* grasshoppers   **24–5.** 1* cool day; ~~and~~ but • *3 4* cool-
day; but   **30.** *3 4* Nahum, Chap. III.   **144.** *3**A pride⫫,   **145.** *3* corn fields
146. *6–8* joined   *8* famine   *5–7* Blood! • *8* blood!   **147.** *5* thee, • *6–8* thee!
6–8 wondering   **148.** *8* Destruction,   *6 7* Vulture,   **149.** *5–7* DESTRUCTION! •
8 Destruction!   **150.** *6–8* through   *6–8* upthundering   **151.** 1 Solitude: •
3* 3–8 solitude;   1 *3* 3 4* yet, as • *5–8* yet as   **154.** *5–8* dragon-eyes,   **155.** *5–*
8 Albion!   *6–8* predestined   **156.** *5–8* fiend-hag   **157.** *5–8* Muttering
6–8 distempered   **159.** *5–8* vain the   *5–7* Birds   **160.** *6–8* famished
162. *3* 3–8* soul,   **164.** *3**A prayer/ • *5–8* prayer   *3**A–B toil/   **165.** 1 soil
166. *5–8* wailed   *5–8* Lament.   **167.** *6–8* recentre   **169.** *6–8* Cleansed
170. *5–8* sister

    title/divisional title. Actually the title-page in PR *2* and the divisional title in PR *3* 3–*
7. The PR *8* title derives from the PR *5–7* divisional title. In the PR *3* list of Contents the
title is given as *"Ode to the New Year,"*.
    additional title/title. Follows the Epigraph, prefatory verses, and Argument where
present, heading a separate page in all except PR *8*.
    epigraph. Given on the title-page of PR *2* and the divisional title of PR *3–7*. The
diacritics were introduced at the proof stage of PR *5*.
    In PR *3**A, on the reverse of the title-page, C wrote: "The Motto—! where is the
Motto—? I would ⟨not⟩ have lost the MOTTO for a kingdom I twas the best part of the
Ode". In PR *3**B he wrote in the same place: "Motto I I beseech you, let the Motto be
printed; and printed accurately."
    argument. Given a separate page, separately headed, in PR *3**A *3 5–7*; not present in

PR *3*B*; in PR *4* it is distributed through the text as footnotes; in PR *8* it is separately headed, but follows on the epigraph and leads directly to the text.

1, 4, 6–7. These and other lines are indented in PR *1*. The pattern of indentation varies in the different versions, and is not detailed here.

6. In RS's (?) copy of PR *3* C emended "a bowed" to "submitted".

6, 8. In AG's and Francis Wrangham's (?) copies of PR *5* C restored the earlier readings. He added in AG's copy: "In deference to the taste of my friend, the Rev^d. Mr Cary, our English Dante, I have restored this stanza to it's original form." He added in Wrangham's copy: "I have restored this stanza to it's original form—& have this to record: that I have never made an alteration in compliment to the Taste and Opinion of another, without finding it complained of and regretted by one (often by several) of far higher claims to decide a question in poetry—(Thus, Mr Carey, the excellent *Englisher* of Dante, was, I found, vexed and almost indignant at the substitution of 'submitted' and 'train' for 'bowed' and 'skirts'.—On the other, I never corrected a poem on the impulse of my own feelings without manifest improvements, as in the Ancient Mariner & Christabel.—ˌS.T.C.ˌ," (the end is worn away).

17–18. Quoted (var) in *The Friend* xv (30 Nov 1809) (*CC*) ii 202 (also i 253).

18. In PR *3*A* C has written alongside "illumine*l*s": "illumine's! that villainous apostrophe ' belongs to the *Genitive case of Substantives* only—it should be illumines. O that Printers were wise! O that they would read Bishop Lowth!—". The reference is to Robert Lowth *A Short Introduction to English Grammar* (2nd ed 1763) 105–6fn—a favourite book of C's father.

22⁺. Line-space in PR *8*.

31. The line—reading "with" for "in"—was printed after line 32 in PR *3**. The correction in PR *3*A* is made in C's hand, and again in PR *3*B* in Joseph Cottle's.

37.1.2⁺. Line-space in PR *6*, though this may be caused by loose type.

40fn. In MS 1 C asked Cottle to omit the note.

44. PR *7* luric] Corrected to "lurid" in JG's (?) copy.

51. C was explicit in PR *3*B*: "the ' put *after* the s' in infants'".

64–73. The whole passage, along with the replacement note on line 71, is deleted in PR *3*B*—as C instructed Cottle to do in his letter of 8 Jun 1797 (*CL* i 325).

71. C wrote the following note to "One cloud, O Freedom!" in PR *3*B*, in place of the note on line 67, which was subsequently deleted: "At the time our Ambassador delivered in his ultimatum, the French had received a check from the Arch-duke Charles."

75fn. In MS 1 C instructed Cottle to omit the note.

88–9. The PR *4* text reapproaches the lines C originally drafted in the Gutch Notebook (*CN* i 207):

> terrible and loud
> As the strong Voice that from the Thunder-cloud
> Speaks to the startled Midnight.

94fn. PR *3* corse-impeded*] The hyphen is inserted in both sets of proofs, A and B.

94–5. Repeated (var) from **132** *Poetical Address for Horne Tooke* 31–2.

106fn. PR *1* wrongly cues the footnote to line 108. In MS 1 C asked Cottle to omit the note, in favour of the note he added to line 143.

106⁺. In RS's (?) copy of PR *3* C inserted and then deleted "And still those Bolts unhurl'd?"

109–10. In RS's (?) copy of PR *3* C deleted the lines and inserted:

And still those Bolts unhurl'd?
Nor thy awaken'd Wrath [??]to vengeance slow,
Open it's eyes of Fire, amid the storm-black skies?
Hark! how wide Nature joins her groans below!
Rise, God of Nature, rise!

111. In RS's (?) copy of PR *3* C deleted "Phantoms" and substituted "Vision".

114. In RS's (?) copy of PR *3* C deleted "vision" and substituted "Phantom".

128⁺. PR *3**A–B are marked for insertion of a line-space here, as given in PR *3–8*. PR *5–8* number the new paragraph "VII."

129–42. Quoted (var) in *The Friend* xv (30 Nov 1809) (*CC*) II 205 (also I 258) and *Church and State* ch 2 (*CC*) 23–4.

141. In RS's (?) copy of PR *3* C altered to: "Nor e'er the proud Invader's rage".

142⁺. PR *3**B is marked for insertion of a line-space here, as given in PR *3–8*. PR *5–8* number the new paragraph "VIII."

143fn Deleted in PR *3**B.

C added at the end of MS 1*: "The *gourds*—alluding to Jonah—do not let it be printed *guards*". The quotation is from Nahum 3.18–19, with omissions and minor variations. A later note on Eichhorn (*CM*—*CC*—II 514–15) associates the passage with Rev.

143–6. In RS's (?) copy of PR *3* C emended lines 143–4 to conform to PR *4* (with a comma after "Guide"), and lines 145–6 to conform to PR *5*.

147. In Thomas Hutchinson's and RS's (?) copies of PR *3* C substituted "The" for "All".

Erratum in PR *5*: "r. (*They*) for (*and.*)". The correction is made by AG and JG in the copies listed under TEXT PR *5* above.

152. In Thomas Hutchinson's and RS's (?) copies of PR *3* C emended the text to conform to PR *4–8*.

153. Joseph Cottle responded in PR *3**B: "That this line was to be omitted is not ~~to be~~ clearly expressed in your directions as I will show you—".

158–70. The variant state of PR *2* represented by Ashley 4766 concludes the poem as follows (with no break at line 157⁺):

Enough. With thee departing Year! shall roll
The floods of Tumult which have whelm'd my soul,
And all these clouds of Passion that bedim
God's Image, Sister of the Seraphim.
In vain, in vain, the birds of warning sing—
And hark! I hear the famin'd brood of prey
Flap their lank pennons on the groaning wind!
    Away, my soul, away!
I unpartaking of the evil thing,
With daily prayer, and daily toil
Soliciting my scant and blameless soil,
Have wail'd my country with a loud lament;
Now I recenter my immortal mind
In the long sabbath of blest self-content.

161. In PR *3**A C wrote: "I suspect, almost suspect, that the word 'dark' was *intentionally* substituted for 'lank'—if so, 'twas the most *tasteless* thing thou ever didst, dear Joseph!—" Cottle rejoined in PR *3**B: "I cannot but think now that you gave me direction to alter this or I am unaccountably mistaken because I like lank so much better than dark myself. | J.C."

168. In William Bowles's copy of PR *3* C emended the text to conform to PR *4*.

170. The line was drafted separately in the Gutch Notebook (*CN* I 272 (g)).

143. LINES TO A YOUNG MAN OF FORTUNE
WHO ABANDONED HIMSELF TO AN
INDOLENT AND CAUSELESS MELANCHOLY

A. DATE

11 Dec 1796? See vol I headnote.

B. TEXTS

1 [=RT]. HEHL HM 12290. Two conjoint leaves, 20.9×26.3 and 20.7× 26.3 cm; wm WATT & CO. | PATENT COPYING | PAPER | 1796; no chain-lines. Signed "S. T. COLERIDGE. | *Bristol, Dec. 11ᵗʰ·, 1796*". Included in an als to Benjamin Flower, 11 Dec 1796 (*CL* I 268).

C introduces the lines into his letter with the comment: "The following Lines are at your service, if you approve of them." Flower was editor of the *Cambridge Intelligencer* (see PR *1* below).

1. Cambridge Intelligencer (17 Dec 1796). Signed "S. T. COLERIDGE. | *Bristol, December* 11."

2. NYPL Berg Collection. Four leaves, now separately mounted, each approx 40×26 cm; wm CR | 1794 and fleur-de-lis within shield; chain-lines 3 cm. Included at the end of a long als to John Thelwall, 17 Dec 1796 (*CL* I 286–7).

This version has been reduced to the length of a sonnet, although C also gives Thelwall the omitted lines 6–7 in an adjacent part of the letter. C's own comment is deprecating: "I love Sonnets; but *upon my honor* I do not love *my* Sonnets."

3. BPL B 21074. Single leaf, 26.7×15.7 cm; wm (partial, faint) oval with small circles at the circumference; no chain-lines; verso blank. Transcript in C's hand. The bottom edge has been torn away immediately following line 13, perhaps by someone seeking an autograph; lines 14–16 are written perpendicular to the other lines, in the hand of John Prior Estlin.

The form of the title is shared by MS 2 only, and a number of small variations are unique. The ms might have been given by C to Estlin any time during during Dec or afterwards—they were regularly in touch at this time—and it is impossible to tell whether it should be placed earlier or later in the sequence of texts. The visual separation of lines 6–7 might suggest that it dates from about the same time as MS 2.

2. Included at the end of C's quarto pamphlet *Ode on the Departing Year* (1796). Signed "𝕾. 𝕿. 𝕮𝖔𝖑𝖊𝖗𝖎𝖉𝖌𝖊." The preface is dated "*BRISTOL,* | *December* 26, 1796."

A variant—represented by V&A Dyce Collection L4° 2293—records what appears to be an earlier, uncorrected state of this same printing which affects line 9. See **142** *Ode on the Departing Year* TEXT PR 2 and commentary on lines 158–70 for a later, trial state.

An untitled transcript in the hand of Mrs C (VCL LT.28) has no textual significance.

3. *M Chron* (5 Jan 1797). Signed "S. T. COLERIDGE. | Bristol, Dec. 11." PR 3—and indeed PR 2 above—could be a reprinting of PR *1* with no textual significance.

Rpt *Russell's New Gentleman's Pocket Magazine* III (1797) 28, over C's name but giving no place or date, and reading "Oppressors" for "THRON'D Murd'rers" in the last line.

4. *SL* (1817).

5. *PW* (1828).

6. *PW* (1829).

7. *PW* (1834).

title. 1 *1 3* LINES *to a Young Man of Fortune who abandoned himself to an indolent and causeless Melancholy.•* 2 𝓛Sonnet | to a young Man who abandoned himself to a causeless & indolent Melancholy.• 3 To a Young Man, who abandoned himself to an indolent and causeless Melancholy.• 2 LINES | *Addressed to a young man of Fortune who abandoned himself to* | *an indolent and causeless Melancholy.•* 4–7 ADDRESSED | *TO A YOUNG MAN OF FORTUNE* | Who abandon'd himself to an indolent and causeless Melancholy.

1	⊠3	Hence that fantastic w̶Wantonness of Woe,
	3	with that morbid
2	1ⁱᵐᵖ	O Youth to partial Fortune vainly dea͚r!͚
	⊠1	dear!
3	☐	To plunder'd WANT⟨'⟩s⟋half-shelter'd Hovel go,
4	☐	Go, and some hunger-bitten Infant hear⸺
5	☐	Moan haply in a dying Mother's Ear;
6	⊠2	Or when the cold and dismal fog-damps brood
7	⊠2	O'er the rank Church-yard with sear elm-leaves strew'd
8	1	Pace a̶r̶ round some WIDOW's grave, whose dearer p̶Part
	⊠1 2	round
	2	Or seek
9	☐	Was slaughter'd͚/ where o'er his uncoffin'd limbs
10	☐	The flocking Flesh-birds scream'd! Then, while thy Heart

11 ⊠*4–7* Groans, and thine eyes a fiercer Sorrow dims,
    4–7   eye
12 □   Know (and the Truth shall kindle thy young Mind)
13 □   What Nature makes thee mourn, she bids thee heal:
14 □   O Abject! if to sickly *d*Dreams resign'd
15 ⊠*4–7* All effortless thou leave Earth's Common weal
    4–7   life's
16 ⊠*4–7* A prey to the thron'd Murderers of Mankind!
    4–7   Tyrants,

title. *1* LINES | *To a young Man of Fortune, who abandoned himself to* | *an indolent and causeless melancholy.* • *3* LINES. | TO A YOUNG MAN OF FORTUNE, WHO ABANDONED | HIMSELF TO AN INDOLENT AND CAUSELESS ME-| LANCHOLY. • *5 6* ADDRESSED TO A YOUNG MAN OF | FOR-TUNE | WHO ABANDONED HIMSELF TO AN INDOLENT AND | CAUSELESS MELANCHOLY. • *7* ADDRESSED TO A YOUNG MAN OF FORTUNE | WHO ABANDONED HIMSELF TO AN INDOLENT | AND CAUSELESS MELAN-CHOLY.   **1.** *2* Hence, *1 3 3–7* wantonness • *2 2* Wantonness *1 3–7* woe, • *2* Woe. **2.** *3* O, *1 3* fortune *3* dear!—   **3.** *5–7* plundered *1* WANT'S • *2 3 4–6* Want's • *2 3* WANT'S • *7* want's *5–7* half-sheltered *1 4–7* hovel *3* go;   **4.** *1 7* infant ⊠*1* hear   **5.** *1 7* mother's *1 3 3* ear; • *4–7* ear: **6.** *3* Or,   **7.** *1 3 2 4–7* church-yard *1 3 2–4* strew'd, • *5–7* strewed,   **8.** *1* WIDOW's • *3 2 3* Widow's • *4–7* widow's *3* Grave, *1 3–7* part • *2 3 2* Part   **9.** *1 2 3 2 4* slaughter'd, • *5–7* slaughtered, *5–7* uncoffined *2* Limbs   **10.** *4–7* flesh-birds *5–7* screamed! *1 3* then, *1 3–7* heart   **11.** *1 3 3–7* sorrow   **12.** *1* Know, (and • *2* Know, and *1 3 4–7* truth *1 3 2 4–7* mind) • *2* Mind, • *3* mind)—   **13.** *1 4–7* nature • *3* NATURE *3 3* heal. • *2 4–7* heal!   **14.** *3* O, *1 2 4–7* abject! • *3* abject • *3* abject, *3–7* if, *1 3 3–7* dreams • *2 2* Dreams *3* resigné'd • *3 4* resign'd, • *5–7* resigned,   **15.** *3* effortless, *1* earth's *1* common weal, • *3* common weal • *2 4–7* common-weal • *3* Commonweal   **16.** *2* Prey *3* THRON'D *7* tyrants *1 7* murderers • *3* Murd'rers *1* mankind! • *4–6* Mankind. • *7* mankind.

title. It seems that C may have decided to reduce his lines to the length of a sonnet in the time it took to write the first letter of the MS 2 title: "Sonnet" is written above the middle line of the rest of the title.

2, 4–7, 9, 11, 13, 15. Indented in PR *1 3*. Different lines are indented in TEXTS *2 2 4–7.*

3. MS 2 Want's] Written as if to be printed bold.

6–7. In MS 2, after copying out the sonnet version of the poem, C added:

After the five first lines these two followed,

> Or when the cold & dismal fog-damps brood
> O'er the rank Church-yard with sear Elm-leaves strew'd,
> Pace round some WIDOW's grave &c ——

Were they rightly omitted?

6–7. In MS 3 these lines are set off from the preceding and following lines by two short rules.

7. Developed from an observation in the Gutch Notebook: "Leaves already on the walk scattered—" (*CN* I 60).

9. The variant state of PR 2 represented by V&A Dyce Collection L4° 2293 reads "slaughter'd. Where".

11. In MS 3 set off from the lines that follow by a short rule.

13. What Nature] In MS 2 C wrote the words, then deleted them and began the line again, so as to maintain the pattern of indentation he had established in this text.

143.X1. PROSPECT OF PEACE

The title *Prospect of Peace* is ascribed to C by Watt *Bibliotheca Britanica* I 246q, where it is dated 1796. The usual details of size and price are absent, which might be cause for suspicion. The title is included in H. G. Bohn's revision of Lowndes *The Bibliographer's Manual of English Literature* I 493, where it is specified as quarto; and it is included in the bibliography added to Caine's *Life of Samuel Taylor Coleridge* by John P. Anderson (p iiiB). Anderson cites Watt and Lowndes, and gives London as the place of publication.

No poem of this title has been traced, and it is almost certain that Watt intended to refer to **142** *Ode on the Departing Year* (1796, in quarto). The details added by Bohn and Anderson are probably derived, in each case, from their predecessor's method of bibliographical description.

144. ON QUITTING OXFORD STREET, BRISTOL, FOR NETHER STOWEY, NEW YEAR'S DAY 1797

A. DATE

1 Jan 1797, early morning and evening. The date given in the title, when the lines were written down many years afterwards, is mistaken.

B. TEXT

NYPL Berg Collection. Two conjoint leaves, 18.5×22.2 cm; wm HAGAR & SON I 1828; no chain-lines; written on all four sides. Fair copy in C's hand.

It is not known for whom C made the copy, or on what occasion, although he used the same paper in 1828–9. See **654** *Exemplary Epitaph on a Black Cat*; **655** *Alice du Clós* VAR TEXT MS 3; **656** *The Accomplishments Most Desirable in an Instructress* VAR TEXT MS 1. The lines are carefully indented.

The RT reproduces the ms except for minor points, chiefly deletions and insertions:

title. ms On quitting Oxford Street, Bristol, for Nether Stowey, New | Years Day 1795, with Mrs C. and Hartley then an infant. | Addressed to M^r M̶o̶r̶r̶i̶saurice our medical friend, | w̶i̶t̶h̶ at whose House we had passed the preceding Evening, and sent off | from Cross, about 19 miles from Bristol.   **1.** ms A̶n̶d̶ With   **3.** ms ⟨And Jokes and Gibes and Fal de ral⟩   **4.** ms ⟨Of Youths most gay and Musical;⟩   **10.** ms a-w̶a̶r̶m̶ buz   **12.** ms M̶o̶r̶r̶i̶s̶.aurice,   **20.** ms ⟨St⟩   **26.** ms t̶h̶e̶ my   **35.** ms she   **41.** ms ?w̶e̶ she   **44.** ms d̶need   **56⁺.** ms Part the Second | sent by the Post the same evening, from Bridgewater.   **57.** ms M̶o̶r̶r̶i̶s̶.aurice!

68⁺. C squeezed in the following comment at the foot of the page: "*Cætera desunt* [tr "The rest is wanting"]. I have tried—hithertoo in vain—to recollect the remaining 7 or 8 Stanzas."

145. THE RAVEN

A. DATE

Late 1796? Jan 1797? Perhaps revised for inclusion in *LB*. In the Preface to *SL* = PR *3* below (see vol I annex B 5) C described the poem as having been written during his schooldays, a description echoed in the subtitle of PR *3–6* and in the PR *4–6* classification among "Juvenile Poems" (between **64** *Songs of the Pixies* and **39** *Absence: An Ode*). None the less, CL refers to the poem in a letter of 5–6 Feb 1797 as C's "dream" and in a way that implies it was a new composition (*LL*—M—I 95–6, cf 225). The earliest texts date from over a year later.

The PR *3–6* subtitle is in any case a fiction, since C was never at home over Christmas during his Christ's Hospital schooldays, and had only elder brothers and sisters. Given his evident self-consciousness about the poem, it is likely to have been written in late 1796–Jan 1797 and passed off as a schoolboy composition almost to disguise its real, political import.

B. TEXTS

1 [=RT]. NYPL Berg Collection. Two leaves (trimmed), 16.1×20.5 cm; no wm; chain-lines 2.6 cm. Transcript in C's hand. Subscribed in another hand "S T C." Endorsed "Coleridges Raven" on the blank verso of f 2, in the hand that subscribed "S T C."

The paper appears to match that on which DW transcribed **152** *The Foster-mother's Tale* (HUL fMS Eng 870 (80B)). This is reinforced by Cottle's late endorsements (trimmed) at the head of f 1^r: "38̕' or "30̕', "2", "⟨Coleridge⟩".

Indeed, the subscribed initials on f 2^r and the endorsement on f 2^v could be in Cottle's earlier hand. *The Foster-mother's Tale* is endorsed by Cottle in a similar way, and if the first reading is correct ("38"), Cottle received the two mss in rapid succession.

If *The Raven* was transcribed with *LB* in mind, MS 1 is likely to date from May 1798 (see Reed I 235n, 238) and thus might postdate PR *1* below. Perhaps it was recalled for WW at a time when they were occupied with ballad and archaising material, written down, and then judged more suitable for newspaper publication. The end of lines 22, 24, 25, and 34 is lost through trimming.

1. M Post (10 Mar 1798). The prefatory epistle is signed "CUDDY".

2. Annual Anthology ed RS (2 vols Bristol 1799–1800) II 240–2. The poem is one of several which C marked "S. T. C." in his own copy (Yale Tinker 1953 2). The text differs from PR *1* only in a few details of punctuation.

3. SL (1817). The poem is one of three added in the preliminary matter of *SL* (sig A), between May and Aug 1817. There are important annotations in two copies: JG's (HUL *EC8 C6795 817s (C)) and a copy reported to have been in the possession of Stuart M. Samuel (*PW*—JDC—564–5), since lost (see vol I annex A 7).

Rpt *Metrical Romances &c. By S. T. Coleridge* (Isleworth 1825).

4. PW (1828).

5. PW (1829).

6. PW (1834).

C. GENERAL NOTE

Besides the copy sent to CL which CL lost (*LL*—M—I 95–6, 225), George Bellas Greenough made a copy when C was in Germany, which has not survived. *C in Germany* 230 reports that it had "in all forty-one lines with slight variants from the final form". It is of interest because, while PR *2* appears to be set from PR *1*, it seems that C had arrived at the PR *3* reading of line 1 before PR *2* was printed.

title. 1 2 The Raven • *3–6 THE RAVEN. I A Christmas Tale, told by a School-boy to his little Brothers I and Sisters.*

prefatory epistle

1 To the EDITOR of The MORNING POST.
1 2 SIR,
    I am not absolutely certain that the following Poem was written by EDMUND SPENSER, and found by an angler, buried in a fishing-box—

> "Under the foot of Mole, that mountain hoar,   ⁻1.5
> "'Mid the green alders, by the Mulla's shore."

But a learned Antiquarian of my acquaintance has given it as his opinion, that as it resembles SPENSER's minor Poems as nearly as *Vortigern and Rowena* the Tragedies of WILLIAM SHAKESPEARE.—This Poem must be read *in recitative*, in the same manner as the Ægloga Secunda of the Shepherd's Calendar. ‾1.10

CUDDY

1 1	Beneath a goodly old Oak-tree
1 2	Under the arms of a goodly
3–5	Underneath a huge
6	an old
2 1 *1 2*	There was of Swine a large company.
3–6	huge
3 1 *1 2*	They were making a rude repast
4 1 *1 2*	Grunting as they crunch'd the mast.
4.1 *3–6*	That grunted as they crunch'd the mast:
4.1.1 *3–6*	For that was ripe, and fell full fast.
5 1 *3–6*	Then they trotted away, for the wind grew high.
1 2	blew
6 1 *3–6*	One acorn they left & no more mote you spy.
1 2	ne
7 1	But soon came a Raven, who lik'd not such folly:
1 2	Next
3–6	that
8 1 *1 2*	He belong'd, I believe, to the Witch Melancholy!
3	it was said,
4–6	they did say,
9 □	Blacker was he than blackest jet—,
10 1 *1 2*	Flew low in the rain, his feathers were wet:
3–6	and his not
11 □	He pick'd up the acorn & buried it strait
12 □	By the side of a River both deep and great.
13 □	Where then did the Raven go?
14 □	He went high and low:
15 □	Over hill, over dale did the black Raven go.
16 □	Many Autumns, many Springs
17 1	Travell'd he on wandering wings:
⊠1	with

17fn *3*   Seventeen or eighteen years ago, an artist of some celebrity was so pleased with this doggerel, that he amused himself with the thought of making a Child's Picture Book of it; but he could not hit on a picture for these four lines. I suggested a *round-about* with four seats, and the four seasons, as children, with Time for the shew-man.   5

18 □	Many ꜱSummers, many ᵥᵥWinters—
19 □	I can't tell half his adventures!
	[*Line-space*]
20 1 *1 2*	At length he return'd, & with him a She:
3–6	came back,
21 1 *1 2*	And the Acorn was grown a large Oak-tree.
3–6	to a tall

22	1^{imp}	They built them a nest on the uppermost bough,
	⊠1	in topmost bough,
23	1	And young Ones they had, & were happy now.
	1 2	jolly enow.
	3–6	happy
24	1^{imp}	But soon came a Woodman, who lik'd in leathern guise,
	⊠1	←—in—→ guise:
25	1^{imp}	His brow, like a pent-house, hung over his eyes,
	⊠1	eyes.
26	1 *1 2*	He'd an ax in his hand, & he nothing spoke,
	3–6	not a word he
27	☐	But with many a hem, & a sturdy stroke
28	1	Ah Wel a day! he brought down the poor Raven's own Oak!
	1 2	At last
	3–6	length
29	1	The His Young Ones were kill'd, for they could not depart:
	⊠1	His
30	1 *1 2*	And his Wife, she did die of a broken heart!
	3–6	their mother

[*Line-space*]

31	1	The boughs from the trunk then the Woodman did sever,
	1 2	branches from off it
	3–6	boughs from the trunk
32	1	And floated it down on the course of the River.
	⊠1	And they
33	1	They saw'd it to planks & its bark they did strip;
	1 2	rind
	3–6	in bark
34	1^{imp}	And with this tree & others they made a good Ship,
	1 2	built up a ship.
	3–6	made a good ship.
35	1	The *I*Ship it was launch'd, but in sight of the Land
	⊠1	ship
36	1 *1 2*	A Tempest arose which no Ship could withstand.
	3–6	Such a storm there did rise as
37	☐	It bulg'd on a rock, & the Waves rush'd in fast:
38	1	The Old Raven flew round & round, & caw'd [?]to the Blast.
	1–5	to
	6	Round and round flew the Raven,
39	1 *1 2*	He heard the sea-shriek of their perishing Souls:
	3–6	last shriek the
40	1	See, she sinks! O'er the top mast the mad water rolls!
	1 2	They be sunk!
	3–6	See! see!
41	1	Very glad was the Raven, that this fate they did *meet*:
	1 2	The Raven was glad that such
42	1 *1 2*	They had taken his all, & REVENGE WAS SWEET!
41.1	*3–6*	Right glad was the raven, and off he went fleet,
41.1.1	*3–6*	And Death riding home on a cloud he did meet,

41.1.2 *3–6*   And he thank'd him again and again for this treat:
42.1 *3–5*   They had taken his all, and revenge was sweet!
    6   it was
42.1.1 *3*   We must not think so; but forget and forgive,
42.1.2 *3*   And what Heaven gives life to, we'll still let it live?

title. *2 The RAVEN.* • *4* THE RAVEN. I A CHRISTMAS TALE, TOLD BY A SCHOOL-BOY TO I HIS LITTLE BROTHERS AND SISTERS. • *5* THE RAVEN. I A CHRISTMAS TALE, TOLD BY A SCHOOL-BOY TO I HIS LITTLE BROTHERS, AND SISTERS. • *6* THE RAVEN. I A CHRISTMAS TALE, TOLD BY A SCHOOL-BOY TO HIS I LITTLE BROTHERS AND SISTERS.   ⁻**1.3–10.** *2* reverses italic and roman in the body of the letter   ⁻**1.4.** *2 Angler, 2 fishing box—*   ⁻**1.6.** *2 "Mid*
1. *1 2* oak-tree, • *3–6* oak tree   **2.** *3–5* was, *3–5* swine, • *6* swine *3–6* company,
3. *1 2* repast,   **4.1.** *4–6* crunched   **5.** *1 2* away: *1 2* high— • *3–6* high:
6. ☒*1* left, *3–6* and *3–6* might *2* spy,   **7.** *3* raven, *3–6* liked *1* folly;
8. *3–6* belonged, ☒*1* witch *1 2* MELANCHOLY!   **9.** *1 2* jet; • *3–6* jet,
10. *1 2* rain; ☒*1* wet.   **11.** *4–6* picked ☒*1* and *1 2* strait, • *4–6* straight
12. ☒*1* river   **13.** *3* raven   **14.** *1* low • *2–6* low,   **15.** *1* O'er *1* o'er
2–6 dale, *3* raven *1 2* go!   **16.** *3* autumns, *1 2* Springs, • *3* springs   **17.** *4–6* Travelled *1* wand'ring *1 2* wings; • *3* wings.   **18.** ☒*1 3* Summers, • *3* summers, ☒*1 3* Winters • *3* winters—   **19.** ☒*1* adventures.   **20.** ☒*1* and *1 2* she; • *3* she, • *4–6* She,   **21.** ☒*1* acorn *1 3–6* oak tree. • *2* oak-tree.   **23.** ☒*1* ones ☒*1* and   **24.** *2 4–6* woodman • *3* woodman, *2–6* guise,   **25.** *1 2* brow *1 2* pent-house   **26.** ☒*1 3* axe *1 2* and   **27.** ☒*1* hem! and ☒*1* stroke,
28. *3* be *3* raven's ☒*1* oak.   **29.** ☒*1* young ones *3* kill'd: • *4–6* killed; ☒*1* depart,   **30.** *1 2* wife *3–6* heart.   **31.** *3–6* woodman *2* sever • *3* sever— • *4–6* sever;   **32.** *3* tne *1* River: • *2* river: • *3–6* river.   **33.** *4–6* sawed ☒*1* planks, and *1* it's ☒*1* strip,   **34.** ☒*1* and others   **35.** *3–6* ship, *1–3* launch'd; • *4–6* launched; *1 2* land, • *3–6* land   **36.** *1 2* tempest ☒*1* ship
37. *4–6* bulged ☒*1* and ☒*1* waves *4–6* rushed *1 2* fast—   **38.** *1 2* auld • *3–5* old *3* raven *1–5* round and ☒*1* and *4–6* cawed ☒*1* blast.   **39.** *1 2* souls! • *3–6* souls—   **40.** *6* See! See! *2–6* o'er *1 2* top-mast • *3–6* topmast *1 2* rolls.
41. *1 2* meet—   **42.** *1 2* and REVENGE *1 2* SWEET.   **41.1.** *4–6* Raven,
42.1. *4 5* REVENGE WAS SWEET! • *6* Revenge was sweet!

1. In the version copied by G. B. Greenough in May 1799 the poem began with a mixture of PR *3–5* and TEXTS 1 *1 2* readings:

> Underneath a huge Oak tree
> There was of Swine a large Company.

(*C in Germany* 230).
8. PR *3* witch] A comma was added after the word in JG's copy at HUL—in ink and perhaps by JG.
13–14 etc. Lines 13–14 indented in PR *1–3*; lines 16–19, 22–8, 41.1, 42.1 also indented in PR *3*. Lines 13–14, and perhaps 16–19, 24–5, 29–30, may be indented in MS 1. Lines 13–14, 16–19, 41.1, and 42.1 indented in PR *4–6*.
20⁺. No line-space in PR *1 2*. The line-space in PR *3–6* coincides with the turn-over from recto to verso of f 1 in MS 1.

30. PR *3* did die] Emended to "she died" in JG's copy at HUL—ink over C's (?) pencil. The full point at the end of the line has also been changed to an exclamation-mark.

30⁺. No line-space in PR *1 2 6*.

32. PR *3* And they floated it down] Emended to "And it went down afloat" in JG's copy at HUL—ink over C's (?) pencil.

38⁺. Line-space in PR *3*. In PR *4 5* there is a page-break at this point, which may explain the absence of a line-space in PR *6*.

42.1. In JG's copy of PR *3* at HUL C double-underlined "and revenge was sweet!", and added a word in the RH margin which looks like "*Extremely*". Underlining and comment are both in pencil, faint and difficult to decipher.

42.1.2⁺. In JG's copy of PR *3* at HUL C appears to have keyed in a further eight lines, but the traces which now remain are too faint to read, or even determine whether the eight lines were in verse or prose. Only a few words are legible: "Faith" (towards the end of the third line), "Fear" and "hath a slander" (at the beginning and middle of the fourth line), "So" (at the beginning of the fifth line). All other pencil annotations by C in this copy have been gone over in ink, whereas these appear to have been erased.

The import of C's pencilled addition is probably the same as his comment in the copy of PR *3* which belonged to Stuart M. Samuel, now lost: see vol I 42–3EC.

146. TO THOMAS POOLE:
INVITATION TO DINE

A. DATE

Early Jan 1797. The lines are endorsed by TP "Fr Col: | Jany 97 | Invitation to dine—". C had moved to Stowey on 1 Jan, and the lines are likely to have been written before Charles Lloyd arrived, in the middle of the month.

B. TEXT

BM Add MS 35343 f 71ᵛ. Written in C's hand on the verso of a Prospectus for Six Lectures on the English Rebellion under Charles I and the French Revolution (given in Bristol, 1795) (*CL* I 296).

The RT reproduces the ms exactly, except for:

title. ms To T. Poole   **13⁺.** ms ~~With which if you'd wish to~~   **17.** ms ~~the~~ said
19. ms B P.S.

19. C at first intended the line to follow line 18 directly, before making it the start of a postscript.

146.X1. OSORIO

DATE

Early Feb 1797 (after 4 Feb)–14 Oct 1797.

See vol III.

147. ON THE CHRISTENING OF
A FRIEND'S CHILD

A. DATE

Feb–Mar 1797.

B. TEXT

Supplement to *Poems* (1797).

The poem was not included in the list C sent Joseph Cottle (BM Ashley 408 f 4^r = *JDC facsimile* 5). It was incorporated into the volume apparently after 10 Mar 1797, when the preliminary arrangements were confirmed (*CL* I 313: to J. Cottle [10 Mar 1797]), and before mid-Jun, when Charles Lloyd's and CL's poems were added and the volume printed.

The RT reproduces the 1797 text exactly, except for the typography of the title:

title. *On the CHRISTENING of a Friend's* | *CHILD.*

148. TO AN UNFORTUNATE WOMAN,
WHOM I KNEW IN THE DAYS OF HER
INNOCENCE: COMPOSED AT THE THEATRE

A. DATE

Early Mar 1797. In his letter to Joseph Cottle of 10 Mar (*CL* I 312) C refers to the poem as his "last-born", and again, a few days later (*CL* I 316: to J. Cottle 16 Mar 1797), as a "recent composition".

1 [=RT]. HUL fMS Eng 947.2. Folded leaf, 24.8×39.0 cm; wm R WIL-
LIAMS; chain-lines 3.0 cm. Transcribed as part of an als to Joseph Cottle, 10
Mar 1797, with emendations in Cottle's hand (*CL* I 313–14).

1. M Post (7 Dec 1797). Signed "ALBERT."
This version, like PR *3–6* below, expands the original five stanzas to eight.

2. Annual Anthology ed RS (2 vols Bristol 1799–1800) II 291–2. Unsigned.
C's copy at Yale (Tinker 1953 2) supplies the initials "S. T. C.", and two
corrections in his hand.

3. SL (1817).
Rpt *Spirit of Contemporary Poetry* (3 vols Boston, Mass 1827) I 5–6.

4. PW (1828).

5. PW (1829).

6. PW (1834).

C sent the poem to Joseph Cottle for inclusion in *Poems* (1797), "immediately
following the Kiss" (=poem **76**), or to be sent with his compliments to the
editor of the *New Monthly Magazine* (*CL* I 312–13: [10 Mar 1797]). Cottle's
reply is given in *E Rec* I 219–24, and C's response in *CL* I 316 [15 Mar 1797]:
"This first poem is but a so so composition—I wonder, I could be so blinded by
the ardor of recent composition, as to see any thing in it.—I will send it myself
to the Editor.—" When C decided to omit the poem from the 1797 collection,
he transposed the larger part of the title to poem **149** (see VAR title below).

title. 1 To an unfortunate Woman, whom I knew in the days of her I Innocence.
Composed at the Theatre. • *1* LINES TO AN UNFORTUNATE WOMAN,
IN I THE BACK SEATS OF THE BOXES AT THE I THEATRE. • *2 To
an unfortunate WOMAN,* I *Whom the Author knew in the days of her Innocence.* I
Composed at the THEATRE. • *3–6* TO I *AN UNFORTUNATE WOMAN* I *At the
Theatre.*

1 1	~~Maid~~ Maiden! that with sullen brow	
1 3–6	Maiden,	
2	Sufferer,	
2 ☐	Sit'st behind those Virgins gay,	
3 ☐	Like a scorch'd and mildew'd bough	
4 ☐	Leafless mid the blooms of May;	
	[*Line-space*]	
5 1 2	Inly-gnawing, thy Distresses	
6 1 2	Mock those starts of wanton glee,	
7 1 2	And thy inmost soul confesses	

8 1   Chaste Affection's Majesty.
  2   affliction's
     [Line-space]

8.1.1 *1 3–6* Him who lur'd thee and forsook,
8.1.2 *1 3–6* Oft I watch'd with angry gaze;
8.1.3 *1 3–6* Fearful saw his pleading look,
8.1.4 *1 3–6* Anxious heard his fervid phrase.
     [Line-space]

8.1.5 *1 3–6* Soft the glances of the Youth,
8.1.6 *1 3–6* Soft his speech and soft his sigh;
8.1.7 *1 3–6* But no sound like simple Truth,
8.1.8 *1 3–6* But no *true* love in his eye.
     [Line-space]

9 ☐   Loathing thy polluted Lot,
10 ☒2 Hie thee, Maiden! hie thee hence:
  2   Sufferer,
11 ☐   Seek thy weeping Mother's cot
12 ☐   With a wiser Innocence!
     [Line-space]

12.1.1 *1 3–6* Thou hast known deceit and folly:
12.1.2 *1 3–6* Thou hast *felt* that vice is woe:
12.1.3 *1 3–6* With a musing melancholy
12.1.4 *1 3–6* Inly arm'd, go, Maiden! go.
     [Line-space]

12.1.5 *1 3–6* Mother sage of Self-dominion,
12.1.6 *1*   Firm are thy steps, O Melancholy!
  3–6   thy
12.1.7 *1 3–6* The strongest plume in Wisdom's pinion
12.1.8 *1 3–6* Is the memory of past folly.
     [Line-space]

13 1 2 Mute the Lavrac and forlorn,
  1 3–6   sky-lark
14 1   When she moults those firstling plumes,
  1 2   While
  3–6   the
15 1 2–6 That   had skimm'd the tender corn
  1   Which late
16 ☐   Or the Beanfield's od'rous blooms:
     [Line-space]

17 ☐   Soon with renovated Wing
18 ☐   Shall She dare a loftier flight,
19 1 2 Upwards to the Day-star sing
  1 3–6   spring,
20 ☐   And embathe in heavenly Light!

---

title. *4 5* TO AN UNFORTUNATE WOMAN | AT THE THEATRE. •
6 TO AN UNFORTUNATE WOMAN AT | THE THEATRE.   **1.** *1* brow,
2. *1 3 6* Sitt'st • *4 5* Sittest *1–6* virgins   **3.** *4–6* scorched *1 4–6* mildewed
1 bow, • *2–6* bough,   **4.** *3–6* 'mid *1 3–6* May!   **5.** *2* Inly *2* distresses

8. *2* majesty.   **8.1.1.** *3–6* lured   **8.1.2.** *4–6* watched   *3–6* gaze,   **8.1.5.** *3–*
6 youth,   **8.1.6.** *3–6* speech,   **8.1.7.** *3–6* truth,   **8.1.8.** *4–6* true   **9.** *1–*
6 lot,   **10.** *1 3–6* Maiden,   *1 3–6* hence! • *2* hence;   **11.** *2–6* cot,   **12.** *1 3–*
6 innocence. • *2* innocence!   **12.1.1.** *3–6* folly,   **12.1.2.** *4–6* felt   **12.1.4.** *4–*
6 armed,   **12.1.5.** *6* self-dominion,   **12.1.7.** *3–6* wisdom's   **12.1.8.** *4* folly
14. *2* plumes   **15.** *4–6* skimmed   *1 3–6* corn, • *2* Corn,   **16.** *1 3 4* bean-field's •
2 Bean-field's • *5 6* beanfield's   *2–6* odorous   *1 3–6* blooms.   **17.** *1* wing, • *2–*
6 wing   **18.** *1–6* she   **19.** *1 3–6* Upward   *1 3–6* day-star   *2* sing,   *3–5* spring
20. *1* light! • *2–6* light.

title. A ms list of poems made in 1799–1800 (?) (VCL S MS F2.7) gives the title as
"Prostitute in the Theatre".
2, 4, 6, etc. Alternate lines indented in TEXTS ☒1.
12. In MS 1 Joseph Cottle deleted "a wiser" and substituted "the wreck of".
13. In MS 1 C added in the margin "the Lark". In the Yale copy of PR 2 he emended
"Lavrac" to "Sky-lark".
14. In MS 1 Joseph Cottle emended "When" to "While".

149. ALLEGORICAL LINES ON
THE SAME SUBJECT

A. DATE

Early Mar 1797. See **148** *To an Unfortunate Woman at the Theatre* sec A.

B. TEXTS

1 [=RT]. HUL fMS Eng 947.2. Folded leaf, 24.8×39.0 cm; wm R WIL-
LIAMS; chain-lines 3.0 cm. Transcribed in an als to Joseph Cottle, 10 Mar 1797
(*CL* I 314).
Cottle's reply is given in *E Rec* I 219–24, and C's response to Cottle's
suggestions in *CL* I 315–16 [15 Mar 1797] (see sec C below). Cottle has written
in the emendations on the ms.

1. Poems (1797).
C asked Cottle to make changes in the printed version in a list of errata
which he sent c 3 Jul 1797 (*CL* I 331), but his request arrived too late. Five
copies contain emendations or corrections in C's hand: William Bowles's (in
the possession of Erwin Schwarz, 1982); the Abbé Barbey's (BM C 126 b
1); GC's (Princeton University Library Robert H. Taylor Collection); William
Roskilly's (in the possession of J.C.C. Mays, 1999); RS's (?) (Yale In 678 797
Copy 1).

2. Poems (1803).

2. Colorado College Library Special Collections. Two leaves, each 32.4×
19.8 cm; wm (leaf 1) Britannia; (leaf 2) 180?0; chain-lines 2.5 cm; signed
"S. T. C." The ms contains some pencilled notes by EHC. Transcribed in an als
to John Whitaker, 30 Apr 1811 (*CL* III 322).

John Whitaker (1776–1847), organist of St Clement's, Eastcheap, was also a
composer and member of a music-publishing firm. C, as the letter explains, sent
him three poems ("Songs") in the hope that Whitaker would set them to music;
cf poems **190, 275.**

3. SL (1817).

4. PW (1828).

5. PW (1829).

6. PW (1834).

C. GENERAL NOTE

This poem, like the previous one, was sent to Cottle to be included in *Poems*
(1797). When Cottle replied with his criticisms, C responded as follows:

> The first poem on the Unfortunate Woman will do well for the monthly
> Magazine—the second therefore only shall be printed in my poems—with
> this title—
>
> Allegorical Lines to an unfortunate Woman,
> whom I had known in the days of her Innocence.

Your remarks are perfectly just on it—except that, in this country, T. P.
informs me, Corn is *as often* cut with a Scythe, as with a hook. How-
ever for Scythesman read Rustic—for "poor fond thing—read—foolish
Thing—& for Flung to fade & rot & die—read Flung to wither & to
die!—Ill-besped is indeed a sad blotch—but after having tried at least a
hundred ways before I sent the poem to you, and as many more since,—I
find it incurable. (*CL* I 315–16: to J. Cottle [15 Mar 1797])

title. 1 Allegorical Lines on the same subject • *1–6* TO AN | *UNFORTUNATE
WOMAN,* | Whom the Author had known in the days of her | Innocence. • 2 The
Myrtle Leaf, or Innocence Seduced: ⟨(an *allegory*)addressed to an unfortunate
Woman.⟩

1	□	Myrtle-Leaf, that ill-besped
2	1	Pinest in the glдadsome ray,
3	⊠2	Soil'd beneath the common tread
2		vulgar
4	⊠2	Far from thy protecting Spray;
2		maternal
	[*Line-space*]	

5	1	When the Scythesman o'er his sheaf	
	1	Rustic	
	☒1 *1*	Partridge	the
6	1 *1*	Caroll'd in the yellow Vale,	
	☒1 *1*	Whirr'd along	
7	☐	Sad I saw thee, heedless Leaf!	
8	☐	Love the dalliance of the Gale.	
		[*Line-space*]	
9	1	Lightly didst thou, poor fond Thing!	
	1–6	foolish	
	2	thoughtless	
10	☐	Heave and flutter to his sighs;	
11	☐	While the Flatt'rer, on his wing	
12	☐	Woo'd and whisper'd thee to rise.	
		[*Line-space*]	
13	☒2	Gaily from thy mother stalk	
	2	parent	
14	☐	Wert thou danc'd and wafted high;	
15	☒2	Soon on this unshelter'd walk	
	2	neglected	
16	1	Flung to fade, and rot, and die!	
	1–6	to	
	2	waste, to	

title. *2* TO AN | *UNFORTUNATE WOMAN* | *Whom the Author had known in the days of her Innocence.* • *3 TO AN UNFORTUNATE WOMAN,* | *Whom the Author had known in the days of her Innocence.* • *4 5* TO AN UNFORTUNATE WOMAN, | WHOM THE AUTHOR HAD KNOWN IN THE DAYS | OF HER INNOCENCE. • *6* TO AN UNFORTUNATE WOMAN, | WHOM THE AUTHOR HAD KNOWN IN THE DAYS OF | HER INNOCENCE.   **1.** *1 2* Myrtle leaf, that • 2 Myrtle Leaf, that • *3–6* Myrtle-leaf that,   *1 2* ill besped • *3–6* ill besped, **2.** ☒1 gladsome   2 Ray,   **3.** *4–6* Soiled   2 Tread • *3–6* tread,   **4.** *1– 6* spray!   **5.** *6* partridge   2 Sheaf   **6.** *4–6* Whirred   *1–6* vale,   **7.** *1 2* Sad, *1* headless   *1–6* leaf!   **8.** *1–6* gale.   **9.** *1–6* thing!   **10.** *1–6* sighs, • 2 Sighs: **11.** *1 2* Flatt'rer • 2 Flatterer • *3–6* flatterer,   2 Wing • *3–6* wing,   **12.** *3–6* Wooed *4–6* whispered   **13.** 2 parent Stalk • *3–6* mother-stalk   **14.** *3–6* danced   2 high, • *3–6* high—   **15.** *4–6* unsheltered   2 Walk   **16.** *1–6* rot   *3–6* die.

    title. The PR *1–6* title derives from the time that C decided to exclude poem **148** from *Poems* (1797). Cf *CL* I 315: to J. Cottle [15 Mar 1797].

    2, 4, 6, etc. Alternate lines indented in PR *3–6*.

    5. In MS 1 Joseph Cottle substituted "Rustic" for "Scythesman", as C instructed.

    5–7, 8. In RS's (?) copy of PR *1* C emended 5 "Rustic" to "Partridge"; 5 "his" to "the"; 6 "Caroll'd" to "whirr'd along"; 7 "headless" to "heedless". In GC's and Roskilly's copies of PR *1* C deleted the comma after 7 "Sad". He had instructed Cottle to do this in the errata he sent c 3 Jul 1797 (*CL* I 331), and also told him to print "Gale" with initial capital in the following line. In Bowles's and Barbey's copies of PR *1* C corrected 7 "headless" to "heedless". Curiously, in Bowles's copy there is no comma after "Sad".

9. In MS 1 Cottle substituted "foolish" for "poor fond", as C instructed.

12. In MS 1 Cottle underlined "thee to rise".

16. In MS 1 Cottle substituted "wither and to die" for "fade, and rot, and die", as C instructed.

150. TO THE REV GEORGE COLERIDGE
OF OTTERY ST MARY, DEVON,
WITH SOME POEMS

A. DATE

PR *1 2* supply the date 26 May 1797, and there is every reason to believe that the poem was written not long before.

B. TEXTS

1. Poems (1797). Signed "*S. T. COLERIDGE.* | May 26th, 1797. | *Nether-Stowey, Somerset.*"

RS's (?) copy (Yale In 678 797 Copy 1) contains emendations to the poem in C's hand, as well as two comments (see vol I headnote and 32EC).

2. Poems (1803). Signed "*S. T. COLERIDGE.* | May 26th 1797. | *Nether-Stowey, Somerset.*"

The transcript in JTC's Commonplace Book (University of Pennsylvania (Special Collections) MS Eng 13) pp 29–30 is of no textual significance.

3 [=RT]. *SL* (1817).

There is a minor correction in JG's copy (HUL *EC8 C6795 817s (C)) and HNC's copy (HUL *AC85 L8605 Zy 817c), neither of which is certainly in C's hand.

4. PW (1828).

5. PW (1829).

6. PW (1834).

title. *1 2* DEDICATION. | *To the Reverend GEORGE COLERIDGE,* | OF | OT-TERY ST. MARY, | DEVON. • *3–6* TO | *THE REV. GEORGE COLERIDGE,* | *Of Ottery St. Mary, Devon.* | WITH SOME POEMS.

⁻**1.1** □   Notus in fratres animi paterni.

⁻**1.2** *1 2* Hor. Carm. Lib. II. 2.

　　　3–6 HOR. *Carm.* Lib. I. 2.

　　1 □   A BLESSED Lot hath he, who having past

2	□	His youth and early manhood in the stir
3	□	And turmoil of the world, retreats at length,
4	□	With cares that move, not agitate the heart,
5	□	To the same Dwelling where his Father dwelt;
6	□	And haply views his tottering little ones
7	□	Embrace those aged knees and climb that lap,
8	□	On which first kneeling his own Infancy
9	□	Lisp'd its brief prayer. Such, O my earliest Friend!
10	⊠2	Thy Lot, and such thy Brothers too enjoy.
	2	Thine and thy Brothers' favorable lot.
11	□	At distance did ye climb Life's upland road,
12	□	Yet cheer'd and cheering: now fraternal Love
13	□	Hath drawn you to one centre. Be your days
14	□	Holy, and blest and blessing may ye live!

[*Line-space*]

15	□	To me th' Eternal Wisdom hath dispens'd
16	□	A different fortune and more different mind—
17	□	Me from the spot where first I sprang to light,
18	□	Too soon transplanted, ere my soul had fix'd
19	□	Its first domestic loves; and hence through life
20	□	Chacing chance-started Friendships. A brief while
21	□	Some have preserv'd me from life's pelting ills;
22	□	But, like a Tree with leaves of feeble stem,
23	*1 2*	If the clouds lasted, or a sudden breeze
	3–6	and
24	□	Ruffled the boughs, they on my head at once
25	□	Dropt the collected shower: and some most false,
26	□	False and fair-foliag'd as the Manchineel,
27	□	Have tempted me to slumber in their shade
28	□	E'en mid the storm; then breathing subtlest damps,
29	□	Mix'd their own venom with the rain from heaven,
30	⊠2	That I woke poison'd! But, all praise to Him
	2	the praise be His
31	□	Who gives us all things, more have yielded me
32	□	Permanent shelter: and beside one Friend,
33	⊠2	Beneath th' impervious covert of one Oak,
	2	I, as beneath the an
34	⊠2	I've rais'd a lowly shed, and know the names
	2	Have
35	⊠6	Of Husband and of Father; nor unhearing
	6	not
36	□	Of that divine and nightly-whispering VOICE,
37	□	Which from my childhood to maturer years
38	□	Spake to me of predestinated wreaths,
39a	□	Bright with no fading colours!

[*Line-space*]

39b	□	Yet at times
40	□	My soul is sad, that I have roam'd through life
41	□	Still most a Stranger, most with naked heart

42 ☐ At mine own home and birth-place: chiefly then,
43 ☐ When I remember thee, my earliest Friend!
44 ☐ Thee, who didst watch my boy-hood and my youth;
45 ☐ Didst trace my wanderings with a father's eye;
46 ☐ And boding evil yet still hoping good
47 *1 2* Rebuk'd each fault and wept o'er all my woes.
　　3–6　　　　　　　←over→
48 *3–6* Sorrow'd in Silence! He who counts alone
49 *1 2* Who counts the beatings of the lonely heart,
　　3–6 The　beatings　of　the　solitary　heart,
50 ☐ That Being knows, how I have lov'd thee ever,
51 ☐ Lov'd as a Brother, as a Son rever'd thee!
52 ☐ O tis to me an ever-new delight,
52.1.1 *1* My eager eye glist'ning with mem'ry's tear,
53 ☐ To talk of thee and thine; or when the blast
54 ☐ Of the shrill winter, ratt'ling our rude sash,
55 ☐ Endears the cleanly hearth and social bowl;
56 ☐ Or when, as now, on some delicious eve,
57 ☐ We in our sweet sequester'd Orchard-plot
58 ☐ Sit on the Tree crook'd earth-ward; whose old boughs,
59 ☐ That hang above us in an arborous roof,
60 ☐ Stirr'd by the faint gale of departing May
61 ☐ Send their loose blossoms slanting o'er our heads!
　　[*Line-space*]
62 ☐ Nor dost not *thou* sometimes recall those hours,
63 ☐ When with the joy of hope thou gav'st thine ear
64 ☐ To my wild firstling lays. Since then my song
65 ☐ Hath sounded deeper notes, such as beseem
66 ☐ Or that sad wisdom, folly leaves behind;
66.1.1 *1 2* Or the high raptures of prophetic Faith;
67 ☐ Or such, as tun'd to these tumultuous times
68a ☐ Cope with the tempest's swell!
　　[*Line-space*]
68b *1 2*　　　　　　　　　　These various songs,
　　3–6　　　　　　　　　　　　　strains,
69 ☐ Which I have fram'd in many a various mood,
70 ☐ Accept my Bʀᴏᴛʜᴇʀ! and (for some perchance
71 ☐ Will strike discordant on thy milder mind)
72 ☐ If aught of Error or intemperate Truth
73 ☐ Should meet thine ear, think thou that riper Age
74 ☐*3* Will calm it down, and let thy Love forgive it!
　　3　　　　　　　　　　they

title. *2* DEDICATION |　*4 5* TO THE REV. GEORGE COLERIDGE
OF | OTTERY ST. MARY, DEVON. | ᴡɪᴛʜ sᴏᴍᴇ ᴘᴏᴇᴍs.•*6* TO THE
REV. GEORGE COLERIDGE | ᴏғ ᴏᴛᴛᴇʀʏ sᴛ. ᴍᴀʀʏ, ᴅᴇᴠᴏɴ. ᴡɪᴛʜ sᴏᴍᴇ
ᴘᴏᴇᴍs.　⁻*1.2. 4–6* Carm. lib. 1.　　**1.** *2* blessed　*3–6* lot　*4–6* passed　　**4.** *3–*
5 Heart,　　**5.** *6* dwelling　*6* father　　**6.** *3* tott'ring　　**7.** *2* knees,　　**8.** *6* infancy
9. *4–6* Lisped　　**10.** *3–6* lot,　*3–6* brothers　*5* enjoy　　**11.** *6* life's　　**12.** *4–*

6 cheered   *6* love   **15.** *4–6* the   *4–6* dispensed   **17.** *4–6* light   **18.** *4–6* fixed
19. *3–5* Life   **20.** ⊠*1* Chasing   *6* friendships.   **21.** *4–6* preserved   *3–*
5 Life's   **22.** *6* tree   **25.** *4–6* Dropped   *3–6* shower;   **26.** *3–6* fair
4–6 foliaged   **29.** *3* Mixt • *4–6* Mixed   *3–6* Heaven,   **30.** *4–6* poisoned!
2 But (the   **31.** *2* things) more   **32.** *3–6* shelter;   *6* friend,   **33.** *4–6* the
6 oak,   **34.** *3–6* raised   **35.** *6* husband   *6* father;   **36.** *2–5* Voice, •
6 voice,   **40.** *4–6* roamed   **41.** *6* stranger,   **43.** *6* friend!   **44.** *3* did'st
4–6 boyhood   **45.** *3* Did'st   *3–5* Father's   **46.** *6* good,   **47.** *4–6* Rebuked
3–6 fault,   *3–6* woes   **48.** *4–6* Sorrowed   *6* silence!   **50.** *6* being   *4–6* loved
51. *4–6* Loved   *3–6* brother,   *6* son   *4–6* revered   **52.** *3–6* Oh!   *2 4–6* 'tis
⊠*1* ever   *3* delight   **53.** *4–6* thine: **54.** *3–6* rattling   **56.** *3–6* when
57. *4–6* sequestered   *3–5* Orchard-Plot • *6* orchard-plot   **58.** *6* tree   *4–6* crooked
60. *4–6* Stirred   *2–6* May,   **62.** *6* thou   **63.** *4 5* gavest   **64.** *3–6* firstling-
lays.   **66.** *4–6* wisdom   *4–6* behind,   **67.** *3–6* such as,   *4–6* tuned   *3–6* times,
69. *4–6* framed   **70.** *2–6* Accept,   *2* BROTHER; • *3–5* Brother! • *6* brother!
72. *6* error   *6* truth   **73.** *3–6* age   **74.** *6* love

23. In RS's (?) copy of PR *1* C emended "or" to "and".
47–9, 52–52.1.1. C emended RS's (?) copy of PR *1* to conform to PR *3* (giving
"silence! He, who counts," in line 48).
74. PR *3* they] Corrected to "thy" in JG's and HNC's copies.

151. SONG FROM *OSORIO/REMORSE*

A. DATE

Apr–Aug 1797. See the introduction to **146.X1** *Osorio* in vol III.

B. TEXTS

1 [=RT]. HEHL HM 361, described at vol III **146.X1** *Osorio* TEXT MS 3.
Part of a transcript of *Osorio* in Mrs C's hand, ff 48ʳ, 49ʳ.

The words were published, with a musical setting, by William Carnaby in
May 1802: see vol III **502.X2** *Remorse* (Stage) appendix B 1. Carnaby had been
lent the ms by R. B. Sheridan, and the publication has no textual significance.

2. HEHL HM 362, described at vol III **146.X1** *Osorio* TEXT MS 4. Part of a
transcript of *Osorio* in an unknown hand, f 101ʳ.

3. HUL MS Eng 947.9, described at vol III **146.X1** *Osorio* TEXT MS 5. Part
of a transcript of *Osorio* in the hand of George Bellas Greenough, f 39ʳ, with a
correction in C's hand.

4. HEHL HM 1753, described at vol III **502.X2** *Remorse* (Stage) introduction
sec D. Part of a transcript of *Remorse* submitted to the censor, James Larpent,

on 5 Jan 1813, probably in the hand of the regular DL copyist, Mr Stokes, f 19^{r-v} (pp 34–5).

1. M Post (25 Jan 1813), at the end of a review of the DL production.

2. *Courier* (25 Jan 1813), at the end of a review of the DL production, related to but not identical with the review in *M Post*.

3. *The Invocation, as Sung with Unbounded Applause by Mrs Bland, at the New Theatre Royal, Drury Lane, in the Popular Tragedy of Remorse, Written by —— Coleridge Esqr. The Music Composed by Mich^l. Kelly* (n.d.).

The text must, like PR *1 2* above, derive from the companion to the Larpent copy in use at DL, which was eventually superseded by the prompt copy. Only the last of Kelly's repeats is included in the collation, and this version omits the second stanza. Cf vol III **502.X2** *Remorse* (Stage) appendix B 2.

4. M Chron (25 Jan 1813), at the end of a review of the DL production, which C ascribed on hearsay to Hazlitt (*CL* III 429: to J. Rickman 25 Jan 1813).

Cf *H Works* XVIII 463 et seq, and for Hazlitt's later comments on the play see v 247, 368, XI 35, XVII 122, XVIII 304. The review itself overlaps in a number of phrases with those printed in *M Post* and *Courier* (PR *1 2* above). The variant in line 12 derives from a compositor's error in PR *5*, as C noted, although this was not on sale before 5 Feb.

5. Remorse (1st ed 1813).

The different states of this edition do not affect the text of the song.

C made minor changes to the text in copies presented to J. G. Raymond (HRC Wn C678 813r Copy 1) and Alexander Pope (BM Ashley 2847). PR *5*'s version of the song was reprinted in the review of the production in *Literary Panorama* XIII (1813) 462, and of the printed text in *The Christian Observer* XII (1813) 236.

6. Remorse (2nd and 3rd eds 1813).

The different states of the second edition do not affect the song; the third edition is a reprint of the second, with an emended title-page.

5. State Historical Museum, Moscow, Department of Written Sources, fund No 166. Transcript of stanza 2 in the hand of JG, in a letter dictated by C addressed to R. W. Elliston, 12 Jul 1821 (in part in *CL* v 161).

7. PW (1828).

The copy owned by Erwin Schwarz (1982) contains an emendation to the song and a comment, both in C's hand (in pencil).

8. PW (1829).

9. PW (1834).

title. 1–3 The Song. • 4 5–9 SONG • *1 2* INVOCATION. • *3 THE INVOCATION,* *etc.* • *4* SONG TO A SPIRIT IN MR. COLERIDGE'S TRA-|GEDY OF REMORSE.

1	⊠5	Hear, sweet Spirit! hear the Spell
2	⊠5	Lest a blacker Charm compel!
3	⊠5	So shall the midnight breezes swell
4	⊠5	With thy deep long-lingering Knell.
		[*Line-space*]
5	⊠*3*	And at Evening evermore
6	⊠*3*	In a Chapel on the Shore
7	⊠*3 9*	Shall the Chaunters sad and saintly,
	9	chaunter,
8	⊠*3 9*	Yellow Tapers burning faintly,
9	⊠*3 9*	Doleful Masses chaunt for thee,
10	⊠*3 9*	Miserere, Domine!
		[*Line-space*]
11	⊠5	Hark! the Cadence dies away
12	⊠5 *4–8*	On the quiet moonlight Sea,
	4–8	yellow
13	⊠5	The Boatmen rest their Oars, and say,
14	⊠5	Miserere, Domine!
14.1.1	*1–4 5*	Wand'ring Dæmon! hear the Spell
	3 6–9	Demons
	4	spirit,
14.1.2	⊠*3 4*	Lest a blacker Charm compel!

title. 2 Song— • *3* Song • *5–9* SONG.   **1.** *3 3* Hear   *3 1 2* spirit! • *3* Spirit • *4–9* spirit,   *3 3* spell • *4 1 2 4–9* spell,   **2.** 4 *1–9* charm   *3* compel. • *1 2* compel; • *3* compel   **4.** *4* deep,   *4 5* long lingering • *3* long ling'ring • *4* long, lingering   *3 4 5–9* knell. • *1 2* knell: • *3* knell • *4* knell;   **5.** *4 1 2 5 6 5 7–9* evening • *4* evening,   *4 1 2* ever more • *4–9* evermore,   **6.** *3 4 9* chapel   *3* shore • *1 2 4–9* shore,   **7.** *4* chaunters, • *1* Chaunters, • *4* chanters,   *3 4* &   **8.** *3 4 1 2 4–9* tapers   *4 5* faintly   **9.** *3 4 2 4 9* masses   *3 4* chant   *4 1 2 5* thee   **10.** *3 4 5–9* Miserere Domine! • *4 Miserere Domine!*   **11.** *3 4 1–9* cadence   **12.** *1* moon light • *2* moon-light   *7* yellow,   *3 2* sea, • *4* sea; • *1 5–9* sea: • *3* sea • *4* sea:—   **13.** *3 2 4–9* boatmen • *1* boat-men   *3 1 2 4* oars, • *4* Oars • *3 5–9* oars   *3 &* 4 Say • *3* say   **14.** *3 4 5–9* Miserere Domine! • *1* Miserere, D mine! • *3* Miserere Domine • *4 Miserere Domine!*   **14.1.1.** 3 Wand'ring • *4 4–6* Wandering   4 demon • *5* Demon • *6* Demons! • *7 8* Demons • *9* demons   *3* spell • *4* spell, • *5 6* spell!   **14.1.2.** 4 *3 5 6* charm   *4 3* compel. • *4* compel! • *5 6* compel—

4⁺. No line-space in TEXTS 1–4 *1 2 4*.

9. MS 3 chant] C has written "chaunt" alongside, in the margin.

10⁺. No line-space in TEXTS 4 *1–4*.

11. PR *3* repeats "Hark!"

12. PR *7* yellow] C has substituted "quiet" in Erwin Schwarz's copy (in pencil), and has added at the foot of the page (also in pencil): "Strange misprint! *Yellow* instead of Quiet! But the Compositor's Eye had caught the antecedent 'yellow' three lines above.—Many Errors from the same cause still deform Shakespere."

An asterisk has been inserted at the RH end of this line in MS 2, apparently by RHS.

12, 14. Indented in TEXTS 1 *5–9*.

14. PR *3* repeats "Miserere Domine" (three times in all), which is then taken up by the Chorus.

14.1.1–2. Added at vol III **146.X1** *Osorio* III i 111–12 (following "The whole Orchestra crashes into one Chorus"); **502.X2** *Remorse* (Stage) III ii 98–9; **502.X3** *Remorse* (Printed) III i 132–3. In PR *3* the lines are introduced by "Let me hear more Music."; in PR *4* they run on directly. They are not present in PR *1 2*.

14.1.1. PR *5* Demon] C added an exclamation-mark in Raymond's copy. In Pope's copy he altered the text to conform to the PR *6* reading "Demons!"

152. THE FOSTER-MOTHER'S TALE:
A DRAMATIC FRAGMENT

A. DATE

Apr–Sept 1797. The poem is excerpted from vol III **146.X1** *Osorio* IV ii 3–83 (var). If WW is reckoned to be a formative influence, it probably dates from Jun, when C visited Racedown, or after. C first mentions printing it as a fragment in a letter to Joseph Cottle of 18 Feb 1798 (*CL* I 387), and by 28 May had come to think of it as a separate "Tale in itself" (*CL* I 412: to J. Cottle). The emendation of the title and other changes made in 1800 are intended to bolster its independent status.

B. TEXTS

1. HUL fMS Eng 870 (80B). Three leaves, glued together along LH edge, each 17×21 cm; wm (partial) top of crown at LH edge; chain-lines 2.6 cm; written on both sides. Fair copy in DW's (?) hand taken from *Osorio*, with emendations and notes by Joseph Cottle.

DW's fair copy is from MS 3 of *Osorio* (HEHL HM 361) ff 78ʳ–81ʳ, in which she changed the wording in three lines: 13 "Troubled" for "Wilder'd" and "the" for "yon"; 16 "entrance" for "entrances"; 54 "made" for "made a". Her copy was perhaps made from C's dictation. Joseph Cottle has written at the head of the first leaf: "This to be kept clean & strait." and on the verso of the same: "(Wordsworth's Coleridge's writing J.C.)" His emendations of the text have no authority, and appear to have been made for the reprinting in *E Rec* I 235–8. He has also numbered the ms at the head of the first leaf "39", "29", and "133"—a fact which is important in the dating of the ms of **145** *The Raven*. The number "97" which follows the last line of the text might have been written by DW.

1. LB (1798).

Foster Mother's Tale

(Scene Spain)
Foster Mother

Now blessings on the man, whoe'er he be,
That joined your names with mine! O my sweet Lady,
As often as I think of those dear times,
When you two little ones would stand, at eve,
On each side of my chair, and make me learn
All you had learnt in the day; and how to talk
In gentle phrase, then bid me sing to you —
'Tis more like 'heaven to come than what has been

Maria

O my dear Mother! this strange man has left us
Troubled with wilder fancies, than the moon
Breeds in the love-sick maid who gazes at it,
Till lost in inward vision, with wet eye
She gazes idly! — But that entrance. Mother!

4. Fair copy of *The Foster-mother's Tale* which served as copy for *Lyrical Ballads* (1798), in the hand of Dorothy Wordsworth with instructions to the printer by Joseph Cottle. Dorothy Wordsworth has characteristically picked up features of Mrs Coleridge's handwriting as she copied from it. Cottle's classificatory numbering is visible at the head of the page (see vol I annex A 8 on the Rugby Manuscript)

2. *LB* (1800).

C's letter to Biggs and Cottle of mid-Jul 1800 (*CL* I 593–4) makes it clear that copy was provided by PR *1* altered according to the instructions given in the letter. They have not been recorded in the textual notes, except for one instruction which was not followed.

C's copy at the State Library of Victoria, Melbourne (*821.71L) contains three emendations in his hand, and he has signed the poem "S. T. Coleridge".

The Philadelphia reprint of 1802 has no textual significance.

3. *LB* (1802).

4. *LB* (1805).

5. *Remorse* (2nd and 3rd eds 1813), Appendix (referred to in a footnote at the beginning of Act IV sc ii, which also appears in PR 7–9).

The two editions are identical apart from the title-page, and might even have been printed at the same time. There are variant states of this printing which affect one word of the text: see vol III **502.X3** *Remorse* (Printed) TEXT PR 2. Some of the changes introduced in this printing are anticipated in C's later revisions to the *Osorio* ms (MS 3ʳ): see vol III **146.X1** *Osorio* IV ii 3–83TN.

The copies of the second edition presented to SH (HUL HEW 2.1.18) and to Sir George Beaumont (Yale In C 678 813B) contain small emendations in C's hand.

6 [=RT]. *SL* (1817).

C made a correction to line 59 in the copies he gave to Francis Wrangham (?) (sold at Christie's 13 Jun 1979 lot 126) and AG (Stanford V 821.6 C69s). JG made the same correction in his own copy (HUL *EC 8 C6795 817s (C)), William Hood's copy (Columbia X825C67 W3 1817), and Martha Fricker's copy (HUL Lowell *EC8 C6795 817s). AG made the same correction in WW's copy (Cornell WORDSWORTH PR 4480 S5 1817 Copy 1), TP's copy (Brown PR 4478 A1 1817 Koopman Collection), and a copy now at Yale (In C678 817s Copy 2).

7. *PW* (1828), Appendix to *Remorse*.

8. *PW* (1829), Appendix to *Remorse*.

9. *PW* (1834), Appendix to *Remorse*.

title. 1 Foster Mother's Tale. • *1 6* THE | *FOSTER-MOTHER'S TALE,* | A DRAMATIC FRAGMENT. • *2–4* THE | *FOSTER-MOTHER's TALE.* | *A Narration in Dramatic Blank Verse.* • *5 7–9* APPENDIX.

prefatory note

1   (Scene Spain)

5 7 8 The following Scene, as unfit for the Stage, was taken from the Tragedy, in the year 1797, and published in the Lyrical Ballads. But this work having been long out of print, and it having been determined, that this with my other Poems in that

collection (the NIGHTINGALE, LOVE, and the ANCIENT MARINER) should be
omitted in any future edition, I have been advised to reprint it, as a Note to the 5
second Scene of Act the Fourth, p. 55.

9   The following Scene, as unfit for the stage, was taken from the tragedy, in the
year 1797, and published in the Lyrical Ballads.

⁻1 *1 6*   FOSTER-MOTHER.
1 *1 6*   I never saw the man whom you describe.
1⁺ *5 7–9*   *Enter* TERESA *and* SELMA.
                  [*Line-space*]
⁻2 *1 6*   MARIA.
  5 7–9   *Ter.*
2 *1 6*   'Tis strange! he spake of you familiarly
  5 7–9   'Tis   said,
3 *1 6*   As mine and Albert's common Foster-mother.
  5 7–9   Alvar's
                  [*Line-space*]
⁻4 *1 6*   FOSTER-MOTHER.
  5 7–9   *Sel.*
4 ⊠*2–4*   Now blessings on the man, whoe'er he be,
5 ⊠*2–4*   That joined your names with mine! O my sweet Lady
6 ⊠*2–4*   As often as I think of those dear times,
7 ⊠*2–4*   When you two little ones would stand, at eve,
8 ⊠*2–4*   On each side of my chair, and make me learn
9 ⊠*2–4*   All you had learnt in the day; and how to talk
10 ⊠*2–4*   In gentle phrase, then bid me sing to you—
11 ⊠*2–4*   'Tis more like heaven to come than what *has* been
                  [*Line-space*]
⁻12 1 *1 6*   Maria
12 1 *1 6*   O my dear Mother! this strange man has left me
13 1 *1 6*   Troubled with wilder fancies, than the moon
14 1 *1 6*   Breeds in the love-sick maid who gazes at it,
15 1 *1 6*   Till lost in inward vision, with wet eye
16 1 *1 6*   She gazes idly!—But that entrance, Mother!
   2–4   But   that   entrance,   Mother!
                  [*Line-space*]
⁻16 *5 7–9*   *Ter.*
16 *5 7–9*   But   that   entrance,   Selma?
                  [*Line-space*]
⁻17 1 *1–4 6*   Foster-mother
   5 7–9   *Sel.*
17 □   Can no one hear? It is a perilous tale!
                  [*Line-space*]
⁻18a 1 *1–4 6*   Maria
    5 7–9   *Ter.*
18a □   No one.
                  [*Line-space*]
⁻18b 1 *1–4 6*   Foster-mother
    5 7–9   *Sel.*

18b ☐		My husband's father told it me,
19 1 *1–4* 6	Poor old Leoni—Angels rest his soul!	
5 7–9		Sesina—
20 ☐	He was a woodman, and could fell and saw	
21 ☐	With lusty arm. You know that huge round beam	
22 ☐	Which props the hanging wall of the old Chapel?	
23 ☐	Beneath that Tree, while yet it was a Tree,	
24 ☐	He found a baby wrapt in mosses, lined	
25 ☐	With thistle-beards, and such small locks of wool	
26 ☐	As hang on brambles. Well, he brought him home,	
27 1 *1–4* 6	And reared him at the then Lord Velez' cost.	
5 7–9		Valdez'
28 ☐	And so the babe grew up a pretty boy,	
29 ☐	A pretty boy but most unteachable—	
30 ☐	And never learnt a prayer, nor told a bead,	
31 ☐	But knew the names of birds, and mocked their notes,	
32 ☐	And whistled, as he were a bird himself:	
33 ☐	And all the autumn 'twas his only play	
34 1 *1* 2	To get the seeds of wild-flowers, and to plant them	
3–9		gather
35 ☐	With earth and water on the stumps of trees.	
36 ⊠*3* 4 6	A Friar who gathered simples in the wood,	
3 4		sought for
6		oft cull'd
37 ☐	A grey-haired man—he loved this little Boy,	
38 ☐	The Boy loved him—and, when the Friar taught him,	
39 ☐	He soon could write with the pen: and from that time	
40 ☐	Lived chiefly at the Convent or the Castle.	
41 1 *1–4* 6	So he became a very learned youth.	
5 7–9		rare and
42 ☐	But O! poor wretch!—he read, and read, and read,	
43 ☐	'Till his brain turned—and ere his twentieth year,	
44 ☐	He had unlawful thoughts of many things:	
45 ☐	And though he prayed, he never loved to pray	
46 ⊠*6*	With holy men, nor in a holy place—	
6		or
47 ☐	But yet his speech, it was so soft and sweet,	
48 1 *1–4* 6	The late Lord Velez ne'er was wearied with him.	
5 7–9		Valdez
49 ☐	And once as by the North side of the Chapel	
50 ☐	They stood together, chained in deep discourse,	
51 ☐	The earth heaved under them with such a groan,	
52 ☐	That the wall tottered, and had well-nigh fallen	
53 ☐	Right on their heads. My Lord was sorely frightened;	
54 ☐	A fever seized him; and he made confession	
55 ☐	Of all the heretical and lawless talk	
56 ☐	Which brought this judgment: so the youth was seized	
57 ⊠*2–4*	And cast into that hole. My husband's father	
2–4		cell.

58 □	Sobbed like a child—it almost broke his heart:			
59 1 *1 2 6*	And once as he was working in	the	cellar,	
3 4		near the	cell	
5 7–9			this dungeon,	

60 □ He heard a voice distinctly; 'twas the Youth's,
61 □ Who sung a doleful song about green fields,
62 1 *1–4 6* How sweet it were on Lake or wild Savannah
5 7–9   wide
63 □ To hunt for food, and be a naked man,
64 □ And wander up and down at liberty.
65 1 *1 5–9* He always doted on the Youth, and now
2–4 Leoni
66 □ His love grew desperate; and defying death,
67 □ He made that cunning entrance, I described:
68a □ And the young man escaped.
            [*Line-space*]
⁻**68b** 1 *1–4 6*   Maria
5 7–9   *Ter.*
68b ☒   'Tis a sweet tale:
69 1 *1 5–9* Such as would lull a listening child to sleep
70 1 *1 5–9* His rosy face besoiled with unwiped tears
71a □ And what became of him?
            [*Line-space*]
⁻**71b** 1 *1–4 6*   Foster-mother
5 7–9   *Sel.*
71b □   He went on Ship-board
72 □ With those bold voyagers, who made discovery
73 1 *1–4* Of golden lands: Leoni's younger brother
5 7–9   Sesina's
6 Leoni's youngest
74 □ Went likewise, and when he returned to Spain,
75 1 *1–4 6* He told Leoni, that the poor mad Youth,
5 7–9   Sesina,
76 □ Soon after they arrived in that new world,
77 □ In spite of his dissuasion seized a boat,
78 □ And all alone, set sail by silent moonlight
79 □ Up a great river, great as any sea,
80 □ And ne'er was heard of more: but 'tis supposed,
81 □ He lived and died among the Savage Men.

title. *6 THE FOSTER-MOTHER's TALE. | A Dramatic Fragment.*
pref n [*5 7 8* version] **6.** *5* p. 55. • *7* p. 202. • *8* p. 226.   ⁻**1.** *6* FOSTER-MOTHER.
1⁺. *9* Teresa *9* Selma.   ⁻**2.** *6* MARIA. • *7 8* TERESA.   **2.** *6* strange,
5–9 familiarly,   **3.** *5 7–9* foster-mother. • *6* Foster-Mother.   ⁻**4.** *6* FOSTER-
MOTHER. • *7 8* SELMA.   **4.** *8 9* be   **5.** *5* join'd *1* lady, • *5 7–9* Lady, •
6 lady!   **6.** *1* times   **7.** *6* little-ones *1 6* stand *1 6* eve   **9.** *6* day,
10. *5 7–9* phrase;   **11.** *5* heav'n *5 7–9* come, *6 9* has *1 6* been. • *5 7–9* been!
⁻**12.** *1* MARIA. • *6* MARIA.   **13.** *6* Moon   **16.** *6* idly— *6* Mother!—
⁻**16.** *7 8* TERESA.   ⁻**17.** *1–4* FOSTER-MOTHER. • *6* FOSTER-MOTHER. •

7 8 SELMA.　　**17.** *6* hear.　　⁻**18a.** *1–4* MARIA.•*6* MARIA.•*7 8* TERESA.
18a. *6* one?　　⁻**18b.** *1* FOSTER-MOTHER•*2–4* FOSTER-MOTHER.•
6 FOSTER-MOTHER.•*7 8* SELMA.　　**19.** *1–4* Leoni!—•*6* Leoni:　*5 7–*
9 angels•*6* Angels,　*7–9* soul;　　**20.** *6* fell,　*6* saw,　　**22.** *6* hanging-wall
1 2 9 chapel?•*3 4* chapel;•*6* chapel?—　　**23.** *1–9* that tree,　*1–3* a tree•*4–9* a
tree,　　**24.** *6* baby,　*4 6* mosses　*5* lin'd　　**25.** *2 3* thistle beards,　　**27.** *5* rear'd
6 Valez' cost;　　**28.** *6* boy—　　**29.** *1–9* boy,　　**30.** *9* learn'd　*6* prayer
6 bead;　　**31.** *5* mock'd　　**32.** *6* himself!•*9* himself.　　**34.** *1–5 9* wild flowers,
35. *1–3* water,　　**36.** *1–9* Friar,　*5* gather'd　　**37.** *4* gray-haired•*5* grey-hair'd
5 7–9 man,　*5* lov'd　*1–4* boy,•*5–9* boy:　　**38.** *1–9* boy　*5* lov'd him:•*7–9* loved
him,　*5 7–9* friar　　**39.** *4–9* pen;　*1–3* time,　　**40.** *5* Liv'd　*9* convent　*9* castle.
41. *5 7–9* youth:　　**42.** *4* But,　*1–4* Oh!•*6* oh!　*3 4* wretch—he•*5–9* wretch!
he　*5* aud　*1–9* read,　　**43.** *4 6 9* Till　*5* turn'd;•*7–9* turned;　*4 5 7–9* year
45. *5* pray'd,　*5* lov'd　　**46.** *5 7–9* place.•*6* place;—　　**48.** *6* Valez　*6* him:
49. *1–9* once,　*1–9* north　*5–9* chapel　　**50.** *9* together　*5* chain'd　　**51.** *5* heav'd
52. *5* totter'd,　*5–9* well nigh　*5* fall'n　　**53.** *5* frighten'd;　　**54.** *5* seiz'd
1–9 him,　　**56.** *6* judgment. So　*5* seiz'd,•*7–9* seized,　　**58.** *5* Sobb'd　*6* heart;
59. *6* once,　　**60.** *6* hear'd　*1 4 9* youth's,•*2 3* youth's　　**61.** *2–4* Who
sang　　**62.** *1–9* lake　*1–4* savannah,•*5–8* savannah•*9* savanna　　**65.** *1–9* youth,
67. *1–9* entrance　*5* describ'd,•*6* described;•*7–9* described,　　**68.** *5* escap'd.
⁻**68a.** *1–4* MARIA.•*6* MARIA.•*7 8* TERESA.　　**68b.** *2–4* tale.　　**69.** *5* list'ning
1 5–9 sleep,　　**70.** *5* besoil'd　*5* unwip'd　*1 6* tears.—•*5 7–9* tears.　　⁻**71b.** *1–*
4 FOSTER-MOTHER.•*6* FOSTER-MOTHER.•*7 8* SELMA.　　**71b.** *1–3* ship-
board•*4 6* ship-board,•*5 7–9* shipboard　　**72.** *4–9* voyagers　　**73.** *1–9* lands.
74. *4 6* likewise;　*5* return'd　　**75.** *1–9* youth,　　**77.** *1–9* dissuasion,　*5* seiz'd
78. *4 6* And,　*5 7–9* alone　　**80.** *6* more;　*4* supposed•*5* suppos'd,　　**81.** *5* liv'd
1–9 savage men.

⁻**4.** In MS 1 Joseph Cottle inserted "Foster Mother" as speaker of the opening line.
　　12. MS 1 me] Cottle substituted "us,".
　　13. MS 1 Troubled] Possibly written over a deleted word. (The *Osorio* ms here reads "Wilder'd".)
　　34. PR 2 get the] C emended the Melbourne copy to "gather".
　　36. PR 2 gathered] C emended the Melbourne copy to "sought for".
　　41. MS 1 youth.] Cottle substituted "man."
　　42. MS 1 wretch] Cottle substituted "youth".
　　44. PR 5 things:] C emended the punctuation in SH's copy of the second edition to "things!".
　　54. MS 1 him] Cottle substituted "the youth".
　　57. PR *1* cast into that hole] C told Cottle and Biggs to emend "hole" to "cell" when he was preparing the text of PR 2 (*CL* I 594); some states of PR 5 have "den" (see vol III **502.X3** *Remorse* (Printed) TEXT PR 2). C emended the phrase in SH's copy of the second edition to "fetter'd in that Den."; and in Sir George Beaumont's copy of the same to "in that Den chain'd down!"
　　59. PR *2 6* in the cellar] C emended the Melbourne copy of PR 2 and AG's copy of PR 6 to "near the cell", and Francis Wrangham's (?) copy of PR 6 to "near the Cell,". The same emendation is carried over in the copies corrected by JG and AG given above (TEXT PR 6). C emended Sir George Beaumont's copy of PR 5 to "the dungeon,".
　　60. PR 5 distinctly;] C altered SH's copy of the second edition to "distinctly—".

153. THE DUNGEON

A. DATE

Apr–Sept 1797, probably during Jun or after. The lines are taken from vol III
146.X1 *Osorio* v ii 1–30 = **502.X3** *Remorse* (Printed) v i 1–30.

B. TEXTS

1. LB (1798).

2 [=**RT**]. *LB* (1800).

C's letter to Biggs and Cottle of mid-Jul 1800 (*CL* I 593–4) makes it clear
that copy was provided by PR *1* altered according to the instructions in the letter.
Three minor alterations constitute the only difference between the texts.

C's copy at the State Library of Victoria, Melbourne (*821.71L) has his
signature at the end of the poem: "S. T. Coleridge".

C. GENERAL NOTE

The PR *1* printing derives from MS 3 of *Osorio* (HEHL HM 361) ff 102^r–103^r,
in Mrs C's hand corrected by C. The *Osorio* text differs at three points (1 "my"
for "our"; 15 "steam and Vapours" for "steams and vapour"; no space at line
19$^+$). The ms also suggests that the PR *2* punctuation is closer to C's intention. C
reverted to the *Osorio* text of lines 1 and 15 in *Remorse*, but included the space
at line 19$^+$.

The reprintings in *The Courier* (12 Sept 1800), *The Albion* (27 Sept 1800),
and *Cambridge Intelligencer* (27 Oct 1800) follow PR *1* in the first two vari-
ants and PR *2* in the third. They use apostrophes instead of "-ed" in past par-
ticiples, and the two later texts have identical misprints in lines 15 and 19
("streams" for "steams", and "sighs" for "sights"). *The Albion* adds the subtitle
"RECOMMENDED TO THE PERUSAL OF THE DEFENDERS OF BASTILES
IN EVERY COUNTRY.", which *Cambridge Intelligencer* drops. There is no tex-
tual significance in these reprints, or in the Philadelphia reprint of PR *2* and the
version included in *The American First Class Book* ed John Pierpont (Boston,
Mass 1831) 207–8.

The words of the two collated texts of the poem are identical. The RT reproduces
PR *2* exactly, and here the readings of the earlier PR *1* are, exceptionally, given
as variants:

title. *1* THE DUNGEON. • *2 THE DUNGEON.*   **2.** *1* wisdom,
10. *1* plague-spot;   **14.** *1* hour

6–9. Quoted (var) *M Post* (22 Jan 1800) (*EOT—CC—*I 120).

153.X1. THE BROOK

In *BL* C described how, when he was at Stowey, he projected and worked on a loosely structured meditative poem resembling Cowper's *The Task*. He reckoned that the poem would be held together more satisfactorily than Cowper's by following the progress of a stream from its source to the sea (*BL* ch 10—*CC*—I 195–7). His description of the poem also echoes the title of a poem by John Thelwall, who visited him in Stowey during Jul 1797: *The Peripatetic; or, Sketches of the Heart, of Nature and Society* (3 vols 1793). C claims in *BL* to have made studies for the poem, "often moulding my thoughts into verse, with the objects and imagery immediately before my senses" (196). His claim is independently corroborated by Home Office reports, which were prompted by the impression that C was making notes to facilitate a French invasion (A. J. Eagleston "Wordsworth, Coleridge, and the Spy" in *Coleridge: Studies by Several Hands on the Hundredth Anniversary of his Death* ed Edmund Blunden and Earl Leslie Griggs—1934—73–87; Bertram R. Davis "Wordsworth, Coleridge, Southey and the Spy" *TLS*—7 Nov 1968—1261). Fragments in the Gutch Notebook also bear witness to the beginnings of such a poem: for instance, the description which KC gives as *CN* I 213 is of Butterfly Combe, and other fragments might be connected with the same brook, as it flows on past the water-wheel down to Ashford Glen, over the fields to the sea at Kilve. Cf *CN* I 213 and n; **122** *Fragments from the Gutch Notebook* (*n*) EC. WW recorded that even the epigraph had been selected. It was to have been Burns's *Epistle to William Simpson* stanza 15 (*WPW* III 504).

The Home Office reports on how both C and WW were so "very attentive to the River near them" are both dated 11 Aug 1797 (*Studies* 80). A larger part of the poem might have been written than the fragments copied into the Gutch Notebook—e.g. the fragments associated with the course of the stream through Holford Glen which found a place in **156** *This Lime-tree Bower my Prison*, and other descriptions which found their way into this and other poems. But the project appears to have been overtaken and dispersed into shorter pieces after WW arrived at Alfoxden and became C's neighbour. C relinquished the ambition to write such a poem even as he bequeathed it to WW. His poem of "impassioned reflections on men, nature, and society", moving from natural origins to rural cultivation to urban society (*BL* ch 10—*CC*—I 196) left its mark not just on WW's *River Duddon* sonnets, but on WW's plans for *The Recluse*, which he began to articulate in Mar 1798 (*WPW* III 503–4; cf *WL*—*E* rev—212, 214; *CL* IV 574–5: to WW 30 May 1815; *TT* 21 Jul 1832—*CC*—I 307–8).

C's project must be reckoned to date from the period just before and after WW's arrival at Alfoxden, centring on Jul–Aug 1797.

154. MELANCHOLY: A FRAGMENT

Jul–Aug 1797? There are several possibilities. (1) C told William Sotheby, "I wrote the lines at 19" (*CL* II 855: to W. Sotheby 26 Aug 1802)—i.e. in 1790–1, presumably in the summer vacation of 1791 between Christ's Hospital and Cambridge, which C spent at Ottery. (2) In a footnote to the PR 2 version he claimed that they were first published in 1794: this is possible, even though they were not published in *M Chron*, as he said. (3) In a letter dated 13–16 Jun 1796 CL thanked C for a "masterly . . . image of melancholy", which he conjectured had been "disbranched" from one of C's projected hymns (*LL*—M—I 28). If CL refers to these lines, they were probably written in May–early Jun 1796. (4) The *terminus ante quem* is Sept 1797, when C repeated the lines to William Bowles at Donhead (see C's note in Francis Wrangham's (?) copy of PR 2, relating to line 4).

It should be noted that the lines were included in the "Sibylline Leaves" section of PR *3–5*, without any appended date to suggest that they more properly belong to "Juvenile Poems". The probability is that they were written in 1797, some time after the Wordsworths arrived at Stowey in Jul—this on the basis of the particular interest taken by C in hart's tongue from this time, an interest shared by the Wordsworths (see line 6EC). With reference to the remaining possibilities, (1) appears in a context of apology, (2) appears to be a mistake, and (3) is too vague to be conclusive. With reference to the last, though the word "disbranched" is from **101** *Religious Musings* 266, the fragment is in some ways closer to C's contribution to and development beyond **110** *Contributions to "Joan of Arc"*, which he had been discussing with TP and CL at this time (*CL* I 207: to TP 5 May 1796; *LL*—M—I 3, 6, 11, 15–16); and it must be stressed that CL's reference is not certainly to this fragment. From another perspective, the fragment has a good deal in common with a poem like **180** *The Nightingale*.

1. M Post (12 Dec 1797). Unsigned.

1. University of Kentucky Library, Lexington W. Hugh Peal Collection. Single leaf, 38.8×23.9 cm, folded to make four pages; wm bugle within shield, below a crown, above LVG; chain-lines 2.4 cm. Included in an als to William Sotheby, 26 Aug 1802 (*CL* II 855–6).

2. SL (1817).

The proof copy at Yale (In C678 817sa) shows that C at first attempted to substitute "Hart's Tongue" for "Adder's Tongue", but cancelled the substitution and provided a different footnote, apologising for the mistake, in proof. Francis

Wrangham's (?) copy of PR 2 (sold at Christie's 13 Jun 1979 lot 126) contains a comment on the poem.

3 [=RT]. *PW* (1828).

4. PW (1829).

5. PW (1834).

title. *1–5 MELANCHOLY.* | A FRAGMENT.

title fn. *2* First published in the Morning Chronicle, in the year 1794.

1	*1–5*	Stretch'd on a moulder'd Abbey's broadest wall,
	1	Upon
2	*1*	Whose running Ivies propp'd the ruins steep;
	1	Where ruining prop
	2–5	propt
3	☐	Her folded arms wrapping her tatter'd pall,
4	☐	Had MELANCHOLY mus'd herself to sleep
5	☐	The Fern was press'd beneath her hair,
6	☐	The dark green Adder's-tongue was there;
6fn	*1*	A Plant found on old walls, and in wells and mois edges.—It is oftener called the Hart's-tongue.
	1	Asplenium Scolopendrium, more commonly called the Hart's Tongue.
	2	A botanical mistake. The plant, I meant, is called the Hart's Tongue; but this would unluckily spoil the poetical effect. *Cedat ergo Botanice.*
	3 4	A botanical mistake. The plant which the poet here describes is called the Hart's Tongue.
7	*1*	And still, as pass'd the flagging sea-gales weak,
	1	came
	2–5	past sea-gale
8	☐	The long lank leaf bow'd flutt'ring o'er her cheek.
		[*Line-space*]
9	*1–5*	That pallid cheek was flush'd: her eager look
	1	Her
10	☐	Beam'd, eloquent in slumber! Inly wrought
11	☐	Imperfect sounds her moving lips forsook;
12	☐	And her bent forehead work'd with troubled thought.
13	*1 2*	Strange was the dream that fill'd her soul,
	3–5	Strange was the dream—
13.1.1	*1 2*	Nor did not whisp'ring spirits roll
13.1.2	*1 2*	A mystic tumult, and a fateful rhyme,
13.1.3	*1 2*	Mix'd with wild shapings of the unborn time!

title. *3–5* MELANCHOLY. | **1.** *3–5* mouldered   1 Wall,   **2.** *2–5* ivies *3–5* propped   1 Ruins steep, • *2–5* ruins steep—   **3.** 1 Arms   *3–5* tattered 1 Pall   **4.** *2–4* MELANCHOLY • *5* melancholy   **5.** 1 FERN • *2–5* fern   1 Hair; **6.** 1 dark-green   1 ADDER's tongue • *2–4* Adder's Tongue • *5* adder's tongue **7.** *2–5* still   1 Sea-gales   **8.** 1 Leaf   *3–5* bowed   1 *2–5* fluttering   **9.** 1 Cheek *3–5* flushed: 1 Look   **10.** 2 Beam'd • *3–5* Beamed   1 slumber.   *2–5* wrought,

11. 1 Sounds   1 Lips   1 *2–5* forsook,   **12.** 1 Forehead   *3–5* worked
1 Thought.—   **13.1.1.** *2* whispering   **13.1.2.** *2* rhyme   **13.1.3.** *2* Mixt
2 time.

title. Introducing the lines to William Sotheby in ms 1, C got the newspaper right but again gave an almost certainly wrong date: "I wrote the lines at 19—& published them many years ago in the Morning Post as a fragment . . . a school-boy performance" (*CL* ii 855, 856).

2, 4, etc. In PR *1–5* lines 2, 4, 10, 12 are indented, and lines 5–6, 13 have a deeper indent; in PR *1 2* line 13.1.1 has the deeper indent. In ms 1 only lines 5–6 are indented.

4. C marked the line in Francis Wrangham's (?) copy of PR *2*, and added the note: "Bowles borrowed this line, unconsciously I doubt not—I had repeated the poem to him, in my first visit." C also refers to the borrowing in his letter to Sotheby (ms 1). His first visit to Bowles was in Sept 1797, and the borrowing refers to lines 36–7 (var) of Bowles's *Coombe Ellen* (written Sept 1798; pub Bath 1798).

6fn. PR *2 Cedat ergo Botanice.*] Tr "Away therefore with Botany."

155. CONTINUATION OF
THE THREE GRAVES,
BY WILLIAM WORDSWORTH

A. DATE

Jul 1797–Apr 1798. Reed i 189–90 describes WW working towards the poem which eventually became *The Three Graves*, writing stanzas related to but not part of the poem which now exists, between Nov 1796 and Jun 1797; and WW probably handed over this work, and *The Three Graves* generally, to C between 4 Jun and Jul 1797 (see *WPW* i 374; Reed i 198). C said in PR *1* below that the poem had been written more than twelve years earlier, i.e. during the summer of 1797, and several places alluded to were favourites of his from that time onward.

It is possible that the "ballad of about 300 lines" which C told Joseph Cottle in Nov 1797 that he had written (*CL* i 357) refers to this poem and not, as is usually assumed, to **161** *The Rime of the Ancient Mariner*. C mentions the ballad again, as if it was complete, in Jan 1798 and describes it in Feb as having 340 lines (*CL* i 368, 387), whereas the 1798 text of poem **161** has 658. However, the usual assumption is probably correct, for reasons given in VAR **161** sec A.

The last lines of the poem appear to have been written during and after the foggy days of early Mar 1798 and the sudden burst of warmth on 8 Apr, Easter Sunday: see vol i headnote.

B. TEXTS

1. V&A Forster MS 112 ff 32^r–44^r. The first two pages of the Preface and the entire text of the poem are on twelve leaves measuring 11.0/11.3 × 14.2 cm; wm EDMEADS & PINE | 1802; chain-lines 2.7 cm. The third page of the Preface is on the recto of a single leaf, 19.6 × 32.5 cm; wm 1807; chain-lines 2.6 cm; verso blank. Transcript in Sarah Stoddart's hand, corrected by C, preceded by a draft of the Preface in C's hand. Both in ink, on pages numbered 1–3, 3–22.

The size of the paper, the watermarks, and the chain-lines of the smaller leaves are the same as in N18, in use in Malta from Feb 1805: see *CN* II General Note and Errata. (The leaves in N17—in use at the same time for more quotidian entries—are 14.5 cm high, but otherwise identical.) In addition, the LH (inner) margin of several leaves shows signs of having been removed from such a notebook (stitching holes, irregularly trimmed edge), and C remarks in a note inscribed between the title and the text (f 33^v): "N.B. Written by Sarah Stoddart for me, while the book was yet an entire *Blank*. I have not *voluntarily* been guilty of any desecration of holy *Names*." There is slight evidence that the transcript was made at C's dictation (see the errors in lines 110, 230; and cf **176** *Christabel* VAR TEXT MS 6). It must date from some time in the last six months of 1804 and the first two of 1805.

C had reason to consult the volume by Bryan Edwards referred to in his Preface during Dec 1804 (*CN* II 2297), but the Preface was not drafted until 1809, when C thought to incorporate the poem in *The Friend*. The corrections and insertions in Sarah Stoddart's transcript were also made at the later time. Several of them are merely clarifications and overwritings for the sake of the printer.

1. The Friend VI (21 Sept 1809) 89–96 (without stanza-breaks) (*CC*) II 88–96 (var).

Rpt *The Friend* (1812), with a number of typographical errors and variations of capitalisation and punctuation which are not recorded here. The copy of the 1812 reprint which C presented to Hugh J. Rose (Bodleian Arch A A d 111) contains a comment quoted in vol I headnote.

A large part of the 1809 *Friend* text was reprinted in the anonymous, hostile "Commentary on Coleridge's Three Graves" *The Monthly Mirror* NS VIII (1810) 26–31, 98–105, 186–96.

2 [=RT]. *SL* (1817).

Two copies contain corrections in C's hand: JG's (HUL *EC8 C6795 817s (C)) and HNC's (HUL *AC85 L8605 Zy 817c). SC's copy (NYPL Berg Collection Copy 5) contains a correction that may be in C's hand. Francis Wrangham's (?) copy (sold at Christie's 13 Jun 1979 lot 126) contains a long comment on the Preface: see line ⁻1.7EC.

The proofs at Yale (In C678 817sa) are relatively clean. At the same time, the printer claimed in his own "Waste Office Copy" (see vol I annex c 17.2) that C rewrote at least one whole stanza, apparently on p 225 (lines 117–36).

It is impossible to tell from the extant texts which stanzas might have been submitted in a different form.

Rpt *Metrical Romances &c. By S. T. Coleridge* (Isleworth 1825).

3. PW (1828).

4. PW (1829).

5. PW (1834).

The date "1818" is added at the end of the Preface.

C. GENERAL NOTE

There is an untitled, undivided transcript of parts I and II of the poem in DW's hand, with corrections possibly by WW, in the NYPL (Berg Collection). This is the "autograph" ms first published by JDC and afterwards by EHC (var), when it was owned by Lucy E. Watson (née Gillman). It was described as being in C's hand at the Hodgson Sale 20–1 Jun 1929 (when it fetched £590), and is now catalogued as C's by the NYPL. However, there is no doubt about the hand, and other peculiarities such as punctuation are decidedly not C's. The DW transcript overlaps a transcript of part II (only) in WW's and in MH's hand in the Racedown Notebook (DCL MS Verse 11; see *WPW* I 308–12; *WEPF* 305–12, 345–6, 842–66).

divisional title. 2 𝕿𝖍𝖊 | 𝕿𝖍𝖗𝖊𝖊 𝕲𝖗𝖆𝖛𝖊𝖘. • *3 4* THE THREE GRAVES.

title. 1 ~~Fragment~~ The Three Graves, a Sexton's Tale, a Fragment. • *1 THE THREE GRAVES,* | A SEXTON'S TALE. | A FRAGMENT. • *2–5 THE THREE GRAVES.* | A FRAGMENT OF A SEXTON'S TALE.

preface
  1 *1* As I wish to commence the important Subject of—The *Principles* of political
    Justice with a separate Number of THE FRIEND, and shall at the same time
    comply with the ~~wishes~~ communicated to me by ⱡone of my female Readers who
    writes as the representative of many others; I shall conclude this Number with the
    following Fragment, ~~consisting of~~ or the second and third ~~Cantos~~ Parts of a Tale   ⁻1.0.5
    consisting of six. The two last parts may be given hereafter, if the present should
    ?ⱡhappear to have ~~given~~ afforded pleasure, and to have answered the purpose of
    ~~an~~ ?ⱡam a relief and amusement to ~~the Reader's att~~ my Readers. The story ~~retold~~
    as far as it is contained in the first and second parts is, as follows:
  2–5 (The Author has published the following humble fragment, encouraged by
    the decisive recommendation of more than one of our most celebrated living
    Poets. The language was intended to be dramatic; that is suited to the narrator;
    and the metre corresponds to the homeliness of the diction. It is therefore pre-
    sented as the fragment, not of a Poem, but of a common Ballad-tale. Whether   ⁻1.5
    this is sufficient to justify the adoption of such a style, in any metrical com-
    position not professedly ludicrous, the Author is himself in some doubt. At all
    events, it is not presented as Poetry, and it is in no way connected with the Au-
    thor's judgement concerning Poetic diction. Its merits, if any, are exclusively

Pschycological. The story which must have been supposed to have been narrated
    in the ⁻1.10
first and second parts is as follows.

1 *1–5*   Edward₍, a young farmer, meets, at the house of Ellen, her bosom-friend, Mary,
and commences an acquaintance which ends in a mutual attachment. With her
consent and by the advice of their common friend, Ellen, he announces his
hopes and intentions to Mary's Mother, a widow-woman bordering on ~~forty years~~
    her forti- ⁻1.15
eth year, ~~and still retaining a comeliness of person,~~ and ~~indeed~~ from constant
    Health, ~~and~~ the possession of a competent property ~~run~~ and
from having had no other children, but Mary and ~~a Sister~~ another Daughter (the
    Father
dy~~inge~~d in their infancy) ~~possessing~~ retaining for the greater part ~~of~~ her personal
    attractions and
comeliness of appearance; but ~~at the same~~ yet a woman of low education and
    violent temper.

1 *1–5*   The answer, which she at once returned to Edward's application, was remark- ⁻1.20
able—"Well, Edward! you are a handsome young fellow: and you shall have
my Daughter.—From *this* time all their Wooing passed under the Mother's Eyes:
and in fine, she became herself enamoured of ⟨her⟩ future Son in law, and ~~she~~
    prac-
tised every art, both of endearment and of calumny, to transfer his affections
from her daughter to herself. (The outlines of the Tale are positive Facts and of ⁻1.25
no very distant date, tho the author has purposely altered the names and the
scene of action, as well as invented the characters of the parties and the detail of
the Incidents.) Edward however, tho' perplexed by her strange detractions
from her daughter's good qualities, yet in the innocence of his own heart still
mistaking her increasing fondness for motherly affection; she at length, over- ⁻1.30
come by her miserable passion, after much abuse of Mary's Temper & moral
tendencies, exclaimed with violent emotion—O Edward! indeed, indeed, she
is not fit for you—she has not a heart to love you, as you deserve. It is I that
love you! Marry me, Edward! and I will this very day settle all my property on
you.—The Lover's Eyes were now opened: and thus taken by ?~~her~~ surprize,
    whether ⁻1.35
from the effect of the horror, which he felt, acting as it were hysterically on
his nervous ~~g~~ system, or that at the first moment he lost the ⟨sense of the⟩ guilt of
    the
proposal in the feeling of it's strangeness and absurdity, he flung her from him
and burst into a fit of Laughter.—Irritated by this almost to frenzy, the Woman
    fell
on her knees, and in a loud voice, that approach⟨ed⟩ to a Scream, she prayed for a ⁻1.40
Curse both on him and on her own Child. Mary happened to be in the room di-
rectly above them, heard Edward's Laugh, and her Mother's blasphemous Prayer,
and fainted away—He hear~~d~~ing the fall, ran up stairs, and taking her in his arms,
carried her off to ~~his own~~ Ellen's Home; and after some fruitless attempts on her
    part
toward a reconciliation with her Mother, she was married to him.—And here ⁻1.45
the third part of the Tale begins.—

1 *1–5*   I was not led to chuse this story from any partiality to tragic, much less, to

monstrous, events (tho' at the time that I composed the ~~poem, if it may be so called, in~~ verses, somewhat

more than twelve years ago, I was less averse to such subjects than at present)

but from finding in ~~the occurrence~~ it a striking proof of the ⟨possible⟩ effect on

    the imagination   ‾1.50

from an Idea violently and suddenly imprest on it. I had been reading Bryan

Edwards's account of the effects of the *Oby* Witch-craft on the Negros in the

West Indies, and Hearne's deeply interesting Anecdotes of similar workings on

the imagination of the Copper Indians: **T**(those of my Readers, who have ~~the~~ it in

their power, will be well repayed for the trouble of referring to those Works for   ‾1.55

the passages alluded to.) and I conceived the design of shewing that instances

of this kind are not peculiar to savage or barbarous tribes, and of illustrating

the mode, in which the mind is affected in these cases, and the progress and

symptoms of the morbid action on the fancy from the beginning.—

1 *1–5*   The Tale is supposed to be ~~told~~ narrated by an old Sexton in a country Church- ‾1.60

yard to a Traveller, whose curiosity had been awakened by the appearance of

three Graves, close by each other, ~~the first with the name~~ to two only of which

    there were Grave-stones.

On the first of these was the Name, and Dates, as usual: on the second no name,

but only a Date, and the Words: The Mercy of God is infinite.

5

                                                               1818. ‾1.65

1 *1*   The language was intended to be *dramatic*, that is, suited to the narrator, and

the metre to correspond to the homeliness of the Diction: and for this reason

I here present ⟨it⟩ not as the Fragment of a *Poem*, but of a Tale in ~~Metre~~ the

common ballad-metre.)

‾1.70 1   IIII

‾1.71 1   1

‾1.72 *3 4*   THE THREE GRAVES.

  1 □   The Grapes upon the vicar's wall

  2 1 *1*   Were ripe as they could be;

    2–5   ripe

  3 □   And yellow Leaves in sun and wind

  4 □   Were falling from the Tree.

           [*Line-space*]

 ‾5 1   2

  5 1   ~~High o~~On the hedge-elms in the ⟨narrow⟩ lane

   ⊠1   On   narrow

  6 ⊠2   Still swung the spikes of Corn:

    2   strikes

  7 □   Dear Lord! it seems but yesterday—

  8 1   Youn~~d~~g Edward's marriage-morn.

   ⊠1   Young

           [*Line-space*]

 ‾9 1   3

  9 □   Up thro' that wood behind the Church

 10 □   There leads from Edward's door

 11 □   A mossy Track, all overbough'd

 12 □   For half a mile or more.

[*Line-space*]
⁻13 1   4
13 ☐   And from their House-door by that Track
14 ☐   The Bride and Bride groom went:
15 ☐   Sweet Mary, tho' she was not gay,
16 ☐   Seem'd chearful and content.
[*Line-space*]
⁻17 1   5
17 ☐   But when they to the Church yard came,
18 ☐   I've heard poor Mary say,
19 ☐   As soon as she stepp'd into the Sun,
20 ☐   Her heart—it died away.
[*Line-space*]
⁻21 1   6
21 ☐   And when the Vicar join'd their hands,
22 ☐   Her limbs did creep and freeze;
23 1 *1*   But when he pray'd, she thought she saw
   2–5   they
24 ☐   Her Mother on her knees.
[*Line-space*]
⁻25 1   7
25 ☐   And o'er the Church-path they return'd—
26 ☐   I saw poor Mary's back
27 ☐   Just as she stepp'd beneath the boughs
28 ☐   Into the mossy track.
[*Line-space*]
⁻29 1   8
29 ☐   Her feet upon the mossy track
30 ☐   The Married Maiden set:
31 ☐   That moment—I have heard her say—
32 ☐   She wish'd she could forget.
[*Line-space*]
⁻33 1   9
33 ☐   The Shade o'erflush'd her limbs with heat—
34 ☐   Then came a chill like Death:
35 ☐   And when the merry Bells rang out,
36 ☐   They seem'd to stop her Breath.
[*Line-space*]
⁻37 1   10
37 ☐   Beneath the foulest Mother's curse
38 ☐   No child could ever thrive:
39 ☐   A Mother is a Mother still,
40 ☐   The holiest Thing alive!
[*Line-space*]
⁻41 1   11
41 1   So five Months pass'd: ~~this~~e Mother ~~foul~~ still
   ⊠1   the   still
42 ☐   Would never heal the strife;
43 ☐   But Edward was a loving Man

44 □   And Mary a fond wife.
        [*Line-space*]
⁻45 1   12
45 □   "My Sister may not visit us,
46 □   "My Mother says her, nay:
47 □   "O Edward! you are all to me,
48 □   "I wish for your sake, I could be
49 1   "More lifesome and more ~~glad~~ gay.
⊠1   gay.
        [*Line-space*]
⁻50 1   13
50 □   "I'm dull and sad! indeed, indeed
51 □   "I know, I have no reason!
52 □   "Perhaps, I am not well in health,
53 □   "And 'tis a gloomy season.
        [*Line-space*]
⁻54 1   14
54 □   'Twas a drizzly Time—no ice, no snow!
55 □   And on the few fine days
56 □   She stirr'd not out, lest she might meet
57 □   Her Mother in the ways.
        [*Line-space*]
⁻58 1   15
58 □   But Ellen, spite of miry ways
59 1 *1* And weather dank and dreary,
   2–5   dark
60 □   Trudg'd every day to Edward's house
61 □   And made them all more cheary.
        [*Line-space*]
⁻62 1   16
62 □   O! Ellen was a faithful Friend,
63 □   More dear than any Sister!
64 □   As chearful too, as singing Lark;
65 □   And she ne'er left them till twas dark,
66 □   And then they always miss'd her.
        [*Line-space*]
⁻67 1   17
67 □   And now Ash wednesday came—that day
68 □   But few to Church repair:
69 □   For on that day you know, we read
70 □   The Commination Prayer.
        [*Line-space*]
⁻71 1   18
71 □   Our late old Vicar, a kind Man
72 □   Once, Sir! he said to me,
73 □   He wish'd that service was clean out
74 □   Of our good Liturgy.
        [*Line-space*]

```
⁻75  1                    19
75  □    The Mother walk'd into the Church—
76  □    To Ellen's seat she went:
77  □    Tho' Ellen always kept her Church
78  □    All Church-days during Lent.
```
         [*Line-space*]
```
⁻79  1                    20
79  □    And gentle Ellen welcom'd her
80  □    With courteous looks and mild:
81  □    Thought she, "what if her heart should melt
82  □    And all be reconcil'd!
```
         [*Line-space*]
```
⁻83  1                    21
83  □    The Day was scarcely like a Day—
84  □    The Clouds were black outright:
85  □    And many a night with half a moon
86  □    I've seen the Church more light.
```
         [*Line-space*]
```
⁻87  1                    22
87  □    The wind was wild; against the Glass
88  □    The rain did beat and bicker;
89  1 1  The Church-tower  singing  over head—
     2                     swaying
     3–5                   swinging
90  1 1  You could     not hear the Vicar!
     2–5          scarce could
```
         [*Line-space*]
```
⁻91  1                    23
91  □    And then and there the Mother knelt
92  □    And audibly she cried—
93  □    "O may a clinging curse consume
94  □    "This woman by my side!
```
         [*Line-space*]
```
⁻95  1                    24
95  □    "O hear me, hear me, Lord in heaven,
96  1 1 2  "Altho thou take my life—
     3–5          you
97  □    "O curse this woman at whose house
98  □    "Young Edward woo'd his wife.
```
         [*Line-space*]
```
⁻99  1                    25
99   □    "By night and day, in bed and bower,
100  □    "O let her cursed be!
101  □    So having pray'd, steady and slow
102  □    She rose up from her knee;
103  □    And left the Church, nor e'er again
104  □    The Church-door enter'd she.
```
         [*Line-space*]

⁻105 1   26
105 ☐   I saw poor Ellen kneeling still,
106 ☐   So pale! I guess'd not why:
107 ☐   When she stood up, there plainly was
108 ☐   A Trouble in her Eye.
        [*Line-space*]

⁻109 1   27
109 ☐   And when the Prayers were done, we all
110 1   Came r?award and ask'd her, why:
  ⊠1   round
111 ☐   Giddy she seem'd and, sure, there was,
112 ☐   A Trouble in her eye.
        [*Line-space*]

⁻113 1   28
113 ☐   But ere she from the Church-door stepp'd,
114 1   She smil'd and told ?me us why:
  ⊠1   us
115 ☐   "It was a wicked Woman's curse,
116 ☐   "Quoth she, and what care I?
        [*Line-space*]

⁻117 1   29
117 ☐   She smil'd and smil'd, & pass'd it off
118 ☐   Ere from the door she stepp'd—
119 ☐   But all agree, it would have been
120 ☐   Much better, had she wept.
        [*Line-space*]

⁻121 1   30
121 ☐   And if her heart was not at ease,
122 ☐   This was her constant cry—:
123 ☐   "It was a wick⟨e⟩d Woman's curse—
124 ☐   "God's good! and what care I?
        [*Line-space*]

⁻125 1   31
125 ☐   There was a Hurry in her Looks,
126 ☐   Her struggles she redoubled:
127 ☐   "It was a wicked Woman's curse,
128 ☐   "And why should I be troubled?
        [*Line-space*]

⁻129 1   32
129 ☐   These tears will come! I dandled her,
130 ☐   When 'twas the merest fairy!—
131 ☐   Good creature!—and she hid it all—
132 ☐   She told it not to Mary.
        [*Line-space*]

⁻133 1   33
133 ☐   But Mary heard the Tale—her arms
134 ☐   Round Ellen's neck she threw:
135 ☐   "O Ellen, Ellen! She curs'd me,

| 136 | 1 *1* | "And now she has curs'd you! |
| | *2–5* | hath |

[*Line-space*]

⁻137	1	34
137	☐	I saw young Edward by himself
138	☐	Stalk fast adown the lea:
139	☐	He snatch'd a stick from every Fence,
140	☐	A Twig from every Tree.

[*Line-space*]

⁻141	1	35
141	☐	He snapt them still with hand or knee,
142	☐	And then away they flew!
143	☐	As if with his uneasy Limbs
144	☐	He knew not what to do!

[*Line-space*]

⁻145	1	36
145	☐	You see, good Sir! that single Hill?
146	⊠*1*	His Farm lies underneath:
	1	This
147	☐	He heard it there—he heard it all,
148	☐	And only gnash'd his teeth.

[*Line-space*]

⁻149	1	37
149	1	~~Nonow~~ Ellen was a darling Love
	⊠1	Now
150	☐	In all his joys and cares;
151	☐	And Ellen's name and Mary's name
152	☐	Fast link'd they both together came,
153	☐	Whene'er he said his prayers.

[*Line-space*]

⁻154	1	38
154	☐	And in the moment of his Prayers
155	☐	He lov'd them both alike:
156	☐	Yea, both sweet names with one sweet Joy
157	☐	Upon his heart did strike.

[*Line-space*]

⁻158	1	39
158	☐	He reach'd his home, and by his looks
159	☐	They saw his inward strife;
160	☐	And they clung round him with their arms,
161	☐	Both Ellen and his Wife.

[*Line-space*]

⁻162	1	40
162	☐	And Mary could not check her tears,
163	☐	So on his breast she bow'd,
164	☐	Then frenzy melted into grief
165	☐	And Edward wept aloud.

[*Line-space*]

⁻166 1   41
166 □   Dear Ellen did not weep at all,
167 1 *1*   But closelier she did cling;
    2–5   did she
168 □   And turn'd her face, and look'd as if
169 □   She saw some frightful Thing!
           [*Line-space*]
⁻170.1 1   ₦ The Three Graves, a Sexton's Tale | Part the IVth.
     1   *THE THREE GRAVES,* | A SEXTON'S TALE. | PART IV.
     2   PART IV.
     3–5   THE THREE GRAVES. | PART IV.
           [*Line-space*]
⁻170.2 1   1
170 □   To see a man tread over Graves
171 □   I hold it no good mark:
172 □   'Tis wicked in the Sun and Moon
173 □   And bad luck in the dark.
           [*Line-space*]
⁻174 1   2
174 □   You see that Grave? The Lord he gives,
175 □   The Lord he takes away!
176 ⊠*2*   O   Sir! the Child of my old Age,
    2   Oh! 'tis
177 □   Lies there, as cold as clay.
           [*Line-space*]
⁻178 1   3
178 □   Except that Grave, you scarce see one
179 □   That was not dug by me:
180 1 *1*   I'd rather dance upon them all
    2–5   'em
181 □   Than tread upon these Three!
           [*Line-space*]
⁻182 1   4
182 □   "Aye Sexton! tis a touching Tale—
183 □   You, Sir! are but a Lad:
184 □   This month I'm in my seventieth year
185 □   And still it makes me sad.
           [*Line-space*]
⁻186 1   5
186 □   And Mary's Sister told it me
187 □   For three good hours and more;
188 □   Tho' I had heard it in the main
189 □   From Edward's self before.
           [*Line-space*]
⁻190 1   6
190 □   Well, it pass'd off—the gentle Ellen
191 □   Did well-nigh dote on Mary;
192 □   And she went oftner than before,
193 □   And Mary lov'd her more and more;

194 ☐   She manag'd all the Dairy.
         [*Line-space*]
⁻195 1   7
195 ☐   To market She on Market days,
196 ☐   To church on Sundays came:
197 ☐   All seem'd the same—all seem'd so, Sir!
198 ☐   But all was not the same.
         [*Line-space*]
⁻199 1   8
199 ☐   Had Ellen lost her mirth? O no!
200 ☐   But she was seldom chearful;
201 ☐   And Edward look'd as if he thought
202 ☐   That Ellen's mirth was fearful.
         [*Line-space*]
⁻203 1   9
203 ☐   When by herself she to herself
204 ☐   Must sing some merry rhyme—
205 ☐   She could not now be glad for hours
206 ☐   Yet silent all the time.
         [*Line-space*]
⁻207 1   10
207 ☐   And when she sooth'd her friend, thro' all
208 ☐   Her soothing words twas plain
209 ☐   She had a sore grief of her own,
210 ☐   A Haunting in her brain.
         [*Line-space*]
⁻211 1   11
211 ☐   And oft she said, "I'm not grown thin!
212 ☐   And then her wrist she spann'd *l*:
213 ☐   And once when Mary was downcast,
214 ☐   She took her by the hand,
215 ☐   And gaz'd upon her, and at first
216 ☐   She gently press'd her hand,
         [*Line-space*]
⁻217 1   12
217 ☐   Then harder, till her Grasp at length
218 ☐   Did gripe like a convulsion:
219 ☐   "Alas! said she—"we ne'er can be
220 ☐   "Made happy by compulsion.
         [*Line-space*]
⁻221 1   13
221 ☐   And once her both arms suddenly
222 ☐   Round Mary's neck she flung:
223 ☐   And her heart panted, and she felt
224 ☐   The words upon her tongue.
         [*Line-space*]
⁻225 1   14
225 ☐   She felt them coming, but no power
226 ☐   Had she the words to smother;

227 ☐   And with a kind of shriek she cried,
228 1   "O Christ! ~~how~~ you're like your Mother!—
   ☒1   you're
         [*Line-space*]
⁻229 1   15
229 ☐   So gentle Ellen now no more
230 1   C?~~auld~~ould make this sad house cheary;
   ☒1   Could
231 ☐   And Mary's melancholy ways
232 ☐   Drove Edward wild and weary.
         [*Line-space*]
⁻233 1   16
233 ☐   Lingering he rais'd his latch at eve
234 ☐   Tho' tir'd in heart and limb:
235 ☐   He lov'd no other place, and yet
236 ☐   Home was no home to Him.
         [*Line-space*]
⁻237 1   17
237 ☐   One evening he took up a book
238 ☐   And nothing in it read;
239 ☐   Then flung it down, and groaning cried,
240 ☐   "O Heaven! that I were dead!
         [*Line-space*]
⁻241 1   18
241 ☐   Mary look'd up into his face,
242 ☐   And nothing to him said;
243 ☐   She try'd to smile and on his arm
244 ☐   Mournfully lean'd her head!
         [*Line-space*]
⁻245 1   19
245 ☐   And he burst into tears, and fell
246 ☒*1* Upon his knees in prayer:
   1   prayers;
247 ☐   "Her heart is broke—O God! my Grief—
248 ☐   "It is too great to bear!
         [*Line-space*]
⁻249 1   20
249 ☐   'Twas such a foggy time, as makes
250 ☐   Old Sextons, Sir! like me,
251 ☐   Rest on their spades to cough: the Spring
252 ☐   Was late uncommonly.
         [*Line-space*]
⁻253 1   21
253 ☐   And then the hot days, all at once
254 1 *1* They came, one knew not how:
   2–5   we
255 ☐   You look'd about for shade, when scarce
256 ☐   A Leaf was on a Bough.
         [*Line-space*]

⁻257	1	22
257	□	It happen'd then (—twas in the bower
258	□	A furlong up the wood—
259	□	Perhaps you know the place, and yet
260	□	I scarce know how you should.)
		[*Line-space*]
⁻261	1	23
261	□	No path leads thither: 'tis not nigh
262	□	To any pasture plot;
263	□	But cluster'd near the chattering brook
264	1 *1*	Some Hollies mark the spot.
	2–5	Lone mark'd
		[*Line-space*]
⁻265	1	24
265	□	Those Hollies, of themselves, a shape
266	□	As of an arbour took;
267	□	A close round Arbour, and it stands
268	1 *1*	Not three strides from the Brook.
	2–5	a
		[*Line-space*]
⁻269	1	25
269	□	Within this Arbour, which was still
270	□	With scarlet berries hung,
271	1	Were these three ~~Dears,~~ Friends, one Sunday Morn,
	☒1	Friends,
272	□	Just as the first bell rung—
		[*Line-space*]
⁻273	1	26
273	□	'Tis sweet to hear a brook: 'tis sweet
274	□	To hear the Sabbath Bell!
275	□	'Tis sweet to hear them both at once
276	□	Deep in a woody Dell.
		[*Line-space*]
⁻277	1	27
277	□	His Limbs along the moss, his head
278	□	Upon a mossy heap,
279	□	With shut-up senses Edward lay:
280	□	That Brook, e'en on a working-day,
281	□	Might chatter one to sleep.
		[*Line-space*]
⁻282	1	28
282	□	And he had pass'd a restless night
283	□	And was not well in health!
284	□	The Women sate down by his side
285	□	And talk'd as twere by stealth.
		[*Line-space*]
⁻286	1	29
286	□	"The Sun peeps thro' the close thick Leaves,
287	□	"See, dearest Ellen! see—

288 1   "'Tis ~~in~~ *in* the Leaves! a little Sun,
   ⊠1   in
289 □   "No bigger than your ee.
          [*Line-space*]
⁻290 1   30
290 □   A tiny Sun! and it has got
291 □   A perfect glory too:
292 1   ⟨Ten thousands threads and hairs of light⟩
   ⊠1   Ten thousand threads and hairs of light
293 □   Make up a glory gay and bright
294 □   Round that small orb so blue!
          [*Line-space*]
⁻295 1   31
295 □   And then they argued of those Rays
296 □   What colour they might be:
297 ⊠*1*   Says this, "they're mostly green! says that,
   1   say
298 □   "They're amber-like to me.
          [*Line-space*]
⁻299 1   32
299 □   So they sate chatting, while bad thoughts
300 □   Were troubling Edward's rest;
301 □   But soon they heard his hard quick pants
302 □   And the thumping in his breast.
          [*Line-space*]
⁻303 1   33
303 □   "A Mother too"! these self-same words
304 □   Did Edward mutter plain;
305 □   His face was drawn back on itself
306 □   With horror and huge pain.
          [*Line-space*]
⁻307 1   34
307 □   Both groan'd at once, for both knew well
308 □   What thoughts were in his mind
309 □   When he wak'd up, and star'd like one
310 □   That hath been just struck blind.
          [*Line-space*]
⁻311 1   35
311 1   He sate upright; and ~~with quick voice~~ ere the Dream
   ⊠1   ⟵———e're———⟶
312 1   ~~Which his eyes seem'd to start;~~ Had had time to depart,
   ⊠1   ⟵—————Had—————⟶
313 □   "O God, forgive me! (he exclaim'd)
314 □   "I have torn out her heart!—
          [*Line-space*]
⁻315 1   36
315 □   Then Ellen shriek'd, and forthwith burst
316 □   Into ungentle laughter;
317 □   And Mary shiver'd, where she sate

318 □   And never she smil'd after!
318⁺ *2–5*   Carmen reliquum in futurum tempus relegatum. To-morrow!
    and To-Morrow and To-morrow!—

title. *3–5* THE THREE GRAVES. | **preface.** ⁻**1.0.3.** *1* wishes *1* by one
1 Readers,   ⁻**1.0.4.** *1* others: ⁻**1.0.5.** *1* Fragment, or   1 second and third
~~Cantos~~ Parts • *1* third and fourth parts   ⁻**1.0.7.** *1* should appear to have afforded
⁻**1.0.8.** *1* of a *1* to my   ⁻**1.0.9.** *1* story, as   *1* parts, is   ⁻**1.8.** *5* poetry,
⁻**1.9.** *3–5* judgment   *5* poetic   ⁻**1.10.** *3 4* Psychological. • *5* psychological.
2 must have been • *3–5* must be   ⁻**1.12.** *1–5* Edward,   *1–5* meets   *3–5* Ellen
2–5 bosom-friend   ⁻**1.13.** *1–5* acquaintance,   ⁻**1.14.** *1–5* consent,   *2–5* friend
⁻**1.15.** *5* mother,   *1–5* on her   ⁻**1.16.** *1–5* year, and from   *2–5* health,   1 ~~and~~
the • *1–5* the   *1–5* property, and   ⁻**1.17.** *1–5* children   *1–5* and another   *3–*
5 daughter   *5* father   ⁻**1.18.** *1–5* died   *1–5* infancy,) • *5* infancy),   1 ~~possessing~~
retaining • *1–3* retaining, • *4 5* retaining   *1–5* part, her   ⁻**1.19.** *1–5* but a
⁻**1.20.** *1–5* answer   *2–5* application   ⁻**1.21.** *2–5* fellow,   ⁻**1.22.** *2–4* Daughter."
From • *5* daughter." From   *3–5* this   *2–5* wooing   *5* mother's   1 *1* Eyes: •
2 eyes; • *3–5* eye;   ⁻**1.23.** *2 5* and,   *1–5* her   *2–4* Son-in-law, • *5* son-in-law,
⁻**1.23–4.** *1–5* and practised   ⁻**1.25.** *1–4* Facts, • *5* facts,   ⁻**1.26.** *1–5* though
⁻**1.28.** *2–5* incidents.)   *1–5* Edward,   *1–5* though   ⁻**1.30.** *1* encreasing *4 5* length
⁻**1.31.** *2–5* temper   *1–5* and   ⁻**1.32.** *5* "O   ⁻**1.33.** *1–5* love you   ⁻**1.34–**
5. *5* on you."   ⁻**1.35.** *1–5* eyes *3 4* opened • *5* opened;   *1–4* by surprize, •
5 by surprise,   ⁻**1.36.** *1–5* horror   ⁻**1.37.** 1 *ẛ* system, • *1–5* system,   *1* the
sense of the guilt • *2–5* the sense of guilt   ⁻**1.38.** *2–5* its   ⁻**1.39.** *1* Laughter. •
2–5 laughter.   *2–5* woman   ⁻**1.40.** *3 5* voice   *1–5* approached   *2–5* scream,
⁻**1.41.** *5* curse   *5* child.   ⁻**1.42.** *2–4* laugh • *5* laugh,   *5* mother's   *2–5* prayer,
⁻**1.43.** *2–5* away. He,   *1–5* hearing   *1* upstairs,   ⁻**1.44.** *1–5* to Ellen's   *2–5* home;
1 part,   ⁻**1.45.** *5* mother,   ⁻**1.46.** *1–5* begins.   ⁻**1.47.** *5* choose   *2–5* less
⁻**1.48.** *1–5* monstrous   *1–5* (though *1–5* the verses,   ⁻**1.49.** *1–5* present),
⁻**1.50.** *1–5* in it   *1–5* possible   *1–5* imagination,   ⁻**1.51.** *3–5* impressed
⁻**1.52.** 1 *1* effects • *2–5* effect   *5* Oby *1 4* Witchcraft • *2 3* Witchraft • *5* witchcraft
1–5 Negroes   ⁻**1.53.** *2–4* West-Indies,   *5* anecdotes   ⁻**1.54.** *2–5* Indians
1–5 (those   *2–4* Readers • *5* readers   *1–5* have it   ⁻**1.55.** *2–5* power   *1–5* repaid
1 Works, • *2–5* works   ⁻**1.56.** *1 3–5* alluded to) • *2* alluded to);   *1* shewing, •
5 showing   ⁻**1.58.** *1–5* mode   ⁻**1.59.** *1–5* beginning.   ⁻**1.60.** *1–5* be
narrated   *1–5* Sexton,   ⁻**1.60–1.** *2–5* church-yard,   ⁻**1.61.** *2–4* Traveller •
5 traveller   ⁻**1.62.** *2–5* graves,   *1–5* other, to   ⁻**1.62–3.** *2–5* grave-stones.
⁻**1.63.** *2–5* name,   *2–5* dates,   *2–5* second,   ⁻**1.64.** *2–5* date,   *2–5* words,
5 "The   *2–4* infinite.) • *5* infinite.")   ⁻**1.67.** *1* reason,   ⁻**1.68.** *1* it *1* in the
⁻**1.69.** *1* ballad   **1.** *5* grapes   *2–5* Vicar's   **3.** *1–5* leaves   *2–4* Sun   *2–4* Wind
4. *1 5* tree.   **6.** *2–5* corn: **9.** *2–5* through   *2–5* church,   **11.** *2–5* track,
1 over-bough'd • *2* over bough'd, • *3–5* over boughed,   **13.** *2–5* house-door   *2–*
5 track   **14.** *5* bride *1* Bride-groom • *2–4* Bridegroom • *5* bridegroom   *2–5* went;
15. *3–5* though   **16.** *3–5* Seemed *1 3–5* cheerful   **17.** *2–5* church-yard
19. *2* stept • *3–5* stepped   *5* sun,   **20.** *2 3 5* heart • *4* Heart   **21.** *3–5* joined
23. *3–5* prayed   **24.** *2–5* mother   **25.** *2–5* church-path   *3–5* returned—
26. *2–5* back,   **27.** *2* stept • *3–5* stepped   **28.** *3* track   **30.** *2–5* married
maiden   **32.** *3–5* wished   **33.** *2 3 5* shade *1 2* o'er-flush'd • *3–5* o'er-flushed
34. *2–5* death: **35.** *2–5* bells   **36.** *3–5* seemed   *2–5* breath.   **37.** *5* mother's

39. *5* mother . . . mother   *1* still;   **40.** *1–5* thing alive.   **41.** *2–5* months
3–5 passed: *5* mother   **43.** *2–4* man • *5* man,   **45.** *2–5* sister   **46.** *2–5* My
2–5 mother   *2–5* her   **47.** *2–5* O   **48.** *2–5* I wish   *2–5* sake   **49.** *2–5* More
lifesome   **50.** *2–4* I'm   **51.** *2–5* I know   **52.** *2–5* Perhaps   *4* health.
53. *2–5* And   *1–5* season."   **54.** *1* Twas   *2–5* time—   **56.** *3–5* stirred   *1* out
57. *2 5* mother   **60.** *3–5* Trudged   *2–5* house,   **61.** *3–5* cheery.   **62.** *2–5* Oh!
5 friend,   **63.** *5* sister!   **64.** *2–5* cheerful too   *2–5* lark;   **65.** *1–5* 'twas
66. *3–5* missed   **67.** *1* Ash-wednesday • *2–5* Ash-Wednesday   **68.** *5* church
69. *2–5* know   **70.** *1–5* prayer.   **71.** *1* Man, • *2–5* man,   **72.** *3–5* Sir,
73. *3–5* wished   **74.** *5* liturgy.   **75.** *5* mother   *3–5* walked   *2–5* church—
77. *3–5* Though   *2–5* church   **78.** *2–5* church-days   **79.** *3–5* welcomed
80. *4* mild.   **81.** *1 3–5* she   *2–5* melt,   **82.** *1 2* reconcil'd!" • *3–5* reconciled!"
83. *2–5* day . . . day—   **84.** *2–5* clouds   **85.** *2–5* night,   *2–4* Moon, • *5* moon,
86. *2–5* church   **87.** *2–5* glass   **89.** *2–5* church-tower   *2* head • *3–5* head,
91. *5* mother   *2–5* knelt,   **93.** *2* Oh! • *3–5* "Oh!   **94.** *2 5* This   **95.** *2–5* O
1–5 Heaven,   **96.** *2* Altho • *3–5* Although   **97.** *2–5* O   *2–5* woman,   **98.** *2–
5* Young   *2* wooed • *3* woe'd   **99.** *2–5* By   **100.** *2–5* O   *1 5* be!" • *2* be!!! •
3 4 be!!!"   **101.** *1* pray'd • *3–5* prayed,   *1–5* slow,   **102.** *2–4* knee! • *5* knee,
103. *2–5* church,   **104.** *2–5* church-door   *1 3–5* entered   **106.** *5* pale,   *3–
5* guessed   **108.** *2–5* trouble   *2–5* eye.   **109.** *2–5* prayers   **110.** *3–5* asked
2–5 her   **111.** *2* seem'd, • *3–5* seemed,   *3* and, • *4 5* and   *2–5* was   **112.** *2–
5* trouble   **113.** *2–5* church-door   *2* stepp'd • *3–5* stepped   **114.** *3–5* smiled
115. *2–5* woman's   *2* curse" • *3–5* curse,"   **116.** *2–5* Quoth   *2–5* "and   *1–
5* I?"   **117.** *2* smil'd, and smil'd, • *3–5* smiled, and smiled,   *1–5* and   *3–5* passed
118. *2* E'er   *2–5* stept—   **119.** *1–5* agree   **120.** *2–5* better   **122.** *2–5* cry—
123. *1–5* wicked   *2–5* woman's   **124.** *2–5* God's good,   *1–5* I?"   **125.** *2–
5* hurry   *2–5* looks,   **127.** *2–5* woman's   **128.** *2–5* And   *1–5* troubled?"
129. *2–5* come—   *2–5* her   **130.** *2–5* fairy—   **131.** *2–5* creature!   *2–5* all:
133. *2–5* tale.   **134.** *2–5* threw;   **135.** *2–5* Ellen, she   *3–5* cursed   **136.** *2–
5* And   *3–5* cursed   *1–5* you!"   **138.** *2–5* lee,   **139.** *2* snatcht • *3–5* snatched
2–5 fence,   **140.** *2–5* twig   *2–5* tree.   **141.** *3–5* snapped   **143.** *2–5* limbs
145. *2–5* sir!   *2–5* hill?   **146.** *2–5* farm   **147.** *2–5* there,   **148.** *3–5* gnashed
149. *2–5* love   **150.** *2–5* cares: **152.** *2* Fast-link'd • *3–5* Fast-linked
154. *1* Moment   *2–5* prayers   **155.** *3–5* loved   **156.** *2–5* joy   **157.** *2–
5* strike!   **159.** *2–5* strife: **161.** *2–5* wife.   **163.** *2* bow'd; • *3–5* bowed;
164. *2–4* Frenzy   *2–4* Grief, • *5* grief,   **167.** *2–5* cling,   **168.** *3–5* turned
2–5 face   *3–5* looked   **169.** *2–5* thing.   **170.** *5* graves   **171.** *2–5* mark;
172. *5* sun   *1–4* Moon, • *5* moon,   **173.** *2–5* dark!   **174.** *5* grave?   *2* Lord,
175. *2–4* Lord,   *2–5* away: **176.** *2–5* child   *1* Age • *2–5* age   **177.** *2–5* there
178. *2–5* grave,   **179.** *2–4* me • *5* me;   **181.** *2–5* three!   **182.** *2–4* "Aye, •
5 "Ay,   *1–5* 'tis   *2–5* tale."   **183.** *2* "You,   *2–5* lad;   **184.** *2–5* year,
186. *2–5* sister   *2–5* me,   **188.** *3–5* Though   *2–5* it,   *2–5* main,   **189.** *2–4* self,
190. *2–5* Well!   *3–5* passed   *2–5* off!   **191.** *2–5* well nigh   **192.** *1* oft'ner •
2–5 oftener   **193.** *3–5* loved   *2–5* more: **194.** *3–5* managed   *2–5* dairy.
195. *2–5* she   *1* Market Days, • *2–5* market-days,   **196.** *2–5* came;   **197.** *3–
5* seemed   *2–5* same: *3–5* seemed   **198.** *2–5* same!   **199.** *2–5* Oh!
200. *2–5* cheerful;   **201.** *3–5* looked   **203.** *2–5* by herself,   **204.** *2* rhime; •
3–5 rhyme;   **205.** *2–5* hours,   **207.** *3–5* soothed   *3–5* through   **208.** *1–
5* 'twas   **210.** *2–5* haunting   **211.** *2–5* I'm   *1* thin!"   **212.** *1* spann'd; •

2 spann'd: • *3* spanned: • *4 5* spanned;   **213.** *2–5* down-cast,   **215.** *3–5* gazed
216. *3–5* pressed   *2–5* hand;   **217.** *2–5* grasp   **218.** *2–5* convulsion!
219. *1* Alas!" • *2–5* Alas!   *2–5* she, we   **220.** *2–5* Made   *1* compulsion." •
2–5 compulsion!   **222.** *2–5* flung,   **228.** *2–5* "Oh   *2* Mother!' • *3 4* Mother!" •
5 mother!"   **230.** *3–5* cheery;   **233.** *3–5* raised   *2–5* eve,   **234.** *2–5* Though
tired   **235.** *3–5* loved   **236.** *2–5* him.   **237.** *2–5* book,   **240.** *2* Oh! •
3–5 "Oh!   *2* dead. • *3–5* dead."   **241.** *3–5* looked   **243.** *2–5* tried   *1–5* smile,
244. *2–5* leaned   *2–5* head.   **247.** *2* Her   *2–5* broke!   *2–5* grief,   **248.** *2–5* It
1 3–5 bear!"   **249.** *1–5* time   **250.** *1* Sexton's • *5* sextons,   **251.** *1–5* cough;
2–5 spring   **253.** *2–5* once,   **255.** *3–5* looked   **256.** *2–5* leaf   *2–5* bough.
257. *3–5* happened   *2–5* ('twas   **258.** *2–5* wood: **260.** *1* should). • *2* shou'd) •
3 4 should) • *5* should,—)   **261.** *2–5* thither,   **262.** *2–5* pasture-plot;   **263.** *3–*
5 clustered   *2–5* brook,   **264.** *2–5* hollies   *3–5* marked   **265.** *2–5* hollies   *2–*
5 themselves   **266.** *2* arbor   *2–5* took,   **267.** *2–5* close,   *2* arbor; • *3–5* arbour;
268. *2–5* brook.   **269.** *2* arbor, • *3–5* arbour,   **271.** *2–5* friends,   *2 3* morn, •
4 5 morn   **272.** *2–5* rung.   **273.** *2–5* brook,   **274.** *2–5* Sabbath-bell,
275. *2–5* once,   **276.** *2–5* dell.   **277.** *2–5* limbs   **279.** *2–5* senses,   **280.** *2–*
5 brook   *2–5* working day   **282.** *3–5* passed   *2 5* night,   **283.** *2–5* health;
284. *2–5* women sat   *2–5* side,   **285.** *3–5* talked   *1–5* 'twere   **286.** *5* sun
3–5 through   *2–5* leaves,   **287.** *5* See,   *2–5* Ellen! see!   **288.** *5* 'Tis   *2–*
5 in   *2–5* leaves,   *5* sun,   **289.** *5* No   *2–5* ee;   **290.** *2–5* "A   *2–4* Sun, •
5 sun,   **291.** *2–4* "A   *4 5* too;   **292.** *2–4* "Ten   *2–5* light,   **293.** *3 4* "Make
2–5 glory,   *2–5* bright,   **294.** *2–4* "Round   *2–5* orb,   *2–5* blue."   **295.** *2–*
5 rays,   **296.** *5* be;   **297.** *2–5* green;"   **298.** *1–5* me."   **299.** *1–5* sat
2–4 thoughts,   **301.** *2–5* pants,   **303.** *2 3* Mother, • *5* mother   *2–5* too!"
305. *2–5* itself,   **307.** *3–5* groaned   **308.** *2–5* mind;   **309.** *3–5* waked   *3–*
5 stared   **311.** *2–5* sat   *2–5* ere   *2–5* dream   **313.** *3–5* exclaimed)   **314.** *5* I
1 heart!" • *2–5* heart."   **315.** *3–5* shrieked,   **317.** *3–5* shivered,   *2 5* sat, • *3 4* sat
318. *3–5* smiled   *2–5* after.   **318⁺.** *3–5* reliquum   *3–5* To-morrow! and

title. The deleted heading "~~Fragment~~" precedes the Preface in MS 1 on f 32ʳ. The title
"The Three Graves, a Sexton's Tale, a Fragment" was inserted at the beginning of the
text on f 33ᵛ when C renumbered each part III and IV (see the heading to part IV at line
⁻170.1, which appears on f 39ʳ). PR *1* follows MS 1 in giving the title after the Preface,
and again between the two parts.

⁻**1.10.** Erratum to PR *2*: "r. *psychological*."

⁻**1.12.** PR *1* does not begin a new paragraph with "Edward,".

⁻**1.20.** PR *2 5* do not begin a new paragraph with "The answer,".

2, 4, 6, etc. All texts indent lines as in the RT.

4⁺, 8⁺, etc. PR *1* lacks line-spaces throughout.

6. PR *2* strikes] Corrected to "spikes" in JG's and SC's copies, the first in ink over
C's pencil and the second not certainly in C's hand.

290–4. C quoted a perhaps earlier version in a letter to Mrs C of 16 Nov 1802 (PML
MA 1489=*CL* II 883):

> "A small blue Sun! and it has got
> A perfect Glory too!
> Ten thousand *Hairs* of Color'd Light

Make up a Glory gay & bright
Round that small orb so blue!—

318⁺. PR *2* religuum] C corrected to "reliquum" in HNC's copy. The Postscript was first introduced in the PR *2* proofs (Yale In C678 817sa).

156. THIS LIME-TREE BOWER MY PRISON

A. DATE

Jul 1797. The exact date of the Wordsworths' arrival at Stowey is not altogether certain. Reed I 199–200n reviews the evidence and suggests Sunday, 2 Jul 1797. The dates of the Lambs' visit are also uncertain, but it most probably extended from 7 to 14 Jul. The nominal date of the poem (contrary to the Advertisement) is thus the second week of Jul, although it might not have been drafted until after the Lambs had left.

B. TEXTS

1. PML MA 1848 (20). 2 leaves, 21×34 cm; wms (1) GR within a circle, above 1794; (2) seated knight with lance, sceptre, and shield; chain-lines 2.6 cm. Transcribed in an als to RS, c 17 Jul 1797 (*CL* I 334–6). The ms is reproduced in part (to line 46) in Verlyn Klinkenborg, Herbert Cahoon, and Charles Ryskamp *British Literary Manuscripts* (2 vols New York 1981) II 12.

2. NYPL Berg Collection. Single leaf, 15.7×25.7 cm (imperfect); counter-mark TH; written on both sides. Transcript in C's hand addressed to Charles Lloyd at Birmingham, signed "S. T. Coleridge", being part of a letter stamped Bridgewater. The beginnings of eight lines (61–2, 64–5, 74–7) have been torn away.

CL complained on Lloyd's behalf, in mid-Sept 1797, that C had not written to him for some time (*LL*—M—I 123), although Lloyd's complaint to CL may not have been justified. Internal evidence such as the variants in lines 38–44 suggests a date after C's letter to Thelwall of Oct 1797, perhaps between Feb and Apr 1798.

There is a transcript by Sophia Lloyd, untitled and subscribed by her "Coleridge.", at VCL (uncatalogued in 1976). It consists of a single leaf, 20×32 cm; wm 1794; written on both sides. The endorsement in Sophia Lloyd's married name may suggest that the transcript was made after her marriage on 24 Apr 1799. It supplies readings where MS 2 is imperfect—at the beginning of lines 61–2, 64–5, 74–7. It varies in spelling and punctuation, and contains verbal miscopyings in lines 6 ("see" for "meet"), 31 ("and thro' pain" for "and pain"), 50–1 (omits "and lov'd . . . the Leaf"), 56 ("branches" for "foliage"). The last of these, an anticipation of the PR *1–5* reading in line 56, appears to be accidental, although it is curious.

1. Annual Anthology ed RS (2 vols Bristol 1799–1800) II 140–4. Signed "*ESTEESI*". C's copy at Yale (Tinker 1953 2) contains his ms corrections. The reprintings in W. F. Mylius *Poetical Class-book* (1810 etc) have no textual significance.

2 [=RT]. *SL* (1817).
The revised proofs (Yale In C678 817sa) show that printer's copy was provided by PR *1*, partly revised. Further revisions were made in proof (no attempt is made here to record this interim stage).

Two copies contain C's ms corrections: HNC's (HUL *AC85 L8605 Zy 817c) and one of JG's (HUL *EC8 C6795 817s (C)). WW's copy (Cornell WORDSWORTH PR 4480 S5 1817 Copy 1) contains two minor corrections in ΛG's hand.

3. PW (1828).
Printer's copy was provided by a part copy of PR *2*, emended in JG's hand (HUL *EC C6795 817s (D)). No attempt is made here to record this interim stage.

4. PW (1829).

5. PW (1834).
The HEHL copy (109531) contains a ms note by C on the poem, given in vol I Advertisement EC. It is reproduced in facsimile in the John Pearson *Catalogue of a Unique Coleridge Collection* (C. Whittingham & Co., London 1913) 74.

title. *1* THIS LIME-TREE BOWER MY PRISON, | A POEM, | Addressed to CHARLES LAMB, *of the India-House, London.* • *2–5* THIS LIME-TREE BOWER MY PRISON.

1 2		ADVERTISEMENT.
1–5		*In the June of* 1797, *some long-expected Friends paid a visit to the*
		Author's Cottage; and on the morning of their arrival he met with
		an accident, which disabled him from walking during the whole
		time of their stay. One evening, when they had left him for a few ⁻1.5
		hours, he composed the following lines, in the Garden Bower.

1 □		Well—they are gone: and here must I remain,
1.1.1 1		Lam'd by the scathe of fire, lonely & faint,
2 1 2		This lime-tree bower my prison. They, meantime,
	1–5	I have lost
3 *1 2*		Such beauties and such feelings, as had been
	3–5	Beauties and Feelings, such as would have been
4 *1*		Most sweet to have remember'd, even when age
	2–5	my remembrance,
5 *1*		Had dimm'd my eyes to blindness! They, meanwhile,
	2–5	mine

6	⊠*3–5*	My Friends, whom I may never meet again,
	3–5	Friends, whom I never more may
7	□	On springy heath, along the hill-top edge,
8	*1*	~~Wand'ring well-pleas'd, look down on grange or dell~~
	1	Wander delighted, and look down, perchance,
	2	Delighted wander,
	1–5	Wander in gladness, and wind
12a.1	*1*	~~Or *that deep gloomy* deep fantastic Rift,~~ where many an Ash
	1	On that same rifted Dell,
	2	the wet Ash
12b.1	*1*	Twists its wild limbs beside ~~the some~~ the ferny rock,
	2	above the
12.1.1	*1 2*	Whose plumy ferns for ever nod and drip
16.1	*1 2*	Spray'd by the waterfall: But chiefly Thou,
9	*1–5*	To that still roaring dell, of which I told;
10	*1–5*	The roaring dell, o'erwooded, narrow, deep,
11	*1–5*	And only speckled by the mid-day sun;
12	*1–5*	Where its slim trunk the Ash from rock to rock
13	*1–5*	Flings arching like a bridge; that branchless Ash
14	*1–5*	Unsunn'd and damp, whose few poor yellow leaves
15	*1–5*	Ne'er tremble in the gale, yet tremble still
16	*1–5*	Fann'd by the water-fall! And there my friends,
17	*1–5*	Behold the dark-green file of long lank weeds,
17fn	*1–5*	*Of long lank weeds.*—The Asplenium scolopendrium, called in some coun-
		tries the Adder's tongue, in others the Hart's tongue: but Withering gives the
		Adder's tongue, as the trivial name of the Ophioalossum only.
18	*1–5*	That all at once (a most fantastic sight!)
19	*1–5*	Still nod and drip beneath the dripping edge
20a	*1*	Of the dim clay-stone.
	2–5	blue
		[*Line-space*]
20b	*1–5*	Now my friends emerge
21	*1–5*	Beneath the wide wide Heaven, and view again
22	*1–4*	The many-steepled track magnificent
	5	tract
23	*1–5*	Of hilly fields and meadows, and the sea
24	*1*	With some fair bark perhaps which lightly touches
	2–5	whose Sails light up
25	*1–5*	The slip of smooth clear blue betwixt two isles
26	*1–5*	Of purple shadow! Yes! they wander on
27	*1–5*	In gladness all; but thou, methinks, most glad
28	*1 2*	My gentle-hearted CHARLES! thou, who hast pin'd
	1	for thou had'st
	2–5	hast
29	□	And hunger'd after Nature many a year
30	□	In the great City pent, winning thy way,

31 1 2   With sad yet bowed soul, thro' evil & pain
   1–5   patient

32 ☐   And strange calamity.—Ah slowly sink

33 1   Behind the western ridge; ⊘Thou glorious Sun!
   ⊠1   thou

34 ☐   Shine in the slant beams of the sinking orb,

35 ☐   Ye purple Heath-flowers! Richlier burn, ye Clouds!

36 ☐   Live in the yellow Light, ye distant ⸎Groves!

37 ☐   And kindle, thou blue Ocean! So my friend

38 1   Struck with Joy's deepest calm, and gazing round
   2   deep calm may stand, as I have stood,
   1–5   joy

39 ⊠1   Silent, with swimming sense; yea, gazing round

40 1   On the wide view, may gaze till all doth seem
   ⊠1 2   landscape,
   2   wild

41 ⊠*3–5* Less gross than bodily, a   living Thing
   3–5   ·   and of such hues

42 1 2   That acts upon the mind, and with such hues
   1 2   Which

43 ⊠*3–5* As cloathe the Almighty Spirit, when he   makes
   3   veil
   4 5   yet he

44a ☐   Spirits perceive his presence!
        [*Line-space*]

44b ☐   A Delight

45 ☐   Comes sudden on my heart, and I am glad

46 ☐   As I myself were there! Nor in this bower

49b.1 1   Want I sweet sounds or pleasing shapes. I watch'd

49a.1 1   The sunshine of each broad transparent Leaf

51.1 1   Broke by the shadows of the Leaf or Stem,

52.1 1   Which hung above it: and that Wall-nut Tree

47 2   This little lime-tree bower, have I not seen
   1–5   mark'd

48 2   Much that has sooth'd me. Pale beneath the Light
   1–3 5   blaze
   4   as

49 ⊠1   Hung the transparent foliage; and I watch'd

50 2   Many   a sunny Leaf, and lov'd to mark
   1–5   Some broad and   see

51 2   The shadows of the Leaf & Stem above
   1–5   shadow

52 ⊠1   Dappling its sunshine! And that Wall-nut Tree

53 ☐   Was richly ting'd: and a deep radiance lay

54 ☐   Full on the ancient ivy which usurps

55 ☐   Those fronting elms, and now with blackest mass

56 1   Makes their dark foliage gleam a lighter hue
   2   ⟨foliage⟩
   1–5   branches

57 1 2   Thro' the late twilight.—And tho' the rapid bat
1–5   now the
58 □   Wheels silent by and not a swallow twitters,
59 □   Yet still the solitary humble-bee
60 □   Sings in the beanflower. Henceforth I shall know
61 1   That nature ne'er ~~the~~ deserts the wise & pure,
⊠1   deserts
62 ⊠2–5 No scene so narrow, but may well employ
2–5   Plot   be but Nature there,
63 2–5   No waste so vacant, but may well employ
64 □   Each faculty of sense, and keep the heart
65 □   Awake to Love & Beauty: and sometimes
66 1   'Tis well to be bereav'd of promis'd good
⊠1   bereft
67 □   That we may lift the soul, & contemplate
68 □   With lively joy the Joys, we cannot share.
69 1   My Sister & my Friends! when the last Rook
2   Sara,
1–5   gentle-hearted CHARLES!
70 □   Beat its straight path along the dusky Air
71 □   Homewards, I bless'd it; deeming, its black wing
72 *1 2* (Now a dim speck, now vanishing in the light)
3–5   light)
73 1   ~~Had cross'd the~~ ***órb*** ~~flood & blaze of setting day,~~
1   Cross'd, like a speck, the blaze of setting day,
2   [?]Had cross'd the mighty Orb's dilated blaze,
1–5   Had   glory
74 1 2   While ye   stood gazing; or when all was still,
1–5   thou stood'st
75 1 2   Flew creaking o'er your heads, & had a charm
1–5   thy   head,
75fn *1–5* *Flew creeking.*—Some months after I had written this line, it gave me plea-
        sure to observe that Bartram had observed the same circumstance of the Savannah
        Crane. "When these birds move their wings in flight, their strokes are slow,
        moderate and regular; and even when at a considerable distance, or high above
        us, we plainly hear the quill feathers, their shafts and webs upon one another   5
        creek as the joints or working of a vessel in a tempestuous sea.
76 1   For you, my Sister & my Friends! to whom
2   Sara
1–5   thee, my gentle-hearted CHARLES!
77 □   No sound is dissonant, which tells of Life!

title. *3–5* THIS LIME-TREE BOWER MY PRISON.   **advertisement.** *2–5*
print in roman type   ⁻**1.1.** *2* ADVERTISEMENT.   ⁻**1.3.** *5* author's cottage;

2–5 arrival,   ‾1.5. *2–4* Evening,   ‾1.6. *2–5* lines *2–4* Garden-Bower. •
5 garden-bower.   **1.** *1–5* Well, *2* gone! • *1–5* gone, *2* remain   **2.** *2–*
4 Lime-Tree Bower *2* Prison. • *1 5* prison! • *2–4* Prison!   **3.** *5* feelings,
4. *3–5* remembrance   **5.** *2–5* dimmed   **6.** *1* friends,   **7.** *2* springey
Heath • *1* springy heath *2* Edge • *1* edge   **8.** *1* perchance   **12.1.1.** *2* plumey
16.1. *2* waterfall. *2* thou,   **11.** *2–4* Sun;   **12.** *5* ash   **13.** *2* Bridge;— •
3–5 bridge;— *2–4* Ash, • *5* ash,   **14.** *3–5* Unsunned   **15.** *2–5* still,   **16.** *3–*
5 Fanned *2–5* and *2–5* friends   **17.** *2–5* dark green *2 4* Weeds, • *3* Weeds.
17fn1. *2 Of long lank Weeds.* • *3 4* OF LONG LANK WEEDS. *5* asplenium
2–4 Scolopendrium,   **17fn2.** *2–5* Adder's Tongue, *2–5* Hart's Tongue:
17fn3. *2–5* Tongue *2–4* Ophioglossum • *5* ophioglossum   **20.** *2–5* Now,
2–4 Friends   **21.** *2–5* Heaven—   **23.** *2–5* sea,   **24.** *2–5* bark, perhaps,
5 sails   **25.** *2–5* Isles   **27.** *2–5* glad,   **28.** *2 2–5* Charles! *2–5* pined
29. *3–5* hungered *2 1* nature • *2–5* Nature, *2–5* year,   **30.** *1* city *1–5* way
31. *2–5* through *2 1–5* and   **32.** *2 1–5* calamity! *2–5* Ah!   **33.** *2 1–5* ridge,
5 sun!   **34.** *2* Orb, • *2 3* orb   **35.** *1–5* heath-flowers! *1–5* richlier *1–5* clouds!
36. *2 1–5* light, *2* Groves! • *1–5* groves!   **37.** *1* ocean!— • *5* ocean! *2 1–*
5 Friend   **39.** *1–5* Silent   **40.** *2* All   **41.** *2* bodily— • *2–5* bodily; *1 2* thing
42. *2 1 acts 1 2* mind—   **43.** *1 2* cloath   **44a.** *2* presence!— • *1–5* presence.
44b. *1–5* delight   **46.** *2 1–5* bower,   **47.** *1* bower *3–5* marked   **48.** *3–*
5 soothed   **49.** *3–5* watched   **50.** *1–5* leaf, *3–5* loved   **51.** *1–5* leaf and
stem   **52.** *1* Wallnut tree • *2–4* Walnut-tree • *5* walnut-tree   **53.** *1* richly ting'd; •
2 richly-ting'd. • *2* richly ting'd, • *3 5* richly tinged,   **54.** *2 2–4* Ivy, • *1* Ivy •
5 ivy, *1 usurps*   **55.** *2* Elms, *2–5* now,   **57.** *2–5* Through *2 1* Twilight: •
2–5 twilight: *2 1–5* and *2–5* though *2 1–4* Bat   **58.** *2 1–5* by, *1–*
4 Swallow   **59.** *2* Humble-bee • *1* humble Bee, • *2–4* humble Bee • *5* humble
bee   **60.** *2* bean-flower.—Hence-forth • *1–5* bean-flower! Henceforth   **61.** *1–*
5 Nature *2* Wise and pure; • *1–4* wise and pure, • *5* wise and pure;   **62.** *4 5* plot
1 narrow   **64.** *2* Heart   **65.** *2* Love & Beauty! and • *1* love and beauty! And •
2–5 Love and Beauty! and   **66.** *2* Tis *2–5* promised *2* Good, • *1–5* good,
67. *2–5* Soul, *2 1–5* and   **68.** *2* Joy *2* Joys • *1–5* joys   **69.** *2* and *2–*
5 Charles! *5* rook   **70.** *1–5* air   **71.** *1–5* blest it! • *2* bless'd it— *1* deeming
2 Wing   **73.** *3–5* crossed *1 5* orb's *2–5* glory,   **74.** *2* or, • *1–5* or *1* still
75. *2 creaking* • *1 creeking* • *2–5* creeking *2 1–5* and   **75fn1.** *3 4* FLEW
CREAKING.   **75fn2.** *1–4* to observe • *5* to find *2–5* Savanna   **75fn3.** *2–5* Birds
75fn4. *2–5* distance   **75fn5.** *2–5* quill-feathers;   **75fn6.** *2–4* sea."   **76.** *2* you
2–5 Charles,   **77.** *2–4* Sound *2 2–5* dissonant *2 1–5* Life.

advertisement. In MS *1* C noted at the start of the text: "Charles Lamb has been with me for a week—he left me Friday morning.—/ ~~f~~The second day after Wordsworth came to me, ~~dear~~ dear Sara accidentally emptied a skillet of boiling milk on my foot, which confined me during the whole time of C. Lamb's ~~residence~~ stay & still prevents me from all *walks* longer than a furlong.—While Wordsworth, his Sister, & C. Lamb were out one evening;/ sitting in th arbour of T. Poole's Garden, which communicates with mine, I wrote these lines, with which I am pleased—"

2–5. I have lost . . . to blindness!] C deleted this passage in the Yale copy of PR *1*.

3. Erratum in PR *2*: "substitute *Beauties and Feelings, such as would have been.*"

6. Erratum in PR *2*: "substitute *Friends whom I never more may meet again.*"

7. In MS *1* C noted: "*elastic*, I mean.—"

8–26. and wind down, perchance . . . Of purple shadow!] C deleted this passage in the Yale copy of PR *1*, and substituted:

> Wander in gladness, pausing oft to view
> The many-steepled Track magnificent
> Of hilly Lawn and Pasture, and the Sea
> With all its shadows. Yes! they wander
> In gladness all; &c

12.1.1. In MS 1 C noted: "The ferns, that grow in moist places, grow five or six together & form a complete 'Prince of Wales's Feathers'—i.e. plumy.—" In MS 2 C noted: "the Ferns in high to dry situations are branchy" (the beginning of the note may have been torn away). Sophia Lloyd's transcript does not have the note.

9–20. The description in the published versions is developed from vol III **146.X1** *Osorio* IV i 18–20, which C had been working on at the time he wrote the poem but had despaired of seeing produced or published by 1800.

33–7. Anticipated by a fragment copied into the Gutch Notebook (*CN* I 157):

> The Sun (for now his Orb
> Gan slowly sink) ~~behind the Western Hill~~,
> Shot half his rays aslant the heath, whose flowers
> Purpled the mountain's broad & level top,
> Rich was his bed of Clouds: & wide beneath
> Expecting Ocean smiled with dimpled face.

38–44. Quoted (var) in a version between MSS 1 and 2, in a letter to John Thelwall of 14 Oct 1797 (PML MA 77–10–; *CL* I 349–50):

> Struck with ~~deep~~ the deepest calm of Joy I stand
> Silent, with swimming sense; and gazing round
> On the wide Landscape gaze till all doth seem
> Less gross than bodily, a living Thing
> Which acts upon the mind, & with such Hues
> As cloath th' Almighty Spirit, when he makes
> Spirits perceive his presence!—

40. In MS 1 C noted: "You remember, I am a *Berkleian*?"
40. Erratum in PR *2*: "for *wild* r. *wide*: and the two following lines thus:

> Less gross than bodily: and of such hues
> As veil the Almighty Spirit."

40, 41–4. In HNC's copy of PR *2* C corrected "wild" to "wide", and substituted the word "Presence" for the passage "; a living thing . . . his presence." The correction of "wild" to "wide" (only) was made by AG, and in JG's copy by JG himself.
41–4. In the Yale copy of PR *1* C deleted these lines and substituted:

> Less gross than bodily, within ~~the~~ his soul
> Kindling unutterable Thanksgivings
> And Adorations, such perchance as rise
> Before the Almighty Spirit, when he makes
> Spirits perceive his presence.

44. No line-space in MS 2 (or in Sophia Lloyd's transcript).

59. There is a note, ink over what appears to be C's hand, in JG's copy of PR *2*: "Cows without horns are called Hummel cows; In the Country as the Hummel bee, as stingless, unless it be a corruption of *humming*, from the sound observable." "Hummel" for "hornless", is Scottish or northern dialect, and C presumably picked up this piece of lore from the Wordsworths.

61–2, 64–5. The beginnings of the lines have been torn away in MS 2, and the readings supplied from Sophia Lloyd's transcript.

65–9. And sometimes . . . My gentle-hearted CHARLES] C deleted this passage in the Yale copy of PR *1*, and capitalised the succeeding "W".

71. its black] C deleted the words in the Yale copy of PR *1*, and substituted "that its wings".

72. Erratum in PR *2*: "omit *the* before *Light*." AG made the correction in the copy sent to WW.

74–7. The beginnings of the lines have been torn away in MS 2, and the readings supplied from Sophia Lloyd's transcript.

75. MS 2^{imp} has a note (written at the end of the poem): "$^\ulcorner$. . .$^\urcorner$ observe the *creek*! *creek*! *creek*! which the $^\ulcorner$. . .$^\urcorner$ with its wings, I believe)—when fly[?]ing *high*$^\ulcorner$. . .$^{\urcorner}$" Sophia Lloyd underlined the word "creaking" in her transcript—which provides the reading here—doubtless so as to attach a note to it (which she did not in fact supply).

157. SONNET: TO WILLIAM LINLEY, ESQ., WHILE HE SANG A SONG TO PURCELL'S MUSIC

A. DATE

12 Sept 1797.

B. TEXTS

1. Buffalo and Erie County Library, Buffalo, NY, James Fraser Gluck Collection. Single leaf, 18.5×21.2 cm; wm 1796; verso blank. Transcript in C's hand, signed "S. T. Coleridge I Donhead I September 12th. I 1797".

EHC (*PW—EHC—*I 236n) cites a ms dated 14 Sept 1797, but appears to be relying on *PW* (JDC) 624B, whom he misreports. JDC perhaps saw the ms as it changed hands, before it was acquired by the Buffalo and Erie County Library in 1887. EHC's readings are identical with MS 1, and, besides, since Lloyd reported C being "unwell with a sore throat" but writing letters at WW's on Friday 15 Sept (cf *CL* I 345–6n), it is likely that he travelled on the Wednesday or Thursday previously. He probably presented the poem to Linley on Tuesday, his last day at Donhead, where he had been staying with Bowles since 6 or 7 Sept.

1 [=**RT**]. *Annual Anthology* ed RS (2 vols Bristol 1799–1800) II 156. Unsigned.

C's copy at Yale (Tinker 1953 2) contains an insertion in his hand.

2. DCL MS 14/10a. Single leaf, 19.2×23.7 cm; no wm or chain-lines (wove); verso blank. Transcript in the hand of Sir George Beaumont. The paper has been folded several times.

The transcript appears not to have been copied from any known version. It might have been dictated by C or written down from a memory of C reciting it, before or after C's time in Malta. Beaumont made what appears to be a later copy of this same version to enclose in a letter to G. A. Ellis dated 13 Mar 1824 (Chatsworth, Devonshire Collections, Sixth Duke's Series, Nos 915–915A).

2. SL (1817).

HNC's copy (HUL *AC85 L8605 Zy 817c) contains an annotation in C's hand, and a comment in another hand, for which see vol I headnote.

3. PW (1828).

4. PW (1829).

JG's (?) copy at NYPL (Berg Collection) contains a single small correction.

5. PW (1834).

title. 1 To Mr William Linley • *1 SONNET XII.* | *To W.L. Esq. while he sung a Song to Purcell's Music.* • 2 On hearing ——— Linley play an air | of Purcels by S. T. Coleridge • *2 LINES* | *To W.L. Esq. while he sang a Song to Purcell's Music.* • *3 4* LINES TO W.L. ESQ. | WHILE HE SANG A SONG TO PURCELL'S MUSIC. • *5* LINES TO W.L. | WHILE HE SANG A SONG TO PURCELL'S MUSIC.

1 1	While my young cheek preserves its healthful hues	
⊠1		retains
2 □	And I have many friends, who hold me dear—	
3 □	LINLEY! methinks, I would not *often* hear	
4 □	Such melodies as thine, lest I should lose	
5 □	All memory of the wrongs and sore distress	
6 □	For which my miserable brethren weep:	
7 ⊠2	But should uncomforted misfortunes steep	
2		misfortune
8 ⊠2	My daily bread in tears and bitterness,	
2	want wretchedness,	
9 1	And if in ~~my last~~ Death's dread moment I should lie	
⊠1 2	at ◄——Death's——►	
2	◄——life's——► last	
10 1 *1*	With no beloved face by my bed side	
2	friend	
2–5	face at	
11 1	To catch the last glance of my closing eye—	
⊠1 2	fix	
2	watch	

12 1	O, such an O God! such songs breath'd by my angel guide
1	O God! such strains
2	some
2–5	←—Methinks,—→ my
13 □	Would make me pass the cup of anguish by,
14 □	Mix with the blest, nor know that I had died!

1. 2 Whilst *2–5* hues, **2.** ⊠1 2 friends *1–5* dear; • 2 dear **3.** *1–5* L——!
methinks, • 2 Linley—methinks ⊠1 2 often **4.** 2 loose **5.** 2 & *1–
5* distress, **6.** 3 brethren *1–5* weep! • 2 weep. **7.** *4* steep, **8.** 2 &
1–5 bitterness; **9.** *2–5* death's **10.** *1* bed-side • *2–5* bed-side, **11.** ⊠1 2 eye,
12. *2–5* strains, *3–5* breathed *2–5* angel-guide, **14.** 2 died.

title. C enlarged the title in his copy of PR *1* at Yale, to read "W. Linley".
2–3, 6–7, 10, 12. Indented in PR *1*. Line 2 and perhaps lines 4–14 might be indented
in MS 2. Lines 2–3, 6–7, 10, 12, 14 indented in PR *2–5*.
3. PR 2 L——!] In the RH margin of HNC's copy C wrote "Linley".
7. PR *4* steep,] The comma is deleted in JG's (?) copy.
12. The new reading in PR 2 and later was introduced by C in proof (Yale In C678
817sa).

158. SONNETS ATTEMPTED IN THE MANNER OF "CONTEMPORARY WRITERS"

A. DATE

Perhaps between late Aug 1797, when the *Monthly Visitor* reviewed C's *Poems*
(1797) and described a "Coleridgean school", and about 20 Nov, when C refers
to the sonnets in a letter to Joseph Cottle (*CL* I 357–8).

B. TEXTS

1 [=RT]. *Monthly Magazine* IV (Nov 1797) 374, where the first two sonnets
are each signed "NEHEMIAH HIGGINBOTTOM.", and the third "NEHEMIAH
HIGGINBOTHAM."
There is no textual significance to the reprintings in *M Chron* (16 Dec 1797)
(sonnet I only); *The Spirit of the Public Journals for 1797* I (1798) 364 (sonnet
I only); *The Annual Register for 1797* XXXIX (1800) 454–5; *Poetical Register
for 1803* (1804) 346–8.

2. *BL* ch 1 (1817) I 27–8fn (*CC*) I 27–8fn.

title. *1* SONNETS, | *attempted in the manner of* | 'CONTEMPORARY
WRITERS.'

I ‾1 □   SONNET I.
I 1 □ Pensive, at eve, on the hard world I mus'd,
I 2 □ And my poor heart was sad: so at the moon
I 3 □ I gaz'd—and sigh'd, and sigh'd!—for, ah! how soon
I 4 *1* Eve darkens into night. Mine eye perus'd
    2   saddens   eyes
I 5 □ With tearful vacancy, the *dampy* grass,
I 6 *1* Which wept and glitter'd in the paly ray:
    2   That
I 7 □ And I did pause me on my lonely way,
I 8 *1* And mus'd me on those wretched ones, who pass
    2   the   that
I 9 *1* O'er the black heath of SORROW. But, alas!
    2   bleak
I 10 □ Most of MYSELF I thought: when it befell,
I 11 □ That the sooth SPIRIT of the breezy wood
I 12 □ Breath'd in mine ear—"All this is very well;
I 13 □ But much of *one* thing is for *no* thing good."
I 14 *1* Ah! my poor heart's inexplicable swell!
    2   Oh
        [*Line-space*]
II ‾1.1 □   SONNET II.
II ‾1.2 □   TO SIMPLICITY.
II 1 □ O! I do love thee, meek *Simplicity!*
II 2 □ For of thy lays the lulling simpleness
II 3 □ Goes to my heart, and soothes each small distress,
II 4 □ Distress tho' small, yet haply great to me!
II 5 □ 'Tis true, on lady Fortune's gentlest pad
II 6 *1* I amble on; yet, tho' I know not why,
    2   and yet
II 7 □ *So* sad I am!—but should a friend and I
II 8 *1* Grow cool and *miff*, O! I am *very* sad!
    2 Frown, pout and part, then
II 9 □ And then with sonnets and with sympathy
II 10 □ My dreamy bosom's mystic woes I pall;
II 11 □ Now of my false friend plaining plaintively,
II 12 □ Now raving at mankind in general;
II 13 □ But whether sad or fierce, 'tis simple all,
II 14 □ All very simple, meek SIMPLICITY
        [*Line-space*]
III ‾1.1 □   SONNET III.
III ‾1.2 *1* ON A RUINED HOUSE IN A ROMANTIC
III ‾1.3 *1*   COUNTRY.
III 1 □ And this reft house is that, the which he built,
III 2 □ Lamented Jack! Ánd here his malt he pil'd,
III 3 □ Cautious in vain! These rats that squeak so wild,
III 4 □ Squeak, not unconscious of their father's guilt.
III 5 *1* Did ye not see her gleaming thro' the glade!
    2   he

III 6 □ Belike, 'twas she, the maiden all forlorn.
III 7 □ What tho' she milk no cow with crumpled horn,
III 8 □ Yet, *aye*, she haunts the dale where *erst* she stray'd:
III 9 □ And, *aye*, beside her stalks her amorous knight!
III 10 □ Still on his thighs their wonted brogues are worn,
III 11 □ And thro' those brogues, still tatter'd and betorn,
III 12 □ His hindward charms gleam an unearthly white;
III 13 *1* As when thro' broken clouds at night's high noon
    2 Ah! thus
III 14 □ Peeps in fair fragments forth the full-orb'd harvest-moon!

I ⁻1.1. *2* SONNET 1.   I 1. *2* Pensive *2 hard* *2* mused,   I 2. *2 my poor*
2 sad; *2* MOON   I 3. *2* gazed, *2* sighed, and sighed; *2* for ah   I 4. *2* night!
mine *2* perused   I 5. *2* vacancy *2* grass   I 6. *2 paly*   I 7. *2 did*
pause me, *2* way   I 8. *2 mused me*, *2 wretched ones*   I 9. *2* sorrow.
But   I 10. *2 myself* *2* thought! *2* befel,   I 11. *2 soothe* spirit *2 breezy*
I 12. *2* ear: *2* well,   I 13. *2* ONE thing, *2* NO   I 14. *2 my poor heart's*
INEXPLICABLE SWELL!   II ⁻1.1. *2* SONNET II.   II 1. *2* Oh *2* SIMPLICITY!
II 4. *2* me,   II 5. *2* true *2* Lady   II 6. *2* why   II 7. *2* am!   II 8. *2* sad.
II 14. *2* SIMPLICITY!   III ⁻1.1. *2* SONNET III.   III 3. *2* these rats,
III 4. *2* Squeak   III 6. *2* Belike   III 8. *2 aye*   III 9. *2* And *2* amarous
III 12. *2* glean *2* white.   III 13. *2* Noon

I 1–4. Quoted (var) ("Wandering at Eve" in the first line) to EC, 8 Feb 1826 (*CL* VI 564), to describe a bad portrait of DC. "Had Cruikshanks made a drawing purposely for the visible impersonation of this Sonnet, he could not have hit off so felicitous a Fac simile."

159. SONNET: TO A LADY

A. DATE

Nov 1797?

B. TEXT

HUL fMS Eng 947.8. Single leaf, 19.1×20.3 cm; wm (fragmentary) top of crown; chain-lines 2.4 cm. Transcript in C's hand; the verso is addressed (in C's hand) "Mʳ Cottle". Cottle has added his classification number "41" on the recto, top right, and the date "1797" alongside in pencil. He also appears to have made two emendations to the text (in pencil). He endorsed the verso, above his name, "Coleridge I Novʳ 1797". A wax seal and the lack of a full address and franks suggest that it was delivered, as a letter, by hand.

There is some doubt about C's authorship, while the occasion and purpose of the poem remain obscure. See vol I headnote.

The RT reproduces the ms exactly, except for:

title. ms Sonnet | To a Lady   **2fn.** ms her Eyes.

2fn. Written alongside, in the RH margin
11. "And"] Probably obscured by the wax used to seal the letter, so Cottle inserted "&" (in pencil) after it.
that] Cottle deleted the word and altered "on" to "upon" (both in pencil).

160. THE WANDERINGS OF CAIN

A. DATE

Early Nov 1797 and 1807. C's work on the poem falls into two phases: his working plan for the whole and the writing of canto I, and his later attempt to renew work on the poem.

The poem was conceived (MS 1) during the short walking tour made by WW, DW, and C to Lynton and the Valley of the Rocks (Prefatory Note to PR *3–5; H Works* XVII 120). Canto II (MS 2) was written in the week following, before their walking tour of about 12–20 Nov, when **161** *The Rime of the Ancient Mariner* was begun instead (see Reed I 208–11).

There are hints that the poem continued to occupy C's mind to some extent (*CN* II 2468, 2501, 2799 and nn; **370** *Lines on Hearing a Tale = CN* II 2644), and the attempt to renew work on it in 1807 resulted in a brief draft for its continuation beyond canto II (MS 3), as well as the brief versified account of events preceding (TEXTS 4 5 *1*). C's allusion (early 1807?) to "the Wandering of Cain, a well-known Work of the Poet Coleridge" (quoted in *CN* III 3422n and *CN* V Addenda) is none the less ironic, and the announcement of its publication in the *London Magazine* and by Taylor and Hessey, in Jan and in May 1824 respectively, appears to have been caused by misunderstanding (Walter Jerrold "Coleridge's 'The Wanderings of Cain'" *N&Q* NS VI (17 Nov 1906) 386; *CL* V 337: to J. Anster 18 Feb 1824; Edmund Blunden *Keats's Publisher: A Memoir of John Taylor*—1936—154n).

Specifically, there is no evidence that C worked on the poem in 1815–16 or in 1824–5, beyond having it recalled to his mind by the publication of **176** *Christabel* and fortuitous circumstances. He seems, however, not to have reconciled himself to the impossibility of completing it until 1828 (PR *2* et seq), and an apologetic preface was retained, albeit in truncated form, even in the year of his death (PR *5*).

1. BM Egerton 2800 f 1. Single leaf, 24.2×40.0 cm; rough heavy paper; no wm; chain-lines 2.5 cm; written on both sides. Working plan of the complete (?) poem, with numerous corrections and insertions, headed "Book 3rd", in C's loose and scrawling hand. Two words and some characters—"?[Ger]many", "Governments", "ma en am"—are written at random on both sides, the first and last in HC's (?) childish hand.

The plan is divided into three sections by lines across the page, and concludes with a shorter line ending with the symbol ⊠. The relation of the three sections to each other is uncertain, and it is unclear whether other episodes were intended to precede or follow. The heading "Book 3rd" is also problematic, since the completed canto II picks up incidents selectively, from the middle and last sections of the plan. Possibly a working plan, as here, was followed by a verbal agreement between WW and C as to how to divide up work on cantos I and II; or possibly the present working plan is a background only to canto II, and WW's working plan has not survived, if it ever existed. Either way, the heading "Book 3rd is most probably a memorandum concerning future use of the plan, in the event of the poem being continued.

A brief fragment in the Gutch Notebook (*CN* I 130) is possibly related to the poem, but it cannot be fitted to MS 1 with certainty.

If HC used the ms for writing practice, it was with C in 1807 at Coleorton, London, and/or Bristol. A ms at VCL (F2.12) subscribed "18 Berkeley Square [Bristol] I 30 May 1807", suggests that HC was kept busy with writing practice at this time.

Divergences from EHC's transcription (*PW*—EHC—I 285–6n) are noted here only when there is room for doubt.

2. NYPL Berg Collection. Seven leaves, 21.5×25.0 cm; wm (ff 1, 7) 1795 and portions of a shield (?) or fleur-de-lis design; chain-lines 2.4 cm; written on rectos only. Transcript of canto I in C's hand. In ink, with one pencil deletion and two pencil emendations.

Folios 1^{v} and 5^{v} are addressed in an unknown hand to "Mrs Wordsworth I Basil Montagu's Esqre I Upper Thornhaugh S^{t} I London", and on f 1^{v} DW added "I will send the Poem tomorrow DW". MW stayed at Basil Montagu's (36 Lower Thornhaugh Street, in fact) during the latter half of Apr 1807. She had travelled down to London with WW, SH, C, and HC from Coleorton, where DW remained (Reed II 351).

The transcript appears to be a fair copy, incorporating minor improvements made at the time of copying, probably the "portion executed" referred to in PR 3–5. There is no way of knowing whether this was the ms ("which came from Poole") which CL sent to Keswick in a brown-paper parcel on 6 Aug 1800 (*LL*—M—I 217). There is a copy at DCL (MS 14 I 10), on four conjoint leaves, wm SE & Co I 1819, which follows the original carefully, and observes the pencil deletions and emendations, with only a few differences of spelling and punctuation—although the copyist omitted one full page of the transcript, and had to add it at the end (f 5ʳ is keyed to f 3ᵛ, and corresponds to f 5ʳ of the transcript). It is most probably the copy made for EC, between 30 Jan and 8 Feb 1826 (*CL* vi 549: to EC 30 Jan 1826; 566: to EC 8 Feb 1826), and it is likely that the pencil deletions and emendations in C's transcript were made at this later time.

3. BM Add MS 47520=Notebook 22 ff 89ʳ–88ʳ (*CN* ii 2780). Draft for a paragraph.

The paragraph appears to connect with the last section of the working plan (ms 1), concerning Cain's sacrifice of Enos.

4. In the possession of Sir John Murray (Jan 1979). Introductory stanza quoted in an als to Lord Byron, 22 Oct 1815 (*CL* iv 602).

The stanza was probably composed in 1807, during or after C's stay at Coleorton. He told Byron in the letter that Beaumont thought the poem "the most impressive of my compositions", and Beaumont is undoubtedly the friend referred to in pr *3–5* below, through whose encouragement C decided to begin anew, "composing the whole in stanzas". It describes events prior to those of the completed canto ii, corresponding to those at the beginning of the second section of the working plan. C describes it in pr *3–5* as "the introductory stanza".

1. The same stanza printed as a footnote to *AR* (1825) 383 (*CC*) 390. The lines are quoted "at once to illustrate and relieve" the subject of "enthusiastic Mystics", and described as "the first stanza" of "WANDERINGS OF CAIN, *a MS. Poem.*"

5. HUL fMS Eng 947. Single leaf, 17.9×19.8 cm; no wm or chain-lines (wove). The same stanza quoted in an als to Frederic Reynolds, 12 May 1825 (*CL* v 449). The verso contains the address.

Frederic Reynolds (1764–1841), popular comic dramatist connected with CG, was the father of Frederic M. Reynolds, to whose *Keepsake* C later contributed. As the brief letter makes clear, the stanza was copied out to be given to a "phil-autographic Friend" of Reynolds's.

2. Canto ii, described as "a fragment", in *The Bijou for 1828* ed William Fraser (1827) 17–23. Signed "By S. T. Coleridge, Esq."

The *Bijou* text is one of several by C printed without his permission and to his annoyance. They were obtained from JG, who was seeing *PW* (1828) though the press, by William Pickering, publisher both of *PW* and of the newly launched annual. See *CL* vi 710–12: to A. A. Watts 24 Nov 1827.

The same text is reprinted complete in the review appearing in *The Literary Magnet* ns iv (1827) 333–5; and in *Literary Magnet . . . in Three Volumes* (1829) iii 333–5; *The Cameo* (1831) 150–5.

3. PW (1828).

Canto ii is introduced by a long Prefatory Note, which contains TEXTS 4 *1* 5.

4. *PW* (1829).
Canto II, as in PR *3*.

5 [=RT]. *PW* (1834).
The Prefatory Note of PR *3 4* is curtailed.

C. GENERAL NOTE

An entry in the Gutch Notebook appears to have some connection with what became *The Wanderings of Cain*, although it would be misleading to connect it with any particular passage of the surviving text:

> Wherefore art thou come?
> doth not the Creator of all things know all things?
> And if thou art come to seek him, know that where thou wast, there *he was*.
>
> (*CN* I 130)

title. 2 4 2–5 The Wanderings of Cain • *1* WANDERINGS OF CAIN. •
5 WANDERINGS OF CAIN, *a MS. Poem.*—

working plan [MS 1 only]

Book 3rd

He falls down in a trance. When he awakes he sees a luminous body coming before him. It stands before him. an orb of fire. It goes on. he moves not. It returns to him again. Again retires as if wishing him to follow it. It then goes on & he follows. [?] They are led to a seat near the bottoms of the roaring woods brooks forests &c &c The [?] Fire gradually shapes itself, retaining its luminous appearance, into the lineaments WP 5
of a Man: a dialogue between the fiery shape & Cain. In which the being presses upon Cain the enormity of his guilt, & that he must make some expiation to the true deity who is a severe God, & persuades him to burn out his eyes. Cain opposes this idea & says that God himself who had inflicted this punishment upon him had done it be cause he neglected to make a proper use of his senses &c The evil spirit answers him that God WP 10
is indeed a God of Mercy & that an example must be given to Mankind & that again ills must be given to mankind. That this end will be answered by his terrible appearance at the same time that his senses he will be gratified, with the most Delicious Sights and feelings. Cain overpersuaded, consents to do it but wishes to go to the top of the rocks to take a farewell of the earth. . His farewell Speech concluding with an abrupt address WP 15
to the promised redeemer & he abandons the idea of which the being had ƿaccompanied him, & turning round to declare this to the being, he sees him dancing from rock to rock in his former shape down those interminable precipices.—

Child influenced by his father's ⟨Cain⟩ ravings goes out to pluck the fruits in the moon-light wildness.—Cain's soliloquy—Child returns with ?soup a pitcher of water & a cake WP 20
Cain wonders what kind of beings dwell in that place—whether any created since Man or whether this world had any beings rescued from the chaos wandering like shipwrecked beings [?]rescued from the former world—
Midnight on the Euphrates cedars palms pines—Cain ?roses discovered sitting on the upper part of the ragged rock where is caverns overlooking the Euphrates the moon WP 25

rising on the horizon. * His soliloquy. The Beasts are out on the romp ~~He determines to rush out amongst them~~ & oppose himself ~~to be destroyed by him. A multitude of these beasts come roaring up to him. Walking among the beasts~~ he hears the screams of ⟨a⟩ Woman & children—surrounded by tigers. ⟨Cain makes a soliloquy debating whether he shall save the woman⟩ Cain advances wishing Death—& the tigers rush off. It proves to be Cain's wife with her two children, determined to follow her husband. She prevails upon him at last to tell his story. ⟨Cain's wife tells him that her son Enoch was placed suddenly by his side.⟩   wp 30

Cain addresses all the elements to cease for a while to persecute him while he tells his story. He begins with telling her that he had first after his leaving her found out a dwelling in the desart under a juniper tree &c &c. how he meets in the desart a young man whom upon a nearer approach he perceives to be Abel, ~~Cain was overwhel~~ on whose countenance appear marks of the greatest misery—the power of another being who had power after this life, greater than Jehovah—He is going to offer sacrifices to this being & persuades Cain to follow him, to come to an immense Gulph filled out with water whither they descend followed by Alligators &c. They go till they come to an immense meadow, so surrounded as to be inaccessible & from its depth so vast that you could not see it from above. Abel offers sacrifice from the blood of his arm. A gleam of light illumines the meadow & ~~a being of terrible majesty appears.~~ The countenance of Abel becomes more beautiful & his arms glistering, he then persuades Cain to of-fer sacrifice for himself & his son Enoch by ~~letting~~ cutting his Child's arm & letting the blood fall from it. Cain is about to do it when Abel himself ~~with~~ in his Angelic appearance. Attended by Michael is seen ~~in~~ the heavens whence they sail slowly down. Abel addresses Cain with terror warning him not to offer up his innocent child. The Evil spirit throws off the countenance of Abel. & assumes his own shape, flies off pursuing a flying battle with Michael, & Abel carries off the Child.   wp 35 ... wp 40 ... wp 45 ... wp 50

draft for a continuation? [MS 3 only]

The Child is born, the Child must die/ Among the desert Sands/ And we too all must die of Thirst/ for not a Drop remains. But whither do we retire/ to Heaven or possibility of Heaven/ But this to darkness, Cold, & tho' not positive Torment, yet positive Evil— Eternal Absence from Communion with the Creator. O how often have the [??] Sands at night roar'd & whitened like a burst of waters/ O that indeed they were! Then full of enthusiastic faith kneels & prays, & in holy frenzy covers the child with sand. In the name of the Father &c &c/—Twas done/ the Infant died/ the blessed Sand retired, each particle to itself, conglomerating, & shrinking from the profane sand/ the Sands shrank away from it, & left a pit/ still hardening & hardening, at length shot up a fountain large & mighty/   DR 5 ... DR 10

How wide around its Spray, the rain-bow played upon the Stream & the Spray—but lo! another brighter, O far far more bright/ it hangs over the head of a glorious Child like a floating veil (vide Raphael's God)—the Soul arises/ they drink, & fill their Skins, & depart rejoicing—O Blessed the day when that good man & all his Company came to Heaven Gate & the Child—then an angel—rushed out to receive them—   DR 15

prefatory note

I‾**1.1** *3 4* PREFATORY NOTE I TO THE WANDERINGS OF CAIN. • *5* THE WANDERINGS OF CAIN. I PREFATORY NOTE.

3–5   A prose composition, one not in metre at least, seems *prima facie* to require explanation or apology. It was written in the year 1798, near Nether Stowey in Somersetshire, at which place (*sanctum et amabile nomen!* rich by so many associations and recollections) the Author had taken up his residence in order $1^-1.5$ to enjoy the society and close neighbourhood of a dear and honoured friend, T. Poole, Esq. The work was to have been written in concert with another, whose name is too venerable within the precincts of genius to be unnecessarily brought into connection with such a trifle, and who was then residing at a small distance from Nether Stowey. The title and subject were suggested by myself, $1^-1.10$ who likewise drew out the scheme and the contents for each of the three books or cantos, of which the work was to consist, and which, the reader is to be informed, was to have been finished in one night! My partner undertook the first canto; I the second: and which ever had *done first*, was to set about the third. Almost thirty years have passed by; yet at this moment I cannot without $1^-1.15$ something more than a smile moot the question which of the two things was the more impracticable, for a mind so eminently original to compose another man's thoughts and fancies, or for a taste so austerely pure and simple to imitate the Death of Abel? Methinks I see his grand and noble countenance as at the moment when having dispatched my own portion of the task at full finger-speed, $1^-1.20$ I hastened to him with my manuscript—that look of humourous despondency fixed on his almost blank sheet of paper, and then its silent mock-piteous admission of failure struggling with the sense of the exceeding ridiculousness of the whole scheme—which broke up in a laugh: and the Ancient Mariner was written instead. $1^-1.25$

Years afterward, however, the draft of the Plan and proposed Incidents, and the portion executed, obtained favor in the eyes of more than one person, whose judgment on a poetic work could not but have weighed with me, even though no parental partiality had been thrown into the same scale, as a makeweight: and I determined on commencing anew, and composing the whole in $1^-1.30$ stanzas, and made some progress in realizing this intention, when adverse gales drove my bark off the "Fortunate Isles" of the Muses; and then other and more momentous interests prompted a different voyage, to firmer anchorage and a securer port. I have in vain tried to recover the lines from the Palimpsest tablet of my memory: and I can only offer the introductory stanza, which had been $1^-1.35$ committed to writing for the purpose of procuring a friend's judgment on the metre, as a specimen.

4 1 5 3–5   Encinctur'd with a twine of Leaves,
                   That leafy Twine his only Dress!

A lovely Boy was plucking fruits
In a moon-light Wilderness.
The Moon was bright, the Air was free,   I 5
And Fruits and Flowers together grew
On many a Shrub and many a Tree:
And all put on a gentle Hue
Hanging in the shadowy Air
Like a Picture rich and rare.   I 10
It was a Climate where, they say,
The Night is more belov'd than Day.
But who that beauteous Boy beguil'd
That beauteous Boy to linger here?
Alone, by Night, a little Child,   I 15
In place so silent and so wild—
Has he no *Friend*, no loving Mother near?

3 4   I have here given the birth, parentage, and premature decease of the
"Wanderings of Cain, a poem,"—intreating, however, my Readers not to
think so meanly of my judgment as to suppose that I either regard or offer
it as any excuse for the publication of the following fragment, (and I may
add, of one or two others in its neighbourhood) in its primitive crudity. But I 17[+].5
I should find still greater difficulty in forgiving myself, were I to record pro
tædio publico a set of petty mishaps and annoyances which I myself wish
to forget. I must be content therefore with assuring the friendly Reader,
that the less he attributes its appearance to the Author's will, choice, or
judgment, the nearer to the truth he will be.   I 17[+].10

S. T. COLERIDGE.

II ⁻**1.1.** 2 Book the Second • *2* A FRAGMENT. • *3 4* THE WANDERINGS OF
CAIN. | CANTO II. • *5* CANTO II.

2 2–5   "A little further, O my Father! yet a little further; and we shall come
out into the open moonlight." It runs on a narrow path, Their road was thro' a
forest of fir-trees. At
its entrance ⟨the Trees⟩ stood at distances from each other; and the path was
broad; and the moonlight and the moonlight shadows reposed upon it,
and appeared quietly to inhabit that solitude. But soon the path winded   II 5
and became narrow; and the Sun at high noon sometimes speckled but never
illumined it: and now it was dark as a Cavern.
It is dark, O my Father! said Enos—but the path under our feet is
smooth and soft—and we shall soon come out into the open moonlight. Ah why
dost thou groan so deeply?—
Lead on, my child, ℂ said Cain: guide me, little child. And the   II 10
innocent little child clasped a finger of the hand, which had murdered
the righteous Abel—and he guided his father. The fir-branches drip upon
thee, my son. Yea, pleasantly, Father: for I ran fast and eagerly to bring
thee the pitcher and the cake, and my body is not yet cool. How happy
the Squirrels are that feed on these fir trees! they leap from bough to   II 15
bough; and the old Squirrels play round their young ones in the nest. I
clomb a tree yesterday noon, O my father! that I might play with them;

but they leapt away. From the branches even to the slender twigs did
they leap, and in a moment I beheld them on another Tree. Why, O my
Father! would they not play with me? Is it, because we are not so happy as they?   II 20
~~Is it because I groan sometimes even as thou groanest? /~~   II 21
Then Cain stopped, and   II 23
stifling his groans he sank to the Earth; and the child Enos stood in the
darkness beside him.—   II 25
    And Cain lifted up his voice, and cried bitterly, & said—The Mighty
one, that persecuteth me, is on this side and that: he pursueth my soul,
like the wind: like the sand-blast, he passeth thro' me: he is around me.
even as the air.—I that I might be utterly no more! I desire to die—yea,
the things that never had life, neither move they upon the earth, behold   II 30
they seem precious to mine eyes. O that a man might live without the
breath of his nostrils, ~~that~~ so I might abide in darkness, and blackness, and
an empty space! Yea, I would lie down, I would not rise, neither would I
stir my limbs, till I became as the rock in the den of the Lion on which the
young Lyon resteth his head while he sleepeth. For the Torrent, that roareth   II 35
far off, hath a voice; and the Clouds in heaven look terribly on me; ~~and the wind~~
    ~~in the Cedar grove telleth of judgment~~ the
Mighty One who is against me, speaketh in the wind of the Cedar-grove;
and in silence I am dried up.—Then Enos ~~said /~~ spake to his Father: Arise,
my Father! arise: we are but a little way from the place where I found
the cake and the pitcher. And Cain said, How knowest thou? And the   II 40
Child answered—Behold, the bare rocks are a few of thy strides' distant
from the forest; and while even now thou wert lifting up thy voice, I
heard the echo.—Then the Child took hold of his father, as if he would
raise him; and Cain, being faint & feeble, rose slowly on his knees, and
pressed ⟨himself⟩ against the trunk of ~~the Tree~~ a Fir, and stood upright, & followed   II 45
the Child.—
    The path was dark, till within three strides' length of its termination,
when it ~~made a sudden turn, and~~ turned suddenly; the thick black trees ~~made~~
    formed a low arch, and
the moonlight appeared for a moment like a dazzling portal. Enos ran
before, and stood in the open air: and when Cain, his ~~emer~~ father, emerged   II 50
from the darkness, the Child was affrighted: for the mighty limbs of
Cain were wasted as by fire; ~~and~~ his hair was black & matted into loathly curls,   II 52
and his countenance was dark, and wild, and ~~spake~~ told, in a strange & terrible   II 56
language, of agonies that had been and ~~still~~ were, and were still to continue
to be.—
    The scene around was desolate: as far as the eye could reach, it was
desolate. The bare rocks faced each other, and left a long & wide inter-   II 60
val of thin white sand. You might wander on, and look round and
round, and peep into the crevices of the rocks, and ~~behold~~ discover nothing that ack-
nowledged the influence of the Seasons. There was no Spring, no Sum-
mer, no Autumn; and the winter's snow, that would have been lovely,
~~came~~ fell not on these hot rocks & scorching sands. Never morning Lark   II 65
had poised himself over this desart; but the huge serpent often hissed
there beneath the talons of the vulture, and the Vulture screamed, his
wings imprisoned within the coils of the ~~snake.~~ Serpent. The pointed & shat-

tered summits of the ridges of ⟨the⟩ rocks made a ~~strange~~ rude mimicry of human
concerns & seemed to prophecy mutely of things that then were not: II 70
~~steeples~~ spires, & battlements, & ~~ship~~ ships with naked masts.—As far from the
wood as a boy might sling a pebble of the brook, ⟨there was⟩ one ~~rocks stood~~ by
itself, at a small distance from the main ridge. It had been precipitated
thither, ~~by some~~ perhaps, by the terrible Groan which the Earth gave when our
   first Father

fell. Before you approached, it appeared to lie flat on the ground; but its   II 75
base slanted from its ~~extremity,~~ point: and between it⟨s point⟩ & the sands a tall
man might stand upright. It was here that Enos had found the pitcher
& cake; and to this place he ~~leadd~~ his father. But ere ~~he~~ they arrived there
~~he~~ they beheld a human shape: ~~and~~ his back was towards them, and they
were coming up unperceived when they heard him smite his breast &   II 80
cry aloud—Wo is me! Wo is me!—I must never die again, and yet I am
perishing with thirst & hunger.
    The face of Cain turned pale;
But Enos said, Ere yet I could speak, I am sure, O my father!   II 84–6
that I heard that voice. Have I not often said that I remembered a sweet
voice—O my Father! this is it. And Cain trembled exceedingly. The voice
was sweet indeed; but it was thin & querulous like that of a feeble
slave in misery who despairs altogether, yet cannot refrain himself   II 90
from weeping & lamentation. Enos
crept softly round the base of the rock, & stood ~~suddenly~~ before the stranger, and
looked up into his face—and the ~~Man~~ Shape shrieked and turned round, and
Cain beheld him that his limbs and his face were those of his Brother
Abel's whom he had killed: and Cain stood like one who struggles in his   II 95
sleep because of the exceeding terribleness of a dream;
and ere he had recovered himself from the tumult of his agitation, the Shape fell
   at his
feet, and embraced his knees, & cried ~~out~~ out with a bitter ~~cry~~ outcry—~~Son of~~
   ~~my Mother,~~ †Thou
eldest born of Adam, whom Eve, my mother, brought forth, cease to tor-
ment me! I was feeding my flocks in green pastures by the side of quiet
rivers, and thou killedst me; and now I am in misery. Then Cain closed   II 100
his eyes and hid them with his hands: and again he opened his eyes,
and looked around him, and said to Enos—What ~~see~~ beholdest thou? Didst
thou hear a voice, my Son?—Yes, my Father! I behold a man in unclean
garments, and he uttered a sweet voice full of lamentation.—Then Cain   II 105
raised up the Shape that was like Abel and said—The Creator of our
father, who had respect unto thee and to thy offering—wherefore hath
he forsaken thee? Then the Shape shrieked a second time, and rent his
garment—~~and~~ & his naked skin was ~~of the color of Ashes~~ like the white sands
   beneath their feet.
And he shrieked yet a third time, and threw himself on his face upon the   II 110
sand that was black with the shadow of the rock; and Cain and Enos sate
beside him, the Child by his right hand & Cain by his left. They were
all three under the rock, and within the shadow. The Shape that was like
Abel raised himself up & spake to the child—I know where the cold
waters are; but I may not drink. Wherefore didst thou take away my   II 115

pitcher?—But Cain said—Didst thou not find favor in the eyes of the
Lord thy God?—~~And~~ the Shape answered, The Lord is God of the living
only—the Dead have another God. ~~And~~ Then the child Enos lifted up his eyes
& prayed; but Cain rejoiced secretly in his heart.—Wretched shall they
be all the days of their mortal life, exclaimed the Shape, who sacrifice   II 120
worthy & acceptable sacrifices to the God of the Dead; but after Death
their toil ceaseth. Woe is me—for I ⟨was⟩ well-beloved by the God of the
Living: and cruel wert thou, O my Brother! who didst snatch me away
from his power and his dominion. Have uttered these words he rose
suddenly & fled over the sands—and Cain said in his heart The curse   II 125
of the Lord is ~~in~~ on me—but who is the God of the Dead?—And he ran ~~over~~
　　after
the Shape; and the Shape fled shrieking over the ~~plain~~ sands; and the Sands
rose, like white mists, behind the steps of Cain, but the feet of him that
was like Abel disturbed not the Sands. He greatly outran Cain; and turn-
ing short he wheeled round and came again to the rock where they had   II 130
been sitting; and where Enos still stood:—and the child caught hold of his
garment, as he passed by, and he fell upon the ground—And Cain stopped,
and beholding him not, said, He is passed into the dark woods! And
he walked slowly back to the rock, and when he reached it, the Child
told him that he had caught hold of his garment as he passed by and   II 135
that the Man had fallen upon the ground. And Cain once more sat be-
side him, and said—Abel, my Brother! I would lament for thee; but that
my spirit within me is withered & burnt up with extreme agony. Now
I pray thee, by thy flocks, and thy pastures, and by the quiet rivers
which thou lovedst, that thou tell me all that thou knowest. Who is the   II 140
God of the Dead? ~~And w~~Where doth he make his dwelling? What sacrifices are
acceptable to him? For I have offered, and have not been received; I
have prayed and have not been heard; and how can I be afflicted ⟨more⟩
than I already am?—Then the Shape arose and answered—O that thou hadst
had pity on me as I will have pity on thee. Follow me, Son of Adam!   II 145
and ~~I~~ bring thy child with thee.
　　And they three passed over the white sands between the rocks, silent
as their Shadows.

canto I. ⁻1.2 *5* prima facie　　⁻1.3. *5* Stowey,　　⁻1.4. *5* sanctum et amabile nomen!
⁻1.5. *5* author　　1.14. *4 5* canto:　*5* done first,　　⁻1.20. *5* despatched
⁻1.21. *5* humorous　　⁻1.26. *5* plan　*5* incidents,　　⁻1.27. *4 5* favour
⁻1.32. *4 5* Muses:　　⁻1.34. *5* palimpsest　　1. *3–5* Encinctured　*3–5* leaves,
2. *1 5 3–5* twine　*3–5* dress!　　3. *3–5* fruits,　　4. *4* In a moon-light • *1* In
a moonlight • *5* In a Moonlight • *3–5* By moonlight, in a　*1 5 3–5* wilderness.
5. *4 1 5* Moon • *5* moon • *3 4* morn　*1 5 3–5* air　*5* free—　　6. *3–5* fruits
3–5 flowers　　7. *3–5* shrub　*3–5* tree:　　8. *1 5 3–5* hue,　　9. *1 5 3–5* air
10. *3–5* picture　　11. *5* ₵Climate • *3–5* climate　　12. *1* night, • *3–5* night
1 5 beloved　*3–5* day.　　13. *1 5 3–5* beguil'd,　　14. *1 5* Boy!　　15. *1 5 3–*
5 night,　*1 3–5* child,　　17. *1 5 3–5* friend,　*1 5* mother

canto II. 1. *2–5* father,　*2–5* further,　　1–2. *2* come out • *2–5* come into
2. *2 3* moonlight!" Their • *4 5* moonlight." Their　*2–5* through　*2–5* fir-trees;

at   **3.** *2–5* the trees   *2–5* other,   **4.** *2–5* broad,   *2–4* moonlight, and   **6.** *2–5* narrow; the   *2–5* sun   *2–5* speckled,   **7.** *2–5* it, and   *2–5* cavern.   **8.** *2–5* "It *2–5* father!"   *2–5* Enos, "but   **9.** *2–5* soft,   *3–5* moonlight."   2 2 Ah . . . deeply?—] *3–5* omit   2 Ah,   2 deeply?"   **10.** *2–5* "Lead   2 on   2 child," said • *3–5* child!" said   2 Cain,   *2–5* "guide   2 child." • *3–5* child!"   **11.** *2–5* hand **12.** *2–5* Abel,   *2–5* "The fir branches   **13.** 2 thee   2 son."— • *3–5* son." *2–5* "Yea,   *2–5* father,   **15.** *2–5* squirrels   5 fir-trees!   **15–16.** *2–5* bough to bough,   **16.** *2–5* squirrels   **17.** 2 yesterday noon, • *2–5* yesterday at noon,   *2–5* father,   *2–5* them,   **18.** 5 leaped   *2–5* away from   *2–5* branches, **19.** *2–5* tree.   **20.** *2–5* father,   **20–3.** 2 with me? Is it because we are not as happy as they? Is it because I groan sometimes even as thou groanest?" Then • *3–5* with me? I would be good to them as thou art good to me: and I groaned to them even as thou groanest when thou givest me to eat, and when thou coverest me at evening, and as often as I stand at thy knee and thine eyes look at me?" Then **24.** 2 groans,   *2–5* earth,   **25–6.** 2 him; and • *3–5* him. And   **26.** *3–5* voice and   *2–5* and said, "The   **27.** *2–5* One   *2–5* me   2 and that: • *2–5* and on that; *2–5* soul   **28.** *2–5* wind,   *2–5* sand-blast   *2–5* through me;   **28–9.** *2–5* me even   **29.** 2 air, • *3–5* air!   2 I that • *2–5* O that   **30.** *2–5* earth—   *3–5* behold! **32.** 2 nostrils, so • *3–5* nostrils. So   2 darkness   **34.** *2–5* limbs   *2–5* lion, on **35.** *2–5* young lion   *2–5* whilst   *2–5* torrent   **36.** *2–5* off   *4* 5 voice: *2–5* clouds *2–5* me; the   **37.** *2–4* mighty one   *2–5* me   *2–5* cedar grove;   **38.** 2 I am • *2–5* am I   *2–5* up." Then   *2–5* Enos spake   *2–5* father,   *2–4* "Arise • *5* "Arise, **39.** *2–5* father, arise, we   **40.** 2 pitcher;" and • *3–5* pitcher." And   *2–5* "How *2–5* thou?" and   **41.** *2–5* child   2 —"Behold, • *3–5* —"Behold   *2–5* strides **43.** *2–5* echo." Then   *2–5* child   **44.** 2 him, • *3–5* him: *2–5* Cain   *2–5* and feeble *2–5* knees   **45.** *2–5* himself   *2–5* of a fir,   *2–5* upright and   **46–7.** *2–5* child. The   **47.** *2–5* dark   2 termination   **48.** *2–5* it turned   *2–5* trees formed **50.** *2–5* before   *2–5* air;   *2–5* his father,   **51.** 2 darkness   *2–5* child   2 affrighted, for • *3–5* affrighted. For   **52.** *2–5* fire; his   2 black, and   **52–8.** 2 2 hair . . . be.— • *3–5* hair was as the matted curls on the Bison's [5 bison's] forehead, and so glared his fierce and sullen eye beneath: and the black abundant locks on either side, a rank and tangled mass, were stained and scorched, as though the grasp of a burning iron hand had striven to rend them; and his countenance told in a strange and terrible language of agonies that had been, and were, and were still to continue to be.   **56.** 2 dark   2 and told   **56–7.** 2 and terrible language   **57.** 2 been, 2 and were,   **58.** 2 be.   **59.** *2–5* desolate; as   *3–5* reach   **60.** 2 desolate; the • *3–5* desolate: the   *2–5* and wide   **61.** 2 *3–5* thin • 2 their   *2–5* on   **62.** *3–5* rocks   *2–5* and discover   **63.** *2–5* seasons.   *2–5* spring,   **63–4.** *2–5* summer, **64.** 2 autumn, • *3–5* autumn: 2 snow   **64–5.** *2–5* lovely, fell   **65.** *2–5* and scorching   *2–5* lark   **66.** *2–5* desert;   **67.** *2–5* vulture screamed,   **68.** *2–5* the serpent.   *2–5* pointed and   **69.** *2–5* the rocks   *2–5* a rude   **70.** *2–5* concerns, and   5 prophesy   *2–5* not;   **71.** 2 steeples spires, • *2–5* steeples,   *2–5* and battlements, and ships   *2–5* masts. As   **72.** *2–5* there was one rock   **73.** 2– 5 itself   **73–4.** 2 precipitated thither, by some perhaps, • *2–5* precipitated there perhaps   **74.** 2 the terrible Groan which the • 2 the terrible groan the • *3–5* the groan which the   2 earth   2 2 gave • *3–5* uttered   *2–5* father   **75.** *2–5* ground, **76.** *2–5* from its point,   2 its points and the • *3–5* its point and the   **78.** *2–5* and cake,   *2–5* he led   **78–9.** 2 they arrived there they • *3–5* they had reached the rock they   **79.** 2 shape; his • *3–5* shape: his   **80.** 2 2 were coming up unperceived •

3–5 were advancing unperceived, *2–5* and **81.** *2–4* aloud, "Wo, • *5* aloud, "Woe *2–4* wo, • *5* woe *2–5* me! I **82–6.** *2* and hunger." I The face of Cain turned pale; but Enos said, • *3–5* and hunger." I Pallid, as the reflection of the sheeted lightning on the heavy-sailing Night-cloud, [*5* night-cloud,] became the face of Cain; but the child Enos took hold of the shaggy skin, his Father's [*5* father's] robe, and raised his eyes to his Father, [*5* father,] and listening whispered, **86.** *2–5* "Ere *2–5* father, **87.** *2* I not • *2–5* not I **88.** *2–4* voice. O • *5* voice? O *2–5* father! *2* it;" • *3–5* it:" *2–5* and **89.** *2–5* indeed, *2–5* and *5* querulous, **90.** *2–5* misery, *2–5* can not **91.** *2–5* weeping and **91–2.** *2* 2 lamentation. Enos crept softly • *3–5* lamentation. And, behold! Enos glided forward, and creeping softly **92.** *2* and stood before • *3–5* stood before **93.** *2–5* face. And the Shape shrieked, **94.** *2–5* him, *2–5* brother **95.** *2 5* Abel • *3 4* A B E L *2* killed; and • *3–5* killed! And **96–7.** *2* 2 dream; . . . his agitation, • *3–5* dream. I Thus as he stood in silence and darkness of Soul, [*5* soul,] **97.** *3 4* S H A P E **98.** *2–5* knees, and *2–5* cried out *2–5* bitter outcry, "Thou **101.** *2–5* misery." **102.** *2–5* eyes, *2* hands— • *3–5* hands; **103.** *2* Enos "What beholdest • *3–5* Enos, "What beholdest **104.** *3 4* voice *2–5* son?" "Yes, *2–5* father, *2* behold • *2–5* beheld **105.** *2–5* voice, *2–5* lamentation." **106.** *2* shape *2–5* Abel, *2* said, "The • *3* said. "The • *4 5* said:—"The *2* creator **107.** *2–5* thee, *2* and to thy offering— • *2–5* and unto thy offering, **108.** *2 3 5* thee?" • *4* thee?', **109.** *2–5* garment, and *2–5* like **109–10.** *2–5* feet; and **111.** *2 5* rock, **112.** *2–5* him; *2–5* child *2–5* hand, and **114.** *2–5* up, and *2 3* child; "I • *4 5* child: "I **115.** *2 5* are, • *3 4* are *2–5* drink, wherefore *2* thou take • *2–5* thou then take **116.** *2–5* pitcher?" But *2–5* said, "Didst *2–5* favour *2* eyes • *2–5* sight **117.** *2–5* God?" The *2–5* "The Lord **118.** *2–5* only, *2–5* dead *2–5* God." Then **119.** *2–5* and *2–5* heart. "Wretched **120.** *2–5* life," *2–5* "who **121.** *2–5* and *2–5* dead; *2–5* death **122.** *2–5* me, *2–5* was well beloved **123.** *2–5* living, *2–5* brother, **124.** *2* dominion. Have • *2–5* dominion." Having *2–5* words, **125.** *2–5* suddenly, and *2–4* sands; • *5* sands: *2–5* heart, "The **126.** *2–5* is on *3–5* me; *2–4* dead?" and • *5* dead? and *2–5* ran after **127.** *2–5* Shape, and *2–5* over the sands, **127–8.** *2–5* sands rose **128.** *2–5* mists **129.** *2–5* sands. *2–5* outrun *2–5* Cain, **130.** *2–5* short, *2–5* round, **131.** *2–5* sitting, *2–5* stood; and *2* Child **132.** *2–5* garment *2* ground; and • *3–5* ground. And **133.** *2* He is • *2–5* "he has *2–5* woods," **133–4.** *2* And he walked • *2* and walked • *3–5* and he walked **134.** *2* rock, • *2* rocks, • *3– 5* rocks; *2–5* it *2–5* child **135.** *2–5* by, **136.** *2–5* man *2 3* ground; and • *4 5* ground: and *4 5* sate **137.** *3–5* said, *2–5* "Abel, *2–5* brother, *2–5* thee, **138.** *2* my spirit • *2–5* the spirit *2–5* withered, and *2–5* Now, **139.** *2* flocks *2* and thy • *2–5* and by thy **140.** *2* lovest, **141.** *2–5* dead? where *2–5* what **142.** *2* to • *2–5* unto *2–5* for *2* offered, and • *2 3 5* offered, but • *4* offered,. but **143.** *2–5* prayed, *2–5* more **144.** *2* am?—Then the Shape. • *2–5* am?" The Shape *3–5* answered, *2–5* "O **145.** *2* son **146.** *2–5* and bring **146–7.** *2* thee:" and • *3–5* thee!" And **148.** *2* 2 their • *3–5* the *2–4* shadows.

WP 4. roaring] EHC reads "wild", which appears less likely.

WP 19. influenced] EHC reads "affeared", which appears less likely.

WP 23. the former] EHC reads "another", which is possible.

WP 26. * His soliloquy.] The completed canto II (TEXTS 2 2–5) possibly fits in at about this point.

romp] EHC reads "ramp", which is possible.

WP 33. his] EHC reads "her", which appears less likely.

WP 38. power] EHC leaves blank; perhaps "face", "form".

WP 45. glistering] EHC has the same reading; possibly "glistening".

I 1.17⁺.6–7. pro *tædio* publico] Tr "for the *boredom* of the public" (a play on "pro bono publico").

II 2. PR *3* moonlight!"] The exclamation-mark is cast in faulty type, which makes it resemble a colon.

II 8. It is dark] No new paragraph in MS 2.

II 10. Lead on] No new paragraph in MS 2.

II 21. The MS 2 deletion is in pencil.

II 26. And Cain] No new paragraph in TEXTS 2 *2*.

II 45. MS 2 a Fir] The substitution is in pencil.

II 47. The path] No new paragraph in TEXTS 2 *2*.

II 71. MS 2 spires] The substitution is in pencil.

II 83. No new paragraph in MS 2; PR *2* begins a new paragraph with "The face", PR *3–5* with "Pallid".

II 97. PR *3–5* Thus] No new paragraph in TEXTS 2 *2*.

II 108. PR *4* thee?',] The apparent comma appears like a dropped piece of type from a double quotation-mark.

II 125. PR *4* sands;] The semicolon is cast in faulty type, which makes it resemble a colon.

II 147. And they] No new paragraph in TEXTS 2 *2*.

161. THE RIME OF THE ANCIENT MARINER

A. DATE

Nov 1797–23 Mar 1798, with subsequent revisions (1800, 1806–7, 1815–17, etc) to 1834. The poem was planned jointly with WW on ?12 Nov 1797, to defray the expenses of the walking tour they embarked upon that day. They abandoned the attempt to compose the poem conjointly perhaps the same evening, and certainly before they returned on 20 Nov (Reed I 210).

C wrote to Joseph Cottle, immediately following his return from the tour, informing him that he had written "a ballad of about 300 lines" (*CL* I 357: [c 20 Nov 1797]), a ballad he claimed to have finished, by 18 Feb 1798, in 340 lines (*CL* I 387: to J. Cottle 18 Feb 1798). While such a description might cover C's contribution to *The Three Graves* (see poem **155** sec A), this is less likely than the supposition that C is referring to an early form of *The Rime of the Ancient Mariner*. Almost certainly the 340-line version was close to the narrative situation described by George Shelvocke *A Voyage round the World by Way of the Great South Sea, Performed in the Years 1719–1722* (1726), brought to C's notice by WW, and it centred on the mariner's voyage to the South Pole, his killing of the albatross, and his return to his own country.

DW describes C coming to Alfoxden on 23 Mar 1798 and bringing his ballad "finished" (*DWJ* I 13)—that is, if in the version which was soon afterwards printed—658 lines long. One can only suppose that the bulk of C's additions were to the supernatural machinery, together with the new Parts V and VI. The supposition rests on several features and kinds of evidence. These parts of the poem interrupt the sweep of the narrative and modify the original joint conception; they differ slightly in their rhythm and style; their concern with the Mariner's guardian saint, and with how the Mariner is redeemed, looks forward to **176** *Christabel*, which was gestating in the early months of 1798 and which C began to work on immediately afterwards; Charles Lloyd quoted the two stanzas which open Part VI in his notes on **146.X1** *Osorio* III i 59–60, 165–8 (Appendix), which he probably made in Feb–Mar 1798, and he does not quote other parallels to other parts which are equally obvious (e.g. between *Osorio* V ii 97–100 and *Ancient Mariner* 257–60).

In the copies of *LB* (1798) and (1800) which C emended, Parts V and VI receive his attention in ways which suggest that they were least digested, more recent, and more personally pressing. WW's criticism of the poem, in his own *Peter Bell* and in the note he appended to PR 2 below, point to the same conclusion. And finally, Stephen Parrish has pointed out that the number of lines in Parts I–IV total 284; and that when a closing section of about the same length as one of Parts I–IV is added, the total comes to 340 lines. Parts V and VI are a quite different length from earlier sections and, taken along with the difference in length between the present Part VII and other, earlier sections, they total the 300 and more lines which bring the poem up to 658 ("'Leaping and Lingering': Coleridge's Lyrical Ballads" in *Coleridge's Imagination: Essays in Memory of Pete Laver* ed Richard Gravil, Lucy Newlyn, and Nicholas Roe—Cambridge 1985—102–16 at 110–11). Two different strata in the poem are evident, though it is impossible to reconstruct the phases of which the inconsistencies are, as it were, the fossils.

C tinkered with the poem in its first printed version, but substantially revised it in Jul 1800 for the new edition of *LB* (*CL* I 598–602: to Biggs and Cottle [mid-Jul 1800]). It seems that its particular relevance to his own concerns was borne in on him during the Scottish Tour of 1802 and, even more, the voyage to Malta in 1805 (*CN* II 1996, 1997, 2001, 2002, 2048, etc); and he attempted further revision on his return (*CN* II 2880).

The origins of the marginal gloss are evident in an annotated copy of *LB* (1800), perhaps as early as 1800–2, but it is unlikely to have been written in its present form until C submitted copy for *SL* late in 1815. The additions to the gloss, in particular, in annotated copies of PR 5 below might be evidence that its composition was then relatively recent. This version of the poem, which included further revisions, appeared in 1817, and C made further adjustments just before and after publication. Minor improvements in the versions of *PW* (1828, 1829, 1834) show C's continued interest in the poem.

1 [=RT LH pp]. *LB* (1798).

A copy of the first issue at Trinity College Cambridge (TCL RW 38 28–29) is annotated in C's hand, in ink and pencil. The ink annotations are illustrated in *The Rothschild Library* (2 vols Cambridge 1954) II facing 704. The pencil annotation (passed over in the *Rothschild Library* description) is now faint, and partly obliterated readings are supplied by RHS in *PW* (4 vols 1877–80) II 54, to whose publisher, Basil Montagu Pickering, the volume once belonged. There is good reason to believe that C's annotations were made soon after the book was printed—that is, in or soon after Sept 1798—and certainly before the end of Jun 1800. EHC (*PW* II 1030, 1032, 1039 nn) records annotations from a copy of the cancelled state of the first issue presented by C to his sister-in-law, Martha Fricker, which has not been recovered.

SC's transcript of the PR *1* text, from line 220 onwards, now at VCL (BT 31 Nos 2 and 3), has no textual significance. (Her copy of PR *1*—VCL Book No 4—is inscribed to her by her friend Archdeacon Bailey, 11 Sept 1851.) The PR *1* text is reprinted—with the substitution of the PR *2* epigraph and subtitle ("A POET'S REVERIE")—in *The American Poetical Miscellany* (2 vols Philadelphia 1809) I 282–304, where it is said to be "believed to be from the pen of the Rev. Mr. *Coleridge*".

2. *LB* (1800) vol I.

Printer's copy was provided by PR *1* revised according to a list of instructions which C sent to Biggs and Cottle in mid-Jul 1800 (Yale MS Vault Shelves + Wordsworth; *CL* I 598–602). The stage represented by these instructions is not recorded here, but two conclusions emerge: C's deletions and recastings show him thinking the revisions as he writes them out, and the revisions were the last before PR *2* was printed—that is, no further stages of revision intervened.

C's revisions prune the archaism and Gothicisms of PR *1*, extending from the form of individual words to the excision and recasting of stanzas. Some (e.g. in line 62) were prompted by reviewers, but the majority must have been encouraged by WW's belief that "the old words and the strangeness of it" deterred readers from going on with the volume (*WL—E* rev—264). C takes in two errata from PR *1* (lines 77 and 612), but not the third (lines 185, 187). A new title and a new argument were provided, and both are perhaps related to the ungenerous note on the poem included on pp [214–15] of PR *2* by WW.

A copy of PR *2* (vol I only), with corrections and additions by C, was given to the State Library of Victoria in Melbourne by Professor M. H. Irving, son of C's friend Edward Irving, who emigrated to Australia in 1856 (Victoria State Library *821.71L). C has signed the *Ancient Mariner* on the half-title "by S. T. Coleridge", corrected the text at line 583, added to the Argument, and provided a prose gloss at lines 345–53. The first, third, and fourth of these annotations are reproduced in Geoffrey Little "Coleridge's Copy of *Lyrical Ballads*, 1800 and his Connection with the Irving Family" *The Book Collector* XXXIII (1984) 457–

69 at 467–9. C's first impulse was evidently to elaborate the Argument, and the similarity between what he added here and the added prose gloss suggests that one followed directly from the other, both being suggested by phrases in the poem. His additions might have been prompted by WW's note on the poem in PR 2, on the poem's lack of purpose etc; or they might have accompanied his tinkering with the poem in 1806–7, as he projected a new collection to be published by Longman.

The two 1800 volumes were reprinted in one at Philadelphia in 1802, with unauthorised changes, particularly of punctuation.

3. LB (1802) vol I.

Substantially identical with PR 2. The Argument and WW's note are omitted, there is an emendment in line 198.1.3, and there are refinements of capitalisation and punctuation (lines 28, 106, 108, 178, 521, etc). The (slight) changes are unlikely to possess C's authority.

Reprinted with intercalated, appreciative critical commentary in *Whitby Repository* v (1829) 114–18, 140–2, 182–5, 205–7, 263–6, 315–18.

4. LB (1805) vol I.

The same pagination as PR *3* and superficially identical, but easily differentiated by changes in capitalisation and punctuation, expansion of apostrophes, and the like. A good many—though not all—of the PR *4* changes are motivated by a spirit of improving tidiness and logic, which suggests that they are not C's.

5. SL (1817).

Rpt *Select British Poets* ed William Hazlitt (1824) 619–25 (without epigraph or gloss); *Metrical Romances &c. By S. T. Coleridge* (Isleworth 1825); *Spirit of Contemporary Poetry* (3 vols Boston, Mass 1827) II 49–84 (with an introduction on pp 47–8 made up from [J. G. Lockhart] "Essays on the Lake School of Poetry, No. III: Coleridge" *Bl Mag* VI—Oct 1819—3–12).

PR 5 is most probably based on a revision of PR 2. The evidence is line 198.1.3, where the PR *3 4* emendation is ignored in PR 5 (as is the case in other C poems from PR 2); and PR 2 is the last text in the *LB* sequence with which C was directly concerned. At the same time, there are connections between PR 5 and PR *3* (e.g. lines 106, 108, 171; in line 171 the PR *3* reading appears to be the result of broken type, but it continues into PR *4 5* and thereafter). In some instances (lines 97, 517, 578, and see 62) PR *1* readings are restored. There are no connections between PR *4* and PR 5.

PR 5 is a careful and thoroughgoing revision, extending to details. It includes the epigraph for the first time, along with the (nearly full) gloss. While some capitals are removed, others are added—like "Moon" in lines 321, 329, etc. *CN* II 2880 (Oct 1806), being a draft for the revised lines 201–12, suggests that PR 5 developed some time after 1806–7, and this version is unlikely to have been written down until 1814–15. The evidence of the gloss added to the Irving copy of PR 2, which is connected in style and phrasing, suggests that the PR 5 gloss was added on a different occasion: although it springs from the same impulse, C takes care in PR 5 to differentiate it from the poem. WW's later remarks on the gloss support the same conclusion: his disclaimer that he and C ever discussed it (Christopher Wordsworth *Memoirs of William Wordsworth*—2 vols 1851—I 108) suggests that the gloss was added after 1804, or after 1806–7, or after 1812. The epigraph from Burnet, on the other hand, was copied into a notebook perhaps as early as 1801–2 (*CN* I 1000H).

The first, important stage of the PR 5 revision was reached in the months before Nov–Dec 1815, when proofs were submitted and returned to John Mathew Gutch and to John Evans, the Bristol printer. The quarrel which arose over printing arrangements is charted in the editorial apparatus to *BL* (*CC*), and the proofs of *SL* are now at Yale (In C678 817sa). No attempt has been made to record this proof stage in the apparatus, but the following points may be noted. The signatures containing the *Ancient Mariner* contain very few corrections, which are of a minor sort, and the text is substantially as published in PR 5 (complete with gloss and other revisions of PR 2–4). The first signature, B, in particular is very lightly marked, and at the same time is endorsed in the hand of the printer, John Evans, "Nov. 26—" in a way which is not characteristic of the rest (with their postmarks, overstamps, etc). Again, sig D, containing the last part of the poem, is missing—the only signature absent from the set which Gutch printed. Taking all this into consideration, there is enough which is not entirely straightforward to make one think that there might after all be something in the claim C made, in notes added to JG's and Francis Wrangham's (?) copies, that he and the printer disagreed as early as in the printing of the first signatures, containing the *Ancient Mariner* (see note on lines 198.1.1– 4).

A lesser stage of minor revisions was reached in the months just before and after publication. Some changes were introduced in the Errata, which were printed off in sig A between May and Jul 1817; others were copied out by hand in the months and years following publication.

The following copies contain annotation to the *Ancient Mariner* in C's hand, dating from just before or soon after the time of publication: JG's (HUL *EC8 C6795 817s (C)); HNC's (HUL *AC L8605 Zy 817c); Francis Wrangham's (?) (sold at Christie's 13 Jun 1979 lot 126); J. H. Frere's (Princeton University Library Robert H. Taylor Collection); Thomas Middleton's (sold at Sotheby's 4 Aug 1939 lot 325).

A further group of copies contain emendations in the hand of JG or AG, apparently copied from an original in C's hand, in the months following publication (Jul, Aug, Sept 1817); or possibly all were copied in Jul and sent to friends in the months following. Of this group, WW's (Cornell WORDSWORTH PR 4480 S5 1817 Copy 1), TP's (Brown PR 4478 A1 1817 Koopman Collection), and an unnamed person's (Yale In C678 817S Copy 2) have emendations in AG's hand. William Hood's copy (Columbia X825C67 W3 1817) and Martha Fricker's (HUL Lowell *EC8 C6795 817s) have emendations copied by JG.

The copies given by C to AG (Stanford V 821.6 C69s) and to Miss Ford

(HUL *EC8 C6795 817s (A)) appear to have been emended, and were certainly presented, at a later stage again. All the copies cited take in different selections of the printed Errata, and of other emendations and comments. The reasons for ordering them thus are given in vol I annex C 17, along with information on untraced copies which are reported to carry annotations.

6. *PW* (1828).

PR 6 takes in the Errata to PR 5 and the gloss to lines 199–202, added in many annotated copies. It corrects a few minor errors of punctuation, fills out contractions, and makes a few slight improvements. At the same time, it introduces a few very minor errors of its own.

Two brief pencilled emendations to the PR 6 text—possibly by C—are cited in *PW* (EHC) I 198, 206 nn. This copy has not been traced.

7. *PW* (1829).

PR 7 has the same pagination as PR 6, and the texts of the poem are very similar. PR 7 corrects minor errors, and introduces a considerable number of changes to the punctuation.

8 [=RT RH pp]. *PW* (1834).

PR 8 introduces a few more corrections, in punctuation and capitalisation, but at the same time some errors creep back in.

divisional title. *1 5–8* THE RIME I OF THE I ANCYENT MARINERE, I IN I SEVEN PARTS.• *2–4* THE I ANCIENT MARINER, I A POET'S REVERIE.

argument [present in PR *1 2* only]

1 2   ARGUMENT.

1 How a Ship having passed the Line was driven by Storms to
the cold Country towards the South Pole; and how from thence
she made her course to the tropical Latitude of the Great Pacific
Ocean; and of the strange things that befell; and in what manner   ⁻1.5
the Ancyent Marinere came back to his own Country.

2 How a Ship, having first sailed to the Equator, was driven by Storms, to the cold
Country towards the South Pole; how the Ancient Mariner cruelly, and in contempt
of the laws of hospitality, killed a Sea-bird; and how he was followed by many and
strange Judgements; and in what manner he came back to his own Country.

epigraph [present in PR *5–8* only]
Facile credo, plures esse Naturas invisibiles quam visibiles in re-
rum universitate. Sed horum omnium familiam quis nobis enarra-
bit? et gradus et cognationes et discrimina et singulorum munera?
Quid agunt? quæ loca habitant? Harum rerum notitiam semper
ambivit ingenium humanum, nunquam attigit. Juvat, interea, non   ⁻1.5
diffiteor, quandoque in animo, tanquam in Tabulâ, majoris et me-
lioris mundi imaginem contemplari: ne mens assuefecta hodierniæ
vitæ minutiis se contrahat nimis, & tota subsidat in pusillas cogita-
tiones. Sed veritati interea invigilandum est, modusque servandus,
ut certa ab incertis, diem a nocte, distinguamus.   ⁻1.10

T. BURNET: *Archæol. Phil.* p. 68.

title. *1* 5–7 THE RIME I OF THE I ANCYENT MARINERE, I IN SEVEN PARTS. • *2 The ANCIENT MARINER.* I A *POET'S REVERIE.* • *3 4* THE I *ANCIENT MARINER.*

⁻1 *1–4*		I.
8		PART I.
1gl *5–8*		An ancient Mariner meeteth three Gallants bidden to a wedding-feast, and detaineth one.
1 □		It is an ancyent Marinere,
2 □		And he stoppeth one of three:
3 *1–4*		"By thy long grey beard and thy glittering eye
5 6 8		glittering
7	the	
4 *1–4*		"Now wherefore stoppest　me?
5–8		thou me?

[*Line-space*]

5 □	"The Bridegroom's doors are open'd wide
6 □	"And I am next of kin;
7 □	"The Guests are met, the Feast is set,—
8 □	"May'st hear the merry din.

[*Line-space*]

8.1.1 *1–4*	But still he holds the wedding-guest—
8.1.2 *1–4*	There was a Ship, quoth he—
8.1.3 *1–4*	"Nay, if thou'st got a laughsome tale,
8.1.4 *1–4*	"Marinere! come with me."

[*Line-space*]

9 □	He holds him with his skinny hand,
10 *1–4*	Quoth he, there was a Ship—
5–8	"There was a ship," quoth he.
11 *1–4*	"Now get thee hence, thou grey-beard Loon!
5–8	"Hold off! unhand me, grey-beard loon!"
12 *1–4*	"Or my Staff shall make thee skip.
5–8	Eftsoons　his　hand　dropt　he.

[*Line-space*]

13gl *5–8*	The wedding-guest is spell-bound by the eye of the old sea-faring man, and constrained to hear his tale.
13 □	He holds him with his glittering eye—
14 □	The wedding guest stood still
15 □	And listens like a three year's child;
16 □	The Marinere hath his will.

[*Line-space*]

17 □	The wedding-guest sate on a stone,
18 □	He cannot chuse but hear:
19 □	And thus spake on that ancyent man,
20 □	The bright-eyed Marinere.

[*Line-space*]

21 □	The Ship was cheer'd, the Harbour clear'd—
22 □	Merrily did we drop

23 □	Below the Kirk, below the Hill,
24 □	Below the Light-house top.
	[*Line-space*]
25gl *5–8*	The Mariner tells how the ship sailed southward with a good wind and fair weather, till it reached the line.
25 □	The Sun came up upon the left,
26 □	Out of the Sea came he:
27 □	And he shone bright, and on the right
28 □	Went down into the Sea.
	[*Line-space*]
29 □	Higher and higher every day,
30 □	Till over the mast at noon—
31 □	The wedding-guest here beat his breast,
32 □	For he heard the loud bassoon.
	[*Line-space*]
33gl *5–8*	The wedding-guest heareth the bridal music; but the mariner contin-ueth his tale.
33 □	The Bride hath pac'd into the Hall,
34 □	Red as a rose is she;
35 ☒*4*	Nodding their heads before her goes
4	go
36 □	The merry Minstralsy.
	[*Line-space*]
37 □	The wedding-guest he beat his breast,
38 □	Yet he cannot chuse but hear:
39 □	And thus spake on that ancyent Man,
40 □	The bright-eyed Marinere.
	[*Line-space*]
41.1 *1*	Listen, Stranger! Storm and Wind,
42.1 *1*	A Wind and Tempest strong!
42.1.1 *1*	For days and weeks it play'd us freaks—
41.2 *2–4*	But now the Northwind came more fierce,
42.2 *2–4*	There came a Tempest strong!
42.2.1 *2–4*	And Southward still for days and weeks
44.1 *1–4*	Like Chaff we drove along.
41gl *5–8*	The ship drawn by a storm toward the south pole.
41 *5–8*	And now the STORM-BLAST came, and he
42 *5–8*	Was tyrannous and strong:
43 *5–8*	He struck with his o'ertaking wings,
44 *5–8*	And chased us south along.
	[*Line-space*]
45 *5–8*	With sloping masts and dipping prow,
46 *5–8*	As who pursued with yell and blow
47 *5–8*	Still treads the shadow of his foe
48 *5–8*	And forward bends his head,
49 *5–8*	The ship drove fast, loud roar'd the blast,
50 *5–8*	And southward aye we fled.
	[*Line-space*]

51	*1*	Listen, Stranger! Mist and Snow,
	⊠*1*	And now there came both
52	☐	And it grew wond'rous cauld:
53	☐	And Ice mast-high came floating by
54	☐	As green as Emerauld.

[*Line-space*]

55gl	*5–8*	The land of ice, and of fearful sounds, where no living thing was to be seen.
55	⊠*5*	And thro' the drifts the snowy clifts
	5	clift
56	☐	Did send a dismal sheen;
57	☐	Ne shapes of men ne beasts we ken—
58	☐	The Ice was all between.

[*Line-space*]

59	☐	The Ice was here, the Ice was there,
60	☐	The Ice was all around:
61	☐	It crack'd and growl'd, and roar'd and howl'd—
62	*1*	Like noises of a swound.
	2–4	A wild and ceaseless sound.
	5–8	Like noises in a swound!

[*Line-space*]

63gl	*5–8*	Till a great sea-bird, called the Abaltross, came through the snow-fog, and was received with great joy and hospitality.
63	☐	At length did cross an Albatross,
64	☐	Thorough the Fog it came;
65	*1*	And an it were a Christian Soul,
	⊠*1*	As if it had been
66	☐	We hail'd it in God's name.

[*Line-space*]

67	*1–4*	The Marineres gave it biscuit-worms,
	5–8	It ate the food it ne'er had eat,
68	☐	And round and round it flew:
69	☐	The Ice did split with a Thunder-fit;
70	☐	The Helmsman steer'd us thro'.

[*Line-space*]

71gl	*5–8*	And lo! the Albatross proveth a bird of good omen, and followeth the ship as it returned northward, through fog and floating ice.
71	☐	And a good south wind sprung up behind,
72	☐	The Albatross did follow;
73	☐	And every day for food or play
74	⊠*6*	Came to the Marinere's hollo!
	6	mariners'

[*Line-space*]

75	☐	In mist or cloud on mast or shroud
76	☐	It perch'd for vespers nine,
77	*1*	Whiles all the night thro' fog smoke-white
	⊠*1*	fog-smoke white
78	☐	Glimmer'd the white moon-shine.

[*Line-space*]

79gl	*5–8*	The ancient Mariner inhospitably killeth the pious bird of good omen.
79	□	"God save thee, ancyent Marinere!
80	□	"From the fiends that plague thee thus—
81	□	"Why look'st thou so?"—with my cross bow
82	□	I shot the Albatross.
		[*Line-space*]
⁻**83**	*1–4*	II.
	5–7	*THE RIME OF THE ANCIENT MARINER.* | PART THE SECOND.
	8	PART II.
83	*1*	The Sun came up upon the right,
	⊠*1*	now rose
84	□	Out of the Sea came he;
85	*1*	And broad as a weft upon the left
	⊠*1*	Still hid in mist; and on
86	□	Went down into the Sea.
		[*Line-space*]
87	□	And the good south wind still blew behind,
88	□	But no sweet Bird did follow
89	□	Ne any day for food or play
90	*1–4*	Came to the Marinere's hollo!
	5–8	mariners'
		[*Line-space*]
91gl	*5–8*	His shipmates cry out against the ancient Mariner, for killing the bird of good luck.
91	□	And I had done an hellish thing
92	□	And it would work 'em woe:
93	□	For all averr'd, I had kill'd the Bird
94	□	That made the Breeze to blow.
95	*5–8*	Ah wretch! said they, the bird to slay,
96	*5–8*	That made the breeze to blow!
		[*Line-space*]
97gl	*5–8*	But when the fog cleared off, they justify the same- and thus make themselves accom,plices in the crime.
97	*1 5–8*	Ne dim ne red, like God's own head,
	2–4	an Angel's
98	□	The glorious Sun uprist:
99	□	Then all averr'd, I had kill'd the Bird
100	□	That brought the fog and mist.
101	□	'Twas right, said they, such birds to slay
102	□	That bring the fog and mist.
		[*Line-space*]
103gl	*5–8*	The fair breeze continues; the ship enters the Pacific Ocean and sails northward, even till it reaches the Line.
103	*1–4*	The breezes blew, the white foam flew,
	5–8	fair breeze
104	⊠*5*	The furrow follow'd free:
	5	stream'd off
104fn	*5*	In the former edition the line was,

The furrow follow'd free;

but I had not been long on board a ship, before I perceived that this was the image as seen by a spectator from the shore, or from another vessel. From the ship itself the *Wake* appears like a brook flowing off from the stern.

105 ☐	We were the first that ever burst
106 ☐	Into that silent Sea.

[*Line-space*]

107gl	*5–8*	The ship hath been suddenly becalmed.
107 ☐		Down dropt the breeze, the Sails dropt down,
108 ☐		'Twas sad as sad could be
109 ☐		And we did speak only to break
110 ☐		The silence of the Sea.

[*Line-space*]

111 ☐	All in a hot and copper sky
112 ☐	The bloody sun at noon,
113 ☐	Right up above the mast did stand,
114 ☐	No bigger than the moon.

[*Line-space*]

115 ☐	Day after day, day after day,
116 ☐	We stuck, ne breath ne motion,
117 ☐	As idle as a painted Ship
118 ☐	Upon a painted Ocean.

[*Line-space*]

119gl	*5–8*	And the Albatross begins to be avenged.
119 ☐		Water, water, every where
120 ☐		And all the boards did shrink;
121 ☐		Water, water, every where,
122 ☐		Ne any drop to drink.

[*Line-space*]

123	*1–4*	The very deeps did rot: O Christ!
	5–8	deep
124 ☐		That ever this should be!
125 ☐		Yea, slimy things did crawl with legs
126 ☐		Upon the slimy Sea.

[*Line-space*]

127 ☐	About, about, in reel and rout
128 ☐	The Death-fires danc'd at night;
129 ☐	The water, like a witch's oils,
130 ☐	Burnt green and blue and white.

[*Line-space*]

131gl *5–8* A spirit had followed them; one of the invisible inhabitants of this planet, neither departed souls nor angels; concerning whom the learned Jew, Josephus, and the Platonic Constantinopolitan, Michael Psellus, may be consulted. They are very numerous, and there is no climate or element without one or more.

131 ☐	And some in dreams assured were
132 ☐	Of the Spirit that plagued us so:

133 □		Nine fathom deep he had follow'd us
134 □		From the Land of Mist and Snow.
		[*Line-space*]
135 □		And every tongue thro' utter drouth
136 □		Was wither'd at the root;
137 □		We could not speak no more than if
138 □		We had been choked with soot.
		[*Line-space*]
139gl	5–8	The ship-mates, in their sore distress, would fain throw the whole guilt on the ancient Mariner: in sign whereof they hang the dead sea-bird round his neck.
139 □		Ah wel-a-day! what evil looks
140 □		Had I from old and young;
141 □		Instead of the Cross the Albatross
142 □		About my neck was hung.
		[*Line-space*]
⁻143	1–4	III.
	5–7	*THE RIME OF THE ANCIENT MARINER.* | PART THE THIRD.
	8	PART III.
148.1/143	1	I saw a something in the Sky
	2–4	So past a weary time; each throat
	5–8	There
148.1.1/144	1	No bigger than my fist;
	⊠1	Was parch'd, and glaz'd each eye,
145	5–8	A weary time! a weary time!
146	5–8	How glazed each weary eye!
147gl	5–8	The ancient Mariner beholdeth a sign in the element afar off.
147	⊠1	When, looking westward, I beheld
148	⊠1	A something in the sky.
		[*Line-space*]
149 □		At first it seem'd a little speck
150 □		And then it seem'd a mist:
151 □		It mov'd and mov'd, and took at last
152 □		A certain shape, I wist.
		[*Line-space*]
153 □		A speck, a mist, a shape, I wist!
154 □		And still it ner'd and ner'd;
155	1	And, an it dodg'd a water-sprite,
	2–5	as if
	6–8	As if
156 □		It plung'd and tack'd and veer'd.
		[*Line-space*]
157gl	5–8	At its nearer approach, it seemeth him to be a ship; and at a dear ransom he freeth his speech from the bonds of thirst.
157	1–5	With throat unslack'd, with black lips bak'd
	6–8	throats
158	1	Ne could we laugh, ne wail:
	⊠1	We nor nor

159 *1*   Then while thro' drouth all dumb they stood
☒*1*   Thro'   utter   we
160 *1*   I   bit my arm and suck'd the blood
2–4   Till I
5–8   I   I
161 □   And cry'd, A sail! a sail!
[*Line-space*]
162 *1–5*   With throat unslack'd, with black lips bak'd
6–8   throats
163 □   Agape they hear'd me call:
164gl *5–8*   A flash of joy.
164 □   Gramercy! they for joy did grin
165 □   And all at once their breath drew in
166 □   As they were drinking all.
[*Line-space*]
167gl *5–8*   And horror follows. For can it be a *ship* that comes onward without wind or tide?
167 *1*   She doth not tack from side to side—
☒*1*   See! See! (I cry'd) she tacks no more!
168 □   Hither to work us weal
169 *1*   Withouten wind, withouten tide
☒*1*   Without a breeze, without a
170 □   She steddies with upright keel.
[*Line-space*]
171 □   The western wave was all a flame,
172 □   The day was well nigh done!
173 □   Almost upon the western wave
174 □   Rested the broad bright Sun;
175 □   When that strange shape drove suddenly
176 □   Betwixt us and the Sun.
[*Line-space*]
177gl *5–8*   It seemeth him but the skeleton of a ship.
177 □   And strait the Sun was fleck'd with bars
178 □   (Heaven's mother send us grace)
179 □   As if thro' a dungeon grate he peer'd
180 □   With broad and burning face.
[*Line-space*]
181 □   Alas! (thought I, and my heart beat loud)
182 □   How fast she neres and neres!
183 □   Are those *her* Sails that glance in the Sun
184 □   Like restless gossameres?
[*Line-space*]
185gl *5–8*   And its ribs are seen as bars on the face of the setting Sun.
185 *1*   Are those *her* naked ribs, which fleck'd
☒*1*   Ribs, thro' which the Sun
186 *1*   The sun that did behind them peer?
☒*1*   Did   peer,   as   thro'   a   grate?

187	*1*	And are those two all, all the crew,
	2–4	her
	5–8	is that Woman
188gl	*5–8*	The spectre-woman and her death-mate, and no other on board the skeleton-ship.
188	*5–8*	Is that a DEATH? and are there two?
189	*1*	That woman and her fleshless Pheere?
	2–4	←——Mate?——→
	5–8	Is DEATH that woman's
		[*Line-space*]
189.1.1	*1–4*	*His* bones were black with many a crack,
189.1.2	*1–4*	All black and bare, I ween;
189.1.3	*1–4*	Jet-black and bare, save where with rust
189.1.4	*1–4*	Of mouldy damps and charnel crust
189.1.5	*1*	They're patch'd with purple and green.
	2–4	They were
		[*Line-space*]
190gl	*5–8*	Like vessel, like crew!
190	*1*	*Her* lips are red, *her* looks are free,
	⊠*1*	were were
191	*1*	*Her* locks are yellow as gold:
	⊠*1*	were
192	*1*	Her skin is as white as leprosy,
	⊠*1*	was
193.1	*1*	And she is far liker Death than he;
	2–4	was
194.1	*1*	Her flesh makes the still air cold.
	2–4	made
193	*5–8*	The Night-Mair LIFE-IN-DEATH was she,
194	*5–8*	Who thicks man's blood with cold.
		[*Line-space*]
195gl	*5–8*	DEATH, and LIFE-IN-DEATH have diced for the ship's crew, and she (the latter) winneth the ancient Mariner.
195	□	The naked Hulk alongside came
196	*1–4*	And the Twain were playing dice;
	5–8	casting
197	*1–4*	"The Game is done! I've won, I've won!"
	5–8	I've,
198	*1–4*	Quoth she, and whistled thrice.
	5–8	whistles
		[*Line-space*]
198.1.1	*1–5*	A gust of wind sterte up behind
198.1.2	*1–5*	And whistled thro' his bones;
198.1.3	*1 2 5*	Thro' the holes of his eyes and the hole of his mouth
	3 4	hole
198.1.4	*1–5*	Half-whistles and half-groans.
		[*Line-space*]
199gl	*6–8*	No twilight within the courts of the sun.
199	*5–8*	The Sun's rim dips; the stars rush out:

200	*5–8*	At one stride comes the dark;
201	*5–8*	With far-heard whisper, o'er the sea,
202	*5–8*	Off shot the spectre-bark.
		[*Line-space*]
201.1	*1–4*	With never a whisper in the Sea
202.1	*1*	Oft darts the Spectre-ship;
	2–4	Off
203	*5–8*	We listen'd and look'd sideways up!
204	*5–8*	Fear at my heart, as at a cup,
205	*5–8*	My life-blood seem'd to sip!
206	*5–8*	The stars were dim, and thick the night,
207	*5–8*	The steersman's face by his lamp gleam'd white;
208	*5*	From the sails the dews did drip—
	6–8	dew
209gl	*5–8*	At the rising of the Moon,
209	*1–4*	While clombe above the Eastern bar
	5–8	Till
210	□	The horned Moon, with one bright Star
211	*1*	Almost atween the tips.
	2–4	between
	5–8	Within the nether tip.
		[*Line-space*]
212gl	*5–8*	One after another,
212	*1–4*	One after one by the horned Moon
	5–8	star-dogg'd
213	*1–4*	(Listen, O Stranger! to me)
	5 7 8	Too quick for groan or sigh,
	6	sight,
214	□	Each turn'd his face with a ghastly pang
215	□	And curs'd me with his ee.
		[*Line-space*]
216gl	*5–8*	His shipmates drop down dead;
216	□	Four times fifty living men,
217	*1–4*	With never a sigh or groan,
	5–8	(And I heard nor sigh nor groan)
218	□	With heavy thump, a lifeless lump
219	□	They dropp'd down one by one.
		[*Line-space*]
220gl	*5–8*	But LIFE-IN-DEATH begins her work on the ancient Mariner.
220	*1–4*	Their souls did from their bodies fly,—
	5–8	The
221	□	They fled to bliss or woe;
222	□	And every soul it pass'd me by,
223	□	Like the whiz of my Cross-bow.
		[*Line-space*]
⁻**224**	*1–4*	IV.
	5–7	*THE RIME OF THE ANCIENT MARINER.*	PART THE FOURTH.
	8	PART IV.
224gl	*5–8*	The wedding-guest feareth that a spirit is talking to him;

224 □   "I fear thee, ancyent Marinere!

225 □   "I fear thy skinny hand;

226 □   "And thou art long and lank and brown

227 □   "As is the ribb'd Sea-sand.

227fn *5–8*   For the two last lines of this stanza, I am indebted to Mr. WORDS-

        WORTH. It

        was on a delightful walk from Nether Stowey to Dulverton, with

        him and his

        sister, in the Autumn of 1797, that that this Poem was planned, and

        in part composed.

        [*Line-space*]

228 □   "I fear thee and thy glittering eye

229 □   "And thy skinny hand so brown—

230gl *5–8*   But the ancient Mariner assureth him of his bodily life, and pro-

        ceedeth to relate his horrible penance.

230 □   Fear not, fear not, thou wedding guest!

231 □   This body dropt not down.

        [*Line-space*]

232 □   Alone, alone, all all alone

233 *1–4*   Alone on the wide wide Sea;

    5–8   a

234 *1–4*   And Christ would take no pity on

    5–8   never a saint took

235 *1–8*   My soul in agony.

        [*Line-space*]

236gl *5–8*   He despiseth the creatures of the calm,

236 □   The many men so beautiful,

237 □   And they all dead did lie!

238 *1–4*   And a million   million slimy things

    5–8   thousand thousand

239 □   Liv'd on—and so did I.

        [*Line-space*]

240gl *5–8*   And envieth that *they* should live, and so many lie dead.

240 □   I look'd upon the rotting Sea,

241 □   And drew my eyes away;

242 *1*   I look'd upon the eldritch deck,

    2–4   ghastly

    5–8   rotting

243 □   And there the dead men lay.

        [*Line-space*]

244 □   I look'd to Heaven, and try'd to pray;

245 □   But or ever a prayer had gusht,

246 □   A wicked whisper came and made

247 □   My heart as dry as dust.

        [*Line-space*]

248 □   I clos'd my lids and kept them close,

249 *1–4*   Till the balls like pulses beat;

    5–8   And

250 □   For the sky and the sea, and the sea and the sky

251 ⊠5   Lay like a load on my weary eye,
    5   cloud,
252 □   And the dead were at my feet.
          [*Line-space*]
253gl *5–8* But the curse liveth for him in the eye of the dead men.
253 □   The cold sweat melted from their limbs,
254 □   Ne rot, ne reek did they;
255 □   The look with which they look'd on me,
256 □   Had never pass'd away.
          [*Line-space*]
257 □   An orphan's curse would drag to Hell
258 □   A spirit from on high:
259 □   But O! more horrible than that
260 *1–5* 8 Is the curse in a dead man's eye!
    6 7   a
261 □   Seven days, seven nights I saw that curse,
262 □   And yet I could not die.
          [*Line-space*]
263gl *5–8* In his loneliness and fixedness, he yearneth towards the journeying
          Moon, and the stars that still sojourn, yet still move onward; and
          every where the blue sky belongs to them, and is their appointed
          rest, and their native country, and their own natural homes, which
          they enter unannounced, as lords that are certainly expected, and yet
          there is a silent joy at their arrival.
263 □   The moving Moon went up the sky
264 □   And no where did abide:
265 □   Softly she was going up
266 □   And a star or two beside—
          [*Line-space*]
267 □   Her beams bemock'd the sultry main
268 *1*   Like morning frosts yspread;
    ⊠*1*   April hoar-frost spread;
269 □   But where the ship's huge shadow lay,
270 □   The charmed water burnt alway
271 □   A still and awful red.
          [*Line-space*]
272gl *5–8* By the light of the Moon he beholdeth God's creatures of the great
          calm.
272 □   Beyond the shadow of the ship
273 □   I watch'd the water-snakes:
274 □   They mov'd in tracks of shining white;
275 □   And when they rear'd, the elfish light
276 □   Fell off in hoary flakes.
          [*Line-space*]
277 □   Within the shadow of the ship
278 □   I watch'd their rich attire:
279 □   Blue, glossy green, and velvet black
280 □   They coil'd and swam; and every track
281 □   Was a flash of golden fire.

		[*Line-space*]
282gl	5–8	Their beauty and their happiness.
282	□	O happy living things! no tongue
283	□	Their beauty might declare:
284	□	A spring of love gusht from my heart,
285gl	5–8	He blesseth them in his heart.
285	□	And I bless'd them unaware!
286	□	Sure my kind saint took pity on me,
287	□	And I bless'd them unaware.
		[*Line-space*]
288gl	5–8	The spell begins to break.
288	□	The self-same moment I could pray;
289	□	And from my neck so free
290	□	The Albatross fell off, and sank
291	□	Like lead into the sea.
		[*Line-space*]
⁻292	1–4	V.
	5–7	*THE RIME OF THE ANCIENT MARINER.*	PART THE FIFTH.
	8	PART V.
292	□	O sleep, it is a gentle thing
293	□	Belov'd from pole to pole!
294	□	To Mary-queen the praise be yeven
295	□	She sent the gentle sleep from heaven
296	□	That slid into my soul.
		[*Line-space*]
297gl	5–8	By grace of the holy Mother, the ancient Mariner is refreshed with rain.
297	□	The silly buckets on the deck
298	□	That had so long remain'd,
299	□	I dreamt that they were fill'd with dew
300	□	And when I awoke it rain'd.
		[*Line-space*]
301	□	My lips were wet, my throat was cold,
302	□	My garments all were dank;
303	□	Sure I had drunken in my dreams
304	□	And still my body drank.
		[*Line-space*]
305	□	I mov'd and could not feel my limbs,
306	□	I was so light, almost
307	□	I thought that I had died in sleep,
308	□	And was a blessed Ghost.
		[*Line-space*]
309gl	5–8	He heareth sounds, and seeth strange sights and commotions in the sky and the element.
309	1	The roaring wind! it roar'd far off,
	2–8	And soon I heard a roaring wind,
310	□	It did not come anear;
311	□	But with its sound it shook the sails
312	□	That were so thin and sere.

[*Line-space*]

313	*1*	The upper air bursts into life,
	⊠*1*	burst
314	□	And a hundred fire-flags sheen
315	*1*	To and fro they are hurried about;
	⊠*1*	were
316	□	And to and fro, and in and out
317	*1*	The stars dance on between.
	⊠*1*	wan stars danc'd

[*Line-space*]

318	*1*	The coming wind doth roar more loud;
	⊠*1*	And the did
319	*1*	The sails do sigh, like sedge:
	⊠*1*	And the did
320	*1*	The rain pours down from one black cloud
	⊠*1*	And the pour'd
321	*1*	And the Moon is at its edge.
	⊠*1*	The was

[*Line-space*]

322	*1*	Hark! hark! the thick black cloud is cleft,
	⊠*1*	The thick black cloud was cleft, and still
323	*1*	And the Moon is at its side:
	⊠*1*	The was
324	□	Like waters shot from some high crag,
325	*1*	The lightning falls with never a jag
	⊠*1*	fell
326	□	A river steep and wide.

[*Line-space*]

327gl	*5–8*	The bodies of the ship's crew are inspirited, and the ship moves on;
327	*1*	The strong wind reach'd the ship: it roar'd
	⊠*1*	loud never reach'd the Ship,
328	*1*	And dropp'd down, like a stone!
	⊠*1*	Yet now the Ship mov'd on!
329	□	Beneath the lightning and the moon
330	□	The dead men gave a groan.

[*Line-space*]

331	□	They groan'd, they stirr'd, they all uprose,
332	□	Ne spake, ne mov'd their eyes:
333	□	It had been strange, even in a dream
334	□	To have seen those dead men rise.

[*Line-space*]

335	□	The helmsman steerd, the ship mov'd on;
336	□	Yet never a breeze up-blew;
337	□	The Marineres all 'gan work the ropes,
338	□	Where they were wont to do:
339	□	They rais'd their limbs like lifeless tools—
340	□	We were a ghastly crew.

[*Line-space*]

| 341 | □ | The body of my brother's son |

342 ☐		Stood by me knee to knee:
343 ☐		The body and I pull'd at one rope,
344 ☐		But he said nought to me—
344.1.1 *1*		And I quak'd to think of my own voice
344.1.2 *1*		How frightful it would be!

[*Line-space*]

345gl *5–8* But not by the souls of the men, nor by dæmons of earth or middle air, but by a blessed troop of angelic spirits, sent down by the invocation of the guardian saint.

345 ☒*1*		"I fear thee, ancient Mariner!
346 ☒*1*		Be calm, thou wedding guest!
347 ☒*1*		'Twas not those souls, that fled in pain,
348 ☒*1*		Which to their corses came again,
349 ☒*1*		But a troop of Spirits blest:

[*Line-space*]

350 *1*		The day-light dawn'd—they dropp'd their arms,
	☒*1*	For when it
351 ☐		And cluster'd round the mast·
352 ☐		Sweet sounds rose slowly thro' their mouths
353 ☐		And from their bodies pass'd.

[*Line-space*]

354 ☐		Around, around, flew each sweet sound,
355 ☐		Then darted to the sun:
356 ☐		Slowly the sounds came back again
357 ☐		Now mix'd, now one by one.

[*Line-space*]

358 ☐		Sometimes a dropping from the sky
359 *1*		I heard the Lavrock sing;
	☒*1*	Sky-lark
360 ☐		Sometimes all little birds that are
361 ☐		How they seem'd to fill the sea and air
362 ☐		With their sweet jargoning,

[*Line-space*]

363 ☐		And now 'twas like all instruments,
364 ☐		Now like a lonely flute;
365 ☐		And now it is an angel's song
366 ☐		That makes the heavens be mute.

[*Line-space*]

367 ☐		It ceas'd: yet still the sails made on
368 ☐		A pleasant noise till noon,
369 ☐		A noise like of a hidden brook
370 ☐		In the leafy month of June,
371 ☐		That to the sleeping woods all night
372 ☐		Singeth a quiet tune.

[*Line-space*]

372.1.1 *1*		Listen, O listen, thou Wedding-guest!
372.1.2 *1*		"Marinere! thou hast thy will:
372.1.3 *1*		"For that, which comes out of thine eye, doth make
372.1.4 *1*		"My body and soul to be still."

[*Line-space*]

372.1.5 *1*	Never sadder tale was told
372.1.6 *1*	To a man of woman born:
372.1.7 *1*	Sadder and wiser thou wedding-guest!
372.1.8 *1*	Thou'lt rise to morrow morn.

[*Line-space*]

372.1.9 *1*	Never sadder tale was heard
372.1.10 *1*	By a man of woman born:
372.1.11 *1*	The Marineres all return'd to work
372.1.12 *1*	As silent as beforne.

[*Line-space*]

372.1.13 *1*	The Mariners all 'gan pull the ropes,
372.1.14 *1*	But look at me they n'old:
372.1.15 *1*	Thought I, I am as thin as air—
372.1.16 *1*	They cannot me behold.

[*Line-space*]

373 *1–4*	Till noon we silently sail'd on
5–8	quietly
374 □	Yet never a breeze did breathe:
375 □	Slowly and smoothly went the ship
376 □	Mov'd onward from beneath.

[*Line-space*]

377gl *5–8* The lonesome spirit from the south-pole carries on the ship as far as the line, in obedience to the angelic troop, but still requireth vengeance.

377 □	Under the keel nine fathom deep
378 □	From the land of mist and snow
379 □	The spirit slid: and it was He
380 □	That made the Ship to go.
381 □	The sails at noon left off their tune
382 □	And the Ship stood still also.

[*Line-space*]

383 □	The sun right up above the mast
384 □	Had fix'd her to the ocean:
385 □	But in a minute she 'gan stir
386 □	With a short uneasy motion—
387 □	Backwards and forwards half her length
388 □	With a short uneasy motion.

[*Line-space*]

389 □	Then, like a pawing horse let go,
390 □	She made a sudden bound:
391 □	It flung the blood into my head,
392 *1–4*	And I fell into a swound.
5–8	down in

[*Line-space*]

393gl *5–8* The Polar Spirit's fellow-dæmons, the invisible inhabitants of the element, take part in his wrong; and two of them relate, one to the other, that penance long and heavy for the ancient Mariner hath been accorded to the Polar Spirit, who returneth southward.

393 ☐		How long in that same fit I lay,
394 ☐		I have not to declare;
395 ☐		But ere my living life return'd,
396 ☐		I heard and in my soul discern'd
397 ☐		Two voices in the air,
		[*Line-space*]
398 ☐		"Is it he? quoth one, "Is this the man?
399 ☐		"By him who died on cross,
400 ☐		"With his cruel bow he lay'd full low
401 ☐		"The harmless Albatross.
		[*Line-space*]
402 ☐		"The spirit who 'bideth by himself
403 ☐		"In the land of mist and snow,
404 ☐		"He lov'd the bird that lov'd the man
405 ☐		"Who shot him with his bow.
		[*Line-space*]
406 ☐		The other was a softer voice,
407 ☐		As soft as honey-dew;
408 ☐		Quoth he the man hath penance done,
409 ☐		And penance more will do.
		[*Line-space*]
⁻410.1	*1–4*	VI.
	5–7	*THE RIME OF THE ANCIENT MARINER.*	PART THE SIXTH.
	8	PART VI.
⁻410.2 ☐		FIRST VOICE.
410 ☐		"But tell me, tell me! speak again,
411 ☐		"Thy soft response renewing—
412 ☐		"What makes that ship drive on so fast?
413 ☐		"What is the Ocean doing?
		[*Line-space*]
⁻414 ☐		SECOND VOICE.
414 ☐		"Still as a Slave before his Lord,
415 ☐		"The Ocean hath no blast:
416 ☐		"His great bright eye most silently
417 ☐		"Up to the moon is cast—
		[*Line-space*]
418 ☐		"If he may know which way to go,
419 ☐		"For she guides him smooth or grim.
420 ☐		"See, brother, see! how graciously
421 ☐		"She looketh down on him.
		[*Line-space*]
⁻422 ☐		FIRST VOICE.
422gl	*5–8*	The Mariner hath been cast into a trance; for the angelic power causeth the vessel to drive northward, faster than human life could endure.
422 ☐		"But why drives on that ship so fast
423 *1*		"Withouten wave or wind?
☒*1*		"Without or

⁻424 ☐   Second Voice.
424 ☐   "The air is cut away before,
425 ☐   "And closes from behind.
             [*Line-space*]
426 ☐   "Fly, brother, fly! more high, more high,
427 ☐   "Or we shall be belated:
428 ☐   "For slow and slow that ship will go,
429 ☐   "When the Marinere's trance is abated."
             [*Line-space*]
430gl 5–8   The supernatural motion is retarded; the Mariner awakes, and his
             penance begins anew.
430 ☐   I woke, and we were sailing on
431 ☐   As in a gentle weather:
432 ☐   'Twas night, calm night, the moon was high;
433 ☐   The dead men stood together.
             [*Line-space*]
434 ☐   All stood together on the deck,
435 ☐   For a charnel-dungeon fitter:
436 ☐   All fix'd on me their stony eyes
437 ☐   That in the moon did glitter.
             [*Line-space*]
438 ☐   The pang, the curse, with which they died,
439 ☐   Had never pass'd away:
440 ☐   I could not draw my een from theirs
441 ☐   Ne turn them up to pray.
             [*Line-space*]
442gl 5–8   The curse is finally expiated.
442 *1*   And in its time the spell was snapt,
⊠*1*   now this spell was snapt: once more
443 *1*   And I could move my een:
⊠*1*   I view'd the ocean green,
444 *1*   I   look'd far-forth, but little saw
⊠*1*   And   yet
445 *1*   Of what might else be   seen.
⊠*1*   had   been
             [*Line-space*]
446 *1*   Like one, that on a   lonely   road
⊠*1*   lonesome
447 ☐   Doth walk in fear and dread,
448 ☐   And having once turn'd round, walks on
449 ☐   And turns no more his head:
450 ☐   Because he knows, a frightful fiend
451 ☐   Doth close behind him tread.
             [*Line-space*]
452 ☐   But soon there breath'd a wind on me,
453 ☐   Ne sound ne motion made:
454 ☐   Its path was not upon the sea
455 ☐   In ripple or in shade.
             [*Line-space*]

456 □		It rais'd my hair, it fann'd my cheek,
457 □		Like a meadow-gale of spring—
458 □		It mingled strangely with my fears,
459 □		Yet it felt like a welcoming.
		[*Line-space*]
460 □		Swiftly, swiftly flew the ship,
461 □		Yet she sail'd softly too:
462 □		Sweetly, sweetly blew the breeze—
463 □		On me alone it blew.
		[*Line-space*]
464gl	*5–8*	And the ancient Mariner beholdeth his native country.
464 □		O dream of joy! is this indeed
465 □		The light-house top I see?
466 □		Is this the Hill? Is this the Kirk?
467 □		Is this mine own countrée?
		[*Line-space*]
468 □		We drifted o'er the Harbour-bar,
469 □		And I with sobs did pray—
470 □		"O let me be awake, my God!
471 □		"Or let me sleep alway!"
		[*Line-space*]
472 □		The harbour-bay was clear as glass,
473 □		So smoothly it was strewn!
474 □		And on the bay the moon light lay,
475 □		And the shadow of the moon.
		[*Line-space*]
475.1.1	*1*	The moonlight bay was white all o'er,
475.1.2	*1*	Till rising from the same,
475.1.3	*1*	Full many shapes, that shadows were,
475.1.4	*1*	Like as of torches came.
		[*Line-space*]
475.1.5	*1*	A little distance from the prow
475.1.6	*1*	Those dark-red shadows were;
475.1.7	*1*	But soon I saw that my own flesh
475.1.8	*1*	Was red as in a glare.
		[*Line-space*]
475.1.9	*1*	I turn'd my head in fear and dread,
475.1.10	*1*	And by the holy rood,
475.1.11	*1*	The bodies had advanc'd, and now
475.1.12	*1*	Before the mast they stood.
		[*Line-space*]
475.1.13	*1*	They lifted up their stiff right arms,
475.1.14	*1*	They held them strait and tight;
475.1.15	*1*	And each right-arm burnt like a torch,
475.1.16	*1*	A torch that's borne upright.
475.1.17	*1*	Their stony eye-balls glitter'd on
475.1.18	*1*	In the red and smoky light.
		[*Line-space*]
475.1.19	*1*	I pray'd and turn'd my head away

475.1.20 *1*		Forth looking as before.
475.1.21 *1*		There was no breeze upon the bay,
475.1.22 *1*		No wave against the shore.
		[*Line-space*]
476 ☐		The rock shone bright, the kirk no less
477 ☐		That stands above the rock:
478 ☐		The moonlight steep'd in silentness
479 ☐		The steady weathercock.
		[*Line-space*]
480gl *5–8*		The angelic spirits leave the dead bodies,
480 ☐		And the bay was white with silent light,
481 ☐		Till rising from the same
482 ☐		Full many shapes, that shadows were,
483 ☐		In crimson colours came.
		[*Line-space*]
484gl *5–8*		And appear in their own forms of light.
484 ☐		A little distance from the prow
485 ☐		Those crimson shadows were:
486 ☐		I turn'd my eyes upon the deck—
487 ☐		O Christ! what saw I there?
		[*Line-space*]
488 ☐		Each corse lay flat, lifeless and flat;
489 ☐		And by the Holy rood
490 ☐		A man all light, a seraph-man,
491 ☐		On every corse there stood.
		[*Line-space*]
492 ☐		This seraph-band, each wav'd his hand:
493 ☐		It was a heavenly sight:
494 ☐		They stood as signals to the land,
495 ☐		Each one a lovely light:
		[*Line-space*]
496 ☐		This seraph-band, each wav'd his hand,
497 ☐		No voice did they impart—
498 ☐		No voice; but O! the silence sank,
499 ☐		Like music on my heart.
		[*Line-space*]
500 *1*		Eftsones I heard the dash of oars,
☒*1*		But soon
501 ☐		I heard the pilot's cheer:
502 ☐		My head was turn'd perforce away
503 ☐		And I saw a boat appear.
		[*Line-space*]
503.1.1 *1*		Then vanish'd all the lovely lights;
503.1.2 *1*		The bodies rose anew:
503.1.3 *1*		With silent pace, each to his place,
503.1.4 *1*		Came back the ghastly crew.
503.1.5 *1*		The wind, that shade nor motion made,
503.1.6 *1*		On me alone it blew.
		[*Line-space*]

504 ☐	The pilot, and the pilot's boy
505 ☐	I heard them coming fast:
506 ☐	Dear Lord in Heaven! it was a joy,
507 ☐	The dead men could not blast.
	[Line-space]
508 ☐	I saw a third—I heard his voice:
509 ☐	It is the Hermit good!
510 ☐	He singeth loud his godly hymns
511 ⊠7	That he makes in the wood.
7	he
512 ☐	He'll shrieve my soul, he'll wash away
513 ☐	The Albatross's blood.
	[Line-space]
⁻514 *1–4*	VII.
5 *7*	*THE RIME OF THE ANCIENT MARINER.* | PART THE SEVENTH.
6	THE ANCIENT MARINER. | PART THE SEVENTH.
8	PART VII.
514gl *5–8*	The Hermit of the Wood,
514 ☐	This Hermit good lives in that wood
515 ☐	Which slopes down to the Sea.
516 ☐	How loudly his sweet voice he rears!
517 ☐	He loves to talk with Marineres
518 ☐	That come from a far Contrée.
	[Line-space]
519 ☐	He kneels at morn and noon and eve—
520 ☐	He hath a cushion plump:
521 ☐	It is the moss, that wholly hides
522 ☐	The rotted old Oak-stump.
	[Line-space]
523 ☐	The Skiff-boat ne'rd: I heard them talk,
524 ☐	"Why, this is strange, I trow!
525 ☐	"Where are those lights so many and fair
526 ☐	"That signal made but now?
	[Line-space]
527gl *5–8*	Approacheth the ship with wonder.
527 ☐	"Strange, by my faith! the Hermit said—
528 ☐	"And they answer'd not our cheer.
529 *1–5*	"The planks look warp'd, and see those sails
6–8	looked
530 ☐	"How thin they are and sere!
531 ☐	"I never saw aught like to them
532 ☐	"Unless perchance it were
	[Line-space]
533 *1–5*	"The skeletons of leaves that lag
6–8	Brown
534 ☐	"My forest brook along:
535 ☐	"When the Ivy-tod is heavy with snow,
536 ☐	"And the Owlet whoops to the wolf below
537 ☐	"That eats the she-wolf's young.

[*Line-space*]

538 *1–4* "Dear Lord! it has a fiendish look—
   5–8   hath
539 ☐ (The Pilot made reply)
540 ☐ "I am a-fear'd.—"Push on, push on!
541 ☐ Said the Hermit cheerily.

[*Line-space*]

542 ☐ The Boat came closer to the Ship,
543 ☐ But I ne spake ne stirr'd!
544 ☐ The Boat came close beneath the Ship,
545 ☐ And strait a sound was heard!

[*Line-space*]

546gl *5–8* The ship suddenly sinketh.
546 ☐ Under the water it rumbled on,
547 ☐ Still louder and more dread:
548 ☐ It reach'd the Ship, it split the bay;
549 ☐ The Ship went down like lead.

[*Line-space*]

550gl *5–8* The ancient Mariner is saved in the Pilot's boat.
550 ☐ Stunn'd by that loud and dreadful sound,
551 ☐ Which sky and ocean smote:
552 ☐ Like one that hath been seven days drown'd
553 ☐ My body lay afloat:
554 ☐ But, swift as dreams, myself I found
555 ☐ Within the Pilot's boat.

[*Line-space*]

556 ☐ Upon the whirl, where sank the Ship,
557 ☐ The boat spun round and round:
558 ☐ And all was still, save that the hill
559 ☐ Was telling of the sound.

[*Line-space*]

560 ☐ I mov'd my lips: the Pilot shriek'd
561 ☐ And fell down in a fit.
562 ☐ The Holy Hermit rais'd his eyes
563 ☐ And pray'd where he did sit.

[*Line-space*]

564 ☐ I took the oars: the Pilot's boy,
565 ☐ Who now doth crazy go,
566 ☐ Laugh'd loud and long, and all the while
567 ☐ His eyes went to and fro,
568 ☐ "Ha! ha!" quoth he—"full plain I see,
569 ☐ "The devil knows how to row."

[*Line-space*]

570 *1–4* And now all in mine own Countrée
   5–8   my
571 ☐ I stood on the firm land!
572 ☐ The Hermit stepp'd forth from the boat,
573 ☐ And scarcely he could stand.

[*Line-space*]

574gl *5–8*   The ancient Mariner earnestly entreateth the Hermit to shrieve him;
and the penance of life falls on him.

574 ☐   "O shrieve me, shrieve me, holy Man!

575 ☐   The Hermit cross'd his brow—

576 ☐   "Say quick," quoth he, "I bid thee say

577 *1–4*   "What manner man   art thou?
  5–8   of man

[*Line-space*]

578 *1 5–8*   Forthwith this frame of mine was wrench'd
  2–4   mind

579 ☐   With a woeful agony,

580 ☐   Which forc'd me to begin my tale

581 ☐   And then it left me free.

[*Line-space*]

582gl *5–8*   And ever and anon throughout his future life an agony constraineth
him to travel from land to land,

582 ☐   Since then at an uncertain hour,

582.1.1 *1*   Now oftimes and now fewer,

582.1.2 *1*   That anguish comes and makes me tell

582.1.3 *1*   My ghastly aventure.

583 *2*   That agency returns;
  3–8   agony

584 ☒*1*   And till my ghastly tale is told

585 ☒*1*   This heart within me burns.

[*Line-space*]

586 ☐   I pass, like night, from land to land;

587 ☐   I have strange power of speech;

588 *1–4*   The moment that his face I see
  5–8   That

589 ☐   I know the man that must hear me;

590 ☐   To him my tale I teach.

[*Line-space*]

591 ☐   What loud uproar bursts from that door!

592 ☐   The Wedding-guests are there;

593 ☐   But in the Garden-bower the Bride

594 ☐   And Bride-maids singing are:

595 ☐   And hark the little Vesper-bell

596 ☐   Which biddeth me to prayer.

[*Line-space*]

597 ☐   O Wedding-guest! this soul hath been

598 ☐   Alone on a wide wide sea:

599 ☐   So lonely 'twas, that God himself

600 ☐   Scarce seemed there to be.

[*Line-space*]

601 ☐   O sweeter than the Marriage-feast,

602 ☐   'Tis sweeter far to me

603 ☐   To walk together to the Kirk

604 ☐   With a goodly company.

[*Line-space*]

605 ☐	To walk together to the Kirk
606 ☐	And all together pray,
607 ☐	While each to his great father bends,
608 ☐	Old men, and babes, and loving friends,
609 ☐	And Youths, and Maidens gay.

[*Line-space*]

610gl *5–8* And to teach by his own example, love and reverence to all things
that God made and loveth.

610 ☐	Farewell, farewell! but this I tell
611 ☐	To thee, thou wedding-guest!
612 ☐	He prayeth well who loveth well,
613 ☐	Both man and bird and beast.

[*Line-space*]

614 ☐	He prayeth best who loveth best,
615 ☐	All things both great and small:
616 ☐	For the dear God, who loveth us,
617 ☐	He made and loveth all.

[*Line-space*]

618 ☐	The Marinere, whose eye is bright,
619 ☐	Whose beard with age is hoar,
620 ☐	Is gone; and now the wedding-guest
621 ☐	Turn'd from the bridegroom's door.

[*Line-space*]

622 ☐	He went, like one that hath been stunn'd
623 ☐	And is of sense forlorn:
624 ☐	A sadder and a wiser man
625 ☐	He rose the morrow morn.

divisional title. *5* THE RIME | OF THE | ANCIENT MARINER. | *IN SEVEN PARTS.* • *6 7* THE RIME | OF | THE ANCIENT MARINER. | IN SEVEN PARTS.   EP⁻1.2–3. *8* enarrabit,   EP⁻1.6. *8* tabulâ,   EP⁻1.7. *6–8* assuefacta   *6–8* hodiernæ   EP⁻1.8. *6–8* et   EP⁻1.10–11. *8* distinguamus T.   EP⁻1.11. *6 7* ARCHÆOL. PHIL. • *8* ARCHÆOL. PHIL.   **title.** *5* 𝕿𝖍𝖊 𝕽𝖎𝖒𝖊 | 𝖔𝖋 𝖙𝖍𝖊 | 𝕬𝖓𝖈𝖎𝖊𝖓𝖙 𝕸𝖆𝖗𝖎𝖓𝖊𝖗. | *IN SEVEN PARTS.* • *6 7* THE RIME | OF | THE ANCIENT MARINER. | IN SEVEN PARTS. • *8* THE RIME OF THE ANCIENT MARINER. | IN SEVEN PARTS.   **1gl.** *8* gallants   **1.** ☒*1* ancient Mariner,   **2.** *5–8* three.   **3.** *4* gray   *5–8* eye,   **4.** *4 8* Now   *5–8* stopp'st   **5.** *4* The   *4 6–8* opened   *4–8* wide,   **6.** *4 8* And   **7.** *4 8* The   *5–8* guests   *5–8* feast   *5–8* set: **8.** *4 8* May'st   *3–8* din."   **8.1.1.** *2 3* wedding guest—   **8.1.2.** *4* "There   *4* Ship,"   **8.1.4.** *2 3* "Mariner! • *4* Mariner!   **10.** *4* "There *4* Ship—"   **11.** *4* gray-beard   **12.** *4* Or   *3 4* skip."   **13gl.** *8* wedding guest   **14.** *4–8* wedding-guest   *5–8* still,   **15.** *4 8* years' • *5–7* years   *5–8* child: **16.** ☒*1* Mariner   **17.** *5–8* sat   *5–8* stone: **18.** *5* can not *4 8* choose   *5–8* hear;   **19.** ☒*1* ancient   **20.** *2–4 8* Mariner. • *5–7* mariner.   **21.** *4* "The   *5–8* ship   *4 6–8* cheered,   *5–8* harbour   *4* cleared— • *5* clear'd, • *6–8* cleared,   **23.** *5–8* kirk,   *5–8* hill,   **24.** *5* light-house • *6–8* light house   **25.** *8* sun   **26.** *5–8* sea   *5* he; • *6–8* he!   **28.** *3–8* sea.   **30.** *4* noon—"   **31.** *5–8* Wedding-Guest   **33gl.** *7 8* wedding guest   **33.** *5–8* bride   *4–8* paced   *5–8* hall,   **36.** *4* Minstrelsy. • *5–8* minstrelsy.   **37.** *5–8* Wedding-

Guest   **38.** *5* can not *4 8* choose *5–8* hear;   **39.** ⊠*1* ancient *5–8* man,
40. ⊠*1 4* Mariner. • *4* Mariner: **41.2.** *4* "But *4* North wind   **41.** *8* storm-
blast   **47.** *8* foe,   **49.** *6–8* roared   **51.** *5–8* mist *5 6 8* snow, • *7* snow
52. *4 6–8* wondrous • *5* wonderous *2 3* cold; • *4–8* cold: **53.** *5–8* ice, mast-high,
5–8 by,   **54.** *2–4* Emerald. • *5–8* emerald.   **55gl.** *8* sounds   **55.** *4–8* through
56. *5–8* sheen: **57.** ⊠*1* Nor . . . nor   **58.** *5–8* ice   **59.** *5–8* ice . . . ice
60. *5–8* ice   **61.** *4–8* cracked *4–8* growled, *4 6–8* roared *4 6–8* howled, •
5 howl'd,   **63gl.** *6–8* Albatross,   **63.** *5–7* Albatross: **64.** *5–8* fog
65. *5–8* soul,   **66.** *4–8* hailed   **67.** *2–4* Mariners   **68.** *5–8* flew.   **69.** *5–*
8 ice *5–8* thunder-fit;   **70.** *5–8* helmsman *4 6–8* steered *4* through. •
5–8 through!   **71gl.** *7 8* northward   **71.** *4* South *2* behind. • *5–8* behind;
72. *5–8* follow,   **73.** *5–8* day, *5–8* play,   **74.** *2–5* Mariner's • *7 8* mariner's
75. *5–8* cloud, *5–8* shroud,   **76.** *4 6–8* perched *5–8* nine;   **77.** *5–8* night,
4–8 through *5–8* white,   **78.** *4–8* Glimmered *4* moon-shine." • *5–7* Moon-
shine.   **79.** ⊠*1 4* ancient • *4* antient ⊠*1* Mariner!   **80.** *4–8* From *5–8* fiends,
4–8 thus!—   **81.** *4–8* Why *3* so? *4* —"With • *5–8* —With *5–8* cross-bow
82. *4* Albatross." • *5* ALBATROSS! • *6 7* ALBATROSS.   ‾**83.** *6 7* THE RIME I
OF I THE ANCIENT MARINER. I PART THE SECOND.   **83.** *4* "The *5–*
8 right: **84.** *5–8* sea *5–8* he,   **85.** *5–8* mist,   **86.** *5–8* sea.   **87.** *4* South
88. *5–8* bird *4–8* follow,   **89.** ⊠*1* Nor   **90.** *2–4* Mariner's   **91.** *8* a *4–*
8 thing,   **92.** *2* e'm   **93.** *4–8* averred, *4–8* killed *5–8* bird   **94.** *5–8* breeze
97gl. *6–8* same, *6–8* accomplices   **97.** ⊠*1* Nor dim nor   **99.** *4–8* averred,
4–8 killed *5 8* bird   **101.** *5–8* slay,   **103gl.** *8* Ocean,   **104.** *4 6–*
8 followed *7 8* free;   **106.** *3 5–8* sea.   **107.** *5–8* sails   **108.** *3 4* be, •
5–8 be;   **110.** *5–8* sea!   **111.** *5–8* sky,   **112.** *5–8* Sun,   **114.** *5–8* Moon.
116. ⊠*1* nor breath nor *6–8* motion;   **117.** *5–8* ship   **118.** *5–8* ocean.
119. *1* w here • *3–8* where,   **121.** *5* Water water,   **122.** ⊠*1* Nor   **126.** *5–*
8 sea.   **128.** *5–8* death-fires *4–8* danced   **130.** *5–8* green,   **132.** *5–8* spirit
7 8 so;   **133.** *4 8* followed   **134.** *5–8* land *5–8* mist *5–8* snow.   **135.** *5–*
8 tongue, *4–8* through *5–8* drought,   **136.** *4 6–8* withered   **137.** *5–8* speak,
138. *5* choak'd   **139.** *5–8* Ah! *3 4* well-a-day! • *5–8* well a-day!   **140.** *4–*
8 young!   **141.** *5–8* cross,   ‾**143.** *6 7* THE RIME I OF I THE ANCIENT
MARINER. I PART THE THIRD.   **143.** *4* "So pass'd • *5–8* So passed *5–*
8 time. Each   **144.** *4–8* parched, *4–8* glazed *5–8* eye.   **146.** *6–8* eye,
147. *5–8* When   **149.** *4 6–8* seemed *4–8* speck,   **150.** *4 6–8* seemed
7 8 mist;   **151.** *4–8* moved and moved,   **154.** *5* near'd and near'd: • *6–8* neared
and neared: **155.** *4 5* And *4–8* dodged   **156.** *4 8* plunged *4 6–8* tacked
4 6–8 veered.   **157.** *4 6–8* unslaked, *4* baked • *5–8* baked,   **158.** ⊠*1* laugh
⊠*1* wail;   **159.** *4–8* Through *5–8* drought *5–8* stood!   **160.** *5–8* arm,
4–8 sucked ⊠*1* blood,   **161.** *4–8* cried,   **162.** *4 6 8* unslaked, • *5 7* unslacked,
4 baked • *5–8* baked,   **163.** ⊠*1* heard   **164.** *8* joy;   **164.** *4–8* grin,
165. *5–8* in,   **167gl.** *6–8* ship   **167.** *5 6 8* See! see! *4–8* cried)   **168.** *5–*
8 weal;   **169.** *5–8* tide,   **170.** *6–8* steadies ⊠*1* keel!   **171.** *3 4* a flame. •
5–8 a-flame.   **177.** *4–8* straight *4–8* flecked *5–8* bars,   **178.** *3–8* Mother
4–8 grace!)   **179.** *4–8* through *5–8* dungeon-grate *4 7 8* peered • *5* peer'd, •
6 peered,   **182.** *5–8* nears and nears!   **183.** *8* her *5–8* sails *5–8* Sun,
184. *5–7* gossameres!   **185.** *8* her *5–8* ribs *4–8* through   **186.** *4–8* through
187. *5–8* crew?   **188.** *8* Death?   **189.** *2–4* Woman, *8* Death *5–8* mate?
189.1.5. *4* patched   **190.** *8* Her . . . her   **191.** *5–8* Her   **193.** *6 7* Night-Mare •

8 Night-mare   *8* Life-in-Death   **195gl.** *8* Death and Life-in-death   **195.** *5–8* hulk   *5–8* came,   **196.** *5–8* twain   **197.** *5–8* game   **198.1.2.** *4 5* through   **198.1.3.** *5* Through   *5* mouth,   **198.1.4.** *3 5* Half whistles   *5* half groans.   **200.** *7* Dark;   **203.** *6–8* listened   *6–8* looked   **205.** *6–8* seemed   **207.** *6–8* gleamed   **209gl.** *8* Moon.   **209.** *7 8* clomb   *5–8* eastern   **210.** *5–8* star   **212.** *5–8* one,   *6–8* star-dogged   *7 8* Moon,   **213.** *7* sigh   **214.** *4 6–8* turned   *5–8* pang,   **215.** *4 6–8* cursed   *5–8* eye.   **216gl.** *8* dead.   **218.** *5–8* lump,   **219.** *4–8* dropped   **220gl.** *8* Life-in-Death   **221.** *5–8* woe!   **222.** *5–8* soul,   *4–8* passed   **223.** *6–8* whizz   *4* Cross-bow." • *5–7* CROSS-BOW! • *8* cross-bow!   ‾**224.** *6 7* THE RIME I OF I THE ANCIENT MARINER. I PART THE FOURTH.   **224gl.** *7 8* wedding guest   *8* him.   **224.** ⊠*1* ancient Mariner!   **225.** *4–8* I   *5–8* hand!   **226.** *4–8* And   *5–8* long,   *5–8* lank,   *5–8* brown,   **227.** *4–8* As   *4–8* ribbed   *5–8* sea-sand.   **227fn1.** *8* Wordsworth.   **227fn3.** *8* autumn   *5* that that this • *6–8* that this   *8* poem   **228.** *4–8* I   *5–8* eye,   **229.** *4–8* And   *5–8* hand,   *3 4* brown"—• *5–8* brown."—   **230.** *4* "Fear *4 8* wedding-guest! • *5–7* Wedding-Guest!   **232.** *5–8* all, all   *3–8* all alone,   **233.** *5–8* sea!   **236gl.** *6–8* calm.   **236.** *5–8* men,   *5–8* beautiful!   **237.** *5–8* lie: **239.** *4 6–8* Lived   *5–8* on;   **240gl.** *6–8* they   **240.** *4 6–8* looked   *5–8* sea,   **242.** *4 6–8* looked   **244.** *4 6–8* looked   *8* heaven,   *4–8* tried   **246.** *5–8* came,   **248.** *4–8* closed   *5–8* lids,   **251.** *5* Lay,   **254.** ⊠*1* Nor *4–8* rot   ⊠*1* nor reek   *5–8* they: **255.** *4 6–8* looked   *5–8* me   **256.** *4 6–8* passed   **257.** *8* hell   **258.** *5–8* high;   **259.** *5–8* oh!   **261.** *5–8* nights, **263gl.** *6–8* fixedness   *6* sky,   *6–8* country   *6–8* expected   **263.** *5–8* sky, **265.** *5–8* up,   **267.** *4 6–8* bemocked   *5–8* main,   **269.** *3 4* Ship's   **272.** *5–8* ship,   **273.** *4 6–8* watched   **274.** *4–8* moved   *5–8* white,   **275.** *4–8* reared, **278.** *4 6–8* watched   **279.** *5–8* black,   **280.** *4–8* coiled   **284.** *6–8* gushed **285.** *4–8* blessed   *6* unaware? • *7 8* unaware: **287.** *4–8* blessed   **288.** *5–7* self same • *8* selfsame   ‾**292.** *6 7* THE RIME I OF I THE ANCIENT MARINER. I PART THE FIFTH.   **292.** *4* "O • *5–8* Oh   *5–8* sleep!   *5–8* thing,   **293.** *4 6–8* Beloved   **294.** *5–8* Mary Queen   *2 3* given • *4* given, • *5–8* given!   **295.** *5–8* Heaven,   **297.** *5–8* deck,   **298.** *4–8* remained, **299.** *4–8* filled   *4* dew, • *5–8* dew;   **300.** *5–8* awoke,   *4–8* rained.   **303.** *4–8* dreams,   **305.** *4* moved • *5–8* moved,   *5–8* limbs: **306.** *5–8* light— **308.** *5–8* ghost.   **309gl.** *7 8* sounds   **309.** *5–8* wind: **311.** *5–8* sails, **313.** *2 3* life • *5–8* life!   **314.** *5–8* sheen,   **315.** *6–8* about!   **316.** *5–8* out, **317.** *4–8* danced   **318.** *5–8* loud,   **319.** ⊠*1* sigh   *5–8* sedge;   **320.** *4 6–8* poured   *5–8* cloud;   **321.** *2–4* moon   **325.** *5–8* jag,   **327gl.** *5* inspirited, • *6–8* inspired,   **327.** *4–8* reached   *5–8* ship,   **328.** *5–8* ship   *4–8* moved **329.** *5 6* Moon   **331.** *4 6–8* groaned,   *4 6–8* stirred,   **332.** ⊠*1* Nor spake, nor *4–8* moved   *5–8* eyes;   **333.** *5–8* dream,   **335.** *3* steer'd, • *4–8* steered,   *4–8* moved   **336.** *5–8* up blew;   **337.** *2–4* Mariners • *5–8* mariners   **338.** *7 8* do; **339.** *4–8* raised   **342.** *5–8* me,   **343.** *4–8* pulled   **344.** ⊠*1 4* me. • *4* me." **345gl.** *8* demons   **345.** *3–8* Mariner!"   **346.** *4* "Be   *4* wedding-guest! • *5–8* Wedding-Guest!   **347.** *5–8* souls   **349.** *5–8* spirits   **350.** *4–8* dawned— *4–8* dropped   **351.** *4–8* clustered   *5–8* mast;   **352.** *4–8* through   *4–8* mouths, **353.** *4–8* passed.   **355.** *5–8* Sun;   **356.** *5–8* again,   **357.** *4–8* mixed, **358.** *4–8* a-dropping   **359.** *5–8* sky-lark   **360.** *5–8* are,   **361.** *4 6–8* seemed   **362.** *2 3* jargoning. • *4–8* jargoning!   **364.** *4* flute: **365.** *5–8* song, **366.** *5–7* Heavens   **367.** *4* ceased: • *5–8* ceased;   **373.** *4–8* sailed on,   **375.** *2–*

4 Ship • *5–8* ship, **376.** *4–8* Moved **377.** *5–8* deep, **378.** *5–8* snow,
379. *4* Spirit *5–8* he **380.** *5–8* ship *6* go **381.** *4–8* tune, **382.** *5–*
8 ship **383.** *4* Sun • *5–8* Sun, *5–8* mast, **384.** *4 6–8* fixed • *5* fixt *5* ocean;
385. *5–8* stir, **387.** *4 5* length, **389.** *5–8* Then **393gl.** *6 7* fellow
dæmons, • *8* fellow demons, **395.** *4–8* returned, **396.** *8* heard, *4–8* discerned
397. *5–7* VOICES ⊠*1* air. **398.** *4* 'Is *3 5–8* he?" • *4* he?' *4* 'Is this **399.** *4–*
8 By **400.** *4–8* With *4–8* laid *5 6* low, **401.** *4–8* The **402.** *4–7* The
4 Spirit *4–8* bideth **403.** *4–8* In **404.** *4–8* loved . . . loved **405.** *4–*
8 Who *3 5–8* bow." **408.** *4–8* he, *4* 'The • *5–8* "The **409.** *4* do.' •
5–8 do." ⁻**410.1.** *6 7* THE RIME | OF | THE ANCIENT MARINER. |
PART THE SIXTH. ⁻**410.2.** *5–8* FIRST VOICE. **410.** *4* "'But • *5–8* But
411. *4–8* Thy **412.** *4–8* What **413.** *4–8* What *5–7* OCEAN • *8* ocean
4 doing?' ⁻**414.** *5–8* SECOND VOICE. **414.** *4* 'Still • *5–8* Still *5–8* slave
5–8 lord, **415.** *4–8* The *5–7* OCEAN • *8* ocean *5–8* blast; **416.** *4–*
8 His **417.** *4–8* Up *5–8* Moon **418.** *4–8* If *5–8* go; **419.** *4–8* For
420. *4–8* See, brother, **421.** *4–8* She *4* him.' ⁻**422.** *5–8* FIRST VOICE.
422gl. *6 8* northward **422.** *4* 'But • *5–8* But *5–8* fast, **423.** *4–8* Without
4 wind?' ⁻**424.** *5–8* SECOND VOICE. **424.** *4* 'The • *5–8* The **425.** *4–8* And
426. *4–8* Fly, brother, *5–8* high, more high! **427.** *4–8* Or **428.** *4–8* For
429. *4–8* When ⊠*1* Mariner's *4* abated.' • *6–8* abated. **430gl.** *8* anew
430. *4* "I **432.** *5–7* Moon **436.** *4–8* fixed *5–8* eyes, **437.** *5–8* Moon
439. *4–8* passed *2–4* away; **440.** ⊠*1* eyes *4–8* theirs, **441.** ⊠*1* Nor
443. *4–8* viewed **444.** *4–8* looked ⊠*1* far forth, **445.** *4–8* seen—
448. *4 6–8* turned *6–8* round *5–8* on, **449.** *4–8* head; **452.** *4–8* breathed
453. ⊠*1* Nor sound nor **454.** *5–8* sea, **456.** *4–8* raised *4–8* fanned *5–*
8 cheek **460.** *2 3* ship **461.** *4–8* sailed **464.** *5–8* Oh! **466.** *5–8* hill?
is *5–8* kirk? **467.** *5–8* countree? **468.** *5–8* harbour-bar, **470.** *4* 'O •
5–8 O **471.** *4–8* Or *3* alway." • *4* alway.' • *5–8* alway. **474.** ⊠*1* moonlight
476. *5–8* less, **478.** *4–8* steeped **481.** *5–8* same, **486.** *4–8* turned
487. *5–8* Oh, *5–8* there! **488.** *5–8* and flat, **489.** *5–8* And, *5–8* holy
rood! **492.** *4–8* waved **493.** *5–8* sight! **495.** *7 8* light; **496.** *4–8* waved
3 haud, **498.** *5–8* oh! *4–8* sank **501.** *5–8* Pilot's cheer; **502.** *4 6–*
8 turned *4–8* away, **504.** *5 6* The Pilot, and • *7 8* The Pilot and *4* pilot's
boy, • *5–8* Pilot's boy, **506.** *4–8* joy ⁻**514.** *7* THE RIME | OF | THE AN-
CIENT MARINER. | PART THE SEVENTH. **514gl.** *8* wood, **514.** *4* "This
515. *5–8* sea. **517.** *2–4* Mariners • *5–8* marineres **518.** *2 3* countreé. •
4 countrée. • *5–8* countree. **519.** *5–8* morn, *8* noon, **521.** *3–8* moss
522. *5–8* oak-stump. **523.** *6–8* skiff-boat *2–4* ner'd: • *5* near'd: • *6–8* neared:
524. *4* 'Why, • *5–7* "Why **525.** *4–8* Where *5–8* fair, **526.** *4–8* That
4 now?' • *5–8* now?" **527.** *4* 'Strange, *4* faith!' • *5–8* faith!" **528.** *4* 'And
4–8 answered *5–8* cheer! **529.** *4–8* The *4* warped, • *5–8* warped! *5–*
8 sails, **530.** *4–8* How **531.** *4–8* I *5* ought *5–8* them, **532.** *4–8* Unless
533. *4 5* The *8* "Brown **534.** *4–8* My *5–8* forest-brook *6–8* along; **535.** *4–*
8 When *5–8* ivy-tod **536.** *4–8* And *5–8* owlet *5–8* below, **537.** *4–8* That
3 5–8 young." • *4* young.' **538.** *4* 'Dear • *5* Dear **539.** *4* pilot **540.** *4–8* I
3 a-fear'd."— • *4* a-fear'd.'— • *5* a-feared— • *6–8* a-feared"— *4* 'Push • *5* Push
3 6–8 on!" • *4* on!' **541.** *2* "Said *6* hermit **542.** *5–8* boat *5–8* ship,
543. ⊠*1* nor spake nor *4* stirred: • *5–8* stirred; **544.** *5–8* boat *5–8* ship,
545. *4–8* straight *4–8* heard. **548.** *4 6–8* reached *4–8* ship, **549.** *4–8* ship

550. *4–8* Stunned   **551.** *4–8* smote,   **552.** *4 6–8* drowned • *5* drown'd,
553. *5–8* afloat;   **554.** *5–8* But   **556.** *5–8* ship,   **557.** *3 4* and round, •
5–8 and round;   **560.** *4–8* moved   *5–8* lips—   *4–8* shrieked   **561.** *5–8* fit;
562. *5–8* holy   *4–8* raised   *5–8* eyes,   **563.** *4–8* prayed   **566.** *4–8* Laughed
567. *5–8* fro.   **568.** *4* 'Ha! ha!'   *5–8* he,   *4* 'full   **569.** *4–8* The   *5–8* Devil
4 row.'   **570.** *5–8* now,   *4* countrée • *5–8* countree,   **572.** *4–8* stepped
574. *4* 'O   *2 3* Man!" • *4* Man!' • *5–8* man!"   **575.** *4 6–8* crossed   *4–8* brow.
576. *4* 'Say quick,'   *2 3* I • *4* 'I   *5–8* say—   **577.** *4–8* What   *3 5–8* thou?" •
4 thou?'   **578.** *4 6–8* wrenched   **579.** *8* woful   **580.** *4–8* forced   *4* tale, • *5–
8* tale;   **582gl.** *6 7* land. • *8* land;   **582.** *4–8* then,   *4* hour   **583.** *7 8* returns:
584. *5–8* told,   **588.** *5–8* see,   **589.** *5–8* me: **592.** *4–8* wedding-guests
6–8 there: **593.** *4–8* garden-bower   *4–8* bride   **594.** *4–8* bride-maids   *3–7* are;
595. *4* vesper-bell • *5–8* vesper bell,   **596.** *5–8* prayer!   **597.** *4* wedding-guest! •
5–8 Wedding-Guest!   **601.** *4–8* marriage-feast,   **602.** *5–8* me,   **603.** *5–8* kirk
604. *4* company:— • *5–8* company!—   **605.** *5–8* kirk,   **607.** *4–8* Father
609. *4* youths, • *5–8* youths   *4–8* maidens   *5–8* gay!   **610gl.** *6–8* teach,
610. *4* But   **611.** *5–8* Wedding-Guest!   **612.** *5–8* prayeth well,   ⊠*1* loveth well
614. *5–8* prayeth best,   ⊠*1* loveth best   **615.** *5–8* small;   **616.** *5–8* God
617. *4–8* all."   **618.** ⊠*1* Mariner,   **620.** *6–8* gone: *5–8* Wedding-Guest
621. *4–8* Turned   **622.** *5–8* went   *4* stunned • *5–8* stunned,   **624.** *5–8* man,

divisional title. PR *8* does not have a separately paged divisional title: the title precedes the epigraph on the same recto page, and the poem follows. (The PR *8* title is collated out of sequence above.)

argument. PR *1 2* print the Argument on a separate recto page following the half-title. PR *2* and in what manner . . . Country.] C deleted this clause in the Irving copy at Melbourne, and expanded the Argument as follows (the RH margin has been cropped): "the Spirit, who loved the Sea-bird‿, pursuing him & his Companions, & sti‿rring‿ up against them two Spectres; and how all his Companions perished, & he wa‿s‿ left alone in the becalmed Vessel; h‿ow‿ his ⟨guardian⟩ Saint took pity on him; and ho‿w‿ a choir of Angels descended, and entered into the bodies of the Men who died; & in what manner he ca‿me‿ back to his own Country."

epigraph. PR *5–7* print the epigraph on a separate page, on the verso of the half-title; PR *8* prints it immediately following the title—the initial "T." given after "distinguamus" and detached from the surname and source, which are ranged right on the same line. C transcribed the passage from Thomas Burnet's *Archaeologiae Philosophicae* as early as 1801–2 (*CN* I 1000H).

⁻1 etc. In PR *1* the part-numbers are placed between a pair of paired rules, in PR *2–4* above a single set of paired rules.

1. In PR *5–7* line 1 follows directly after the title, from which it is separated by a rule.
2, 4, 6, etc. Alternate lines indented in PR *1–4* (see RT LH pp).
62. C undoubtedly made the change in PR *2–4* in deference to a reviewer's complaint that the line in PR *1* was nonsensical (see *British Critic* XIV—Oct 1799—364–9 at 364–5).
65. PR *1* And an] C emended to "As if" in the copy he gave to Martha Fricker (*PW*—EHC—II 1032n).
77. Erratum in PR *1*: "for 'fog smoke-white,' read 'fog-smoke white.'"
83–122. There is a very faint pencilled bracket round these lines in HNC's copy of PR *5* at HUL.

85. PR *1* weft] Deleted by C in the copy he gave to Martha Fricker (*PW*—EHC—II 1032n).

95. PR *5* slay,] The "y" and the comma are missing in some copies, because of poor inking or loose type.

104fn. The occasion C refers to here is described in *CN* II 1996.

149. In PR *1* the line follows directly after 144, as part of the same six-line stanza.

171. The full point at the end of the line in PR *3* appears to be the result of broken type. If it is, the punctuation in PR *4–8* is accidentally derived.

185gl, 188gl. PR *8* runs together as a continuous gloss attached to line 185.

185, 187. Erratum in PR *1*: "'those,' read 'these.'"

185–9. C emended the stanza in copy of PR *1* at Trinity College Cambridge to read as follows:

> Are those *her* ribs, which fleck'd the Sun,
> Like the bars of a dungeon grate?
> And are these two all, all the crew,
> That woman and her Mate?

He also keyed in the following stanza, to be inserted between lines 189 and 189.1.1, which he wrote out at the foot of the page:

> This Ship, it was a plankless Thing,
> A bare Anatomy!
> A plankless Spectre—and it mov'd
> Like a Being of the Sea!
> The Woman and a fleshless Man
> Therein sate merrily.

193. PR *5* Night-Mair] Emended by C to "Night-Mare" in the copy he gave to JG (at HUL).

197. PR *5–8* I've,] Since SC's and DC's edition of *Poems of Samuel Taylor Coleridge* (1852), it has been customary to assume that the PR *1–4* reading should be restored.

198.1.1–4, 199–202. C struck out lines 198.1.1–4 in a number of copies of PR *5*—Middleton's, HNC's, J. H. Frere's, Miss Ford's—adding in HNC's copy (in pencil): "To be struck out. | S. T. C.", in Frere's "Omitted", in Miss Ford's "Struck out by the Author". In the copy of PR *5* he gave JG, now at HUL, he deleted the stanza and added the footnote: "This stanza was struck out by the Author, and reprinted either by the Oversight or the Self-opinion of the Printer, to whom the Author was indebted for various *intended* improvements of his Poems. | S. T. Coleridge." In Wrangham's (?) copy C deleted the stanza and wrote around and beneath it: "This Stanza I had earnestly charged the Printer to omit, but he was a coxcomb, & had an opinion of his own, forsooth! the Devil daub him! (i.e. his own Devil.)"

In Gutch's defence, C did not mark the passage at all in the proof copy now at Yale, though he did correct details on the facing page. He might have changed his mind some time between Nov–Dec 1815 and 1817, when it was too late for the passage to be reset. Against this, there is something odd about the proof signatures of the *Ancient Mariner* which Gutch chose to retain. Sig B is uncharacteristically lightly marked, and might be a second or alternative proof. Sig D is missing—the only one missing from the sequence Gutch printed.

C added the following gloss to lines 199–202 in Wrangham's (?) copy: "Between the Tropics there is no Twilight. As the Sun's last Segment dips down, and the evening-Gun is fired, the Constellations appear arrayed." He added a similar gloss to AG's copy (in which he also struck out lines 198.1.1–4): "Within the Tropics there is no Twilight. As the Sun sinks, the Evening Gun is fired, and the starry Heaven is at once over all, like men in ambush that have been listening for the signal—& Hark! *Now*." And in Miss Ford's: "Within the Tropics there is no Twilight. At the moment, the *second*, that the Sun sinks, the Stars appear all at once as if at the word of command announced by the evening Gun, in our W. India Islands.—" J. L. Lowes (*RX* 167, 505 n 62) reported a similar gloss in a copy which has not been traced: "Within the Tropics there is no Twilight."

A group of copies of PR 5, sent to friends soon after publication, are emended by JG (those sent to Miss Fricker and W. Hood) and AG (those sent to WW, TP, and a person unknown)—apparently from a single copy marked up by C. In all five copies lines 198.1.1–4 have been deleted, and the gloss added to lines 199–202 is in all but three cases the same: "No Twilight within the Courts of the Sun." The exceptions are WW's copy, in which AG wrote "in" for "within"; TP's, in which she wrote "course" for "Courts"; and Miss Fricker's, in which JG copied the fuller version: "No Twilight where there is no Latitude nor yet on either side within the Park & Race-course of the Sun.—"

In addition to the changes noted, in line 199 of Miss Ford's copy of PR 5 C emended "stars" to "Stars"; and in line 200 of HNC's, Wrangham's (?), and Middleton's he emended "dark" to "Dark" (in pencil in HNC's); in Miss Ford's and AG's copies he emended "dark" to "Dᴀʀᴋ".

The PR 5–8 reading in lines 199–200 does not result from C's Malta journey alone: a similar observation occurs in **146.X1** *Osorio* III i 245–6.

198.1.1–4. Erratum in PR 5 [for p 15]: "erase the 2d stanza, *A gust of wind. &c.*"

201–12. C drafted lines towards the PR 5 reading, perhaps in Oct 1806, in N 11 f 5ʳ (*CN* II 2880 var):

> With never a whisper on the main
> Off shot the spectre ship:
> And stifled words & groans of pain
> Mix'd on each ~~trembling~~ murmuring lip/
> ⟨And⟩ We look'd round & we look'd up
> And Fear at our hearts as at a Cup
> The Life-blood seem'd to sip
>
> The Sky was dull & dark the Night,
> The Helmsman's Face by his lamp gleam'd bright,
>   From the Sails the Dews did drip/
> Till ~~rose~~ clomb above the Eastern Bar
> The horned moon, with one bright Star
>   Within its nether Tip.
>
> One after one, by the star-dogg'd moon,
>   &c—

The division between stanzas in the draft, if any was intended, is uncertain.

202.1. The PR *1* misprint "Oft" is very neatly corrected with a pen to "Off" in many copies of the Bristol and London issues, evidently by the printer or publisher. References to discussions of this feature are provided in vol I annex c 7.

209gl. PR *6–8* position the gloss at line 203. The terminal comma in PR *6 7* is faint, and easily misread as a full point.

210. PR *1* The horned Moon] C added the following footnote in the copy at Trinity College Cambridge: "It is a common superstition among Sailors, 'that something evil is about to happen whenever a star dogs the Moon.'"

215. PR *5* me with his eye.] C had to write the words into AG's copy because his deletion of lines 198.1.1–4 (on the reverse) had obscured the printed text.

251. Erratum in PR *5*: "for *cloud* read *load*." C corrected "cloud" to "load" in JG's copy (ink over pencil); and to "Load" in HNC's and Wrangham's (?) copies. JG corrected it to "Load" in Hood's and Miss Fricker's copies; AG corrected it to "load" in TP's copy, and to "Load" in WW's copy and the copy, now at Yale, belonging to a person unknown.

285. The punctuation in PR *6* is clearly a mistake. The punctuation in PR *7 8* was possibly substituted without referring to previous texts.

300. PR *7* awoke] *PW* (EHC) I 198n reports a copy in which the word has been emended in pencil to "woke", perhaps by C.

344.1.2–345. C inserted a row of asterisks between the stanzas in the copy of PR *1* he gave to Martha Fricker (*PW*—EHC—II 1039n).

345–53. In the Irving copy of PR *2* C wrote the following prose gloss in the margin (the RH margin has been cropped): "By the interception of his kind Saint⌟, a Choir of Angels desc⌞ended⌟, from Heaven, & entered into the dead bodi⌞es⌟, using the bodies a⌞s⌟ material Instrum⌞ents⌟,"

402. PR *1* 'bideth] Some copies do not have the apostrophe.

480gl. PR *6–8* position the gloss at line 482.

503.1.1–6. In the copy of PR *1* at Trinity College Cambridge C deleted all but the first line of the stanza, in pencil, and wrote the following four lines in pencil at the foot of the page (the writing is faint and the RH margin has been cropped; use has been made of the transcription supplied by RHS in *P&DW*—1877–80—II 54):

> Then vanish'd all the lovely Lig⌞hts⌟,
> The Spirits of the Air,
> No Souls of mortal men ⌞were they⌟,
> But Spirits bright & fair.

511. PR *7* makes] *PW* (EHC) I 206n reports a copy in which the word has been emended in pencil to "maketh", perhaps by C.

529–30, 531–2, 533. In Wrangham's (?) copy of PR *5* C inserted quotation-marks at the beginning of lines 529 and 530, deleted lines 531–2, and emended 533 "The" to "Like". In WW's copy of PR *5* 533 "The" has been emended to "Brown" (as in the Errata), probably by AG.

533. Erratum in PR *5*: "for *The* r. *Brown*."

541. PR *1* Said] Some copies have opening quotation-marks before the word.

583. PR *2* agency] C corrected to "agony" in the Irving copy.

594. PR *7* are;] The type is broken, so that the semicolon appears almost like a colon.

612. Erratum in PR *1*: "Omit the comma after 'loveth well.'"

161.X1. TRANSLATION FROM
WIELAND'S *OBERON*

C told Joseph Cottle in Nov 1797: "I am translating the Oberon of Wieland—it is a difficult Language, and I can translate at least as fast as I can construe" (*CL* I 357). C's interest was probably prompted by the series of articles on Wieland by William Taylor of Norwich in the *Monthly Review*, beginning in Dec 1795. The last article had appeared shortly before he wrote to Cottle—in *Monthly Review* NS XXIII (Aug 1797) 575–84—and it had devoted some ten pages to an enthusiastic summary of *Oberon*. The fact that WW knew *Oberon* well enough to discuss it with Klopstock when he arrived in Germany (*W Prose* I 93–4; *Friend—CC—*II 245; *BL Satyrane's Letters* III—*CC—*II 202–3) probably depends on the same article, or on William Sotheby's subsequent translation (1798).

It is likely that C was expressing an ambition rather than reporting an achievement when he wrote to Cottle. A case can be made for Wieland's influence on his poems of this time and afterwards, but it does not depend on whether or not he made the translation or wrote it down. When he was certainly in a position to assess the style of *Oberon*, he "was severe on the want of purity" in it (*Misc C* 387). C was probably overstating his assiduousness when he wrote to Cottle, but it is still possible that a translation was embarked upon and fragments written down.

William Sotheby—whom C was to meet through John Rickman in the summer of 1802—published a translation of *Oberon* in 1798. C referred to it in elliptical terms in a letter written ten years later (*CL* III 94: to W. Sotheby [28 Apr 1808]; cf *Misc C* 387).

162. PARLIAMENTARY OSCILLATORS

A. DATE

Dec 1797. The date "1794" is appended to PR *3* below, which is clearly misleading; but in the proofs of PR *3* at Yale (In C678 817sa) it was actually confirmed when it was deleted from the LH side of the page and written in on the RH side.

B. TEXTS

1. M Post (30 Dec 1797). Signed "LABERIUS."

2. Cambridge Intelligencer (6 Jan 1798). Signed "LABERIUS."

3 [=RT]. *SL* (1817).

title. *1 To Sir* JOHN SINCLAIR, *Alderman* LUSHING- | TON, *and the whole Troop of Parliamentary* | OSCILLATORS.• *2 To Sir* JOHN SINCLAIR, S. THORNTON, | *Alderman* LUSHINGTON, *and the whole* | *Troop of Parliamentary* OSCILLATORS.• *3* PARLIAMENTARY OSCILLATORS.

1 ☐	Almost awake? Why, what is this, and whence,	
2 ☐	O, ye right loyal men, all undefiled?	
3 *1*	It is not possible, that Common-sense	
2	It's hardly	
3	Sure, 'tis not	
4 ☐	Has hitch'd her pullies to each heavy eye-lid:	

[*Line-space*]

5 ☐	Yet, wherefore else that start, which discomposes	
6 ☐	The drowsy waters lingering in your eye?	
7 ☐	And are you *really* able to descry	
8 ☐	That precipice three yards beyond your noses?	

[*Line-space*]

9 *1 2*	But yet I cannot flatter you, your wit	
3	Yet flatter you I cannot, that	
10 ☐	Is much improv'd by this long loyal dozing:	
11 ☐	And I admire, no more than Mr. PITT,	
12 ☐	Your jumps and starts of patriotic prosing.	

[*Line-space*]

13 ☐	Now cluttering to the Treasury cluck, like chicken;	
14 *1 2*	Now with small beeks his ravenous *Bill* opposing;	
3	the	
15 ☐	With serpent tongue now stinging, and now licking,	
16 ☐	Now semi-sibilant, now smoothly glozing:	

[*Line-space*]

17 ☐	Now having faith implicit, that he can't err,	
18 ☐	Hoping his hopes, alarm'd with his alarms;	
19 ☐	And now believing him a sly inchanter,	
20 ☐	Yet still afraid to break his brittle charms;	

[*Line-space*]

21 ☐	Lest some mad devil, suddenly unhamp'ring,	
22 ☐	Slap dash the imp should fly off with the steeple,	
23 ☐	On revolutionary broomstick scamp'ring,	
24 *1 2*	O ye soft-hearted and soft-headed people!	
3	soft-headed soft-hearted	

[*Line-space*]

25 ☐	If you can stay so long from slumber free,	
26 ☐	My Muse shall make an effort to salute ye;	
27 ☐	For lo! a very dainty simile	
28 ☐	Flash'd sudden thro' my brain, and 'twill just suit ye.	

[*Line-space*]

29 *1 2*	You know that water-fowl which cries quack! quack!	
3	that	

30 *1*   Ditch-full often have I seen a waggish crew
    2   oft
    3   Full   often
31 ☐   Fasten the bird of wisdom on its back,
32 ☐   The ivy-haunting bird that cries, tu-whoo!
        [*Line-space*]
33 ☐   Both plung'd together in the deep mill-stream,
34 ☐   (Mill-stream, or farm-yard pond, or mountain lake)
35 ☐   Shrill, as a *church and constitution* scream,
36 ☐   Tu-whoo! quoth Broad-face; and down dives the Drake!
        [*Line-space*]
37 ☐   The green-neck'd Drake once more pops up to view,
38 ☐   Stares round, cries quack! and makes an angry pother:
39 ☐   Then shriller screams the Bird with eye-lids blue,
40 ☐   The broad-fac'd Bird! and deeper dives the other!
41 ☐   Ye *quacking* Statesmen! 'tis even so with you—
42 ☐   One Pease-cod is not liker to another.
        [*Line-space*]
43 ☐   Even so on loyalty's decoy-pond each
44 ☐   Pops up his head as fir'd with British blood,
45 ☐   Hear's once again the ministerial screech,
46 ☐   And once more seeks the bottom's blackest mud.

2. *3* O   **3.** *3* possible   *3* Common Sense   **4.** *3* eye-lid?   **5.** *3* Yet
10. *3* improved   *3* dosing;   **11.** *2* PITT,   **12.** *3* prosing—   **13.** *2* cluck •
3 Cluck,   *3* chicken,   **14.** *2 3* beaks   **15.** *3* serpent-tongue   **16.** *3* glozing—
17. *2 3* implicit   **20.** *3* charms,   **21.** *3* Devil   *2* unhampring,   **22.** *3* Slap-
dash!   **23.** *3* broom-stick scampering.—   **24.** *3* people,   **26.** *3* muse
3 'e: **28.** *3* through   *3* 'e!   **29.** *3* cries, Quack! quack!?   **31.** *3* Bird
3 Wisdom   *3* it's   **32.** *3* bird,   *3* Tu-whoo!   **33.** *3* plunged   **34.** *3* mountain-
lake,)   **35.** *3 Church   3 Constitution*   **36.** *3* TU-WHOO!   *2* Broad face: •
3 BROAD-FACE,   **38.** *3* Quack!   *3* pother;   **39.** *3* bird   **40.** *3* broad-faced
bird!   *3* other.   **42.** *3* peasecod   **43.** *3* Loyalty's Decoy-pond,   **44.** *3* head,
45. *2 3* Hears   *3* Ministerial   **46.** *3* mud!

2, 4, 6–7, etc. Rhyming lines are indented in PR *1 3*, alternate lines in PR *2*.

163. STUDIES IN CLOUD EFFECTS

A. DATE

21–31 Dec 1797 (KC's dating).

B. TEXT

BM Add MS 47518 = Notebook 21 f 3ᵛ (*CN* I 315, 316, 317, 318).

The RT reproduces the untitled Notebook text exactly, apart from the parenthetical lettering of the fragments.

164. ON DEPUTY —— ——

A. DATE

Late Dec 1797.

B. TEXT

M Post (2 Jan 1798). Signed "LABERIUS."

The RT reproduces the *M Post* text exactly.

165. THE APOTHEOSIS
OR, THE SNOW-DROP

A. DATE

28 or 29 Dec 1797? The poem by Mary Robinson to which C's was an immediate reply was published in *M Post* (26 Dec), and London newspapers took one or two days to reach Stowey.

B. TEXTS

1. NYPL Berg Collection. Single leaf, 25.0×37.8 cm; countermark I V; chain-lines 2.5 cm; written on both sides. Draft in C's hand, the introductory note signed "ZAGRI." *CL* I 639–42 (ELG dates [late Oct 1800]). Facsimile of recto in David V. Erdman "Lost Poem Found: The Cooperative Pursuit and Recapture of an Escaped Coleridge 'Sonnet' of 72 Lines" *BNYPL* LXV (1961) 249–68 facing 249.
  The draft is introduced as follows:

~~Lines written immediately after the perusal of~~ Mʳˢ ~~Robinson's "Snow Drop."~~—To the Editor of The Morning Post.

Sir

I am one among your many readers, who have been highly gratified by your extracts from Mrs Robinson's Walsingham; you will oblige ~~my~~ me by inserting the following lines immediately on the perusal of her beautiful poem, the Snow Drop—.

ZAGRI.

1 [=RT]. *M Post* (3 Jan 1798). Signed "FRANCINI." Rpt *Express and Evening Chronicle* (6–9 Jan 1798).

No copy of *M Post* for this date has been located, but a reference in the following issue (4 Jan) confirms that it did appear carrying C's poem. RS himself failed to locate a copy when he searched only two years later, and C was unable or unwilling to supply him with the ninth stanza as printed (see vol I headnote).

The *Express and Evening Chronicle* was another of Daniel Stuart's newspapers, and was made up largely of selections and abridgements of matter from *M Post*. It appeared three times a week, and was printed in the same shop. To judge from other articles and items—including its reprinting of **174** *France: An Ode* (under the title *The Recantation*) on 15–17 Apr 1798 from *M Post* of 16 Apr—it is likely to be an exact reproduction and even to have been printed from the same standing type; although, as happened with poem **174,** it is likely that the *M Post* version carried some introductory text (as in MS 1), which was dropped to fit the narrower confines of the provincial digest.

title. 1 To the Snow Drop • *1* THE APOTHEOSIS, OR THE SNOW-DROP.

‾1.1	1	1
1.1	1	Fear thou no more the wintry storm,
1.1.1	1	Sweet Flowret, blest by LAURA's song!
11.1	1	She gaz'd upon thy slender form,
11.1.1	1	The mild Enchantress gaz'd so long;
13.1	1	That trembling as she saw thee droop,
13.1.1	1	Poor Trembler! o'er thy snowy bed,
15.1	1	With imitative sympathy
16.1	1	She too inclin'd her head.
		[*Line-space*]
‾17.1	1	2
17.1	1	She droop'd her head, she stretch'd her arm,
18.1	1	She whisper'd low her witching rhymes:
19.1	1	A gentle Sylphid heard the charm,
20.1	1	And bore thee to Pierian Climes!
21.1	1	Fear thou no more the ~~Tempest's Howl,~~ sparkling Frost,
21.1.1	1	The ~~silent~~ Tempest's howl, the Fog-damp's gloom:
23.1	1	For there mid laurels ever-green
24.1	1	Immortal thou shalt bloom!
		[*Line-space*]
‾1	1	1
1	□	Fear no more, thou timid Flower!
2	□	Fear thou no more the winters might;

3	1	The ~~tempest stern, howling Blast,~~ whelming thaw, the ponderous shower,
	1	←————————whelming————————→
4	□	The silence of the freezing night!
5	□	Since Laura murmur'd o'er thy leaves
6	□	The potent sorceries of song,
7	1	To thee, ~~sweet~~ meek Flowret! gentler gales
	1	meek
8	□	And cloudless skies belong.

[*Line-space*]

            2

⁻9	1	
9	1	With ~~steady eye & brooding thought~~ eager feelings ~~pity~~ unreprov'd
	1	On thee with feelings unreprov'd,
10	1	~~My Fancy saw her gaze at thee~~
	1ⁱᵐᵖ	Her eye with tearful meanings fraugh⌐t,⌐
	1	fraught,
11	1	~~Till all the moving body, caught~~
	☒	She gaz'd till all the body mov'd
12	1	~~The Spirit's eager sympathy~~
	☒	Interpreting the Spirit's thought—
13	1	~~She~~ Now trembled with thy trembling stem,
	1	Now
14	□	And while thou drooped'st o'er thy bed
15	1	With ~~sweet unconscious portraiture~~ fair sweet unconscious sympathy
	1	←————————imitative————————→
16	1	~~She too i~~ Inclin'd ~~the her~~ the drooping head
	1	←—Inclin'd—→ ←—the—→

[*Line-space*]

            3

⁻17	1	
17	□	She droop'd her head, she stretch'd her arm,
18	□	She whisper'd low her witching rhymes:
19	1	~~A gentle Sylphid~~ Fame unreluctant heard the charm,
	1	FAME unrebellious
20	□	And bore thee to Pierian climes!
21	□	Fear thou no more the matin frost
22	1	That ~~glitter'd~~ sparkled on thy bed of snow:
	1	←—sparkled—→
23	□	For there mid laurels evergreen
24	⊓	Immortal thou shalt blow.

[*Line-space*]

            4

⁻25	1	
25	1	Thy petals boast a ~~richer white /~~ White more soft,
	1	←————white————→
26	□	The spell hath so perfumed thee,
27	1	~~LOVE's careless eye~~ That careless LOVE shall deem thee oft
	1	←————That————→
28	□	A Blossom from his myrtle tree.
29	1	~~Now~~ Then laughing at the fair deceit
	1	Then

30 1   ~~He races~~ Shall race with ~~the western~~ some Etesian wind
    1   ←—Shall—→   ←—some—→
31 □   To seek the woven arboret
32 1   Where L A U R A ~~'s~~ lies reclin'd.
    1   L A U R A
    [*Line-space*]

    1   5
33 1   ~~For then,~~ All them whom Love and Fancy grace,
    1   ←—For—→
34 1   When grosser eyes are clos'd in sleep
    1   human
35 1   The   gentle Spirits of the place
    1   Them oft the
36 1   Waft up the' ~~unvoyageable~~ insuperable steep
    1   that   strange   unpathway'd
37 1   On whose ~~strange~~ vast summit broad & smooth
    1   ←—vast—→   smooth   broad,
38 1   Her nest the Phoenix Bird conceals;
    1   His
39 1   And ~~there~~ where by cypresses o'erhung
    1   where
40 1   ɅThe heavenly Lethe steals.
    1   A
    [*Line-space*]
¯**41** 1   6
41 □   A sea-like sound the branches breathe
42 □   Stirr'd by the Breeze that loiters there:
43 1   And, all ~~who~~ that stretch their limbs beneath
    1   who
44 □   Forget the coil of mortal care—
45 1   ~~Such~~ ~~Strange~~ Such mists ~~of magic odour~~ along the margin rise
    1   ←—Such—→   ←—along—→
46 1   ~~To~~ As heal the guests who thither come,
    1   As
47 □   And fit the soul to re-endure
48 □   Its earthly Martyrdom.
    [*Line-space*]
¯**49** 1   7
49 1   The margin dear to ~~midnight~~ moonlight elves
    1   That marge, how dear to moonlight
50 1   ~~When~~ Where zephyr-trembling Lilies grow
    1   ←—There—→   blow,
51 □   And bend to kiss their softer *s*Selves
52 □   That tremble in the stream below—
53 1   ~~Along that marge~~ There, nightly born, does Laura lie
    1   ←——There,——→
54 1   ~~Full oft, when~~ A magic slumber heaves her breast:
    1   ←——A——→
55 □   Her arm, white wanderer of the Harp,

56 ☐   Beneath her cheek is prest.—
      [*Line-space*]

⁻57 1

57 ☐   The Harp, uphung by golden chains,

58 1   Of that low ~~sound that~~ wind which whispers round

    1   ←—wind—→

59 ☐   With coy reproachfulness complains

60 ☐   In snatches of reluctant sound.

61 ☐   The music hovers half-perceiv'd

62 ☐   And only moulds the slumberer's dreams:

63 1   Remember'd LOVES ~~reillume~~ her cheek

    1   light up

64 1   With ~~Beauty's morning~~ Youth's returning gleams.

    1   ←——youth's——→

      [*Line-space*]

65 *1*   The LOVES trip round her all the night;

66 *1*   And PITY hates the morning's birth,

67 *1*   That rudely warns the ling'ring SPRITE

68 *1*   Whose plumes must waft her back to earth!

69 *1*   Meek PITY, that foreruns relief,

70 *1*   Yet still assumes the hues of woe;

71 *1*   Pale promiser of rosy Spring,

72 *1*   A SNOW-DROP mid the snow.

1. *1* flower!   **2.** *1* Winter's   **3.** *1* thaw;   *1* shower;   **5.** *1* LAURA

7. *1* flow'ret!   **12.** *1* spirit's thought: **13.** *1* stem;   **14.** *1* And,   *1* bed,

16. *1* head.   **20.** *1* climes.   **23.** *1* there,   *1* ever green,   **25.** *1* soft—

28. *1* blossom   *1* myrtle-tree: **31.** *1* aboret,   **32.** *1* reclin'd!   **33.** *1* them,

1 LOVE   *1* FANCY   **34.** *1* sleep,   **35.** *1* spirits   **36.** *1* steep;

37. *1* summit,   *1* and   **38.** *1* phœnix bird conceals,   **41.** *1* breathe,

42. *1* breeze   *1* there;   **43.** *1* And all,   *1* beneath,   **44.** *1* care.   **45.** *1* rise,

46. *1* guests,   *1* come;   **48.** *1* It's   *1* martyrdom.   **49.** *1* elves!   **50.** *1* lilies

51. *1* selves   **52.** *1* below!   **53.** *1* borne,   *1* LAURA lie—   **54.** *1* breast!

55. *1* harp,   **56.** *1* prest!   **57.** *1* harp,   **58.** *1* round,   **60.** *1* sound!

61. *1* half-perceiv'd,   **63.** *1* loves

1.1–24.1. The two stanzas were deleted together, with a single cross and line. Lines 1 16 were drafted alongside them, making a second, rather cramped column at the right. Stanzas 3 and 4 were then written side by side at the foot of the same page, separated from each other by a vertical line. Stanzas 5–8 were written in sequence down the LH side of the verso.

15. PR *1* "imitative" replaces the two adjectives following the deletions.

16.1, 24.1, etc. In MS 1 the last line of each stanza is indented; in PR *1* alternate lines are indented throughout (as in the RT).

9. MS 1 feelings] C deleted the word in favour of "pity" and then, by means of crosses above and below the deleted word, indicated that it should be restored.

166. TO A WELL-KNOWN MUSICAL CRITIC, REMARKABLE FOR HIS EARS STICKING THRO' HIS HAIR

A. DATE

Late Dec 1797.

B. TEXT

M Post (4 Jan 1798). Signed "LABERIUS."

The RT reproduces the *M Post* text exactly, except for the typography of the title:

To a well-known MUSICAL CRITIC, *remarkable* | *for his ears sticking thro' his hair.*

167. FIRE, FAMINE, AND SLAUGHTER: A WAR ECLOGUE, WITH AN APOLOGETIC PREFACE

A. DATE

Dec 1797? See vol I headnote on references in the poem to events in Ulster in Mar 1797. The date appended to PR *3–6* below is likely to be inaccurate, though it is possible that the poem was conceived at the earlier time.

B. TEXTS

1. M Post (8 Jan 1798). Signed "LABERIUS."
C used the same pseudonym in *M Post* on 30 Dec 1797 and 2 and 4 Jan 1798: see poems **162, 164, 166.**

2. Annual Anthology ed RS (2 vols Bristol 1799–1800) II 231–5. Unsigned.
C told RS on 18 Feb 1800: "Fire & Famine do just what you like with—I have no wish either way" (*CL* I 573). The changes in this version are none the less extensive, and likely to have been supplied by C. He did not comment on or emend the revised text in his own copy of PR *2* now at Yale (Tinker 1953 2).
Rpt *Cambridge Intelligencer* (22 Nov 1800); *The Examiner* (24 Nov 1816) 744; *The Apostate Bard* (1817) 45–8 (with "Bob Northey" [=RS]). The tran-

script made by Mary Godwin (Shelley) in 1815–16 (*Shelley and his Circle 1773–1822* ed Kenneth Neill Cameron and Donald H. Reiman—8 vols Cambridge, Mass 1961–86—VII 4–8) has no textual authority.

3. *SL* (1817). Dated at the end "1796".

The poem is printed with a separate divisional title, followed on the verso by two epigraphs, facing the start of a long prose introduction ("AN APOLOGETIC PREFACE"). The Preface appears to have been projected as early as Dec 1799 (see VCL S MS F2.2 f 1ʳ).

Rpt *Select British Poets* ed William Hazlitt (1824) 628–9; *Metrical Romances &c. By S. T. Coleridge, Esq.* (Isleworth 1825).

The proof copy of PR *3* at Yale (In C678 817sa) contains an additional ms stanza, which C at once thought better of. Ten copies contain corrections and emendations: JG's (HUL *EC8 C6795 817s (C)), in C's hand and JG's; HNC's (HUL *AC85 L8605 Zy 817c), in C's hand; Francis Wrangham's (?) (sold at Christie's 13 Jun 1979 lot 126), in C's hand; WW's (Cornell WORDSWORTH PR 4480 S5 1817 Copy 1), in AG's (?) hand; TP's (Brown PR 4478 A1 1817 Koopman Collection), in AG's hand; an unknown person's (Yale In C678 817s Copy 2), in AG's hand; William Hood's (Columbia X 825 C67 W3 1817), in JG's hand; Miss Fricker's (HUL Lowell *EC8 C6795 817s), in JG's hand; DC's copy (HRC, uncatalogued in Oct 1978), in C's hand and DC's, partly trimmed; emended part copy (HUL *EC8 C6795 817s (D)), in JG's hand.

The bulk of the annotations are minor, and merely take in the Errata. The annotations in the last two copies listed above are more extensive and of a different kind. In DC's copy almost all the annotation is concentrated on this text, and it may be linked to the claim that C made to DC in late Nov 1818 (?) that the Preface "is my happiest performance in respect of *Style*" (*CL* IV 885): the emendations are improving, though not all were carried across into later texts. Many but not all of the emendations in DC's copy are shared with the part copy at HUL.

4 [=RT]. *PW* (1828). Dated at the end "1796".

PR *4–6* drop the half-title and epigraphs, and print the Preface at the end of the volume. The copy in the Fitzwilliam Museum, Cambridge (Marlay Bequest 1912) contains a single emendation of the Preface, in C's hand.

5. *PW* (1829). Dated at the end "1796".

JG's (?) copy at NYPL (Berg Collection) contains several small corrections and an emendation.

6. *PW* (1834). Dated at the end "1796".

C. GENERAL NOTE

George Bellas Greenough copied out a version—presumably from C's holograph or at C's dictation—into his diary during their walking tour of the Harz

mountains, which has since been lost (*C in Germany* 230). C remarked in 1830
that he thought the poem had been published in an Irish miscellany, where it
was attributed to Porson (*CL* VI 830: to H. W. Montagu Apr 1830). This reprint-
ing has not been traced, and it is possible that C is referring in a muddled way
to the "Bob Northey" reprinting of PR 2.

divisional title. *3 𝔉𝔦𝔯𝔢, 𝔉𝔞𝔪𝔦𝔫𝔢, 𝔞𝔫𝔡 𝔖𝔩𝔞𝔲𝔤𝔥𝔱𝔢𝔯.* | *A WAR-ECLOGUE.* | WITH | AN
APOLOGETIC PREFACE.

epigraphs [present in PR *3* only]

ME DOLOR INCANTUM, ME LUBRICA DUXERIT ÆTAS,
ME TUMOR IMPULERIT, ME DEVIUS EGERIT ARDOR:
TE TAMEN HAUD DECUIT PARIBUS CONCURRERE TELIS.
EN ADSUM: RENIAM, CONFESSUS CRIMINA, POSCO.
                                   CLAUD. *Epist. ad Had.*

  THERE IS ONE THAT SLIPPETH IN HIS SPEECH, BUT NOT
FROM HIS HEART; AND WHO IS HE THAT HATH NOT OFFENDED
WITH HIS TONGUE?
                              Ecclesiasticus, xix. 16.

preface [present in PR *3–6*]

At the house of a gentleman, who by the principles and corresponding virtues of
a sincere Christian consecrates a cultivated genius and the favorable accidents
of birth, opulence, and splendid connexions, it was my good fortune to meet,
in a dinner-party, with more men of celebrity in science or polite literature,
than are commonly found collected round the same table. In the course of   ⁻1.5
conversation, one of the party reminded an illustrious Poet, then present, of
some verses which he had recited that morning, and which had appeared in
a newspaper under the name of a War-Eclogue, in which Fire, Famine, and
Slaughter, were introduced as the speakers. The gentleman so addressed replied,
that he was rather surprised that none of us should have noticed or heard of the   ⁻1.10
Poem, as it had been, at the time, a good deal talked of in Scotland. It may
be easily supposed, that my feelings were at this moment not of the most
comfortable kind. Of all present, one only knew, or suspected me to be the
author; a man who would have established himself in the first rank of England's
living Poets, if the Genius of our country had not decreed that he should rather   ⁻1.15
be the first in the first rank of its Philosophers and scientific Benefactors. It
appeared the general wish to hear the lines. As my friend chose to remain
silent, I chose to follow his example, and Mr. ***** recited the Poem. This
he could do with the better grace, being known to have ever been not only a
firm and active Anti-Jacobin and Anti-Gallican, but likewise a zealous admirer   ⁻1.20
of Mr. Pitt, both as a good man and a great Statesman. As a Poet exclusively,
he had been amused with the Eclogue; as a Poet, he recited it; and in a spirit,
which made it evident, that he would have read and repeated it with the same
pleasure, had his own name been attached to the imaginary object or agent.
  After the recitation, our amiable host observed, that in his opinion Mr. *****   ⁻1.25
had over-rated the merits of the poetry; but had they been tenfold greater, they
could not have compensated for that malignity of heart, which could alone

have prompted sentiments so atrocious. I perceived that my illustrious friend became greatly distressed on my account; but fortunately I was able to preserve fortitude and presence of mind enough to take up the subject without exciting even a suspicion, how nearly and painfully it interested me.

⁻1.30

What follows, is substantially the same as I then replied, but dilated and in language less colloquial. It was not my intention, I said, to justify the publication, whatever its author's feelings might have been at the time of composing it. That they are calculated to call forth so severe a reprobation from a good man, is not the worst feature of such poems. Their moral deformity is aggravated in proportion to the pleasure which they are capable of affording to vindictive, turbulent, and unprincipled readers. Could it be supposed, though for a moment, that the author seriously wished what he had thus wildly imagined, even the attempt to palliate an inhumanity so monstrous would be an insult to the hearers. But it seemed to me worthy of consideration, whether the mood of mind, and the general state of sensations, in which a Poet produces such vivid and fantastic images, is likely to co-exist, or is even compatible with, that gloomy and deliberate ferocity which a serious wish to *realize* them would pre-suppose. It had been often observed, and all my experience tended to confirm the observation, that prospects of pain and evil to others, and in general, all deep feelings of revenge, are commonly expressed in a few words, ironically tame, and mild. The mind under so direful and fiend-like an influence, seems to take a morbid pleasure in contrasting the intensity of its wishes and feelings, with the slightness or levity of the expressions by which they are hinted; and indeed feelings so intense and solitary, if they were not precluded (as in almost all cases they would be) by a constitutional activity of fancy and association, and by the specific joyousness combined with it, would assuredly themselves preclude such activity. Passion, in its own quality, is the antagonist of action; though in an ordinary and natural degree the former alternates with the latter, and thereby revives and strengthens it. But the more intense and insane the passion is, the fewer and the more fixed are the correspondent forms and notions. A rooted hatred, an inveterate thirst of revenge, is a sort of madness, and still eddies round its favourite object, and exercises as it were a perpetual tautology of mind in thoughts and words, which admit of no adequate substitutes. Like a fish in a globe of glass, it moves restlessly round and round the scanty circumference, which it can not leave without losing its vital element.

⁻1.35

⁻1.40

⁻1.45

⁻1.50

⁻1.55

⁻1.60

There is a second character of such imaginary representations as spring from a real and earnest desire of evil to another, which we often see in real life, and might even anticipate from the nature of the mind. The images, I mean, that a vindictive man places before his imagination, will most often be taken from the realities of life: they will be images of pain and suffering which he has himself seen inflicted on other men, and which he can fancy himself as inflicting on the object of his hatred. I will suppose that we had heard at different times two common sailors, each speaking of some one who had wronged or offended him; that the first with apparent violence had devoted every part of his adversary's body and soul to all the horrid phantoms and fantastic places that ever Quevedo dreamt of, and this in a rapid flow of those outrè and wildly combined execrations, which too often with our lower classes serve for *escape-valves* to carry off the excess of their passions, as so much superfluous steam that would endanger the vessel if it were retained. The other, on the contrary,

⁻1.65

⁻1.70

⁻1.75

with that sort of calmness of tone which is to the ear what the paleness of anger
is to the eye, shall simply say, "If I chance to be made boatswain, as I hope I
soon shall, and can but once get that fellow under my hand (and I shall be upon
the watch for him), I'll tickle his pretty skin! I won't hurt him! oh no! I'll only   ⁻1.80
cut the —— —— to the *liver!*" I dare appeal to all present, which of the two
they would regard as the least deceptive symptom of deliberate malignity? nay,
whether it would surprize them to see the first fellow, an hour or two afterward,
cordially shaking hands with the very man, the fractional parts of whose body
and soul he had been so charitably disposing of; or even perhaps risking his   ⁻1.85
life for him. What language Shakespear considered characteristic of malignant
disposition, we see in the speech of the good-natural Gratiano, who spoke "an
infinite deal of nothing more than any man in all Venice;"

> "—— Too wild, too rude and bold of voice,"

the skipping spirit, whose thoughts and words reciprocally ran away with each   ⁻1.90
other;

> "—— O be thou *damn'd*, inexorable dog!
> And for thy life let justice be accused!"

and the wild fancies that follow, contrasted with Shylock's tranquil "*I stand
here for Law.*"   ⁻1.95

Or, to take a case more analogous to the present subject, should we hold it
either fair or charitable to believe it to have been Dante's serious wish, that all
the persons mentioned by him, (many recently departed, and some even alive at
the time,) should actually suffer the fantastic and horrible punishments, to which
he has sentenced them in his *hell and purgatory?* Or what shall we say of the   ⁻1.100
passages in which Bishop Jeremy Taylor anticipates the state of those who,
vicious themselves, have been the cause of vice and misery to their fellow-
creatures. Could we endure for a moment to think that a spirit, like Bishop
Taylor's, burning with Christian love; that a man constitutionally overflowing
with pleasurable kindliness; who scarcely even in a casual illustration introduces   ⁻1.105
the image of woman, child, or bird, but he embalms the thought with so rich
a tenderness, as makes the very words seem beauties and fragments of poetry
from a Euripides or Simonides;—can we endure to think, that a man *so* natured
and so disciplined, did at the time of composing this horrible picture, attach a
sober feeling of reality to the phrases? or that he would have described in the   ⁻1.110
same tone of justification, in the same luxuriant flow of phrases, the tortures
about to be inflicted on a living individual by a verdict of the Star-Chamber?
or the still more atrocious sentences executed on the Scotch anti-prelatists and
schismatics, at the command, and in some instances under the very eye of the
Duke of Lauderdale, and of that wretched bigot who afterwards dishonored and   ⁻1.115
forfeited the throne of Great Britain? Or do we not rather feel and understand,
that these violent words were mere bubbles, flashes and electrical apparitions,
from the magic cauldron of a fervid and ebulient fancy, constantly fuelled by
an unexampled opulence of language?

Were I now to have read by myself for the first time the Poem in question,   ⁻1.120
my conclusion, I fully believe, would be, that the writer must have been some
man of warm feelings and active fancy; that he had painted to himself the
circumstances that accompany war in so many vivid and yet fantastic forms, as

proved that neither the images nor the feelings were the result of observation, or in any way derived from realities. I should judge, that they were the product of his own seething imagination, and therefore impregnated with that pleasurable exultation which is experienced in all energetic exertion of intellectual power; that in the same mood he had generalized the causes of the war, and then personified the abstract and christened it by the name which he been accustomed to hear most often associated with its management and measures. I should guess that the minister was in the author's mind at the moment of composition, as completely ἀπαθής, ἀναιμόσαρκος, as Anacreon's grasshopper, and that he had as little notion of a real person of flesh and blood,   ⁻1.125   ⁻1.130

> "Distinguishable in member, joint, or limb,"

as Milton had in the grim and terrible phantoms (half person, half allegory) which he has placed at the gates of Hell. I concluded by observing, that the Poem was not calculated to excite *passion* in *any* mind, or to make any impression except on *poetic* readers; and that from the culpable levity, betrayed in the grotesque union of epigrammatic wit with allegoric personification, in the allusion to the most fearful of thoughts, I should conjecture that the "rantin Bardie," instead of really believing, much less wishing, the fate spoken of in the last line, in application to any human individual, would shrink from passing the verdict even on the Devil himself, and exclaim with poor Burns,   ⁻1.135   ⁻1.140

> But fare ye weel, auld Nickie-ben!
> Oh! wad ye tak a thought an' men!
> Ye aiblins might—I dinna ken—
>   Still hae a *stake*—
> I'm wae to think upon yon den,
>   Ev'n for your sake!

  ⁻1.145   ⁻1.150

I need not say that these thoughts, which are here dilated, were in such a company only rapidly suggested. Our kind host smiled, and with a courteous compliment observed, that the defence was too good for the cause. My voice faultered a little, for I was somewhat agitated; though not so much on my own account as for the uneasiness that so kind and friendly a man would feel from the thought that he had been the occasion of distressing me. At length I brought out these words: "I must now confess, Sir! that I am the author of that Poem. It was written some years ago. I do not attempt to justify my past self, young as I then was; but as little as I would now write a similar poem, so far was I even then from imagining, that the lines would be taken as more or less than a sport of fancy. At all events, if I know my own heart, there was never a moment in my existence in which I should have been more ready, had Mr. Pitt's person been in hazard, to interpose my own body, and defend his life at the risque of my own."   ⁻1.155   ⁻1.160

[*Line-space*]

I have prefaced the Poem with this anecdote, because to have printed it without any remark might well have been understood as implying an unconditional approbation on my part, and this after many years consideration. But if it be asked why I re-published it at all? I answer, that the Poem had been at-   ⁻1.165

tributed at different times to different other persons; and what I had dared beget, I thought it neither manly nor honorable not to dare father. From the same motives I should have published perfect copies of two Poems, the one entitled *The Devil's Thoughts*, and the other *The Two Round Spaces on the Tomb-Stone*, but that the four first stanzas of the former, which were worth all the rest of the poem, and the best stanza of the remainder, were written by a friend of deserved celebrity; and because there are passages in both, which might have given offence to the religious feelings of certain readers. I myself indeed see no reason why vulgar superstitions, and absurd conceptions that deform the pure faith of a Christian, should possess a greater immunity from ridicule than stories of witches, or the fables of Greece and Rome. But there are those who deem it profaneness and irreverence to call an ape an ape, if it but wear a monk's cowl on its head; and I would rather reason with this weakness than offend it.

The passage from Jeremy Taylor to which I referred, is found in his second Sermon on Christ's Advent to Judgement; which is likewise the second in his year's course of sermons. Among many remarkable passages of the same character in those discourses, I have selected this as the most so. "But when this Lion of the tribe of Judah shall appear, then Justice shall strike and Mercy shall not hold her hands; she shall strike sore strokes, and Pity shall not break the blow. As there are treasures of good things, so hath God a treasure of wrath and fury, and scourges and scorpions; and then shall be produced the shame of Lust and the malice of Envy, and the groans of the oppressed and the persecutions of the saints, and the cares of Covetousness and the troubles of Ambition, *and the insolencies of traitors and the violences of rebels*, and the rage of anger and the uneasiness of impatience, and the restlessness of unlawful desires; and by this time the monsters and diseases will be numerous and intolerable, when God's heavy hand shall press the *sanies* and the intolerableness, the obliquity and the unreasonableness, the amazement and the disorder, the smart and the sorrow, the guilt and the punishment, out from all our sins, and pour them into one chalice, and mingle them with an infinite wrath, and make the wicked drink off all the vengeance, and force it down their unwilling throats with the violence of devils and accursed spirits."

That this Tartarean drench displays the imagination rather than the discretion of the compounder; that, in short, this passage and others of the same kind are *in a bad taste*, few will deny at the present day. It would doubtless have more behoved the good bishop not to be wise beyond what is written, on a subject in which Eternity is opposed to Time, and a death threatened, not the negative, but the *positive* Opposite of Life; a subject, therefore, which must of necessity be indescribable to the human understanding in our present state. But I can neither find nor believe, that it ever occurred to any reader to ground on such passages a charge against BISHOP TAYLOR's humanity, or goodness of heart. I was not a little surprized therefore to find, in the Pursuits of Literature and other works, so horrible a sentence passed on MILTON's moral character, for a passage in *his* prose-writings, as nearly parallel to this of Taylor's as two passages can well be conceived to be. All his merits, as a poet, forsooth—all the glory of having written the PARADISE LOST, are light in the scale, nay, kick the beam, compared with the atrocious malignity of heart expressed in the offensive paragraph. I remembered, in general, that Milton had concluded one of his works on Reformation, written in the fervour of his youthful imagination, in a high

⁻1.170

⁻1.175

⁻1.180

⁻1.185

⁻1.190

⁻1.195

⁻1.200

⁻1.205

⁻1.210

⁻1.215

poetic strain, that wanted metre only to become a lyrical poem. I remembered
that in the former part he had formed to himself a perfect ideal of human virtue,
a character of heroic, disinterested zeal and devotion for Truth, Religion, and ⁻1.220
public Liberty, in Act and in Suffering, in the day of Triumph and in the hour
of Martyrdom. Such spirits, as more excellent than others, he describes as hav-
ing a more excellent reward, and as distinguished by a transcendent glory: and
this reward and this glory he displays and particularizes with an energy and
brilliance that announced the Paradise Lost as plainly, as ever the bright purple ⁻1.225
clouds in the east announced the coming of the Sun. Milton then passes to the
gloomy contrast, to such men as from motives of selfish ambition and the lust
of personal aggrandizement should, against their own light, persecute truth and
the true religion, and wilfully abuse the powers and gifts entrusted to them, to
bring vice, blindness, misery and slavery, on their native country, on the very ⁻1.230
country that had trusted, enriched and honored them. Such beings, after that
speedy and appropriate removal from their sphere of mischief which all good
and humane men must of course desire, will, he takes for granted by parity
of reason, meet with a punishment, an ignominy, and a retaliation, as much
severer than other wicked men, as their guilt and its consequences were more ⁻1.235
enormous. His description of this imaginary punishment presents more distinct
pictures to the fancy than the extract from Jeremy Taylor; but the *thoughts* in
the latter are incomparably more exaggerated and horrific. All this I knew; but
I neither remembered, nor by reference and careful re-perusal could discover,
any other meaning, either in Milton or Taylor, but that good men will be re- ⁻1.240
warded, and the impenitent wicked punished, in proportion to their dispositions
and intentional acts in this life; and that if the punishment of the least wicked be
fearful beyond conception, all words and descriptions must be so far true, that
they must fall short of the punishment that awaits the transcendently wicked.
Had Milton stated either his ideal of virtue, or of depravity, as an individual ⁻1.245
or individuals actually existing? Certainly not! Is his representation worded
historically, or only hypothetically? Assuredly the latter! Does he express it as
his own *wish*, that after death they *should* suffer these tortures? or as a gen-
eral consequence, deduced from reason and revelation, that such *will* be their
fate? Again, the latter only! His wish is expressly confined to a speedy stop ⁻1.250
being put by Providence to their power of inflicting misery on others! But did
he name or refer to any persons, living or dead? No! But the calumniators of
Milton *daresay* (for what will calumny not dare say?) that he had LAUD and
STAFFORD in his mind, while writing of remorseless persecution, and the en-
slavement of a free country, from motives of selfish ambition. Now, what if a ⁻1.255
stern anti-prelatist should *daresay*, that in speaking of the *insolencies of traitors
and the violences of rebels*, Bishop Taylor must have individualized in his mind,
HAMDEN, HOLLIS, PYM, FAIRFAX, IRETON, and MILTON? And what if he
should take the liberty of concluding, that in the after-description the Bishop
was feeding and feasting his party-hatred, and with those individuals before the ⁻1.260
eyes of his imagination enjoying, trait by trait, horror after horror, the picture
of their intolerable agonies? Yet this Bigot would have an equal right thus to
criminate the one good and great man, as these men have to criminate the other.
Milton has said, and I doubt not but that Taylor with equal truth could have
said it, "that in his whole life he never spake against a man even that his skin ⁻1.265
should be grazed." He asserted this when one of his opponents (either Bishop

Hall or his nephew) had called upon the women and children in the streets to
take up stones and stone *him* (Milton). It is known that Milton repeatedly used
his interest to protect the royalists; but even at a time when all lies would have
been meritorious against him, no charge was made, no story pretended, that   ⁻1.270
he had ever directly or indirectly engaged or assisted in their persecution. Oh!
methinks there are other and far better feelings, which should be acquired by
the perusal of our great elder writers. When I have before me on the same table,
the works of Hammond and Baxter; when I reflect with what joy and dearness
their blessed spirits are now loving each other: it seems a mournful thing that   ⁻1.275
their names should be perverted to an occasion of bitterness among *us*, who are
enjoying that happy mean which the *human* TOO-MUCH on both sides was per-
haps necessary to produce. "The tangle of delusions which stifled and distorted
the growing tree of our well-being have been torn away; the parasite-weeds that
fed on its very roots have been plucked up with a salutary violence. To us   ⁻1.280
there remain only quiet duties, the constant care, the gradual improvement, the
cautious unhazardous labours of the industrious though contented gardener—to
prune, to strengthen, to engraft, and one by one to remove from its leaves and
fresh shoots the slug and the caterpillar. But far be it from us to undervalue with
light and senseless detraction the conscientious hardihood of our predecessors,   ⁻1.285
or even to condemn in them that vehemence, to which the blessings it won for
us leave us now neither temptation nor pretext. We ante-date the *feelings*, in
order to criminate the *authors*, of our present Liberty, Light and Toleration."
(THE FRIEND, p. 54.)

If ever two great men might seem, during their whole lives, to have moved in   ⁻1.290
direct opposition, though neither of them has at any time introduced the name
of the other, Milton and Jeremy Taylor were they. The former commenced
his career by attacking the Church-Liturgy and all set forms of prayer. The
latter, but far more successfully, by defending both. Milton's next work was
then against the Prelacy and the then existing Church-Government—Taylor's,   ⁻1.295
in vindication and support of them. Milton became more and more a stern re-
publican, or rather an advocate for that religious and moral aristocracy which,
in his day, was *called* republicanism, and which, even more than royalism it-
self, is the direct antipode of modern jacobinism. Taylor, as more and more
sceptical concerning the fitness of men in general for power, became more and   ⁻1.300
more attached to the prerogatives of monarchy. From Calvinism, with a still
decreasing respect for Fathers, Councils, and for Church-Antiquity in general,
Milton seems to have ended in an indifference, if not a dislike, to *all* forms
of ecclesiastic government, and to have retreated wholly into the inward and
spiritual church-communion of his own spirit with the Light, that lighteth every   ⁻1.305
man that cometh into the world. Taylor, with a growing reverence for authority,
an increasing sense of the insufficiency of the Scriptures without the aids of
tradition and the consent of authorized interpreters, advanced as far in his ap-
proaches (not indeed to Popery, but) to Catholicism, as a conscientious minister
of the English Church could well venture. Milton would be, and would utter the   ⁻1.310
same, to all, on all occasions: he would tell the truth, the whole truth, and noth-
ing but the truth. Taylor would become all things to all men, if by any means he
might benefit any; hence he availed himself, in his *popular* writings, of opinions
and representations which stand often in striking contrast with the doubts and
convictions expressed in his more philosophical works. He appears, indeed, not   ⁻1.315

too severely to have blamed that *management* of truth (*istam fatsitatem dispen-sativam*) authorized and exemplified by almost all the fathers: Integrum omnino Doctoribus et cœtus Christiani Antistitibus esse, ut dolos versent, falsa veris intermisceant et imprimis religionis hostes fallant, dummodo veritatis commodis et utilitati inserviant.

⁻1.320

The same antithesis might be carried on with the elements of their several intellectual powers. Milton, austere, condensed, imaginative, supporting his truth by direct enunciation of lofty moral sentiment and by distinct visual representations, and in the same spirit overwhelming what he deemed falsehood by moral denunciation and a succession of pictures appalling or repulsive. In his prose, so many metaphors, so many allegorical miniatures. Taylor, eminently discursive, accumulative, and (to use one of his own words) *agglomerative;* still more rich in images than Milton himself, but images of Fancy, and presented to the common and passive eye, rather than to the eye of the imagination. Whether supporting or assailing, he makes his way either by argument or by appeals to the affections, unsurpassed even by the Schoolmen in subtlety, agility and logical wit, and unrivalled by the most rhetorical of the fathers in the copiousness and vividness of his expressions and illustrations. Here words that convey feelings, and words that flash images, and words of abstract notion, flow together, and at once whirl and rush onward like a stream, at once rapid and full of eddies; and yet still, interfused here and there, we see a tongue or islet of smooth water, with some picture in it of earth or sky, landscape or living group of quiet beauty.

⁻1.325

⁻1.330

⁻1.335

Differing, then, so widely, and almost contrariantly, wherein did these great men agree? wherein did they resemble each other? In Genius, in Learning, in unfeigned Piety, in blameless Purity of Life, and in benevolent aspirations and purposes for the moral and temporal improvement of their fellow-creatures! Both of them wrote a Latin Accidence, to render education more easy and less painful to children; both of them composed hymns and psalms proportioned to the capacity of common congregations; both, nearly at the same time, set the glorious example of publicly recommending and supporting general Toleration, and the Liberty both of the Pulpit and the Press! In the writings of neither shall we find a single sentence, like those *meek deliverances to God's mercy,* with which LAUD accompanied his votes for the mutilations and loathsome dungeoning of Leighton and others!—no where such a pious prayer as we find in Bishop Hall's memoranda of his own Life, concerning the subtle and witty Atheist that so grievously perplexed and gravelled him at Sir Robert Drury's, till *he prayed to the Lord to remove him,* and behold! his prayers were heard; for shortly afterward this philistine-combatant went to London, and there perished of the plague in great misery! In short, no where shall we find the least approach, in the lives and writings of John Milton or Jeremy Taylor, to that guarded gentleness, to that sighing reluctance, with which the holy Brethren of the Inquisition deliver over a condemned heretic to the civil magistrate, recommending him to mercy, and *hoping* that the magistrate will treat the erring brother with all possible mildness!—the magistrate, who too well knows what would be his own fate, if he dared offend them by acting on their recommendation.

⁻1.340

⁻1.345

⁻1.350

⁻1.355

⁻1.360

The opportunity of diverting the reader from myself to characters more worthy of his attention, has led me far beyond my first intention; but it is not unimportant to expose the false zeal which has occasioned these attacks on our

elder patriots. It has been too much the fashion, first to personify the Church ⁻1.365
of England, and then to speak of different individuals, who in different ages
have been rulers in that church, as if in some strange way *they* constituted its
personal identity. Why should a clergyman of the present day feel interested in
the defence of Laud or Sheldon? Surely it is sufficient for the warmest partizan
of our establishment, that he can assert with truth,—when our Church perse- ⁻1.370
cuted, it was on mistaken principles held in common by all Christendom; and
at all events, far less culpable were the Bishops, who were
maintaining the existing laws, than the persecuting spirit afterwards shewn by
their successful opponents, who had no such excuse, and who should have been
taught mercy by their own sufferings, and wisdom by the utter failure of the ex- ⁻1.375
periment in their own case. We can say, that our Church, apostolical in its faith,
primitive in its ceremonies, unequalled in its liturgical forms; that our Church,
which has kindled and displayed more bright and burning lights of Genius and
Learning, than all other protestant churches since the reformation, was (with the
single exception of the times of Laud and Sheldon) least intolerant, when all ⁻1.380
Christians unhappily deemed a species of intolerance their religious duty; that
Bishops of our church were among the first that contended against this error;
and finally, that since the reformation, when tolerance became a fashion, the
Church of England, in a tolerating age, has shewn herself eminently tolerant,
and far more so, both in Spirit and in Fact, than many of her most bitter oppo- ⁻1.385
nents, who profess to deem toleration itself an insult on the rights of mankind!
As to myself, who not only know the Church-Establishment to be tolerant, but
who see in it the greatest, if not the sole safe *bulwark* of Toleration, I feel
no necessity of defending or palliating oppressions under the two Charleses, in
order to exclaim with a full and fervent heart, ESTO PERPETUA! ⁻1.390

title. *1–3 FIRE, FAMINE, AND SLAUGHTER:* | A WAR ECLOGUE. •
4–6 FIRE, FAMINE, AND SLAUGHTER. | A WAR ECLOGUE. | WITH AN
APOLOGETIC PREFACE.* **title fn.** *4–6* Printed at the end of this volume.

scene-description. *1* SCENE—A depopulated tract in La Vendee. FAMINE is
discovered stretched on the ground: to her enter SLAUGHTER and FIRE. • *2–6 The*
SCENE, *a desolated Tract in La Vendee.*—FAMINE *is discovered lying on the ground:*
to her enter FIRE *and* SLAUGHTER.

⁻1 □		FAMINE.
1 □	Sisters! Sisters! who sent you here?
	[*Line-space*]
⁻2 *1*		←—SLAUGHTER.—→
⊠*1*		SLAUGHTER (to FIRE)
2 *1*	I will name him in your ear.
⊠*1*	whisper it　　her
	[*Line-space*]
⁻3 □		FIRE.
3 □	No! No! No!
4 □	Spirits hear what spirits tell!
5 □	'Twill make an holiday in hell.
6 □	No! no! no!
7 □	Myself I nam'd him once below,

8 ☐   And all the souls that damned be,
9 ☐   Leap'd up at once in anarchy;
10 ☐   Clapp'd their hands and danc'd for glee;
11 ☐   They no longer heeded *me*;
12 ☐   But laugh'd to hear hell's burning rafters
13 ☐   Unwillingly re-echo laughters.
14 ☐   No! no! no!
15 ☐   Spirits hear what spirits tell:
16 ☐   'Twill make an holiday in hell.
      [*Line-space*]

⁻17 ☐   FAMINE.
17 *1*   Then sound it not, yet let me know;
   ⊠*1*   Whisper it, Sister! so and so!
18 *1*   Darkly hint it—soft and low!
    2   In a dark hint,
    3 6   slow.
      [*Line-space*]

⁻19 ☐   SLAUGHTER.
19 *1*   Four   letters form his name.
   ⊠*1*   Letters four do
20a ☐   And who sent you?
      [*Line-space*]

⁻20b *1*   FAMINE.
   ⊠*1*   BOTH.
20b ☐   The same! the same!
      [*Line-space*]

⁻21 ☐   SLAUGHTER.
21 ☐   He came by stealth and unlock'd my den,
22 *1*   And I have spill'd the blood since then
   ⊠*1*   drank
23 *1*   Of thrice ten hundred thousand men.
   ⊠*1*   three
      [*Line-space*]

⁻24a *1*   FIRE AND FAMINE.
   ⊠*1*   ◄——BOTH.——►
24a ☐   Who bade you do 't?
      [*Line-space*]

⁻24b ☐   SLAUGHTER.
24b ☐   The same! the same!
25 *1*   Four   letters form his name.
   ⊠*1*   Letters four do
26 ☐   He let me loose, and cry'd Halloo!
27 ☐   To him alone the praise is due.
      [*Line-space*]

⁻28 ☐   FAMINE.
28 *1*   Thanks, Sisters, thanks! the men have bled,
   ⊠*1*   Sister!
29 *1*   Their wives and   children   faint for bread;
   ⊠*1*   their children

30 ☐   I stood in a swampy field of battle,
31 ☐   With bones and skulls I made a rattle,
32 *1 2* To frighten the wolf and the carrion crow,
   3–6   ←carrion-crow→
33 ☐   And the homeless dog—but they would not go.
34 ☐   So off I flew; for how could I bear
35 ☐   To see them gorge their dainty fare.
36 ☐   I heard a groan, and a peevish squall,
37 ☐   And thro' the chink of a cottage wall,
38 ☐   Can you guess what I saw there?
     [*Line-space*]
⁻39 *1*   SLAUGHTER AND FIRE.
  ⊠*1*   ←———BOTH.———→
39 ☐   Whisper it, Sister! in our ear!
     [*Line-space*]
⁻40 ☐   FAMINE.
40 ☐   A baby beat its dying mother—
41 ☐   I had starv'd the one, and was starving the other!
     [*Line-space*]
⁻42a *1*   SLAUGHTER AND FIRE.
  ⊠*1*   ←———BOTH.———→
42a ☐ Who bade you do 't?
     [*Line-space*]
⁻42b ☐   FAMINE.
42b ☐   The same! the same!
43 *1* Four   letters form his name.
  ⊠*1* Letters four do
44 ☐   He let me loose, and cry'd Halloo!
45 ☐   To him alone the praise is due.
     [*Line-space*]
⁻46 ☐   FIRE.
46 ☐   Sisters! I from Ireland came—
47 *1*   Huts and corn-fields all on flame,
  ⊠*1* Hedge
48 ⊠*2* I triumph'd o'er the setting Sun;
49 ⊠*2* And all the while the work was done.
  2   Halloo!   halloo!
50 *1*   As   on I strode with mons'trous strides,
  2   And on as   my   great
  3–6 On   as   huge
51 *1 2* I flung back my head, and held my sides;
  3–6   I held
52 ☐   It was so rare a piece of fun,
53 ☐   To see the swelter'd cattle run,
54 *1*   With uncouth gallop, all the night,
  ⊠*1*   thro'
55 ☐   Scar'd by the red and noisy light!
56 ☐   By the light of his own blazing cot,
57 ☐   Was many a naked Rebel shot:

58	*1*	The house-stream met the fire, and hiss'd
	2	flames,
	3–6	flame
59	*1*	While, crash! the roof fell in, I wish
	⊠*1*	fell in the roof, wist,
60	☐	On some of those old bed-rid nurses,
61	☐	That deal in discontent and curses!

[*Line-space*]

⁻**62a**	*1*	SLAUGHTER AND FAMINE.
	⊠*1*	←———BOTH.———→
62a	☐	Who bad you do 't?
⁻**62b**	☐	FIRE.
62b	☐	The same! The same!
63	*1*	Four letters form his name
	⊠*1*	Letters four do
64	☐	He let me loose, and cry'd Halloo!
65	*1*	How shall I give him honour due?
	⊠*1*	To him alone the praise is

[*Line-space*]

⁻**66**	☐	ALL.
66	☐	He let us loose, and cry'd Halloo!
67	*1*	How shall I give him honour due?
	⊠*1*	we yield

[*Line-space*]

⁻**68**	☐	FAMINE.
68	☐	Wisdom comes with lack of food,
69	☐	I'll gnaw, I'll gnaw the multitude,
70	☐	Till the cup of rage o'er brim,
71	*1*	They shall seize him of his brood.
	⊠*1*	and
⁻**72**	☐	SLAUGHTER.
72	☐	They shall tear him limb from limb!

[*Line-space*]

⁻**73**	☐	FIRE.
73	☐	O thankless Beldames, and untrue!
74	☐	And is this all that you can do
75	*1*	For him that did so much for you?
	⊠*1*	who

[*Line-space*]

⁻**75.1.1**	*1*	TO SLAUGHTER.
75.1.1	*1*	For *you* he turn'd the dust to mud,
75.1.2	*1*	With his fellow creatures' blood!

[*Line-space*]

⁻**75.1.3**	*1*	TO FAMINE.
75.1.3	*1*	And hunger scorch'd as many more,
75.1.4	*1*	To make *your* cup of joy run o'er.

[*Line-space*]

⁻76 *1*   TO BOTH.
76 *1*   Full many moons, he by my troth,
    ⊠*1*   Ninety   months
77 □   Hath richly cater'd for you both;
78 *1*   And in an hour you would repay,
    ⊠*1*   would you
79 *1*   An eight years debt, away! away!
    ⊠*1*   work?—
80 □   I alone am faithful, I
81 □   Cling to him everlastingly!

preface title [in texts printing Preface at end of volume]. *4–5* APOLOGETIC
PREFACE I TO I "FIRE, FAMINE, AND SLAUGHTER." • *6* APO-
LOGETIC PREFACE. I TO "FIRE, FAMINE, AND SLAUGHTER."*
preface. ⁻**1.1.** *6* who,   ⁻**1.2.** *6* Christian,   *4–6* favourable   ⁻**1.6.** *6* poet,
⁻**1.9.** *6* Slaughter   ⁻**1.11.** *4–6* poem,   ⁻**1.15.** *6* poets,   ⁻**1.16.** *6* philosophers
6 benefactors.   ⁻**1.18.** *6* poem.   ⁻**1.19.** *6* he   ⁻**1.21.** *6* statesman. *6* poet
⁻**1.22.** *6* poet   ⁻**1.31.** *5 6* suspicion   ⁻**1.32.** *3–5* is substantially the same as
I • *6* is the substance of what I   ⁻**1.42.** *6* poet   ⁻**1.44.** *6* realize   ⁻**1.48.** *4–*
6 influence   ⁻**1.59.** *5 6* favorite   ⁻**1.62.** *4–6* cannot   ⁻**1.71.** *5 6* him:
⁻**1.73.** *3–5* outrè • *6* outrageous   ⁻**1.74–5.** *6* escape-valves   ⁻**1.76.** *4–*
6 other   ⁻**1.80.** *4–6* him,)   *4–6* wont   ⁻**1.81.** *6* liver!"   ⁻**1.83.** *4–6* surprise
6 afterwards,   ⁻**1.86.** *5 6* Shakespeare   *4* cnsidered   ⁻**1.87.** *4–6* good-
natured   ⁻**1.89.** *4–6* —— "Too *4–6* voice!"   ⁻**1.92.** *4–6* —— "O
4–6 damn'd,   ⁻**1.94–5.** *6* "I stand here for Law."   ⁻**1.100.** *4 Hell and
Purgatory?* • *5 Hell and Purgatory?* • *6* Hell and Purgatory?   ⁻**1.108.** *3* from
a • *4 5* from an • *6* from *6* so   ⁻**1.115.** *5 6* dishonoured   ⁻**1.118.** *4–*
6 ebullient   ⁻**1.119.** *5 6* language.   ⁻**1.120.** *6* poem   ⁻**1.132.** *6* ἀπαθὴς,
4 5 ἀναιμόσαρκος   ⁻**1.137.** *6* poem *6* passion *6* any   ⁻**1.138.** *6* poetic
⁻**1.138–9.** *3* betray'd in • *4 5* betrayed at the close of the Eclogue by • *6* betrayed
at the close of the eclogue by   ⁻**1.141.** *4–6* "rantin'   ⁻**1.148.** *4–6* stake—
⁻**1.154.** *6* faltered   ⁻**1.157.** *6* poem.   ⁻**1.163.** *4–6* risk   ⁻**1.165.** *6* poem
⁻**1.167.** *6* years'   ⁻**1. 168.** *6* all, *6* poem   ⁻**1.170.** *4–6* honourable
5 farther.   ⁻**1.171.** *6* poems,   ⁻**1.172.** *6* The Devil's Thoughts, *6* The
Two round Spaces on the Tomb-Stone,   ⁻**1.173.** *3* four first • *4 5* three first •
6 first three   ⁻**1.183.** *4–6* Judgment;   ⁻**1.186.** *6* strike,   ⁻**1.189.** *6* lust
⁻**1.190.** *6* envy,   ⁻**1.191.** *6* covetousness   ⁻**1.191–2.** *3* Ambition, *and the
insolencies of traitors and the violences of rebels,* • *4* Ambition, *and the insolences
of traitors and the violences of rebels,* • *5* Ambition, *and the indolence of traitors
and the violences of rebels,* • *6* ambition, and the indolence of traitors and the
violences of rebels,   ⁻**1.195.** *6* sanies   ⁻**1.202.** *5* compounder: ⁻**1.203.** *6* in
a bad taste, *6* would, doubtless,   ⁻**1.204.** *6* written   ⁻**1.206.** *6* positive
3 6 Opposite • *4 5* Oppositive   ⁻**1.207.** *5* indiscribable   ⁻**1.209.** *6* Bishop
Taylor's   ⁻**1.210.** *6* surprised *5* pursuits   ⁻**1.211.** *6* Milton's   ⁻**1.212.** *6* his
prose writings,   ⁻**1.213.** *3 4 6* well • *5* will   ⁻**1.214.** *6* Paradise Lost,
⁻**1.215.** *5 6* heart,   ⁻**1.221.** *6* act *6* suffering, *6* triumph   ⁻**1.222.** *6* martyrdom.
⁻**1.223.** *6* transcendant   ⁻**1.237.** *6* pictures *6* thoughts   ⁻**1.244.** *6* transcendantly
⁻**1.246.** *6* not. *3* Is his • *4–6* Is this   ⁻**1.247.** *6* latter.   ⁻**1.248.** *6* wish, *6* should
⁻**1.249.** *6* will   ⁻**1.250.** *6* only.   ⁻**1.251.** *6* others.   ⁻**1.252.** *6* persons

6 No. ⁻**1.253.** *5* Milon *6* dare say *6* Laud ⁻**1.254.** *6* Strafford
⁻**1.256.** *6* dare say, ⁻**1.256–7.** *6* insolencies of traitors and the violences of
rebels, ⁻**1.257.** *4–6* individualised ⁻**1.258.** *6* Hampden, Hollis, Pym,
Fairfax, Ireton, and Milton? ⁻**1.259.** *4–6* that, *4–6* after description,
⁻**1.262.** *6* bigot ⁻**1.268.** *6* him ⁻**1.274.** *5 6* Baxter: ⁻**1.276.** *6* us,
⁻**1.277.** *6* human too-much ⁻**1.279.** *3* have • *4–6* has ⁻**1.284.** *5* caterpiller.
⁻**1.287.** *6* feelings, ⁻**1.288.** *6* authors, *6* liberty, light and tolera-
tion." ⁻**1.289.** *6* The Friend, ⁻**1.295.** *5 6* Taylor's ⁻**1.298.** *6* called
⁻**1.301.** *5 6* Calvinism ⁻**1.302.** *6* Church-antiquity ⁻**1.303.** *6* all
⁻**1.304.** *5* ecclesiatic ⁻**1.308–9.** *6* approaches, ⁻**1.309.** *3–5* Catholicism, •
6 Roman-Catholicism, ⁻**1.313.** *6* popular ⁻**1.315.** *5* appears ⁻**1.316.** *6* too
severely *6* management ⁻**1.316–17.** *4 5 (istam falsitatem dispensitivam)* •
6 (istam falsitatem dispensitivam) ⁻**1.317.** *6* authorised ⁻**1.318.** *6* doctoribus
6 antistitibus ⁻**1.327.** *5 agglomerative;* • *6* agglomerative; ⁻**1.328.** *6* fancy,
⁻**1.331.** *6* schoolmen *6* agility, *3* logical • *4–6* logic ⁻**1.334–5.** *3–5* and at once
whirl • *6* and whirl ⁻**1.336.** *4–6* still *3 6* islet • *4 5* isle ⁻**1.339.** *6* genius,
6 learning, ⁻**1.340.** *6* piety, *6* purity of life, ⁻**1.342.** *3–5* education more
easy and less • *6* education less ⁻**1.345.** *6* toleration, ⁻**1.346.** *6* liberty
6 pulpit *6* press! ⁻**1.347.** *6* meek deliverances to God's *4 5* mercy, • *6* mercy,
⁻**1.348.** *6* Laud ⁻**1.350.** *6* life, ⁻**1.351.** *6* atheist ⁻**1.352.** *4–6* Drury's *6* he
prayed to the Lord to remove him, ⁻**1.353.** *6* heard: *6* Philistine-combatant
⁻**1.357.** *6* brethren ⁻**1.358.** *6* hoping ⁻**1.367.** *6* they ⁻**1.372.** *3* were
the • *4–6* was this intolerance in the ⁻**1.373.** *6* shown ⁻**1.378–9.** *6* genius
and learning, ⁻**1.384.** *6* England *6* shown ⁻**1.385.** *6* spirit *6* fact,
⁻**1.388.** *6* bulwark of toleration, ⁻**1.390.** *6* Esto perpetua! **title.** *2 FIRE,*
FAMINE, & SLAUGHTER. | A *WAR-ECLOGUE.* • *3* 𝕱𝕚𝕣𝕖, 𝕱𝕒𝕞𝕚𝕟𝕖, 𝕒𝕟𝕕 𝕊𝕝𝕒𝕦𝕘𝕙𝕥𝕖𝕣. |
A WAR-ECLOGUE. • *6* FIRE, FAMINE, AND SLAUGHTER. | A WAR
ECLOGUE. WITH AN APOLOGETIC PREFACE.* **scene-description.** *3* Scene, •
4–6 Scene *3–6* lu *3* Vendee. • *4 6* Vendée. *3–6* ground; ⁻*1* etc. *3–*
5 print part-ascriptions in spaced capital plus small capitals ("FAMINE." etc),
except where noted below • *6* gives abbreviated forms in capital plus lower-case
italic ("*Fam.*" etc), to the left of the first line of the speech **1.** *3–6* sisters!
who ⁻**2.** *3 4 (To Fire.)* • *5 6 (to Fire).* **3.** ☒*1* No! no! no! **4.** *2* what
Spirits *2* tell, • *3–6* tell: **5.** *6* a ☒*1* Hell. **7.** *3–6* Myself, *4–6* named
8. ☒*1* souls, **9.** *2 3* Leapt • *4–6* Leaped ☒*1* anarchy, **10.** *4–6* Clapped
☒*1* danced ☒*1* glee. **11.** *2* ME; • *3–6* me; **12.** *4–6* laughed ☒*1* Hell's
13. ☒*1* laughters! **15.** *2* Spirits tell, **16.** *6* a ☒*1* Hell! **17.** *3–6* sister!
18. *2* low **19.** ☒*1* name— ⁻**20b.** *3 6 Both.* **21.** ☒*1* stealth, *4–*
6 unlocked **22.** *6* drunk ⁻**24a.** *3 6 Both.* **24a.** *5 6* it! **26.** *3* cried, •
4–6 cried **28.** *3–6* sister, **29.** ☒*1* bread. **30.** ☒*1* battle; **31.** *2* Bones
2 Skulls **32.** *2* crow **33.** *2* go: **34.** *2* flew, • *3–6* flew: **35.** *3–*
6 fare? **36.** ☒*1* groan **37.** *3–6* through *2* cottage wall— • *3–6* cottage-wall—
⁻**39.** *3 6 Both.* **39.** *3–6* sister! ☒*1* ear. **40.** *2* mother, • *3–6* mother:
41. *4–6* starved *3–6* one ⁻**42.** *3 6 Both.* **44.** *3–6* cried, **46.** *2* came •
3–6 came! **48.** *4–6* triumphed *3* Sun! • *4–6* sun! **49.** *2* done— • *3–*
6 done, **51.** ☒*1* head ☒*1* sides, **52.** ☒*1* fun **53.** *4–6* sweltered ☒*1* run
54. ☒*1* gallop *3–6* through **55.** *3–6* Scared *2* light. **56.** *2* Cot • *3–6* cot
57. *6* rebel **58.** *2 3* hiss'd, • *4–6* hissed, **59.** ☒*1* While **61.** ☒*1* curses.
⁻**62a.** *3 6 Both.* • *4* BOTH. • *5* BOOTH. **62a.** ☒*1* bade **62b.** *2 3 6* same!

the   **63.** 2 name, • *3–6* name.   **64.** 2 loose   *3* cried, • *4–6* cried   **65.** ☒*1* due.
⁻**66.** *3 All.*   **66.** 2 loose   *3* cried, • *4–6* cried   **67.** 2 honor   **68.** *3–*
6 food.   **70.** 2 o'erbrim, • *3–6* o'erbrim: **71.** ☒*1* brood—   **73.** 2 Beldames •
3–6 beldames   2 untrue,   **75.** *3–6* him,   **76.** ☒*1* he,   ☒*1* troth!   **77.** *4–*
6 catered   **78.** ☒*1* repay   **79.** 2 year's • *3–6* years'   *3–6* Away! away!
80. ☒*1* faithful!   **81.** ☒*1* everlastingly.

epigraphs. Erratum in PR *3*: "r. *incautum* and *veniam*." The correction is made in
C's hand in JG's copy at HUL and in DC's copy at HRC; in AG's (?) hand in WW's
copy at Cornell; in AG's hand in TP's copy at Brown and in an unknown person's copy
at Yale; in JG's hand in William Hood's copy at Columbia, in Miss Fricker's copy at
HUL, and in the emended part copy at HUL. In HNC's copy at HUL C made only the
second correction (to "VENIAM,").

preface title. The PR *4 5* titles continue with a third line: "See page 154.)"; PR *6* cues
the following fn to the second line: "See page 141."

⁻**1.1,** ⁻**1.6,** ⁻**1.14.** In HNC's copy of PR *3* at HUL C identified the three individuals
in the margins: "*W. Sotheby*," "Sir W. Scott.", and "H. Davy". The identifications are
independently confirmed by Scott and DeQ: Scott to Mrs Fletcher, 18 Dec 1831, in
Fragmentary Remains, Literary and Scientific, of Sir Humphry Davy ed John Davy
(1858) 113; "Coleridge and Opium-Eating" *DeQ Works* v 191.

⁻**1.86 et seq.** In DC's copy of PR *3* at HRC C marked this sentence and added in the
margin: "ˌWiˌth the exception ˌofˌ this slovenly ˌsenˌtence, I ˌholdˌ this ˌPreˌface to be
ˌmˌy happiest ˌeffˌort in ˌpˌrose comˌpˌosition."

⁻**1.87.** Erratum in PR *3*: "r. *good-natured*." The correction is made by C in DC's copy
at HRC; by AG in WW's copy at Cornell; and by JG in the emended part copy at HUL.

⁻**1.87,** ⁻**1.91.** In the emended part copy of PR *3* at HUL JG inserted parentheses:
"(who . . . other;)".

⁻**1.89.** In JG's copy of PR *3* at HUL C emended to "voice!"

⁻**1.90.** In JG's copy of PR *3* at HUL C emended to "—the skipping spirit,".

⁻**1.91.** In JG's copy of PR *3* at HUL C replaced "other;" with "other! Contrast, I say,
Gratiano's tempestuous".

⁻**1.94.** contrasted] Deleted by C in JG's copy of PR *3* at HUL.

⁻**1.96.** subject, should] Emended by C in JG's copy of PR *3* at HUL to "subject!
Should".

⁻**1.100.** In the emended part copy of PR *3* at HUL JG noted in the RH margin: "See
p. 98." Page 98 of *SL* contains lines ⁻1.170–89. Perhaps the note refers to **214** *The
Devil's Thoughts* and **267** *The Two Round Spaces on the Tombstone*, which, C might
have argued, he had been led into writing by RS.

⁻**1.118.** PR *3* ebuliant] In DC's copy at HRC C corrected to "ebullient". JG made the
same correction in his own copy and in the emended part copy, both now at HUL.

⁻**1.138–9.** Erratum in PR *3*: "for *betrayed in* r. *betrayed by*." In TP's copy of PR *3*
at Brown AG deleted "in" and substituted "at the close of the Eclogue by". The same
substitution is made by JG in Hood's copy at Columbia and Miss Fricker's copy at HUL.
In the emended part copy at HUL JG substituted only "by".

⁻**1.163.** own] Deleted by C in DC's copy of PR *3* at HRC.

⁻**1.164⁺.** The extra space is present in all versions.

⁻**1.170.** PR *5* farther] In JG's copy emended to "father".

⁻**1.172.** PR *3* Tomb-Stone] In Francis Wrangham's (?) copy, sold at Christie's 13 Jun
1979, C added an asterisk and wrote a note at the foot of the page: "This is an Epitaph

on Sir James Mackintosh, written of course many years before his Death". DC copied the same note into his own copy, now at HRC. PR *6* adds the footnote "See post 2nd volume."

⁻**1.173.** Erratum in PR *3*: "for *four* r. *three*." C himself made the correction in JG's copy at HUL, in Wrangham's (?) copy sold at Christie's 13 Jun 1979, and in DC's copy at HRC. It was made by AG in WW's copy at Cornell; and by JG in the emended part copy at HUL.

⁻**1.185–200.** In PR *3–5* each line of the quotation begins with quotation-marks.

⁻**1.192.** PR *5 indolence*] Corrected in JG's (?) copy to "*insolence*".

⁻**1.202.** PR *4* compounder;] The tail of the semicolon is broken away.

⁻**1.207.** PR *5* indiscribable] Corrected in JG's (?) copy to "indescribable".

⁻**1.219.** PR *3* former] Emended by C in the copy he gave to DC, now at HRC, to "preceding".

⁻**1.223.** PR *3* and as] C deleted "and" in the copy he gave to DC, now at HRC.

⁻**1.289.** PR *6* prints the reference to *The Friend* in a footnote, without parentheses.

⁻**1.301,** PR *5* Calvinism] In JG's (?) copy a comma is added.

⁻**1.304.** PR *5* ecclesiatic] Corrected in JG's (?) copy to "ecclesiastic".

⁻**1.316.** PR *3 fatsitatem*] Corrected by C in the copy he gave to DC, now at HRC, to "*falsitatem*". The same correction was made by JG in the emended part copy at HUL.

⁻**1.335.** PR *3* at once] Deleted by C in the copy he gave to DC, now at HRC.

⁻**1.370.** PR *3* truth,—when] Altered by JG in the emended part copy at HUL to "truth:—When".

1.372. PR *3* were the Bishops,] In the emended part copy at HUL JG deleted "were" and substituted "was the violence of".

⁻**1.383.** PR *3* reformation] C altered to "revolution in 1688," in DC's copy, now at HRC. In the Fitzwilliam copy of PR *4* he altered to "revolution". In JG's (?) copy of PR *5* "reformation" is underlined and "lution" written in the margin.

3, 6, 14. Indented in all six texts. The RT reproduces the pattern of indentation found in PR *3–6*.

27⁺. C inserted and then deleted an extra ms stanza in the proof copy of PR *3* now at Yale (In C678 817sa):

ALL.
He let us loose and cried Halloo!
How shall we yield him honour due?

76. In all texts except PR *1* this follows line 75 without a break.

167.X1. IDEAS OR LINES FOR A POEM

The lines, written in C's hand, appear in BM MS Egerton 2800 f 3ʳ, following a prose introduction to a fictitious tale (presumably verse) about Sæmund's travels and associated with the translation of the *Edda* in Amos Cottle's *Icelandic Poetry* (Bristol 1797). Thus:

Scald by the northern Sea in ocean Cave—

Bard in the center of the Lonely Forest—

The $ Minstrel at the City ⌜. . . .⌝

Genius of Italy—Boccaccio—

SW&F (*CC*) 68 prints the lines (var) under the heading "Ideas for a Poem?"

168. THE OLD MAN OF THE ALPS

A. DATE

Dec 1797?–early Mar 1798.

B. TEXT

M Post (8 Mar 1798). Signed "NICIAS ERYTHRÆUS."
   There is a transcript by Francis Wrangham in a letter to C, dated 5 Apr 1802, now at DCL (MS A Wrangham 1).

C. GENERAL NOTE

The extent of C's authorship is discussed in vol I headnote.

The RT reproduces the *M Post* text exactly.

169. MODIFICATION OF *TRANSLATION OF A CELEBRATED GREEK SONG*, BY WILLIAM WORDSWORTH

A. DATE

Jan–early Feb 1798.

B. TEXT

M Post (13 Feb 1798). Signed "PUBLICOLA." (lit "Cultivator of the Public").

C. GENERAL NOTE

The relation of the *M Post* version to WW's original is discussed in vol I headnote.

The RT reproduces the *M Post* version exactly, except for the typography of the title:

TRANSLATION | OF A CELEBRATED GREEK SONG.

D. APPENDIX: WORDSWORTH'S POEM

The first known version by WW possibly dates from c 1793–4 and was subsequently sent to his Quaker friend Thomas Wilkinson: see *WEPF* 315–18. A later version was written in the Windy Brow Notebook c May–Jun 1794: see *WEPF* 270–1; *WPW* I 299–300 (var). The two versions are collated with the *M Post* version in *WEPF* 711–16, where C is described as "probably . . . responsible in this instance for both the pseudonym and the revisions" (711).

WW's earlier version (DCL MS 169: a single leaf, 18.3×22.7 cm; no wm or chain-lines; signed "W. Wordsworth") is designated below as MS 1. The later version (DC MS 10 ff 17ᵛ and 18ᵛ: 15.6×20.0 cm; wm Britannia within a circular band surmounted by a shield) is designated below as MS 2. (The later version is followed in the Windy Brow Notebook by WW's version of *Inscription for a Seat*: cf poem **270** below.)

title. 2 From the Greek

			Equivalent RT lines
1	□	And I will bear my vengeful blade	1
2	□	With the myrtle's boughs array'd	2
3	□	As Harmodius before	3
4	□	As Aristogiton bore	4
5	□	When the Tyrant's breast they gor'd	5
6	□	With the myrtle braided sword	6
7	□	Gave to triumph freedom's cause	7
8	⊓	Gave to Athen's equal laws	8
		[*Line-space*]	
9	□	Where unnumber'd with the dead	10
10	□	Dear Harmodius art thou fled	9
11	1	Athens sings 'tis thine to rest	11
	2	says	
12	□	In the islands of the blest	12
13	□	Where Achilles swift of feet	15
14	□	And the brave Tydides meet	—
		[*Line-space*]	
15	□	I will bear my vengeful blade	17
16	□	With the myrtle's boughs array'd	18

17 ☐	As Harmodius before		19
18 ☐	As Aristogiton bore		20
19 1	When in Athen's festal time		—
20 1	The tyrant felt their arm sublime		—
18.1.1 2	Towering mid the festal ~~plain~~ train		—
18.1.2 2	Oer the man Hipparchus slain		—
18.1.3 2	Tyrant of his brother men		—
	[Line-space]		
22 ☐	Let thy name Harmodius dear		21
23 ☐	Live thro' heaven's eternal year—		22
24 ☐	Long as heaven ~~et~~ & earth survive		23
25 ☐	Dear Aristogiton live		24
26 ☐	With the myrtle-braided sword		25
27 ☐	Ye the tyrant's bosom gor'd		26
28 ☐	Gave to triumph freedom's cause		27
29 ☐	Gave to Athens equal laws.		28

1. 2 —And   **2.** 2 myrtles   2 arrayed   **5.** 2 tyrants   2 gored   **7.** 2 Triumph
Freedom's   **8.** 2 Athens   2 laws.   **9.** 2 unnumbered   **11.** 2 tis   **14.** 2 meet.
16. 2 myrtles   2 arrayed   **23.** 2 through heavens   2 year   **24.** 2 and
26. 2 myrtle braided   **27.** 2 tyrants   2 gored   **28.** 2 freedoms

9, 15, 22. MS 2 is not divided into stanzas. Line 22 heads the verso in MS 1: it is not
indented and may not be meant to begin a new stanza.

170. DE PAPA:
VATICINIUM HAUD VALDE OBSCURUM,
NEC INCREDIBILE, 1798

A. DATE

Late Jan–early Feb 1798.

B. TEXT

M Post (12 Feb 1798). Unsigned. *EOT* (*CC*) III 16–17.

C. GENERAL NOTE

The case for C's authorship is made by David V. Erdman in *EOT* (*CC*) III
16–17; see also vol I headnote. There is still room for doubt.

The RT reproduces the *M Post* text, except for:

title. *M Post* DE PAPA | Vaticinium haud valde obscurum, | nec incredibile, 1798. **3.** *M Post* "Iterum cantante." **4.** *M Post* "Alter **5.** *M Post "Ultimus Romanorum!"*

171. FROST AT MIDNIGHT

A. DATE

C returned to Nether Stowey from Shrewsbury on 9 Feb 1798 (*CL* I 383: to GC 8 [=9] Feb 1798; 385: to J. P. Estlin [13 Feb 1798]). There was a deep snow on 17 Feb (*DWJ* I 8–9), while the moon was beginning to move into its first quarter, and the last of C's autobiographical letters to TP—in which he describes the school experiences depicted in the poem—is endorsed 19 Feb (*CL* I 387–9); lines 54–64 are paralleled by lines written by WW in Jan–Mar (see vol I headnote and lines 54–64EC). The likely date of composition is at this time or soon afterwards. DW in her journal describes the second half of Feb as a time of bright moonlight and frosty beauty.

B. TEXTS

1. The third of the three poems published in *Fears in Solitude, Etc* (1798). Signed "BY S. T. COLERIDGE." Dated (at the end) "February 1798."

The apostrophisation of "its" and other peculiarities might suggest that the text was set from C's holograph. Sir George Beaumont's copy (PML Book No 47225) contains a ms comment made c 1807 (see vol I line 74⁺EC).

The last two paragraphs from this version are reprinted in *The Parnassian Garland* (1807) 66–7; *The Bristol Gazette* (24 Mar 1808); *The Weekly Entertainer* (Sherborne) XLVIII (2 May 1808) 360.

2. The Poetical Register for 1808–1809 VII (1812) 530–2. Signed "BY S. T. COLERIDGE, ESQ."

3. The third of three poems published in *Poems* (1812). Signed "BY S. T. COLERIDGE, ESQ."

RS's copy (V&A Forster Collection P. 97) contains three minor emendations in his hand. See **174** *France: An Ode* TEXT PR 5, concerning the authority which RS's emendations might possess.

4. SL (1817).

C protested vigorously when the printer first included the poem among "Poems Occasioned by Political Events", and insisted that it should be transferred to the section of "Meditative Poems in Blank Verse", with the result that it appears in both sig F and sig P of the proofs (Yale In C678 817sa).

Four copies contain emendations in C's hand: Francis Wrangham's (?) (sold at Christie's 13 Jun 1979 lot 126); HNC's (HUL *AC85 L8605 Zy817c), in pencil and ink; one of JG's copies at HUL (*EC8 C6795 817s (C)), in which C's pencil has been gone over in ink; and SC's (NYPL Berg Collection Copy 5). AG copied out the Errata in WW's copy (Cornell WORDSWORTH PR 4480 S5 1817 Copy 1), as did SC in her own copy. In TP's copy (Brown PR 4478 A1 1817 Koopman Collection) the third paragraph (only) is numbered.

Rpt *Spirit of Contemporary Poetry* (3 vols Boston, Mass 1827) I 29–31.

5. PW (1828).

6 [=RT]. *PW* (1829).

7. PW (1834).

title. □ FROST AT MIDNIGHT.   **title fn.** *2* This poem, which was first published with "Fears in Solitude," and "France an Ode," has been since enlarged and corrected, and with the other poems, is now inserted in the Poetical Register, by the kind permission of Mr. Coleridge.

1 □	The Frost performs it's secret ministry,
2 □	Unhelp'd by any wind. The owlet's cry
3 □	Came loud—and hark, again! loud as before.
4 □	The inmates of my cottage, all at rest,
5 □	Have left me to that solitude, which suits
6 □	Abstruser musings: save that at my side
7 □	My cradled infant slumbers peacefully.
8 □	'Tis calm indeed! so calm, that it disturbs
9 □	And vexes meditation with it's strange
10 □	And extreme silentness. Sea, hill, and wood,
11 □	This populous village! Sea, and hill, and wood,
12 □	With all the numberless goings on of life,
13 □	Inaudible as dreams! The thin blue flame
14 □	Lies on my low-burnt fire, and quivers not:
15 □	Only that film, which flutter'd on the grate,

15fn *1–3* *Only that film.* In all parts of the kingdom these films are called *strangers*, and supposed to portend the arrival of some absent friend.

16 □	Still flutters there, the sole unquiet thing,
17 □	Methinks, it's motion in this hush of nature
18 □	Gives it dim sympathies with me, who live,
19 □	Making it a companionable form,
19.1.1 *1*	With which I can hold commune. Idle thought!
2 3	haply hence,
19.1.2 *1*	But still the living spirit in our frame,
2 3	That
19.1.3 *1*	That loves not to behold a lifeless thing,
2 3	Which
19.1.4 *1*	Transfuses into all it's own delights
2 3	things its own Will,
19.1.5 *1*	It's own volition, sometimes with deep faith,
2 3	And its own pleasures;

19.1.6	*1*	And sometimes with fantastic playfulness.
	2 3	a wilful
19.1.7	*1*	Ah me! amus'd by no such curious toys
19.1.8	*1*	Of the self-watching subtilizing mind,
19.1.9	*1*	How often in my early school-boy days,
19.1.10	*1*	With most believing superstitious wish
19.2.7	*2 3*	That stealing pardon from our common sense
19.2.8	*2 3*	Smiles, as self-scornful, to disarm the scorn
19.2.9	*2 3*	For these wild reliques of our childish Thought,
19.2.10	*2 3*	That flit about, oft go, and oft return
19.2.11	*2 3*	Not uninvited. Ah there was a time,
19.2.12	*2 3*	When oft, amused by no such subtle toys
19.2.13	*2 3*	Of the self-watching Mind, a child at school,
19.2.14	*2 3*	With most believing superstitious wish
19.3.2	*4 5*	To which the living spirit in our frame,
19.3.3	*4 5*	That loves not to behold a lifeless thing,
19.3.4	*4 5*	Transfuses its own pleasures, its own will.
20	*6 7*	Whose puny flaps and freaks the idling Spirit
21	*6 7*	By its own moods interprets, every where
22	*6 7*	Echo or mirror seeking of itself,
23a	*6 7*	And makes a toy of Thought.
		[*Line-space*]
23b	*6 7*	But O! how oft,
24	*4–7*	How oft, at school, with most believing mind,
25	□	Presageful have I gaz'd upon the bars,
26	*1–3*	To watch the *stranger* there! and oft belike,
	4–7	that fluttering *stranger!* and as oft
27	⊠*2 3*	With unclos'd lids, already had I dreamt
	2 3	have
28	□	Of my sweet birthplace, and the old church-tower,
29	□	Whose bells, the poor man's only music, rang
30	□	From morn to evening, all the hot fair-day,
31	□	So sweetly, that they stirr'd and haunted me
32	⊠*4*	With a wild pleasure, falling on mine ear
	4	sweet
33	□	Most like articulate sounds of things to come!
34	□	So gaz'd I, till the soothing things, I dreamt,
35	□	Lull'd me to sleep, and sleep prolong'd my dreams!
36	□	And so I brooded all the following morn,
37	□	Aw'd by the stern preceptor's face, mine eye
38	□	Fix'd with mock study on my swimming book:
39	□	Save if the door half-open'd, and I snatch'd
40	□	A hasty glance, and still my heart leapt up,
41	□	For still I hop'd to see the *stranger's* face,
42	□	Townsman, or aunt, or sister more belov'd,
43	□	My play-mate when we both were cloth'd alike!
		[*Line-space*]
44	□	Dear babe, that sleepest cradled by my side,

45	*1–4*	Whose gentle breathings, heard in this dead calm,
	5–7	deep
46	⊠*4*	Fill up the interspersed vacancies
	4	Fill'd
47	☐	And momentary pauses of the thought!
48	*1–4*	My babe so beautiful! it fills my heart
	5–7	thrills
49	☐	With tender gladness, thus to look at thee,
50	☐	And think, that thou shalt learn far other lore,
51	☐	And in far other scenes! For I was rear'd
52	☐	In the great city, pent mid cloisters dim,
53	☐	And saw nought lovely but the sky and stars.
54	☐	But *thou*, my babe! Shalt wander, like a breeze,
55	☐	By lakes and sandy shores, beneath the crags
56	☐	Of ancient mountain, and beneath the clouds,
57	☐	Which image in their bulk both lakes and shores
58	☐	And mountain crags: so shalt thou see and hear
59	☐	The lovely shapes and sounds intelligible
60	☐	Of that eternal language, which thy God
61	☐	Utters, who from eternity doth teach
62	☐	Himself in all, and all things in himself.
63	☐	Great universal Teacher! he shall mould
64	☐	Thy spirit, and by giving make it ask.
		[*Line-space*]
65	☐	Therefore all seasons shall be sweet to thee,
66	☐	Whether the summer clothe the general earth
67	*1–3*	With greenness, or the redbreasts sit and sing
	4–7	redbreast
68	☐	Betwixt the tufts of snow on the bare branch
69	*1*	Of mossy apple-tree, while all the thatch
	⊠*1*	the nigh
70	*1*	Smokes in the sun-thaw: whether the eave-drops fall
	⊠*1*	eve-drops
71	⊠*4*	Heard only in the trances of the blast,
	4	traces
72	*1*	Or whether the secret ministery of cold
	⊠*1*	if frost
73	☐	Shall hang them up in silent icicles,
74	☐	Quietly shining to the quiet moon,
74.1.1	*1*	Like those, my babe! which, ere to-morrow's warmth
74.1.2	*1*	Have capp'd their sharp keen points with pendulous drops,
74.1.3	*1*	Will catch thine eye, and with their novelty
74.1.4	*1*	Suspend thy little soul; then make thee shout,
74.1.5	*1*	And stretch and flutter from thy mother's arms
74.1.6	*1*	As thou would'st fly for very eagerness.

title. *4 FROST AT MIDNIGHT.*   **1.** *7* frost   ⊠*1* its   **2.** *5–7* Unhelped
9. ⊠*1* its   **13.** ⊠*1* the   **14.** *4–7* low burnt   *4–7* not;   **15.** *5–*
7 fluttered   **15fn.** *2 3* kingdom,   **16.** ⊠*1* thing.   **17.** ⊠*1* its   **18.** *4–7* me

19.1.1. *2 3* commune: **19.1.6.** *2 3* playfulness,   **19.2.11.** *3* Ah!   **25.** *4–7* Presageful,   *5–7* gazed   **26.** *5 stranger!* • *7* stranger!   **27.** *4–7* unclosed **28.** ⊠*1* birth-place,   *2 3* church tower,   **30.** *4* fair day, • *5–7* Fair-day, **31.** *4–7* stirred   **32.** *2 3* ear,   **34.** *5–7* gazed   *7* things I dreamt   **35.** *5–7* Lulled   *5–7* prolonged   **37.** *5–7* Awed   **38.** *5–7* Fixed   **39.** *4* half open'd, • *5–7* half opened,   *5–7* snatched   **40.** *5–7* leaped   **41.** *5–7* hoped *4 stranger*'s • *7* stranger's   **42.** *4–7* beloved,   **43.** *2 3* playmate   *5–7* clothed **44.** *4–7* Babe,   **48.** *4 5* Babe   **50.** *4–7* think   *4–7* lore   **51.** *5–7* reared **52.** ⊠*1* 'mid   **54.** *7* thou,   ⊠*1* shalt   *4–7* wander   *4–7* breeze   **56.** *4* clouds **70.** *4–7* sun-thaw;   *4* fall,   **71.** *2 3* blast;   **72.** ⊠*1* ministry   **74.** *2 3* moon. • *4–7* Moon.

11. PR *3* village!] In the V&A copy RS emended the punctuation to "village,".

19.1.4. PR *3* Will,] In the V&A copy RS emended to "soul,".

19.2.11. PR *3* Ah] Begins a new paragraph.

19.3.4⁺. Line-space in PR *4 5*.

30. Erratum in PR *4*: "for *fair day* r. *Fair-day.*" C made the correction himself in Wrangham's (?) and JG's copies; AG made it in WW's copy.

32. Erratum in PR *4*: "for *sweet* r. *wild.*" C made the correction himself in Wrangham's (?), JG's, and HNC's copies; AG made it in WW's copy, and SC for herself.

44–58. Quoted (var) in a draft of a letter to Edward Coppleston, provost of Oriel College Oxford, c 11 Oct 1820, in which C explains and defends HC's habits and dispositions (*CL* v 111–12).

45. Erratum in PR *4*: "for *dead* r. *deep.*" AG made the correction in WW's copy, and SC for herself.

46. Erratum in PR *4*: "for *Fill'd* r. *Fill.*" AG made the correction in WW's copy, and SC for herself.

PR *4* interspersed] In HNC's copy C accentuated the word (in pencil) "interspérsed", emphasising that the final "ed" is to be sounded.

48. Erratum in PR *4*: "for *fills* r. *thrills.*" JG made the correction in his own copy, AG in WW's, and SC for herself.

59–62. Applied (var) to "the Heart of our Reason" in *The Friend* VI (21 Sept 1809) (*CC*) II 81. They were added by C to the main body of the ms (in SH's hand), V&A Forster Collection MS 112, between ff 24 and 27.

64–5. TP's copy of PR *4* has the number "3", in pencil, at this point in the LH margin.

69–70. Notebook 21 (*CN* I 329) contains the undated lines:

> The reed-roof'd Village, still bepatch'd with snow
> Smok'd in the sun-thaw.

70. PR *3* eave-] In the V&A copy RS emended to "eave's-".

71. Erratum in PR *4*: "for *traces* r. *Trances.*" In HNC's copy, besides inserting the "n" (at first in pencil), C added (in ink): "*Trances*—i.e. the brief intervals of profound silence." C also made the correction in JG's and SC's copies; AG made it in WW's copy.

74.1.1–6. C drew a line round the passage in the Beaumont copy of PR *1*, and wrote alongside: "Omitted. S. T. C." The comment he wrote beneath the cancelled lines is given in vol I line 74⁺EC. A remark to RS in Dec 1799 (*CL* I 552) suggests that C thought of deleting the passage soon after the poem was first published.

172. LEWTI
OR, THE CIRCASSIAN LOVE-CHANT

A. DATE

Dec 1797–Apr 1798; probably Feb–Mar 1798. C's experiments to describe cloud effects—written in a notebook in Dec 1797 (*CN* I 315–18=poem **163**)— appear to precede similar descriptions in the poem. Daniel Stuart wrote to C in Jan 1798, urging him to fulfil his contract by sending more verse contributions for *M Post* (*Poole* I 261; *EOT—CC*—III 162–3), an obligation in which WW appears to have assisted C by making available his juvenilia (MS 1 below).

B. TEXTS

1. BM Add MS 27902. On ff 1^v–2^v of four conjoint leaves, 20.0×12.5 cm; no wm; chain-lines 2.6 cm. The second of five poems copied in DW's hand. Type facsimile in *JDC facsimile* 132–4; photographic reproduction in *WEPF* 328–30.

2. BM Add MS 35343 f 2^r. Single leaf, 11.8×20.2 cm; wm (partial) 95; chain-lines 2.5 cm; verso blank. Draft in C's hand. Type facsimile in *PW* (EHC) II 1050–1.

The bottom of the leaf has been torn away, and it is likely that the lines originally continued in this draft.

3. BM Add MS 35243 f 3^r. Single leaf, 11.8×42.3 cm; no wm; chain-lines 2.5 cm; verso blank. Further drafts in C's hand. Type facsimile in *PW* (EHC) II 1051–2; photographic reproduction in *English Poetical Autographs* ed Desmond Flower and A.N.L. Munby (1938) 21.

1. M Post (13 Apr 1798). Signed "NICIAS ERYTHRŒUS." (for "ERY-THRÆUS.").

The lines are preceded by the following recommendation:

It is not amongst the least pleasing of our recollections, that we have been the means of gratifying the public taste with some exquisite pieces of Original Poetry. For many of them we have been indebted to the Author of the *Circassian's Love Chant*. Amidst images of war and woe, amidst scenes of carnage and horror, of devastation and dismay, it may afford the mind a temporary relief to wander to the magic haunts of the Muses; to bowers and fountains which the despoiling power of war has never visited, and where the lover pours forth his complaint, or receives the recompence of his constancy. The whole of the subsequent Love Chant is in a warm and impassioned strain. The fifth and last stanzas are, we think, the best.

2. LB (Bristol 1798), as originally printed. The poem appeared on pp 63–7, but was suppressed before publication and replaced by **180** *The Nightingale*. The original, uncancelled leaves bearing *Lewti* exist in five known copies of the book: BM (C. 58. c 12 (1)); NYPL Berg Collection; Yale (2 copies: In W890 798; In W890 798c); Princeton University Library Robert H. Taylor Collection. EHC (*PW* II 1030n) reported a sixth copy which C presented to his sister-in-law, Martha Fricker. The poem might have been suppressed either to preserve anonymity or because it did not fit the purpose of the joint volume.

The lack of stanza-breaks (at lines 4$^+$, 14$^+$, 27$^+$, 41$^+$, perhaps 52$^+$) might suggest that copy was provided by PR *1*, where the breaks are obscure.

3. Annual Anthology ed RS (2 vols Bristol 1799–1800) II 23–6. Unsigned.

C's copy (Yale Tinker 1953 2) has a note and substitution in his hand. It is also signed "Esteesi." See *CM* (*CC*) I 91. After Feb 1803 C also rewrote several lines in TP's copy (James B. Clemens Sale, Parke–Bernet Galleries, 8 Jan 1945 lot 180), but this has not been traced. RS wrote, somewhat misleadingly, in his copy (HUL 10493. 27. 25*): "W. Wordsworth when a boy, corrected by S. T. C."

RS owned the copy of PR *2* now at BM, and the PR *3* version undoubtedly derives from it.

4 [=RT]. *SL* (1817). Described at the end as being *"(From the Morning Post,* 1795.*)"*

The Erratum correction in line 53 is made in the following copies in C's hand: JG's (HUL *EC8 C6795 817s (C)) (ink over pencil); HNC's (HUL *AC85 L8605 Zy 817c); J. H. Frere's (Princeton University Library Robert H. Taylor Collection); AG's (Stanford V 821.6 C69s); Francis Wrangham's (?) (sold at Christie's 13 Jun 1979 lot 126). The correction is made in AG's hand in an unknown person's copy (Yale In C678 817s Copy 2), in TP's copy (Brown PR 4478 A1 1817 Koopman Collection), and in WW's copy (Cornell WORDSWORTH PR 4480 S5 1817 Copy 1); and in JG's hand in William Hood's copy (Columbia X825C67 W3 1817), Miss Fricker's copy (HUL Lowell *EC8 C6795 817s), and the emended part copy (HUL *EC8 C6795 817s (D)). There are two notes in Wrangham's (?) copy, both in C's hand, and a note in JG's hand in the emended part copy. These are given in the commentary following the text.

Rpt *Metrical Romances &c. By S. T. Coleridge* (Isleworth 1825).

5. PW (1828). Dated at the end "1795."

6. PW (1829). Dated at the end "1795."

7. PW (1834). Dated at the end "1795."

C. GENERAL NOTE

See the appendix following the commentary below for the MSS 1–3 versions.

title. *1* LEWTI, OR, THE CIRCASSIAN'S LOVE | CHANT. • *2–7* LEWTI; | OR, | *THE CIRCASSIAN LOVE CHANT.*

1 *1–7* At midnight, by the stream I rov'd,
2 *1–7* To forget the form I lov'd.
3 *1–7* Image of LEWTI! from my mind
4 *1–7* Depart; for LEWTI is not kind.
　　　[Line-space]
5 *1–7* The moon was high, the moonlight gleam,
6 *1–7* And the shadow of a star
7 *1–7* Heav'd upon Tamaha's stream;
8 *1–7* But the rock shone brighter far,
9 *1–7* The rock half-shelter'd from my view,
10 *1–7* By pendent boughs of tressy yew.
11 *1–7* So shines my LEWTI's forehead fair,
12 *1–7* Gleaming thro' her sable hair.
13 *1–7* Image of LEWTI! from my mind
14 *1–7* Depart; for LEWTI is not kind.
　　　[Line-space]
14.1.1 *1* I saw the white waves, o'er and o'er,
14.1.2 *1* Break against the distant shore.
14.1.3 *1* All at once upon the sight,
14.1.4 *1* All at once they broke in light:
14.1.5 *1* I heard no murmur of their roar,
14.1.6 *1* Nor ever I beheld them flowing,
14.1.7 *1* Neither coming, neither going;
14.1.8 *1* But only saw them, o'er and o'er,
14.1.9 *1* Break against the curved shore;
14.1.10 *1* Now disappearing from the sight,
14.1.11 *1* Now twinkling regular and white,
14.1.12 *1* And LEWTI's smiling mouth can shew
14.1.13 *1* As white and regular a row.
14.1.14 *1* Nay, treach'rous image! from my mind
14.1.15 *1* Depart; for LEWTI is not kind.
　　　[Line-space]
15 *1–7* I saw a cloud of palest hue,
16 *1–7* Onward to the moon it pass'd.
17 *1–7* Still brighter and more bright it grew,
18 *1–7* With floating colours not a few,
19 *1–7* Till it reach'd the moon at last.
20 *1–7* Then the cloud was wholly bright,
21 *1–7* With a rich and amber light;
22 *1–7* And so with many a hope I seek,
23 *1–7* And with such joy I find my LEWTI;
24 *1–7* And even so my pale wan cheek
25 *1–7* Drinks in as deep a flush of beauty!
26 *1–7* Nay, treach'rous image! leave my mind,
27 *1–7* If LEWTI never will be kind.
　　　[Line-space]

28	*1–7*	The little cloud—it floats away,
29	*1–7*	Away it goes—away so soon!
30	*1–7*	Alas! it has no pow'r to stay:
31	*1–7*	Its hues are dim, its hues are grey—
32	*1–7*	Away it passes from the moon,
33	*1–7*	How mournfully it seems to fly,
34	*1–7*	Ever fading more and more,
35	*1–7*	To joyless regions of the sky—
36	*1–7*	And now 'tis whiter than before,
37	*1–7*	As white as my poor cheek will be,
38	*1–7*	When, LEWTI! on my couch I lie
39	*1–7*	A dying man, for love of thee.
40	*1–7*	Nay, treach'rous image! leave my mind—
41	*1–7*	And yet thou didst not look unkind!

[*Line-space*]

42	*1–7*	I saw a vapour in the sky,
43	*1–7*	Thin and white and very high.
44	*1–7*	I ne'er beheld so thin a cloud—
45	*1–7*	Perhaps the breezes, that can fly
46	*1–7*	Now below, and now above,
47	*1 7*	Have snatch'd aloft the lawny shroud
48	*1–7*	Of Lady fair, that died for love:
49	*1–7*	For Maids, as well as Youths, have perish'd
50	*1–7*	From fruitless love, too fondly cherish'd!
51	*1–7*	Nay, treach'rous image! leave my mind—
52	*1*	Tho' LEWTI never will be kind;
	2–7	For
52.1.1	*1*	This hand should make his life blood flow,
52.1.2	*1*	That ever scorn'd my LEWTI so!

[*Line-space*]

52.1.3	*1*	I cannot chuse but fix my sight
52.1.4	*1*	On that small vapour, thin and white!
52.1.5	*1*	So thin, it scarcely, I protest,
52.1.6	*1*	Bedims the star that shines behind it:
52.1.7	*1*	And pity dwells in LEWTI's breast,
52.1.8	*1*	Alas! if I knew how to find it.
52.1.9	*1*	And O! how sweet it were, I wist,
52.1.10	*1*	To see my LEWTI's eyes to-morrow
52.1.11	*1*	Shine brightly thro' as thin a mist
52.1.12	*1*	Of pity and repentant sorrow!
52.1.13	*1*	Nay, treach'rous image! leave my mind—
52.1.14	*1*	Ah, LEWTI! why art thou unkind?

[*Line-space*]

53	*1–7*	Hush! my heedless feet from under
54	*1–7*	Slip the crumbling banks for ever;
55	*1–7*	Like echoes to a distant thunder.
56	*1–7*	They plunge into the gentle river:
57	*1–7*	The river-swans have heard my tread,
58	*1–7*	And startle from their reedy bed.

59 *1–7* O beauteous birds! methinks ye measure
60 *1–7* Your movements to some heav'nly tune!
61 *1–7* O beauteous birds! 'tis such a pleasure
62 *1–7* To see you move beneath the moon;
63 *1–7* I would, it were your true delight
64 *1–7* To sleep by day, and wake all night.
65 *1–7* I know the place where LEWTI lies,
66 *1–7* When silent night has clos'd her eyes—
67 *1–7* It is a breezy jasmin bow'r,
68 *1–7* The Nightingale sings o'er her head;
69 *1–3* Had   I   the   enviable pow'r
    4–7 VOICE of the Night! had I the
70 *4–7* That leafy labyrinth to thread,
71 *1–3* To creep unseen with noiseless tread,
    4–7 And   like   thee,   soundless
72 *1–3* Then should I view her bosom white,
    4–7 I then might
73 *1–3* Heaving lovely to the sight,
    4–7   my
74 *1 2* As those two swans together heave
    3–7   these
75 *1–7* On the gently-swelling wave.
76 *1–7* O that she saw me in a dream,
77 *1–7* And dreamt that I had died for care!
78 *1–7* All pale and wasted I would seem,
79 *1–7* Yet fair withal, as spirits are.
80 *1–7* I'd die indeed, if I might see
81 *1–7* Her bosom heave, and heave for me!
82 *1–7* Sooth, gentle image! sooth my mind!
83 *1–7* To-morrow LEWTI may be kind.

title. *2* LEWTI; OR, THE CIRCASSIAN'S LOVE | CHANT. • *3 LEWTI,* |
Or the CIRCASSIAN LOVE-CHANT. • *4 LEWTI,* | OR | THE CIRCASSIAN
LOVE-CHANT. • *5 6* LEWTI, OR THE CIRCASSIAN | LOVE-CHAUNT. •
7 LEWTI, | OR THE CIRCASSIAN LOVE-CHAUNT.   **1.** *3–7* midnight
2 3 rov'd • *4–7* roved,   **2.** *4–7* loved.   **3.** *3–7* Lewti!   **4.** *3–7* Lewti   **5.** *4–*
7 Moon   *4–7* gleam   **7.** *4–7* Heaved   **8.** *2* far.   **9.** *2* half-sheltered • *3* half
shelter'd • *4–7* half sheltered   *4* form   *4–7* view   **10.** *3* pendant   *2–4* yew.— • *5–*
7 yew—   **11.** *3–7* Lewti's   **12.** *2* gleaning   *4–7* through   **13.** *3–7* Lewti!
14. *5* Depart   *3–7* Lewti   **16.** *4–6* Moon   *4* passed. • *5–7* passed;   **19.** *4–*
7 reached   *4–6* Moon   *3 4* last; • *5–7* last: **21.** *4–7* light!   **22.** *4–6* seek
23. *3–7* Lewti;   **26.** *4–7* treacherous   **27.** *3–7* Lewti   **29.** *4–7* goes; away
4–7 soon?   **30.** *3–7* power   **31.** *5* dim, it   **32.** *2 3* moon. • *4–6* Moon! •
7 moon!   **36.** *4–7* before!   **38.** *6* When   *3–7* Lewti!   *2–7* lie,   **39.** *3–7* man
40. *4–7* treacherous   **41.** *4–7* yet,   *4–7* did'st   *4–7* unkind.   **43.** *3–7* Thin,
3–7 white,   *4* high: • *5–7* high;   **44.** *4* cloud. • *5–7* cloud: **45.** *2–7* breezes
46. *4–7* below   **47.** *5–7* snatched   **48.** *2 3* lady   *3–7* fair—   *3* love; •
4–7 love.   **49.** *4–7* maids,   *4–7* youths,   *5–7* perished   **50.** *3–7* love
4 cherish'd. • *5–7* cherished.   **51.** *5–7* treacherous   **52.** *3–7* Lewti   *2–7* kind.

53. *4* Slush!   **54.** *4–7* ever: **55.** *2–7* thunder,   **56.** *3–7* river.   **57.** *3* river
swans   **59.** *4–6* Birds!   **60.** *3–7* heavenly   **61.** *4–6* Birds!   **62.** *3 7* moon, •
4–6 Moon,   **63.** *3–7* would   **64.** *2–7* day   **65.** *3–7* Lewti   **66.** *4–7* closed
5–7 eyes: **67.** *3* jasmin bower, • *4–7* jasmine-bower,   **68.** *3 7* nightingale
4–7 head: **69.** *7* Voice   *7* night!   *3–7* power   **71.** *4–7* creep,   **72.** *3–*
7 white   **75.** *2 4–7* gently swelling   **76.** *4–7* Oh!   *6* dream   **77.** *6 7* care;
79. *4–7* are!   **82.** *2–7* Soothe,   *2–7* soothe   **83.** *3–7* Lewti

4⁺. No line-space in PR *2 3*.

6, 8, 16, 19, etc. The RT gives the pattern of indentation found in all printed versions.

8–9. C added a fn to the Yale copy of PR *3*: "Two lines expressing the wetness of the Rock—".

14⁺. No line-space in PR *2 7*. In PR *7* this is undoubtedly a mistake carried over from PR *5 6*, where the gap coincides with a page-break (vol I p 168) (as it does in PR *4* at p 125).

27⁺. No line-space in PR *2*.

41⁺. No line-space in PR *2*.

47–8. C wrote in the LH margin of Wrangham's (?) copy of PR *4*: "This image was borrowed by Miss Bailey in her Basil: as the dates of the Poems prove." There is a related note in JG's hand in the margins of the emended part copy at HUL: "Miss Baillie has done me the honor of adopting this image in her 'Basil' at least, has flattered me by the coincidence."

Joanna Baillie's *Count Basil* was published in her anonymous *Series of Plays* in 1798, and over her own name in 1799. C might have been struck by Basil's description of his beloved's "robe, and tresses floating on the wind, I Like some light figure in a morning cloud" (I ii 128–9), or of clouds as being "As tho' an angel, in his upward flight, I Had left his mantle floating in mid-air" (IV v 41–2); but the borrowing is doubtful and the resemblance tenuous.

53. The line heads a new page in PR *2* (p 66), and it is not clear whether it is meant to be thought of as beginning a new paragraph.

53. Erratum in PR *4*: "for *Slush* I. *Hush*." C—and AG and JG acting as amanuenses—made the correction in the copies of PR *4* listed in sec B above. In Wrangham's (?) copy C also added an asterisk in the LH margin and the following note at the foot of the page and of the page facing:

> This Leaf the Publisher had promised to cancel together with 3 or 4 others made ludicrous by blunders of the Press, and still worse by the presumptuous ignorance and coxcombry of the Bristol Printer, who perpetrates verses himself, forsooth! and *lets* a Sonnet (see Boyers' French and English Dictionary) ever and anon & ~~gratuitous~~. Tho' this promise, however, was not kept, still this ⟨ridiculous⟩ blunder was marked in the Errata—& yet the Monthly Reviewer adduces it as one of the hundred new coined barbarous and mock-imitative *s*words or rather letters representing *noises* that disfigure my poems. Except one ~~instance,~~ *quoted from Shakespear* (tu-whit, tu-whoo) in the Christabel, there is not a single instance in all my works!
>
> S.T.C.

C corrected the mistake—which was one of a particularly large number in this poem—in the proofs (Yale In C678 817sa). The *Monthly Review* (NS LXXXVIII—Jan 1819—24–38 at 36) had said about the word "Slush": "There is no end to these imitative sounds."

Earlier articles (*The Champion* CLXXVII—26 May 1816—166–7 at 167; *Monthly Review* NS LXXXII—Jan 1817—22–5 at 23) had mentioned the owl's call in *Christabel* in disparaging terms. The reference to the standard French–English dictionary of the time is presumably intended to compound the scatological insult of "*lets* a Sonnet" (cf *CL* III 502: to J. J. Morgan 2 [=1] Jun 1814; IV 554: to R. H. Brabant [13 Mar 1815]; etc).

55. PR *1* thunder.] The punctuation at the end of the line looks like a full point, but could be a broken comma.

57–64. Quoted (var) in the Appendix to C's "On the Principles of Genial Criticism concerning the Fine Arts" (*SW&F—CC*—385; *BL*—1907—II 245).

64⁺. Line-space in PR *4–7*; line 65 heads a new page in PR *3* (p 26). It is just possible that the space is correct; or else line 65's position in PR *3* led to a misunderstanding in the later editions.

69. PR *3* enviable] The epithet was singled out and condemned by CL—it "would dash the finest poem" (*LL*—M—I 217). In the Yale copy of PR *3* C deleted the line heavily and substituted: "(O beating Heart!) had I the power".

75⁺. Line-space in PR *4–7*.

D. APPENDIX: THE EARLY MS VERSIONS

C's poem is based on an early thirty-six-line fragment by WW, *Beauty and Moonlight* (DCL MS 2 ff 14ʳ, 15ʳ, 16ʳ, 17ʳ: photographic reproduction in *WEPF* 38, 40, 42, 44, cf 383–4; *WPW* I 263–4; Woof 170). Reed I 16–17 and n, 65 dates this to 1786. The other four poems which accompany MS 1 are WW juvenilia, one of which was published in *M Post* (11 Apr 1798), signed "MORTIMER."

MS 1 is a revision of the WW original, and the significantly light punctuation suggests that it might be from WW's (or C's) dictation. MSS 2 and 3 appear to be independent reworkings, and the three drafts together make up a kind of prior text, on which subsequent printed texts draw.

title. 2 The ~~wild Indian's~~ Circassian's Love-chaunt. • 3 *1* LEWTI, or the Circassian's Love-chant.

1 1	High o'er the silver	rocks I roved	
2	~~silver~~ rocks at night		
3	rocks		
2 1–3	To forget the form I loved		
2.1.1 1	In hopes fond fancy would be kind		
2.1.2 1	And steal my Mary from my mind		
3 2	Image of ~~Cora~~ LEWTI! from my mind		
3	LEWTI!		
4 2	Depart! for ~~Cora~~ LEWTI is not kind!		
3	LEWTI		
	[*Line-space*]		
5 1	'Twas twilight & the lunar beam		
2 3ⁱᵐᵖ	Bright was the Moon: the Moon's bright		
6 2 3	Speckled with many a moving Shade,		

7	1	Sailed slowly o'er Tamaha's stream
	2 3	Danc'd upon
7.1.1	1	As down its sides the water strayed
8	1^{imp}	Bright on a rock the moonbeam play'ed,
	2 3	But brightlier on the Rock it play'd,
9	1	It shone, half-sheltered from the view
	2 3	The Rock, my
10	1–3	By pendent boughs of tressy yew
11	1	True, true to love but false to rest,
	2 3	True
12	1	So fancy whispered to my breast,
	2 3	My in
13	1	So shines her forehead smooth & fair
	2	my ~~Cora's~~ LEWTI's forehead
	3	←—LEWTI's—→
14	1–3	Gleaming through her sable hair
14.1.1	1	I turned to heaven—but viewed on high
14.1.2	1	The languid lustre of her eye
14.1.3	1	The moons mild radiant edge I saw
14.1.4	1	Peeping a black-arched cloud below
14.1.5	1	Nor yet its faint & paly beam
14.1.6	1	Could tinge its skirt with yellow gleam
		[*Line-space*]
14.1.7	1	I saw the white waves o'er & o'er
14.1.8	1	Break against a curved shore
14.1.9	1	Now disappearing from the sight
14.1.10	1	Now twinkling regular & white
14.1.11	1	Her mouth, her smiling mouth can shew
14.1.12	1	As white & regular a row
14.1.13	1	Haste ~~h~~haste, some God indulgent prove
14.1.14	1	And bear me, bear me to my love
14.1.15	1	Then might—for yet the sultry hour
14.1.16	1	Glows from the sun's oppressive power
14.1.17	1	Then might her bosom soft & white
14.1.18	1	Heave upon my swimming sight
14.1.19	1	As yon two swans together heave
14.1.20	1	Upon the gently-swelling wave
14.1.21	1	Haste—haste some God indulgent prove
14.1.22	1	And bear—oh bear me to my love
15	2	Image of ~~Cora~~ LEWTI! from my mind
	3	LEWTI!
16	2	Depart! for Cora LEWTI is not kind.
	3	LEWTI
		[*Line-space*]
17	2 3	I saw a cloud of whitest hue;
18	2 3	Onward to the Moon it pass'd!
19	2 3	Still brighter and more bright it grew
20	2 3	With floating colours not a few,
21	2 3	Till it reach'd the Moon at last.

22	3	Then the Cloud was wholly bright
23	3	With a ~~deep~~ rich and amber light!
24	3	And so with many a hope I seek,
25	3	And so with joy I find my LEWTI:
26	3	And even so my pale wan cheek
27	3	Drinks in as deep a flush of Beauty
28	3	Image of LEWTI! leave my mind
29	3	If LEWTI never will be kind!

[*Line-space*]

30	3	Away the little Cloud, away.
31	3	Away it goes—~~alone~~ away so soon!
32	3	Alas! it has no power to stay:
33	3	Its hues are dim, its hues are grey
34	3	Away it passes from the Moon.
35	3	And now tis whiter than before—
36	3	As white as my poor cheek will be,
37	3	When, LEWTI! on my couch I lie
38	3	A dying Man for Love of thee!
39	3	~~Thou living Image~~ Image of LEWTI in my mind,
40	3	Methinks thou lookest not ~~kin~~ unkind!

1. 2 3 rov'd   **2.** 2 3 form,   2 3 lov'd.   **4.** 3 Depart: 3 kind.   **5.** 3 bea⌐.⌐
6. 3 shade,   **7.** 3 TAMAHA'S   2 3 stream;   **9.** 2 3 half-shelter'd
10. 2 3 Yew!   **11.** 2 3 Love,   2 3 Rest,   **12.** 2 3 whisper'd   2 3 breast—
14. 2 3 thro'   2 hair. • 3 hair!   **16.** 3 Depart—   **17.** 3 Cloud   3 hue—
18. 3 pass'd.   **21.** 3 last:

2.1.2. Mary] WW's original verses were addressed to an idealised Mary, a name "to [his] ear the most musical and truly English in sound we have" (*WL—E* rev—499); C's lines reinvent the kind of feeling he had earlier felt for Mary Evans.

3, 4, etc. Cora] Perhaps the heroine of Marmontel's romance *Les Incas, ou la destruction de l'Empire du Pérou* (1777; anon English tr same year: *The Incas; or, The Destruction of the Empire of Peru*). An Italian operatic version followed in 1778; a German operatic version, entitled *Cora*, in 1781; and a play based on the novel, Thomas Morton's *Columbus; or, A World Discovered*, was performed at CG in 1792. Alternatively, the name might derive from an intermediate source, such as John Thelwall's ms play *The Incas; or, The Peruvian Virgin*, or Kotzebue's *Die Sonnenjungfrau* (1791) or *Der Spanier in Peru* (1796). (Though the earliest translations and adaptations date from 1799, C discussed Kotzebue with a Cambridge undergraduate at the time he was involved with the *Lewti* drafts: *CL* I 378: to WW [23] Jan 1798.)

5. MS 3 bea] If any text or punctuation followed, it has been lost.

8. MS 1 play] If any text or punctuation followed, it has been lost.

173. WELCOMING LINES TO LAVINIA POOLE

A. DATE

31 Mar 1798 (see MS 1 below). The PR *1* 2 date must be an attempt to bring the poem up to the moment for newspaper readers (C was in Germany in spring 1799).

B. TEXTS

1 **[=RT]**. BM Add MS 35343 f 68ʳ. "Copied from the Original for Thomas Poole Esqʳᵉ·" Subscribed "S. T. Coleridge March 31ˢᵗ, 1798". Transcript by J. Draper, North Down, Yeovil, in an als to TP, 22 Oct 1836.

The writer of the letter says that he or she is sending a copy and retaining the original in memory of the parent to whom it is addressed. The Draper family lives at Yeovil even now (1978), but the original cannot be traced. The writer also says that there is an instruction in pencil at the end of the poem, at the foot of the page, "Turn over". And overleaf the same hand has written (in pencil):

> "To gaze on thee is Death
> "but oh how sweet that
> "Death when 'tis the lightning
> "of thine Eye which gives the
> "Wound"—

It is not possible without the original to say whether C is the author of the pencilled note.

1. M Post (9 Dec 1799). Signed "LABERIUS."

2. Annual Anthology ed RS (2 vols Bristol 1799–1800) II 32–3. Signed "*LA-BERIUS.*"

C wrote in his copy (Yale Tinker 1953 2), above the pseudonym, "S. T. C."

3. SL (1817).

4. PW (1828).

5. PW (1829).

6. PW (1834).

title. 1 To Lavinia Poole • *1* 2 TO A YOUNG LADY, ON HER FIRST APPEAR- I ANCE AFTER A DANGEROUS ILLNESS. I *Written in the Spring*, 1799. • *3–6 TO A YOUNG LADY.* I *On her Recovery from a Fever.*

‾1 *1 2*   I.
1 1   Why need I say, Lavinia dear!
   1 2   OPHELIA
   3–6   Louisa
2 ☐   How glad I am to see you here,
3 ☐   A lovely convalescent
4 ☐   Risen from the bed of pain and Fear,
5 ☐   And fev'rish Heat incessant!
           [*Line-space*]
‾6 *1 2*   II.
6 1   The fields so green, the Sun, the Sky,
   1 2   breezy   air,
   3–6   sunny Showers,   dappled
7 1 1 *1 2* The little Birds that sing on high
   3–6   warble
8 ☐   Their vernal loves commencing,
9 ☐   Will better welcome you than I
10 ☐   With their sweet influencing.
           [*Line-space*]
‾11 *1 2*   III.
11 1   Believe me, while in pain you lay,
    ☒1   bed
12 1   Your dangers taught us how to pray;
    1 2   danger
    3–6   all
13 1 1 *1 2* You made us   all devouter!
    3–6   grow
14 ☐   Each eye look'd up, and seem'd to say,
15 ☐   "How can we do without her?
           [*Line-space*]
‾16 *1 2*   IV.
16 ☒*1 2* Besides (what vex'd us worse) we knew,
    1 2   (which
17 1 1 *1 2* They had no need of such as you
    3–6   have
18 ☐   In the place where you were going:
19 ☐   This world has Angels all too few
20 ☐   And Heaven is overflowing!

title. *2 To a YOUNG LADY,* | *On her first Appearance* | *AFTER A DANGEROUS ILLNESS.* | *Written in the Spring,* 1799. • *4–6* TO A YOUNG LADY. | ON HER RECOVERY FROM A FEVER.   **3.** *1* convalescent—• *2* convalescent:—• *3–6* convalescent;   **4.** *1* Ris'n *3 4* pain, ☒1 fear,   **5.** *3–6* feverish ☒1 heat *3–6* incessant.   **6.** *6* showers, *1 2* sun, *1 2 6* sky,   **7.** *1 2 6* birds ☒1 high, **9.** *1–3* I,   **12.** *1 3–6* pray: **13.** *2* devouter: **14.** *4–6* looked ☒1 up *3–6* seemed   **15.** *3–6* How *1 2* her?"   **16.** *3–6* Besides, what *4–6* vexed *3–6* worse, *1 2* knew   **18.** *1 2* going.   **19.** *3–6* World *3–6* angels ☒1 few, **20.** *1 2* Heav'n *1 2* overflowing.

3, 5, 8, etc. All texts have the indentation given in the RT.

174. FRANCE: AN ODE

A. DATE

Late Mar–early Apr 1798. News of the final Swiss defeat at Berne was not reported in England until late Mar, and PR *1* appeared on 16 Apr. PR *2 4–6* append the date Feb 1798; PR *3* describes it as having been published "in the beginning of the year 1798"; PR *7–9* append the date Feb 1797. The latter is probably, though not necessarily, a genuine mistake (see on lines 85–98 below). Predating the poem by a few months connects it with earlier protests at the invasion of Switzerland and disengages it from the late recantation and somewhat embarrassed disavowal by the Opposition of earlier commitments.

B. TEXTS

1. M Post (16 Apr 1798). "By S. T. COLERIDGE."
The poem is preceded by the following notice:

The following excellent Ode will be in unison with the feelings of every friend to Liberty and foe to Oppression: of all who, admiring the French Revolution, detest and deplore the conduct of France towards Switzerland. It is very satisfactory to find so zealous and steady an advocate for Freedom as Mr. COLERIDGE concur with us in condemning the conduct of France towards the Swiss Cantons. Indeed his concurrence is not singular; we know of no Friend to Liberty who is not of his opinion. What we most admire, is the *avowal* of his sentiments, and public censure of the unprincipled and atrocious conduct of France. The Poem itself is written with great energy. The second, third, and fourth stanzas, contain some of the most vigorous lines we have ever read. The lines in the fourth stanza,

> To scatter rage and trait'rous guilt,
> Where Peace her jealous home had built,

to the end of the stanza, are particularly expressive and beautiful.

This version was reprinted—without the prefatory notice—in *Express and Evening Chronicle* (15–17 Apr 1798) and *The Spirit of the Public Journals for 1798* II (1799) 357–9. There is a transcript of lines 1–12a, in an unknown hand, in the album of Mary Barker, Greta Lodge, Keswick (Bodleian MS Eng poet d 36 f 12ʳ), but this has no textual significance.

2. The second of the three poems published in *Fears in Solitude, Etc* (1798). "BY S. T. COLERIDGE." Dated at the end "February 1798."

The text differs from PR *1*, but not as much as C soon claimed that it should, and he complained of printing errors (see on line 46 below). The copy at PML (Book No 47225) contains corrections to and comments on this text, as on the others, made at Coleorton c 1807. Three of C's comments—on lines 53–4, 84, and the last stanza—are quoted in vol I EC. The transcript made by Mary Godwin (Shelley) in 1815–16 (*Shelley and his Circle 1773–1822* ed Kenneth Neill Cameron and Donald H. Reiman—8 vols Cambridge, Mass 1961–86—VII 1–4) has no textual significance.

3 [=RT]. *M Post* (14 Oct 1802). "By S. T. COLERIDGE." The poem is preceded by the following notice:

The following ODE was first published in this paper (in the beginning of the year 1798) in a less perfect state. The present state of France, and Switzerland, gives it so peculiar an interest at this present time, that we wished to re-publish it, and accordingly have procured from the Author, a corrected copy.

This version was reprinted—without the prefatory notice—in *The Courier* (14 Oct 1802). It is considerably revised. David V. Erdman (*EOT—CC—*I 367n) explains why the poem was thought worth reprinting in 1802.

4. The Poetical Register for 1808–1809 VII (1812) 332–5. "BY S. T. COLE-RIDGE, ESQ." Dated at the end "*February,* 1798."
The text is almost identical with PR *2*, and differs only in details of spelling and punctuation (lines 12, 17, 20, 32, 39, 45, 83, 94).

5. The second of the three poems published in *Poems* (1812). "BY S. T. COLERIDGE, ESQ." Dated at the end "*February,* 1798."
The text is almost identical with PR *4*, differing only in details (lines 5, 32, 39, 45, 83). The copy which belonged to RS (V&A Forster Collection P.97) has emendations in RS's hand. These partly coincide with C's corrections to the copy of PR *2* at PML, partly bring PR *5* into line with PR *3*, and are partly unique: they clearly have authority, although their precise source is unknown.

6. SL (1817). Dated at the end "February 1798."
PW (JDC) 588, 608B quotes a comment on the poem from the copy once belonging to Stuart M. Samuel, since lost (see vol I lines 54–5EC).

7. PW (1828). Dated at the end "February, 1797."
Two copies—C's at the Fitzwilliam Museum, Cambridge (Marlay Bequest 1912) and AG's (in the possession of Erwin Schwarz)—contain the same emendation in line 104. Neither is in C's hand.

8. PW (1829). Dated at the end "February, 1797."
JG's (?) copy at NYPL Berg Collection contains a single correction.

9. PW (1834). Dated at the end "February, 1797."

title. *1 THE RECANTATION,* | AN ODE. • ⊠*1* FRANCE. | AN ODE.

argument [present in PR *3* only]

First Stanza. An invocation to those objects in Nature, the contemplation of which had inspired the Poet with a devotional love of Liberty. Second Stanza. The exultation of the Poet at the commencement of the French Revolution, and his unqualified abhorrence of the Alliance against the Republic. Third Stanza. The blasphemies and horrors during the domination of the Terrorists, regarded by the Poet as a transient storm, and as the natural consequence of the former despotism, and of the foul superstition of Popery. Reason, indeed, began to suggest many apprehensions; yet still the Poet struggled to retain the hope, that France would make conquests by no other means, than by presenting to the observation of Europe, a people more happy, and better instructed, than under other forms of Government. Fourth Stanza. Switzerland, and the Poet's recantation. Fifth Stanza. An address to Liberty, in which the Poet expresses his conviction, that those feelings, and that grand *ideal*, of freedom, which the mind attains by its contemplation of its individual nature, and of the sublime surrounding objects (see Stanza the First), do not belong to men, as a society, nor can possibly be either gratified, or realised, under any form of human government; but belong to the individual man, so far as he is pure, and inflamed with the love and adoration of God in Nature.

⁻1.5

⁻1.10

⁻1.15

⁻1.20

⁻**1.24** ⊠*4*		I.
1 ⊠*3*		Ye clouds, that far above me float and pause,
3		or
2 ⊠*3*		Whose pathless march no mortal may controul!
3		Veering your pathless march without
3 ⊔		Ye ocean waves, that whereso'er ye roll,
4 □		Yield homage only to eternal laws!
5 *1–5*		Ye woods, that listen to the night-bird's singing,
6–8		night-birds'
9		night-birds
6 *1–5*		Midway the smooth and per'lous steep reclin'd;
6–9		slope
7 □		Save when your own imperious branches swinging,
8 □		Have made a solemn music of the wind!
9 □		Where, like a man belov'd of God,
10 □		Thro' glooms which never woodman trod;
11 □		How oft pursuing fancies holy,
12 *1*		By moonlight way o'er flow'ry weeds I wound,
⊠*1 3*	My	flow'ring
3		path
13 □		Inspir'd beyond the guess of folly,
14 □		By each rude shape, and wild unconquerable sound!
15 □		O ye loud waves, and O ye forests high,

16 ☐	And O ye clouds, that far above me soar'd!
17 ☐	Thou rising sun! thou blue rejoicing sky!
18 ☐	Yea, every thing, that is and will be free,
19 ☐	Bear witness for me, whereso'er ye be,
20 ☐	With what deep worship I have still ador'd
21 ☐	The spirit of divinest Liberty!

[*Line-space*]

⁻22 ☐   II.

22 ☐	When France in wrath her giant limbs uprear'd,
23 *1 2 4 5*	And with that oath, which smote earth, air, and sea,
3	shook
6–9	smote air, earth
24 *1*	Stamp'd her strong feet and said, she would be free,
⊠*1*	foot
25 ☐	Bear witness for me, how I hop'd and fear'd!
26 ⊠*3*	With what a joy my lofty gratulation
3	eager
27 ☐	Unaw'd I sung amid a slavish band:
28 ☐	And when to whelm the disenchanted nation,
29 ☐	Like fiends embattled by a wizard's wand,
30 ⊠*3*	The Monarchs march'd in evil day,
3	mov'd
31 ☐	And BRITAIN join'd the dire array!
32 ☐	Though dear her shores, and circling ocean,
33 ☐	Though many friendships, many youthful loves
34 ⊠*3*	Had swol'n the patriot emotion,
3	that
35 ⊠*3*	And flung a magic light o'er all her hills and groves;
3	spread
36 ☐	Yet still my voice unalter'd sang defeat
37 ☐	To all that brav'd the tyrant-quelling lance,
38 ☐	And shame too long delay'd, and vain retreat!
39 ☐	For ne'er, O Liberty! with partial aim
40 ☐	I dimm'd thy light, or damp'd thy holy flame;
41 ⊠*1 3*	But blest the Pæans of deliver'd France,
1 3	I
42 ☐	And hung my head and wept at BRITAIN's name!

[*Line-space*]

⁻43 ☐   III.

43 ☐	"And what (I said) tho' blasphemy's loud scream
44 ⊠*3*	"With that sweet music of deliv'rance strove?
3	those Pæans
45 ☐	"Tho' all the fierce and drunken passions wove
46 *1 2 4 5*	"A dance more wild than ever Maniac's dream?
3 6–9	e'er was
47 ☐	"Ye storms, that round the dawning East assembled,
48 ⊠*8*	"The sun was rising, tho' ye hid his light!"
8	he
49 ☐	And when to sooth my soul, that hop'd and trembled,

50 □	The diss'nance ceas'd, and all seem'd calm and bright;	
51 □	When France, her front deep-scar'd and gory,	
52 □	Conceal'd with clust'ring wreaths of glory;	
53 ⊠*3*	When insupportably advancing,	
3	irresistibly	
54 *1–6*	Her arm made mock'ry of the warrior's ramp,	
7–9	tramp;	
55 *1*	While timid look of fury glancing	
⊠*1*	looks	
56 □	DOMESTIC TREASON, crush'd beneath her fatal stamp,	
57 □	Writh'd, like a wounded dragon in his gore;	
58 ⊠*3*	Then I reproach'd my fears that would not flee,	
3	rebuk'd	
59 ⊠*3*	"And soon (I said) shall wisdom teach her lore.	
3	cried)	
60 □	"In the low huts of them that toil and groan!	
61 □	"And conqu'ring by her happiness alone,	
62 ⊠*3*	"Shall FRANCE compel the nations to be free,	
3	persuade	
63 ⊠*3*	"'Till LOVE and JOY look round, and call the earth their own!"	
3	lo! earth's	

[*Line-space*]

⁻**64** □	IV.	
64 ⊠*2 4 5*	Forgive me, Freedom! O forgive those dreams!	
2 4 5	these	
65 □	I hear thy voice, I hear thy loud lament,	
66 ⊠*9*	From bleak HELVETIA's icy caverns sent—	
9	cavern	
67 □	I hear thy groans upon her blood-stain'd streams!	
68 □	Heroes, that for your peaceful country perish'd;	
69 *1*	And ye, that flying spot the mountain snows	
2 4 5	fleeing	
3	flying your	
6–9	fleeing,	
70 □	With bleeding wounds; forgive me that I cherish'd	
71 □	One thought, that ever bless'd your cruel foes!	
72 □	To scatter rage and trait'rous guilt,	
73 □	Where PEACE her jealous home had built;	
74 □	A Patriot race to disinherit	
75 ⊠*3*	Of all that made their stormy wilds so dear;	
3	native	
76 □	And with inexpiable spirit,	
77 ⊠*3*	To taint the bloodless freedom of the mountaineer—	
3	stain	
78 □	O FRANCE! that mockest Heav'n, adult'rous, blind,	
79 *1 3*	And patient only in pernicious toils!	
⊠*1 3*	patriot	
80 ⊠*3*	Are these thy boasts, champion of human kind?	
3	Was this boast,	

81 ⊠*3*		To mix with Kings in the low lust of sway,
3		Monarchs in the
82 □		Yell in the hunt, and share the murd'rous prey;
83 □		T' insult the shrine of Liberty with spoils,
84 □		From freemen torn; to tempt and to betray!

[*Line-space*]

¯**84.1.1** ⊠*3*	V.
84.1.1 *1*	* * * * * * * * * *
84.1.2 *1*	* * * * * * * * * * * *
84.1.3 *1*	The fifth Stanza, which alluded to the African Slave-
84.1.4 *1*	Trade, as conducted by this Country, and to the present
84.1.5 *1*	Ministry and their supporters, has been omitted; and
84.1.6 *1*	would have been omitted without remark, if the commencing
84.1.7 *1*	lines of the sixth Stanza had not referred to it.
84.1.8 *1*	* * * * * * * * * * * * *
84.1.9 *1*	* * * * * * * * * * * * * * *

[*Line-space*]

¯**84.1.10** *1*	VI.
84.1.10 *1*	Shall I with *these* my patriot zeal combine?
84.1.11 *1*	No, Afric, no! They stand before my ken,
84.1.12 *1*	Loath'd as th' Hyænas, that in murky den
84.1.13 *1*	Whine o'er their prey, and mangle while they whine!
85 ⊠*1*	The sensual and the dark rebel in vain,
86 ⊠*1*	Slaves by their own compulsion! In mad game
87 ⊠*1 3*	They burst their manacles, and wear the name
3	break
88 ⊠*1*	Of freedom graven on a heavier chain!
89 *1*	Divinest Liberty! with vain endeavour,
⊠*1*	O Liberty! with profitless
90 □	Have I pursued thee many a weary hour—
91 □	But thou nor swell'st the victor's strain; nor ever
92 ⊠*3*	Didst breathe thy soul in forms of human pow'r,
3	on
93 □	Alike from all, howe'er they praise thee—
94 ⊠*7 8*	(Nor pray'r, nor boastful name delays thee)
7 8	(Not
95 *1 2 4 5*	Alike from priesthood's harpy minions,
3 6–9	priestcraft's
96 □	And factious blasphemy's obscener slaves,
97 □	Thou speedest on thy subtle pinions,
98 *1 2 4 5*	To live amid the winds, and move upon the waves!
3	among brood
6–9	The guide of homeless winds, and playmate of
99 *1 6–9*	And *there* I felt thee—on that sea-cliff's verge,
2 4 5	then
3	there yon
100 ⊠*3*	Whose pines, scarce travell'd by the breeze above,
3	just
101 □	Had made one murmur with the distant surge.

102 ⊠*3*	Yes! while I stood and gaz'd, my temples bare,	
3	as	forehead
103 ☐	And shot my being thro' earth, sea, and air,	
104 ⊠*3*	Possessing all things with intensest love,	
3	by	
105 ☐	O Liberty, my spirit felt thee there!	

title. *3 FRANCE.* I AN ODE: • *4 5* FRANCE, I AN ODE • *6 FRANCE.* I *An Ode.* • *9* FRANCE. AN ODE.   **1.** *2 4 5* Clouds, • *3* clouds! • *6–9* Clouds! **2.** *2 4 5 9* control!   **3.** *6–9* Ocean-Waves! *2 4–9* that,   **5.** *3* woods! • *5* woods • *6–9* Woods!   *3* night bird's singing   **6.** ⊠*1* perilous   *3 6* recln'd, • *7–9* reclined, **7.** *2–7* swinging   **9.** *7–9* beloved   **10.** *6–9* Through   ⊠*1* glooms,   ⊠*1* trod, **11.** *2 4–9* oft,   *3* holy   **12.** *4 5* moon-light   *7–9* flowering   **13.** *4 5* Inspired • *6–9* Inspired,   *3* folly • *7* folly.   **14.** *6–9* shape   **15.** *2 4 5* O,   *3* waves! • *6–9* Waves!   *2 4 5* and O,   *6–9* Forests   ⊠*1 4 5* high!   **16.** *2 4 5* O,   *3–5* clouds • *6–9* Clouds   *7–9* soared!   **17.** *4 5* sun, • *6–9* Sun!   *6–9* Sky! **18.** *2 4–9* thing   *6–9* free!   **19.** *2 4 5* me   *6* wheresoe'r • *7–9* wheresoe'er **20.** *4 5* ador'd, • *7–9* adored   **21.** *2 4 5* liberty • *3 6–9* Liberty.   **22.** *3* FRANCE *6–9* giant-limbs upreared,   **23.** *2 4 5* oath   **24.** *7–9* Stamped   *3* foot,   *6–9* said   **25.** *7–9* hoped   *7–9* feared!   **27.** *7–9* Unawed   *3* sang • *6–9* sang, **29.** *3* Wizard's • *6* wizzard's   **30.** *2 4 5* monarchs   *7–9* marched   **31.** *2 4–9* Britain   *7–9* joined   ⊠*1* array;   **32.** *3 4* Tho'   *3 6–9* shores   **33.** *3* 'Tho' *3* loves,   **34.** *2–8* swoln   *3* Patriot   *6–9* emotion   **36.** *6–9* voice,   *6* unalter'd, • *7–9* unaltered,   **37.** *3* all,   *7–9* braved   **38.** *3 6* delay'd • *7–9* delayed *3* retreat.   **39.** *4* ne'er   *3* Liberty,   **40.** *7–9* dimmed   *6–9* light   *7–9* damped *3* flame!   **41.** *7–9* blessed   *2 4–9* pæans   *7–9* delivered   **42.** *2 4 5* head, ⊠*1* Britain's   *3 6–9* name.   **43.** *3* And what? (I said) tho' blasphemy's • *6–9* "And what," I said, "though Blasphemy's   **44.** *3 9* With   *6–9* deliverance *2 4 5* strove; • *7–9* strove!   **45.** *3* Tho' • *6–8* "Though • *9* Though   *4* wove, **46.** *3 9* A   *3* wild,   *2 4–9* maniac's   *2 4 5* dream; • *7–9* dream!   **47.** *3 9* Ye *3* storms!   *2 4–9* east   **48.** *3 9* The   *3 6 9* Sun   *6–9* though   *3 8* light! **49.** *3 6–9* when,   *3 9* soothe   *6–9* hoped   **50.** ⊠*1* dissonance   *7–9* ceased, *5 7–9* seemed   *3* bright: **51.** *3* FRANCE, • *6–9* France   *3 9* deep-scarr'd *6–9* gory   **52.** *7–9* Concealed   *6–9* clustering   *3* glory,   **53.** *6–9* When, **54.** *6–9* mockery   *6* ramp;   **55.** *2–5* While,   ⊠*1* glancing,   **56.** ⊠*1* Domestic treason,   *7–9* crushed   **57.** *6* Writh'd • *7–9* Writhed   **58.** *7–9* reproached *3* fears,   *6–9* flee;   **59.** *3* And   *6–9* soon," I said, "shall Wisdom   ⊠*1* lore **60.** *3 9* In   *3* groan,   **61.** *3* And • *6–8* "And, • *9* And,   *6–9* conquering **62.** *3 9* Shall   ⊠*1* France   **63.** *2 4 5 8* "Till • *3* 'Till • *6 7 9* 'Till   *2–5* love • *6–9* Love   *2–5* joy • *6–9* Joy   *6–9* Earth   *3* own! • *6–9* own."   **65.** *3* lament **66.** ⊠*1* Helvetia's   **67.** *7–9* blood-stained   **68.** *3* Heroes!   *6* perish'd, • *7–9* perished,   **69.** *6–9* ye that, fleeing,   *6–9* mountain-snows   **70.** ⊠*1* me, *7–9* cherished   **71.** *6–9* thought   *3* blest • *7–9* blessed   **72.** *3 6–9* rage, *6–9* traitorous   *2 4 5* guilt   **73.** ⊠*1* Peace   **74.** *2–5* patriot race • *6–9* patriot-race   **75.** *2–5* dear,   **76.** ⊠*1* spirit   **77.** *2 4 5* mountaineer.— **78.** *2 4 5* France! • *6–9* France,   *2 4 5* heav'n, adult'rous, • *6–9* Heaven, adulterous,   **79.** *3 9* toils,   **80.** *6–9* Champion   *2 4 5* kind: • *3* kind! • *6 7* kind;   **81.** *2 4 5* kings   **82.** *7–9* murderous   *3* prey—   **83.** *4 6–9* To *2 4 5* liberty   ⊠*1* spoils   **84.** *3* torn!   *6–9* betray?   **85.** *6–9* Sensual   *6–9* Dark

87. *6–9* manacles   **88.** *3* Freedom • *6–9* Freedom,   *3* chain.   **89.** *3* LIBERTY!
☒*1* endeavour   **90.** *6–9* thee,   *2 4 5* hour: • *3 6–9* hour;   **91.** ☒*1* strain,
92. *3* huma   *2 4 5* pow'r. • *3* Pow'r! • *6–9* power.   **93.** *2 4–9* thee, • *3* thee
94. *4 5* pray'r • *6–9* prayer,   *3* thee), • *4 5* thee,)   **95.** *6–9* Priestcraft's   **96.** *6–*
9 Blasphemy's   **97.** *3* pinions   **99.** *6–9* there   *2 4 5* thee on • *3* thee! On •
6–9 thee!—on   **100.** *3* pines   *7–9* travelled   **101.** *2 4–9* surge! • *3* surge—
102. *6–9* Yes,   *7–9* gazed,   **103.** *6–9* through   *6–9* sea   **104.** *3* love—
105. *3* LIBERTY! • *6–9* Liberty!   *6 8 9* there. • *7* there,

2, 3, 6, etc. PR *3* indents as shown in the RT; the pattern of indentation varies slightly in PR *1* and differently again in PR *6–9*. No lines are indented in PR *2 4 5*.

41. PR *2* deliver'd] Some copies lack the apostrophe.

46. PR *2 5* ever] This is corrected by C and RS, in the copies cited in sec B, to "e'er was" (the reading of PR *3 6–9*). C wrote in the margin of PR *2*, alongside the correction: "this poem was PRINTED in my absence from my Country."

48. PR *8* he] Corrected to "ye" in JG's (?) copy.

51. C deleted both marks of punctuation in the corrected copy of PR *2*; RS deleted the comma after "France" and added a comma after "front" in his corrected copy of PR *5*.

52. PR *5* with] RS emended to "in" (a unique reading) in his corrected copy.

55. PR *1* look] It seems that PR *1* dropped an "s" after the "k".

59. PR *1* lore.] The full point might be a defect in the type.

64. PR *5* these] RS emended to "those" (the reading of PR *1 3 6–9*) in his corrected copy.

77. PR *2* mountaineer—] C added another dash beneath the existing one in his corrected copy. His intention is unclear.

79. PR *2* patriot] C underlined the word in his corrected copy, and added in the margin: "—I wrote it 'patient'—who altered it, I know not; but it seems to me an improvement. S. T. C.—"

80. PR *5* kind:] RS emended to "kind?" (the reading of PR *1 8 9*) in his corrected copy.

82. PR *5* prey;] RS emended to "prey!" (a unique reading) in his corrected copy.

84. PR *5* torn;] RS emended to "torn!" (the reading of PR *3*) in his corrected copy.

84.1.10–13. There is no evidence that PR *1* ever contained an intervening stanza from which these lines develop.

85. This line begins stanza V in PR *2 4–9*; it follows line 84, after a line-space, in PR *3*.

85–98. Quoted in a version close to PR *6* in *BL* ch 10 (1817) I 194 (*CC*) I 199–200:

> "The sensual and the dark rebel in vain,
> Slaves by their own compulsion! In mad game
> They break their manacles, to wear the *name*
> Of freedom, graven on an heavier chain.
> O liberty! with profitless endeavor
> Have I pursued thee many a weary hour;
> But thou nor swell'st the victor's pomp, nor ever
> Didst breathe thy soul in forms of human power!
>   Alike from all, howe'er they praise thee
>   (Nor prayer nor boastful name delays thee)
>   From superstition's harpy minions
>   And factious blasphemy's obscener slaves,

> Thou speedest on thy cherub pinions,
> The guide of homeless winds and playmate of the waves!"
> FRANCE, *a Palinodia.*

It should be noted that the lines are quoted in *BL* to illustrate C's feeling about political events when he retired to Stowey, in a way which might suggest that they were written at that time. Cf the date of Feb 1797 appended to PR *7–9.*

92. PR *1* pow'r,] So PR *1* appears; but the tail of the comma is broken, and it is just possible that the line ends with a full point.

99. In his corrected copy of PR *5* RS emended the line to read: "And there I felt thee! On that sea-cliff's verge," (which brings it closer to PR *1 3 6–9*).

104. PR *7* with] An unidentified Gillman (?) hand substituted "through" (a unique reading) in both annotated copies.

174.X1. TO —— ——
("I MIX IN LIFE, AND LABOUR
TO SEEM FREE")

LR I 280: "I mix in life, and labour to seem free,". 4 lines, untitled, included among other short pieces and fragments "communicated by Mr. Gutch". *PW* (JDC) 64B; *PW* (EHC) I 292.

The lines in fact comprise the first stanza of William Preston's *The Diffident Lover*, probably from the review of Preston's *Poetical Works* in *Critical Review* (Feb 1795). See *CN* I 11 and n.

175. FEARS IN SOLITUDE:
WRITTEN IN APRIL 1798,
DURING THE ALARM OF AN INVASION

A. DATE

20 or 28 Apr 1798 (see line 233⁺). It is unclear why the date was emended in *SL* and thereafter, and the later date is probably an error. (The proofs of this poem in PR *6* contain an unusually large number of errors.) The significance of the two dates in C's life is that, between them, he completed **161** *The Rime of the Ancient Mariner*; they appear to have no special significance in political history.

1. The first of the three poems published in *Fears in Solitude, Etc* (1798). "BY S. T. COLERIDGE."

The apostrophisation of "its" and other peculiarities suggest that the text might have been set directly from C's holograph. C complained, apropos of another poem in the same pamphlet, that the printing had gone unrevised because of his departure for Germany (a letter to Mrs C of 18 Sept 1798—*CL* I 417–18—refers to it being in the printer's hands; cf **174** *France: An Ode* VAR 46).

Sir George Beaumont's copy (PML Book No 47225) contains comments and corrections in C's hand, dating from 1807, three of which are quoted in vol I EC. Lines 42–130 were reprinted in *The Microscope* (Belfast) I (1799) 182–4 ("TRANSCRIBED BY G. I LISBURN, 8mo 20TH, 1799").

1. PML MA 837. Six conjoint leaves, each 12.11×18.3 cm; wm (partial) crown or fleur-de-lis device in the corner of several leaves; chain-lines 2.6 cm. All but the first leaf written on both sides. Initialled at the end "S.T.C.—". Transcript in C's hand, made in Germany for Clement Carlyon.

The transcript omits one short passage and introduces several variants. It is identified as Carlyon's in correspondence between JDC and EHC, dating from 1891–2, now at HRC (uncatalogued in 1978). JDC describes borrowing the ms from Edward Dowden, when it accompanied the transcript of **146.X1** *Osorio* which is now at HUL. Carlyon I 141 refers to it as follows: "He not only recited this beautiful poem to us, but gave us copies of it; and much as I admired it then, it has lost nothing in my estimation since"; again (II 93): "I lately found, among my papers, a manuscript copy of 'His Fears in Solitude,' . . .". The transcript must have been made in Mar–Jun 1799, perhaps c 6 Apr, when C quoted line 221 in a letter to TP (*CL* I 478), though some of the variants suggest an effort to recollect which was not always successful.

A note following C's initials, at the end, is quoted in vol I headnote.

2. Extract (lines 130–60, 162.1.1–167, 173–98) in *M Post* (14 Oct 1802).

The extract differs from TEXTS *1* 1, and accompanies "a corrected copy" of **174** *France: An Ode*.

2. DCL (uncatalogued in Mar 1979). Two conjoint leaves, each 24.0× 38.5 cm; wm JOHN HALL I 1805; no chain-lines. Each leaf written on both sides. Transcript of the complete text of PR *1* in SH's hand.

The variations from PR *1* are few and minor: the text illustrates SH's accuracy as a copyist. It is just possible, however, that SH was copying from a corrected copy of PR *1*; the variant at line 108 is matched only in MS 1.

3. Extract (lines 130–67, 172–98) in *The Friend* II (8 Jun 1809) 19–20fn (*CC*) II 24–5fn.

The extract differs from PR 2 and other texts, and coincides with MS 1 at line 151. It was reprinted in *The Friend* (1812) with three misprints, not recorded here. The ms for this second number of *The Friend* is not among those at the V&A.

4. *The Poetical Register for 1808–1809* VII (1812) 227–34. "BY S. T. COLERIDGE, ESQ."

5. The first of three poems published in *Poems* (1812). "BY S. T. COLERIDGE, ESQ." Apart from the title, which may be a mistake, the text differs from PR *4* only in three matters of punctuation.

6 [=RT]. *SL* (1817).
Three comments have been cited from the proof sheets (Yale In C678 817sa); cf on lines 120, 133, 215 below. A copy reported in *PW* (JDC) 610B as being in the possession of Stuart M. Samuel, and since lost, contains an emendation in C's hand; and TP added a comment in his own copy (Brown PR 4478 A1 1817 Koopman Collection), given at lines 223–4EC.
Rpt *Select British Poets* ed William Hazlitt (1824) 626–8; *The Living Poets of England: Specimens of the Living British Poets* (2 vols Paris 1827) I 446–53.

7. *PW* (1828).
Lines 1–28 were reprinted in *Berkshire Chronicle and Windsor Herald* (20 Sept 1828), entitled "A RUSTIC SCENE" and signed "COLERIDGE" (with "he" for "had" in line 15, and differences of punctuation).

8. *PW* (1829).
JG's (?) copy at NYPL (Berg Collection) contains two minor corrections.

9. *PW* (1834).

title. *1* 2 5 FEARS IN SOLITUDE. | WRITTEN, APRIL 1798, DURING THE ALARMS OF AN INVASION. • 1 Fears in Solitude, written April, 1798, during | the Alarm of the Invasion.—The Scene, the Hills near | Stowey.— • 2 *The following Extracts are made from a Poem by the | same Author written in April, 1798, during the Alarm respecting the threatened Invasion.* • 3 *Fears of Solitude, a Poem.* • *4* FEARS IN SOLITUDE. | *Written, April 1798, during the Alarm of an Invasion.* • *5* FEARS IN SOLITUDE. | *Written, April 1798, during the Alarms of an Invasion.* • *6–9 FEARS IN SOLITUDE.* | *Written in April 1798, during the Alarm of an* Invasion.

1	⊠2 *3*	A green and silent spot amid the hills!
2	⊠1 *2 3*	A small and silent dell!—O'er stiller place
	1	Scene
3	⊠2 *3*	No singing sky-lark ever pois'd himself!
4	⊠2 *3*	The hills are heathy, save that swelling slope,
5	⊠2 *3*	Which hath a gay and gorgeous covering on,
6	⊠2 *3*	All golden with the never-bloomless furze,
7	⊠2 *3*	Which now blooms most profusely; but the dell,
8	⊠1 *2 3*	Bath'd by the mist, is fresh and delicate,
	1	Mists,
9	⊠2 *3*	As vernal corn field, or the unripe flax,

10	⊠*2 3*	When thro' its half-transparent stalks, at eve,
11	⊠*2 3*	The level sunshine glimmers with green light.
12	⊠*2 3*	O 'tis a quiet spirit-healing nook,
13	⊠*2 3*	Which all, methinks, would love; but chiefly he,
14	⊠*2 3*	The humble man, who in his youthful years
15	⊠*2 3*	Knew just so much of folly as had made
16	⊠*2 3*	His early manhood more securely wise:
17	⊠*1 2 3*	Here he might lie on fern or wither'd heath,
	1	rest
18	⊠*2 3*	While from the singing lark (that sings unseen
19	*1 2 4 5*	The minstrelsy which solitude loves best)
	1	That
	6–9	The that
20	⊠*2 3*	And from the sun, and from the breezy air,
21	⊠*2 3*	Sweet influences trembled o'er his frame;
22	⊠*2 3*	And he with many feelings, many thoughts,
23	⊠*2 3*	Made up a meditative joy, and found
24	⊠*2 3*	Religious meanings in the forms of nature!
25	⊠*2 3*	And so, his senses gradually wrapp'd
26	⊠*2 3*	In a half-sleep, he dreams of better worlds,
27	⊠*2 3*	And dreaming hears thee still, O singing lark!
28	⊠*2 3*	That singest like an angel in the clouds.
		[*Line-space*]
29	⊠*1 2 3*	My God! it is a melancholy thing
	1	And ah!
30	⊠*2 3*	For such a man, who would full fain preserve
31	⊠*2 3*	His soul in calmness, yet perforce must feel
32	⊠*1 2 3*	For all his human brethren— O my God,
	1	Ah,
33	⊠*2 3 7–9*	It is indeed a melancholy thing,
34	*1 1 2 4–6*	And weighs upon the heart, that he must think
	7–9	It
35	⊠*1 2 3*	What uproar and what strife may now be stirring
	1	Tumult may
36	⊠*1 2 3*	This way or that way o'er these silent hills—
	1	~~and~~ or
37	⊠*2 3*	Invasion, and the thunder and the shout,
38	⊠*2 3*	And all the crash of onset; fear and rage
39	⊠*2 3*	And undetermined conflict—even now,
40	⊠*2 3*	Ev'n now, perchance, and in his native Isle,
41	*1 1 2 4 5*	Carnage and screams beneath this blessed sun!
	6–9	groans
42	⊠*2 3*	We have offended, O my countrymen!
43	⊠*2 3*	We have offended very grievously,
44	*1 1 2 4 5*	And have been tyrannous. From east to west
	6–9	been most
45	⊠*1 2 3*	A groan of accusation pierces heaven!
	1	The pleads against us.
46	⊠*1 2 3*	The wretched plead against us, multitudes

47	☒1 *2 3*	Countless and vehement, the sons of God,
48	☒1 *2 3*	Our brethren! like a cloud that travels on,
49	☒1 *2 3*	Steam'd up from Cairo's swamps of pestilence,
50	☒1 *2 3*	Ev'n so, my countrymen! have we gone forth
51	*1 4–9*	And borne to distant ~~tribes~~ slavery and pangs,
2		~~climes~~ tribes
52	☒1 *2 3*	And, deadlier far, our vices, whose deep taint
53	☒1 *2 3*	With slow perdition murders the whole man,
54	☒*2 3*	His body and his soul! Meanwhile, at home,
60.1	*1* 1 *2 4 5*	We have been drinking with a riotous thirst
61.1	*1* 1 *2 4 5*	Pollutions from the brimming cup of wealth,
54.1.1	*1* 1 *2 4 5*	A selfish, lewd, effeminated race,
55	*6–9*	All individual dignity and power
56	*6–9*	Engulph'd in Courts, Committees, Institutions,
57	*6–9*	Associations and Societies,
58	*6–9*	A vain, speech-mouthing, speech-reporting Guild,
59	*6–9*	One Benefit-Club for mutual flattery,
60	*6–9*	We have drunk up, demure as at a grace,
61	*6–9*	Pollutions from the brimming cup of wealth;
62	☒1 *2 3*	Contemptuous of all honourable rule,
1		Sway
63	☒*2 3*	Yet bartering freedom, and the poor man's life,
64	☒*2 3*	For gold, as at a market! The sweet words
65	☒*2 3*	Of christian promise, words that even yet
66	☒*2 3*	Might stem destruction, were they wisely preach'd,
67	☒*2 3*	Are mutter'd o'er by men, whose tones proclaim,
68	☒*2 3*	How flat and wearisome they feel their trade.
69	☒*2 3*	Rank scoffers some, but most too indolent,
70	☒*2 3*	To deem them falsehoods, or to *know* their truth.
71	☒1 *2 3*	O blasphemous! the book of life is made
1		Blasphemy! Word
72	☒*2 3*	A superstitious instrument, on which
73	☒1 *2 3*	We gabble o'er the oaths we mean to break,
1		mutter
74	☒*2 3*	For all must swear—all, and in every place,
75	☒1 *2 3*	College and wharf, council and justice-court,
1		Senate
76	☒*1 ? 3*	All, all must swear, the briber and the brib'd,
1		~~Old Man and the Young,~~ Briber & the Drib'd,
77	☒1 *2 3*	Merchant and lawyer, senator and priest,
78	☒1 *2 3*	The rich, the poor, the old man, and the young,
1		~~Old,~~ Rich, the ~~young~~ Poor, the ~~rich~~ old Man & the ~~poor~~ Young,
79	☒*2 3*	All, all make up one scheme of perjury,
80	☒*2 3*	That faith doth reel; the very name of God
81	☒*2 3*	Sounds like a juggler's charm; and bold with joy,
82	☒1 *2 3*	Forth from his dark and lonely hiding-place
1		obscure
83	☒*2 3*	(Portentous sight) the owlet, Atheism,

84　☒1 *2 3*　Sailing on obscene wings athwart　　the　　noon,
1　　　　　　　　　~~across~~ athwart the ~~Moon~~ Noon
85　*1 4–9*　←—Drops—→ his blue-fringed lids, and holds them close,
1　　　　　　~~Lets fall~~ Drops
2　　　　　　←—Drops—→　　　　　　hold
86　☒*2 3*　And, hooting at the glorious sun in heaven,
87a　☒*2 3*　Cries out, "where is it?"
　　　　　　　[Line-space]

87b　☒*2 3*　　　　　　　　　Thankless too for peace,
88　☒*2 3*　(Peace long preserv'd by fleets and perilous seas)
89　☒1 *2 3*　Secure from actual warfare, we have lov'd
1　　　　　　~~We~~ Impatient of the Blessing,
90　☒1 *2 3*　To　swell　the war-whoop, passionate for war!
1　　　　　　　~~roar~~ swell
91　☒*2 3*　Alas! for ages ignorant of all
92　☒*2 3*　It's ghastlier workings (famine or blue plague,
93　☒*2 3*　Battle, or siege, or flight thro' wintry snows)
94　☒*2 3*　We, this whole people, have been clamorous
95　☒*2 3*　For war and bloodshed, animating sports,
96　☒*2 3*　The which we pay for, as a thing to talk of,
97　☒*2 3*　Spectators and not combatants! no guess
98　☒*2 3*　Anticipative of a wrong unfelt,
99　*1* 1 2 *4–6*　No speculation on contingency,
7–9　　　　　　　　or
100　☒1 *2 3*　However dim and　vague,　too vague and dim
1　　　　　　　　　ð vague,
101　☒*2 3*　To yield a justifying cause: and forth
102　☒*2 3*　(Stuff'd out with big preamble, holy names,
103　☒*2 3*　And adjurations of the God in heaven)
104　☒*2 3*　We send our mandates for the certain death
105　☒*2 3*　Of thousands and ten thousands! Boys and girls,
106　☒*2 3*　And women that would groan to see a child
107　☒1 *2 3*　Pull　off an insect's leg, all read of war,
1　　　　　　　Pluck
108　*1 4–9*　The best amusement for our morning meal!
1 2　　　　　　　　　　　　　of
109　☒1 *2 3*　The poor wretch, who has learnt ←———his———→ only prayers
1　　　　　　　　　　hath　　　~~his Maker's Name~~ his
110　☒1 *2 3*　From curses,　who　knows scarcely words enough
1　　　　　　　　　　& who
111　*1* 1 2 4 5　To ask a blessing　of　his heavenly Father,
6–9　　　　　　　　　from
112　☒*2* 2 *3*　Becomes a fluent phraseman, absolute
2　　　　　　　　phrasemen,
113　☒*2 3* 6 7　And technical in victories and defeats,
6 7　　　　　　　　　　deceit,
114　☒*2 3*　And all our dainty terms for fratricide,
115　☒*2* 2 *3*　Terms which we　trundle　smoothly o'er our tongues
2　　　　　　　　⟨trundle⟩

116	☒2 3	Like mere abstractions, empty sounds to which
117	☒2 3	We join no feeling and attach no form,
118	☒2 3	As if the soldier died without a wound;
119	☒2 3	As if the fibres of this godlike frame
120	☒2 3	Were gor'd without a pang: as if the wretch,
121	☒2 3	Who fell in battle doing bloody deeds,
122	☒2 3	Pass'd off to heaven, *translated* and not kill'd;
123	☒2 3	As tho' he had no wife to pine for him,
124	☒2 3	No God to judge him!—Therefore evil days
125	☒2 3	Are coming on us, O my countrymen!
126	☒2 3	And what if all-avenging Providence,
127	☒2 3	Strong and retributive, should make us know
128	☒2 3	The meaning of our words, force us to feel
129	☒2 3	The desolation and the agony
130a	☒2 3	Of our fierce doings?—

[*Line-space*]

130b	☐	Spare us yet a while,
131	☐	Father and God! O spare us yet a while!
132	☒3	O let not English women drag their flight
	3	speed
133	☐	Fainting beneath the burden of their babes,
134	☒2 3	Of the sweet infants, that but yesterday
	2 3	who
135	*1 2 4–9*	Laugh'd at the breast! Sons, brothers, husbands, all
	1	Bosom!—
	2	Husbands, fathers,
	3	Smiled	Brothers,
136	☐	Who ever gaz'd with fondness on the forms,
137	☒1 2	Which grew up with you round the same fire side,
	1 2	That
138	☐	And all who ever heard the sabbath bells
139	☒2 3 8	Without the infidel's scorn, make yourselves pure!
	2	stand forth! be men!
	3	make yourselves strong,
	8	infidels's	pure!
140	☒2 3	Stand forth! be men! repel an impious foe,
	2	Make yourselves strong!
	3	Stand forth, be men,	race,
141	☒2	Impious and false, a light yet cruel race,
	2	and
142	☒6–9	That laugh away all virtue, mingling mirth
	6–9	Who
143	☐	With deeds of murder; and still promising
144	☐	Freedom, themselves too sensual to be free,
145	☐	Poison life's amities, and cheat the heart
146	☐	Of Faith and quiet Hope, and all that soothes
147	☒3	And all that lifts the spirit! Stand we forth;
	3	ye
148	☐	Render them back upon th' insulted ocean,

149	⊠*3*	And let them toss as idly on it's waves,
	3	float
150	*1 2 4 5*	As the vile sea-weeds, which some mountain blast
	1 3	Sea weed th
	2 6–9	some
151	⊠*1 3*	Swept from our shores! And O! may we return
	1 3	Sweeps
152	*1 2 4–9*	Not with a drunken triumph, but with fear,
	1 2	awe
	3	in
153	⊠*3*	Repenting of the wrongs, with which we stung
	3	Repentant
154a	⊠*3*	So fierce a foe to frenzy!
	3	race

[*Line-space*]

154b	☐	I have told,
155	⊠*3*	O Britons! O my brethren! I have told
	3	men of England! Brothers!
156	*1 2 4–9*	Most bitter truth, but without bitterness.
	1 2 3	Truths
157	☐	Nor deem my zeal or factious or mistim'd;
158	⊠*2*	For never can true courage dwell with them,
	2	freedom
159	☐	Who, playing tricks with conscience, dare not look
160	⊠*2*	At their own vices. We have been too long
	2	At their own vices. [*incomplete line*]
161	⊠*2*	Dupes of a deep delusion! Some, belike,
162	⊠*2 3*	Groaning with restless enmity, expect
	3	Restless in enmity, have thought all change
162.1.1	*2*	[*incomplete line*] Fondly some expect
163	⊠*2 3*	All change from change of constituted power:
	2	delegated
	3	Involv'd in constituted
164	⊠*2 3*	As if a government had been a robe,
	2 3	were but
165	*1 2 4–9*	On which our vice and wretchedness were tagg'd
	1	Misery
	2	To crimes mis'ries affix'd,
	3	On Vice Wretchedness sewn
166	⊠*2*	Like fancy-points and fringes, with the robe
	2	fringe or epaulet, and
167	⊠*2 3*	Pull'd off at pleasure. Fondly these attach
	2	Others, the mean time,
	3	Pull'd off at pleasure. [*incomplete line*]
168	⊠*2 3*	A radical causation to a few
169	⊠*2 3*	Poor drudges of chastising Providence,
170	⊠*2 3*	Who borrow all their hues and qualities
171	⊠*2 3*	From our own folly and rank wickedness,

172	*1 2 4–6*	Which gave them birth, and nurse them. Others, meanwhile,
	1	meantime
	3	[*incomplete line*] others, meantime,
	7–9	nursed Others, meanwhile,
173	☐	Dote with a mad idolatry; and all,
174	⊠2	Who will not fall before their images,
	2	bow their heads, and close their eyes,
175	⊠2	And yield them worship, they are enemies
	2	worship bluntly—these
176	⊠2	Ev'n of their country!—Such have I been deem'd.
	2	they deem'd *me*.
177	*1–9*	But, O dear Britain! O my mother Isle!
	1	~~Broth~~itain!
	2	Briton!
178	*1 2 4–9*	Needs must thou prove a name most dear and holy
	1 2 3	be
179	☐	To me, a son, a brother, and a friend,
180	⊠3	A husband and a father! who revere
	3	Parent,
181	⊠2	All bonds of natural love, and find them all
	2	natural bonds of
182	⊠2 3	Within the limits of thy rocky shores.
	2 3	circle
183	*1–9*	O ⟵—native⟶ Britain! O my mother Isle!
	1	~~native~~ dear dear
	2	⟵—native⟶ Briton!
184	⊠2 3	How should'st thou prove aught else but dear and holy
	2	could'st be
	3	should'st
185	⊠2 3	To me, who from thy lakes and mountain-hills,
	2	brooks
	3	seas rocky shores,
186	*1 2 4–9*	Thy clouds, thy quiet dales, thy rocks, and seas,
	1 2	quiet Fields, thy Clouds, thy
	3	streams and wooded Hills
187	☐	Have drunk in all my intellectual life,
188	☐	All sweet sensations, all ennobling thoughts,
189	☐	All adoration of the God in nature,
190	☐	All lovely and all honourable things,
191	☐	Whatever makes this mortal spirit feel
192	☐	The joy and greatness of it's future being?
193	☐	There lives nor form nor feeling in my soul
194	☐	Unborrow'd from my country! O divine
195	☐	And beauteous island, thou hast been my sole
196	☐	And most magnificent temple, in the which
197	☐	I walk with awe, and sing my stately songs,
198a	⊠3	Loving the God that made me!—
	3	who

[*Line-space*]

198b	⊠*2 3*	May my fears,
199	⊠*1 2 3*	My filial fears, be vain! and may the vaunts
	1	Vaunt,
200	⊠*2 3*	And menace of the vengeful enemy
201	⊠*2 3*	Pass like the gust, that roar'd and died away
202	⊠*2 3*	In the distant tree, which heard, and only heard;
203	⊠*2 2 3*	In this low dell bow'd not the delicate grass.
	2	mov'd
204	⊠*2 3*	But now the gentle dew-fall sends abroad
205	⊠*2 3*	The fruitlike perfume of the golden furze:
206	⊠*2 3*	The light has left the summit of the hill,
207	⊠*1 2 3*	Tho' still a sunny gleam lies beautiful
	1	Glǽeam
208	*1 1 2*	On the long-ivied beacon.—Now, farewell,
	4–9	Aslant the ivied
209	⊠*2 3*	Farewell, awhile, O soft and silent spot!
210	⊠*2 3*	On the green sheep-track, up the heathy hill,
211	⊠*2 3*	Homeward I wind my way; and lo! recall'd
212	⊠*2 2 3*	From bodings, that have well nigh wearied me,
	2	well nigh have
213	⊠*2 3*	I find myself upon the brow, and pause
214	*1 2 4–9*	Startled! And after lonely sojourning
	1	For
215	*1 1 2 4 5*	In such a quiet and surrounded scene,
	6–9	nook,
216	*1 2 4–9*	This burst of prospect, here the shadowy main,
	1	(here *there*
217	*1 2 4–9*	Dim-tinted, there the mighty majesty
	1	*here*
218	⊠*2 3*	Of that huge ampitheatre of rich
219	⊠*2 3*	And elmy fields, seems like society,
220	⊠*2 3*	Conversing with the mind, and giving it
221	⊠*2 2 3*	A livelier impulse, and a dance of thought;
	2	←a→
222	⊠*2 3*	And now, beloved STOWEY! I behold
223	⊠*2 3*	Thy church-tower, and (methinks) the four huge elms
224	⊠*2 3*	Clust'ring, which mark the mansion of my friend;
225	⊠*2 3*	And close behind them, hidden from my view,
226	⊠*2 3*	Is my own lowly cottage, where my babe
227	⊠*2 3*	And my babe's mother dwell in peace! With light
228	*1 2 4–9*	And quicken'd footsteps thitherward I tend,
	1	bend,
229	⊠*2 3*	Rememb'ring thee, O green and silent dell!
230	⊠*2 3*	And grateful, that by nature's quietness
231	⊠*2 3*	And solitary musings all my heart
232	⊠*2 3*	Is soften'd, and made worthy to indulge
233	⊠*2 3*	Love, and the thoughts that yearn for human kind.

233⁺ *1 4 5*   Nether Stowey, April 20th, 1798.
     2   17**8**
    6–9   28th, 1798.

title. 2 Fears in Solitude | Written, April 1798, during the alarms of an Invasion •
5 Written, April 1798, *during the Alarms of an Invasion.* • *7* FEARS IN SOLI-
TUDE. | Written in April 1798, during the Alarm of an Invasion. • *8* FEARS IN
SOLITUDE. | Written in April, 1798, during the Alarm of an Invasion. • *9* FEARS
IN SOLITUDE. | WRITTEN IN APRIL, 1798, DURING THE ALARM | OF
AN INVASION.   **1.** 1 Spot • *6–9* spot,   1 Hills!— • *6–9* hills,   **2.** 1 Dell!
O'er • *6–9* dell! O'er   **3.** 1 Sky-lark *7–9* poised *6–9* himself.   **4.** 1 Hills
1 Slope   **5.** 1 Covering   **6.** 1 Furze,   **7.** 1 profusely! But • *7–9* profusely:
but 1 Dell,   **8.** *7–9* Bathed 1 *6–9* delicate   **9.** 1 Corn-field, • *6–9* corn-field,
1 Flax   **10.** *6–9* When, through 1 Stalks 1 eve   **11.** 1 *6–8* Sunshine
1 Light.   **12.** 1 O— • *6–9* Oh! 1 tis 1 Nook, • *6–9* nook!   **13.** 1 2 all
1 methinks 1 love, 1 He,   **14.** 1 Man, *6–9* who, 1 *y*Years • *6–9* years,
15. 1 Folly, • *6–9* folly,   **16.** 1 *m*Manhood 1 wise. • *6–9* wise!   **17.** 1 *he*
1 Fern *7–9* withered 1 Heath   **18.** 1 *S*singing Lark, that • *6–9* singing-lark
(that   **19.** 1 *m*Minstrelsy 1 Solitude 1 best, • *6–9* best,)   **20.** 1 Sun • *6–8* Sun,
1 Air • *6–8* Air,   **21.** 1 Influences 1 *f*Frame,   **22.** 1 He • *6–9* he, 1 Feelings, •
2 feelings 1 Thoughts   **23.** 1 *j*Joy,   **24.** 1 Meanings 1 Forms 1 Nature:
25. 1 Senses 1 *6–9* wrapt   **26.** *6–9* half sleep, 1 Worlds,   **27.** 1 singing
Lark! • *6 7* singing-lark, • *8 9* singing-lark;   **28.** 1 singest, 1 Angel 1 Clouds.— •
6–9 clouds!   **29.** 1 Thing   **30.** 1 Man   **31.** 1 Calmness,   **32.** 1 Brethren, •
4 5 brethren,— 1 *6–9* God!   **33.** 1 Thing   **34.** 1 Heart, 1 *He*   **35.** 1 Uproar
4 stirrin   **36.** 2 that Way 2 Hills—   **37.** 1 INVASION, and • *7* Invasion,
amd 1 Thunder 1 Shout   **38.** 1 Crash 1 Onset—Fear 1 Rage • *6–9* rage,
39. 1 *4–6* undetermin'd 1 Conflict—   **40.** *4–9* Even 1 now 2 perchance
1 Isle— • *6–9* isle: **41.** 1 Screams 1 *6–8* Sun!   **42.** *6–9* Oh! 1 Countrymen!
43. 1 grievously   **44.** 1 tyrannous! 1 East 1 West   **45.** 1 Groan 2 6–
9 Heaven!   **46.** *6–9* us;   **47.** *6–8* Sons   **48.** 2 bretheren! • *6–8* Brethren!
6–9 Like   **49.** *7–9* Steamed   **50.** *7–9* Even 2 so   **54.** 1 Meanwhile
1 home   **60.1.** 1 Thirst   **61.1.** 1 Cup 1 Wealth,   **54.1.1.** 2 selfish
1 Race,   **56.** *7–9* Engulfed *9* courts, committees, institutions,   **57.** *9* societies,
58. *9* guild,   **59.** *9* benefit-club   **62.** 1 *6* honorable   **63.** 1 Freedom •
6–9 freedom 1 Man's Life • *6–9* man's life   **64.** 1 Gold, • 2 gold 1 Market!
1 Words   **65.** 1 *6–9* Christian 1 Promise, Words   **66.** 1 Destruction, •
2 *4* destruction *5* preach d • *7 9* preached, • *8* preached   **67.** *7–9* muttered
1 Tones 1 *6–9* proclaim   **68.** 1 Trade— • *4–9* trade: **69.** 1 Scoffers
1 *6–9* indolent   **70.** 1 *f*Falsehoods • *6–9* falsehoods *6–9* know 1 Truth.
71. *6–9* Oh! 1 Life   **72.** 1 Instrument,   **73.** 1 Oaths, 1 break. • *4 5* break: •
6–9 break;   **74.** 1 swear, 1 *6–9* all and   **75.** 1 Wharf, 1 & Justice-court, •
6–9 and justice-court;   **76.** 1 swear— *6–9* bribed,   **78.** *6–9* man 6–
9 young;   **79.** 1 Perjury   **80.** 1 Faith 1 reel—   **81.** 1 Juggler's Charm;
6–9 and, 1 Joy   **82.** 1 Hiding-place, • *6–9* hiding-place,   **83.** 1 Portentous
Sight! • *6–9* (Portentous sight!) 1 Owlet • *8 9* owlet *9* Atheism,   **83.** 1 Wings
85. 1 Lids &   **86.** 1 2 *4–9* And 1 *6–8* Sun 1 Heaven • 2 *4 5* heaven, •
6–9 Heaven,   **87a.** *4 5* out 1 *4–9* "Where 1 it?—   **87b.** 1 Peace, •
6 peace;   **88.** 1 Peace *7–9* preserved 1 Fleets 1 Seas,   **89.** *4* lov'd, • *7–*

9 loved   **90.** 1 Warwhoop, • *5* war whoop, 1 War!   **92.** 2 *7–9* Its 1 Workings, Famine • *4 5* workings (famine, • *6–9* workings, (famine 1 Plague,   **93.** 1 Battle 1 Siege 1 Flight 2 *6–9* through 1 wintry Snows, • *6* wintry snows,) • *7–9* wintry-snows,)   **94.** 1 People,   **95.** 1 War & ƀBloodshed, • *6–9* war and bloodshed; 1 Sports   **96.** *6–9* for 1 Thing   **97.** 1 & 1 Combatants! 1 *6–9* No 1 *6–8* Guess   **98.** 1 Wrong   **99.** 1 Speculation 1 Contingency   **100.** 1 & dim   **101.** 1 Cause; & • *6–9* cause; and *6–9* forth,   **102.** 1 Stuff'd • *7–9* (Stuf-fed 1 Preamble, 1 Names,   **103.** 1 Adjurations 1 Heaven • *6–9* Heaven,) **104.** 1 Mandates 1 Death   **105.** 1 Thousands & 1 Thousands!—   *4 5* boys 1 & Girls,   **106.** 1 Women • *6–9* women, 1 Child   **107.** 1 Insect's Leg, • 2 insects leg, 1 War,   **108.** 1 Amusement 1 Morning Meal. • *6–9* morning-meal! **109.** 1 Wretch,   **110.** 1 Curses,   **111.** *6–9* Heavenly   **112.** 1 Phraseman, **113.** 1 Victories & Defeats,   **114.** 1 Terms 1 Fratricide, • *6–9* fratricide; **115.** 1 Tongues   **116.** 1 Abstractions, 1 Sounds   **117.** 1 Feeling 1 Form, • *6–9* form!   **118.** 1 Soldier 1 Wound.—   **119.** 1 Fibres 1 Frame   **120.** *7–9* gored 1 pang, • *6–9* pang; 1 Wretch   **121.** 1 Battle, • 2 *6–9* battle, 1 Deeds,   **122.** *7–9* Passed 1 *4–9* Heaven, 1 *6–9* translated 1 & 1 kill'd, • *6* kill'd;— • *7* killed;— • *8 9* killed;   **123.** 2 *6–9* though 1 Wife   **124.** *6–9* him! Therefore, 1 Evil Days   **125.** 1 Countrymen!   **127.** 1 &   **129.** 1 & **130a.** 1 Doings?— • *4–6* doings? • *7–9* doings!   **130b.** 1 2 *4–9* awhile, • *3* awhile! **131.** 1 &   *3* God, *6 7* Oh! • *8 9* O!   ⊠*1 3* awhile! • *3* awhile.   **132.** *6–9* Oh!   1 *2 3* Women 1 Flight, • *2* flight,   **133.** 1 Burthen • 2 *3 6–9* burthen 1 *3* Babes,   **134.** 1 Infants • *2* infants • *3* Infants,   **135.** *7–9* Laughed 2 bosom. • *3* bosom! 1 Brothers, 1 Husbands,   **136.** *3 7–9* gazed 1 Forms • *2 3 6–9* forms **137.** 1 Fire-side, • *2* fireside. • *3 6–9* fire-side,   **138.** 1 All • *2* all, 1 *3* Sabbath Bells • *6–9* sabbath-bells   **139.** 1 *2* Infidel's • *3* Infidels' 1 Scorn, • *2 3* scorn; 1 pure,   **140.** 1 forth, 1 men, *1* Foe,   **141.** 1 & false, 1 Race • *3* race **142.** 1 Virtue, 1 Mirth   **143.** 1 Murder, • *3* murder! 1 &   **145.** 1 *3* Life's 1 Amities & • *3* amities and 1 Heart • *3–5* heart,   **146.** 2 *6–9* faith 1 & quiet Hope • 2 *6–9* and quiet hope, • *3* and quiet Hope 1 & all 1 sooths **147.** 1 Spirit!—   1 *3* forth, • *2* forth!   **148.** *6–9* the 1 Insulted Ocean, • *3* insulted ocean   **149.** ⊠*1* 1 *6* its   ⊠*1 2 4 5* waves   **150.** 2 *3 6–9* sea-weed, *3* the 1 Mountain Blast • *6–9* mountain-blast   **151.** 1 Shores—and • *3* Shores! And 1 o! • *6–9* oh! 2 return,   **152.** 1 Triumph, 2 *3* awe,   **153.** 1 Wrongs, • 2 *6–9* wrongs   **154a.** 1 Frenzy!— • *2* frenzy. • *3* Frenzy.   **155.** 1 2 Britons, 1 o 1 Brethren, • 2 Brethren! • 2 bretheren!   **156.** 2 truths,   **157.** 1 Zeal 1 2 mistim'd: • *3* mistimed: • *6* mis-tim'd; • *7–9* mis-timed;   **158.** 1 *3* Courage 2 *3* them   **159.** 1 *3* Who 1 Tricks 1 *3* Conscience   **160.** 1 Vices.— **161.** 1 Delusion— • *3* delusion. 2 Some   **162.** 1 Enmity   **163.** 1 Constituted 1 Power • 2 *3* power, • *6–9* power;   **164.** 1 *3 6–9* Government 1 *3* Robe • 2 robe   **165.** 1 Vice & *7–9* tagged   **166.** 1 Fancy-points & Fringes, 1 *3* Robe   **167.** *7–9* Pulled   **168.** 1 Causation   **169.** 1 Drudges 1 Providence **170.** 1 Hues & Qualities   **171.** 1 Folly & 1 Wickedness   **172.** 1 Birth & • 2 *4 6–9* birth and 1 them!— 1 *Others*   **173.** 2 Doat 1 Idolatry, • 2 idolat y, • *3* Idolatry! ⊠*1 2 4 5* all   **174.** 1 *3* Images   **175.** 1 Worship, 1 Enemies   **176.** ⊠*1 2 4 5* Even 1 Country!— • *2* country. • *3* Country! • *6–9* country! 1 Such have *1* been deem'd. • *3 Such have I been deem'd.* • *6* Such have I been deem'd— • *7–9* Such have I been deemed—   **177.** 1 *2 3* But *3* O! *3 6–9* Mother 2 isle!   **178.** 1 &   **179.** *3* me 1 *3* Son, 1 *3* Brother,

1 & 1 *3* Friend, **180.** 1 Husband & • *2 6–9* husband, and • *3* Husband, and
1 Father, • *2* father, **181.** 1 *3* Bonds 1 Love & • *3* Love, and **182.** 1 Limits
1 Shores! • *3* shores! **183.** 1 *3 6–9* Mother 2 isle! **184.** *6–9* shouldst
1 [?]aught 1 & **185.** 1 Lakes & Mountain Hills, • *2* brooks and mountain
hills, **186.** *2 3* fields, 2 clouds, 1 Rocks, • *6–9* rocks 1 Seas, **187.** 1 drank
1 Life, **189.** 1 Adoration • *2* adorati n 1 *6 7* Nature, **190.** 1 lovely,
1 *3 6* honorable 1 Things, **191.** 1 Spirit **192.** 1 Joy & Greatness
2 *6–9* its • *3* its' 1 *3* Being! • *2* being. **193.** 1 *3* Form 1 *3* Feeling
1 *3* Soul **194.** *3 7–9* Unborrowed 1 Country! • *2 6–9* country. • *3* Country.
195. 1 *3* Island! • *2* Island, • *6–9* island! **196.** 1 *3* Temple, **197.** 1 &
1 Songs • *3* songs **198a.** *3* God, 1 *6–9* me! • *2* me. • *3* me." **198b.** 1 Fears,
199. 1 Fears, 1 vain/ & **200.** 1 Menace 1 Enemy, **201.** 1 Gust 7–
9 roared 1 & **202.** 1 Tree, • *6–9* tree: 1 heard & 1 *6–9* only heard • *4 5* only
heard, **203.** 1 Dell • *6–9* dell, *7–9* bowed 1 Grass. **204.** 1 Dewfall
205. *6–9* fruit-like 1 Perfume 1 Furze: **206.** 1 Light 1 Hill **207.** *6–*
9 Though *7–9* beautiful, **208.** 1 Beacon.— • *6–9* beacon. 1 *2 6–9* Now
209. 1 Farewell 1 & 1 Spot! **210.** 1 Sheeptrack 1 Hill **211.** 1 & • *6* and,
7–9 recalled **212.** 1 Bodings, • *4–9* bodings **213.** 1 Brow, & • *4 5* brow and
214. 1 Startled!— 1 Sojourning **215.** 1 & 1 Scene **216.** 1 Burst 1 Prospect
1 Main • *6–8* Main, **217.** *6–9* Dim tinted, 1 Majesty **218.** 1 Ampitheatre
219. 1 Fields) • *6 8* Fields, 1 Society, • *6–9* society— **220.** 1 Mind,
221. 1 Impulse • *6–9* impulse 1 Thought. • *6–9* thought! **222.** 2 now *6–*
9 Stowey! **223.** 1 Church-tower, & (methinks) • *6 7 9* church-tower, and,
methinks, • *8* church-tower, and, methinks 1 Elms **224.** *6–9* Clustering,
1 Friend. **226.** 1 Cottage, 1 Babe **227.** 1 Babe's Mother 1 peace. *4 5* with
228. *4 5 7–9* quickened 1 Footsteps *6* tend. **229.** *6–9* Remembering 1 &
1 Dell! **230.** 1 grateful 1 Nature's Quietness **231.** 1 Musings • *6–9* musings,
1 Heart **232.** 1 *7–9* softened, 1 & **233.** 2 Love 1 & 1 Kind. • 2 kind
233⁺. *4 5 Nether-Stowey*, April • *6 9* Nether Stowey, | April 2 20th. • *4 5* 20th. • *7* 28th.

title. The lists of Contents in PR *7 8* give "Tears in Solitude", a mistake shared by the
Microscope reprinting of PR *1*.

33–4. *PW* (JDC) 610B reports that in Stuart M. Samuel's copy of PR *6* (since lost) C
revised the lines to conform to the text of PR *7–9*.

41⁺. Line-space in MS 1.

46–54. In MS 1 line 45 is followed by a broken rule and the phrase "Desunt ali-
qua" ("Some [words] are missing"); the text resumes, after another rule, with line 54
"Meanwhile".

106. PR *8* women,] The comma is deleted in JG's (?) copy.

113. MS 2 technical] Written over an erasure.

120. PR *6* gor'd] C added in the margin of the proof copy at Yale: "To *gore* is to
wound so as the same to mangle—hence applied to a a bull's horn, &c".

121. MS 2 bloody deeds,] Written over an erasure.

124–5. Thomasina Dennis quoted the phrase "Evil days O my Country men are
coming on us" in a letter of 15 Aug 1798. See Francis Doherty "Some First-hand
Impressions of Coleridge in the Correspondence of Thomasin Dennis and Davies Giddy"
Neophilologus LXIII (Apr 1979) 300–8 at 303; cf R. S. Woof "Coleridge and Thomasina
Dennis" *UTQ* XXXII (1962) 37–54 at 42–3.

133. PR *6* burthen] The Yale proof copy originally read "burden", which C corrected with the exclamation: "Why burden instead of burthen! Why, the flat dull german *d* instead of the soft *th*, the pride of English and Greek orthoëpy? I never even in common talk say burden; but always *burthen*. Because of the copy ⌜ . . . .⌝" (the conclusion of C's remark has been trimmed away).

139. PR *8* infidels's] The first "s" is deleted in JG's (?) copy.

143–7. Quoted in *SM* (*CC*) 22.

160. vices.] The first part of the extract from PR *2* ends here.

167–72. PR *2* omits lines 168–72 with no indication that any text has been excluded. The incomplete lines 167, 172 in PR *3* are preceded and followed by rows of dots. In MS 1 line 172 is preceded by a line-space.

176. PR *6–9* Such] Preceded by a line-space.

198a. PR *2* me. • PR *3* me."] PR *2 3* end here.

199–203. Quoted (var) (e.g. with "Vaunt" for "vaunts") in a letter to Mariana Starke of 28 [=30] Oct 1819 (HEHL HM 12100; *CL* IV 963).

202, 203. In Sir George Beaumont's copy of PR *1* C deleted the semicolon at the end of line 202 and inserted a comma after line 203 "dell".

203⁺. Line-space in TEXTS 1 *6–9*.

215. PR *6* nook] The Yale proof copy originally read "scene," which C corrected with the following comment: "*Scene* should never be used but either *properly* or by metaphorical allusion to the Theatre. Mr Pope was the first to introduce this with 500 other barbarisms in his Homer. At least, it is only in Dryden's most careless verses that he has used it as an idle Synomen of Place."

222. MS 1 Stowey] Written larger, perhaps to be read as bold.

176. CHRISTABEL

A. DATE

Feb–Apr 1798; Aug–Oct 1800. C said several times that Part I was written in 1797 (*CL* IV 601: to Lord Byron 22 Oct 1815; 1816 Preface; *C Life*—G—280–1). There are parallels and anticipations dating from late 1797 and even from the year before (*CN* I 161g, 170, 188, 216, 316, etc and nn). None the less, the number of exact coincidences between Part I and entries in DW's journal for the first three months of 1798 (*DWJ* I 4, 5, 8–9, 11–12), taken along with C's literary interests at that time (specifically his interest in Matthew Lewis's *Castle Spectre* and Bishop Percy's *Reliques*: *CL* I 378–9: to WW [23] Jan 1798) suggest a later date.

Work must have proceeded alongside the enlargement of **161** *The Rime of the Ancient Mariner* after the 340-line version had been completed—i.e. after 18 Feb (*CL* I 387)—the theme of polar guardian spirits being shared. Work on *Christabel* intensified when the enlarged *Ancient Mariner* was complete—i.e. after 23 Mar (*DWJ* I 13)—and Part I was well in hand during the next two months, before the Wordsworths departed from Alfoxden in late Jun 1798 (Reed I 241). WW refers to C reading it, along with the *Ancient Mariner*, "That summer . . . Upon smooth Quantock's airy ridge" (*Prelude*—1850—XIV 395–6). C's retrospective statement that the quarrel with Charles Lloyd prevented his finishing the poem (*CN* III 4006 f 23ʳ) tends to confirm the date Mar–May 1798, even while it confuses this time with recollections of Sept–Nov 1797 (cf **178** *Kubla Khan* VAR sec A). The claim that the beginnings date from 1797 might reflect his sense of the poem as a contribution to *LB*, differing in kind from WW's contribution—a difference which had been broached in Nov 1797 (Reed I 210)—or his sense of themes carried forward from **155** *Continuation of "The Three Graves"*.

Carlyon I 138–9 records C explicating part of *Christabel* at Göttingen early in 1799; and RS requested it, on C's return, for publication in his *Annual Anthology* (*S Letters*—Curry—I 203; cf 207). RS's request might have prompted C to return to the poem in Oct–Nov (*CL* I 540: to RS 15 Oct 1799; 545: to RS 10 Nov [1799]): the word *tairn* (line 306) is specifically a Lake District word, and the note on it in MS 2 relates to places visited on the tour C took with WW in Nov 1799 (Reed I 277–81); see also the word *fell* in line 310. However, by Dec C appears to have put the poem aside again (*CL* I 549: to RS [19 Dec 1799]). But there is in fact no certainty that C worked on the poem at this time. If analogues are evidence, lines 315–18 might reflect HC's being quieted by the moon earlier, in autumn 1797 (*CN* I 219), or DC's reaction to wind later, in autumn 1800 (*CN* I 835). The interest in tarns could also be taken to reflect C's later walks during Aug 1800 (e.g. *CN* I 793, 797); the note in MS 2 appears to have been added at the time the transcript was made.

The next stage of the evolution of the poem is unclear in several respects, probably because C was uncertain about its development himself. He was in London with CL from Dec 1799 to the end of Mar 1800, and the poem was on his mind (see *CN* I 720, 753n). He left behind an incomplete copy of Part I, and CL's repeated request for the missing passages (*LL*—M—I 200, 216) shows that he had no idea, up to the end of Jul, that C intended to publish the poem shortly; from his later comment to JG (*C Life*—G—302–3) it appears that C gave him no inkling that he intended to add a second part. RS wrote from Lisbon in May (*S Life*—CS—II 65), asking for a copy in a way that has similar implications. Meanwhile, when C was in Bristol in May he made arrangements with Humphry Davy for Davy to see a new edition of *LB* through the press (Cottle *E Rec* II 46; *CL* I 588. to W. Godwin 21 May 1800; etc). It would appear from later letters, which assume that the printing of *Christabel* might have begun (*WL*—E rev—302; *CL* I 649: to H. Davy 2 Dec 1800), that C either left behind copy for *Christabel* with Davy or had it sent to Davy from Keswick. In either case, it is clear that Davy knew only Part I of the poem (*CL* I 549; Davy to C 26 Nov 1800, at PML, cited by Reed II 65–6n).

C told Josiah Wedgwood that he took up *Christabel* again immediately he arrived in the north (*CL* I 643: 1 Nov 1800). Part II is likely to have been written at one stretch during the last two weeks of Aug 1800, at least in its first form, and DW records a reading at the very end of the month (*DWJ* I 58). C spoke of the poem to J. W. Tobin, during Sept, in terms which suggest he had drafted a continuation beyond Part I (*CL* I 623: 17 Sept 1800), and at the end of Sept he told Daniel Stuart that the poem was to be published soon (*CL* I 627: [28 Sept 1800]). He read Part II, in what was undoubtedly a revised and polished version, to WW and DW on 4 Oct and again on 5 Oct (*DWJ* I 64; cf *CN* I 821). Although there is no certain evidence that he read William Hutchinson's *History of the County of Cumberland* (2 vols Carlisle 1794) before Jul 1802 (*CN* I 1205, 1206), Hutchinson appears to have supplied the name of Sir Leoline and perhaps of Geraldine (see vol I lines 6EC, 80EC, 407EC), perhaps via WW.

What happened next marks the beginning of a long interval in the evolution of the poem. On 6 Oct 1800 it was decided that *Christabel* had so developed in size and changed in character that it was more suitable for separate publication, and should therefore be dropped from the *LB* printing (*DWJ* I 64; *CL* I 631: to H. Davy 9 Oct 1800; *WL—E* rev—304, 309). C agreed to the decision, but it removed the sense of support and encouragement he needed to continue, and even while he told friends like Davy and TP that he was busy with it (*CL* I 631, 634: to TP [c 11 Oct 1800]), he exaggerated the amount he was doing and in fact did less. This pattern of behaviour was repeated and confirmed in succeeding months and years. C's publicly expressed plans for completing the poem became more grandiose (*CL* I 649; II 662: to TP 7 [=6] Jan 1801; 707: to TP [16 Mar 1801]; 715: to W. Godwin 25 Mar 1801; 716: to T. N. Longman 26 [=27] Mar 1801; *WL—E* rev—324), and his privately expressed resolutions to pick up the threads became less frequent and more forlorn (see e.g. *CN* I 1577 f 53ᵛ). He recited the poem on numerous occasions, and it circulated in ms and clandestine versions, but in a form essentially the same as the text which C had reached in 1801 (MS 2 below).

Such was the situation when Byron intervened to encourage the publication of *Christabel* in Oct 1815 (*BL&J* IV 318–19; cf *CL* IV 601–6: to Lord Byron 22 Oct 1815; *BL&J* IV 321–2, 331–2). Although C told Byron that he had written two Books "and a part of the third Book" (*CL* IV 601), no portion of the latter has been traced or identified. A Conclusion to Part II was added to the ms versions, by drawing on verses written in a letter to RS of 6 May 1801 (MS 1 below). It has thematic and poematic connections—for example, its rhymes echo the description of Sir Leoline's speech—although C himself recognised that the connection needed to be enlarged upon (*CL* IV 634: to J. Murray 23 Apr 1816). The addition is *ad hoc*, and C's concern with the poem continued for some months after publication, as the number of annotated copies shows. Thereafter, although further changes were introduced in later years, they are either minor or tangential.

When C's thoughts returned to composing the third part of the poem in Oct 1823 (*CN* IV 5032), it was with the proviso "Were I free to do so." There is a possibility that *Christabel* is the "Ballad" he promised JG he would finish in Oct 1824, but other interpretations of what C meant are equally plausible (*CL* V 375: to J. Gillman [6 Oct 1824]; cf **598.X1** *Ballad*). The final version of the gloss added to the Ramsgate copy of PR *1* in 1824 is, for all its interest, a commentary on an abandoned poem.

B. TEXTS

1. PML MA 1848 (37). Conclusion to Part II, transcribed in an als to RS, 6 May 1801 (*CL* II 728).

The unheaded lines are not part of any ms version or copy thereof: MSS 2–6 below comprise only Part I, the Conclusion to Part I, and Part II. It would seem that they were not taken into the poem until shortly before publication (see *CL* IV 634 and sec A above).

2. VCL S MS 1. Hand-made album of 46 folios of blue-grey paper, the last 8 blank; each leaf c 16×20 cm; wm Britannia in oval; chain-lines 2.6 cm; written on rectos only, except for ff 7ᵛ and 16ᵛ. The folios were sewn together with coarse thread before being sewn into a notebook whose cover measured 17.0×20.8 cm (since removed). Transcript in C's hand, made for SH. Facsimile edition by EHC (1907).

The sonnet on the inside front cover (**295** *Sonnet to Asra*) is on white paper, with a large double oval wm and chain-lines 2.6 cm apart; it was once folded in four and was pasted in later. There is also an inscription from Dora Quillinan to SC, and Edith C's signature, and the whole is contained in a handsome green cover of later date.

The date of the transcript must be conjectural, connected with the relation between this ms and MSS 3 4. One possibility is the period of C's visit to the Hutchinsons, 16 or 17 Jul–23 Aug 1801, or shortly thereafter. Or C might have left it with SH on his way from Keswick to London, on 13–14 Nov 1801. KC notes SC's hand in N 21, on the same page used by C to draft lines later used in the Preface to *Christabel* (*CN* I 1003 and 1007nn), and this strengthens the case for the later date.

There is a copy of MS 2 in the Bodleian Library (MS Eng poet e 26), but it has no textual significance. The paper bears an 1812 wm, and the copy was probably made before publication in 1816. The date at the end, "Grasmere Augᵗ 18ᵗʰ 1800", might refer to the conjectural date of composition, and has been tampered with. It appears to be in the hand of SH's niece, Dora W, the initials "S.T.C" on p 15 and an insertion on p 27 (line 493 "Flood,") being in SH's hand. The copy is endorsed with the signature of William Jackson, son of the rector of Grasmere, tutor of George Hutchinson and Johnny Wordsworth, and later provost of The Queen's College, Oxford, in whose family it remained until 1919. Perhaps it was a writing exercise and/or a gift: William Jackson was well liked by the Wordsworth household, and not least by SH, who called him "Mentor". A cartoon head of WW in pencil hovers above the opening line, and suggests the atmosphere in which the copy was given and received. There are traces of pencil guidelines for the transcriber, and a page has been removed before the first page of text; possibly it contained a dedication. More than half the pages follow MS 2 page for page. It omits lines and phrases, and misspells, misreads, and changes others. The blotting of facing pages suggests that it was done hurriedly, and the flourish at the end suggests relief at a task completed. Some misreadings (e.g. at lines 590 and 601) conclusively prove that the copy derives from MS 2, although at line 559 it concurs with MS 4 in reading "seems".

The copy of MS 2 which fills the first half of a small paper-covered album at HRC (MS (Coleridge, S T) Works) likewise has no textual significance. It is in Mrs C's hand, on paper bearing a wm of Britannia in a circular frame, crowned, and the remaining material in the book (by HC, SC, and Mrs C) is dated variously 1816, 1824–30, and 1829. It is inaccurate in several respects (individual words, spellings, lack of punctuation), and it omits line 590 (which in MS 2 is difficult to read). Only line 277 might give pause, since the reading coincides with the printed version, and the fact that the wm suggests that the paper might date from before 1800. (According to a librarian at HRC, it most resembles W. A. Churchill *Watermarks in Paper*—Amsterdam 1935—No 232; but later analogues might well be found.)

3. DCL MS 15 = WW's "Christabel Notebook". The notebook is described by Reed I 322–5, II 615–16; the poem is written in from the end, on ff 89^r–88^v, 85^r–72^v (f 78^r is blank). DW transcribed *Christabel* up to line 294 (interrupted by some pages of WW poems); MH completed the transcript, apparently on the same occasion. Photographic reproduction of ff 89^r–88^v (= lines ⁻1.31–54) in Reynold Siemens *The Wordsworth Collection: A Catalogue of Dove Cottage Papers Facsimiles* (Edmonton 1971) pl IV.

Reed II 616 comments that because of MH's involvement the transcript is unlikely to have reached completion before 6 Nov 1801, unless, as seems improbable, C carried WW's notebook to Gallow Hill the previous summer. C arrived at Dove Cottage, probably with MH, on 6 Nov and departed on 9 Nov. Was the poem copied hurriedly by DW and MH on 7–8 Nov? It is possible that MS 3 somehow derives from a conflation of MS 2 and MS 4, possibly from dictation (see lines 25, 96; MH's share is significantly more careful with punctuation and capitalisation), in which case the question of the date is more open; but this is not likely.

The relation of MS 3 to MSS 2 and 4 is close but problematic. DW's transcript overlaps with MS 4 (only) at line 52, and MH's with MS 2 (only) at lines 444 and 559. A number of other readings are unique to this ms, but since a proportion are demonstrably erroneous it is impossible to tell what authority the remainder possess. Lines 220.1 and 397.1 indicate care over stanza divisions, and again might suggest dictation.

4. Yale MS Vault Shelves Coleridge. Seven elongated folios 13.0×31.9 cm; wm Britannia within oval, surmounted by crown; A BLACKWELL | & | G JONES | 1801; all but the last written on both sides, and numbered 1–13; page 2 is on the verso of page 1; pages 5 and 6 on the verso of pages 4 and 3; pages 10, 11, and 12 on the verso of pages 9, 8, and 7; and the verso of page 13 is

blank except for a "Morgan classification" number, added later and described below. Transcript in SH's hand. The pattern of pagination reveals the systematic way in which SH worked, as she warmed to her task, writing (after pages 1–2) in adjacent columns on the rectos and versos of larger sheets, which were subsequently divided.

The transcript is connected with MS 2 but has independent interest. There are a few pen trials in the margins ("Sara", "Thom‚as‚", "Mary"), which are identical with pen trials appearing on the margins of MS 2 in SH's hand; and the two versions are very close. None the less, MS 4 differs from MS 2 at line 52 in a way paralleled only by MS 3; at line 559 in a way paralleled only by Dora W's transcript of MS 2 (Bodleian) and PR *1–4*; and line 444 is unique. It appears to be a particularly careful and accurate transcript, and its peculiar variations are likely to possess authority. (The several occasions on which a wrong reading has been erased and the correct one written over it are not recorded below.)

The occasion and provenance of the transcript are almost straightforward, but not quite. Lady Beaumont's interest in the poem had been roused by hearing Scott recite it (*CL* IV 601: to Lord Byron 22 Oct 1815), and this might be the copy SH made for her, at C's request, in late Feb 1804 (*CL* II 1075: to J. Rickman [28 Feb 1804]; 1076: to Lady Beaumont 5 Mar 1804; 1094–5: to J. Rickman 17 Mar [1804]). Possibly SH had made the transcript some time before. It appears to have come into the possession of Mary Morgan (the wife of C's friend J. J. Morgan), since it bears on the verso of f 7 the Morgan "classification number" M. M. 28. If it is the transcript sent to Lady Beaumont, it is likely to have passed into the Morgans' hands after C's visit to Coleorton at Christmas 1806. The pages are numbered in a hand which wrote C's name on the first and "(last Page)" on the last, and which might belong to one of the Morgans or to Mary Morgan's sister, Charlotte Brent. It was perhaps the version "in the form and as far as it existed before my voyage to the Mediterranean" sent to Byron on 22 Oct 1815 (*CL* IV 602). Since it was owned in EHC's time by A. H. Hallam Murray (1854–1947), grandson of the publisher John Murray II, it is reasonable to assume that it is the same ms that Byron forwarded to Murray (*BL&J* IV 331–2), which was used—with alterations and the addition in proof of the Preface and Conclusion to Part II—as copy for PR *1* and which Murray did not return to Byron as requested.

5. Boston University (Special Collections). Pages 1–33 of an album made up of 41 numbered pages and 2 unnumbered blank leaves; each leaf measures 18.5×15.8 cm; wm Britannia | 1804; chain-lines 2.7 cm; written on both sides, parallel to the album hinge. Transcript in the hand of Sarah Stoddart. *Christabel* is followed by a transcript in another contemporary hand of **293** *Dejection: An Ode* and of WW's sonnet "I griev'd for Bonaparte". The cardboard cover (19.0×15.9 cm) is endorsed "Mr Coleridge's Gift at Parndon. Winter of 1806". There is an electrostatic copy in BM (RP 580 (3)).

Sarah Stoddart (1774–1840) was the sister of Dr John Stoddart, to whom C had recited his poem in Oct 1800 (*DWJ* I 69; see also sec C below). It has sometimes been assumed that she made a copy at this time, for Stoddart to read to Scott, but she did not accompany her brother to Grasmere. The copy must have been made some time between C's arrival in Malta during the summer of 1804 and the summer of the following year, when Sarah Stoddart left Malta, where her brother was then the King's and admiralty advocate, to care for her mother; the most likely date is Dec 1804–Feb 1805, when she is likely also to have transcribed **155** *Continuation of "The Three Graves"*.

The transcript is obviously painstaking but it is not altogether accurate. Despite its care over punctuation and capitalisation, it omits lines 160 and 458, and the variations in lines 102, 158, 349, 379, 380, 457, 485, and 602 are probably mistakes on Sarah Stoddart's part. The name Christabel appears to be written "Christobel", although the handwriting makes it slightly ambiguous. The latter spelling is found in several contemporary reviews and references; see also MS 6. The interest of the transcript lies in the fact that the version C took with him to Malta was essentially the same as MS 2, except for line 254 (where it coincides with MS 3) and line 579 (where it coincides with TEXTS 4 *1–4*).

C visited Parndon in Essex—the seat of William Smith (1756–1835), MP for Norwich—several times on his return from Malta, during Sept–Oct 1806. He brought with him "only two pocket-books" (*CL* II 1177: to RS 19 [=20] Aug 1806), but recovered more in a trunk bearing Thomas Russell's name just before his last visit to Parndon. The transcript might have been given to William Smith at this time, 9–10 Oct, but it is more likely that it was given to Mrs Clarkson. She had been staying with William Smith, had brought C to Parndon in the first place, and afterwards brought him backwards and forwards as he recovered his property (see *CL* II 1180, 1182: to Mrs C 16 Sept 1806; 1190: to Mrs C [9 Oct 1806]; 1193: to G. Fricker [9 Oct 1806]). She had a copy in her possession in 1811, which she read to HCR (*CRB* I 47; see sec C below).

CN II 2890 proves that C was thinking of Stoddart on this same, last visit in Oct 1806; and the talk of Scott's having stolen C's metrical thunder made the poem especially topical (see *CN* II 2880–2 and nn, 2900, 2915). C also reports Mrs Clarkson mentioning Scott's obligations in a letter of 9 Oct (*CL* II 1191: to Mrs C)—as indeed she later did to HCR.

6. NYPL Berg Collection. Sarah Stoddart's Commonplace Book pp 41–76 (pp 74 and 75 were missing before the poem was transcribed); each leaf 11.1 × 18.0 cm; wm crown above oval design, above 1795; chain-lines 2.5 cm; written on both sides. Transcript in the hand of Sarah Stoddart.

The transcript undoubtedly derives from MS 5: it contains the same errors (e.g. omission of lines 160 and 458) and adds others; as in MS 5, the name Christabel appears to be spelt "Christobel" throughout. Considered alongside the careful capitalisation of MS 5, and in view of the variations of wording and stanza division that exist, it appears to have been taken down by Sarah Stoddart hurriedly from dictation. Variations can be classified either as misreadings ("he" for "it", "that" for "whom", etc) or mishearings (singulars for plurals, "morn" for "dawn", etc). Line 551 is preceded by a line-space, which almost certainly derives from the fact that the line begins a new page in MS 5, the pause in the reader's voice being mistaken by Sarah Stoddart for a break in the sense. Some variants in which MS 6 is closer to other readings (line 158 "But" where MS 5 has "And"; line 485 "thou" where MS 5 has "then"; etc) could be due to a misreading of MS 5, where the words can easily be confused. Others (in lines 6, 78, 379–80, etc) can only be fortuitous.

It could be argued that C dictated MS 6 (he may have dictated **155** *Continuation of "The Three Graves"* to Sarah Stoddart: see **155** VAR TEXT 1), and that MS 5 was subsequently prepared as a corrected fair copy. The relation between the variants makes this unlikely, however, and MS 6 appears to be a hasty copy that Sarah Stoddart made for her own use afterwards.

MS 6 merits inclusion not because of its authority as a text which represents C's meaning, but because in 1811 it was collated by John Payne Collier against an original, unrecovered ms in C's hand. Collier described MS 6 in the Preface to *Seven Lectures on Shakespeare and Milton, by the Late S. T. Coleridge* (1856) as "made some years before by a lady of Salisbury" (p xxxix), and the Commonplace Book does indeed carry the bookplate "S. Stoddart, St. Anne's Street, Sarum." It was given to Collier by William Hazlitt soon after he married Sarah Stoddart in May 1808, and Hazlitt recalled it to quote in his *Examiner* review of 2 Jun 1816 ("The manuscript runs thus, or nearly thus: 'Hideous, deformed, and pale of hue'"). Collier meanwhile ticked and annotated 38 lines where MS 6 differed from the ms C had lent him; the ticks, and Collier's comments on some of the differences in his Preface, suggest an unrecovered ms closer to PR *1* and later versions than to any earlier ms (including MS 4).

Some of Collier's ticks appear to pick up mistakes (lines 78, 232, 457, 602). Others appear to mark readings which were altered in PR *1* (lines 34, 65, 81, 83, 137, 145, 161, 191, 193.1.1, 219, 252.1.1, 254, 277, 360, 453, 463, 507). Others again, readings altered only in emended copies of PR *1* and in PR *2–4* (lines 11, 32, 37, 62, 92, 106, 107.1.1, 112, 114, 115, 120, 166, 166.1.1, 254.1.1). Yet others—the most interesting category—suggest variants which were never carried forward into any text which has been recovered (lines 39, 118, 306; and perhaps some categorised above as mistakes, such as 78 and 232). The variants Collier printed in his Preface are a selection from these categories: they affect lines 32, 65, 81, 92, 114–17, 160, 191, 193.1.1–2, 219, 453, 463), and they are described in the notes to the Variorum Text below.

Collier is not a wholly trustworthy witness, and it should be emphasised that the diary entry for 6 Nov 1811, printed long afterwards in 1856, has no equivalent in the original ms diary (Folger MS M a 219). One detail that proves his collation was more sophisticated than a simple comparison with MSS 5 and 6 is a note he added to line 219 (in MS 6). He has written in the later reading, commenting at the foot of the page: "So in the printed Copy—". However, while Collier might have invented or distorted details, there is no reason to doubt the substance of his claim.

She folded her arms beneath her cloak,
And stole to the other side of the oak.
What sees she there?

There she sees a damsel bright,
Drest in a silken robe of white ,
~~Her neck, her feet, her arms were bare,~~
~~And the jewels disorder'd in her hair~~
I guess, 'twas frightful there to see
A lady so richly clad as she—
Beautiful exceedingly!

Mary mother, save me now!
(Said Christabel,) And who art thou?

The lady strange made answer meet,
And her voice was faint and sweet :—
Have pity on my sore distress,
I scarce can speak for weariness.

That shadowy in the moonlight shone:
The neck that made that white robe wan,
Her stately neck, and arms were bare;
Her blue-vein'd feet unsandal'd were
And, wildly glitter'd here and there
The jems entangled in her hair

5(*a*). Page 7 of *Christabel* (1816) corrected by Anne Gillman

She folded her arms beneath her cloak,
And stole to the other side of the oak.
    What sees she there?

There she sees a damsel bright,
Drest in a silken robe of white ;
~~Her neck, her feet, her arms were bare,~~
~~And the jewels disorder'd in her hair~~.
I guess, 'twas frightful there to see
A lady so richly clad as she—
Beautiful exceedingly!

Mary mother, save me now!
(Said Christabel,) And who art thou ?

The lady strange made answer meet,
And her voice was faint and sweet :—
Have pity on my sore distress,
I scarce can speak for weariness.

That shadowy in the moonlight shone
The neck that made that white robe wan
Her stately Neck & Arms were bare
Her blue vein'd feet unsandal'd were
And wildly glitter'd here & there
The Gems entangled in her Hair.

5(*b*). Page 7 of *Christabel* (1816) corrected by James Gillman

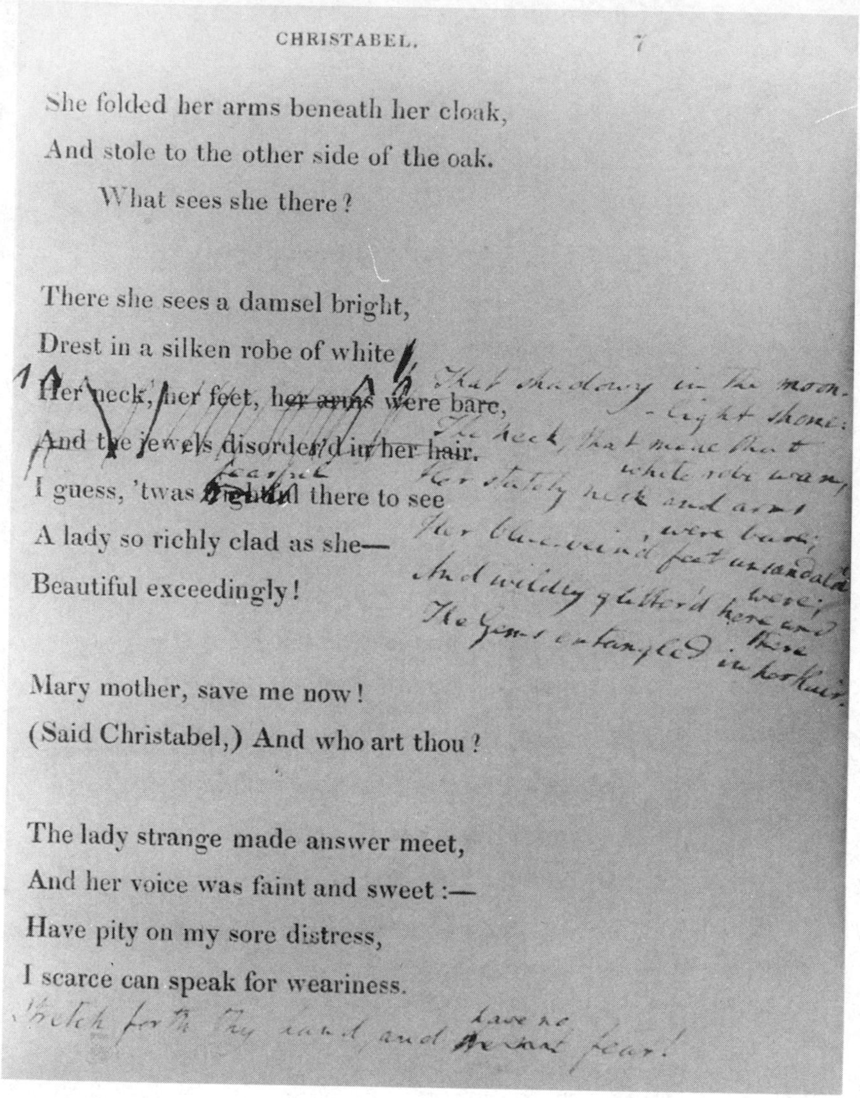

She folded her arms beneath her cloak,
And stole to the other side of the oak.

What sees she there?

There she sees a damsel bright,
Drest in a silken robe of white,
Her neck, her feet, her ~~arms~~ were bare,
And the jewels disorder'd in her hair.
I guess, 'twas ~~frightful~~ *fearful* there to see
A lady so richly clad as she—
Beautiful exceedingly!

Mary mother, save me now!
(Said Christabel,) And who art thou?

The lady strange made answer meet,
And her voice was faint and sweet :—
Have pity on my sore distress,
I scarce can speak for weariness.

[handwritten marginal additions by Coleridge]
That shadowy in the moon-light shone:
The neck that made that white robe wan,
Her stately neck and arms were bare;
Her blue-vein'd feet unsandal'd were,
And wildly glitter'd here and there
The gems entangled in her hair.

Stretch forth thy hand, and have no fear!

5(c). Page 7 of *Christabel* (1816) corrected by Coleridge

~~So up she rose, and forth they pass'd,~~
~~With hurrying steps, yet nothing fast;~~
~~Her lucky stars the lady blest,~~
~~And Christabel she sweetly said—~~
~~All our household are at rest,~~
~~Each one sleeping in his bed~~ ;
~~Sir Leoline is weak in health,~~
~~And may not well awaken'd be~~ ;
~~So to my room we'll creep in stealth,~~
~~And you to-night must sleep with me.~~

They cross'd the moat, and Christabel
Took the key that fitted well;
A little door she open'd straight,
All in the middle of the gate;
The gate that was iron'd within and without,
Where an army in battle array had march'd out.

Her grenwood stand the lady blest
And thus spake on sweet Christabel
All our household are at rest,
The hall as silent as the cell
Sir Leoline is weak in health,
And may not well awaken'd be
But we will move as if in stealth
And I beseech your courtesy
This night to share your couch with me.

6(*a*). Page 10 of *Christabel* (1816) corrected by Anne Gillman

So up she rose, and forth they pass'd,
With hurrying steps, yet nothing fast ;
Her lucky stars the lady blest,
And Christabel she sweetly said—
All our household are at rest,
Each one sleeping in his bed ;
Sir Leoline is weak in health,
And may not well awaken'd be ;
So to my room we'll creep in stealth,
And you to-night must sleep with me.

They cross'd the moat, and Christabel
Took the key that fitted well ;
A little door she open'd straight,
All in the middle of the gate ;
The gate that was iron'd within and without,
Where an army in battle array had march'd out.

She rose & forth with steps they pass'd
That strove to be & were not fast
Her gracious stars the Lady blest.
And then spake on sweet Christabel
All our Household are at rest
The Hall as silent as the Cell—
But we will move as if in stealth
and I beseech your Courtesy
This night to share your bed with me.

6(*b*). Page 10 of *Christabel* (1816) corrected by James Gillman

So ... he rose: and ... they pass'd, *fort / ... with slip*

That stone to lie, ... yet were not fast;

Her ... stars the lady blest, *gracious*

And Christabel she sweetly said— *thus spake on sweet Christabel —*

All our household are at rest,

The Hall as silent as the Cell;
Each one sleeping in his bed ;

Sir Leoline is weak in health,

And may not well awaken'd be ;
But we will move, as if in stealth,
So to my room we'll creep in stealth,
And I beseech your courtesy
And ...
This night to share your bed with me.

They cross'd the moat, and Christabel

Took the key that fitted well ;

A little door she open'd straight,

All in the middle of the gate ;

The gate that was iron'd within and without,

Where an army in battle array had march'd out.

6(*c*). Page 10 of *Christabel* (1816) corrected by Coleridge

Thy power to declare
That in the dim forest
Thou heard'st a low moaning
And found'st a bright Lady surpassingly fair
And did'st bring her home with thee with love...
To shield her & shelter her & shelter her from the damp air.

The Conclusion of
Book the first

It was a lovely sight to see
The Lady Christabel when she
Was praying at the old Oak Tree.
Amid the jagged shadows
Of mossy leafless Boughs
Kneeling in the moonlight
To make her gentle Vows;
Her slender palms together prest
Heaving sometimes on her Breast
Her face resigned to Bliss or Bale
Her face Oh call it fair not pale
And both blue eyes more bright than clear
Each about to have a tear.

With open eyes (Ah woe is me)
Asleep & dreaming fearfully
Fearfully dreaming, yet I wis
Dreaming that alone which is —
O Sorrow and Shame! Can this be she
The Lady that knelt at the old Oak...

7(*a*). Fair copy of *Christabel* in the hands of Dorothy Wordsworth and Mary Hutchinson, in William Wordsworth's so-called "Christabel Notebook" (Mary Hutchinson apparently took over at line 295, with the same pen and ink). See TEXT MS 3

and lo! the Worker of these Harms,
That holds the Maiden in her Arms,
Seems to slumber still and mild,
As a Mother with her Child.

A Star hath set, a Star hath risen,
O Geraldine! since arms of thine
Have been the lovely Lady's Prison.
O Geraldine! One Hour was thine —
Thou'st had thy will! By Tairn & Rill
The night-birds all that Hour were still
But now they are jubilant anew,
From Cliff and Tower, Tu-whoo! Tu-whoo!
Tu-whoo! tu-whoo! from wood and Fell

And see! the Lady Christabel
Gathers herself from out her Trance;
Her Limbs relax, her Countenance
Grows sad and soft; the smooth thin lips
Close o'er her Eyes; and Tears she sheds —
Large Tears that leave the Lashes bright.
And oft the while she seems to smile
As Infants at a sudden Light!

Yea she doth smile and she doth weep
Like a youthful Hermitess

6

He took two Paces, and a Stride,
And lay down by the Maiden's Side:
And in her arms the Maid she took,
          Ah wel-a-day!
And with sad Voice and doleful Look
These Words did say:

In the Touch of my Bosom there worketh a Spell,
Which is Lord of thy Utterance, Christabel!
Thou knowest to night and wilt know to morrow
The mark of my Shame, the Seal of my Sorrow;
          But vainly thou warrest,
          For this is alone in
     Thy Power to declare,
          That in the dim Forest
          Thou heardst a low Moaning
And foundst a bright Lady, surpassingly fair:
And didst bring her home with thee with love &
To shield her & shelter her from the damp air. with charity

          The Conclusion to
               Book the First

It was a lovely Sight to see
The Lady Christabel, when she
Was praying at the old Oak Tree.
          Amid the jagged Shadows
          Of mossy leafless Bows
          Kneeling in the Moonlight
          To make her gentle Vows;
Her slender Palms together prest,
Heaving sometimes on her Breast,
Her Face resign'd to Bliss or Bale —
Her Face, oh call it fair not pale,
And both blue Eyes more bright than clear,
Each about to have a Tear!

With open eyes (ah woe is me!)
Asleep, and dreaming fearfully,
Fearfully dreaming, yet I wis,
Dreaming that alone, which is —
O Sorrow and Shame! Can this be She,
The Lady, that knelt at the old Oak Tree?
And lo! the Worker of these Harms,
That holds the Maiden in her Arms,
Seems to slumber still and mild,
As a Mother with her Child.

A Star hath set, a Star hath risen,
O Geraldine! since arms of thine
Have been the lovely Lady's Prison.
* Thou'st had thy Will! By Tairn and Rill
The Night-birds all that Hour were still.
But now they are jubilant anew
From Cliff and Tower, Tu — whoo! Tu - whoo!
Tu - whoo! tu - whoo! from Wood and Fell!

* O Geraldine! one Hour was thine —

7(*b*). The passage of *Christabel* given in Fig. 7(*a*),
in the hand of Sara Hutchinson. See TEXT MS 4

1. The first of three poems in a separately published volume (1816), "B Y
S. T. COLERIDGE, ESQ." Though C at first intended to exclude the poem
from *SL* (*LL*—M—III 188; *CL* IV 585: to J. M. Gutch [17 Sept 1815]), he
appears to have been encouraged by Byron's reception to insert it; and it was
removed from *SL* only at the last moment in May 1815, when an agreement
was reached with Murray (see the letter by J. J. Morgan to J. M. Gutch of 6
May 1816 q *BL*—*CC*—II 286–7). Three editions were published in the same
year, the second and third differing from the first only in their title-pages. It is
possible that the second and third appeared almost simultaneously, as part of
Murray's scheme of advertising, since he appears to have lost money on the
publication (*BL&J* v 108, 208).

    The printed text of *Christabel* seems to have been set from MS 4, which C
sent to Byron in Oct 1815 and which Byron passed on to Murray (see TEXT MS
4 above), probably because it was the neatest, cleanest ms C could find. The
text must have been emended in proof, if not before MS 4 went to the printer,
but not to the extent of bringing it into line with the improved ms reported by
Collier in 1811 (see TEXT MS 6 above).

    The two extracts from PR 1 (lines 23–103, 154–254) printed in *Felix Farley's
Bristol Journal* (29 Jun and 20 Jul 1816) have no textual significance; the poem
was reprinted entire in *Metrical Romances &c. By S. T. Coleridge* (Isleworth
1825).

    C presented a number of copies of the first edition to neighbours and friends
at Highgate, but did not correct or emend the text of the poem. He appears to
have worked on the text of later editions during his holiday at Mudeford, which
began on 19 Sept 1816—a task in which he was aided by JG and perhaps AG,
and very much influenced by the reviews which had begun to appear: Hazlitt's
in *The Examiner* (2 Jun 1816) 348–9; Thomas Moore's in *Ed Rev* XXVII (Sept
1816) 58–67—which C believed was also by Hazlitt. Four annotated copies
derive from this period, copies which C gave to an assorted group, comprising
David Hinves (in the possession of Sir John Murray, 1979), his new friend
J. H. Green (NYPL Berg Collection), and the visiting Ludwig Tieck (Princeton
University Library Robert H. Taylor Collection), and C's own copy, used as the
basis for PR 2 below (HUL *EC8 C 6795 817s (C)). Two further copies—given
to his old schoolfriend Bishop Middleton (in private hands, 1982), and to his
son DC (St John's College, Cambridge, Class 15 Shelf 53)—were corrected
either at this time or a little later (before early 1819). A seventh annotated
copy (Princeton University Library Robert H. Taylor Collection) dates from C's
Ramsgate holiday in Nov 1824, and is especially notable for its development
of the marginal gloss present in a rudimentary (and severely cropped) form in
Middleton's copy. However, the manner in which annotations were inscribed
and abandoned in this copy, contained in a circulating library, again exhibits an
element of the adventitious and dispirited, as in the earlier copies.

2. PW (1828).
Lines 564–96 were reprinted with an engraving by T. Stothard in *The Bijou*

for 1829 (1828) 285–6, which has no textual authority. The copy of PR 2 at the Fitzwilliam Museum, Cambridge (Marlay Bequest 1912) contains corrections of the poem in C's hand, and also in a hand which appears not to be C's.

3. *PW* (1829).

4 [=RT]. *PW* (1834).

C. GENERAL NOTE

C recited or read the poem frequently. Besides the readings to WW, Byron, Carlyon, and Davy already mentioned, others are recorded by Richard Warner *Literary Recollections* (2 vols 1830) II 155–6n and Thomas Noon Talford in *The Letters of Charles Lamb, with a Sketch of his Life* (2 vols 1837) II 28. Davy also records C in a large company reciting "the poem of *Christabel* unfinished, as I had heard it before" (*Fragmentary Remains, Literary & Scientific, of Sir Humphry Davy* ed John Davy 74). The occasion, before C left for Keswick, was perhaps 4 Apr 1803, when C dined with William Sotheby and Sotheby asked him to finish *Christabel*: see *CL* II 941: to Mrs C 4 Apr 1803 (cf 1094: to W. Sotheby 17 Mar 1804); see *CL* I 549: to RS [19 Dec 1799] for Davy's earlier hearing of the poem.

At the same time, C's friends read and lent the transcripts in their possession. WW read MS 3 to John Wilson, along with *The White Doe of Rylstone* (*WL—M* rev—I 326); SH (and DW) read MS 2 to Johnny Wordsworth, and had Dora Wordsworth make a copy for William Jackson (see TEXT MS 2 above); Sarah Stoddart's copy (MS 6) passed to William Hazlitt on her marriage to him, and from Hazlitt to Collier. There are a particularly large number of untraced mss of the poem—associated with CL, Davy, C himself, and others—all of them circulating or in some way available to interested persons. The way in which the poem circulated in one such group is illustrated by HCR. Mrs Clarkson read the version C gave her at Parndon (MS 5 above) to him on 9 Oct 1811; by 1814 he had his own copy, and he read it at the Flaxmans' and the Pordens' on 3 Dec, at Dr Aikin's on 4 Dec, to the Flaxmans and Miss Vardel on 19 Dec, to the Pattissons and Mr Murray on 28 Dec, and at the Nashes' on 14 Mar 1815 (*CRB* I 47, 155, 156, 157, 164).

One particularly significant reading, or possibly untraced copy, concerns John Stoddart. Stoddart had called at Grasmere on 22 Oct 1800, on which evening C read the then new poem to him and the Wordsworths (*DWJ* I 69). Stoddart accompanied C to Keswick the next day, sufficiently impressed by the poem to write to Scott two months later: "Coleridge is engaged in a poetical Romance called Christabel, of very high merit" (als, 26 Dec 1800: National Library of Scotland MS 3874 f 89ʳ). He seems not to have taken a copy of the poem while he was with C, or to have committed it to memory, since he wrote on 12 Jan 1801 urging C to come to London and to bring *Christabel* with him (PML MA 1857 (13), from The Joanna Langlais Collection).

How Stoddart obtained a copy or refreshed his memory is not known: he could have acquired, copied, or memorised CL's incomplete copy of the very first, unrevised version, since he was in CL's company a good deal during 1801–2. Or Stoddart might have had the poem in his memory from the first, and urged C to bring a copy to London so that it could be circulated more widely or published. At all events, Stoddart was able to recite it to Scott during his next visit to Edinburgh during Sept–Oct 1802. Scott claimed thereafter to be able to repeat much of the poem (so he told WW and DW when they visited him in Sept 1803: *WL—E* rev—633). Scott repeated it to Lady Beaumont, and was thus the cause of SH copying out MS 4 (see TEXT MS 4 above); and to Francis Jeffrey (see the note, signed with Jeffrey's initials, in the review of *BL* in *Ed Rev* XXVIII—Aug 1817—488–515 at 509–10). Scott also repeated it to Byron, who claimed that the whole of the poem had been recited to him (Thomas Medwin *Conversations of Lord Byron* ed E. J. Lovell—Princeton 1966—177). See also C's note in the front flyleaves of the copy he gave to Bishop Middleton (vol I annex C 16.8).

half-title/divisional title/title. *1* 𝕮𝖍𝖗𝖎𝖘𝖙𝖆𝖇𝖊𝖑, &c. • *2–4* CHRISTABEL.

epigraph [present in MS 2 only]

> Are there two things, of all which Men possess,
> That ~~seem~~ are so like each other and so near
> As mutual Love seems like to Happiness?
> Dear Asra, Woman beyond utterance dear!
> This Love, which ever welling at my heart   EP 5
> Now in its living fount doth heave and fall,
> Now overflowing pours. thro' every part
> Of all my Frame, and fills and changes all,
> Like vernal waters springing up thro' Snow—
> This Love, that seeming ~~greater~~ beyond the power   EP 10
> Of Growth, yet seemeth evermore to ~~grow~~—
> Could I transmute the whole to the rich dower
> Of Happy Life, and give it all to Thee,
> Thy Lot, methinks, were Heaven, thy Age Eternity!

preface [present in PR *1–4*]

PREFACE.

The first part of the following poem was written in the year one thousand seven hundred
 and ninety seven, at Stowey in
the county of Somerset. The second part, after my return from Germany, in the
 year one thousand eight hundred, at Keswick, Cumberland. Since the latter date, my
 poetic powers have been, till very lately, in a state of suspended animation. But as,
 in my very first conception of the tale, I had the whole present to my mind, with
 the wholeness, no less than with the liveliness of a vision; I trust that I shall be able
 to embody in verse the three parts yet to come, in the course of the present year.
 It is probable, that if the poem had been
finished at either of the former periods, or if even the first and second part had   ⁻1.5
been published in the year 1800, the impression of its originality would have

been much greater than I dare at present expect. But for this, I have only my
own indolence to blame. The dates are mentioned for the exclusive purpose of
precluding charges of plagiarism or servile imitation from myself. For there is
among us a set of critics, who seem to hold, that every possible thought and ⁻1.10
image is traditional; who have no notion that there are such things as fountains
in the world, small as well as great; and who would therefore charitably derive
every rill, they behold flowing, from a perforation made in some other man's
tank. I am confident however, that as far as the present poem is concerned,
the celebrated poets whose writings I might be suspected of having imitated, ⁻1.15
either in particular passages, or in the tone and the spirit of the whole, would
be among the first to vindicate me from the charge, and who, on any striking
coincidence, would permit me to address them in this doggrel version of two
monkish Latin hexameters:

> 'Tis mine and it is likewise your's, ⁻1.20
> But an if this will not do;
> Let it be mine, good friend! for I
> Am the poorer of the two.

I have only to add, that the metre of the Christabel is not, properly speaking,
irregular, though it may seem so from its being founded on a new principle: ⁻1.25
namely, that of counting in each line the accents, not the syllables. Though
the latter may vary from seven to twelve, yet in each line the accents will
be found to be only four. Nevertheless this occasional variation in the number of
syllables is not introduced wantonly, or for the mere ends of convenience, but
in correspondence with some transition in the nature of the imagery or passion. ⁻1.30

pref fn. *2–4* To the edition of 1816.

⁻1.31	2–5	*Christabel* | *Book the First.*
	6	*Christabel* Book 1
	1	CHRISTABEL. | PART I.
	2 3	CHRISTABEL. | PART THE FIRST.
	4	PART I.
		[*Line-space*]
1	⊠1	Tis the middle of Night by the Castle Clock,
2	⊠1	And the Owls have awaken'd the crowing Cock:
3	2–6	Tu-u-whoo! Tu-u-whoo!
	1–4	Tu—whit! —— Tu—whoo!
4	⊠1	And hark, again! the crowing Cock,
5	⊠1 6	How drowsily it crew.
	6	he
		[*Line-space*]
6	⊠1	Sir Leoline, the Baron rich,
7	⊠1 2 3	Hath a toothless mastiff Bitch:
	2 3	which
8	⊠1	From her ₭Kennel beneath the Rock
9	2–6 *1*	She makes Answer to the Clock,
	2 3	Maketh
	4	She maketh
10	⊠1	Four for the Quarters and twelve for the Hour,

11	2–6 *1*	Ever and aye, Moonshine or Shower,
	2–4	by shine and
12	☒1	Sixteen short Howls, not overloud;
13	☒1	Some say, she sees my Lady's Shroud.
		[*Line-space*]
14	☒1	Is the Night chilly and dark?
15	☒1	The Night is chilly but not dark.
16	☒1	The thin grey Cloud is spread on high,
17	☒1	It covers but not hides the Sky.
18	☒1	The Moon is behind, and at the Full,
19	☒1	And yet she looks both small and dull.
20	☒1	The Night is chill, the ¢Cloud is grey:
21	☒1	Tis a Month before the Month of May,
22	☒1	And the Spring comes slowly up this way.
		[*Line-space*]
23	☒1	The lovely Lady, Christabel,
24	☒1	Whom her Father loves so well,
25	☒1 3	What makes her in the Wood so late
	3	Woods
26	☒1	A furlong from the Castle Gate?
27	☒1	She had dreams all yesternight
28	☒1	Of her own betrothed Knight,
28.1.1	*1*	Dreams, that made her moan and leap,
28.1.2	*1*	As on her bed she lay in sleep;
29	☒1	And She in the Midnight Wood will pray
30	☒1	For the Weal of her Lover, that's far away.
		[*Line-space*]
31	☒1	She stole along, ʃShe nothing spoke,
32	2–6 *1*	The Breezes they were still also;
	2–4	sighs she heaved were soft and low,
33	☒1	And nought was green upon the Oak,
34	2–6	But the Moss and Misletoe:
	1–4	moss and rarest
35	2–6	She knelt beneath the huge Oak Tree,
	1–4	kneels
36	☒1 6	And in Silence prayeth She.
	6	prayed
		[*Line-space*]
37	2–6 *1*	The Lady leaps up suddenly,
	2–4	sprang
38	☒1	The lovely Lady, Christabel!
39	☒1	It moan'd as near, as near can be,
40	☒1	But what it is, She cannot tell—
41	☒1	On the other Side it seems to be
42	☒1	Of the huge broad-breasted old Oak⸗Tree.
		[*Line-space*]
43	☒1	The Night is chill; the Forest bare;
44	☒1	Is it the Wind that moaneth bleak?
45	☒1 3	There is not Wind enough in the Air

46 ⊠1 3	To move away the ringlet Curl	
47 ⊠1 3	From the lovely Lady's Cheek—	
48 ⊠1 3	There is not Wind enough ←——to——→ twirl	
3	~~in the air to tw~~ to	

49 ⊠1   The One red Leaf, the last of its Clan,

50 2   That dances as ~~d~~ often as dance it can,

⊠1 2   often

51 ⊠1   Hanging so light and hanging so high

52 ⊠1 3 4   On the topmost Twig that looks up at the Sky.

3 4   out

[*Line-space*]

53 ⊠1   Hush, beating Heart of Christabel!

54 ⊠1   Iesu Maria, shield her well!

[*Line-space*]

55 ⊠1   She folded her Arms beneath her Cloak,

56 ⊠1   And stole to the other side of the Oak.

57 2   What ~~sa~~sees She there?

⊠1 2   sees

[*Line-space*]

58 ⊠1 3   There ~~s~~She sees a Damsel bright

3   A   Damsel

59 ⊠1 3 6   Drest in a silken Robe of White;

3   Clad

6   Drest   silver

60 2–4   That shadowy in the moonlight shone:

61 2–4   The neck that made that white robe wan,

62 2–6 *1*   Her ~~n~~Neck, her Feet, her Arms were bare,

2–4   stately   neck,   and

63 2–4   Her blue-veined feet unsandal'd were

64 2–4   And wildly glittered here and there

65 2–6   And the Jewels were tumbled in her Hair.

1   disorder'd

2–4   The   gems   entangled

66 ⊠1   I guess, 'twas frightful there to see

67 2   A Lady ⟨so⟩ richly-clad, as She,

⊠1 2   so

68 ⊠1   Beautiful exceedingly!

[*Line-space*]

69 ⊠1   Mary Mother, save me now!

70 ⊠1   Said Christabel, And who art thou?

[*Line-space*]

71 ⊠1   The Lady strange made ~~d~~Answer meet,

72 ⊠1   And her ~~v~~Voice was faint and sweet:

73 ⊠1   Have ~~p~~Pity on my sore ~~d~~Distress,

74 ⊠1   I scarce can speak for ~~w~~Weariness.

75 ⊠1   Stretch forth thy Hand, and have no fear—

[*Line-space*]

76 ⊠1   Said Christabel, How cam'st thou here?

77 ⊠1   And the Lady, whose Voice was faint and sweet,

78 ☒1 6   Did thus pursue her answer meet.
  6   return
      [*Line-space*]
79 ☒1   My Sire is of a noble Line,
80 ☒1   And my Name is Geraldine.
81 2 4–6   Five ←—Ruffians—→ seiz'd me yestermorn,
  3   g̷[?]*ΙΙ*[?] Ruffians
  1–4   ←—warriors—→
82 ☒1   Me, even me, a Maid forlorn;
83 2–6   They chok'd my ℓCries with wicked Might,
  1–4   force and fright,
84 ☒1   And tied me on a Palfrey white;
85 2   The̷y Palfrey was as fleet as ꝥWind,
  ☒1 2   The
86 ☒1   And they rode furiously behind.
87 ☒1   They spurr'd amain, their Steeds were white,
88 2–6   And twice we cross'd the Shade of Night.
  1–4   once
89 ☒1   As sure as Heaven shall rescue me,
90 ☒1   I have no Thought what Men they be,
91 ☒1   Nor do I know how long it is
92 2–6 *1*   (For I have lain in fFits, I wis)
  2–4   entranced
93 ☒1   Since One, the tallest of the five,
94 2   Took me from the Palfrey's [?]Back,
  ☒1 2   Back,
95 ☒1   A weary Woman scarce alive.
96 ☒1 3   Some mutter'd ꝥWords his Comrades spoke,
  3   *1* Comrade
97 ☒1   He plac'd me underneath this Oak,
98 2   ~~And~~ He swore ~~he sh~~ they would return ~~in~~ with ħHaste;
  ☒1 2   He   they   with   haste;
99 2   ~~But he~~ Whither they went, I cannot tell—
  ☒1 2   ←—Whither—→
100 ☒1   I thought I heard, some minutes past,
101 2   ꞓSounds as of a Castle Bell.
  ☒1 2   Sounds
102 ☑1 5 6   ~~Stretch forth thy Hand~~ (thus ended She)
  5 6   endeth
103 ☒1   And help a wretched Maid to flee.
      [*Line-space*]
104 ☒1   Then Christabel stretcht forth her Hand
105 ☒1   And comforted fair Geraldine,
106 2–6 *1*   Saying, that she should command
  2–4   O well bright dame may you
107 ☒1   The ꞩService of Sir Leoline;
107.1.1 2–6 *1*   And straight be convoy'd, free from Thrall,
108 *2–4*   And gladly our stout chivalry
109 *2–4*   Will he send forth and friends withall

110	*2–4*	To guide and guard you safe and free
111	*2–6 1*	Back to her noble Father's Hall.
	2–4	Home your
		[*Line-space*]
112	*2–6 1*	So up she rose and forth they pass'd
	2–4	She rose: and forth with steps
113	*2–5 1*	With hurrying steps yet nothing fast.
	6	step
	2	That strovad to be, and were not,
	3 4	strove
114	*2–6 1*	Her lucky Stars the Lady blest,
	2–4	gracious
115	*2–6 1*	And Christabel she sweetly said—
	2–4	thus spake on sweet Christabel;
116	☒1	All our Household are at rest,
116.1.1	*2–6 1*	Each one sleeping in his bed;
117	*2–4*	The hall as silent as the cell,
118	☒1	Sir Leoline is weak in health,
119	*2–5*	And may not awaken'd be,
	6	he may
	1–4	may well
120	*2–6 1*	So to my Room we'll creep in stealth,
	2–4	But we will move as if
121	*2–4*	And I beseech your courtesy
122	*2–6 1*	And you to night must sleep with me.
	2–4	This night, to share your couch
		[*Line-space*]
123	*2*	They ~~reach'd~~ cross'd the Moat, and Christabel
	☒1 *2*	←—cross'd—→
124	☒1	Took the Key that fitted well;
125	☒1	A little Door she open'd straight
126	☒1	All in the middle of the Gate,
127	☒1	The Gate, that was iron'd within and without,
128	☒1	Where an Army in Battle Array had march'd out.
		[*Line-space*]
129	☒1 *6*	The Lady sank, belike thro' Pain,
	6	with
130	☒1	And Christabel with mMight and mMain
131	☒1	Lifted her up, a weary Weight,
132	☒1	Over the Threshold of the Gate:
133	☒1	Then the Lady rose again,
134	☒1	And mov'd, as She were not in Pain.
		[*Line-space*]
135	*2*	~~Thus~~ So free from dDanger, free from fFear
	☒1 *2*	So
136	☒1	They cross'd the Court: right glad they were.

137 2   And Christabel ~~devoutedly~~ she sweetly   cried
    3 4 6   ←—she—→
    5   ~~said~~ cried
    1–4   devoutly   cried,
138 ⊠1   To the Lady by her side,
139 2–6   O   praise the Virgin all divine
    1–4   Praise we
140 ⊠1   Who hath rescued thee from thy Distress!
141 ⊠1   Alas, alas! said Geraldine,
142 ⊠1   I cannot speak for Weariness.
143 ⊠1   So free from Danger, free from Fear,
144 ⊠1   They cross'd the Court: right glad they were.
              [*Line-space*]
145 2 4–6 Beside   her   Kennel the Mastiff old
    3   ~~the~~ her
    1–4   Outside   her
146 ⊠1 6 Lay fast asleep in   moonshine cold.
    6   the
147 ⊠1   The Mastiff old did not awake,
148 ⊠1   Yet she an angry moan did make.
149 ⊠1   And what can ail the Mastiff Bitch?
150 ⊠1   Never till now she utter'd Yell
151 ⊠1   Beneath the eye of Christabel.
152 ⊠1   Perhaps, it is the Owlet's Scritch:
153 ⊠1   For what can ail the Mastiff Bitch?
              [*Line-space*]
154 ⊠1   They pass'd the Hall, that echoes still
155 ⊠1   Pass as lightly as you will.
156 ⊠1   The Brands were flat, the Brands were dying
157 ⊠1   Amid their own white Ashes lying;
158 ⊠1 5 But when the Lady pass'd, there came
    5   And
159 ⊠1   A Tongue of Light, a Fit of Flame,
160 ⊠1 5 6 And Christabel saw the Lady's Eye,
161 2–6   And nothing else she saw thereby
    1–4   saw she
162 ⊠1   Save the Boss of the Shield of Sir Leoline tall,
163 ⊠1   Which hung in a murky old Nitch in the Wall.
164 ⊠1   O softly tread, said Christabel,
165 ⊠1   My Father seldom sleepeth well.
              [*Line-space*]
166 2–6 *1* Sweet Christabel her feet she bares,
    2–4   doth bare
166.1.1 2–6 *1* And they are creeping up the stairs,
167 2–4   And jealous of the listening air
168 2–4   They steal their way from stair to stair
169 ⊠1   Now in Glimmer, and now in Gloom,
170 ⊠1   And now they pass the Baron's Room,
171.1 4   ~~And now have~~ As still as Death, with ~~stifled Breath~~

171	⊠1	As still as Death with stifled Breath!
172	2	And ~~now they~~ now have reach'd her Chamber Door,
	⊠1 2 6	◄—now—►
	6	they've
173	2–6	And now they with their Feet press down
	1	with eager
	2–4	◄—doth—► Geraldine
174	2–6 *1*	The Rushes of her Chamber Floor.
	2–4	the

[*Line-space*]

174.1.1	2	A ~~Breeze~~ Night-wind thwarts the Owlet's Cry,
174.1.2	2	The far Owl's Scream came on as the Night,
175	⊠1	The Moon shines dim in th' open Air,
176	⊠1 5	And not a Moonbeam enters here.
	5	there.
177	2	But they without its Light can ~~chamber~~ see
	⊠1 2	◄—see—►
178	⊠1	The Chamber carv'd so curiously,
179	⊠1	Carv'd with figures strange and sweet
180	⊠1	All made out of the Carver's Brain
181	⊠1	For a Lady's Chamber meet:
182	⊠1	The Lamp with twofold silver Chain
183	2	Is fasten'd to ~~An~~ an Angel's Feet.
	⊠1 2	an

[*Line-space*]

184	⊠1 6	The silver Lamp burns dead and dim;
	6	burnt
185	⊠1	But Christabel the Lamp will trim—
186	⊠1	She trimm'd the Lamp, and made it bright,
187	⊠1	And left it swinging to and fro,
188	⊠1	While Geraldine in wretched Plight
189	⊠1	Sank down upon the Floor below.

[*Line-space*]

190	⊠1	O weary Lady, Geraldine,
191	2–6	I pray you, drink this spicy Wine.
	1–4	cordial
192	⊠1	It is a Wine of virtuous powers,
193	⊠1	My Mother made it of wild flowers.
193.1.1	2–6	Nay, drink it up, I pray you, do!
193.1.2	2–6	Believe me, it will comfort you.

[*Line-space*]

194	⊠1	And will your Mother pity me,
195	⊠1	Who am a Maiden most forlorn?

[*Line-space*]

196	⊠1	Christabel answer'd—Woe is me!
197	⊠1	She died the hour, that I was born.
198	⊠1	I have heard the grey-hair'd Friar/ tell,
199	⊠1	How on her Death-bed she did say
200	⊠1	That she should hear the Castle Bell

201 ☒1	Strike twelve upon my Wedding Day.
202 ☒1	O Mother dear/! that thou wert here!
203 ☒1	I would, said Geraldine, She were!
	[Line-space]
204 ☒1	But soon with alter'd Voice said She—
205 ☒1 3	"Off, wandering Mother! Peak and pine!
206 ☒1 3	"I have power to bid thee flee.
207 ☒1 3	Alas! what ails poor Geraldine?
208 2	Whaty stares she with unsettled Eye?
☒1–3	Why
209 ☒1 3	Can she the bodiless Dead espy?
210 ☒1 3	And why with hollow Voice cries she,
211 ☒1	"Off, Woman, off! this Hour is mine—
212 ☒1 3	"Though thou her Guardian Spirit be,
213 ☒1	"Off, Woman, off! tis given to me.
	[Line-space]
214 ☒1	Then Christabel knelt by the Lady's Side,
215 ☒1	And rais'd to heaven her eyes so blue—
216 ☒1	Alas, said she, this ghastly Ride—
217 ☒1	Dear Lady! it hath wilder'd you!
218 ☒1	The Lady wip'd her moist cold brow,
219 2–6	And faintly said, I am better now.
1–4	"'Tis over now!"
	[Line-space]
220 ☒1	Again the wild flower Wine she drank,
220.1 3	Again the Wild-flower Wine she drank,
221 ☒1	Her fair large Eyes 'gan glitter bright,
222 ☒1	And from the Floor, whereon she sank,
223 ☒1	The lofty Lady stood upright:
224 ☒1	She was most beautiful to see,
225 ☒1	Like a Lady of a far Countreè.
	[Line-space]
226 ☒1	And thus the lofty Lady spake—
227 ☒1	All they, who live in th' upper Sky,
228 ☒1	Do love you, holy Christabel!
229 ☒1	And you love them, and for their sake
230 ☒1	And for the Good which me befel,
231 ☒1	Even I in my Degree will try,
232 ☒1 6	Fair Maiden, to requite you well.
6	"Dear
233 ☒1	But now unrobe yourself: for I
234 ☒1	Must pray, ere yet in bed I lie.
	[Line-space]
235 ☒1	Quoth Christabel, So let it be!
236 ☒1	And as the Lady bade, did she.
237 ☒1	Her gentle Limbs did she undress,
238 ☒1	And lay down in her Loveliness.
	[Line-space]
239 ☒1	But thro' her Brain of Weal and Woe

240	2	So many Thoughts ~~went~~ mov'd to and fro,
	⊠1 2	←mov'd→
241	⊠1	That vain it were her lids to close;
242	⊠1	So half way from the Bed she rose,
243	⊠1	And on her Elbow did recline
244	⊠1	To look at the Lady Geraldine.
		[*Line-space*]
245	⊠1	Beneath the Lamp the Lady bow'd
246	⊠1	And slowly roll'd her eyes around,
247	⊠1 5 6	Then drawing in her Breath aloud,
	5 6	And
248	⊠1	Like one that shudder'd, she unbound
249	⊠1	The Cincture from beneath her Breast:
250	⊠1 6	Her silken Robe and inner Vest
	6	silver
251	⊠1	Dropt to her feet, and full in View,
252	⊠1	Behold! her Bosom and half her Side
252.1.1	2–6	Are lean and old and foul of Hue—
253	⊠1	A ʃSight to dream of, not to tell!
254	2 4 *1*	And she is to sleep by Christabel.
	3 5 6	with
	2–4	O shield her! shield sweet
		[*Line-space*]
254.1.1	2	She took two ?ʃPaces, and a Stride,
	3–6 *1*	Paces,
255	2–4	Yet Geraldine nor speaks nor stirs:
256	2–4	Ah! what a stricken look was hers!
257	2–4	Deep from within she seems half-way
258	2–4	To lift some weight with sick assay,
259	2–4	And eyes the maid and seeks delay;
260	2–4	Then suddenly as one defied
261	2–4	Collects herself in scorn and pride,
262	⊠1	And lay down by the Maiden's Side:
263	⊠1	And in her arms the Maid she took,
264	⊠1	Ah weladay!
265	2–6	And with sad Voice and doleful Look
	1–4	low
266	⊠1	These Words did say:
		[*Line-space*]
267	2–6	In the ʄTouch of my Bosom there worketh a Spell,
	1–4	this
268	⊠1	Which is Lord of thy Utterance, Christabel!
269	⊠1	Thou knowest to night and wilt know tomorrow
270	2–6	The Mark of my Shame, the Seal of my Sorrow;
	1–4	This this
271	⊠1	But vainly thou warrest,
272	⊠1	For this is alone in
273	⊠1	Thy Power to declare,
274	⊠1	That in the dim Forest

275	⊠1	Thou heard'st a low Moaning,
276	⊠1	And found'st a bright Lady, surpassingly fair.
277	2–6	And didst bring her home with thee with Love & with Charity
	1–4	in in
278	⊠1 3	To shield her and shelter her ⟵——from——⟶ the damp Air.
	3	& shelter her from

[*Line-space*]

⁻279	2 4	The I Conclusion I to I Book the First.
	3	The Conclusion ~~to~~, I Book the first
	1–3	THE CONCLUSION I TO I PART THE FIRST.
	4	THE CONCLUSION TO PART I.

[*Line-space*]

279	⊠1	It was a lovely Sight to see
280	⊠1	The Lady Christabel, when She
281	⊠1	Was praying at the old Oak Tree.
282	⊠1	Amid the jagged Shadows
283	⊠1	Of mossy leafless Boughs
284	⊠1	Kneeling in the Moonlight
285	⊠1	To make her gentle Vows;
286	⊠1	Her slender Palms together prest,
287	⊠1	Heaving sometimes on her Breast;
288	⊠1	Her Face resign'd to Bliss or Bale—
289	⊠1	Her Face, Oh call it fair not pale,
290	⊠1	And both blue Eyes more bright than clear,
291	⊠1	Each about to have a Tear.

[*Line-space*]

292	⊠1	With open eyes⁄ (ah woe is me!)
293	⊠1	Asleep, and dreaming fearfully,
294	⊠1	Fearfully dreaming, yet, I wis,
295	⊠1	Dreaming that alone, which is—
296	⊠1	O Sorrow and Shame! Can this be She,
297	2–6	The Lady, that knelt at the old Oak Tree?
	1–4	who
298	2	And ~~She~~ lo! the Worker of these Harms,
	⊠1 2	lo!
299	⊠1	That holds the Maiden in her Arms,
300	⊠1	Seems to slumber still and mild,
301	⊠1	As a Mother with her Child.

[*Line-space*]

302	⊠1	A Star hath set, a Star hath risen,
303	⊠1	O Geraldine! since Arms of thine
304	⊠1	Have been the lovely Lady's Prison.
305	2	O Geraldine! One Hour was [??]thine—
	⊠1 2	thine—
306	⊠1	Thou'st had thy Will! By Tairn and Rill
307	⊠1	The Night-birds all that Hour were still.
308	⊠1	But now they are jubilant anew,
309	⊠1	From Cliff and Tower, Tu-whoo! Tu-whoo!
310	⊠1	Tu-whoo! tu-whoo! from Wood and Fell!

[*Line-space*]

311 ⊠1   And see! the Lady Christabel
312 ⊠1   Gathers herself from out her Trance;
313 ⊠1   Her Limbs relax, her Countenance
314 ⊠1   Grows sad and soft; the smooth thin Lids
315 ⊠1   Close o'er her Eyes; and Tears she sheds—
316 ⊠1   Large Tears, that leave the Lashes bright!
317 ⊠1   And oft the while she seems to smile
318 ⊠1   As Infants at a sudden Light!

[*Line-space*]

319 ⊠1   Yea, she doth smile and she doth weep,
320 ⊠1   Like a youthful Hermitess
321 ⊠1   Beauteous in a Wilderness,
322 ⊠1   Who, praying always, prays in ʃSleep.

[*Line-space*]

323 ⊠1   And if she move unquietly,
324 2   Perchance, tis but ~~her~~ the Blood so free
    ⊠2 3   the
325 ⊠1   Comes back and tingles in her Feet.
326 2   No doubt, she ~~sees~~ hath a Vision sweet.
    ⊠1 2   hath
327 ⊠1   What if her guardian Spirit twere?
328 ⊠1   What if She knew her Mother near?
329 ⊠1   But this she knows, in Joys and Woes,
330 ⊠1   That Saints will aid if Men will call,
331 ⊠1   For the blue Sky bends over all!

[*Line-space*]

⁻332 2 4   Christabel | Book the Second.
    3 5 6   Book the Second
    1   CHRISTABEL. | PART II.
    2 3   CHRISTABEL. | PART THE SECOND.
    4   PART II.

[*Line-space*]

332 ⊠1   Each matin Bell, the Baron saith,
333 ⊠1   Knells us back to a World of Death.
334 ⊠1   These Words Sir Leoline first said,
335 ⊠1   When he rose and found his Lady dead:
336 ⊠1   These Words Sir Leoline will say
337 ⊠1   Many a Morn to his dying Day.

[*Line-space*]

338 ⊠1   And hence the Custom and Law began,
339 ⊠1 6   That still at Dawn the Sacristan,
    6   morn
340 ⊠1   Who duly pulls the heavy Bell,
341 ⊠1   Five and forty Beads must tell
342 ⊠1   Between each Stroke—a warning Knell,
343 ⊠1 3   Which not a Soul can chuse but hear
    3   to
344 ⊠1   From Bratha Head to Wyn'dermere.

[*Line-space*]
345 ⊠1   Saith Bracy the Bard, So let it knell!
346 ⊠1   And let the drowsy Sacristan
347 ⊠1   Still count as slowly as he can!
348 ⊠1   There is no Lack of such, I ween,
349 ⊠1 4–6 As   well   fill up the Space between.
    4   w̶i̶l̶l̶ well
    5 6   will
350 ⊠1   In Langdale Pike and Witch's Lair
351 ⊠1   And Dungeon-ghyll so foully rent,
352 ⊠1   With Ropes of Rock and Bells of Air
353 ⊠1 3 6 Three sinful Sextons' Ghosts are pent,
    3   simple
    6   sinful   Souls
354 ⊠1   Who all give back, one after t'other,
355 ⊠1   The Death-note to their living Brother;
356 2–6   And oft too by their Knell offended,
    1–4   the
357 ⊠1   Just as their One——! Two——!——Three!——is ended,
358 2   The Devil mocks the̶i̶r̶ doleful Tale
    ⊠1 2   the
359 ⊠1   With a merry Peal*l* from Borrodale.
    [*Line space*]
360 2–6   The Air is still: thro'   many   a Cloud
    1–4   mist and
361 ⊠1   That merry Peal comes ringing loud:
362 ⊠1   And Geraldine shakes off her dread
363 2–6   And rises lightly from her Bed;
    1–4   the
364 ⊠1 3 Puts on her silken Vestments white,
    3   simple
365 ⊠1   And tricks her Hair in lovely Plight,
366 ⊠1   And nothing doubting of her Spell
367 ⊠1   Awakens the Lady Christabel.
    [*Line-space*]
368 ⊠1   "Sleep you, sweet Lady Christabel?
369 ⊠1   "I trust, that you have rested well.
    [*Line-space*]
370 ⊠1   And Christabel awoke and spied
371 ⊠1   The Same, who lay down by her Side—
372 ⊠1   O rather say, the Same whom She
373 ⊠1   Rais'd up beneath the old Oak Tree!
374 ⊠1   Nay, fairer yet! and yet more fair!
375 ⊠1 4 For She, belike,   hath   drunken deep
    4   h̶a̶d̶ hath
376 ⊠1   Of all the Blessedness of Sleep;
377 ⊠1   And while she spake; her Looks, her Air
378 ⊠1   Such gentle Thankfulness declare,

379 ☒1 5   That (so it seem'd) her girded Vests
   5   Vest
380 ☒1 5   Grew tight beneath her heaving Breasts.
   5   Breast.
381 ☒1   "Sure I have sinn'd! said Christabel,
382 ☒1   "Now Heaven be prais'd, if all be well!
383 ☒1   And in low faltering Tones, yet sweet
384 ☒1 3   Did She the lofty Lady greet
   3   he
385 ☒1   With such Perplexity of Mind
386 ☒1   As Dreams too lively leave behind.
     [*Line-space*]
387 ☒1   So quickly she rose, and quickly array'd
388 ☒1   Her maiden Limbs, and having pray'd
389 ☒1   That He, who on the Cross did groan,
390 ☒1   Might wash away her Sins unknown,
391 ☒1   She forthwith led fair Geraldine
392 ☒1   To meet her Sire, Sir Leoline.
     [*Line-space*]
393 ☒1   The lovely Maid and the Lady tall
394 ☒1   Are pacing both into the Hall,
395 ☒1   And pacing on thro' Page and Groom
396 ☒1   Enter the Baron's Presence Room.
     [*Line-space*]
397 ☒1   The Baron rose and while he prest
397.1 3   The Baron rose and while he prest
398 ☒1   His gentle Daughter to his Breast,
399 ☒1   With chearful Wonder in his Eyes
400 ☒1   The Lady Geraldine espies,
401 2   ~~And gave~~ And gave such Welcome to the Same,
   ☒1 2   ⟵——And——⟶
402 ☒1 4   As might beseem so   bright   a Dame!
   4   ?~~great~~ bright
     [*Line-space*]
403 ☒1   But when he heard the Lady's Tale
404 ☒1   And when she told her Father's Name,
405 ☒1   Why wax'd Sir Leoline so pale,
406 ☒1   Murmuring o'er the Name again,
407 ☒1   Lord Roland de Vaux of Tryermaine?
     [*Line-space*]
408 ☒1   Alas! they had been Friends in Youth;
409 ☒1   But whispering Tongues can poison Truth;
410 ☒1   And Constancy lives in Realms above;
411 ☒1   And Life is thorny; and Youth is vain;
412 ☒1   And to be wroth with one, we love,
413 ☒1   Doth work, like madness in the Brain:
414 ☒1   And thus it chanc'd, as I divine,
415 ☒1   With Roland and Sir Leoline.
416 ☒1   Each spake words of high Disdain

417	⊠1	And Insult to his Heart's best Brother,
418	2–6	And parted—ne'er to meet again!
	1–4	They
419	⊠1 3	But never either found Another
	3	And
420	⊠1	To free the hollow Heart from Paining——
		[*Line-space*]
421	⊠1	They stood aloof, the scars remaining,
422	2	Like Cliffs, which ha~~ve~~d been rent asunder;
	⊠1 2	had
423	⊠1	A dreary Sea now flows between,
424	⊠1	But neither Heat, nor Frost, nor Thunder
425	⊠1	Shall wholly do away, I ween,
426	⊠1	The Marks of that, which once hath been.
		[*Line-space*]
427	⊠1	Sir Leoline a moment's Space
428	⊠1	Stood gazing on the Damsel's Face,
429	⊠1	And the youthful Lord of Tryermaine
430	⊠1	Came back upon his Heart again.
		[*Line-space*]
431	⊠1 3	O then the Baron forgot his Age,
	3	Ra Age,
432	2	His noble ⟨Heart⟩ swell'd high with Rage;
	⊠1 2	Heart
433	⊠1 6	He swore by the wounds in Jesu's Side,
	6	wound
434	⊠1	He would proclaim it far and wide
435	⊠1	With Trump and solemn Heraldly,
436	⊠1	That they, who thus had wrong'd the Dame,
437	⊠1	Were base as spotted Infamy!
438	⊠1	"And if they dare deny the Same,
439	⊠1	"My Herald shall appoint a Week
440	⊠1	"And let the recreant Traitors seek
441	⊠1	"My Tournay Court—that there and then
442	⊠1	"I may dislodge their Reptile Souls
443	⊠1 3	"From the Bodies and Forms of Men!
	3	?~~Hearts~~ Forms
444	⊠1 4	He spake: his eye in lightning rolls!
	4	like
445	⊠1	For the Lady was ruthlessly seiz'd; and he kenn'd
446	⊠1	In the beautiful Lady the Child of his Friend!
		[*Line-space*]
447	⊠1	And now the Tears were on his Face,
448	⊠1	And fondly in his Arms he took
449	⊠1	Fair Geraldine, who met th' Embrace
450	⊠1	Prolonging it with Joyous Look.
451	⊠1	Which when she view'd, a Vision fell
452	⊠1	Upon the Soul of Christabel,

453	2–6	The Vision foul of fFear and Pain!
	1–4	of fear, the touch
454	☒1	She shrunk, and shudder'd, and saw again
455	☒1	(Ah woe is me! Was it for thee,
456	☒1	Thou gentle Maid! such Sights to see?)
457	☒1 5 6	Again she saw that Bosom old,
	5 6	cold,
458	☒1 5 6	Again she felt that Bosom cold,
459	☒1	And drew in her Breath with a hissing Sound:
460	☒1	Whereat the Knight turn'd wildly round,
461	☒1	And nothing saw but his own sweet Maid
462	☒1	With Eyes uprais'd, as one that pray'd.

[*Line-space*]

463	2–5	The Pang, the Sight, had pass'd away,
	6	was
	1–4	touch, had
464	☒1	And in its Stead that Vision blest,
465	☒1 3	Which comforted her After rest,
	3	⟨her⟩
466	☒1	While in the Lady's Arms she lay,
467	☒1	Had put a Rapture in her Breast,
468	☒1	And on her Lips and o'er her Eyes
469a	☒1	Spread Smiles, like Light!

[*Line-space*]

469b	☒1	With new Surprize,
470	☒1 6	"What ails then my beloved Child?
	6	thee
471	☒1	The Baron said—His Daughter mild
472	☒1	Made answer, "All will yet be well"!
473	☒1	I ween, She had no Power to tell
474	☒1	Aught else: so mighty was the Spell.

[*Line-space*]

475	☒1	Yet He, who saw this Geraldine,
476	☒1	Had deem'd her sure a Thing divine,
477	☒1	Such Sorrow with such Grace she blended,
478	☒1	As if she fear'd, she had offended
479	☒1	Sweet Christabel, that gentle Maid!
480	☒1	And with such lowly Tones she pray'd,
481	☒1	She might be sent without Delay
482a	☒1	Home to her Father's Mansion.

[*Line-space*]

482b	☒1	"Nay!
483	☒1	"Nay, by my Soul! said Leoline.
484	☒1	"Ho! Bracy, the Bard, the Charge be thine!
485	☒1 4 5	"Go thou with Music sweet and loud
	4	~~with~~ thou
	5	then
486	☒1 6	"And take two Steeds with fTrappings proud
	6	trapping

487	☒1	"And take the Youth, whom thou lov'st best,
488	☒1	"To bear thy Harp, and learn thy Song,
489	☒1	"And cloath you both in solemn Vest,
490	☒1 3	"And over the Mountains haste along,
491	☒1	"Lest wandering Folk, that are abroad,
492	☒1	"Detain you on the Valley Road.

[*Line-space*]

493	☒1	"And when He has cross'd the Irthing Flood,
494	2	"My merry Bard! He hastes, ~~and~~ he hastes
	☒1 2	he
495	☒1	"Up Knorren Moor thro' Halegarth Wood,
496	☒1	"And reaches soon that Castle good
497	☒1 6	"Which stands and threatens Scotland's Wastes.
	6	~~moors~~ wastes

[*Line-space*]

498	☒1	"Bard Bracy! Bard Bracy! Your Horses are fleet,
499	☒1	"Ye must ride up the Hall, your Music so sweet
500	☒1	"More loud than your Horses' echoing Feet!
501	☒1	"And loud, and loud, to Lord Roland call,
502	☒1	"Thy Daughter is safe in Langdale Hall!
503	☒1 3	"Thy beautiful Daughter is safe and free—
	3	beauteous
504	☒1	"Sir Leoline greets thee thus thro' me.
505	☒1	"He bids thee come without Delay
506	☒1	"With all thy numerous Array
507	2–6	"And fetch thy lovely Daughter home,
	1–4	take
508	☒1	"And He will meet thee on the way
509	☒1	"With all his numerous Array
510	☒1	"White with their panting Palfreys' Foam;
511	☒1	"And, by mine Honor! I will say,
512	☒1	"That I repent me of the Day
513	☒1 6	"When I spake words of fierce Disdain
	6	word
514	☒1	"To Roland de Vaux of Tryermain!—
515	☒1	—"For since that evil hour hath flown,
516	2–6	"Many a Summer's Suns have shone;
	1 2	sun
	3 4	hath
517	☒1	"Yet ne'er found I a Friend again
518	☒1	"Like Roland de Vaux of Tryermain.

[*Line-space*]

519	☒1	The Lady fell and clasp'd his Knees,
520	☒1	Her Face uprais'd, her Eyes o'erflowing;
521	☒1	And Bracy replied, with faltering Voice,
522	☒1	His gracious Hail on all bestowing.
523	☒1	Thy Words, thou Sire of Christabel,
524	☒1	Are sweeter than my Harp can tell;
525	☒1	Yet might I gain a Boon of thee,

526	⊠1	This Day my Journey should not be,
527	⊠1	So strange a Dream hath come to me,
528	⊠1 6	That I had vow'd with Music loud
	6	have
529	⊠1	To clear yon Wood from Thing unblest
530	⊠1	Warn'd by a Vision in my Rest.

[*Line-space*]

531	⊠1	For in my Sleep I saw that Dove,
532	⊠1 6	That gentle Bird, whom thou dost love,
	6	that
533	⊠1	And call'st by thy own Daughter's Name,
534	⊠1	Sir Leoline! I saw the Same
535	⊠1	Fluttering and uttering fearful Moan
536	⊠1	Among the green Herbs in the Forest alone.
537	⊠1	Which when I saw and when I heard
538	⊠1	I wonder'd what might ail the Bird:
539	⊠1	For nothing near it could I see
540	⊠1 3	Save the Grass and green Herbs underneath the old Tree.
	3	the

[*Line-space*]

541	⊠1	And in my Dream methought I went
542	⊠1	To search out what might there be found,
543	⊠1	And what the sweet Bird's Trouble meant
544	⊠1	That thus lay fluttering on the Ground.
545	⊠1	I went, and peer'd, and could descry
546	⊠1 4	No cause for her distressful Cry;
	4	~~the~~ her
547	⊠1	But yet for her dear Lady's sake
548	⊠1 4	I stoop'd, methought, the Dove to take,
	4	~~Bird~~ Dove
549	⊠1	When lo! I saw a bright green Snake
550	⊠1	Coil'd around its wings and neck.
551	⊠1^{imp}	Green as the Herbs, on which it couch'd‿
552	⊠1	Close by the Dove's its Head it crouch'd,
553	⊠1	And with the Dove it heaves and stirs,
554	⊠1	Swelling its Neck as she swell'd her's!
555	⊠1	I woke; it was the Midnight Hour,
556	⊠1	The Clock was echoing in the Tower;
557	⊠1	But tho' my Slumber was gone by,
558	⊠1	This Dream it would not pass away—
559	2 3 5 6	It seem'd to live upon my Eye!
	4 *1–4*	seems
560	⊠1 3	And thence I vow'd this self-same Day
	3	the
562.1	2	~~To wander thro' the Forest bare~~
561	⊠1	With ~~th~~Music strong and saintly Song
562	⊠1	To wander thro' the Forest bare,

563 ☒1 3 6   Lest aught unholy loiter there.
    3   wander
    6   loiter'd
        [*Line-space*]
564 ☒1   Thus Bracy said: the Baron, the while,
565 ☒1   Half-list'ning, heard him with a Smile;
566 ☒1   Then turn'd to Lady Geraldine,
567 ☒1   His Eyes made up of Wonder and Love;
568 ☒1   And said in courtly accents fine,
569 ☒1 4   "Sweet Maid, Lord   Roland's beauteous Dove,
    4   ~~Ro~~ Lord
570 ☒1   With arms more strong than Harp or Song
571 ☒1   Thy Sire and I will crush the Snake:
572 ☒1   He kiss'd her Forehead, as he spake,
573 ☒1   And Geraldine in maiden wise
574 ☒1   Casting down her large bright Eyes
575 ☒1   With blushing Cheek and Courtesy fine
576 ☒1   She turn'd her from Sir Leoline,
577 2   Softly gathering up her ~~Vest~~ Train
    ☒1 2   Train
578 2   ~~Across~~ That o'er her Right Arm fell again,
    ☒1 2   ←—That—→
579 2   And   folded her arms ~~upon~~ across her Chest,
    3   ~~She~~ And   across
    4 5 *1–4*   And
    6   arm
580 ☒1   And couch'd her Head upon her Breast,
581 ☒1   And look'd askance at Christabel—
582 ☒1   Iesu Maria, shield her well!
        [*Line-space*]
583 ☒1 4   A Snake's small Eye blinks dull and shy;
    4   ~~clea~~ shy;
584 ☒1   And the Lady's Eyes they shrunk in her Head,
585 ☒1   Each shrunk up to a Serpent's Eye,
586 ☒1   And with somewhat of Malice & more of Dread
587 ☒1   At Christabel she look'd askance!—
588 ☒1   One moment—and the Sight was fled!
589 ☒1   But Christabel in dizzy Trance
590 2   ⟨Stumbling on the unsteady Ground—⟩
    ☒1 2   Stumbling on the unsteady Ground
591 2–6   Shudder'd aloud with hissing Sound;
    1–4   with a
592 ☒1   And Geraldine again turn'd round,
593 ☒1   And like a Thing, that sought Relief,
594 ☒1   Full of Wonder and full of Grief,
595 ☒1   She roll'd her large bright Eyes divine
596 ☒1 3   Wildly on Sir Leoline.
    3   o'er
        [*Line-space*]

597 ⊠1   The Maid, alas! her thoughts are gone
598 2   ⟨She nothing see—no sight but one!⟩
   ⊠1 2 2   She nothing sees—no sight but one!
   2   But
599 2   ~~But she~~ The Maid, devoid of Guile and Sin,
   ⊠1 2   ←—The—→
600 2   ~~Sweet Christabel~~ I know not how, in fearful wise
   ⊠1 2   ←———I———→
601 2   So deeply ~~now had~~ had she drunken in
   ⊠1 2   ←—had—→
602 2   That Look, those ~~dull and treacherous serpent~~ shrunken serpent Eyes,
   3 4 *1–4*   ←————shrunken————→
   5 6
                                ←—Eyes,—→
603 ⊠1   That all her Features were resign'd
604 ⊠1   To this sole Image in her Mind:
605 ⊠1   And passively did imitate
606 ⊠1   That Look of dull and treacherous Hate.
606.1.1 2   ~~The ?Ground flow'd with her, like a Stream,~~
606.1.2 2   ~~She seems to float, as in a dream~~
607 2   And ~~thus standing~~ thus ⟨she stood⟩ in dizzy Trance
   ⊠1 2   ←——thus——→ she stood
608 2   ~~She~~ Still ~~pictur'ding~~ ~~still~~ that Look askance
   ⊠1 2   Still   picturing   that
609 ⊠1   With forc'd unconscious Sympathy
610 ⊠1   Full before her Father's View—
611 ⊠1   As far as such a Look could be
612 ⊠1   In ~~t~~Eyes so innocent and blue!
   [*Line-space*]
613 2   But when ~~this~~ ~~Spell~~ Trance was o'er, the Maid
   3–6 *1*   the   Trance
   2–4   And
614 ⊠1   Paus'd awhile and inly pray'd,
615 ⊠1 *3 4*   Then falling at her Father's Feet,
   3 4   the Baron's
616 ⊠1 4   "By My Mother's Soul do I intreat
   4   *I* do
617 ⊠1   "That Thou this Woman send away!
618 ⊠1   She said; and more she could not say,
619 ⊠1   For what she knew, she could not tell
620 ⊠1 3   O'ermaster'd by the mighty Spell.
   3   that
   [*Line-space*]
621 ⊠1   Why is thy Cheek so wan and wild,
622 ⊠1   Sir Leoline?—Thy only Child
623 ⊠1   Lies at thy Feet, thy Joy, thy Pride,
624 ⊠1   So fair, so innocent, so mild;
625 ⊠1   The same, for whom thy Lady died!
626 ⊠1   O by the Pangs of her dear Mother
627 ⊠1   Think thou no evil of thy Child!

628 ☒1	For her and thee and for no other
629 ☒1	She pray'd the moment, ere she died,
630 ☒1	Pray'd, that the Babe for whom she died,
631 ☒1	Might prove her dear Lord's Joy & Pride!
632 ☒1	That Prayer her deadly Pangs beguil'd,
633 ☒1	Sir Leoline!
634 ☒1	And would'st thou wrong thy only child,
635 ☒1	Her Child & thine!

[*Line-space*]

636 ☒1	Within the Baron's Heart & Brain
637 ☒1	If Thoughts, like these, had any Share,
638 ☒1	They only swell'd his Rage & Pain
639 ☒1 3	And did but work Confusion there.
3	not
640 ☒1 3	His Heart was cleft with Pain & Rage,
3	~~Rage~~ Pain
641 ☒1	His Cheeks they quiver'd, his Eyes were wild,
642 ☒1	Dishonouŕ'd thus ın his old Age,
643 ☒1 3	Dishonour'd by his only Child,
3	on only
644 ☒1	And all hıs Hospitality
645 ☒1 *4*	To th' insulted Daughter of his Friend
4	wrong'd
646 ☒1	By more than woman's Jealousy
647 2	Brought thus to a disgraceful ~~End~~ End—
☒1 2	End—
648 ☒1	He roll'd his Eye with stern Regard
649 ☒1	Upon the gentle Minstrel Bard
650 ☒1	And said in tones abrupt, austere—
651 ☒1	Why, Bracy! dost thou loiter here?
652 ☒1	I bade thee hence! The Bard obey'd;
653 ☒1	And turning from his own sweet Maid
654 ☒1	The aged Knight, Sir Leoline,
655 ☒1	Led forth the Lady, Geraldine!

[*Line-space*]

‾**656** *1–3*	THE CONCLUSION I ᴛᴏ I PART THE SECOND.
4	THE CONCLUSION TO PART II.

[*Line-space*]

656 1 *1–4*	A little Child, a limber Elf
657 1 *1–4*	Singing, dancing to itself;
658 1 *1–4*	A faery Thing with red round Cheeks,
659 1 *1–4*	That always *finds*, and never *seeks*—
660 1	Doth make a Vision to the Sight,
1–4	Makes such
661 1	Which fills a Father's Eyes with Light!
1–4	As
662 1 *1–4*	And Pleasures flow in so thick & fast
663 1 *1–4*	Upon his Heart, that he at last
664 1 *1–4*	Must needs express his Love's Excess

665 1   In   Words of Wrong and Bitterness.
 1–4   With   unmeant
666 1 *1–4*   Perhaps 'tis pretty to force together
667 1 *1 3 4* Thoughts so all unlike each other;
 2   unlike
668 1 *1–4*   To mutter and mock a broken Charm;
669 1 *1–4*   To dally with Wrong, that does no Harm—
670 1 *1–4*   Perhaps, tis tender too & pretty
671 1 *1–4*   At each wild Word to feel within
672 1 *1–4*   A sweet Recoil of Love & Pity.
673 1 *1–4*   And what if in a World of Sin
674 1 *1–4*   (O sorrow & shame! should this be true)
675 1 *1–4*   Such Giddiness of Heart & Brain
676 1 *1–4*   Comes seldom, save from Rage & Pain,
677 1 *1–4*   So talks, as it's most us'd to do.— —

Note. MS 1 (=lines 656–77 only) is not reported in the following register. Its readings are given verbatim in the preceding main sequence.

preface. ⁻**1.2.** *4* year 1797,   *4* Stowey,   ⁻**1.4.** *4* year 1800,   *1–3* Cumberland. . . . |
It is • *4* Cumberland. It is   *3* lately   *1* liveliness • *2 3* loveliness   *3* vision,   *1* I
trust . . . the present year. • *2 3* I trust that I shall yet be able to embody in verse
the three parts yet to come.   ⁻**1.10.** *3 4* amongst   ⁻**1.13.** *2–4* rill   ⁻**1.14.** *2–*
4 confident,   *1 2 4* far • *3* for   ⁻**1.18.** *4* doggerel   ⁻**1.19.** *3 4* hexameters.
⁻**1.20.** *2 3* your's • *4* yours;   ⁻**1.24.** *3* not   ⁻**1.28.** *1* in the number • *2–*
4 in number   ⁻**1.30.** *3 4* transition,   ⁻**1.31.** 3 Christabel—Book the first •
4 Christabel | Book the first. • 5 Christabel. Book the First,   **1.** ⊠2 5 'Tis   3 6 *1–*
4 night   *1–4* castle   3 Clock • 6 *1–4* clock,   **2.** 6 *1–4* owls   *2–4* awakened
3 Cock • 6 cock: • *1–4* cock;   **3.** 3 Tu—u—whoo!—Tu—u—whoo! • 4 Tu—
u—whoo! Tu—u—whoo! • 6 Tu—u—whoo! —— Tu—u—whoo!   **4.** 6 hark
6 *1–4* cock,   **5.** 6 crew!   **6.** 4 5 rich   **7.** *2 3* mastiff,   6 bitch: • *1 4* bitch;
8. 3 4 Kennel • 5 *1–4* kennel • 6 kennel,   5 *1–4* rock • 6 rock,   **9.** 3 4 6 *1–*
4 answer   3 *1–4* clock, • 6 clock: **10.** 3 quarters • 6 *1–4* quarters,   3 &
3 6 hour, • *1–4* hour;   **11.** 3 6 *1* moonshine   3 6 *1–4* shower,   **12.** 3 6 *1–*
4 howls,   5 overloud: • 6 over loud: • *1–4* over loud;   **13.** 6 say   *1–4* lady's
6 shroud— • 3 *1–4* shroud.   **14.** 3 6 *1–4* night   6 chilly,   **15.** 3 6 *1–4* night
3 6 *1–4* chilly,   3 dark,   **16.** *1–4* gray   3 6 *1–4* cloud   6 high: **17.** 6 covers,
3 6 *1–4* sky.   **18.** 3 6 *1–4* moon   5 Full • 6 full, • *1–4* full;   **19.** 5 dull •
6 dull: **20.** 3 6 *1–4* night   3 6 *1–4* cloud • 4 5 Cloud   3 grey; • *1–4* gray:
21. ⊠2 4 'Tis   ⊠2 4 a month   ⊠2 4 month of   3 May • 6 May.   **23.** 6 Lady • *1–*
4 lady,   **24.** *1–4* father   3 well   **25.** ⊠2 wood   6 *1–4* late,   **26.** 3 Furlong
6 Castle-gate? • *1–4* castle gate?   **27.** 6 dreams,   6 yesternight,   **28.** *1–4* knight;
29. ⊠2 4 she   ⊠2 3 midnight   6 *1–4* wood   **30.** 6 *1–4* weal   3 Lover • *1–4* lover
31. 6 along: 3 4 6 She nothing • 5 *1–4* she nothing   6 spoke: **32.** 5 6 *1* breezes
3–5 also, • 6 also: **33.** 5 6 *2–4* naught   4 *6*Oak, • 6 *1–4* oak,   **34.** 6 *1–4* moss
3 &   5 Missletoe: • 6 missletoe: • *1–4* misletoe: **35.** 6 *1–4* oak tree,   **36.** 6 *1–*
4 silence   3 6 *1–4* she.   **37.** *1–4* lady   **38.** 6 Lady • *1–4* lady,   6 Christabel!—
39. *2–4* moaned   6 be;   **40.** 6 is   3 6 *1–4* she   5 *1–4* tell.—   **41.** ⊠2 5 side
1–4 be,   **42.** *1–4* huge, broad-breasted,   3–5 Oak Tree. • 6 *1–4* oak tree.

43. 6 *1–4* night   3 chill, • 5 6 chill: 6 *1–4* forest   4 bare, • 5 6 bare: **44.** 3 6 *1–4* wind   **45.** 3 6 *1–4* wind   6 *1–4* air   **46.** 6 *1–4* curl   **47.** *1–4* lady's   6 Cheek • *1–4* cheek—   **48.** 3 6 *1–4* wind   **49.** ⊠2 5 one   3 leaf • 6 *1–4* leaf, 6 *1–4* clan,   **51.** 3 *1–4* light,   3 & *1–4* high,   **52.** 6 *1–4* twig   6 *1–4* sky. **53.** 6 *2 3* Hush   3 6 *1–4* heart   **54.** *1–4* Jesu,   **55.** ⊠2 5 *1–4* arms   *1–4* cloak, **56.** *1–4* oak.   **57.** ⊠2 4 she   **58.** ⊠2 3 she   6 *1–4* damsel   *1–4* bright, **59.** ⊠2–4 robe   3 White, • 6 *1* white; • *2–4* white,   **62.** 3–5 Neck, • 6 *1* neck, 6 *1* feet,   6 *1–4* arms   *2–4* bare;   **63.** 4 were,   **65.** 3 6 *1* jewels   3 *1–4* hair. • 5 Hair, • 6 hair,   **66.** 6 guess   5 twas   **67.** *1–4* lady   3 6 *1–4* richly clad • 4 richly-clad   3 she • 6 she, • *1–4* she—   **69.** 6 "Mary   *1–4* mother,   6 now!" **70.** *1–4* (Said   4 Christabel • *1–4* Christabel,)   3 *f*And • 6 "and   6 thou?"   **71.** *1– 4* lady   3 6 *1–4* answer • 4 5 Answer   **72.** 3 6 *1–4* voice • 4 5 Voice   6 sweet. • *1–4* sweet:—   **73.** 6 "Have   3 6 *1–4* pity • 4 5 Pity   3 6 *1–4* distress, • 4 5 Distress,   **74.** 6 "I   3 6 *1* 2 weariness. • 4 5 Weariness. • 3 4 weariness: **75.** 6 "Stretch   3 *1–4* hand, • 6 hand   3 & 6 fear."— • *1* 2 fear, • *3 4* fear! **76.** 4–6 Christabel.   6 "How   3 *2 4* camest   6 here?"   **77.** 3 6 Lady • *1– 4* lady,   3 6 *1–4* voice   3 6 & 5 sweet   **78.** 4 5 Answer   *1–4* meet:— **79.** 6 "My   *1–4* sire   4 Line • 6 *1–4* line,   **80.** 6 *1–4* name   *2–4* Geraldine: **81.** 6 ruffians   3 *2–4* seized   3 yestermorn. • 4 yestermorn   **82.** 6 *1–4* maid   ⊠*1– 4* forlorn: **83.** 3 *2–4* choked • 5 6 choak'd   3 6 *1–4* cries • 4 5 Cries   3 might • 6 might,   **84.** 6 *1–4* palfrey   5 6 white: • *1 4* white.   **85.** 6 *1–4* palfrey 4 5 Wind, • 6 *1–4* wind,   **87.** *2–4* spurred   3 amain; • 6 amain   6 *1–4* steeds 5 6 white • *1–3* white; • *4* white: **88.** *2–4* crossed   6 *1–4* shade   3 Night • 6 *1–4* night.   **89.** 3 me   **90.** ⊠2 4 thought • 4 *f*Thought   ⊠2–4 men   *1– 4* be;   **92.** 3 6 fits • 4 5 Fits • *1* fits,   **93.** 3 6 *1–4* one, • 5 One   3 Tallest 3 five   **94.** ⊠2–5 palfrey's back,   **95.** 6 woman • *1–4* woman,   3 6 alive, • 5 alive   **96.** *2–4* muttered   3 6 *1–4* words • 4 5 Words   6 *1–4* comrades   *1– 4* spoke: **97.** 4 place'd • *2–4* placed   5 6 Oak • *1–3* oak, • 4 oak;   **98.** 4 Haste; • 5 Haste: • 6 haste: **99.** ⊠2–4 went   **100.** 6 heard   5 past   **101.** *1– 4* castle   3–5 Bell • 6 *1–4* bell.   **102.** 6 "Stretch   ⊠2 4 hand (thus   3 6 she) • *1 4* she), • *2 3* she,)   **103.** 6 *1–4* maid   6 flee"   **104.** 3 5 6 *1* stretch'd • *2–4* stretched   ⊠2 5 hand   **105.** *2–4* Geraldine: **106.** *3 4* well,   *3 4* dame! **107.** 3 6 *1–4* service • 4 5 Service   **107.1.1.** 6 strait   5 6 convoy'd   6 *1* thrall, **109.** *4* withal   **111.** 6 *1–4* father's hall.   **112.** 4 She   *1* rose,   3 & *1* pass'd, • *2–4* passed   **113.** *1* steps,   3 fast • *1* fast;   **114.** 3 6 *1 4* stars • 2 3 STARS   *1–4* lady   3 bless'd   **115.** *3 4* Christabel: 6 said,   **116.** 6 "All 3 Houshold • 5 6 houshold • *1–4* household   **116.1.1.** 3 5 6 bed,   **117.** *3 4* cell; **118.** 3 *2 3* health   **119.** *2–4* awakened   *3* he • *1* be;   **120.** 3 6 *1* room 6 *2 3* stealth   **121.** *3 4* courtesy,   **122.** 5 6 *1* to-night   6 me."   **123.** *2– 4* crossed   ⊠2–4 moat,   3 &   **124.** ⊠2–4 key   3 well,   **125.** ⊠2–4 door *2–4* opened   *1–4* straight,   **126.** 3 6 gate, • *1–4* gate;   **127.** 3 gate, • 5 Gate • 6 *1–4* gate   *2–4* ironed   3 & 6 without   **128.** 6 *1–4* army   3 Battle Arr*y*ay • 6 *1–4* battle array   *2–4* marched   **129.** *1–4* lady   4 sank • 5 6 sunk,   5 *2– 4* through   3 *1–4* pain, • 5 Pain • 6 pain   **130.** 3 4 Might • ⊠2–4 might   3 & 3–5 Main • 6 *1–4* main   **131.** 5 6 up   6 weight • 3 *1–4* weight,   **132.** ⊠2– 4 threshold   3 Gate. • 6 gate; • *1–4* gate: **133.** *1–4* lady   3 again • 6 again. **134.** 3 mov'd • 6 *2–4* moved,   ⊠2 4 she   ⊠2 4 5 pain.   **135.** ⊠2 4 6 danger, • 4 Danger, • 6 danger   3 6 fear • 4 5 Fear • *1–4* fear,   **136.** *2–4* crossed   6 court • *1–4* court: 3 6 were   **137.** 6 Christabel,   *3 4* cried   **138.** 4 *f*Lady • *1–*

3 lady   5 side. • *4* side;   **139.** 6 "O   3 ⫽Virgin   **140.** 6 "Who   3 distress •
6 distress!" • *1–4* distress!   **141.** 3 Alas, alas, • 5 Alas! alas! • 6 "Alas! Alas!
3 6 Geraldine   **142.** 6 "I   3 *1–4* weariness. • 5 Weariness • 6 weariness."
143. 3 *1–4* danger, • 6 danger   3 fear • 6 *1–4* fear,   **144.** *2–4* crossed
6 court • *1–4* court: **145.** 6 *4* kennel • *1–3* kennel,   6 *1–4* mastiff   **146.** *1–
4* asleep,   4 Moonshine   **147.** ⊠2–4 mastiff   **148.** *1–4* make!   **149.** ⊠2–
5 mastiff bitch?   **150.** 4 'till   *2–4* uttered   ⊠2 4 5 yell   **151.** 6 Christabel
152. ⊠2 4 Perhaps   ⊠ 2–5 owlet's   3 6 scritch • 4 5 Scritch • *1–4* scritch:
153. ⊠2–5 mastiff bitch?   **154.** *2–4* passed   6 hall • *1–4* hall,   3 *1–4* still,
155. 5 6 will, • *1–4* will!   **156.** ⊠2 4 5 brands   6 flat   ⊠2 4 5 brands   *1–
4* dying,   **157.** ⊠2–4 ashes   5 lying: **158.** *1–4* lady   5 pass'd • *2–4* passed,
159. ⊠2–5 tongue   ⊠2 4 5 light,   ⊠2 4 5 *3* fit of • *3* fit af   3 flame, • 6 flame • *1–
4* flame;   **160.** *1–4* lady's   3 *1–4* eye,   **161.** *1–4* thereby,   **162.** ⊠2–5 boss
⊠2–5 shield   4–6 tall   **163.** 3 6 *1* nitch • *2–4* niche   6 *1–4* wall.   **164.** 6 "O
5 tread   3 Christabel   **165.** 6 "My   ⊠2–5 father   6 well."   **166.** 3 bares
4 bare,   **166.1.1.** 4–6 stairs • *1* stairs;   **167.** *4* And,   4 air,   **168.** *4* stair,
169. ⊠2 4 5 glimmer,   3 &   ⊠2 4 5 gloom,   **170.** 3 Room • 6 *1–4* room,
171. 3 *1–4* death • 6 death,   3 breath, • 5 6 breath: • *1–4* breath!   **172.** *2–4* reached
⊠2 4 5 chamber   3 door • 6 door, • *1–4* door;   **173.** 3 6 *1* feet   **174.** ⊠2–
5 rushes   ⊠2 4 5 chamber floor.   **175.** ⊠2 4 5 moon   ⊠2 5 the   ⊠2 4 air,
176. 3 *1–4* moonbeam • 6 moon beam   **177.** ⊠2 4 5 light   **178.** ⊠2–
5 chamber   *2–4* carved   **179.** *2–4* Carved   3 &   *1–4* sweet,   **180.** ⊠2–
5 carver's   3 5 6 brain • *1–4* brain,   **181.** *1–4* lady's   ⊠2 4 5 chamber   6 meet.
182. ⊠2–5 lamp   ⊠2 4 chain   **183.** *2–4* fastened   *1–4* angel's   ⊠2 4 5 feet.
184. 5 Silver   ⊠2 4 5 lamp   3 &   5 dim: • 6 dim,   **185.** ⊠2–5 lamp   4 trim •
1–4 trim.   **186.** 6 trim'd • *2–4* trimmed   6 lamp • *1–4* lamp,   3 &   **187.** 3 &
188. *1–4* Geraldine,   3 6 plight • *1–4* plight,   **189.** ⊠2 4 floor   **190.** 6 "O
3 5 6 Lady • *1–4* lady,   5 Geraldine   **191.** 6 "I   5 6 you   3 wine. • 4 Wine •
6 wine, • *1–4* wine!   **192.** 6 "It   ⊠2 4 wine   3 5 powers • *1–4* powers;
193. 6 "My   *1–4* mother   5 Wild   4 Flowers   **193.1.1.** 5 Nay • 6 "Nay   5 up.
5 6 you   **193.1.2.** 6 "Believe   5 6 me   4 you • 6 you."   **194.** 6 "And   ⊠2–
5 mother   **195.** 6 "Who   ⊠2–5 maiden   6 forlorn?"   **196.** *2–4* answered—
5 6 "Woe   6 me   **197.** 6 "She   ⊠2 4 hour   **198.** 6 "I   *1* gray-hair'd • *2* gray-
haired • *3 4* grey-haired   3–5 Friar • ⊠2–5 friar   3 5 6 tell   **199.** 6 "How   6 death
bed • *1–4* death-bed   *1–4* say,   **200.** 6 "That   6 *1 2* castle bell • *3 4* castle-bell
201. 6 "Strike   6 wedding day • *1–4* wedding day.   **202.** 6 "O   3 ⋔Mother • *1–
4* mother   ⊠2 6 dear! • 6 dear,   6 here!"   **203.** 6 "I   4–6 would   5 Geraldine
⊠2 3 she   6 were."   **204.** 3 *2–4* altered   3 6 voice • *1–4* voice,   3 She • 5 *1–
4* she— • 6 she   **205.** 4 "Off • 6 "Off! • *4* Off,   ⊠2–5 mother!   6 peak   4 &
206. *4* I   ⊠2 3 5 flee."   **208.** ⊠2–5 eye?   **209.** ⊠2–5 dead   **210.** ⊠2–5 voice
211. 3 Off,   4 "Off Woman, • 5 6 "Off woman, • *1–4* "Off, woman,   ⊠2 4 5 hour
3 6 mine   **212.** *4* Though   ⊠2–5 guardian spirit   **213.** 3 Off • 5 *4* Off, •
6 "Off   3 Woman • ⊠2–4 *3* woman, • *3* woman   ⊠2 'tis   3 me • ⊠2–5 me."
214. *1–4* lady's   3 Side • 4 side • ⊠2–4 side,   **215.** *2–4* raised   3–5 Heaven
3 blue   **216.** 6 "Alas, • *1–4* Alas!   3 Ride • ⊠2–4 ride—   **217.** 6 "Dear
1–4 lady!   *2–4* wildered   3 you • 6 you!"   **218.** *1–4* lady   *2–4* wiped
3 Brow   **219.** 3 I'm   6 "I   *2–4* "'tis   5 now • 6 now"   **220.** 3 *1–4* wild-
flower   ⊠2 4 wine   3 drank • 5 6 drank. • *1–4* drank: **221.** ⊠2 4 eyes   3 gan
222. 3 *1–4* floor • 4 5 Floor • 6 floor,   4 sank   **223.** *1–4* lady   3 upright. •

6 *2–4* upright;   **225.** *1–4* lady   5 6 Countree. • *1–4* countrée.   **226.** *1–4* lady
227. 6 "All   5 6 they   ☒2 the   ☒*2–5* sky,   **228.** 6 "Do   **229.** 6 "And you
3 & for   5 6 sake,   **230.** 6 "And   ☒2 4 5 good   6 *4* befell,   **231.** 6 "Even
6 I,   5 in,   3 *1–4* degree • 6 degree,   6 try   **232.** 3 Maiden • 6 *1–4* maiden,
233. 6 "But   3 *1–4* yourself;   **234.** 6 "Must   6 lie."   **235.** 3 *1–4* so • 6 "so
6 be!"   **236.** *1–4* lady   5 6 bade   4 She.   **237.** ☒2 4 limbs   6 undress
238. ☒2 4 loveliness.   **239.** *2–4* through   3 Brain, • ☒*2–5* brain   ☒*2–5* weal   3 &
☒*2–5* woe   **240.** ☒2 4 5 thoughts   6 *2–4* moved   3 &   **241.** 3 Lids   3 close, •
5 6 close: **242.** 3 *1–4* half-way   6 *1–4* bed   **243.** ☒*2–4* elbow   **244.** *1–*
4 lady   **245.** ☒*2–5* lamp   *1–4* lady   *1* bow'd, • *2–4* bowed,   **246.** *2–4* rolled
6 around • *1–4* around;   **247.** ☒*2–4* breath   3 5 6 *4* aloud   **248.** *2–4* shuddered,
249. 3 *1–4* cincture   3 breast, • 5 *1–4* breast: • 6 breast;   **250.** 3 Robe, • 6 robe • *1–*
4 robe,   3 &   6 vest • *1–4* vest,   **251.** 3 &   ☒*2–4* view,   **252.** ☒*2–5* bosom
3 &   5 6 side • *1–4* side——   **252.1.1.** 3 & old &   3 6 hue—   **253.** 3 4 Sight •
☒*2–4* sight   3 tell   **254.** 3 She   *2–4* Christabel!   **254.1.1.** 6 paces •
1 paces,   3 &   6 *1* stride,   **255.** 3 *4* stirs;   **262.** 6 *1 4* maiden's   3 Side •
5 6 side, • *1* side: • *2–4* side!—   **263.** ☒*2–5* maid   3 took   **264.** 6 wcll a
day! • *1–3* wel-a-day! • *4* well-a-day!   **265.** ☒2 *4* voice   3 &   ☒2 4 look
266. ☒2 4 5 words   3 say   **267.** ☒2 4 touch • 4 Touch   ☒*2–5* bosom   6 spell •
1–4 spell,   **268.** *1–4* lord   3 6 utterance • 4 ūUtterance, • 5 Utterance • *1–*
4 utterance,   **269.** 3 6 tonight, • 5 tonight • *1–4* to-night,   3 6 &   5 6 will
5 *1–4* to-morrow   **270.** ☒*2–4* mark   ☒*2–5* shame,   ☒*2–5* seal   3 Sorrow •
5 Sorrow, • 6 sorrow, • *1–4* sorrow;   **271.** 6 warrest   **273.** ☒2 4 5 power
5 6 declare   **274.** ☒2 4 5 forest   **275.** 4 heardst • *2 3* heardest   3 5 *1–*
4 moaning, • 4 ṁMoaning • 6 moaning   **276.** *2 3* foundest   *1–4* lady,   3 fair •
4 *1–4* fair: **277.** 3 dids • 5 did'st   5 thee,   ☒*2–5* love   *1–4* and   6 charity • *1–*
4 charity,   **278.** 3 4 her &   3 Air • 5 *1–4* air. • 6 air   ⁻**279.** 4 The Conclusion
to I Book the First • *2 3* THE I CONCLUSION TO PART THE FIRST.
279. ☒*2–5* sight   **280.** *1–4* lady   3 5 6 Christabel   ☒*2–4* she   **281.** ☒*2–5* oak
6 tree • *1–4* tree.   **282.** ☒*2–5* shadows   **283.** 3 Mossy   4 Bows • 6 boughs •
1–4 boughs,   **284.** 6 moonlight • *1–4* moonlight,   **285.** 5 Vows: • 6 vows •
1–4 vows;   **286.** ☒2 4 5 palms   3 press'd • 5 6 prest   **287.** 3 Breast •
☒*2–5* breast;   **288.** ☒2 4 5 face   *2–4* resigned   ☒*2–5* bliss   ☒*2–5* bale—
289. 3 face • ☒*2–5* face,   4 *1–4* oh   6 O   5 6 fair,   3 pale   **290.** ☒2 4 5 eyes
3 clear   **291.** ☒2 4 tear.   **292.** ☒2 eyes   3 (Ah   **293.** 3 5 6 Asleep
3 &   **294.** ☒2 yet   3 wis   **295.** 5 alone   *1* is——   **296.** ☒*2–5* sorrow
☒*2–5* shame!   5 6 can   ☒*2–4* she,   **297.** 3 5 6 Lady • *1–4* lady,   3 Oak
Tree • ☒*2–5* oak tree?   **298.** 4 wWorker • ☒*2–5* worker   ☒*2–5* harms,
299. ☒*2–5* maiden   5 *1–4* arms, • 6 arms   **300.** 5 mild   **301.** ☒*2–5* mother
☒*2–5* child.   **302.** ☒*2–5* star   ☒*2–5* star   5 6 risen   **303.** ☒*2–5* arms
6 thine,   **304.** *1–4* lady's   5 *1–4* prison. • 6 prison   **305.** 6 Geraldine
☒2 3 one   ☒*2–5* hour   5 6 thine   **306.** ☒*2–4* will!   6 Tarin • *1–4* tairn   3 &
6 rill • *1–4* rill,   **307.** ☒*2–5* night-birds   ☒*2–5* hour   3 still   **309.** ☒*2–5* cliff
☒*2–5* tower,   5 Tu whoo! Tu-whoo! • 6 tu whoo! tu whoo! • *1–4* tu—whoo!
tu—whoo!   **310.** 5 Tu-whoo! Tu-whoo! • 6 Tu whoo! tu whoo! • *1–4* Tu—whoo!
tu—whoo!   ☒*2–5* wood   3 Fell • ☒*2–5* fell!   **311.** *1–4* lady   **312.** 5 Trance, •
6 trance, • *1–4* trance;   **313.** ☒*2–5* limbs   ☒*2–5* countenance   **314.** 5 6 soft:
☒*2–5* lids   **315.** 5 6 eyes: • *1–4* eyes;   ☒*2–4* tears   **316.** 5 6 tears, • *1–4* tears
☒*2–4* lashes   3 bright.   **318.** ☒*2–5* infants   ☒*2–5* light!   **319.** 3 5 6 Yea

⊠2–4 smile,   3 weep   **320.** *1–4* hermitess,   **321.** 6 wilderness • *1–4* wilderness,   **322.** 3 5 6 Who   3–5 Sleep. • ⊠2–5 sleep.   **323.** *1–4* And, **324.** 5 6 Perchance   ⊠2 5 'tis   ⊠2–5 blood   4 free free • *1–4* free,   **325.** 6 feet, • *1–4* feet.   **326.** 3 5 6 doubt   ⊠2–5 vision   3 sweet • 6 sweet,   **327.** ⊠2–5 spirit   3 4 6 *4* 'twere? • 5 t'were? • *1* 'twere • *2 3* 'twere,   **328.** ⊠2 3 she ⊠2–5 mother   **329.** 5 Ioys • ⊠2–5 joys   3 & ⊠2–5 woes,   **330.** ⊠2–5 saints ⊠2–5 men   *1–4* call: **331.** ⊠2–5 sky   3 all • 5 6 all.   **332.** 6 "Each 6 bell" • *1–4* bell,   **333.** 6 "Knells   ⊠2 4 5 world   6 death." • *1–4* death. **334.** ⊠2–4 words   3 said   **335.** *1–4* lady   **336.** ⊠2–4 words   *2–4* say, **337.** ⊠2–5 morn   5 *1* day. • 6 day • 2 day, • *3 4* day!   **338.** ⊠2–5 custom ⊠2–5 law   **339.** *1–4* dawn   *1–4* sacristan,   **340.** 3 Bell • ⊠2–5 bell, **341.** ⊠2–5 beads   **342.** ⊠2–4 stroke—   6 knell! • *1–4* knell,   **343.** ⊠2–5 soul *1–4* choose   **344.** ⊠2–4 *1* Wyndermere.   **345.** 3 Bard. • 6 Bard,— • *1–4* bard, 6 "so   **346.** *1–4* sacristan   **348.** ⊠2 4 5 lack • 4 Ilack   5 6 such   4 6 *1–3* ween **349.** ⊠2–5 space   3 between, • 6 between   **350.** 5 Pike, • 6 pike   6 witches lair • *1–4* Witch's Lair,   **351.** 3 5 Dungeon-gill • 6 dungeon-Gill   **352.** ⊠2–5 ropes ⊠2–5 rock   ⊠2–5 bells   ⊠2–5 air   **353.** 5 6 Sexton's • *1 2 4* sextons' • *3* sexton's *1–4* ghosts   **354.** 5 6 back   **355.** ⊠2–5 death-note   3–5 Brother, • 6 brother, • *1– 4* brother;   **356.** *1–4* too,   ⊠2–4 knell   **357.** 4 *6*One—! • *1–4* one!   3 Two!— • 6 two—! • *1–4* two!   4 5 Three—! • 6 three—! • *1–4* three!   **358.** *1–4* devil ⊠2–5 tale   **359.** 3 4 Peal • ⊠2–4 peal   3 4 *1–3* Borrowdale. • 4 Borodale. **360.** ⊠2 4 air   *1–4* still!   3 2–4 through   ⊠2–4 cloud   **361.** ⊠2–5 peal   *1– 4* loud;   **362.** *3* of   *1–4* dread,   **363.** 4 Bed, • ⊠2–5 bed;   **364.** ⊠2– 5 vestments   **365.** ⊠2–5 hair   ⊠2–5 plight,   **366.** ⊠2–5 spell   **367.** *1–4* lady 6 Christabel,   **368.** *1–4* lady   **369.** *4* I   ⊠2 3 trust   ⊠2–5 well."   **371.** 3 *1– 4* same • 4 Same • 6 same,   ⊠2–5 side—   **372.** 5 Say,   ⊠2–5 same   ⊠2–5 she **373.** *2–4* Raised   3 Oak-tree! • ⊠2–5 oak tree!   **374.** 3 Nay   **375.** 4 She • ⊠2–4 she   ⊠2 3 5 belike   **376.** ⊠2–5 blessedness   3 Sleep, • 6 sleep; • *1–4* sleep! **377.** ⊠2 5 6 spake,   6 looks • *1–4* looks,   ⊠2–5 air   **378.** ⊠2–5 thankfulness **379.** ⊠2 4 5 *1* seemed)   ⊠2–5 vests   **380.** ⊠2–5 breasts.   **381.** 3 sinned! • *1* sinn'd! • *2–4* sinned!"   **382.** 3 Now   ⊠2–5 heaven   4 *1* prais'd • *2–4* praised ⊠2–5 well!"   **383.** ⊠2–5 tones,   *1–4* sweet,   **384.** ⊠2–5 she   *1–4* lady **385.** ⊠2 3 5 perplexity   ⊠2–5 mind   **386.** ⊠2–5 dreams   **387.** 6 qu⟨i⟩ckly *2–4* arrayed   **388.** ⊠2–5 limbs,   *2–4* prayed   **389.** 6 he,   *1–4* cross **390.** ⊠2–5 sins   *3* unknwon,   **392.** *1–4* sire,   **393.** 5 Maid, • ⊠2–5 maid ⊠2–5 lady   **394.** ⊠2–5 hall,   **395.** 3 *2–4* through   ⊠2–5 page   6 *1–3* groom • *4* groom,   **396.** 3 Presense Room • ⊠2–5 presence room.   **397.** *1–4* rose, **398.** ⊠2–5 daughter   ⊠2–5 breast,   **399.** *1–4* cheerful   ⊠2 4 wonder   ⊠2–5 eyes **400.** *1–4* lady   **401.** 4 ⱴWelcome • ⊠2–5 welcome   5 Same; • ⊠2–5 same, **402.** ⊠2–5 dame!   **403.** *1–4* lady's   6 tale • *1–4* tale,   **404.** ⊠2–5 father's 5 ᴎName, • ⊠2–5 name,   **405.** *2–4* waxed   **406.** ⊠2–5 name   **408.** 3 Alas ⊠2–5 friends   5 Youth: • 6 youth: • *1–4* youth;   **409.** ⊠2–5 tongues   ⊠2–5 truth; **410.** ⊠2–5 constancy   ⊠2–5 realms   **411.** ⊠2–5 life   ⊠2–5 youth   *3* vain; **412.** ⊠2 5 6 one • 5 One,   **413.** ⊠2 work   3 Madness   6 brain: • *1–4* brain. **414.** 3 *2–4* chanced,   **416.** ⊠2–5 disdain   **417.** ⊠2–4 insult   3 hearts • ⊠2– 5 heart's   6 brother, • *1–4* brother: **418.** 6 parted   3 neer   **419.** ⊠2 4 another **420.** ⊠2–5 heart   3–5 Paining— • *1–4* paining—   **421.** 6 aloof   3 6 remaining **422.** 5 Cliffs • ⊠2–5 cliffs   3 asunder • 5 6 asunder: **423.** ⊠2–5 sea   *3* between. • *4* between;—   **424.** ⊠2–5 heat,   ⊠2–5 frost,   6 thunder • *1–4* thunder,

425. 5 6 away   **426.** ⊠2–5 marks   *1–4* that   3 been   **427.** *1–4* Leoline,
6 space • *1–4* space,   **428.** ⊠2–5 damsel's   6 face, • *1 2* face; • *3 4* face:
430. 5 ⱧHeart • ⊠2–5 heart   3 again   **431.** 6 age. • *1–4* age,   **432.** ⊠2–
5 heart   *2–4* swelled   6 rage. • *1–4* rage;   **433.** 5 6 Iesu's   6 side • ⊠2 4 6 side,
435. ⊠2–5 trump   3–5 Heraldry, • ⊠2–5 heraldry,   **436.** 5 6 *4* they   *2–4* wronged
⊠2–5 dame,   **437.** ⊠2–5 infamy!   **438.** ⊠2–5 same,   **439.** *4* My   ⊠2–
5 herald   6 week • *1–4* week,   **440.** *4* And   • ⊠2–5 traitors   **441.** *4* My
4 5 Tourney Court— • 6 Tourney-court— • *1 2* tournay court— • *3 4* tourney
court—   6 then,   **442.** *4* I   ⊠2–4 reptile   ⊠2–5 souls   **443.** *4* From
⊠2–5 bodies   ⊠2–5 forms   6 men! • *1–4* men!"   **444.** 4 Eye   5 6 light'ning
3 rolls   **445.** *1–4* lady   4 2 *4* seized; • *3* seized: 4 &   *2–4* kenned   **446.** ⊠2–
5 lady   ⊠2–5 child   3 5 Friend; • 6 friend; • *1–4* friend!   **447.** ⊠2–5 tears
⊠2–5 face,   **448.** ⊠2–5 arms   **449.** ⊠2–5 *1* the   6 embrace • *1–4* embrace,
450. 5 Ioyous Look • ⊠2 4 5 joyous look.   **451.** 4–6 view'd • *2–4* viewed,   ⊠2–
5 vision   **452.** ⊠2–5 soul   **453.** ⊠2–5 vision   3–5 Fear • 6 fear   ⊠2–5 pain!
454. ⊠2 5 6 shrunk   *2–4* shuddered,   3 & saw   *4* again—   **455.** *1–4* (Ah,
5 6 was   **456.** ⊠2–5 maid!   ⊠2 3 sights   5 6 see!)   **457.** ⊠2–5 bosom
458. *1–4* bosom   4 cold   **459.** ⊠2–5 breath   ⊠2–5 sound: **460.** *2–4* turned
461. *1–4* saw,   ⊠2–5 maid   **462.** ⊠2–5 eyes   5 6 uprais'd • *2–4* upraised,
2–4 prayed.   **463.** 6 pang,   6 sight • *1–4* sight,   3 *2–4* passed   5 6 away;
464. ⊠2–4 stead   ⊠2–5 vision   **465.** ⊠2–5 after-rest,   **466.** *1–4* lady's
⊠2–5 arms   **467.** ⊠2–5 rapture   ⊠2–5 breast,   **468.** 5 Lips, • 6 lips, •
1–4 lips   ⊠2–5 eyes   **469.** 4 Smiles • 6 smiles, • *1–4* smiles   ⊠2–5 light!
469. 3 Surprize • 6 surprise • *1–4* surprise,   **470.** 3 5 What   ⊠2–5 child?"
471. 6 his   ⊠2–5 daughter   **472.** 3 well! • ⊠2 3 well!"   **473.** 5 6 ween
⊠2–4 she   ⊠2 4 5 power   **474.** ⊠2–4 spell.   **475.** ⊠2–4 he,   **476.** *2–*
4 deemed   ⊠2–5 thing   *3 4* divine.   **477.** ⊠2 4 5 sorrow   3 ⱨGrace • ⊠2–5 grace
478. 3 feared • 5 6 fear'd • *2–4* feared,   **479.** ⊠2–5 maid!   **480.** ⊠2–5 tones
6 pray'd • *2–4* prayed,   **481.** ⊠2 5 delay   **482.** ⊠2–5 father's   4 Mansion •
⊠2–5 mansion.   **483.** 5 "Nay • *4* Nay,   6 soul! • *1–4* soul!"   5 6 Leoline,
484. ⊠2 5 *4* Bracy   *1–4* bard,   ⊠2–5 charge   3 thine   **485.** *4* Go   *1–*
4 thou,   ⊠2–5 music   *1–4* loud,   **486.** *4* And   *1–4* steeds   3–5 Trappings
proud • *1–4* trappings proud,   **487.** *4* And   6 youth, • *1–4* youth   ⊠2–5 best
488. *4* To   6 harp • *1–4* harp,   ⊠2–5 song,   **489.** *4* And   *1–4* clothe   ⊠2–5 vest,
490. *4* And   ⊠2–5 mountains   5 6 along   **491.** *4* Lest   *1* wand'ring   6 folk •
1–4 folk,   **492.** *4* Detain   ⊠2–5 valley   6 road • *1–4* road.   **493.** *4* And
⊠2 4 he • *4* ⱧHe   *2–4* crossed   ⊠2–5 flood,   **494.** *4* My   *1–4* bard!   5 He
hastes he • 6 he hastes he • *1–4* he hastes, he   **495.** *4* Up   6 moor • *1–4* Moor,
3 *2–4* through   6 wood,   **496.** *4* And   4 *ₜ*Castle • *1–4* castle   **497.** *4* Which
1–4 wastes.   **498.** 6 Bard Bracy! your • *1–4* bard Bracy! your   ⊠2–5 horses
499. *4* Ye   ⊠2–5 hall,   5 Your   ⊠2 4 5 music   *1–4* sweet,   **500.** *4* More   3 *1–*
4 horses' • 6 horses   ⊠2 4 5 feet!   **501.** *4* And   4 *1–4* loud and   ⊠2 3 loud
to   **502.** *4* Thy   ⊠2–5 daughter   *1–4* hall!   **503.** *4* Thy   ⊠2 4 5 daughter
504. *4* Sir   3 *2–4* through   **505.** *4* He   ⊠2 4 5 delay   **506.** *4* With   6 array •
1–4 array;   **507.** *4* And   ⊠2–5 daughter   *3 4* home: **508.** *4* And   ⊠2 4 5 he
509. *4* With   ⊠2–5 array   **510.** *4* White   4 5 Palfrey's • 6 palfrey's • *1–*
4 palfreys'   3 5 Foam: • 4 Foam. • 6 *1 2* foam, • *3 4* foam: **511.** 5 6 3 "And •
4 And   6 Honour! • *1–4* honour!   **512.** *4* That   ⊠2–5 day   **513.** 2 'When •
4 When   3 Words   ⊠2–5 disdain   **514.** 2 'To • *4* To   ⊠2 Tryermaine!—

515. 6 "For • *1–3* "—For • *4* —For   3 Hour   **516.** *4* Many   ⊠2–5 summer's
6 suns   5 6 shone: **517.** *4* Yet   ⊠2–5 friend   **518.** *4* Like   3–6 Tryermaine. •
1–4 Tryermaine."   **519.** *1–4* lady fell,   4 *1–4* clasped   6 knees • *1–4* knees,
520. ⊠2 4 5 face   3 *2–4* upraised, • 6 uprais'd   ⊠2–5 eyes   3 5 o'erflowing:
521. 3 *2 3* faultering   4 Voice • ⊠2–5 voice,   **522.** ⊠2–5 hail   *1 2* bestow-
ing:— • *3* bestowing;— • *4* bestowing!—   **523.** *4* "Thy   4 Words • 6 words •
1–4 words,   *1–4* sire   4–6 Christabel   **524.** ⊠2–5 harp   3 5 6 tell,   **525.**
⊠2 3 5 boon   5 6 thee   **526.** ⊠2–5 day   4 *j*Journey • 5 Iorney • ⊠2–
5 journey   **527.** ⊠2–5 dream   *1 2* me: • *3 4* me;   **528.** 5 6 vow'd, • *2–4* vowed
⊠2–5 music   **529.** ⊠2 4 5 wood   3 *f*Thing • ⊠2–5 thing   *1–4* unblest,   **530.** *2–*
4 Warned   ⊠2–5 vision   6 rest. • *1–4* rest!   **531.** ⊠2–4 sleep   ⊠2–5 dove,
532. 3 Bird • ⊠2–5 bird,   **533.** 3 calles't • 6 callst   ⊠2–5 daughter's   6 name •
1–4 name—   **534.** 6 *4* same • *1–3* same,   **535.** *1–4* Fluttering,   6 moan • *1–*
4 moan,   **536.** ⊠2–5 herbs   ⊠2–5 forest   3 alone   **537.** 3 &   5 *1–4* heard,
538. 3 wondered   ⊠2–5 *4* bird: • *4* bird;   **539.** *1–4* see,   **540.** ⊠2–5 grass
3 6 &   ⊠2–4 herbs   5 Old   3 Tree • ⊠2–5 tree.   **541.** *4* "And   6 *4* dream
methought • *1–3* dream, methought,   **542.** 3 found. • 4 6 found • *1–4* found;
543. 3 Birds • ⊠2–5 bird's   ⊠2 4 trouble   *1–4* meant,   **544.** 3 Ground • ⊠2–
5 ground.   **545.** 4 *1–4* went   *2–4* peered   **546.** ⊠2–5 cry;   **547.** *1–4* lady's
548. 3 stoop't, • *2–4* stooped,   *1–3* methought   ⊠2–5 dove   **549.** 5 6 *1–4* snake
550. *2–4* Coiled   3 *w*Wings   3 Neck • 6 *4* neck,   **551.** 3–5 Herbs • ⊠2–5 herbs
3–5 *1* couch'd, • 6 couch'd • *2–4* couched,   **552.** ⊠2–5 dove's   ⊠2–5 head
3 crouched, • 6 crouch'd; • *1* crouch'd; • *2–4* crouched;   **553.** ⊠2–5 dove   3 &
6 stirs • *2* stirs.   **554.** ⊠2 4 5 neck   *2–4* swelled   ⊠2–5 hers!   **555.** 3 woke,
⊠2 3 midnight   ⊠2–5 hour,   **556.** ⊠2 4 5 clock   ⊠2–5 tower;   **557.** *2–*
4 though   ⊠2–5 slumber   **558.** ⊠2–5 dream   **559.** ⊠2–5 eye!   **560.** 3 *2–*
4 vowed   6 self same day • *1–4* self-same day,   **561.** 3–5 Music • ⊠2–5 music
3 strong,   3 Saintly   3 Song, • ⊠2–5 song   **562.** *2–4* through   ⊠2–5 forest
3 6 bare   **563.** *4* there."   **564.** 3 said   3 Baron   **565.** 3 Half-listening, •
4 Half-list'ning • 6 Half listening, • *1–4* Half-listening   3 Smile: • ⊠2–4 smile;
566. 3 *2–4* turned   **567.** 4 *t*Eyes • ⊠2–5 eyes   ⊠2–5 wonder   3 &   3 Love •
⊠2–5 love;   **568.** 5 6 fine   **569.** 4 *1–3* Sweet   6 maid • *1–4* maid,   6 *1–*
4 dove,   **570.** 6 "With   ⊠2–5 harp   6 song • *1–4* song,   **571.** 6 "Thy   *1–*
4 sire   3 &   3 Snake • 6 snake:" • *1–3* snake! • *4* snake!"   **572.** 3 *2–4* kissed
3–5 Forehead • ⊠2–5 forehead   **573.** *4* Geraldine,   3 Maiden   *1–4* wise,
574. 6 eyes • *1–4* eyes,   **575.** ⊠2–5 cheek   3 & curtsey • 6 and curtesy • *1–4* and
courtesy   **576.** 3 *2–4* turned   3 Leoline • *1–4* Leoline;   **577.** 5 6 train • *1–*
4 train,   **578.** ⊠2 4 right   ⊠2 3 arm · *1–4* again;   **579.** 3 Arms   4 5 Chest •
⊠2–5 chest,   **580.** 3 *2–4* couched   ⊠2–5 head   ⊠2–5 breast,   **581.** *2–*
4 looked   3 asknane   *1–4* Christabel——   **582.** 4 *4* Jesu • *1–3* Jesu,   6 Maria
583. 5 Snakes • ⊠2–5 snake's   ⊠2–5 eye   6 & shy: • *1–4* and shy,   **584.** *1–*
4 lady's   ⊠2–5 eyes   5 6 head • *1–4* head,   **585.** ⊠2–4 serpent's   5 Eye •
6 eye • *1–4* eye,   **586.** 6 malice • *1–4* malice,   5 *1–4* and   3 6 *1–3* dread •
4 dread,   **587.** *2–4* looked   *1* askance!——   **588.** 3 —&   ⊠2–5 sight
589. 6 *4* trance • *1–3* trance,   **590.** 4   Ground— • 5 *g*Ground • 6 *3 4* ground •
1 2 ground—   **591.** *2–4* Shuddered   *1–4* aloud,   3 6 sound: • 5 Sound: •
1–4 sound;   **592.** *2–4* turned   3 round   **593.** 3 5 Thing • 6 thing • *1–*
4 thing,   ⊠2 4 relief,   **594.** 6 wonder, • *1–4* wonder   3 &   ⊠2–5 grief,
595. *2–4* rolled   ⊠2–5 eyes   **596.** 3 Sir Leoline   **597.** ⊠2–5 maid,   *1–*

4 gone,   **599.** 3 5 Maid • ⊠2–5 maid,   ⊠2–5 guile   3 &   ⊠2–5 sin,
600. 3 how— • 5 6 how   **602.** ⊠2–5 look,   ⊠2–5 eyes,   **603.** ⊠2–5 features
2–4 resigned   **604.** ⊠2–5 image   ⊠2–5 4 mind: • 4 mind;   **606.** ⊠2 3 5 look
3 &   6 hate • 1 hate. • 2 hate, • 3 4 hate!   **607.** 4 1–4 stood,   6 trance • 1–
4 trance,   **608.** ⊠2–5 look   1 2 askance,   **609.** 2–4 forced   ⊠2–5 sympathy
610. 6 1–4 father's   3 5 6 view— • 1–4 view——   **611.** ⊠2 4 5 look •
4 *l*Look   1–4 be,   **612.** ⊠2 4 5 eyes • 4 5 Eyes   3 &   **613.** ⊠2–5 trance
⊠2–5 maid   **614.** 2–4 Paused   1–4 awhile,   3 &   3 pray'd • 2 prayed, •
3 4 prayed: **615.** 6 1 2 father's   ⊠2 4 5 feet,   **616.** ⊠2 4 my   ⊠2–5 mother's
⊠2–5 soul   4 1–4 entreat   **617.** 4 That   ⊠2–4 thou   ⊠2–5 woman   3 away •
⊠2–5 away!"   **618.** 5 6 3 4 said: 3 &   3 4 say: **619.** ⊠2 3 knew   1–
4 tell,   **620.** 3 O'ermastered • 1 O'er-master'd • 2–4 O'er-mastered   ⊠2–5 spell.
621. 3 *t*Cheek • ⊠2–5 cheek   **622.** 4 1–4 Leoline? Thy • 6 Leoline?—thy
⊠2–5 child   **623.** ⊠2–5 feet,   5 Ioy, • ⊠2–5 joy,   ⊠2–5 pride,   **624.** 5 6 mild:
625. 5 6 same   1–4 lady   **626.** ⊠2–5 pangs   6 1–4 mother   **627.** ⊠2–5 child!
628. 1–4 her,   3 & thee & • 1–4 and thee, and   1–4 other,   **629.** 2–4 prayed
⊠2 4 1 moment   4–6 1 died; • 2–4 died: **630.** 4–6 1 Pray'd • 2–4 Prayed
⊠2–5 babe   **631.** 1–4 lord's   5 Ioy • ⊠2–5 joy   ⊠2 3 and   3 Pride. •
⊠2–5 pride!   **632.** ⊠2–4 prayer   ⊠2–4 pangs   4 beguil*é*'d, • 2–4 beguiled,
634. 4 4 wouldst   3 Child • 4 Child,   **635.** ⊠2–5 child   ⊠2 3 and   1–4 thine?
636. ⊠2–5 heart   ⊠2 3 and   ⊠2–5 brain   **637.** 5 6 thoughts • 1–4 thoughts,
⊠2–4 share,   **638.** 2–4 swelled   4 *t*Rage • ⊠2–5 rage   ⊠2 3 and   6 pain • 1–
4 pain,   **639.** ⊠2–4 confusion   **640.** ⊠2 4 5 heart   ⊠2–5 pain   ⊠2 3 and
⊠2–5 rage, • 3 Rage   **641.** ⊠2–5 cheeks   3 2–4 quivered, • 6 quiver'd   ⊠2–
5 eyes   **642.** 3 Dishonored • 4–6 1 Dishonour'd • 2–4 Dishonoured   3 Old
5 6 age, • 1–4 age;   **643.** 3 Dishonored • 2–4 Dishonoured   ⊠2–5 child,
644. 5 Hospitality, • ⊠2–5 hospitality   **645.** 2–4 the   ⊠2–5 daughter   ⊠2–5 friend
646. 3 Woman's Jealousy. • 5 woman's Iealousy • 6 3 4 woman's jealousy •
1 2 woman's jealousy,   **647.** 1 disgracful   ⊠2–5 end—   **648.** 2–4 rolled
⊠2–5 eye   ⊠2–5 regard   **649.** ⊠2–5 minstrel   1–4 bard,   **651.** 3 5 6 Why •
4 "Why,   3 Bracy   4 here   **652.** 4 hence!"   6 the   1–4 bard   5 6 obey'd: •
2–3 obeyed; • 4 obeyed;—   **653.** 6 maid • 1–4 maid,   **654.** 3 Aged   5 6 Knight •
1–4 knight,   **655.** 3–6 Lady • 1–4 lady   3 Geraldine   ‾656. 2 3 THE |
CONCLUSION TO PART THE SECOND.   **656.** 1–4 child,   1–4 elf,
657. 1–4 itself,   **658.** 1–4 fairy thing   1–3 cheeks • 4 cheeks,   **659.** 1–
4 finds,   1–4 seeks,   **660.** 1–4 vision   1–4 sight   **661.** 1–4 father's eyes   1–
4 light;   **662.** 1–4 pleasures   1–4 and   **663.** 1–4 heart,   **664.** 1–4 love's
excess   **665.** 1–4 words   1–4 bitterness.   **668.** 1–4 charm,   **669.** 1–4 wrong
1–4 harm.   **670.** 1–4 Perhaps 'tis   1–4 and   **671.** 1–4 word   1 within,
672. 1–4 recoil   1–4 love and pity.   **673.** 1–4 what,   1–4 world   1–4 sin
674. 1–4 and shame   1–4 true!)   **675.** 1–4 giddiness   1–4 heart and brain
676. 1–4 seldom   1–4 rage and pain,   **677.** 1–4 talks   1–4 used   1–4 do.

half-title/divisional title/title. In PR 1 the half-title is followed by a title-page with the title in roman capitals ("CHRISTABEL: etc"). The divisional title appears on a separate recto in PR 2 3. In PR 4 the title heads a verso.

epigraph (=**295** *Sonnet to Asra*). It is not certain that C ever intended the sonnet to be prefixed to *Christabel*: it might have been added on SH's initiative, or even by a later owner of the album. Certainly, it was added after MS 2 was transcribed (see TEXTS MS 2 above).

preface. The Preface appears on a recto facing the blank verso of the title-page in PR *1* and facing the blank verso of the divisional title in PR *2 3*. It follows on directly after the title in PR *4*.

PR *2–4* add an asterisk to the preface title, and add the footnote: "To the edition of 1816."

⁻**1.4.** PR *4* does not begin a new paragraph.

preface fn. Cued in PR *2–4* to the title "PREFACE."

⁻**1.31.** PR *1* gives the part-title on a separate recto (verso blank) and repeats the title "CHRISTABEL." with rule beneath, before line 1. PR *2 3* give the part-title at the head of a recto. In PR *4* it follows on directly after the Preface.

3 etc. Indented in MS 2 but not in other texts. The varying patterns of indentation are not recorded here.

5⁺. No line-space in MS 6.

7. The PR *2 3* reading has been supplied in all seven known corrected copies of PR *1*. In Hinves's copy C first experimented by substituting "bold" and "old;" (for "rich," and "bitch;") in lines 6–7.

9. The PR *2 3* reading has been supplied in all seven known corrected copies of PR *1*. In Tieck's copy C first made the correction in pencil, then went over it in ink. In Hinves's copy he also emended the comma at the end of the line to an exclamation-mark, and the semicolon at the end of line 10 to a comma.

11. In Hinves's copy of PR *1* C first emended the line to read "Ever and aye, by Shine and Shower," (which is the emended reading, in AG's hand, in his own copy). He then altered the line again in the Hinves copy, to read "Ever and aye, by Shine or Shower," (which is the emended reading in Green's, Tieck's, Middleton's ["Shine or Shower"], and the Ramsgate copies). In Tieck's copy he made the emendation first in pencil, later in ink. In Hinves's copy he also emended the semicolon at the end of line 12 to a colon. In DC's copy he emended the line to read "Ever and aye, in shine or shower,".

16–17. Compare the draft in the Gutch Notebook (*CN* I 216); also *DWJ* I 4, 5, 13; *WPW* II 208–9.

25. MS 3 Woods so] The error suggests that DW was copying from dictation (see also line 96).

281.1–2. Deleted in Hinves's, Tieck's, and the Ramsgate copies, and in C's own copy of PR *1*.

29. PR *1* she] Deleted by C in the Ramsgate copy.

32. The PR *2 3* reading has been supplied in all seven known corrected copies of PR *1*. C's own capitalisation (in Hinves's, Tieck's, Middleton's, DC's, and the Ramsgate copies) is: "The Sighs, she heav'd, were soft and low;". Collier Preface to *Seven Lectures* xl records the following version of the line in the ms that C lent him in 1811: "The breezes they were whispering low:".

37. The PR *2–4* reading is substituted in Hinves's, Green's, Middleton's, DC's, and C's own copy of PR *1*.

39. PR *1* can] Emended by C to "could" in Hinves's copy.

41. PR *1* be,] C deleted the comma in Hinves's copy.

49. In MS 3 DW omitted lines 45–7. For similar mistakes in this ms see lines 205–10, 212, 490.

52⁺. No line-space in MS 6.

54. Jesu Maria] No punctuation separates the words in what are likely to have been

C's sources: Monk Lewis *The Castle Spectre* (1798) III iii p 57; George Shelvocke *A Voyage round the World* (1726), where it is the name of a vessel in which Shelvocke sailed; Thomas Gray *A Long Story* (1750) 133. The exclamation was made much of by the parodists, of whom there is a convenient list in EHC's facsimile ed of MS 2 (1907) appendix II p 103.

54⁺. No line-space in TEXTS 6 *2–4*. The error in PR *2–4* arises from a misunderstanding of PR *1*, where the line heads a new page (p 7).

62, 65. Deleted in Hinves's, Green's, Middleton's, DC's, and the Ramsgate copies, and in C's own copy of PR *1*. Lines 60–5 are rewritten (var). Hinves's copy reads:

> That shadowy in the moonlight shone:
> The Neck, that made that white robe wan,
> Her stately neck and arms were bare;
> Her blue-vein'd feet unsandal'd were;
> And wildly glitter'd here and there
> The Gems entangled in her Hair.

Middleton's and DC's copies read: "The Neck, which . . .", and the last two lines of C's substitution have been cropped from the Middleton copy. There are also differences of capitalisation and punctuation: "shone!" (DC's copy); "Neck which", "bare:", and "were," (Middleton copy); "stately Neck and Arms" and "Feet" (Middleton's, DC's, and the Ramsgate copies); "hair." (DC's copy), "hair!" (Ramsgate copy).

Both Hinves's and the Ramsgate copies emend the semicolon at the end of line 59 to a comma (line 59 already ends with a comma in C's own copy; in Green's copy the semicolon is left unchanged). DC's copy adds a dash.

The ms reading of line 65 recorded by Collier Preface to *Seven Lectures* xl–xli is: "And the jewels were tangled in her hair." Collier also wrote "tangled" above "tumbled", which he underlined, in MS 6.

66. PR *1* frightful] C substituted "fearful" in the Hinves copy.

70¹. No line-space in MS 6.

75. In the Ramsgate copy of PR *1* C corrected the comma at the end of the line to an exclamation-mark.

75⁺. No line-space in TEXTS 6 *1–4*.

76. C revised the line in Hinves's copy of PR *1* to read "Alas!—But say, how cam'st thou here?", and added the instruction: "This Line to be printed as a Paragraph by itself."

In further elucidating how the line should be printed, he wrote line 74 as "I cannot speak for weariness." and line 75 as "Stretch forth thy hand, and have no fear!"

79–103. In the margins of Tieck's copy of PR *1* a pencil-line and a cross are written alongside. In Hinves's copy C deleted (somewhat indecisively) lines 82–4, 89–90.

81–98. C drew a line in the margin of the copy of PR *1* he gave to DC, and added the following note: "This paragraph I purpose to re-write, with the exception of two or perhaps three Lines. As it stands, it might be placed in any one's mouth, appropriately therefore in no one's, and in Geraldine's it falls flat."

81. The ms reading recorded by Collier Preface to *Seven Lectures* xli conforms to the text of PR *1–4*.

88. twice/once] The revision sacrifices sound for plausible consistency with Part II. Tryermaine Castle is some 50 miles from Langdale: even over rough terrain, a journey extending across two nights is unlikely to have been "furious".

92. PR *1* in fits,] In Hinves's copy C substituted "entranced" ("entranc'd," in the Ramsgate copy). The substitution—which conforms to the PR *2–4* reading—is also made in

Green's and in C's own copy. The ms reading recorded by Collier Preface to *Seven Lectures* xli also conforms to PR *2–4*.

106–11. C marked the lines in pencil in the margins of Tieck's copy of PR *1*, writing against them "8 lines instead". He then inserted, in ink, at the foot of the page, here and in the Ramsgate copy, the PR *2–4* version of the lines. JG wrote them into Hinves's and Green's copies, and AG into C's own copy. In Tieck's copy, after emending the comma at the end of line 105 to a colon (as in Hinves's and the Margate copies; JG in Green's copy gives a full point), C proceeds:

> O well, bright Dame! may you command
> The service of Sir Leoline—
> And gladly our stout Chivalry
> Will he send forth and friends withall
> To guide and guard you, safe and free,
> Home to your noble Father's Hall.

DC's copy has "Dame," DC's and the Ramsgate copies have "Leoline:" (Middleton's has "Leoline;"). Middleton's has "⟨stout⟩". DC's has "forth and friends withal,"; Middleton's and the Ramsgate copies have "forth, and Friends withal". DC's and Middleton's copies have "you safe and free". The Ramsgate copy has "Hall!" The other three copies, corrected in the hands of JG and AG, differ in further details of capitalisation and punctuation.

112–22. C marked the lines in pencil in the margin of Tieck's copy of PR *1*, writing against them "Altered". He then corrected the printed text, in ink, to read:

> She rose, and forth with steps they pass'd,
> That strove to be, and were not fast.
> Her gracious stars the lady blest,
> And thus spake on sweet Christabel—
> All our household are at rest,
> The Hall as silent as the Cell;
> Sir Leoline is weak in health,
> And may not well awaken'd be;
> But we will move as if in stealth,
> And I beseech your Courtesy
> This Night to share your Couch with me.

C corrected the lines in both Hinves's and DC's copies in a similar way. Hinves's copy has: "She rose:"; "That strove to be, ~~and~~ yet were not, fast:"; "we will move,"; "courtesy | This night to share your bed with me." The version in the Hinves copy was transcribed by JG into the copy belonging to J. H. Green. DC's copy reads:

> She rose: and forth with steps they pass'd
> That seem'd to be yet were not fast.
> Her gracious Stars the Lady blest,
> And thus spake on sweet Christabel:
> All our Household . . .
> . . . .
> This night to share your bed with me.

AG copied the last nine of the eleven lines into C's own copy of PR *1*. It appears that she copied them from Middleton's copy, where they also appear, or from another lost copy which precedes both of them. In Middleton's copy the last two lines, at the foot of the page, have been cropped, and there are slight differences of punctuation: "*Stars* the Lady blest—"; "Christabel:"; "Household"; "rest"; "Cell."; "health".

In the Ramsgate copy (continuing on from the previous page, where he wrote "turn over") C deleted the lines and wrote the following substitution at the foot of the same and of the facing page:

> She rais'd the Dame: and forth they pass'd
> With hurringying steps yet nothing fast,
> Her lucky *Stars* the Lady blest:
> And thus spake on sweet Christabel—
> All our Household are at rest,
> The Hall as silent as the Cell.
> Sir Leoline is weak in health,
> And may not well disturbed be;
> So to my room we'll creep in stealth,
> And I beseech your courtesy
> This night to share your couch with me!

> They cross'd the moat &c.

Middleton's copy of PR *1* also contains the following marginal note alongside the deleted lines 115–16: "the first suspicious circumstance, of the evil & præternatural character of Geraldine." Alongside the deleted lines in the Ramsgate copy C wrote the first of nine more developed marginal glosses: "The Strange Lady cannot rise, without the touch of Christabel's Hand: and now she blesses her *Stars*. She will not praise the *Creator* of the Heavens, or name the Saints".

113. PR 2 strovad] Corrected to "strove" in the Fitzwilliam copy.

114–116.1.1/117. Collier Preface to *Seven Lectures* xli–xlii records the following version of the lines in the ms C lent him:

> Her smiling stars the lady blest,
> And thus bespake sweet Christabel:
> All our household is at rest,
> The hall as silent as a cell.

124, 127. In Tieck's copy of PR *1* C (?) marked the stresses in pencil:

> Toók the kéy that fítted wéll;

and

> The gáte that was íron'd withín and withoút,

123–8. C wrote Alongside the lines in Middleton's copy of PR *1* the following cropped note: "the secon⌜. . . .⌝ but nothing". Its purport is clarified in the corresponding gloss on lines 129–32 which he wrote in the Ramsgate copy: "The strange Lady may not pass the threshhold without Christabel's help and will."

128⁺. No line-space in PR *2–4*, an error arising from the fact that line 129 heads a new page in PR *1* (p 11).

129–34. In MS 2 the lines are written on the blank verso (f 7ᵛ) opposite the main text, with a series of crosses to indicate their place between the two other paragraphs on f 8ʳ.

It cannot be determined whether C omitted them when he first made his transcript, or whether he composed them afterwards.

136, 144. AG (?) wrote a pencilled "A" alongside the first of these lines in C's copy of PR *1*, and a cross alongside the second.

141–2. Alongside these lines in Middleton's copy of PR *1* C wrote the following cropped note: "the thiᵗ. . . .ʰ". Its purport is again clarified by the third of the nine glosses he added in the Ramsgate copy: "The strange Lady makes an excuse, not to praise the Holy Virgin."

144. PR *1* were.] Some copies lack the full point.

146. PR *1* Lay fast] JG substituted "Was stretch'd" in Hinves's copy.

151. There is a cross, in pencil, at the end of the line in C's copy of PR *1*.

154–5. In C's copy of PR *1* line 154 "echoes" is underlined; all of line 155 is underlined and there is a cross beside the line.

159. In C's copy of PR *1* "flash" is written against the line in pencil, possibly in C's hand.

160. Collier Preface to *Seven Lectures* xlii supplies the line, omitted in MS 5, from the ms C lent him.

166. PR *1* she bares,] In C's and Green's copies the text is corrected to conform to the PR *2–4* reading, by AG and JG respectively. In this they follow C's own correction in Middleton's copy (which reads "bare,"). In the Ramsgate copy C corrected the text to "will bare,".

166.1.1. Deleted in Hinves's copy of PR *1*. In C's own copy of PR *1* AG replaced it with the PR *2–4* reading (lines 167–8) . In this she follows the correction in Middleton's copy (which reads "Air" and "stair,").

In the Ramsgate copy C replaced the line with: "And jealous of the listning Air, I They cheat the echo, stair by stair—"; in the same copy he emended the comma at the end of line 169 to a semicolon. In Green's copy JG replaced the line with: "Stealing the way from stair to stair;".

171.1. In MS 4 SH first began to copy line 172, deleted it and copied line 171 alongside, then deleted both and copied line 171 afresh on a new line.

171. Deleted in Hinves's copy of PR *1*, where JG substituted "With stifled breath I As still as death!" In the Ramsgate copy C simply inserted a comma in the middle of the line: "As still as death, with stifled breath!"

173–4. The PR *2–4* reading of line 173 is substituted in the following copies of PR *1*: Hinves's and Green's (by JG); C's own copy (by AG); DC's, Middleton's, and the Ramsgate copies (by C). The PR *2–4* reading of line 174 is substituted in C's own copy (by AG) and the Middleton and Ramsgate copies (by C).

183⁺. No new paragraph in PR *4*; clearly an error arising from the fact that in PR *2 3* line 184 heads a new page (p 51).

191. The ms reading recorded by Collier Preface to *Seven Lectures* xlii conforms to the PR *1–4* text.

193.1.1–2. Collier Preface to *Seven Lectures* xlii records that in the ms C lent him these lines had been cancelled.

195⁺. There is clearly a line-space in MS 4, less clearly in MS 2, but none is given in TEXTS 3 5 6 *2–4*. PR *1* is an ambiguous instance because line 196 heads a new page (p 15).

204–9. Alongside these lines in Middleton's copy of PR *1*, C wrote the following cropped note: "Geraldine beholdᵗ. . . .ᵀ the mateᵗ. . . .ᵀ Spirit." Alongside the lines in the Ramsgate copy, he wrote the fourth of nine marginal glosses: "The Mother of

Christabel, who is now her ₰Guardian Spirit, appears to Geraldine, as in answer to her wish. Geraldine fears the Spirit, but yet has power over it for a time."

205. PR *4* Off,] The line is indented and the quotation-marks are omitted.

213⁺. No line-space in MS 3.

219. The PR *1–4* reading is inserted in MS 6; the ms reading recorded by Collier Preface to *Seven Lectures* xlii–xliii also conforms to the text of PR *1–4*.

219⁺. No line-space in MSS 5 6.

220.1. A mistake on DW's part, deriving from her wish to maintain the stanza-division. Line 220 is the last line on f 82ᵛ, 220.1 heads f 82ʳ. Cf line 397.1, at ff 78ᵛ–77ᵛ.

231–6. The lines are deleted in Hinves's copy of PR *1*. In DC's copy C drew a line in the LH margin alongside lines 229–34 and added the footnote: "These six lines must likewise be changed, for the same reason as the §§ p. 8." See on lines 81–98 above.

238⁺. No line-space in MS 6.

252. In C's copy of PR *1* there is a caret-mark alongside the line, and someone (RHS? JDC?) has written in the upper margin: "It was dark and rough as the Sea Wolf's hide." The same line is inserted in the Fitzwilliam copy of PR *2*—whether or not in C's hand is debatable. Curiously, the sea-wolf appears in Anna Niven's anonymous "continuation" of the poem in *European Magazine* XLVII (Apr 1815) 345–6.

254, 254.1.1, 262. In Hinves's copy of PR *1* C replaced line 254.1.1 with: "She gaz'd upon the maid, she sigh'd!" and corrected "And" in line 262 to "Then". In the same copy JG replaced line 254 with: "And must *she* ~~with~~ sleep by Christabel?"

Both sets of substitutions were then deleted by JG, who keyed in the following lines, written by him at the foot of the opposite page:

~~And she is alone with Christabel~~
O shield her, shield sweet Christabel

Deep from within she seems half-way
To lift some weight, with sick assay,
And eyes the Maid, and seeks delay
Then suddenly as one defied
Collects herself in scorn and pride
And lay down by the Maiden's side

C marked the passage in Tieck's copy of PR *1*, writing alongside in pencil "9 Lines". He afterwards copied the revised set of emendations given in Hinves's copy, and JG did likewise in Green's copy. The only differences are of capitalisation and punctuation, Tieck's copy reading:

O shield her, shield, sweet Christabel!

Deep from within she seems half way
To lift some weight with ~~som~~eick Assay   (Assay = Attempt.
And eyes the Maid and seeks delay:
Then suddenly, as one defied
Collects herself in scorn and pride
And lay down by the Maiden's side.—

In DC's copy of PR *1* C revised line 254 to read "O shield her, shield sweet Christabel!" He then deleted line 254.1.1, and indicated the following insertion between the two stanzas:

Two or more Lines, by which the pronoun "She" is made refer to Geraldine—

> A woman she: and in her mood
> Still wrought the soul of Womanhood,

are to be added: and then as follows:

> Deep from within she [?]seems half-way
> To lift some weight with sick Assay,
> And eyes the Maid and seeks delay:
> Then suddenly, as one defied,
> Collects herself in scorn and pride
> And lay down &c.

In C's own copy AG copied out the revised set of emendations, as given in Hinves's, Tieck's, and Green's copies. C afterwards inserted in his own hand, above AG's transcription, lines 255–6, thereby making up the full PR *2–4* text (except that C wrote "Look" in line 256). In the copy C gave Middleton the same revisions appear, all in C's hand, with the following minor differences from the PR *2–4* text: "shield her—"; "Look". C added the gloss "effort" alongside line 258, and lines 259–60 have been cropped by the binder.

The Ramsgate copy of PR *1* revises the text in a slightly different way. C deleted lines 254 and 254.1.1, and himself inserted:

> O shield her! Shield meek Christabel!
>
> But Geraldine nor moves nor stirs—
> Ah! what a stricken Look was her's!
> Deep from within she seems half way
> To lift some weight with faint Essày,
> And eyes the Maid, and seeks delay:
> Then suddenly, as one defied,
> Collects herself in scorn and pride

262–8. C wrote the fifth marginal gloss alongside the lines in the Ramsgate copy of PR *1*: "As soon as the wicked Bosom, with the mysterious sign of *t*Evil stamped thereby, touches Christabel, she is deprived of the power of disclosing what has occurred."

266⁺. No line-space in PR *1–4*.

278⁺. MSS 5 6 have a line-space only.

⁻279. The title of the Conclusion is given at the head of a verso in PR *1–3*. It follows on directly after line 278 in PR *4*.

291⁺. No line-space in MSS 5 6.

295. PR *1* is——] The word is underlined in Hinves's copy, and "in Italic" written alongside. The changes are probably by C.

296. PR *2 3* she,] The tail of the comma is defective, especially in PR *2*, making it resemble a full point.

297. PR *1* who] JG substituted "that" in Hinves's copy.

305. Originally omitted in MS 4, and keyed in by SH at the foot of the page.

306. MS 2 Tairn] C added a note on the blank page opposite (f 16ᵛ): "Tairn or Tarn (derived by Lye from the Icelandic ?T[. . .] *Tiorn*, stagnum, palus) is ~~explained~~ ⟨rendered⟩ in our Dictionaries as synonimous with ~~Lake; / It~~ Mere or Lake; but it is properly a ~~small Lake~~ large Pool or Reservoir in the Mountains, commonly the Feeder of some Mere ~~(or Lake)~~ in the Valleys. Tarn Watling & Blellum Tarn, tho' on lower Ground than Tother Tarns, are yet not exceptions—for ~~Tarns~~ both are on elevations, and Blellum Tarn feeds the Wynander Mere." C's reference is to Edward Lye *Dictionarium Saxonico et Gothico-Latinum* (2 vols 1772), a work to which his attention might have been drawn by Horne Tooke. He appended a more succinct note on the word to *293 Dejection: An Ode* 100 in *M Post* (4 Oct 1802) and subsequent printed versions.

310⁺. No line-space in MSS 5 6.

318⁺. No line-space in PR *4*, almost certainly an error arising from the fact that line 319 heads a new page in PR *2 3* (p 58).

322⁺. No line-space in PR *2–4*, an error arising from the fact that in PR *1* line 323 heads a new page (p 23).

⁻332. PR *1* gives the part-title on a separate recto (verso blank) and repeats the title "CHRISTABEL." with rule beneath, before line 332. PR *2 3* give the part-title at the head of a recto. In PR *4* it follows on directly after line 331.

337⁺. No line-space in TEXTS 6 *2*. The error in PR *2* arises from a misunderstanding of PR *1*, where the line heads a new page (p 28); it is one of the few such errors which was noticed and corrected in PR *3 4*.

367⁺. No line-space in TEXTS 5 6 *1–4*.

383–6. C wrote the sixth marginal gloss alongside the lines in the Ramsgate copy of PR *1*: "Christabel is made to believe, that the fearful Sight had taken place only in a Dream."

396⁺. No line-space in MS 6. The repetition in MS 3 (line 397.1) appears to derive from an intention to begin a new stanza with the line. Cf line 220.1 above.

408–26. C quoted the lines before publication in a letter to TP of 13 Feb 1813 (BM 35343 f 374ʳ=*CL* III 435–6), with the following variations in wording: 414 "so it chanc'd"; 418 "They" (as in PR *1–4*); 424 "But neither Frost, nor Heat, nor Thunder,".

411. PR *3* vain:] The tails of the semicolons at the end of the three preceding lines are imperfect, and the present reading may be due to faulty type.

420⁺. No line-space in PR *1–4*.

430⁺. No line-space in MS 6; line 430 comes at the foot of a page (f 11ʳ) in MS 5.

445. PR *3* seized:] The colon may in fact be a semicolon with a broken tail.

446⁺. No line-space in MSS 5 6, and the gap is doubtful in MS 3.

451–6. C wrote the seventh marginal gloss alongside the lines in the Ramsgate copy of PR *1*: "Christabel then recollects the whole, and knows that it was not a Dream; but yet cannot disclose the fact, that the strange Lady is a supernatural Being with the stamp of the Evil Ones on her."

453. The ms reading recorded by Collier Preface to *Seven Lectures* xliii conforms to the text of PR *1–4*.

456⁺. Line-space in PR *2 3*. This is almost certainly an error arising from a misunderstanding of PR *1*, where line 457 heads a new page (p 35); cf line 475 below. But it is just possible that a stanza-division is intended in MS 2.

457–8. MSS 5 6 have coalesced the two lines, apparently in error.

463. The ms reading recorded by Collier Preface to *Seven Lectures* xliii conforms to the text of PR *1–4*.

463–6. C wrote the eighth marginal gloss alongside the lines in the Ramsgate copy of PR *1*: "Christabel for a moment sees her Mother's Spirit."

474⁺. No line-space in PR *1 2*. This may well result from a misunderstanding concerning stanza-division at line 457 above.

492⁺. No line-space in PR *2–4*.

493–7. C wrote the ninth marginal gloss in the Ramsgate copy of PR *1*, keyed by a cross against these lines: "How gladly Sir Leoline repeats the names and shows, how familiarly he had once been acquainted with all the spots and paths in the neighborhood of his former Friend's Castle & Residence."

530⁺. No line-space in TEXTS 5 6 *1–4*.

550⁺. Line-space in MS 6.

554⁺. It is possible, even probable, that a gap is intended in MS 2.

590. Squeezed in at the bottom of the page in MS 2.

612⁺. No line-space in PR *4*, clearly an error arising from the fact that line 613 heads a new page in PR *2 3* (p 71).

635⁺. No line-space in PR *1 2*.

⁻656. The title of the Conclusion is given at the head of a recto in PR *1–3*. It follows on directly after line 655 in PR *4*.

664. JG (?) added the following instruction to Hinves's copy of PR *1*: "in two lines".

667. PR *2* so unlike] C inserted "all" after "so", in pencil, in the Fitzwilliam copy.

677⁺. Following the text C wrote, in pencil, in Tieck's copy of PR *1*:

about sixty added to complete the Conclusion

The additional preface should be a Sheet; but *might* be perhaps by omissions comprest to ½ a Sheet—

177. THE STORY OF THE MAD OX

A. DATE

Apr–May 1798. Sheridan and Tierney were reported as having "recanted" (line 126VAR) in the newspapers of 20–1 Apr; the duel between Tierney and Pitt (line 125) took place on 27 May. C's ms note on PR *2* (see on the prefatory note below) suggests that the lines were indeed written at this time, "when fears were entertained of an Invasion".

B. TEXTS

1 [=RT]. *M Post* (30 Jul 1798). Unsigned.

2. Annual Anthology ed RS (2 vols Bristol 1799–1800) II 59–66. "*By S. T. COLERIDGE.*"

C told RS on 18 Feb 1800: "Let my Mad Ox keep my name" (*CL* I 573). C's own copy (Yale Tinker 1953 2) contains a note by C, a large part of which has been cut away.

3. *SL* (1817).

An unlocated copy, of unverified authenticity, offered for sale by Rosenbach on three occasions between 1916 and 1942, contains corrections centred on the poem (see vol I annex C 17A).

title. *1* A TALE. • *2 3 RECANTATION,* | *Illustrated in the STORY of the MAD OX.*   **prefatory note.** *1* The following amusing Tale, gives a very humorous description of the French Revolution, which is represented as an OX.

‾1.3 *2 3*   I.

  1 *1*   An Ox, long fed on musty hay,
      2 3   with
  2 ☐   And work'd with yoke and chain,
  3 *1*   Was loosen'd on an April day,
      2 3   turn'd out
  4 ☐   When fields are in their best array,
  5 ☐   And growing grasses sparkle gay
  6 ☐   At once with sun and rain.
      [*Line-space*]

‾7 *2 3*   II.

  7 *1*   The grass was sweet, the sun was bright—
      2 3   fine,
  8 ☐   With truth I may aver it;
  9 *1*   The beast was glad, as well he might,
      2 3   Ox
 10 ☐   Thought a green meadow no bad sight,
 11 ☐   And frisk'd—to shew his huge delight,
 12 ☐   Much like a beast of spirit.
      [*Line-space*]

‾13 *2 3*   III.

 13 ☐   "Stop, neighbours, stop! Why these alarms?
 14 ☐   "The ox is only glad!
 15 ☐   —But still they pour from cots and farms—
 16 ☐   "Halloo!" the parish is up in arms,
 17 ☐   (A *haoxing* hunt has always charms)
 18 ☐   "Halloo! the ox is mad!"
      [*Line-space*]

‾19 *2 3*   IV.

 19 *1*   The frighted ox scamper'd about—
      2 3   beast
 20 ☐   Plunge! thro' the hedge he drove:
 21 *1*   The mob pursued with hideous rout,
      2 3   pursue
 22 *1*   A bull-dog fasten'd on his snout—
      2 3   fastens
 23 ☐   "He gores the dog! his tongue hangs out!
 24 ☐   "He's mad, he's mad, by Jove!
      [*Line-space*]

⁻25 *2 3*   V.
25 □   "Stop, neighbours, stop!" aloud did call
26 □   A sage of sober hue:
27 *1*   "You cruel dog!" at once they bawl,
   2 3 But all at once on him they fall,
28 □   And women squeak and children squall
29 □   "What? would you have him toss us all?
30 □   "And, dam'me, who are you?"
          [*Line-space*]
⁻31 *2 3*   VI.
31 *1 2* Ah hapless sage! his ears they stun,
   3   Oh!
32 □   And curse him o'er and o'er!
33 □   "You bloody-minded dog! (cries one)
34 □   "To slit your wind-pipe were good fun—
35 □   "Od bl–st you for an *impious* son
35fn *2 3* One of the many *fine* words which the most uneducated had about this time
          a constant opportunity of acquiring from the sermons in the pulpit, and the
          proclamations on the —— corners.
36 □   "Of a *Presbyterian* wh–re!"
          [*Line-space*]
⁻37 *2 3*   VII.
37 *1*   "You'd have him gore our Parish-priest,
   2 3   the
38 *1*   "And drive against the altar!
   2 3   run
39 *1*   "You rogue"—the sage his warnings ceas'd,
   2 3   Fiend!"—
40 □   And north and south, and west and east,
41 □   Halloo! they follow the poor beast,
42 *1*   Mat, Tom, Bob, Dick, and Walter.
   2 3   Dick, Tom, Bob,
          [*Line-space*]
⁻43 *2 3*   VIII.
43 □   Old LEWIS ('twas his evil day)
44 □   Stood trembling in his shoes.
45 □   The ox was his—what cou'd he say?
46 □   His legs were stiffen'd with dismay;
47 □   The ox ran o'er him 'mid the fray,
48 □   And gave him his death's bruise!
          [*Line-space*]
⁻49 *2 3*   IX.
49 *1*   The baited ox drove on (but here
   2 3   frighted beast ran
50 *1 2* The   Gospel   scarce more true is,
   3   (No tale, tho' in print,   is)
51 □   My Muse stops short in mid career—
52 □   Nay, gentle Reader, do not sneer!

53	*1*	I could not chuse but drop a tear,
	2 3	cannot
54	□	A tear for good old LEWIS!)
		[*Line-space*]
⁻55	*2 3*	X.
55	*1*	The Ox drove on right thro' the town;
	2 3	frighted beast ran
56	□	All follow'd, boy and dad,
57	□	Bull-dog, parson, shopman, clown!
58	□	The publicans rush'd from the crown—
59	□	"Halloo! hamstring him! cut him down!"—
60	□	—They drove the poor Ox mad!
		[*Line-space*]
⁻61	*2 3*	XI.
61	□	Should you a rat to madness teize,
62	□	Why, ev'n a rat might plague you!
63	□	There's no philosopher but sees,
64	□	That rage and fear are one disease—
65	*1*	Tho' that may burn, and this may breeze,
	2 3	freeze,
66	□	They're both alike the ague!
		[*Line-space*]
⁻67	*2 3*	XII.
67	□	And so this ox in frantic mood
68	*1*	Fac'd round, like mad bull!
	2 3	any
69	□	The mob turn'd tail, and he pursued,
70	*1*	Till they with flight and fear were stew'd,
	2	fright
	3	heat fright
71	*1*	And not a chick of all the brood
	2 3	this
72	□	But had his belly full!
		[*Line-space*]
⁻73	*2 3*	XIII.
73	*1*	Old Nick's astride the ox, 'tis clear!
	2 3	beast,
74	□	Old Nicholas to a tittle!
75	*1*	And all agreed, he'd disappear,
	2 3 But	agree,
76	*1*	Would but the Parson venr e near,
	2 3	venture
77	□	And thro' his teeth right o'er the steer,
77fn	*1*	According to the common superstition, there are two ways of fighting with the Devil. You may cut him in half with a straw; or he will vanish, if you spit over his horns with fasting spittle
	2 3	According to the superstition of the West Countries, if you meet the Devil, you may either cut him in half with a straw, or you may cause him instantly to disappear by spitting over his horns.

78 □   Squirt out some fasting spittle.
        [*Line-space*]
⁻79 *2 3*   XIV.
79 □   Achilles was a warrior fleet,
80 □   The Trojans he could worry:
81 *1* The Parson too was swift of feet,
    2 3 Our
82 □   But shew'd it chiefly in retreat—
83 *1* The victor ox drove down the street,
    2 3   scour'd
84 □   The mob fled hurry-skurry!
        [*Line-space*]
⁻85 *2 3*   XV.
85 □   Thro' gardens, lanes, and fields new-plough'd,
86 □   Thro' *his* hedge, and thro' *her* hedge
87 □   He plung'd and toss'd, and bellow'd loud—
88 *1* And in his madness he grew proud
    2 3 Till
89 □   To see this helter-skelter crowd,
90 □   That had more wrath than courage!
        [*Line-space*]
⁻91 *2 3*   XVI.
91 *1* Alack! to mend the breaches wide,
    2 3 Alas!
92 □   He made for these poor ninnies,
93 □   They all must work, whate'er betide,
94 □   Both days and months, and pay beside
95 □   (Sad news for Av'rice and for Pride)
96 □   A *sight* of golden guineas!
        [*Line-space*]
⁻97 *2 3*   XVII.
97 *1* But now once more to view did pop
    2 3   here
98 □   The man that kept his senses—
99 *1* And now he bawl'd—"Stop, neighbours, stop!
    2 3   cried—
100 □   "The ox is mad! I would not swop,
101 □   "No, not a school-boy's farthing top
102 □   "For all the parish fences.
        [*Line-space*]
⁻103 *2 3*   XVIII.
103 *1* "The ox is mad! Tom!   Walter! Mat!
    2 3   Ho! Dick, Bob,
104 □   "What means this coward fuss?
105 □   "Ho! stretch this rope across the plat—
106 □   "'Twill trip him up!—or if not that,
107 □   "Why, dam'me! we must lay him flat—
108 □   "See! here's my blunderbuss.
        [*Line-space*]

‾**109** *2 3*   XIX.

109 *1*   "A barefac'd dog! just now he said,

      2 3   lying

110 ☐   "The ox was only glad!

111 ☐   "Let's break his Presbyterian head—

112 ☐   "Hush!" quoth the sage, "you've been misled;

113 ☐   "No quarrels now! let's all make heed,

114 ☐   "You *drove* the poor ox mad!

[*Line-space*]

‾**115** *2 3*   XX.

115 *1*   But lo, to interrupt my chat,

      2 3   As thus I sat in careless

116 ☐   With the morning's wet newspaper,

117 ☐   In eager haste, without his hat,

118 ☐   As blind and blund'ring as a bat,

119 *1*   In rush'd that fierce aristocrat,

      2 3   came

120 *1*   The pursy woollen-draper.

      2 3 Our

[*Line-space*]

‾**121** *2 3*   XXI.

121 *1*   And so per force, my muse drew bit,

      2 3   my Muse perforce

122 *1*   And he rush'd in and panted!

      2 3   in he rush'd

123 ☐   "Well, have you heard,"—"no, not a whit,

124 ☐   "What! han't you heard?—come, out with it!

125 *1*   "That TIERNEY's wounded Mr. PITT,

      2 3   Tierney   votes   for

126 *1*   "And his fine tongue enchanted?"

      2 3   Sheridan's   *recanted.*"

title. *3 RECANTATION.* | *Illustrated in the Story of the Mad Ox.*   **1.** *2 3* Ox,
5. *2* gay,   **6.** *3* Sun   **7.** *3* Sun   *2* bright, • *3* bright: **11.** *2* frisk'd • *3* frisked,
13. *2* "Stop, neighbours! stop! why these alarms? • *3 Stop, Neighbours! stop!*
why these alarms?   **14.** *3 The*   *2* Ox is only glad."—. • *3 Ox is only glad—*
15. *2 3* But   **16.** *2 3* Halloo!   *2* Parish   *2* arms   **17.** *2 hoaxing* hunt •
3 hoaxing-hunt   **18.** *2* HALLOO! • *3* Halloo!   *2* THE OX IS MAD. • *3* the Ox is
mad.   **19.** *2* about, • *3* about;   **20.** *3* through   *2 3* drove—   **22.** *2* snout, •
3 snout;   **23.** *2 3* He   *2 3* dog,   *2* out— • *3* out;   **24.** *2* He's mad, he's • *3* He's
mad! he's   **25.** *3 "Stop, Neighbours, stop!"*   **26.** *2 3* hue.   **27.** *3* all,   *3* once,
28. *2 3* squall,   **29.** *2 3* "What!   *2* all!   **30.** *2 3* "And damme!   **31.** *3* sage,
32. *2 3* and o'er—   **33.** *2* dog!"   *3* cries one,   **34.** *2 3* windpipe   *3* fun,—
35. *2 3* "'Od   *2* bl— • *3* blast   **35fn1.** *3* fine   **35fn2.** *3* acquiring,   *3* pulpit
35fn3. *2* on • *3* in   **36.** *2 3* presbyterian   *2* w—re! • *3* w—re."   **37.** *2* parish
priest, • *3* parish-priest,   **38.** *2 3* altar—   **39.** *3* fiend!"   *2 3* The   **40.** *2* North,
2 South,   *2* West,   *2* East,   **43.** *2 3* Lewis,   *2* 'twas   *2* day,   **44.** *2 3* shoes;
45. *2 3* Ox   *2 3* could   **46.** *3* stiffened   *2 3* dismay,   **47.** *2 3* Ox   *2 3* mid
48. *2 3* bruise.   **49.** *2 3* on—but here,   **50.** *2* gospel   *2* is—   **51.** *2* muse

52. *2* Nay!   *2 3* reader!   *2* sneer,   **53.** *3* choose   **54.** *2* Lewis. • *3* Lewis!
55. *3* through   *2* town,   **57.** *2* Bulldog,   *2 3* Parson, Shopman,   *2* Clown, •
3 Clown: **58.** *2 3* Publicans   *2 3* Crown,   **59.** *2 3* down!"   **60.** *2 They
drove the poor Ox mad.* • *3* THEY DROVE THE POOR OX MAD.   **61.** *2 3* Rat
62. *2 3* Why   *2* even • *3* e'en   *2 3* Rat   *2 3* you: **63.** *2 3* Philosopher   *2 3* sees
64. *2 3* Rage   *2 3* Fear   *2 one*   **65.** *3* Though   *2 3* burn   **66.** *2* ague. •
3 Ague.   **67.** *2* Ox • *3* Ox,   *3* mood,   **68.** *2 3* Faced round   *2 3* Bull—
70. *3* stewed,   **71.** *2* brood,   **72.** *2 3* full.   **73.** *2 3* clear—   **74.** *3* Nicholas,
76. *2* parson   **77.** *3* through   *3* teeth,   **77fn** [2nd version] **1.** *3* West-Countries,
77fn [2nd version] **2.** *2* or you may cause him instantly to • *3* or force him to
78. *3* fasting-spittle.   **80.** *2 3* worry—   **81.** *2* parson   **82.** *2* retreat! •
3 retreat: **83.** *2 3* Ox   **84.** *2* hurry-skurry. • *3* hurry-scurry.   **85.** *3* Through
3 lanes   *3* new plough'd,   **86.** *3* Through his   *2* hedge   *3* through her
2 3 hedge,   **87.** *2* plung'd,   *3* toss'd   *2 3* loud,   **88.** *2 3* proud,   **89.** *2* helter
skelter   **90.** *2 3* courage.   **91.** *2 3* wide   **94.** *2 3* beside,   **95.** *2 3* Avarice
96. *2 3* sight   *2* guineas.   **98.** *2* senses. • *3* senses;   **99.** *2 3* neighbours!
3 stop;   **100.** *2 3* Ox   **101.** *3* "No!   *2* farthing top, • *3* farthing-top,
102. *3* parish-fences."   **103.** *2 3* Ox   *3* Mat!"   **104.** *3* What   **106.** *2 3* up—
107. *2* "Why   *2 3* damme!   **108.** *2 3* "See,   *2* blunderbuss!"   **109.** *3* "*A lying
dog! just now he said*   **110.** *2* "*The Ox was only glad.* • *3* "*The Ox was only glad*—
111. *3* "*Let's break his*   *2* presbyterian • *3 presbyterian*   *2* head!"— • *3 head!*"
112. *2* "Hush! (quoth   *2* sage) you've   *2* misled,   **113.** *2 3* now—   *2 3* head—
114. *2* "*You drove the poor Ox mad!*" • *3* "YOU DROVE THE POOR OX MAD."
115. *3* sat,   **118.** *2 3* blundering   **119.** *3* Aristocrat,   **120.** *2 3* Woollen-
draper.   **121.** *3* bit;   **122.** *2 3* panted—   **123.** *2* heard?"—"No! • *3* heard?"
No,   *2* whit." • *3* whit.   **124.** *2 3* "What,   *2* ha'nt • *3 ha'nt*   *2* heard?"—
"Come • *3* heard?" Come,   *2* it—" • *3* it!—   **125.** *3* TIERNEY   *2 3* Mister Pitt,
126. *3* SHERIDAN's *recanted!*"

prefatory note. C wrote a note, now partly cut away, in his copy of PR *2*: "Written
when fears were entertained of an Invasion—& Mr Sheridan & Mr Tierney were absurdly
represented as having *recanted*, because tho' ⌜. . . .⌝ to the ⌜. . . .⌝ in its origin, they ⌜. . . .⌝"
2, 6, 8, etc. All texts indent the lines as in the RT.
63–6. The PR *2 3* version is quoted in *BL* ch 2 (1817) I 30 (*CC*) I 31, to illustrate the
connection between fear and anger ("the first defence of weak minds is to recriminate").

177.X1. TO LESBIA

M Post (11 Apr 1798): "*LINES* I IMITATED FROM CATULLUS I My
Lesbia, let us love and live,". 18 lines. Signed "MORTIMER." Included in
LR I 274; *PW* (JDC) 28–9; *PW* (EHC) I 60–1.

The lines are in fact by WW. See Woof 169–70; *WEPF* 299–300, 327, 375–7.

177.X2. THE DEATH OF THE STARLING

LR I 274–5: "Pity! mourn in plaintive tone". 10 lines. Included in *PW* (JDC) 29A; *PW* (EHC) I 61.

The lines are in fact by WW. See Woof 170–2; *WEPF* 33–5, 331, 371–4.

177.X3. MORIENS SUPERSTITI

M Post (10 May 1798): "The hour-bell sounds, and I must go;". 2 8-line stanzas, untitled. Signed "MORTIMER." Included in *LR* I 275; *PW* (JDC) 29; *PW* (EHC) I 61–2.

The lines are in fact by WW. See Woof 170–2; *WEPF* 100, 115–16, 827–30.

177.X4. MORIENTI SUPERSTES

LR I 275–6: "Yet art thou happier far than she". 8 lines. Included in *PW* (JDC) 29B; *PW* (EHC) I 62.

The lines are in fact by WW. See Woof 170–2; *WEPF* 35, 332, 371–4.

178. KUBLA KHAN
OR, A VISION IN A DREAM

A. DATE

The date is disputed and will probably remain so. Three possibilities have been canvassed, and each is plausible. Firstly, if the poem was written in "the fall of the year, 1797", or "the summer of the year 1797" (Preface TEXTS 1 *1*), this might have taken place in the days following 15–18 Sept, when Charles

Lloyd, staying at Alfoxden, may have told DW that C was a villain and, by his generally estranged behaviour, prompted C's retirement (see *CN* III 4006 f 23^r; C Lloyd to RS [15 Sept 1797] q *CL* I 345–6n)—the scenery around Porlock fitting the poem better than Bristol. Or it might have been before 14 Oct 1797, when a letter to Thelwall appears to recall the Porlock scenery (*CL* I 349–52: [14 Oct 1797]; though the absence of "a day or two", immediately preceding, was less probably spent at Porlock than at Bristol, where C returned two folio volumes of a county history on 13 Oct—*Bristol LB* No 96—and the passages quoted from **146.X1** *Osorio* in the latter appear to have been written by the end of Aug, if not some time before). Or it might have been during early Nov 1797, when WW, DW, and C made a walking tour to Lynton via Porlock (Reed I 208–9).

Secondly, the poem might have been written during May 1798, either between the 8th and the 12th or (less likely) between the 20th and the 22nd, following the intensification of C's quarrel with Lloyd and at a time when he was perhaps working to finish **176** *Christabel* (see *CN* III 4006 f 23^r). It should be noted that the latter reference also supports the earlier date of 1797: C consistently thought of *Christabel* Part I as having been composed in autumn 1797. However, the evidence suggests that *Christabel* was composed in spring 1798, and the autumn and spring dates appear to have occupied a fluid, interchangeable relation in his mind.

Thirdly, the poem might have been written in either Oct 1799 or (less likely) May–Jun 1800, depending on later references to the quarrel with Lloyd, coincidences with C's reading in 1799, and the fact that no conclusive earlier references can be found (Elisabeth Schneider *Coleridge, Opium and "Kubla Khan"*—Chicago 1953—ch IV and nn).

Attempts to adjudicate between these three possibilities quickly come to depend on large considerations affecting C's relations with his contemporaries and literary values. The story of his retirement to a distant farmhouse, along with the person from Porlock, may of course be a fiction. If it is, the date of a tour which would take C to Porlock is unimportant. The suggestion that he either carried or found there a heavy volume of Purchas is complicated by the accompanying phrase "or words of the same substance", in which he might acknowledge that the words were read figuratively or in recollection.

There are possible allusions to the poem in Jan 1798 (Woodring 124–5) and Oct of the same year (*DWJ* I 34; cf Schneider *Coleridge, Opium and "Kubla Khan"* appendix III 298–305), but the first certain references are in the poem *Mrs. Robinson to the Poet Coleridge*, dated Oct 1800 (Mary Robinson *Memoirs*—4 vols 1801—IV 145–9). Thereafter, John Payne Collier recorded C reciting it in 1811, Thomas Noon Talford in 1815–16, on both occasions at CL's, and Leigh Hunt at Byron's house in Piccadilly in late Mar–early Apr 1815 or perhaps Apr 1816 (*Seven Lectures on Shakespeare and Milton by the Late S. T. Coleridge* ed John Payne Collier—1856—xlvi; *The Letters of Charles Lamb, with a Sketch of his Life* ed Talford II 28; cf also *LL*—M—III 215; Leigh

Hunt *Lord Byron and Some of his Contemporaries*—2nd ed 2 vols 1828—II 53; *The Autobiography of Leigh Hunt* ed J. E. Morpurgo—1949—288).

B. TEXTS

1. BM Add MS 50847. Single leaf, 18.6×29.4 cm; wm Britannia in oval frame, surmounted by a crown, with the letter C or G (or the numeral 6) in the frame below the crown; chain-lines 2.5 cm. Transcript in C's hand, signed "S. T. Coleridge". The paper has a distinctive blue-grey tinge, like some leaves in the Rugby Manuscript or the Advertisement for *Poems* (1797) in Ashley 408, or C's own holograph of *Christabel* (MS 2). Photographic reproductions in *British Museum Quarterly* XXXVI (Spring 1963) pls XXX and XXXI; *Review of English Literature* VII (1966) between 32 and 33; John Spencer Hill *A Coleridge Companion* (1983) pls 8–9; Jonathan Wordsworth, Michael C. Jaye, and Robert Woof *William Wordsworth and the Age of English Romanticism* (Brunswick, NJ 1987) 184–5. (The last of these is the most satisfactory.)

The ms shows traces of folding (from its conveyance by post?) and glue (from being mounted in an album?) and is endorsed in pencil "Sent by Mr. Southey, as an Autograph of Coleridge", in the hand of Elizabeth Smith of Bownham House, Gloucestershire. Hilton Kelliher makes this identification and describes the occasion (2 Feb 1804) in "The *Kubla Khan* Manuscript and its First Collector" *British Library Journal* XX (1994) 184–98. C's poem had been described in a ms letter of RS sent to another correspondent the day before as a "fragment". Although the resemblance between the paper and that used in SH's transcript of **176** *Christabel* is indeed very close, the "C", "G", or "6" within the frame of the oval in the wm is not present in the *Christabel* paper. Kelliher considers the possibility that *Kubla Khan* is written on paper in use at Greta Hall in the period before Jan 1804, but his researches have so far proved inconclusive.

1 [=RT]. The second poem in the volume *Christabel* (1816).

The second and third editions of the volume, which appeared during the same year, are textually identical, although *Kubla Khan* (and **335** *The Pains of Sleep*) are omitted from the title-page.

A copy of the first edition (HUL *EC8 C6795 817s (C)), which appears to have served as copy for PR *2* below, contains a correction to the poem (perhaps in RHS's or JDC's hand: apparently the same hand that occurs in the margins of *Christabel*, on p 18). David Hinves's copy of the second edition (in the possession of Sir John Murray) contains the same correction in pencil, and an emendation to the Preface in JG's hand.

There is a transcript of PR *1* in the hand of Jane Reynolds Hood (?) in the Reynolds–Hood Commonplace Book ff 9r–10r (BPL B 27744). Besides differing in details of spelling and punctuation, this omits the first paragraph and the last one-and-a-half paragraphs of the Preface; it has the corrected reading "Enfolding" in line 11; and it has the unique (mis)reading "plaints" for "pants"

In Xanadù did Cubla Khan
A stately Pleasure-Dome decree;
Where Alph, the sacred River, ran
Thro' Caverns measureless to Man
Down to a sunless Sea.
So twice six miles of fertile ground
With Walls and Towers were compass'd round:
And here were Gardens bright with sinuous Rills
Where blossom'd many an incense-bearing Tree,
And here were Forests ancient as the Hills
Enfolding sunny spots of Greenery.
But o! that deep romantic Chasm, that slanted
Down a green Hill athwart a cedarn Cover,
A savage Place, as holy and inchanted
As e'er beneath a waning Moon was haunted
By Woman wailing for her Daemon Lover.
From forth this Chasm with hideous Turmoil seething,
As if this Earth in fast thick Pants were breathing,
A mighty Fountain momently was forc'd,
Amid whose swift half-intermitted Burst
Huge Fragments vaulted like rebounding Hail,
Or chaffy Grain beneath the Thresher's Flail:
And mid these dancing Rocks at once & ever
It flung up momently the sacred River.
Five miles meandring with a mazy Motion
Thro' Wood and Dale the sacred River ran,
Then reach'd the Caverns measureless to Man
And sank in Tumult to a Lifeless Ocean;
And mid this Tumult Cubla heard from far
Ancestral Voices prophesying War.
     The Shadow of the Dome of Pleasure
     Floated midway on the Wave
     Where was heard the mingled Measure
     From the Fountain and the Cave.
It was a miracle of rare Device
A sunny Pleasure-Dome with Caves of Ice!
     A Damsel with a Dulcimer

8. Coleridge's fair copy of *Kubla Khan*, with Robert Southey's appended note on the circumstances of its composition

In a vision once I saw:
It was an Abyssinian Maid,
And on her Dulcimer she play'd,
Singing of Mount Amara.
Could I revive within me
Her Symphony & Song,
To such a deep Delight 'twould win me,
That with Music loud and long
I would build that Dome in Air,
That sunny Dome! those Caves of Ice!
And all, who heard, should see them there,
And all should cry, Beware! Beware!
His flashing Eyes! his floating Hair!
Weave a circle round him thrice,
And close your Eyes in holy Dread:
For He on Honey-dew hath fed
And drank the Milk of Paradise.——

This fragment with a good deal more, not
recoverable, composed, in a sort of Reverie brought
on by two grains of Opium, taken to check a
dysentery, at a Farm House between Porlock &
Linton, a quarter of a mile from Culbone Church,
in the fall of the year, 1797.——

S. T. Coleridge

in line 18. On the date of the transcription see the description of the Reynolds–Hood Commonplace Book in vol I annex A 11, where reasons are given for thinking that it has no textual significance. The poem was reprinted in *Metrical Romances &c. By S. T. Coleridge* (Isleworth 1825); *The Casquet of Literary Gems: Second Series* ed Alexander Whitelaw (2 vols Glasgow 1836) II 235.

   2. PW (1828).

   The poem is included, with a separate divisional title, at the close of the section of "Odes and Miscellaneous Poems" (it is followed by **335** *Pains of Sleep* in PR *3* and by **335** along with **478** *Limbo* and **479** *Ne Plus Ultra* in PR *4*). It might have been originally intended for this section of *SL* in 1815–16, and removed at the last moment when *Christabel* was removed, just as sigs T and U went to press (see on *SL* in vol I annex B 5).

   3. PW (1829).

   4. PW (1834).

divisional/preliminary title. ⊠1 𝕶𝖚𝖇𝖑𝖆 𝕶𝖍𝖆𝖓: I OR I A VISION IN A DREAM.

preface/postscript

1   This fragment with a good deal more, not recoverable, composed, in
            a sort of Reverie brought on by two grains of Opium, taken to check
            a dysentery, at a Farm House between Porlock & Linton, a quarter
            of a mile from Culbone Church, in the fall of the year, 1797.—S. T.
            Culeridge

⁻1.1 *1–3*   OF THE I FRAGMENT OF KUBLA KHAN.
    4   A FRAGMENT.

   ⊠1 *4* The following fragment is here published at the request of a poet of
            great and
            deserved celebrity, and as far as the Author's own opinions are con-
            cerned,
            rather as a psychological curiosity, than on the ground of any supposed
            poetic
            merits.   ⁻1.5
   ⊠1   In the summer of the year 1797, the Author, then in ill health, had
            retired to
            a lonely farm-house between Porlock and Linton, on the Exmoor con-
            fines of
            Somerset and Devonshire. In consequence of a slight indisposition, an
            anodyne
            had been prescribed, from the effects of which he fell asleep in his
            chair at
            the moment that he was reading the following sentence, or words of
            the same   ⁻1.10
            substance, in "Purchas's Pilgrimage:" "Here the Khan Kubla com-
            manded a

palace to be built, and a stately garden thereunto. And thus ten miles of fertile
ground were inclosed with a wall." The author continued for about three hours
in a profound sleep, at least of the external senses, during which time he has
the most vivid confidence, that he could not have composed less than from   ‾1.15
two to three hundred lines; if that indeed can be called composition in which
all the images rose up before him as *things*, with a parallel production of the
correspondent expressions, without any sensation or consciousness of effort. On
awaking he appeared to himself to have a distinct recollection of the whole, and
taking his pen, ink, and paper, instantly and eagerly wrote down the lines that   ‾1.20
are here preserved. At this moment he was unfortunately called out by a person
on business from Porlock, and detained by him above an hour, and on his return
to his room, found to his no small surprise and mortification, that though he still
retained some vague and dim recollection of the general purpose of the vision,
yet, with the exception of some eight or ten scattered lines and images, all the   ‾1.25
rest had passed away like the images on the surface of a stream into which a
stone has been cast, but, alas! without the after restoration of the latter:

>   Then all the charm
> Is broken—all that phantom-world so fair
> Vanishes, and a thousand circlets spread,   ‾1.30
> And each mis-shape the other. Stay awhile,
> Poor youth! who scarcely dar'st lift up thine eyes—
> The stream will soon renew its smoothness, soon
> The visions will return! And lo, he stays,
> And soon the fragments dim of lovely forms   ‾1.35
> Come trembling back, unite, and now once more
> The pool becomes a mirror.

Yet from the still surviving recollections in his mind, the Author has frequently
purposed to finish for himself what had been originally, as it were, given to
him. Σαμερον αδιον ασω: but the to-morrow is yet to come.   ‾1.40
    As a contrast to this vision, I have annexed a fragment of a very different

character, describing with equal fidelity the dream of pain and disease.

⁻1.43⁺ ☒1   KUBLA KHAN

1 ☐   In Xannadù did Cubla Khan

2 ☐   A stately Pleasure-Dome decree;

3 ☐   Where Alph, the sacred River, ran

4 ☐   Thro' Caverns measureless to Man

5 ☐   Down to a sunless Sea.

6 1   So twice six miles of fertile ground
    ☒1   five

7 1   With Walls and Towers were compass'd round:
    ☒1   girdled

8 ☒*4*   And here were Gardens bright with sinuous Rills
   4   there

9 ☐   Where blossom'd many an incense-bearing Tree,

10 ☐   And here were Forests ancient as the Hills

11 ☒*1*   Enfolding sunny Spots of Greenery.
   1   And folding

12 1   But o! that deep romantic Chasm, that slanted
    ☒1   which

13 1   Down a green Hill athwart a cedarn Cover,
    ☒1   the

14 ☐   A savage Place, as holy and inchanted

15 ☐   As e'er beneath a waning Moon was haunted

16 ☐   By Woman wailing for her Dæmon Lover:

17 1   ~~And from~~ From forth this Chasm with hideous Turmoil seething,
    ☒1   And   from   ceaseless

18 ☒*2*   As if this Earth in fast thick Pants were breathing,
   2   think

19 ☐   A mighty Fountain momently was forc'd,

20 ☐   Amid whose swift half-intermitted Burst

21 ☐   Huge Fragments vaulted like rebounding Hail,

22 ☐   Or chaffy Grain beneath the Thresher's Flail:

23 ☐   And mid these dancing Rocks at once & ever

24 ☐   It flung up momently the sacred River.

25 ☐   Five miles meandring with a mazy Motion

26 ☐   Thro' Wood and Dale the sacred River ran,

27 ☐   Then reach'd the Caverns measureless to Man

28 ☐   And sank in Tumult to a lifeless Ocean;

29 1   And mid this Tumult Cubla heard from ~~fea~~far
    ☒1   far

30 ☐   Ancestral Voices prophesying War.

31 1   The Shadow of the Dome of ?M Pleasure
    ☒1   pleasure

32 1   Floated midway on the Wave
    ☒1   waves;

33 ☐   Where was heard the mingled Measure

34 1   From the Fountain and the Cave.
    ☒1   caves.

35 ☐   It was a miracle of rare Device,
36 ☐   A sunny Pleasure-Dome with Caves of Ice!
        [*Line-space*]
37 ☐   A Damsel with a Dulcimer
38 ☐   In a Vision once I saw:
39 ☐   It was an Abyssinian Maid,
40 ☐   And on her Dulcimer she play'd
41 1   Singing of Mount Amøara.
   ☒1   Abora.
42 ☐   Could I revive within me
43 ☐   Her Symphony & Song,
44 ☐   To such a deep Delight 'twould win me,
45 ☐   That with Music loud and long
46 ☐   I would build that Dome in Air,
47 ☐   That sunny Dome! those Caves of Ice!
48 ☐   And all, who heard, should see them there,
49 ☐   And all should cry, Beware! Beware!
50 ☐   His flashing Eyes! his floating Hair!
51 ☐   Weave a circle round him thrice,
52 1   And close your Eyes   in   holy Dread:
   ☒1   with
53 ☐   For He on Honey-dew hath fed
54 ☐   And drank the Milk of Paradise.—

title. *2 3* KUBLA KHAN I OR, I A VISION IN A DREAM. • *4* KUBLA KHAN: OR, A VISION I IN A DREAM.   **preface.** ‾**1.7.** *2–4* farm house   ‾**1.9.** *1–3* effects • *4* effect   ‾**1.12.** *3 4* thereunto: and   ‾**1.17.** *4* things, ‾**1.20.** *2* pen   ‾**1.22.** *2* Parlock,   ‾**1.23.** *4* found,   ‾**1.24.** *1* purpose • *2–4* purport   ‾**1.27.** *1* has • *2–4* had   ‾**1.32.** *2 3* darest   ‾**1.34.** *4* lo! ‾**1.40.** *4* Αὔριον ᾄδιον ᾄσω: ‾**1.42.** *1* disease. • *2 3* disease.—Note to the first Edition, 1816 • *4* disease.—1816.   **1.** ☒1 Xanadu   *1–3* KUBLA • *4* Kubla   *1–3* KHAN   **2.** ☒1 pleasure-dome decree: **3.** *1–3* ALPH, ☒1 river,   **4.** ☒1 Through caverns   ☒1 man   **5.** ☒1 sea.   **7.** ☒1 walls ☒1 towers   *1* round;   **8.** ☒1 gardens   ☒1 rills   **9.** *2–4* blossomed   ☒1 tree; **10.** ☒1 forests   ☒1 hills,   **11.** ☒1 spots   ☒1 greenery.   **12.** *1–3* oh • *4* oh! ☒1 chasm   **13.** ☒1 hill   ☒1 cover!   **14.** ☒1 place!   *2–4* enchanted **15.** ☒1 moon   **16.** ☒1 woman   ☒1 demon-lover!   **17.** ☒1 chasm, ☒1 turmoil   **18.** ☒1 earth   ☒1 pants   **19.** ☒1 fountain   ☒1 forced: **20.** *4* burst   **21.** ☒1 fragments   ☒1 hail,   **22.** ☒1 grain   ☒1 thresher's flail: **23.** ☒1 rocks   ☒1 and   **24.** ☒1 river.   **25.** ☒1 meandering   ☒1 motion **26.** ☒1 Through wood   ☒1 dale   ☒1 river   **27.** ☒1 reached   ☒1 caverns ☒1 man,   **28.** ☒1 tumult   ☒1 ocean: **29.** ☒1 'mid   ☒1 tumult   ☒1 Kubla **30.** ☒1 voices   ☒1 war!   **31.** ☒1 shadow   ☒1 dome   **33.** ☒1 measure **34.** ☒1 fountain   **35.** ☒1 device,   **36.** ☒1 pleasure-dome   ☒1 caves ☒1 ice!   **37.** ☒1 damsel   ☒1 dulcimer   **38.** ☒1 vision   **39.** *1–3* maid • *4* maid,   **40.** ☒1 dulcimer   *1* play'd, • *2–4* played,   **43.** ☒1 symphony and song,   **44.** ☒1 delight   **45.** ☒1 music   ☒1 long,   **46.** ☒1 dome   ☒air, **47.** ☒1 dome!   ☒1 caves   ☒1 ice!   **48.** ☒1 all   ☒1 heard   **50.** ☒1 eyes,

⊠1 hair! **52.** ⊠1 eyes *1* dread: • *2 3* dread • *4* dread, **53.** ⊠1 he ⊠1 honey-dew *1 4* fed, **54.** *4* drunk ⊠1 milk ⊠1 Paradise.

title. PR *1–3* have a separately paged divisional title, the verso blank and the Preface beginning on the facing recto. In PR *4* the equivalent preliminary title heads a LH page and is followed immediately by the title of the preface.

preface/postscript. In MS 1 it follows the text of the poem.

⁻**1.41.** PR *1* I have] In Hinves's copy JG substituted "there is".

1–5. Leigh Hunt "thought he recollected a variation of this stanza" over forty years later, in which the second line read "A stately *pleasure-house ordain*" and the fifth line ended with the word "*main*" (*Imagination and Fancy*—1845 [for 1844]—288). For the original occasion, which must have been in 1815 or 1816, see sec A above.

5. Indented in PR *1–4*.

5⁺. It is just possible (but unlikely) that MS 1 intends a gap at this point.

11. PR *1* And folding] Hinves's copy and the corrected copy at HUL (perhaps in RHS's or JDC's hand) are emended to "Enfolding", the first in pencil.

11⁺. Line-space in PR *1–4*. It is just possible that MS 1 also intends a gap.

30⁺. Line-space in PR *1–4*. It is just possible (but unlikely) that MS 1 also intends a gap.

31–4. Indented in all texts.

36⁺. No line-space in PR *2–4* (although it heads p 269 in PR *4*).

37–8, 41. Indented in MS 1.

37–44. Indented in PR *1–4*.

179. CONTRIBUTION TO
WE ARE SEVEN,
BY WILLIAM WORDSWORTH

A. DATE

Early Mar–c 16 May 1798 (Reed I 32, 221).

B. TEXT

LB (1798), restored according to the note dictated to Isabella Fenwick in 1843 (*WPW* I 236, 361–2); cf *The Fenwick Notes of William Wordsworth* ed Jared Curtis (Bristol 1993) 3.

Vol I headnote describes how the RT version was arrived at.

180. THE NIGHTINGALE:
A CONVERSATION POEM

A. DATE

18 Apr–10 May 1798. Entries that surround others relating to this poem in the Gutch Notebook (*CN* I 219, 231) show that it was gestating at the time C was working on **171** *Frost at Midnight*, particularly the ending of that poem. All versions of the title give Apr 1798, which probably alludes to one or several late-night rambles with WW and DW after C returned from Ottery on 18 Apr, on at least one of which they heard nightingales and saw glow-worms (*DWJ* I 16; Reed I 233–5). The complete poem was not sent to WW until 10 May (*CL* I 406).

B. TEXTS

1. LB (1798).
The poem was inserted at the last moment to replace **172** *Lewti*, which appears in only five known copies of the earlier Bristol printing.

2. LB (1800).
C's letter to Biggs and Cottle of mid-Jul 1800 (*CL* I 594) makes it clear that printer's copy was provided by PR *1* altered according to these instructions: that is, to omit a phrase from the title and also lines 64–9.
In the copy at the State Library of Victoria, Melbourne (*821.71L), C added his signature at the end, "S. T. Coleridge".

3. LB (1802).

4. LB (1805).

5 [=RT]. *SL* (1817).
Four copies contain corrections in C's hand: Francis Wrangham's (?) (sold at Christie's 13 Jun 1979 lot 126); HNC's (HUL *AC 85 L 8605 Zy 817c); Miss Ford's (HUL *EC C6795 817s (A)); J. H. Frere's (Princeton University Library Robert H. Taylor Collection). The emendations in TP's copy (Brown PR 4478 A1 1817 Koopman Collection), WW's copy (Cornell WORDSWORTH PR 4480 S5 1817 Copy 1), and an unknown person's copy (Yale In C678 817s Copy 2) are in AG's hand. The emendations in Miss Fricker's copy (HUL Lowell *EC8 C 6795 817s) and William Hood's copy (Columbia *825 C 67 W 3 1817) are in JG's hand.

6. PW (1828).

7. PW (1829).

8. PW (1834).

The following reprintings have no textual significance: *Spirit of Contemporary Poetry* (3 vols Boston, Mass 1827) II 90–4; *The Beauties of the British Poets* ed George Croly (1828) 227–30; *The Diadem* (1830?) 139–41; *The Cabinet Album* (1830) 374–6; *The Naturalist's Poetical Companion* (1833) 96–7; *The Casquet of Literary Gems: Second Series* ed Alexander Whitelaw (2 vols Glasgow 1836) I 373–4; *The Book of Gems* ed S. C. Hall (3 vols 1836–8) III 55–7.

title. *1* THE NIGHTINGALE; I A CONVERSATIONAL POEM, WRITTEN IN APRIL, I 1798. • *2–4 The NIGHTINGALE.* I *Written in April, 1798.* • *5–7 THE NIGHTINGALE;* I A CONVERSATION POEM. I *Written in April 1798.* • *8* THE NIGHTINGALE; I A CONVERSATION POEM. APRIL, 1798.

1 ☐		No cloud, no relique of the sunken day
2 ☐		Distinguishes the West, no long thin slip
3 ☐		Of sullen Light, no obscure trembling hues.
4 ☐		Come, we will rest on this old mossy Bridge!
5 ☐		You see the glimmer of the stream beneath,
6 ☐		But hear no murmuring: it flows silently
7 ☐		O'er its soft bed of verdure. All is still,
8 ☐		A balmy night! and tho' the stars be dim,
9 ☐		Yet let us think upon the vernal showers
10 ☐		That gladden the green earth, and we shall find
11 ☐		A pleasure in the dimness of the stars.
12 ☐		And hark! the Nightingale begins its song,
13 ☐		"Most musical, most melancholy" Bird!

13fn ☐ *"Most musical, most melancholy."* This passage in Milton possesses an excellence far superior to that of mere description: it is spoken in the character of
the melancholy Man, and has therefore a *dramatic* propriety. The Author makes
this remark, to rescue himself from the charge of having alluded with levity to
a line in Milton: a charge than which none could be more painful to him, except   5
perhaps that of having ridiculed his Bible.

14 ☐		A melancholy Bird? O idle thought!
15 ☐		In nature there is nothing melancholy.
16 ☐		—But some night-wandering Man, whose heart was pierc'd
17 ☐		With the remembrance of a grievous wrong,
18 ☐		Or slow distemper or neglected love,
19 ☐		(And so, poor Wretch! fill'd all things with himself
20 ☐		And made all gentle sounds tell back the tale
21 *1–4*		Of his own sorrows) he and such as he
5–8		sorrow)
22 ☐		First nam'd these notes a melancholy strain;
23 ☐		And many a poet echoes the conceit,
24 ☐		Poet, who hath been building up the rhyme

25 ☐	When he had better far have stretch'd his limbs
26 ☐	Beside a brook in mossy forest-dell
27 ☐	By. sun or moonlight, to the influxes
28 ☐	Of shapes and sounds and shifting elements
29 ☐	Surrendering his whole spirit, of his song
30 ☐	And of his fame forgetful! so his fame
31 ☐	Should share in nature's immortality,
32 ☐	A venerable thing! and so his song
33 ☐	Should make all nature lovelier, and itself
34 ☐	Be lov'd, like nature!—But 'twill not be so;
35 ☐	And youths and maidens most poetical
36 ☐	Who lose the deep'ning twilights of the spring
37 ☐	In ball-rooms and hot theatres, they still
38 ☐	Full of meek sympathy must heave their sighs
39 ☐	O'er Philomela's pity-pleading strains.
40 *1 4*	My Friend, and my Friend's Sister! we have learnt
5–8	thou, our
41 ☐	A different lore: we may not thus profane
42 ☐	Nature's sweet voices always full of love
43 ☐	And joyance! 'Tis the merry Nightingale
44 ☐	That crowds, and hurries, and precipitates
45 ☐	With fast thick warble his delicious notes,
46 ☐	As he were fearful, that an April night
47 ☐	Would be too short for him to utter forth
48 ☐	His love-chant, and disburthen his full soul
49 ☐	Of all its music! And I know a grove
50 ☐	Of large extent, hard by a castle huge
51 ☐	Which the great lord inhabits not: and so
52 ☐	This grove is wild with tangling underwood,
53 ☐	And the trim walks are broken up, and grass,
54 ☐	Thin grass and king-cups grow within the paths.
55 ☐	But never elsewhere in one place I knew
56 ☐	So many Nightingales: and far and near
57 ☐	In wood and thicket over the wide grove
58 *1–5*	They answer and provoke each other's songs—
6–8	song,
59 ☐	With skirmish and capricious passagings,
60 ☐	And murmurs musical and swift jug jug
61 ⊠*5*	And one low piping sound more sweet than all—
5	one, low piping, sounds
62 ⊠*8*	Stirring the air with such an harmony,
8	a
63 ☐	That should you close your eyes, you might almost
64 ☐	Forget it was not day! On moonlight bushes,
65 ⊠*2–4*	Whose dewy leafits are but half disclos'd,
66 ⊠*2–4*	You may perchance behold them on the twigs,
67 ⊠*2–4*	Their bright, bright eyes, their eyes both bright and full,
68 ⊠*2–4*	Glistning, while many a glow-worm in the shade
69a ⊠*2–4*	Lights up her love-torch.

[*Line-space*]

69b □		A most gentle maid
70 □	Who dwelleth in her hospitable home
71 □	Hard by the Castle, and at latest eve,
72 □	(Even like a Lady vow'd and dedicate
73 □	To something more than nature in the grove)
74 □	Glides thro' the pathways; she knows all their notes,
75 □	That gentle Maid! and oft, a moment's space,
76 □	What time the moon was lost behind a cloud,
77 □	Hath heard a pause of silence: till the Moon
78 □	Emerging, hath awaken'd earth and sky
79 *1–4*	With one sensation, and those wakeful Birds
5–8	these
80 ⊠*3 4*	Have all burst forth in choral minstrelsy,
3 4	with
81 *1–5*	As if one quick and sudden Gale had swept
6–8	some sudden Gale had swept at once
82 ⊠*8*	An hundred airy harps! And she hath watch'd
8	A
83 *1–5*	Many a Nightingale perch giddily
6–8	perched
84 □	On blosmy twig still swinging from the breeze,
85 □	And to that motion tune his wanton song,
86 □	Like tipsy Joy that reels with tossing head.

[*Line-space*]

87 □	Farewell, O Warbler! till to-morrow eve,
88 □	And you, my friends! farewell, a short farewell!
89 □	We have been loitering long and pleasantly,
90 □	And now for our dear homes.—That strain again!
91 □	Full fain it would delay me!—My dear Babe,
92 □	Who, capable of no articulate sound,
93 □	Mars all things with his imitative lisp,
94 □	How he would place his hand beside his ear,
95 □	His little hand, the small forefinger up,
96 □	And bid us listen! And I deem it wise
97 □	To make him Nature's playmate. He knows well
98 □	The evening star: and once when he awoke
99 □	In most distressful mood (some inward pain
100 □	Had made up that strange thing, an infant's dream)
101 □	I hurried with him to our orchard plot,
102 *1–4*	And he beholds the moon, and hush'd at once
5–8	beheld
103 □	Suspends his sobs, and laughs most silently,
104 □	While his fair eyes that swam with undropt tears
105 □	Did glitter in the yellow moon-beam! Well—
106 □	It is a father's tale. But if that Heaven
107 □	Should give me life, his childhood shall grow up
108 □	Familiar with these songs, that with the night
109 □	He may associate Joy! Once more farewell,

110 □   Sweet Nightingale! once more, my friends! farewell.

title. *6* THE NIGHTINGALE; | A CONVERSATION POEM. | WRITTEN IN APRIL 1798.• *7* THE NIGHTINGALE; | A CONVERSATION POEM. | WRITTEN IN APRIL, 1798.   3. *5–8* light,   4. *5* old,   *5–8* bridge!   6. *6–8* silently, 8. *4 6–8* though   13. *8* bird!   13fn1. *5 8 "Most musical, most melancholy."]* • *6 7* "MOST MUSICAL, MOST MELANCHOLY."]   13fn2. *5–8* description. It   13fn3. *5–8* man,   *5–8* dramatic   *5–8* author   13fn4. *5–8* levity, 13fn5–6. ☒*8* Milton: . . . Bible. • *8* Milton.   13fn5. *4* except,   14. *8* bird! *5–8* Oh!   16. *5–8* But   *5–8* man,   *4–8* pierced   18. *3–8* distemper,   19. *5– 7* so   *3 4 8* wretch!   *4 6–8* filled   *3 4 8* himself,   21. *5–8* he, and   *5–8* as he,   22. ☒*1* named   *2–6* strain: • *7 8* strain.   23. ☒*1* conceit;   24. *5– 8* Poet   25. ☒*1 2 5* stretched   26. *5–8* forest-dell,   27. *4* sun- • *5–7* Sun *3 4 8* moon-light, • *5–7* Moon-light,   31. *5–8* Nature's   33. *5–8* Nature 34. *4* loved, • *5* lov'd • *6–8* loved   *5–8* Nature! But   35. *5–8* poetical, 36. *6–8* deepening   42. *5–8* voices,   46. *4–8* fearful   50. *5–8* huge, 51. *5–8* not;   56. *5–7* Nightingales; • *8* nightingales;   *5–8* near,   57. *5– 8* thicket,   *5–8* grove,   60. *5–8* jug jug,   61. *6 7* Sound   63. *4* That, 64. *3 4* day.   *6 7* Moonlight • *8* moon-lit   65. *6–8* leaflets   *5–8* disclosed, 68. *5–8* Glistening,   69. *3 4* Maid • *5–8* Maid,   71. *5–8* castle,   *4–8* eve 72. *4 6–8* vowed   73. *5–8* Nature   *6* grove   74. *4 6–8* through   75. *5–8* oft 76. *5–7* Moon   77. *5–8* silence;   *7* Moo • *8* moon   78. *4 6–8* awakened 79. *8* birds   80. *5 6* Choral   *5* ministrelsy,   81. *8* gale   82. *4 6–8* watched 83. *8* nightingale   84. *6–8* blossomy   85. *5–8* song   86. *5–8* joy 89. *3* pleasantly   90. *5–7* again?   91. *3–8* me! My   *5–8* babe,   97. *5– 7* Play-mate. • *8* play-mate.   98. *5–8* evening-star;   *5–8* once,   100. *8* dream.—) 101. *5–8* orchard-plot,   102. *5–7* Moon,   *5–8* and,   *4 6–8* hushed   *5–8* once, 104. *5–8* eyes,   *6–8* undropped   *8* tears,   105. *5–8* Well!—   106. *5–8* tale: 109. *5 6* joy! • *7* joy? • *8* joy.—   *8* more,   110. *5–8* Once   *6 7* more

title. Omitted from the PR *6 7* list of Contents.

39+. PR *5–8* have a line-space.

40. *1–4* My Friend, and my Friend's Sister!] A phrase remembered by Thomasina Dennis in Aug 1798: see Francis Doherty "Some First-hand Impressions of Coleridge in the Correspondence of Thomasin Dennis and Davies Giddy" *Neophilologus* LXIII (1979) 300–8 at 303; R. S. Woof "Coleridge and Thomasina Dennis" *UTQ* XXXII (1962) 37–54 at 42.

40–1. An adapted version of the lines makes up the first two of four which conclude a prose tribute to Edward Irving in *AR* (1825) 373fn (*CC*) 378fn (=poem **602**).

43–9. the merry Nightingale . . . Of all its music!] Taken verbatim from the Gutch Notebook (*CN* I 231).

44. PR *5* hurries] Underlined in TP's copy, in which "gurgles" has been written, in pencil, in the LH margin.

49. PR *5–8* split the line, giving a line-space before "And".

61. Erratum in PR *5*: "punctuate thus, reading *Sound* for *sounds;*

And one low piping Sound more sweet than all—".

In a note to Gutch with the proofs C asked that the line should read: "And one low, piping sound more sweet than all" (*CL* IV 645–6: [6 Jun 1816]). This uncertainty as to punctuation carries over into the corrected copies. "Sound" is corrected thus, to the singular, in all copies, but Wrangham's (?) is altered so that there is no punctuation; Hood's has commas after "one" and "low"; WW's has commas after "one", "low", and "piping"; Frere's has a comma after "low" only; Miss Fricker's has commas after "low" and "piping"; Miss Ford's has commas after "low" and "sound"; HNC's has commas after "low" and "*ʃ*Sound", and above it C has written out the line differently as "And one low, *piping* Sound more sweet than a,ll—,". A notebook entry of 1810 gives the line differently again, as "the one ~~sweet~~ low piping note more sweet than all" (*CN* III 3766).

64. The line ends with "day" in PR *2–4*.

81. In WW's, Miss Fricker's, and Hood's copies of PR *5* JG and AG have emended the line to read: "As if some sudden Gale had swept at once". AG has made the same emendation in TP's copy and the copy belonging to an unknown person at Yale, except that "and" before "sudden" has been left undeleted.

181. TO WILLIAM WORDSWORTH,
WITH *THE NIGHTINGALE*

A. DATE

10 May 1798.

B. TEXT

DCL MS 14/1. Recto of a single leaf, folded, 31.2×19.4 cm; wm (imperfect) ₗMA,TTHEWS. Transcript in C's hand, signed "S. T. Coleridge | May 10ᵗʰ | 1798". The verso is addressed in C's hand "Mʳ Wordsworth | Allfoxden". There are no seals or stamps, so it must have been delivered by hand. *CL* I 406.

The RT reproduces the untitled ms exactly, except for:

8. ms small ⌐. . .⌐ space   **13.** ms sure~~ly~~,   **16.** ms ⌐. . .⌐ Æolio crepitûʃ, ⌐. . .⌐ non carmine.

182. THE BALLAD OF THE DARK LADIÈ:
A FRAGMENT

A. DATE

Mar–summer 1798, and afterwards to 1800?, or possibly 1802? In *BL* ch 14 (*CC*) II 7 C said that the poem was "prepared" after **161** *The Rime of the*

Ancient Mariner, at the same time as **176** *Christabel*, by which he appears to mean that it was conceived and worked on but not brought to a finished state. A draft version of two stanzas attached to the NYPL ms of **253** *Love* (MS 3) proves that substantial reworking continued after Nov–Dec 1799, and the poem was positioned after *Love* when it was collected in 1834. C recited what he had composed, and resolved to continue beyond the first part he had written, on various occasions from Jul 1802 onwards (*CL* II 812: to W. Sotheby 13 Jul 1802; *CN* I 1577 f 53ᵛ; *CL* II 1094: to W. Sotheby 17 Mar 1804; see also *CL* III 324–5: to T. N. Longman [2 May 1811]). He did not write out what he had composed until Sept 1827 (MS 1 below).

B. TEXTS

1 [=RT]. Bodleian MS Eng Misc e 181 = the album of Louisa Powles, Summit House, Stamford Hill, Middlescx, ff 9ʳ–12ʳ. A fair copy in C's hand, signed "S. T. Coleridge." Written on the rectos only.

Louisa Powles's married name was Plummer. She was a friend of HNC and SC, and SC obtained the poem from her father (on the evidence of letters and surrounding entries in the album) in early Sept 1827. C's own note on the title-heading, to the effect that this is the first full-length version "committed to writing", is here taken to be literally true, in the absence of evidence to the contrary.

2. The album of Lady Hannah Ellice (?) pp 4–6, sold at Phillips (London) Sale No 29,111 (12 Nov 1992) lot 115 (for £4,600); formerly in the possession of Ian Ramsay (Aug 1991). The album measures 19×24 cm overall, and is in an ornately tooled and high-quality contemporary binding. Fair copy in C's hand, signed "S. T. Coleridge | 30, July 1831." Written on pp 4–6 (ff 4ʳ–5ʳ).

C's fair copy is prefaced by two pages related to "A Prologue or Introduction to the Tale of the Dark Ladiè", i.e. **253** *Love*. The remarks preceding the stanzas from *Love* are given at **253** TEXT MS 6. The remarks following the stanzas from *Love* are quoted in the EC to the present poem in vol I.

The original ownership of the album is a matter of speculation. C's contribution makes up the first entry. Subsequent autographs comprise verses on Charles Lambton, who died aged 14 on 24 Sept 1831 (pp 7–10); he was the elder son of John Lambton, earl of Durham (1792–1840), and Louisa, eldest daughter of Earl Grey. The verses were evidently written by someone who knew the family well; they might be in the hand of and even have been composed by the father, John, but it has not been possible to verify this. Then follow (p 11) verses by John Bowring, editor of the *Westminster Review* (written on 24 Oct 1831); then (p 12) prose advice from Jeremy Bentham (also 24 Oct 1831). These last two autographs are paste-ins. Subsequent entries, by Maria G. Ross and J. Burns, appear to date from c 1844. Further bound-in stubs are present to allow for sheets to be affixed without overfilling the album, but have not been used. The later entries appear to reflect a change of use and/or a less eminent owner.

Ian Ramsay told the present editor that the provenance of the album connects it with the Queensberry family household, but it is here suggested that Lady Hannah Ellice was the original owner because, when Bowring included the Bentham lines in his edition of Bentham's *Works* (11 vols Edinburgh 1838–43) XI 71, he said it had originally been written for her. She was Earl Grey's younger daughter, i.e. the aunt of the elegised Charles Lambton; and she died in Jul 1832, which would explain the break in entries.

An explanation of how C came to inscribe the first contribution might be as follows. Lady Ellice was married to the Right Hon Edward Ellice, who was Joint Secretary of the Treasury 1830–2. CL, Thomas Pringle, and others had negotiated with Edward Ellice on C's behalf in Jun 1831, apropos of a grant from the Treasury (*LL*—III—315–16; *CL* VI 862n; etc). Was CL, or one of the other people involved in applying for a grant, inveigled by Lady Ellice into acquiring C's autograph? or did they decide to present her with a new album so inscribed on their own initiative? HNC spoke to his uncle at some length on 30 Jul 1831 (*TT*—*CC*—I 233–5), and, though himself removed from the Whig-Reformist-Utilitarian circles which C deplored in his conversation that day, might have acted as go-between. The similar circumstances in which the MS 1 album was inscribed might even have suggested the choice of poem.

3. Yale MS Vault Shelves Coleridge. Two conjoint leaves, 18.6×22.7 cm; stamped paper (no wm or chain-lines), the stamp being an oval enclosing a cross within a shield, which is surmounted by the words ⌜. . .⌝R FIVE; written on both sides of each leaf. Fair copy in C's hand, signed "S. T. Coleridge".

Though it is here assumed that MS 3 follows MSS 1 2 in time, because of C's note in MS 1, MS 3 is closer to the presumably earlier drafts of the last stanzas.

4. Yale MS Vault Shelves Coleridge. Recto of a single leaf, 15.1×22.2 cm; wm (imperfect) R BARNARD; verso blank. Fair copy of stanzas 1, 2, 4, and 5 in C's hand, signed "S. T. Coleridge".

This selected and adapted version is presumably a response to a request for an autograph. Its place in the sequence of texts does not rest on certain evidence.

1. PW (1834).

C made several corrections in one stanza (lines 49–52) in the HEHL copy (Book No 109531). PR *1* coincides in all but one reading (in line 59) with MS 1, which may have supplied printer's copy.

C. GENERAL NOTE

The reference to a 190-line version of "The Black Ladie" in a ms list of poems now at VCL (S MS F2.7) is puzzling. It has been suggested that such a version existed, at least in C's head, and is to be associated with 200 lines written on 25 Sept 1798 at Ratzeburg (*CN* I 343 and n). The reference is not to the present version of the poem plus the earlier version of **253** *Love* (viz "Introduction to the Tale of the Dark Ladie"), which together add up to 192 lines, because the

96-line revised version of *Love* is so listed immediately beforehand in the same VCL ms—unless C set down the possibilities of presenting the "Introduction" by itself and combined, side by side, in the same list. The 200 lines referred to in the notebook might just as plausibly refer to the earlier part or full version of **184** *Lines Describing "The silence of a City"*. The reference is also unlikely to be to **655** *Alice du Clós*, which traverses similar themes in 193 lines, because, among other things, Alice is fair.

The ms list was added to at different times, but the group of poems in which "The Black Ladie" appears must date from 1799–1800, when the second edition of *LB* was in preparation. The title might have been copied down at a time when C had decided not to include **176** *Christabel* but was hopeful that he could finish the other, related poem. There are reasons for thinking, however, that the line-count might have been added afterwards, during or after 1802. See also **256** *Hexametrical Version of Isaiah* secs A and B.

Two ms versions of the last three stanzas—one at the NYPL (Berg Collection), the other reported by EHC but unlocated—are described below in the commentary on lines 53–60.

title. 1 Introductory Stanzas of the Ballad of the "Dark Ladie", to which the Poem in the Sibylline Leaves entitled, LOVE, was originally composed as *the Preface. • 2–4 The DARK LADIÈ: a fragment. • *1* THE BALLAD OF THE DARK LADIE. I A FRAGMENT.   **title fn.** 1 * And in this form it has been preserved by Sir Walter Scott in a Collection of Poems published by Ballantine. "The DARK LADIE" itself was never finished—& this is the first time that these Stanzas have been committed to Writing. I S. T. Coleridge.

1	1 *1*	Beneath yon Birch with Silver Bark
	2–4	Beside
2	□	And Boughs so pendulous and fair
3	□	The Brook falls scatter'd down the Rock:
4	□	And all is mossy there!
		[*Line-space*]
5	1	And there upon the moss she ?all sits,
	⊠1	sits,
6	□	The **Dark Ladie** in silent pain:
7	□	The heavy Tear is in her eye,
8	□	And drops, and swells again,
		[*Line-space*]
9	⊠2 4	Three times she sends her little Page
	2	Thrice hath she sent
10	⊠4	Up the castled Mountain's breast,
11	1 2 *1*	If he might find the Knight, that wears
	3	To seek the stately
12	⊠4	The Griffin for his Crest.
		[*Line-space*]
13	1 2 *1*	The Sun was sloping down the Sky,
	3	hast'ning
	4	sinking in the West,

14 □   And She had linger'd there all day,
15 □   Counting Moments, dreaming fears—
16 □   O wherefore can he stay?
　　　　　　[*Line-space*]
17 □   She hears a rustling o'er the Brook,
18 □   She sees far off a swinging Bough!
19 1 2 *1* Tis He! Tis my betrothed Knight!
　 3 4　　　　　　　　　　　Lord!
20 ⊠4   Lord Falkland, it is thou!
　 4　　　　　Albert!
　　　　　　[*Line-space*]
21 1 2 *1* She springs, she clasps him round the Neck,
　 3　　　　leaps,　　　　in her　Arms!
22 ⊠4   She sobs a thousand hopes and fears.
23 1 *1*   Her kisses glowing on his Cheeks
　 2　　　　Her glowing kisses
　 3　　　　She fastens kisses
24 1 2 *1* She　　quenches with her tears.
　 3　　　　And drowns them
　　　　　　[*Line-space*]
24⁺ 1   * * * * * * * * * * * * * *
　　　　　A Stanza, which has dropt from
　　　　　　　　　　my Memory.
　 2　　* * * —a stanza wanting.
　 1　　*　 *　 *　 *　 *
　　　　　　[*Line-space*]
25 ⊠4   "My Friends with rude ungentle Words,
26 ⊠4   "They scoff and bid me fly to thee!
27 1 *1*   "O give me shelter in thy breast,
　 2 3　　　　　　　　　　　heart!
28 ⊠4   "O shield and shelter me!
　　　　　　[*Line-space*]
29 ⊠4   "My Henry! I have given thee much!
30 1 2 *1* ◄——— "I——► gave what I can ne'er recall!
　 3　　　　"~~Have given~~ I
31 1 2 *1* "I gave my Heart, I gave my Peace—
　 3　　　　　　　Love,
32 ⊠4   "O heaven! I gave thee all.
　　　　　　[*Line-space*]
33 ⊠4   The Knight made answer to the Maid,
34 ⊠4   While to his heart he held her Hand:
35 ⊠4   "Nine Castles hath my noble Sire,
36 1 2 *1* "None statelier in the Land.
　 3　　　　"The stateliest of
　　　　　　[*Line-space*]
37 ⊠4   "The fairest one shall be my Love's,
38 1 2 *1* "The fairest　Castle　of the Nine!
　 3　　　　　　　　Mansion

39 1 2 *1*   "Wait only till the Stars peep out,
3   "Or ere the waning Moon have risen,
40 ☒4   "The fairest shall be thine.
      [*Line-space*]
41 ☒4   "Wait only till the Hand of Eve
42 ☒3 4 "Hath wholly closed yon Western Bars;
3   "Have
43 ☒4   "And thro' the Dark we two will steal
44 ☒4   "Beneath the twinkling Stars!
      [*Line-space*]
45 ☒4   The Dark? the Dark? No! not the Dark?
46 1 2 *1*   The twinkling Stars? How, Henry? How?
3   Beneath   the
47 ☒4   O God! 'twas in the eye of Noon
48 1 2 *1*   He pledged his sacred Vow!
3   solemn
      [*Line-space*]
49 ☒4   And in the Eye of Noon my Love
50 1 *1*   Shall lead me from my Mother's Door,
2 3   Father's
51 ☒4   Sweet Boys and Girls all cloath'd in White
52 ☒4   Strewing Flowers before.
      [*Line-space*]
53 1 2 *1*   But first the nodding Minstrels ←——— go ——→
3   ~~pace~~ ~~march~~ pace,
54 ☒4   With Music meet for lordly bowers:
55 1 2 *1*   The Children next in snow-white Vests,
3   robes,
56 ☒4   Strewing buds and flowers!
      [*Line-space*]
57 1 2 *1*   And then my Love and I shall pace,
3   go,
58 ☒4   My jet-black Hair in pearly braids
59 1   Between the comely Bachelors
2 3 *1*   our
60 ☒4   And blushing Bridal Maids.
      [*Line-space*]
60⁺ ☒2 4   *   *   *   *   *   *   *
2   Cætera desunt.

title. 3 The DARK LADIE | a fragment. • 4 The Dark Ladiè, a Fragment.
1. *1* birch   ☒1 silver   3 *1* bark, • 2 4 bark   **2.** ☒1 boughs   ☒1 fair,   **3.** *1* brook
2 *1* rock: • 4 rock—   **4.** 3 4 there.   **5.** 2–4 Moss   **6.** 2 *DARK LADIE* •
3 4 Dark Ladiè • *1* Dark Ladie   4 pain— • *1* pain;   **7.** 2 *1* tear   3 Eye, •
4 eye   **8.** 2 4 *1* drops   2 3 again!   **9.** 3 She   *1* page   **10.** *1* mountain's
3 breast   **11.** 3 *1* Knight   **12.** *1* crest.   **13.** *1* sun   2 Sky • 3 Sky: • *1* sky,
14. *1* she   *1* lingered   **15.** ☒1 moments,   3 fears: • 4 fears,   **16.** 2 Oh! •
4 O!   **17.** 3 Brook; • *1* brook,   **18.** 2 4 Bough— • 3 Bough: • *1* bough!
19. 2 'Tis • 3 "Tis • *1* "'Tis   2 'tis my • 3 4 tis my • *1* 'Tis my   **20.** 3 "Lord

2 3 Falkland!   2 3 Thou! • *1* Thou!"   **21.** 2 *1* neck,   **22.** 2 3 fears! •
1 fears,   **23.** 2 3 *1* cheeks   **25.** 2 friends, • *1* friends 2 *1* words   **26.** *1* They
3 thee: **27.** *1* O   *1* breast!   3 Heart!   **28.** 2 *1* O   2 me.   **29.** *1* Henry,
2 much— • *1* much,   **30.** *1* I gave *1* recall,   **31.** *1* I gave 2 heart— • *1* heart,
2 peace— • *1* peace,   **32.** *1* O   2 3 *1* Heaven!   2 3 All! • *1* all."   **34.** 2 Heart
2 3 hand: • *1* hand,   **35.** *1* castles 3 Noble *1* sire,   **36.** *1* None   3 Land! •
1 land.   **37.** 2 3 One   3 Loves, • *1* love's,   **38.** *1* The   *1* castle 3 Nine. •
1 nine!   **39.** *1* Wait   *1* stars   **40.** *1* The   2 3 thine! • *1* thine: **41.** 3 only,
2 *1* hand   *1* eve   **42.** *1* Hath   2 3 *1* western 2 3 bars; • *1* bars,   **43.** *1* And
through   *1* dark   **44.** *1* Beneath   2 Stars. • *1* stars!"—   **45.** 3 *1* "The   *1* dark?
2 Dark?—No—Not • *1* dark? No! not 3 Dark! • *1* dark?   **46.** 3 "Beneath
2 *Stars?*— • *1* stars?   2 how? Henry! how? • 2 3 How, Henry! how?   **47.** 3 "O
3 twas   3 Eye   *1* noon   **48.** 3 "He pledg'd 2 Vow. • *1* vow!   **49.** 3 *1* "And
1 eye   *1* noon,   *1* love,   **50.** 3 "Shall   *1* mother's door,   **51.** 3 "Sweet   *1* boys
2 3 Girls, • *1* girls   *1* clothed   2 3 white, • *1* white   **52.** 3 "Strewing   2 3 flowers •
1 flow'rs   3 before! • *1* before: **53.** 3 *1* "But   3 Nodding   *1* minstrels 2 go,
54. 3 "With   2 *1* music   2 bowers— • 3 Bowers! • *1* bow'rs,   **55.** 3 "The
3 *1* children   3 next,   2 vests • *1* vests,   **56.** 3 "Strewing   2 flowers. •
1 flow'rs!   **57.** 3 *1* "And   *1* love   **58.** 3 "My   *1* jet black hair 2 braids; •
3 *1* braids,   **59.** 3 "Between   2 3 Batchelors • *1* bachelors   **60.** 3 "And   *1* bridal
2 maids.— • *1* maids."   **60⁺.** 3 *1* *   *   *   *   *

4, 8, etc. All texts indent the last line of each stanza, as in the RT.

20⁺. In MS 4, where line 20 is the final line, there follows a row of asterisks.

22–3. In MS 3 C wrote alongside, in the LH margin: "*d*".

33. MS 1 Knight] C keyed in the following note in the RH margin, with an asterisk:
"N.B. a *solemn* Scoundrel. | *S. T. C.*"

48. MS 2 sacred] C underlined the word and wrote alongside, in the RH margin:
"??*knightly?*"

49. In the HEHL copy of PR *1* C corrected the line to read: "And in the eye of noon
my Love".

50. PR *1* door,] C emended the punctuation in the HEHL copy to "door;".

52. PR *1* before:] C emended the punctuation in the HEHL copy to "before!"

53–60. A draft version of these two stanzas appears thus, after the NYPL (Berg
Collection) ms of **253** *Love* (MS 3):

> ~~But first~~ And then my Love and I shall go,
> 2 My jet-black Hair in pearly Braids,
> Between our comely Batchelors
> And blushing bridal Maids—
>
> And ~~next~~ first the nodding Minstrels
> 1 With Music fit for lordly Bowers
> FThe Children then in snowy robes
> Strewing Buds & Flowers

The numbers to the LH of each stanza, putting them in their later order, are C's. The
unlocated ms of the last three stanzas reported in *PW* (EHC) I 293–5nn is a variation of
the draft above. EHC gives, for lines 53–6:

> And first the nodding Minstrels go
> With music fit for lovely Bowers,
> The children then in snowy robes,
> Strewing Buds and Flowers.

In the same ms EHC reports "go" for TEXTS 1 *1* "pace" in line 57.
60⁺. Tr "The rest is wanting."

183. TRANSLATION OF AN INSCRIPTION IN STOWEY CHURCH

A. DATE

1797–8?

B. TEXT

NYPL Berg Collection. TP's 1800 Letter Book, written on the front pastedown. Transcript in the hand of Thomas Ward, with two insertions into the title by TP.

Ward's transcript is followed by an initialled note in TP's late hand, probably addressed to HNC (who printed the poem in *LR*): "I will copy the original latin and send it to you—".

The RT reproduces the transcript exactly, except for the title, which contains insertions in TP's shaky hand):

title. ms Translation ⟨by Coleridge⟩ of the Inscription ⟨written by Bowles the Poet⟩ in Stowey Church

183.X1. EPIGRAM: "TO BE RULED LIKE A FRENCHMAN THE BRITON IS LOTH"

Annual Anthology ed RS (2 vols Bristol 1799–1800) II 271: "To be rul'd like a Frenchman the Briton is loath,". Two lines, untitled. Unsigned. Included in *P&DW* (RHS) II 166; *PW* (EHC) II 953 No 6.

The epigram is in fact by James Tobin. C has so marked the copy of *Annual Anthology* at Yale (*CM—CC—*I 98).

183.X2. CONTRIBUTIONS TO
THE MORNING POST

In Sept 1798 C told TP in a letter from Hamburg: "I have not been idle—you will soon see in the Morning Post the Signature of *Cordomi*" (*CL* I 419). No contributions to *M Post* at the time are signed in this way—a signature C used for **189** *Something Childish but very Natural* and **196** *Homesick* in the *Annual Anthology* (1800). Either C did not in fact submit the poems to *M Post*, or they were submitted but not printed, or they were printed without a pseudonym and so cannot now be identified.

184. LINES DESCRIBING "THE SILENCE
OF A CITY"

A. DATE

Sept 1798? Certainly before 27 Sept 1802 (KC's dating).

B. TEXT

BM Add MS 47518 = Notebook 21 ff 5ᵛ–6ʳ (*CN* I 348). Untitled draft.

　　1 The silence of a City—How awful at midnight—
　2a.1 ~~As silent as a sleeping Hermit's cell,~~
2a.2/5.2 ~~Mute as the cell of a sleeping anchoret,~~
　　2a.3 ~~As silent~~
　　　2 Mute as the battlements & crags & towers
　　　3 That fancy makes in the clouds—yea as mute
　　　4 As the moonlight that sleeps on the steady Vanes,—
　　　5 The cell of a departed Anchoret,
　　　6 His skeleton & flitting ghost are there,
　　　7 Sole tenants—
　　　8 And ~~the huge~~ all the City, silent as the moon
　　　9 That steeps in quiet light ~~her~~ the steady Vanes
　　10 Of her huge temples—

185. ENGLISH HEXAMETERS

A. DATE

Perhaps early Dec 1798 (see ELG's note in *CL* I 450); or possibly Nov 1798 (see on MS 3 below and *CL* I 443: to TP 20 Nov 1798).

B. TEXTS

1. MS untraced. Part of an undated letter from Ratzeburg to WW at Goslar, preceded by 27 and followed by 2 further hexameter lines, apparently impromptu. Printed in Christopher Wordsworth *Memoirs of William Wordsworth* I 140–1; *CL* I 452: to WW [early Dec 1798]. The 29 extra lines are given in vol I headnote, along with C's accompanying comments.

2 [=RT]. HEHL HM 12123. Single leaf (imperfect), 20.0×32.6 cm; wm COLES | 1795; chain-lines 2.5 cm; written on both sides. Transcript in C's hand, being the first of four metrical examples entitled "Specimen" (viz of hexameters). Numbered in Joseph Cottle's hand "194", and endorsed "This written by S. T. Coleridge ⟨for J. C.⟩". Printed (var) in Cottle *E Rec* I 226.

C's introductory remarks are given in vol I headnote.

3. BM C. 126. k. 1. Part of a marginal note by C on a back flyleaf of Jakob Böhme *Works* (4 vols 1764–81) II ⁺1 (*CM—CC—*I 672). Signed "S. T. Coleridge".

In the note C writes out a hexameter line, dated 20 Jul 1822, arising from his distress at DC's fever ("Eye! the Micranthrope thou in the marvellous Microcosmos!"), followed by a discussion which alternates between metrics and physiology; he concludes with the reflection: "Already in 1799 I had written the following Lines (then blind from weeping about little Berkley, I being absent & at Ratzeburg, 35 miles N.W. of Hamburg)". His distress arose from Mrs C's letter to him of 1 Nov 1798, not at this stage from learning of Berkeley's death, which did not occur till 10 Feb 1799 and which he learned of later still at Göttingen (*CL* I 478: to TP 6 Apr 1799).

4. VCL S MS F3.57. Recto of single leaf, 18.6×23.0 cm; no wm. Transcript in HNC's (?) hand. The verso is addressed in C's hand from Highgate to HNC at Lincoln's Inn, and endorsed 30 Jul 1833, being part of a letter.

The transcript is scribbled, which may be an indication of the writer's age, or else simply a sign of haste. It is not possible to determine whether it was sent as part of the letter or written on to the letter at a later date. It did not provide copy for PR *1* 2 below.

1. *Friendship's Offering for 1834* ed Thomas Pringle (1833) 167. The second of five "FRAGMENTS FROM THE WRECK OF MEMORY: OR, POR-

TIONS OF POEMS COMPOSED IN EARLY MANHOOD: BY S. T. COLE-
RIDGE."

A set of loose annotated pages from this volume at PML (Book No 49359)
contains a correction by C to the lines. The fragments are introduced with a
note on metre.

5. VCL S MS 20=*Table Talk* Workbook ff 90ᵛ–91ʳ. Transcript in HNC's
hand, dated 10 Aug 1833. Cf *TT* (*CC*) I 414 n 4.

Although the ms is struck through with a vertical line, it was not printed in
TT; nor did this version provide copy for PR *2*.

2. *PW* (1834).

title. *1* ENGLISH HEXAMETERS, WRITTEN DURING A TEM- I
PORARY BLINDNESS, IN THE YEAR 1799.•*2* WRITTEN DURING A
TEMPORARY BLINDNESS, I IN THE YEAR 1799.

1 1–3	O! what a life is the eye! what a fine and inscrutable essence!	
4 5 2	strange	
1	EYES!	
2 ☐	Him that is utterly blind, nor glimpses the fire that warms him;	
3 ☒4	Him that never beheld the swelling breast of his mother;	
4	heart	
4 1	Him that ne'er smiled at the bosom as babe that smiles in its slumber;	
2	⟨Him that smil'd at the Bosom, as Babe that smiles in its slumber—⟩	
3	(Smiling awake at the bosom as a Babe that smiles in its Slumber)	
4	(Yea & be content at the breast as the babe that smiles in her slumber)	
1 2	Him, that smil'd in his gladness, as a babe that smiles in its slumber;	
5	(Yea, & he smil'd at the breast as the babe that smiles in his slumber)	
5 1	Even to him it exists, it stirs and moves in its prison;	
2	moves	stirs
3 4	for	stirs moves
1 5 2	moves stirs	
6 ☒3 *1 2*	Lives with a separate life, and "Is it the spirit?" he murmurs:	
3 *1 2*	a	
7 1	Sure, it has thoughts of its own, and to see is only its language.	
☒1	a	

1. 3–5 O•*1 2* O, 2 3 Life 2 3 5 Eye!•4 eye— 3 5 What 2–5 & 2 Essence!, •
3 Essence!•4 essence **2.** *1 2* Him, 3 blind 2 3 Fire 2 3 him,•4 him
3. *1* Him, 3 Breast 2 Mother,•3 Mother•4 5 mother **4.** 2 Him 2 smiled
2 gladness **5.** 3 *1* Him 2 3 *1 2* exists!•4 exists—•5 exists!— 3 *1 5 2* It
2 4 5 & 2 3 Prison,•4 prison•*1 2* prison!•5 prison— **6.** 2 separate
Life/ "& is•3 Separate Life: and "Is•4 separate life, & "is•*1 2* separate life:
and—"Is•5 separate life—& "is 2 3 *1* Spirit?"•4 spirit"•5 spirit"— 2 mur-
murs—•4 5 murmurs, **7.** 2 4 5 "Sure•3 *1 2* "Sure, 2 3 Thoughts 2 4 5 &
3 *to see*•*1* TO SEE•4 5 to see, 3 *Language*!"•4 *1* language!•5 *2* language!"

1. C marked the scansion in MS 2 (see vol I headnote).

PR *l* EYES!] C deleted the "s" in the corrected pages at PML.
3. MS 4 heart] Written carelessly: it could be construed as "breast".

186. ENGLISH DUODECASYLLABLES, ADAPTED FROM MATTHISSON

A. DATE

Nov–Dec 1798? Friedrich von Matthisson's *Gedichte* (4th ed Zurich 1797), from which the original of C's poem comes, was one of the first books C bought on arriving in Germany (*CN* I 340). The translation was probably made soon afterwards, in Ratzeburg, as C exercised his German by exploring metrical equivalents in English.

B. TEXTS

1 [=RT]. HEHL HM 12123. Single leaf (imperfect), 20.0×32.6 cm; wm COLES | 1795; chain-lines 2.5 cm; written on both sides. Transcript in C's hand, being the last of four metrical examples. Numbered in Joseph Cottle's hand "194", and endorsed "This written by S. T. Coleridge ⟨for J. C.⟩". Printed (var) in Cottle *E Rec* I 227–8.

1. PW (1834).

title. *1* CATULLIAN HENDECASYLLABLES.

1 1 Heard, my Beloved an old Milesian Story—
  1 Hear,
2 1 High and embosom'd in ~~consecrated~~ congregated Laurels
  1   ←——congregated——→
3 □ Glimmer'd a Temple upon a Bbreezy Headland.
4 □ In the dim Distance amid the skiey Billows
5 1 Rose a fair Island—the God of Flocks had blest it.
  1   plac'd
6 1 From the dim shores of this bleat-resounding Island
  1   far   the bleak resounding
7 1 Oft in the moon light a little Boat came floating,
  1   by
8 □ Came to the sea-cave beneath the breezy Headland
9 1 Where between Myrtles a Pathway stole in Mazes
  1   amid
10 □ Up to the Groves of the high embosom'd Temple.
11 1 There in a Thicket of consecrated Roses
  1   dedicated

12 ☐ Oft did a Priestess, as lovely as a Vision,
13 ☐ Pouring her soul to the son of Cytherea
14 1 Pray him to hover around the light Canoe boat,
    1   slight
15 ☐ And with invisible Pilotage to guide it
16 1 Over the dusky waves, till the nightly Sailor
    1   dusk wave, until   mighty
17 ☐ Shiv'ring with extacy sank upon her Bosom.
18 1 Now by th*é*' Immortals! he was a beauteous Stripling,
19 1 Worthy to dream the ~~sweet~~ Dream of young Endymion.

1. *1* beloved, *1* story!—   **2.** *1* High, *1* laurels,   **3.** *1* temple *1* breezy
1 headland;   **4.** *1* distance *1* billows   **5.** *1* island; *1* god *1* flocks
6. *1* island   **7.** *1* moonlight *1* boat   **8.** *1* headland,   **9.** *1* myrtles
1 pathway *1* mazes   **10.** *1* groves *1* temple.   **11.** *1* thicket *1* roses,
12. *1* priestess, *1* vision,   **13.** *1* Cytherea,   **14.** *1* canoe-boat,   **15.** *1* pilotage
16. *1* sailor   **17.** *1* Shivering *1* ecstasy *1* bosom.

⁻1. In MS 1 the lines are preceded by the note: "The English ~~Hen~~ Duodecasyllable consists of two Dactyls and three Trochees—the two Dactyls first, the Trochees following—".
1. C's scansion of the line is given in vol I headnote.

187. THE HOMERIC HEXAMETER
DESCRIBED AND EXEMPLIFIED,
ADAPTED FROM SCHILLER

A. DATE

Nov–Dec 1798 (when C was interested in translating German hexameters into English)? Aug–Oct 1799 (on the basis of MS 1 below, containing on the recto joint plans of RS and C for a hexametrical poem about Mahomet)? Feb–Mar 1802 (when C was reading Schiller's *Musen-Almenach* for 1797—*CN* I 1127, 1128—and soon after which he conceived his plan for translating Voss into English hexameters, a specimen of which accompanies MS 1)?

B. TEXTS

1. Mitchell Library, State Library of New South Wales, Sydney, A 27 p 26. Verso of single leaf, 15.7×20.0 cm; wm crown on semicircle. Transcript in C's hand, endorsed by DC.
The verso also contains an example of an Ovidian elegiac and of a translation

from Voss's *Luise*, in C's hand (poems **188, 215**). The recto contains notes for **216** *Mahomet* in C's and RS's hands.

2 [=**RT**]. HEHL HM 12123. Single leaf (imperfect), 20.0×32.6 cm; wm COLES ǀ 1795; chain-lines 2.5 cm; written on both sides. Transcript in C's hand, being the second of four metrical examples. Numbered in Joseph Cottle's hand "194", and endorsed "This written by S. T. Coleridge ⟨for J. C.⟩". Printed (var) in Cottle *E Rec* ɪ 226.

1. Friendship's Offering for 1834 ed Thomas Pringle (1833) 168. The third of five "FRAGMENTS FROM THE WRECK OF MEMORY: OR, POR-TIONS OF POEMS COMPOSED IN EARLY MANHOOD: BY S. T. COLE-RIDGE."

2. PW (1834).

title. 1 Of the Hexameter • 2 Another Specimen describeding the Hexameter in Hexameters. • *1 2* THE HOMERIC HEXAMETER DESCRIBED AND ǀ EXEMPLIFIED.

1 1   Proudly it drives us along thro' leaping & limitless Billows
  2   Strongly   tilts   o'er
  1 2   bears   in swelling
2 □   Nothing before and nothing behind but the Sky & the Ocean.

title. *2* DESCRIBED ǀ AND EXEMPLIFIED.   **1.** *1 2* and   *2* Billows, •
1 2 billows,   **2.** *2* behind,   *1 2* sky and   *1* ocean.

188. THE OVIDIAN ELEGIAC METRE
DESCRIBED AND EXEMPLIFIED,
FROM SCHILLER

A. DATE

Nov–Dec 1798? Aug–Oct 1799? Feb–Mar 1802? See **187** *The Homeric Hexa-meter* sec A.

B. TEXTS

1 [=**RT**]. Mitchell Library, State Library of New South Wales, Sydney, A 27 p 26. Verso of single leaf, 15.7×20.0 cm; wm crown on semicircle. Transcript in C's hand, endorsed by DC.
The verso also contains an example of the hexameter and a translation from

Voss's *Luise*, in C's hand (poems **188, 215**). The recto contains notes for **216** *Mahomet* in C's and RS's hands.

2. HEHL HM 12123. Single leaf (imperfect), 20.0×32.6 cm; wm COLES | 1795; chain-lines 2.5 cm; written on both sides. Transcript in C's hand, being the third of four metrical examples. Numbered in Joseph Cottle's hand "194", and endorsed "This written by S. T. Coleridge ⟨for J. C.⟩". Printed (var) in Cottle *E Rec* I 227.

1. *Friendship's Offering for 1834* ed Thomas Pringle (1833) 168. The fourth of five "FRAGMENTS FROM THE WRECK OF MEMORY: OR, POR-TIONS OF POEMS COMPOSED IN EARLY MANHOOD: BY S. T. COLE-RIDGE."

2. *PW* (1834).

title. 1 Of the Hexameter & Pentameter | from Schiller • 2 Specimen of English Elegiac • *1 2* THE OVIDIAN ELEGIAC METRE DESCRIBED | AND EXEMPLIFIED.

1 □   In the Hexameter rises the Fountain's silvery Column
2 1 2 In the Pentameter still falling melodious down.
 1 2   aye   in melody back.

1. *1 2* hexameter   *1 2* fountain's   *1 2* column;   **2.** *1 2* pentameter

2. Indented in TEXTS ⊠2. C's scansion of MS 2 "melodious" is given in the vol I headnote.

189. SOMETHING CHILDISH BUT VERY NATURAL, FROM THE GERMAN

A. DATE

Early Oct 1798–6 Feb 1799. In introducing the poem in MS 1 below, C says that it was written "one wintry night in bed" at Ratzeburg, "but never sent" (*CL* I 488: to Mrs C 23 Apr 1799). The German folk song on which it is based is to be found in the Herder collection he bought on arriving in Hamburg (*CN* I 346; see vol I headnote). The pseudonym used in PR *1* was in his mind as soon as he arrived in Germany (see **183.X2** *Contributions to "The Morning Post"*).

B. TEXTS

1 [=RT]. NYPL Berg Collection. Transcript in C's hand in an als to Mrs C, 23 Apr 1799 (*CL* I 488–9).

1. Annual Anthology ed RS (2 vols Bristol 1799–1800) II 192; signed "*COR-DOMI.*"

C's annotated copy (Yale Tinker 1953 2) contains the explanation "Cordomi (i.e. Heart at home) S. T. Coleridge" on the front flyleaf. Cf **196** *Homesick* TEXT PR *1*.

2. BM Add MS 47499=Notebook 3½ f 126ᵛ (*CN* I 625). Transcript in C's hand. The poem is the penultimate in a long sequence of transcribed poems, and is headed "⟨Printed⟩".

2. *SL* (1817).
Rpt *Metrical Romances &c. By S. T. Coleridge* (Isleworth 1825).

3. PW (1828).

4. PW (1829).

5. PW (1834).

title. *1–5 Something childish, but very natural. | Written in GERMANY.*

The words of all seven texts are identical with the RT (MS 1), except that MS 1 inserts numbers before each stanza ("⟨1⟩", "⟨2⟩", and "⟨3⟩") amd MS 2 has "dawn" for "break" in line 12. The only other variations are in accidentals, as recorded below.

title. *2 SOMETHING CHILDISH, BUT VERY | NATURAL. | Written in Germany.* • *3 4 SOMETHING CHILDISH, BUT VERY | NATURAL. | WRITTEN IN GERMANY.* • *5 SOMETHING CHILDISH, BUT VERY NATURAL. | WRITTEN IN GERMANY.*   **1.** ☒1 wings,   **2.** *1–5 feathery 1–5* bird, • *2* bird—   **3.** ☒1 you *3 4* fly ☒1 dear!   **4.** *1–5* thoughts • *2* Thoughts ☒1 these *1* things • ☒1 *1* things,   **6.** ☒1 you *2* fly—! • *2–5* fly: **7.** *1* sleep, • *2* sleep; • *3–5* sleep!   **8.** ☒1 world   **9.** *1–5* wakes, *2* &   **10.** ☒1 alone.   **11.** *2–5* not, *1–5* though *2–5* monarch *2–5* bids: **12.** *1* 'ere *1* day; • ☒1 *1* day: **13.** *1–5* though ☒1 sleep   **14.** *2–4* Yet, *1* dark *1* lids • *2* Lids,   **15.** *1–5* on. • *2* on!

3, 5, 8, etc. The RT shows the indentation of MSS 1 2. Lines 2–3, 5, 7–8, etc are indented to the same extent in PR *1*; lines 2, 3, 5, etc. have progressive indentation in PR *2–5*.

190. THE VISIT OF THE GODS, IMITATED FROM SCHILLER

A. DATE

C made a note—"Send for Schiller's Götter des Greekenlandes—& remember W's remark"—in Oct 1799 (*CN* I 494 f 57ᵛ). The lines might therefore date from Nov–Dec 1798, soon after WW and C arrived in Germany, at a time when they were exchanging samples of hexameters; or it might reflect C's interest in Oct–Dec 1799, at a time when he was pursuing the same interest with RS and by himself. Alternatively, since he quotes the opening stanza of Schiller's poem with a comment on metre in Feb–Mar 1802 (*CN* I 1128), his version might date from this later time. When he quoted it again in Nov 1810, he added that he had translated it: HCR *Blake, Coleridge, Lamb, Etc.: Selections from the Remains* ed E. J. Morley (Manchester 1922) 31.

B. TEXTS

1. Colorado College, Colorado Springs, Special Collections. Two leaves, each 32.4×19.8 cm; wm (first leaf) Britannia, (second leaf) 180?0; chain-lines 2.5 cm. Transcribed in an als to John Whitaker of [30 Apr 1811] (*CL* III 321–2). The first letter of line 8 "fills" and of line 19 "him" have been worn away by creasing.

The poem is the first of three transcribed with evident care in the letter, the others being **149** *Allegorical Lines on the Same Subject* and **275** *After Bathing in the Sea at Scarborough*. C describes all three as "Songs" of his own composition, and initials each of them "S. T. C." They were sent to Whitaker for him to set to music, apparently by previous arrangement. On Whitaker see poem **149** TEXT MS 2.

1 [=RT]. *SL* (1817).

2. PW (1828).

3. PW (1829).

4. PW (1834).

C numbered each of the three stanzas in the copy now at HEHL (Book No 109531).

title. 1 The Visit of the Gods • *1–4 THE VISIT OF THE GODS.* | Imitated from Schiller.

1 □   Never, believe me!
2 □   Appear the Immortals,
3 □   Never alone.
4 □   Scarce had I welcom'd the Sorrow-beguiler,
5 □   Iacchus; but in came Boy Cupid, the Smiler!
6 □   Lo! Phœbus, the Glorious, descends from his Throne!
7 □   They advance! They float in! The Olympians all!
8 □   With Divinities fills my
9 □   Terrestrial Hall.
    [*Line-space*]
9⁺ 1   ————————

    [*Line-space*]

10 □	How shall I yield you
11 □	Due Entertainment,
12 □	Celestial Quire?
13 1	Me rather, bright Guests! with delicious Upbuoyance
⊠1	your wings of upbuoyance
14 1	Bear aloft to *your* Home, to your Banquet of Joyance,
⊠1	homes, banquets
15 □	That the Roofs of Olympus may echo my Lyre!
16 □	Hah!—we mount! On their pinions they waft up my Soul!
17 □	O give me the Nectar!
18 □	O fill me the Bowl!
18⁺ 1	————————

[*Line-space*]

19 1	Give, give him the Nectar!
⊠1	Give him
20 □	Pour out for the Poet!
21 □	Hebe! pour free!
22 1	Moisten his Eyes with celestial Dew,
⊠1	Quicken
23 1	That S T Y X the desttested no more he may view,
⊠1	detested
24 1	But like one of us Gods may conceit him to be!
⊠1	And
25 □	Thanks, Hebe! I quaff it! Io Pæan, I cry!
26 □	The Wine of the Immortals
27 □	Forbids me to die.
27⁺ 1	————————

title. *2–4* THE VISIT OF THE GODS. | IMITATED FROM SCHILLER.
1. ⊠1 me,   **3.** ⊠1 alone: **4.** *2–4* welcomed   *4* sorrow-beguiler,
5. ⊠1 Iacchus!   *4* boy   *2–4* Cupid   *1–3* Smiler; • *4* smiler;   **6.** *2–4* Phœbus
1–3 Glorious • *4* glorious   *4* throne!   **7.** ⊠1 advance, they   ⊠1 in, the
8. *4* divinities   **9.** *1–3* Hall! • *4* hall!   **11.** *1 4* entertainment, • *2 3* entertainment
12. *4* quire?   **13.** ⊠1 guests!   **14.** ⊠1 your   ⊠1 joyance,   **15.** ⊠1 roofs
⊠1 lyre!   **16.** ⊠1 Hah! we   ⊠1 on   *4* soul!   **17.** *4* nectar!   **18.** *4* bowl!
19. *4* nectar!   **20.** *3* Poet, • *4* poet,   **21.** *2* free?   **22.** ⊠1 eyes   ⊠1 dew,
23. ⊠1 Styx   *1* detested   **26.** *4* wine   **27.** ⊠1 die!

title. The list of contents in PR *2 3* gives "The Vision of the Gods."
1–2, 3, 8, 9, etc. The RT gives the indentation found in all texts, although much less clearly in MS 1.
19. The line does not begin a new stanza in PR *2–4*. The mistake arises from the fact that the third stanza heads a new page in PR *1* (p 275). C marked the division in the HEHL copy of PR *4*.
25, 26. The words "Io Pæan", and (less prominently) "Wine of the Immortals" are written larger in MS 1, as if to be printed bold.

191. TRANSLATION OF OTFRID

A. DATE

Feb–May 1799? See vol I headnote.

B. TEXT

BL ch 10 (1817) I 204fn (*CC*) I 208fn. HNC included the poem in *TT* (1835) II 363–4, having not included it in *PW* (1834).

The RT reproduces the untitled *BL* text exactly, except that in *BL* the first line is indented.

192. ALCAEUS TO SAPPHO
(REVISING WILLIAM WORDSWORTH)

A. DATE

Feb 1799–Oct 1800. As described in vol I headnote, C appears to have made clear his response to the poem—and presumably suggested how it might be improved—at the time WW sent it to him in 1799. The application of the poem to Mrs Robinson appears to have been made at the later date, to cheer her in her illness.

B. TEXTS

1 [=RT]. BM Add MS 34046 f 7ᵛ. Portion of a single leaf, 23.5×20.5/ 22.6 cm; wm (fragmentary) bugle in shield, surmounted by crown; chain-lines 2.2 cm. Transcript included at the end of a letter to Daniel Stuart, 7 Oct 1800 (*CL* I 629).

C introduces the poem with the comment "I shall fill up these Blanks with a few Poems—. It grieves me to hear of poor Mrs Robinson's illness.—" The remainder of the letter, after the present poem, was trimmed away and has not survived.

1. M Post (24 Nov 1800). Unsigned.

The RT reproduces MS 1 exactly, except for the title and the deletion in line 7 recorded below:

title. 1ⁱᵐᵖ A⌊LC⌋AEUS to SAPPHO. • *1* ALCÆUS TO SAPPHO.   **1.** *1* colours

5. *1* Heav'n *1* blush,   **6.** *1* soul   **7.** 1 ℬ Flush • *1* flush   **8.** *1* cheek!
9. *1* eyes, eyes *1* roll'd,   **10.** *1* shades *1* blue,   **12.** *1* sight *1* you!
13. *1* And, *1* lip *1* glow,   **15.** *1* world   **16.** *1* SAPPHO!   **17.** *1* smile,
18. *1* thing *1* birth,   **19.** *1* eyes   **20.** *1* face *1* earth!

1. The first (and only) line quoted by WW in his letter to C of 27 Feb 1799 (*WL—E* rev—256) is: "How sweet where crimson colours".
2, 4, 6, etc. Alternate lines indented in both texts.

193. ON AN INFANT WHO DIED BEFORE ITS CHRISTENING, PERHAPS INSPIRED BY LESSING

A. DATE

Late Mar 1799. In MS 1 below C says that the letter was written "a few weeks ago".

B. TEXTS

1 [=RT]. NYPL Berg Collection. Thomas Poole's 1800 Letter Book p 42. Transcript in the hand of Thomas Ward of an als to Mrs C, 8 Apr 1799 (*CL* I 483).

2. BM Add MS 47499=Notebook $3\frac{1}{2}$ f 124^r (*CN* I 625 var). Numbered "20" in a long sequence of transcribed verses, mostly deriving from German authors.

3. PML MA 2832. Recto of a single leaf, 18.4×22.6 cm; embossed wove paper; verso blank. Transcript in C's hand, signed "S. T. Coleridge". Electrostatic reproduction in BM RP 143.
This version may postdate MS 4 below. Before the ms was exported, it was sold along with MS 1 of **682** *My Baptismal Birth-day*, in J. H. Green's hand, now at Yale, which dates from 1832 (Sotheby's 18 Jul 1967 lot 548).

4. HUL *AC 85 L8605 Zy 817c. Fair copy in C's hand, written into HNC's copy of *SL* p 261, following the printed text of **448** *Another Epitaph on an Infant.*

1. PW (1834).

title. 1 2 On an Infant, who died before it's Christening— • 3 On an Infant that died unbaptized. • 4 On an Infant who died suddenly before Baptism. • *1* ON AN INFANT I WHICH DIED BEFORE BAPTISM.

1 ⊠4 Be rather than be *call'd*   a Child of God!
4   *nam'd*, the
2 □   Death whisper'd. With assenting Nod
3 ⊠*1* It's head upon the Mother's breast
1   its
4 ⊠*1* The baby bow'd, and went without demur,
1   ←—without—→
5 □   Of the Kingdom of the blest
6 □   Possessor, not Inheritor!

title. 2 Infant   **1.** 2 "Be • 3 4 "*Be*, • *1* "Be,   2 call'd • 3 *call'd*, • *1* called,   *1* child 2 God— • 3 God!" • *1* God,"   **2.** 2 whisper'd! with • *1* whispered!—with   2 nod • *1* nod,   **3.** ⊠1 3 Its • 3 Its'   *1* mother's   2 Breast • *1* breast,   **4.** 2–4 Baby 4 bow'd: • *1* bowed,   2 &   4 demur₍₎ • *1* demur—   **5.** 4 *1* kingdom   ⊠1 Blest **6.** 2 Inheritor. • *1* inheritor.

4, 6. Line 4 is indented in PR *1*, line 6 in TEXTS 2 3 *1*.

194. METRICAL ADAPTATION OF GESSNER

A. DATE

Feb–May 1799 (KC's dating).

B. TEXT

BM Add MS 47499 = Notebook $3\frac{1}{2}$ f 37ᵛ (*CN* I 396). Transcript in C's hand.

The RT reproduces the untitled ms exactly, except for the addition of a question-mark to line 14 "verstehen".

195. LINES IN A GERMAN
STUDENT'S ALBUM

A. DATE

May–Jun 1799. C set off with Chester on the first stage of their journey to England on 24 Jun, though his university studies had begun to relax more than a month earlier. Carlyon had arrived in Göttingen in Apr or early May.

Reported by Carlyon I 68.

The RT reproduces Carlyon's text exactly, with the addition of a title.

196. HOMESICK: WRITTEN IN GERMANY, ADAPTED FROM BÜRDE

A. DATE

5–6 May 1799. C introduced the poem to TP in MS 1 with the words: "O Poole! I am homesick.—Yesterday, or rather, yesternight, I dittied the following hobbling Ditty."

B. TEXT

1 [=RT]. BM Add MS 35343 f 208ʳ. Two conjoint leaves, each 23.2 × 39.0 cm; wm bugle within shield, surmounted by crown, above inverted V I VAN DER LEY; countermark ͺVAͺN DER LEY; chain-lines 2.5 cm. Transcript in an als to TP, 6 May 1799 (*CL* I 493). Lines 13–15 of the poem are imperfect because of a hole in the paper.

2. Recorded in Carlyon I 66, omitting the second stanza.

Carlyon describes how the lines were dictated by C and inscribed by one of the party (Greenough, apparently: *C in Germany* 229) in the Brocken Stammbuch in the Wernigerode Inn. Cf *CN* I 412 f 26ʳ, where C wrote "here insert the Poem" into the account of his tour. The poem was evidently written into the album at the Brocken, on 13 May, not at Elbingerode on 14 May, as KC assumes.)

1. Annual Anthology ed RS (2 vols Bristol 1799–1800) II 193. Signed "*CORDOMI.*" See **189** *Something Childish but Very Natural* TEXT PR *1* for C's gloss on the pseudonym; he adopted it as soon as he arrived in Germany (**183.X2** *Contributions to "The Morning Post"*).

2. *SL* (1817). The proof copy at Yale (In C678 817sa) is cited in the commentary on line 13 below.

Rpt *The Casquet of Literary Gems: Second Series* ed Alexander Whitelaw (2 vols Glasgow 1836) II 139 (the Advertisement is dated Jan 1829).

3. PW (1828).

4. PW (1829).

5. *PW* (1834).

title. *1–5* HOME-SICK. | *Written in GERMANY.*

1	☐	Tis sweet to him, who all the week
2	☐	Thro' city crowds must push his way,
3	⊠2	To stroll alone thro' fields and woods
2		woods fields,
4	☐	And hallow thus the Sabbath day.

    [*Line-space*]

5	⊠2	And sweet it is, in summer bower
6	⊠2	Sincere, affectionate, and gay,
7	⊠2	One's own dear Children feasting round,
8	⊠2	To celebrate one's marriage day.

    [*Line-space*]

9	☐	But what is all to *his* delight,
10	1	Who having long been ~~driven~~ doom'd to roam
	⊠1	doomed
11	☐	Throws off the Bundle from his Back
12	☐	Before the Door of his own Home?

    [*Line-space*]

13	1[imp]	H⌐ome sickne⌐ss is no baby pang,
	2 *1*	Home sickness
	2–5	a wasting
14	1[imp]	T⌐hat feel⌐, I hourly more and more:
	2	That feel
	1–5	This
15	1[imp]	The⌐re's healing⌐ only in thy wings,
	⊠1	There's healing
16	☐	Thou Breeze, that play'st on Albion's shore!

title. *2* HOME-SICK | *Written in Germany.* • *3–5* HOME-SICK. | WRITTEN IN GERMANY. **1.** ⊠1 'Tis 2 *1* him   **2.** ⊠1 *1* Through *2–5* city-crowds **3.** ⊠1 *1* through *2–5* woods,   **4.** *1–4* Sabbath-Day. • *5* Sabbath-day.   **5.** *1* is *1–5* bower,   **6.** *2–5* affectionate   **7.** *1–5* children *1* round   **8.** *2–5* marriage-day.   **9.** *2–5* all, ⊠1 his *1* delight   **10.** 2 Who, *1* 2 doom'd ⊠1 roam, **11.** ⊠1 bundle 2 *1* back • *2–5* back,   **12.** ⊠1 door 2 home. • *1* home! • *2–5* home?   **13.** *1–5* Home-sickness 2 baby-pang— • *2–5* wasting pang; **14.** 2 more; • *1* more,   **15.** *2–4* Healing *1* wings   **16.** 2 breeze • *1–5* Breeze *3 4* playest 2 *1* shore.

2, 4, 6, 8, etc. Indented in all texts in which they appear.
13. PR *2–5* a wasting] The new reading was introduced at the proof stage of PR *2*.

197. ADAPTED LINES ON FLEAS

A. DATE

Before May 1799.

B. TEXTS

1 [=RT]. Reported by Carlyon I 214n.

2. VCL BT 23 No 2 f 22^r. Reported in C's second Philosophical Lecture. *P Lects* (1949) 96.

The RT reproduces the untitled MS 1 exactly. MS 2 (also untitled) reads as follows:

Fleas bite little Dogs and less fleas bite them
And so you go on ad infinitum

The version quoted by HC to Branwell Brontë in 1840 (*The Hartley Coleridge Letters: A Calendar and Index* ed Fran Carlock Stephens—Austin, Tex 1978—29) is as follows:

Fleas that bite little dogs have lesser fleas
that bite em,
The lesser fleas, have fleas still less, so on,
ad infinitum.

198. EXTEMPORE COUPLET ON GERMAN ROADS AND WOODS

A. DATE

11 May 1799.

B. TEXTS

1 [=RT]. Recorded by George Bellas Greenough, *C in Germany* 222, in a diary which is now lost.

2. Recorded in Carlyon I 33.

1 1 We walk'd: the younger Parry bore our goods,
    2   went,

2 1   On damn'd bad roads thro' damn'd delightful woods.
    2 O'er

1 2 goods   **2.** 2 d——   2 through d——

    2. Indented in MS 1.

199. THE VIRGIN'S CRADLE-HYMN, COPIED FROM A PRINT OF THE VIRGIN IN A CATHOLIC VILLAGE IN GERMANY

A. DATE

Probably 11 May 1799. The Catholic village where C copied the Latin appears to have been Womarshausen, which he and his companions passed through on that day: see *CN* I 410; *CL* I 498–9: to Mrs C 17 May 1799.

B. TEXTS

1. BM Add MS 47499=Notebook $3\frac{1}{2}$ f 53^v (*CN* I 409). Transcript in C's hand, with the following introductory note: "At the bottom of a little Print in a Roman Catholic Village in the electorate of Mentz—May 1799". Deleted with a single vertical line and endorsed in pencil by C (?) "⟨Printed⟩".
    The Latin original and C's translation are written with different pens, perhaps at different times or even on different days.

1. Latin lines only in *M Post* (26 Dec 1801), with the following introductory note: "A correspondent, in Germany, transcribed the following elegant Latin rhymes from the bottom of a small print, in an Inn, in a Roman Catholic village. We communicate them to our readers with great pleasure:—" Unsigned.

2. The Courier (30 Aug 1811), with the following introductory note: "About 13 years ago, or more, travelling through the middle parts of Germany, I saw a little print of the Virgin and Child, in the small public-house of a Catholic Village, with the following beautiful Latin Lines under it, which I transcribed. They may be easily adapted to the air of the famous Sicilian Hymn, '*Adeste fideles, læti, triumphantes,*' by the omission of a few notes. I send you the words, with an English Imitation:" Unsigned.

3. Rpt *The Bristol Gazette and Public Advertiser* (5 Sept 1811), with the following note appended: "The critical reader will recognise in this happy imitation the pen of Mr. COLERIDGE." The subtitle, as well as the note concerning C's authorship, suggest that the text might have independent authority.

4 [=RT]. *SL* (1817).
HNC copied some parallel lines, dated "April 2nd. 1838—Dundalk", into his copy now at HUL (*AC 85 L8605 Zy 817c). The English lines only are reprinted in *Specimens of Sacred and Serious Poetry* ed John Johnstone (Edinburgh 1827) 476; *Spirit of Contemporary Poetry* (3 vols Boston, Mass 1827) II 87.

5. PW (1828).

6. PW (1829).

7. PW (1834).

title. *2* THE VIRGIN'S CRADLE-HYMN. • *3–6* THE VIRGIN's CRADLE HYMN, | *Copied from a Print of the Virgin, in a Catholic | Village in Germany.* • *7* THE VIRGIN'S CRADLE-HYMN. | COPIED FROM A PRINT OF THE VIRGIN, IN A ROMAN | CATHOLIC VILLAGE IN GERMANY.

1 ☐	Dormi Jesu, mater ridet
2 ☐	Quæ tam dulcem somnum videt—
3 ☐	Dormi Jesu blandule.
4 ☐	Si non dormis mater plorat—
5 ☐	Inter fila cantans orat,
6 ☐	Blande veni Somnule!
	[*Line-space*]
⁻**7** *2–7*	ENGLISH.
7a.1/8.1 1	Sleep, my Jesu!—Mother's smiling,
7.2 1	Sweetest Sleep thy sense beguiling,
9.1/12b.1 1	Sleep, my Jesu! balmily—
7 *2–7*	Sleep, sweet Babe! my cares beguiling:
8 *2–7*	Mother sits beside thee smiling:
9 *2–7*	Sleep, my darling, tenderly!
10 ⊠*1*	If thou sleep not, Mother mourneth,
11 1	Singing while her Wheel she turneth,
2–7	as
12 1	Stay, sweet Slumber, hov'ringly.
2–7	Come, soft slumber! balmily!

title. *4 THE VIRGIN's CRADLE-HYMN.* | Copied from a Print of the Virgin, in a Catholic village in Germany. • *5 6* THE VIRGIN'S CRADLE-HYMN. | COPIED FROM A PRINT OF THE VIRGIN, IN A | CATHOLIC VILLAGE IN GERMANY. **1.** ⊠1 Dormi, Jesu! Mater *1–6* ridet, **2.** *3* tum *1* videt: • *2–7* videt, **3.** ⊠1 Dormi, *2–7* Jesu! ⊠1 blandule! **4.** ⊠1 dormis, Mater *1* plorat: • *2–7* plorat, **5.** *4–6* orat **6.** *2–7* Blande, veni, *2 3* somnule! • *4–7* somnule. **7.** *3* Babe, • *4–7* babe! **8.** *3 7* smiling; **10.** *2–7* mother **11.** *2–7* wheel *4–7* turneth: **12.** *3–7* slumber,

3, 6, 9.1/12b.1, 9, 12. Indented in all texts in which they appear.

200. LINES WRITTEN IN THE ALBUM AT ELBINGERODE, IN THE HARZ FOREST

A. DATE

14 May 1799. It seems that the lines were inscribed on the morning C and his party left Elbingerode, not during the evening on which they arrived (see *CL* I 504: to Mrs C 17 May 1799).

B. TEXTS

1. Copied by Clement Carlyon from the Elbingerode Album: Carlyon I 64–5. George Bellas Greenough also copied the lines into his diary (*C in Germany* 230), but the diary is now lost.

2. NYPL Berg Collection. Two leaves, perhaps once conjugate, each 24 × 38 cm; wm crown above bugle within shield above G (?) W (?); chain-lines 2.5 cm. Transcribed in an als to Mrs C, 17 May 1799 (*CL* I 504–5). The letters and punctuation at the end of lines 37, 38, and 39 have been worn away.

1. M Post (17 Sept 1799). Unsigned.

2. Annual Anthology ed RS (2 vols Bristol 1799–1800) II 74–6. Signed "*C.*" C's copy at Yale (Tinker 1953 2) expands the signature to "S. T. Coleridge", and has two emendations. TP's copy—sold in the James B. Clemens Sale (Parke–Bernet Galleries 8 Jan 1945 lot 180)—also contained C's autograph corrections to this poem, made some time after Feb 1803 (cf *CL* II 924: to RS 15 Feb 1803).

3 [=RT]. *SL* (1817).
Emendations are cited from the proof copy at Yale (In C678 817sa) and from the emended part copy at HUL (*EC8 C6795 817s (D)) used as copy for PR *4*. (The emendations in the HUL copy are in JG's hand, and were not carried forward into later printed versions.)

4. PW (1828).

5. The Amulet for 1829 (1828) 130–1.
The poem is incorporated into a prose piece assembled from C's letters home from Germany, entitled "FRAGMENTS I OF A I JOURNEY OVER THE BROCKEN, &c. I BY S. T. COLERIDGE." It was reprinted from this source in *C Life* (G) 132–3; also in *SW&F* (*CC*) 1476–7.

6. PW (1829).

7. PW (1834).

C. GENERAL NOTE

Lines 1–33 of the PR *1 2* text were reprinted under the title "THE GRAND-
EST SCENES IMPERFECT, IF UNASSOCIATED WITH AFFECTIONATE RE-
COLLECTIONS", signed "COLERIDGE", in *The Poetical Class-book* ed W. F.
Mylius (1810) 194–5. The complete PR *3* text was reprinted in *Spirit of Con-
temporary Poetry* (3 vols Boston, Mass 1827) II 95–6; and the complete PR *6 7*
text in *The Book of Gems* ed S. C. Hall (3 vols 1836–8) III 58. The last three
lines were reprinted in *The Cynosure, Being Select Passages from the Most
Distinguished Writers* (1837) 135. None of these reprintings has any textual
significance.

title. *1–4 6 7* LINES, | WRITTEN IN THE ALBUM AT ELBINGERODE, | IN THE
HARTZ FOREST.

1 □		I stood on Brocken's sovran height, and saw
1fn *1–4 6 7*		The highest Mountain in the Hartz, and indeed in North Germany.
2 □		Woods crowding upon woods, hills over hills,
3 □		A surging scene, and only limited
4 ⊠2 *5*		By the blue distance. Heavily my way
	2 5	Wearily
5 ⊠*1 2*		Downward I dragged through fir-groves evermore,
	1 2	Homeward
6 ⊠2 *5*		Where bright green moss heaves in sepulchral forms
	2	heav'd
	5	moved
7 □		Speckled with sunshine; and, but seldom heard,
8 ⊠*5*		The sweet bird's song became an hollow sound;
	5	become
9 ⊠2 *5*		And the breeze, murmuring indivisibly,
	2 5	Gale
10 ⊠*5*		Preserved its solemn murmur most distinct
	5	Reserved more
11 ⊠2 *5*		From many a note of many a waterfall,
	2 5	Waterbreak,
12 ⊠2 *5*		And the brook's chatter; 'mid whose islet stones
	2 5	on
13 □		The dingy kidling with its tinkling bell
14 □		Leapt frolicsome, or old romantic goat
15 □		Sat, his white beard slow waving. I moved on
16 ⊠2 *5*		In low and languid mood; for I had found
	2 5	With thought:
16fn1 *1–4 6 7*		——————— ——————— When I have gaz'd
16fn2 *1–4 6 7*		From some high eminence on goodly vales,
16fn3 *1–4 6 7*		And cots and villages embower'd below,
16fn4 *1–4 6 7*		The thought would rise that all to me was strange
16fn5 *1–4 6 7*		Amid the scene so fair, nor one small spot
16fn6 *1–4 6 7*		Where my tir'd mind might rest, and call it *home*.
16fn7 *1–4 6 7*		SOUTHEY's Hymn to the Penates.

17 1 *3* 4 6 7 That outward forms, the loftiest, still receive
18 1 *3* 4 6 7 Their finer influence from the life within;
19 1 *3* 4   Fair cyphers of vague import, where the eye
  6 7   else: fair, but of import vague
20 1 *3* 4   Traces no spot, in which the heart may read
  6 7   Or unconcerning, where the Heart not finds
21 1 *3* 4 6 7 History or prophecy of friend or child,
17.1 2 *1* 2 5 That grandest Scenes have but imperfect Charms,
19.1 2   Where the ~~eye~~ sight vainly wanders nor beholds
  1 2   sight
  5   eye
20.1 2 *1* 2 5 One spot, with which the Heart associates
21.1 2 5   Holy Remembrances of Child or Friend,
  1 2   Friend,   Child,
22 ☐   Or gentle maid, our first and early love,
23 ☐   Or father, or the venerable name
24 ☐   Of our adored country! O, thou queen,
25 ☐   Thou delegated deity of earth,
26 1 5   O dear, dear England! how my longing eyes
  ☒1 5   Eye
27 ☐   Turned westward, shaping in the steady clouds
28a ☐   Thy sands and high white cliffs!
28b 1 *3* 4 6 7   My native land!
  2 5   Sweet Native Isle,
  1 2   O native land,
29 ☒2 5   Filled with the thought of thee this heart was proud,
30 1   Yea, mine eyes swam with tears; that all the view
  ☒1 2 5   eye
29b.1/30a.1 2 This Heart was proud, ~~this Eye was~~ yea, mine Eyes swam with Tears
  5   ←——yea,——→
29a.1/30b.1 2 5 To think of Thee; & all the goodly view
31 ☐   From sovran Brocken, woods and woody hills,
32 ☐   Floated away, like a departing dream,
33 ☐   Feeble and dim! Stranger, these impulses
34 ☐   Blame thou not lightly; nor will I profane,
35 ☐   With hasty judgment or injurious doubt,
36 ☐   That man's sublimer spirit, who can feel
37 ☒2   That God is every where! the God who framed
  2^imp   fram
38 ☒2 5   Mankind to be one mighty   family,
  2   Brotherhoo⌊d,⌋
  5   brotherhood,
39 ☒2   Himself our father, and the world our home.
  2^imp   Ho⌊me.⌋

title. *2 LINES | Written in the Album at Elbingerode, in the | Hartz Forest.* •
3 LINES | Written in the Album at Elbingerode, in the Hartz Forest. • *4 6* LINES |
WRITTEN IN THE ALBUM AT ELBINGERODE, IN | THE HARTZ FOREST.•
7 LINES | WRITTEN IN THE ALBUM AT ELBINGERODE, | IN THE HARTZ

FOREST. **1.** 2 height & • *1* height; and **1fn.** *3 4 6 7* mountain *3* Hartz
2. *1* hills over hills— • *4* hills, over hills, • *5* hills over hills; **3.** 2 *1 2 surging*
2 Scene **4.** 2 Distance. **5.** 2 *1–3* dragg'd • *5* dragged, 2 *1 2* thro'
2 Fir-groves • *4–7* fir groves **6.** 2 bright-green Moss 2 *1 2 5* forms,
8. 2 Bird's Song *5 7* a 2 Sound; **9.** *1 2* breeze *5* gale *1* murm'ring
2 indivisibly **10.** 2 *1 2* Preserv'd 2 Murmur • *5* murmur, **11.** 2 Note
5 waterbreak, **12.** 2 Brook's *Chatter*; *1* islet-stones **13.** 2 Kidling •
5 kidling, 2 Bell • *5* bell, **14.** *4 6 7* Leaped *1 5* frolicksome, 2 Goat
15. 2 Beard slow-waving! *2 1 2* mov'd **16.** 2 & *1 2* mood, • *3 4 6 7* mood:
5 thought, **16fn1.** *1 2* —————— • *3 4 6 7* .... *3 4 6 7* gazed
16fn3. *3 4 6 7* embowered **16fn5.** *1* scene • *2–4 6 7* scenes **16fn6.** 2–
4 6 7 tired *3 4 6 7* home. **16fn7.** *7 Southey's 2–4 6 7 Hymn to the*
Penates. **17.** *3 4 6* Forms, **18.** *3 4 6 7* Life *3 4 6* within: • *7* within;—
19. *3 4* Cyphers *3 4* Eye **20.** *3 4 6* Heart • *7* heart **21.** *3 4 6* Prophecy
3 4 6 Friend, • *7* friend, *3 4 6* Child, **17.1.** *1 2 5* scenes *1 2* charms, • *5* charms
19.1. *1 2 5* wanders, **20.1.** *1 2 5* spot *1 2 5* heart **21.1.** *1 2 5* remembrances
5 child 2 Friend • *5* friend, **22.** ⊠*1 5 7* Maid, 2 & 2 Love, • *1* love;
23. ⊠*1 5 7* Father, 2 Name **24.** 2 Country. • *1 3 4 6* Country! • 2 Coun-
try!— • *5* country. ⊠*1* O ⊠*1* Queen, **25.** ⊠*1* Deity ⊠*1 1* Earth, • *1* Earth!
26. 2 "dear dear" England; • *1 2* dear, dear, England! • *5* "dear, dear" England!
1 2 How ⊠*1 2 5* eye **27.** 2 *1 2* Turn'd 2 Westward, 2 Clouds **28.** 2 &
2 Cliffs! **28.** *5* native 2 Land, • *3 4 6 7* Land! *5* isle, **29.** *1 2* Fill'd
1 thee, • 2 Thee, **30.** *1* tears • 2 tears, • *3 4 6 7* tears: **29b.1/30a.1.** *5* heart
5 eyes *5* tears **29a.1/30b.1.** *5* thee; and **31.** 2 sov'ran *1 2* woods, 2 Hills, •
5 hills **32.** 2 Dream, **33.** 2 dim.— • *1 2* dim!— • *5* dim. 2 Stranger!
2 Impulses **34.** 2 I 2 *1 2* profane **35.** 2 Judgment • 2 judgement 2 Doubt •
1 2 doubt **36.** 2 Spirit, **37.** *1 2* GOD is *1* ev'ry where! • *4 6 7* everywhere! •
5 every where, *1 2* GOD who *1 2* fram'd **38.** *1* family— • *2–4 6* Family,
39. 2 Father & • *1–7* Father, and ⊠*1 5* World *3 4 6 7* Home.

5. PR 2 Homeward] C substituted "Downward" in the copy at Yale.
17–21. The proof copy of PR *3* at Yale reveals that the poem was initially set in the PR
2 form (see lines 17.1–21.1), and that the PR 3 reading was substituted at this, the proof
stage.
19. PR *3* where] JG substituted "if" in the emended part copy at HUL.
26. PR *3* eye] JG substituted "Sight" in the emended part copy at HUL.
28. The line is not split in TEXTS 2 *1 2 5*. C introduced the break in the proofs of
PR *3* at Yale, and indicated that he also wanted a line-space (which the printer failed to
provide). The line-space appears only in PR *4 6 7*.
28b. PR 2 O] C substituted "My" in the copy at Yale.

200.X1. GERMAN ALBUM VERSES

Carlyon I 67 introduces **195** *Lines in a German Student's Album* as follows:
"The Germans, of all mortals the most imaginative, take extraordinary delight

in their albums; and Coleridge being a NOTICEABLE ENGLANDER, and a poet withal, was not infrequently requested to favour with a scrap of verse persons who had no very particular claims upon his muse." Cf C to Mrs C, describing how poem **200** was written at Elbingerode: "At the Inn they brought us an Album, or Stamm Buch, requesting that we w⸤ould write⸥ our names, & something or other as a remembrance that we had been there" (*CL* I 504: 17 May 1799). The only such verses known were preserved by Greenough and Coleridge himself, besides Carlyon. It is conceivable that others, as well as other versions of those already known, exist somewhere in the original albums and guest-books of inns.

201. EPIGRAM ON GOSLAR ALE, FROM THE GERMAN

A. DATE

May 1799. C was in Goslar on 15–16 May.

B. TEXTS

1 [=RT]. BM Add MS 47499 = Notebook 3½ f 43ᵛ (*CN* I 429 var). Draft in C's hand.

The draft follows C's transcript of the German original, which is given in vol I headnote.

2. BM C 45 a 4 = JG's copy of *Omniana* II 38. Written in C's hand and signed "S. T. C." *CM* (*CC*) III 1072.

The *Omniana* passage which prompted C's lines is given in vol I headnote. C added the following footnote, of which his own lines form the conclusion: "I remember a similar German Epigram on the Goslar Ale, ~~of~~ which may be englished thus— . . ."

1 1 This Goslar̸ ~~Gose! good and~~ staunch Ale is strong & staunch,
  2   Goslar   ale ~~is~~ stout
2 1 Yet ~~strangely one by~~ sure 'twas brew'd by by Witches:
  2 But   sure   'tis   by
3 1 For ~~scarce you launch it down~~ ere you think, 't has reach'd the Paunch
  2 Scarce   do   you   feel   it   warm   in
4 1 Odd's fish! tis in your Breeches!
  2   blood!

1. 2 and staunch;   **2.** 2 Witches!   **3.** 2 paunch,   **4.** 2 Ods

1. MS 1 staunch] C evidently meant to delete the word, which ran over on to a following line.

202. EPITAPH ON JOHANN REIMBOLD OF CATLENBURG, FROM THE GERMAN

A. DATE

16–19 May 1799. C copied the original into Notebook 3 f 28ᵛ (*CN* I 418) on 16 May.

B. TEXT

BM Add MS 35343 f 211ᵛ. Two conjoint leaves, each 23.7×39.1 cm; wm bugle within shield, surmounted by crown, above inverted V I VAN DER LEY; countermark VAN DER LEY; chain-lines 2.5 cm. Quoted in an als to TP, 19 May 1799. (*CL* I 515).

The RT reproduces the ms exactly, except for:

⁻**1.** ms Johann Reimbold of Catlenberg   **4.** ms He was more ~~to me~~ than ʃMany!

203. EPIGRAM ON KEPLER, FROM KÄSTNER

A. DATE

May 1799 (KC's dating).

B. TEXTS

1. BM Add MS 47499=Notebook 3½ f 49ᵛ (*CN* I 432). Numbered "1" in a series of some 30 or so such epigrams or notes for epigrams, mostly adapted from German authors.

1 [=RT]. *The Friend* XV (30 Nov 1809) 231fn (*CC*) II 201fn.

2. The Friend (1818) II 95fn (*CC*) I 252fn.

2. J.M.?B.'s notebook album (see vol I annex A 13) f 126ᵛ. One of several epigrams by C transcribed in the hand of J.H.B. Williams.

In the possession of J.C.C. Mays (1999).

1 1   No mortal Genius yet had clomb so high
   1 2   spirit
   2   ever
2 1   As Kepler, and his Country ~~let~~ saw him die
   ⊠1   yet   saw
3 1   For very want! The ~~Souls~~ minds alone he fed
   ⊠1   *Minds*
4 ⊠2 And so the Bodies left him without   bread!
   2   ~~head~~ bread

2. *1 2* Kepler—   2 country   **3.** *1* Want! • 2 want—   *1 2* the   *2 minds* • 2 minds
1 2 fed,   **4.** *1 Bodies* • *2 bodies* • 2 bodies   *1 2* bread.

204. EPIGRAM: "JACK DRINKS FINE WINES", FROM KÄSTNER

A. DATE

May–Sept 1799 (KC's dating).

B. TEXTS

1. BM Add MS 47499=Notebook $3\frac{1}{2}$ f 49ᵛ (*CN* I 432). Numbered "2" in a series of some 30 or so such epigrams or notes for epigrams, mostly adapted from German authors.

1 [=RT]. *M Post* (16 Nov 1799). Unsigned.
Rpt *The Spirit of the Public Journals for 1800* IV (1801) 88.

2. Annual Anthology ed RS (2 vols Bristol 1799–1800) II 268; marked "S. T. C." by C in his own copy (Yale Tinker 1953 2). The fifth in a series of 17 epigrams, 12 of them by C.

title. *1 EPIGRAM.*

1 1   Jack drinks the costliest wines, wears splendid Clothing
   1 2   ←fine→   modish
2 1   ~~What is his future? Where lies his~~ How much &c—Estate?—
   1 2 But   prithee   where   lies   JACK'S   estate?
3 □   In Algebra; for there I found of late
4 □   A Quantity call'd less than nothing.

1. *1* clothing; • *2* clothing, **2.** *2* Jack's **3.** *1 2* Algebra, **4.** *1 2* quantity
2 nothing,

title. In the PR *2* sequence the poem is numbered "V."
2–3. Indented in PR *1 2.*

205. EPIGRAM ON MR ROSS,
USUALLY COGNOMINATED "NOSY"

A. DATE

May 1799 (KC's dating).

B. TEXT

BM Add MS 47499=Notebook $3\frac{1}{2}$ f 50^r (*CN* I 432). Numbered "4" in a series of some 30 or so such epigrams or notes for epigrams, mostly adapted from German authors.

The RT reproduces the ms exactly, except for the typography of the title:

ms On Mr Ross, usually cognominated *Nosy.*

206. EPIGRAM: "O WOULD
THE BAPTIST COME AGAIN",
FROM LOGAU

A. DATE

May–Sept 1799.

B. TEXTS

1. BM Add MS 47499=Notebook $3\frac{1}{2}$ f 50^v (*CN* I 432). Numbered "8" in a series of some 30 or so such epigrams or notes for epigrams, mostly adapted from German authors.

1 [=RT]. *M Post* (2 Sept 1799). Unsigned.

2. *Annual Anthology* ed RS (2 vols Bristol 1799–1800) II 267; marked

"S. T. C." by C in his own copy (Yale Tinker 1953 2). The first in a series of 17 epigrams, 12 of them by C.

In the Yale copy C deleted the poem, together with the epigram following (**207** *On the United Irishmen*), describing both in the RH margin as "Dull & profane".

title. *1 EPIGRAM.*

1.1	1	Should John the Baptist come again,
1.1.1	1	He'd still repeat his ancient strain—
3.1	1	O vip'rous Race! O race of lies!
3.1.1	1	And so I venture to advise
5a.1	1	That ere on mortal
1	□	O would the Baptist come again
2	1	And cry aloud his ancient Strain, preach aloud with might & main,
	1 2	◄——————preach——————►
3	1	Repent, / repent! / Ahance to our vip'rous Race!
	1 2	◄———Repentance———►
4	1	And Yet should this ever be the case,
	1 2	But should this miracle take place,
5	1	I hope ere mortal Irish ground he treads
	1 2	Irish
6	□	He'll lay in a good stock of Heads.

1. *1* again,   **2.** *1 2* and main   **3.** *2* viperous   *1* race!   **5.** *1 2* hope,
1 2 treads,   **6.** *2* Stock   *1* heads! • *2* Heads!

title. In the PR *2* sequence the poem is numbered "I."

207. ON THE UNITED IRISHMEN

A. DATE

May–Sept 1799.

B. TEXTS

1. BM Add MS 47499=Notebook $3\frac{1}{2}$ ff 50^v–51^r (*CN* I 432 var). Numbered "9" in a series of some 30 or so such epigrams or notes for epigrams, mostly adapted from German authors.

1 [=RT]. *M Post* (3 Sept 1799). Unsigned.

2. *Annual Anthology* ed RS (2 vols Bristol 1799–1800) II 267; marked "S. T. C." by C in his own copy (Yale Tinker 1953 2). The second in a series of 17 epigrams, 12 of them by C.

For C's marginal note in the Yale copy see **206** *"O would the Baptist come again"* TEXT PR 2.

title. *1* EPIGRAM. • *2 Occasioned by the Former.*

1 ☐	I hold of all our vip'rous Race	
2 1	The servile greedy Things in Place	
1 2	greedy creeping	
3 1	Most vile, most dangerous; & then	
1 2	venomous;	
4 ☐	The United Irishmen.	
4.1.1 1	Now by miraculous deeds to stir men	
5 ☐	To come on earth should John determine	
6 1	Imprimis we'd excuse his sermon	
1 2	we'll	
7 ☐	With out a word the good old Dervis	
8 1	Might do incalculable service,	
1 2	work	
9 ☐	At once from tyranny & riot	
10 ☐	Save laws, lives, liberties, & moneys,	
11 1	If ~~taking~~ sticking to his ancient diet	
1 2	sticking	
12 ☐	He'd but eat up our locusts & wild Honeys.	

1. *2* viperous *1* race,   **2.** *1* place   **3.** *1 2* and   **4.** *1 2* Irishmen!
5. *1* JOHN   *1 2* determine,   **6.** *1 2* Imprimis,   *1 2* sermon.   **7.** *1 2* Without
8. *1* service;   **9.** *2* Tyranny   *1 2* and   *2* Riot   **10.** *2* Laws, Lives, Liberties,
1 2 and   *2* Moneys,   **11.** *1* antient   *2* Diet   **12.** *1* locusts • *2 Locusts*   *1 2* and
1 wild honeys! • *2 wild Honeys!*

title. In the PR *2* sequence the poem is numbered "II."
4. Indented in MS *1*.
10, 12. Indented in PR *1*.

208. EPIGRAM ON A READER
OF HIS OWN VERSES,
INSPIRED BY WERNICKE

A. DATE

May–Sept 1799.

B. TEXTS

1. BM Add MS 47499 = Notebook $3\frac{1}{2}$ f 52^r (*CN* I 432). Numbered "16" in a series of some 30 or so such epigrams or notes for epigrams, mostly adapted from German authors.

2. Recorded by Cottle *E Rec* II 65.
The lines are the first in a group of five epigrams translated from the German which Cottle says C gave him together on the same occasion. Presumably they were in ms.

1 [=RT]. *M Post* (7 Sept 1799). Unsigned.
Rpt *The Spirit of the Public Journals for 1800* IV (1801) 84.

2. *Annual Anthology* ed RS (2 vols Bristol 1799–1800) II 268; marked "S. T. C." by C in his own copy (Yale Tinker 1953 2). The third in a series of 17 epigrams, 12 of them by C.
C made an emendation in the Yale copy.

3. *The Keepsake for 1829* ed F. M. Reynolds (1828) 122. The first of three "EPIGRAMS. | BY S. T. COLERIDGE."

title. 2 ON A BAD READER OF HIS OWN VERSES.• *1* 2 ON A READER OF HIS OWN VERSES.

1 □   Hoarse Mævius reads his hobbling Verse
2 □   To all & at all times;
3 *1 3*   And finds them both divinely smooth,
  2 *1* 2   deems
4 □   His Voice as well as Rhymes.
5 1   Yet folks say; Mævius is no Ass;
  ⊠1   But
6 □   But Mævius makes it clear,
7 □   That he's a Monster of an Ass,
8 □   An Ass without an ear.

title. *2 On a READER of his own VERSES.*   **1.** *1* MÆVIUS *2 1 3* verse
2. *2 1 3* all, ⊠1 and *2 1* 2 times,   **4.** 2 voice,• *1* 3 voice *2 1 3* rhymes.
5. *2 1 3* say • *2* say, *1* MÆVIUS 2 ass! • *2* Ass! • *3* ass;   **6.** *1* MÆVIUS *3* clear
7. *2 1 3* monster 2 ass, • *2* Ass— • *3* ass—   **8.** *2 3* ass 2 Ear. • *3* ear!

title. In the PR *2* sequence the poem is numbered "III."
2, 4, 6, 8. Indented in all texts.
4+. Line-space in TEXTS 2 *1* 2.
5. PR *2* But] In the Yale copy C substituted "Yet".

209. EPIGRAM ON NEAERA'S PORTRAIT, INSPIRED BY LESSING

A. DATE

May 1799.

B. TEXT

BM Add MS 47499 = Notebook $3\frac{1}{2}$ f 52^r (*CN* I 432). Numbered "18" in a series of some 30 or so such epigrams or notes for epigrams, mostly adapted from German authors.

The RT reproduces the untitled ms exactly.

210. EPIGRAM ON EXCHANGING FRIENDS, FROM LOGAU

A. DATE

May 1799.

B. TEXT

BM Add MS 47499 = Notebook $3\frac{1}{2}$ f 53^r (*CN* I 432). Numbered "26" in a series of some 30 or so such epigrams or notes for epigrams, mostly adapted from German authors.

The RT reproduces the untitled ms exactly.

211. EPIGRAM ON A SLANDERER, FROM LESSING

A. DATE

May 1799 (KC's dating).

1. BM Add MS 47499=Notebook $3\frac{1}{2}$ f 146^v (*CN* I 441 var). Draft of an adaptation of a Lessing epigram.

2 [=RT]. BM Add MS 47499=Notebook $3\frac{1}{2}$ f 147^r (*CN* I 441). Second draft of the same, following on directly in the same notebook entry.

3. BM Add MS 47524=Notebook 26 f 106^r (*CN* v). Third draft of the same, being the last of a series of four drafts headed "For *Autographs*"; signed "S. T. C."

The four poems follow immediately on an entry (ff 104^r–105^r) dated 16 May 1827; for the three others see poems **631–3.**

1. The Keepsake for 1829 ed F. M. Reynolds (1828) 122. The second of three "EPIGRAMS. I BY S. T. COLERIDGE." A shortened and radically revised version.

title. 1 ~~Hic jacet~~ On a Slanderer • 2 On a Slander • *1* Hic jacet FETID BACK-BITE, Armiger.

1	1 3	From yonder ~~grave~~ Tomb of recent date
	2	Tomb
2	1 3	There comes a strange mephitic Blast!
	2	most
3.1	1	Here lies—Ha! *Backbite!* ~~gone at last!~~
3.2	1	'Tis He indeed: and Sure as fate
5.1	1	~~Into the Earth He has been cast,~~ They buried him in over-haste
6.1	1	~~Before the Man had~~ And in this Grave he breath'd his last
3	2	Here lies—Ha! Backbite!—Sure as Fate
4.1	2	~~The Undertaker was in haste~~ They buried him ere Life was past,
6.1	2	And in this Grave *He breath'd his last!*
3.3	3	~~Ha!~~ Ha! Backbite's ~~grave~~ gone! ~~As~~ And sure as fate,
3.4	3	Tis Backbite's Grave.
4	2	The W⟨retch⟩ ere yet the Life had past,
	3	~~Ere yet the Wretch's life had past,~~
5	2	Into the earth, they must have cast,
	3	~~they him have~~ cast, he has been cast.
6	2	And left him, there to breathe his last.
	3	~~And left him here~~ Ere the poor Wretch had *breath'd his last.*
1.1/2a.1	*1*	There comes from old Avaro's grave
2b.1	*1*	A deadly stench—why, sure, they have
5.2	*1*	Immured his *soul* within his grave?

1. 3 ~~Grave~~ Tomb   2 Date   **2.** 2 Blast:

3.4. The words are written directly beneath the second half of line 3.3, and may be intended as an alternative or a substitution.

212. THE BRITISH STRIPLING'S WAR-SONG, FROM STOLBERG

A. DATE

Late Jul–mid Aug (?) 1799. Preparations for war with France had been in the air for some months, but intensified dramatically from mid-Jul onwards. However, the poem might have been undertaken earlier in Germany in a mood of homesick patriotism.

B. TEXTS

1. BM Add MS 27902 ff 4ʳ–5ʳ. Two leaves, 18.7×22.7 cm; wm PIETER DE VRIES | & | COMP surmounted by a shield device (fragmentary); chain-lines 2.7 cm; verso of second leaf blank. Draft in C's hand, signed "S. T. Coleridge". Type facsimile in *JDC facsimile* 129–31.

The draft is on the same paper as two drafts of **253** *Love* (MSS 1 2), but in a slightly different hand, as if it had been made at another time.

1. M Post (24 Aug 1799). Unsigned.
Rpt *The Spirit of the Public Journals for 1799* III (1800) 251.

2 [=RT]. *Annual Anthology* ed RS (2 vols Bristol 1800) II 173–4. Signed "*ESTEESI.*"

C emended the poem in the copy now at Yale (Tinker 1953 2). The PR 2 version was reprinted in *The Poetical Class-book* ed W. F. Mylius (1810) 152; *The Universal Piece Writer* ed J. Blake (Chester 1811) 286.

3. The Bath Herald (21 Apr 1804). Signed "S. T.COLERIDGE."

C's poem is a late contribution to the volunteer frenzy of the previous summer and autumn. RS told John May in a letter from Bristol on 20 Jul 1803: "All Bristol is up in arms and volunteering—cool sport for the dog-days. The Duke of Cumberland is to be here to-day, to form a camp upon Leigh Down: . . . A few days more, and England will be in a formidable state of preparation, if they arm the people as is talked of" (*S Letters*—Warter—I 221). Poems on the subject of invasion and on the Bath Volunteers filled *The Bath Herald* in Aug–Sept 1803, and less often in the months thereafter.

C had left England in Apr 1804, and was at Gibraltar on the day his poem was published. The same newspaper published **77** *Epitaph on an Infant* on 8 Sept 1804 and, subsequently, poems by WW and RS (24 Nov 1804, 16 Mar 1805, 6 Apr 1805). The text appears to include patent errors (e.g. the misreading of a printed "f" as an "s" in line 9), as well as readings which have only ms parallels (line 13). It is possible that a revised version of PR 2, now lost, was submitted by one of RS's friends in the Bath–Bristol area—perhaps the "E. T. T. Y." of Hyde who sent in the poem to *Gentleman's Magazine* NS XXIX (1848) 160.

title. 1 The Stripling's War-song | imitated from the German of Stolberg •
1 2 THE BRITISH STRIPLING's WAR SONG. • *3* THE VOLUNTEER
STRIPLING. | A SONG.

  1 1   My noble old Warrior! this Heart has beat high
     ⊠1 Yes,
  2 1   Since you told of the Deeds that   our Countrymen wrought—
     1   which your
     2   our
     3 When
  3 1   Ah! give me the F̶a̶l̶c̶h̶i̶o̶n̶ Sabre, that h̶a̶n̶g̶sung by thy Thigh,
     ⊠1 O lend   ←—sabre—→   hung
  4 ☐ And I too will fight as my Forefathers fought.
     [*Line-space*]
  5 1   O despise not my Youth/ for my Spirit is steel'd
     ⊠1 Despise
  6 ☐ And I know, there is strength in the grasp of my Hand:
  7 1   Yea, as firm as thyself would I move to the Field
     ⊠1   march
  8 ⊠*3* And as proudly would die for my dear Native-land!
     3   our
     [*Line-space*]
  9 ⊠*3* In the sports of my Childhood I mimick'd the Fight;
     3   sight—
 10 1   A̶n̶d̶ ̶tThe s̶o̶u̶n̶d̶ Shrill of a Trumpet suspended my breath;
     1   The   sound   the
     2 3   a
 11 ☐ And my fancy still wander'd by d̶Day and by Night
 12 1   Amid tumults and   perils,   'mid Conquest and Death!
     1   battle,   tumult,   and
     2   mid
     3 Mid battles   bloodshed,
     [*Line-space*]
 13 1   My own eager   Shout w̶h̶e̶n̶ ̶t̶h̶e̶ ̶A̶r̶m̶i̶e̶s̶ ̶a̶d̶v̶a̶n̶c̶e̶ in the Heat of my Trance
     1 2   shout of onset, when   th'   armies   advance,
     3   in   the   heart   of   my   trance,
 14 1   How oft it awakes me from dreams full of Glory,
     1 2   visions
     3   has wak'd
 15 1   W̶h̶e̶n̶ ̶A̶s̶ When I meant to have leapt on the Hero of France
     1 2 ←—When—→
     3   dreamt, that I'd rush'd
 16 ⊠*3* And have dash'd him to earth pale and breathless and gory!
     3   dash'd   breathless,
     [*Line-space*]
 17 1   W̶h̶e̶n̶ As late thro' the City with bannerets streaming
     1 2 As   banners all
     3   our

18 1   ~~With a terrible beauty~~ ~~The~~ To the ~~sound~~ music of ~~the~~ Trumpets the
                                                                    Warriors flew by:

   ⊠1   To the music of trumpets
19 ⊠2   (With helmet & scymitar naked and gleaming
   2   scymetars
20 □   On their proud trampling thunder-hoof'd Steeds did they fly;)
       [*Line-space*]
21.1.1 1   ~~And the~~ Host pacing after in gorgeous parade
21.1.2 1   All mov'd to one measure in front and in rear;
21.1.3 1   And the ~~Flute Pipe, Drum,~~ & Trumpet such harmony made
21.1.4 1   As the Souls of the Slaughter'd would loiter to hear!
       [*Line-space*]

21 □   I sped to yon Heath that is lonely & bare—
22 1   ~~For my Soul~~ ~~And~~ For each nerve was unquiet, each pulse in alarm!
 1 2 For   each
 3   ←——————Each——————→
23 1   I   hurl'd my Mock-lance thro' the   objectless   Air
 1 And I
 2   the
 3   my   mind-peopled
24 ⊓   And in open-ey'd Dream prov'd the strength of my Arm.
       [*Line-space*]
25 □   Yes! noble old Warrior! this Heart has beat high,
26 ⊠*3* Since you told of the Deeds that our Countrymen wrought:
 3   When
27 1   Ah! give me the Falchion that hung by thy ~~Leg~~ Thigh
  ⊠1 O   lend   sabre   thigh,
28 1   And I too will fight as my ~~own~~ Forefathers fought!
  ⊠1   forefathers

---

title. *2 The BRITISH STRIPLING's WAR-SONG.*   **1.** *3* Yes!   *3* warrior!
⊠1 heart   *1 3* high,   **2.** ⊠1 deeds   ⊠1 countrymen wrought;   **3.** *3* sabre,
⊠1 thigh,   **4.** *1* I, too,   *1 3* forefathers   **5.** *1 2* youth, • *3* youth;   ⊠1 spirit
⊠1 steel'd,   **6.** *1 2* know   *1* hand, • *2* hand; • *3* hand!   **7.** *3* firm,   *3* thyself,
1 breath, • *3* breath!   **9.** ⊠1 childhood   *1 2* fight,   **10.** ⊠1 trumpet
1 breath, • *3* breath!   **11.** *2* wandered   ⊠1 day   ⊠1 night,   **12.** *2* battle
1 conquest, • *2 3* conquest   ⊠1 death.   **13.** *2* the Armies   **14.** ⊠1 glory;
15. *3* hero   ⊠1 France,   **16.** ⊠1 earth,   *3* pale,   *1 3* breathless,   *1 2* gory.
17. *1* City, • *2 3* city   ⊠1 streaming,   **18.** *3* warriors   *1 2* by, • *3* by—
19. ⊠1 With   ⊠1 and   *1* scymeter   ⊠1 gleaming,   **20.** *2 3* proud-trampling,
⊠1 steeds   *1 3* fly. • *2* fly;   **21.** *1 2* heath • *3* heath,   ⊠1 and   *1 2* bare,
22. *3* unquiet—   *1* alarm, • *2* alarm;   **23.** *1* mock lance • *2 3* mock-lance   ⊠1 air,
24. *2* open-eyed   ⊠1 dream   *2* proved   *1 2* arm. • *3* arm!   **25.** ⊠1 Yes,
3 warrior!   ⊠1 heart   **26.** ⊠1 deeds   *1 3* countrymen   ⊠1 wrought;
27. *2* Sabre • *3* sabre,   **28.** *1* I, too,   *2* Forefathers   *1* fought.

2, 4, 6, etc. Alternate line indented in all three printed texts.
13. PR *2* when the Armies advance] In the corrected copy at Yale C substituted "In
the heat of my Trance,".

213. EPIGRAM ON HIPPONA,
FROM LESSING

A. DATE

May–Aug 1799.

B. TEXTS

1 [=RT]. *M Post* (29 Aug 1799). Unsigned.
Rpt *The Spirit of the Public Journals for 1800* IV (1801) 92.

2. Annual Anthology ed RS (2 vols Bristol 1799–1800) II 269; marked
"S. T. C." by C in his own copy (Yale Tinker 1953 2). The eighth in a se-
ries of 17 epigrams, 12 of them by C.

The RT reproduces PR *1* exactly, apart from the title. In other respects the two
texts are identical except for accidentals:

title. *1* EPIGRAM.   **2.** *2* cheek,   **4.** *2* titters   *2* gay.   **5.** *2* Oh Shame
2 flush   **6.** *2* this,—

   title. In the PR *1* sequence the poem is numbered "VIII."

214. THE DEVIL'S THOUGHTS

A. DATE

The first version of the poem was a collaboration between C and RS while
they were together at Nether Stowey and Exeter in Aug–early Sept 1799. RS
describes how the poem was begun in his continuation (stanza 38):

> Then, while the one was shaving,
>   Would he the song begin;
> And the other, when he heard it at breakfast,
>   In ready accord join in.

The poem developed differently in the hands of each writer thereafter, C's
version being affected by the attribution to Richard Porson. These matters are
explained in the sec C below. Texts by RS and attributed to Porson are included
in the collation, alongside texts by or deriving from C of obviously greater
authority, because they have a general bearing on the evolution of C's text.

1. BM Add MS 47887 ff 6^r–8^r. Two leaves, the first 20.3×16.1 cm., folded to make four pages (ff 6^r–7^v); the second 12.6×9.8 cm; no wm; chain-lines 2.6 cm; the second leaf written on one side only (f 8^r); the RH end of lines 40, 44, and 60 is imperfect. Rough draft in RS's hand.

In the LH margin of f 6^r RS added the note: "This is the original for rough draught of the Devil's Thoughts—begun at Stowey & finished in Exeter. 1799 RS."

The leaves are preceded by another (f 5), of a different paper and dating from a later occasion, describing them as "The original rough draft of the D. W.—". There is no trace of C's hand but, in view of the obvious haste of transcription, it is possible that RS wrote at C's dictation. Some of the abbreviations (e.g. "th" for "the") were habitual with RS, but other mistakes are revealing (e.g. in line 45).

The rough draft is followed by later drafts in RS's hand (f 9^r) and (ff 10–9) a fair copy of his expanded version, with variants. The opening stanzas of the original and the expanded versions (ff 6^r and 11^r) are reproduced in P. J. Croft (ed) *Autograph Poetry in the English Language* (2 vols 1973) II 99, with a facing transliteration.

1 [=RT]. *M Post* (6 Sept 1799). Unsigned.

C claimed in 1830 that this version had been set from mss submitted by himself (he was in Ottery and Exeter at the time it must have been submitted). Daniel Stuart reports that several hundred extra copies were struck off, and that "the paper was in demand for days and weeks afterwards" ("Anecdotes of the Poet Coleridge" *Gentleman's Magazine* NS IX—May 1838—485–92 at 488).

2. University of Rochester Library, Robert Southey Papers, A S727, Box 4. Two conjugate leaves, each 18.0×22.5 cm, written on all four sides; no wm or chain-lines; holes along the fold suggest that the leaves have been removed from a bound volume (an album?). Fair copy in RS's hand, signed "1798. S. T. C.— R. S." Endorsed on the last page, in pencil: "Written by Southey when on a visit at Greenbank & been in the possession of the family from that time. Wm. Reynolds."

If Greenbank was Green Bank at Ambleside (subsequently the Charlotte Mason College), William Reynolds might be a descendant of the Knott family, who lived there until the late 1820s; or of WW's cousin, Dorothy Wordsworth of Whitehaven (1801–90), who had married Benson Harrison, an ironmaster, in 1823, and who moved in after the Knotts.

3. Bodleian Dep b 229/5. Single leaf, 18.4×22.7 cm; wm MOLINEUX JOHNSTON; chain-lines 2.7 cm; written on both sides. Incomplete transcript in the hand of William Godwin.

The authority of this transcript is uncertain. Several readings appear corrupt; others, it seems, could only have come only from C. Several mistakes and corrections are evidence that the transcript was copied. If it was copied from a version supplied by C, it might have been made on one of many occasions in the early 1800s, when C and Godwin met regularly. The transcript ends a third of the way down the verso, at the end of stanza 9, and it is followed by a string of ten asterisks.

4. DCL DC MS 41 ff 11ᵛ–13ʳ=*SH's Poets* pp 20–3 (*C&SH* 20–3). Transcript in C's hand "⟨by Σουθει & ΕΣΤΗΣΜΕ⟩" (viz Southey and "Esteesi"= STC in Greek characters). Pages 20–1 (title+stanzas 1–4) are reproduced in *C&SH* between pp 32 and 33.

C marked lines 1–12 and 34–7 as being by RS. The reference to Burrard in line 66 places this version pretty definitely in the period of *The Friend* (1809–10) and WW's interest in the Convention of Cintra.

2. *Felix Farley's Bristol Journal* (31 Mar 1810), "BY A LATE EMINENT PROFESSOR." Signed ******.

The proprietor of the newspaper was C's schoolfriend J. M. Gutch, although C was in Keswick when the stanzas were published. It is difficult to say whether Gutch knew the identity of the author.

There is a transcript in an unknown hand, unattributed and unsigned, among the West papers (BM Add MS 34744 ff 130ʳ–131ʳ). It is on two conjoint leaves, 16.8×21.1 cm; wm crown surmounting shield device; chain-lines 2.5 cm; first leaf written on both sides. The transcript is anomalous in the context of the 21 volumes of papers, which are mainly those of James West (d 1772), Secretary of the Treasury 1741–62, MP for St Albans 1741–68, President of the Royal Society, etc. It differs from the newspaper version only once (in line 37, where it reads "For . . . dungeons" instead of "Of . . . dungeon").

5. Dr Williams's Library, London, Bundle 1 vi 29(l). Single leaf, 20.3× 25.0 cm; no wm or chain-lines (laid). Transcript in the hand of HCR, with corrections and alternative readings by JTC. Unattributed and unsigned. The transcript in two columns fills the recto; JTC has used the verso for alternative readings of two stanzas.

The verso contains, in one corner, the following note in HCR's hand: "11 Linc Inn Squ. Coote." Richard Holmes Coote, a conveyancer, lived at 11 Lincoln's Inn, New Square, in the period 1817–19, and JTC was called to the bar at the Middle Temple in 1819. The transcript probably dates from this period. JTC's corrections correspond with no other version entirely, and were probably carried across from a version that has been lost. They are recorded in the commentary.

Another 12-stanza version, which also appears to follow from PR 2, was printed in the Owenite periodical *The Mirror of Truth* II (1817) 67–8, where it is attributed to Porson. The order of the stanzas is, in the order of the conspectus collation, 1 2 4 5 6 9 10 11 7 E X4 17. Some divergent readings are supported by other versions, but many of those which are unique are patently corrupt.

6. A version "BY THE LATE PROFESSOR PORSON", in *The Literary Journal* I (29 Mar 1818) 15–16. A headnote claims that the text reproduces the ms in a fellow guest's hand at Dr and Mrs Vincent's house, taken from Porson's dictation and corrected by Porson himself. (Hannah, wife of William Vincent—1739–1815—who expelled RS from Westminster School in 1792, died in Feb 1807.)

Rpt (without headnote) in *The Yellow Dwarf* XIX (9 May 1818) 152. There is also a transcript (including the headnote, slightly abbreviated) by R. H. Barham in his holograph commonplace book pp 134–9 (NYPL Berg Collection). This is likely to have been made late 1819–early 1820. The political verses that follow in the commonplace book, *The Devil's Day in London*, were inspired by C's poem.

If the printed report is what it claims to be, this version is earlier than PR 2. Its position at this point of the sequence is determined by its relation to surrounding texts.

7. HRC MS (Coleridge, D) Works = DC's Maroon Commonplace Book ff 3ᵛ–4ʳ. Transcript in DC's hand, subscribed "S. T. C—". The lines are written out continuously, without stanza-breaks or indentation.

The transcript is followed by an additional stanza "From an idea of an S. T. Cs—", dated "D. C. June 1820". The next transcript in the book is of **267** *The Two Round Spaces on the Tombstone*. DC's transcript is matched—in the number and sequence of the stanzas it includes—only by a transcript from "a manuscript copy" supposed to be by Porson, printed by "H. N." in *The Literary Journal* I (24 May 1818) 133. Particular readings of this published text coincide with other versions (line 66 names General Gascoigne, for example), while other readings which are unique appear to be corrupt.

3. *The Cambridge Tart: Epigrammatic and Satiric-poetical Effusions* ed "Socius" (1823) 22–5; "ASCRIBED I TO THE LATE PROFESSOR POR-SON".

Socius was Richard Gooch, who matriculated from St John's College Cambridge in 1820. He was admitted to the Inner Temple in 1827, edited various newspapers (as well as publishing *Facetiae Cantabrigienses* in 1825), and died in 1849. For an unsigned review of this anthology, which quotes yet another version of the poem claiming to derive from the original in C's hand, see below on line 66.

8. *Bl Mag* XIX (Feb 1826) 135–6. Printed as "a complete copy" of "the joint composition of Coleridge and Southey in some playful moments" (to refute claims made on behalf of Porson), presumably from a ms copy.

The Wellesley Index to Victorian Periodicals 1824–1900 ed Walter E. Houghton and Jean Harris Slingerland (5 vols Toronto 1966–89) I No 284 gives the anonymous contributor as the physician Robert Gooch, whose acquaintance with RS began in 1811 and who attended C in 1812 (*CL* III 414–15: to D. Stuart 7 Aug 1812).

This version may predate several of those which are here placed earlier in the sequence. It was reprinted without Gooch's comments in *St James's Chronicle* (31 Jan–2 Feb 1826); and in *The Common-place Book of Humorous Poetry* (1826) 105–8. A ms variant of the same version, in small-album format with illustrations by Margaret Scott, was exported from Britain in 1987; there is a photocopy in the BM (RP 3062). The BM catalogue dates it c 1825, perhaps on the evidence of the paper; the style of the illustrations might suggest a later date.

4. *PW* (1828).

5. *The Poetical Works of Robert Southey* (Paris 1829) 723.

A note to the title reads: "This has been attributed to Professor Porson; but as in the last edition of Coleridge's Works, it is given as his joint production with Mr Southey, we insert it here." The text was not authorised by RS (*S Letters—*Curry—II 335, 339–40), and has more in common with e.g TEXTS 6 7 than MSS 2 8 or the enlarged version RS had been working on in 1826–7.

6. *PW* (1829).

7. Cornell WORDSWORTH PR 4480 D4 1830r: *The Devil's Walk* (n.d.). A separate edition of the poem, being one folded leaf in wrappers, the text extending on to the inside wrapper. The front wrapper contains the title; there is no title-page or indication of a printer or date of publication.

The text bears some resemblance to MS 4. The preliminary account differs slightly: it attributes the poem to Porson, but says that it was written at Mr Beloe's at the request of Dr and Mrs Vincent. The circumstances (claiming to derive from William Beloe *Anecdotes*—6 vols 1807–12) coincide with the account given in the Preface to PR 8, although there is reason to think that they are deliberately misleading (see sec C below). Variants to the text are given in the same form as in PR 8 9, though they are not identical; they are not recorded here. There are no illustrations and no explanatory notes (in contrast to PR 8 9), and it should be noted that PR 8 9 contain an extra stanza on schoolboys.

8. *The Devil's Walk* (1830) ed H. W. Montagu, with designs by R. Cruikshank; "BY I PROFESSOR PORSON." There were two issues: the incorrect pagination of the first is corrected in the second, but the text is otherwise the same. A second edition appeared later in the same year, reprinting the first state of the first edition.

H. W. Montagu comments on Porson as author in his Preface, and the text is accompanied by variant readings and notes, which are not recorded here.

9. *The Devil's Walk* (1830) ed H. W. Montagu, with designs by R. Cruikshank; "BY I S. T. COLERIDGE, Esq. I AND I ROBERT SOUTHEY, ESQ. LL. D. &c." A second edition—a straightforward reprint—appeared later in the same year.

The PR 8 Preface is modified to include an apology for the error respecting authorship, and the text of the poem is also modified. The variant readings of this edition are not recorded here.

10. PW (1834).
The reading "Unfetter" in line 39 is patent nonsense; lines 54–61 appear first in a version which claims to be from Porson's dictation (MS 5), though if they are by C their obscurity might explain why he had not previously laid claim to them; lines 62–5 express an attitude he might privately have found sympathetic, though his ascription of them to RS in the note to PR *10* line 28 indicates some embarrassment. (Cf **267** *The Two Round Spaces on the Tombstone* sec C for similar embarrassment concerning spite against the Scots.) Because of the doubts these matters raise, the RT of vol I follows the shorter and differently ordered PR *1*, even though PR *10* is the most complete version that C acknowledged, and forms the basis of the line-numbering in the main sequence below.

C. GENERAL NOTE

The collated texts are unusually heterogeneous. Besides versions of the poem by RS, the previous section includes versions which circulated under the name of Richard Porson and which contain details for which C was obviously not responsible. The versions ascribed to RS and Porson have a place for two reasons: they are the form in which the poem circulated most widely during C's lifetime, when it was most influential; and C appears to have been influenced by such versions when he took the poem into his last three collections.

The beginnings of the poem are clear, even though C and RS acknowledged each other's contributions in different ways. RS's account was printed along with his enlarged 57-stanza version in 1838 (*Poetical Works* III 83–100). It describes how he began the poem and showed what he had written to C, who helped revise what had been written and added to it. The suggestion is that the poem was essentially his, though C helped improve it, and this appears to be confirmed by other considerations. RS had previously discussed with William Taylor the possibility of imitating Voss's "diabolic idyll", *The Devil in Ban* (Robberds I 228, 233), and he sketched an idea for the whole in his commonplace book (*SCB* IV 199). It may be significant that, whereas C claimed not to have even a copy of the version published in *M Post* when he came to gather materials for *PW* (1828) (*CL* VI 672–3: to D. Stuart [25 Feb 1827]), RS retained the original ms.

C's view of the collaboration was that each had contributed different stanzas to the poem, and that RS had contributed by far the fewer. In *SH's Poets* (MS 4) he marked stanzas 1, 2, 3, and 9 as RS's work. In the "Apologetic Preface" to **167** *Fire, Famine, and Slaughter* in *SL* (lines ⁻1.173–4) he allowed RS to have written the first three stanzas ("which were worth all the rest of the poem") "and the best stanza of the remainder". In a note to the version included in *PW* (1828 and 1829) he attributed to RS "the first three stanzas, which are worth all the rest, and the ninth"; and he revised this in *PW* (1834) to read "the 1st, 2d,

3d, 9th, and 16th stanzas". Whatever the count, C reckoned himself to be "the principal author" (*CL* VI 830: to H. W. Montagu Apr 1830). Apart from RS's interest in Voss's *The Devil in Ban*, an equally plausible source of inspiration for the poem is Hans Sachs *Der Teufel und das alte Weib*, in which the Devil goes for a walk with the old woman. C had recently discovered Sachs's writings in Germany, and was full of enthusiasm for them (see *RX* 542–4 n 19, 604n–r).

While RS retained the original ms, he appears to have lent it, or copies of it, to his acquaintances. Theodore Hook records making a copy "when a boy"— i.e. probably c 1806, when, at the age of 16, he began to write for the stage; certainly before 1813, when he took up residence in Mauritius. It was copied from "a MS. of Southey's, which he himself gave to the friend, who lent it to me" (E. H. Barker *Literary Anecdotes and Contemporary Reminiscences, of Professor Porson and Others*—2 vols 1852—I 224–5). MSS 2 and 8 above represent slightly different improvements of the original by RS. It will be noted that the first was transcribed for friends, and the second reported by a friend: RS does not appear himself to have given the poem a wide circulation. It will also be noted that their relation to the original represented by MS 1 is fairly close, especially in the sequence of stanzas. The presence of stanza 3—it is not present in TEXTS 1 *1* or several other early versions—might indicate that it was added by RS after the poem was first published.

Such was the situation, as far as RS took notice of it, until the mid-1820s. Caroline Bowles wrote to request the poem on 8 Dec 1825, but RS could not lay hands on the "rough draft" he knew he had (*The Correspondence of Robert Southey with Caroline Bowles* ed Edward Dowden—Dublin 1881—92, 93). He found the original in Sept 1826 (ibid 110), and was moved to enlarge on it during the following months (ibid 111–12; also *S Letters*—Curry—II 307– 8). The stanza following stanza 5 in MS 8 was taken forward as stanza 13 of the new version, and the stanza describing the Lord of the North Country (in MSS 2 8) was taken forward in a modified form as stanza 5. It appears that Caroline Bowles's encouragement was largely responsible for the full-scale enlargement at this time. RS refers to it as her "favourite poem" (*S Letters*— Curry—II 308), and made a present to her of the original ms and presumably the enlarged version along with it (*S Letters*—Warter—IV 52fn). The version in 57 stanzas is a quite separate development, having much less to do with the version finally acknowledged by C than with TEXTS 2, 8, and 5. But besides interpolating and adding stanzas, it does leave stanza 7 close to its original position, and it preserves the unrevised and out-of-date version of stanza 8, as well as incorporating the new version; curiously, it drops stanza 16, which C specifically attributed to RS in *PW* (1834).

C appears not to have promulgated the poem any more widely than RS. A solitary instance of him reciting the poem is recorded in 1803 (Carlyon I 239); he claimed not to remember it in 1811 (John Payne Collier's diary, in *Coleridge on Shakespeare: The Text of the Lectures of 1811–1812* ed R. A. Foakes— 1971—42–3); he might or might not have been responsible for the version copied by Godwin (MS 3); the version in *SH's Poets* (MS 4) would have had a very limited circulation. Notwithstanding, during the larger part of his lifetime he was perhaps even more aware than RS that the author was commonly taken to be Richard Porson. Porson had an extraordinarily tenacious memory, and was in the habit of repeating humorous poems he had read or heard, which he did not actively repudiate when they were ascribed to him (see J. S. Watson *The Life of Richard Porson*—1801—289–93). There is no reason to doubt the story which accompanies MS 6—that the poem was copied down from his dictation at Dr Vincent's—and after Porson died in Sept 1808 the legend of his authorship was dominant for another twenty years. It was accepted by Byron and Shelley, who both imitated the poem, and by others who made copies and embellishments and who reprinted it.

C laid claim to authorship in the Preface to **167** *Fire, Famine, and Slaughter* in 1817, but though there was some public discussion of the matter at this time the misattribution continued. C again claimed the poem in *PW* (1828, 1829), only to be met with the counter-claim that there was a holograph ms in Porson's hand (PR 7 8). The counter-claim was desperate: sceptics would have expected such a ms to have been made available earlier, in 1818, when the authorship was first publicly debated; the reference to a party at Dr Beloe's (in prefaces to PR 7 8) is not to be found in the six volumes of Beloe's *Journals* (the advertisement to PR 9 talks of the verses being produced at a different party, at Mr Lodge's); the "nephew", R. C. Porson, who in 1830 claimed to possess the Porson holograph did not exist and no such person was traceable at the address he gave. The discussion continued briefly in the pages of *John Bull*, *M Post*, and the *Court Journal*; it is summarised by E. H. Barker in *Monthly Magazine* NS XXV (1838) 169–71, 311–14, 402–10, 481–8. It was not finally settled until C intervened, between the first and second editions of the pamphlet edited by H. W. Montagu, in Apr 1830 (PR 8 9: see *CL* VI 829–30: to H. W. Montagu Apr 1830).

The attribution to Porson raises the question of why C did not assert his authorship earlier, and then more strongly. Again, the versions attributed to Porson differ in complicated ways from those they might have derived from, and from each other. For example, what are we to make of the way they incorporate improvements, subsequently taken over by C, as well as obvious corruptions? The versions attributed to Porson set out the stanzas in an order which cannot have derived from the published *M Post* version (PR 1) or from RS, whose early transcripts kept close to that order. Porson must have based his on one he heard C recite, or someone else report, or on an interim ms which has not survived; or the *M Post* version Porson repeated at an early stage was superseded by other versions connected with his name, curiously incorporating authentic Coleridgean features. Versions attributed to Porson thereafter take over improvements, such as the rewritten stanza 8, which C either made himself or adopted. They again incorporate stanzas which C had earlier rejected—e.g. stanzas 14 and 15—though later transcripts by RS had also found a place for them.

The way the original C–RS text developed and changed while it was attached to the dead Porson's name is curious. One might guess that neither was averse to being set at a distance from political attitudes they might for some years have found embarrassing. C might have allowed the confusion to continue at the same time that he added to the poem, or allowed his detachment from the poem to decide in favour of retaining improvements and additions made by others. In short, the evidence suggests that the evolution of the poem was as improvised as its beginnings, sometimes obscure in ways that might not be unintended. The sequence of stanzas changed, their phrasing was revised, one stanza was dropped, and several others were added according to circumstance. References were modified and others introduced, during a span of twenty years, and C's responsibility for the changes cannot always be determined. One can only say that "Porson's" contribution to the reordering and revision of the stanzas must have been as substantial as RS's contribution of particular stanzas.

One result is that the collated texts vary greatly in their authority. The usual method of presenting the texts has been modified by giving all versions of a line together regardless of the order in which the stanzas appeared in the reported texts. For this purpose the most complete text authorised by C, PR *10*, is used as the basis for the ordering of stanzas in the main sequence. The accompanying table gives a résumé of the contents and ordering of all the collated texts (plus RS's expanded version of 1826–7, which is not collated below).

The collation of versions attributed to Porson is necessarily incomplete: other holograph versions circulated, combining readings which are recorded here in various other combinations, and are known or will come to light. Thus, there is a transcript in J.M.?B.'s notebook album (see vol I annex A 13) ff 68^v–70^r, in the "earlier" hand. The context suggests it was copied in the period 1828–30, and a comparison of texts suggests the copy was made from a version current during the 1820s. It is headed "The Devils walk by Porson. I A wrong edition", and the sequence of stanzas is 1 2 3 6 4 5 7 9 8 17. The sequence 6 4 5 is paralleled only in MS 8; yet unlike MS 8, the text has the later form of stanza 8 and of course fewer stanzas overall. Other versions have the same number of stanzas and the later form of stanza 8, but in a different order. Similarly, individual readings are closest to MS 5, but elsewhere coincide with other texts and are in a few cases unique (corrupt?). To incorporate such texts in the collation would obscure the already complicated picture, but a last example is worth including here.

A ms commonplace book belonging to Henry Goulburn (1784–1856; see *DNB*), in the possession of Hilton Kelliher (1991), contains on pp 45–7 a version of the poem which combines a curious mixture of elements. It is headed "Song ?⟨written⟩ by M^r. Porson—?⟨^{r}. . . .^{T}⟩" (the inserted words are indecipherable).

1 [=I]

From his brimstone bed at break of Day
A walking the Devil is gone
To visit his snug little farm of the earth
And see how his stock goes on.

Conspectus of the Collated Texts

TEXT *PW* (1834) stanza-number (in roman numerals in the original)

TEXT	1	2	3	4	5	6	7	8	9	10	11	12	13	14	15	16	17	X1	X2	X3	X4	X5
MS 1	✓	✓	–	✓	✓	✓	✓	E	✓	✓	✓	✓	✓	✓	✓	–	✓	✓	–	–	✓	–
PR 1	✓	✓	–	✓	✓	✓	✓	E	✓	✓	✓	✓	✓	–	–	–	✓	–	–	–	✓	–
MS 2	✓	✓	✓	✓	✓	✓	✓	E	✓	✓	✓	✓	✓	–	–	–	✓	–	–	–	✓	✓
MS 3	✓	✓	✓	✓	✓	✓	✓	–	✓	–	–	–	–	–	–	–	–	–	–	–	–	–
MS 4	✓	✓	✓	✓	✓	✓	✓	–	✓	–	–	–	✓	–	–	–	✓	–	–	–	–	–
PR 2	✓	✓	–	✓	✓	✓	✓	E	✓	✓	✓	–	–	–	–	–	✓	–	–	–	✓	–
MS 5	✓	✓	–	✓	✓	✓	✓	E	✓	✓	✓	–	–	–	–	–	✓	–	–	–	✓	–
MS 6	✓	✓	✓	✓	✓	✓	✓	✓	✓	✓	✓	–	–	✓	✓	–	✓	–	–	–	–	–
MS 7	✓	✓	✓	✓	✓	✓	✓	✓	✓	–	–	–	–	–	–	–	✓	–	–	–	–	–
PR 3	✓	✓	✓	✓	✓	✓	✓	✓	✓	✓	✓	–	–	–	–	–	✓	–	✓	–	✓	–
MS 8	✓	✓	✓	✓	✓	✓	✓	E	✓	✓	✓	✓	✓	✓	✓	–	✓	–	–	✓	✓	✓
PR 4	✓	✓	✓	✓	✓	✓	✓	✓	✓	–	–	–	–	–	–	–	✓	–	–	–	–	–
PR 5	✓	✓	✓	✓	✓	✓	✓	✓	✓	✓	✓	–	–	✓	✓	–	✓	–	–	–	–	–
PR 6	✓	✓	✓	✓	✓	✓	✓	✓	✓	–	–	–	–	–	–	–	–	–	–	–	–	–
PR 7	✓	✓	✓	✓	✓	✓	✓	✓	✓	✓	✓	–	–	✓	✓	–	✓	–	–	–	–	–
PR 8	✓	✓	✓	✓	✓	✓	✓	✓	✓	✓	✓	–	–	✓	✓	–	✓	–	✓	–	–	–
PR 9	✓	✓	✓	✓	✓	✓	✓	✓	✓	✓	✓	–	–	✓	✓	–	✓	–	✓	–	–	–
PR 10	✓	✓	✓	✓	✓	✓	✓	✓	✓	✓	✓	✓	✓	✓	✓	✓	✓	–	–	–	–	–

✓ stanza present   – stanza absent   E early version of stanza 8 (always followed by stanza X4)   X1 extra stanza on vipers   X2 extra stanza on the behaviour of school/college boys   X3 extra stanza on Brothers the prophet   X4 extra stanza on taxation   X5 extra stanza on the Lord of the North

Order of Stanzas in Each Collated Text ("+" indicates absence of line-space)

MS 1: 2 1 4 X1 5 7 10 11 9 6 E+X4 14 15 12 13 17; stanzas X1, 14, 15 are cancelled.
PR 1: 1 2 4 5 7 10 11 9 6 E X4 12 13 17.
MS 2: 1 3 2 4 5 7 10 11 9 6 E X4 12 13 X5 17.
MS 3: 1 2 3 4 5 6 7 9.
MS 4: 1 2 3 4 5 6 7 9 13 17.
PR 2: 1 2 4 5 6 7 E X4 9 10 11 17.
MS 5: 1 2 4 5 6 7 E X4 9 10 11 17; the verso contains the later form of stanza 8.
MS 6: 1+2 3+4 5+6 7+9 10+11 8 14+15 17.
MS 7: 1+2+3+4+5+6+7+9+8+17.
PR 3: 1+2 3+4 5+7 X2+6 8+9 10+11 17+X4.
MS 8: 1 3 2 6 4 5 X3 7 9 10 11 12 13 E X4 X5 14 15 17.
PR 4: 1 2 3 4 5 6 7 8 9 17.
PR 5: 1+2 3+4 5+6 7+9 10+11 8 14+15 17.
PR 6: 1 2 3 4 5 6 7 8 9.
PR 7: 1 2 3 4 5 6 7 9 10 11 8 14+15 17; stanzas E and X4 are included in a footnote, as if to precede stanza 17.
PR 8: 1 2 3 4 5 6 7 X2 9 10 11 8 14+15 17; stanzas E and X4 as PR 7.
PR 9: 1 2 3 4 5 6 7 X2 9 10 11 8 14+15 17; stanzas E and X4 as PR 7.
PR 10: 1 2 3 4 5 6 7 8 9 10 11 12 13 14 15 16 17.

Robert Southey's Version of 1826–7 (*pub 1838*)

This 57-stanza expansion is made up as follows (superior numbers indicate RS's stanza-numbering, and "S" indicates a new stanza composed by RS): 1^1 2^2 3^3 S^4 S^5 4^6 5^7 6^8 E^9 $X4^{10}$ S^{11} 8^{12} S^{13} S^{14} 9^{15} 10^{16} 11^{17} 12^{18+23} 13^{19} . . . 17^{57}. (The RS stanzas following stanza 13^{19} concern Scottish preachers, Roman Catholics, and Utilitarians.)

2 [=II]

Over the hill and over the Dale
    And he walk'd over the plain
And backwards & forwards he switch'd his long tail
    As a Gentleman switches his Cane.

3 [=IV]

He saw a lawyer killing a Viper
    On a dunghill beside the stable
Oh ho! quoth he: for it put him in mind
    Of the story of Cain & Abel

4 [=VII]

He peep'd into a rich Booksellers shop
    Cries he "we are both of one College"
For I sat myself like a Cormorant once
    Upon the Tree of knowledge

5 [=V]

An apothecary on a White horse
    Rode by on his vocations
And it put him in mind of his old friend
    Death in the Revalations.

6 [=IX]

As he pass'd by the Cold Bath fields
    He peep'd in a Solitary Cell
And the Devil was pleas'd for it gave him a hint
    For improving his Dungeons in Hell.

7 [=X]

He saw a Turnkey in a Trice
    Handcuff a troublesome Blade
"How Nimbly", quoth he, "the fingers move"
    If a man be but us'd to his trade

8 [=XI]

He saw the same turnkey unfetter a man
    With but little expedition
And it put him in mind of the long debates
    On the slave trade Abolition

9 [=VIII(*a*)]

He saw a Pig right rapidly
    Adown the river float

The Pig swam well, but ev'ry stroke
Was cutting his own throat.

10 [=vⁱⁱⁱ(b)]

Old Nick then grinn'd & switch'd his tail
With joy & admiration
For he thought of his ~~darling~~ daughter Victory
And his darling babe Taxation—

11

12 [=xvⁱⁱ]

General ——'s fiery face
He view'd with consternation
Then back to Hell his way did take
For the Devil thought by a slight mistake
T'was yᵉ general conflagration—

Goulburn was an undergraduate at Trinity while Porson was resident, and early entries in the commonplace book appear to date from this time; an earlier ballad on pp 25–7, *Hell's Holiday*, claims also to be from Porson. The version of the present poem would appear to position itself between MS 4 and PR 2, which is where one would expect it to fall from the date of surrounding entries in the book. However, Goulburn's version is unique in omitting stanza 6, positioning stanza 7 before stanza 5, and positioning stanzas 9–11 before the early version of stanza 8. Various features connect it with Porson, and a case could be made for including it in the collation, but it appears none the less to represent, on balance, a version which was either severely edited by Porson or was imperfectly recalled by his auditor; and it departs too far from the central configuration of texts to be reckoned to contribute to their evolution. At the same time, it possesses features which uncannily coincide with those arrived at by C. As indicated above, one must suppose that C took over suggestions which evolved while the text floated free in the public domain.

Finally, numerous imitations and extensions of C's and RS's poem(s) did not contribute at all to the enlarging, modifying process here described. Among these offshoots one might mentioned Anon "The Devil's Walk" *The Times* (16 Aug 1827) rpt *The Standard* (16 Aug 1827); J.H. "The Devil's Ramble" *True Sun* (9 Apr 1832); Anon "The Retort" *True Sun* (17 May 1832), of which there is a ms copy in Dr Williams's Library, Bundle 1 vi 29(r).

title. *1 2 2 7 4 6 10* THE DEVIL's THOUGHTS. • 3 The Devil's Visit to his Farm • 4 The Devil's Thoughts— I A Fragment from the Wreck I of Memory.— originally revealed I to ΑΡΣΟΥΘΕΙ & ΕΣΤΗΣΕ. I ~~to which is now~~ I added I ~~The Angel's Thoughts I as thought by Seraph~~ I ΑΣΡΑ ~~ΨΩΝΘΙΝΫ~~ I ——————— I The Devils' Thoughts I ⟨by Σουθει & ΕΣΤΗΣΜΕ⟩ • 5 6 8 5 7 The Devils Walk. •

3 EXTEMPORANEOUS LINES, | ascribed | TO THE LATE PROFESSOR PORSON. • *8 9* THE DEVIL'S WALK; A POEM.

<pre>
‾1 10   I.
 1 1   At break
   ⊠5 7   From his brimstone bed at   break of day
   5 7   the
 2 ⊠5 3   A walking th Devil is gone—
   5   The Devil a walking
   3   devil's   gone;
 3 1   To spy look at his little snug farm upon of th earth
   1 2   look   of
   3 4   visit
   2
   5   snug little
   6 7 3 5   of   the
   8   look   at   the   world,
   4 6   visit   little snug
   7–10   snug little   earth,
 4 1 1 2 4 7 8 4 6 And see how his stock   went on.
   3   the
   2 5 6 5 7–10   his   goes
   3   there goes
                   [Line-space]
‾5 10   II.
 5 1   The Devil came over the heath & th hils he went
   ⊠1 3 6 3 5 7 8 Over the   hill   and   over   the dale,
   3   He flew over hill, over mountain &
   6 3 5 7 8   And over the hill, and over the
 6 1   And the Devil came he went over the plain—
   1 2 4 7 8 4 6 10   ←——he——→
   3   Over   lake,   river,   forest   &
   2 5   And   he shuffled across   the
   6 5 7–9   He   walked,   and   over
   3   rambled,
 7 ⊠2 2 5 8   And backward & forward he swishd his long tail
   2 8   tail
   2   Backwards   long tail
   5   tail
 8 □   As a Gentleman swishes his cane
                   [Line-space]
‾9 10   III.
 9 2 8   How   then   was   the   Devil drest
   3   You'll ask me perhaps ɏhow the Devil was
   4 4 6 10   And how   then   was   the   Devil
   6 5 7–9   pray   how
   7   ←——how——→
   3   pray now, how
</pre>

10 ⊠1 *1* 3 2 5 8	Oh he was in his Sundays best;
3	Why, faith, holiday
8	He was Sunday's
11 2 6–8 *5*	His coat was red & his breeches were blue
3	it ⟨red⟩
3	red
4 *4* 6 9 *10*	Jacket
7	coat trowsers blue,
8	breeches
12 2 8	And there was a hole where his tail came through.
3	for to come
4 *4* 6 *10*	where the came
6 7	With a little hole behind, his
7	And there was a hole went
3	With a hole behind, which
5	that
8 9	where came
	[*Line-space*]
⁻**13** *10*	IV.
13 1	~~He put his hand in the vipers hole~~
⊠3	He saw a Lawyer killing a viper
3	A lawyer he spied, who was
14 1	On the dung heap beside his stable
1 2 8	dunghill
3	a pil'd up near
4 *4* 6	Dungheap beside
2 *5* 9	dunghill,
6 *5* 7 8	his own
7	⟵—near—⟶
3	⟵—by—⟶
10	hard by
15 1	Oh ho! quoth he for it put him in mind
1 2	Oh—oh;
3	And the Devil was pleas'd,
4	smil'd, ~~his~~ it
6 7 *4–10*	it
2	Oh, Oh, says the Devil,
5	Old Nicholas laughed
3	And the devil he smiled,
8	Devil was shock'd,
16 1 *1* 2 2 5 8	Of the story of Cain & Abel
3 4 6 7 *3–10*	Cain & his brother
	[*Line-space*]
⁻**17** *10*	V.
17 ⊠3 2 *3* 9 *10*	An Apothecary on a whit horse
3	A doctor of physic upon
2	An Apothecary on his
3 9 *10*	He saw an apothecary on a

18 1	Went by on his ←—vocation—→
1 2 5 8	Rode
3	trade & vocation;
4	Vocations/
2 7 4 6	←—vocations;—→
6 5 7 8	avocations—
3 9	Ride ←—vocation;—→
10	←—vocations;—→
19 ⊠5–7 *3 5* 7–9	And th Devil thought of his old friend
5	he smiled for it put him in mind
6 5 7–9	"Oh!" says the Devil, "there's my old friend
7	And the Devil thought of his
3	again he smiled, for it put him in mind
20 ⊠5 *3*	Death in the Revelation.
5 3	Of Death
20fn *1*	And I looked, and behold a pale horse: and his name that sat on him was
	death. Revel. vi. 8.
	[*Line-space*]
⁻**21** *10*	VI.
21 1 *1* 2	He past a Cottage with a double coach house
3	A cottage he saw
4	But Lo!—A [??]Cot
2 5–7 *3–10*	He saw a Cottage,
8	pass'd by
22 ⊠3 *4 5 3*	A Cottage of ←—Gentility—→
3	Full of ton, pride &
4	A cottage of high
5	~~hostility~~ gentility
3	←—quality:—→
23 1 *1* 2 8	And he grinnd at the sight for his favourite vice
3	the Devil he grinn'd,
4 7 3 4 6 10	did Grin: darling Sin
2	Oh, he grinn'd, vice
5	And Sin
6 5 7–9	was pleas'd, vice
24 ⊠3 6 *5* 7–9	Is Pride that apes Humility.
3	affects
6 5 7–9	the apes
	[*Line-space*]
⁻**25** *10*	VII.
25 1 *1* 2 4 7 3 8 4 6	He went into a rich booksellrs shop
3	next popp'd his horns in a
2	←—stepp'd—→ into
5	←—walked—→
6 5 7–9	←—stepp'd—→ a rich
10	←—peep'd—→

26 1 *1* 2–4 8 *4 6* 10	Quoth he we are both of one College
2 5 6 *3* 5 7–9	Says
7	Quoth he, friend we ~~are~~ are
27 ⊠3 6 7 *3–9*	For I sate myself like a Cormorant once
3	in cormorant's shape,
6 7 *3–9*	myself sat like Cormorant once
28 1 *1* 2 8	Upon th Tree of Knowledge.
3 2 5	Perch'd on
4 7 3 *8–10*	Hard by
6 5 7	by on
4 6	Fast by
28fn *1*	This anecdote is related by that most interesting of the Devil's Biographers, Mr. John Milton, in his Paradise Lost, and we have here the Devil's own testimony to the truth and accuracy of it.
4 6 10	And all amid them stood the TREE OF LIFE High eminent, blooming ambrosial fruit Of vegetable gold (query *paper-money:*) and next to Life *Our* Death, the TREE OF KNOWLEDGE, grew fast by.—

    *   *   *   *   *   *   5

    *   *   *   *   *   *

So clomb this first grand thief—
Thence up he flew, and on the tree of life
Sat like a cormorant.—PAR. LOST. IV.

The allegory here is so apt, that in a catalogue of *various* 10 *readings* obtained from collating the MSS. one might expect to find it noted, that for "LIFE" *Cod. quid. habent*, "TRADE." Though indeed THE TRADE, i.e. the bibliopolic, so called κάτ' ἐξόχην may be regarded as LIFE sensu *eminentiori*; a suggestion, which I owe to a young retailer in the hosiery line, 15 who on hearing a description of the net profits, dinner parties, country houses, &c. of the trade, exclaimed, "Ay! that's what I call LIFE now!"—This "Life, *our* Death," is thus happily contrasted with the fruits of Authorship.—Sic nos non nobis mellificamus Apes. 20

Of this poem, which with the Fire, Famine and Slaughter first appeared in the Morning Post, the three first stanzas, which are worth all the rest, and the ninth, were dictated by Mr. Southey. See Apologetic Preface. Vol. 1. p. 337. Between the ninth and the concluding stanza, two or three are omitted, 25 as grounded on subjects that have lost their interest—and for better reasons.

If any one should ask, who General —— meant, the Author begs leave to inform him, that he did once see a red-faced person in a dream whom by the dress he took for a General; but 30 he might have been mistaken, and most certainly he did not hear any names mentioned. In simple verity, the Author never

meant any one, or indeed any thing but to put a concluding
stanza to his doggerel.
[*Line-space*]

<pre>
‾29 10   VIII.
29.1 1   He saw a Pig a̶d̶o̶w̶n̶ ̶t̶h̶ ̶t̶h̶o̶r̶ m̶o̶s̶t̶ ̶r̶a̶p̶i̶
      1 2 2 5   right   rapidly
      8   As he stood near Somerset House, he saw
29.2 1   t̶h̶a̶t̶ ̶r̶i̶g̶h̶t̶ adown th river float
      1 2   ⟵—Adown—⟶
      2 5
      8   a
                A pig down the
30.1 1 1 2 8   The   Pig swam well but   every stroke
      2   at
      5   And the
32.1 1 1 2 2 5 8   Was cutting his own throat.
                [*Line-space*]
31.1 1   T̶h̶e̶n̶ ̶s̶h̶o̶e̶d̶ ̶h̶i̶s̶ ̶t̶e̶e̶t̶h̶ ̶B̶e̶e̶l̶z̶e̶ Old Nicholas grinnd & w̶a̶v̶d̶
                                                       swishd his tail
      1 2 5   Old Nicholas grinn'd, and   swish'd his tail
      2   he
      3   Sir
      8   switch'd
                He view'd the sight with gloating eyes
32.1.1 1   F̶a̶s̶t̶e̶r̶ ̶w̶i̶t̶h̶ For joy   admiration
      1   ⟵—For—⟶   and
      2 3   ⟵—With—⟶
      2 5   joyful
      8   ⟵—Of—⟶ joy and exultation;
32.1.2 1   And thought of c̶e̶r̶t̶a̶i̶n̶ ̶v̶i̶c̶t̶o̶r̶y̶ t̶h̶ ̶g̶o̶d̶d̶e̶s̶s̶ his daughter Victory
      1   he   thought   of
      2 3   For
      2   As
      5   For   own child
      8
                                                 daughter, War,
32.1.3 1 1 2 2 5 3   And her darling babe Taxation.
      8   child,
                [*Line-space*]
29 6 5 7 10   Down the river did glide, with wind and with tide,
      7 8 9   ⟵tide,⟶
      3   He saw swim down the river,
      4 6   Down the river there plied,
30 6 7 3–10   A pig, with vast celerity!
31 6 7 5 7   And the Devil grinn'd,   for he saw all the while
      4 6 10   look'd wise as   how
32.2 3   Oh, it cut its own throat, and he thought   the while
      8 9   Ah!—   all
32 6 7 5 7   How it cut its own throat, and he thought, with a smile,
      4 6 10   ⟵It⟶   There! quoth he
</pre>

33 6 *3* 5 7–9   Of "England's commercial prosperity!"
7   On
4 6 10   Goes
                   [*Line-space*]
⁻34 *10*   IX.
34 1   As he went thro Cold Bath fields he ~~peep~~ lookd
1   look'd
2   Cold-Bath
3   In   Cold Bath Fields he call*e*'d & peep'd in
4 6 5   As he   pass'd   thro' Coldbath Fields he saw
2   by the C*** B*** F****,
5   Cold-bath   fields
7   through
3   He   pass'd   Cold-Bath-Fields, and   saw
8   As he   pass'd by   he   look'd
4 *6* 10   went through   saw
7–9   pass'd   by
35 1 *1* 2 8   At   a solitary cell
3   To   a
4 6 *3–10*   ←——A——→
2   He peep'd into a
5   passed
7   saw
36 1 *1* 2 4 5 4 6 10   And the Devil was · pleasd, for it gave him a   hint
3   ←smil'd,→
2   was   pleas'd, as
6 5 7–9   charm'd, for
7   pleased   put   in mind
3   he   paused,   gave   a   hint
8   he   was pleased—
37 1 *1* 2 6 8 7 8   For improving the   prisons of hell.
3   confinement in
4   his Dungeons
2   Of   the dungeon
5   For   Dungeons of
7   Of   his   prisons   in
3 4 6 9 10   For
5   the
                   [*Line-space*]
⁻38 *10*   X.
38 ⊠3 4 5 7 *4 6* He saw a turnkey   in   a trice
5   ~~fetter~~ in
39 1 *1* 2 2   Handcuff a troublesome blade
5 3 8   Fetter
6 5 7–9   jade;
10   Unfetter   blade;

40 1^{imp}
1 2
2 5
6 5 7–9
3 10
8
41 1 *1* 2 8
2
5
6 5 7–9
3 10

Nimbly   quoth ←—he—→   th   fingers mov₁e.₁
                                                        move,
                            the Devil,
"Ah! nimble,"   he,   "do the
      Nimbly,
How   nimbly,   the
   If   a man is but   used to   his trade
When   best pleas'd with
                 pleased
         they're   used   to their
   If   a man be but   used   his
[*Line-space*]

                    XI.

⁻**42** *10*
42 1
1 2
2 3 8 *10*
5
6 5 7 8
9
43 1
1 2 2 5 3 8 *10*
6 5 7–9
44 1^{imp}
1 2
2 5 *3*
6 5
8
7–9
10
45 1
☒1 3 7 *4 6*

He saw   th   turnkey unfetterin a   man
               the same
                                     unfetter
                             ~~fett~~ unfetter
                                     unfetter   the same,
                   the   Turnkey
      With   little expedition
With but
But with
And he laughd for he thought of th long deba₁tes₁
                                                        debates
Which   put   him   in   mind
And the   Devil   thought on
      he laughed—for he thought of   debate
      the   Devil   thought
Which   put   him   in   mind
On th slave trade exhibition
                 Abolition.
[*Line-space*]

                    XII.

⁻**46** *10*
46 1 *1* 2
8
10
47 1 *1* 2
8
10
48 1
1
2 8
10
49 1^{imp}
1
2
8
10

He   met   an old acquaintance
            met with
            saw
Just   by   th Methodist meetin
Close
As he pass'd by a
She held a consecrated Key—
                 flag,
      bore
      holds   key,
He   nods   familiar greati₁ng.₁
And the   Devil   nods   a greeting.
      he nodded a friendly
      she gave him a nod of
      the Devil nods her a
[*Line-space*]

```
⁻50 10                          XIII.
 50 1          She tippd him th wink &     then    she     cried
     1                                then frown'd and
     2 4                                        cried        aloud,—
     8                                       and     then      cried
    10                       turned   up    her   nose,   and   said,
 51 1 2 4 8 10   Avaunt my names Religion
     1                          ──────
 52 1              Then    turns  to Mr  Wilberforce
     1             And     turn'd        W──  ──
     2             And   she               Wilberforce
     4             And  Then
     8             And   she  leer'd on
    10                     looked to        ──────────
 53 1            And leerd like a love Sick pigeon
     1 2 4 10                 love-sick
     8                 ←──Like──→
                    [Line-space]
⁻54 10                          XIV.
 54 1 6 8 5 7–10  He saw a certain Minister
 55 1             A minister of to his mind—
     6 5 7–10                to
     8                       of
 56 1             Who went   into   a certain house
     6 5 10            Go       up
     8 7–9                   into
 57 1 6 8 5 7–10  With a Majority behind
                    [Line-space]
⁻58 10                          XV
 58 1 6 8 5 7–10  Th Devil quote Genesis
 59 1ⁱᵐᵖ          Like a   learne,d,   eerk Clerk
     6 5 7–10           very learned    clerk,
     8                       learned
 60 1ⁱᵐᵖ          How Noah & his creepin thin,gs,,
     6 8 5 7–10                        things,
 61 1 8           Went   into   th Ark.
     6 5 7–10           up into
                    [Line-space]
⁻62 10                          XVI.
 62 10            He took from the poor,
 63 10            And he gave to the rich,
 64 10            And he shook hands with a Scotchman,
 65 10            For he was not afraid of the ──
                    [Line-space]
```

‾66 *10*

66 1   XVII.

     ~~He saw~~   General   ——'s   ~~red face~~ burning face

   1 2 4 6 10   ←——General——→   ←—burning—→

   4   Burrard's

   2   G********'s ←—fiery—→

   5   Gascoyne's

   6 5 7

   7   ←—burning—→

   3   Tarleton's

   3   He   saw General   ——'s

   8   When he

   8 9   ←——face,——→

          ←——General——→ ********'s ←—burning—→ face,

67 *1 1 2 4 6 4–10* He   saw   with consternation

   2   view'd

   5 7   beheld

   3   Which put him into a

   8   He   fled   with

68 *1 1 6 5 7–9* And back to hell his way did   take

   2 4 7 4 6 10   did he

   2   Then   he did

   5   did he

69 ⊠*3 5 3 8* For the Devil   thought by a ~~slight~~ mistake

   5   he

   3   So he hied to his lake, for,

   8   For the Devil thought,   small

70 *1*   ~~it~~   Twas   ~~th~~ general Conflagration.

   1 4 2 4 6 10 It   was

   2 6 8 5 7–9 Twas   the

   5   He   was

   7   ~~Of Cam~~ 'Twas

   3   He thought 'twas a

title. *2* The Devils Thoughts • *6 8 5 7* THE DEVIL'S WALK. • *7* The Devil's thoughts. • *4 6 10* THE DEVIL'S THOUGHTS   **1.** *3 5* brimstone-bed • *4* Brimstone Bed • *2 6 3 8 5 7* brimstone bed, *1 2 6 7 3 8 5 7–9* day, • *4* Day   **2.** *2 6 8* A-walking ⊠*1 5 3* the *4 6* DEVIL *1 3 6–8 4–10* gone, • *2 2 5* gone • *4* gone/   **3.** ⊠*1 2 5* the *4* Snug *4 2* Farm • *8* farm, *1–3* earth, • *3 4 6 7 5 7–10* Earth,   **4.** *4 2* Stock *5* on; • *7–9* on: **5.** *4* Hill • *8 9* hill, • *5* hill *2 7 &* *2 3 5 7 3–9* dale • *4* Dale   **6.** *7–9* walk'd, *1 3 7 4–6 10* plain, • *2 5* plain • *4* Plain • *2 6 8 7–9* plain; • *3* plain: **7.** *2 3 6 3 5 7–9* backwards • *5* Backward *1 2 6 3 8 4–10* and *2 3 2 6 3 5 7–9* forwards *1* swish'd • *2 4 4 6* swished • *3* switcht • *2 5 3 8 7–9* switch'd • *6 5 10* switched • *7* ~~sw~~swished *1 3 2 6 3 8 5 7–9* tail, • *4* Tail   **8.** ⊠*1 1 4 5* gentleman ⊠*1 1 2 4 4 6* switches ⊠*1 2 4 7* cane. • *2* ~~tail~~ cane. • *4* Cane. • *7* cane—   **9.** *3* "And *3* devil *3 5* dress'd. • *4 6–8 4–10* drest? • *3* drest?"   **10.** *4 6 5* O! • *3* Oh, • *4 6–10* Oh! *4–8 4–10* Sunday's • *3* sunday's *3 4 6–10* best: • *4* Best. • *5* best,   **11.** *4 6 9 10* jacket *4 6 3 8 5 7–9* red, *6 3 8 4–10* and *4* Breeches *3 4 6 7 3 8 5 7–10* blue,   **12.** *4* Hole *5* behind *7* were *4* Tail *4 7* thro'.   **13.** *1 2 7 3* lawyer • *4 4 6* LAWYER *4 2 5 4 6* Viper • *6–8 5 7–9* viper,   **14.** *5 3* dunghill • *7 10* dung hill • *4 6* dung heap *5* besides *1 3 2 6 3 8 5 7–10* stable; • *4* Stable • *7* stable: • *4 6* stable,

15. 2 Oh oh— *1* he, • *2* he,— 7 smiled • *4–10* smiled, 7 mind, **16.** 5 Story ⊠1 2 3 7 and *4 6 9 his* 4 Brother • *4 6* brother, ⊠1 5 7 8 Abel. • 5 Able. • 7 *8* Abel: **17.** *1 3* apothecary • 4 A 'Pothecary • 6 8 7 8 Apothecary, • 7 A potecary • *4 6* A POTHECARY • *9* a Pothecary, • *10* Apothecary ⊠1 *2* 5 white • 2 5 White *1 6 3 8 7–9* horse, • *4 2* Horse **18.** *1* vocation, • 5 Vocation • 7 *4 6* vocations, • 8 vocation; • *5* avocations, • *7 8* avocations; **19.** 7–9 Oh! ⊠1 *3* the 3 thɾought *7–9* there's 3 8 friend, • 4 *4 6* Friend **20.** *1 2* 8 Death, • 4 *4 6* DEATH • 5 6 "Death • *3* death 2 *7 4 6 8 10* Revelations. • 5 Revelations • 6 Revelations!" • *3* revelation. • *5 7* Revelations." **21.** *1 7 3 8 4–10* cottage • 5 Cottage • 6 cottage, *1 3* 8 *4–6 10* coach-house, • 2 *2* Coach-house, • 4 Coach House, • 5 7 coach-house • 6 *3* coach-house; • 7 coach house— • *8 9* coach-house— **22.** ⊠1–3 7 cottage *1 2* 7 *7–9* gentility, • 3 2 8 5 *10* gentility; • 6 *4 6* gentility! **23.** *1* 8 grinn'd *1* 2 sight, • 8 sight— 5 grinned • 7 grin • *3* grin; • *4 6 10* grin, 5 *7–9* pleased, 7 sin, • *3 4 6 10* sin **24.** ⊠1 *1* 4 2 5 7 pride • *1* 2 pride, ⊠1 4 5 7 5 humility. • 5 humility— • 7 humility • 5 humility! **25.** 7– 9 stept *1 3* 7 *3 4 6–10* bookseller's • 2 5 booksellers • 4 2 6 8 5 Bookseller's *1 2* 7 *3 4 6 10* shop, • 3 2 6 8 shop; • 4 Shop • *5 7–9* shop: **26.** ⊠1 *4 6 10* he, • *4 6 10* he! *1* 3–5 We • 6 *3* 5 *10* "We *1* college, • 2 7 College, • 3 college: • 4 College! • 2 6 5 college; • 5 *4 6* college • *3* college;" • 8 college— • *1–* 9 College; • *10* college! **27.** 6 "For I, 2 3 5 8 sat • 6 *3* 5 sat, • *4 6* sate 4 6 *10* myself, *1* 2 7 8 *4–9* cormorant • 6 *3* 5 *10* cormorant, 2 4 6 7 5 *7–9* once, **28.** 5 Perched 6 5 "Hard 6 by, ⊠1 the 5 7 *3 4 6 10* tree 4 Knowlege. • 6 5 Knowledge." • 7 *4 6* knowledge. • *3 10* knowledge." **28fn1.** *10* tree of life **28fn3.** *10* paper money: **28fn4.** *10* Our *10* tree of know- ledge, **28fn9.** *10* cormorant. PAR. LOST. IV. **28fn10–11.** *10* various readings **28fn12.** *10* "life" Cod. quid. habent, "trade." **28fn13.** *10* the trade, **28fn14.** *10* κατ' ἐξόχην *10* Life *10* eminentiori; **28fn18.** *10* call Life **28fn19.** *10* authorship.— **28fn20.** *10* apes. **28fn21.** *10* Famine, and Slaughter, **28fn22–4.** *10* the Morning Post, the 1st, 2d, 3d, 9th, and 16th stanzas were dictated by Mr. Southey. **28fn24.** *4 6* Preface. Vol. 1. p. 337. • *10* Preface, vol. i. **28fn24–7.** *4 6* Between . . . reasons.] *10* omits **28fn25.** 6 omitted **28fn28.** *10* ask **28fn32.** *10* author **29.1.** *1* 5 pig **29.2.** *1* 2 8 the *1* float, • 2 float. • 2 8 float; **30.1.** *1 2* 5 8 pig *1 2* 2 5 8 well, **32.1.** 5 throat **31.1.** 2 grinnd • 5 grinned 2 5 & 2 swished • 2 *3* switch'd • 5 switched **32.1.1.** 2 & *1* admiration— • 2 2 admiration, • 5 admiration • *3* admiration; **32.1.2.** *1* daughter, *1–3* Victory, • 5 victory **32.1.3.** *1 3* babe, Taxation. • 5 babe—Taxation— **29.** 7 glide 7 & **30.** 7 Pig • *5 7 10* pig 7 4–7 celerity, • *3* celerity: • *8 9* celerity,— • *10* celerity; **31.** 7 grinn'd • 7 grinn'd— *4 6 10* while, **32.** 7 throat & • *4 6* throat. There! • *10* throat. "There!" 7 *5* 7 thought *7 4 6 7* smile **33.** *10* "Goes *7 3 7–10* England's 7 Prosperity. • *3 7–9* prosperity. • *4 6 10* prosperity." **34.** 7 *8 9* passed *1* thro' • 6 7 5 through 2 Cold-Bath Fields • 6 *3* 8 Cold-Bath-Fields, • *4 6 10* Cold-Bath Fields • 5 Cold Bath Fields • *7–9* Cold Bath Fields, 2 lookd **35.** *1* 7– 9 cell— • *3* Cell; • *4* Cell— • 2 8 *5 10* cell; • 6 *3* cell: • 7 cell. • *4 6* cell, **36.** *3 4* devil *1* pleas'd, • 2 *4 6 10* pleased, • *4* pleased: • *5* 7 pleased *1* hint, • 4 Hint **37.** ⊠1 *3* 5 *7 3* 8 Hell. **38.** 2 2 5 6 8 5 *7–10* Turnkey *7–9* trice, **39.** *1* blade— • *2 3* 8 *10* blade; **40.** *1* 2 2 5 *3* Nimbly, • *10* "Nimbly" 7– 9 Ah! nimble (quoth he) do *1* 2 6 *3* 8 *5 10* he, *3* do ⊠1 *3* 4 *7 4 6* the fingers 2 5 6 *3* 5 *10* move **41.** 6 "When *1* us'd *1* 2 2 3 8 *7–9* trade. •

6 *5 10* trade." 42. 2 *2* 5 6 *5* 7–*10* Turnkey *1* 2 unfettering 5 Man • 8 man, 43. *1* 2 6 *3* 8 *7–9* expedition; • 2 *10* expedition, • *5* expedition: 44. *1* laugh'd, • 2 laughed,— ⊠1 3 4 7 *4* 6 the 45. ⊠1–4 7 *4* 6 the *1* 2 6 Slave Trade • 5 *10* Slave-trade • 8 *7–9* slave-trade • 5 Slave-Trade 2 *3* 8 *7–10* abolition. • 5 Abolition 47. *1* 2 8 the *1* Meeting; • 2 Meeting, • 8 meeting, • *10* meeting;— 48. 2 flag 50. *1* tip'd • 2 4 tipt • 8 tipp'd *1* 2 4 8 the *1* 2 8 wink, • 4 wink/ *1* cri'd 4 aloud, 51. *1* 2 8 Avaunt! • 4 *10* "Avaunt! 4 *My* *1* 2 4 8 *10* name's 2 Religion. • 4 Religion!" • 8 Religion; • *10* Religion," 52. 2 turnd *1 10* Mr. • 4 Mister 4 8 Wilberforce, 53. *1* 2 4 leer'd • *10* leered *1* 2 8 *10* pigeon. • 4 Pigeon. 54. 8 Minister, • *7–9* minister— • *10* minister 55. 6 *5 10* (A • *7–9* (a 6 8 *5* Minister 6 *5* 7–*10* mind) • 8 mind, 56. 6 *10* House, • 8 house, • 5 House • *7–9* house— 57. *7–9* with 6 8 *5* 7–*10* majority 6 8 *10* behind. • 5 behind; • *7–9* behind: 58. 6 8 *5* 7–*10* The 6 8 *5* 7–*10* quoted 6 8 *10* Genesis, • *7–9* Genesis— 59. *7–9* like 8 clerk: 60. 6 "Noah, • 5 *10* "Noah 6 8 *5* 7–*10* and 6 *5* 7–*10* creeping • 8 *creeping* 8 5 *10* things • *7–9* things— 61. 6 "Went • *7–9* went 6 8 *5* 7–*10* the 6 Ark!" • *5 10* Ark." • *7–9* ark. 66. 6 GENERAL GASCOIGNE's burning • *5* 7 General Gascoigne's burning • 4 *6 10* General —— burning 3 8 *7–9* face, 67. *1* 6 4–6 *10* consternation, • 2 consternation. • 4 7 consternation— • 2 consternation: • *3* 8 *7–9* consternation; 68. *1* 2 4 2 6 *5* 7–*9* Hell *1* 4 2 7 4 6–*10* take, • 6 take; 69. 4 devil *1* 4 2 5 6 8 *5* 7–*9* thought, *1* 4 2 6 7 3 8 *5* 7–*9* mistake, 70. 6 8 *7–9* 'Twas • 5 'T was *1* 4 2 5 5 General • 6 GENERAL • 8 *general* 5 Conflagration • 6 CON- FLAGRATION! • 7 conflagration— • *3* 8 4 6–*10* conflagration. • 5 Conflagration!

title. RS's endorsement of MS 1 describes it as "the Devil's Thoughts"; while his later, added description in MS 1 is "The D. W——".

There is a facsimile of the MS 4 title in *C&SH*, facing 32. The authors' names, translit- erated from the Greek, become "ARSOUTHEI" or "Southei" and "ESTEESE", i.e. RS and STC. The deleted name, made up of Greek characters and one Hebrew charac- ter, transliterates into "ASRA SCHONTHINU"—which is an exact anagram of Sara Hutchinson if ש is transliterated "Sch", German style. For SH as "My Angel" see *CN* III 3406; for C's use of the initial Hebrew letter of this anagram, ש, to indicate SH see *CN* II 3222 and *CN* II appendix C, as well as the General Note on N 18 in *CN* II; also *CN* III 3428, 3429, etc.

‾**1 etc.** The stanzas are numbered only in TEXTS 5 *10* (and their numbering of course differs). The PR *10* sequence is followed here; the numbers appearing in MS 5 (in arabic numerals) may be calculated from the conspectus in sec C above.

2, 4, 6, etc. Alternate lines are indented in TEXTS ⊠7 *4* 6, as in the RT, though the pattern varies slightly in some versions and transcripts.

5–7. In MS 5 JTC underlined both occurrences of "the" in line 5, putting a cross in the margin; he gave an alternative to line 6 on the verso: "He wanderd & over plain"; and he inserted "long" before "tail" in line 7, putting another cross in the margin.

13. The cancelled line in MS 1 is also the first line of a stanza which follows stanza 4 (in the PR *10* numeration) in that ms, and which was subsequently deleted. Thus:

> He put his hand in the vipers hole
> And counted the young ones there
> Fear nothing ~~my~~ you dear little ~~darlings~~ orphans, he said

Sting while you live & when you are dead
Your souls shall make for a fury head

14–16. In MS 5 JTC gave the alternative "near his own" above "besides his" in line 14; he gave the alternative "And the Devil he" for "Old Nicholas" in line 15; he underlined "the Story of" in line 16, and expanded "Able." to "his brother Abel."

17. In MS 1 stanza 5 is preceded at the head of the page (f 6ᵛ) by a line which may or not have anything to do with the poem: "Her ~~hall & her drawing room~~ favourit lock of hair."

17–18. In MS 5 JTC wrote "He saw" before "An Apothecary" in line 17; in line 18 he wrote "Ride" alongside "Rode", which he underlined, and added an "s" to "Vocation".

20⁺. In MS 8 stanza 5 is followed by a stanza on Brothers the Prophet. This became stanza 13 (var) in the expanded version by RS published in 1838.

28⁺. The following stanza appears in PR *3* between stanzas 7 and 6:

He saw school-boys acting prayers at morn,
And naughty plays at night;
And, "Oho Mr Dean," he shouted, "I ween
My own good trade goes right."

PR *8 9* insert the same stanza (var) between stanzas 7 and 9. It was printed alone—from "one of the Cambridge Papers"—as evidence to support the claim that Porson wrote it at Dr Vincent's, by "CANTAB." in *The Literary Journal* I (1818) 183.

28fn1–9. PL IV 218–21, 192, 194, 196 (in that order).

28fn12. Cod[ices] quid[am] habent] Tr "Some mss have". The point C makes is that the bookselling trade is called *the* trade, pre-eminently (κατ᾽ ἐξόχην), and that in turn may be regarded as life in the higher sense ("sensu eminentiori").

28fn19–20. Sic nos non nobis mellificamus Apes] Tr "We bees make honey, but not for ourselves." C has substituted "nos . . . nobis" for "vos . . . vobis" (first person for second) in a line said to be Virgil's in the *Life* attributed to Aelius Donatus: see *BL* ch 2 (*CC*) I 46.

28⁺. In MS 4 line 28 is followed by a rule and the explanation "Hiatus. | Multa desiderantur | in hoc loco" tr "A gap. Much is missing at this point."

29.1–33. JTC wrote the later form of the stanza on the verso of MS 5, thus:

Down a river did glide with wind & tide
A pig with vast celerity
And the Devil was tickled for he saw all the while
How it cut its own throat and He thought with a smile
On Englands commercial prosperity

PR *7–9* give the earlier form of the two stanzas (var) in a footnote, as if they came before stanza 17.

29.2. In MS 1 the line is continuous with line 29.1.

32.1⁺. MS 1 has no line-space.

35. MS 5 passed] JTC deleted the word and substituted "peeped".

37⁺. In MS 4 the line is followed by the summary "Here he meets one of the Furies, an old Acquaintance of his, with a consecrated Banner in her Hand—and gives her a familiar Greeting—". This is followed by line 50.

44. PR *1* debates] The last letter is smudged in all the copies examined, making it easy to read the word as "debate".

53⁺. In MS 4 the line is followed by a rule, presumably to register C's memory of stanzas not brought forward from earlier versions.

In MSS 2 8 stanza 13 is followed by a 6-line additional stanza, beginning "He met a Lord of the North country I The Lord of the Dale was his name". It was adapted to become stanza 5 in the expanded version which RS published in 1838.

54–61. Stanzas 14 and 15 are cancelled with a single cross in MS 1 (f 7ᵛ), which explains why they do not appear in TEXTS *1 2* etc.

54–7. The reference is not entirely clear. Cruikshank's illustration to PR *8 9* shows Wellington, who became leader of the government in Jan 1828, moving to the Lower House at the time of the King's Speech with two rats in a cage. The Lords smirk behind him as the King's Speech announces "No Distress." MS 6, on the other hand, dates from a decade earlier. If the minister is Pitt, the reference might be to the Act of Union with Ireland in 1800 and the first imperial (united) parliamentary session of 1801 before the Peace of Amiens, by which time Pitt had fallen from office.

55. In PR *7–9* the line is continuous with line 54.

57. In PR *7–9* the line is continuous with line 56.

58–61. The image bears a relation to C's comment on Burke, that he "found himself, as it were, in a Noah's Ark, with a very few Men and a great many Beasts!" (*The Friend* IX 12 Oct 1809—*CC*—II 124; cf I 188–9); the source of the comparison is Robert South *Sermons* (1737) (cf *CN* I 325). To this extent the likelihood of C's authorship of lines 54–61 is strengthened, though it should be noted that the two stanzas are not included, as are all but one of the others, in RS's continuation published in 1838.

59. In PR *7–9* the line is continuous with line 58.

61. In PR *7–9* the line is continuous with line 60.

65⁺. In the PR *4 6 10* versions stanza 16 is followed by a row of six asterisks, to indicate the "two or three" stanzas omitted "as grounded on subjects that have lost their interest—and for better reasons" (C's note to line 28 in PR *4 6*). There is no record of any additional stanzas.

66. An unsigned review of PR *3*, which claims to be based on "the rough draft of these very lines in the handwriting of their real author, Mr Coleridge", fills the blank with the name Gage. The review appeared on pp 575–8 of the vol XIX (Jun 1828) issue of an unnamed journal, and is preserved among the EHC papers at HRC (uncatalogued in 1978).

A note among RHS's materials for a third edition of C's poems at HEHL (HM 16083 vol III p 11) records that the blank is filled in, in "Lord Coleridge's MS. Book", with the name Fitzpatrick, "'Notorious,' says a note, 'for his copious libations to the ruddy God.'" The name Fitzpatrick is also supplied as a variant in the voluminous editorial surround to PR *7–9*.

JTC supplied the name Laurie as a correction to MS 5 (see the next note).

66–9. In MS 5 JTC wrote "Laurie's" above "Gascoyne's" in line 66; he inserted "And it filled him" alongside the beginning of line 67, and "huge" before "consternation"; he wrote "And" before "Then" in line 68, and transposed "did" and "he"; and he wrote "'Twas" before "He was" in line 69.

215. BEFORE GLEIM'S COTTAGE: ELEGIACS FROM VOSS

A. DATE

Late Aug 1799? The verso of MS 1 contains notes for **216** *Mahomet* in C's and RS's hands.

B. TEXTS

1. Mitchell Library, State Library of New South Wales, Sydney, A 27 p 26. Recto of a single leaf, 15.7×20.0 cm; wm crown on a semicircle. Draft in C's hand, endorsed by DC.

The draft is followed by examples of metres deriving from Schiller (**187** *The Homeric Hexameter* and **188** *The Ovidian Elegiac Metre*) and, on the verso, by notes for **216** *Mahomet* in C's and RS's hands.

2 [=RT]. DCL Letters Coleridge (2 iʳ). Recto of a single leaf, 20.0×31.7 cm; wm ?RK I 1798. Another draft in C's hand, in ink and pencil.

The draft is preceded by a note on elegiac verse, with an example derived from Ossian (**217** *Specimen Elegiacs*). The verso contains notes on metre and metrical feet, followed by a fragment of **216** *Mahomet*.

title. 1 The prefatory Verses to Voss's Louise translated ~~nearly~~ almost verbally, & in the original metre. I Before Gleim's Cottage. • 2 Voss before Gleim's Cottage

1 ☐ Up, up! noble old Man! *Who knocks there?* Friend & Acquaintance.
2 1 *Friends should more quietly knock.* True! but ~~thou hearedst us not~~ you would not
have heard.

2   thou hearedst us not.
3 ☐ *Hush! ye'll awaken the Maidens.* They love us. *Hush! it is Midnight.*
4 1 ~~*Must I*~~ *And could ye wish them to rise?* Rise & receive the Belov'd.
 2 *And*   *would*
5 1 *Whom,* ~~*pray*~~ *prithee? Knowst* ~~*thou*~~ you the Vicar of Greeno? What? & Luisa?*
 2   *prithee?* Know'st   thou
6 ☐ She and her Husband. *But where's Mother?* And Mother, to boot.
7 ☐ *Up up, Girls! make ready the Best!* Nay, nothing but Shelter—
8 1 Shelter and welcoming Smiles. *Dear Souls! come in—it is cold!*
 2   *it freezes—come in!*

1. 2 Up up, 2 man! **3.** 2 *H USH*! *it* 2 *midnight.* **4.** 2 *you* 2 *'em*
6. 2 She & her Husband. **7.** 2 *Up, up,* 2 *best.* Nay! **8.** 2 Smiles!—

title. The MS 2 title supersedes a previous pencil heading "Elegiacs".
1–2. C has scanned the lines in MS 2. This, together with a note at the end of the draft, is quoted in vol I headnote.

1. The first part of the line in MS 2—up to "*there?*"—is in ink over pencil.
2, 4, 6, 8. Alternate lines are indented in MS 1. Only line 2 is indented in MS 2.
6. In MS 2 "She & her Husband." was underlined, but the line was cancelled.

216. MAHOMET: A FRAGMENT

A. DATE

The plan for RS's and C's joint poem was apparently "squeezed into a sufficient oneness" by 1 Sept 1799 (Robberds I 294). C's lines were undoubtedly written at that time or very soon afterwards. See vol I headnote.

B. TEXTS

1. DCL Letters Coleridge (2 i^v). Verso of a single leaf, 20.0×31.7 cm; wm ?RK I 1798. Draft in C's hand, in ink, pencil, and ink over pencil. Lines 1–2 are in ink, lines 9–14 in ink over pencil. The recto contains C's translation from Voss's *Luise* (=**215** *Before Gleim's Cottage*) and **217** *Specimen Elegiacs*.
    The lines are preceded and followed by examples of metrical feet, and there is a note on metre in the space occupied by lines 2–8 of PR *1* (given in vol I headnote). These examples and notes are variously written in pencil, ink over pencil, and ink.

1 [=RT]. *PW* (1834).

C. GENERAL NOTE

Vol I headnote gives the text of a ms outline of the proposed poem, in C's and RS's hands, along with C's comments on continuing the poem and some related verses, as well as references to RS's plans for continuing the poem and to what he wrote and published.

title. *1* MAHOMET.

1 1 Utter in Song, o my Soul, the Flight and Return of Mohammed
     1   the
2 1 Prophet and Chief: which scatter'd abroad both Evil & Blessing
     1   priest,   who
3 *1* Huge wasteful empires founded and hallow'd slow persecution,
4 *1* Soul-withering, but crush'd the blasphemous rites of the Pagan
5 *1* And idolatrous Christians.—For veiling the Gospel of Jesus,
6 *1* They, the best corrupting, had made it worst than the vilest.
7 *1* Wherefore Heaven decreed th' enthusiast warrior of Mecca,
8 *1* Choosing good from iniquity rather than evil from goodness.

[*Line-space*]

9 1   Loud the Tumult in Mecca surrounding the Fane of the Idols
   1   idol;—

10 1   Naked and Prostrate the Priesthood were stretch'd: the People with mad shouts
   1   laid—

11 1   Thundering now, and now with saddest Ululations
   1   ululation

12 ☐   Flew, as over the channel of rock-stone the ruinous River

13 ☐   Shatters its waters abreast: & in mazy uproar bewilder'd

14 ☐   Rushes dividduous all, all rushing impetuous onwards

1. *1* song, O *1* soul! *1* flight *1* return *1* Mohammed,   **2.** *1* evil and blessing,
9. *1* tumult *1* fane   **10.** *1* prostrate *1* priesthood *1* people   **12.** *1* river
13. *1* abreast, and *1* bewilder'd,   **14.** *1* dividuous all—all *1* onward.

1, 9, 10, etc. The metrical scansion in MS 1 is given in vol I headnote.

217. SPECIMEN ELEGIACS, ADAPTING OSSIAN

A. DATE

The other pieces in the same ms date from Aug–Sept 1799 (see sec B), and C had adapted specimen elegiacs from Schiller and shown an interest in hexameters in Nov–Dec 1798 (see poems **185, 187, 188**). The present specimen probably dates from the later of the two occasions; *CN* I 377 f 13ᵛ (see vol I headnote) is evidence of his interest in Ossian at the later time.

B. TEXT

DCL Letters Coleridge 2 (iʳ). Recto of a single leaf, 20.0×31.7 cm; wm ?RK I 1798. Draft in C's hand.

The draft is followed by C's translation from Voss's *Luise* (**215** *Before Gleim's Cottage*) and (on the verso) a note on hexameters and a specimen from **216** *Mahomet*.

The RT reproduces the untitled ms exactly.

217.X1. RIGMAROLE VERSES
ABOUT SAMUEL JACKSON PRATT

In a letter to RS from Stowey dated 30 Nov [1799] C reported: "I have found the long rigmarole Verses which I wrote about Pratt &c/ but there's nothing in 'em, save facility of Language & oddity of Rhyme—. If however I go to Bristol, I will leave it with Cottle to be sent with any parcel that may be moving towards you— (*CL* I 536). The verses have not survived, indeed it is not even known if they got as far as Cottle in Bristol.

Samuel Jackson Pratt (1749–1814) wrote under the pseudonym of Courtney Melmoth and was the author of *The Triumph of Benevolence; Occasioned by the National Design of Erecting a Monument to John Howard* (Cambridge 1786). The title of his compilation, *Gleanings* (1795–9), had irritated RS a year before, when he had hoped to use the same title for the collection which eventually became the *Annual Anthology* (see *LL*—M—I 151; Robberds I 239; etc). C's verses were presumably an extempore satirical composition, dating from the time he spent in RS's company when he returned from Germany and when they also wrote **214** *The Devil's Thoughts*.

218. EPIGRAM ON A REPORT
OF A MINISTER'S DEATH,
FROM LESSING

A. DATE

May 1799 (KC's dating); certainly before Sept 1799.

B. TEXTS

1. BM Add MS 47499=Notebook $3\frac{1}{2}$ f 120^r (*CN* I 625). Numbered "4" (though actually the first entry) in a series of some 30 or so such epigrams or notes for epigrams, mostly adapted from German authors.

1 [=RT].   *M Post* (18 Sept 1799). Unsigned.
Rpt *The Spirit of the Public Journals for 1800* IV (1801) 67.

2. *The Courier* (22 Aug 1800). Unsigned.

3. *The Keepsake for 1829* ed F. M. Reynolds (1828) 122. The last of three "EPIGRAMS. I BY S. T. COLERIDGE."

title. *1* ON A REPORT OF A MINISTER's DEATH. I WRITTEN IN
GERMANY.• *2 CITY NEWS.*

  1 □   Last Monday all the Papers said,
  2 1 *3* That M^r   was ←—dead! —→
  1   Mr. ——   surely dead;
  2   B I L L Y P I T T
  3 1   ~~Portentous news~~ Ah then! What said the City?
  1 2 ←——Ah—→
  3 ←——Why, —→
3.1.1 1   ~~What said the nation?~~
3.1.2 1   ~~With pious Resignation~~
  4 1 *3* The tenth Part sadly shook their head,
  1 2   the
  5 □   And shaking sigh'd, & sighing said—
  6 □   Pity! indeed 'tis Pity!
          [*Line-space*]
 ⁻**7** 1   2
  7 1   But wh~~at~~en the sad Report was found
  1 3   when   said
  2   sad
  8 □   A Rumour wholly without ground,
  9 ⊠*3* Ah then, what said the City?
  3 Why,
9.1.1 1   ~~What said the nation?~~
9.1.2 1   ~~With pious Resignation~~
 10 1 *3* The other nine Parts shook their head
  1 2   the
 11 1   Repeating what the tenth ~~part~~ had said—
  ⊠*1*   ←tenth→
 12 □   Pity! indeed 'tis pity.

1. *3* papers *1 2* said   **2.** *3* Mr. —— ⊠1 dead;   **3.** *1 2* then • *3* then,
⊠1 what *3* city?   **4.** *1 3* tenth part • *2* T E N T H P A R T   **5.** ⊠1 and ⊠1 said,
6. *3* "Pity, ⊠1 indeed, *1 2* pity! • *3* pity!"   **7.** ⊠1 report   **8.** *1 2* rumour, •
3 rumour   **9.** *1 2* Ah—then *3* city?   **10.** *2* N I N E • *3 nine* *1 3* parts • *2* P A R T S
⊠1 head,   **11.** *2 tenth* ⊠1 said,   **12.** *3* "Pity, ⊠1 indeed, *1 2* pity! • *3* pity!"

3, 6, 9, 12. Indented in all texts. In MS 1 lines 3.1.1–2 and 9.1.1–2 are also indented.

219. EPIGRAM TO A PROUD PARENT,
FROM LESSING

A . DATE

May–Sept 1799.

B. TEXTS

1. BM Add MS 47499 = Notebook $3\frac{1}{2}$ f 120^r (*CN* I 625). The second, labelled "(a)", in a series of some 30 or so such epigrams or notes for epigrams, mostly adapted from German authors.

1 [=RT]. *M Post* (29 Aug 1799). Unsigned.
Rpt *The Spirit of the Public Journals for 1800* IV (1801) 89.

2. *Annual Anthology* ed RS (2 vols Bristol 1799–1800) II 269; marked "S. T. C." by C in his own copy (Yale Tinker 1953 2). The seventh in a series of 17 epigrams, 12 of them by C.

title. *1 2* TO A PROUD PARENT.

1 □   Thy Babes ne'er greet thee with the Father's Name
2 1   My Lord, they lisp—. ~~And~~ Now whence can this arise?
 1 2   Now
3 1   ~~Think~~ Perhaps their Mother feels an honest shame
 1 2   Perhaps
4 1   And will not leave her Infants to tell Lies.
 1   teach
 2   Infant

title. *2 To a PROUD PARENT.*   **1.** *1* babes *1* father's *1* name, • *2* name;
2. *1 My Lud!* • *2* My Lud! *1 2* lisp. *1* arise!   **3.** *2* Perhaps, *1* mother
1 2 shame,   **4.** *1* infants *1* lies.

title. In the PR *2* sequence the poem is numbered "VII."
2, 4. Indented in PR *1 2*.

220. EPIGRAM ON A NOTORIOUS LIAR, FROM LESSING

A. DATE

May–Sept 1799.

B. TEXTS

1. BM Add MS 47499 = Notebook $3\frac{1}{2}$ f 120^v (*CN* I 625). Numbered "6" in a series of some 30 or so such epigrams or notes for epigrams, mostly adapted from German authors.

2. Cottle *E Rec* II 66.
The lines are the third in a group of five epigrams translated from the German

which Cottle says C gave him together on the same occasion. Presumably they were in ms.

> *1* [=RT]. *Annual Anthology* ed RS (2 vols Bristol 1799–1800) II 269; marked "S. T. C." by C in his own copy (Yale Tinker 1953 2). The sixth in a series of 17 epigrams, 12 of them by C.

title. 1 On a notorious Liar, in *rough* Verse.

```
1  1    As Dick & I in Cheapside late were walking,
   2 1               at Charing Cross
2  1    At On th' other side o' th' street whom should we spy
   2 1   Whom should we see on t' other side pass by,
3  □    But Informator, with a stranger talking—
4  1    And So I exclaim'd at once—Heavens! what a Lye!
   2    So              ←———"O,———→
   1                    ←———Lord———→
5  1    Says Dick—What? can you hear him?—Hear him? Stuff!
   2    Quoth                      ←———Stuff!———→
   1                              —hear him! stuff!
6  1    I see him open his mouth. An't that enough?
   2 1   saw
```

1. 2 "As   2 *1* and   *1* walking   **2.** *1* by   **3.** 2 INFORMATOR • *1* Informator
2 *1* talking,   **4.** 2 exclaimed— • *1* exclaim'd,   2 lie!"   **5.** 2 Dick, "What can •
1 Dick—what can   2 him?"   **6.** 2 *1* mouth—an't   2 enough?"

title. In the PR *1* sequence the poem is numbered "VI."
2, 4. Indented in TEXTS 2 *1*.